THE INTERNATIONAL FOUNDATION DIRECTORY 2003

THE INTERNATIONAL FOUNDATION DIRECTORY 2003

Europa Publications
Taylor & Francis Group
LONDON AND NEW YORK

First published 1974
12th edition 2003

11 New Fetter Lane, London EC4P 4EE, United Kingdom
(A member of the Taylor & Francis Group)

ISBN 1 85743 140 5
ISSN 1366-8048

Editor: Cathy Hartley
Directory updated and compiled by: Karina Holly

Typeset by Ignition UK Limited,
printed by Unwin Brothers Limited
and bound by MPG Books Ltd

Foreword

Since it was first published in 1974, *The International Foundation Directory* has undergone many revisions, and has now, for this twelfth edition, been expanded to include in the region of 2,300 directory entries. These, together with the three introductory essays and comprehensive indexes, aim to provide a thorough and up-to-date overview of civil society and the third sector world-wide.

The distinction between foundations, trusts and foundation-type organizations and other non-governmental organizations (NGOs) is, to some extent, unclear; thus it was decided that, from its tenth edition, the Directory should formally include grant- and non-grant-making NGOs and similar third-sector organizations. As a result, the Directory now includes not only foundations and trusts (private, operating, grant-making and corporate), but also charities and other NGOs, some of which make grants to organizations and individuals, while others carry out their own programmes and projects.

To gain entry to the publication, an organization must be international, or, where operating on a purely national basis, must be important enough to have a widespread impact; it must have charitable or public benefit status; and must have significant funds available, or make significant charitable donations, or run its own projects of importance (however, the Editors have no pre-determined figure to establish inclusion, as the importance of an organization's funds is relative, depending on the wealth of the country in which it is located). The Editors have excluded foundations established purely for the benefit of a particular named hospital or school; moreover, governmental bodies may only be included if they are independent of political control.

The Directory contains introductory essays, a directory section and three indexes. The essays inform on the development, and current state, of foundations and the third sector in a global context, along with details of how to approach such organizations for funding. The Directory section is organized by country, with organizations arranged alphabetically under the appropriate heading: Foundation Centres and Co-ordinating Bodies, or Foundations, Trusts and Non-Profit Organizations. A Bibliography is followed by three indexes: a full index of foundations, an index by main activity (where organizations are listed under headings including conservation and the environment, education, medicine and health, and social welfare), and an index by geographical area of activity. This latter index allows the reader to find organizations active in, for example, South America, Central America and the Caribbean, Central and South-Eastern Europe, or Asia and the Pacific.

The Editors would like to acknowledge the interest and co-operation of all the contributors to this publication, and the assistance of the organizations included in providing up-to-date material is much appreciated.

May 2003

Acknowledgements

The Editor and publishers of *The International Foundation Directory* are greatly indebted to the many people who advised and helped with its compilation, and offer their sincere thanks.

They gratefully acknowledge the assistance of the foundations, trusts, NGOs and other non-profit organizations which replied to the questionnaires sent to them, and which provided up-to-date information for the Directory, and would like to thank the governmental bodies and other national and international institutions, foundation centres and co-ordinating bodies which have helped provide information on foundations and NGOs in all parts of the world.

In particular, they are grateful to Karina Holly, Editor of *Philanthropy in Europe,* who updated the Directory section for this edition.

Contents

Indexes

Abbreviations

AB	Alberta
AC	Companion of the Order of Australia
ACT	Australian Capital Territory
Admin	Administration
Admin.	Administrative, Administrator
AG	Aktiengesellschaft (Joint Stock Company)
AIDS	Acquired Immune Deficiency Syndrome
al.	aleja (alley, avenue, Spanish)
Amb.	Ambassador
Apdo	Apartado (apartment, Spanish)
Approx.	approximately
Apt	Apartment
AR	Arkansas
Assoc.	associate
Asst	assistant
Aug.	August
Av.	Avenida (Portuguese)
Avda	Avenida (Spanish)
Ave	Avenue
AZ	Arizona
BC	British Columbia
Bldg	Building
Blvd	Boulevard
BP	Boîte Postale
Bte	Boîte (P.O. Box)
bul.	bulvar (boulevard)
CA	California
CEO	Chief Executive Officer
Chair.	Chairman/woman, Chairmen/women
CIS	Commonwealth of Independent States
Cnr	Corner
CO	Colorado
Co.	Company, County
Col	Colonel
Col.	Colonia
Corpn	Corporation
CP	Case (Casa) Postale
Cres.	Crescent
Ct	Court
CT	Connecticut
Cttee	Committee
DC	District of Columbia
DE	Delaware
Dec.	December
Dept	Department
DF	Distrito Federal
Dir(s)	Director(s)
DNA	deoxyribonucleic acid
Dott.	Dottore
Dr	Doctor
Dr.	Drive
Drs	Doctorandus
ECOSOC	Economic and Social Council (United Nations)
Edif.	Edificio (building)
e-mail	electronic mail
Emer.	Emeritus
Eng.	Engineer
etc.	et cetera
EU	European Union
eV	eingetragener Verein
Exec.	Executive
Fax	facsimile
FL	Florida
Fr	Father
GA	Georgia
Gen.	General
GmbH	Gesellschaft mit beschränkter Haftung
h.c.	honoris causa (honorary)
HE	His (Her) Excellency
HI	Hawaii
HIV	Human immunodeficiency virus
HM	His (Her) Majesty
Hon.	Honourable; honorary
HRH	His (Her) Royal Highness
IA	Iowa
i.e.	id est (that is to say)
IL	Illinois
IN	Indiana
Inc	Incorporated
Ing.	Engineer (German, Spanish)
Int.	International
Ir	Engineer (Dutch)
Izq.	Izquierda (left, Spanish)
Jan.	January
Jr	Junior
km	kilometre
Lic.	Licenciado (Spanish)
Lt	Lieutenant
Ltd	Limited
m.	million
MA	Massachusetts
Maj.	Major
Man.	Manager, Managing
MBA	Master of Business Administration
MB	Manitoba
MD	Maryland
Mgr	Monseigneur, Monsignor
MI	Michigan
MN	Minnesota
MO	Missouri
MP	Member of Parliament
MS	Mississippi
n.a.	not available
Nat.	National
NC	North Carolina
NGO	non-governmental organization
NH	New Hampshire
NJ	New Jersey
No(.)	Numero, Number
Nov.	November
NSW	New South Wales
NV	Naamloze Vennootschap
NW	North West
NY	New York
Of.	Oficina (Spanish)
OH	Ohio
On.	Honourable (Italian)
ON	Ontario
PA	Pennsylvania
per.	pereulok (lane, alley, Russian)
Pl.	Place
PLC	Public Limited Company
POB	Post Office Box
PQ	Québec
PR	Public Relations
Preb.	Prebendal, Prebendary
Pres(.)	President, Presidents
Prof.	Professor
Pty	Proprietary
QC	Queen's Counsel
Qld	Queensland
q.v.	quod vide (see)
qq.v.	quae vide (see—plural)
Rd	Road
Rep.	Representative
Retd	Retired
Rev.	Reverend
RI	Rhode Island
Rm	Room
Rt Hon.	Right Honourable
Rt Rev.	Right Reverend
SA	South Australia
Sec.	Secretary
Sec.-Gen.	Secretary-General
Sq.	Square
Sr	Senior
St	Saint, Street
Str.	Strasse (street, German)
Treas.	Treasurer
TX	Texas
u./út	utca (street, Hungarian)
UK	United Kingdom (of Great Britain and Northern Ireland)
ul.	ulitsa (street, Polish, Russian)
UN	United Nations

ABBREVIATIONS

UNESCO	United Nations Educational, Scientific and Cultural Organization
UNHCR	United Nations High Commissioner for Refugees
UNICEF	United Nations Children's Fund
USA	United States of America
USSR	Union of Soviet Socialist Republics
UT	Utah
VA	Virginia
Vic	Victoria
vul. (vulitsa)	Street (Ukrainian)
WA	Washington (state), Western Australia
WHO	World Health Organization
WI	Wisconsin
YMCA	Young Men's Christian Association
YWCA	Young Women's Christian Association

International Telephone Codes

The following codes should be added to the relevant telephone and fax numbers listed in *The International Foundation Directory*. The code and number must be preceded by the International Dialling Code of the country from which you are calling.

Country	Code
Albania	355
Algeria	213
Argentina	54
Armenia	374
Australia	61
Austria	43
Azerbaijan	994
Bangladesh	880
Belarus	375
Belgium	32
Benin	229
Bermuda	1 441
Bolivia	591
Bosnia and Herzegovina	387
Botswana	267
Brazil	55
Brunei	673
Bulgaria	359
Burkina Faso	226
Canada	1
Chile	56
China (People's Republic)	86
Colombia	57
Costa Rica	506
Côte d'Ivoire	225
Croatia	385
Cyprus	357
Czech Republic	420
Denmark	45
Dominica	1 767
Dominican Republic	1 809
Ecuador	593
Egypt	20
El Salvador	503
Estonia	372
Finland	358
France	33
Gambia	220
Georgia	995
Germany	49
Ghana	233
Greece	30
Guatemala	502
Haiti	509
Honduras	504
Hong Kong	852
Hungary	36
Iceland	354
India	91
Indonesia	62
Iran	98
Ireland	353
Israel	972
Italy	39
Japan	81
Jordan	962
Kazakhstan	7
Kenya	254
Korea (Republic)	82
Kuwait	965
Kyrgyzstan	996
Latvia	371
Lebanon	961
Liechtenstein	423
Lithuania	370
Luxembourg	352
Macedonia	389
Malawi	265
Malaysia	60
Malta	356
Mexico	52
Moldova	373
Monaco	377
Mongolia	976
Morocco	212
Mozambique	258
Namibia	264
Nepal	977
Netherlands	31
Netherlands Antilles	599
New Zealand	64
Nicaragua	505
Nigeria	234
Norway	47
Pakistan	92
Palestinian Autonomous Areas	970
Panama	507
Paraguay	595
Peru	51
Philippines	63
Poland	48
Portugal	351
Puerto Rico	1 787
Romania	40
Russian Federation	7
Saudi Arabia	966
Senegal	221
Serbia and Montenegro	381
Slovakia	421
Slovenia	386
South Africa	27
Spain	34
Sri Lanka	94
Sweden	46
Switzerland	41
Taiwan	886
Tajikistan	992
Tanzania	255
Thailand	66
Trinidad and Tobago	1 868
Turkey	90
Ukraine	380
United Kingdom	44
United States of America	1
Uruguay	598
Uzbekistan	998
Vatican City	39
Venezuela	58
Zambia	260
Zimbabwe	263

Currencies and Exchange Rates

(at 31 December 2002, unless otherwise indicated)

Country	Unit	Value (1,000 units) £ sterling	US $	Euro €
Albania*	Lek	4.673	7.253	7.306
Algeria	Dinar (AD)	7.782	12.543	11.961
Argentina	New peso	186.875	301.205	287.217
Armenia	Dram	1.061	1.710	1.630
Australia	Dollar ($A)	351.284	566.200	539.907
Austria	Euro	650.639	1,048.700	1,000.000
Azerbaijan	Manat	0.127	0.204	0.195
Bangladesh	Taka	10.715	17.271	16.469
Belarus	Rouble	0.323	0.521	0.497
Belgium	Euro	650.639	1,048.700	1,000.000
Benin	CFA franc	0.992	1.599	1.524
Bermuda	Bermuda dollar (B$)	620.424	1,000.000	953.562
Bolivia	Boliviano	82.834	133.511	127.311
Bosnia and Herzegovina	Convertible Marka	302.487	487.548	511.292
Botswana	Pula	113.476	182.900	174.406
Brazil	Real	175.593	283.022	269.878
Brunei	Brunei dollar	357.284	575.871	549.128
Bulgaria	Lev	329.138	530.504	505.868
Burkina Faso	CFA Franc	0.992	1.599	1.524
Canada	Dollar (C$)	392.773	633.072	603.673
Chile	Peso	0.871	1.404	1.339
China, People's Repub. of	Yuan	74.955	120.812	115.202
Colombia	Peso	0.217	0.349	0.333
Costa Rica	Colón	1.638	2.640	2.518
Côte d'Ivoire	CFA franc	0.992	1.599	1.524
Croatia	Kuna	86.824	139.944	133.445
Cyprus	Cyprus pound	1,134.570	1,828.700	1,743.778
Czech Republic	Koruna	20.584	33.177	31.637
Denmark	Krone	87.603	141.199	134.642
Dominica	East Caribbean dollar	229.787	370.370	353.171
Dominican Republic	Peso	29.274	47.184	44.992
Ecuador	US dollar (US $)	620.424	1,000.000	953.562
Egypt	Egyptian pound	137.872	222.222	211.903
El Salvador	Colón	70.906	114.286	108.978
Estonia	Kroon	41.539	66.952	63.843
Finland	Euro	650.639	1,048.700	1,000.000
France	Euro	650.639	1,048.700	1,000.000
Gambia†	Dalasi	34.001	52.260	52.391
Georgia	Lari	296.854	478.469	456.250
Germany	Euro	650.639	1,048.700	1,000.000
Ghana	New cedi	0.074	0.119	0.113
Greece	Euro	650.639	1,048.700	1,000.000
Guatemala	Quetzal	79.468	128.087	122.139
Haiti	Gourde	16.497	26.589	25.354
Honduras	Lempira	36.661	59.090	56.460
Hong Kong	Hong Kong dollar (HK $)	79.562	128.238	122.283
Hungary	Forint	2.755	4.441	4.235
Iceland	Króna	7.699	12.410	11.834
India	Indian rupee	12.917	20.820	19.853
Indonesia	Rupiah	0.069	0.112	0.107
Iran	Rial	0.078	0.126	0.120
Ireland	Euro	650.639	1,048.700	1,000.000
Israel	New shekel	130.974	211.104	201.301
Italy	Euro	650.639	1,048.700	1,000.000
Japan	Yen	5.175	8.340	7.953
Jordan	Dinar (JD)	875.070	1,410.437	1,344.939
Kazakhstan	Tenge	4.013	6.468	6.168
Kenya	Kenya shilling	8.050	12.975	12.372
Korea, Repub. of	Won	0.523	0.843	0.804
Kuwait	Dinar (KD)	2,071.101	3,338.200	3,183.179
Kyrgyzstan	Som	13.460	21.694	20.687
Latvia	Lats	1,044.485	1,683.502	1,605.322
Lebanon	Lebanese pound	0.412	0.663	0.633
Liechtenstein	Swiss franc	447.378	721.085	687.598
Lithuania	Litas	187.360	301.987	289.620
Luxembourg	Euro	650.639	1,048.700	1,000.000

Country	Unit	Value (1,000 units)		
		£ sterling	US $	Euro €
Macedonia	New denar	10.541	16.991	16.202
Malawi	Kwacha	7.120	11.476	10.943
Malaysia	Ringgit	163.270	263.158	250.937
Malta	Maltese lira	1,555.652	2,507.400	2,309.960
Mexico	Peso	60.162	96.970	92.467
Moldova	Leu	44.887	72.348	68.989
Monaco	Euro	650.639	1,048.700	1,000.000
Mongolia	Tögrög (tugrik)	0.551	0.889	0.848
Morocco	Dirham	61.023	98.357	93.790
Mozambique	Metical	0.026	0.042	0.040
Namibia	Namibian dollar	71.808	115.741	110.366
Nepal	Nepalese rupee	7.924	12.771	12.783
Netherlands	Euro	650.639	1,048.700	1,000.000
Netherlands Antilles	Guilder (NA Fl.)	346.606	558.659	532.716
New Zealand	Dollar ($NZ)	326.653	526.500	502.050
Nicaragua	Gold córdoba	42.289	68.161	64.995
Nigeria	Naira	4.908	7.911	7.544
Norway	Krone	89.068	143.561	136.894
Pakistan	Pakistani rupee	10.599	17.084	16.291
Palestinian Autonomous Areas	n.a.	n.a.	n.a.	n.a.
Panama	Balboa	620.424	1,000.000	953.562
Paraguay	Guaraní	0.087	0.141	0.134
Peru	New sol	176.558	284.576	271.361
Philippines	Peso	11.685	18.834	17.959
Poland	New złoty	160.769	249.513	251.348
Portugal	Euro	650.639	1,048.700	1,000.000
Puerto Rico	US dollar (US $)	620.424	1,000.000	953.562
Romania	Leu	0.019	0.030	0.028
Russian Federation	New rouble	19.520	31.462	30.001
Saudi Arabia	Saudi riyal	165.667	267.023	254.623
Senegal	CFA franc	0.992	1.599	1.524
Serbia and Montenegro‡	Yugoslav dinar	10.204	16.447	15.684
Slovakia	Koruna	15.497	24.978	23.818
Slovenia	Tolar	2.806	4.523	4.313
South Africa	Rand	71.808	115.741	110.366
Spain	Euro	650.639	1,048.700	1,000.000
Sri Lanka	Sri Lanka rupee	6.414	10.339	9.858
Sweden	Krona	70.303	113.314	108.052
Switzerland	Swiss franc	447.378	721.085	687.598
Taiwan§	New Taiwan dollar (NT $)	17.849	28.769	27.433
Tajikistan¶	Somoni	217.098	338.673	343.343
Tanzania*	Tanzanian shilling	0.654	1.016	1.023
Thailand	Baht	14.378	23.174	22.098
Trinidad and Tobago	Trinidad and Tobago dollar (TT $)	98.714	159.106	151.718
Turkey‖	Turkish lira	0.000	0.001	0.001
Ukraine	Hryvnya	116.350	187.533	178.824
United Kingdom	Pound sterling (£)	1,000.000	1,611.800	1,536.951
United States of Amercia	US dollar (US $)	620.424	1,000.000	953.562
Uruguay	Peso uruguayo	22.810	36.765	35.057
Uzbekistan	Som	0.687	1.108	1.056
Vanuatu	Vatu	4.659	7.509	7.160
Vatican City	Euro	650.639	1,048.700	1,000.000
Venezuela	Bolívar	0.443	0.714	0.681
Zambia	Kwacha	0.143	0.231	0.220
Zimbabwe**	Zimbabwe dollar (Z.$)	11.702	18.170	18.479

* Figures refer to 29 November 2002.
† Figures refer to 28 June 2002.
‡ Montenegro uses the Euro.
§ Source: Directorate General of Budget, Accounting and Statistics, Executive Yuan.
¶ Figures refer to 31 October 2002.
‖ £ sterling: 0.00037746; US $ 0.00060838; Euro 0.00058013.
** Figures refer to 30 August 2002.

PART ONE
Introductory Essays

Foundations and the Third Sector in International Perspective—an Overview

HELMUT ANHEIER

Introduction

In recent years there has been a renewed interest in the broad range of philanthropic institutions that operate outside the confines of the market and the state (Salamon et al., 1999). Referred to as the 'voluntary', 'non-profit', 'non-governmental', or 'third' sector, this set of institutions includes a vast array of entities—charities and social service providers, interest and lobby organizations of all kinds, universities, social clubs, professional organizations, museums, human rights organizations, environmental groups, international development and relief organizations, sports clubs, marriage counselling centres, art history societies, and many more.

Foundations are part of this third sector, but are none the less seen as a separate category. Like the third sector, foundations seem to have experienced a veritable renaissance and increased attention paid to them by policy-makers (Renz, Mandler and Tran, 1997; Anheier and Toepler, 1999). Already by the mid-1980s, and in countries as different as the United Kingdom, the USA, Japan, Italy, Germany, Sweden, Turkey and Brazil, observers had begun to report the end of the relative decline in the overall size and importance of the foundation sector—a trend that had characterized the previous two decades (Leat, 1992; Odendahl, 1987; Boris, 1987; Neuhoff, 1992; Biermann, Cannon and Klainberg, 1992; Arias Foundation, 1992). Some analysts suggested the possibility of a new, third 'foundation wave', after a first growth period in the late middle ages, alongside the rise of commerce and finance, and a second period of growth in the late 19th century, following the industrial revolution.

What are the reasons behind the growth in the importance and scale of foundations, and the third sector more generally? Political stability, an increase in demand for social, educational and cultural services of all kinds, and economic prosperity are certainly significant factors behind this growth. Yet a more immediate reason is the way in which foundations and voluntary organizations have been suggesting themselves as alternatives to, or instruments of, the modern welfare state. In this context, foundations have become more attractive options in recent years. Politically, they appear more acceptable tools to governments that are less certain about their own roles and ambitions, and willing to have institutions like foundations occupy more 'institutional space'. In contrast to previous historical periods, the state seems less challenged by foundations—to the contrary, national governments and international organizations alike welcome foundation involvement in a broad range of activities and fields. Economically, foundations seem an appropriate vehicle to solve a number of corporate challenges. For the German, Austrian or Swiss *Mittelstand* (middle class), foundations are one way to solve the succession problem for owner-managers of medium-scale enterprises, and to help provide stability in terms of ownership and control. For large international corporations, foundations are a tool to express corporate citizenship and concerns for the public good. And for government and corporations alike, foundations may be a more neutral way to handle specific problems, e.g. the issue of how to deal with assets of Holocaust victims, which have been held in Swiss banks for many decades.

Culturally, foundations are an expression of what could be called 'bourgeois confidence', particularly among private citizens. The vastly expanded middle class in most developed countries seems to have regained the self-confidence and institutional trust it lost during the first half of the 20th century, particularly in Europe. There appears to be a greater acceptance of private actors in the provision of public goods and quasi-public goods. At the same time, the state is no longer expected to be the sole provider of social security, culture, education and many other areas that previously have been lodged with the public sector.

Thus, foundations and third-sector institutions more generally have been discovered and rediscovered by policy-makers, corporations and private citizens alike. For the state, non-profit organizations and foundations tend to be vehicles either for privatizing certain tasks that are not as easily or as efficiently accomplished within the bounds of the regular state administration, or for leveraging private money for public purposes. Accordingly, some countries have begun to enact legislation to encourage the establishment of foundations. At the European level, the European Commission of the European Union supports the establishment and operations of foundations in fostering a 'New Europe' (European Commission, 1997). Moreover, the European Commission calls for the introduction of the European Foundation and Association Statute as a legal instrument that would allow foundations to operate at a European-wide level (Kendall and Anheier, 1999).

Yet, it is not only national and international government agencies that have discovered foundations. Local communities and municipalities in Europe are increasingly turning to the idea of foundations to deliver services. Indeed, community foundations have been among the fastest growing segments of American philanthropy over the past two decades (Renz et al., 1997), and are spreading in most European countries as well (Walkenhorst, 2000). Corporations, too, are making more frequent use of foundations. They may establish foundations as part of their corporate giving and outreach strategy. Less frequently, foundations may assume legal ownership of significant parts of corporate assets, and, in some cases, they even officially become owner of the profit-making enterprise.

Of course, the most frequent founders of foundations are private citizens. In the USA and in the United Kingdom, virtually all foundations are set up by individuals; in Switzerland, individuals founded 95% of foundations under federal jurisdiction, of which 5% are primarily grant-making, with the great majority either operating or of a mixed type. In Germany, likewise, the great majority of foundations are founded by individuals, followed by those established by public authorities and corporations.

The Modern Foundation: An American Phenomenon?

Historically, foundations are among the oldest existing social institutions, and show great longevity. It is, however, difficult to point to the precise moment when the first foundation was established, or which of the existing foundations today can look back farthest in time. Scholars, however, do not see the origin of foundations in early medieval times, but trace the 'genealogy' of foundations back to antiquity (Coing, 1981). These roots include Plato's Academy in Greece (Whitaker 1974, p. 31), and the library of Alexandria in Egypt (Coon 1938, p. 20).

THE EUROPEAN EXPERIENCE

Throughout the Middle Ages, foundations were largely synonymous with religious institutions operating in the fields of health and education, and operating as orphanages, hospitals, schools, colleges and the like. Integral part of the feudal social structures, the governance and operations of foundation boards frequently combined both aristocracy and clergy. Indeed, foundations were the prototypical institutional mechanism for the delivery of educational, health and social services under the feudal order. From the High Middle Ages on, however, could be found an increasing presence in the emerging urban middle class among founders of foundations, which were often linked, and dedicated, to particular trades or crafts guilds (Schiller, 1969). Gradually, the emerging bourgeoisie began to replace gentry and clergy as the dominant founder group—a trend the process of industrialization amplified throughout the 19th century.

As Smith and Borgmann (2001) suggest, the role and *raison d'être* of foundations in Europe underwent several dramatic changes between the 16th and the 20th centuries. The Reformation era did away with the medieval ideal of community and triggered the complex process of state-building, in which foundations were no longer part of a *res publica christiania*.[1] Instead, foundations had to compete for space in an increasingly secular public sphere. Only some foundations succeeded in this task, and many, if not most, became victims of secularization and state expansion. At the same time, new foundations emerged, fuelled by the interests of the crown, landed élite and the emerging middle class, particularly urban merchants and craftsmen.

As the nation state developed, the role of foundations changed from that of a traditional, religion-based charitable institution to a somewhat more pluralist provider of quasi-public goods, used by special groups and for particular interests. The numerous guild-based and trade-related foundations in the growing cities of the 17th and 18th centuries are perhaps the best example to illustrate how foundations became a private tool for serving public needs. This re-positioning, however, had the result that, throughout the 19th and early 20th centuries, the role of foundations continued to be challenged to the extent that the consolidated nation state assumed responsibility for and over other parts and groups of society.

During much of the 19th century, the development of foundations depended on the political solution, if any, that could be found between the aspirations of an expanding, and frequently struggling, nation state on the one hand, and the interests of a more pluralist civil society on the other. The latter included, in particular, the new economic élite, the urban middle class and the professions as the major force in the establishment of foundations. From a supply-side perspective, the development of foundations also depended on the extent to which the proceeds of market transactions could be transformed into philanthropic assets. In other words, even where public 'space' for foundations existed, countries and regions differed in terms of philanthropic entrepreneurship, whereby public-minded merchants, industrialists or professionals set up foundations.

While the potential supply of founders is difficult to estimate, the 19th century growth of foundations in Britain, Scandinavia and the Netherlands, and even in countries with autocratic regimes like Germany, the Austro-Hungarian Empire and Italy, suggest that the supply-side considerations were much less of a constraint than restrictive state policies. The urban middle class at the local level supported much of the growth in the number of foundations under aristocratic and autocratic regimes. Most foundations remained local in character, often with well-defined circles of beneficiaries. For example, the foundation directory for the city of Vienna from the late 19th century lists 2,148 foundations, the great majority of which serve highly specialized and localized needs ranging from welfare provisions to education support (Markhoff, 1895).

In other countries, however, such as France, the state succeeded in establishing itself as the primary representative of the public will *and* in keeping foundations at bay through the use of anti-clerical, anti-liberal policies (Archambault, 1996). Yet not all nation states were as successful as France in establishing a hegemonic regime across and against diverse political and cultural interests. More frequently, the emerging nation state remained weak, failed in its attempt to consolidate power, and had to forge political compromises with existing power bases and their institutions. As a result, traditional foundations remained strong (for example in Italy and Spain) and many new ones emerged (for example in Switzerland and Germany).

In other cases, early forms of private-public partnerships began to emerge between state and foundations, with Sweden and the Netherlands as prime examples, leading to a general expansion and consolidation. Only in Britain, however, did the formation of a relatively independent set of foundations develop without too much state interference. The 19th century philanthropists and industrialists provided welfare services, supported the arts, and even championed causes overseas, for example the Anti-Slavery Society (Leat, 1992).

Two key insights emerge from this tour through European foundation history. First, at least since the reformation period, foundations have operated at or close to the major 'fault lines' of society: secularization in the 17th century, republicanism and political liberalization in the 18th century, industrialization and the social upheavals

[1] The history of foundations in the Islamic world is substantially different and shows more continuity from the Middle Ages to the early modern period.

of the 19th and early 20th centuries. Depending on the sustainability and extent of the political compromises that were found or that emerged, foundations occupied more or less public space, either flourished or declined in numbers and importance, and either helped shape the social order or moved to more marginal positions.

Second, throughout this historical development, certain patterns or path dependencies emerged that accounted for more or less distinct national or regional traditions. Britain and France offer perhaps the best examples for the extreme range of persistent policy patterns across Europe. In the British case, the Statute of Charitable Uses of 1601 has functioned for 400 years to delineate the purpose and limitations of charity even though its actual definition and legal application continues to be shaped by prevailing practices and common law traditions. The Protestant gentry of the 17th century found the Statute appealing for its philanthropic aspirations, as did the industrialists of the 19th century who wanted to support educational institutions to improve the living standards of the poor. In France we find a different pattern that essentially sought to prevent the development of foundations as a modern tool of civil society. The *Loi de Chapelier* of 1791 established state monopoly over the public interest, which meant that foundations lost their legal status altogether; it was only at the end of the 19th century that foundation regained some ground, albeit under strict state supervision (Archambault et al., 1999).

In most European countries, foundations were caught in a complicated political conundrum, from which few foundation sectors managed to escape unharmed. It would have taken a consolidated state, a self-confident middle class and enlightened élite, in addition to the increasing economic prosperity of the 19th century, to bring about a full renaissance of foundations. Concerns over the *main morte* remained (France, Belgium, Luxembourg), as did social-democratic reservations that saw foundations as undemocratic (Finland, Sweden), or as paternalistic instruments of the Victorian age (Ireland, Britain). Yet whatever patterns and path dependencies had developed until the early 20th century, nothing could have prepared European foundations for the upheavals that two world wars, economic crises, the Holocaust, and the establishment of communist regimes in the central and eastern parts of the continent would bring to most countries.

Of course, foundations in some countries such as Switzerland or Sweden were spared the devastation, but unknown numbers of foundations across the continent did not manage to survive confiscation, destruction, capital depletion or loss of property, and many faced legal and frequently illegal dissolution. In other words, the variations of foundation sector size (Table 1) reflect not only long-term developments, but significantly also the impact of the two major wars in the last century. It is no historical accident that, of the countries with large foundation sectors, most escaped the destructive force of the Second World War, e.g. Sweden, Switzerland and Liechtenstein.

The impact of war was perhaps nowhere greater than in the central and eastern parts of the continent. The philanthropic élite and much of the middle class that had been central in building and maintaining foundations in the late 19th and early 20th centuries were displaced and often killed. The Stalinist and state socialist regimes that followed saw no need for foundations, and, with few exceptions, confiscated the remaining foundation property that war and Nazism had not yet destroyed. It is therefore not surprising that much of the current impetus to create and re-establish foundation communities in this part of Europe relies on external support, capital and know-how, at least initially, and perhaps for some time to come.

THE AMERICAN EXPERIENCE

By contrast, the American experience has been very different. Significantly, while Europe's foundations faced great uncertainty and frequent decline, the American foundation moved to the forefront of organized philanthropy. While foundations in various forms have existed throughout American history, perhaps the most important development occurred in the USA at the beginning of the 20th century, with the emergence of large-scale philanthropic foundations associated with names like Carnegie and Rockefeller. Historians like Karl and Katz (1981; 1987) have shown that the first of these new foundations did not adopt the more traditional charity approach of directly addressing social and other public problems, but aimed at exploring the causes of such problems systematically, with the aim of generating long-term solutions rather than just alleviating them (see Bulmer, 1999; McCarthy, 1989). Given the significance of this new orientation of foundation work and the large amount of resources that went into it, the first of these foundations came to symbolize a new era of institutional philanthropy pushing the more traditional aspects of foundation work to the background.

Perhaps because of the importance of these developments, the modern foundation is often perceived as a genuinely American invention, as a 'unique American answer' to the problem of excess wealth in a society with limited income redistribution. Although foundations existed before, it was suggested that 'in no other civilization have such instruments been utilized so widely as in the United States. It may even be said that the foundation had become the ascendant American device for disposing of large accumulations of surplus wealth' (Lindeman, 1988, p.8).

It becomes clear that the rise of the American foundation in the early part of the 20th century highlights their financial redistributive function, and neglects, if not outright discards, the service delivery function that was, and indeed remains, one of the major *raisons d'être* of the European foundations. It would indeed appear that Americans in the past have shown a high propensity to transfer excess wealth to private foundations serving public purposes; moreover, against the backdrop of low government social spending and a rudimentary social welfare system, foundations in the USA occupy a more prominent role in public life than in other countries. In addition, the international presence of such philanthropic giants as the Ford and Rockefeller Foundations has further emphasized this particular variant of 'American Exceptionalism' not only in the USA, but all over the globe.

However, public and scholarly concentration on a limited number of large grant-makers as the 'prototypical' American foundations has led to a monolithic view of the US foundation community, and may have contributed to a certain mystification of the American foundation phenomenon. In this still widespread view, there are numerous large-scale foundations in the US that are professionally organized, and which thrive in the absence of competition from an activist state. Compared to the perceived lack of proper incentives and the administrative barriers that foundations face in other parts of the world (see van der Ploeg, 1999), the USA appears to be the *El Dorado* of foundation activity.

The tendency to emphasize the US foundation experience holds two potential dangers. First, the actual economic importance of foundations relative to government spending may be over-estimated. Although US foundations held nearly $449,000m. in assets in 1999 (Foundation Center, 2001), total foundation assets none the less represent only a very small fraction of the national wealth (see Margo, 1992). Against this background, Salamon (1992a, p. 17) observed that 'although the overall scale of foundation assets seems quite large, it pales in comparison to the assets of other institutions in American society'. The second potential danger lies in downplaying other philanthropic traditions and styles. Other countries have developed a rich tapestry of foundation types, and can look back to a long history of philanthropic traditions, as is the case of Europe. How then does the US experience compare internationally? The following sections will attempt to summarize what is known about foundations internationally in terms of size, prevailing types, and relationship with the state. To do this, a brief look at the different forms foundations and related organizations can take needs to be taken.

Definitions and Types

Our understanding of foundations is complicated by a highly complex, sometimes confusing, terminology: what is defined as a foundation in one country may not qualify as such in another (Anheier, 2001). Moreover, not all organizations labelled 'foundation' are in fact foundations. In Central and Eastern Europe, many foundations are either membership associations or corporations. The German political foundations such as the Friedrich-Ebert-Stiftung or the Konrad-Adenauer-Stiftung are registered associations with no significant assets of their own; their operating budgets are largely covered by annual subventions from the German government (Beise, 1998). In the Netherlands, the distinction between foundation (asset-based) and association (membership-based) has become largely indistinguishable in the field of education and social services. In Switzerland, some foundations are primarily investment trusts for families, pension schemes for corporations, or local sickness funds.

The definition of foundations varies from one country to another (Anheier, 2001; Anheier and Toepler, 1999), not along one primary axis, but frequently in several dimensions. There are legal definitions that reflect either common law traditions with an emphasis on trusteeship (e.g. the USA, the United Kingdom), or civil law traditions (e.g. Switzerland and Germany), with the important distinction between legal personalities based on either membership or assets (Van der Ploeg, 1999). Other definitions bring in additional aspects, such as type of founder (private or public), purpose (charitable or other), activities (grant-making or operating), revenue structure (single or multiple funding sources), asset type (own endowment or regular allocations), and the degree of independence from either the state, business or family interest.

To cut across this terminological tangle, a modification of the structural/operational definition developed by Salamon and Anheier (1997) for non-profit organizations generally was proposed by Anheier (2001). Accordingly, a foundation has the following characteristics:

1. It must be an asset-based entity, financial or otherwise. The foundation must rest on an original deed, typically a charter that gives the entity both intent of purpose and relative permanence as an organization.
2. It must be a private entity. Foundations are institutionally separate from government, and are 'non-governmental' in the sense of being structurally separate from public agencies. Therefore, foundations do not exercise governmental authority and are outside direct majoritarian control.
3. It must be a self-governing entity. Foundations are equipped to control their own activities. Some private foundations are tightly controlled either by governmental agencies or corporations, and function as parts of these other institutions, even though they are structurally separate.
4. It must be a non-profit-distributing entity. Foundations are not to return profits generated by either use of assets or commercial activities to their owners, members, trustees or directors. In this sense, commercial goals neither principally nor primarily guide foundations.
5. It must serve a public purpose. Foundations should do more than serve the needs of a narrowly-defined social group or category, such as members of a family, or a closed circle of beneficiaries. Foundations are private assets that serve a public purpose.[2]

Grant-making foundations are usually regarded as the prototype of the modern foundation, which is largely a reflection of the US experience and its post-war dominance in the field of philanthropy (Toepler, 1999). Whereas in the USA more than 99% of the existing 50,000 foundations are grant-making, the majority of foundations in Europe are either operating, or pursue their objectives by combining grant-making activities with the running of their own institutions, programmes and projects. Historically, of course, foundations were operating institutions primarily, e.g. hospitals, orphanages, schools and universities, although many did distribute money (alms-giving) and contributions in kind (food or wood, for example). By contrast, the sharp distinction between grant-making and operating foundations emerged much later historically, and is for both the USA and Europe largely a product of the 19th and early 20th centuries (Karl and Katz 1987; Bulmer, 1999). Behind the complexity of forms, are none the less several basic categories:

Firstly, grant-making foundations, i.e. endowed organizations that primarily engage in grant-making for specified purposes. Examples include the Ford Foundation in the USA, the Leverhulme Trust in the United Kingdom, the Volkswagen Stiftung in Germany, the Bernard van Leer Foundation in the Netherlands and the Carlsbergfondet in Denmark.

Secondly, operating foundations, i.e. foundations that primarily operate their own programmes and projects. Examples include the Institut Pasteur in France, the Pescatore Foundation in Luxembourg, which runs a home for senior citizens, and the Calouste Gulbenkian Foundation in Portugal (although this could also fall into the mixed category—see below).

Thirdly, mixed foundations, i.e. foundations that operate their own programmes and projects and engage in grant-making on a significant scale. Examples include the Fundación BBV in Spain and the Robert Bosch Stiftung in

[2] Of course, as with any comparative definition, some problems remain. Specifically, there are three major areas where the definition proposed here encounters difficulties: firstly, where foundations engage with a market economy and change into primarily economic actors; secondly, where foundations become instruments of the state; and thirdly, where they become a dynastic means of asset protection and control (see Anheier, 2001, pp 42–47).

Germany.

Non-governmental organizations (NGOs) would differ from a foundation in the sense that no asset base or original deed would be required. They would be either based on membership, i.e. associations, or some other corporate form such as limited liability corporation or co-operative. Like foundations, however, NGOs have no owners as such (see Salamon and Anheier, 1997). Operating foundations are closer to the NGO form than they are to grant-making foundations.

A Profile of Foundations

There is great variation in the number of foundations (see Table 1), ranging from a high of more than 50,000 in the USA, 20,000–30,000 in Sweden, around 14,000 in Denmark, 13,500 in Japan, to a low of 30 in Ireland. The data suggest that there are around 80,000–90,000 foundations in Europe (including Greece and Turkey), or an average of around 4,500 per country. However, only foundations in the USA and the United Kingdom are almost exclusively grant-making. Around 50% of foundations in Finland and Germany are grant-making. In most other countries we find that the majority of foundations are of a mixed type. They are both operating institutions and grant-making, thereby combining service delivery with philanthropic giving.[3]

Clearly, the economic weight of running institutions, programmes and projects tends to be more important than the actual grant-making activities. For example, estimates of employment in German grant-making foundations in 1995 ranged between 3,000–5,000 employees, whereas operating foundations employed over 90,000. The majority of German foundations, however, employ no staff at all: nine out of 10 foundations are run and managed by volunteers only. In Scandinavia, similar results can be found: only a few of Denmark's 14,000 foundations have paid employment at all, and only eight of the over 2,500 Finnish foundations have more than 10 full-time staff.

[3] The data reported in this section draw on a comparative analysis by Anheier (2001), which itself uses data from individual country reports in Schlüter, Then and Walkenhorst (2001). The authors of the country studies are W. Bachstein and C. Badlet (Austria), M. Maree and S. Mousny (Belgium), G. Hellman and J. Parving (Denmark), K. Herbets (Finland), E. Archambault (France), R. Strachwitz (Germany), S. Tsakraklides (Greece), F. Donoghue (Ireland), G. Barbetta and M. Demarie (Italy), M. Wanger (Liechtenstein), A. Bonn and A. Schmitt (Luxembourg), A. Burger, P. Dekker and V. Veldheer (the Netherlands), H. Lorentzen (Norway), C. Monjardino (Portugal), J. Olabuenaga (Spain), F. Wijkstroem (Sweden), M. Steinert (Switzerland), D. Aydin (Turkey), Diana Leat (United Kingdom) and Francis Pinter (Central and Eastern Europe). These reports are in Schlüter et al. (2001, pp. 83–317). Data for Canada are from the Canadian Centre for Philanthropy; for Japan from the Japan Foundation Center; for the USA from the Foundation Center, New York.

Table 1: Number and Types of Foundations

Country	Number of Foundations	Relative Share of Grant-making Foundations	Relative Share of Operating Foundations	Mixed Type of Foundations
Austria	803			majority
Belgium	310	few		majority
Canada	1,353	great majority		very few
Denmark	*c.* 14,000			
Finland	2,522	50%	30%	20%
France	404		majority	
Germany	8,312	*c.* 50%	*c.* 25%	*c.* 25%
Greece	*c.* 500	few	majority	few
Ireland	30	27%	70%	3%
Italy	*c.* 1,300	15%	39%	43%
Japan	13,553	not known		
Liechtenstein	*c.* 600		majority	
Luxembourg	143		majority	
Netherlands	*c.* 1,000	majority		
Norway	2,989			majority
Portugal	664		majority	
Spain	*c.* 6,000	5%	95%	
Sweden	*c.* 20,000–30,000			
Switzerland	*c.* 8,000	5%	majority	
Turkey	9,326			majority
UK	*c.* 8,800	almost 100%	very few	
USA	50,201	majority	5.7%	

c. = approximately.

Asset estimates are the most difficult data to obtain on foundations, especially cross-nationally, given the influence of different valuation measures and techniques. Irrespective of these difficulties, available estimates reveal significant cross-national variations. For example, the assets held by the 20 largest Japanese foundations amount to 443,000m. yen, whereas the 20 largest US foundations are, with 12,000,000m. yen, about 28 times larger (Japan Foundation Center, 2002). The assets of German foundations are €354 per head; the figure is higher for foundations in the United Kingdom (€536), and over €1,000 for foundations in Italy, Sweden and Switzerland. Finally, the highest per head assets are reported for Liechtenstein, with a figure that exceeds €12,000 because of offshore foundation assets. The high amount of assets per head for Italian foundations is a function of the privatization of the banking sector in Italy (Law 218/1990, or Amato law). Most public savings banks were previously quasi-public, 'nationalized' non-profit organizations, and became stock corporations as a result of the 1990 reforms (see Barbetta, 1999). The shares in the privatized banks became the endowment for the new 'foundations of banking origin', which, not surprisingly, have significant assets, of between €50,000m.–€75,000m. combined.

Foundation sectors by country can be grouped into three classes: small, medium and large, with the middle group further divided into subcategories. Given the data situation, it is not possible to construct a strict and consistent ranking of countries in terms of foundation sector size. Yet, taken together, the various size indicators suggest three groups or clusters, and even such an admittedly crude classification involves some qualitative judgements. The relative size of the foundation sectors of European countries can be classified as follows:

1. Countries with a small foundation sector: Austria, Belgium, France, Greece, Ireland, Luxembourg, and countries of Central and Eastern Europe.
2. Countries with a medium–small foundation sector: Portugal, Spain and Turkey; and countries with a medium–large foundation sector: Denmark, Finland, Germany, the Netherlands, Norway, Japan, Canada and the United Kingdom.
3. Countries with a large foundation sector: the USA, Italy, Liechtenstein, Sweden and Switzerland.

Foundation Areas of Activity

Yet, what do foundations do? Two fields clearly dominate the profile of foundation activity: education and research, with an average of 30% of foundation activity, and social service (25%). Together, both fields account for over one-half of foundation activities so measured. In fact, education and research, and social services are the main categories of foundation activity in eight of the 15 countries studied. Adding health care, with an average of 17% of foundation activity, pushes the total share up to 71%. In other words, two-thirds of foundations operate in just three fields, the same fields that also dominate the non-profit sector at large (Salamon et al., 1999).

The field of art and culture accounts for the next largest share of foundation activities. It is the most important area of activity of foundations in Spain, with 44% of all foundations involved in this field, and is relatively prominent in Finland, Germany, Italy, Portugal and Switzerland. Some countries show clear concentration in one field in particular: this is the case for health-care foundations in France, housing foundations in Ireland, international activities in the Netherlands, and cultural foundations in Spain. Such concentrations are the result of specific historical developments, e.g. urgent demand for affordable housing in early 20th century Ireland, or institutional effect, such as the prominence of large health-care research foundations in France, e.g. the Institut Pasteur and Institut Curie (Archambault et al., 1999).

Growth Patterns of Foundations

Foundations are largely a product of the period following the Second World War, and a veritable foundation 'boom' seems to have set in, beginning in the late 1980s. More foundations were created in the 1980s and 1990s than in the three preceding decades, and more of the foundations existing in the early 2000s were established after 1950 than prior to that date. However, this growth is not evenly spread across countries.

1. *High-Growth Countries, such as the USA, Italy, Spain, Turkey and Portugal.* From 1980 onwards, the USA experienced one of the most sustained expansions in the growth in the number of foundations as well as the amounts of assets held. In Europe, with the exception of Turkey, high-growth countries are those in which foundation law underwent a major reform: in Italy, Law 218/1990 (or Amato law), in Spain, the Foundation Act, 1994, and in Portugal, Law 460/1977, with the proven effect that foundations increased sharply in number. In Portugal, where 56% of all foundations were established after 1980, and Spain (over 90% of cultural foundations and 70% of educational foundations), the rapid growth could also be a delayed effect of the democratization in the 1970s, when both countries shed their autocratic regimes. The high growth is also a reflection of the rapid economic development of the countries of Europe's south, in particular Portugal, Spain and Turkey (see Baloglu, 1996).
2. *Medium-Growth Countries, such as Finland, Germany, Greece, Switzerland and the United Kingdom.* With the exception of Belgium and Greece, these are countries with already sizeable foundation sectors, and recent growth rates of 20–30 per decade add to a relatively high base. Finland, Germany, Switzerland and the United Kingdom are high-income countries with stable political systems. We can assume that the foundation boom of recent years is in large measure a function of political stability and economic prosperity, amplified by a more self-confident middle class. Greece has a small foundation sector, and the expansion is probably the result of increased economic prosperity and greater political stability.
3. *Low-Growth Countries, such as Austria, Belgium and France.* All three of these countries have relatively small foundation sectors. Japanese foundations grew significantly between 1980 and the early 1990s, but they have largely stagnated since, due to difficult economic conditions. At the same time, however, the regulatory environment has become more encouraging for foundations in Japan generally. The same cannot be said for countries like France. The country's relatively few foundations are, on average, older, with one-half pre-dating the post-war period, and with fewer foundations being established during the expansion period

that began in the 1980s. Similarly, growth rates have changed little in Austria and Belgium over the last four decades, even though a slight upward trend is discernible. The reasons for the slow growth are legal and procedural, as the establishment of foundations in France or Belgium is highly regulated and complicated, providing relatively few incentives for potential founders.

The Third Sector

How do the profile and growth patterns of foundations compare to that of the third sector at large?[4] Of particular interest were four critical dimensions of such organizations: paid full-time equivalent employment, volunteer employment converted to full-time equivalent, operating expenditures and revenue sources (government payments, private fees and charges, and private philanthropy). There are a number of major conclusions about the scope, structure and financing of non-profit activity in the more than 20 countries covered by the Johns Hopkins Comparative Nonprofit Sector Project (see Salamon et al., 1999).

In the first place, the third sector was found to be a major economic force. In the 22 countries covered by the Johns Hopkins Project, the sector constitutes a US $1,100,000m. industry that employs close to 19m. full-time equivalent employees. Moreover, the sector attracts a considerable amount of volunteer effort. Indeed, within the countries studied, an average of 28% of the population report contributing their time to non-profit organizations. This translates into another 10.6m. full-time equivalent employees, increasing the total number of full-time equivalent non-profit employees in the 22 project countries to 29.6m.

As shown in Figure 1, the third sector is larger in the more developed countries and much less in evidence in Central and South America and Central Europe. Perhaps one of the most surprising outcomes is that the USA, commonly thought to be the seedbed of non-profit activity, ranks only fifth in terms of paid employment as a percentage of non-agricultural employment, after the Netherlands, Ireland, Belgium, and Israel. The developed Western European countries turned out to have the largest third sectors among all project countries, surpassing their Eastern European neighbours by a ratio of about 7:1. In fact, the size of the third sectors in former communist

[4] The data reported in this section are from the Johns Hopkins Comparative Non-profit Sector Project, Salamon et al. (1999), and the following paragraphs draw from the overview chapter by Salamon and Anheier in that volume. For more information about the data collection methodology see Salamon et al., 1999.

Figure 1: Economic Size of the Third Sector, 1995

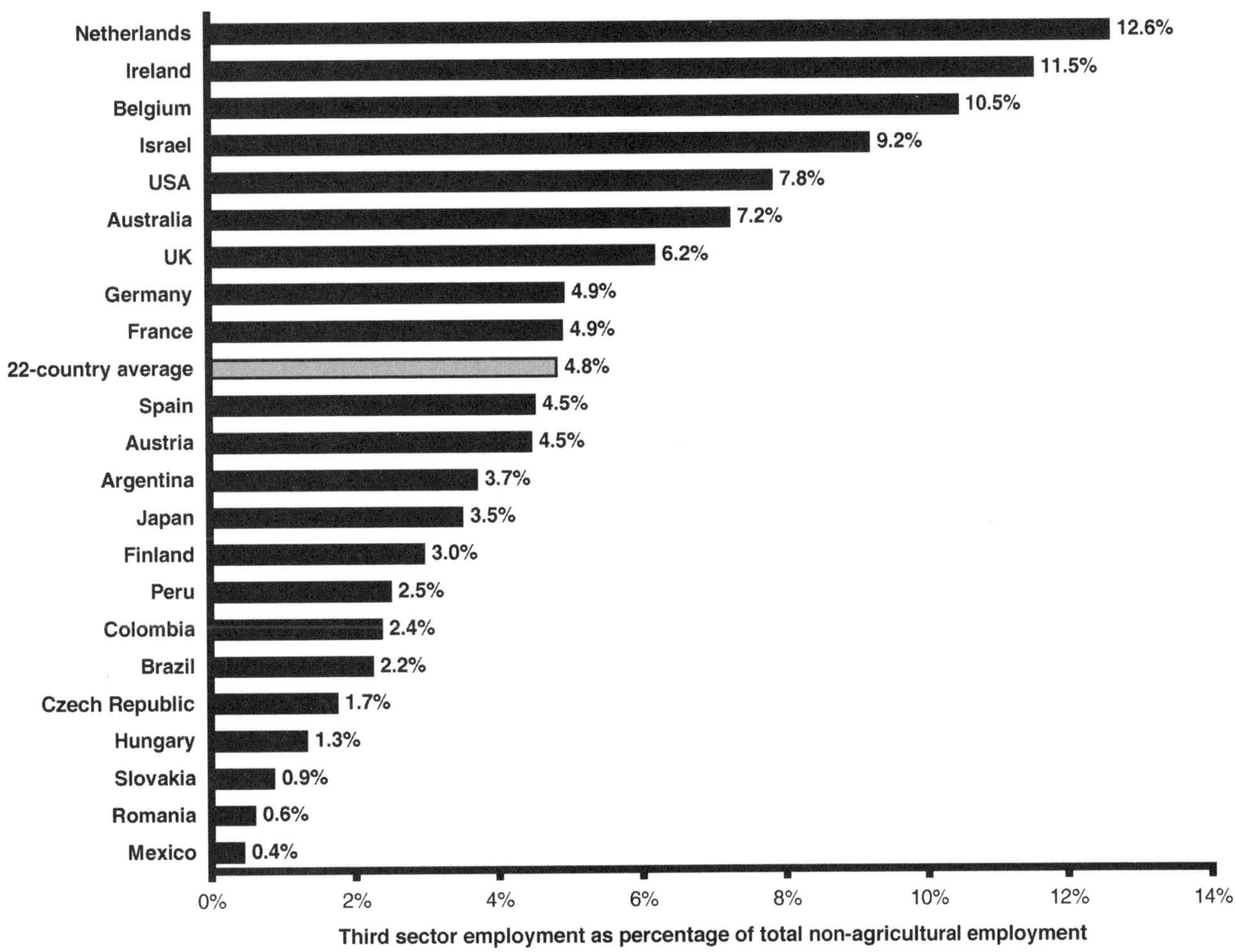

Source: Johns Hopkins Comparative Nonprofit Sector Project

countries turned out to be surprisingly low, accounting for a mere 1% of non-agricultural labour.[5]

By comparison, Central and South American countries are located in-between, as far as the size of their third sectors is concerned, but there is also substantial variability among them. On the one hand, Argentina has a third sector that is only slightly smaller than that of many Western European countries on the employment measure, and on a par with Western Europe on the value added measure. On the other hand, Mexico falls below even the Eastern European level on both measures.

Two-thirds of all non-profit employment is concentrated in the three traditional fields of welfare services: education (accounting for 30% of total non-profit employment), health (20%) and social services (18%), as shown in Figure 2. Western Europe in particular displays a significant concentration of non-profit employment in welfare services, in large part a reflection of the historic prominence organized religion traditionally maintained in this particular field. In Central and Eastern Europe, on the other hand, the recreation and culture field plays a much more important part in the employment base of the third sector, constituting one-third of all full-time equivalent workers employed in non-profit associations in the region. In Central and South America the education field dominates the employment base of the third sector, again an indication of the strong influence the Catholic Church historically maintained in the field. Finally in the USA, Japan, Australia and Israel, the major area of non-profit employment is in the health field, which accounts, on average, for 35% of total non-profit employment in these countries, followed closely by education (accounting for 29% of total non-profit employment.

[5] Since these countries have relatively larger agrarian employment than their Western European counterparts, the gap between East and West would widen even further if total employment were used as the basis for a comparison.

Figure 2: Composition of the Third Sector, by Region, 1995

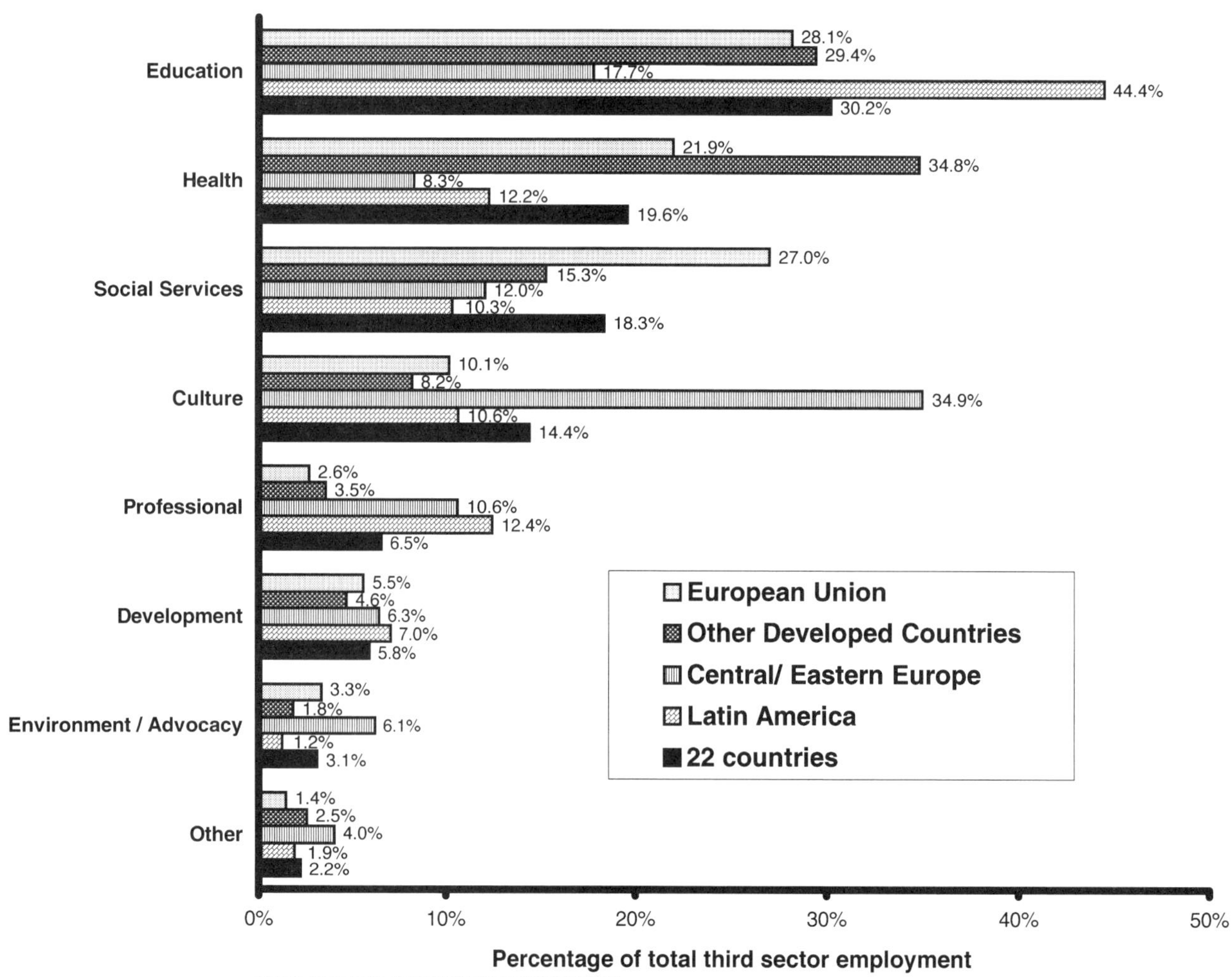

Source: Johns Hopkins Comparative Nonprofit Sector Project

Figure 3: Third sector Cash Revenue, by Country, 1995

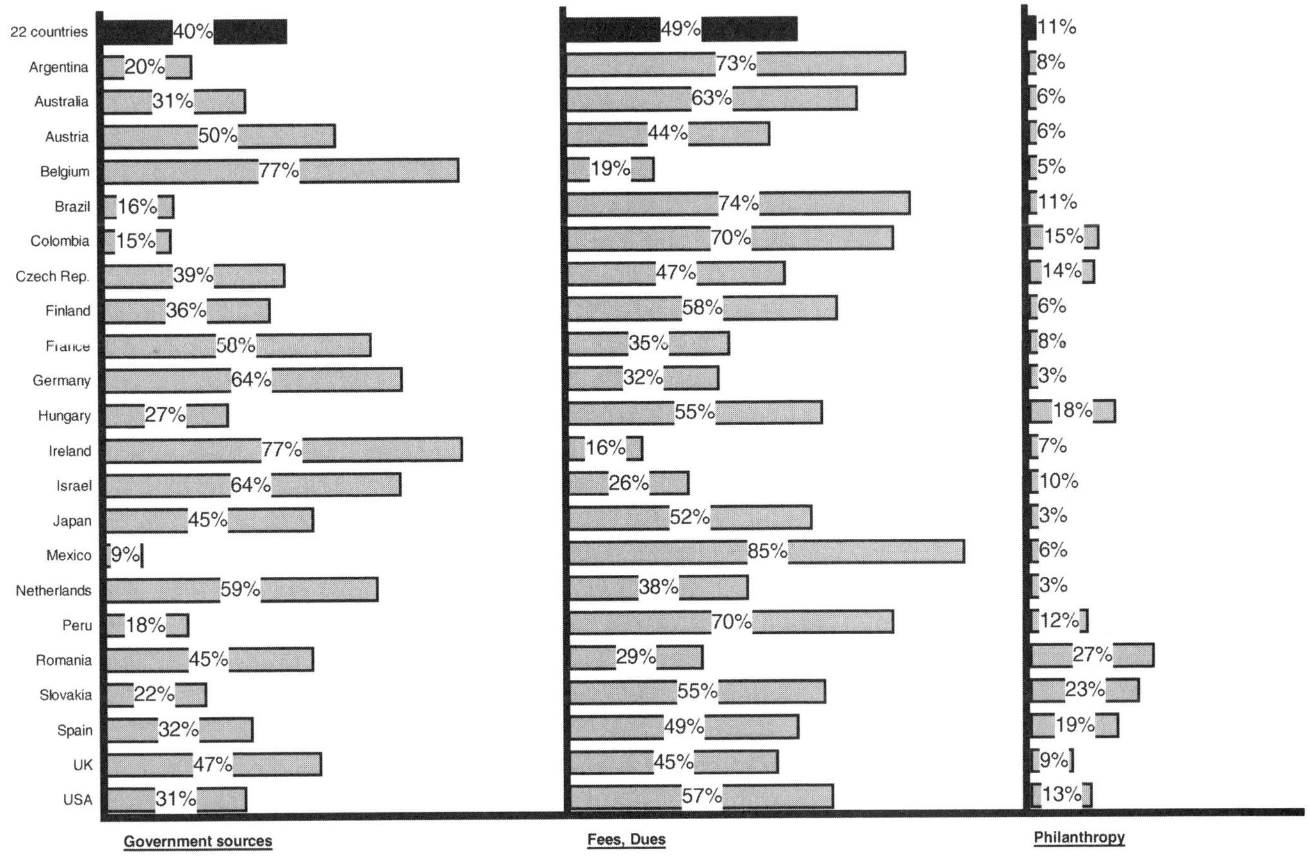

Source: Johns Hopkins Comparative Nonprofit Sector Project

The major sources of non-profit income in the 22 countries of the Johns Hopkins project are fees and public support. As shown in Figure 3, fees and other commercial income alone account for nearly one-half of all non-profit revenue (49%), while public-sector payments amount to 40% of the total. By contrast, private philanthropy—from individuals, corporations and foundations combined—constitutes only 11% of total non-profit income. This pattern varies somewhat, however, by country and region. Whereas fee income is predominant in Central and South America and Central and Eastern Europe, as well as in the USA, Australia and Japan, public grants and third-party payments, primarily from public social insurance funds, are the most important sources of income for the third sector in the Western European region.

Not only is the non-profit sector a major economic force, but it has also been an unusually dynamic one in recent years, surpassing the general economies in most of the Johns Hopkins Project countries in generating employment growth. Non-profit employment in Belgium, France, Germany and the United Kingdom grew by an average of 24%, or by more than 4% a year, between 1990 and 1995. In comparison, overall employment in these same countries grew at a considerably slower rate during this same period: 6%, or barely 1% a year. The non-profit sector therefore outpaced the overall growth of employment in these countries by a ratio of almost 4:1. Social services accounted for the largest share of non-profit employment growth in Western Europe.

More generally, the growth in non-profit employment evident in these figures has been made possible not chiefly by a surge in private philanthropy or public-sector support, but by a substantial increase in fee income. In the eight countries for which Salamon et al. (1999) report revenue data going back to 1990, fees accounted for 58% of the real growth in non-profit revenue between 1990 and 1995. In comparison, the public sector accounted for 34%, and private giving, which includes foundation grants, 8% of the growth in non-profit income. Thus, while both non-profit and foundation sectors increased in size and number, the relative importance of foundation revenue for voluntary associations declined, relative to more 'commercial' forms of revenue.

Non-governmental Organizations and Globalization[6]

Next to the national third sectors in the various countries covered above, a somewhat different phenomenon took place, particularly in the 1990s: the rise of international NGOs, or INGOs. This led to the emergence of a supranational sphere of social and political participation in which NGOs, groups and individuals engage in dialogue, debate, confrontation and negotiation with each other and with various governmental bodies—international, national, and local—as well as with the business world. Many INGOs employ staff and are professional organizations. They can include campaigning groups like Amnesty International or Greenpeace, the famous 'brand names' of global civil society; professional societies like international

[6] This section draws on Anheier, Glasius and Kaldor, 2001.

employers' federations or trades unions; charities like Christian Aid or CARE International; and 'think tanks' and international commissions.

Of course historically, elements of a supra-national non-governmental sphere have existed: INGOs are not new. They date back to the 19th century, but the term itself is of more recent origins, coined during the League of Nations period. The earliest INGO is generally said to be the Anti-Slavery Society, formed as the British and Foreign Anti-Slavery Society in 1839, although there was a transnational social movement against slavery much earlier. Henri Dunant founded the International Committee of the Red Cross (ICRC) in 1863 after his experiences at the battle of Solferino.

What seems new, however, is the sheer scale and scope that international and supranational institutions and organizations of many kinds have achieved in recent years. The number of organizations and individuals that are part of global civil society has probably never been bigger, and the range and type of fields in which they operate never been wider: from United Nations (UN) conferences about social welfare or the environment to conflict situations in Kosovo, and from media corporations spanning the globe to indigenous peoples' campaigns over the internet.

By 1874 there were 32 registered INGOs and this number had increased to 1,083 by 1914 (Chatfield 1997). INGOs grew steadily after the Second World War, but there was an acceleration in the 1990s. Around one-quarter of the 13,000 INGOs in existence in 2000 were created after 1990. Moreover, membership by individuals or national bodies of INGOs has increased even faster; well over one-third of the membership of INGOs joined after 1990. (These figures include only NGOs narrowly defined as 'international'; they do not include national NGOs with an international orientation.) Moreover, during the 1990s INGOs became much more interconnected, both to each other and to international institutions such as the UN or the International Bank for Reconstruction and Development (World Bank). Thus, not only did the global range of INGO presence grow during the 1990s and early 2000s, but the networks linking these organizations became denser as well. In Held's terms (Held et al., 1999), the data suggest that networking of INGOs is becoming 'thicker' and is increasingly becoming part of globalization more generally.

The growth of INGOs has been facilitated by the growth of resources available, i.e. technology and money. Increases in internet usage and in both mobile or cell phones and land-lines have greatly facilitated the construction of networks and have allowed greater access for groups outside the main centres of international power. Thus, even just taking membership of INGOs, membership of INGOs of low- and middle-income regions (70% and 98% respectively) increased faster between 1990 and 2000 than membership in high-income regions (56%). The biggest increases were for Eastern Europe and Asia.

Likewise, during the 1990s and early 2000s there was a big increase in the economic importance of NGOs. Specifically, governments and international institutions greatly increased the amount of development funds channelled through NGOs (OECD, 1997). In addition, private giving also increased from both foundations and corporations. Pinter (2001) estimates that global civil society receives approximately US $7,000m. in development funds and $2,000m. in funds from US foundations. Salamon et al. (1999) show that the number of full-time equivalent employees in INGOs for France, Germany, Japan, the Netherlands, Spain and the United Kingdom alone amounts to over 100,000 and that volunteers in INGOs represent an additional 1.2m. full-time jobs in these countries. Even without precise and comprehensive figures, available data suggest the significant economic scale of INGO activities.

Conclusion

The political stability and economic prosperity of the USA, Japan, Europe and other parts of the developed world are closely related to the renaissance of foundations in recent decades. The rise of the third sector and INGOs is closely related to this process, additionally fuelled by an opening of institutional space for private activities and self-organization among citizens. These expansions are fairly recent phenomena, and their continued growth and sustainability by no means a foregone conclusion. At the very least such pronounced and prolonged growth brings policy options and dilemmas to the political agenda. For instance, to what extent can governments, national as well as international, allow private actors, be they foundations or NGOs, to influence the political agenda? Who is responsible for delivering public and quasi-public good? If governments no longer see themselves as the party primarily responsible for social security, welfare, education, culture, etc., who has legitimacy to act in the public interest? Should the fate of fortunes, large and small, be left primarily to individuals, or can government express some moral or political priority? Ultimately, foundations and NGOs, unlike democratic governments, are not answerable to the electorate, which creates profound accountability problems. Moreover, unlike interest and lobby groups, foundations are typically not answerable to specific members and stakeholders who might control or own them.

Of course, to some extent, the answers to these dilemmas and questions depend on the relevant policies and laws in place, but they are also shaped by the prevailing political climate. Across much of the developed world, this climate currently favours a reduced role for government and greater responsibility lodged with individuals—yet, what theoretical case can be made for foundations and NGOs more generally? Why do they exist, and why are they expanding? While a fuller answer to these questions is beyond the scope of this chapter, it may be useful, in conclusion, to examine briefly some of the answers suggested in the literature (see Anheier and Toepler, 1999, for an overview).

Foundations and NGOs, like all non-profit institutions, exist for several basic reasons. More specifically, foundations and non-profit organizations exist because markets and government may fail, as Hansmann (1996) and Weisbrod (1988) have pointed out. Under conditions of demand heterogeneity and information asymmetries, markets, because of moral hazard problems inherent in such transactions, fail to supply some public and quasi-public goods in efficient and equitable ways (Anheier and Ben-Ner, 1997). Moreover, such goods cannot be supplied by the state because of government failure, i.e. the inability of the state to meet and safeguard minority demands. Correcting for such failures would otherwise run into conflict with the inherent constitutional doctrine of limited state interference in liberal democracies.

This reasoning implies that diverse societies have needs that neither market nor state can provide at reasonable economic costs and acceptable political risks. And it is in this context, that, according to Prewitt (1999), foundations make their truly distinct contribution to modern society: pluralism. By promoting diversity and differentiation in thought, approaches and practice of advocacy and service provision, foundations create and preserve pluralism, and thereby increase the problem-solving capacity of societies. In other words, modern societies both require and reflect the pluralism generated by foundations and NGOs.

References

Anheier, H. 'Foundations in Europe: A Comparative Perspective', in Schlüter, A. et al. (Editors), *Foundations in Europe,* pp 35-81. Directory of Social Change, London and Bertelsmann Foundation, Gütersloh, 2001.

Anheier, H. 'Das Stiftungswesen in Zahlen: Eine sozialökonomische Strukturebeschreibung deutscher Stiftungen', in Bertelsmann Foundation (Editor), *Handbuch Stiftungen* pp 47-82. Gabler, Wiesbaden, 1998.

Anheier, H. and Ben-Ner, A. 'The Shifting Boundaries: Long-term Changes in the Size of the For-profit, Nonprofit, Co-operative and Government Sectors', in *Annals of Public and Cooperative Economics,* 68 (3), 1997, pp 335-354.

Anheier, H. and Toepler, S. 'Philanthropic Foundations: An International Perspective', in Anheier, H. and Toepler, S. (Editors), *Private Funds, Public Purpose: Philanthropic Foundations in International Perspective,* pp 3-23. Kluwer Academic/Plenum Publishers, New York, 1999.

Anheier, H., Glasius, M. and Kaldor, M. (Editors), *Global Civil Society 2001.* Oxford University Press, Oxford, 2001.

Archambault, E., Bournendil, J. and Tsyboula, S. 'Foundations in France', in Anheier, H. and Toepler, S. (Editors), *Private Funds, Public Purpose: Philanthropic Foundations in International Perspective,* pp 185-198, as above.

Arias Foundation For Peace And Human Progress. *The State of Philanthropy in Central America.* San José, 1992.

Baloglu, Z. (Editor). *The Foundations of Turkey.* TÜSEV, Istanbul, 1996.

Barbetta, G. 'Foundations in Italy', in Anheier, H. and Toepler, S. (Editors), *Private Funds, Public Purpose: Philanthropic Foundations in International Perspective,* pp 199–218, as above.

Beise, M. 'Politische Stiftungen', in Bertelsmann Foundation (Editor), *Handbuch Stiftungen.* Gabler, Wiesbaden, 1998.

Bertelsmann Foundation (Editor). *Handbuch Bürgerstiftungen.* Bertelsmann Foundation, Gütersloh, 2000.

Biermann, B., Cannon, L. and Klainberg, D. *A Survey of Endowed Grantmaking Development Foundations in Africa, Asia, Eastern Europe, Latin America, and the Caribbean.* Synergos Institute, New York, 1992 (mimeo).

Boris, E. 'Creation and Growth: A Survey of Private Foundations', in Odendahl, T. (Editor), *America's Wealthy and the Future of Foundations,* pp 65–126. Foundation Center, New York, 1987.

Bulmer, M. 'The History of Foundations in the United Kingdom and the United States: Philanthropic Foundations in Industrial Society', in Anheier, H. and Toepler, S. (Editors), *Private Funds, Public Purpose: Philanthropic Foundations in International Perspective,* pp 27–53, as above.

Coing, H. (1981). 'Remarks on the History of Foundations and their Role in the Promotion of Learning', in *Minerva,* XIX(2), pp 271-181.

European Commission. *Communication from the Commission on Promoting the Role of Voluntary Organizations and Foundations in Europe* (COM 97/241). EUR-OP, Luxembourg, 1997.

Foundation Center. *Foundation Yearbook 2001.* Foundation Center, New York, 2001.

Hansmann, H. *The Ownership of Enterprise.* Harvard University Press, Cambridge, MA, 1996.

Held, D, McGrew, A. Goldblatt, D. and Perraton, J. *Global Transformations.* Polity Press, Cambridge, 1999.

Karl, B. and Katz, S. 'Foundations and the Ruling Class', in *Daedalus,* 116 (1), 1987, pp 1–40.

Kendall, J. and Anheier, H. 'The third sector and the European Union policy process: an initial evaluation', in *Journal of European Public Policy,* 6 (2), 1999, pp 283–307.

Leat, D. *Trusts in Transition: The Policy and Practice of Grant-making Trusts.* Joseph Rowntree Foundation, York, 1992.

Lindeman, Eduard C. *Wealth and Culture.* Reprint, Society and Philanthropy Series. Transaction Books, New Brunswick and Oxford, 1988 [1936].

Margo, R., 'Foundations', in Clotfelter, C. T. (Editor), *Who Benefits from the Nonprofit Sector?* pp 207–234. University of Chicago Press, Chicago, 1992.

Neuhoff, K. *Kommentar zum Bürgerlichen Gesetzbuch,* (11th edn), *Band 1: Allgemeiner Teil.* Sonderdruck aus SOERGEL, Stifterverband für die Deutsche Wissenschaft, Essen, 1978.

Neuhoff, K. 'Stiftung und Stiftungsrecht', in Bauer, R. (Editor), *Lexikon des Sozial- und Gesundheitswesens,* pp. 1967–1974. R. Bauer, Munich and Vienna, 1992.

Odendahl, T. 'Independent Foundations and the Wealthy Donors: An Overview', in Odendahl, T. (Editor), *America's Wealthy and the Future of Foundations,* pp1–26. Foundation Center, New York, 1987.

Pharaoh, C. 'The growth of community trusts and foundations', in CAF (Editor), *Dimensions of the Voluntary Sector,* pp 70–73. CAF Publications, West Malling, 1996.

Pinter, F. 'Funding Global Civil Society', in Anheier, H. K., Glasius, M. and Kaldor, M. (Editors), *Global Civil Society 2001.* Oxford University Press, Oxford, 2001.

Prewitt, K. 'The Importance of Foundations in an Open Society', in Bertelsmann Foundation (Editor), *The Future of Foundations in an Open Society,* pp 17–29. Bertelsmann Foundation, Gütersloh, 1999.

Renz, L., Mandler, C. and Tran, T. *Foundation Giving. Yearbook of Facts and Figures on Private, Corporate and Community Foundations.* Foundation Center, New York, 1997.

Salamon, L. M. *America's Nonprofit Sector: A Primer.* Foundation Center, New York, 1992a.

Salamon, L. and Anheier, H. *The Emerging Nonprofit Sector: An Overview.* Manchester University Press, Manchester, 1996.

Salamon, L. and Anheier, H. (Editors). *Defining the Nonprofit Sector: A Cross-National Analysis.* Manchester University Press, Manchester, 1997.

Salamon, L., Anheier, H., List, R., Toepler, S. and Sokolowski, W. (Editors). *Global Civil Society: Dimensions of the Nonprofit Sector.* Johns Hopkins Institute for Policy Studies, Baltimore, MD, 1999.

Schiller, T. *Stiftungen im gesellschaftlichen Prozeß* Nomos, Baden-Baden, 1969.

Schlüter, A. et al. (Editors). *Foundations in Europe.* Directory of Social Change, London and Bertelsmann Foundation, Gütersloh, 2001.

Schlüter, A., Then, V. and Walkenhorst, P. (Editors). *Foundations in Europe: Society, Management and Law.* Directory of Social Change, London, 2001.

Smith, J. and Borgmann, K. 'Foundations in Europe: the Historical Context', in Schlüter, A., Then, V., and Walkenhorst, P. (Editors), *Foundations in Europe: Society, Management and Law.* Directory of Social Change, London, 2001.

Smith, J., Chatfield, C. and Pagnucco, R. (Editors). *Transnational social movements and global politics: solidarity beyond the state.* Syracuse University Press, Syracuse, NY, 1997.

Strachwitz, R. and Toepler, S. 'Traditional Methods of Funding: Endowments and Foundations', in Doyle, L. (Editor), *Funding Europe's Solidarity,* pp 100–108. AICE, Brussels, 1996.

Strachwitz, R. 'Foundations in Germany and Their Revival in East Germany after 1989', in Anheier, H. and Toepler, S. (Editors), *Private Funds, Public Purpose: Philanthropic Foundations in International Perspective,* pp 219–233, as above.

Toepler, S. 'Operating in a Grantmaking World: Reassessing the Role of Operating Foundations', in Anheier, H. and Toepler, S. (Editors), *Private Funds, Public Purpose: Philanthropic Foundations in International Perspective,* pp 163–185, as above.

UIA (Union of International Associations). *Yearbook of International Organizations: Guide to civil society networks.* K. G. Saur, Munich, 1905–1999/2000.

Van der Ploeg, T. 'A Comparative Legal Analysis of Foundations: Aspects of Supervision and Transparency', in Anheier, H. and Toepler, S. (Editors), *Private Funds, Public Purpose: Philanthropic Foundations in International Perspective,* pp 55–78, as above.

Walkenhorst, P. (Editor). *Building Philanthropic and Social Capital: The Work of Community Foundations.* Bertelsmann Foundation, Gütersloh, 2001.

Weisbrod, B. *The Nonprofit Economy.* Harvard University Press, Cambridge, MA, 1988.

Whitaker, Benjamin. *The Philanthropoids.* William Morrow, New York, 1974.

Ylvesaker, P. 'Foundations and Nonprofit Organizations', in Powell, W. (Editor), *The Nonprofit Sector: A Research Handbook,* pp 360–379. Yale University Press, New Haven, CT, 1987.

Helmut Anheier is Professor of Social Welfare and Center Director, UCLA (University of California, Los Angeles) Center for Civil Society, which is part of the School of Public Policy and Social Research. From 1998–2002 he was the founding Director of the Centre for Civil Society at the London School of Economics (LSE), and a member of the LSE's Department of Social Policy, where he now holds the title of Centennial Professor. Prior to this he was a Senior Research Associate and Project Co-Director at the Johns Hopkins University Institute for Policy Studies, and Associate Professor of Sociology at Rutgers University. He has been Social Affairs Officer with the United Nations, and has held research appointments at Yale University, the University of Cologne and the Science Centre in Berlin.

Foundations and Global Change

CATHERINA PHAROAH

The Importance of Global Issues

Most international foundations, operating within an atmosphere of heightened international tension following the terrorist attacks on New York on 11 September 2001 and military action in Iraq in 2003, have placed global political, social and economic concerns high on their agenda. Just as they thus sought to widen their focus, increased pressure has arisen from a more constrained financial position because of the global economic downturn. For example, corporate charitable giving in the USA fell by 14.5% in real terms in 2001, and in the United Kingdom by 21%. US foundation giving grew at a modest 2.5% in real terms, although international grant-making itself continued to increase, perhaps revealing a growing preoccupation with global challenges.

A further pressure is that the environment for cross-border foundation giving has become more complex, one of the many effects of the terrorist attacks on New York, as foundations seek assurance that international funding flows are properly directed. The US Internal Revenue Service, for example, has developed an extended voluntary code of good practice for grant-makers to follow when making international grants, involving greater scrutiny of grantees' management and use of funds, to ensure that all monies flow to appropriate causes and are not diverted to terrorist organizations. Though important, this policy increases compliance costs and the time taken to make grants. Similarly there has been an accelerating interest in—and growth of—the role of intermediaries which can provide information, validation or accreditation in relation to beneficiaries, for example GuideStar, the Top Foreign 500 and the BBB (Better Business Bureau) Wise Giving Alliance. While such services are of great value to foundations, they represent a trend that risks excluding the many organizations which, for perfectly good reasons (for example, that they are new organizations with no previous experience, small, unknown, informal or perhaps working in more contentious or risky areas) do not feature on lists of validated beneficiaries.

International grant-makers are also having to develop a much more finely tuned cultural understanding of the distinctions between the faith-based, ethnic, national and political allegiances of local communities, and become aware of the links between local and global needs. The Bertelsmann Foundation summed up the challenges in its newsletter of July 2002, in which it stated that it aimed 'to de-escalate conflicts and work on finding practical solutions beyond the restrictions imposed by daily politics . . . As geographical borders are de-emphasized local problems and crises are having an impact on a wider scale'. The Report on the Proceedings of the 2002 European Foundation Centre (EFC) conference commented that 'A common (foundation) concern was expressed for the world of the excluded, many of whom are attracted by populist and fundamentalist movements. Poverty and exclusion seem to play a major role in many questions related to fundamentalist movements and terrorism'. This report also picked up the theme, noted above, that 11 September also led to some suspicion of non-governmental organizations (NGOs), stating that 'Faith-based organizations, in particular, need to rebuild their credibility and introduce new models of transparency and accountability'.

It is unfortunate that this mistrust has arisen just when there was a growing re-discovery of the very important role that faith-based organizations still play today in acting as a catalyst for both generating NGO funds and providing NGO services. In the United Kingdom the conditions for making grants from the National Lottery funds to faith-based organizations were relaxed, while in the USA, President George W. Bush put forward an initiative to allow more faith-based groups to access federal funding.

Mistrust of another type arose from the enormous challenges faced by NGOs involved in organizing aid to victims of the 2001 terrorist attacks. While a huge contribution was made by the NGO sector (the September 11th Fund, for example, provided help to 100,000 people in 26 different countries), none the less the effort exposed some fault-lines in the capacity of NGOs to co-ordinate their work, provide accessible and speedy relief to all needs groups, and raise appropriately targeted funds. The EFC published new guide-lines for foundations on co-ordinated disaster relief.

One global issue that has finally won wide international foundation support, however, is the need to address HIV/AIDS: there are around 36m. people living with AIDS around the world, and 1,300 new cases being diagnosed every day. The United Nations (UN) has played an important role in bringing the issue to the attention of the international community; UNAIDS aims to play a campaigning and co-ordinating role for funders' efforts, and there have been many grants for HIV/AIDS programmes in the areas of prevention, care and treatment. Examples range from small preventative local initiatives such as SYGA in Ethiopia to affinity groups such as the FCAA group of large US foundations, major programmes such as the US $100m. given by the Gates Foundation for an AIDS initiative in India and the initiative from the United Nations Foundation Global Fund, which is a government/NGO/private sector partnership, for work in Haiti and Tanzania.

This united effort represents an example of what can be achieved when global intermediary organizations sponsor issues alongside the third sector. The need for such approaches was acknowledged in the International Bank for Reconstruction and Development's (World Bank) 2000/01 report, which claimed that the 10 years of global strategy based on economic restructuring in developing countries had made little impact on global poverty. In a new approach, funded by the Development Gateway Foundation (USA), it established its ambitious and extensive internet knowledge-management project, Development

Gateway, a portal for development issues, providing access to knowledge, donors, projects and needs through a range of intermediary organizations. The World Bank also appointed a new co-ordinator for partnership work with foundations. Community foundations continue to be an attractive model to funders, with their scope for stimulating indigenous philanthropy.

The Challenge of Creating Sustainable Change

A specific challenge in Europe is to promote the development of philanthropy in the newly independent states of Central and Eastern Europe, especially given plans for the enlargement of the European Union. This involves both ensuring that the non-profit communities in these countries are enabled to access mainstream European Communities and foundation opportunities, as well as building on the embryonic indigenous philanthropy, largely developing in Russia and Ukraine, through funders such as the Yukos Oil Company and the Eurasia Foundation. Indigenous support is essential to the sustainability of civil society in these regions, as international funding moves to other areas of the globe. Developments such as the creation of the Foundation Investment Fund (FIF) in the Czech republic with 1% of the stocks from privatization of state property have proved invaluable for local foundations, although it took nine years for the first funds to be distributed. In Croatia the Council for the Development of Civil Society was established in 2002 to work with the Government in the area of allocation of public funds to non-profit organizations, and successfully lobbied for 50% of lottery proceeds to be allocated to non-profits. Six US foundations combined to set up the Trust For Civil Society in Central and Eastern Europe with funding to stimulate local sustainable infrastructure initiatives, as an 'exit strategy' from the region.

There are plenty of emerging areas across the globe for funder attention. Civil society in Afghanistan is beginning to emerge and, facilitated by the Swiss Peace Foundation, had first meetings in Germany and in Kabul in 2001 resulting in the Afghan Civil Society Forum framing a set of messages to government and to the international community. Since the late 1990s, NGOs have been emerging in many countries of Central Asia, including Kyrgyzstan, which is estimated to have at least 1,000 organizations, followed by Kazakhstan, Tajikistan, Uzbekistan and Turkmenistan. In all these areas there is an almost total dependence on international agencies. One result of this is that NGOs in these countries still need to develop their own agenda and legislative regimes, and are still heavily influenced by concepts brought in from the international community. The People's Republic of China too is struggling to resolve these issues in the development of an NGO community.

Civil society has begun to ask whether international foundations should *define* or *follow,* lead or work alongside national and international programmes of activities and interventions. An increasing number of funders see the need to find innovative ways of developing local partnerships as the only way to identify need, target funds directly and achieve sustainable interventions. For example, a large portion of the US Ford Foundation's special 50th Anniversary in India programme was given to NGO capacity-building through the Society for the Promotion of Area Resource Centres, which aims to persuade local organizations to work with public authorities to improve local housing and employment. For large international foundations, finding out how to work at the local level continues to be the single most important condition for a successful global strategy. Delegating the management of funds to local areas is one—possibly risky—way of doing this, although at a workshop aimed at sharing funder experience in relation to tackling poverty in the urban areas through innovative uses of local funds, sponsored by the United Kingdom Department for International Development and the Swiss Agency for Co-operation and Development, a number of successful case-studies in Zambia, Uganda, Thailand and Central America, Pakistan, South Africa, Cambodia, Zimbabwe, Namibia and the Philippines were presented.

The development of appropriate partnerships to tackle the complexity of international challenges is now a key element of foundation strategy, with new initiatives between government and foundations, between foundations themselves, and between foundations and other types of agency constantly emerging. Partnerships with government are widely recognized across many countries as a crucial feature of civil society, and there have been significant recent initiatives to develop a framework for third sector–government relationships. The European Commission of the EU published its consultation paper on European governance, the White Paper on European Governance (see http://europa.eu.int/comm/governance/index_en.htm) in July 2001, which called for a formalization of the EU relationship with civil society, a code of conduct for consultation, and greater responsibility and accountability. One emerging issue has been the need for foundations to have their own European legislation embodying main principles for foundations such as independence and tax incentives. Many countries have begun or have continued to review their laws in relation to NGOs, and while it is generally beneficial to develop the legal and fiscal environment for philanthropy, in some countries, particularly formerly communist regimes, greater deregulation at state level has led, paradoxically, to increased regulation of NGOs, which still lacked public trust.

Networking

Somewhat looser but none the less powerful forms of partnership are the emerging networks for the sharing of resources, expertise, ideas and influence. Some networks, of which many examples could be cited, consist of intermediary organizations providing support and capacity building to sections of the NGO community, some are 'virtual' or internet-based networks for knowledge and information, and some are based on links of mutual local or topical interest. New local and regional networks for funders and other infrastructure or support organizations include CERES, the Ecuadorian Consortium for Social Responsibility, which had its first meeting in Quito, with representatives of 11 foundations; and the Fes-Saiss Association, which in 2002 brought together civil society organizations from Jordan, Palestinian Autonomous Areas, Tunisia and Morocco alongside Western European and US foundations to promote more collaborative working. With joint funding from the Fes-Saiss Association, the EFC and the Luso-American Foundation, a resource centre for civil society organizations has been established in Casablanca. The International Network on Strategic Philanthropy (INSP) was established by three European and three US foundations to generate discussion on the role of foundations as agents of change. Participants include the Bertelsmann Foundation (Germany), the Charles Stewart Mott Foundation (USA), the Compagnia di San Paolo (Italy), the Ford Foundation (USA), the German Marshall Fund of the United States and the King Baudouin Foundation (Belgium), and a rolling programme of events and publications was launched, attempting to present the best of contemporary foundation thinking and practice on topics including new donors, venture- and e-philanthropy, communications and innovative programme design, evaluation, governance and stakeholder involvement.

Regional NGO internet-based support networks continue to expand. The 'digital divide' challenges access to such facilities, and a new joint initiative by a group of telecommunications companies, the CEO Charter for Digital Development, aims to divert 20% of their corporate philanthropy budgets to technology programmes in developing countries to ensure that the latter are not excluded from internet and telephone services. Networks include the RealNetworks Foundation, endowed by the internet media company RealNetwork, which donates 5% of its annual net income to philanthropy, supports free speech, access to technology and innovative use of the internet in areas poorly served by electronic communications. In Spain the Professional Associations Network Foundation was, in early 2002, developing an internet portal to serve many information and communication needs for professional associations (see www.recol.es). An important development is the emergence of on-line NGO news services. OneWorld on Yahoo! is one example. OneWorld, an on-line network for human rights and sustainable development, has set up a news service in the world news section of Yahoo! News (see http://news.yahoo.com). All the major foundation intermediaries, such as the Foundation Center and the Council on Foundations in the USA, the EFC and, in the United Kingdom, the Association of Charitable Foundations (ACF) and CAF (Charities Aid Foundation), provide major services over the internet to their members or to other potential donors and grant-seekers.

Intermediaries and Umbrella Groups

Other forums operate to support foundation work at an international level: the International Youth Federation, for example, works mainly as a co-ordinating network for local country developments. CIVICUS (World Alliance for Citizen Participation) emerged as a global platform for foundations and associations, and has developed a tool, known as the CIVICUS Index, for countries to measure the development of their civil society and benchmark themselves against others. A Resource Alliance, based in Amsterdam, emerged from the previous International Fundraising Group, with a wider remit for developing international funding. WINGS (Wordwide Initiatives for Grantmaker Support), which has moved from the USA to Brussels, aims to support grant-making activity throughout the world, and has begun to generate regional forums for grant-makers, for example, in Central and South America, and has made the bulk of its website available in Spanish (www.wingsweb.org). The International Center for Not-for-Profit Law is an important resource for funders on the different legal and fiscal regimes existing in different countries for third-sector organizations: many funders grapple with the difficulties of transferring funding from one national regime to another. Various initiatives focus on legal reform and the establishment of some common global principles.

Regional Forums

Fast-growing regional networks are proving to be further evidence of the rapid growth of interest in developing the role of philanthropy world-wide. A new bi-national network is the Border Philanthropy Partnership for the development of community philanthropy along the Mexico–USA border, funded by the Ford Foundation. CAFO (Conference of Asian Foundations), which was established in 1996, holds annual conferences for representatives from 11 countries and territories. The Asia Pacific Philanthropy Consortium was established in 1993 to support grant-making organizations in the Asia-Pacific region and continues to develop and grow. In Thailand and Indonesia Synergos convenes workshops to bring together community foundations from across the country. The Sasakawa Southeast Asia Co-operation Fund was set up in 1992 by the Sasakawa Peace Foundation (Japan) to advance reconstruction in Vietnam, Laos and Cambodia. Moreover, the Sasakawa Peace Foundation has pledged to connect local Japanese communities with the rest of the world. INTERFUND, a consortium of European and Canadian NGOs and foundations started operating in South Africa in 1986. The Non-Profit Partnership in South Africa provides a forum for broad coalitions around areas of common interest such as tax reform. The EFC, established in 1989, continues to expand its spheres of interest and operation, providing a bridge for foundations wanting to begin to operate internationally.

Corporate Social Responsibility

Many of the inherent challenges involved in the partnership between NGOs and companies were demonstrated at the World Summit on Sustainable Development in Johannesburg, South Africa, held in 2002, when civil society struggled to ensure it would be involved in the discussion process alongside governments and multinational corporations, and when NGOs took differing stances on relationships with corporations. Few major multinational corporations have not become engaged in corporate social responsibility (CSR) programmes as they increasingly grapple with the challenges of global capitalism in countries experiencing huge disparities of wealth and power. The EU's 'Green Paper Promoting a European framework for Corporate Social Responsibility' prompted responses from more than 300 organizations and individuals, and has led to the EU's official communication on CSR. (See www.europa.eu.int/comm/employment_social/soc-dial/csr/csr_index.htm.) In addition to well-established corporate support for the international third sector from companies such as BP, Royal Dutch/Shell Group, Rio Tinto, Diageo and Levi-Strauss, new CSR programmes have emerged particularly in the energy, pharmaceutical and banking industries. CSR programmes are also emerging amongst corporates in Russia, e.g. the Yukos Oil Company, and in Hungary, emulating the example of many of the US and European multinational companies established in the area. Companies, important funders of non-profit organizations in South Africa, still, however, have a long way to go in relation to developing fully-fledged social investment programmes, as a report from the African Institute of Corporate Citizenship has shown. In regions from Central and South America to South-East Asia, corporate philanthropy is of major importance.

Foundations: An Expanding Role in an Expanding Sphere of Operation

The growth of foundations on a country by country basis has been stimulated in part by the growth in investment in international giving of major US foundations, such as the Carnegie Corporation of New York, the Ford Foundation, the Andrew W. Mellon Foundation, the Charles Stewart Mott Foundation, the Rockefeller Brothers Fund, the Pew Charitable Trusts and the various foundations and organizations established by George Soros (which include the Central European University, the Open Society Institute—New York and various foundations and institutes mainly in Central and Eastern Europe and the Republics of Central Asia). Large international European foundations include the Bertelsmann Foundation and the Robert Bosch Stiftung in Germany, and the Italian banking foundations such as the Compagnia di San Paolo and the Fondazione Monte dei Paschi di Firenze, which was to sell off 65% of its parent bank shares. The Science Foundation Ireland was established by the Irish Government to administer the Technology Foresight Fund of €711m., which was set up in 2000 to consider research applications on an international basis.

Some major foundations in Western Europe and Mediterranean countries such as Portugal, Spain and Turkey have established an international profile similar to that of the large-scale foundations in Japan, whose government in recent years increased its use of foundations to dispense international grants. The number of foundations in Eastern Europe expanded rapidly in the 1990s and early 2000s, particularly in Hungary, where there were in the early 2000s about 6,300 foundations. Eastern European emigrants to the USA, such as George Soros, played an important role in promoting and funding this development. This encouraged similar activity in successful second-generation entrepreneurs in the new international information technology (IT) industries in, for example, Silicon Valley, CA, where there is considerable interest in support for foundation developments in countries of origin. The impact of the decline in value of 'dot.com' internet-based companies in the late 1990s and early 2000s was closely monitored by those seeking grants.

In the Middle East and North Africa the Ford Foundation supports educational, social and cultural programmes. The Bernard van Leer Foundation (Netherlands) runs projects in Morocco and other countries, and the International Youth Foundation (USA) planned to extend its network to this region. The Fundación Banco Bilbao Vizcaya (BBV, Spain) and the Luso-American Development Foundation are also partner organizations. There are few civil society organizations based in this region, although major local funders include the Fondation du Roi Abdul-Aziz Al Saoud (Morocco) and the Third Sector Foundation of Turkey.

In Central and South America foundations such as Riva Aguero, Larco Herrera and Fernandini, founded on the legacies of wealthy individuals or families, have a long history. There are also business foundations, such as the Carvajal Foundation in Ecuador. In Argentina, the Fundación José Maria Aragón provides information on Argentine foundations, of which there were some 1,600 in the early 2000s.

Elsewhere, foundations such as the Fundación Grupo ESQUEL—Ecuador are part of a widespread growth in indigenous philanthropy that aims to reduce dependence on external sources and boost local traditions in philanthropy. New examples of organizations aimed at strengthening indigenous resources in other countries include the Bangladesh Philanthropy Resource Centre, the Pakistan Centre for Philanthropy, the Philippines Council for NGO Certification, the Mozambique Child, Family and Development Association and the Nicaraguan Development Centre. The Mwalimu Nyerere Foundation based in Tanzania was established in 1996 as a permanent tribute to Dr Julius Nyerere, the country's first President. The Carnegie Corporation of New York and the Rockefeller Foundation also operate in sub-Saharan Africa. The indigenous Nelson Mandela Foundation was established in South Africa in 1999.

Sustainability

As foundations increasingly tackle the need to build civil society on a global scale, the general fragility of the NGO funding structure remains a huge problem. Increasing efforts to develop local sustainability either through indigenous philanthropy, building up local government/NGO sector partnerships and more experimental use of funding at the community level, as noted above, are some responses to this. The World Economic Forum, founded by Charles Schwab, has given significant encouragement to the concept of social investment as a way of extending the resources available to develop civil society organizations. Its Schwab Foundation for Social Entrepreneurship has drawn up a blueprint for a Global Exchange for Social Investment (GEXSI, see www.gexsi.org) to encourage potential funders to come together to create new funding networks and principles and a new type of intermediary funder. From the late 1990s onwards the United Kingdom saw the development of many initiatives related to social enterprise, from government support agencies to a range of both government and philanthropic funds, including CAF's charity bank which was launched in October 2002, and tax credits. The NESsT Venture Fund (Fondo Nido) was launched in Chile in 2002 (www.nesst.org). Venture philanthropy is an interesting new departure with huge potential, but it remains to be seen whether it has the ability to attract funds to projects where social need is high and the risks significant.

What is clear, is the fact that global challenges are prompting many international foundations to begin to work in new ways, and that what will be needed is increasing evidence of how real social change can be achieved.

Catherina Pharoah is Director of Research, CAF (Charities Aid Foundation); also Editor of CAF's annual report on the United Kingdom voluntary sector, Dimensions of the Voluntary Sector, *and author of several reports on voluntary sector resource issues, including financial management, partnerships, civil society, the role of foundations, tax-effective giving and social enterprise.*

A Journey without Borders—Researching and Applying to Foundations

KARINA HOLLY

Introduction

Grant-making foundations are notoriously eclectic. Some publish detailed information on their grant-making policies and how to apply for funding, and actively seek out applicants; many are less than happy to reveal any information at all, preferring to distribute funds without regard to basic notions of accountability and openness. Available resources for researching funders are as varied. In some countries, for example Switzerland, the United Kingdom and the USA, where foundations are required to register with the appropriate authorities, and financial and grant information is publicly available, there is a correspondingly large amount of information accessible to fundraising researchers. Elsewhere, where there may be the barest requirements to provide information to the public, researching foundations and other funders can be as much an art as a science.

Why Apply to a Foundation or Trust?

However, despite the obstacles, fundraising from foundations is worthwhile. There are estimated to be approximately 200,000 foundations in Central, Eastern and Western Europe, at least a further 100,000 foundations in the English-speaking world, and 400,000 world-wide. In 1997 research commissioned by CAF (the Charities Aid Foundation) and the Association of Charitable Foundations in the UK discovered grants by an estimated 8,800 foundations totalling £1,850m. in the United Kingdom alone. The 56,582 independent, corporate, community and grant-making operating foundations in the USA known to the Foundation Center in New York donated a total of US $27,563m. in 2000, and held assets of $486,085m. Targeting foundations and trusts is now, more often than not, also the most effective way of accessing the philanthropic munificence of the world's wealthiest individuals, the majority of whom choose to direct their philanthropic giving through foundations. *Forbes* magazine reported that approximately 75% of the wealthiest individuals in the USA give to non-profits through their own foundations.

The Importance of Research

When applying, one must be aware of the differences, rather than the similarities, between funders. Some foundations are legally restricted to giving within a geographical area, while others are simply not interested in giving elsewhere. However, some grant-makers (and significantly, some of the biggest) do make grants across national borders.

> 'Successful funding from foundations and corporate citizenship programmes should be based on the development of a deliberate organizational strategy and a linked project proposal.'[1]

The vital ingredient in a successful fundraising campaign is good research. Luck and good timing are also crucial, but if the research is done properly, then grant-seekers can help make their own timing and luck.

As the vast majority of grant-makers limit their giving to the country in which they are based, it is important for grant-seekers to look closely at the resources available in their own country. Local foundations are likely to be organizations' keenest supporters. Many local and national grant directories are available, ranging from simple listings of funders with contact information, to more detailed critical guides, which give examples of funded projects and details on how best to apply for a grant. A huge variety of national grant directories now exists world-wide: the *Directory of Grantmaking Foundations* in Japan, the *Directory of 300 Major Foundations in Taiwan,* the *Fondsenboek* in the Netherlands, the *Directory of Donors in the Czech Republic,* the *Australian Directory of Philanthropy,* the *Directory of Donors in Jamaica,* etc. International directories are also an invaluable source of information on funders world-wide—see for example the *World Guide to Foundations,* edited by Michael Zils, and this *International Foundation Directory*—as is the small number of magazines offering an international perspective on grant-making, for example *Philanthropy in Europe* (www.philanthropyineurope.com).

The expansion of the internet has completely transformed fundraising research over the last few years. Researchers can now access thousands of websites useful for their task from the 40m. or so now on-line: foundations, charities, non-governmental organizations (NGOs), companies, networking organizations, on-line databases, fundraising newsletters, fundraising research, newspapers, etc. However, the information on a foundation website, just like any information material published by the foundation, is no more than a starting point for a fundraiser, and caution needs to be exercised. A search for 'foundation' on the Google search engine, for example, yields around 21m. responses. The vast amount of data now on the internet can prove an obstacle unless grant-seekers have a clear idea of where to begin, what they are looking for, and how they plan to use the information they find. Publications like the *Directory of Grantmakers' Websites,* published

[1] *Independent Funding—A Directory of Foundation and Corporate Members of the EFC.* European Foundation Centre, 2002.

by Chapel and York in 2001, offer a starting point for researchers looking to access funders' sites, as it includes information on sites in Australia, Canada, India, Japan, New Zealand, South Africa, the United Kingdom, the USA and Western Europe.

National and International Foundation Centres and Co-ordinating Bodies

Many of the organizations set up to either co-ordinate the activities of foundations or to provide information on their activities, can also prove an invaluable starting point for research. Some are country- or region-specific, while others are subject-specific, and often provide either guidelines or details of funding directories.

Researching funders must be done meticulously, and an invaluable source of information on a country's foundations can be found in the growing number of foundation co-ordinating bodies and membership organizations, which act as an interface between grant-seeker and grant-maker. The Worldwide Initiatives for Grantmaker Support (WINGS) network is an organization set up to facilitate the work of national grant-making organizations, and to support the strengthening of global philanthropy. The WINGS website (www.wingsweb.org) includes information on the activities of each of its 87 member organizations: 41 organizations serving grant-makers and a further 46 general purpose organizations serving philanthropy, ranging from the Centre on Philanthropy in Bermuda to the Southern African Grantmakers Association; from the Jamaican Foundations and Corporate Donors group to the China Association of Science Foundations. The site contains links to national organizations' websites, which contain a huge variety of information useful to grant-seekers; codes of good grant-making practice; listings of publications relevant to both grant-makers and grant-seekers; advice and guidance for fundraisers; initiatives to encourage philanthropy; and on-line foundation searches.

On-line databases are an increasing feature of fundraising research. There is a growing number of, often free, resources giving on-line access to details on foundation operations both nationally and internationally. They are many and varied: some on-line databases are free, while others charge a fee. Some provide limited information and are updated infrequently, while others carry extensive descriptions and links to foundation websites. The most extensive on-line foundation database (on more than 70,000 US foundations and over 150,000 grants) is available (at a price) from the Foundation Center in the USA: the *Foundation Directory,* on-line at www.fconline.fdncenter.org), while the *Chronicle of Philanthropy* on-line edition includes a searchable database of deadlines for US foundation grants and awards (http://philanthropy.com/deadlines); but there is a growing number of other on-line databases or sites with links to foundations, including Israel's Giving Wisely database (Internet Directory of Israeli Non-Profit and Philanthropic Organizations—www.givingwisely.org); the Swiss Federal Register of Foundations (www.esv2000.admin.ch/e/verzeich.asp); the German Foundation Register (German Charities Institute—www.dsk.de); foundations operating under the aegis of the Fondation de France (www.fdf.org); the United Kingdom's official Government register of charities, the Charity Commission register of charities (which since the end of 2001 includes financial information on registered charities—www.charitycommission.org.uk); Charities Direct, also in the United Kingdom (www.caritasdata.co.uk); the European Foundation Centre's database (www.fundersonline.org); NGO Net, which covers Central and Eastern Europe (www.ngonet.org); international grant-makers in the USA (www.usig.org); the Canadian Directory to Foundations and Grants (www.ccp.ca); charity search of the Centre on Philanthropy in Bermuda (www.charity.bm/cop/cop.nsf/main4); Grant Tracker, an on-line searchable database of approximately 800 funding sources in Northern Ireland, launched in 2003 by NICVA—Northern Ireland Council for Voluntary Action (www.grant-tracker.org); and an increasing number of others.

Grantmakers Without Borders is another initiative aiming to encourage the growth of progressive international philanthropy. A collaborative effort of the International Donors' Dialogue and the International Working Group of the National Network of Grantmakers in the USA, Grantmakers Without Borders (www.internationaldonors.org) provides free advice to donors on how to give internationally, as well as encouraging communication and dialogue between funders. The organization also runs a unique service, whereby member donors recommend projects to be posted on the website for other funders to consider funding. Projects can be searched for by name, issue or region, and the relevant page contains a brief description of the project's goal, impact and contact details. There is also an NGO Board allowing non-profits to post short messages about international projects needing funding. In 2003 a further initiative to match foundations with projects seeking funding was established by two former International Bank for Reconstruction and Development (World Bank) employees. Development Space (www.developmentspace.com) enables non-profits to post their projects on-line in the hope of finding interested donors.

It is important for grant-seekers to look for information on foundations in every available outlet in order to build as full a picture as possible of their target funders. Increasingly, the internet provides the most direct access to invaluable information. A Foundation Center initiative, FC Stats (http://fdncenter.org/fc_stats/index.html), launched in October 2000, offers free on-line access to data on more than 50,000 US foundations and their funding patterns. It includes more than 1,300 listings, giving the most frequently-requested types of summary data on foundations and their grants.

Another new resource invaluable for the time-squeezed fundraiser, available via the internet, is e-mail newsletters. Regularly delivered to a chosen computer, monthly or even weekly e-mail newsletters tend to offer a summary of the news and information carried on the website, along with links direct to the full article, e.g. the e-mail newsletters of the US Philanthropy News Network (www.pnnonline.org) and UK Fundraising (www.fundraising.co.uk).

There is a growing desire amongst funders and individual philanthropists, which originates in the USA, towards putting a greater investment in the projects that they fund. The venture philanthropy model of giving, originating in Silicon Valley, CA is one of the latest developments in giving. It applies the venture capital concept of investing in start-up companies to non-profits striving to find solutions to social problems. The USA's new breed of venture philanthropists measure a project's success in terms of its 'social return', i.e. they invest in social entrepreneurs. The financial returns for the non-profit can be significant, but a venture philanthropist is more likely to request a seat on the non-profit's board than an annual report after the project's conclusion.

Venture philanthropy has been slow to move across the Atlantic, but at the end of 2001 it had made its first inroads into Europe, with an international conference held in Budapest in November, organized by the Nonprofit Enterprise and Self-sustainability Team (NESsT—www.nesst.org), a non-profit based in Chile and Hungary. Other new funding developments, which emphasize the need for fundraisers to look outside traditional methods of applying for funds, include a radical initiative by the IT (Information Technology) company Social Ecology. Founded to develop IT products for non-profits, Social Ecology donated 100,000 of its shares to 10 non-profits. Equivalent to 1% of Social Ecology's total stock, the shares were to become tradable in the event of an IPO (initial public offering). Fundraisers need to be attentive to this kind of innovative and long-term approach to grant-making. Fundraisers also need to carry out research in as many different places as possible: many business magazines and websites regularly carry information about foundations linked either through a shareholding or by the founder to companies; moreover, many profiles of individuals in either newspapers or magazines will highlight any charitable giving either individually or through a foundation. Another initiative, this time aimed at donors seeking information on development projects to fund, was launched in 2002 by the Swiss-based Schwab Foundation for Social Entrepreneurship (www.schwabfound.org). Its Global Exchange for Social Investment (GEXSI), provides information, including evaluation on approximately 100 projects operated by non-profits.

The application process is also evolving to take advantage of technological changes, with a few foundations pioneering the use of on-line applications. In the USA fundraisers are able to submit part of their application to the Pew Charitable Trusts on-line, while in the United Kingdom organizations from seven European countries can apply directly over the internet for the first time to a Levi Strauss Foundation fund managed by CAF.

Asking for Funds

'Approaching a funder for support is a highly individualized process that should be conducted in a businesslike manner.'[2]

Fundraising is a competitive activity. Funds are scarce and every funder receives many times the number of applications than it can afford to grant. The European Foundation Centre estimates that 90% of applications are rejected immediately by funders.

The secret is to identify what each individual funder's requirements are, and that consequently the form of approach for a grant-seeking organization is correct. For some, this may mean sending a single-page letter outlining the basic proposal, how much it will cost, the amount requested from the funder and why the funder should fund a particular project. Other funders request rather more, which may mean sending audited accounts, full project budgets and detailed outlines. It may also mean meetings with the funder, either person-to-person or by telephone. Grant-seekers need to be aware that no two funders are the same, and consequently no two applications produced should ever be completely identical. Fundraising can appear a very pedestrian activity; long-term relationships need to be built with funders, and this can only be done over time. It is vital to make follow-up phone calls, meet with possible foundation donors and cultivate these contacts—to go out and seek funders.

Submitting unsolicited proposals carries no guarantee of success. Far better than indiscriminately mailing huge numbers of foundations which might be interested in a grant-seeker's proposal, is to invest valuable resources in building a relationship with several carefully-targeted funders. The directories and other resources referred to above can be used to identify a shortlist of possible funders (i.e. 10–15). This list should then be narrowed down to a target group of three or four probable funders. Then more research should be carried out. A good rule of thumb is that at least 60% of the time spent developing a proposal should be spent in research and planning.

However, proposals also need to be submitted in order to achieve any success. This may sound obvious, but despite the age-old fundraising advice of the need to target funders and avoid making large numbers of inappropriate applications, many groups simply do not submit an adequate number of proposals. Recent research carried out by the National Committee for Responsive Philanthropy in the USA found that a sample of grassroots organizations interviewed were submitting proposals in 1999 which were achieving a 63% success rate. While this might seem to be a pretty good success rate, it might not be as successful as it seems. A 63% rate probably means that the organizations were simply not submitting enough proposals. Even an experienced fundraiser operating conservatively, only approaching foundations thought likely to fund the organization, would expect to submit two to three times as many proposals as were ultimately funded, at a 33%–50% success rate. Again, a general rule of thumb for professional fundraisers is to submit six to ten proposals for every one they expect to be funded, an apparently less impressive 10%–17% success rate.

Building a relationship with a funder takes patience. Sometimes it is as easy as making a phone call, as many foundations will be happy to discuss a proposal with a potential grantee. Often this is as much to save themselves valuable time, but it can also prove invaluable. Once a contact has been found at a foundation, he or she should not be misused. The art is to maintain a delicate balance between developing a funder/grantee relationship and being irritating. If a proposal is submitted to the funder and it is rejected, do not give up. The contact at the foundation should be called to try and ascertain why the application for funds was unsuccessful. Was it bad luck or could the proposal have been stronger? Defensiveness should be avoided, and the grant-seeker should be open to honest and critical advice, but let them know the organization will reapply. The next proposal should hopefully fulfil all their requirements.

Experienced fundraisers frequently reiterate the basic rules of foundation fundraising. Be flexible to both proactive and reactive funders, and never assume anything on the part of funders. Keep meticulous records of everything: telephone conversations, meetings, invitations to events, even likes and dislikes of particular organizations. Do not write an appeal more than once a year, as foundation administrators get immensely irritated when they see a non-profit wasting money on unnecessary appeals. Always remember to ask the funder if the organization wants to be mentioned in publicity. Finally, if after a funder has

[2] *A Message to Grantseekers.* Online Library, Foundation Center, 2000.

been located, researched and eventually applied to, a grant is actually awarded, possibly the most obvious but important rule of fundraising should not be forgotten. Say thank you. Even a small donation now could turn into a much larger donation in the future.

Karina Holly is the editor of Philanthropy in Europe, *a magazine appearing every two months informing on fundraising and philanthropy across Europe.*

PART TWO

Directory

Albania

FOUNDATION CENTRE AND CO-ORDINATING BODY

Albanian Civil Society Foundation

Established in 1995 to support the development of civil society, through offering support to Albanian NGOs.

Activities: Provides grants, fellowships, information, assistance and training to NGOs and their staff. Maintains a database of NGOs in Albania, and Citizens' and Information centres.

Geographical Area of Activity: Albania.

Restrictions: No funding for individuals for social assistance or medical requirements, nor for political parties or foreign non-profit organizations operating in Albania.

Publications: Annual Report; directories of Albanian NGOs; newsletter (every two months).

Finance: Expenditure 21,505,000 Lek (1998).

Trustees: Violanda Thedhori (Chair.); A. Gusho; A. Kocollari; V. Leskaj; F. Lubonja; A. Mandro; A. Minga; M. Muco; V. Sala; S. Sampson.

Principal Staff: Exec. Dir Rolanda Dhimitri.

Address: Rruga Asim Vokshi, Vila 137, Tirana.

Telephone and Fax: (42) 38-056; **Internet:** www.acsf.org.al; **e-mail:** shoqciv@ngo.org.al.

FOUNDATIONS, TRUSTS AND NON-PROFIT ORGANIZATIONS

Open Society Foundation for Albania

Established in January 1992 as an independent foundation, and part of the Soros foundations network, aiming to foster political and cultural pluralism, and to reform economic structures in order to encourage private enterprise and a market economy.

Activities: The Foundation operates mainly in the areas of economic reform, education (including a fellowship programme), information and youth and strengthening public institutions, although grants are also made in the areas of the arts and culture, women's programmes, public health, ethnic minorities and civil society. The Foundation co-operates with other foundations in the Soros network on international programmes, including the regional Higher Education Support Programme and the East–East Programme.

Geographical Area of Activity: Albania.

Finance: Funded by the Open Society Institute (q.v.). Annual expenditure US $5,149,000 (2001).

Board of Directors: Milva Ekonomi (Chair.); Artan Santo (Vice-Chair.); Diana Culi; Artan Hajdari; Edmond Leka; Mira Meksi; Natasha Sheshi.

Principal Staff: Exec. Dir Capajev Gjokutaj; Programme Dir Mimoza Gjika.

Address: Rruga 'Pjeter Bogdani', Pallati 23/1, Tirana.

Telephone: (42) 34-621; **Fax:** (42) 35-855; **Internet:** www.soros.al; **e-mail:** soros-al@osfa.soros.al.

Algeria

FOUNDATIONS, TRUSTS AND NON-PROFIT ORGANIZATIONS

African Youth Network for Sustainable Development

Activities: Active in the field of sustainable development, particularly where it relates to children and young people, through networking and representation at international level at conferences and symposia. Also organizes media campaigns in Algeria, volunteer programmes to support elderly people and environmental clean-up activities.

Geographical Area of Activity: Algeria and international.

Address: 22 rue Matiben, El-Mouradia, Algiers 16000.

Telephone: (21) 505-368; **Fax:** (21) 860-573; **Internet:** www.aynsd.org; **e-mail:** redamgueni@yahoo.fr.

Argentina

FOUNDATION CENTRE AND CO-ORDINATING BODY

Grupo de Fundaciones (Association of Foundations)

Established to promote the development of foundations in Argentina.

Activities: Promotes the development of philanthropy; offers information to foundations about philanthropy in Argentina, including news on foundations' activities. Also maintains on-line databases on foundations and projects operated by not-for-profit organizations.

Geographical Area of Activity: Argentina.

Publications: Bulletin (monthly); *Proyectos Aprobados* (quarterly publication on projects funded by foundations).

Principal Staff: Fernando Esnaola.

Address: Sánchez de Bustamante 191, PB 'C', 1173 Buenos Aires.

Telephone and Fax: (11) 4865-3648; **Internet:** www.gdf.org.ar; **e-mail:** gdf@gdf.org.ar.

FOUNDATIONS, TRUSTS AND NON-PROFIT ORGANIZATIONS

Comité de América Latina y el Caribe para la Defensa de los Derechos de la Mujer—CLADEM (Latin American Committee for the Defence of Women's Rights)

A network of individual women and women's organizations, established in 1987, aiming to defend the rights of women in Central and South America and the Caribbean.

Activities: Operates in the field of women's rights, through education and information, proposals for legislative change and campaigning, solidarity activities, and through prizes awarded in recognition of women's achievements. Maintains offices in 17 countries of Central and South America and the Caribbean, and a regional office in Peru.

Geographical Area of Activity: Central and South America and the Caribbean.

Publications: Books; reports; pamphlets; videos.

Principal Staff: Regional Co-ordinator Susana Chiarotti.

Address: España 225, Dpto C, 2000 Rosario.

Telephone: (341) 425-2242; **Fax:** (341) 425-2242; **Internet:** www.cladem.org; **e-mail:** coordie@cladem.org.

Fundación Acíndar (Acíndar Foundation)

Founded in 1962 by Arturo Acevedo, J. M. Aragón, J. E. Acevedo, A. F. A. Acevedo, M. Ezcurra, Rogelio A. Galarce, R. S. Pujals, J. José Ré, Thomas Jefferson Williams and C. A. Acevedo to provide social, cultural, educational and philanthropic assistance and to promote scientific investigation and professional and technical training in Central and South America and the Caribbean.

Activities: Operates mainly in the areas of education, health and the environment, including grants to hospitals, multimedia education projects and training schemes.

Geographical Area of Activity: Central and South America and the Caribbean.

Publications: Annual Report.

Administrative Council: Arturo Tomás Acevedo (Pres.); Guillermo Carlos Acevedo (Vice-Pres.); Lola Acevedo; Ana María Acevedo; Rafael Pablo Acevedo; Jorge Carlos Acevedo; Fernando Manuel Calvente.

Principal Staff: Exec. Pres. Arturo Tomás Acevedo; Exec. Vice-Pres. Guillermo Carlos Acevedo; Exec. Dir Teresa A. U. de Acevedo.

Address: Estanislas Zeballos 2739, B1643AGY Beccar, Buenos Aires.

Telephone: (11) 4719-8311; **Fax:** (11) 4719-8501; **Internet:** www.acindar.com.ar/fundacion/default.htm; **e-mail:** fundacion@acindar.com.ar.

Fundación Ambiente y Recursos Naturales—FARN (Environment and Natural Resources Foundation)

Founded in 1985 to promote the conservation of natural resources and the environment, and sustainable development in South America.

Activities: Operates in the fields of agriculture, energy, conservation and forestry, through campaigning on environmental policy and law, and public participation and the promotion of public debate; maintains a library and database.

Geographical Area of Activity: South America (mainly Argentina).

Publications: *Suplemento de Derecho Ambiental* (quarterly, in Spanish); articles, reports, papers and other publications; Annual Report.

Principal Staff: Exec. Dir Daniel A. Sabsay.

Address: Monroe 2142, 1428 Buenos Aires.

Telephone: (11) 4788-4266; **Fax:** (11) 4788-4266; **Internet:** www.farn.org.ar; **e-mail:** info@farn.org.ar.

Fundación Antorchas (Antorchas Foundation)

Established in 1985 by the Hochschild Group of companies for general philanthropic activities.

Activities: Operates mainly in Argentina in the fields of education, science and the humanities, the arts and conservation of cultural heritage, and social welfare and community development, through self-conducted programmes, scholarships and grants to individuals and institutions, and publications. Awards the US$100,000 Antorchas Fellowship for outstanding scientific research, as well as making awards for scientific collaboration between Argentinian and overseas scientists and researchers.

Geographical Area of Activity: Mainly Argentina.

Publications: *Archivo Fotográfico del Ferrocarril de Santa Fe 1891–1948* (1991); *Juan Pi—Fotografías* (1994); *Los años del daguerrotipo 1843–1870* (1995); *Imágenes de Buenos Aires 1915–1940* (1997); other history and photography publications; Annual Report.

Finance: Financed by the Lampadia Foundation in Liechtenstein. Total grants approx. US$7,000,000 (2000–2001).

Trustees: Josef E. Oppenheimer (Pres.); José Xavier Martini (Exec. Dir); Máximo Bomchil; Guillermo Jaim Etcheverry; Fabián Lebenglik; Leiser Madanes.

Address: Chile 300, 1098 Buenos Aires.

Telephone: (11) 4331-9905; **Fax:** (11) 4331-5673; **Internet:** www.fundantorchas.retina.ar; **e-mail:** info@fundantorchas.retina.ar.

Fundación José María Aragón (José María Aragón Foundation)

Founded in 1962 by Ing. José María Aragón to promote university education and scientific and technological research, and to make available information on professional training opportunities throughout the world.

Activities: Provides information about Argentine foundations, postgraduate studies, international courses and scholarships (national and international), and Argentine social sciences publications.

Geographical Area of Activity: International.

Publications: Annual report and financial statement; monthly reports on scholarships and international courses.

Directors: R. Aguirre (Pres.); N. Alesso; Ing. Carlos F. Aragón; Luis Alberto Aragón; Dr R. Sanguinetti; Dr José María Zamora; Pascual E. Zamora.

Principal Staff: Exec. Dir Guillermo Battro; Admin. Officer F. Aragón.

Address: Casilla de Correo 2870, 1000 Buenos Aires.

Telephone: (11) 4331-6300; **Fax:** (11) 4331-6300; **Internet:** www.aragon.org.ar; **e-mail:** info@aragon.org.ar.

Fundación Bariloche (Bariloche Foundation)

Founded in 1963 to improve the quality of life in Central and South America; to stimulate creative thinking in these areas; to conduct research and teaching programmes; and to offer activities of a similar type to leaders of social groups and to promote the exchange of ideas and information among them, as well as among scientists and intellectuals.

Activities: In 1978, as a result of changed socio-political conditions in Argentina, the Foundation changed its style of operation to become primarily a promotional rather than an executive institution for teaching and research. Since then the Foundation has concentrated on four main fields of interest: energy economics and planning, with an emphasis on developing countries; environmental policy and sustainable development; quality of life; and philosophy. The Foundation assists with the planning of government programmes relating to these areas. The Foundation promotes scientific meetings and the publication of a series of books in various languages to give world-wide diffusion to Central and South American intellectual activity; and maintains a library.

Geographical Area of Activity: Argentina.

Publications: *Boletín Bibliografico* (2 a year); *Revista Desarrollo y Energía* (2 a year); *Revista Patagónica de Filosofia* (journal); and publications relating to foundation programmes.

Finance: Budget of Fundación Bariloche and its associated groups approx. US $1,100,000.

Governing Board: Carlos E. Suárez (Pres.); J. C. Secondi (Vice-Pres.); D. Bouille; N. Di Sbroiavacca; J. Jorquera; A. Lattes; J. Legisa; O. Nudler; H. Pistonesi.

Principal Staff: Exec. Pres. Carlos E. Suárez.

Address: Casilla de Correo 138, 8400 Bariloche.

Telephone: (2944) 422050; **Fax:** (2944) 422050; **Internet:** www.bariloche.com.ar/fb; **e-mail:** fb@bariloche.com.ar.

Fundación Bunge y Born (Bunge y Born Foundation)

Founded in 1963 by the Bunge group of companies to promote and facilitate studies and investigations that will be of benefit to the community as a whole, through financial aid in the broad fields of social welfare, culture and science; and to award prizes to those who have best distinguished themselves in the field of scientific investigation.

Activities: Operates nationally in the fields of education, research, health and culture, chiefly through grants to institutions and the allocation of prizes and scholarships for research, or to attend conferences. Also provides emergency disaster aid.

Geographical Area of Activity: Argentina.

Publications: *Memoria* (Annual report and financial statement); *Humor in Rural Argentine Schools; 25 Years with Rural Argentine Schools*.

Finance: Receives contributions from the Bunge Group, private donations and bequests. Annual expenditure approx. US $1,500,000—US $1,800,000.

Board of Directors: Salvador L. Carbó (Pres.); Octavio Caraballo; Juan Cristian Born; Alejandro de La Tour d'Auvergne; Jorge Cóppola; Raúl Padilla.

Principal Staff: Exec. Dir María L. Herrera Vegas.

Address: 25 de Mayo 501, 2°, 1002 Buenos Aires.

Telephone: (11) 4318-6600; **Fax:** (11) 4318-6610; **Internet:** www.fundacionbyb.org; **e-mail:** fundbyb@fundacionbyb.org.

Fundación Ecológica Universal—FEU (Universal Ecological Foundation)

Founded in Buenos Aires in 1990 to disseminate information and link fields of ecological information.

Activities: Operates in the field of conservation and the environment in Bolivia, Brazil, Chile, Mexico, Paraguay and Uruguay. Organizes environmental education projects in conjunction with schools, training workshops and conferences, and conducts research. Works in partnership with international organizations.

Geographical Area of Activity: Central and South America.

Principal Staff: Pres. Gabriel Andrés Juricich.

Address: Sarmiento, 1041 Buenos Aires.

Telephone: (11) 4373-0522; **Fax:** (11) 4373-1243; **Internet:** www.feu999.org; **e-mail:** info@feu999.org.

Fundación para Estudio e Investigación de la Mujer—FEIM (Foundation for Women's Research and Studies)

Established in 1989 to promote the rights of women and the enhancement of their social and economic position in society.

Activities: Operates in Argentina in the area of women's rights, through providing services such as health-care and health education (especially AIDS and reproductive health); promotes the development of small enterprises; conducts research; maintains a library.

Geographical Area of Activity: Argentina.

Publications: *Desidamos* (quarterly, in Spanish); *Safe Motherhood* (in Spanish); books and videos.

Finance: Annual budget approx. US $120,000.

Principal Staff: Pres. Dr Mabel Bianco; Sec. Alejandra Perrone; Treas. Catalina Abifadel.

Address: Paraná 135, 3°, Of. 13, 1017 Buenos Aires.

Telephone: (11) 4372-2763; **Fax:** (11) 4375-5977; **Internet:** www.feim.org.ar; **e-mail:** feim@ciudad.com.ar.

Fundación de Investigaciones Económicas Latinoamericanas (Foundation for Latin American Economic Research)

Founded in 1964 by the Chamber of Commerce of Argentina, the Stock Exchange of Buenos Aires, the Union Industrial Argentina and the Cattle Breeders' Association, to analyse economic problems.

Activities: Operates in the field of economic affairs, by conducting research on business trends and structural problems of the Argentine and Central and South American economies. Co-operates with similar Central and South American organizations; runs a computerized data bank and maintains a library.

Geographical Area of Activity: Central and South America (mainly Argentina).

Publications: *Indicadores de Coyuntura* (monthly); *Documentos de Trabajo* (monthly); *Indicadores de Actividad y Precios* (monthly); *Resena Anual de la Industría* (annually); surveys and studies.

Finance: Monthly donations are made by the four founding institutions and a number of large and medium-sized firms operating in Argentina.

Board of Directors: Dr Juan P. Munro (Pres.); Ing. Víctor L. Savanti, Federico J. L.Zorraquín (Vice-Pres.); Juan C. Masjoan (Sec.); Dr. Mario E. Vázquez (Treas.); and 22 others.

Principal Staff: Exec. Dir Juan Luis Bour; Chief Economists Fernando Navajes, Daniel A. Artana.

Address: Córdoba 637, 4°, 1054 Buenos Aires.

Telephone: (11) 4314-1990; **Fax:** (11) 4314-8648; **Internet:** www.fiel.org; **e-mail:** postmaster@fiel.org.ar.

Fundación Mediterránea (Mediterranean Foundation)

Founded in 1977 by a number of industrial concerns to promote national economic research and to contribute to a better understanding of and solution to Central and South American economic problems.

Activities: Sponsors a regional economic research institute, the Instituto de Estudios Económicos sobre la Realidad Argentina y Latinoamericana (IEERAL); organizes conferences and publishes the results of investigations.

Geographical Area of Activity: Central and South America.

Publications: *Estudios* (quarterly); *Novedades Económicas* (monthly); newsletter (quarterly).

Principal Staff: Pres. Nadin Arganaraz.

Address: Juan del Campillo 394, Casilla de Correo 1311, CP 5001, Córdoba.

Telephone: (351) 472-6523; **Fax:** (351) 472-4625; **Internet:** www.fundmediterranea.org.ar.

Fundación Mujeres en Igualdad (Women's Equality Foundation)

Founded in August 1989 by Zita C. Montes de Oca.

Activities: Aims to support women's empowerment, principally in Argentina, through coalition building, political training and by creating public awareness of gender issues, operating a range of awareness raising initiatives, including national and international seminars and workshops, a scholarship for a female graduate to study at Dartmouth College in the USA, political campaigning and debates. Active in networks in the fields of health, ecology, civil and political rights, human rights, and domestic violence. Also maintains a database of women active in the field of social and political empowerment.

Geographical Area of Activity: Mainly Argentina.

Publications: *Mujeres en Politica* (3 a year); series of handbooks.

Board of Trustees: Zita C. Montes de Oca (Founder); Monique Thiteux-Altschul (Pres.); Hebe Molinuevo (Vice-Pres.); Blanca Kaschapava (Sec.); Raquel Rebaudi-Alonso (Treas.); María Celia González Gay-Ulloa; Kendra Langlie; Maria Pía Rizzotti-Veiravé; Mercedes Emma Piccoli.

Address: Urquiza 1835, 1602 Florida, Buenos Aires.

Telephone: (11) 4791-0821; **Fax:** (11) 4791-0821; **Internet:** www.mei.com.ar.

Fundación Paz, Ecologia y Arte—Fundación PEA (Foundation for Peace, Ecology and the Arts)

Established in 1997 for the promotion of peace throughout the world.

Activities: Promotes the peaceful resolution of war, and works towards world peace and a culture of peace through supporting ecology and the arts, and peace education.

Geographical Area of Activity: International.

Principal Staff: Pres. Nancy Ducuing de Martorelli; Sec. Prof. Elsa Peña; Treas. Prof. Isabel Susana Guzzo; Dir-Gen. Prof. Marcelo G. Martorelli.

Address: Córdoba 2069, 13°, Depto A, 1120 Buenos Aires.

Telephone: (11) 4961-7941; **Fax:** (11) 4961-7941; **Internet:** www.fundacionpea.org; **e-mail:** info@fundacionpea.org.

Fundación Raúl Prebisch (Raúl Prebisch Foundation)

Founded in 1986 by Eliana de Prebisch and Enrique García Vázquez to promote development studies in developing countries.

Activities: Operates nationally and internationally in the fields of economic affairs and social welfare. The Foundation provides grants to institutions and individuals (including research grants made to citizens of Argentinian nationality for study at the Harvard Institute for International Development, USA, in any area of development studies); awards prizes and scholarships; carries out its own research; organizes training courses and conferences.

Geographical Area of Activity: International.

Publications: *Cuadernos de Trabajo; Boletín de noticias; Documentos de Trabajo.*

Principal Staff: Dir Dr Gustavo Ferrari Wolfensen.

Address: Pasaje de la Piedad 24, 1037 Buenos Aires.

Telephone: (11) 4384-8044.

Fundación Schcolnik (Schcolnik Foundation)

Founded in 1964 by Dr Enrique Schcolnik, Dr Manuel Schcolnik, José Schcolnik and Juan Schcolnik.

Activities: Operates nationally in the fields of education and social welfare, through self-conducted programmes, grants to individuals and institutions, scholarships, publications and lectures.

Geographical Area of Activity: Argentina.

Publications: List of schools and libraries assisted by the Schcolnik Foundation.

Principal Staff: Pres. Dr E. Schcolnik; Vice-Pres. Dr F. Loyudice; Treas. J. Acevedo; Auditor Dr H. R. Della Rocca.

Address: Avda Jujuy 425, 1083 Buenos Aires.

Telephone: (11) 4957-0350; **Fax:** (11) 4956-1368; **Internet:** www.fundacionschcolnik.org.ar; **e-mail:** fundacionschcolnik@infovia.com.ar.

Fundación SES—Sustentabilidad, Educación, Solidaridad (SES Foundation—Sustainability, Education, Solidarity)

Established to assist disadvantaged youth in Argentina, promote improvement to the education system, and support other NGOs operating in these areas.

Activities: Aims to promote educative strategies towards the social inclusion of disadvantaged adolescents. Lends financial and technological support to other NGOs and community organizations working on related issues, as well as funding projects in school and universities. Also provides technical and evaluation expertise to funded projects.

Geographical Area of Activity: Argentina.

Restrictions: No grants to individuals; grants only to partner organizations.

Publications: Report of innovative educational experiences; *Bóletin* (electronic newsletter).

Officers and Trustees: Prof. Alberto Cesar Croce (Pres.); Roque Grunauer; Dr Daniel Ernesto Siben; Alejandra Esther Solla; Elizabeth Diana Wanger.

Address: Vuelta de Obligado 2667, 1428 Buenos Aires.

Telephone: (11) 4896-1921; **Fax:** (11) 4896-1920; **Internet:** www.fundses.org.ar; **e-mail:** info@fundses.org.ar.

Fundación Dr J. Roberto Villavicencio (Dr J. Roberto Villavicencio Foundation)

Established in 1982 by Dr Roberto L. Villavicencio and family to promote teaching, research and assistance in the medical sciences.

Activities: Operates in Rosario and its surrounding area in the fields of education, medicine and health, and science and technology, through self-conducted programmes, research, grants to institutions and individuals, scholarships and fellowships, prizes, conferences, training courses and publications.

Geographical Area of Activity: Argentina (Rosario).

Publications: Annual Report.

Trustees: Roberto L. Villavicencio (Pres.); Fernando Villavicencio (Vice-Pres.); Zulema B. de Villavicencio (Sec.); Ramón Parmigiani (Treas.).

Principal Staff: Dir Dr Juan Pablo-Recagno Cepeda.

Address: Alvear 854, 2000 Rosario, Santa Fe.

Telephone: (341) 449-0152; **Fax:** (341) 449-0152; **Internet:** www.villavicencio.org.ar; **e-mail:** info@villavicencio.org.ar.

Instituto para la Integración de América Latina y el Caribe—BID-INTAL (Institute for Latin American and Caribbean Integration)

Founded in 1965 as a result of an agreement between the Inter-American Development Bank and the Government of Argentina to promote regional integration.

Activities: Undertakes research on all aspects of regional integration and co-operation related to international trade, hemispheric integration and international relations with other regions and countries world-wide. There are four principal areas of activity: regional and national technical co-operation projects on integration; policy forums; integration forums; and the REDINT Integration Research Centres Network. Also provides journals, information and documentation centre services, which include 100,000 documents, 12,000 books and 400 periodicals, as well as updated bibliographies on integration and on-line searches on specific subjects.

Geographical Area of Activity: North, Central and South America, Europe and the Asia-Pacific region.

Publications: *Integration and Trade* (3 a year, in English and Spanish); *INTAL Monthly Newsletter* (monthly, in English and Spanish); *Central American Report* (annually, in Spanish); *Visión microeconómica de los impactos de la integración regional en las inversiones inter e intrarregionales: El caso de la CAN* (in Spanish); working papers and dissemination papers.

Principal Staff: Dir Juan José Taccone.

Address: Esmeralda 130, 17°, 1035 Buenos Aires.

Telephone: (11) 4320-1850; **Fax:** (11) 4320-1865; **Internet:** www.iadb.org/intal; **e-mail:** int/inl@iadb.org.

Instituto Torcuato di Tella (Torcuato di Tella Institute)

Founded in 1958 by the Fundación Torcuato di Tella, Siam di Tella Ltda, María Robiola di Tella, Torcuato di Tella, Guido di Tella, Guido Clutterbuck, Antonio Sudiero, Torcuato Sozio, Mario Robiola and Arturo Uriarte, as an entity of public benefit with the purpose of serving the community, promoting educational and intellectual activities in general, and scientific research in particular.

Activities: Operates nationally and internationally in the fields of economics, sociology, epistemology and methodology of the social sciences, political science, history and educational science, through self-conducted research, fellowships, scholarships, conferences, courses, seminars, publications and lectures. The Institute creates, directs and administers centres of investigation such as the Centro de Investigaciones Económicas and the Centro de Investigaciones Sociales. It also supports an associated centre: the Centro de Investigaciones en Ciencias de la Educación. Training courses are held for graduate students, in economics, public policy and history. Maintains a library.

Geographical Area of Activity: International.

Publications: Annual report and financial statement; each Centre publishes the results of its research work in the form of books, papers and articles in specialized journals. The Institute Press publishes books and working-papers.

Principal Staff: Dir Adolfo Canitrot.

Address: Miñones 2177, 1428 Buenos Aires.

Telephone: (11) 4783-8680; **Fax:** (11) 4783-3061; **Internet:** www.itdt.edu.

International Confederation of Family Support—CIAF

Founded in 1986 by Dr Ana Mon to support families in need and to help children living on the streets.

Activities: Operates internationally in the field of social welfare. Supports children, women and families in need through a network of day-care centres. Children are given education and training, including craft workshops and micro-enterprise training, and women are offered programmes in literacy, self-esteem and skills training, as well as support for drug and alcohol problems. Support is also offered to older members of the family. Currently operates 165 support centres in Argentina, with a further five scheduled to open, and has a further 8 centres operating in Haiti, India, Mexico, Peru, South Africa, Uruguay and Venezuela.

Geographical Area of Activity: Mainly Argentina, but also Haiti, India, Mexico, Peru, South Africa, Uruguay and Venezuela.

Restrictions: No grants for individuals and only to organizations working in the area of social promotion amongst children and young people, women and families in need.

Publications: Various reports and publications.

Finance: Each National Federation has its own budget. Argentina Federation of Family Support: total revenue US $177,648, expenditure US $196,536 (2000).

Board of Trustees: Dr Ana Mon (Pres.); Sabina Carranza (Sec.); Ma. Del Carmen Gibert (Treas.).

Address: Calle 33, No 1118, 1900 La Plata.

Telephone: (221) 422-9328; **Fax:** (221) 422-3734; **Internet:** www.esperanza.org.ar; **e-mail:** info@esperanza.org.ar.

Armenia

FOUNDATIONS, TRUSTS AND NON-PROFIT ORGANIZATIONS

AREGAK—Sun/Soleil

Established in 1996 to assist in the social development of orphan Armenian children.

Activities: Helps children in need through providing essential day-to-day assistance, assists pensioners, orphans and people with disabilities, organizes medical care for children in need, improves the provision of medical services and aims to increase philanthropic giving. Programmes include a micro-credit programme for women.

Geographical Area of Activity: Armenia.

Principal Staff: Contact: Varduhi Khachikyan.

Address: Chaikina st. 49, Yerevan 375082.

Telephone: (2) 52-22-93; **e-mail:** sun1@intarnet.am.

Open Society Institute Assistance Foundation Armenia

Established in 1996; an independent foundation, part of the Soros foundations network.

Activities: Promotes reform in the fields of education, information and the media, social welfare, public health, law and human rights, ethnic minorities and the arts and culture. Collaborates with other Armenian NGOs. Also operates on a regional level through the East–East programme.

Geographical Area of Activity: Armenia.

Finance: Annual expenditure US $1,889,000 (2001).

Board of Trustees: Boris Navasardyan (Chair.); Anahit Bayandour; Avetik Ishkhanyan; Marine Janoyan; Lana Karlova; Karen Mikaelyan; Igor Mkrtumyan.

Principal Staff: Exec. Dir Larisa Minasian.

Address: 375010 Yerevan, 1 Pushkin St, Apt 2.

Telephone: (2) 54-17-19; **Fax:** (2) 54-17-19; **Internet:** www.eurasianet.org/resource/armenia/index.shtml; **e-mail:** office@osi.am.

Australia

FOUNDATION CENTRE AND CO-ORDINATING BODY

Philanthropy Australia Inc

Established in 1975, and formerly known as the Australian Association of Philanthropy, the organization is a national membership organization representing grant-making private, family and corporate trusts and foundations.

Activities: Aims to promote responsible and effective philanthropy; assist member organizations to achieve their charitable goals; represent the views of its member organizations to policy-makers, the media and the public; encourage the development of organized philanthropy; and enhance the understanding of philanthropy. The organization operates nationally and internationally through research, conferences, training courses, networking and publications. Offers an advisory service for foundations and for those wishing to set up foundations, and a research service. Promotes and protects the interests of private and corporate giving in Australia. The organization has more than 130 member trusts and foundations, which hold assets worth over $A10,000m. and which assist the community, principally in the areas of welfare, health and medical research, education, the environment and the arts. Maintains a library, database and statistical information service.

Geographical Area of Activity: Australia.

Publications: *Australian Philanthropy* (journal, 3 a year); *The Australian Directory of Philanthropy* (every 2 years); *A Guide to Informed Giving; Successful Submission Writing for Business and Non-Profit Organizations; The Community Foundation Kit; Working with Foundations in Australia;* Annual Report.

Finance: Total assets $A513,766 (2001); annual revenue $A1,023,127, expenditure $A1,021,907 (2001).

Principal Staff: Pres. Lady Southey; Vice-Pres. Dur-e Dara; Treas. Prof. Tom Healy; National Dir Elizabeth Cham.

Address: Level 10, 530 Collins St, Melbourne, Vic 3000.

Telephone: (3) 9620 0200; **Fax:** (3) 9620 0199; **Internet:** www.philanthropy.org.au; **e-mail:** pa@philanthropy.org.au.

FOUNDATIONS, TRUSTS AND NON-PROFIT ORGANIZATIONS

Activ Foundation

Established in 1951 by a group of parents to support services for people with intellectual disability and their families.

Activities: Operates nationally to assist people with learning disabilities and their families, by providing support services including short- and long-term accommodation, respite care, employment opportunities, community access programmes, holiday and leisure programmes, transport, and a library service specific to intellectual disability.

Geographical Area of Activity: Western Australia.

Publications: *ACTIVNEWS* (newsletter, monthly); Annual Report.

Finance: Total assets $A9,466,732 (June 2002); total budget approx. $A40,000,000 (2002).

Principal Staff: Exec. Dir John S. Groves.

Address: POB 446, Wembley, WA 6913.

Telephone: (8) 9387 0555; **Fax:** (8) 9387 0599; **Internet:** www.activ.org.au.

AMP Foundation

Established in 1992 by the AMP Group, a financial services company, for general charitable purposes in the areas of health and welfare.

Activities: Operates in the fields of health care and community welfare, through offering grants to charitable and community organizations carrying out projects designed to improve health and health-care services, relieve disadvantage, and support families and young people at risk. Also offers scholarships to talented New Zealanders in any field and supports community projects in New Zealand,supports community initiatives in the United Kingdom through an employee participation scheme, and promotes academic and cultural exchanges with the People's Republic of China. In 2002, the Foundation helped establish Social Ventures Australia, in association with three leading Australian social sector organizations, which aims to find new, innovative solutions to entrenched social issues, and supporting these ideas with business mentoring and seed funding, as well as operating a $A250,000 Challenge fund, to support the most innovative ideas to address issues in the social sector, from the environment and education to employment and indigenous issues. The Foundation also operates an employee volunteering programme.

Geographical Area of Activity: Australia, New Zealand, the United Kingdom and the People's Republic of China.

Finance: Annual expenditure approx. $A3,000,000.

Principal Staff: Contact Lynn McClelland.

Address: 33 Alfred St, Sydney, NSW 2000.

Telephone: (2) 9257 7601; **Fax:** (2) 9257 2864; **Internet:** www.ampgroup.com; **e-mail:** helen_cook@amp.com.au.

Anzac Day Trust

Founded in 1960 under the Anzac Day Act for the purposes of the preservation, alteration and improvement of existing homes and the construction of new homes for aged ex-servicemen and women and their maintenance in such homes; for the welfare of widows and children of deceased ex-servicemen who were members of the forces of Her Majesty or of the Commonwealth of Australia or who, now resident in Western Australia, were members of any force of any foreign power allied or associated with Her Majesty or with the Commonwealth during any war in which Her Majesty or the Commonwealth was or is engaged, or who were allocated for navy, military or air force duty in a prescribed special area outside Australia.

Activities: Operates in the field of social welfare through grants to ex-service institutions and associations.

Geographical Area of Activity: Australia.

Publications: Annual Report.

Finance: Annual expenditure $A885,052 (2001).

Trustees: Lt Col. M. W. Farmer (retd, Chair.); Peter Ferguson; Judy Hunter; Sam Komarowski.

Address: GPO Box 69, Brisbane, Qld 4001.

Apex Foundation for Research into Intellectual Disability, Ltd

Founded by the Association of Apex Clubs to support research workers in any field which may relate to the causes, diagnosis, treatment or prevention of intellectual disability.

Activities: Provides grants to institutions and individuals and awards scholarships.

Geographical Area of Activity: Australia.

Restrictions: Researchers may be of any nationality but research must be undertaken in Australia.

Finance: Total annual funds approx. $A60,000.

Principal Staff: Pres. G. A. Angus; Sec. K. E. Morrish; Treas. P. Matthews.

Address: POB 311, Mount Evelyn, Vic 3796.

Telephone: (3) 9736 1261; **e-mail:** morrish@c031.aone.net.au.

Appropriate Technology for Community and Environment, Inc—APACE

Established in 1976 by Dr Robert Waddell and other senior academics from Sydney-based universites to seek socially-sustainable solutions to escalating global environmental degradation.

Activities: Operates in the small island states of the Pacific region, Papua New Guinea, the People's Republic of China and South-East Asia, in the fields of aid to less-developed countries, and conservation of the environment, providing technical assistance, research facilities, project design, and management and evaluation services in the fields of appropriate technology, micro-hydro-electricity and sustainable agriculture. Operates in partnership with village communities, carries out research, and offers training courses and publications.

Geographical Area of Activity: South-East Asia and the Pacific.

Publications: *APACE Newsletter* (quarterly); *Replanting the Banana Tree: a study in ecologically sustainable development; SAPA: the natural way of growing food; Rural Electrification: assessing the impacts; Micro-hydro Systems for Small Communities; Community-based Electrification Models;* and other publications.

Trustees: Prof. Paul Bryce (Pres.); Prof. Steve Johnston; Colin Lennox; John Newsom; Dr Robert Waddell.

Principal Staff: Exec. Officer Donnella Bryce; Financial Officer Peter Vail.

Address: c/o UTS, POB 123, Broadway, NSW 2007.

Telephone: (2) 9514 2554; **Fax:** (2) 9514 2611; **e-mail:** apace@uts.edu.au.

Fred P. Archer Charitable Trust

Founded for the advancement of public purposes beneficial to the community, education and the relief of poverty.

Activities: Operates nationally and in Papua New Guinea in the fields of education and social welfare.

Geographical Area of Activity: Australia and Papua New Guinea.

Principal Staff: Trust Admin. Megan McHardy.

Address: Permanent Trustee Company Ltd, 23–25 O'Connell St, GPO Box 4270, Sydney, NSW 2001.

Telephone: (2) 8295 8151; **Fax:** (2) 8295 8694.

Arthritis Foundation of Australia

Established to provide information and support to people with arthritis and related conditions, and to promote medical and scientific research in the field. Acts as the national secretariat for affiliated foundations throughout Australia.

Activities: Operates in Australia, the United Kingdom and the USA in the field of medicine and health, in particular arthritis research and education; provides assistance to the medical, scientific and allied health professions.

Geographical Area of Activity: Australia, the United Kingdom and the USA.

Finance: Annual disbursements approx. $A500,000.

National Executive: Dr John Hewson (Pres.); Sue Knowles (Vice-Pres.); Peter Hocking (Treas.); Richard Dennis (Sec.).

Principal Staff: Chief Exec. Bridget Kirkham.

Address: POB 121, Sydney, NSW 2001.

Telephone: (2) 9552 6085; **Fax:** (2) 9552 6078; **Internet:** www.arthritisfoundation.com.au.

Australasian Spinal Research Trust

Established with the aim of finding a cure for paralysis.

Activities: Operates in the field of health, through funding and promoting research into curing paralysis, fostering co-operation between all disciplines involved in central nervous system research, disseminating information about research progress, and co-operating with international efforts in the same field.

Geographical Area of Activity: Australia.

Board of Directors: Gary F. Allsop; Dr Perry F. Bartlett; A. David Cooper; Perry Cross; Bill Gibson; Joanna M. Knott; David Prast; Bob Turner; Stewart Yesner.

Address: POB 131, Artarmon, NSW 1570; Sydney Fish Market, 1st Floor, Cnr Bank St and Pyrmont Bridge Rd, Pyrmont, NSW 2009.

Telephone: (2) 9660 1040; **Fax:** (2) 9410 1539; **Internet:** www.spinetrust.com.au; **e-mail:** spinetrust@ozemail.com.au.

Australia Business Arts Foundation

Aims to increase the level of private-sector resources available to the arts, culture and humanities, and to encourage reflection on what it is to be Australian. The Foundation is an Australian government company directed by an independent board.

Activities: Encourages and promotes private-sector support for the arts and humanities in Australia and develops partnerships between the arts and business.

Geographical Area of Activity: Australia.

Publications: *Partnerships News* (quarterly newsletter); *AbaF E-News* (on-line newsletter); *The Gold Book of Business Arts Partnerships; Business Arts Partnerships—a Guide to the Business Case Approach for the Cultural Sector*; research reports.

Principal Staff: Chair. James Strong; Exec. Dir Winsome McCaughey.

Address: Level 2, 405 Collins St, Melbourne, Vic 3000.

Telephone: (3) 9616 0300; **Fax:** (3) 9614 2550; **Internet:** www.abaf.org.au; **e-mail:** information@abaf.org.au.

Australia–Japan Foundation

Founded in 1976 by the Australian Government as an independent statutory body, to strengthen relations between Australia and Japan.

Activities: Operates in Australia and Japan in the fields of education, science and the arts, by developing projects which enhance understanding. Projects include a Japanese language website and a public access Australian Resource Centre, as well as support for Australian community groups to gain access to a Japanese audience. The Sir Neil Currie Memorial Australian Studies Awards offer funding to Japanese postgraduate scholars and academics.

Geographical Area of Activity: Australia and Japan.

Publications: Annual Report.

Board of Trustees: J. Ellis (Chair. and CEO); Dr D. Carter; G. Hiscock; M. Hollands; Dr R. I. Mair; H. Nugent; M. Seares; I. Williams; A. Wynn.

Principal Staff: CEO J. Ellis; Dir, Canberra Office Don Smith; Dir, Tokyo Office Leonie Boxtel.

Address: POB E500, Kingston, ACT 2604.

Telephone: (2) 6261 3898 (Australia); (3) 5232-4063 (Japan); **Fax:** (2) 6261 2143 (Australia); (3) 5232-4064 (Japan); **Internet:** www.ajf.australia.or.jp/english/index.htm; **e-mail:** foundation.ajfcanberra@dfat.gov.au.

Australian Academy of the Humanities

Founded in 1969 by the Australian Humanities Research Council to advance scholarship and research in the humanities.

Activities: The Academy conducts research and makes grants to institutions for research. It awards grants to Australian scholars for short-term travel abroad connected with research being undertaken in the humanities.

Geographical Area of Activity: Australia.

Publications: *Proceedings* (annual report); symposium papers, monographs, occasional papers.

Finance: Maximum grant disbursed $A2,500.

Council members: Prof. Iain McCalman (Pres.); Dr Ann Kumar (Treas.); Graeme Clarke (Sec.); Prof. Robin Jeffery (Int. Sec.); Prof. Bruce Bennett (Editor); Prof. Ian Ang; Prof. Barbara Caine; Prof. Peter Cryle; Prof. Malcolm Gillies (immediate past Pres.); Prof Nerida Newbigin; Prof. Graeme Turner.

Principal Staff: Exec. Dir Dr Lawrence Warner.

Address: 3 Liversidge St, Canberra, ACT 2601; GPO Box 93, Canberra, ACT 2601.

Telephone: (2) 6125 9860; **Fax:** (2) 6248 6287; **Internet:** www.humanities.org.au; **e-mail:** aah@anu.edu.au.

Australian Academy of Science

Founded in 1954 to promote and disseminate scientific knowledge; to establish and maintain standards of scientific endeavour and achievement in the natural sciences in Australia; to recognize outstanding contributions to the advancement of science; and to establish and maintain associations and relations between Australian scientists and the International Council of Scientific Unions and other international groups of scientists, as well as between Australian scientific activities and the activities of scientists in other countries.

Activities: Operates nationally in the field of education, and both nationally and internationally in the fields of natural science, through programmes, scholarships, awards, international collaboration and publications. There are more than 300 Fellows. Maintains a library. Established the Australian Foundation for Science in 1990, which aims to promote science and technology in Australia.

Geographical Area of Activity: Mostly Australia.

Publications: *The Australian Journals of Scientific Research;* Newsletter (3 a year); various textbooks and academic publications; Annual Report.

Finance: Total assets approx. $A20,000,000 (2000).

Council Executive Committee: Dr Jim Peacock (Pres.); Prof. Bruce McKellar (Sec., Physical Sciences); Prof. John Shine (Sec., Biological Sciences); Dr Michael Barber (Sec., Science Policy); Prof. John McKenzie (Sec. Education and Public Awareness); Prof. Kurt Lambeck (Foreign Sec.); Prof. Ian McDougal (Treas.).

Principal Staff: Pres. Dr Jim Peacock.

Address: POB 783, Canberra, ACT 2601.

Telephone: (2) 6247 5777; **Fax:** (2) 6257 4620; **Internet:** www.science.org.au; **e-mail:** eb@science.org.au.

Australian–American Fulbright Commission

Founded in 1949 by the Governments of Australia and of the USA to further mutual understanding between the people of the two nations through educational and cultural exchanges.

Activities: Operates in the field of education by operating the Fulbright Scholarship programme for Americans and Australians to undertake research, study or lecturing assignments in Australia or the USA respectively. Awards cover all academic disciplines and professions.

Geographical Area of Activity: USA and Australia.

Restrictions: Scholarships are open to Australian and US citizens only.

Publications: Annual Report; *The Fulbrighter* (newsletter).

Finance: Annual government grants from Australia and the USA, and additional funding from private sources. Grants range from $A20,000 to $A50,000.

Principal Staff: Exec. Dir Mark Darby.

Address: POB 9541, Deakin, ACT 2600.

Telephone: (2) 6260 4460; **Fax:** (2) 6260 4461; **Internet:** www.fulbright.com.au; **e-mail:** fulbright@fulbright.com.au.

Australian Cancer Research Foundation

Established in 1984 by Sir Peter Abeles and Lady Sonia McMahon, the Foundation is committed to national excellence in cancer research.

Activities: Operates nationally in the field of cancer research. Funding for capital projects and equipment is provided by the Foundation, which raises funds through corporate sponsorship, donations, bequests and committee fundraising activities.

Geographical Area of Activity: Australia.

Publications: Newsletter (annual).

Finance: Raises funds through donations, corporate sponsorships and bequests; it does not raise funds from overseas. Annual disbursements approx. $A2,000,000.

Board of Trustees: T. S. Dery (Chair.); J. Boettcher; D. Boling; E. Cameron; G. Camm; T. Crommelin; C. Ganter; S. Gerlach; H. Kerr; G. Kryger; Lady McMahon; S. Perrott; Sir I. Turbott; R. Valentine.

Principal Staff: Exec. Dir Helen M. Kerr; Chair., Medical Research Cttee Prof. M. A. Vadas.

Address: Strand Arcade, Ste 409, 412 George St, Sydney, NSW 2000.

Telephone: (2) 9223 7833; **Fax:** (2) 9223 1800; **Internet:** www.acrf.com.au.

Australian Conservation Foundation

Founded in 1965 to promote the understanding and practice of conservation throughout Australia and its territories.

Activities: Operates in the field of conservation and the environment through campaigning, research, policy development, enterprises, membership services and promotion of public awareness. Operates campaign offices in South Australia and New South Wales, and a national lobby office in Canberra. Maintains a library of 11,000 volumes.

Geographical Area of Activity: Australia and the Asia-Pacific region.

Restrictions: Not a grant-making organization.

Publications: Annual Report; *Habitat* (6 a year); monthly on-line newsletter; reports, policy statements and discussion papers.

Finance: Provided by membership subscriptions, donations and government grants (10%). Total annual revenue $A4,852,258, expenditure $A4,814,035 (June 2001/02).

Principal Staff: Pres. Peter Garrett; Exec. Dir Don Henry.

Address: Floor 1, 60 Leicester St, Carlton, Vic 3053.

Telephone: (3) 9345 1111; **Fax:** (3) 9345 1166; **Internet:** www.acfonline.org.au; **e-mail:** acf@acfonline.org.au.

Australian Council for Overseas Aid—ACFOA

Founded in 1965 to provide for consultation and co-operation between member organizations concerning their work at home and abroad, with the Federal and State Governments, the United Nations and its specialized agencies, and in the field of overseas aid both nationally and internationally; to bring the needs for, and the purposes and results of, overseas aid before member organizations, the Australian community and Governments and the United Nations and its agencies; to prepare and disseminate information on aid activities and issues of development, including refugee and migrant services; and to promote research into aid activities.

Activities: The Council co-ordinates the activities of its numerous member organizations during international disasters or emergencies through the International Disaster Emergencies Committee, and has sub-committees co-ordinating activities in areas such as North–South relations, the Pacific, Indo-China and regional human rights. A development education programme co-ordinates the educational activities of member agencies, and informs and educates particular groups in the community who have a special opportunity to promote international development and co-operation, such as teachers, students and those engaged in voluntary aid administration. The Council holds specialized conferences and consultations and, in addition, promotes more stringent self-regulation by the aid sector, particularly through its development of a Code of Conduct for NGOs.

Geographical Area of Activity: International.

Publications: *ACFOA Research and Information Series; Development Issues* (occasional); *ACFOA Directory* (annually); campaign brochures; other publications related to research and development.

Finance: In addition to annual subscriptions from member organizations, the Council receives contract payments from the Federal Government, calculated on a ratio basis. The education programme is financed by special contributions from most member organizations, as well as from part of the annual grant from the Federal Government. Total accumulated funds $A795,761 (June 2002).

Executive Committee: Gaye Hart (Pres.); John Deane, Wendy Rose, David Syme (Vice-Pres.); Lynn Arnold; Jack de Groot; Andrew Hewett; Conny Lenneberg; Paul Mitchell; Veronica Ross; Heather Saville; Greg Thompson.

Principal Staff: Exec. Dir Graham Tupper.

Address: 14 Napier Close, Private Bag 3, Deakin, ACT 2600.

Telephone: (2) 6285 1816; **Fax:** (2) 6285 1720; **Internet:** www.acfoa.asn.au; **e-mail:** acfoa@acfoa.asn.au.

The Australian Elizabethan Theatre Trust—AETT

Founded in 1954 to promote independent drama, opera, ballet and the performing arts in general.

Activities: Sponsors national tours for Australian and overseas works. Conducts research, training courses and conferences, and awards prizes and grants within Australia; also awards grants and scholarships for international programmes.

Geographical Area of Activity: Mostly Australia.

Publications: *Trust News* (6 a year).

Address: 139 Regent St, Chippendale, NSW 2008.

Telephone: (2) 698 1688; **Fax:** (2) 699 1618.

Australian Foundation for the Peoples of Asia and the Pacific

Established in 1968, originally to co-ordinate philanthropic programmes in the Pacific region, now expanded to include Africa and Asia; formerly known as the Foundation for the Peoples of the South Pacific.

Activities: Supports the economic and social development of communities in Africa, Asia and the Pacific Islands, through grants to projects in the fields of health, education, rural development and the environment. Funded initiatives include HIV awareness, water and sanitation projects, literacy programmes, and training of health-care workers. Funding is currently directed towards projects in Afghanistan, Cambodia, Timor Leste, Fiji, India, Iran, Kazakhstan, Kenya, Kyrgyzstan, Laos, Malawi, Mozambique, Nepal, Philippines, Papua New Guinea, Samoa, Sri Lanka, Tajikistan, Tonga, Turkmenistan, Uzbekistan, Vietnam, Zambia and Zimbabwe. Also donates medical equipment and supplies.

Geographical Area of Activity: Africa, Asia and the Pacific.

Publications: *2000–2001 Program Report.*

Address: POB 12, Crows Nest, NSW 2065.

Telephone: (2) 9906 3792; **Fax:** (2) 9436 4637; **Internet:** www.pnp.com.au/afap; **e-mail:** afsp@mpx.com.au.

Australian Institute of International Affairs

Founded in 1933 to stimulate interest in, and provide a forum for the discussion of international affairs and foreign policy, both among its members and the general public. The Institute provides a wide range of opportunities for the dissemination of information and the free exchange of views in this field; it does not itself hold or express any opinions.

Activities: The Institute's work covers international relations, economics, trade, strategic and defence studies, and international law, through research, publications, lectures and national and international conferences. There are branches in all States. Membership of the Institute is restricted to persons over 18 years of age who are normally resident in Australia. Non-residents are eligible for associate membership, and corporate membership is available to companies and similar institutions. Companies are eligible to become 'National Supporters' of the Institute.

Geographical Area of Activity: Australia.

Publications: *Australian Journal of International Affairs—(AJIA)* (journal, 3 a year); *Australia in World Affairs* (series); *Regime Change and Regime Maintenance.*

Finance: Financed mainly through membership subscriptions, a modest government subvention, private benefactions and rental income.

National Executive Board: Neal Blewett (Pres.); Robert Clarke; David Goldsworthy; Clive Hildebrand; Doug Hunt; Aynsley Kellow; Geoffrey Miller; Felix Patrikeef; Peter Sim; Leo Teller.

Principal Staff: Exec. Dir Ross Cottrill; Chair., Research Cttee Prof. David Goldworthy.

Address: Stephen House, 32 Thesiger Court, Deakin, ACT 2600.

Telephone: (2) 6282 2133; **Fax:** (2) 6285 2334; **Internet:** www.aiia.asn.au; **e-mail:** ceo@aiia.asn.au.

Australian Multicultural Foundation

Established in 1988 to promote a commitment to Australia as one people drawn from many cultures.

Activities: Operates in Australia in the fields of the arts and humanities, education, law and human rights, medicine and health, and social welfare and social studies, through self-conducted programmes, research, grants to institutions, conferences, training courses and publications. Priority areas of interest to the Foundation are: assisting the participation of Australians in organizations important for citizenship and community responsibility; promoting an awareness of diverse cultures through English language and literacy programmes and increasing foreign language skills; and increasing tolerance through improving community relations, overseas links and social justice.

Geographical Area of Activity: Australia, with ties to the People's Republic of China, Europe and the United Kingdom.

Restrictions: No grants to individuals or outside Australia.

Publications: Annual Report; newsletter; project reports.

Board of Directors: Sir James Gobbo (Chair.); K. Lee Dow; W. McCarthy; J. Nieuwenhuysen; V. Suit-Cheng Hope; R. Tzannes.

Principal Staff: Exec. Dir B. (Hass) Dellal.

Address: POB 538, Carlton South, Vic 3053.

Telephone: (3) 9347 6622; **Fax:** (3) 9347 2218; **Internet:** www.amf.net.au; **e-mail:** info@amf.net.au.

Australian Spinal Research Foundation

Established in 1977, to contribute to the improvement of the health of Australians through research into spinal health care.

Activities: Supports research into the causes, diagnosis, prevention and treatment of syndromes and diseases of the spine. The Foundation makes grants to facilitate spinal research, in particular basic research, and research which relates to the practices and principles of chiropractic care. The Dynamic Growth (DG) Congress, a major fundraising activity, is conducted annually by the Foundation on the Gold Coast, in Queensland.

Geographical Area of Activity: Australia.

Restrictions: Priority is given to applicants from Australia.

Publications: Annual report; newsletters; brochures.

Finance: Annual disbursements approx. $A100,000.

Directors: Dr Brian Kelly (Pres.); Dr David Cahill (Vice-Pres.).

Principal Staff: Exec. Admin. Noel Culbert.

Address: POB 1047, Springwood, Qld 4127.

Telephone: (7) 3808 4098; **Fax:** (7) 3808 8109; **Internet:** www.spinalresearch.com.au; **e-mail:** asrf@spinalresearch.com.au.

Australian Volunteers International

Founded in 1961 and previously known as the Overseas Service Bureau, to encourage the transference of technical expertise from Australia to people of the developing world, particularly countries of Africa, Asia and the Pacific.

Activities: Promotes exchanges between experts in international development; recruits, prepares and sends volunteers to work in less-developed countries, in partnership with local communities. The organization has placed approximately 6,000 Australian volunteers in more than 50 countries of Africa, Asia, the Pacific and Central and South America, and in Australian Aboriginal communities. Maintains a library.

Geographical Area of Activity: Africa, Asia and the Pacific, and Central and South America.

Publications: *Australian Volunteers* (newsletter, 3 a year); Annual Report.

Finance: Total assets $A8,301,216 (June 2002); total revenue $A21,260,149, total expenditure $A20,406,875 (2002).

Management Committee: Prof. Bob Meyenn (Chair.); Alan Davis; John Ingram; Hugh O'Neill; Barbara Spalding; Jean Ker Walsh; Dr Katrina Watson.

Principal Staff: CEO Bill Armstrong.

Address: POB 350, Fitzroy, Vic 3065.

Telephone: (3) 9279 1788; **Fax:** (3) 9419 4280; **Internet:** www.ozvol.org.au; **e-mail:** ccr@ozvol.org.au.

Jack Brockhoff Foundation

Founded in Victoria to provide financial assistance to agencies offering support services to the aged, disabled, homeless and disadvantaged, and to people with long-term health problems dependent on support programmes.

Activities: Provides funding for community groups, hospitals, youth support organizations, special schools, research institutes and charitable organizations in Victoria. Funds are primarily directed at people with disabilities, particularly children, elderly people, people with debilitating illnesses, severely disadvantaged families, homeless young people at risk and those recovering from substance abuse.

Geographical Area of Activity: Victoria, Australia only.

Restrictions: Funding is restricted to organizations in Victoria, Australia; no funding for the arts, museums, environment, conservation, travel, seminars, conferences, sporting clubs, and salaries.

Finance: Annual disbursements approx. $A2,500,000.

Principal Staff: Exec. Officer Ken Mayberry.

Address: POB 1580, Doncaster East, Vic 3109.

Telephone: (3) 9842 0667; **Fax:** (3) 9842 0663; **e-mail:** kem@brockhoff.info.

The Cancer Council of Victoria

Founded in 1936 by the State Government of Victoria and governed by the Cancer Act 1958; it is now an independent, volunteer-based charity whose mission is to lead, co-ordinate, implement and evaluate action to minimise the human cost of cancer for all Victorians.

Activities: Promotes research into the causes and treatment of cancer; encourages prevention; organizes public education campaigns; provides support services for cancer patients and their carers; and raises funds for the provision of grants for relevant study in institutions in Victoria. The Cancer Control Research Institute of the Cancer Council carries out behavioural research in cancer, especially sun exposure and tobacco consumption and regulations.

Geographical Area of Activity: Victoria, Australia.

Publications: Annual Report; *Canstat* (quarterly); *Cancer News* (quarterly).

Finance: Funded through donations, bequests and corporate sponsorship, and through fundraising events. Annual expenditure on research projects approx. $A10,000,000.

Principal Staff: Dir Prof. David Hill; Council Sec. Nicole Prosper.

Address: 1 Rathdowne St, Carlton, Vic 3053.

Telephone: (3) 9635 5000; **Fax:** (3) 9635 5270; **Internet:** www.cancervic.org.au; **e-mail:** enquiries@cancervic.org.au.

Children's Medical Research Institute

Established in 1958 to initiate and carry out research in the field of paediatrics; to collate and assess the results of current paediatric research and to make available knowledge so obtained to those concerned in the care of the nation's children and to the medical profession. It is affiliated with the University of Sydney and the Children's Hospital Westmead.

Activities: Provides funds for students undertaking research which will lead to postgraduate degrees, and for post-doctoral research. Main areas of research are childhood diseases, with special reference to neurosciences, cancer, leukaemia and genetic disorders, utilizing recombinant DNA technology. Awards are open to Australian residents for graduate studies and to postgraduates from outside Australia for fellowships.

Geographical Area of Activity: Australia and international.

Restrictions: Grants to students who are Australian residents and internationally to postgraduate students.

Publications: Annual Report.

Finance: Total net assets $A65,131,274 (June 2001).

Board of Directors: Dr Frank Martin (Pres.); Carolyn Forster (Vice-Pres.); Rod Atfield (Treas.); John Bevins; Christopher Cullen; Prof. Anthony Cunningham; John Dunlop; Elizabeth Hallett; Prof. Craig Mellis; Vicki Miller; Assoc. Prof. Kathryn North; Patricia Payne; Prof. Peter Rowe; Prof. John Turtle.

Principal Staff: Dir Prof. Peter B. Rowe.

Address: Locked Bag 23, Wentworthville, NSW 2145.

Telephone: (2) 9687 2800; **Fax:** (2) 9687 2120; **Internet:** www.cmri.com.au; **e-mail:** prowe@cmri.usyd.edu.au.

Winston Churchill Memorial Trust

Founded in 1965 to perpetuate and honour the memory of Sir Winston Churchill, who died that year, by the award of Memorial Fellowships, known as 'Churchill Fellowships'.

Activities: Churchill Fellowships are awarded each year to Australians from all walks of life to undertake an overseas investigative project of a kind for which facilities are not available in Australia. There are no prescribed qualifications, academic or otherwise, for the award of a fellowship. Merit is the primary test, whether based on past achievements or on demonstrated ability for future achievement in any field. The value of an applicant's work to the community and the extent to which it will be enhanced by the applicant's overseas study project are also important criteria.

Geographical Area of Activity: Australia.

Restrictions: Grants normally only to individuals who are Australian citizens.

Publications: Annual report and financial statement.

Finance: Total assets $A52,552,721 (Jan. 2002). About 100 Churchill Fellowships are awarded annually, with a value of approx. $A20,000 (2001).

Board of Directors: R. L. Martin (Nat. Pres.); Hon. Justice Cox (Nat. Chair.); E. Alexander, Dr B. Appleton (Deputy Chair.); Ian Castles (Hon. Treas.); W. R. R. Beggs; C. J. Brazier; J. H. Byth; L. F. Guthrey; J. P. Kennedy; R. A. Layton; A. G. McGregor; K. McInnes; Sir David Smith; Justice S. G. Thomas; A. S. Trethewey; M. J. White; Dr J. Wilson.

Principal Staff: Chief Exec. Paul Tys; Senior Exec. Officer Margaret Bell; Fellowship Officer Meg Martin.

Address: Churchill House, 30 Balmain Crescent, Acton ACT 2601; GPO Box 1536, Canberra, ACT 2601.

Telephone: (2) 6247 8333; **Fax:** (2) 6249 8944; **Internet:** www.churchilltrust.com.au; **e-mail:** churchilltrust@bigpond.com.

Clean Up the World

Founded by Ian Kiernan in 1993 as a global outreach programme of Clean Up Australia, to help communities make a positive impact on the health of their environment.

Activities: Operates internationally in the field of conservation and the environment, through supporting community-based environmental projects. The emphasis is on simple activities, such as rubbish collection and removal, tree-planting, education initiatives such as schools-focused lectures and activities, worm-farming and composting. Clean Up events are currently held in 124 countries.

Geographical Area of Activity: International.

Restrictions: Acts as a sponsorship facilitator; no direct grants.

Publications: *Clean Up the World Activity Report* (annual); Regional Bulletin (quarterly); Newsletter (bi-annual).

Finance: Funding comes from private sponsorship and donations.

Clean Up the World Board: Ian Kiernan (Chair.); Kim McKay (Deputy Chair.); Simon Balderstone; John Buttle; Dr Jane Hall; Molly Harriss Olson; Victor Kelly; Richard Osborn; Alan Tippett.

Principal Staff: Gen. Man. Rose Read.

Address: Level 1, 18 Bridge Rd, Glebe, NSW 2037.

Telephone: (2) 9552 6177; **Fax:** (2) 9552 4468; **Internet:** www.cleanup.com.au; **e-mail:** foundation@cleanup.com.au.

Ian Clunies Ross Memorial Foundation

Established in 1959 to promote and further the development of science and its communication and application to best benefit a developing Australia and the challenges of the global environment.

Activities: Administers the annual Clunies Ross National Science and Technology Award awarded to people who have made important contributions to science and its application for the benefit of Australia. Also established the Queensland Clunies Ross Centre for Science and Industry in collaboration with the Queensland Government.

Geographical Area of Activity: Australia.

Restrictions: Not a grant-making organization.

Publications: *Outside the Square;* Annual Report.

Governors: Dr John Zillman (Chair.).

Principal Staff: Foundation Sec. Mary Bolger.

Address: 89 High St, Ste 505, Kew, Vic 3101.

Telephone: (3) 9854 6266; **Fax:** (3) 9853 5267; **Internet:** www.cluniesross.org.au; **e-mail:** mbolger@cluniesross.org.au.

Collier Charitable Fund

Founded in 1954 by the wills of Annette Collier, Alice Collier and Edith Collier to support various charitable purposes in Australia.

Activities: Grants are made at the discretion of the trustees for the benefit of hospitals and institutions for the sick or elderly in Victoria, public education, the relief of poverty, to the Australian Red Cross and for other causes thought worthy of consideration in Australia.

Geographical Area of Activity: Australia.

Restrictions: Grants made within Australia only.

Finance: Annual disbursements $A2,282,000 (2002).

Principal Staff: Sec. Judith Robertson.

Address: Marland House, 31st Floor, 570 Bourke St, Melbourne, Vic 3000.

Telephone: (3) 9670 1647; **Fax:** (3) 9670 2474.

Council for the Encouragement of Philanthropy in Australia—CEPA

Founded by Ron Clarke with the purpose of encouraging Australians to consider and assist disadvantaged people. Membership organization open to the community, public and business sectors.

Activities: Aims to support disadvantaged people in Australia, through encouraging and channelling donations from individuals, foundations and companies to not-for-profit organizations. Grants are made in the fields of education and research, including educational scholarships; the environment; health; and social services.

Geographical Area of Activity: Australia.

Restrictions: No unsolicited appeals accepted; no grants to individuals except educational scholarships.

Publications: *CEPA Trust Newsletter* (electronic newsletter, quarterly).

Principal Staff: Pres. Ron Clarke; Exec. Dir Mike Strauss.

Address: Locked Bag 120, 600 St Kilda Rd Central, Melbourne, VIC 8008.

Telephone: (3) 9526 8916; **Fax:** (3) 9526 8922; **Internet:** www.cepatrust.com.

Credit Union Foundation Australia—CUFA

Founded in 1971 as the international development agency of the Australian Credit Union Movement, to assist the development of credit unions in South-East Asia, the South Pacific and Australia.

Activities: Supports the development of credit unions in communities in the Asia-Pacific region, and amongst Australian Aboriginals and Torres Strait Islanders. Co-operates with credit union movements, governments and NGO development agencies.

Geographical Area of Activity: South-East Asia and the Pacific.

Publications: *CUFA Advocate* (newsletter); Annual Report.

Trustees: Neville Parsons (Chair.); Bill Field (Deputy Chair.); Ashley Jennings; Rob Nicholls.

Principal Staff: Man., Int. Development Grahame Mehrtens.

Address: 51 Druitt St, Level 3, NSW 2000.

Telephone: (2) 9333 7841; **Fax:** (2) 9267 5415; **Internet:** www.cu.net.au; **e-mail:** gmehrten@cuscal.com.au.

The Foundation for Young Australians

Established in June 2000 following the merger of the Queen's Trust for Young Australians and the Australian Youth Foundation; aims to create positive opportunities and outcomes for children and youth by leading the development of innovative strategies that enable young people to reach their potential and participate fully in society.

Activities: Fifty per cent of funding is spent on programmes to benefit disadvantaged young people in the fields of education, law and human rights, employment, health and mental health, housing and homelessness, and civic and youth participation. The remaining 50 per cent is spent on programmes to develop leadership potential and promote the pursuit of excellence. The Foundation is an affiliated partner of the International Youth Foundation (USA, q.v.) and a member of the International Youth Foundation Global Network of Partners.

Geographical Area of Activity: Australia.

Restrictions: Funding is only provided to benefit young Australians.

Publications: *Social Marketing for the New Millennium* (2000); *Any Which Way You Can; The START Do-it-Yourself Evaluation Manual; Young People and Police Powers; Public Spaces for Young People*; reports and evaluations; Annual Report.

Finance: Assets $A53,091,593 (2001); annual expenditure more than $A3,000,000.

Board of Governors: William J. Conn (Chair.); J. Ralph (Deputy Chair.); W. Bailey; R. H. Barry; R. Campbell; Hon. G. Crafter; Capt. D. Eldridge; S. Hewlett; J. Horne; B. Lancken; K. F. Lim; A. McDonald; Rev. Dr D. Merritt; Prof. R. Moodie; B. Nguyen; R. Oliver; J. Reichstein; M. Sullivan; T. Williams.

Principal Staff: CEO Mary Wooldridge.

Address: GPO 239E, Melbourne, Vic 3001.

Telephone: (2) 9357 2344; **Fax:** (2) 9358 5635; **Internet:** www.youngaustralians.org; **e-mail:** nsw@youngaustralians.org.

The Heart Foundation

Founded in 1960 to co-ordinate and correlate the efforts of organizations and individuals interested in the causes, diagnosis, prevention and treatment of diseases of the heart with a view to reducing the resulting disability and mortality in Australia; to assist the study of and the acquisition, dissemination and application of information concerning such diseases; and to stimulate public interest in the prevention and treatment of diseases of the heart.

Activities: Operates in the fields of science, medicine and community education on a nationally co-ordinated basis, through self-conducted programmes, research, grants to individuals and institutions, fellowships and scholarships, conferences, courses, lectures and publications. The Foundation offers the Warren McDonald International Fellowship to bring researchers in its field of interest to Australia; the Overseas Research Fellowship for research abroad and in Australia, open to Australian nationals or permanent residents; medical and scientific research scholarships for Australian nationals or permanent residents; and travel grants for Australian residents.

Geographical Area of Activity: Australia.

Publications: Report of operations and financial statement; research reports; Annual Report.

Finance: Annual disbursements approx. $A5,600,000.

Principal Staff: Dir of Health, Medical and Scientific Affairs Prof. Andrew Tonkin.

Address: Cnr Geils Court and Denison St, Deakin, ACT 2600.

Telephone: (2) 6282 2144; **Fax:** (2) 6282 5147; **Internet:** www.heartfoundation.com.au; **e-mail:** heartlinesa@heartfoundation.com.au.

The Fred Hollows Foundation

Established in 1992 the Foundation works throughout the world to prevent unnecessary and avoidable blindness. Aims to help establish a world where no one is needlessly blind and where indigenous people enjoy the same health outcomes as all Australians; draws on the values and beliefs inspired by the work of the late Prof. Fred Hollows.

Activities: Provides funding, training and expertise to assist with the treatment of the cataract blind in developing countries; works with local agencies to develop programmes to provide modern cataract surgery and support local health infrastructure relating to eye health in these countries. The Foundation is active in Australia, Africa, Asia and the Pacific and has links with various international blindness-prevention programmes, including Vision 2020: The Right to Sight. It does not offer regular grants or scholarships.

Geographical Area of Activity: Australia, Africa, Asia and the Pacific.

Restrictions: No grants or scholarships available.

Publications: *Sharing the Vision* (quarterly newsletter); *Strategic Framework: 2002–2005*; Annual Report.

Finance: Funded through public donations, government grants, corporate and foundation support, bequests, research and development and merchandise proceeds; total assets $A3,629,834 (2001); total revenue $A8,348,826, total expenditure $A7,758,066 (2001).

Board of Trustees: Nigel Milan (Chair.); Howard Davies (Treas.); Victoria Rubensohn (Sec.); Fessehaie Abraham; John Dawkins; Tim Fischer; Mark Gillies; Gabi Hollows; Brent Impey; Michael Johnson; Ray Martin; Hugh Taylor.

Principal Staff: Chief Exec. Mike Lynskey; Deputy Chief Exec. Chip Morgan.

Address: 4 Mitchell St, Enfield, NSW 2136; Locked Bag 3100, Burwood, NSW 1805.

Telephone: (2) 8741 1900; **Fax:** (2) 8741 1999; **Internet:** www.hollows.org; **e-mail:** fhf@hollows.org.

James N. Kirby Foundation

Founded in 1967 by Sir James Norman Kirby, chair of the James N. Kirby group of companies, for broad charitable and community welfare purposes.

Activities: Operates nationally in the fields of education, medicine, social welfare, science, technology, art, culture, and the conservation, maintenance and development of Australia's natural resources, through grants to charitable, educational and technical institutions, particularly in support of technical education projects for young people. Also supports the annual James N. Kirby Award, made by the Institution of Industrial Engineers.

Geographical Area of Activity: Australia.

Restrictions: No grants are made to individuals, nor outside Australia. Grants only to charitable organizations.

Publications: Annual report and financial statement.

Finance: Annual disbursements approx. $A350,000.

Governing Board: K. J. Kirby (Chair.).

Principal Staff: Exec. Asst J. Sinfield.

Address: Locked Bag 6501, Milperra, Sydney, NSW 1891.

Telephone: (2) 9212 2711; **Fax:** (2) 9211 4474.

Law and Justice Foundation of New South Wales

Founded in 1967, seeks to improve access to justice, particularly for socially- and economically-disadvantaged people.

Activities: The Foundation identifies the needs, in particular of socially- and economically-disadvantaged people with regard to access to justice; conducts rigorous, independent research to inform policy development; contributes to the availability of understandable legal information; and supports organizations and projects that improve access to justice.

Geographical Area of Activity: Australia.

Restrictions: Grants only in Australia.

Publications: *Bulletin* (quarterly); Annual Report.

Finance: Publicly funded. Annual disbursements vary but approx. $A750,000.

Board of Governors: G. E. (Tony) Fitzgerald (Chair); Geoff Mulherin; Annette O'Neill; Kevin Rozzoli; Janelle Saffin; Bret Walker; Pauline Wright.

Principal Staff: Dir Geoff Mulherin; Grants Man. Catherine M. Lloyd.

Address: GPO Box 4264, Sydney, NSW 2001.

Telephone: (2) 9221 3900; **Fax:** (2) 9221 6280; **Internet:** www.lawfoundation.net.au; **e-mail:** lf@lawfoundation.net.au.

Macquarie Charitable Foundation

Established in 1984 by Macquarie Bank, to illustrate the company's commitment to the society in which it operates and to contribute toward the betterment of society.

Activities: Foundation support focuses on five main areas: the arts; education; the environment; welfare; and health-care and medical research.

Geographical Area of Activity: Australia.

Restrictions: No grants to individuals; grants made to Australian-based initiatives.

Publications: Annual Report.

Principal Staff: Man. Julie White.

Address: Macquarie Bank Ltd, GPO Box 4294, Sydney, NSW 1164.

Telephone: (2) 8232 9673; **Fax:** (2) 8232 6346; **Internet:** www.macquarie.com.au; **e-mail:** julie.white@macquarie.com.

Medical Research Endowment Fund

Founded to provide support nationally to universities, institutions, Federal or State departments and individuals involved in medical research.

Geographical Area of Activity: Australia.

Publications: Numerous publications.

Finance: Annual disbursements approx. $A6,000,000.

Address: c/o National Health and Medical Research Council, GPO Box 9848, Canberra, ACT 2601.

Telephone: (2) 6289 7178; **Fax:** (2) 6289 4117; **Internet:** www.health.gov.au/nhmrc.

The Sir Robert Menzies Memorial Foundation Ltd

Founded in 1979 by the Sir Robert Menzies Memorial Trust using funds raised in memory of Sir Robert Menzies.

Activities: The Foundation provides funding for postgraduate scholarships in the discipline of law (one or two annually); applicants must be Australian citizens. Awards are tenable at all United Kingdom universities; however, priority is given to those wishing to study at the Universities of Oxford, Cambridge, St Andrews or Edinburgh. Part funds the Menzies Centre for Australian Studies at the University of London.

Geographical Area of Activity: Australia.

Restrictions: Scholarship applicants must be Australian citizens.

Publications: Annual Report; *Transactions of the Menzies Foundation* (report series).

Finance: Total assets $A14,315,304 (Dec. 2001); total revenue $A593,591, total expenditure $A999,306 (2001).

Board of Directors: Hon. Sir Daryl Dawson (Chair.).

Principal Staff: Gen. Man. S. Mackenzie.

Address: 210 Clarendon St, East Melbourne, Vic 3002.

Telephone: (3) 9419 5699; **Fax:** (3) 9417 7049; **Internet:** www.vicnet.net.au/~menzies; **e-mail:** menzies@vicnet.net.au.

R. G. Menzies Scholarship Fund

Founded in 1967 by the Harvard Club of Australia to 'honour a great Australian statesman', and to further Australian–American relations through the establishment of a fund to help Australians undertake study at Harvard, and Americans at The Australian National University (ANU). Present sponsors are the Harvard Club of Australia, the ANU and the Sir Robert Menzies Memorial Trust (q.v.).

Activities: Operates in the field of education, through the allocation of one or more scholarships annually for a graduate of an Australian university to attend a graduate school at Harvard University, or from time to time for a Harvard graduate to attend the ANU. To be eligible for consideration, a candidate must be a graduate of an Australian university; an Australian citizen or permanent resident of Australia; normally resident in Australia; intending to return to Australia after studies at Harvard or to represent directly Australia overseas; not previously or currently enrolled in a postgraduate course at a US university; eligible for and in the process of directly applying, or have applied, for admission to a degree programme in a graduate school of Harvard University.

Geographical Area of Activity: Australia and the USA.

Finance: Annual scholarship budget approx. $A50,000 (2003/2004).

Principal Staff: Cttee Sec. Karen Holt.

Address: c/o ANU, Rm 1.09, Chancelry Bldg 10, Canberra, ACT 0200.

Telephone: (2) 6125 2825; **Internet:** www.anu.edu.au/cabs/scholarships/; **e-mail:** cabs.admin@anu.edu.au.

Murdoch Children's Research Institute

Established originally as the Royal Children's Hospital Research Foundation in 1960, merged with the Murdoch Institute (established in 1984) in 2000, the Institute conducts, supports and promotes research to improve the health of children and adolescents.

Activities: Operates in the field of medicine and health, nationally and internationally through carrying out and funding research in a number of themed areas, including bone disorders, addiction, cerebral palsy and chromosome abnormalities, each area encompassing biomedical and public health research and community education. All research is carried out at the Institute; however, the Institute maintains strong international links and encourages visits by overseas students.

Geographical Area of Activity: Australia.

Restrictions: No outside grants available.

Publications: Annual Report.

Board of Directors: Laurence G. Cox (Chair.); W. H. Hodgson (Deputy Chair.); Kathy Alexander; Martin Armstrong; Janet Calvert-Jones; Assoc. Prof. Anthony Dart; Helen Davison; Jane Fenton; Peter Griffin; Judy Paterson; Prof. David Penington; Prof. Richard Smallwood; Prof. Peter Smith; Prof. Geoff Tregear; Prof. Bob Williamson.

Principal Staff: Chief Operating Officer and Assoc. Dir Anne Cronin.

Address: Royal Children's Hospital, Flemington Rd, Parkville, Melbourne, Vic 3052.

Telephone: (3) 8341 6200; **Fax:** (3) 9348 1391; **Internet:** www.murdoch.rch.unimelb.edu.au; **e-mail:** murdoch@cryptic.rch.unimelb.edu.au.

Myer Foundation

Founded in 1959 by Kenneth B. Myer and S. Baillieu Myer to support programmes responding to community needs.

Activities: Works nationally through self-conducted programmes and grants to institutions, particularly in the five following areas selected for specific focus: the arts and humanities, developing the Australian and Aboriginal cultural identity; 'beyond Australia' projects, supporting Australian organizations that work in the Asia-Pacific region, and assisting refugees and asylum seekers; social justice, funding research and organizations in the field; water and the environment, empowering communities to engage actively in environmental protection, and improving water resources; and the development of Australian philanthropy. Also supports special projects, including the annual Sydney Myers Performing Arts Awards, collectively worth $A105,000, and research into the future needs of elderly people in Australia.

Geographical Area of Activity: Australia and the Asia-Pacific region.

Restrictions: No support is given for medical research, scholarships, travel, film or video, nor to individuals.

Publications: Annual Report.

Finance: Total grants $A5,625,142 (2000/2001).

Directors: Marigold Southey (Pres.); Carrillo Gantner, Andrew Myer, Rupert Myer (Vice-Pres); Joanna Baevski; Sandy Clark; Baillieu Myer; Emily Myer; Sidney Myer; Stephen Shelmerdine.

Principal Staff: CEO Charles R. Lane.

Address: 55 Collins St, 44th Floor, Melbourne, Vic 3070.

Telephone: (3) 9207 3040; **Fax:** (3) 9207 3070; **Internet:** www.myerfoundation.org.au; **e-mail:** christine@myerfoundation.org.au.

Sidney Myer Fund

Founded by Sidney Myer in 1934, to support programmes which respond to community needs.

Activities: The Fund operates nationally in all areas relating to community needs, including the fields of human rights, law, welfare, the environment and personal services. Emphasis is placed on social development and innovation. Limited support is available for building programmes and general appeals.

Geographical Area of Activity: Australia.

Restrictions: No support is given for scholarships, travel, films or videos, nor for individuals.

Publications: Annual Report.

Finance: Total grants $A4,457,540 (2000/2001).

Trustees: Carrillo Gantner (Chair); Sandy Clark; Geoffrey Cohen; Sidney Myer.

Principal Staff: Exec. Officer Helen Morris; Office Man. Irene Tury.

Address: 55 Collins St, Level 45, Melbourne, Vic 3000.

Telephone: (3) 9207 3040; **Fax:** (3) 9207 3070; **Internet:** www.myerfoundation.org.au; **e-mail:** enquiries@myerfoundation.org.au.

National Health and Medical Research Council

Founded in 1936 to inquire into, advise and make recommendations to the Federal and the State governments on matters of public health legislation and administration; to advise on the application of the Medical Research Endowment Fund (q.v.); and to advise and make recommendations on the expenditure of money on medical research.

Activities: Operates nationally and internationally in the field of science and medicine, through research fellowships, publications and support of research projects. In the field of education, support is given to nationals for training in medical research. Grants are made to universities, independent institutions and individuals engaged in medical research. Projects are also carried out through self-conducted programmes and conferences. The Council makes annual awards to assist in the appointment of distinguished expatriate medical and dental researchers, who have been overseas for at least seven years, to an academic position in Australia; the Awards are valued at up to $A150,000 per year. R. Douglas Wright Awards are made annually to 'outstanding' researchers, to give an opportunity for independent research together with improved security; the Awards provide a salary plus an allowance of $A10,000 payable to the department where the awardee is working; the Award is tenable for four years.

Geographical Area of Activity: Australia.

Publications: *Report of Council Session* (3 a year); reports from Council's Committees relating to medical care, medical research and public health.

Finance: Total grants awarded $A369,764,410 (2001).

Council: Prof. Nicholas Saunders (Chair.).

Principal Staff: CEO Alan Pettigrew.

Address: POB 9848, Canberra, ACT 2601.

Telephone: (2) 6289 9184; **Fax:** (2) 6289 9197; **Internet:** www.nhmrc.health.gov.au; **e-mail:** exec.sec@nhmrc.gov.au.

New South Wales Cancer Council

Founded in 1955, the Council funds research into the causes, treatment, early diagnosis and prevention of cancer, assists with the education of public and health professionals and gives practical and emotional support to people who have cancer and to their families.

Activities: Disseminates information on cancer; organizes cancer education and publicity programmes throughout New South Wales; co-ordinates cancer-related services for patients, relatives and health professionals; raises funds to support activities. Funding is provided for projects in New South Wales which investigate the causes and control of cancer at fundamental and applied levels, and for resources or programmes in professional education in New South Wales. The Council runs breast and cervical screening programmes. Travel grants are awarded to workers in palliative care and other health professionals.

Geographical Area of Activity: New South Wales, Australia.

Publications: Annual Report; Research Report; Guidelines.

Finance: Research budget approx. $A5,100,000 (2002).

Principal Staff: Man., Corporate Services David Penny.

Address: 153 Dowling St, Woolloomooloo, NSW 2011; POB 572, Kings Cross, NSW 1340.

Telephone: (2) 9334 1900; **Fax:** (2) 9357 2676; **Internet:** www.nswcc.org.au; **e-mail:** feedback@nswcc.org.au.

Oxfam Community Aid Abroad

Established in 1953 to work with communities for social justice, environmental sustainability and the eradication of poverty. Merged with the Australian Freedom From Hunger Campaign in 1992.

Activities: Operates in the area of assistance to less-developed countries, through self-conducted programmes, research, publications and advocacy; supports innovative and imaginative development projects in Aboriginal Australia and overseas, and acts to mobilize the Australian community and influence key policy- and decision-makers. Launched the Ethical Investment Trust, which in 2000 established the first Ethical Investment Deposit Account. The organization is a member of Oxfam International (q.v.).

Geographical Area of Activity: Africa (the Horn and Southern), South and South-East Asia, Central America, the Pacific, Indo-China, Aboriginal Australia, and the Middle East.

Publications: *Oxfam Horizons* (quarterly); *Oxfam Connections* (quarterly); *The Globalisation Challenge; Breaking the Banks; Setting Things Right: Ending Poverty by Achieving Basic Human Rights;* Annual Report; other books and publications for schools, background reports, briefing papers, reports on issues in development, etc.

Finance: Total assets $A17,791,000 (June 2001); annual revenue $A23,654,000, expenditure $A27,127,000 (2001).

National Executive Committee: Judy Mitchell (Chair.).

Principal Staff: Exec. Dir Andrew Hewett.

Address: 156 George St, Fitzroy, Vic 3065.

Telephone: (3) 9289 9444; **Fax:** (3) 9419 5318; **Internet:** www.caa.org.au; **e-mail:** enquire@caa.org.au.

Oz Child: Children Australia Inc

Established in 1993, through the merger of Family Action (established 1851), Family Focus (established 1893) and the National Children's Bureau of Australia (established 1971), for the protection of children.

Activities: Operates nationally in the areas of children's rights and welfare, including the protection of children from abuse, disability, juvenile justice and educational support services; internationally, through the Oz Child International Program (a separate trust fund), the organization is involved in reducing the effects of environmental degradation, the alleviation of poverty, and the protection of children from abuses such as child labour and sexual exploitation, in Southern and South-East Asia and the Pacific region. The types of international projects supported include micro-financing initiatives and vocational training programmes.

Geographical Area of Activity: Australia and the Asia-Pacific region.

Publications: Newsletter; Annual Report.

Address: Level 3, 150 Albert Rd, South Melbourne, NSW 3205.

Telephone: (3) 9695 2200; **Fax:** (3) 9696 0507; **Internet:** www.childrenaustralia.com.au; **e-mail:** ozchild@ozchild.com.au.

Perpetual Foundation

The Foundation was established by Perpetual Trustees Australia, a trustee company operating throughout Australia.

Activities: The Foundation administers about 270 charitable trusts and foundations operating in Australia. Income generated from the capital of these foundations is distributed annually to charitable organizations, in accordance with the wishes of the founders of the managed trusts, supporting initiatives in the areas of social and community welfare, education, medical and scientific research, arts and culture and the environment.

Geographical Area of Activity: Australia.

Restrictions: No grants are made to individuals.

Finance: Assets of managed trusts and foundations approx. $A12,200,000 (June 2001); total grants $A526,971 (2001).

Principal Staff: Chair. Graham J. Bradley.

Address: Perpetual Trustee Co Ltd, GPO Box 4712, Sydney, NSW 2001.

Telephone: (2) 9229 3951; **Fax:** (2) 9229 3957; **Internet:** www.perpetual.com.au; **e-mail:** foundations@perpetual.com.au.

Ian Potter Foundation

Founded in 1964 by Sir Ian Potter for the establishment, endowment, maintenance and support of any public charitable purposes in Australia such as universities, colleges, schools, laboratories, research and experimental stations, libraries and statistical bureaux, and eleemosynary institutions, by any means or methods which to the trustees seem desirable.

Activities: Operates nationally in many spheres of charity, through research, grants to institutions, fellowships, scholarships, conferences, courses, publications and lectures. Extensive grants have been awarded in the fields of education, scientific and medical research, health, the arts, environmental research, and social welfare; travel grants are available to help young staff members attend conferences or study overseas; and the Ian Potter Cultural Trust also provides grants to individuals for education, travel and a range of cultural activities.

Geographical Area of Activity: Australia.

Restrictions: No grants to individuals. Organizations must have Deductible Gift Recipient status.

Publications: Annual distribution report.

Finance: Assets approx. $A200,000,000 (2001); annual disbursements approx. $A7,600,000 (2001).

Principal Staff: Exec. Sec. Dr Dorothy Scott; Admin. C. Mackieson.

Address: 111 Collins St, Level 3, Melbourne, Vic 3000.

Telephone: (3) 9650 3188; **Fax:** (3) 9650 7986; **Internet:** www.ianpotter.org.au; **e-mail:** admin@ianpotter.org.au.

Queensland Cancer Fund

Founded in 1961 to foster investigation and assist research into the causes, prevention and treatment of cancer.

Activities: Provides funding for cancer research projects at major research institutions in Queensland; finances development and improvement of treatment facilities in Queensland hospitals and treatment centres; provides a broad-based education for the community on cancer; awards scholarships and fellowships; maintains hospital and residential accommodation for patients receiving treatment for cancer; establishes and maintains a network of cancer support services for cancer sufferers, their immediate families and friends.

Geographical Area of Activity: Queensland, Australia.

Restrictions: No grants made outside Queensland.

Publications: *Cancer News* (quarterly newsletter); *Impact;* Annual Report.

Finance: Annual disbursements $A14,500,000 (2002).

Board of Trustees: Anti-Cancer Council.

Principal Staff: Exec. Dir Dr J. Dunn; Finance Dir A. Hooper.

Address: POB 201, Spring Hill, Qld 4004.

Telephone: (7) 3258 2200; **Fax:** (7) 3257 1306; **Internet:** www.qldcancer.com.au; **e-mail:** qldcf@qldcancer.com.au.

Clive and Vera Ramaciotti Foundation

Founded in 1970 by Vera Ramaciotti to support biomedical research, particularly in new fields.

Activities: The Foundation awards grants to biomedical institutions and administers the Ramaciotti Travel Grants.

Geographical Area of Activity: Australia.

Finance: Annual disbursements $A1,400,000 (Nov. 2000).

Trustees: Perpetual Trustee Co., Ltd (see Perpetual Foundation).

Address: c/o Perpetual Trustee Co Ltd, GPO Box 4712, Sydney, NSW 2001.

Telephone: (2) 9229 3951; **Fax:** (2) 9229 3957; **Internet:** www.perpetual.com.au; **e-mail:** foundations@perpetual.com.au.

Reichstein Foundation

Established with the aim of facilitating structural change in society and community development.

Activities: Aims to support community development and facilitate structural change in society in Australia, through grants to community organizations, within the priority areas of indigenous peoples, people with disabilities, and refugees and asylum seekers. Support is also available for community organizations working in the field of social justice related causes, for projects concerning violence against women, criminal justice, the environment, rural communities. Also organizes workshops and training sessions aimed at raising awareness and understanding.

Geographical Area of Activity: Mainly Australia.

Restrictions: No grants for direct service provision, unless it facilitates community development; only Australian not-for-profit organizations are eligible to apply.

Publications: *Reichstein News* (quarterly newsletter).

Finance: Annual grant distributions approx. $A700,000.

Board of Trustees: Jill Reichstein (Chair.); Jenny Florence; Rhonda Galbally; Lucy Larkins; Peter Norden; Barbara Spalding; Jane Tewson.

Principal Staff: Exec. Officer Christa Momot.

Address: 2nd Floor, 172 Flinders St, Melbourne, Vic 3000.

Telephone: (3) 9650 4400; **Fax:** (3) 9650 7501; **Internet:** www.reichstein.org.au; **e-mail:** info@reichstein.org.au.

R. E. Ross Trust

Founded in 1970 under the terms of the will of the late R. E. Ross.

Activities: Operates through awarding grants for projects in the fields of the arts, social welfare, health, nature conservation and the education of foreign students, through a teacher exchange programme, with particular regard to students from Timor Leste and the South-Pacific Islands. Makes several major grants each year and funds an annual travel scholarship awarded by the Royal Australasian College of Physicians. Grants are restricted to charitable organizations based within the State of Victoria.

Geographical Area of Activity: Australia, South-East Asia and the South Pacific.

Restrictions: Grants are only made in the Victoria area. Generally no funding for projects deemed to be the responsibility of government, general appeals, long-term support, travel expenses or conferences, or for projects too rigid in application to groups defined by religion or ethnic origin, social surveys or social research. No grants for individuals.

Publications: Annual report and financial statement.

Finance: Annual disbursements approx. $A2,500,000.

Board of Trustees: Colin J. Harper; George E. Limb; Frank H. Osborn; Ian A Renard; Edna N. Ritchie.

Principal Staff: Exec. Officer Sylvia J. Geddes.

Address: 24 Albert Rd, 7th Floor, South Melbourne, Vic 3205.

Telephone: (3) 9690 6255; **Fax:** (3) 9690 5497; **Internet:** www.rosstrust.org.au; **e-mail:** information@rosstrust.org.au.

Royal Australasian College of Physicians

Founded in 1938 to promote the study of the science and art of medicine; to encourage research in clinical science and the institutes of medicine; to bring together physicians for their common benefit and for scientific discussions and clinical demonstrations; and to disseminate knowledge of the principles and practice of medicine. Established the Research and Education Foundation in 1991 to increase funding to its medical research awards programme.

Activities: Through its Boards and Committees, the College presents the views of physicians and paediatricians on questions of medical importance to the Government and other bodies; it encourages continuing education for qualified physicians; conducts a training and examination programme for admission of trainees to Fellowship; makes grants for research and overseas study; provides lecturers for medical teaching in the Asia-Pacific region; maintains a library on the history of medicine; and publishes the results of research and study. There are 70 Honorary Fellows and over 9,000 Fellows and Trainees. Maintains a library of 30,000 volumes, including the Ford Collection. Awards over 40 fellowships and awards annually.

Geographical Area of Activity: Australia and the Asia-Pacific region.

Publications: Annual Report; *Internal Medicine Journal; The Journal of Paediatrics and Child Health* ; Research Reports.

Council: Dr Robin Mortimer (Pres.).

Principal Staff: CEO D. W. Swinbourne.

Address: 145 Macquarie St, Sydney, NSW 2000.

Telephone: (2) 9256 5444; **Fax:** (2) 9252 3310; **Internet:** www.racp.edu.au; **e-mail:** racp@racp.edu.au.

Royal Flying Doctor Service of Australia

Established in 1928 by the Very Rev. John Flynn as a charitable service to provide emergency medical care, primary health-care services and education assistance by air to people in remote areas of Australia.

Activities: Provides 24 hour emergency health services; primary health-care clinics at remote sites; tele-health radio and telephone consultations; medical chests to be stored in isolated areas; inter-hospital transfers; and female health clinics. Currently operates from 22 bases throughout Australia.

Geographical Area of Activity: Australia.

Restrictions: Not a grant-making organization.

Finance: Funded by the Australian Federal Government, State and Territory Governments and donations; assets $A2,986,569 (2000).

Council: T. Crook (Nat. Pres.); C. Kitchen (Vice-Pres.); D. Burrough; J. Fahey; G. Gannon; P. Kronborg; J. Milhinch; L. Miller; J. Scott; R. Young.

Address: 15–17 Young St, Level 5, Sydney, NSW 2000.

Telephone: (2) 9241 2411; **Fax:** (2) 9247 3351; **Internet:** www.flyingdoctor.net; **e-mail:** enquiries@rfdsno.com.

SEARCH Foundation

Founded in October 1990 to promote greater understanding in the community of the main factors affecting social life, influencing social development and advancing social well-being.

Activities: Works through operating national and international campaigns and supporting networks related to social justice, democracy and environmental sustainability. Carries out research and public education initiatives and awards scholarships and grants.

Geographical Area of Activity: International, with an emphasis on Australia, South-East Asia and Africa.

Restrictions: No grants for publications.

Publications: *Political Education for Trade Unionists; How Green has Australia Become?*.

Finance: Net assets $A3,200,000; annual expenditure $A185,000 (2001).

Foundation Committee: Richard Walsham (Pres.); Louise Connor (Vice-Pres.); Adam Farrar (Treas.); Peter Murphy (Sec.); Brian Aarons; Greg Giles; Don Jarrett; Judith Klepner; Sally McManus; Brendan O'Kane; Leonie Short.

Principal Staff: Co-ordinator Peter Murphy.

Address: Rm 610, 3 Smail St, Broadway, NSW 2007.

Telephone: (2) 9211 4164; **Fax:** (2) 9211 1407; **Internet:** www.search.org.au; **e-mail:** search@magna.com.au.

Tear Australia

Set up to support non-profit organizations in less-developed countries involved in relief and development work.

Activities: Operates internationally in the field of aid to less-developed countries. Supports indigenous Christian development projects that aim for long-term, sustainable change in the life circumstances of poor communities, in the fields of agriculture and livestock, fisheries and aquaculture, forestry, water resources, income generation, health, children's care and education, community organization, non-formal education, vocational training, and relief and rehabilitation. Also provides emergency relief assistance.

Geographical Area of Activity: International.

Publications: *Target Magazine; Harambee* (newsletter for artist network).

Finance: Total revenue $A7,011,235, expenditure $A6,089,389 (June 2002).

Board of Trustees: Tony McCarthy (Chair.); Dr Deborah Storie (Vice-Chair.); David Andrews (Treas.); Steve Bradbury (Sec.); Cheryl Catford; Carlyn Chen; Colin Duthie; Jane Furniss; Adam Murray; Sara Parrott; William Stent; Trevor Thomas.

Principal Staff: Dir Steve Bradbury; Overseas Programme Co-ordinator Peter Fitzgerald.

Address: 4 Solwood Lane, Blackburn; POB 164, Blackburn, Vic 3130.

Telephone: (3) 9877 7444; **Fax:** (3) 9877 7944; **Internet:** www.tear.org.au; **e-mail:** vice@tear.org.au.

Union Aid Abroad—APHEDA

Established in 1984 by ACTU (the Australian Council of Trade Unions) as ACTU's charitable humanitarian overseas aid operation.

Activities: Operates about 60 projects in collaboration with local organizations in countries of South-East Asia, the Far East, the Middle East, the Pacific, South Africa and in Cuba. Projects are concerned with skills training, literacy training, campaigns against child labour, and workers' rights. Also offers study tours. Maintains offices in Cambodia, Timor Leste and Laos.

Geographical Area of Activity: South-East Asia, the Far East, the Middle East, the Pacific, South Africa and Cuba.

Restrictions: Projects are initiated locally.

Publications: *Solidarity Partnerships* (quarterly newsletter); Annual Report; reports and submissions.

Finance: Total assets $A1,716,889 (June 2002); total revenue $A3,200,333, total disbursements $A3,072,409 (2002).

Management Committee: Tas Bull (Chair.); Sharan Burrow (Vice-Chair.); Sandra Moait (Hon. Treas.); Paul Bastian; Cathy Bloch; Phil Davey; Laurie Ferguson; Janet Hunt; Greg Sword.

Principal Staff: Exec. Officer Peter Jennings.

Address: Level 3, 377 Sussex St, Sydney NSW 2000.

Telephone: (2) 9264 9343; **Fax:** (2) 9261 1118; **Internet:** www.apheda.org.au; **e-mail:** apheda@labor.net.au.

Charles and Sylvia Viertel Charitable Foundation

Established under the terms of Charles Viertel's Will in 1992 for the benefit of charitable organizations throughout Australia, especially operating in the areas of medical research and support for the aged and infirm.

Activities: Operates in Australia, through two principal programmes: the General Programme, which offers grants to organizations working with the aged, children and young people, the disadvantaged, people with cancer or sight impairment, and projects supporting Aboriginal and Torres Strait Islander people; and the Medical Programme, which supports outstanding Australian medical researchers, through offering Senior Medical Research Fellowships to Australian nationals or permanent residents, and grants to clinical investigators.

Geographical Area of Activity: Australia.

Restrictions: Grants are not given to charities with high administrative expenses, nor, under the General Programme, to individuals or for medical research.

Trustees: George Curphey; Rex Freudenberg; James Kennedy; ANZ Executors & Trustee Co Ltd.

Address: c/o ANZ Charitable Trusts, Level 18, 530 Collins St, Melbourne, Vic 3000.

Fax: (3) 9273 2929.

Austria

FOUNDATION CENTRE AND CO-ORDINATING BODY

The World of NGOs

Founded in 1997 by Christiana Weidel and Christian Pichler-Stainern to promote and support the non-profit sector in Austria.

Activities: Operates nationally and internationally in the fields of education, law and human rights, social welfare and social studies and the provision of information, through self-conducted programmes, research, conferences, training courses and publications.

Geographical Area of Activity: Austria and Europe.

Restrictions: No grants made.

Publications: Annual Report (1998); documentation of the first 'NGO internet fiesta' (1998); annual brochure about the development of the Third Sector.

Finance: Funded through membership fees, public funds and project finance.

Trustees: Christiana Weidel; Christine Hapale; Edith Denman; Gerhard Wagner; and others.

Principal Staff: Man. Dir Christiana Weidel; Deputy Dir Christian Pichler-Stainern.

Address: Spiegelgasse 8/5, 1010 Vienna.

Telephone: (1) 513-17-28; **Fax:** (1) 512-60-89; **Internet:** www.ngo.at; **e-mail:** info@ngo.at.

FOUNDATIONS, TRUSTS AND NON-PROFIT ORGANIZATIONS

Afro-Asiatisches Institut in Wien (Afro-Asian Institute in Vienna)

Founded in 1959 by Cardinal Dr Franz König, Archbishop of Vienna, for the promotion of contacts between Austrians and Africans and Asians; the promotion of research concerning African and Asian countries; to assist economic co-operation between Austria and African and Asian countries; to encourage students from developing countries to complete postgraduate education; and for the promotion of understanding among Austrians of the interests of these countries.

Activities: Operates internationally in the fields of education, social welfare, economic affairs, science and medicine, the arts and humanities, religion, international relations and aid to less-developed countries, through self-conducted programmes, courses, conferences, publications and lectures, both in Austria and abroad, and through grants, fellowships and scholarships to Africans and Asians. Maintains a library.

Geographical Area of Activity: Africa, Asia, Central and South America and Austria.

Principal Staff: Contacts Dr Ruth Gamsjäger, Markus Pleschko.

Address: Türkenstr. 3, 1090 Vienna.

Telephone and Fax: (1) 310-51-45; **Internet:** www.aai-wien.at/; **e-mail:** office@aai-wien.at.

Entwicklungshilfe-Klub

Supports community development initiatives in the developing world.

Activities: Supports community development initiatives in less-developed countries, through grants to small grassroots projects and through work with partner organizations. In 2002, grants were made to projects working in Africa, Asia, Central and South America, Eastern Europe and North Africa, including Albania, Algeria, Angola, Bangladesh, Bolivia, Brazil, Cambodia, the Congo, Ecuador, Egypt, El Salvador, Ethiopia, Ghana, Guatemala, Haiti, India, Madagascar, Malawi, Mozambique, Nicaragua, Peru, Senegal, Sri Lanka, Sudan, Tanzania and Uganda.

Geographical Area of Activity: Africa, Asia, Central and South America, Eastern Europe and North Africa.

Publications: Annual Report.

Finance: Total project expenditure €1,131,656 (2002).

Principal Staff: Dir Gabriele Tabatabai.

Address: Böcklinstr. 44, 1020 Vienna.

Telephone: (1) 720-51-50; **Fax:** (1) 728-37-93; **Internet:** www.eh-klub.at; **e-mail:** info@eh-klub.at.

Fonds zur Förderung der Wissenschaftlichen Forschung—FWF (Austrian Science Fund)

Founded in 1967 with the aim of supporting scientific research.

Activities: Provides finance for basic research in all fields of science, including the humanities. The Fund is also responsible for assisting in the formulation and implementation of national science policy, for public relations work relating to science, and for the promotion of the internationalization (in particular Europeanization) of the scientific sector in Austria. Awards include support for non-Austrian scientists working at Austrian science institutes and for Austrian postgraduate students wishing to carry out scientific research abroad.

Geographical Area of Activity: Austria.

Publications: Annual Report; *Info* (magazine in German); statistical publications.

Principal Staff: Pres. Georg Wick; Sec.-Gen. Dr Eva Gluck.

Address: Weyringergasse 35, 1040 Vienna.

Telephone: (1) 505-67-40; **Fax:** (1) 505-67-39; **Internet:** www.fwf.ac.at; **e-mail:** office@fwf.ac.at.

International Helsinki Federation for Human Rights—IHF

Founded in 1982 to defend the right of organizations and individuals to monitor human rights, according to the provisions of the 1975 Helsinki Final Act.

Activities: Promotes human rights within the 54 signatory countries of the Helsinki Final Act; aims to establish Helsinki monitoring committees in these countries, and undertakes activities in co-operation with one or more of the 39 member Helsinki committees and associated groups of the Federation. The Federation also conducts research, organizes projects in Eastern and South-Eastern Europe, the countries of the former USSR and Central Asia, and holds symposia.

Geographical Area of Activity: Europe, the USA, Central Asia and countries of the former USSR.

Restrictions: No grants available.

Publications: Annual Report; *Women 2000: An Investigation into the Status of Women's Rights in Central and South Eastern Europe and the Newly Independent States;* books, conference proceedings and report updates.

Finance: Annual budget approx. US $1,100,000.

Advisory Board: Yuri Orlov (Hon. Chair.); Karl v. Schwarzenberg (Chair.); Ludmilla Alexeyeva (Pres.); Ulrich Fischer (Vice-Pres.); Stein-Ivar Aarsaether (Treas.).

Principal Staff: Exec. Dir Aaron Rhodes; Deputy Exec. Dir Brigitte Dufour.

Address: Wickenburggasse 14/7, 1080 Vienna.

Telephone: (1) 408-88-22; **Fax:** (1) 408-88-22-50; **Internet:** www.ihf-hr.org; **e-mail:** office@ihf-hr.org.

International Institute for Applied Systems Analysis—IIASA

Founded in 1972 as a non-governmental interdisciplinary research institute by the Academies of Sciences or equivalent institutions in 12 countries in both East and West. Since 1972 several scientific institutions from Europe and the USA have joined the Institute.

Activities: IIASA's three main areas of research are: energy and technology; environment and natural resources; and population and society. Its research activities are dedicated to the study of global change, and its main areas of concern in the investigation of environmental, economic, social and technological developments are sustainability and the human dimensions of global change.

Geographical Area of Activity: International.

Publications: Annual Report; *Options* (quarterly); *Quarterly Report* (update on IIASA's activities); *Population and Climate Change; Transboundary Risk Management.*

Finance: Operating budget of approx. US $9,000,000 (2001), from the 16 national member organizations. The Institute also receives funds from external sources.

Council: The Institute is governed by a Council composed of one permanent representative from each member institution.

Principal Staff: Dir Prof. Leen Hordijk.

Address: Schlossplatz 1, 2361 Laxenburg.

Telephone: (2) 236-80-70; **Fax:** (2) 236-71-31-3; **Internet:** www.iiasa.ac.at; **e-mail:** inf@iiasa.ac.at.

International Press Institute

Founded in New York in 1950 to promote and safeguard the freedom of the press.

Activities: The Institute's main objectives are to defend and promote the freedom of the press; to publish studies of governmental pressure on the media; to ensure the safety of journalists and allow them to work without interference; to improve the practice of journalism; to promote the free exchange of news and the free flow of information; and to encourage co-operation and communication between its members. Organizes training courses and seminars in Africa, Asia, the countries of the former USSR and Eastern Europe; conducts editorial research; arranges conferences; and disseminates information. The Institute has members in over 110 countries.

Geographical Area of Activity: International.

Publications: *IPI Global Journalist* (4 a year, in English); *IPI Newsletter* (monthly); *IPI World Press Freedom Review* (annual); *The Kosovo News and Propaganda War; Putin and the Press; IPI World Annual Congress Reports.*

Finance: Financed through membership fees.

Executive Board: Jorge E. Fascetto (Chair.); Hugo Butler, Hans Erik Matre, Lyle Turnball (Vice-Chair.).

Principal Staff: Dir Johann P. Fritz; Editor David Dadge; Press Freedom Advisor Michael Kudlak, Barbara Trionfi; Documentation Antony Lowstedt.

Address: Spiegelgasse 2, 1010 Vienna.

Telephone: (1) 512-90-11; **Fax:** (1) 512-90-14; **Internet:** www.freemedia.at; **e-mail:** ipi@freemedia.at.

Bruno Kreisky Forum for International Dialogue

Aims to bring together politicians, academics, businesspeople and others from all over the world to create international dialogue.

Activities: Operates in five areas: the Middle East, Unemployment and the Global Economy, New Europe, North–South Dialogue and Human Rights, through research projects, discussions, symposia, lectures and seminars. Maintains the Bruno Kreisky Archives, established the Bruno Kreisky Foundation for Outstanding Achievements in Human Rights, and awards the Bruno Kreisky European Scholarship.

Geographical Area of Activity: Austria.

Publications: Annual Report; Newsletter; Dialogue Series; *La rôle de la Social-Democratie dans la Nouvelle Europe; From Cancún to Vienna. International Development in a New World; The Social Left: The Present and the Prospect*; and other publications.

Board of Directors: Franz Vranitzky (Pres.); Ferdinand Lacina, Brigitte Ederer (Vice-Pres.); Rudolf Scholten (Treas.); Eva Nowotny (Sec.); and others.

Principal Staff: Sec.-Gen. Margit Schmidt.

Address: Armbrustergasse 15, 1190 Vienna.

Telephone: (1) 318-82-60; **Fax:** (1) 378-51-11; **Internet:** www.kreisky.org; **e-mail:** kreiskyforum@kreisky.org.

MEDIACULT—International Research Institute for Media, Communication and Cultural Development

Founded in 1969, on the initiative of the International Music Council under the auspices of UNESCO, for research in the field of cultural development, with special reference to the audio-visual media.

Activities: Operates in the fields of the arts and humanities, and science and technology, especially in the areas of the digital technologies of production and distribution, and the globalization of culture and culture industries. Carries out research in three main areas: new communication technologies, art and culture; the global music market and music in Austria; and cultural policy and cultural development. Publishes the results of its research; advises on cultural policy; and holds congresses, symposia and workshops.

Geographical Area of Activity: International.

Publications: *MEDIACULT Newsletter* (2 a year); books and research reports.

Finance: Regular subsidies are provided by the Austrian Government and the City of Vienna; the Institute also receives donations and grants from other sources, and income is also derived from payment for research services.

Board of Directors: Prof. Raymond Weber (Pres.); Prof. Irmgard Bontinck; Prof. N. de Camargo; L. del Grosso Destreri; Prof. P. Etzkorn; Prof. Michael Hruby; R. Hummel; K. Malm; Prof. D. Mark; M. M. Markhof; Prof. J. P. L. Roberts; W. Scheib; Prof. Alfred Smudits; Dr J. Trappel; R. Wangermée; A. Wiesand.

Principal Staff: Sec.-Gen. Alfred Smudits; Dir Robert Harauer.

Address: Anton von Webern-Platz 1, 1030 Vienna.

Telephone: (1) 711-55-88-00; **Fax:** (1) 711-55-88-09; **Internet:** www.mdw.ac.at/mediacult; **e-mail:** mediacult@mediacult.mdw.ac.at.

Österreichische Forschungsstiftung für Entwicklungshilfe (Austrian Foundation for Development Research)

Founded in 1967 by the Afro-Asiatisches Institut in Wien (q.v.) and the Österreichischer Auslandsstudentendienst to support research in connection with developing countries.

Activities: Operates in the field of aid to less-developed countries, through grants to individuals and institutions, and issuing publications. Provides documentation and information on development aid and policy, developing countries and international development, particularly relating to Austria. The Foundation maintains a library of approximately 40,000 volumes, of which 30,000 are monographs and 10,000 periodicals, as well as 140 regularly-available subscription magazines.

Publications: *Österreichische Entwicklungspolitik; ÖFSE-Forum; ÖFSE Edition.*

Finance: Total budget approx. 24,400,000 Austrian schillings (2000).

Principal Staff: Man. Gerhard Bittner.

Address: Berggasse 7, 1090 Vienna.

Telephone: (1) 317-40-10; **Fax:** (1) 317-40-15; **Internet:** www.oefse.at; **e-mail:** office@oefse.at.

Österreichische Gesellschaft für Außenpolitik und Internationale Beziehungen (Austrian Association for Foreign Policy and International Relations)

Founded in 1958 by Prof. Dr Alfred Verdross and Prof. Dr Rudolf Blühdorn to increase and widen interest in and knowledge of foreign policy, particularly Austrian foreign policy.

Activities: Operates internationally in the fields of foreign affairs and international relations, through international conferences, lectures, panel discussions and publications on foreign policy.

Geographical Area of Activity: Austria.

Publications: Annual Report; *Österreichisches Jahrbuch für Internationale Politik* (annually).

Principal Staff: Pres. Dr Wolfgang Schallenberg; Sec.-Gen. Michael F. Pfeifer.

Address: Hofburg/Schweizerhof/Brunnenstiege, 1010 Vienna.

Telephone: (1) 535-46-27; **Fax:** (1) 532-26-05; **Internet:** http://start.at/oega; **e-mail:** oega@start.at.

South East Europe Media Organization—SEEMO-IPI

Established in Zagreb in 2000 to promote and safeguard the freedom of the press in South-Eastern Europe, and as a leading media organization in the region.

Activities: Seeks to promote and safeguard press freedom, including freedom of access to news, freedom of transmission of news, freedom of publication of newspapers and freedom of expression. Its activities include fostering understanding between journalists and other media professionals; improving standards and practices; ensuring safety of journalists; and promoting co-operation. Programmes include a Media Aid Programme, Media Law Programme and a Media in Transition Programme. Through the SEEMO South-East Europe Media Foundation for Emergency Help, the organization offers support for projects in the region. The Organization maintains national offices in all countries in the region. It also awards the annual SEEMO Award for Better Understanding, a prize of €2,000, made to a journalist, editor or media executive in South-Eastern Europe, who, through the media, has promoted a climate of better understanding amongst peoples and worked toward ending minority problems, ethnic divisions, racism and xenophobia, as well as the Award for Mutual Co-operation in South East Europe. Also makes awards from the SEEMO Emergency Fund to provide direct help to journalists in need in South-Eastern Europe.

Geographical Area of Activity: South-Eastern Europe.

Publications: *SEEMO Media Handbook* (annually, in English); *SEEMO Review*.

Principal Staff: Sec.-Gen. Oliver Vujovic.

Address: IPI, Spiegelgasse 2/29, 1010 Vienna.

Telephone: (1) 513-39-40; **Fax:** (1) 512-90-15; **Internet:** www.seemo.at; **e-mail:** seemo@freemedia.at.

Wiener Institut für Entwicklungsfragen und Zusammenarbeit (Vienna Institute for Development and Co-operation)

Founded in 1987 as successor to the Vienna Institute for Development (founded in 1962 by Bruno Kreisky); aims to disseminate information on the cultural, social and economic life of the countries of Asia, Africa and Central and South America, in order to increase public awareness of the problems of economic development and international co-operation. The Institute also conducts research programmes.

Activities: The Institute conducts research programmes, holds conferences, seminars and workshops on development policy and developing countries, and issues publications relating to international development. Members come from 20 countries.

Geographical Area of Activity: International.

Publications: *Report Series* (in English and German).

Principal Staff: Pres. Franz Vranitzky; Dir Erich Andrlik.

Address: Möllwaldplatz 5/3, 1040 Vienna.

Telephone: (1) 713-35-94; **Fax:** (1) 713-35-94-73; **Internet:** www.vidc.org; **e-mail:** office@vidc.org.

Azerbaijan

FOUNDATIONS, TRUSTS AND NON-PROFIT ORGANIZATIONS

Open Society Institute—Assistance Foundation (Azerbaijan)

Established in 1996; an independent foundation, part of the Soros foundations network.

Activities: Promotes the development of an open society by supporting programmes in the fields of education, information and the media, women, the arts and culture, law and human rights, and public health. Encourages the creation and development of NGOs in Azerbaijan as well as developing community information centres in regional public libraries.

Geographical Area of Activity: Azerbaijan.

Finance: Annual expenditure US $3,138,000 (2001).

Board of Trustees: Sabit Bagiroul (Chair.); Mehman Aliyer; Farhad Badalbeyei; Irada Bagirova; Ndir Ibadov; Lliudmila Mamedova.

Principal Staff: Exec. Dir Farda Asadov.

Address: Academician Hasan Aeiyer Str. 117a, 370110 Baku.

Telephone: (12) 41-27-22; **Fax:** (12) 98-69-34; **Internet:** www.osi-az.org; **e-mail:** fasadov@osi-az.org.

Bangladesh

FOUNDATIONS, TRUSTS AND NON-PROFIT ORGANIZATIONS

Action in Development—AID

Founded by Tarikul Islam Palash in 1992 to promote development.

Activities: Operates in the fields of education, law and human rights, community health-care and social welfare through self-conducted programmes including the Disabled programme, the Human Development programme, and the Income-Generating programme and through conferences and seminars. Collaborates internationally with similar organizations.

Finance: Assets 506,443 taka (2000); annual revenue and expenditure 619,956 taka (2000).

Executive Committee: Shahidul Islam Latu (Pres.); Sheikh Selim (Vice-Pres.); Tarikul Islam Palash (Gen. Sec.); Farzana Ahmed Neela (Asst Gen. Sec.); Nurun Nahar Kusum (Treas.); Chandan Kumar Maulik; Sayada Nasima Akther.

Principal Staff: Exec Dir Tarikul Islam Palash.

Address: POB 3, Jhedidah.

Telephone: (451) 3094; **Fax:** (451) 3272; **e-mail:** aid@bdoneline.com.

Antarjatik Beshamarik Sheba Sangstha—ABESH

Founded by Chowdhury Anwar Husain in 1962 for general philanthropic purposes.

Activities: Operates in the fields of disaster relief, education, health care, environmental conservation and peace studies, through networking, organizing its own programmes and training courses, conducting research, giving grants to individuals, organizing work camps and holding conferences; advocates peace and seeks the creation of an international agency to foster increased confidence between nations; maintains a library.

Publications: *Joti* (Bengali, quarterly); *Social Spectrum* (English, annually); *State of the Environment in Bangladesh.*

Finance: Budget approx. 280,000 taka.

Principal Staff: Pres. Chowdhury Anwar Husain.

Address: Zohura Mansion, 1st Floor, Rm 18, 27/1 Mymensingh Rd, Dhaka 1000.

Telephone: (2) 502071; **Fax:** (2) 863060; **e-mail:** omasis@citerhco.netaltabesh.

Bangladesh Freedom Foundation

Established in May 1999 to make grants to not-for-profit organizations concerned with problems of fundamental freedoms of the citizens of Bangladesh, and to promote and strengthen indigenous philanthropy in Bangladesh.

Activities: Provides funding support to programmes promoting three fundamental freedoms: freedom from poverty, freedom from ignorance and freedom from oppression. Other areas of interest include freedom of expression, freedom of the press and media, human rights and equality before the law. Groups prioritized for funding under these interest areas include those working with women, children and minority groups in poverty and disadvantage; and habitable and sustainable ecology and environment.

Geographical Area of Activity: Bangladesh.

Restrictions: Preference is given to small-scale initiatives.

Finance: Total assets 194,070,754 taka (2001); total expenditure 18,323,730 taka (2001).

Board of Trustees: Mahfuz Anam (Chair.); Dr. Debapriya Bhattacharya; Syed Manzur Elahi; Angela Gomes; Prof. Meghna Guhathakurta; Prof. Muhammad Zafar Iqbal; Sultana Kamal; Prof. Naila Khan; Prof. Wahiduddin Mahmood; Kazi Fazlur Rahman; Rokia A. Rahman; Raja Devashis Roy; Prof. Rehman Sobhan; Prof. Muhammad Yunus.

Principal Staff: Exec. Dir Iftek Haruzzarnan.

Address: Rd 15, House 30, Dhanmondi R/A, Dhaka 1209.

Telephone: (2) 8114532; **Fax:** (2) 8116200; **Internet:** www.freedomfound.org; **e-mail:** edbff@bdcom.com.

Mukti Lawrence Foundation

Founded in 1990 by Dr A. A. Quoreshi to establish a voluntary social welfare organization to help in the formation of a drug-free generation of people and to campaign for justice for women.

Activities: Operates in the fields of social welfare and health care, particularly the reduction of drug abuse and the treatment of mental health problems related to drug abuse. Established *Mukti*, a centre for the treatment of drug addicts in Bangladesh, in 1988. This currently holds 100 beds and provides treatment and rehabilitation for drug users, as well as a number of other services, including psychiatric treatment, advice and counselling, a drug help-line, and research and campaigns for drug prevention and education. Also runs projects, conferences and produces a number of publications. In the field of women's justice, the Foundation recently campaigned for government action on sexual abuse of garment workers.

Geographical Area of Activity: Asia and Europe.

Publications: *Human Rights; Awareness, Prevention and Treatment of Drug Addicts.*

Finance: Funded by its own sources, donations and subscriptions.

Executive Committee: Prof. M. A. Hussain (Chair.); Dr A. A. Quoreshi (Sec.-Gen.); Ausaful Hoque (Treas.).

Principal Staff: Exec. Dir Dr A. A. Quoreshi.

Address: Rd 49, House No. 2, Gulshan-2, Dhaka.

Telephone: (2) 9983991; **Fax:** (2) 8827147; **e-mail:** muktilwf@bdmail.net.

World Legal Aid Organization

Established by Liberty International in 1993. Aims to ensure that legal advice and representation is available to everyone whose life, liberty, property or reputation are under threat and who lack the resources to pay for it, particularly in developing countries.

Activities: Operates in the field of law, through offering legal advice and representation, especially to people who are unable to afford it in less-developed countries, and provides legal services to asylum seekers. Has members in Austria, Bangladesh, Belgium, Bolivia, Canada, Cyprus, Ecuador, Ethiopia, France, India, Indonesia, Japan, Republic of Korea, Malaysia, Nepal, Nigeria, Pakistan, Peru, Philippines, Saudi Arabia, Singapore, Sri Lanka, Sweden, Switzerland, Syria, Thailand, and the USA.

Geographical Area of Activity: International.
Finance: Funded by the Chair.
Directors: M. A. Mutaleb (Chair.).
Principal Staff: 10 volunteer staff members.
Address: Bar Asn Bldg, Ste No 1, 1st Floor, Mymensingh.
Telephone: (91) 54527; **Fax:** (91) 53804.

Belarus

FOUNDATION CENTRE AND CO-ORDINATING BODY

Support Centre for Associations and Foundations—SCAF

Founded in 1996; a member of the European Foundation Centre (q.v.) network of NGO resource centres under the EFC Orpheus Programme and a think tank focusing on education, peace building and civil society development.

Activities: Acts as an education and information support centre and think tank for NGOs in Belarus. Maintains a database of Belarusian NGOs; provides advisory services and workshops for representatives of organizations, relating to grant management, proposal writing, leadership and staff development; promotes the exchange of knowledge and information between NGOs.

Geographical Area of Activity: Belarus.

Publications: *Grantmanship* (journal); *Belarus Civil Society: In Need of a Dialogue; The State of Civil Society in Belarus; Index on Civil Society in Belarus; Fundraising and Grantsmanship; Organizational Management and Development of NGOs; Partnership Building Between NGOs and Local Government*; and other publications.

Principal Staff: CEO Dr Iouri Zagoumennov; Asst Dir Ludmila Shelkovich, Ihar Zahumionau.

Address: 220004 Minsk, 16 Korolia St, Rm 414.

Telephone: (17) 210-57-51; **Fax:** (17) 210-57-51; **Internet:** www.dialogue.unibel.by; **e-mail:** izag@user.unibel.by.

FOUNDATIONS, TRUSTS AND NON-PROFIT ORGANIZATIONS

Belarusian Charitable Fund 'For the Children of Chernobyl'

Established in 1990 by Gennady V. Grushevoy as a charitable fund to aid the victims of the Chernobyl disaster.

Activities: Operates in the fields of ecology, research into the consequences of the Chernobyl disaster, social and humanitarian aid, medical aid, rebuilding of community, cultural and educational exchanges, information, youth policy and alternative power supplies, through the following main programmes: Medical Programme (including co-operation with hospitals and research institutes); Charitable Recuperation Programme (for the recuperation of mothers and children in families and rest homes abroad); Educational Programme (projects include arranging postgraduate medical education or further training for Belarusian doctors, nurses and medical specialists abroad); Resettlement (the development of partnership between regions, towns and institutions with institutions abroad, and construction and economic projects); Information and Cultural Programme (publishing, international congresses, seminars and conferences, cultural projects and cultural exchanges); Youth Programmes (creation of regional youth centres and educational, informational, international exchanges); and Social Programmes (legal aid, assistance for 'street children', orphanages, 'weekend clubs' for elderly people, social rehabilitation of under-age delinquents). The Foundation has also established the Social Medical Consulting Centre. The Foundation collaborates with organizations and institutions in 26 countries and maintains local branches in more than 70 cities and districts in Belarus.

Geographical Area of Activity: International.

Publications: *DEMOS* (magazine); *World after Chernobyl; Chernobyl Digest*.

Finance: The Foundation is financed through charitable donations and subscriptions.

Board of Directors: Prof. Dr Gennady V. Grushevoy (Chair.).

Principal Staff: Technical Secretariat Olga Dashkevich, Irina Pobyazhina.

Address: 220029 Minsk, Starovilenskaya 14.

Telephone: (17) 234-12-15; **Fax:** (17) 234-34-58; **Internet:** http://bbfchernobyl.iatp.by/; **e-mail:** bbf@charity.belpak.minsk.by.

International Humanitarian Foundation

Founded in 1992 as a programme of the Sabre Foundation (q.v.).

Activities: Promotes education and the study of humanitarian issues in Belarus; provides textbooks and educational materials; supports arts educational activities; maintains a library. Founding member of the the European Humanities University, in Minsk, Belarus.

Geographical Area of Activity: Belarus.

Principal Staff: Contact Prof. Anatoli Mikhailov.

Address: 220004 Minsk, Masherov Ave 1-2-5.

Telephone: (17) 239-34-64; **Fax:** (17) 239-31-63; **e-mail:** info@ehu.minsk.by.

Belgium

FOUNDATION CENTRES AND CO-ORDINATING BODIES

Association internationale des charités—AIC (International Association of Charities)

Founded by Saint Vincent de Paul in 1617, as Confraternity of Ladies of Charity. Re-established under Belgian law in 1986.

Activities: Operates internationally in the field of welfare. Works with member organizations in 50 countries to eliminate poverty and sustain the promotion and development of the underprivileged. Encourages voluntary work for, with, and of the poor. Develops various kinds of social work, including support for drug addicts and alcoholics, care for the elderly and the sick, help to single mothers, assistance to the lonely, defence of human rights, and working towards a culture of solidarity, respect and peace. Runs literacy and other forms of educational workshops, provides technical training, as well as making loans to individuals in need.

Geographical Area of Activity: International.

Publications: *Initiation to Associative Life; AIC Volunteers Today*; and other publications.

Principal Staff: Int. Pres. Anne Sturm; Vice-Pres. Uca de Gonzalez, Rose de Lima Ramanankavana; Treas. Christine de Cambray; Sec.-Gen. Agnès Dandois.

Address: 23 Rampe des Ardennais, 1348 Louvain La Neuve.

Telephone: (1) 045-63-53; **Fax:** (1) 045-80-63; **Internet:** www.famvin.org/aic; **e-mail:** aic@euronet.be.

EURODAD—European Network on Debt and Development

A network of 48 NGOs in 15 European countries, dedicated to developing a comprehensive debt strategy to combat the problem of Third World debt.

Activities: Co-ordinates the activities of member organizations working in the areas of Third World debt, structural adjustments and financial markets, in order to bring their views to the attention of the relevant decision-making governments and institutions, such as the International Bank for Reconstruction and Development (World Bank) and the International Monetary Fund (IMF). The Network is also working to increase the accountability of international financial institutions to further debt relief, and has initiated, developed and promoted global networking on debt, development and alternatives to adjustment.

Geographical Area of Activity: International.

Finance: Funded by member organizations (60%) and Directorate-General VIII of the European Commission of the European Union (40%). Total assets €218,189 (2001); total income €644,783 (2001).

Directors: Rudy de Meyer (Chair.); Pieter van Veenen (Treas.); Marta Arias; Bogdan van den Berghe; Bart Bode; Morten Emil Hansen; Stefan Hochhuth; Jürgen Kaiser; Martin Koehler; Paul Ladd; Annika Otterstedt; Jean Somers.

Principal Staff: Co-ordinator Ted van Hees, Jacqueline Woodman.

Address: 46 rue Dejoncker, 1060 Brussels.

Telephone: (2) 543-90-60; **Fax:** (2) 544-05-59; **Internet:** www.eurodad.org; **e-mail:** info@eurodad.org.

European Environmental Bureau

Established in 1974, a federation of 134 environmental organizations based in 25 countries in Western and Eastern Europe, which aims to protect the environment in Europe and to enable European citizens to play a part in its defence.

Activities: Operates in Europe in the area of conservation and the environment, through providing member organizations with information, producing reports, representing member organizations in relations with European Union institutions, and organizing working groups and conferences. Works as an advocate for improved environment and conservation protection policies, and co-ordinates workshops and seminars. Operates in a number of environmental areas, including agriculture, air pollution, global warming, noise pollution, waste and tourism.

Geographical Area of Activity: Europe.

Publications: Annual Report; conference reports; memoranda.

Principal Staff: Sec.-Gen. John Hontelez.

Address: 34 blvd de Waterloo, 1000 Brussels.

Telephone: (2) 289-10-90; **Fax:** (2) 289-10-99; **Internet:** www.eeb.org; **e-mail:** info@eeb.org.

European Federation of National Organizations Working with the Homeless—FEANTSA

A non-profit association of more than 70 organizations, founded in 1989 to improve the quality of life of homeless people in Europe.

Activities: An association of organizations that provide a range of services to homeless people throughout Europe. Works to promote and support the activities of these organizations at local, regional, national and European levels in order to develop a successful infrastructure of services to improve living conditions for low-income groups. Carries out research, communicates with European institutions and national governments, advocating the development and implementation of effective policies facilitating access to affordable and reasonable housing, and raises awareness of the situation of homeless people. Organizes seminars, and holds a General Assembly every two years.

Geographical Area of Activity: Europe.

Publications: *Homeless in Europe* (quarterly newsletter); *European Observatory on Homelessness;* national and international research reports.

Executive Committee: Thomas Specht-Kittler (Pres.); Michel Mercadié (Vice-Pres.); Rina Beers (Vice-Pres.); Stefano Galliani (Treas.); Hannu Puttonen (Sec.); René Kneip.

Principal Staff: Sec.-Gen. Freek Spinnewijn.

Address: 194 Chaussée de Louvain, 1210 Brussels.

Telephone: (2) 538-66-69; **Fax:** (2) 539-41-74; **Internet:** www.feantsa.org; **e-mail:** office@feantsa.org.

European Foundation Centre—EFC

Established in 1989 by seven of Europe's leading foundations; a membership association dedicated to strengthening organized philanthropy in Europe and internationally.

Activities: Provides membership services in three areas: monitoring European institutions and assisting members in the representation of their interests at European level; aiding members to form interest groups and business committees, according to common sectoral interests, to enable independent funders to share experience and begin joint projects; and providing information services through publications, a database on foundations and corporate funders, and an extensive library collection. Thirty-seven Networking Centres, national or regional associations and forums of foundations throughout Europe participate in the EFC Orpheus Programme, which provides a public record and a public information service on foundations and corporate funders active in Europe. The Civil Society Project assists in increasing the capacity of resource centres serving foundations and associations in Central and Eastern Europe, and EFC members include 'special guests' from the region. A committee of EFC members, Corporate Citizenship in Europe, is committed to quality initiatives for corporate social responsibility and corporate giving. The EFC holds an annual meeting and conference. There are more than 200 members and associate members throughout Europe and internationally.

Geographical Area of Activity: Europe.

Restrictions: Not a grant-making organization.

Publications: *Selected Bibliography on Foundations and Corporate Funders in Europe* (1994); *Typology of Foundations in Europe* (1994–95); *Environmental Funding in Europe* (1998); *Education Funding in Europe* (1998); *European Grants Index* (1998); *Mediterranean Funding* (1999); *European Foundation Fundamentals* (1999); *Independent Funding—A Directory of Foundation and Corporate Members* (2002); *Youth Funding in Europe* (2000); *Working With Foundations: Why and How?* (2001); *Funding Minorities and Multiculturalism in Europe* (2001); *efc bookshelf* (quarterly newsletter, updating the bibliography); *efc newsline* (newsletter); *efc partners europe* (newsletter); *efc alerts* (information bulletins); other books, conference and meeting reports and annual reports.

Finance: Assets €1,350,000 (Sept. 2000); annual revenue €1,870,000 (2000).

Management Committee: Luc Tayart de Borms (Chair.); Dario Disegni, Carlos Monjardino (Vice-Chair.).

Principal Staff: Chief Exec. John Richardson.

Address: 51 rue de la Concorde, 1050 Brussels.

Telephone: (2) 512-89-38; **Fax:** (2) 512-32-65; **Internet:** www.efc.be; www.fundersonline.org; **e-mail:** efc@efc.be.

Union of International Associations

Founded in 1907 (present name 1910) to assist the activities of non-profit organizations throughout the world, especially non-governmental or voluntary organizations.

Activities: The Union maintains contact with a wide variety of organizations in both developed and developing countries, collects and makes available information on their activities, and promotes research on the legal, administrative and other problems common to these organizations, especially in their contacts with government bodies. It maintains a database which provides information on international organizations and issues relevant to their work, and from which various reference books are generated. A general assembly is held every two years, and meetings of international congress organizers are held. The Union has consultative status with the United Nations (ECOSOC), UNESCO and the International Labour Organisation (ILO).

Geographical Area of Activity: International.

Publications: *Transnational Associations* (quarterly, in English and French); *International Congress Calendar* (quarterly); *Yearbook of International Organizations; Who's Who in International Organizations; Encyclopedia of World Problems and Human Potential;* and a number of other publications.

Finance: Budget approx. 25,000,000 Belgian francs.

Principal Staff: Pres. Anne-Marie Boutin; Sec.-Gen. André Onkelinx.

Address: 40 rue Washingtonstraat, 1050 Brussels.

Telephone: (2) 640-18-08; **Fax:** (2) 643-61-99; **Internet:** www.uia.org; **e-mail:** uia@uia.be.

WINGS—Worldwide Initiatives for Grantmaker Support

Established in 2000 to support networking between, and development of, grant-making organizations world-wide.

Activities: Aims to strenghten philanthropy world-wide and promote collaboration, networking and support between philanthropic organizations. Offers resources for grant-makers and organizations supporting them; organizes meetings, conferences and networks; offers internships and technical assistance. Created the WINGS-CF (Community Foundations) initiative in 2000 to support the development and work of community foundations world-wide. Currently has more than 95 member organizations, which are themselves membership organizations for grant-makers and support organizations.

Geographical Area of Activity: International.

Publications: *WINGS* (newsletter).

Principal Staff: Dir Gaynor Humphreys.

Address: c/o European Foundation Centre (EFC), 51 rue de la Concorde, 1050 Brussels.

Telephone: (2) 512-89-38; **Fax:** (2) 512-32-65; **Internet:** www.wingsweb.org; **e-mail:** wings@efc.be.

FOUNDATIONS, TRUSTS AND NON-PROFIT ORGANIZATIONS

Alamire Foundation

Founded in July 1991 by the Catholic University of Leuven and Musica (the Flemish Early Music Centre), to stimulate research in the musical history of Belgium, Southern Netherlands and Northern France before 1800.

Activities: Organizes conferences and exhibitions, carries out research, publishes books, and has created a database of publications relevant to the Foundation's research.

Geographical Area of Activity: Europe and the USA.

Restrictions: Grants made to specific international research projects only.

Publications: *Yearbooks of the Alamire Foundation; Monumenta Flandriae Musica;* facsimile editions and monographs.

Finance: Receives funding from the Government of the Flemish region, from the University of Leuven and the Belgian National Lottery.

Board of Directors: Prof. Dr H. Vanden Berghe (Pres.); Prof. Dr I Bossuyt (Vice-Pres.); Dr H. Baeten (Treas.); Dr E. Schreurs.

Principal Staff: Man. Dir Dr Eugeen Schreurs; Dr B. Bouckaert; K. Steelandt; P. Lenaers.

Address: Universiteitsbibliotheek, Mgr Ladeuzeplein 21, 3000 Leuven.

Telephone: (16) 32-46-61; **Fax:** (16) 32-47-06; **Internet:** fuzzy.arts.kuleuven.ac.be/alamire; **e-mail:** alamire .foundation@arts.kuleuven.ac.be.

ASMAE—Association Sociale et Médicale d'Action et d'Education (Social and Medical Action and Education Association)

Established in 1981 to promote an equality of exchange between countries in the Northern and Southern hemispheres, in particular in the areas of action and education.

Activities: Operates in the fields of aid to less-developed countries and education, working in partnership with local organizations in Djibouti, Egypt, Romania and Senegal, to give financial and material aid. Operates volunteer exchange programmes for young people from Belgium to work in less-developed countries. Also promotes the establishment of links between partner associations for North–South and South–North co-operation.

Geographical Area of Activity: Mainly Djibouti, Egypt, Romania and Senegal.

Publications: *Passerelles* (quarterly); *Les Cahiers asmae; Passe-Partout*.

Council of Administration: Thierry Lebrun (Pres.); Jean Verhelst (Treas.); Gérard Kuyper (Sec.); Claire Delforge; Marc Van den Haute; Yves Robeet.

Address: Ave de Woluwé-St-Lambert 14, 1200 Brussels.

Telephone: (2) 742-03-01; **Fax:** (2) 742-03-13; **Internet:** www.asmae.org; **e-mail:** info@asmae.org.

CARE International

Founded in November 1945 in Washington, DC, as Co-operative for American Remittances to Europe, registered under present name in 1981. An association of 12 national member organizations, it provides disaster relief and aims to improve social and economic conditions in developing countries.

Activities: The organization promotes the use of indigenous resources, and provides disaster relief and rehabilitation support. Development activities include: agriculture and environment; small business development; health, including immunization, water and sanitation, family planning services and AIDS education; and food security.

Geographical Area of Activity: Eastern Europe, Asia, Africa, Middle East, and Central and South America.

Restrictions: Does not normally award grants; funds its own programmes.

Publications: *CI Strategic Report 2001–2006;* Annual Reports and other member publications.

Finance: The organization is financed through: donations from individuals and the private sector; grants from CARE member governments and multilateral agencies; host government support; donations-in-kind.

Board of Trustees: Lydia Marshall (Chair.).

Principal Staff: Sec.-Gen. Denis Caillaux.

Address: International Secretariat, 58/10 blvd du Régent, 1000 Brussels.

Telephone: (2) 502-43-33; **Fax:** (2) 502-82-02; **Internet:** www.care.org; **e-mail:** info@care-international.org.

Damien Foundation

Founded in 1964 to promote the eradication of leprosy and tuberculosis in developing countries.

Activities: Operates in developing countries to provide specialist medical assistance, aiming to eradicate leprosy and tuberculosis, through long-term projects, research and international co-operation. The Foundation also supports field training and formal training in specialized institutions; operates charitable programmes; supports local people in developing countries both medically and morally; and maintains a library.

Geographical Area of Activity: Bangladesh, Burundi, People's Republic of China, Democratic Republic of the Congo (formerly Zaire), Comoros, Egypt, Guatemala, India, Laos, Nicaragua, Nigeria, Panama, Peru, Rwanda and Vietnam.

Publications: *Perspectives* (quarterly, in Dutch and French).

Finance: Annual revenue €13,254,618, expenditure €14,440,487 (2003).

Trustees: M. De Doncker (Pres.); L. Ceyssens; M. Colruyt-Hemeryckx; A. De Schutter; Dr E. Eeckhout; Fr J.-P. Holemans; J. Juspin; E. Krings; B. Meganck; T. Nagels-Coune; Dr D. Porignon; J.-P. Salmon; E. Schacht; Dr P. Stes; A. Vanhoutte; S. Wodon-van Lidth.

Principal Staff: Sec.-Gen. Rigo Peeters.

Address: 263 blvd Léopold II, 1081 Brussels.

Telephone: (2) 422-59-11; **Fax:** (2) 422-59-00; **Internet:** www.damien-foundation.be; **e-mail:** secret@damien-foundation.be.

EMonument

Set up to assist NGOs and communities run programmes in the area of 'Quality Assurance Management' of the environment.

Activities: Operates internationally in the area of conservation and the environment by encouraging technological and scientific co-operation internationally; strengthening networking capacities in the fields of technology and science; fostering the accomplishments of scientific merit within the wider international framework; and contributing to the implementation of infrastructure development in the area of policy management world-wide. Projects include development of Proper Chemical Disposal Fact Sheets (PCDFS) and a Division for Water and Human Resources which maintains a Quality Assurance Data Management web-linked database; maintenance of the Stewardship Program (STEP), a networking system that monitors environmental developments, and of HACCP Overview (Hazard Analysis Critical Control Point); co-ordination of the Aral Sea Project; and the development of a balanced guide for establishing a proficient food, safety and hygiene programme in agriculture. Also co-operates with European Union (EU) environmental programmes.

Geographical Area of Activity: International.

Restrictions: Not a grant-making organization.

Publications: Proper Chemical Disposal Fact Sheets (PCDFS).

Principal Staff: Contact Ian Muse.

Address: Goedmoedstraat 18, 8310 Assebroek, Bruges.

Telephone: (476) 67-07-81; **Fax:** (50) 67-54-75; **Internet:** www.environmonument.com; **e-mail:** contact@environmonument.com.

European Anti-Poverty Network

Independent coalition of national and international NGOs established in 1990; aims to eliminate poverty and social exclusion in the member states of the European Union.

Activities: Works in the countries of the European Union, combating poverty, through campaigning for the issue to be dealt with by the institutions of the EU, promoting action against poverty and supporting existing campaigns against social exclusion; and providing advocacy services for people and groups affected by poverty.

Geographical Area of Activity: Europe.

Publications: *Network News* (newsletter in English, French, German, Italian and Spanish); *Poverty in Europe: the figures for the Member States; Combating Poverty and Social Exclusion: a new momentum in the EU?; Making a Decisive Impact on Poverty and Social Exclusion*; position papers and reports.

Executive Committee: Ludo Horemans (Pres.); Letizia Cesarini Sforza (Vice-Pres.); Janice Ransom (Treas.); Sergio Aires (Sec.).

Principal Staff: Dir Fintan Farrell.

Address: 37–41 rue du Congrès, bte 2, 1000 Brussels.

Telephone: (2) 230-44-55; **Fax:** (2) 230-97-33; **Internet:** www.eapn.org; **e-mail:** team@eapn.skynet.be.

European Foundation for Management Development

Founded in 1971 to provide an international network of private and public organizations, educational institutions and individuals for promoting management development.

Activities: Organizes annual activities for particular sections of its membership, and an annual conference on a subject of current and prospective importance for all categories; initiates special studies, meetings, seminars, workshops and projects on selected topics; brings relevant issues in the field of management development and education to the attention of national or international representative bodies; sponsors professional associations in specific fields; publishes or sponsors publications for its members. In 2002 the

Foundation had more than 470 members, located in more than 45 countries. Members include major European business schools and management centres, and a large number of companies and consultancy organizations. The Foundation promotes the creation of national networks of members to facilitate the exchange of information on a national basis and the development of transnational activities, and co-operates with management development associations in Central and Eastern Europe, North, Central and South-East Asia and Africa. The Foundation administers management training programmes in the People's Republic of China, India, Algeria, Russia and the Commonwealth of Independent States.

Geographical Area of Activity: International.

Publications: *Forum* (magazine, 3 a year); *Bulletin* (newsletter, 3 a year); *Guide to the EC; Lobbying in the EU; European Directory on Executive Education;* various reports and surveys.

Principal Staff: Dir-Gen. Eric Cornuel.

Address: 88 rue Gachard, 1050 Brussels.

Telephone: (2) 628-08-10; **Fax:** (2) 628-08-11; **Internet:** www.efmd.be; **e-mail:** info@efmd.be.

European Foundation for Quality Management

Founded in 1988 by 14 of Europe's largest companies to promote Total Quality Management (TQM) in Europe.

Activities: The main aim of the Foundation is to support the management of European organizations in making quality the key strategy for achieving global competitive advantage. It has more than 800 member organizations from over 38 countries in Europe. Makes annual European Quality Awards recognizing organizational excellence.

Geographical Area of Activity: Europe.

Publications: *Quality Link* (every 2 months); *The European Quest for Excellence* (10th anniversary book); on-line information brochures.

Principal Staff: CEO Alain de Dommartin.

Address: 15 ave des Pleiades, 1200 Brussels.

Telephone: (2) 775-35-11; **Fax:** (2) 775-35-35; **Internet:** www.efqm.org; **e-mail:** info@efqm.org.

European Network on Street Children Worldwide

Founded in Amsterdam in 1995; a network of European organizations which aim to improve the quality of life of 'street children' world-wide, and especially in Eastern Europe and less-developed countries.

Activities: A networking organization with member organizations world-wide, that works to improve street children's lives and provide better opportunities for them, by addressing the causes of their homelessness and poverty; raising public awareness of the existence of homeless children and their rights and needs; promoting strategies to eliminate this phenomenon; lobbying on behalf of homeless children; seeking financial and technical support for member organizations; and facilitating the exchange of information through workshops and conferences.

Geographical Area of Activity: International.

Publications: Newsletter.

Directors: Maartje van Putten (Chair.); Nicolas Fenton (Vice-Chair.).

Principal Staff: Dir Nikhil Roy.

Address: 137 ave Albert, 1190 Brussels.

Telephone: (2) 347-78-48; **Fax:** (2) 347-79-46; **Internet:** www.enscw.org; **e-mail:** info@enscw.org.

European NGO Council on Drugs and Development—ENCOD

An organization established in 1996 by NGOs from 10 European countries to provide information on the causes of the international traffic in illegal drugs and the consequences of current government anti-narcotics policies.

Activities: Operates in Europe carrying out information campaigns on illegal drugs and development, funded by different sponsors.

Geographical Area of Activity: Europe.

Restrictions: Not a grant-making organization.

Publications: *Drugs and Development* (bi-monthly newsletter); reports.

Principal Staff: Sec. Joep Oomen; Chair. Martin Jelsma; Treas. Sergio Cipolla.

Address: Lange Lozanastraat 14, 2018 Antwerp.

Telephone: (3) 237-74-36; **Fax:** (3) 237-02-25; **e-mail:** encod@glo.be.

Eurostep—European Solidarity Towards Equal Participation of People

Established in 1990; an association of NGOs involved in development established to seek to influence development policies of national governments and of the European Union and other international organizations, and to improve the quality and effectiveness of development initiatives taken by NGOs.

Activities: A group of 15 development NGOs from 11 European countries which seeks to lobby national governments and international organizations in areas such as the eradication of poverty, social development, trade, the Cotonou Agreement and the quality of aid. Also aims to to improve the quality and effectiveness of initiatives taken by NGOs in support of people-centred development. Issues numerous position papers on development issues.

Geographical Area of Activity: Europe.

Restrictions: No grants available.

Publications: *The Reality of Aid* (annual report); *EU Global Player*; briefing papers.

Finance: Annual budget approx. US $25,000.

Steering committee: Bjørn Førde (Chair); Greetje Lubbi (Vice-Chair); Guiseppe Crippa; Luis de França; Folke Sundmann.

Principal Staff: Dir Simon Stocker.

Address: 115 rue Stévin, 1000 Brussels.

Telephone: (2) 231-16-59; **Fax:** (2) 230-37-80; **Internet:** www.eurostep.org/index.html; **e-mail:** admin@europstep.org.

Fédération internationale de services latino-américains et asiatiques de promotion de l'habitation populaire—SELAVIP-International (International Federation of Latin-American and Asian Services for the Promotion of Popular Housing)

Founded in 1976, and previously known as the Latin-American and Asian Low Income Housing Service, to promote the welfare, in its widest sense, of the unfortunate in less-developed countries.

Activities: Operates through forming links with local corporations by specific contracts of affiliation; ensuring by all available means decent accommodation for homeless families in urban areas of the countries concerned; covering with all forms of guarantee and insurance the repayment of loans, contracted in their respective countries with the financial aim of constructing accommodation by corporations so affiliated; taking responsibility, totally or in part, for the interest of said loans; collaborating directly with long-term projects of affiliated corporations and in particular with projects aimed at developing mechanisms of local financing; collecting gifts, donations, loans, subsidies, etc. for the realization of the aims mentioned above, placing them ultimately in permanent foundations and ensuring the administration of this capital and these foundations; establishing contacts with public and private organizations, national and international, for credit and help in less-developed countries; and serving as an intermediary between these organizations and the affiliated corporations. In special conditions, aid and services may also be granted to local non-affiliated institutions. The organization has affiliates and associates in 22 countries.

Geographical Area of Activity: Africa, Asia, and Central and South America.

Publications: *SELAVIP News* (2 a year).

Principal Staff: Pres. R. P. Josse Van der Rest; Sec. J. P. Van der Rest.

Address: c/o J. P. Van der Rest, 82 rue de l'été, 1050 Brussels.

Telephone: (2) 649-68-97; **Fax:** (2) 644-67-15; **e-mail:** selavip@hogardecristo.cl.

Fondation pour l'Architecture (Architecture Foundation)

Founded in 1986, a private cultural institution which supports the interaction of different areas of contemporary design and promotes architectural excellence.

Activities: The Foundation operates internationally through self-conducted programmes. It has established a system of cultural and financial partnership between Belgian and foreign public authorities and private businesses, and also works closely with museums, galleries, publishers and cultural centres. Each year the Foundation stages exhibitions, conferences and public events devoted to all aspects of the built environment—contemporary architecture, history, current affairs, urban planning and design. The Foundation maintains two exhibition halls and a library.

Geographical Area of Activity: International.

Publications: Numerous catalogues.

Board of Trustees: Philippe Bodson (Pres.).

Principal Staff: Dir Diane Hennebert; Sec. Giasmina Giuliana.

Address: 55 rue de l'Ermitage, 1050 Brussels.

Telephone: (2) 644-24-80; **Fax:** (2) 648-24-82; **e-mail:** fondation.architecture@skynet.be.

Fondation Auschwitz (Auschwitz Foundation)

Founded in 1980 by Amicale des Ex-Prisonniers Belge as a study and documentation centre to preserve the memory of the prisoners of Auschwitz.

Activities: The Foundation operates nationally and internationally in the fields of education, the arts, law and human rights, and holocaust studies, through self-conducted programmes, awarding prizes, conferences and issuing publications. Awards the annual Auschwitz Foundation Prize of €2,500 for an original and unpublished text which makes an important contribution to the political, economic, social or historical analysis of the world of the Nazi concentration camps and the processes leading to its creation.

Geographical Area of Activity: Europe.

Publications: *Bulletin Trimestriel de la Fondation Auschwitz / Driemaandelijks Tijdschrift*.

Principal Staff: Pres. Baron Paul Halter; Dir Yannis Thanassekos.

Address: 65 rue des Tanneurs, 1000 Brussels.

Telephone: (2) 512-79-98; **Fax:** (2) 512-58-84; **Internet:** www.auschwitz.be; **e-mail:** fondation@auschwitz.be.

Fondation Bernheim (Bernheim Fund)

Established in 1974 for general charitable purposes.

Activities: Operates in the fields of education, culture, peace, and economic and social issues, through offering grants, awarding prizes, including a biennial literature prize worth 200,000 Belgian francs, holding conferences and seminars, publications, scholarships and student assistance. Also supports entrepreneurial initiatives and medical research, including a chair in entrepreneurial studies at the Université Libre de Bruxelles.

Geographical Area of Activity: Belgium.

Publications: Information brochures.

Finance: Assets approx. 2,000,000,000 Belgian francs.

Directors: Jacques Dopchie (Pres.); Françoise Thys-Clement, Edouard Jakhian (Vice-Pres); Jacques Leduc; André Farber.

Principal Staff: Gen. Delegate Micheline Mardulyn.

Address: 2 place de l'Albertine, 1000 Brussels.

Telephone: (2) 213-14-99; **Fax:** (2) 213-14-95; **e-mail:** michmardulyn.bernheim@online.be.

Fondation Cardiologique Princesse Liliane (Princess Liliane Cardiological Foundation)

Founded in 1952 by HRH Princess Lilian of Belgium to encourage the study of cardiac and cardiovascular diseases and the physiopathology of diseases.

Activities: Operates mainly through the organization of international symposia in the field of diseases and related surgery; symposia held include 'Blood Cells and Leukaemia', 'Brain Repair', 'Gene Therapy' and 'Lymphocyte activation in health and disease'.

Publications: *Symposia* (annually).

Governing Council: M. A. Bodson; J. Willems; A. Oosterlinck; Mr Decoster; E. Witte; J. L. Vanherweghem; M. Crochet; Elected Members: H. De Croo (Pres.); L. Aerts; Baron de Fauconval; Comte J. P. de Launoit; Baron J. Godeaux; J. Goossens; Baron J. Lequime; A. Leysen; P. Meyers; Baron E. Van Dyck; J.-Ch. Velge; A. Verplaetse; Baron L. Wauters.

Principal Staff: Sec.-Gen. C. van Ypersele de Strihou; Admin. Officer A. Van den Bosch.

Address: 5 rue d'Egmont, 1050 Brussels.

Telephone: (2) 510-24-67; **Fax:** (2) 510-25-64.

Fondation Égyptologique Reine Elisabeth (Queen Elisabeth Egyptological Foundation)

Founded in 1923 by Jean Capart to promote studies in the fields of Egyptology and papyrology.

Activities: Operates both nationally and internationally through research, conferences, lectures and publications; sponsors study trips to Egypt. Holds an extensive papyrus archive.

Geographical Area of Activity: International.

Publications: *Chronique d'Egypte* (2 a year).

Trustees: Comte A. d'Arschot (Pres.); J. Bingen (Sec.); W. Clarysse; H. De Meulenaere; E. Haerinck; D. Homès-Fredericq; L. Limme; M. Malaise; A. Martin; A. Mekhitarian; G. Nachtergael; R. Tefnin; P. Theunissen; Baron Cl. Tibbaut; W. Van der Elst; F. Van Noten.

Principal Staff: Sec.-Gen. L. Limme.

Address: 10 Parc du Cinquantenaire, 1000 Brussels.

Telephone: (2) 741-73-64; **Fax:** (2) 733-77-35.

Fondation Europalia International (Europalia International Foundation)

Founded in 1969 to promote and highlight the culture of one European country every year.

Activities: Organizes and finances its own cultural activities and collaborates with other bodies; arranges international conferences; sponsors an annual festival highlighting a specific country—Italy in 2003.

Geographical Area of Activity: Belgium and other European countries.

Publications: Exhibition catalogues.

Administrative Council: Paul De Keersmaeker (Pres.); and 18 other administrators, representatives of Belgian banks, government departments, media and arts organizations, the European Parliament and the Council of Europe.

Principal Staff: Man. Dir Luc Stainier; Financial Man. M. Donnet; External Relations Man. Colette Delmotte; Dir, Exhibitions Kristine de Mulder; Dir, Music Michael Scheck.

Address: 23 rue Ravenstein, 1000 Brussels.

Telephone: (2) 507-85-95; **Fax:** (2) 513-54-88; **Internet:** www.europalia.be; **e-mail:** info@europalia.be.

Fondation Evens Stichting (Evens Foundation)

Founded in 1991 by Georges and Irene Evens to promote increased respect for cultural and ethnic differences in Europe.

Activities: Operates nationally and internationally in the fields of inter-cultural education, the arts and literature, through self-conducted programmes, grants to institutions and schools, conferences and training courses, and awarding prizes. Also has an office in Paris.

Geographical Area of Activity: Europe.

Publications: *Learning for Change in a Multicultural Society; Europe's New Racism? Causes, Manifestations and Solutions.*

Principal Staff: Pres. Corinne Evens; Dir Christine Castille.

Address: Van Breestraat 14, 2018 Antwerp.

Telephone: (3) 231-39-70; **Fax:** (3) 233-94-32; **Internet:** www.evensfoundation.be; **e-mail:** ef@evensfoundation.be.

Fondation Francqui (Francqui Foundation)

Founded in 1932 by Emile Francqui and Herbert Hoover to promote the development of higher education and scientific research in Belgium.

Activities: Operates in the field of higher education. Confers the annual Prix Francqui on a Belgian under 50 years of age, who has made a notable advance in the fields of science, humanities or medicine. Also awards Francqui Professorships each year, inviting two scholars from each Belgian university and three foreign professors to teach in Belgium under the Foundation's auspices. Provides annual fellowships to selected young Belgian academics to enable them to study abroad, mainly in the USA.

Geographical Area of Activity: Belgium.

Restrictions: Grants only available to Belgian nationals.

Publications: Report of operations every five years.

Board of Directors: 20 members.

Principal Staff: Pres. M. Eyskens; Exec. Dir Prof. L. Eyckmans.

Address: 1 rue Defacqz, 1000 Brussels.

Telephone: (2) 539-33-94; **Fax:** (2) 537-29-21; **Internet:** www.francquifoundation.be; **e-mail:** francquifoundation@sbynet.be.

Fondation Marcel Hicter (Marcel Hicter Foundation)

Established in 1980 to promote and carry out activities contributing to the socio-cultural development of the French community in Belgium, and to promote co-operation at a European and international level in the area of culture.

Activities: Operates in the field of the arts and culture, formerly through organizing the European Diploma in Cultural Project Management, which operates in three countries; training cultural managers from 36 countries; and managing, on behalf of the Council of Europe, mobility grants for cultural management experts and trainees. However as of January 2003 the programme had been cancelled due to the withdrawal of Council of Europe funding. The Foundation also organizes conferences, carries out research and issues publications.

Geographical Area of Activity: Central, Eastern and Western Europe, the Russian Federation and Central Africa.

Publications: *Citoyens et Pouvoirs en Europe.*

Board of Directors: Xavier Mabille (Pres.); E. Grosjean (Sec.); J. P. Braine (Treas.).

Principal Staff: Dir Jean-Pierre Deru.

Address: 78 rue Gachard, 1050 Brussels.

Telephone: (2) 641-89-80; **Fax:** (2) 641-89-81; **Internet:** www.fondation-hicter.org; **e-mail:** contact@fondation-hicter.org.

Fondation Pégase (Pegasus Foundation)

Founded in 1991 by individual members of the European Parliament from all countries of the European Community (now the European Union) to promote, disseminate and sponsor educational actions in cultural heritage intended to develop the perception of the European cultural identity in its complex and rich diversity.

Activities: Aims to act as a catalyst in the field of culture between the worlds of business, culture and the European institutions. The Foundation's major project is Schools Adopt Monuments; since 1993 this project has been implemented in 15 European countries, involving over 700 schools; its goal is to acquaint children with their local and European heritage in an innovative way, through adopting a local site or monument and conducting research into it. Other projects are SIMILE, making museum collections available to schools through new technology; ParlEuNet, giving schools information on the European Parliament over the internet; and video conferences between schools and members of the European Parliament.

Geographical Area of Activity: Europe.

Board of Administration: Fernand Herman (Pres.); Willy de Clerc (Founding Member); Eugenio Belloni (Exec. Pres.); and 29 others.

Principal Staff: Gen. Man. Michele Ciavarini Azzi.

Address: c/o European Parliament, Eastman Bldg, 135a rue Belliard, 1047 Brussels.

Telephone: (2) 284-23-27; **Fax:** (2) 284-90-09; **Internet:** www.fondation-pegase.be; **e-mail:** pegase@fondation-pegase.be.

Fondation Royale Père Damien pour la Lutte Contre la Lèpre—FOPERDA (Father Damien Foundation for the Campaign Against Leprosy—Royal Society)

Founded in 1939 by Félicien Cattier to combat leprosy.

Activities: Operates in the Democratic Republic of the Congo (formerly Zaire) in the field of medicine; runs an anti-leprosy centre at Pawa (Haut-Uele), with training courses for paramedical workers; supports about 20 field-teams in Haut- and Bas-Uele, tracing new cases and attending both leprosy and tuberculosis patients; and offers general support to local health-care structures.

Geographical Area of Activity: Africa, mostly the Democratic Republic of the Congo (formerly Zaire).

Restrictions: A grant-seeking, not a grant-making organization.

Finance: Annual revenue and expenditure 10,234,000 Belgian francs (1999).

Trustees: François Eeckhout (Pres.); Prof. René Tonglet, Prof. Stefaan Pattyn (Vice-Pres).

Principal Staff: Dir of Projects Dr Jacques Deverchin.

Address: Société Royale, 263 blvd Leopold II, 1081 Brussels.

Telephone: (2) 422-59-39; **Fax:** (2) 422-59-00; **e-mail:** plec@damien-foundation.be.

Fondation Paul-Henri Spaak—Stichting Paul-Henri Spaak (Paul-Henri Spaak Foundation)

Founded in 1973 by Vicomte Etienne Davignon, Fernand Dehousse, Auguste Edmond De Schryver, André de Staercke, Walter Ganshof van der Meersch, Marcel Grégoire, André Jaumotte, Comte Georges Moens de Fernig, Jean Rey, Paul Smets and Fernand Spaak, to constitute a centre of thought and action to prolong the European work of Paul-Henri Spaak, particularly in the field of the external relations of the European Community (now the European Union); to promote any activity contributing to a better understanding of the European ideal and associating new generations with the construction of Europe.

Activities: The Foundation was established to operate nationally, internationally and on a European level in the field of international relations and economic affairs, through self-conducted programmes, research, conferences and publications. It encourages education and scientific research related to its aims through creating specialized professorships in European Union external affairs to be occupied by distinguished foreigners; international fellowships and scholarships; and the sponsoring of publications and diffusion of documentation and information. Lectures and seminars as well as regional, national and international congresses are organized. Also awards a science prize.

Geographical Area of Activity: International.

Administrative Council: Vicomte Etienne Davignon (Pres.); A. de Staercke (Vice-Pres.); François Danis (Sec.-Gen.); D. M. Abshire; M. Albert; F. Boas; W. de Clercq; H. de Croo; J. Delors; Baron J. Godeaux; A. Jacquemin; Baron A. Jaumotte; Sir M. Palliser; Baron P. de Schoutheete de Tervarent; P.-F. Smets; A. Spaak; G. Spitaels.

Address: 62 ave George Bergmann, bte 4, 1050 Brussels.

Telephone: (2) 672-08-05; **Internet:** www.fondationspaak.org; **e-mail:** fond.spaak@skynet.be.

Fonds National de la Recherche Scientifique (National Fund for Scientific Research)

Founded in 1928 by King Albert I to promote scientific research in Belgium.

Activities: Provides subsidies each year to scientists or research workers to enable them to continue their investigations, and awards about 800 grants annually to university students in the field of science. Also provides more than 200 research posts of limited duration to qualified research workers and supports the attendance at scientific meetings and conferences of Belgian researchers. Enables qualified research workers to undertake short visits abroad to familiarize themselves with new developments and techniques in scientific research. Awards prizes for achievement in the field of research. Also administers the Fund for Medical Scientific Research, the Fund for Fundamental Collective Research, the Inter-University Institute for Nuclear Sciences and the Industry and Agriculture Research Training Fund.

Geographical Area of Activity: Belgium.

Publications: Annual Report.

Board: The Fund and its associated Funds are administered by a Board which consists of representatives of university institutions and from the economic, social and political spheres within French-speaking Belgium.

Principal Staff: Sec.-Gen. M.-J. Simoen.

Address: 5 rue d'Egmont, 1000 Brussels.

Telephone: (2) 504-92-11; **Fax:** (2) 504-92-92; **Internet:** www.fnrs.be; **e-mail:** mjsimoen@fnrs.be.

Fonds voor Wetenschappelijk Onderzoek—Vlaanderen (Fund for Scientific Research—Flanders)

Established in 1928 at the initiative of King Albert I to encourage and support fundamental scientific research in the Flemish community in Belgium. Since 1992, the Flemish Board of Trustees has had fully autonomous powers of decision.

Activities: Promotes and finances fundamental scientific research in the universities of the Flemish community and in research institutions in all fields of science, including medicine, technology, environmental studies, social sciences and the humanities, including law. Provides pre- and postdoctoral fellowships and grants for national and international research projects, contacts and co-operation.

Geographical Area of Activity: Belgium.

Publications: Annual Report.

Finance: Annual expenditure €124,000,000 (2003).

Principal Staff: Sec.-Gen. José Traest.

Address: Egmontstraat 5, 1000 Brussels.

Telephone: (2) 512-91-10; **Fax:** (2) 512-58-90; **Internet:** www.fwo.be; **e-mail:** jose.traest@fwo.be.

Foundation for Scientific Research and Educational Exchange

Founded in 1980 to provide grants to Belgians and Luxembourgeois for postgraduate study in the USA.

Activities: The Foundation offers grants, scholarships, prizes and fellowships to individuals wishing to pursue postgraduate study in any discipline, in the USA.

Geographical Area of Activity: Belgium and Luxembourg.

Finance: The Foundation is supported by donations.

Board of Directors: J. Van den Eynde (Chair.).

Principal Staff: Exec. Dir Margaret Nicholson.

Address: 4 blvd de l'Empereur, 1000 Brussels.

Telephone: (2) 519-57-72; **Fax:** (2) 519-57-73; **e-mail:** fulbright@kbr.be.

Îles de Paix (Islands of Peace)

Founded in 1965 by Father Dominique Pire to ameliorate conditions for people living in the Southern regions of the world through food security and infrastructure development; and to educate people in more developed countries about life in the Southern hemisphere.

Activities: Operates internationally in the field of aid to less-developed countries, through self-conducted programmes carried out with partner organizations in West Africa (including Benin, Burkina Faso, Mali, Niger, and Togo) and South America (Ecuador and Bolivia). Also educates the public in Belgium about life in less-developed countries.

Geographical Area of Activity: West Africa and South America.

Publications: *Transitions* (quarterly); Annual Report; financial statements; reports and news-sheets.

Finance: Annual revenue 67,619,085 Belgian francs, expenditure 73,330,244 Belgian francs (2002).

Trustees: Eric Tilman (Pres.).

Principal Staff: Sec.-Gen. Luc Langouche.

Address: 37 rue du Marché, 4500 Huy.

Telephone: (85) 23-02-54; **Fax:** (85) 23-42-64; **Internet:** www.ilesdepaix.org; **e-mail:** info@ilesdepaix.org.

Institut Royal des Relations Internationales—Koninklijk Instituut voor Internationale Betrekkingen (Royal Institute of International Relations)

Founded in 1947 to further studies into foreign politics, international law and economics, in particular in relation to the foreign policies of Belgium, Luxembourg and the Netherlands. The foundation expresses no official opinion on national or international affairs.

Activities: Operates internationally through self-conducted programmes, including research projects, carried out on an international basis, and through both national and international conferences, lectures and publications; maintains a library.

Geographical Area of Activity: International.

Publications: *Studia Diplomatica* (6 a year, in Dutch, English and French); *Internationale Spectator* (monthly, in Dutch).

Finance: Individual, government and corporate donations.

Principal Staff: Pres. Viscount Etienne Davignon; Dir Gen. François de Kerchave d'Exaedre; Dir, European Studies Franklin Dehousse; Dir, Security Studies Rik Coolsaet.

Address: 69 rue de Namur, 1000 Brussels.

Telephone: (2) 223-41-14; **Fax:** (2) 223-41-16; **Internet:** www.irri-jkiib.be; **e-mail:** info@irri-kiib.be.

Institute of Cultural Affairs International

Established in 1977 to develop and test methods of individual, community and organizational development.

Activities: Operates in collaboration with other organizations in three major areas: sustainable development, lifelong education and organizational transformation. Promotes activities that encourage people to take responsibility for their own lives, development and for society as a whole, including development conferences and projects, leadership training, workshops and seminars, and documentation. Maintains offices in Africa, North, Central and South America, the Asia-Pacific region and Europe.

Geographical Area of Activity: International.

Restrictions: Not a grant-making organization.

Publications: *The Network Exchange* (newsletter, monthly); *The ICAI Location Directory*.

Finance: Funded by membership fees.

Board of Directors: Judy Harvie (Pres.); Eduard Christensen (Vice-Pres.); Martin Gilbraith (Treas.); Hala El Kholy (Sec.); Moses Ogianyo; Tatwa Timsina.

Address: 8 rue Amédée Lynen, 1210 Brussels.

Telephone: (2) 219-00-87; **Fax:** (2) 219-04-06; **Internet:** www.icaworld.org; **e-mail:** icai@linkline.be.

International Coalition for Development Action

Founded in 1976, a coalition of NGOs and other development organizations in Organisation for Economic Co-operation and Development (OECD) countries.

Activities: Operates internationally in the areas of development, economic affairs and international affairs, through supporting social and political change in less-developed countries in the Southern hemisphere; disseminating informative material on trade issues in order to promote people-centred trade policies; monitoring international and regional trade policy negotiation and implementation; and promoting the study of the effect on gender and social status of trade liberalization. The Coalition administers the co-ordination of the Co-ordination of European NGOs Networking on Trade, and the Informal Working group on Gender and Trade (international network).

Geographical Area of Activity: International.

Publications: *ICDA Journal* (2 a year); *ICDA Update* (2 a year).

Principal Staff: Chair. Janice Goodson Foerde.

Address: 115 rue Stévin, 1000 Brussels.

Telephone: (2) 230-04-30; **Fax:** (2) 230-52-37; **Internet:** www.icda.be; **e-mail:** icda@icda.be.

International Co-operation for Development and Solidarity—CIDSE

Established in 1966, under present name in 1981, to facilitate co-ordination and information exchange between Catholic development organizations in Europe and North America; to promote aid to developing countries; and to encourage individuals in those countries to attain economic, social and political rights.

Activities: Aims to be an effective and strong voice in international forums through its advocacy and lobby work, which currently focuses on debt and structural adjustment, coherence of development policies, trade, food security and peace-building. Members aim to promote development and solidarity with partner organizations in the Southern hemisphere through funding of projects and programmes. Members seek to inform and challenge the general public in the Northern hemisphere through development education programmes. There are 15 member agencies in 14 countries and territories. CIDSE seeks strategic alliances with other organizations and networks.

Geographical Area of Activity: International.

Restrictions: Not a grant-making organization.

Publications: *Advocacy Newsletter* (quarterly, in English); Annual Report (in English and French).

Finance: Funded by membership fees. Expenditure on projects US $950,465 (2000).

Executive Committee: Jean-Marie Fardeau (Pres.); Paul Chitnis (Vice-Pres.); Luc Claessens; Hans Kruijssen; Sergio Morelli.

Principal Staff: Sec.-Gen. Christiane Overkamp; Pres. Jean-Marie Fardeau; Vice-Pres. Paul Chitnis; Treas. Norbert Dittrich; Ecclesiastical Advisor Fernando Charrier; Jürgen Nikolai.

Address: 16 rue Stévin, 1000 Brussels.

Telephone: (2) 230-77-22; **Fax:** (2) 230-70-82; **Internet:** www.cidse.org; **e-mail:** postmaster@cidse.org.

International Yehudi Menuhin Foundation

Non-profit organization established in 1991.

Activities: Promotes music and the arts internationally; encourages exchange and encounters between different cultures, through the organization of events; promotes the representation and expression of cultural identities through the arts, particularly of those cultures that are under threat, by the creation of a forum (the Assembly of Cultures of Europe); co-ordinates cultural projects initiated by Yehudi Menuhin, and disseminates them throughout the world.

Geographical Area of Activity: International.

Publications: On-line newsletter.

Finance: Funded by its own activities, and by sponsorships and donations. Also receives local, national and European subsidies. Supported by a number of foundations and institutions, such as the European Union, the Council of Europe and UNESCO.

Directors: Enrique Baron Crespo (Pres.); Gianfranco di Bosio; Guilhermo de Oliveira Martins; Ivan Hodác; Stefano Micossi; Marianne Poncelet; Robert Verrue.

Address: 61 chaussée de la Hulpe, 1180 Brussels.

Telephone: (2) 673-35-04; **Fax:** (2) 672-52-99; **Internet:** www.menuhin-foundation.com; **e-mail:** menuhin.foundation@skynet.be.

Koning Boudewijnstichting/Fondation Roi Baudouin (King Baudouin Foundation)

Founded in 1976 to commemorate the 25th anniversary of King Baudouin's coronation, the Foundation is an independent public welfare institution, which aims 'to carry out initiatives to improve the life of the population, including measures of an economic, social, scientific and cultural nature'; to stimulate solidarity and generosity; and to act as a catalyst for sustainable change.

Activities: From 2002–05 the Foundation was to operate in four main programme areas: social justice; civil society; governance; and philanthropy. Priority is given to projects focusing on exclusion, problems facing young people, the challenges of an ageing society, attention to gender diversity; the stimulation of cultural pluralism in Belgium and South-Eastern Europe, provoking a public debate on the production and application of science and technology, and the creation of a culture of giving oriented around a European perspective. Funds are also available for specific initiatives which fall outside these areas. The Foundation offers individuals, organizations and businesses the opportunity to establish funds to support projects, and supports transnational funding through its Transnational Giving Europe project and the King Baudouin Foundation US, Inc in the USA. Also awards the €150,000 King Baudouin International Development Prize every two years.

Geographical Area of Activity: Europe.

Publications: Annual Report and financial statement; newsletter; publications, reports and studies.

Finance: Receives a grant from the Belgian National Lottery. Annual budget €25,085,248 (2003).

Board of Trustees: Herman Vanden Berghe (Chair.); Camille Paulus, Jean-Louis Six (Vice-Chair.); and 22 other members.

Principal Staff: Hon. Pres. HH Queen Fabiola of Belgium; Man. Dir Luc Tayart de Borms.

Address: rue Brederodestraat 21, 1000 Brussels.

Telephone: (2) 511-18-40; **Fax:** (2) 511-52-21; **Internet:** www.kbs-frb.be; **e-mail:** info@kbs-frb.be.

Médecins Sans Frontières—MSF (Doctors Without Frontiers)

Founded in 1971 in Paris to provide medical care to populations in times of crisis in any part of the world.

Activities: The organization works in the fields of medicine and health, aid to less-developed countries, and law and human rights, through self-conducted programmes, conferences, training courses and publications. It relies on volunteer health professionals, and provides medical aid to those in need world-wide, in countries at war or coping with disaster. It runs missions in refugee camps and long-term operations in countries where health structures have broken down; promotes human rights; helps to secure long-term rehabilitation of health structures; organizes the training of MSF and local staff; and operates two centres for surveillance and applied research in epidemiology and public health. The international MSF network comprises 18 operational sections and delegate offices in Europe, North America and Asia; there are missions in over 80 countries and territories world-wide. MSF was awarded the Nobel Peace Prize in 1999.

Geographical Area of Activity: International.

Publications: *MSF International Newsletter; Développement durable: espace de démocratie et d'intégration citoyenne; Populations in Danger* (annually); bulletins; Activity Report.

Finance: Annual budget approx. US $180,000,000.

Address: International Office, 39 rue de la Tourelle, 1040 Brussels.

Telephone: (2) 280-18-81; **Fax:** (2) 280-01-73; **Internet:** www.msf.org.

Oil Companies' European Organization for Environment, Health and Safety—CONCAWE

Founded in 1963 as the Oil Companies' International Study Group for Conservation of Clean Air and Water in Europe. It aims to collect and disseminate scientific, technical and economic information on all aspects of environmental and health protection related to the petroleum-refining industry (including pollution control, safety advice for workers and customers, and legislation).

Activities: Collects, exchanges and evaluates environmental and health data; initiates and evaluates research; assesses the consequences of proposed environmental legislation in terms of economic feasibility and cost/benefit; promotes co-operation between petroleum companies, industry and governments on all environmental issues concerning the oil-refining industry; publishes reports and other information. Work areas comprise: industrial atmospheric emissions; water protection; packaging, labelling and safe handling of petroleum products; health protection; automotive fuels and vehicle emissions; oil-spill cleaning technology; pipeline integrity; and refinery safety management. The Organization has 29 members in 19 Organisation for Economic Co-operation and Development (OECD) European countries and one associate member in Eastern Europe.

Geographical Area of Activity: Europe.

Publications: *CONCAWE Review* (2 a year); *CONCAWE Reports*.

Principal Staff: Sec.-Gen. Jean Castelein.

Address: 165 blvd du Souverain, 1160 Brussels.

Telephone: (2) 566-91-60; **Fax:** (2) 566-91-81; **Internet:** www.concawe.be; **e-mail:** annemie.hermans@concawe.be.

RedR International

Established in 1979 by Peter Guthrie, and originally known as Registered Engineers for Disaster Relief, to train personnel to work for humanitarian aid agencies internationally; its members are mainly engineers, but other professions are represented.

Activities: Operates world-wide, selecting and training personnel to work for humanitarian aid agencies for short periods. Maintains a register of people who can be called upon at short notice to spend up to three months on secondment from their usual employer to assist in disaster relief. Maintains offices in Australia, Canada, New Zealand and the United Kingdom.

Geographical Area of Activity: International.

Principal Staff: Dir Koen Versavel.

Address: ave Molière 507, 1050 Brussels.

Internet: www.redr.org; **e-mail:** redr.international@brutele.be.

Ruralité-environnement-développement—RED

Founded in 1980 to encourage communication between those involved in rural development throughout Europe.

Activities: Organizes conferences and seminars in the fields of economic development, planning and cultural heritage in rural areas. The organization is President of the European Centre for Rural and Environmental Interests, co-ordinates the European Countryside Movement, and is Vice-President of the Advisory Committee on Rural Development of the European Commission of the European Union. The organization has members in 15 countries.

Geographical Area of Activity: Europe.

Restrictions: No grants are made.

Publications: *RED Dossier* (2 a year); *Eurobrèves* (newsletter); seminar papers.

Board of Directors: G. Peltre (Pres.).

Principal Staff: Dir P. Collignon.

Address: 304 rue des Potiers, 6717 Attert.

Telephone: (63) 23-04-90; **Fax:** (63) 23-04-99; **Internet:** www.ruraleurope.org; **e-mail:** red@skynet.be.

Service Civil International

Founded in 1920 by Pierre Ceresole, to provide opportunities for men and women, young and old, irrespective of their race, nationality, creed or politics, to join together in giving useful voluntary service to the community in a spirit of friendship and international understanding, with the aim of promoting peace, international understanding and solidarity, social justice, sustainable development and concern for the environment.

Activities: Operates internationally through the provision of volunteers for community service and work-camp exchanges world-wide. Projects include the East/West Working Group. A second International Secretariat, serving Asia, is based in Sri Lanka. Service Civil International has 33 branches and groups in Europe, Asia, Africa and North America, plus an affiliate in Australia. The organization has consultative status with UNESCO and the Council of Europe.

Geographical Area of Activity: International.

Restrictions: Not a grant-making organization.

Publications: Newsletter.

Principal Staff: Int. Pres. Ingrid Danckaerts; Vice-Pres. M. N. Ganesh; Int. Treas. Frank Ormel.

Address: International Secretariat, St-Jacobsmarkt 82, 2000 Antwerp.

Telephone: (3) 226-57-27; **Fax:** (3) 232 03 44; **Internet:** www.sciint.org; **e-mail:** info@sciint.org.

Solidar

Established in 1951, and formerly known as Internationales Arbeiter-Hilfswerk (International Workers Aid).

Activities: Solidar is an association of 22 independent development and social welfare agencies, based in 15 European countries, which are linked to the labour and democratic socialist movement and whose main areas of activity are development projects, education and training, environment and conservation issues, health care, rural development, human rights and emergency aid. It is committed to international co-operation, understanding and solidarity as a way of fostering freedom, fundamental human rights and social and economic justice. Its aim is to contribute to the creation of radical models of economic and social development, and to advance practical solutions to enable people to create and control their own future. The organization disseminates information about developing countries; supports the establishment of welfare organizations in Central and Eastern Europe; advocates the development of modern social policies by campaigning for the realization of the European Social Charter (the Charter of Fundamental Social Rights of the European Union), and the improvement of the welfare and social security systems in Europe.

Geographical Area of Activity: Europe.

Publications: *Solidar Bulletin* (six a year); *The Global Network; SOLIDAR in Humanitarian Aid; Towards a Citizen s Europe: Time to Discuss the Future of the European Union; Toolkit for NGOs on the convention on the future of Europe; The Status Quo is Not Enough! The Guide to Good Practice for a non-discriminatory access to services provided by NGOs; At Your Service: NGOs building a Social Europe; Manual for Coordination, Training and Capacity Building in Humanitarian Aid for the SOLIDAR Network*.

Principal Staff: Sec.-Gen. Giampiero Alhadeff.

Address: 22 rue du Commerce, 1000 Brussels.

Telephone: (2) 500-10-20; **Fax:** (2) 500-10-30; **Internet:** www.solidar.org; **e-mail:** solidar@skynet.be.

Speech, Artificial Intelligence and Language Trust—SAIL

Established in 1999 by Jo Lernout and Pol Hauspie, founders of Lernout & Hauspie Speech Products, NV, a Belgian computer software company, to advance research in the area of computer speech and translation technology.

Activities: Operates in collaboration with local governments in Argentina, Belgium, Hungary, Israel, Japan, Norway, Singapore, the USA and in Africa to establish 'ports' or technology campuses to encourage research in computer speech and translation technology. Each port was to be given US $10,000,000 from the Trust, in exchange for a matching amount from local governments. The first port, Flanders Language Valley in Belgium was to be joined by nine other campuses by the end of 2000.

Geographical Area of Activity: Africa, Argentina, Belgium, Hungary, Israel, Japan, Norway, Singapore and the USA.

Finance: Endowed with US $100,000,000 (1999).

Principal Staff: Chair. J.-L. Dehaene.

Address: Ypres.

University Foundation for Development Co-operation

Founded in 1984 by the late Prof. Dr L. Van Bladel to support development co-operation, with special emphasis on the underprivileged in society.

Activities: The Foundation operates nationally and internationally in the fields of development studies, aid to developing countries and education, through self-conducted programmes, research, publications and conferences. Projects are carried out in the Democratic Republic of the Congo (formerly Zaire), India and Nicaragua.

Geographical Area of Activity: Central Africa, Central America and India.

Restrictions: Grants only to specific organizations.

Publications: Reports.

Trustees: The Foundation is governed by the University of Antwerp–UFSIA and the North Flemish Province of the Society of Jesus (Jesuits).

Principal Staff: J. Bastiaensen; H. Cobbaert; H. de Craen; M. Decancq; R. Embrechts; S. Geukens; J. Ghysels; T. de Herdt; S. Marysse; J. Vanhoutte; J. Verschueren.

Address: Prinsstraat 13, 2000 Antwerp.

Telephone: (3) 220-40-37; **Fax:** (3) 220-44-20; **Internet:** www.ufsia.ac.be/usos; **e-mail:** tom.deherdt@ua.ac.be.

World Animal Handicap Foundation—WAHF

Founded in 1992 to care for disabled animals using adapted orthopaedic therapy.

Activities: The Foundation works with veterinary surgeons, pet clinics and hospitals, animal protection associations, pet-owners and others to further its aims.

Geographical Area of Activity: International.

Finance: Funded by charities, gifts, membership fees, etc.

Principal Staff: Chair. Michelle Mommer-Horikoshi; Vice-Chair. G. de Beauffort; Sec. M.-P. Moulin.

Address: 40 square Marie-Louise, bte 22, 1000 Brussels.

Telephone: (2) 230-79-12; **Fax:** (2) 230-53-68; **e-mail:** sdmedia@skynet.be.

Benin

FOUNDATIONS, TRUSTS AND NON-PROFIT ORGANIZATIONS

Centre Pan-Africain de Prospective Sociale (Pan-African Centre for Social Prospects)

Founded in 1987 by Prof. Albert Tevoedjre.

Activities: Undertakes research and training programmes linked to social and development issues; trains young professionals as future leaders in Africa in the areas of social policy, economics, communication, consumer protection, environmental protection and management; facilitates the exchange of business and technological information; and supports NGOs involved in development projects and programmes, and socio-economic projects. The Centre also helped found the African Humanitarian Initiative to assist refugees with food and medicines.

Geographical Area of Activity: Africa.

Principal Staff: Dir Albert K. Ekue.

Address: BP 1501, Porto Novo.

Telephone: 21-44-36; **Fax:** 21-39-65; **e-mail:** cpps@elodia.intnet.bj.

Fondation de l'Entrepreneurship du Bénin (Enterprise Foundation of Benin)

Aims to help establish and promote new businesses and private companies in Benin.

Activities: Provides assistance and support to entrepreneurs (both nationals and foreigners) who wish to invest in Benin. Organizes seminars, offers advice on marketing and management skills and strategies, training, and the opportunity to contact other suppliers and potential customers around the world. Runs an annual entrepreneurial competition for young people, funded by the Benin National Lottery and the Canadian International Development Agency. Manages the Place du Québec socio-cultural centre.

Geographical Area of Activity: Benin.

Principal Staff: Dir Pierre Dovonou Lokossou.

Address: 08 BP 1155, Cotonou.

Telephone: 30-53-52; **Fax:** 31-37-26; **Internet:** www.placequebec.org; **e-mail:** fonda@intnet.bj.

Groupe d'Action pour la Justice et l'Egalité Sociale—GAJES (Action Group for Justice and Social Equality)

Founded in 1990, a pressure group dedicated to achieving equality for all women in society.

Activities: Operates in the field of social justice, primarily in the field of social justice for women. Programmes include education of girls in the Mono department; the development and support of Parents–Teachers associations; and the L'Unité Documentaire Femmes et Développement, a documentation centre providing information sources for women on sustainable development and empowerment.

Geographical Area of Activity: Benin.

Council of Administration: Thècla Midiohouan Gbikpi (Founding Pres.); Marie-Odile Comlanvi-Hountondji (Pres.); Victoire Idossou Atihou Kegue (Vice-Pres.); Anne-Marie Falade Gandji (Treas.); Gisèle Agboton (Sec.-Gen.); and 13 others.

Principal Staff: Sec.-Gen. Gisèle Agboton.

Address: BP 04-778, Cotonou.

Telephone: 33-61-05; **Internet:** www.bj.refer.org/benin_ct/cop/gajes/accueil.htm; **e-mail:** ongajes_99@yahoo.com.

Groupe de Recherche et d'action pour le Bien-Être Social—GRABS

Established and run by women to support the development of women in Benin.

Activities: Promotes popular participation, primary health care, literacy and improved education for rural populations. Dedicated to eliminating poverty and malnutrition. Works for women's participation and rights, and for sustainable development. Collaborates with international organizations, including co-ordinating conferences.

Geographical Area of Activity: Benin.

Principal Staff: Pres. Christophe Denadi.

Address: BP 04-0172, Cotonou.

Telephone: 30-29-32; **Fax:** 30-28-73.

Bermuda

FOUNDATION CENTRE AND CO-ORDINATING BODY

Centre on Philanthropy

Membership organization set up in 1991 to promote a philanthropic philosophy in the community, and an attitude of giving, through information, seminars and dialogue with charities, the public, government and the business sector.

Activities: Acts as a resource and advocacy centre for Bermuda's charities and volunteers, promoting a philosophy of philanthropy in the community, through information, seminars and dialogue with its member charities, the public, the government and the corporate sector. Provides information, training workshops and seminars for its members. Resources include databases of charities and volunteers and a library of educational and reference materials.

Geographical Area of Activity: CEO G. Peters.

Publications: *Accounting for Bermuda Charities; A Portrait of Charities in Bermuda; ABC Booklet; Ready-Set-Go; Charity Tip-Sheets; Bermuda Donor Directory; The Registered Charity Directory.*

Board of Trustees: Cummings V. Zuill (Chair.); André J. Dill (Vice-Chair.).

Principal Staff: CEO Greg Peters.

Address: Russell Eve Bldg, 21 Church St, POB 3217, Hamilton HM NX.

Telephone: 292-5320; **Fax:** 295-8679; **Internet:** www.charity.bm; **e-mail:** info@charity.bm.

FOUNDATIONS, TRUSTS AND NON-PROFIT ORGANIZATIONS

International Charitable Fund of Bermuda

Formed in 1994 and co-sponsored by the Centre on Philanthropy (q.v.) and PricewaterhouseCoopers (formerly Price Waterhouse), to promote and support the purposes and activities of not-for-profit charitable organizations in Bermuda through tax-deductible gifts from US taxpayers.

Activities: Makes grants to non-profits in Bermuda operating exclusively for charitable, scientific or educational purposes.

Geographical Area of Activity: Bermuda.

Board of Trustees: Thomas Conyers (Pres. and Treas.); Nancy Smythe (Vice-Pres.); Margaret Hern; Lady Swan.

Address: POB HM 1624, Hamilton HM GX.

Telephone: 295-4271; **Fax:** 295-9797.

Bolivia

FOUNDATIONS, TRUSTS AND NON-PROFIT ORGANIZATIONS

Fundación Amigos de la Naturaleza (Friends of Nature Foundation)

Founded in November 1988 by a small group of naturalists located in Santa Cruz for the conservation of biodiversity in Bolivia.

Activities: The Foundation is a private non-profit organization aiming to protect biodiversity in Bolivia and countries bordering Bolivia, through self-conducted programmes, research, offering scholarships and fellowships, and through conferences.

Geographical Area of Activity: South America.

Trustees: Jaime Rozenmann Attie (Pres.); Victor Hugo Jiménez, Hermes Justiniano Suárez (Vice-Pres.).

Principal Staff: Exec. Dir Karin Columba.

Address: Km 7 Carretera antigua a Cochabamba, Casilla 2241.

Telephone: (3) 3556800; **Fax:** (3) 3547383; **Internet:** www.fan-bo.org; **e-mail:** fan@fan-bo.org.

Fundación San Gabriel (San Gabriel Foundation)

Activities: Operates in the field of women's rights in Bolivia, through maintaining women's centres, promoting a national women's movement, and providing training and educational courses, credit assistance for small enterprises, grants and health services for women and children and publishing and supporting research. Also operates a private women's hospital in a poor district of La Paz.

Geographical Area of Activity: Bolivia.

Principal Staff: Contact: Maritza Jiménez.

Address: Avda Tito Yupanqui 1205, Casilla 8061, La Paz.

Telephone: (2) 332276; **Fax:** (2) 331112.

Fundación Sartawi (Sartawi Foundation)

Founded in 1989 by the Lutheran Church, and part of Oikocredit, the Ecumenical Development Co-operative Society; aims to help the rural population of Bolivia.

Activities: Provides technical assistance to groups of people with little access to resources, with an emphasis on rural areas, facilitating economic initiatives and strengthening the artisan industry in order to increase job opportunities for women. Runs programmes relating to agricultural forestation in valleys and areas of the *altiplano*, micro-enterprises and providing easier access to credit for those in need.

Geographical Area of Activity: Bolivia.

Publications: Annual Report.

Principal Staff: Pres. Arend Smid; Dir Irene Sievers.

Address: 2013 Avda Jaime Freire, Casilla 1862, La Paz.

Telephone: (2) 420341; **Fax:** (2) 2419598; **e-mail:** sartawi@ceibo.entelnet.bo.

Bosnia and Herzegovina

FOUNDATIONS, TRUSTS AND NON-PROFIT ORGANIZATIONS

Open Society Fund—Bosnia-Herzegovina

Founded in November 1992 to restore a belief in the values of an open society; encourage individuals important to the preservation of an open society to remain in the country; foster an atmosphere in which the prospect of a new and valuable society remains viable; and offer hope and a sense of perspective to younger generations. The fund is an independent foundation, part of the Soros foundations network, which aims to foster political pluralism and reform economic structures in order to encourage private enterprise and a market economy.

Activities: Provides financial support to assist institutions working towards the development of an open society. Funds educational programmes, including the printing of textbooks, awarding scholarships to university students and initiating alternative educational programmes. Supports media institutions, and has established an e-mail network. Its humanitarian programme provides medical assistance, food parcels and employment opportunities. In the field of the arts and culture, the Fund supports local artists, and promotes visits to Sarajevo by famous foreign artists. Also operates grant programmes within the fields of women's rights and empowerment and the development of the Roma community. Collaborates with other Soros institutions on projects such as the Open Society City of Sarajevo Project to restore damaged schools and cultural institutions. Maintains an office in Banja Luka.

Geographical Area of Activity: Bosnia and Herzegovina.

Publications: Reports.

Finance: Annual expenditure US $4,061,000 (2001).

Board of Trustees: Senka Nozica (Pres.); Zarko Papic (Vice-Pres.); Milivoj Gagro; Mirza Kusljugic; Ljiljana Miovic; Sevima Sali-Terzic; Ugo Vlaisavljevic.

Principal Staff: Exec. Dir Dobrila Govedarica.

Address: Marsala Tita 19/III, 71000 Sarajevo; Ranke Sipke 4, 78000 Banja Luka.

Telephone and Fax: (33) 472580 (Sarajevo); (51) 301230 (Banja Luka); **Internet:** www.soros.org.ba; **e-mail:** osf@soros.org.ba.

Botswana

FOUNDATION CENTRE AND CO-ORDINATING BODY

Botswana Council of NGOs—BOCONGO

Established in 1995. Aims to assist and support NGOs in Botswana, in order to further the development process.

Activities: Facilitates the development of NGOs, and works to ensure their participation in the on-going development process in Botswana; enables NGOs, the Government, the private sector and other development partners to network effectively, and promotes improved communication and the dissemination of information; aims to take on a leading role in policy advocacy and lobbying, in order to allow NGOs to work as a united body on issues of national interest.

Geographical Area of Activity: Botswana.

Publications: Downloadable programme reports.

Executive Committee: Rev. Rupert Hambira (Chair.); Koketso Rantona (Vice-Chair.); Rev. Mpho Moruakgomo (Treas.); Monica Tabengwa (Sec.); Thapelo Leareng (Vice-Sec.); James Olesitse; Wazha Tema.

Principal Staff: Exec. Sec. Gaogakwe Phorano.

Address: Private Bag 00418, Gaborone.

Telephone: 311319; **Fax:** 312935; **Internet:** www.bocongo.bw; **e-mail:** bocongo@bocongo.bw.

FOUNDATIONS, TRUSTS AND NON-PROFIT ORGANIZATIONS

Chobe Wildlife Trust

Founded in 1988 to assist in the conservation of the Chobe National Park and its immediate surroundings.

Activities: Works to achieve a local response to global sustainability as described at the Rio 1992 summit by way of environmental education, community-based natural resources management and conservation research and management in North Eastern Botswana, including the protection of the rhinoceros; assists the Botswana Department of Wildlife; campaigns against poaching.

Geographical Area of Activity: Carobe District, North Eastern Botswana.

Publications: *Serondella News* (newsletter).

Trustees: S. Griesel (Chair.); H. Almendinger; J. Carr-Hartley; P. Carr-Hartley; K. van Essyn; J. Gibson; P. Hepburn; D. Joubert; R. Randall; G. Williams; T. Williams.

Principal Staff: CEO Stephen Austin.

Address: POB 55, Kasane.

Telephone: 650516; **Fax:** 650223; **e-mail:** cwt@botsnet.bw.

International Foundation for Education with Production—FEP International

Founded in 1980 by Patrick Van Rensburg with the purpose of encouraging closer links between educational establishments and workplaces in order to make education more relevant to careers in industry; formerly known as the Foundation for Education with Production.

Activities: Encourages curriculum reform; supports democratic management of schools and workplaces; has established the FEP-CORDE Programme to promote co-operative research and education programmes; organizes courses; and produces research reports.

Geographical Area of Activity: Africa.

Publications: *FEP Newsletter* (quarterly); *Education With Production* (2 a year); various books and textbooks.

Principal Staff: Dir Patrick Van Rensburg.

Address: POB 20906, Gaborone.

Telephone and Fax: 314311.

Brazil

FOUNDATION CENTRE AND CO-ORDINATING BODY

Grupo de Institutos, Fundações e Empresas—GIFE (Group of Institutions, Foundations and Private Enterprises)

Established in 1995 as a membership organization representing companies and foundations in Brazil. Aims to improve and disseminate the concepts and practical means of using private funds for the good of the community.

Activities: Composed of institutes, foundations and corporations which are active within the third sector in Brazil. Provides member organizations with information and a centre in which they can exchange knowledge and experience through meetings, seminars, courses and forums. Establishes links between similar local and national organizations, aiming to create an environment to enable private businesses to invest in community development. Maintains a national reference centre, which contains materials on philanthropic knowledge and practices. Trains third-sector professionals through its GIFE Trainee Programme.

Geographical Area of Activity: Brazil.

Governing Board: Léo Voigt (Pres.).

Principal Staff: Exec. Dir Rebecca Raposo; Sec. Margareth Silva.

Address: Av. Doutor Cardoso de Melo 1666, 9th Floor, Vila Olímpia, CEP 04.548-005 São Paulo, SP.

Telephone: (11) 3849-2022; **Fax:** (11) 3849-2022; **Internet:** www.gife.org.br; **e-mail:** diretoria@gife.org.br.

FOUNDATIONS, TRUSTS AND NON-PROFIT ORGANIZATIONS

Brazil Foundation

Established in 2001 by Leona Forman to encourage Brazilian philanthropic activity in the USA.

Activities: Supports and encourages Brazilian philanthropic activity in the USA and channels resources to social projects in Brazil in the areas of education, health, human rights, citizenship and culture. Operates in partnership with other philanthropic organizations.

Geographical Area of Activity: Brazil.

Restrictions: Grants are made only in Brazil.

Finance: Annual revenue US $325,000, expenditure $120,000 (2002/03).

Board of Governors: Edmar Lisboa Bacha; Ruth Cardoso; Claudius Ceccon; Nancy Englander; Gelson Fonseca, Jr; Gilberto Gil; Hélio Matter; Kenneth Maxwell; Marcilo Marques Moreira.

Principal Staff: Pres. Leona Shluger Forman; Vice-Pres. Susana Woreman.

Address: Rua Santa Luzia 735, Sala 1201, 20.030-040 Rio de Janeiro, RJ.

Telephone: (21) 2532-3029; **Fax:** (21) 2532-2998; **e-mail:** info@brazilfoundation.org.

ChildHope Brasil

Founded in 1986 in Guatemala, to provide information about the problems of 'street children'—homeless young people living and working in the streets—and previously known as the Childhope International Foundation. Now a network of independent regional and national groups operating in the United Kingdom and Europe, Asia and Central and South America.

Activities: ChildHope (q.v.) provides support to other agencies involved in the provision of services and the operation of programmes, such as AIDS prevention, which cater for children in their own communities. Projects include support for pre-school care facilities.

Geographical Area of Activity: Brazil.

Publications: *Let Us Speak* (2 a year); *Our Child-Our Hope* (2 a year); *Study Ideas* (2 a year); numerous books.

Principal Staff: Exec. Dir Dr Jorge Barros.

Address: Rua Senador Correia 48, Laranjeiras, 22231-180 Rio de Janeiro, RJ.

Telephone: (21) 225-1044; **Internet:** www.alternex.com.br /~childhope/; **e-mail:** childhope@ax.apc.org.

Fundação Abrinq pelos Direitos da Criança (Abrinq Foundation for Children's Rights)

Established in 1990 to protect the fundamental rights of children.

Activities: Supports projects aiming to protect the fundamental rights of children and young people, provides technical assistance and promotes intersectoral cooperation. Also provides information and documentation for NGOs, community groups, international agencies and government agencies.

Finance: Annual grants approx. US $1,000,000.

Principal Staff: Pres. Hélio Mattar.

Address: Rua Lisboa 224, 05.413-000 São Paulo, SP.

Telephone and fax (11) 881-0699; Internet: www.fundacaoabrinq.org.br; **e-mail:** fundabrinq@ax.apc.org.

Fundação Acesita para o Desenvolvimento Social (Acesita Foundation for Social Development)

Private, non-profit organization founded in 1994 by Acesita, a Brazilian business.

Activities: Operates in the Vale do Aço and Timóteo areas, funding social and economic development projects, including educational, cultural, environmental and community work. Created a Cultural Centre in Timóteo.

Geographical Area of Activity: Brazil (Vale do Aço).

Principal Staff: Pres. Anfilófio Salles Martins.

Address: Av. João Pinheiro 580, Centro, 30.130180 Belo Horizonte, MG.

Telephone: (31) 3235-4200; **Fax:** (31) 3235-4294; **Internet:** www.acesita.com.br; **e-mail:** facesita@gtc.com.br.

Fundação Banco do Brasil (Bank of Brazil Foundation)

Founded in 1985, dedicated to social community work in Brazil.

Activities: Promotes, assists and financially supports initiatives in a number of areas within urban and rural communities, including education, culture, health, social welfare, recreation and sports, and science and technology. Provides credit and technical support to other non-profit organizations and grass-roots groups in Brazil, and promotes volunteerism and philanthropy.

Geographical Area of Activity: Brazil.

Finance: Annual expenditure approx. 75,000 reais.

Principal Staff: Pres. Heloisa Helena Silva de Oliveira; Exec. Dir Fernanda M.B. de M. de Oliveira, José Fernando Romano Furné.

Address: SCN Quadra 1, Bloco A-9° e 10° andares-Asa Norte, 70711-900 Brasília, DF.

Telephone: (61) 310-1951; **Fax:** (61) 310-1966; **Internet:** www.cidadania-e.com.br; **e-mail:** cidadania-e@fbb.org.br.

Fundação O. Boticario

Established in 1990 to support nature conservation projects in Brazil.

Activities: Operates three principal programmes in the area of nature conservation. The Nature Conservation Incentive Programme funds the creation, implementation and maintenance of natural protected areas, research and protection of species and important or endangered populations and their habitats; the stimulation, creation, implementation and maintenance of green areas and urban tree planting; and recuperation of altered or degraded ecosystems. The Natural Areas Protection Programme maintains the Salto Morato Preserve. The Mobilization and Education Programme promotes involvement in nature conservation activities through a series of training courses and publications.

Geographical Area of Activity: Brazil.

Board of Directors: Miguel Gellert Krigsner (Pres.); Bernardo Fedalto; Antônio Carlos Sanches; Artur Noêmio Grynbaum; Ibsen de Gusmão Câmara; Maria Tereza Jorge Pádua; Marcos Sá Côrrea; Michael Jenkins; Vladimir Passos de Freitas.

Principal Staff: Technical Dir Miguel Serediuk Milano; Financial Admin. Dir Maria Carolina Zani; Communications Dir Silvana Cassol.

Address: Av. Rui Barbosa, 3450 Afonso Pena, 83.065-360, São José dos Pinhais, PR.

Internet: www.fbpn.org.br.

Fundação Brasileira para a Conservação da Natureza (Brazilian Foundation for Nature Conservation)

Founded in August 1958 by José Cândido de Melo Carvalho to promote management and conservation of natural areas and endangered species; environmental education; reforestation and aforestation projects; sustainable development projects; and scientific research applied to conservation.

Activities: The Foundation operates nationally, through self-conducted programmes, research, awarding prizes and offering training courses. It carries out projects in conjunction with national and international organizations; executes management plans for various national parks and ecological stations; co-ordinates campaigns for the preservation of endangered species, such as whales, turtles, Amazon manatees, the golden lion tamarin and woolly spider monkeys; and maintains an extensive library. The Foundation has about 5,000 members nationally and internationally.

Geographical Area of Activity: Brazil.

Publications: *Informativo FBCN* (newsletter); *Boletim FBCN* (annually).

Finance: Annual budget variable.

Board of Trustees: Ibsen de Gusmão Câmara (Pres.).

Principal Staff: Pres. Jairo C. Costa.

Address: Rua Miranda Valverde 103, Botafogo, 22281-000 Rio de Janeiro.

Telephone: (21) 2537-7565; **Fax:** (21) 2537-1343; **e-mail:** fbcnbr@uol.com.br.

Fundação Gaia (Gaia Foundation)

Established in June 1987 by José A. Lutzenberger, Augusto C. Cunha Carneiro, Magdalena K. Lutzenberger and others to promote sustainable development.

Activities: Operates in the Brazilian state of Rio Grande do Sul in the field of protection of the environment, by providing advisory services, participating in conferences, offering training courses and issuing publications. Promotes sustainable development, working with regenerative agriculture, environmental education, protection of biodiversity, conservation of the cultural identity of minorities, and the use of 'soft' technologies.

Geographical Area of Activity: Brazil.

Restrictions: No grants available.

Publications: *Ecológica; Fruticultura; Sanidade Animal na Agroecologia; A Teoria da Trofobiose;* and publications in English, German and other languages.

Finance: Financed by private donations, consultancies, projects, courses and sale of products.

Trustees: José A. Lutzenberger (Pres.); Lara Lutzenberger (Vice-Pres.); Alexandre de Freitas; Elisabeth Renck; Marcia Santos.

Address: Rua Jacinto Gomes 39, barrio Santana, 90040-270 Porto Alegre, Rio Grande do Sul.

Telephone: (51) 3330-3567; **Fax:** (51) 3330-3567; **Internet:** www.fgaia.org.br; **e-mail:** sede@fgaia.org.br.

Fundação Iochpe

Established in 1989 by Iochpe-Maxion SA.

Activities: Aims to promote the development of people's full potential and improve the quality of life of the people and communities in which the founding company operates, including funding not-for-profit organizations active in the areas of education, culture and social welfare, with a specific focus on the education of at-risk children and young people. Also provides information and documentation to not-for-profit organizations, grassroots groups, international organizations and government agencies, as well as technical assistance and training for grassroots groups and other not-for-profit organizations.

Geographical Area of Activity: Argentina and Brazil.

Finance: Annual grants approx. US $1,000,000.

Principal Staff: Pres. Evelyn Berg Iochpe.

Address: Al. Tiete, 618 casa 1, 01417-020 São Paulo, SP.

Telephone: (11) 3060-8388; **Fax:** (11) 3060-8388; **e-mail:** fiochpe@osite.com.br.

Fundação Roberto Marinho

Founded in 1977 by the journalist Roberto Marinho.

Activities: Operates nationally, primarily in the area of education, but also in the fields of ecology and conservation, and national heritage. Works in partnership with a number of other organizations to fund and carry out projects, including literacy programmes for children and adults; an annual prize for young scientists; funding for national museums, music and dance; and developing ecological campaigns to protect the environment.

Geographical Area of Activity: Brazil.

Principal Staff: Pres. Roberto Marinho; Dir Gen. José Roberto Marinho.

Address: Av. Paulo de Frontin 568, 20.261-243 Rio de Janeiro, RJ.

Telephone: (21) 273-5020; **Internet:** www.frm.org.br.

Fundação Museu do Homem Americano—FUMDHAM (Museum of American Man Foundation)

Founded in 1986 to promote scientific research, ecological preservation and sustainable development.

Activities: Operates nationally and internationally in the fields of aid to less-developed regions of Brazil and sustainable development studies, conservation and the environment, economic and international affairs, education, medicine and health, and science and technology, through self-conducted programmes, research, prizes, conferences and training courses. The Foundation is a private scientific research institute responsible for the protection of the Serra da Capivara National Park and the Environmental Protection Area.

Geographical Area of Activity: Brazil.

Publications: *Fumdhamentos.*

Principal Staff: Niede Guidon.

Address: Rua Abdias Neves 551, Centro, 64770 São Raimundo Nonato, PI.

Telephone: (86) 582-1612; **Fax:** (86) 582-1293; **Internet:** www.fumdham.com.br; **e-mail:** fumdham@zaz.com.br.

Fundação Armando Alvares Penteado (Armando Alvares Penteado Foundation)

Founded in 1947 by Armando Alvares Penteado and Annie Alvares Penteado for exclusively pedagogical purposes. It aims to contribute, through teaching and related activities, to Brazil's cultural expansion and integration in the technological world of today.

Activities: Operates through the maintenance of a University, a Museum of Fine Arts and various Centres and Institutes. Courses are offered in science and technology, the arts and humanities, economics, business management and international relations. Awards scholarships.

Geographical Area of Activity: Brazil.

Publications: Report of operations.

Principal Staff: Pres. Celita Procopio de Carvalho; Man. Dir Dr Antonio Bias Bueno Guillon; Treas. Dr Américo Fialdini, Jr.

Address: Rua Ceará 2, Higienopolis, 01.243-010 São Paulo, SP.

Telephone: (11) 3662-1717; **Fax:** (11) 3662-1716; **Internet:** www.faap.br; **e-mail:** info@faap.br.

Fundação Romi

Activities: Aims to promote educational, social and cultural development in Brazil, through support for educational initiatives, including computer training.

Geographical Area of Activity: Brazil.

Address: Av. Monte Castelo, 1095, CEP 13.450-285, Santa Bárbara d'Oeste, São Paulo, SP.

Telephone: (19) 3455-1055; **Fax:** (19) 3455-1345; **Internet:** www.fundacaoromi.org.br; **e-mail:** fundacaoromi@fundacaoromi.org.br fundacaoromi@fundacaoromi.org.br.

Fundação José Silveira (José Silveira Foundation)

Activities: Funds a hospital in Santo Amaro, provides social and medical assistance, provides funding for studies at the Universidade Estadual de Campinas, and lobbies the Government on behalf of people in need.

Geographical Area of Activity: Brazil.

Finance: Annual budget approx. 35,620,000 reais.

Principal Staff: Contact: Gilvana Maria Rodrigues Barbosa.

Address: Rua America Silva, S/N, Ondina, Salvador, BA.

Telephone: (71) 245-6119.

Fundação Mauricio Sirotsky Sobrinho

Established in 1987 to defend the rights of children and young people.

Activities: Promotes sustainable self-development aimed at building citizenship and respecting fundamental social rights, with a particular focus on the defence of the rights of children and adolescents, primarily in the states of Rio Grande do Sul, Santa Catarina and Paraná. Also provides information resources to not-for-profit organizations.

Geographical Area of Activity: Brazil.

Finance: Annual grants approx. US $2,000,000.

Principal Staff: Exec. Dir Leo Voigt.

Address: Av. Getúlio Vargas, 1620, 4 Andar, CEP 90.150-004 Porto Alegre, RS.

Telephone: (51) 218-6474; **Fax:** (51) 218-6488; **Internet:** www.fmss.org.br; **e-mail:** fundacao@fmss.org.br.

Fundação SOS Mata Atlantica (Brazilian Foundation for the Conservation of the Atlantic Rainforest)

Founded in 1986 to work towards the protection of the forests of Brazil's Atlantic region, the preservation of the communities inhabiting them and their cultural heritage, and the sustained development of these areas.

Activities: Operates in Brazil in the area of conservation and the environment.

Geographical Area of Activity: Brazil.

Address: Rua Manoel dâ Nóbrega 456, Paraíso, 04001-001 São Paulo, SP.

Telephone: (11) 3887-1195; **Fax:** (11) 3885-1680; **Internet:** www.sosmatatlantica.org.br; **e-mail:** comunicacao@sosmatatlantica.org.br.

FUNDHAS—Fundação de Atendimento à Criança e ao Adolescente Professor Hélio Augusto de Souza (Professor Hélio Augusto de Souza Foundation for Serving Children and Adolescents)

Established in 1987, a non-profit institution aiming to assist children and young people.

Activities: Operates three basic programmes in education, welfare and training: the Child Programme, for children between the ages of seven and 14; the Adolescent Programme, for young people 14–18 years old; and the Supporting/Partnership Programmes. The Foundation currently assists around 5,000 children and young people through its programmes.

Geographical Area of Activity: Brazil, in the city of São José dos Campos.

Publications: *Notícias da Fundhas.*

Principal Staff: Pres. José Omir Veneziani, Jr; Dirs Rosane Ferreira Faria, Hiromiti Yoshiooka.

Address: Fabrícia Santos Santana, R. Santarém 560, 12.235-550 São José dos Campos, SP.

Telephone: (12) 3932-0539; **Fax:** (12) 3931-8416; **Internet:** www.fundhas.org.br; **e-mail:** captacao@fundhas.org.br.

GRUMIN—Grupo Mulher-Educação Indigena (Indigenous Women's Education Group)

Established in 1986 by Eliane Potiguara, to support and assist indigenous women in Brazil, dedicated to promoting indigenous women's economic, political and social self-determination, and to combating social discrimination.

Activities: Operates nationally, encouraging indigenous women to take control of their own lives, through raising their awareness. Funds a variety of projects, including creating community gardens where families who have lost their land can grow food. Holds conferences and seminars, organizes vocational training for indigenous women, provides a forum for on-line dabates, and holds courses on indigenous history and handicrafts.

Geographical Area of Activity: Brazil.

Publications: Journal; bulletin; and other publications.

Address: Daline Braga Av. Heitor Beltrao 71, sala 301, Tijuca, 20550-000 Rio de Janeiro, RJ.

Telephone and Fax: (21) 567-2675; **Internet:** www.grumin.hpg.ig.com.br; **e-mail:** grumin1@terra.com.br.

Instituto Ayrton Senna (Ayrton Senna Institute)

Established in 1995 after the death of the Brazilian racing-car driver Ayrton Senna. Based on Ayrton Senna's life and ideals, the Institute develops programmes in Brazil.

Activities: Operates nationally and internationally in two areas: direct assistance to guarantee the rights of Brazilian children and adolescents; and advocacy work to help stimulate activities to help future generations. Operates in the fields of medicine and health, and education, by supporting small-scale education and relief of poverty work, including nutrition, health, education, sports and cultural projects. The Foundation runs anti-poverty programmes for 'street children' in Brazil. International activities are undertaken by the UK-based Ayrton Senna Foundation.

Geographical Area of Activity: Brazil.

Restrictions: Grants are not made to individuals.

Finance: Receives 100% of the profits obtained from the licensing of the Senna brand and image, and is also financed through alliances with the Brazilian and multinational business community.

Board of Directors: Viviane Senna (Pres.); Fábio da Silva Machado; Leonardo Senna da Silva; Milton Guirado Theodoro da Silva; Neyde Joana Senna da Silva.

Principal Staff: Julian Jakobi.

Address: Rua Dr Olavo Egídio 287, 02.037-000 São Paulo, SP.

Telephone: (11) 6950-0440; **Fax:** (11) 6950-0050; **Internet:** www.senna.com.br.

REDEH—Rede de Desenvolvimento Humano (Network for Human Development)

Set up in 1996 to bring a women's perspective to environmental issues.

Activities: Provides a forum for women to share their views and concerns, through a variety of formats including a daily one-hour radio programme called Fala Mulher (Speak Women), which won an award from *Claudia* magazine. Also runs a training programme for activists, a project to combat desertification, health and prevention initiatives, sustainable development initiatives, as well as programmes to improve practices for integrating women into local councils in cities and towns.

Geographical Area of Activity: Brazil.

Finance: Annual budget approx. 661,000 reais (1999).

Principal Staff: Gen. Co-ordinator Thais Corral.

Address: Rua Alvaro Alvim, 16° Andar, 20.032-010 Rio de Janeiro, RJ.

Telephone: (21) 2262-1704; **Fax:** (21) 2262-6554; **Internet:** www.redeh.org.br; **e-mail:** redeh@redeh.org.br.

Brunei

FOUNDATIONS, TRUSTS AND NON-PROFIT ORGANIZATIONS

Robert and Tini Foundation Company

Activities: Operates in the areas of social welfare and health care, assisting children, the elderly, disabled people, orphans, the underprivileged and the destitute in Asia. Sponsors people who cannot afford necessary medical treatment.

Geographical Area of Activity: Asia.

Address: POB 574, Gadong Post Office, Bandar Seri Begawan 3978.

Bulgaria

FOUNDATION CENTRE AND CO-ORDINATING BODY

Union of Bulgarian Foundations and Associations—UBFA

Founded in 1992 to lend assistance to Bulgarian NGOs and Foundations, working nationally and internationally.

Activities: Facilitates co-operation among non-profit organizations; supports NGOs in their development and work; protects the interests of its member organizations; encourages good practices and high standards in the activities of NGOs; provides information services and issues publications.

Geographical Area of Activity: Bulgaria.

Publications: Annual Report; list of funders; strategic plan.

Principal Staff: Contact: Ognian Lipovski.

Address: 1421 Sofia, 47–51 Tzvetna Gradina St.

Telephone: (2) 65-65-22; **Fax:** (2) 65-76-00; **Internet:** www.ngo.bg/ubfa.htm; **e-mail:** ubfa@techno-link.com.

FOUNDATIONS, TRUSTS AND NON-PROFIT ORGANIZATIONS

Civil Society Development Foundation (Razvitie na Grazhdansko Obshtestvo)

Established in 1995 with the aims of supporting the development of civil society in Bulgaria, through providing support to the non-profit sector; creating a favourable environment for its operation; and extending its capacity, the types of activity, and the participation of NGOs at local, regional and national level.

Activities: The Foundation provides financial assistance to Bulgarian NGOs for the protection and development of minorities; to combat crime and corruption; to protect nature and the environment; to promote social entrepreneurship in marginalized groups; and to inform and train civil society organizations. The Foundation also works to promote effective donor dialogue and collaboration, improving information exchange, networking and research on the Bulgarian NGO sector and bridging private and state resources in community development partnerships.

Geographical Area of Activity: Bulgaria.

Restrictions: No grants to individuals; grants are made depending on programme priorities to NGOs and civic associations registered under Bulgarian law.

Publications: Annual Report; brochures, newsletters.

Finance: Total assets €37,475 (2001); total expenditure €721,098 (2001).

Board of Directors: Georgi Lipovanski (Chair.); Boryana Savova (Deputy Chair.); Yucel Atilla; Sali Ibrahim; Assia Kavrakova; Vergil Marinov; Mihail Mihailov; Iliycho Plachkov; Hristo Tomov.

Principal Staff: Exec. Dir Bouryana Konaklieva.

Address: 1504 Sofia, 23 Shipka St.

Telephone: (2) 944-53-23; **Fax:** (2) 944-53-24; **Internet:** www.civilsoc.org/ece/bulgaria/csdf.htm; **e-mail:** secretary@csdf.bgone.net.

Evrika Foundation

Founded in 1990 to encourage and educate young people in the fields of science, economics, technology and management.

Activities: The Foundation operates nationally and internationally in the fields of economic and international affairs, education, medicine and health, and science and technology, through self-conducted programmes, grants to individuals and institutions, scholarships and fellowships, and conferences. It supports the education of talented young people; works towards implementing scientific and technological ideas and projects; provides equipment and material for creative work; encourages international co-operation in the fields of science, technology and management; disseminates information; organizes events; provides financial support for scientific research undertaken by talented young scholars; awards for innovative young farmers; and credit and loans to young people developing research and technological products and new products and services.

Geographical Area of Activity: Bulgaria.

Publications: Annual Report; *Computer; Do-it-Yourself; EVRIKA* (monthly bulletin); *Andromeda* (magazine); *Telescope*.

Finance: Net assets 2,211 Leva (1999); annual revenue 329,631 Leva, expenditure 252,319 Leva (1999).

Governing Council: Blagovest Sendov (Chair.); Luben Dolapchiev, Dimitar Michev (Vice-Chair.); Georgi Atanasov; Emil Benatov; Valery Borisov; Bozhidar Fotev; Jordan Genchev; Evgheny Golovinski; Georgi Ivanov; Ivan Ivanov; Stefan Kuchukov; Traiko Petkov; Zahari Rajkov; Soloman Rozanis.

Principal Staff: Exec. Dir Vassil Velev; Programme Dirs Boriana Kadmonova, Stoil Kolev.

Address: 1000 Sofia, 1 Patriarch Evtimii Blvd.

Telephone: (2) 981-51-81; **Fax:** (2) 981-54-83; **Internet:** www.evrika.org; **e-mail:** evrika@einet.bg.

Free and Democratic Bulgaria Foundation

Founded in 1991 by Yvonne and John Dimitry Panitza to facilitate the process of democratization of Bulgarian society based on pluralism, free press, free market, tolerance, youth education and open dialogue.

Activities: The Foundation operates in six main programme areas: Street Children, in collaboration with ChildHope (UK, q.v.) and the European Union PHARE (Poland and Hungary Assistance for Economic Restructuring programme), to provide opportunities for homeless children, including a shelter and a national information centre; AIDS and drug abuse prevention and education; Outward Bound, part of the international Outward Bound movement, which runs courses aimed at character-building, care for the environment, serving others and building team spirit; Civil Society, organizing training programmes and seminars for young Bulgarian politicians and functionaries at national and local levels in democratic party and parliamentary practices, election campaigns, etc.; the Centre for Pluralism established in conjunction with the Institute for Democracy in Eastern Europe; and Excellence in Journalism prizes. Maintains an office in Paris.

Geographical Area of Activity: Bulgaria.

Publications: Annual Report; *International Round Table on the Problems of Recommunization* (1993); translations of books on Balkan issues, the media, democracy, etc.

Finance: The Foundation is reliant on personal contributions and grants.

Board of Directors: Radoslav Genchev (Chair.); Vassil Gotzev; Milko Konstantinov; Christo Marinov; Ivan Tatarchev.

Principal Staff: Chair. J. D. Panitza; Exec. Dir Lenko Lenkov.

Address: 1000 Sofia, Venelin St 22; 16 rue de Chazelles, 75017 Paris, France.

Telephone: (2) 988-82-73 (Sofia); 1-44-40-03-77 (Paris); **Fax:** (2) 989-17-84 (Sofia); 1-42-27-41-75 (Paris); **e-mail:** fdbfound@bol.bg.

National Charitable Fund Thirteen Centuries of Bulgaria

Established in 1981 on the anniversary of 13 centuries of the state of Bulgaria, for the development of cultural, social and spiritual life in Bulgaria.

Activities: Operates nationally in the areas of the arts and humanities, historical preservation and education, through grants to art galleries, museums, writers, periodicals on the cinema, theatre and philosophy, and for educational exchange.

Geographical Area of Activity: Bulgaria.

Publications: Annual Report; periodicals.

Principal Staff: Exec. Dir Alexander Milanov; Head, Int. Dept Dr D. Romanov.

Address: 1421 Sofia, Akatzia St 16.

Telephone: (2) 963-26-84.

Open Society Foundation—Sofia (Bulgaria)

Founded in April 1990 to support education and culture and the development of Bulgarian society. An independent foundation, part of the Soros foundations network, which aims to foster political and cultural pluralism and reform economic structures in order to encourage private enterprise and a market economy.

Activities: The Foundation supports projects under the programme areas of economic integration and regional stability; public life and civil participation; democracy and rule of law; education policies; and public health. Initiatives include support for electoral reform and accession to the European Union. Also runs a nation-wide network of 17 information centres offering consultation and funding advice.

Geographical Area of Activity: Bulgaria; some aid to Kosovo.

Publications: *Wide Awake* (newsletter, every 2 months); fortnightly newsletter.

Finance: Annual expenditure US $7,432,000 (2001).

Trustees: Stefan Popov (Chair.); Svetoslav Bozhilov; Roumiana Chervenkova; Marin Delchev; Yonko Grozev; Georgi Koritarov; Nelly Koutskova; Vesselin Metodiev; Svetlana Vassilev.

Principal Staff: Exec. Dir Rayna Gavrilova.

Address: 1000 Sofia, Solunska Str. 56.

Telephone: (2) 930-66-19; **Fax:** (2) 951-63-48; **Internet:** www.osf.bg; **e-mail:** info@osf.bg.

Roma Lom Foundation

Established in 1996 with the aim of changing the traditional attitudes and the way of life of the Roma community.

Activities: Aims to support the development of the Roma community in the areas of education, culture, employment and social protection, through encouraging participation of the Roma community in foundation-initiated projects.

Geographical Area of Activity: Bulgaria.

Principal Staff: Prog. Dir Asen Slavchev.

Address: Lom 3600, 4, Neofit Bozveli St.

e-mail: roma-lom@roma-lom.org.

Saint Cyril and Saint Methodius International Foundation

Founded in 1982 as the Lyudmila Zhivkova International Foundation, dedicated to preserving and popularizing the spiritual heritage of St Cyril and St Methodius; the Foundation aims to encourage cultural co-operation and the creative and educational development of young people, and to assist in the integration of Bulgaria into the 'New Europe' and the world.

Activities: Operates internationally in the fields of the arts and humanities and cultural education; arranges cultural and educational exchanges; promotes cultural exchange, international understanding and the creative development of young people; awards prizes and scholarships; organizes conferences and exhibitions; supports publishing projects; organizes events and seminars; and maintains an art gallery.

Geographical Area of Activity: International.

Publications: Annual Report; brochure; financial report.

Finance: Assets US $3,396,000 (1999).

Board of Governors: Petar Kenderov (Pres.).

Principal Staff: Sec.-Gen. Michael Tachev.

Address: 1504 Sofia, Oborishte St 19.

Telephone: (2) 943-41-85; **Fax:** (2) 44-60-27; **Internet:** www.fundersonline.org/cmfnd; **e-mail:** cmfnd@mgu.bg.

Values Foundation

Founded in 1998 by Antonina Stoyanova to address the issue of sustainable development through culture.

Activities: Operates in Bulgaria, promoting and supporting the development of Bulgarian science, education and culture. Concerned with the integration of Bulgaria into Europe, whilst also preserving the cultural values and cultural diversity of the nation, and works to strengthen projects which work on social integration and communication. Also concentrates on secondary school and university education, awarding prizes and promoting exhanges. Works in collaboration with other Bulgarian organizations.

Geographical Area of Activity: Bulgaria.

Finance: Total income 491,072 Leva, expenditure 255,829 Leva (June 2000).

Directors: A. Stoyanova (Chair.); B. Bogdanov; B. Hadzhiev; B. Karadocheva; M. Nikolchina-Marinova; V. Radinska; N. Subotinov.

Principal Staff: Admin. Dir Aleksandra Vassileva.

Address: 1000 Sofia, 34, Shesti septemvri St.

Telephone: (2) 986-55-07; **Fax:** (2) 980-40-47; **Internet:** www.values.bg; **e-mail:** values@info.unacs.bg.

Manfred Woerner Foundation

Founded by the Atlantic Club of Bulgaria in October 1994 to foster Atlantic values and co-operation.

Activities: Operates nationally and internationally in the fields of education and international affairs, through self-conducted programmes, research, scholarships and fellowships, conferences and publications.

Geographical Area of Activity: International.

Publications: Strategic reports and policy recommendations (occasional).

Finance: Assets US $12,000 (1999); annual revenue US $38,000 (1999), expenditure US $35,000 (2002).

Trustees: Lyubomir Ivanov (Pres.); Milen Milanov; Solomon Passy; Ivanka Petkova; Antoniy Todorov.

Principal Staff: Project Dir Adelina Tomova.

Address: 1000 Sofia, Slavyanska St 29.

Telephone: (2) 981-06-99; **Fax:** (2) 981-57-82; **Internet:** www.natoinfo.bg; **e-mail:** grytvika@yahoo.com.

Dr Zhelyu Zhelev Foundation

Established in 1996 by Dr Zhelyu Zhelev, former President of Bulgaria, to involve young people in social and political life.

Activities: Operates programmes in the Balkan region, other areas of Europe and the USA, through programmes in the following areas: civil society; democratic reforms; social integration; and Balkan integration. Seeks to educate young people in politics and civil society, and form links with similar institutions throughout the world. Organizes seminars and publishes books, research and pamphlets.

Geographical Area of Activity: Western, Central and South-Eastern Europe and the USA.

Restrictions: Not a grant-making organization.

Publications: Conference reports; information brochures; multi-year report.

Principal Staff: Pres. Dr Zhelyu Zhelev; Exec. Dir Antonina Kosseva.

Address: 1000 Sofia, Dunav St 4, 3rd Floor, Apt 4.

Telephone: (2) 988-86-50; **Fax:** (2) 986-21-10; **e-mail:** zhelev@bgnet.bg.

Burkina Faso

FOUNDATIONS, TRUSTS AND NON-PROFIT ORGANIZATIONS

Fédération Panafricaine des Cinéastes—FEPACI

(Pan-African Federation of Film-makers)

Founded in 1970 by African film-makers for the development and promotion of African cinema.

Activities: Operates in almost all African countries to defend democracy in communications as a basic human right, through self-conducted programmes, conferences, training courses and publications. Organizes cinema festivals and campaigns in conjunction with other organizations, for government funding for cultural organizations.

Geographical Area of Activity: Africa.

Publications: *FEPACI-Infos* (quarterly); *Ecrans d'Afrique* (quarterly).

Principal Staff: Sec.-Gen. Gaston Kaboré.

Address: BP 2524, Ouagadougou 01.

Telephone: 31-27-35; **Fax:** 31-16-59.

Fondation Nationale pour le Développement et la Solidarité—FONADES

(National Foundation for Solidarity and Development)

Established in 1973 to promote economic development designed to meet the needs of local populations and their capabilities.

Activities: Promotes sustainable economic development, through supporting locally-administered development programmes. Types of projects include building of anti-erosion constructions to protect fragile areas; organization of local communities in the management and production of manure as a fertilizer; assistance in the production of seeds and tree planting programmes; well building in different villages; and the organization of micro-credit programmes among indigenous women to help them start commercial activities.

Geographical Area of Activity: Burkina Faso.

Address: BP 523, Ouagadougou 01.

Telephone: 36-37-68; **Fax:** 36-10-79.

John Paul II Foundation for the Sahel

Founded in 1984 with the aim of combating desertification and drought in the countries of the Sahel.

Activities: Operates in the Sahel region. Finances and organizes the training of individuals in the control and prevention of desertification, and assists the relief of people in drought-stricken regions, as well as providing practical support to NGOs.

Geographical Area of Activity: Burkina Faso, Cape Verde, Chad, Gambia, Guinea-Bissau, Mali, Mauritania, Niger and Senegal.

Principal Staff: Sec.-Gen. Abbé Fulgence Coly.

Address: 01 BP 4890, Ouagadougou 01.

Telephone: 36-53-14; **Fax:** 36-53-93; **Internet:** www.fjp2-sahel.org; **e-mail:** found.jp2@cenatin.bf.

Canada

FOUNDATION CENTRES AND CO-ORDINATING BODIES

Canadian Centre for Philanthropy

Established in 1981 to assist Canadian charitable and voluntary organizations through research, public affairs, information products and professional development.

Activities: The Centre operates through research into the charitable and voluntary sector and the environment in which they function; issuing publications; and organizing conferences and seminars. It is involved in communicating with government, the media and the public on the voluntary sector, and informs its affiliates on legislative and regulatory initiatives proposed by government.

Geographical Area of Activity: Canada.

Publications: *Canadian Directory to Foundations and Grants; Building Foundation Partnerships; Portrait of Canada's Charities; Give and Take: a resource manual for Canadian Fundraisers; Connecting Companies to Communities; Promoting Corporate Citizenship; Charities and Not-for-Profits Fundraising Handbook; Front and Centre* (newspaper); publications on foundations and fundraising; resource guides, brochures, pamphlets and special papers.

Finance: Annual revenue C $2,331,351 (1999), expenditure C $2,174,037 (1999).

Directors: D. Godsoe (Chair.); S. Herzog (Vice-Chair.); M. De Mara (Treas. and Sec.); E. Atcheson; R. Bailey; J. Crawford; D. Elton; T. Garrard; S. Hicks; D. McCreesh; R. Morin; S. O'Brien; E. Young; Dr D. Zussman.

Principal Staff: Pres. and CEO Patrick Johnston.

Address: 425 University Ave, Ste 700, Toronto, ON M5G 1T6.

Telephone: (416) 597-2293; **Fax:** (416) 597-2294; **Internet:** www.ccp.ca; **e-mail:** general@ccp.ca.

Canadian Co-operative Association

Established in 1987 by the merger of the Co-operative College of Canada and the Co-operative Union of Canada, as the co-ordinating organization for English-speaking co-operatives in Canada.

Activities: Provides leadership and support to its membership organizations in maintaining and improving the co-operative presence in Canada, which works to improve the quality of life of those in all parts of Canada and abroad. Member organizations work in the areas of finance, insurance, agri-food, wholesale and retail, housing, health and day-care. Its international development programme provides technical and financial assistance to credit unions and co-operatives in over 20 countries. Has offices in eight countries other than Canada. Funds are provided through the affiliated Co-operative Development Foundation of Canada (CDF).

Geographical Area of Activity: Mainly Canada.

Publications: *International Development Digest* (3 a year); *InterSector* (3 a year); *Co-operative News Briefs* (fortnightly electronic newsletter); *Concern for Community; Governance Matters* ; Annual Report; research papers and reports; videos.

Finance: Assets C $5,968,880 (March 2002); annual revenue C $11,606,147, expenditure C $11,642,565 (2002).

Directors: L. Arragutainaq; B. Dobson; M. Goldblatt; J. Johnson; W. Lee; L. Losier; P. McNair; F. Nielsen; P. Reeves.

Principal Staff: Pres. G. Tully; Vice-Pres. J. Hoyt; Exec Member P. Graham, W. McLeod; CEO Jean-Yves Lord.

Address: Co-operative House, 275 Bank St, Ste 400, Ottawa, ON K2P 2L6.

Telephone: (613) 238-6711; **Fax:** (613) 567-0658; **Internet:** www.coopscanada.coop; **e-mail:** info@coopscanada.coop.

FOUNDATIONS, TRUSTS AND NON-PROFIT ORGANIZATIONS

Aga Khan Foundation Canada

Established in 1980, and part of the network of foundations established by His Highness Prince Karim Aga Khan, aiming to support social development projects in Africa and Asia in order to benefit the poor, regardless of race, religion or political affiliation.

Activities: Operates internationally in the areas of health, education, employment, gender equality, the environment, and strengthening local NGOs. The Foundation is currently supporting six large programmes in East Africa, and South and Central Asia, as well as awarding smaller grants to educational and primary health-care projects. It also works nationally, strengthening links between Canadian institutes and their counterparts in developing countries, promoting greater understanding of global issues, fundraising to support international co-operation, and providing fellowships, management training and expertise from overseas to young Canadians.

Geographical Area of Activity: Canada, East Africa, and South and Central Asia.

Principal Staff: CEO Nazeer Aziz Ladhani.

Address: 360 Albert St, Ste 1220, Ottawa, ON K1R 7X7.

Telephone: (613) 237-2532; **Fax:** (613) 567-2532; **Internet:** www.akfc.ca; **e-mail:** info@akfc,ca.

Alberta Heritage Foundation for Medical Research

Founded in 1980 by an act of legislation to support biomedical and health research, principally in the province of Alberta.

Activities: The Foundation supports biomedical and health research, by offering awards based on international standards of excellence to researchers and researchers-in-training.

Geographical Area of Activity: Alberta, Canada and international.

Restrictions: Awards only for salary support, equipment costs, student support, renovation costs, construction costs and partnership initiatives.

Publications: *AHFMR Research News* (quarterly); Annual Report; community reports (annually); triennial reports.

Finance: All funding provided by a portion of the annual income of an endowment of C $800,000,000; annual grants expenditure approx. C $50,000,000.

Trustees: Harley Hotchkiss (Chair.); Dr Rod Fraser; Lou Hyndman; David Kitchen; Dr Cledwyn Lewis; Jo-Anne Lubin; Dr Eldon Smith; Gail Surkan; Dr Harvey Weingarten.

Principal Staff: Pres. and CEO Dr Matthew Spence.

Address: Ste 1500, 10104–103 Ave, Edmonton, AB T5J 4A7.

Telephone: (780) 423-5727; **Fax:** (780) 429-3509; **Internet:** www.ahfmr.ab.ca; **e-mail:** ahfmrinfo@ahfmr.ab.ca.

The Alva Foundation

Established in 1965 to support Canadian not-for-profit organizations helping children at risk.

Activities: Aims to help Canadian children at risk, through funding organizations conducting research and/or developing services that address significant risk factors in early childhood development.

Geographical Area of Activity: Canada.

Restrictions: Grants will not be made to individuals, nor for emergency or deficit funding.

Board of Directors: Derek Fisher (Pres., Sec. and Treas.); Graham F. Hallward (Vice-Pres.); Paul Duder; Dr. Sydney Duder; Christopher Kerrigan; Amanda Mathers; Judy McMartin.

Address: c/o Graham Hallward, 199 Albertus Ave, Toronto, ON M4R 1J6.

Internet: www.alva.ca; **e-mail:** donations@alva.ca.

Arctic Institute of North America—AINA

Founded in 1945 by Act of Parliament in Canada; incorporated concurrently in the USA under the laws of the State of New York. The Canadian Corporation became an integral part of the University of Calgary in 1979. The Institute's aims are to advance the study of Arctic and sub-Arctic conditions and problems; to collect material relating to these regions and to make it available for scientific use; to arrange for the publication of relevant material; and to maintain contact with organizations engaged in similar studies.

Activities: The physical, natural and social sciences and the humanities are all represented in AINA's work. Although mainly concerned with the North, its interests also extend to Antarctica and to Alpine environments. Programmes investigating the ecology of the Arctic and the physiology of high altitude and expeditions are typical of the work supported by AINA. The Institute maintains a major library and an automated bibliographic database system, the Arctic Science and Technology Information System (ASTIS). The Institute administers a small grants fund to assist student researchers on field projects and makes travel awards to enable researchers to travel to conferences.

Geographical Area of Activity: Canada and Alaska.

Publications: *Arctic* (quarterly); *KOMATIK Series*; research papers, technical papers, monographs and other occasional publications.

Finance: Budget: C $1,000,000.

Board of Directors: The Directors are appointed by the Board of Governors of the University of Calgary; Murray Todd (Chair.); and 12 others.

Principal Staff: Exec. Dir Karla Jessen Williamson.

Address: University of Calgary, 2500 University Dr., NW, Calgary, AB T2N 1N4.

Telephone: (403) 220-7515; **Fax:** (403) 282-4609; **Internet:** www.ucalgary.ca/aina; **e-mail:** wjkessen@ucalgary.ca.

Asia Pacific Foundation of Canada

Founded in 1984 to enhance economic, social and cultural relationships and networks between Canada and the countries of the Asia-Pacific Region.

Activities: The Foundation is a Canadian leading authority on Canada–Asia relations. It is the site of the Asia-Pacific Economic Co-operation (APEC) Study Centre in Canada, which promotes collaborative research and disseminates information; it also acts as the secretariat for the Asia Pacific Business Network, the Pacific Economic Co-operation Council, the Pacific Basin Economic Council and the APEC Business Advisory Council. It is developing, in partnership with the Federal Government, a network of Canadian Education Centres in Asian cities, including Seoul, Taipei, Kuala Lumpur, Jakarta, Bangkok, Singapore, Hong Kong and New Delhi. The Foundation maintains databases. Further Foundation offices are located in Québec. Through its subsidiary, the GLOBE Foundation, the Foundation manages the GLOBE Series of conferences and trade exhibitions on business and the environment.

Geographical Area of Activity: Canada and the Asia-Pacific region.

Publications: *Canada/Asia Review; Canada Asia Commentary*; and other publications.

Finance: Receives just over 50% of its financial support from the Federal Government, the provinces of British Columbia, Alberta, Saskatchewan, Manitoba and Québec, and from a number of private companies; the balance of its revenues are made up of fees paid for Foundation programmes. Annual budget approx. C $4,000,000.

Board of Directors: Thomas S. Axworthy (Chair.); and 13 other members.

Principal Staff: Pres. and CEO Dr John D. Wiebe; Exec. Editor Ron Richardson.

Address: 666–999 Canada Pl., Vancouver, BC V6C 3E1.

Telephone: (604) 684-5986; **Fax:** (604) 681-1370; **Internet:** www.asiapacific.ca; **e-mail:** info@asiapacific.ca.

E. A. Baker Foundation for the Prevention of Blindness

Founded in 1962 by the Canadian National Institute for the Blind (CNIB) to encourage the prevention, treatment and cure of blindness.

Activities: Supports Canadian hospitals and universities conducting research in ophthalmology and eye diseases. Awards fellowships for advanced training for Canadian ophthalmologists, and one-year grants of up to C $40,000 for research into the prevention of blindness.

Geographical Area of Activity: Canada.

Trustees: National Board of the CNIB; Fran Cutler (Chair.); J. Sanders (Pres. and CEO).

Principal Staff: Exec. Dir Barbara Marjeram.

Address: 1929 Bayview Ave, Toronto, ON M4G 3E8.

Telephone: (416) 480-7586; **Internet:** http://cnib.ca/awards_foundations/eabf/eabf.htm; **e-mail:** marjeram@cnib.ca.

Max Bell Foundation

Founded in 1965 by George Maxwell Bell for general charitable purposes, particularly in the fields of health, medical education and veterinary sciences in Canada and the Asia-Pacific region.

Activities: Operates in Canada and the Asia-Pacific region through research and grants to institutions; currently the Foundation is focusing on health, education and communications in society, especially in relation to public policy and responsible journalism.

Geographical Area of Activity: Canada and the Asia-Pacific region.

Publications: Programme Report.

Finance: Grants disbursed C $1,445,000 (2000); total grants of approx. C $65,000,000 since the foundation's establishment.

Officers and Directors: Ronald Mannix (Chair.); David Elton (Pres.); Carol Hill; Carolyn Hursh; Ken Marra; Dr Bernard Shapiro; Allan Taylor; Dr Michael Walker.

Address: Ste 1230, 639 5th Ave SW, Calgary, AB T2P 0M9.

Telephone: (403) 215-7310; **Fax:** (403) 215-7319; **Internet:** www.maxbell.org; **e-mail:** northcott@maxbell.org.

Berman Family Foundation

Established in 1974 for general charitable and educational purposes.

Activities: Operates in Canada and Israel, making grants for special projects to Jewish organizations, universities and organizations assisting the physically and mentally disabled, children and the aged.

Geographical Area of Activity: Canada and Israel.

Restrictions: Grants will not be made for building funds, deficit financing or endowment funds.

Principal Staff: Pres. Joseph Berman; Vice-Pres. Helen Berman.

Address: 230 Arnold Ave, Thornhill, ON L4J 1B9.

Samuel and Saidye Bronfman Family Foundation

Established in 1952 by the estate of Samuel Bronfman and family members to promote initiative and enterprise in Canada, and the development of new ideas and innovative projects aiming to find solutions to emerging problems in Canada.

Activities: Operates throughout Canada in the fields of the arts and humanities, conservation and the environment, education, human rights and social welfare, through grants to charitable organizations in Canada. There are three main funding programmes: Transitions, promoting positive change in Canadian society, including assistance for the disabled, community development, and supporting arts management training, through funding the Centre for Cultural Management at the University of Waterloo and projects of the Canadian Association of Arts Administration Educators, etc.; Futures, making grants for projects which exhibit potential for lasting national benefit; and Special Initiatives, providing funding for innovative and imaginative projects. Awards the Saidye Bronfman Award for craftwork and funds the Saidye Bronfman Centre for the Arts in Montréal and the Combined Jewish Appeal of Montréal. Established the Urban Issues Program, which supports community projects uniting urban conservation with community development.

Geographical Area of Activity: Canada.

Restrictions: Grants are not made for activities outside Canada, nor to individuals.

Publications: Brochure.

Officers and Directors: Gisele Rucker (Exec. Dir); Phyllis Lambert (Hon. Pres.); Jean de Gunzberg (Pres.); Andrew Parsons (Treas.); Michel Boucher (Asst Treas.); Robert Vineberg (Sec.); Matthew Bronfman; Stephen R. Bronfman.

Principal Staff: Exec. Dir Gisele Rucker; Donations Coordinator Andrea Barile.

Address: 1170 Peel St, Ste 800, Montréal, QC H3B 4P2.

Telephone: (514) 878-5270; **Fax:** (514) 878-5293; **Internet:** www.bronfmanfoundation.org; **e-mail:** info@bronfmanfoundation.org.

The Canada Council for the Arts/Conseil des Arts du Canada

The Canada Council for the Arts is an independent agency created by the Parliament of Canada in 1957 to provide grants and services to professional Canadian artists and arts organizations in dance, media arts, music, theatre, writing and publishing, interdisciplinary work and performance art, and the visual arts.

Activities: The Council provides a wide range of grants, prizes and services to professional Canadian artists and arts organizations in accordance with its aims (see above). The Art Bank of the Canada Council rents contemporary Canadian art to the public and private sectors in Canada. The Council maintains the secretariat for the Canadian Commission for UNESCO, administers the Killam Program of awards and prizes, and offers other awards. It operates the Public Lending Right Commission to administer payments to Canadian writers for their books held in Canadian libraries.

Geographical Area of Activity: Canada.

Publications: Annual Report; other publications describing programmes of assistance.

Finance: Funded by and reports to Parliament through the Minister of Canadian Heritage; its annual appropriation from Parliament is supplemented by endowment income, donations and bequests; grants, payments and awards C $137,000,000 (2001–02).

Members of the Board: Jean-Louis Roux (Chair.); François Colbert (Vice-Chair.); Suzanne Rochon Burnett; Craig Dowhaniuk; Richard Laferrière; David Lui; Nalini Stewart; David Thauberger; Jeannita Thériault.

Principal Staff: Dir Shirley L. Thomson.

Address: 350 Albert St, POB 1047, Ottawa, ON K1P 5V8.

Telephone: (613) 566-4414; **Fax:** (613) 566-4390; **Internet:** www.canadacouncil.ca; **e-mail:** info@canadacouncil.ca.

Canada Foundation for Innovation

Established in 1997 by the Federal Government to strengthen Canadian capability for research, ultimately contributing to economic growth and improvements in employment, health and the environment.

Activities: Invests in research infrastructure, to encourage innovation in universities, colleges, hospitals and other non-profit institutions. Promotes the training of young Canadians for research and other careers, attracts and retains able research workers, and works to ensure the best results in innovation by promoting sharing of information and resources among institutions. Also occasionally launches calls for proposals for international research projects.

Geographical Area of Activity: Canada and international.

Publications: Annual Report.

Finance: Total assets C $1,792,374,569 (March 2001); total income and expenditure C $188,168,235 (2001).

Directors: John R. Evans (Chair.); Michael Gervais (Vice-Chair); Lorne A. Babiuk; Alan Bernstein; Aldée Cabana; Dian Cohen; Bernard Coupal; David Dolphin; Kevin O'Brien Fehr; Monique Frize; Robert A. Phillips; David Pink; Gerri Sinclair; Stella Thompson; Ronald Whelan.

Principal Staff: Pres. and CEO Dr D. W. Strangway.

Address: 230 Queen St, Ste 450, Ottawa, ON K1P 5E4.

Telephone: (613) 947-6496; **Fax:** (613) 943-0923; **Internet:** www.innovation.ca.

Canada Israel Cultural Foundation

Established in 1963 to promote intercultural exchange between Canada and Israel.

Activities: Operates in the field of the arts and humanities, through the organization of cultural, artistic, musical and social events and support for Israeli performers to travel to Canada.

Geographical Area of Activity: Canada and Israel.

Principal Staff: National Pres. Ron Bresler; Sec. Grace Brooker.

Address: 2221 Yonge St, Ste 502, Toronto, ON M4S 2B4.

Telephone: (416) 932-2260; **Fax:** (416) 482-8281; **e-mail:** cicf@look.ca.

Canada Israel Foundation for Academic Exchanges

Established in 1975 to promote academic exchanges between Canada and Israel in the fields of the humanities and social sciences.

Activities: Operates through international exchange programmes in the humanities and social sciences; offers scholarships and bursaries; makes awards; promotes education research. Grants are made to Canadian academics wishing to teach in Israel, and for Israeli academics to teach in Canada.

Geographical Area of Activity: Canada and Israel.

Restrictions: No grants made to individuals.

Officers and Directors: Anne Gross (Pres.); Prof. Alain Goldschlager (Academic Dir); Hillel Becker; Myer Bick; Walter Bick; Irwin Cotler; Jack Cummings; Norma Cummings; Eph Diamond; David Goldberg; Martin Goldberg; David Golden; Edwin A. Goodman; Gerald Granek; John Greenburg; Ralph Halbert; Shira Herzog; James Kay; Sonia

Kizell; Norman May; Aaron Pollack; Cyril Reitman; Jeremy H. Reitman; David Satok; H. Arnold Steinberg; Bleema Steinberg; Stephen Victor; Rose Wolfe.

Address: 112 University of Western Ontario, London, ON N6G 3K7.

Canada World Youth/Jeunesse Canada Monde

Founded in 1971 by the Hon. Jacques Hébert to provide young people from Canada and abroad with the opportunity to travel and learn about local and international development, whilst actively providing support for different communities in developing countries.

Activities: Canada World Youth works on projects internationally. It runs a number of programmes for young people from Canada and other countries to spend time living and working in communities in Canada, and also provides the opportunity to participate actively in the development of healthy, sustainable and peaceful communities and societies in less-developed countries. It runs exchange programmes for young people from 17–20 years old; work experience programmes for people under the age of 30; and themed customized programmes, sending young people to work on projects in developing countries. Maintains five regional offices.

Geographical Area of Activity: Africa, Asia, North, Central and South America and the Caribbean, and Central and Eastern Europe.

Publications: Newsletter (2 a year); Annual Report.

Finance: Funded by the Canadian International Development Agency and by Canadian donors.

Directors: Michel Lamontagne (Chair.); Jacques Hébert (Founding Pres.); Michel Desjardins (Vice-Chair.); Matthew Pearce (Pres., CEO, Sec.); Claude Lemay (Treas.); Darlene Bessey; Jocelyne Bourgon; Jay Godsall; David Hawkins; Ivan Head; Duhane Lam; Anne Leahy; Don Logan; Roger Samson; Alexandre Trudeau.

Principal Staff: Pres., CEO and Sec. Matthew Pearce.

Address: 2330 Notre-Dame St West, 4th Floor, Montréal, QC H3J 1N4.

Telephone: (514) 931-3526; **Fax:** (514) 939-2621; **Internet:** www.cwy-jcm.org; **e-mail:** cwy-jcm@cwy-jcm.org.

Canadian Cancer Society

Founded in 1938 with the mandate to disseminate important information about the early warning signs of cancer to the Canadian public; since 1947 it has also funded research through its research partner, the National Cancer Institute of Canada (q.v.). It is a national, community-based organization of volunteers whose mission is the eradication of cancer and the enhancement of the quality of life of people living with cancer.

Activities: Operates nationally through funding and carrying out research on all types of cancer; providing comprehensive information about cancer care and treatment; giving support to people living with cancer; promoting healthy lifestyles and strategies for reducing cancer risk; and lobbying to prevent cancer and to help those living with it.

Geographical Area of Activity: Canada.

Restrictions: Awards are made for the purpose of clinical training in Canada or abroad and are open only to those who are Canadian citizens or who have status as landed immigrants.

Publications: Annual Report; information on specific cancers, treatment, risk reduction and supportive care.

Finance: The Society contributes about 95% of the budget of the National Cancer Institute of Canada (q.v.). Financed by public donations.

Principal Staff: Chief Exec. Julie White.

Address: 10 Alcorn Ave, Ste 200, Toronto, ON M4V 3B1.

Telephone: (416) 934-5661; **Fax:** (416) 961-4189; **Internet:** www.cancer.ca; **e-mail:** ccs@cancer.ca.

Canadian Catholic Organization for Development and Peace

Established in 1967, aiming to improve living and working conditions world-wide, support initiatives by people in less-developed countries to take control of their future, and to educate Canadians about North–South issues.

Activities: Supports local organizations in less-developed countries, in the fields of human rights, women's rights, community development, housing, education and employment opportunities, and agrarian reform. Provides emergency relief for the victims of natural and man-made disasters, and humanitarian aid for those who need it. Works to inform Canadians about the causes of poverty, and to enlighten them of the alternatives to unjust social, political and economic systems and offering support for democratization.

Geographical Area of Activity: Africa, Asia, Eastern and Western Europe, North, Central and South America, and the Middle East.

Publications: *Global Village Voice* (newsletter, quarterly); Annual Report.

Finance: Annual revenue C $25,527,955, expenditure C $21,806,864 (Aug. 2001).

Principal Staff: Exec. Dir Robert Letendre; Deputy Exec. Dir Richard Renshaw; Exec. Sec. Francine Martineau.

Address: 10 St Mary St, Ste 420, Toronto, ON M4Y 1P9.

Telephone: (416) 922-1592; **Fax:** (416) 922-0957; **Internet:** www.devp.org; **e-mail:** communications@devp.org.

Canadian Centre for International Studies and Co-operation—CECI

Originally founded in 1958, it was officially incorporated under its current name as a non-profit NGO in 1968, with the aim of fighting poverty and injustice in the developing world.

Activities: Works to strengthen the opportunities for development in disadvantaged communities around the world, operating in the fields of human rights and democracy, the environment, humanitarian aid, socio-economic rehabilitation and supporting peace initiatives.

Geographical Area of Activity: Asia and the Far East, Africa, North, Central and South America and the Caribbean, and South-Eastern Europe.

Publications: *Capacity Building: a Manual for NGOs and Field Workers*; Annual Report; other publications in French and Spanish.

Finance: Total assets C $9,970,654 (March 2002); total revenue C $40,406,306, expenditure C $40,266,970 (2002).

Directors: Danielle Sauvage (Chair.); Pierre Pichette (Vice-Chair.); Patricia Borlace (Treas.); Michel Chaurette (Sec. and Exec. Dir); Raymond Batrie; Lucie Blondeau; Bernard Décaluwé; Louis-Joseph Goulet; Caroline Marcel; Monique Vézina.

Principal Staff: Exec. Dir Michel Chaurette.

Address: 3185 Rachel St East, Montréal, QC H1W 1A3.

Telephone: (514) 875-9911; **Fax:** (514) 875-6469; **Internet:** www.ceci.ca; **e-mail:** info@ceci.ca.

Canadian Crossroads International/Carrefour Canadien International—CCI

Incorporated in 1969 to encourage global understanding and cross-cultural awareness through international development.

Activities: There are two main programmes, the Individual Program, comprising the Overseas Program (which organizes exchanges between Canadians and people from developing countries), and the To-Canada Program (which organizes volunteer work placements for people from developing countries); and the Group Program, based in the Province of Québec, which sends groups of volunteers to Francophone countries in West Africa for work placements and organizes placements in Québec for West African volunteers. Partner countries are located in Asia/Oceania, the Caribbean, Latin America, and East, Central, West and Southern Africa. Also organizes South-to-South placements (Interflow) and information technology placements through the Netcorps programme.

Geographical Area of Activity: North, Central and South America and the Caribbean, Africa and Asia/Oceania.

Restrictions: Programmes are available only to Canadian citizens and to volunteers from partner countries; no other organizations or individuals are funded.

Publications: *Sankofa* (newsletter, 2 a year); Annual Report.

Finance: Total assets C $779,145 (March 2002); total revenue C $6,466,540, expenditure C $6,629,888 (2002).

Directors: Lambrina Nikolaou (Chair.); K. O'Brien (Past Chair.); and country representatives.

Principal Staff: Exec. Dir Karen Takacs.

Address: 317 Adelaide St West, Suite 500, Toronto, ON M5V 1P9.

Telephone: (416) 967-1611; **Fax:** (416) 967-9078; **Internet:** www.cciorg.ca; **e-mail:** info@cciorg.ca.

Canadian Cystic Fibrosis Foundation

Founded in 1960, a non-profit, voluntary health organization, which works through its 52 chapters throughout Canada, raising and allocating funds to promote public awareness of cystic fibrosis, conducting research into improved care and treatment, and seeking a cure or control for this disorder.

Activities: The Foundation promotes research on cystic fibrosis in Canadian universities and hospitals by funding research grants and major research development programmes, and gives special grants for training and research to students, fellows, scholars and visiting scientists skilled in such areas as respirology, paediatrics and the behavioural sciences.

Geographical Area of Activity: Canada.

Publications: *Candid Facts* (quarterly newsletter, in English and French); *Circle of Friends* (newsletter, 2 a year, in English and French); *Cyber.Flash* (e-mail newsletter); Annual Report; brochures and reports.

Principal Staff: CEO C. Morrison; Dir, Communications June Pierotti; Dir, Medical/Scientific and Community Programs J. Chiarot; Dir, Development J. Cookson.

Address: 2221 Yonge St, Ste 601, Toronto, ON M4S 2B4.

Telephone: (416) 485-9149; **Fax:** (416) 485-0960; **Internet:** www.cysticfibrosis.ca; **e-mail:** info@cysticfibrosis.ca.

Canadian Executive Service Organization—CESO

A volunteer-based, non-profit organization founded in 1967, aiming to support and increase the economic and social growth of the indigenous peoples of Canada, and of those in the developing world, by lending the services of volunteers to businesses, and other professional and industrial activities.

Activities: Operates nationally and internationally. In Canada, CESO works towards the self-sufficiency and successful growth of indigenous communities, through transference of skills and training in businesses, advising on housing projects and a number of other projects run by volunteers. Internationally, CESO works to improve the quality of life of the inhabitants of many developing countries in Africa, Asia, Central and South America and the Caribbean, and emerging market economies in Eastern Europe and the former USSR, by increasing their capacity to manage and produce goods and services in both the public and private sectors, so that they can achieve economic self-sufficiency.

Geographical Area of Activity: International.

Trustees: Robert Dickson (Chair); Ginette Gagné-Koch, Clifford Moar (Vice-Chair.).

Principal Staff: Pres. and CEO Charles Beer; Treas. Terry Brackenridge; Vice-Pres. Clare Bonnell.

Address: 700 Bay St, Ste 700, Box 328, Toronto, ON M5G 1Z6.

Telephone: (416) 961-2376; **Fax:** (416) 961-1096; **Internet:** www.ceso-saco.com; **e-mail:** toronto@ceso-saco.com.

Canadian Feed the Children

Aims to relieve the effects of hunger, poverty and suffering in Canada and around the world, and to help communities to achieve self-sufficiency successfully.

Activities: Focuses on both long-term solutions to poverty and hunger, and immediate aid to those who are suffering. Works nationally, running and supporting food supply and nutrition programmes in schools, community centres, refugee centres, women's shelters and subsidized housing projects, as well as supporting other programmes throughout the country that work to mitigate the effects of hunger and poverty. Internationally, the organization operates a number of programmes that work with communities to ensure that children have their basic needs fulfilled in terms of food, water, sanitation and education; train and support child-focused charities around the world; provide vegetable seeds to refugees and displaced families to provide them with a self-sufficient lifestyle; provide credit and training to families so that they can begin to break out of the poverty cycle; and provide emergency materials for communities and families in times of crisis.

Geographical Area of Activity: International.

Publications: *Newslink* (newsletter).

Finance: Total revenue C $15,887,535, expenditure C $15,984,503 (2001).

Board of Directors: Dennis Eaton (Chair); Brian Leon (Vice-Chair.); John Irwin (Treas.); Mary Coyle; Charity Lebeanya; Paul MacLaren; Patrick Phillips.

Principal Staff: Exec. Dir Jim Dahl.

Address: 174 Bartley Dr., Toronto, ON M4A 1E1.

Telephone: (416) 757-1220; **Fax:** (416) 757-3318; **Internet:** www.canadianfeedthechildren.ca; **e-mail:** cftc@canadianfeedthechildren.ca.

Canadian Foodgrains Bank

Established in 1983 as a practical way in which Canadian farmers could share their produce with those in less-developed countries, thus helping to alleviate world hunger.

Activities: The organization operates in collaboration with 13 Canadian church partners, collecting donations of money, grain and other agricultural commodities to distribute to those who are hungry in less-developed countries. Conducts a food/grain collection system; provides advice and services regarding food programming; and seeks to develop policy and educate in areas relating to hunger and food security.

Geographical Area of Activity: Less-developed countries.

Publications: Annual Report.

Directors: M. Rempel (Chair.); O. Lofton-Brook (Vice-Chair.); A. Bacon (Sec.); J. Kramer (Treas.); W. Amos; E. Bumstead; P. Brander; S. Cameron; D. Clements; D. Cole; R. Fee; J. Gustafson; M. Humenny; S. Kear; C. King; I. Klassen; H. Matchullis; J. Meyer; E. Oduro; D. Peters; D. Raymer; D. Sefton; B. Slater; B. Syvret; C. Tuin; E. Willcox.

Principal Staff: Exec. Dir Jim Cornelius.

Address: 400-280 Smith St, Box 767, Winnipeg, MB R3C 2L4.

Telephone: (204) 944-1993; **Fax:** (204) 943-2597; **Internet:** www.foodgrainsbank.ca; **e-mail:** cfgb@foodgrainsbank.ca.

Canadian Foundation for World Development

Founded in 1967 to promote environmentally sound and sustainable development world-wide.

Activities: Supports development projects world-wide, particularly community projects aiming to increase self-sufficiency. Also operates in the fields of conservation and the environment, and medicine and health in Central America and the Caribbean. Carries out research and educational projects.

Geographical Area of Activity: International.

Publications: *Grassroots* (periodic); brochures.

Principal Staff: Pres. Kenneth G. Davis.

Address: 2441 Bayview Ave, Willowdale, ON M2L 1A5.

Telephone: (416) 445-4740; **Fax:** (416) 441-4025.

Canadian Friends of the Hebrew University of Jerusalem

Founded in 1943 to identify and maintain the interest of Canadian Jewish communities in Jewish and Hebrew studies, traditions and culture.

Activities: Operates nationally and internationally in the field of education, through speaker-orientated programmes, conferences, publications, and by awarding grants for study at the Hebrew University in Jerusalem.

Geographical Area of Activity: Canada.

Restrictions: Grants only to students studying at the Hebrew University of Jerusalem.

Publications: Newsletter (monthly).

Principal Staff: Nat. Dir Charles Diamond.

Address: 3080 Yonge St, Ste 5024, Toronto, ON M4N 3N1.

Telephone: (416) 485-8000; **Fax:** (416) 485-8565; **Internet:** www.cfhu.org; **e-mail:** inquiry@cfhu.org.

Canadian Hunger Foundation/Fondation canadienne contre la faim—Partners in Rural Development

Founded in 1961 under the auspices of the United Nations Food and Agriculture Organization (FAO) to enable people in poor communities to attain sustainable, healthy livelihoods.

Activities: The Foundation works with NGOs in 38 countries in Africa, Asia, Central and South America and the Caribbean to strengthen the capacity of community-based organizations and support self-help projects. The organization promotes policies that reduce poverty, and programmes that raise public understanding of development issues. Priorities are: subsistence food production and income generation; self-help initiatives—rural infrastructure and services; community-based organization building; NGO partners—institutional capacity development; long-term sustainability; participation of women; ecological practices; and Canadian development education. Projects focus on agriculture (food production and processing), water and sanitation, energy (alternative and renewable), nutrition and health, and capacity building and networking.

Geographical Area of Activity: Africa, Asia, Central and South America and the Caribbean.

Publications: *Dry Zone: Revitalization and Development; Tough to Swallow; Rural Energy Journal* (2 a year); *Global Link* (newsletter, 2 a year); educational materials, reports and papers.

Principal Staff: Exec. Dir Tony Breuer; Chair., Bd of Dirs Nick Hare.

Address: 323 Chapel St, Ottawa, ON K1N 7Z2.

Telephone: (613) 237-0180; **Fax:** (613) 237-5969; **Internet:** www.partners.ca; **e-mail:** info@partners.ca.

Canadian Institute of International Affairs

Founded in 1928 as an independent, non-partisan organization with the aim of providing a nation-wide forum for discussion and analysis of international affairs.

Activities: Operates briefing missions, conferences, lectures and a research and publications programme. The organization maintains a specialized library of 23,000 volumes; there are 1,800 members in 15 branches.

Geographical Area of Activity: Mostly Canada.

Publications: Annual report and financial statement; *International Journal* (quarterly); *Behind the Headlines* (quarterly); *Instituite Affairs* (bi-weekly electronic newsletter); *Canadian Foreign Relations Index; A Bibiliography of Works on Canadian Foreign Relations.*

Finance: Total assets C $2,198,999 (June 2001); annual revenue C $1,509,680, expenditure C $799,717 (2001).

Directors: R. MacLaren (Chair.); Hon. B. McDougall (Pres. and CEO); R. A. Broadbent; M. Côté; A. Ferrari; R. Herbst; L. Herman; Prof. M. MacMillan; R. Morden; S. Mullin; F. Potter; M. Rayfield; J. White.

Principal Staff: Pres. and CEO Hon. Barbara McDougall; Dir, Admin. Services Nancy Snelgrove.

Address: Glendon Manor, 2nd Floor, Glendon College, 2275 Bayview Ave, Toronto, ON M4N 3M6.

Telephone: (416) 487-6830; **Fax:** (416) 487-6831; **Internet:** www.ciia.org; **e-mail:** mailbox@ciia.org.

Canadian Liver Foundation (Fondation Canadienne du Foie)

Founded to support research and education into the causes, diagnosis, prevention and treatment of liver disease.

Activities: The Foundation offers operating grants and studentships to suitably qualified persons wishing to undertake research into the cause, diagnosis, prevention and treatment of liver and biliary tract disorders.

Geographical Area of Activity: Canada.

Restrictions: Organizations must be registered in Canada.

Publications: Pamphlets and information sheets on all forms of liver disease; Annual Report.

Finance: Receives donations. Total assets C $3,391,987 (2001); total revenue C $8,283,669, expenditure C $7,380,838 (2001).

Board of Directors: Eve Roberts (Chair. and CEO); Wesley Armour; Chris Collingwood; Samuel Lee; P. Michael Huet; Pauline Tsang; Joe P. Turkel; Melvin C. Zwaig.

Principal Staff: CEO and Chair. Eve Roberts.

Address: 2235 Sheppard Ave East, Ste 1500, Toronto, ON M2J 5BW.

Telephone: (416) 491-3353; **Fax:** (416) 491-4952; **Internet:** www.liver.ca; **e-mail:** clf@liver.ca.

Canadian Organization for Development through Education—CODE

Founded in 1959, CODE encourages self-sufficiency through literacy in the developing world.

Activities: Supports literacy and education by distributing books from Canadian and US sources (usually new books from publishers) to countries in the developing world, primarily in Africa, although shipments are also made to the Caribbean and the Pacific region. Also funds training of librarians, writers, illustrators and literacy workers.

Geographical Area of Activity: Mainly Africa and Guyana.

Publications: *NGOMA* (bi-annual newsletter); Annual Report.

Finance: Total revenue C $2,586,029, total expenditure C $2,545,425 (March 2001).

Directors: R. Evans (Chair.); C. Bredt (Vice-Chair.); C. Vahey (Treas.); N. Campbell; L. Donaldson; G. Fallon; S. Heckbert; S. Kinsman; C. McNain; K. Mohombu; R. Richardson; N. Salti; B. Vogt.

Principal Staff: Exec. Dir Yvonne Appiah; Dir, Development Sean Maddox; Dir, Fundraising Emily Hutchinson; Dir, Admin and Finance Fernand Mercier.

Address: 321 Chapel St, Ottawa, ON K1N 7Z2.

Telephone: (613) 232-3569; **Fax:** (613) 232-7435; **Internet:** www.codecan.org; **e-mail:** codehq@codecan.org.

Canadian Urban Institute

A non-profit organization that aims to improve the quality of life in urban areas of Canada and abroad.

Activities: Operates nationally and internationally to improve policy-making and management in urban regions, by enhancing understanding of urban issues by government, businesses and other key institutions. Participates in applied research and training, runs seminars and conferences, and produces publications. Identifies emerging economic and social issues that affect the urban sector in the fields of social development, housing, sustainability, the environment, urban infrastructure and economic development. The Institute's annual Brownie Awards recognise leadership, innovation and environmental sustainability.

Geographical Area of Activity: Eastern Europe, South America and the Caribbean, and the Far East.

Publications: *Smart Growth In North America: New Ways To Create Liveable Communities; The Urban Century* (newsletter, quarterly); and other publications.

Directors: J. Berridge; I. D. Clark; M. Entwistle; R. Holloway; S. Hoy; D. Hutcheon; E. Lindquist; P. McCarney; E. Pukonen; D. Richmond; A. Stevenson; E. Stroback.

Address: 100 Lombard St, Ste 400, Toronto, ON M5C 1M3.

Telephone: (416) 365-0816; **Fax:** (416) 365-0650; **Internet:** www.canurb.com; **e-mail:** cui@interlog.com.

Chastell Foundation

Established in 1987 for general charitable purposes.

Activities: Provides general and educational grants to foundations and service clubs; Jewish organizations, schools and cultural organizations; Israeli organizations; hospitals; organizations serving people with health disorders; family services; arts and cultural groups; orchestras; synagogues and temples; and for basic scientific research.

Geographical Area of Activity: Canada.

Restrictions: The Foundation does not accept applications.

Finance: Assets C $143,615,390 (2000); grants disbursed C $13,428,330 (2000).

Officers and Directors: Charles R. Bronfman (Pres.); Michel Boucher (Asst Treas.); Geri Craig (Asst Sec.); Richard P. Doyle (Vice-Pres.); Robert M. Jamieson (Controller); Arnold M. Ludwick (Sec. and Dir.); Andrew J. Parsons (Vice-Pres. and Treas.); Andrea M. Bronfman; Ellen Bronfman; Stephen R. Bronfman;.

Principal Staff: Admin. Susan Spencer.

Address: 1170 Peel St, 8th Floor, Montréal, QC H3B 4P2.

Telephone: (514) 878-5248; **Fax:** (514) 878-5293.

Club 2/3

Founded in 1970 by students concerned about the poverty and injustice that affects around two-thirds of the world's population.

Activities: Works in the field of international development and international solidarity, through supporting projects, mostly concerned with drinking water, education and training, initiated by partner organizations in 10 less-developed countries of Africa, Asia and Central and South America. Particularly focuses on young people between the ages of 12 and 17.

Geographical Area of Activity: Brazil, Burkina Faso, El Salvador, Haiti, Nepal, Paraguay, Peru, the Philippines, Senegal and Togo.

Address: 1259 rue Berri, bureau 510, Montréal, QC H2L 4C7.

Telephone: (514) 382-7922; **Fax:** (514) 382-3474; **Internet:** www.2tiers.org; **e-mail:** club@2tiers.org.

Coady International Institute

Founded by the St Francis Xavier University in 1959 to improve the lives of disadvantaged people by empowering them with knowledge and skills.

Activities: Works in the field of integral development, through research, training and consultancy. Runs five-month training programmes targeted at managers and trainers of regional and national development organizations in less-developed countries and conducts workshops and short courses, as well as offering youth fellowships to promote community development.

Geographical Area of Activity: International.

Restrictions: An educational facility, not a grant-making organization.

Finance: Funded by agencies and individuals in Canada and overseas. Annual revenue and expenditure C $3,200,160 (March 2000).

Principal Staff: Dir Mary Coyle.

Address: St Francis Xavier University, POB 5000, Antigonish, NS B2G 2W5.

Telephone: (902) 867-3960; **Fax:** (902) 867-3907; **Internet:** www.stfx.ca/institutes/coady; **e-mail:** coady@stfx.ca.

Columbia Foundation

Established by Working Enterprises, a group of companies owned by the labour movement, to invest in human and social capital for the benefit of all Canadians.

Activities: Aims to fund innovative social research, to develop and fund new scholarships that promote re-training and life-long learning, and promote the inclusive involvement of citizens in decision-making and community building.

Geographical Area of Activity: Canada.

Board of Directors: Tobi Davidge; Tom Dufresne; Ken Georgetti; David Levi; Ken Neumann; Jerri New; Barry O'Neill; John Shields.

Principal Staff: Exec. Dir Tobi Davidge.

Address: 702–1166 Alberni St, Vancouver, BC V6E 3Z3.

Telephone: (604) 408-2500; **Fax:** (604) 408-2525; **Internet:** www.columbiafoundation.ca; **e-mail:** info@columbiafoundation.ca.

CPAR—Canadian Physicians for Aid and Relief

Established in 1984 in response to famine and poor health conditions suffered by Ethiopian refugees in Sudan. The organization now aims to build health communities for vulnerable people in a number of parts of rural Africa.

Activities: Works to improve the quality of life of people living in Ethiopia, Malawi, Tanzania and Uganda, by operating long- and short-term programmes that focus on primary health care, water and sanitation, food security, community agro-forestry, agricultural rehabilitation, environmental protection, rural feeder road construction, adult training, credit programmes for small-scale entrprises, and peace-buiding. CPAR is also committed to informing Canadians about these causes, engaging them in the global effort for health and development. Has offices in Ethiopia, Malawi, Tanzania and Uganda.

Geographical Area of Activity: Africa.

Publications: Annual Report; Newsletter (quarterly); *Global Perspectives* (annual).

Finance: Funded by government grants and funding, the Canadian public, foundations and other organizations.

Directors: Leonard Bellam (Chair.) and 15 others.

Principal Staff: Exec. Dir Kevin O'Brien; Dir of Finance Zemede Russom; Dir of Development Peter Montgomery.

Address: 1425 Bloor St West, Toronto, ON M6P 3L6.

Telephone: (416) 369-0865; **Fax:** (416) 369-0294; **Internet:** www.cpar.ca; **e-mail:** info@cpar.ca.

CRB Foundation

Founded in 1988 by Charles R. Bronfman to support major initiatives contributing to the enhancement of 'Canadianism' and to strengthening the unity of the Jewish people.

Activities: Operates at national and international levels, seeking partners in the public and private sectors, or national organizations and other foundations with common goals, to run projects in the field of education and alternative education directed at young people; in its programmes, the Foundation emphasizes project innovation rather than on-going projects. Has initiated travelling Heritage Fairs that exhibit student projects.

Geographical Area of Activity: Mainly Canada.

Restrictions: The Foundation does not offer scholarships or academic chairs, nor does it finance annual campaigns, building or capital projects, general operating expenses, deficit funding or endowment funds. No grants are made to individuals.

Publications: Programme brochure.

Officers and Directors: Charles R. Bronfman (Chair.); Andrea M. Bronfman (Co-Chair.); Robert Rabinovitch (Treas.); Arnold M. Ludwick (Sec.); Thomas S. Axworthy (Exec. Dir); Ann Dadson (Admin. Dir); Stephen R. Bronfman; John Hobday; Donna S. Kaufman; E. Leo Kolber.

Address: 1170 Peel St, 8th Floor, Montréal, QC H3B 4P2.

Telephone: (514) 878-5250; **Fax:** (514) 878-5299.

CUSO

Established in 1961, aiming to support alliances that work for global social justice, the elimination of poverty and international development.

Activities: Operates in the fields of development, human rights, the environment and international development, mainly through placing Canadian volunteers in less-developed countries of Asia and the Pacific region, Africa, and Central and South America and the Caribbean; also by disseminating information, human and material resources and promoting policies for developing long-term sustainablility.

Geographical Area of Activity: Asia and the Pacific, Africa, and Central and South America and the Caribbean.

Publications: *CUSO News; Sustainable Times; Kébek News; Health Advice for Living Overseas; A Healthy Stay in Canada*; and other publications.

Finance: Financed by the Canadian International Development Agency and other donors. Net assets C $4,469,000 (March 2001), annual revenue C $25,581,000, expenditure C $25,404,000 (2001).

Directors: Ruth Schneider (Chair.).

Principal Staff: Exec. Dir Claire Dansereau.

Address: 500-2255 Carling Ave, Ottawa, ON K2B 1A6.

Telephone: (613) 829-7445; **Fax:** (613) 829-7996; **Internet:** www.cuso.org; **e-mail:** cuso.secretariat@cuso.ca.

Disabled People's International

Founded in 1981 to promote the integration of physically or mentally disabled people in society.

Activities: Promotes equal opportunities for disabled people; initiates the formation of organizations in developing countries, emphasizing the importance of self-help; maintains a database for the use of interested parties. Has around 135 member organizations.

Geographical Area of Activity: International.

Publications: *Disability International* (2 a year, in English, French and Spanish).

Principal Staff: Chair. Venus Ilagon; Treas. Shoji Nakanishi; Man. Dir Moira Horgan-Jones.

Address: 748 Broadway, Winnipeg, MB R3G 0X3.

Telephone: (204) 287-8010; **Fax:** (204) 783-6270; **Internet:** www.dpi.org; **e-mail:** info@dpi.org.

Donner Canadian Foundation

Founded in 1950 by W. H. Donner to provide financial assistance for innovative research projects, in order to help Canadians solve their social and economic problems.

Activities: Operates nationally, through grants for innovative projects with wide geographical impact in the fields of Canadian–US relations and international affairs, with a focus on applied research on questions of public policy. In 1998, the Foundation created the Donner Prize, awarding C $25,000 to the author of the best book on Canadian public policy and C $10,000 each to the two runners up. Also funds the Donner Canadian Foundation Awards for Excellence in the Delivery of Social Services, administered by the Fraser Institute.

Geographical Area of Activity: Canada.

Publications: Report of operations (annually, in English and French).

Officers and Directors: Allan Gotleib (Chair.); Robert Donner, Jr; Timothy E. Donner; William D. Spencer; Kenneth Whyte; Hon. Curtin Winsor, Jr; Mark Mitchell.

Principal Staff: Exec. Dir Helen McLean; Programme Officer Amy Buskirk; Admin. Asst. Debbie Gosney.

Address: 8 Prince Arthur Ave, 3rd Floor, Toronto, ON M5R 1A9.

Telephone: (416) 920-6400; **Fax:** (416) 920-5577; **Internet:** www.donnerfoundation.org; **e-mail:** mclean@donner.ca.

EJLB Foundation—Fondation EJLB

Established in 1983 to fund scientific research in all areas of neuroscience pertaining to mental illness, and to promote the protection of the environment.

Activities: Operates in two areas: an international Scholar Research Programme in neuroscience, particularly that pertain directly or indirectly to schizophrenia and mental illness, which offers up to seven awards of C $300,000 annually; and grants to support environmental projects in Canada which are working for the preservation of natural areas, and for environmental scientific research. Also funds the EJLB–CIHR Michael Smith Chair in Neurosciences and Mental Health, in conjunction with the Canadian Institutes of Health Research (CIHR), to be awarded annually to a Canadian university, or affiliated research institute, for a scientist in neurosciences and mental health.

Geographical Area of Activity: Canada, with limited international grant-making.

Restrictions: Grants will not be made for building funds, capital funds, endowment funds or equipment funds.

Finance: Net assets C $143,075,674 (2000); grants expenditure C $6,028,156 (2000).

Directors: Edith Low-Beer (Pres.); Robert Alain (Exec. Dir and Sec.).

Address: 1350 Sherbrooke St West, Ste 1050, Montréal, QC H3G 1J1.

Telephone: (514) 843-5112; **Fax:** (514) 843-4080; **Internet:** www.ejlb.qc.ca.

Eldee Foundation

Founded in 1961 for the support of Canadian organizations and charitable institutions.

Activities: Operates nationally in the fields of medicine and health, the environment, and Jewish causes in Canada and Israel, especially medical research and hospital development where it pertains directly or indirectly to schizophrenia and mental illness, and acquiring and preserving natural areas of significance to the urban landscape and funding Canada-based environmental research.

Geographical Area of Activity: Canada and Israel.

Restrictions: No grants are made to individuals for awards, fellowships, scholarships, bursaries or research grants.

Officers and Directors: Neri J. Bloomfield (Pres.); Harry J. F. Bloomfield (Vice-Pres.); Peter K. Johnson (Sec. and Treas.); Evelyn R. Schachter; Raphael Schachter.

Address: 1080 Beaver Hall Hill, Ste 1720, Montréal, QC H2Z 1S8.

Telephone: (514) 871-9261; **Fax:** (514) 397-0816.

EnerGreen Foundation

Founded in 1994 and supported by companies and individuals active in the independent power industry, specifically renewable and clean energy technologies.

Activities: Aims to promote renewable energy and sustainable development in Canada and around the world through support of projects, including reforestation initiatives, micro-hydro projects and renewable energy education programmes.

Geographical Area of Activity: Borneo, Canada, Nicaragua and the Philippines.

Publications: Newsletter.

Board of Directors: Jeff Arsenych (Chair.); David W. Beckwermert; Woon-Chin Chee; Donald O. Downing; J. C. Ireland; Colin F. W. Isaacs; Dr J. A. C. Kentfield; Joanne Phillips; Michael Royce; Dr Erdal Yildirim.

Address: Ste 2610, 645–7 Ave SW, Calgary, AB T2P 4G8.

Telephone: (403) 531-2131; **Fax:** (403) 264-1924; **Internet:** www.energreen.org; **e-mail:** energreen@energreen.org.

ETC Group—Action Group on Erosion, Technology and Concentration

Incorporated in the Netherlands in 1985, and previously known as Rural Advancement Foundation International—RAFI, the organization is an international NGO which dedicates itself to the responsible and sustainable advancement of rural communities world-wide.

Activities: Operates internationally in the field of sustainable development, through supporting community, national and regional NGOs. Provides research and analysis to assist the responsible advancement of technology in rural areas, and provides socio-economic, biological and technological information to aid sustainable self-reliance in rural society. Works to ensure genetic diversity in global agricultural systems.

Restrictions: Not a grant-making organization; cannot undertake grass-roots community or national work.

Publications: *Communique* (research journal published 4–6 times a year); *ETC Century: Erosion, Technological Transformation, and Corporate Concentration in the 21st Century; The Seed Giants: Who Owns Whom?;* Annual Report; other specialist publications and occasional papers.

Finance: Assets C $239,405 (1999); annual revenue C $384,377, expenditure C $360,319 (1999).

Board of Directors: T. Brodhead; E. N. C. Dano; M. J. Guazzelli; A. Mittal; A. Nadal; O. Nordberg; N. Wiebe; Dr G. Wolbring.

Principal Staff: Exec. Dir Pat Roy Mooney; Dir of Research Hope Shand; Programme Man. Jim Thomas.

Address: 478 River Ave., Ste 200, Winnipeg, MB R3L 0C8.

Telephone: (204) 453-5259; **Fax:** (204) 284-7871; **Internet:** www.etcgroup.org; **e-mail:** etc@etcgroup.org.

Fondation Armand-Frappier

Established in 1978 to support scholarship programmes and the purchase of scientific equipment, as well as the Institut Arman-Frappier, which aims to promote the pursuit of excellence and innovative research.

Activities: Operates in the fields of education and science and technology, offering scholarships to pre- and post-doctoral students studying at the Institut Armand-Frappier, and scholarships to students at Québec universities aiming to continue their studies at the Institut Armand-Frappier. Also offers Armand-Frappier prizes in the areas of Health, Innovation and Emerging Businesses in Québec working in relevant areas.

Geographical Area of Activity: Canada.

Publications: Annual Report.

Finance: Assets C $2,300,000 (June 2002); expenditure C $558,000 (2002).

Directors: C. Joly (Pres.); P.-Y. Châtillon; A. Bouchard, J. Chagnon, G. Proulx (Vice-Pres); G. Gélineau (Treas.).

Principal Staff: Dir-Gen. Claude Pichette; Dir of Development Claude Tanguay.

Address: 531 blvd des Prairies, Ville de Laval, QC H7V 1B7.

Telephone: (450) 686-5360; **Fax:** (450) 686-5361; **Internet:** www.fondation afrappier.qc.ca; **e-mail:** fondation .armand-frappier@inrs-iaf.uquebec.ca.

Fondation Marcelle et Jean Coutu

Established to assist those in less-developed countries and the disadvantaged in Canada.

Activities: Operates in Canada, especially Québec, in the field of social welfare, in particular disadvantaged women and children and drug abuse.

Geographical Area of Activity: Mostly Canada.

Directors: Marie-Josée Coutu (Pres.); Jean Coutu; Marcelle Coutu; Sylvie Coutu.

Address: 1374 Mont-Royal est, bureau 101, Montréal, QC H2V 4P3.

Fondation Jean-Louis Levesque

Established in 1961 by Jean-Louis Levesque to promote the development of universities, research institutes and charitable organizations.

Activities: Operates in Québec, Ontario and the Atlantic Provinces of Canada in the fields of education, medical research and social welfare, through making grants for research and special projects.

Geographical Area of Activity: Canada.

Restrictions: All funds are currently committed.

Officers and Directors: Suzanne Levesque (Pres.); Andre Charron; Pierre-Louis Levesque; Louis Page; Yanick Page.

Address: 2000 ave McGill College, Ste 2340, Montréal, QC H3A 3H3.

Fondation Baxter and Alma Ricard

Established by Baxter and Alma Ricard in 1998 to offer French Canadians living in a linguistic minority situation the opportunity to pursue graduate studies in the best schools in the world without having to go into debt.

Activities: The Foundation offers annual graduate and postgraduate scholarships to young French Canadians 21 years old and over, for a period of up to three years. Candidates are evaluated on the basis of academic excellence, leadership, civic pride and their commitment to the community..

Geographical Area of Activity: Canada.

Finance: Total assets approx. C $25,000,000.

Address: 225 rue Metcalfe, Ste 407, Ottawa, ON K2P 1P9.

Telephone: (613) 236-7065; **Fax:** (613) 236-3718; **Internet:** www.fondationricard.com/; **e-mail:** fonricar@cyberus.ca.

Foundation for International Training

Founded in 1976 to enhance self-reliance in developing countries by providing training.

Activities: Operates internationally in providing training and consultancy services and materials. The Foundation works with both private and public sectors, collaborating with local institutions; it concentrates on strengthening the capabilities of those who can then offer training to others. The three main programme areas are: social development, economic development and environmental management.

Geographical Area of Activity: International.

Publications: Annual Report; training materials; and policy and background papers.

Finance: Assets C $2,751,970 (March 2000); total expenditure C $4,804,628 (2000).

Trustees: Don Stevenson (Chair.).

Principal Staff: Exec. Dir Mirabelle Rodrigues.

Address: 7181 Woodbine Ave, Ste 110, Markham, ON L3R 1A3.

Telephone: (905) 305-8680; **Fax:** (905) 305-8681; **Internet:** www.ffit.org; **e-mail:** info@ffit.org.

Frontiers Foundation Inc—Operation Beaver

Established in 1968 by the Rev. Charles R. Catto to contribute to the relief of poverty by supporting tangible community development projects which have enduring significance. The Operation Beaver Program began in 1964; the Frontiers Foundation assumed responsibility for its administration in Canada in 1968 and overseas in 1969.

Activities: Operates through the Operation Beaver Program in Canada, Haiti and Bolivia in the areas of aid to less-developed countries, education and housing, through self-conducted programmes for community development, grants to individuals and institutions, training courses and publications.

Geographical Area of Activity: Canada, Bolivia and Haiti.

Publications: Annual Report; *Beaver Tales;* films, video documentaries, slides, etc.

Finance: Net assets C $169,313 (March 2000); annual revenue C $1,700,000, expenditure C $1,600,000 (2000-2001).

Directors: L. Gladue (Pres.); C. King (Vice-Pres.); G. Jennings (Sec. and Treas.); C. Nabigon (Chair., Operation Beaver Division); E. Carlson; R. Cyr; L. Gisborn; Reid; R. Ross; D. Stark; L. Tabobondung; S. Wheeler.

Principal Staff: Exec. Dir Marco A. Guzman; Founding Dir Charles R. Catto; Office Man. Patsy Cuffy.

Address: 419 Coxwell Ave, Toronto, ON M4L 3B9.

Telephone: (416) 690-3930; **Fax:** (416) 690-3934; **Internet:** www.frontiersfoundation.org; **e-mail:** frontiersfoundation@on.aibn.com.

Gairdner Foundation

Founded in 1957 by James A. Gairdner for the recognition of individuals who have made outstanding contributions in the field of medical science.

Activities: Operates nationally and internationally in the fields of medicine and health, and science and technology, through awards to individuals. Although the Foundation is primarily concerned with medical science, awards may be made to those who have distinguished themselves in other areas of medicine. No restrictions on nationality are observed.

Geographical Area of Activity: International.

Restrictions: Grants are only made on the basis of nominations and peer review.

Trustees: Bren Gairdner (Chair.); Lynne Upton (Vice-Chair); Dr John H. Dirks (Pres.); and others; there is also a Medical Advisory Board.

Principal Staff: Exec. Dir Donna Metcalfe.

Address: 2 Carlton St, Ste 1307, Toronto, ON M5B 1J3.

Telephone: (416) 596-9996; **Fax:** (416) 596-9992; **Internet:** www.gairdner.org; **e-mail:** thegairdner@on.aibn.com.

Mahatma Gandhi Foundation for World Peace

Established in 1988, aims to share the beliefs and philosophies of Mahatma Gandhi to promote international understanding and world peace.

Activities: Conducts and supports research and scholarship to promote Gandhian philosophy in a contemporary context, through supporting exchanges, lectureships and other academic posts; organizing conferences and lectures on the life and thoughts of Gandhi; and other educational projects.

Geographical Area of Activity: Canada.

Directors: Prem Kalia (Chair); Rajinder Abrol; Vijay K. Bhardwaj; Harchand Grewal; Jim Gurnett; Kapil Gurtu; Reva Joshee; Sushil Kalia; Bruce Miller; Madan Mohan; Deborah Morrison; William Pidruchney; Prasad Indira Puri; Jitendra A. Shah.

Address: POB 60002, U of A Postal Outlet, Edmonton, AB T6G 2S4.

Telephone: (780) 492-5504; **Fax:** (780) 492-0113; **Internet:** www.gandhi.ca; **e-mail:** info@gandhi.ca.

Gems of Hope

An NGO that promotes the self-sufficiency of families and communities, with a particular focus on women, in less-developed countries.

Activities: Works with local partners to support community development initiatives in the areas of health, education and local enterprise. Makes loans to small businesses in poor communities, thus providing sustainable development and funds for education, training and community health programmes.

Geographical Area of Activity: Asia, and Central and South America.

Publications: Newsletter.

Principal Staff: Dir of Int. Programs Bella Lam.

Address: 675 King St West, Ste 304, Toronto, ON M5V 1M9.

Telephone: (416) 362-4367; **Fax:** (416) 362-4170; **Internet:** www.gemsofhope.org; **e-mail:** gems@gemsofhope.org.

Globe Foundation of Canada

Founded in 1992 to promote the development of eco-business throughout the world.

Activities: The main focus of the Foundation is the development of business opportunities from environment problems. Programmes include: the creation of small enterprises; institutional development; credit and financial assistance; and the control of pollution and management of waste. Founded the EXCEL group, a forum for Canada's top business executives to share business strategies and improve global competitiveness. Also works in Asia and Eastern Europe. Globe Foundation (Europe) is based in Ireland.

Geographical Area of Activity: Canada, Asia and Eastern Europe.

Finance: Annual budget approx. C $1,850,000.

Principal Staff: Chair. Michael Phelps; Pres. and CEO John D. Wiebe; Admin. Man. Margaret McBride.

Address: 504-999 Canada Pl., World Trade Center, Vancouver, BC V6C 3E1.

Telephone: (604) 775-7300; **Fax:** (604) 666-8123; **Internet:** www.globe.ca; **e-mail:** info@globe.ca.

Walter and Duncan Gordon Charitable Foundation

Established in 1965 by Walter L. Gordon and Duncan L. Gordon to promote the strengthening of Canada and the enhancement of the well-being of all Canadians.

Activities: Operates in four main areas: Secondary Education in Manitoba, Peace and Security (throughout Canada, with an emphasis on demilitarization policy in the Arctic), Northern Affairs (in the Yukon and Northwest Territories) and Art Acquisitions, through making grants to charitable organizations for innovative projects or community initiatives which make an impact on and influence the development of public policy and social action, research projects, conferences and seminars.

Geographical Area of Activity: Canada.

Restrictions: Does not offer scholarships, nor does it offer bursaries or make grants to individuals.

Publications: Brochure.

Officers and Directors: Harvey Sector (Chair.); Dona Harvey (Vice-Chair.); Dr John Evans (Acting Treas.); Jane L. Glasso; Adele Hurley; Kyra Montagu; Tony Penikett; Edward Waitzer.

Principal Staff: Exec. Dir Christine Lee; Programme Dir Annette Tromly.

Address: 11 Church St, Ste 400, Toronto, ON M5E 1W1.

Telephone: (416) 601-4776; **Fax:** (416) 601-1689; **Internet:** www.gordonfn.org; **e-mail:** gordonfn@gordonfn.org.

The Lotte and John Hecht Memorial Foundation

Established in 1962 as the 1945 Foundation with the proceeds of the sale of shares of a company owned by Lotte and John Hecht.

Activities: Provides grants to not-for-profit organizations in two main fields: investigation and support of complementary and alternative medicine, particularly in the treatment of cancer; and economic education that promotes the principles of a free market.

Geographical Area of Activity: Canada.

Finance: Annual distributions approx. C $2,000,000 (2001).

Address: 502–325 Howe St, Vancouver, BC V6C 1Z7.

Telephone: (604) 683-7575; **Fax:** (604) 683-7580; **Internet:** www.hecht.org/index.htm; **e-mail:** info@hecht.org.

HOPE International Development Agency

Established in 1974, HOPE aims to provide support to developing countries where environmental, economic or social circumstances have interfered with communities' ablilities to sustain themselves.

Activities: HOPE endeavours to help less-developed countries in crisis in a number of ways: by providing emergency aid, including clean water and sanitation, shelter, medicine and food, as well as more long-term solutions, such as technological and educational support, training in food production and nutrition, and health-care and community development programmes. In this way, HOPE aims to assist communities to learn the skills necessary to sustain themselves in the long term. Also maintains offices in Bangladesh, Cambodia, Ethiopia, Japan, UK and the USA.

Geographical Area of Activity: Africa, Asia and Central America.

Finance: Annual revenue and expenditure C $15,080,049 (2001).

Principal Staff: Exec. Dir David McKenzie.

Address: 214 Sixth St, New Westminster, BC V3L 3A2.

Telephone: (604) 525-5481; **Fax:** (604) 525-3471; **Internet:** www.hope-international.com; **e-mail:** hope@hope-international.com.

Horizons of Friendship

International development organization founded in 1973 by Tim Coughlan and Christine and David Stewart. Aims to eliminate poverty in Mexico and Central America.

Activities: Works with people living with the effects of poverty in rural and urban communities. Runs development projects to provide clean water and sanitation, health care, housing and skills training. Horizons has given humanitarian assistance to victims of war and political oppression, aided refugees in need of rehabilitation and provided aid to those affected by natural disasters.

Geographical Area of Activity: Mexico and Central America.

Publications: Newsletter; Annual Report.

Finance: Funded by private donors and the Canadian Government. Assets C $1,500,000 (March 2002); annual revenue C $1,505,259, expenditure C $1,493,656 (2002).

Directors: E. Wilson (Pres.); R. Braganca (Vice-Pres.); Rev. T. Coughlan (Past Pres.); B. Lynch (Treas.); Dr P. Caldwell; E. Gervan; Rev. J. Lynch; Dr B. Moebus; Dr D. Morrison; C. Rosene; D. Smith.

Principal Staff: Exec. Dir Patricia Rebolledo.

Address: 50 Covert St, POB 402, Cobourg, ON K9A 4L1.

Telephone: (905) 372-5483; **Fax:** (905) 372-7095; **Internet:** www.horizons.ca; **e-mail:** info@horizons.ca.

Hospital for Sick Children Foundation

Founded in 1972 by, among others, Duncan L. Gordon and John T. Law to provide funds for research, special programmes and public health education at the Hospital for Sick Children, Toronto and throughout Canada.

Activities: Organizes educational and research programmes in two main areas; developing research skills, and knowledge generation and community action. Provides grants to Canadian institutions and individuals; awards fellowships and scholarships (including the Duncan L. Gordon Fellowships for post-doctoral study in child health, and the Visiting Scientists and Foreign Research Fellowship Program for researchers from Canada and abroad); its National Grants Program funds research, conferences, scholarships and fellowships nationally; maintains a Research Institute; and runs a grants programme in youth and child home care.

Geographical Area of Activity: Canada.

Publications: *Handbooks for Parents* (various); *Child Safety; Planning for Kids* (newsletter, 3 a year); Annual Report; conference proceedings.

Finance: Assets C $386,500,000 (1999–2000); annual revenue C $94,000,000 (1999–2000).

Governing Board: J. Pitblado (Chair.); Alexander R. Aird; Patsy Anderson; Jennifer Ivey Bannock; Susan Bassett; Jill Denham; John R. Evans; Paul V. Godfrey; Mitchell Goldhar; Ruth M. Grant; Arthur S. Labatt; Stephen D. MacDonald; Mary Mogford; R. Jeffrey Orr; C. W. M. Scott; Andrew Sheiner; David G. Ward; V. Prem Watsa; Adam Zimmerman.

Principal Staff: CEO Dianne Lister.

Address: 555 University Ave, Toronto, ON M5G 1X8.

Telephone: (416) 813-6166; **Fax:** (416) 813-5024; **Internet:** www.sickkids.on.ca/foundation; **e-mail:** erin.mullin@sickkids.ca.

Imperial Oil Charitable Foundation

Established in 1994 for general charitable purposes in Canada which are compatible with the company's business objectives and activities.

Activities: Operates nationally in the fields of arts and humanities, education, medicine and health, and social welfare (in particular community and social services and sport and recreation), through grants to Canadian charitable organizations for existing facilities and programmes.

Geographical Area of Activity: Canada.

Restrictions: No grants are made to individuals; grants are limited to communities in which the company has employees; no finance for research projects, fellowships or scholarships.

Publications: *Tradition of Giving*; Annual Report.

Finance: Grant expenditure approx. C $6,700,000 (2002).

Officers and Directors: Barbara Hejduk (Pres.); Susan E. Young (Treas.); John Zych (Sec.); Douglas D. Baldwin; J. Bruce Buchanan; Richard J. Currie; Pierre Des Marais, II; William A. Macdonald; Sheelagh D. Whittaker.

Principal Staff: Corporate Contributions Assoc. John E. Mathers; Lorri Swinson.

Address: 111 St Clair Ave West, Toronto, ON M5W 1K3.

Telephone: (519) 319-2168; **Internet:** www.imperialoil.ca.

Inter Pares

Founded in 1975 by Timothy Brodhead and Ian Smiley to support the efforts of self-help groups in developing countries in gaining control over their lives, to create economic alternatives and to find sustainable solutions to poverty.

Activities: Inter Pares ('among equals'), supports local groups in 20 countries in Asia, Africa, Central America and the Caribbean to establish co-operatives and credit schemes; reclaim land for food production; promote reproductive rights; protect the environment; provide community-based health care, education and training; and organize women, farmers and urban poor to improve their lives. In Canada Inter Pares promotes understanding of the causes of poverty and powerlessness, and encourages groups in Canada and developing countries to learn from and support each other in strategies for change. Inter Pares works with local and regional organizations in Canada to support community development and social change.

Geographical Area of Activity: Africa, Asia, Central and South America, and Canada.

Publications: *Bulletin* (quarterly).

Principal Staff: Exec. Dir Molly Kane.

Address: 58 Arthur St, Ottawa, ON K1R 7B9.

Telephone: (613) 563-4801; **Fax:** (613) 594-4704.

International Development and Relief Foundation

Founded in 1985 by a group of Canadian Muslims aiming to empower the world's disadvantaged people.

Activities: Aims to empower the world's disadvantaged people through the provision of emergency relief aid and participatory development programmes. Participates in training of refugees, reconstruction work after natural disasters, economic development programmes, health projects and community development initiatives internationally, including in Afghanistan, Bangladesh, Bosnia, Ethiopia, India, Iran, Iraq, Kenya, Kosovo, Pakistan, Palestine, Somalia, South Africa, Sri Lanka, Sudan and Turkey.

Geographical Area of Activity: International.

Publications: *IDRF Reporter* (annual).

Address: 1063 McNicoll Ave, Scarborough ON M1W 3W6.

Telephone: (416) 497-0818; **Fax:** (416) 497-0686; **Internet:** www.idrf.ca; **e-mail:** office@idrf.ca.

International Institute for Sustainable Development

Founded in 1990 to promote sustainable social and economic development world-wide and to promote innovation.

Activities: Collates and disseminates information on economic development; serves, in an advisory capacity, government agencies and national and international organizations involved in development work; devises business strategies and trade principles; promotes community living and the creation of sustainable economies. Also conducts research, produces educational materials and maintains a library. Maintains offices in Ottawa, Geneva and New York.

Geographical Area of Activity: International.

Publications: Annual Report; various books, brochures and handbooks.

Finance: Annual budget approx. C $5,000,000.

Board of Directors: Jacques Gérin (Chair.); Edward S. Ayensu; James P. Bruce; James Carr; Eleanor Clitheroe; Angela Cropper; Christian Friis Bach; Chuck Hantho; Nicolas Imboden; Aban Marker Kabraji; Ashok Khosla; Rosemarie Kuptana; Huguette Labelle; Elizabeth May; Mark Moody-Stuart; Robert Page; Hon. Edward R. Schreyer.

Principal Staff: Pres. and CEO D. Runnalls; Chair. J. Gérin.

Address: 161 Portage Ave East, 6th Floor, Winnipeg, MB R3B 0Y4.

Telephone: (204) 958-7700; **Fax:** (204) 958-7710; **Internet:** www.iisd.org/default.asp; **e-mail:** info@iisd.ca.

The Richard Ivey Foundation

Established in 1947 by Richard G. and Richard M. Ivey; a private charitable foundation.

Activities: Operates nationally. About one-third of the Foundation's funds are allocated to the General Program, which serves the greater Toronto area, operating in the fields of health and welfare, education, the environment and the arts and humanities. Remaining funds (about 70%) are allocated to two further grants programmes: the Biodiversity in Forest-Dominated Ecosystems Program; and the Telehealth Program.

Geographical Area of Activity: Canada, particularly Ontario.

Restrictions: Grants only to Canadian-based organizations that are registered charities. Grants not normally made for the following: building campaigns; scholarships or student aid; sabbaticals or academic leaves; land acquisitions; seminars, workshops, conferences, tours, competitions or special events; costs of performances; publication of studies and research; operating expenditures, except temporarily for new undertakings; deficits; private foundations or other grant-making organizations; production of films, videos, CD-ROMs or websites.

Publications: Annual Report; programme brochures.

Finance: Assets C $74,360,365 (2001); grants disbursed C $1,760,625 (2001).

Directors: Rosamond A. Ivey (Chair. and Pres.); Richard W. Ivey (Sec. and Treas.); Beryl M. Ivey; Jennifer L. Ivey Bancock; Suzanne E. Ivey Cook.

Principal Staff: Exec. Dir Bruce Lourie.

Address: 11 Church St, Ste 400, Toronto, ON M5E 1W1.

Telephone: (416) 867-9229; **Fax:** (416) 601-1689; **Internet:** www.ivey.org; **e-mail:** info@ivey.org.

Kahanoff Foundation

Established in 1979 by the estate of Sydney Kahanoff for general charitable purposes, in particular innovative projects.

Activities: Operates throughout Canada, with an emphasis on projects in Alberta, and in Israel, in the areas of education, the arts and humanities, medicine and health, research, social welfare, philanthropy and community development, through grants to non-profits in Canada and partner organizations carrying out Foundation projects in Israel.

Geographical Area of Activity: Canada.

Restrictions: Grants are not given to individuals, for conferences, fellowships, bursaries, scholarships, tours, exhibitions or conferences, public works, non-applied research, nor for operating or endowment funds.

Finance: Funded by the estate of Sydney Kahanoff; assets approx. C $100,000,000 (2002).

Officers and Directors: James B. Hume (Pres.); Shira Herzog (Vice Pres.); Alan C. Moon (Sec.); Carol E. Peter (Controller); Clement W. Dumett, Jr.; Frank Kettner; George H. Plewes; Stuart A. Ross.

Principal Staff: Man. Cynthia P. Moore.

Address: Ste 4206, 400 Third Ave SW, Calgary, AB T2P 4H2.

Telephone: (403) 237-7896; **Fax:** (403) 261-9614; **Internet:** www.kahanoff.com; **e-mail:** info@kahanoff.com.

Henry White Kinnear Foundation

Established in 1979 by the estate of Mr and Mrs Henry White Kinnear and others for general charitable purposes.

Activities: Operates throughout Canada in the areas of the arts and humanities, education, medicine and health, and social welfare, through grants to organizations..

Geographical Area of Activity: Canada.

Restrictions: No grants to individuals.

Officers and Directors: Arthur R. A. Scace (Pres.); Marjorie Koren (Sec. and Treas.); Richard H. McCoy; Susan M. Scace.

Address: Toronto Dominion Bank Tower, Ste 4700, Toronto Dominion Centre, Toronto, ON M5K 1E6.

Telephone: (416) 925-9866.

Laidlaw Foundation

Established in 1949 by W. C. Laidlaw, R. A. Laidlaw, R. W. L. Laidlaw and Dr R. G. N. Laidlaw to strengthen the environment for children, young people and families, to promote opportunities for human development and creativity, and to support healthy communities and ecosystems.

Activities: Operates in the fields of the arts and humanities, conservation and the environment, and social welfare. The Foundation's main programmes are: Children at Risk and Contaminants and Child Health (both operating throughout Canada); New Works in the Performing Arts and a Youth Recreation Initiative (Ontario), Youth Engagement, promoting leadership and decision-making skills and the construction of a Children's Agenda based on social inclusion.

Geographical Area of Activity: Canada.

Publications: Annual Report; information brochures; occasional papers.

Finance: Assets C $60,081,255 (Dec. 2001); grants disbursed C $2,848,314 (2001).

Officers and Directors: Paul Zarnke (Pres.); Walter Ross (Past Pres.); Marylon Fallis; Barbara Hall; Jamie Laidlaw; William Laidlaw; Vinay Mehta; Ratna Omidvar; Anver Saloojee; Deborah Senior; David Wheeler.

Principal Staff: Exec. Dir Nathan Gilbert.

Address: 365 Bloor St East, Ste 2000, Toronto, ON M4W 3L4.

Telephone: (416) 964-3614; **Fax:** (416) 975-1428; **Internet:** www.laidlawfdn.org; **e-mail:** ngilbert@laidlawfdn.org.

Daniel Langlois Foundation for Art, Science, and Technology/Fondation Langlois pour l'Art, la Science et la Technologie

Established in 1997 by Daniel Langlois to further artistic and scientific knowledge by promoting the meeting of science and art in the field of technology internationally.

Activities: Operates internationally in the fields of the arts and culture, and science and technology. Supports interdisciplinary research that encourages the co-operation of people from a variety of fields; funds projects by high-level artists and scientists; makes the results of its research public and encourages public exhibition of projects in galleries, museums and other public institutions; promotes the integration of different cultures by providing scholarships to individuals and organizations from less-developed countries, so that they can immerse themselves in technological contexts not usually available to them; and provides research grants to individual artists or scientists.

Geographical Area of Activity: International.

Restrictions: No grants to projects that entertain a commercial approach.

Publications: *Images du Futur Past* by Hervé Fischer; *A Meditation on the Vasulka Archive* by Gene Youngblood; *The Experiments in Art and Technology; The Body of the Line: Eisenstein's Drawings; anarchive 2: Digital Snow.*

Finance: Grants expenditure approx. C $1,500,000 (2002).

Board of Directors: D. Langlois (Pres.).

Principal Staff: Dir of Programmes J. Gagnon; Asst to Dir of Programmes A. Navarre; Programme Officer Jacques Perron, Dominique Fontaine.

Address: 3530 Blvd St-Laurent, Ste 402, Montréal, QC H2X 2V1.

Telephone: (514) 987-7177; **Fax:** (514) 987-7492; **Internet:** www.fondation-langlois.org; **e-mail:** info@fondation-langlois .org.

The Lawson Foundation

Established in 1956 by the Hon. Ray Lawson, to enrich the quality of life of Canadians.

Activities: Aims to enrich the quality of life of Canadians, with a particular focus on early childhood competencies and the strengthening of communities, through support of projects targeting young children, their families and caregivers, and the delivery of community-based, patient-centred health-care services.

Geographical Area of Activity: Canada.

Publications: Annual Report; *Toward the Development of a 'Know-How' Knowledge Diffusion and Utilization Model for Social and Health Programs.*

Finance: Total assets C $62,000,000 (2001); total grants C $2,969,445 (2001).

Principal Staff: Pres. Constance Gardiner.

Address: 252 Pall Mall St, Ste 302, London, ON N6A 5P6.

Internet: www.lawson.on.ca; **e-mail:** inquiry@lawson.ca.

Lifeforce Foundation

Founded in 1980 by Peter Hamilton to support human rights, animal rights and environmental issues and to promote the harmonious coexistence of humans and animals in their environment.

Activities: Operates internationally in the fields of environmental problems and abuses, poverty, racism, sexism, violent crime, and experiments on animals. The Foundation also conducts marine life programmes (Education, Conservation and Research) to further the protection of marine habitats; develops public education programmes; compiles statistics; conducts symposia; provides video cassettes and educational packages; and maintains a library.

Geographical Area of Activity: International.

Restrictions: Not a grant-making organization—seeks grants for its programmes.

Publications: *Lifeforce News* (newsletter); *Orca: A Family Story; Respect Life with Lifeforce*; brochures, booklets and educational materials.

Finance: Annual budget approx. C $40,000.

Principal Staff: Dir Peter Hamilton.

Address: POB 3117, Main Post Office, Vancouver, BC V6B 3X6.

Telephone and Fax: (604) 669-4673; **e-mail:** lifeforcefoundation@hotmail.com.

Samuel Lunenfeld Charitable Foundation

Established in 1954 and funded by the estate of the late Samuel Lunenfeld to support religious, educational and general charitable activities.

Activities: Operates, principally in Ontario, in the fields of medicine and health, and social welfare, through funding medical research projects, the Baycrest Hospital for sufferers of Alzheimer's disease (with the Ontario Government), the Samuel Lunenfeld Research Foundation at the Mount Sinai Hospital and the Samuel Lunenfeld Summer Research Programme at the Hospital for Sick Children, Toronto. Makes grants for research projects, emergency funds, endowment funds, awards, 'seed' money, fellowships and scholarships. Also operates a scholarship scheme for international students at the Raphael Recanati International School in Israel.

Geographical Area of Activity: Canada.

Restrictions: No grants to individuals.

Officers and Directors: Sybil Kunin (Pres.); William Andrews (Sec.).

Principal Staff: Exec. Dir Mitchell Kunin.

Address: 8 King St East, Ste 712, Toronto, ON M5C 1B5.

Telephone: (416) 363-9191; **Fax:** (416) 363-2548.

The J. W. McConnell Family Foundation

Established in 1937 by J. W. McConnell to help Canadians understand, adapt and respond to the forces transforming Canadian and world society.

Activities: Operates throughout Canada in the areas of the arts and humanities, and social welfare and development, through grants to charitable organizations aiming to help communities cater for their needs through the generation and regeneration of community resources; aims to promote learning and the development of new approaches to employment. Grants are made for activities which are carried out principally in Canada. Foundation initiatives include projects aiming to promote student involvement in the arts, engage students in environmental stewardship activities, supporting community-based economic activities and developing support structures for non-formal care-givers.

Geographical Area of Activity: Canada.

Restrictions: No grants for conferences, seminars, scholarships, fellowships, bursaries, research, nor to individuals nor to projects oriented towards third world development. Grants only to organizations that have charitable status in Canada.

Publications: *Should You Sow What You Know?; Foundation Do's and Don'ts*; funding guidelines.

Finance: Grants disbursed C $19,361,608 (2001).

Officers and Directors: Linda M. Leus (Chair.); Tim Brodhead (Pres. and CEO); Joan McCammon (Sec.); Claude David (Treas.); Lyn P. Baptist; Diana M. Hillman; Kathleen M. Laing; Peter G. McConnell; Jill M. Price; C. Sean McConnell; David W. McConnell; Derek A. Price.

Principal Staff: Programme Man. Katherine Pearson.

Address: 1002 Sherbrooke St West, Ste 1800, Montréal, QC H3A 3L6.

Telephone: (514) 288-2133; **Internet:** www.mcconnellfoundation.ca; **e-mail:** inquiries@mcconnellfoundation.ca.

Macdonald Stewart Foundation

Established in 1967 by Macdonald Tobacco Inc for general charitable purposes in the areas of the humanities, education and medicine.

Activities: Operates throughout Canada in the fields of the arts and humanities, in particular assisting museums; education, promoting new and innovative ideas and providing bursaries and scholarships; and medicine and health, supporting projects, short-term research and voluntary medical services. Projects supported must be Canadian or have Canadian content, and be carried out by registered charitable organizations.

Geographical Area of Activity: Canada.

Restrictions: Grants are not made to individuals.

Publications: Annual Report.

Finance: Assets C $73,733,401 (Dec. 1999); grants disbursed C $6,517,990 (1999).

Officers and Directors: Liliane Stewart (Pres.); L. Jacques Ménard, David Johnston (Vice-Pres); James P. Carroll (Vice-Pres., Exec. Dir and Sec.); Douglas Ross (Controller); Andre Bérard; Hartland MacDougall; Diana Stewart; John D. Thompson.

Address: 1195 Sherbrooke St West, Montréal, QC H3A 1H9.

The McLean Foundation

Established in 1945 by J. S. McLean.

Activities: Aims to support projects showing promise of general social benefit, but which may initially lack broad public appeal, within the fields of the arts, education, conservation, health and social welfare.

Geographical Area of Activity: Canada.

Restrictions: Grants only to Canadian registered charities; no grants to individuals.

Finance: Total assets C $34,855,988 (2001); annual revenue C $1,312,462, total grants disbursed C $1,455,550 (2001).

Board of Directors: Mary C. Brown; J. Edward Chamberlin; Carol Gray; Mark F. McLean; Paul S. McLean; Andrew M. Stewart; John S. Stewart; Nigel E. M. Stewart; Patrick D. M. Stewart; Timothy C. Stewart; William G. Stewart.

Principal Staff: Pres. Paul S. McLean; Vice-Pres. Timothy C. Stewart; Treas. Elaine M. Kalm; Sec. Britt M. L. Bengtsson.

Address: 2 St. Clair Ave, W. Ste 1008, Toronto, ON M4V 1L5.

Telephone: (416) 964-6802; **Fax:** (416) 964-2804; **e-mail:** info@mcleanfoundation.on.ca.

Nelson Mandela Children's Fund—Canada (Le fonds Nelson Mandela pour les enfants—Canada)

Established in 1998 by former South African President Nelson Mandela.

Activities: Funds not-for-profit organizations working with disadvantaged children in South Africa and campaigns to raise public awareness in Canada of the plight of disadvantaged and victimized South African children. Works in association with the Nelson Mandela Children's Fund (q.v.) in South Africa.

Geographical Area of Activity: Canada and South Africa.

Board of Directors: Bahadur Madhani (Chair.); Zanana Akande; Dr Jane Arthur; Robin Benger; Hendrikus Bervoets; Harold Brathwaite; Gordon Cressy; Gloria Fallick; Dorothée Gizenga; Dr Jay Govender; Fatimah Jackson; Andre Jaquet; Zeib Jeeva; Joan Jeffers; Cheuk Kwan; Charity Lebeanya; Judith C. Lee; Dr Paks Madikiza; Khwezi Mbolekwa; Lloyd McKell; Sibongile (Bongi) Mkhabela; John Piper; Deborah Turnbull; Hassan Yussuff.

Principal Staff: Exec. Dir Mark Beckles.

Address: 1063 McNicoll Ave, Toronto, ON M1W 3W6.

Telephone: (416) 496-8403; **Fax:** (416) 497-0686; **Internet:** www.mandela-children.ca; **e-mail:** info@mandela-children.ca.

The Ernest C. Manning Awards Foundation

Established in 1982 to encourage innovation in Canada.

Activities: Makes awards to Canadian resident citizens who have demonstrated recent innovative talent in developing and successfully marketing a new concept, process or procedure. Awards are made under the categories of the Principal Award, worth C $100,000; Award of Distinction, worth C $25,000; Innovation Awards, two awards of C $10,000 each; and the Young Canadian program, which makes eight awards totalling C $20,000.

Geographical Area of Activity: Canada.

Finance: Total annual awards C $165,000.

Board of Trustees: Ida Albo; Marjorie E. V. Dawson; Maureen Howe; David W. Kerr; Hon. Donald Macdonald; David B. Mitchell; David E. Mitchell; Dr Claire Laberge-Nadeau; Thomas B. Nickerson; John K. Read; Allan C. Shaw; Marshall M. Williams; Dick Wilson.

Principal Staff: Exec. Dir Donald A. Park.

Address: 2900–421, 7 Ave SW, Calgary, AB T2P 4K9.

Telephone: (403) 645-8277; **Fax:** (403) 645-8320; **Internet:** www.manningawards.ca; **e-mail:** manning@aec.ca.

Maranatha Foundation

Established in 1973 by Dr Donald Miller Alloway for general charitable purposes.

Activities: Operates nationally and internationally in the fields of aid to less-developed countries, education, and medicine and health, through grants to Canadian organizations for research and special projects with an emphasis on Christianity and evangelism, which included founding the Institute of Evangelism at the University of Toronto.

Geographical Area of Activity: International (through Canadian organizations).

Officers and Directors: Dr Donald Miller Alloway (Chair., Treas. and Sec.); D. Miller Alloway, Jr; Graham F. Alloway; Heather E. Alloway; Robert R. Alloway; Ronald C. Knechtel; Wendy J. Macdonald; Robert E. Morris; Dr Clifford C. Pitt.

Address: 12745 7th Concession, King City, ON L7B 1K4.

Match International Centre

International development NGO established in 1976 to promote equal rights for women world-wide, through international solidarity.

Activities: Operates in the fields of gender equality, human rights and sustainable development, working with partner groups in Africa, Asia, South America and the Caribbean in order to improve conditions and quality of life for women. Runs campaigns, awareness training and carries out research in order to work towards the elimination of violence against women in Canada and abroad. Seeks to empower women in developing countries by giving them the opportunities to improve their lives and enhance their roles, through training, community work and networking initiatives.

Geographical Area of Activity: Canada, Africa, Asia, and South America and the Caribbean.

Publications: *Words of Women* (annual publication); *Matchnews* (newsletter, 3 a year); and other publications.

Finance: Assets C $60,000 (March 2002); annual revenue C $768,249, expenditure C $894,887 (2002).

Principal Staff: Exec. Dir Madonna Larbi; Pres. Rosemary Brown; Vice-Pres. Ceta Ramkhalawansingh.

Address: 200 Elgin St, Ste 1102, Ottawa, ON K2P 1L5.

Telephone: (613) 238-1312; **Fax:** (613) 238-6867; **Internet:** www.web.ca/~matchint/; **e-mail:** matchint@web.net.

The Maytree Foundation

Established in 1982 for social welfare purposes; the organization is committed to the reduction of poverty and inequality in Canada and to building strong civic communities; seeks to identify, support and fund ideas, leaders and organizations with the capacity to achieve change and advance the common good.

Activities: Operates in three main areas: the development of social policy, through a grant to the Caledon Institute of Social Policy; a Strategic Partners Initiative, working with leaders who have the capacity to make change and advance the common good; and the Refugee and Immigrant Program, which invests in the capacity of leaders, organizations and solution-oriented ideas that accelerate the settlement of refugees and immigrants in Canada.

Geographical Area of Activity: Canada, primarily large urban areas in Ontario.

Restrictions: No funding for deficit reduction, equipment purchases, building or renovation costs, capital campaigns or endowments, partisan political activities, religious activities, legal challenges, conferences or workshops.

Publications: Annual Report; programme brochures; policy and research papers.

Finance: Assets C $23,807,977 (2002).

Officers and Directors: Alan Broadbent (Chair.); Judy Broadbent (Pres.); Paul J. Gallagher (Vice-Pres.); Colin Robertson (Treas.); Vali Bennett (Sec.); Daniel Burns; Jane Millan.

Principal Staff: Exec. Dir Ratna Omidvar; Admin. Asst Violeta Li; Man., Research and Policy Elizabeth McIsaac; Man., Grants Luna Ramkhalawansingh; Communications Co-ordinator Stephanie Saunders; Man., Leadership Development and Civic Partnership Projects Anita Srinivasan; Writer Carl Warren.

Address: 170 Bloor St West, Ste 804, Toronto, ON M5S 1T9.

Telephone: (416) 944-2627; **Fax:** (416) 944-8915; **Internet:** www.maytree.com; **e-mail:** info@maytree.com.

George Cedric Metcalf Charitable Foundation

Established in 1967 by George Cedric Metcalf for general charitable purposes.

Activities: Operates in Canada and less-developed countries in three programme areas: the performing arts, the environment and community development initiatives.

Geographical Area of Activity: International (through Canadian organizations).

Restrictions: Grants only available to registered charitable organizations in Canada; no grants to individuals or for-profit organizations.

Publications: Annual Report.

Finance: Assets approx. C $110,000,000.

Officers and Directors: Kirsten Hanson (Pres.); Johanna Metcalf (Vice-Pres.); Peter Hanson (Treas.); W.T. Pashby (Sec.); Prof. Joy Cohnstaed; Prof. David Johnston; John Lounds; Luke Metcalf.

Principal Staff: Exec. Dir J. Alexander Houston.

Address: 174 Ave Rd, Toronto, ON M5R 2J1.

Telephone: (416) 926-0366; **Fax:** (416) 926-0370; **Internet:** www.metcalffoundation.com/; **e-mail:** shouston@metcalffoundation.com.

Molson Donations Fund

Established in 1973 by subsidiaries of Molson Companies Ltd for the support of charitable organizations.

Activities: Operates throughout Canada in the fields of the arts and humanities, third-level education, medicine and health, and social welfare, through grants to charitable organizations for projects, awards, grants and research project. The Fund comprises a national committee and five regional committees. Current focus areas are: post-secondary student programs; disenfranchised youth retraining; community centres; hospital trauma units in urban areas; and United Ways across Canada.

Geographical Area of Activity: Canada.

Restrictions: Grants made only to registered charitable organizations.

Finance: Assets C $197,463 (March 2000); grants disbursed C $1,146,973 (2000).

Officers and Directors: Daniel J. O'Neill (Chair.); John Paul Macdonald (Vice-Chair.); Judy McClelland (Sec. and Donations Officer); Fergie Devins; Scott Ellis; Marieke Tremblay.

Principal Staff: CEO Daniel J. O'Neill.

Address: 33 Carlingview Dr., Etobicoke, ON M9W 5E4.

Telephone: (416) 679-1786; **e-mail:** jlmcclelland@molson.com.

Molson Family Foundation

Established in 1958 by T. H. P. Molson, Hartland de Montarville Molson, E. H. Molson and S. T. Molson to support innovative projects in the fields of the humanities, education, health and welfare, and social and national development.

Activities: Operates throughout Canada in the fields of health and welfare, education, social development, national development, and the humanities, through grants to charitable organizations for special projects. Awards the C $50,000 Molson Award for the Arts.

Geographical Area of Activity: Canada.

Restrictions: Grants are not made for conferences, seminars, publications, fellowships or scholarships; only Canadian registered organizations eligible.

Finance: Assets C $40,727,992 (1998).

Officers and Directors: Hon. Hartland de Montarville Molson (Pres.); Eric H. Molson (Vice-Pres.); Stephen T. Molson (Sec.); Rolland A. Peloquin (Treas.); M. G. Huband; M. R. McMaster; Zoe A. Murray.

Address: BP 340, Station C, Montréal, QC H2L 4K3.

Telephone: (514) 521-1786; **Fax:** (514) 598-6866.

The F. K. Morrow Foundation

Activities: Aims to promote religion, charity, education and charitable activities in the interest and welfare of the public, funding projects in the fields of arts and culture; first nations culture; film and video; libraries; education; special education; universities; health; hospitals; Christian and religious organizations; sciences; environment; social services; community services; special needs groups; sports and recreation; and youth.

Geographical Area of Activity: Mainly Canada.

Principal Staff: Contact Fern Densem.

Address: 3377 Bayview Ave, North York, ON M2M 3S4.

Telephone: 416-229-2009.

The Muttart Foundation

Founded in 1953 by Merrill and Gladys Muttart.

Activities: Aims to support the development of not-for-profit organizations in Canada, through grants for infrastructure development. Also provides grants for technological development of not-for-profit organizations, fellowships, training grants and bursaries, and a grant programme for young people, that makes grants to not-for-profit organizations working with young people.

Geographical Area of Activity: Canada.

Finance: Total assets approx. C $60,000,000.

Board of Directors: Dr R. L. Collins-Nakai (Pres.); H.A. Parker (Vice-Pres.); R. M. Claney (Treas.); Dr L. K. Penrod (Asst Treas.); Dr J. D. Calkin; M. F. Gracey; W. L. Hunter; A. L. Knight.

Principal Staff: Exec. Dir Bob Wyatt.

Address: Ste 1150, Scotia Tower One, 10060 Jasper Ave, Edmonton, AB T5J 3R8.

Telephone: (780) 425-9616; **Fax:** (780) 425-0282; **Internet:** www.muttart.org.

National Cancer Institute of Canada

Founded in 1947 to undertake and support cancer research and related programmes that will lead to a reduction in the incidence, morbidity and mortality from cancer.

Activities: Bestows grants on individuals and institutions for research, training and the purchase of equipment. Supports the Canadian Breast Cancer Research Initiative and the Centre for Behavioural Research and Program Evaluation.

Geographical Area of Activity: Canada.

Publications: Annual Report; *Canadian Cancer Statistics* (annually); application manuals.

Finance: Assets C $103,268,000 (2001) raised through its funding partners, the Canadian Cancer Society (q.v.) and the Terry Fox Foundation; annual revenue C $59,630,000, expenditure C $54,910,000 (2001).

Directors: Dr Anthony Fields (Pres.); Norm Achen; Monique Bégin; Pam Crosby; Bernard Cummings; Dr Elizabeth Eisenhauer; Dr Margaret Fitch; Dr Stuart Foster; Bruce Fraser; Dr James Friesen; Dr Abraham Fuks; Dr Brenda Gallie; Carol Hiscock; Dr Gerald C. Johnston; Dr Peter Lansdorp; Dr Victor Ling; Dr Brent Schacter; Dr Simon Sutcliffe; Dr Roy West.

Principal Staff: CEO Julie White; Exec. Officer Michael A. Wosnick.

Address: 10 Alcorn Ave, Ste 200, Toronto, ON M4V 3B1.

Telephone: (416) 961-7223; **Fax:** (416) 961-4189; **Internet:** www.ncic.cancer.ca; **e-mail:** ncic@cancer.ca.

The North–South Institute/Institut Nord–Sud

Founded in 1976, an independent, non-profit and non-partisan institute, focusing on international development; its research aims to help Canadians to understand the problems and opportunities facing countries in the developing world.

Activities: The Institute conducts research on Canada's relations with developing countries and on a wide range of foreign policy issues. The research aims to support efforts around the world to increase co-operation effectiveness, ensure development sustainability, improve global governance and enhance gender equality. The Institute publishes its research findings, and also participates in human resource development activities of the Asia-Pacific Economic Co-operation (APEC) forum.

Geographical Area of Activity: Africa, Asia and the Americas.

Publications: *Canadian Development Report; Review* (3 a year); Annual Report; briefing papers, books.

Finance: Assets C $1,495,083 2001); annual revenue C $2,349,293, expenditure C $2,422,217 (2001).

Directors: Betty Plewes (Chair.); Edward Broadbent (Vice-Chair.); Lloyd LeVan Hall (Treas.);.

Principal Staff: Pres. and CEO Roy Culpeper.

Address: 55 Murray St, Ste 200, Ottawa, ON K1N 5M3.

Telephone: (613) 241-3535; **Fax:** (613) 241-7435; **Internet:** www.nsi-ins.ca; **e-mail:** nsi@nsi-ins.ca.

Operation Eyesight Universal

Founded in 1963 to promote the prevention of blindness and the restoration of sight to people in developing countries.

Activities: The organization conducts programmes of eye care in developing countries, particularly through 'eye camps' in Bangladesh, El Salvador, Guatemala, India, Kenya, Malawi, Nepal, Pakistan, Peru and Zambia, eye care units in hospitals and mobile ophthalmic units, and the establishment of special programmes to combat blindness due to malnutrition. It makes grants to eye hospitals and gives assistance for the training of eye surgeons and ophthalmic auxiliaries in developing countries.

Geographical Area of Activity: Asia, Africa, and Central and South America.

Publications: Annual Report; *Gift of Sight* (quarterly).

Finance: Assets C $10,927,954 (2000); annual revenue C $3,971,239, expenditure C $4,022,527 (2000).

Board of Directors: Dr Art T. Jenkyns (Founder); Kenneth Shelley (Past Chair.); Brian Foster (Chair.); and others.

Principal Staff: Pres. Pat Ferguson.

Address: 4 Parkdale Cres., NW, Calgary, AB T2N 3T8.

Telephone: (403) 283-6323; **Fax:** (403) 270-1899; **Internet:** www.giftofsight.com; **e-mail:** oeuca@giftofsight.com.

Pacific Peoples' Partnership

Founded in 1975, and previously known as the South Pacific Peoples Foundation of Canada, to promote increased understanding of social justice, environment, development, health and other issues of importance to the people of the Pacific islands, and to support equitable, environmentally sustainable development and social justice in the region.

Activities: The Partnership is primarily an educational organization which seeks to raise the profile of the Pacific island nations and territories internationally. It provides and supports educational programmes and print and audio-visual materials on Pacific island issues; encourages links between Canadian and Pacific island organizations working in similar areas, and between indigenous peoples in Canada and the Pacific; holds conferences and training courses; provides direct and indirect support to projects in the Pacific; and operates an international internship programme.

Geographical Area of Activity: Canada and the Pacific islands.

Restrictions: Grants only to specific organizations.

Publications: *Tok Blong Pasifik* (quarterly); videos.

Finance: Budget approx. C $200,000.

Board of Directors: Dr James Boutilier (Emer. Pres.); Jack Lakavich (Pres.); Elaine Monds (Vice-Pres.).

Principal Staff: Exec. Dir Rita Parikh.

Address: 1921 Fernwood Rd, Victoria, BC V8T 2Y6.

Telephone: (250) 381-4131; **Fax:** (250) 388-5258; **Internet:** www.sppf.org; **e-mail:** sppf@sppf.org.

Partnership Africa Canada—PAC

Founded in 1986, PAC is a coalition of Canadian and African NGOs promoting and engaging in research and action to help African countries in need.

Activities: Operates in sub-Saharan Africa in the fields of peace, justice and sustainable development, by helping its

African and Canadian members strengthen their skills in the area of policy and advocacy relating to issues of sustainable human development. Promotes policies that foster sustainable human development and a greater understanding of, and commitment to, sustainable human development in sub-Saharan Africa, among both Canadian and African people.

Geographical Area of Activity: Africa.

Restrictions: No grants available.

Publications: Annual Report; *The Heart of the Matter: Sierra Leone, Diamonds and Human Security; Peace and Development in Northern Somalia—Opportunities and Challenges; Local Initiatives in the Great Lakes—community voices and sustainable development.*

Finance: Total revenue and expenditure C $604,773 (March 2002).

Board of Directors: Flora MacDonald (Pres.); Jacqueline N'Koyok (Vice-Pres.); Marie-Helene Bonin (Sec. and Treas.); Kebede Asrat; Pierre Beaudet; John Mwaniki; Matthew Pearce; Anita Sheth; Aristide Sokambi.

Principal Staff: Exec. Dir Bernard Taylor.

Address: 323 Chapel St, Ottawa, ON K1N 7Z2.

Telephone: (613) 237-6768; **Fax:** (613) 237-6530; **Internet:** www.partnershipafricacanada.org; **e-mail:** pac@web.ca.

Pearson Peacekeeping Centre

Established in 1994 by the Canadian Government, and formerly known as the Lester B. Pearson Canadian International Peacekeeping Centre, the Centre is a division of the Canadian Institute of Strategic Studies. It aims to support and increase the Canadian contribution to international peace and stability.

Activities: Provides research, education and training in international peace-keeping. Conducts seminars and courses on the subjects of world peace, produces a number of related publications each year through its publishing arm The Canadian Peacekeeping Press, and funds mobile training teams in Canada and abroad. Awards scholarships to university students and NGOs, and takes an active role in the New Peacekeeping Partnership (consisting of those organizations and individuals in Canada that work to improve peace-keeping operations).

Geographical Area of Activity: Canada.

Publications: *Peacekeeping and International Relations* (6 a year); Annual Report; booklets; periodicals and 8–10 books a year.

Officers and Directors: Sandra L. Dunsmore (Pres.); Kenneth L. Osman (Chair.); G. Côte-Harper (Vice-Chair.); H. Klepak; L. Marchand; B. Martin; A. P. Rasiulis; E. M. Riddell-Dixon; J. A Simons; Hon. J. J. Blais (Chair. Emer.).

Address: Cornwallis Park, POB 100, Clementsport, NS B0S 1B0.

Telephone: (902) 638-8611; **Fax:** (902) 638-8888; **Internet:** www.cdnpeacekeeping.ns.ca; **e-mail:** info@peaceoperations.org.

Presbyterian World Service and Development

Established as the agency of the Presbyterian Church in Canada, aiming to improve the quality of life in developing countries and to educate congregations about world-wide needs.

Activities: Operates mainly in the field of international development, providing long-term solutions to the problems caused by poverty in communities and villages in Central America, Africa and Asia, promoting self-help and restoring human dignity to those in need. Supports projects in the fields of education, health care, clean water and sanitation, agriculture and food security. Also provides emergency relief to victims of natural and man-made disasters, including work with refugees. Promotes awareness and understanding of development issues within Canada.

Geographical Area of Activity: International.

Publications: *PWS Development* (newsletter, 2 a year).

Finance: Total income C $2,878,464, expenditure C $3,103,988 (2001).

Principal Staff: Dir Richard Fee; Jean-Frédéric Beauchesne; Colleen McCue; Karen Watts Plater; Guy Smagghe.

Address: 50 Wynford Dr., Toronto, ON M3C 1J7.

Telephone: (416) 441-1111; **Fax:** (416) 441-2825; **Internet:** www.presbyterian.ca/pwsd; **e-mail:** pwsd@presbyterian.ca.

Primate's World Relief and Development Fund

Established in 1959 by the General Synod of the Anglican Church of Canada as the official relief and development agency of the Anglican Church of Canada The fund is committed to international development work.

Activities: Operates in the fields of justice, human rights and political advocacy (non-partisan), as well as community development. Helps local partners in developing countries to provide long-term solutions to the causes of suffering and disaster. Also provides emergency relief to victims of crisis, and to protect refugees. A percentage of funds is reserved for work with Canada's indigenous population for land claims, self-determination and aboriginal rights. Works to educate and advocate for change.

Geographical Area of Activity: International.

Publications: Annual Report; *Under the Sun* (quarterly).

Finance: Total revenue C $5,122,850, total expenditure C $4,936,122 (March 2002).

Principal Staff: Exec. Dir Andrew Ignatieff.

Address: 600 Jarvis St, Toronto, ON M4Y 2J6.

Telephone: (416) 924-9199; **Fax:** (416) 924-3483; **Internet:** www.pwrdf.org; **e-mail:** ppakyam@pwrdf.org.

Pueblito Canada

An international development organization that aims to improve the quality of life and build a better future for children in Central and South America and the Caribbean.

Activities: Operates in the fields of child care, health care and education. Funds grass-roots NGOs in Central and South America and the Caribbean that aim to provide long-term sustainable development for families, and especially children, who suffer the effects of poverty, including illiteracy, malnutrition, pollution, abuse and abandonment.

Geographical Area of Activity: Central and South America and the Caribbean.

Publications: *El Puente* (occasional newsletter); Annual Report.

Finance: Funded by donations and by the Canadian International Development Agency.

Principal Staff: Exec. Dir Miriam Castaneda.

Address: 720 Spadina Ave, Ste 304, Toronto, ON M5S 2T9.

Telephone: (416) 963-8846; **Fax:** (416) 963-8853; **Internet:** www.pueblito.org; **e-mail:** pueblito@pueblito.org.

RBC Foundation

Established in 1993 by the Royal Bank of Canada for general charitable purposes. Formerly known as the Royal Bank of Canada Charitable Foundation.

Activities: Operates throughout Canada in the fields of the arts and humanities, conservation and the environment, education, medicine and health, and social welfare, through grants to organizations for programmes, projects, awards, fellowships and scholarships, operating funds, etc. RBC Financial Group is committed to contributing at least one per cent of average annual net income before tax.

Geographical Area of Activity: Canada.

Restrictions: Grants are not made for conferences or seminars, nor to individuals.

Publications: *Community Report*.

Finance: Grants disbursed approx. C $27,000,000 (2001).

Officers and Directors: P. Gauthier (Chair.); J. E. Cleghorn; G. A. Cohon; G. N. Cooper; J. E. Lawson; H.T. Richardson; A. R. Taylor.

Address: Royal Bank Plaza, South Tower, 9th Floor, Toronto, ON M5J 2J5.

Telephone: (416) 974-3113; **Fax:** (416) 974-0624; **Internet:** www.royalbank.com/community.

Richelieu International

Founded in 1944 by Horace Viau to promote the social and cultural needs of the francophone population of Canada. The Richelieu International Foundation was created in 1977.

Activities: Operates in the French-speaking regions of the world in the fields of the arts and humanities, education, and medicine and health, through self-conducted programmes, grants to individuals and institutions, scholarships and fellowships, and prizes.

Geographical Area of Activity: French-speaking communities in North America, Europe, Africa and the Caribbean.

Publications: *Le P'tit Bulletin* (on-line newsletter); and downloadable reports and information leaflets.

Administrative Council: Patrice Forget (Pres.); Raymond Gionet (Pres. Foundation); Jacques Tremblay (Vice-Pres.); Jacques G. Albert; Jean-Luc Bélanger; Roger Brisson; Armand Devoe; Janita Kinowski; Alfred Michel.

Principal Staff: Dir-Gen. Laurier Thériault.

Address: 1010 rue Polytek, bureau 25, Ottawa, ON K1J 9J1.

Telephone: (613) 742-6911; **Fax:** (613) 742-6916; **Internet:** www.richelieu.org; **e-mail:** international@richelieu.org.

Rights and Democracy

Established in 1988 by the Canadian Parliament, and formerly known as the International Centre for Human Rights and Democratic Development; an independent and non-partisan non-profit organization, which aims to promote the universal values of human rights and democracy worldwide.

Activities: Operates internationally, principally in Guatemala, Haiti, Indonesia, Kenya, Mexico, Myanmar, Nigeria, Pakistan, Peru, Rwanda, Thailand and Togo, in the fields of human rights, in four principal areas: democratic development and justice; women's rights; the rights of indigenous peoples; and globalization and human rights, with two additional focus points, International Human Rights Advocacy and Urgent Action and Important Opportunities. Works in collaboration with Canadian and foreign NGOs and governments to support advocacy and capacity building initiatives. Aims to increase public awareness of human rights issues, and sponsors research, conferences and publications. Makes grants as well as managing its own projects and awarding prizes, including the annual John Humphrey Freedom Award, worth C $25,000.

Geographical Area of Activity: International.

Publications: *Libertas* (newsletter); *Democratic Development* (series of publications); Annual Report; occasional papers.

Finance: Total assets C $1,924,879 (March 2002); total revenue C $4,882,126, total expenditure C $5,425,429 (2002).

Board of Directors: Kathleen Mahoney (Chair.); Jean-Louis Roy (Pres.); Rebecca Cook; John Fryer; Lydia A. Hwitsum; Suzanne Laporte; Sofia Macher; Wayne MacKay; David Matas; Vitit Muntarbhorn; Willy Munyoki Mutunga; Michèle Rouleau; Peter C. Turner.

Principal Staff: Pres. Jean-Louis Roy; Regional Officer (Africa) Akouété Akakpo-Vidah, (Americas) Madeleine Desnoyers, (Asia) Micheline Lévesque.

Address: 1001 blvd de Maisonneuve est, bureau 1100, Montréal, QC H2L 4P9.

Telephone: (514) 283-6073; **Fax:** (514) 283-3792; **Internet:** www.ichrdd.ca; **e-mail:** ichrdd@ichrdd.ca.

Rooftops Canada Foundation

Established in 1984 to support community housing projects in developing countries.

Activities: Provides technical assistance to community-based and co-operative housing organizations in less-developed countries; training and capacity building for NGOs; conducts educational programmes; and maintains a library.

Geographical Area of Activity: International.

Restrictions: Grants only to community-based housing organizations.

Publications: *Program Report* (annually).

Finance: Budget C $1,000,000.

Principal Staff: Dir Barry Pinsky.

Address: 2 Berkeley St, Ste 207, Toronto, ON M5A 2W3.

Telephone: (416) 366-1445; **Fax:** (416) 366-3876; **Internet:** www.rooftops.ca; **e-mail:** info@rooftops.ca.

Salamander Foundation

Established in 1965 by Richard G. Ivey; originally known as the Richard and Jean Ivey Fund.

Activities: Makes grants to Canadian registered charities, within the fields of arts and culture, and environmental health, with particular emphasis on resource management and pollution and environmental degradation and their impacts on ecosystems and human health. Consideration is also given to issues and projects which serve as models replicable in other jurisdictions, which could benefit a broad population base; or may be of national significance.

Geographical Area of Activity: Canada, primarily Ontario.

Restrictions: No grants for annual appeals, buildings, capital campaigns, conferences or seminars, deficit financing, emergency funds, seed funding, bursaries, scholarships or individuals.

Finance: Total grants C $518,300 (2002).

Directors and Officers: Nan Shuttleworth (Pres.); Paul O. Gratias (Sec. and Treas.); Peter M. Adamson; Martha Shuttleworth; H. Lorraine Shuttleworth; Keith L. Sumner.

Principal Staff: Pres. Nan Shuttleworth.

Address: 50 Park Rd, Toronto, ON M4W 2N5.

Telephone: (416) 972-9200; **Fax:** (416) 972-9198; **Internet:** www.salamanderfoundation.org; **e-mail:** general@salamanderfoundation.org.

Seagull Foundation

Established by the Seagull Pewter Company to protect the environment.

Activities: Aims to protect the natural world and the environment, through tree planting and land preservation initiatives and environmental education and a range of other conservation and environmental activities.

Geographical Area of Activity: Canada.

Finance: Seagull Pewter Company has pledged to donate 10% of annual profits to the Foundation.

Address: c/o Seagull Pewter, Durham St, POB 370 Pugwash, NS B0K 1L0.

Internet: shop.timwebworks.com/seagull_car1/foundation_main.asp.

The Sharing Way

The relief and development department of Canadian Baptist Ministries. Aims to promote self-reliance, social justice and peace in grass-roots communities in the developing world.

Activities: Provides relief to victims of natural and man-made disasters around the world. The majority of funds, however, are used to support long-term development projects in Central and South America, Africa, Asia and Europe, including Bolivia, Brazil, El Salvador, Ethipia, Ghana, India, Kenya and Rwanda. Programmes include a partnership with the Canadian Foodgrains Bank (CFGB) distributing cash and crops received from farmers, churches and other groups.

Geographical Area of Activity: International.

Publications: *Meet the Neighbours; Food for All.*

Address: 7185 Millcreek Dr., Mississauga, ON L5N 5R4.

Telephone: (905) 821-3533; **Fax:** (905) 826-3441; **Internet:** www.cbmin.org/share/index.html; **e-mail:** thesharingway@cbmin.org.

Shastri Indo-Canadian Institute

Founded in 1968 by the Governments of Canada and India to enhance mutual understanding between the two countries.

Activities: Operates internationally in the fields of development studies, the humanities and social sciences, management and law. Fellowships for research and study, and language training in India, are offered to junior and senior scholars in Canada. The Institute's Library Programme acquires Indian documents and publications for scholarly use in Canada, and Canadian publications are presented to Indian institutions. It also organizes international academic conferences, runs an educational resources programme for Canadian schools and a summer programme when funding is available, co-ordinates a visiting lecturer programme for Canadian universities, and supports the growth of Canadian studies at Indian universities and of development studies at Canadian universities. Twenty-one Canadian universities and the Canadian Museum of Civilization are members of the Institute.

Geographical Area of Activity: South Asia and Canada.

Restrictions: Grants only for Canadians or landed immigrants to go to India, or for Indians from India to go to Canada.

Publications: *Shastri News* (newsletter, 2 a year).

Principal Staff: Pres. Dr Leona Anderson; Vice-Pres. India Dr Om Kamra; Exec. Dir Lavinia Mohr.

Address: University of Calgary, Education Tower, Rm 1402, 2500 University Dr., NW, Calgary, AB T2N 1N4; (India Office) 5 Bhai Vir Singh Marg, New Delhi 110 001, India.

Telephone: (403) 220-7467; (11) 23746417 (New Delhi); **Fax:** (403) 289-0100; (11) 23746416 (New Delhi); **Internet:** www.ucalgary.ca/~sici; **e-mail:** sici@ucalgary.ca.

Steelworkers Humanity Fund

Labour-based NGO, established in 1985 by the United Steelworkers of America, to support development, relief and social justice issues, both nationally and internationally.

Activities: The Fund has four broad main areas of interest: project support, education, exchange, and policy and advocacy. It is involved in social and development issues in Canada, setting up health clinics, credit unions, day-care centres and housing co-operatives for its members and others in the community. Works internationally in the fields of workers' rights, food self-sufficiency, structural adjustment and north/south relations. The Fund is an active member of NGO coalitions with policy and advocacy objectives worldwide.

Geographical Area of Activity: Africa, Central and South America and Canada.

Publications: Bulletins.

Finance: Funded by a wage deduction system, negotiated by the workers. Annual budget approx. C $1,700,000.

Board of Directors: Lawrence McBrearty (Pres.).

Address: 234 Eglington Ave East, 8th Floor, Toronto, ON M4P 1K7.

Telephone: (416) 487-1571; **Fax:** (416) 482-5548; **Internet:** www.uswa.ca/eng/humanity/humanity_fund.htm; **e-mail:** shf@uswa.ca.

Nathan Steinberg Family Foundation

Established in 1967 for general charitable purposes.

Activities: Operates in Canada, Israel and the USA in the fields of the arts and humanities, education, medicine and health (including cancer research and services), and social services (in particular Jewish organizations).

Geographical Area of Activity: Canada, Israel and the USA.

Restrictions: The Foundation does not currently accept applications.

Officers and Directors: Lewis Steinberg (Pres.); Murray Steinberg (Vice-Pres.); H. Arnold Steinberg (Sec. and Treas.); Marc Steinberg.

Address: 3500 de Maisonneuve West, Ste 900, Montréal, QC H3Z 3C1.

Telephone: (514) 931-7500.

Street Kids International

Founded in 1988 by Peter Dalglish; aims to help children living and working on the streets in cities around the world to help themselves.

Activities: Operates in less-developed countries of Africa, Central Asia and South America, by providing training and educational resources to youth workers and educators so that they can help and educate street children about the dangers of HIV and drug abuse, and to deal with problems of sexuality and risk behaviour. Also runs various projects for street children, including business start-up programmes.

Geographical Area of Activity: Africa, Central Asia and South America.

Finance: Total assets C $217,700 (2001); annual revenue C $1,506,000, expenditure C $1,242,000 (2001).

Board of Directors: 12 members.

Principal Staff: Exec. Dir Rosemary McCarney.

Address: 38 Camden St, Ste 201, Toronto, ON M5V 1V1.

Telephone: (416) 504-8994; **Fax:** (416) 504-8977; **Internet:** www.streetkids.org; **e-mail:** ski@streetkids.org.

Joseph Tanenbaum Charitable Foundation

Established in 1967 by Joseph Tanenbaum for general charitable purposes.

Activities: Operates in the fields of aid to less-developed countries, the arts and humanities, education, health and welfare, and social welfare, through grants to organizations involved in the areas of education (including international education and community colleges), disabled children, international relief (including medical services), Jewish social services and medical research.

Geographical Area of Activity: International.

Restrictions: Grants are primarily given to Jewish organizations.

Officers and Directors: Kurt Rothschild (Pres.); Gerald Abramoff; Arthur David Goldwasser; Rabbi Uri Kaufman; Rabbi Nota Schiller; Rabbi Baruch Taub.

Principal Staff: Pres. Kurt Rothschild.

Address: 3101 Bathurst St, Ste 501, Toronto, ON M6A 2A6.

Terre Sans Frontières

Created in 1981 by les Frères de l'instruction chrétienne du Québec; a non-profit organization involved in international development projects.

Activities: Operates in the areas of self-sufficiency and sustainable development, through programmes offered in partnership with associated organizations to groups of individuals in developing countries, particularly in parts of Africa, Haiti and Honduras. Also works to increase the awareness of Canadians of development issues. Support offered includes micro-credit and grants to institutions, as well as providing skilled volunteers.

Geographical Area of Activity: Africa, and Central America and the Caribbean.

Finance: Annual budget approx. C $18,000,000 (2001/02).

Administrative Council: Joseph Bourgeois (Pres.); Denise Favreau (Vice-Pres.); Jacques L'Heureux (Treas.); Laurier Labonté (Sec.).

Principal Staff: Exec. Dir Robert Gonneville.

Address: 399 rue des Conseillers, Ste 23, La Prairie, QC J5R 4H6.

Telephone: (450) 659-7717; **Fax:** (450) 659-2276; **Internet:** www.terresansfrontieres.ca; **e-mail:** tsf@terresansfrontieres.ca.

USC Canada

Established in 1945, an international development organization that works in partnership with people in Africa and Asia to overcome the effects of poverty.

Activities: Operates in collaboration with local organizations in less-developed countries of Africa and Asia (Bangladesh, Timor Leste, Indonesia, Mali and Nepal) in the fields of water, health, income generation, training and education, savings and credit, the environment and food security. One of the main programmes is Seeds of Survival, a sustainable agriculture initiative, which works to provide a long-term solution to hunger in developing countries through the preservation, utilisation and enhancement of farmers' indigenous seeds and traditional practices. USC Canada also works nationally in outreach and community projects, and education to improve awareness of global issues. Maintains offices in Bangladesh, Nepal, East Timor and Mali.

Geographical Area of Activity: Africa, Asia and Canada.

Finance: Financed by donations and grants, and by the Canadian International Development Agency.

Principal Staff: Exec. Dir A. Thomson; Dir of Int. Programmes L. Breuer; Communications Man. M. Trenholm; Fundraising Officer J. S. Luczak.

Address: 56 Sparks St, Ste 705, Ottawa, ON K1P 5B1.

Telephone: (613) 234-6827; **Fax:** (613) 234-6842; **Internet:** www.usc-canada.org; **e-mail:** info@usc-canada.org.

R. Howard Webster Foundation

Established in 1967 to make grants to hospitals, universities and for general charitable purposes.

Activities: Operates throughout Canada in the fields of the arts and humanities, education, medicine and health, and social welfare, funding scholarships and fellowships.

Geographical Area of Activity: Canada.

Officers and Directors: Lorne C. Webster (Chair.); Norman E. Webster (Pres.); W. Ronald Shaw (Sec.); Howard W. Davidson (Treas.); Sherry Eaton; Margaret Gallagher; Lucy Grossman-Hensel; Hugh Hallward; Nancy McFadyen; Anthony Taylor; Meredith Webster; Peter W. Webster; Philip L. Webster.

Address: 1155 René-Levesque Blvd West, Ste 2912, Montréal, QC H3B 2L5.

Telephone: (514) 866-2424; **Fax:** (514) 866-9918.

Wild Rose Foundation

Established in 1984 by the Government of Alberta and financed by Alberta's Lottery Fund, to provide funding to non-profit volunteer organizations providing services to Albertans; to foster or promote the use of volunteers, or assist those who volunteer or use the services of volunteers in Alberta; and to foster or promote charitable, philanthropic, humanitarian or public-spirited acts or assist those who perform them.

Activities: Operates in Alberta and internationally through various volunteer and financial support programmes, including the Quarterly Grants programme, International Volunteer Exchange programme, the International Development Grants programme, the Youth Grant programme, the Volunteerism Awards Programme, the Volunteer Week Initiative, the Youth Initiatives Grant Programme and Vitalize Provincial Volunteer conference.

Geographical Area of Activity: Canada (Alberta) and international (especially developing countries and countries in transition).

Restrictions: No grants are made to individuals.

Publications: Brochures on programmes; international development and quarterly grants programme guidelines.

Finance: The Foundation is financed by the Alberta Lottery Fund. Annual expenditure C $6,600,000 (2002).

Officers and Directors: Krishan C. Joshee (Chair.); Richard Armstrong; Dick Chamney; Michael Lee; Diane Osberg; Georgette Thrasher; Eva Urlacher.

Principal Staff: Exec. Dir Noni J. Heine; Man. Pat Blakney.

Address: 907 Standard Life Centre, 10405 Jasper Ave, Edmonton, AB T5J 4R7.

Telephone: (780) 422-9305; **Fax:** (780) 427-4155; **Internet:** www.cd.gov.ab.ca/wrf.

World Accord

Established in 1980 to provide development assistance in less-developed countries.

Activities: Works in less-developed countries of Asia and Central America, in collaboration with partners in Canada and overseas, to improve the quality of life of individuals and communities in the developing world in the long term, through the building of local institutional and human capacities and encouraging participation in civil society. Funds educational self-help programmes in order to create a better future for disadvantaged people. Runs development education projects in Canada.

Geographical Area of Activity: Asia, Canada and Central America.

Publications: *Global Voice* (newsletter).

Principal Staff: Exec. Dir T. Fielder; Program Specialist S. Heathers; Resource Dir D. Barth; Admin. Asst A. Meinzinger.

Address: 1C-185 Frobisher Dr., Waterloo, ON N2V 2E6.

Telephone: (519) 747-2215; **Fax:** (519) 747-2644; **Internet:** www.worldaccord.org; **e-mail:** waccord@worldaccord.org.

World Literacy of Canada

A non-profit charitable organization, founded in 1955, which aims to promote adult literacy in Canada and abroad, raise public awareness, and to fund community literacy development programmes in Southern Asia.

Activities: Operates internationally, aiming to improve general adult literacy world-wide, in order to improve social, cultural and economic conditions. In Canada, the organization has initiated presentations, forums and national tours; supported the formation of the Movement for Canadian Literacy; and provided resources for schools and literacy groups on effective and innovative strategies. Overseas, it provides financial support for literacy programmes which integrate health, housing, vocational training, and credit and savings programmes; offers funding for teacher training, educational supplies and development of literary resources; and also arranges a variety of capacity-building programmes for human resource development at a grass-roots level. Has a particular focus on the literacy needs of poor women. Also maintains an office in India.

Geographical Area of Activity: Canada and Southern Asia.

Publications: *Worldlit* (newsletter, 2 a year).

Board of Directors: Margie Zeidler (Pres.); Joanne Norris (Vice-Pres.); Doug Shrigley (Treas.); John Monger (Sec.); Rahul Bhardwaj; Mary Fisher; Jane Glassco; Andrew Ignatieff; Alexandra MacLennan; Diane Martin; Barbara Mencke; Arlene Perly Rae; Neil Phillips; Paul Richardson; Gregor Robinson; John Stackhouse; Atul Tolia; Mark Wright; Jamie Zeppa.

Principal Staff: Exec. Dir Mamta Mishra; Assoc. Dir Alicia Homer.

Address: 401 Richmond St West, Studio 236, Toronto, ON M5V 3A8.

Telephone: (416) 977-0008; **Fax:** (416) 977-1112; **Internet:** www.worldlit.ca; **e-mail:** info@worldlit.ca.

Chairman, to support the welfare, education and cultural advancement of Chinese children, and to promote international friendship and world peace.

Activities: Operates in the areas of children's education and culture. The Foundation provides training for kindergarten teachers and scholarships for girls to receive further education. It has established a Children's Science and Technology Pavilion that provides activities for children; the Tianjin Bohai Children's World, an education and recreation centre; and the Huayin Music School. Sponsored the Red Apple Child Development Center in 2000, and promotes children's sporting activities and exchanges. It awards various prizes, including a literary prize given every two years for children's literature in China and a Children's Invention Prize; and sponsors an electric organ competition. Works in co-operation with UNICEF. Sister foundations have been established in Canada, Japan and the USA.

Geographical Area of Activity: People's Republic of China.

Publications: Books for children on a variety of subjects and documents about the life of Soong Ching Ling.

Principal Staff: There is a governing council of 73 members; Pres. Huang Hua.

Address: 46 Houhai Beiyan, Beijing 100009.

Telephone: (10) 4016304; **Fax:** (10) 4011354; **Internet:** www.sclf.org.

Colombia

FOUNDATIONS, TRUSTS AND NON-PROFIT ORGANIZATIONS

Centro Internacional de Agricultura Tropical—CIAT (International Centre for Tropical Agriculture)

Established in 1967 by the Rockefeller Foundation and the Ford Foundation (q.q.v.) to contribute to the alleviation of hunger and poverty in tropical developing countries by applying science to the generation of technology that will lead to lasting increases in agricultural output, while preserving the natural resource base.

Activities: The Centre conducts research in five main areas: crop improvement; conservation of biological diversity; pest and disease management; soil quality and production systems; and land management. It carries out this work in collaboration with a wide range of national partner organizations. While concentrating mainly on tropical America (especially the Andean zone, the Amazon and Central America), the Centre also conducts projects in South-East Asia and Eastern, Central and Southern Africa. Scientists work on a global scale in crop improvement, and in research on soil quality the Centre focuses on three major agro-ecosystems of tropical America: forest margins, hillsides and savannahs.

Geographical Area of Activity: Central and South America, South-East Asia, and Eastern, Central and Southern Africa.

Publications: *Growing Affinities* (2 a year); *CIAT in Perspective* (annual report); *Pasturas Tropicales* (tropical pastures newsletter, 3 a year); Publications Catalogue; research reports.

Finance: Core budget is provided by about 23 donor countries and organizations that are members of the Consultative Group for International Agricultural Research—CGIAR (q.v.). Additional funds for specific projects are provided by some of these and other donors.

Board of Trustees: Chair., Vice-Chair. and 14 others from 10 countries.

Principal Staff: Dir-Gen. Dr Joachim Voss.

Address: Apdo Aéreo 6713, Recta Cali-Palmira, Km 17, Cali.

Telephone: (2) 4450000; **Fax:** (2) 4450073; **Internet:** www.ciat.cgiar.org; **e-mail:** ciat@cgiar.org.

Fundación Amanecer

Established in 1994.

Activities: Proivides grants and financial support, including loans, to not-for-profit organizations in Colombia. Also provides technical suppport in the field of agriculture and agricultural technology to co-operative enterprises and grassroots organizations.

Geographical Area of Activity: Colombia.

Finance: Annual grants approx. US $1,000,000.

Principal Staff: Exec. Dir Cesar Ivan Velosa Proveda.

Address: Carrera 24, 20 A-27, Yopal, Casanare.

Telephone: (87) 554739; **Fax:** (87) 554738.

Fundación Corona

Established in 1963.

Activities: Aims to contribute to the social development of Colombia by improving the management of social processes and through innovative programmes and projects that help the poorest members of the population have access to the benefits of development. Makes grants in the fields of health, education, the environment and the development of micro-enterprises at both local and national levels.

Geographical Area of Activity: Colombia.

Restrictions: Only supports development projects in Colombia.

Publications: *Globalización y crisis económica: Incidencia en la financiación de unidades de pequeña escala; Sistema de evaluación de impacto de los programas de apoyo a la microempresa: Evaluación de los programas de apoyo a la microempresa 1997–1998; Informe de progreso educativo Colombia, entre el avance y el retroceso; Mejoramiento de la Gestión Escolar*; working papers and other publications.

Finance: Total expenditure US $2,668,277 (2002).

Board of Directors: Hernán Echavarría Olózaga; Elena Echavarría de Aparicio; María Eugenia Garcés de Campagna; John Jairo Peláez Botero; Pedro Miguel Navas; Marco Fidel Rocha; Andrés Echavarría Olano; Virginia Garcés de Sanz de Santamaría; María Inés Restrepo de Arango; Alejandro Sanz de Santamaría; Gustavo Bell Lemus; Rodrigo Guerrero Velasco.

Principal Staff: Exec. Dir Jorge Hernán.

Address: Calle 100, No. 8 A-55, Torre C, Piso 9, Santafé de Bogota.

Internet: www.fundacioncorona.org.co; **e-mail:** fundacion@fcorona.org.

Fundación para la Educación Superior y el Desarrollo—Fedesarrollo (Foundation for Higher Education and Development)

Founded in 1970 by Manuel Carvajal Sinisterra, Rodrigo Botero Montoya and Alberto Vargas Martínez to promote cultural and scientific advancement and to stimulate research into Colombia's social, economic and political problems.

Activities: Operates nationally in the fields of social welfare and political science and administration, and both nationally and internationally in the fields of economic affairs and international relations, through research, surveys, publications and lectures on an international level and through conferences and courses conducted in Colombia.

Geographical Area of Activity: Colombia.

Publications: *Coyuntura Económica* (quarterly); *Coyuntura Social* (quarterly); economic and employment statistics; more than 50 social science publications and working papers.

Principal Staff: Exec. Dir Juan José Echavarría Soto.

Address: Calle 78, No 9-91, Bogotá.

Telephone: (1) 3125300; **Fax:** (1) 2126073; **Internet:** www.fedesarrollo.org.co; **e-mail:** fedesarr@openway.com.co.

Fundación Hábitat Colombia (Colombian Habitat Foundation)

Established in 1991, to improve the quality of life.

Activities: Operates in Colombia, through promoting a better quality of life for urban dwellers in collaboration with the Government, the private sector and social organizations. Supports initiatives that encourage envionmental development, the exchange of experience and information, the establishment of strategic alliances and promote sustainability.

Geographical Area of Activity: Colombia.

Principal Staff: Contact: Jair Eduardo Restrepo Pineda.

Address: Calle 36 No 2B-09, Risaralda, 52411 Pereira.

Telephone: (6) 3263569; **e-mail:** habitatcolombia@yahoo.com.

Fundación Herencia Verde (Green Heritage Foundation)

Founded in September 1983 by a group of 30 people to protect Colombia's natural resources.

Activities: The Foundation operates nationally in the Andean and Pacific coast regions in the fields of biodiversity, conservation and the environment, through self-conducted programmes, research and publications. Proprietor of the Natural Reserve of Alto Quindio in the central Andes.

Geographical Area of Activity: Colombia.

Publications: Research findings.

Principal Staff: Exec. Dir Juan Carlos Riascos.

Address: Apdo Aéreo 32802, Cali.

Telephone: (2) 8933052; **Internet:** cali.cetcol.net.co/~fhv/; **e-mail:** fhv-adm@cali.cetcol.net.co.

Fundación Horizontes (Horizons Foundation)

A private foundation established to grant scholarship support to undergraduate students at local universities.

Activities: Operates nationally in the field of education, through providing scholarships and fellowships, and grants to individuals, including a scholarship scheme at the Universidad de Los Andes in Colombia.

Geographical Area of Activity: Colombia.

Directors: Juan Caro; Magdalena Holguín; Cecilia Mejía; Rafael Obregón; María Luisa Ortega.

Principal Staff: Exec. Dir Cecilia Mejía.

Address: Apdo Aéreo 088931, Santafé de Bogotá.

Telephone: (1) 2128962; **Fax:** (1) 2127381.

Fundación Antonio Restrepo Barco

Aims to foster the educational, cultural, and technical development, namely among children and young people.

Activities: Supports projects in the fields of health, family, social participation and income improvement, and publishes books.

Geographical Area of Activity: Colombia.

Publications: *Niños, niñas y conflicto armado en Colombia; Cartilla Prácticas culturales para la educación de la niñez*; and other related publications.

Address: Carrera 7, 73–55, Piso 12, Santafé de Bogota.

Telephone: (2) 3121511; **Fax:** (2) 3121182; **Internet:** www.funrestrepobarco.org.co; **e-mail:** frb@funrestrepobarco.org.co.

Fundación SERVIVIENDA (Housing Services Foundation)

Founded in 1972 by the Society of Jesus to develop housing programmes for low-income families.

Activities: Operates nationally and internationally. Produces, sells, finances and erects over 4,000 concrete prefabricated houses per year; has built over 79,000 houses to date.

Finance: Financed from sale of houses: approx. US $8,000,000 annually.

Principal Staff: Dir Rev. Alberto Jiménez Cadena.

Address: Avda Caracas 37–20, Santafé de Bogotá.

Telephone: (1) 3201595; **Fax:** (1) 2887605; **e-mail:** servivdg@tutopia.com.

Grupo Latinoamericano de Rehabilitación Profesional—GLARP (Latin-American Vocational Rehabilitation Group)

Founded in 1977 by a group of 10 national rehabilitation institutions and nine individuals, to co-ordinate rehabilitation services in Central and South America and the Caribbean and to create new centres, in order to reinstate as active members of the community those incapacitated by illness or other disadvantages.

Activities: The Group encourages co-operation among its members and acts as a centre for the exchange of information. It promotes at an international level the development of rehabilitation programmes, in co-operation with private and governmental bodies. It offers advisory and training services, and finance for specific projects.

Geographical Area of Activity: Central and South America and the Caribbean.

Publications: *Boletín GLARP-CEDIR* (monthly); reports; bibliographies.

Finance: Provided by subscriptions and donations; annual budget approx. US $450,000.

Principal Staff: Exec. Dir Dr Martha Aristizabal Gomez.

Address: Carrera 9A, No 93-93, Apdo Aereo 56208, Santafé de Bogotá.

Telephone: (1) 6135366; **Fax:** (1) 6135124; **e-mail:** glarp@cable.net.co.

Costa Rica

FOUNDATION CENTRE AND CO-ORDINATING BODY

Asociación Latinoamericana de Organizaciones de Promoción (Latin American Association of Development Organizations)

Established in 1979 by 11 Central and South American organizations.

Activities: Works to develop communication and co-operation between members. Promotes the rights of native peoples affected by development projects; supports the use of appropriate technology in development projects; collates and distributes information on projects world-wide; provides technical, legal, medical and emergency assistance in Central and South America and the Caribbean. Also awards prizes, and organizes conferences and training courses.

Geographical Area of Activity: Central and South America and the Caribbean.

Publications: *Tianguez* (quarterly, in Spanish); *Las ONGs y el Foro Económico Global de Davos; Exclusión, Desigualdad y Pobreza en América Latina y el Caribe; Las ONGs Bajo Escrutinio.*

Principal Staff: Pres. Eduardo Ballón; Exec. Sec. Manuel Chiriboga.

Address: Apdo Postal 265, 1350 San José.

Telephone: 283-2122; **Fax:** 283-5898; **Internet:** www.alop.or.cr; **e-mail:** info@alop.or.cr.

FOUNDATIONS, TRUSTS AND NON-PROFIT ORGANIZATIONS

Acceso (Access)

A non-profit, technical assistance organization, which aims to provide training, technical assistance and institution-building services to organizations working towards sustainable development in Central and South America.

Activities: Lends support and assistance to grass-roots development organizations, and regional, national and international institutions, NGOs, private firms and individuals in Central and South America that work in the field of sustainable development. Areas covered include programme planning, human resource development, fundraising, strategic internet use and other related areas.

Geographical Area of Activity: Central and South America.

Publications: A number of reports, booklets and directories.

Directors: Ana Elena Badilla; Stephen Cox; Alfredo Mora; Jorge Nowalski; Yolanda María Rojas; Maria Sáenz.

Principal Staff: Exec. Dir Cristina Nogués.

Address: de Farmacia la Palina (carretera a Sabanilla), 50 oeste y 150 norte, mano derecha, San José.

Telephone: 283-2726; **Fax:** 283-2748; **Internet:** www.acceso.or.cr; **e-mail:** info@acceso.or.cr.

DEMUCA—Fundación para el Desarrollo Local y el Fortalecimiento Municipal e Institucional de Centroamérica y el Caribe (Foundation for Local Development and the Municipal and Institutional Support of Central America and the Caribbean)

Founded in 1990; aims to strengthen the capacity of local governments in Central America and the Caribbean to promote human development.

Activities: Promotes the exchange of experience and information, and international co-operation between Spain, Central America and the Caribbean, in order to improve human development work in the latter two regions. Works to improve municipal finances, and raise the level of efficiency in grant-making and of basic public services in local governments, including clean water supplies and sanitation, rubbish disposal, and public transport. Also provides general support for local and regional governments.

Geographical Area of Activity: Central America and the Caribbean.

Publications: *El Régimen Municipal de Nicaragua; Organización, Funciones y Prácticas Generales de Gestión Pública; La Basura; El Agua como Servicio Público Municipal; La Gestión de los Servicios Públicos Municipales; Qué es una Municipalidad?; Memoria del Seminario Taller 'Municipio, Turismo y Desarrollo'; Contabilidad Municipal; Recolección y Disposición Final de la Basura: Un Servico Público Municipal; Los 10 Años de DEMUCA.*

Address: del Restaurante El Chicote, 100 mts norte, 50 mts este y 175 mts norte, Sabana Norte, San José.

Telephone: 290-8843; **Fax:** 290-8678; **Internet:** www.demuca.or.cr; **e-mail:** info@demuca.or.cr.

Earth Council

Established in 1992 to support and empower people in building a more secure, equitable and sustainable future; its three fundamental objectives are to promote awareness of the needed transition to more sustainable and equitable patterns of development; to encourage public participation in decision-making at all levels of government; and to promote understanding and co-operation between civil society and governments world-wide.

Activities: Operates internationally in the fields of poverty, development, environmental deterioration, population growth and patterns of production and consumption, through disseminating information to NGOs working in these fields, and supporting projects in collaboration with national and international partner organizations world-wide. Its current programme, initiated in 1996, is 'Making Sustainability Work', which includes the Rio+5 project to promote sustainable development, and the 'Towards a Millennium Earth Initiative', in collaboration with partner organizations. Promotes several on-line communication initiatives.

Geographical Area of Activity: International.

Publications: *Earth Fax; UN Fax; NCSD Network Bulletin; Implementing Sustainable Development: Experiences and Recommendations from National and Regional Consultation for the Rio+5 Forum; Implementing Sustainable Development: Summaries of Special Focus Reports prepared for the Rio+5 Forum; Implementing Sustainable Development: Proceedings of the Rio+5 Forum; The Earth Summit: Different Visions; Life Wisdom and Future* (newsletter).

Finance: The Council is funded by the Earth Council Foundation, and is sponsored by several international conservation and development groups.

Trustees: The Council has a governing body comprising 18 members drawn from the world's political, business and non-governmental communities; Amb. Frans van Haren (Pres. and Chief-Exec.); Maurice F. Strong (Chair.).

Principal Staff: Chief-Exec. Amb. Frans van Haren.

Address: POB 319-6100, San José.

Telephone: 205-1600; **Fax:** 249-3500; **Internet:** www.ecouncil.ac.cr; **e-mail:** eci@terra.ecouncil.ac.cr.

Fundación Arias para la Paz y el Progreso Humano (Arias Foundation for Peace and Human Progress)

Established in 1988 by Dr Oscar Arias Sánchez, former president of Costa Rica, to work to build just and peaceful societies in Central America.

Activities: Operates in Central America in the fields of education, law and human rights, and social welfare and social studies, through self-conducted programmes, research, workshops, training courses and publications through three main initiatives: the Center for Human Progress, which carries out work on gender studies; the Center for Peace and Reconciliation, working in the field of demilitarization, conflict prevention and the development of democracy; and the Center for Organized Participation, working in the field of law and civil society. Currently raising funds for a Museum of Peace. Also established the CEIBA database of civil society non-profits in Central America.

Geographical Area of Activity: Central America.

Publications: *Cooperación, Solidaridad y Filantropía: Viejos y Nuevos Significados en Centroamérica; De la Guerra a la Integración: La Transición y Seguridad en Centroamérica; Del Trabajo No Remunerado al Trabajo Productivo; Desafíos Humanitarios en Centroamerica; Desmorilización, Desmilitarización y Democratización en Centroamerica; Directorio de Organismos Costarricenses que trabajan con la Adolescencia; El Accesso de la Mujer a la Tierra en Costa Rica; El Accesso de la Mujer a la Tierra en Guatemala; El Accesso de la Mujer a la Tierra en Honduras; El Accesso de la Mujer a la Tierra en Panamá; Género e Identidad; Horizontes de Paz; Inventario de Organizaciones que Trabajan con la Mujer en Centroamerica; La Transición de la Vida Militar a la Vida Civil en El Salvador; Memoria Taller de Capacitación en Incidencia; Paz en Centroamérica de Nassau a Esquipulas; Relaciones Cívico-Militares Comparadas; Soldados como Empresarios* (in English and Spanish); *Taller Centroamericano de los Derechos de las Mujeres; Taller Centroamericano el Accesso de las Mujeres a la Tierra; The State of Philanthropy in Central America*; and many other publications.

Finance: Annual budget approx. US $1,000,000.

Board of Governors: Rodrigo Aria Sánchez (Pres.); Alvaro Umaña (Vice-Pres.); Olga Brenes Camacho; Rodrigo Madrigal Montealegre; Eduardo Soto Chavcarría.

Principal Staff: Exec. Dir Lara Blanco.

Address: Apdo Postal 8-6410-1000, San José.

Telephone: 255-2955; **Fax:** 255-2244; **Internet:** www.arias.or.cr; **e-mail:** info@arias.or.cr.

Fundación Costarricense de Desarrollo (Foundation for Costa Rican Development)

Established in 1973 to improve the quality of life of the underprivileged.

Activities: Operates nationally in the areas of social welfare and economic affairs, promoting the creation of small businesses, collective effort and supporting education through technical and financial assistance, and conferences and training programmes; co-operates with other national and international organizations.

Geographical Area of Activity: Costa Rica.

Publications: *Correo Gráfico* (monthly); *Ultimas Notícias* (monthly).

Finance: Annual budget approx. US $2,500.

Principal Staff: Exec. Dir William Flores Martínez.

Address: Edif. Trejos González 211, Calle 7, 2°, Oficinas 210 y 211, Avda Central y Primera, Apdo 7-1270, 1000 San José.

Telephone: 223-5735; **Fax:** 222-5770.

Instituto Interamericano de Derechos Humanos (Inter-American Institute of Human Rights)

Founded in 1980, dedicated to the promotion of, and investigation into, human rights in Central and South America.

Activities: Operates in the fields of education and human rights. Promotes human rights and social justice, and works to consolidate democracy through investigation, education, political mediation, technical assistance and the dissemination of relevant information through specialized publications. Organizes conferences, issues publications, and works with a number of other organizations and local governments. Maintains an on-line documentation centre.

Geographical Area of Activity: Central and South America.

Publications: *Boletín Infomativo* (3 a year, in Spanish; published in English as *IIHR Newsletter*); *Boletín Electoral Latinoamericano* (weekly); *Revista IIDH* (weekly); *Estudios Básicos en Derechos Humanos; Estudios Especializados en Derechos Humanos; Exodos en América Latina; Iudicum et Vita;* and more than 250 other titles including books, magazines, manuals, videos and CD-ROMs.

Principal Staff: Exec. Dir Roberto Cuéllar; Admin. Dir Charles Moyer.

Address: POB 10081-1000, San José.

Telephone: 234-0404; **Fax:** 234-0955; **Internet:** www.iidh.ed.cr; **e-mail:** instituto@iidh.ed.cr.

Red de Mujeres para el Desarrollo (Women's Development Network)

Established in 1998 as a strategic alliance among grassroots women's groups, NGO s, churches, development professionals, and international agencies, concerned for the economic development of excluded women in Central and South America and the Caribbean.

Activities: Operates in the field of women's rights by representing women at risk of exclusion in Central and South America and the Caribbean. Promotes communication and collaboration and the development and empowerment of women. Activities include publication of a quarterly newsletter; access to a database providing information on economic projects, bibliographic material and sources of financing and training; support for not-for-profit organizations searching for funding and training; and the formation of local support networks. Maintains offices in Brazil, Colombia, Curaçao (Netherlands Antilles), Dominica, Haiti, Honduras, Puerto Rico, Trinidad and Tobago and the USA.

Geographical Area of Activity: Central and South America and the Caribbean, and the USA.

Publications: Newsletter (quarterly).

Principal Staff: Co-ordination Nancy Boye.

Address: Apdo 692–2070, Sabanilla, San José.

Telephone and Fax: 922-49942; **e-mail:** mujerdp@sol.racsa.co.cr.

Côte d'Ivoire

FOUNDATIONS, TRUSTS AND NON-PROFIT ORGANIZATIONS

Alliance panafricaine pour l'environnement et le développement (Pan-African Alliance for Environment and Development)

Founded in 1991 by Dr Mansour A. Franck to promote environmental protection and sustainable development in Africa.

Activities: Operates throughout Africa in a number of fields, including aid to less-developed countries, conservation and the environment, economic and international affairs, education, medicine and health, and social welfare, through self-conducted programmes, research, grants, scholarships and fellowships, prizes, conferences, training courses and publications. Provides consultancy services. The Alliance has members in 14 countries, mostly in Africa.

Geographical Area of Activity: Africa.

Publications: *Ecodev* (2 a month, in French).

Finance: Annual budget approx. 7,000,000 CFA (francs de la Communauté financière africaine).

Principal Staff: International Affairs Adviser Lord O. Ben Allah; Dr Mansour A. Franck.

Address: c/o RECI, 01 BP 1843, Abidjan 01.

Telephone: 24-14-43; **Fax:** 24-20-33.

Comité International des Femmes Africaines pour le Développement—CIFAD

Established in July 1985; aims to alleviate poverty for women in Africa.

Activities: Provides opportunities for African women through operating in the areas of legal representation and assistance, research, fight against sexual mutilation, agriculture and rural development, micro-enterprise and training. Also aims to involve African women in the process of socio-economic development.

Geographical Area of Activity: Africa.

Publications: *Amugnan* (newsletter, 3 a year).

Principal Staff: Contact: Jeannine Bugain.

Address: 01 BP 5147, Abidjan 01.

Telephone: 22-93-84; **Fax:** 22-70-23.

Croatia

FOUNDATION CENTRE AND CO-ORDINATING BODY

Centre for Development of Non-Profit Organizations—CERANEO

Activities: Promotes the development of NGOs and foundations in Croatia through debates, lobbying, organizing conferences and networking with similar organizations. Also researches the not-for-profit sector in Croatia, contributes to public debate about foundation law, offers resources to Croatian not-for-profit organizations, and promotes the Croatian not-for-profit sector to potential international donors.

Geographical Area of Activity: Croatia.

Governing Board: Sanda Bozic; Sonja Preis-Bedenik; Zoran Pusic,.

Principal Staff: Pres. Prof. Gojko Bezovan; Admin. and Sec. Veronika Borcic.

Address: 1000 Zagreb, Jakova Gotovca 1.

Telephone: (1) 4895829; **Fax:** (1) 4812384; **Internet:** www.geocities.com/CapitolHill/9175/; **e-mail:** ceraneo@zg.tel .hr.

FOUNDATIONS, TRUSTS AND NON-PROFIT ORGANIZATIONS

Budi aktivna, Budi emancipirana—BaBe (Be Active, Be Emancipated)

Founded in 1994 by Vesna Kesic to promote women's rights.

Activities: Operates in the field of human rights, through advocacy and lobbying for the affirmation and implementation of women's rights and gender equality. Supports programmes working to eliminate violence against women; promotes the right to reproductive freedom of choice and adequate health-care; and the right to equal and full participation in all areas of society. Specific projects also include monitoring and influencing laws, women and media, SEELINE—the South Eastern European Women's Legal Initiative, women and ICT, disseminating relevant information to those affected, and providing a free legal advice telephone help-line, covering areas such as sexual violence, divorce, child custody and employment. Holds conferences and workshops.

Geographical Area of Activity: Croatia and South Eastern Europe.

Restrictions: No grants made.

Publications: Newsletter.

Principal Staff: Co-ordinator Martina Belic, Sanja Sarnavka.

Address: 10000 Zagreb, Vlaska 79.

Telephone and Fax: (1) 4611686; **Internet:** www.babe.hr /eng; **e-mail:** babe@zamir.net.

Open Society Institute—Croatia

Established in June 1992 by George Soros to work in the fields of education, the media and humanitarian aid. Part of the Soros foundations network, which aims to foster political and cultural pluralism and reform economic structures in order to encourage private enterprise and a market economy.

Activities: Operates principally in the fields of civil society, education, culture, the media, economic reform, law and public health. The Institute participates internationally in the East–East programme and the South–East programme; otherwise only citizens of Croatia are supported.

Geographical Area of Activity: Croatia; some activity in Central, Eastern and South-Eastern Europe.

Restrictions: Participates internationally only in the East–East and the South–East programmes, run by the Soros foundations.

Publications: Annual Report.

Finance: Annual expenditure US $3,812,000 (2001).

Board of Directors: Josip Kregar (Chair.); Cedo Prodanović (Vice-Chair.); Anna Maria Gruenfelder; Drazen Lalić; Slavica Singer; Aleksandar Stulhofer; Andrea Zlatar.

Principal Staff: Exec. Dir Tomislav Reškovac.

Address: 10000 Zagreb, Ilica 73.

Telephone: (1) 4855578; **Fax:** (1) 4856459; **Internet:** www.soros.hr; **e-mail:** office@soros.hr.

Cyprus

FOUNDATIONS, TRUSTS AND NON-PROFIT ORGANIZATIONS

Bank of Cyprus Cultural Foundation

Founded in 1984 by the Bank of Cyprus Group, the Foundation's policy is to promote studies on Cyprus at a professional and scholarly level. All projects are aimed at extending the study of the history and culture of Cyprus as an island of the wider Hellenic world.

Activities: The Foundation operates four major collections: coins, maps, rare historical documents and contemporary Cypriot art. Each of the collections is linked to a long-term project involving research, publications, lectures, seminars, educational programmes, and temporary and permanent exhibitions. The Foundation's first Museum, the Museum of the History of Cypriot Coinage, was opened in 1995, and the Museum of the Archaelogical Collection of George and Nefeli Tziapra Rierides was inaugurated in 2002.

Geographical Area of Activity: World-wide.

Publications: Guides to archaeological and historical monuments, Cypriot literature, Cypriot coinage, Cyprus studies, exhibition catalogues, texts of lectures on History, Archaeology and Cartography of Cyprus, volumes on the Cultural Foundation Collection, CDs and video publications.

Finance: Contributions by Bank of Cyprus.

Board of Trustees: Yiannis Kypri (Chair.); George Charalambous; Costis Colotas; Prof. Maria Iacovou; Dr Vassos Karageorghis; Nikiforos Orphanos; Dr Theodoros Papadopoullos; Andreas Philippou; Chris Phylactou; Demitris Pierides; Stella Souliotes.

Principal Staff: Dir Lefki Michaelidou; Public Relations Officer Alecia C. Anastasiadou; Curators Eleni Zapiti, Christodoulos Hadjichristodoulou.

Address: POB 21995, Nicosia 1515.

Telephone: 22677134; **Fax:** 22662898; **Internet:** www.bankofcyprus.com/cultural; **e-mail:** info@cultural.bankofcyprus.com.

Foundation Anastasios G. Leventis

Founded in 1980 by the Leventis Family, endowed with the properties of the late Anastasios G. Leventis in Cyprus, as a branch of the A. G. Leventis Foundation (q.v.), which also funds its work.

Activities: Operates in a number of areas in Cyprus, protecting and promoting the cultural heritage of Cyprus, including supporting the creation of new museums; working to preserve the environment; granting scholarships for postgraduate study abroad and at the University of Cyprus (particularly in the fields of education and science); financing publications; and working in the field of social welfare.

Geographical Area of Activity: Cyprus.

Publications: Numerous publications in English, French and Greek on Cypriot and Greek art and civilisation.

Finance: Funded by The A. G. Leventis Foundation.

Governing Board: Constantinos Leventis (Chair.); Tassos Papadopoulos (Alternate Chair.); George David; Andreas Iacovides; Vassos Karageorghis; A. P. Leventis; H. K. Leventis; Fotini Papadopoulos; Patroclos Stavrou; Theofilos Theofilou.

Address: 40 Gladstonos St, POB 2543, 1095 Nicosia.

Telephone: 2667706; **Fax:** 2675002; **Internet:** www.leventisfoundation.org; **e-mail:** leventcy@zenon.logos.cy.net.

Monagri Foundation

Established in 1991 to raise funds for the restoration of the ancient Monastery of the Archangel Michael at Monagri, near Limassol, and to develop it as a residential arts centre, providing visiting artists with access to the cultural and historical environment of the Eastern Mediterranean.

Activities: Operates internationally in the fields of the arts, with an emphasis on individual hosting of mature artists, who seek the time and space to develop their ideas. The Foundation currently provides one self-contained studio with living accommodation, and separate exhibition space. A second studio suite is planned. Applications are also invited from writers, scholars and musicians, although no applications are being accepted in 2003.

Geographical Area of Activity: World-wide.

Restrictions: The Foundation is not yet grant-making.

Publications: Artists' catalogues.

Trustees: Dr Nadia Anaxagorou-Michaelides; Prof. Demetris Michaelides; George Michaelides; Richard Sale; Rita Severis.

Principal Staff: Dir Alison Sale.

Address: Archangelos Monastery, 4746 Monagri.

Telephone: (5) 434165; **Fax:** (5) 434166; **Internet:** www.monagri.org.cy; **e-mail:** info@monagri.org.cy.

George and Thelma Paraskevaides Foundation

Founded in 1980 by George and Thelma Paraskevaides for medical, educational and cultural purposes.

Activities: The Foundation assists indigent Cypriots who need to go abroad for medical treatment, as well as making grants to medical institutions; awarding scholarships for higher studies abroad; and providing grants for cultural purposes in Cyprus (particularly conservation). Also funds the Annual Prize for Journalism and Democracy awarded by the Organization for Security and Co-operation in Europe (OSCE).

Geographical Area of Activity: Cyprus.

Address: Cosmo Bldg, Demosthenis Severis and Griva Dhigheni Aves, POB 2200, Nicosia.

Telephone: 22463798; **Fax:** 22450824.

Pierides Foundation

Established in 1974 to promote Cypriot history and civilization.

Activities: Operates in Cyprus and Greece in the fields of the arts and humanities and conservation, through offering scholarships to postgraduate students for research in archaeology, history of art and museology, financing archaeological excavations, publishing, acquiring Cypriot antiquities from abroad and organizing international symposia on the arts and humanities. Runs an archaeological museum in Larnaca and has helped establish the Contemporary Arts Centre in Nicosia, the Pierides Library of History of Art in Nicosia, the Cycladic Art Gallery and Library on the island of Syros and other museums, including the House of Cyprus in Athens, the Pierides Museum of Contemporary Art in Glyfada (Athens), the Pierides Museum of Ancient Cypriot Art at the Athinaïs Centre (Athens), the Tornaritis–Pierides–Hellenic Bank Paleontology Museum in Larnaca and Marine Life Museum in Aghia Napa. Maintains an office in Athens.

Geographical Area of Activity: Cyprus and Greece.

Finance: Assets US $8,000,000.

Trust: Popular Bank's Cultural Centre—Pierides Foundation.

Principal Staff: Pres. Demetrios Z. Pierides; Vice-Pres. Dr Sofocles Hadjisavvas; Dir Yiannis Toumazis.

Address: 4 Zeno Kitieus, POB 40025, Larnaca 6300.

Telephone: 24651345; **Fax:** 24657227.

Czech Republic

FOUNDATION CENTRES AND CO-ORDINATING BODIES

Council of Humanitarian Associations

Founded in 1990 as the Czechoslovak Council for Humanitarian Co-operation—an independent non-governmental voluntary association of 154 organizations aimed at relieving human suffering which, after the split of Czechoslovakia into the Czech Republic and Slovakia, became the Czech Council for Humanitarian Co-operation and the Slovak Humanitarian Council (q.v.).

Activities: The Council's work focuses on minority groups, the underprivileged and the disabled; it provides a database of humanitarian organizations, training for members, and organizes seminars and workshops. Operates mainly in the Czech Republic, but has worked in Armenia and with organizations active internationally. There are around 180 member organizations.

Geographical Area of Activity: Mainly Czech Republic.

Publications: Monthly review; bulletin; newsletter; conference reports.

Principal Staff: Pres. Ing Pavel Dušek.

Address: Ceskobratrská 9, 130 00 Prague 3.

Telephone: (2) 22587455; **Fax:** (2) 22587455; **Internet:** www.braillnet.cz/crho; **e-mail:** kancelar@crho.cz.

Czech Donors Forum

As association of grant-makers established in 1997 by three Czech citizens and a number of international foundations and governmental organizations, to support donor activity; improve the practice of philanthropy in the Czech Republic; and to promote the interests of donors.

Activities: Operates as a support organization for grant-making organizations in the Czech Republic through three programmes, the Programme for Foundations, the Programme for the Development of Corporate Philanthropy and the Programme for the Development of Philanthropy. Provides advisory and other services to grant-making organizations; issues publications; and organizes conferences. Internationally, the Forum co-operates through international networks of foundation centres and co-ordinating bodies.

Geographical Area of Activity: Western, Central and Eastern Europe.

Restrictions: Not a grant-making organization.

Publications: Newsletter (quarterly); *Directory of Foundations; the Economic Development for the Civil and Not-for-Profit Sector in the Czech Republic: Foundations and Assets; Foundations in the Czech Republic; Strategy for the Development of the Non-Profit Sector in the Czech Republic*; Annual Report.

Finance: Annual revenue US $79,390, expenditure US $80,940 (2000).

Executive Committee: Tána Hlavatá; Marie Kopecká; Tomáš Krejčí; Miroslav Kundrata; Jana Malovičová; Ivo Schötta; Gita Tučna.

Principal Staff: Exec. Dir Pavlina Kalousová.

Address: Štepánská 61, Palác Lucerna, 5° patro, 116 02 Prague 1.

Telephone: (2) 24215385; **Fax:** (2) 24215385; **Internet:** www.donorsforum.cz; **e-mail:** donorsforum@donorsforum.cz.

Hestia—The National Volunteer Centre

Activities: Co-ordinates voluntary work in the Czech Republic. Raises awareness of the voluntary opportunities available to the public, offers training programmes for volunteers, co-ordinators and organizations, and acts as an advice and information source for volunteers. Also helps supervise all existing regional voluntary centres thoughout the Czech Republic, and organizes the national Five Ps/Pet P programme, a mentoring volunteer programme to help children who encounter social or health problems in life and need support.

Geographical Area of Activity: Czech Republic.

Principal Staff: Int. Programmes Co-ordinator Olga Sozanska; Asst Dir Jiri Tosner.

Address: Na Porici 12, 115 30 Prague 1.

Telephone: (2) 24872075; **Fax:** (2) 24872076; **Internet:** www.hestia.ecn.cz; **e-mail:** hestia@ecn.cz.

ICN Foundation

Founded in 1992 to provide information, training and co-ordination services to support the development of non-profit organizations in the Czech Republic.

Activities: The Foundation aims to provide access to information on government regulations and training for organization personnel; to facilitate national and international communication and co-operation; to encourage greater public involvement in the non-profit sector; and to influence government policy with regard to the development of the non-profit sector in the Czech Republic. ICN has a library and an information centre, and maintains a database of financial resources for non-profits.

Geographical Area of Activity: Czech Republic.

Publications: *GRANTIS—Non-Profit Sector Monthly* (monthly in Czech, annually in English); *Directory of Czech NGOs; Compendium of Financial Resources in the Czech Republic; Guide to the Law for Not-for-Profit Organizations;* Annual Report.

Finance: Several international foundations have provided support for the Centre. Total assets 1,225,654 koruny (2001); total revenue 7,404,170 koruny, total expenditure 8,683,582 koruny (2001).

Board of Directors: Charlotte Sommer (Chair.); Roman Branberger; Irena A. Brichta.

Principal Staff: Dir Marek Sedivy; Financial Dir Vera Prevratilova; Sec. Katerina Blahova.

Address: Hradební 3, 110 00 Prague 1.

Telephone: (2) 24827310; **Fax:** (2) 24827345; **Internet:** www.icn.cz; **e-mail:** icn@icn.cz.

FOUNDATIONS, TRUSTS AND NON-PROFIT ORGANIZATIONS

Charta 77 Foundation

Established in 1989 on the initiative of František Janouch, Karel Jan Schwarzenberg and George Soros. It is a non-profit organization, an autonomous branch of the Swedish Charta 77 Foundation, promoting open society, civil society, democracy, and the development of culture, science, technology, education and international co-operation.

Activities: Operates in the Czech Republic in the fields of education, law and human rights, medicine and health, and social welfare (especially for disabled citizens). Annual awards are the literary Jaroslav Seifert and Tom Stoppard prizes; the František Kriegel prize for civil courage; and the Josef Vavroušek environmental prize.

Geographical Area of Activity: Czech Republic and Europe.

Finance: Assets US $3,000,000 (1998).

Governing Board: František Janouch (Chair.); Gita Tučná (Vice-Chair.).

Principal Staff: Exec. Dir Jan Kačer.

Address: Melantrichova 5, 110 00 Prague 1.

Telephone: (2) 24214452; **Fax:** (2) 24213647; **Internet:** www.bariery.cz; **e-mail:** charta77@mbox.vol.cz.

Civic Forum Foundation

Founded in 1990 by the Civic Forum to revive educational, cultural and humanistic ideals in the Czech Republic.

Activities: The Foundation's Board of Directors decided that from 1996 the Foundation's resources would be focused on cultural heritage issues, and that its mission would be to endeavour to aid in the protection and conservation of the Czech Republic's cultural heritage through awareness-building and the promotion of partnerships between the business, non-profit and governmental sectors, with specific attention paid to neglected monuments. The Foundation operates through self-conducted projects, grants to organizations within the Czech Republic and conservation awards. It collaborates with international organizations on several projects. Maintains a cultural heritage database.

Geographical Area of Activity: Czech Republic.

Publications: Newsletter (3 a year); *Children's Guide Book to Třeboň Chateau; Cultural Programme Information Sheet;* Annual Report.

Finance: Programme expenditure 750,000 koruny (2000).

Board of Directors: Dasa Havel (Chair.); Jana Outrata (Vice-Chair.); Olga Bašeová; František Formánek; Vladimír Grégr; Ivan M. Havel; Miroslav Masák; Radim Palous.

Principal Staff: Exec. Dir Sunny A. Stastny.

Address: Hálkova 2, 120 00 Prague 2.

Telephone: (2) 24941305; **Fax:** (2) 24941305; **Internet:** www.radio.cz/nadace-of; **e-mail:** info@nadaceof.cz.

Czech Literary Fund Foundation

Aims to promote literature in the Czech Republic.

Activities: Presents awards for prose, poetry, literary essays and literary research, including the Josef Hlavka Prize for an original piece of academic or specialist literature published in book form in the Czech Republic. Also supports cultural organizations in the fields of translation, film and television, theatre, science and journalism.

Geographical Area of Activity: Czech Republic.

Finance: Annual budget 14,779,000 koruny (2000).

Address: Pod Nuselskymi schody 3, 120 00 Prague 2.

Telephone: (2) 22560081; **Fax:** (2) 22560083; **Internet:** www.nclf.cz; **e-mail:** nclf@vol.cz.

Czech Music Fund Foundation

Founded by the Czech Music Fund in 1994. Aims to support and encourage the development of Czech musical culture.

Activities: Provides grants and scholarships to talented Czech musicians; supports musical activities, such as competitions for composers and performers, workshops and music education; holds public composition competitions to stimulate new works. Has set up two beneficial institutions—the Music Information Centre and the Czech Music Fund, which runs an instrument hire service with branches throughout the Czech Republic, and hires out musical scores and parts from other institutions all over the world.

Geographical Area of Activity: Czech Republic.

Publications: Annual Report (in Czech only).

Finance: Annual expenditure approx.6,000,000 koruny.

Governing Board: Nine members serving three-year terms.

Address: Besední 3, 118 00 Prague 1.

Telephone: (2) 57320008; **Fax:** (2) 57312834; **Internet:** www.nchf.cz; **e-mail:** nchf@gts.cz.

Euronisa Foundation

Founded in 1995 by the Moravian church in Liberec, aims to support cultural pursuits, education and to solve social problems prevalent in the Czech Republic.

Activities: Operates in the fields of health and social welfare, culture and education. Provides support services to the elderly and the infirm; funds projects working to solve health and social problems such as drug abuse, AIDS, abandoned children and alcoholism. Operates mainly in the Czech area of the Nisa Euroregion.

Geographical Area of Activity: Czech Republic (mainly the Czech sectors of the Nisa Euroregion).

Restrictions: No grants to individuals.

Directors: Zdeněk Fejfar.

Principal Staff: Dir Aleš Rozkovec.

Address: Rumjancevova 3, 460 01 Liberec 1.

Telephone: (48) 5251953; **Fax:** (48) 5102753; **Internet:** www.euronisa.cz; **e-mail:** euronisa@nextra.cz.

Foundation Civilia

A grant-making organization that has taken on the activities previously undertaken by the Co-operating Netherlands Foundations for Central and Eastern Europe (q.v.) in the Czech Republic.

Activities: Supports non-profit NGOs working in the fields of social welfare and health care, through grant-making, technical support, and developing links between such organizations. Makes grants to social care projects, including foster-care homes, community centres and retirement homes; and to health-care and crisis intervention programmes for the funding of hospices, day centres, homes for the mentally disabled, drug rehabilitation centres and shelters for the homeless.

Geographical Area of Activity: Czech Republic.

Finance: Total grants awarded 14,090,000 koruny (2000).

Directors: Pavel Bratinka (Chair.); Jiri Heller; Simon Hradilek; Karel Janousek; Miroslav Klipa; Miloslav Kotek.

Principal Staff: Dir Jaroslava Jones.

Address: Jelení 15, 118 00 Prague 1.

Telephone: (2) 33351273; **Fax:** (2) 33354709; **Internet:** www.civilia.cz; **e-mail:** nadace@civilia.cz.

Fund for the Future—Deutsch-Tschechischer Zukunftsfonds

Established in 1998, as an NGO based in the Czech Republic, by the Governments of the Czech Republic and Germany, to compensate Czech victims of Nazism.

Activities: The Fund planned to operate in the field of social welfare, funding social projects for Czech survivors of atrocities committed during the country's occupation by German forces before and during the Second World War, including Jewish and Roma (Gypsy) people, Catholics, Jehovah's Witnesses, homosexuals and political prisoners. The Fund received €84,900,000 between 1998 and 2002, with Germany contributing 84.3% of this amount.

Geographical Area of Activity: Czech Republic.

Address: Na Kazance 634/7, 171 00 Prague 7.

Telephone: (2) 83850512; **Fax:** (2) 83850503; **Internet:** www.zukunftsfonds.cz; **e-mail:** info@fb.cz.

Jan Hus Education Foundation

Founded in 1990 by Miroslav Pospíšil, Jana Kuchtová and Julie Štastná to support the development of higher education in the arts, humanities and law in the Czech Republic and Slovakia. Since 1993, the former branch office in Bratislava has operated as a sister foundation in Slovakia.

Activities: Operates in the Czech Republic in the fields of the development of education, and the development of civil society, through self-conducted programmes, training courses, grants to institutions and publication awards.

Geographical Area of Activity: Czech Republic and Slovakia.

Restrictions: Only open to applicants from the Czech Republic and Slovakia.

Publications: Annual Reports for both the Czech Republic and Slovakia; *Going Abroad to Study; The Velvet Philosophers; Granting—a Process of Grant-Giving in Foundations; Ethical Principles in Foundations' Work; The Management of Foundation Assets, a Way to Self-Sustainability of the Foundation Sector*.

Finance: Assets 35,685,947 koruny (2000); annual revenue 9,532,045 koruny, expenditure 9,134,451 koruny (2000).

Trustees: Dr Vladimir Jochmann (Chair.); Krístina Korená (Vice-Chair.); and nine others.

Principal Staff: Dir Jana Malovičová.

Address: Joštova, 602 00 Brno.

Telephone: (5) 42211577; **Fax:** (5) 42211581; **Internet:** www.vnjh.sk; **e-mail:** vnjh@janhus.anet.cz.

Tereza Maxová Foundation

Founded by Tereza Maxová in 1997 to address the social issues that lead to the abandonment of children, and to provide assistance to children's homes.

Activities: Operates in the Czech Republic in the field of social welfare, specifically that of abandoned children. Works to prevent abandonment through education; provides assistance to adoptive families, thus shortening the time that children must stay in institutions; and raises public awareness of the plight of children who have been abandoned. Also provides material support to children's homes.

Geographical Area of Activity: Czech Republic.

Finance: Total assets 4,098,027 koruny (2000).

Principal Staff: Dir Terezie Plášková.

Address: Na Florenci 19, 110 00 Prague 1.

Telephone: (2) 21733247; **Fax:** (2) 24812689; **Internet:** www.nadacetm.cz; **e-mail:** info@nadacetm.cz.

Nadace Olgy Havlové/Výbor Dobré Vůle—VDV (Olga Havel Foundation/Committee of Good Will)

Founded by the late Olga Havel in 1990, to alleviate suffering through disability and chronic illness; it was originally a clearing-house for health-related aid from the West, but has now expanded to invest in public health with long-term grants and projects, and nine branches.

Activities: The Foundation aims to raise society's awareness of the problems and challenges faced by people with disabilities and chronic illnesses, particularly in the areas of employment, education and housing; to provide organizational and financial support to humanitarian projects and for disaster relief; and to help create an integrated society. Operates the following programmes: Medical Fellowship Programme to send Czech and Slovak medical practitioners on two-month internships to North American hospitals; Sasakawa Asthma Fund, established to address the growing problem of asthma-related diseases; and the Education Fund, which awards scholarships to students with disablilities. The Medical Fellowship Programme, Sasakawa Asthma Fund and Journals Programme operate in both the Czech Republic and Slovakia, the other programmes operate only in the Czech Republic. Also distributes the annual Olga Havel Award.

Geographical Area of Activity: Czech Republic.

Publications: Annual Report; *Life in Black and White*.

Finance: Annual expenditure US $280,487 (1999).

Governing Board: Ivan Douda; Eliška Hranáčová; Jan Kašpar; Václav Malý; Jaroslava Moserová; Dana Nemcová; Diana Sternberg Phipps; Milan Tománek; Ljuba Václavova.

Principal Staff: Exec. Dir Dr Milena Černá; Int. Programmes Co-ordinator Helena Tabakhovová.

Address: Senovažné nám 2, Box 240, 111 21 Prague 1.

Telephone: (2) 24216883; **Fax:** (2) 24217082; **Internet:** www.vdv.cz; **e-mail:** vdv@telecom.cz.

Nadace VIA (VIA Foundation)

Established in October 1997 as the successor to the USA-based Foundation for a Civil Society's (q.v.) Prague office to promote and strengthen active public participation in democratic society in the Czech Republic.

Activities: Operates in the Czech Republic in the fields of conservation and the environment, human rights and social welfare, through community development (in particular the sustainable development of Czech cities and regions), the development of philanthropy, and support for NGOs. The Foundation makes grants to institutions and individuals, offers prizes (the Via Bona awards to philanthropic donors, businesses and individuals), organizes training courses and issues publications. It has also established the DataVia internet database of non-profit organizations.

Geographical Area of Activity: Czech Republic.

Publications: *Místo pro život* (A Place for Life), 1999.

Board of Directors: Ivana Svobodová (Chair.); Ivan Dvorak; Ondrej Klofac; Ludmila Nutilova; Martin Poláček; Romana Poloprutska; Vaclav Sramek.

Principal Staff: Exec. Dir Jiri Barta.

Address: Jelení 200/3, 118 00 Prague 1.

Telephone: (2) 33113370; **Fax:** (2) 33113380; **Internet:** www.nadacevia.cz/; **e-mail:** via@nadacevia.cz.

Open Society Fund—Prague

Founded in 1992 to support the building of civil society, the development of educational and cultural activities, and the promotion of intellectual co-operation between Central and Eastern European countries. The Fund is an independent foundation, part of the Soros foundations network, which aims to foster political and cultural pluralism and reform economic structures in order to encourage private enterprise and a market economy.

Activities: Supports the development of civic society, education and culture, and law reform in the Czech Republic; co-operates with non-governmental and non-profit organizations; offers educational programmes; contributes to the promotion of intellectual co-operation between Central and Eastern European countries; issues publications; and supports other non-profit activities.

Geographical Area of Activity: Czech Republic.

Publications: Annual Report.

Finance: Annual expenditure US $2,959,000 (2001).

Board of Directors: Šimon Pánek (Chair.); Josef Jara; Marie Nemcová; Ivo Sanc; Petr Stepanik; Eva Valentová; Ivan Vesely.

Principal Staff: Exec. Dir Marie Kopecká.

Address: Seifertova 47, 130 00 Prague 3.

Telephone: (2) 22540979; **Fax:** (2) 22540978; **Internet:** www.osf.cz; **e-mail:** osf@osf.cz.

Patrik for Children Foundation

Founded in 1993 by Okresní Úřad Karviná.

Activities: Works nationally, in the fields of medicine and health and social welfare, making grants to organizations that support children in the areas of education and physical rehabilitation.

Geographical Area of Activity: Czech Republic.

Restrictions: No grants to individuals; grants only made to organizations that work in the Czech Republic.

Governing Body: Olga Dlouhá (Pres. and Exec. Dir).

Principal Staff: Dr Anna Salomonová; Dr Zdeněk Moldrzyk; Dr Trina Chmelová; Dr Marie Hamplová; Dr Martin Nogol.

Address: Olga Dlouhá, Phoniatric Dept, General Faculty Hospital, Zitná 24, 120 00 Prague 2.

Telephone: (2) 24941639; **Fax:** (2) 24943051; **Internet:** www.czechdonors.cz; **e-mail:** fonia@lf1.cuni.cz.

People in Need Foundation

Non-profit NGO established in 1992, aiming to help those in need and to promote democratic freedom.

Activities: Provides relief, rehabilitation and support services to people in 20 countries, suffering the effects of disaster, war and other catastrophes. Co-operates with a number of international aid organizations in its projects, as well as working closely with the Czech media which provide free airtime and advertising space to PINF's appeals, and screen documentaries produced by the Foundation focusing on areas of crisis. Also works as an advocate for human rights and democracy, establishing the Belarusian Centre in 1998, funding Roma communities, and supports the annual Central European human rights film festival, *One World*. Awards an annual 'Homo Homini' prize to individuals who display exceptional courage in defence of peace, democracy and human rights.

Geographical Area of Activity: International.

Finance: Annual budget approx. 37,670,000 koruny (Dec. 1999).

Principal Staff: Dir Tomáš Pojar.

Address: Kavčí hory, 140 70 Prague 4.

Telephone: (2) 61134401; **Fax:** (2) 61134137; **Internet:** www.pinf.cz; **e-mail:** pinfcz@czech-tv.cz.

Preciosa Foundation

Founded in 1993 by the Preciosa company, to raise funds to support non-profit and publicly beneficial activities in the Czech Republic.

Activities: Funds projects in the fields of health care, education, the arts and culture, science and research, sports, and humanitarian work. Projects are mainly carried out in the region of northern Bohemia, but some activities are carried out throughout the Czech Republic, often in co-operation with Prague-based organizations. The Foundation has set up seven funds, to support each operational area in which it works, including the Health Fund, the Ecology and Environment Fund and the Education and Re-training Fund. These funds then distribute money to sponsor projects within that particular sphere.

Geographical Area of Activity: Czech Republic.

Finance: Total assets approx. 50,000,000 koruny; total donations since 1996 approx. 31,000,000 koruny.

Administrative Board: Prof. Vìnìk Šilhán (Chair.); Stanlislav Vohlídal (Vice-Chair.).

Principal Staff: Dir Ivo Schötta; Sec. Marcela Vojtíšková.

Address: Opletalova 17, 466 67 Jablonec nad Nisou.

Telephone: (428) 225393; **Fax:** (428) 225306; **Internet:** www.preciosa.com; **e-mail:** info@preciosa.com.

Tolerance Foundation

A non-profit NGO, made up of people who wish to implement positive changes in society through non-violent means, civil activity and honesty. Aims to encourage tolerance and mutual respect between all people.

Activities: Works to eliminate intolerance in any form, and human rights violations, through a number of projects carried out by the Foundation. These include organizing concerts against racism; chairing public meetings and organizing demonstrations to react to immediate need; conducting research, and acting as an advocate for equal rights; giving legal assistance to those sentenced to expulsion under Czech law; providing social and psychotherapeutic treatment to families affected by the Holocaust and to sufferers of other group violence; and promoting tolerance in children and young people through education programmes and publications. Works with the co-operation of other international groups with similar aims.

Geographical Area of Activity: Czech Republic.

Executive Board: Helena Klimová; Milan Pospisil; Vera Roubalová.

Address: Senovazne nám 24, 116 47 Prague 1.

Telephone and Fax: (2) 24102314; **Internet:** www.ecn.cz /tolerance; **e-mail:** tolerance@ecn.cz.

Denmark

FOUNDATIONS, TRUSTS AND NON-PROFIT ORGANIZATIONS

Aktion Børnehjælp (Action Children Aid)

Founded in 1965 to help children in need in India. Part of Emmaüs International (q.v.).

Activities: Provides funding to children's aid projects in India, as well as food and equipment, including powdered milk, blankets and children's clothes. Also distributes handicrafts manufactured in India, as well as disseminating information about the area.

Geographical Area of Activity: India.

Publications: *Aktion Børnehjælp Nyt* (quarterly magazine).

Address: Bellisvej 10, 3450 Allerød.

Telephone: 48-14-21-08; **Fax:** 35-85-03-15; **Internet:** www.aktion-boernehjaelp.dk/in.htm; **e-mail:** children-aid@vip-cybercity-dk.

Alfred Benzon Foundation

Founded by Dr Bøje Benzon in 1952 in memory of his paternal grandfather Alfred Nicolai Benzon, founder of Denmark's first pharmaceutical company, to promote biomedical research.

Activities: The Foundation's main activity is the organization of the Benzon Symposia, which concentrate on medicine and pharmacy and related sciences. It also offers fellowships to Danish research scientists undertaking study at foreign institutions, and to a limited number of foreign scientists wishing to conduct their research in Denmark. Applications for these latter fellowships must be forwarded by a Danish scientist. Grants are also made to the Copenhagen Zoological Garden.

Geographical Area of Activity: Denmark.

Board of Trustees: Prof. Arne Svejgaard (Chair.); Prof. Povl Krogsgaard-Larsen (Vice-Chair.); Prof. Niels Borregaard; Prof. Sven Frøkjær; Prof. Allan Philip.

Principal Staff: Sec. Birgit Dalgaard.

Address: Strandvejen 203, 2900 Hellerup.

Telephone: 39-62-09-37; **Fax:** 39-62-09-33; **Internet:** www.benzon-foundation.dk; **e-mail:** benzon@post1.tele.dk.

Carlsbergfondet (Carlsberg Foundation)

Founded in 1876 by Jacob Christian Jacobsen to contribute to the growth of science in Denmark; to continue and extend the work of the chemical-physiological Carlsberg Laboratory; to further the various natural sciences, together with mathematics, philosophy, history, linguistics and social sciences; and to set up and develop the Museum of National History at Frederiksborg Castle. Tuborgfondet (the Tuborg Foundation), established in 1931, merged with Carlsbergfondet in 1991; it works for socially beneficial purposes, especially those which foster Danish economic life.

Activities: Operates in the fields of science and the arts and humanities, through self-conducted programmes, research, grants to institutions and individuals, fellowships, scholarships, publications and lectures. Activities are carried out through three departments and the New Carlsberg Foundation (founded in 1902 by Carl Jacobsen) as follows: Department A, the Carlsberg Laboratory, studies science with a view to improvements in malting, brewing and fermentation; Department B awards grants to support Danish scholars and various activities including archaeological research, the Academy of Sciences and Letters, and publication of books and papers; Department C supports the Museum of National History; and the New Carlsberg Foundation supports the visual arts and architecture, chiefly through the purchase of works for art galleries and public buildings.

Geographical Area of Activity: Denmark.

Publications: Annual Report; financial statement.

Governing Boards: The Carlsberg Foundation: Prof. P. Krogsgaard-Larsen (Chair.); Prof. T. Andersen; Prof. N. Kaergård; Prof. A. Michelsen; Prof. P. Øhrgaard. **The New Carlsberg Foundation:** H. E. Norregard-Nielsen (Chair.); E. M. Bukdahl; K. Ohrt.

Principal Staff: Head of Admin Gunver Kyhn.

Address: H. C. Andersens Blvd 35, 1553 Copenhagen V.

Telephone: 33-43-53-63; **Fax:** 33-43-53-64; **Internet:** www.carlsbergfondet.dk; **e-mail:** carlsbergfondet@carlsbergfondet.dk.

Carlsbergs Mindelegat for Brygger J. C. Jacobsen (Carlsberg Bequest to the Memory of Brewer J. C. Jacobsen)

Founded in 1938 by the Carlsberg Foundation to serve the community in the practical sphere, especially purposes related to scientific work.

Activities: Operates nationally in the fields of education, science, youth projects and the arts and humanities.

Geographical Area of Activity: Denmark.

Finance: Annual budget approx. US $575,000.

Trustees: Poul Christian Matthiessen (Chair.).

Principal Staff: Sec. Finn Terkelsen.

Address: Gamle Carlsberg Vej 10, 2500 Valby.

Telephone: 33-27-33-20; **Fax:** 33-27-47-03.

Columbus-Fonden (Columbus Foundation)

The aim of the Foundation is to promote international understanding and peaceful relations between all nations of the world.

Activities: Operates through the distribution of grants.

Geographical Area of Activity: International.

Address: Enebaervej 16, 9500 Hobro.

Telephone: 98-52-02-13.

Danish Centre for Human Rights

Founded in 1987. Aims to gain and disseminate human rights information, with a particular focus on sexual and reproductive rights.

Activities: Operates in the field of human rights, engaging in research, education and disseminating information and documentation regionally, nationally and internationally. Co-operates with a number of other human rights organizations, both in Denmark and abroad. Established a student internship programme in collaboration with private companies and the Danish Industrialization Foundation for Developing Countries.

Geographical Area of Activity: International.

Publications: *As If Peoples Mattered: Critical Appraisal of 'Peoples' and 'Minorities' from the International Human Rights Perspective and Beyond; The Declaration* (CD-Rom); *Let's be Careful out there* (video); *Human Rights Education in a European Perspective; Between Culture and Constitution—The Cultural Legitimacy of Human Rights in Nigeria;*

Substantive Equality and Pregnancy (UN) Defined: Some Repercussions; Rwanda 1997: An Analysis of Human Rights and Politics; The Universal Declaration of Human Rights—A Common Standard of Achievement; Political Development and Human Rights in China: Report from Five Seminars at the Danish Centre for Human Rights; UPDATE (newsletter); Annual Report.

Finance: Total revenue 62,700,000 Danish kroner, expenditure 65,100,000 kroner (2000).

Directors: Claus Haagen Jensen (Chair.).

Principal Staff: Dir Morten Kjærum.

Address: Wilders Plads 8H, 1403 Copenhagen K.

Telephone: 32-69-88-88; **Fax:** 32-69-88-00; **Internet:** www.humanrights.dk; **e-mail:** center@humanrights.dk.

Danish Outdoor Council

Founded in 1942 as a membership organization; the Council now has 94 individual member organizations.

Activities: Works in all areas of outdoor recreational facilities and conservation, and lobbies on relevant issues, including sustainable tourism and develops environmental education projects. Operates a small grants programme involving Danish and indigenous organizations in environmental work in Eastern and Southern Europe.

Geographical Area of Activity: Scandinavia, the Baltic Region and Eastern and Southern Europe.

Finance: Small grants available of up to 250,000 Danish kroner.

Principal Staff: International Consultant Finn Bolding Thomsen.

Address: Scandiagade 13, 2450 Copenhagen SV.

Telephone: 33-79-00-79; **Fax:** 33-79-01-79; **Internet:** www.friluftsraadet.dk/; **e-mail:** fr@friluftsraadet.dk.

Danmark–Amerika Fondet (Denmark–America Foundation)

Founded in 1914 to encourage understanding between the peoples of Denmark and the USA.

Activities: Encourages educational exchange between Denmark and the USA through the provision of grants to Danes; organizes programmes; assists Danish academics in finding appointments in US institutes of higher education; awards prizes to Danish citizens. It works in conjunction with the Danish-Fulbright Commission, sharing an administration and a secretariat.

Geographical Area of Activity: Denmark.

Restrictions: Grants only to Danish citizens.

Publications: Reports (annually, in Danish).

Address: Fiolstraede 24/3, 1171 Copenhagen K.

Telephone: 33-12-82-23; **Fax:** 33-32-53-23; **Internet:** www.daf-fulb.dk; **e-mail:** daf-fulb@daf-fulb.dk.

Danmarks Nationalbanks Jubilaeumsfond af 1968 (National Bank of Denmark 1968 Jubilee Fund)

Founded in 1968 to provide financial support for both the promotion and development of artistic design in Denmark.

Activities: The Foundation gives financial support to not-for-profit organizations, and to individuals in the form of grants for the purpose of conducting studies at home or overseas, and provides accommodation expenses for visiting lecturers from abroad.

Geographical Area of Activity: Denmark and international.

Finance: Capital of 35,000,000 Danish kroner.

Principal Staff: Sec. Lillian Karstensen.

Address: Havnegade 5, 1098 Copenhagen K.

Telephone: 33-14-14-11.

Danske Kulturinstitut (Danish Cultural Institute)

Founded in 1940 (originally as Danske Selskab—Danish Institute) to stimulate cultural relations between Denmark and other countries.

Activities: Operates internationally, providing information about prominent Danish cultural, social and educational organizations, in the fields of education, social welfare, architecture, and the arts and humanities, through self-conducted programmes, lectures, conferences, professional study tours, exchange programmes, reference services and publication of books and pamphlets, all of which are organized on an international basis. The Institute's activities are based on the principle of mutuality and its information work is seen as a comparative study of cultural traditions and development. It has offices in Edinburgh, Brussels, Bonn, Poznan and Warsaw (Poland), Kecskemét (Hungary), Rīga, Tallinn, Vilnius and St Petersberg.

Geographical Area of Activity: International.

Finance: Receives a grant from the Danish Ministry of Culture, which is supplemented by donations from foundations, business sponsors and local government organizations.

Principal Staff: Sec.-Gen. Finn Andersen.

Address: Kultorvet 2, 1175 Copenhagen K.

Telephone: 33-13-54-48; **Fax:** 33-15-10-91; **Internet:** www.dankultur.dk; **e-mail:** dankultur@dankultur.dk.

Egmont Fonden (Egmont Foundation)

Founded in 1920 in accordance with the wishes of Egmont Harald Petersen, printer to the Royal Danish Court, to operate the businesses established by him, so as to raise funds for charitable purposes.

Activities: The Foundation is the owner of the Egmont Group, a multi-media group of over 100 companies, operating in the fields of publishing, radio, television, children's games, etc., in 24 countries, including countries in Western and Eastern Europe and the USA. The charitable activities of the Foundation are concentrated on initiatives that can help provide lasting improvements for children and young people. In the social welfare and health area priority is given to initiatives that seek to reduce, and if possible prevent the marginalization of disadvantaged children. In the field of education and leisure efforts are concentrated on initiatives that address and develop curiosity, imagination and creativity, stimulating a broad range of learning and strengthening new ways of acquiring knowledge, developing the communication skills of children and young people. Examples of the Foundation's work include the modernization of the Danish National Museum, a children's art gallery in the Royal Museum of Fine Art, a science centre 'Experimentarium', the establishment of the Children's Centre for Rehabilitation of Brain Injury, the 'Music as Medicine' Music Programme for Intensive Care and Recovery Patients and the Centre for the Prevention of Congenital Malformations. Since 1992 the Foundation has been involved in the 'Democratization of Pre-school Education' project in co-operation with the Open Society Foundation (q.v.) in Lithuania.

Geographical Area of Activity: Denmark and Lithuania.

Restrictions: No grants to individuals.

Publications: Annual Report.

Finance: Annual expenditure approx. €4,000,000.

Trustees: Ivar Samrén (Chair.); Mikael O. Olufsen (Vice-Chair.); Hans Egmont-Petersen; Niels Fisch-Thomsen; Jens Jordan.

Principal Staff: Man. Dir Bente Groth.

Address: Toldbodgade 10A, 2, 1253 Copenhagen K.

Telephone: 33-91-36-44; **Fax:** 33-91-37-36; **Internet:** www.egmont.com.

Fredsfonden (Danish Peace Foundation)

Founded in 1981 by Lise and Niels Munk Plum to support activities intended to promote peace and disarmament both in Denmark and world-wide.

Activities: Operates in the fields of international affairs and human rights, through the provision of grants and prizes to institutions and individuals in Denmark and other countries. Activities include awarding an annual international peace prize.

Geographical Area of Activity: Mainly Denmark.

Restrictions: No scholarships.

Trustees: Helle Hansen (Chair.).

Principal Staff: Admin. Sec. Mille Rode.

Address: Dronningensgade 14, 1420 Copenhagen K.

Telephone: 32-95-44-17; **Fax:** 32-95-44-18; **Internet:** www.fredsfonden.dk.

IBIS

Established in 1966, to provide assistance to people in developing countries.

Activities: Supports development and capacity building projects in less-developed countries; raises awareness in Denmark of problems suffered by people living in developing countries, including HIV and AIDS programmes; promotes ecologically sustainable growth; and campaigns for positive change in Denmark's foreign aid policy. Supports 170 large and small-scale projects in Angola, Bolivia, Ecuador, El Salvador, Ghana, Guatemala, Honduras, Mozambique, Namibia, Nicaragua, Peru and South Africa.

Geographical Area of Activity: Central and South America, and Southern Africa.

Publications: *Zig Zag*; Annual Report.

Principal Staff: Sec.-Gen Vagn Berthelsen.

Address: Nørrebrogade 68B, 2200 Copenhagen N.

Telephone: 35-35-87-88; **Fax:** 35-35-06-96; **Internet:** www.ibis.dk; **e-mail:** ibis@ibis.dk.

International Work Group for Indigenous Affairs

Aims to support and assist indigenous peoples around the world.

Activities: Operates in the field of human rights, specifically the rights of indigenous peoples. Supports their land rights, self-governance and independence, cultural integrity and the right to control their own futures. Works in collaboration with a number of indigenous peoples' organizations; runs development projects all over the world (especially in Africa, Central and South America, Asia and the Pacific, and the Arctic); holds conferences; engages in research; and produces related publications and documentation which it disseminates internationally.

Geographical Area of Activity: International.

Publications: *Indigenous Affairs* (periodical, 4 a year); *The Indigenous World* (annually); an extensive list of books and papers relating to indigenous rights.

Finance: Funded by the Nordic Governments and the European Union.

Principal Staff: Dir Jens Dahl.

Address: Classengade 11E, 2100 Copenhagen Ø.

Telephone: 35-27-05-00; **Fax:** 35-27-05-07; **Internet:** www.iwgia.org; **e-mail:** iwgia@iwgia.org.

IUC-Europe International Education Centre

Founded in 1985 (re-organized in 1991) by Frits Korsgaard, Dr Jacob Christensen, Dr Tom Høyem, Dr Knud Overø, Bent le Févre and Ingolf Knudsen to promote international understanding and co-operation through a variety of interdisciplinary and intercultural programmes that emphasize experiential education.

Activities: The Foundation develops and implements numerous educational programmes, including study missions for students, teachers and business people to the capitals of the Member States and the institutions of the European Union, and for North American students and teachers to Europe and European students and teachers to the USA; exchanges with Central, Eastern and Western Europe, Scandinavia and the Baltic Republics; Holocaust study; and international conferences and seminars. The IUC network includes affiliate offices in Hungary, Poland, Canada, the United Kingdom and the USA; the organization also has partners in most European countries. IUC-Europe has an International Board of Advisers.

Geographical Area of Activity: Western, Central and Eastern Europe, and North America.

Restrictions: Does not sponsor individuals, groups or programmes outside the IUC network.

Publications: *IUC-News* (newsletter).

Trustees: Nina Nørgaard (Chair.); Jette Petersen (Vice-Chair.); Kisten Dalberg; Tina Nedergaard; Ole Visti Petersen; Eigil S. Rasmussen; Bente Sibbernsen.

Principal Staff: Project Man. Kirsten Stribley.

Address: POB 150, 5700 Svendborg.

Telephone: 62-21-68-92; **Fax:** 62-20-28-92; **Internet:** www.iuc-europe.dk; **e-mail:** iuc@iuc-europe.dk.

J. L. Fondet (J. L. Foundation)

Founded in 1945 by Ivar and Knud Lauritzen to promote Denmark, with special emphasis on the support and development of its shipping industry, the arts and humanitarian causes.

Activities: Finances technical and commercial research related to the Danish shipping industry; promotes Danish and Nordic cultural activities; provides funds for social, recreational and cultural purposes; supports the training of young people in Denmark and abroad; organizes humanitarian aid; provides funding for medical research, especially in the field of preventative medicine.

Geographical Area of Activity: Mostly Denmark.

Principal Staff: Man. Laila Rasmussen.

Address: Sankt Annæ Plads 28, 1291 Copenhagen K.

Telephone: 33-11-12-22; **Internet:** www.jl-fondet.dk; **e-mail:** ira@jl-fondet.dk.

Hermod Lannung Foundation in Support of the Work for a Strengthening and Further Development of the United Nations

Founded by Hermod Lannung in November 1970, to support work towards peace, international understanding, an international legal system and arms reduction.

Activities: The Foundation supports studies, research and initiatives aimed at strengthening international peace, human rights, understanding and justice, especially concerning the development of the United Nations, and also international conferences whose aims are in line with those of the Foundation.

Geographical Area of Activity: International.

Board of Directors: The Board consists of three members: one appointed by the Ministry of Foreign Affairs, one by the Radical Liberal Party and the founder or his designate.

Principal Staff: Admin. Hermod Lannung.

Address: Landsretssagfoerer Hermod Lannung, Svinget 18, 3tv, 2300 Copenhagen.

Telephone: 32-95-72-42.

Mellemfolkeligt Samvirke—MS (Danish Society for International Co-operation)

A membership organization aiming to promote understanding and solidarity between people and, by co-operating across national and cultural boundaries, to contribute to sustainable global development and a just distribution of the earth's resources.

Activities: Provides development assistance, political lobbying and grassroots activism; membership organization comprising approximately 5,000 individual and 100 institutional members. Also maintains an on-line searchable database of Southern partner organizations.

Geographical Area of Activity: International, including Kenya, Lesotho, Mozambique, Nepal, Tanzania, Uganda, Zambia, Zimbabwe, and Central America.

Publications: Annual Report; *Kontakt* (magazine).

Address: Borgergrade 14, Copenhagen 1300.

Telephone: 77-31-00-00; **Fax:** 77-31-01-01; **Internet:** www.ms-dan.dk; **e-mail:** ms@ms-dan.dk.

Nordisk Kulturfond (Nordic Cultural Fund)

Founded in 1966 by the Nordic Council to encourage cultural co-operation in all its aspects by the Nordic countries (Denmark, Finland, Iceland, Norway and Sweden).

Activities: Grants are made to support scientific research, education and general cultural activities: for short-term projects such as exhibitions, publications and seminars; for projects of a more permanent character for a limited experimental period; for reports or studies of general Nordic interest; and for disseminating information both within and outside the Nordic region. Carries out research and issues reports and holds conferences. Projects must all involve at least three of the Nordic countries in order to be accepted.

Geographical Area of Activity: Scandinavia.

Finance: Annual expenditure 25,000,000 Danish kroner (2000).

Governing Board: Two members from each country, one appointed by the government, the other by the parliament.

Principal Staff: Special Adviser Mats Jönsson.

Address: Store Kongensgade 36, 4th Floor, Copenhagen K.

Telephone: 33-96-02-00; **Fax:** 33-32-56-36; **Internet:** www.nordiskkulturfond.dk; **e-mail:** kulturfonden@nmr.dk.

Nordita—Nordisk Institut for Teoretisk Fysik (Nordic Institute for Theoretical Physics)

Founded in 1957 by the Governments of Denmark, Finland, Iceland, Norway and Sweden to undertake research, provide training to young physicists from the Nordic countries, and promote co-operation between institutes in member countries. The Foundation operates in conjunction with the Niels Bohr Institute of the University of Copenhagen.

Activities: Promotes scientific research by supporting programmes at this and other institutes in the Nordic countries, and by awarding fellowships to physicists from the member countries. Research fields include nuclear physics, high energy physics, astrophysics and solid state physics.

Geographical Area of Activity: Scandinavia.

Publications: *Nordita News* (bi-monthly newsletter); and research reports.

Finance: Annual budget approx. 17,400,000 Danish kroner (2000).

Trustees: The Institute is governed by a Board comprising two members from each of the Nordic countries. The members are appointed by the Nordic Council of Ministers; Chair. Prof. Ole Hansen (Denmark).

Principal Staff: Dir Prof. P. Hoyer.

Address: Blegdamsvej 17, 2100 Copenhagen Ø.

Telephone: 35-32-55-00; **Fax:** 35-38-91-57; **Internet:** www.nordita.dk; **e-mail:** nordita@nordita.dk.

Novo Nordisk Foundation

Founded in January 1989, on the merger between the Novo Foundation (established in 1951), the Nordisk Insulinfond (Nordic Insulin Foundation, established in 1926) and the Nordisk Insulinlaboratorium (Nordic Insulin Laboratory). The Foundation's purpose is to provide a base for Novo Nordisk A/S, a large biotechnology company.

Activities: The Foundation operates in the Nordic countries, through conducting research into physiology, endocrinology, metabolism and other medical areas. It provides a base for the commercial and research business of Novo Nordisk A/S, and supports various scientific, humanitarian and social programmes. Awards the Novo Nordisk Prize to a Danish scientist for a contribution in the field of biology and medicine.

Geographical Area of Activity: Scandinavia.

Trustees: Mads Øvlisen (Pres); Palle Marcus (Chair.); Jørgen Boe (Vice-Chair.); Niels Borregaard; Kurt Bligaard Pedersen; Tove Funder-Nielsen; Kurt Koch; Preben Kristensen; Jan Lindsten; Mads Øvilsen; Bente Anette Skriver; Stig Strøbæk.

Principal Staff: Dir Gert Almind.

Address: Brogårdsvej 70, POB 71, 2820 Gentofte.

Telephone: 44-43-90-35; **Fax:** 44-43-90-98; **Internet:** www.novonordiskfonden.dk; **e-mail:** nnfond@novo.dk.

Rockwool Foundation (Rockwool Fonden)

Founded in 1981 by the children of the late Gustav Kähler. The Foundation's aim is to support scientific, artistic, social and humanitarian goals, and contribute to the improvement of the environment and social development.

Activities: The Foundation provides funding for a wide range of projects, including research on population and leisure activities, the labour market, immigrants and their living conditions, politicians and credibility, suicide, the shadow economy and environmental problems. It also supports numerous projects in the arts and humanities carried out by small organizations or individuals.

Geographical Area of Activity: Denmark; some grants are made internationally, via Danish organizations.

Publications: *Immigration to Denmark. International and National Perspectives* (1999).

Finance: Assets 757,200,000 Danish kroner (2000); grants disbursed 26,000,000 kroner (2000).

Trustees: The Foundation is run by a board of 10 members, three of whom are chosen by Rockwool International A/S; another one must be appointed by the Federation of Danish Industries; Tom Kähler (Chair.).

Principal Staff: Dir Poul Erik Pedersen.

Address: Hovedgaden 584, 2640 Hedehusene.

Telephone: 46-56-03-00; **Fax:** 46-59-10-92; **Internet:** www.rockwoolfonden.dk; **e-mail:** rockwool.fonden@rockwool.org.

Sonning-Fonden

Founded in 1949 by the late writer and editor C. J. Sonning to award a prize every two years for meritorious work in the promotion of European civilization.

Activities: The Sonning Prize, awarded every two years, amounts to 500,000 Danish kroner; European universities have the right to propose candidates, and the winner is selected by a committee established by the Rector of the University of Copenhagen. Former prizewinners include Sir Winston Churchill (extraordinary award, 1950), Albert Schweitzer (1959), Bertrand Russell (1960), Dominique Pire (1964), Sir Laurence Olivier (1966), Arthur Koestler (1968), Karl Popper (1973), Dario Fo (1981), Simone de Beauvoir (1983), William Heinesen (1985), Ingmar Bergman (1989), Václav Havel (1991), the Polish film director Krzysztof Kieslowski (1994), Günter Grass (1996), Jørn Utzon (1998) and Eugenio Barba (2000). Also sponsors various concerts, exhibitions and festivals.

Geographical Area of Activity: Europe.

Finance: The awards of the Foundation are administered by the Chancellor or Vice-Chancellor of the University of Copenhagen and five of the University's professors.

Principal Staff: Dir E. Davidsen Jensen.

Address: Noørregade 10, POB 2177, 1013 Copenhagen K.

Telephone: 35-32-26-26; **Internet:** www.sonningmusik.dk/; **e-mail:** ns@asc.dk.

Thomas B. Thriges Fond (Thomas B. Thriges Foundation)

Founded in 1934 by Thomas B. Thrige for purposes which benefit Danish business, particularly industry and the trades.

Activities: The Foundation promotes scientific and educational projects which, in the opinion of its Board of Trustees, are of importance to the wellbeing of Danish business and industry. It provides grants to Danish universities and research institutes for specialized equipment, and finances study tours abroad for Danish researchers and participation in international conferences by Danish experts; it also gives grants to visiting professors from abroad.

Geographical Area of Activity: Denmark.

Publications: Annual report and accounts.

Board of Trustees: Poul Svanholm (Chair.).

Principal Staff: Man., Sec. Claus Ehlers.

Address: Tuborg Nord, Strandvejen 64L, 2900 Hellerup.

Telephone: 39-61-50-30; **Fax:** 39-61-50-31.

Folmer Wisti Foundation for International Understanding

Founded in 1974 by Folmer Wisti to contribute to international understanding and co-operation on issues of importance in daily life at local and regional level, the support of decentralization and regionalism, and the exchange of experience and ideas primarily in the fields of culture and general education.

Activities: Operates in Europe. The Foundation sponsors the 'Europe of Regions' conference on decentralization and regional autonomy; and supports activities of the Danish Cultural Institute (q.v.). Institutions eligible for support must be independent of party politics, non-profit-making and non-governmental.

Geographical Area of Activity: Europe.

Restrictions: No grants to individuals.

Publications: *Industrial Life in Denmark, The Faroe Islands and Greenland; Danish Foundations; Regional Contact* (vols 1–16, journal for the exchange of ideas and experiences in regionalism).

Finance: Assets 12,000,000 Danish kroner (2001).

Principal Staff: Chair. Helle Wisti; Deputy Chair. Finn Andersen.

Address: Gammel Vallerødvej 26, 2960 Rungsted Kyst.

Telephone: 45-86-13-36; **Fax:** 45-86-13-46.

Dominica

FOUNDATION CENTRE AND CO-ORDINATING BODY

East Caribbean Organization of Development Foundations—ECODEF

Established in 1987 as a regional organization of national development foundations of Antigua and Barbuda, Barbados, Dominica, Grenada, Montserrat, Saint Christopher and Nevis, Saint Lucia and Saint Vincent and the Grenadines.

Activities: Offers financial and technical assistance to, and aims to foster the institutional development of, national development foundations; promotes the establishment of small businesses and administers a regional Micro/Small Enterprise Credit Programme for its member foundations; promotes women's empowerment; supports networking between its member foundations and between member foundations and other organizations working in the field of economic development in the Eastern Caribbean.

Geographical Area of Activity: Eastern Caribbean.

Publications: Annual Report; *Development* (annually); Newsletter.

Finance: Annual budget approx. US $300,000.

Principal Staff: Regional Dir Milton F. Lawrence.

Address: 9 Great Marlborough St, POB 976, Roseau.

Telephone: 448-8808; **Fax:** 448-4368.

Dominican Republic

FOUNDATION CENTRES AND CO-ORDINATING BODIES

Fundación Solidaridad (Solidarity Foundation)

Established in 1991 to promote sustainable development in urban and rural communities, and to promote democracy.

Activities: Offers education, capacity-building and development services to non-profits in the Dominican Republic. Supports the structural development of community organizations, as well as co-ordinating networking activities between community organizations and the private sector and providing information and resources. Also supports the development of democracy and youth education projects.

Geographical Area of Activity: Dominican Republic.

Publications: Numerous publications on democracy and development issues.

Board of Directors: Claudio Lugo Pérez (Pres.); Mariana Moreno (Sec.); José de Luna (Treas.); Alfredo Alonzo; Juan Castillo; Olga Luciano.

Principal Staff: Exec. Dir Juan Castillo.

Address: Avda Francia 40, Apdo Postal 129-2, Santiago.

Telephone: 971-5400; **Fax:** 587-3656; **Internet:** www.solidaridad.org.do; **e-mail:** f.solidaridad@codetel.net.do.

Solidarios—Consejo de Fundaciones Americanas de Desarrollo (Council of American Development Foundations)

Founded in 1972 by representatives of national development foundations in Central and South American and Caribbean countries to exercise multinational representation of its members; to assist and support the individual and collective work of its members; to co-ordinate joint programmes; to stimulate the participation of the private sector in social development activities; to make available the necessary information to extend and improve the work of its members; and to administer funds for development programmes carried out by its members.

Activities: Provides technical assistance, training services and 'soft' loans to members carrying out social and economic development programmes in their own countries. Consists of 13 members organizations based in 12 Central and South American countries.

Geographical Area of Activity: Central and South America and the Caribbean.

Publications: *SOLIDARIOS* (quarterly); *Catálogo de Fundaciones Latinoamericanas y del Caribe* (2 or 3 a year); Annual Report.

Finance: Budget approx. US $300,000.

Executive Committee: Mercedes Pimentel (Pres.); Edgar Guardia (Vice-Pres.); E. Fernández (Sec.-Gen.); Amalia Arango; Guillermo Martínez; Morella Ramírez.

Address: POB 620, Gustavo A. Mejía Ricart 68, 2nd Floor, Santo Domingo.

Telephone: 567-6131; **Fax:** 566-4641; **e-mail:** solidarios@codetel.net.do.

FOUNDATIONS, TRUSTS AND NON-PROFIT ORGANIZATIONS

Fundación Dominicana de Desarrollo—FDD (Dominican Development Foundation)

Founded in 1962 to stimulate private sector participation in finding solutions to the basic problems encountered by the low-income sector, particularly those problems experienced in rural areas. Promotes the participation of individuals in the process of their own development.

Activities: Operates nationally in the fields of education, social welfare and economic affairs through research and capacity building programmes. Also involved in funding environmental programmes and providing support to micro-enterprises.

Geographical Area of Activity: Dominican Republic.

Publications: Report of operations and financial statement; *Notas de Desarrollo; Catálogo de Organizaciones Voluntarias de Acción Social.*

Counsel: José Manuel Mallén (Pres.); Osvaldo Brugal (Vice-Pres.); Carolina Alorda (Sec.); Magda Dickson (Vice-Sec.); Regina Vitienes (Treas.); Pedro Gamundi (Vice-Treas.); José Luis Alonso; Julio Brache; Alejandro González Cuadra; Marino Inchaustegui; Jaime Roca; Juan Sanoja Rizek; Pedro Pérez; Mario Morles; Eduardo Valcarcel.

Principal Staff: Exec. Dir Ada Wiscovitch Carlo.

Address: Calle Mercedes No 4, Casa de Las Gárgolas, Apdo 857, Santo Domingo.

Telephone: 688-8101; **Fax:** 686-0430; **Internet:** www.fdd.org.do; **e-mail:** fdd@codetel.net.do.

Ecuador

FOUNDATION CENTRE AND CO-ORDINATING BODY

CERES—Ecuadorean Consortium for Social Responsibility

Established in 2002, an association of local grant-making organizations; the secretariat from 2002–04 was to be located at the Fundación Grupo ESQUEL—Ecuador (q.v.), one of CERES' founding organizations.

Activities: There were, in 2003, 11 member organizations—including corporate, private and community foundations—from throughout Ecuador. The organizations aimed to network, promote civil society in Ecuador, through focusing on the following areas: promoting social responsibility in Ecuador; fostering dialogue between foundations and government agencies, the media and the private sector; and increasing the institutional capacity and skills of Ecuadorean foundations.

Geographical Area of Activity: Ecuador.

Principal Staff: Co-ordinator Valentina Ramia.

Address: Avda Colón 1346 y Foch, Edif. Torres de la Colón Mz., Of. 12, Quito.

FOUNDATIONS, TRUSTS AND NON-PROFIT ORGANIZATIONS

Asociación de Corporaciones de Desarrollo de la Microempresa (Association for the Development of Microenterprises)

Established in 1989; aims to bring together and strengthen member foundations with similar principles and purposes that implement microenterprise development programmes.

Activities: Aims to support the development of microenterprises in Ecuador, through the provision of grants, technical assistence and training, with a particular focus on supporting women, children and young people, and ethnic and religious groups.

Geographical Area of Activity: Ecuador.

Finance: Total annual grants approx. US $500,000.

Principal Staff: Exec. Dir Rodrigo López Nieto.

Address: Edif. Metropoli, Mezzanine, Quito.

Telephone: (2) 460-599; **Fax:** (2) 250-075; **e-mail:** corpomi1@corpomicro.com.ec.

Charles Darwin Foundation for the Galapagos Islands

Founded in 1959, under the auspices of the Government of Ecuador, UNESCO and the World Conservation Union (IUCN, q.v.), to administer the Charles Darwin Research Station on the Galapagos Islands, and to provide facilities for research and conservation measures.

Activities: Operates internationally in the fields of science and the conservation of natural resources. The Charles Darwin Research Station, with its research vessel, *Beagle*, provides research facilities to visiting scientists of many nationalities, and undertakes conservation measures for the unique fauna, flora and habitat of the archipelago, including a breeding programme for tortoises and iguanas and the protection of endangered plants and animals. The Foundation supports the Galapagos National Park Service and assists in the management for a marine reserve. It also holds courses in field ecology, offers training to Ecuadorean university students, and publishes the results of research. Maintains a library of books, maps and photographs of the Galapagos Islands. Also maintains fundraising offices in the USA and Europe.

Geographical Area of Activity: Galapagos Islands, Ecuador.

Publications: *Noticias de Galapagos;* Annual Report; and numerous specialist publications.

Finance: Annual revenue and expenditure approx. US $3,790,000 (2000).

Board of Directors: Thomas H. Fritts (Pres.); Roque Sevilla (Vice-Pres.); Padraig Whelan (Sec.); Laura Arcos Terán; Guy Coppois; Grand Duke Henri of Luxembourg; Carlos Valle; Tjitte de Vries.

Principal Staff: Exec. Dir Fernando Espinoza.

Address: Avda 6 de Diciembre, N36-109 y Pasaje California, Casilla 17-01-3891, Quito.

Telephone: (2) 244-803; **Fax:** (2) 443-935; **Internet:** www.darwinfoundation.org; **e-mail:** galapagosinfo@darwinfoundation.org.

EcoCiencia—Fundación Ecuatoriana de Estudios Ecologicos (Ecuadorean Foundation for Ecological Studies)

Founded in September 1989 by Danilo Silva, Patricio Mena, Roberto Ulloa, Mario García, Luis Suárez and Juan Manuel Carrión, to promote wildlife and biodiversity conservation and environmental education.

Activities: The Foundation operates in the field of conservation and the environment, in particular the conservation of biodiversity, through research, environmental education, training programmes and natural resources management; maintains the GIS laboratory, a documentation centre and a publications department; runs a Scholarship Programme for Ecuadorean students.

Geographical Area of Activity: Ecuador.

Publications: Books on conservation, ethnobiology; technical reports and papers.

Finance: Total income US $1,228,162 (2000).

Principal Staff: Pres. Rocio Alarcón; Exec. Dir Mario García.

Address: Isla San Cristóbal N44-495 y Isla Seymour, POB 1712257, Quito.

Telephone: (2) 2451-338; **Fax:** (2) 2249-334; **Internet:** www.ecociencia.org; **e-mail:** info@ecociencia.org.

Fondo Ecuatoriano Populorum Progressio—FEPP

Established in 1970 to promote the development of marginalized rural and urban groups.

Activities: Aims to support the development of marginalized groups in rural and urban areas of Ecuador, through the provision of grants and technical assistance, and by raising awareness. Targeted groups include children and young people, with grants made to projects in the fields of health, social services, development, civil and human rights, and conflict resolution.

Geographical Area of Activity: Ecuador.

Finance: Annual grants approx. US $2,000,000.

Principal Staff: Exec. Dir Jose Tonelo.

Address: Mallorca 427 y Coruña, La Floresta, Casilla 17-110-5202, Quito.

Telephone: (2) 222-5248; **Fax:** (2) 250-4978; **e-mail:** fepp@uio.satnet.net.

Fundación Alternativas para el Desarrollo—Alternativa (Alternatives for Development Foundation)

Established in 1991 by Mónica Hernández de Phillips and Santiago Ribadeneira to promote alternatives for development.

Activities: Operates in Ecuador in the field of economic affairs, principally financial services development, through self-conducted programmes. A programme operates in the North Andean region, promoting rural microfinance services for Andean peasants. The Convivir, or Living Together project is an integral community development service, working towards an organized, productive and pro-active, innovative and sustainable life. The Foundation also gathers information about and informs on the activities of national and international NGOs working in Ecuador through the Sistema de Información de Organizaciones Sociales. The Foundation is the social promoter of Banco Solidario, and administers a training centre specializing in microfinance matters.

Geographical Area of Activity: Ecuador.

Publications: *Directorio de Organizaciones Sociales de Desarrollo 2001* (4th edn).

Finance: Financed by a financial corporation and through the commercialization of the Foundation's services and products; annual revenue US $603,059, expenditure US $424,949 (2001).

Board of Directors: Santiago Ribadeneira Troya; Manuel Romolereux; Mónica Hernández; Roberto Moss; Lourdes Barragán; Lucía Burneo; Juan Vásconez; Eduardo Vintimilla; Patricia Pinto de Baus.

Principal Staff: Exec. Dir Mónica Hernández; Adviser Soledad Burbano; Technical Dir María Soledad Jarrín.

Address: Edif. Grupo Enlace, 7°, Avda Amazonas 3887 y Corea, Quito.

Telephone: (2) 260-260; **Fax:** (2) 262-536; **Internet:** www.siosecuador.org/sios_frame_center.htm; **e-mail:** enmas@enlace.fin.ec.

Fundación para el Desarrollo Agropecuario—FUNDAGRO (Foundation for Agricultural Development)

Founded in 1987 to support the modernization of agriculture and to improve the standard of living of those working in agriculture.

Activities: The Foundation designs and manages projects in the fields of sustainable development, agricultural research and education. Supports innovations in agricultural technology, marketing, financing and organizational schemes. FUNDAGRO is a member of the Consortium for the Sustainable Development of the Andean Ecoregion (CONDESCAN).

Geographical Area of Activity: Ecuador.

Publications: Annual Report.

Trustees: Rodolfo Arámbulo (Pres.); Jorge Muñoz; Adolfo Rodriguez; Herbert Schlenker; Rafael Wong.

Principal Staff: Exec. Dir Jorge F. Chang.

Address: Moreno Bellido E6-168 y Avda Amazonas, Apdo Postal 1716-219 CEQ, Quito.

Telephone: (2) 507-361; **Fax:** (2) 507-422; **e-mail:** fundagro@uio.telconet.net.

Fundación Ecuatoriana de Desarrollo (Ecuadorean Development Foundation)

Established in 1968 to improve the standard of living for the disadvantaged in Ecuador.

Activities: Operates in the fields of aid to less-developed countries, economic affairs and social welfare, through supporting business, economic and social development in micro-enterprise programmes, giving loans to individual borrowers, the majority of whom are women. Also offers training programmes.

Geographical Area of Activity: Ecuador.

Publications: *Fedinforma* (monthly); training materials.

Finance: Money disbursed approx. US $8,535,414 (1999).

Principal Staff: Exec. Dir César Alarcon Costta.

Address: 9 de Octubre 1212 entre Colón y Orellana, Apdo Postal 2529, Quito.

Telephone: (2) 547-864; **Fax:** (2) 209-084; **e-mail:** admin@dialogodegestiones.com.

Fundación Eugenio Espejo (Eugenio Espejo Foundation)

Established in 1978 to work in social welfare and the development of civil society, especially promoting development in rural and urban communities.

Activities: The Foundation supports small enterprises, education and training, special education, health and welfare. Also operates a private health clinic in southern Quito serving disadvantaged people, with plans for a network of similar clinics across Ecuador.

Geographical Area of Activity: Ecuador.

Principal Staff: Exec. Dir Patricia Salvador de Dossman.

Address: Samanes 2nd Floor, Mz 204, Solar P21, Apdo Postal 09014557, Guayaquil.

Telephone: (4) 210-816; **Fax:** (4) 210-813.

Fundación General Ecuatoriana (General Ecuadorean Foundation)

Established in 1980 to assist the disabled in areas such as education, health, housing and culture.

Activities: Operates nationally in the areas of education, medicine and health, and social welfare for disabled people, through conferences and training courses for mentally disabled young people.

Geographical Area of Activity: Ecuador.

Publications: Directory of institutes for people with mental disability, autism, cerebral palsy and Down's Syndrome; diagnostic of the occupational situation of disabled persons.

General Council: Manuel de Guzmán Polanco (Pres.); Mauro Ordáñez Bravo (Vice-Pres.); Rodrigo Moncayo García (Sec.); Ramón Arregui Monreal.

Principal Staff: Exec. Dir Jorge Luna Maldonado.

Address: San Javier N26-63 y Orellana, Casilla 17-17-282, Quito.

Telephone: (2) 221-929; **Fax:** (2) 500-781; **e-mail:** fge5@fge.org.ec.

Fundación Grupo ESQUEL—Ecuador (ESQUEL Foundation—Ecuador)

Established in 1990 to contribute to the sustainable human development of Ecuador, to improve the quality of life of disadvantaged people and to build a democratic society.

Activities: The Foundation operates through the following programmes: the Programme for Children and Youth Development, seeking to improve the lives of children and youth; the Programme for Sustainable Human Development, which aims to improve the quality of life of the rural and low-income urban populations of the coastal region, the highlands and the Amazon region; the Programme for Economic and Social Community Development, aiming to improve the quality of life of low-income groups which have alternative business ideas but cannot access traditional financing sources; the Social Responsibility Programme, which promotes social responsibility through establishing the concept and value of citizenship, building solidarity and forming a new culture of dialogue; the Civic Education Programme, which works through training and the encouragement of civic education; and the Programme for Community Development, which carries out socially-oriented projects emerging from community initiatives and aims to strengthen small NGOs.

Geographical Area of Activity: Ecuador.

Publications: Annual Report; *Esquela* (newsletter, quarterly); *Con los sueños sobre la tierra; Responsabilidad Social: Una empresa de Todos; La Aventura de lo Alternativo; Publicaciones sobre Corrupción; Temas para una sociedad en crisis.*

Finance: Total assets. US $3,643,000 (2000); annual revenue US $3,534,000, expenditure US $1,658,000 (2000).

Principal Staff: Exec. Pres. Cornelio Marchán.

Address: Avda Colón 1346 y Foch, Edif. Torres de la Colón Mz., Of. 12, Quito.

Telephone: (2) 520-001; **Fax:** (2) 554-029; **Internet:** www.esquel.org.ec; **e-mail:** fesquel3@hoy.net.

Fundación Natura—Fundación Ecuatoriana para la Conservación de la Naturaleza (Nature Foundation)

Founded in July 1978 with the aim of conserving the natural environment and encouraging better use of natural resources.

Activities: Promotes environmental education; runs training courses; organizes small-scale environmental projects in the areas of biodiversity, natural resources, solid waste management and urban ecology; seeks to advise policy-makers on environmental matters; and maintains a small library.

Geographical Area of Activity: Ecuador.

Publications: *Boletín Natura* (quarterly newsletter); *Responsbilidad Integral* (quarterly); *El Ambiental* (monthly); *Informe Galápagos* (annually).

Finance: Annual budget approx. US $6,000,000.

Principal Staff: Exec. Dir Abogada Ana Albán Mora.

Address: Avda Carlos Julio, Arosemena km 2, via Daule, Quito.

Telephone: (4) 201-628; **Fax:** (4) 206-777; **e-mail:** naturgye@gu.natura.org.ec.

Egypt

FOUNDATIONS, TRUSTS AND NON-PROFIT ORGANIZATIONS

Arab Fund for Technical Assistance to African and Arab Countries—AFTAAAC

Founded in 1974 (known until 1992 as the Arab Fund for Technical Assistance), to benefit African and Arab countries through the provision of finance for technical assistance programmes organized by the League of Arab States and other bodies. The Fund is part of the League of Arab States but operates independently.

Activities: Finances training programmes in the Arab States; awards grants and scholarships for training; provides a consultancy service; encourages information exchange between technical experts in African and Arab countries. Members of the Fund comprise the governments of 21 African and Middle-Eastern countries.

Geographical Area of Activity: North Africa and the Middle East.

Finance: Assets approx. US $25,000,000.

Board of Directors: The Board comprises seven experts appointed for a three-year term by the Council of the League of Arab States.

Principal Staff: Exec. Dir Mahdi Mostafa El-Hadi; Dir Garril Mattar.

Address: c/o League of Arab States, Maidan At-Tahrir, POB 11642, Cairo.

Telephone: (2) 750511; **Fax:** (2) 750324.

Arab Office for Youth and Environment—AOYE

Established in 1978. Aims to encourage environmental protection.

Activities: Works to raise awareness, particularly among young people, of environmental issues and the need for sustainable development in Egypt. Co-operates with other environmental NGOs, the government, and the United Nations to develop and carry out programmes and projects and to educate young people in order to produce future leaders with an increased awareness of the need to protect the environment and natural resources, as well as collaborating to establish environmental networks. Founded the Arab Union for Youth and Environment in 1983 and is the Secretariat for the Arab Network for Environment and Development (RAED). Also participates in international conferences and networks.

Geographical Area of Activity: Egypt.

Publications: *Montada Elbiah* (RAED monthly newsletter).

Principal Staff: Pres. Dr Emad Adly; Vice-Pres. El Nagdy Hagar; Sec.-Gen. Daliah Lotayef; Treas. Dr Ahmed El Shazly.

Address: POB 2 Magless El-Shaab, Cairo.

Telephone: (2) 3041634; **Fax:** (2) 3041635; **Internet:** www.aoye.org; **e-mail:** aoye@link.net.

Arab Organization for Human Rights—AOHR

Founded in 1983 to defend human rights.

Activities: Works to protect the human rights of those living in Arab countries, and to defend anyone whose rights have been violated. Provides legal assistance and campaigns for people convicted without fair trial, as well as financial assistance to their families; supports improvements in conditions for prisoners of conscience; and fights for amnesty for people sentenced for political reasons.

Geographical Area of Activity: North Africa and the Middle East.

Publications: *Almonazzama Alarabiya Lihoqouq Alinsan–Nashra Ikhbariya* (monthly newsletter); *Arab Organization for Human Rights Newsletter* (monthly); *Hoqouq Alinsan Filwatan Alarabi* (quarterly); Annual report; special bulletins.

Finance: Funded by members' dues and contributions.

Board of Trustees: 25 members.

Address: 91 Al-Marghany St, Heliopolis, Cairo.

Telephone: (2) 4181396; **Fax:** (2) 4185346; **Internet:** www.aohr.org; **e-mail:** aohr@link.com.eg.

Legal Research and Resource Center for Human Rights—LRRC

Established in 1991 to improve human rights in Egypt.

Activities: Operates nationally in the field of human rights, raising public awareness of human rights issues, with a particular interest in women's rights. This is done by liaising with local, regional and national NGOs through national networks, disseminating information and maintaining archives, and creating new education methods to enhance the general understanding of human rights issues in Egypt. Engages in research and runs informative courses for children, NGOs and individuals. Founding member of the Arab NGO Network, Afronet and the African Human Rights Education Network.

Geographical Area of Activity: Egypt.

Publications: *People's Rights* (journal, monthly in Arabic, 6 a year in English); *People's Rights / Women's Rights* (quarterly, in Arabic and English); and various publications on human rights-related subjects.

Address: 7 Al-Higaz St, Roxi, Cairo.

Telephone: (2) 4520977; **Fax:** (2) 2596622; **Internet:** www.geocities.com/lrrc.geo; **e-mail:** lrrc@brainy1.ie-eg.com.

El Salvador

FOUNDATIONS, TRUSTS AND NON-PROFIT ORGANIZATIONS

Fundación Herbert de Sola (Herbert de Sola Foundation)

Founded in 1959 by Herbert de Sola to promote the material, moral, cultural and intellectual welfare of the inhabitants of the Republic of El Salvador.

Activities: Operates nationally in the fields of education and information technology, social welfare and studies, science and medicine, the arts and humanities, ecology and the conservation of natural resources, through grants to individuals and institutions, fellowships, scholarships, publications and lectures; also supports educational programmes and institutions in Honduras, Costa Rica and Nicaragua.

Geographical Area of Activity: El Salvador, Costa Rica, Honduras and Nicaragua.

Trustee: Banco de Comercio de El Salvador.

Principal Staff: Pres. Francisco Ricardo Roberto de Sola; Exec. Dir Francisco Choriego.

Address: Blvd Constitución 339, Colonia Escalón, San Salvador.

Telephone: 279-3666; **Fax:** 298-6399; **Internet:** www.grupodesola.com/fundacion.htm; **e-mail:** hdesola@sal.gbm.net.

Estonia

FOUNDATIONS, TRUSTS AND NON-PROFIT ORGANIZATIONS

Eestimaa Looduse Fond (Estonian Fund for Nature)

Established in February 1991 to raise and distribute funds for nature protection in Estonia.

Activities: The Foundation operates in Estonia in the fields of conservation and the environment, and education, through self-conducted programmes, research, conferences, training courses and publications; it provides financial support for conservation and environmental projects such as scientific research, the application of practical conservation measures, and public information and education.

Geographical Area of Activity: Estonia.

Publications: *Orchid Ecology and Protection in Estonia; Estonian Coastal and Flood Plain Meadows; Estonian Ramsar Wetlands;* Annual Report.

Finance: The Foundation receives donations and finance for specific projects from individuals and other foundations. Total assets €108,197 (2001); total income €376,807, total expenditure €390,229 (2001).

Governing Board: Robert Oetjen (Chair.).

Principal Staff: Exec. Dir Toomas Trapido; Financial Dir Gea Kõverjalg, Irja Pärn.

Address: Riia 185A, POB 245, Tartu 50002.

Telephone: (7) 428-443; **Fax:** (7) 428-166; **Internet:** www.elfond.ee; **e-mail:** elf@elfond.ee.

Estonian National Culture Foundation

Founded in 1991 to promote and preserve Estonia's national culture.

Activities: Operates in the area of the arts and humanities. Offers scholarships and grants to individuals and projects dedicated to developing aspects of Estonian culture; presents Lifetime Achievement Awards to people who have made significant contributions to national culture; and works in co-operation with a number of institutions and individuals that support Estonian culture. Administer 76 special foundations.

Geographical Area of Activity: Estonia.

Finance: Total income 8,356,194 Estonian kroons, expenditure 4,871,651 Estonian kroons (June 2002).

Council: Eri Klas (Chair.); J. Engelbrecht; M. Kolk; J. Kross; R. Maran; I. Normet; I. Rüütel; E. Tamberg; B. Tamm; J. Tamm; M. Unt.

Principal Staff: Man. Dir Toivo Toomemets.

Address: A. Weizenbergi 20 A-13, 10150 Tallinn.

Telephone: 601-3428; **Fax:** 601-3429; **Internet:** www.erkf.ee; **e-mail:** post@erkf.ee.

Open Estonia Foundation

Founded in 1990 to support the development of open society through supporting democratic principles, the creation of non-profit organizations and assisting those working in the areas of human rights and economic and legal reform; it is an independent foundation, part of the Soros foundations network.

Activities: Operates in the areas of civil society, education, information and the media, public health, youth, law and criminal justice, the arts and culture, and ethnic minorities. Plans to concentrate on the development of public policy and programmes concentrating on European integration, civil society and Central and Eastern Europe co-operation, through making awards and grants as well as initiating its own projects. Involved in the CIVICUS (q.v.) Index on Civil Society.

Geographical Area of Activity: Estonia.

Publications: Annual Report; *Courier* (newsletter, monthly, in Estonian, English and Russian); special reports.

Finance: Annual expenditure US $1,468,000 (2001).

Board of Directors: Peep Pruks (Chair.); Vitali Belobrovtsev; Mikko Lagerspetz; Aap Neljas; Barbi Pilvre; Rein Ruutsoo.

Principal Staff: Exec. Dir Mall Hellam.

Address: Estonia Ave 3/5, Tallinn 10143.

Telephone: 631-3791; **Fax:** 631-3796; **Internet:** www.oef.org.ee; **e-mail:** postmaster@oef.org.ee.

Finland

FOUNDATION CENTRE AND CO-ORDINATING BODY

Council of Finnish Foundationskult

Established in 1970, an association of Finnish grant making foundations and associations.

Activities: Assists its 40 member foundations and associations to exchange information and ideas; represents its members; advises members through its Foundation Service, which also provides information on grants and foundations; and issues publications. In 2000/01, the organizations represented by the Council made grants amounting to approximately €65,000,000.

Geographical Area of Activity: Finland.

Publications: *The Finnish Foundation Directory;* and other guides for grant-seekers.

Board of Directors: L. Niinistö (Chair.); A. Alho; K. Asp; L. Elovainio; L. Koivu; A. Mäenmaa; K. Riistama; R. Sunell; H. Wiklund.

Principal Staff: Contact: Eeva-Liisa Palotie; Exec. Dir Ralf Sunell.

Address: c/o Suomen Kulttuurirahasto, Bulevardi 5A, POB 203, 00120 Helsinki.

Telephone: (9) 642174; **Fax:** (9) 640474; **Internet:** www.skr.fi/spalvelu/council; **e-mail:** info@skr.fi.

FOUNDATIONS, TRUSTS AND NON-PROFIT ORGANIZATIONS

Baltic Sea Foundation

Founded in 1989 by Anders Wiklöf to support activities for the protection of the Baltic Sea environment.

Activities: Grants scholarships, prizes and financial support for relevant scientific research, technology, published material and other activities, including the protection of historical ship-wrecks in the Baltic Sea region. The Foundation also aims to establish new economic relationships between countries.

Geographical Area of Activity: The Baltic region.

Publications: Newsletter; *World of the Baltic Sea* (annual).

Principal Staff: Man. Dir. Hasse Svensson.

Address: c/o Ålands Högskola, POB 160, 22101 Mariehamn.

Telephone: 1825256; **Fax:** 1822160; **e-mail:** hasse.svensson@ah.aland.fi.

Foundation for Commercial and Technical Sciences

Founded in 1956 to support study in the fields of commercial and technical sciences, and to support teaching and research activities in these fields.

Activities: Operates nationally in the fields of economic affairs, education and science and technology, through grants to individuals and granting scholarships and fellowships. Member of the Council of Finnish Foundations (q.v.).

Geographical Area of Activity: Finland.

Finance: Grants disbursed €218,644 (1999/2000).

Principal Staff: Officer Sirkku Kuoppamäki.

Address: Ratavartijankatu 2, 00520 Helsinki.

Telephone: (9) 47677277; **Fax:** (9) 47677677.

Signe and Ane Gyllenberg Foundation

Established in 1948 to support medical and scientific research, especially in the area of psychosomatic illness, and research in the field of medicine following the ideas of Rudolf Steiner.

Activities: Operates internationally. Supports medical and scientific research, especially in the area of psychosomatic illness and blood disorders, through awarding grants; also maintains the Villa Gyllenberg Art Museum in Helsinki.

Geographical Area of Activity: International.

Restrictions: Grants are not given for research which involves painful experiments on animals.

Finance: Grants disbursed approx. €1,200,000 (2003/04).

Principal Staff: Chair. of Board Prof. Matti Klockars; Man. Dir Mikael Westerback.

Address: Yrjönkatu 4A, 5, 00120 Helsinki.

Telephone: (9) 647390; **Fax:** (9) 607119; **Internet:** www.gyllenberg-foundation.fi; **e-mail:** stiftelsen@gyllenberg-foundation.fi.

Yrjö Jahnsson Foundation

Founded in 1954 by Mrs Hilma Jahnsson to sponsor Finnish research in economics and medicine as well as to support Finnish educational and research institutes.

Activities: Operates nationally in the field of education, and internationally in the fields of economic affairs and science and medicine, through grants to Finnish institutions and individuals, and fellowships and scholarships for Finnish citizens, and through international research, conferences, courses, publications and lectures. Distributes the Yrjö Jahnsson Award in Economics to a young European economist who has significantly advanced the field of economics research.

Geographical Area of Activity: Finland and Europe.

Publications: Report of operations and financial statement.

Finance: Grants disbursed €1,681,879 (1999/2000).

Address: Ludviginkatu 3–5A, 00130 Helsinki.

Telephone: (9) 6869100; **Fax:** (9) 605002; **Internet:** www.yjs.fi; **e-mail:** toimisto@yjs.fi.

Sigrid Jusélius Foundation

Founded in 1930 by the terms of the will of Fritz Arthur Jusélius to promote and support medical research, independently of language and nationality, with the aim of fighting diseases particularly harmful to humanity.

Activities: Operates in the fields of medicine, pharmacology, biochemistry and genetics. Supports research in those fields and awards grants to both individuals and institutions. Organizes occasional symposia and workshops. Grants are made to medical research projects, conducted by senior researchers in Finland.

Geographical Area of Activity: Finland.

Restrictions: No direct grants for foreign medical research, or for studies or doctoral theses.

Publications: Annual Report (in Finnish and Swedish).

Finance: Assets €637,000 (2001).

Board of Trustees: Edward Andersson (Chair.); Henry Wiklund (Vice-Chair.); H. Andersson; H. Gustav Bjorkstrand; Bo Harald; Elianne Riska; Matti J. Tikkanen;.

Principal Staff: Man. Dir Magnus Savander.

Address: Aleksanterinkatu 48B, 00100 Helsinki.

Telephone: (9) 634461; **Fax:** (9) 634502; **Internet:** www.terkko.helsinki.fi/juselius; **e-mail:** s.juselius@dlc.fi.

KIOS—Finnish NGO Foundation for Human Rights

Established in 1998 by 11 Finnish NGOs. Aims to promote human rights internationally.

Activities: Operates in the field of human rights in developing countries, through a grant-making programme for projects that raise public awareness of human rights issues, and other activities related to human rights—legal aid, technical support and emergency aid. Works in co-operation with locally-based human rights NGOs in less-developed countries.

Geographical Area of Activity: Africa, Central and South America, Asia, Europe and the Middle East.

Restrictions: No grants for scholarships, humanitarian aid, travel or international conferences; no grants to Finnish NGOs; grants only to European and US NGOs if the activity is carried out in a developing country.

Finance: Receives financial support from the Dept for International Development Co-operation of the Finnish Ministry for Foreign Affairs.

Trustees: Eleven representatives from founding organizations.

Principal Staff: Exec. Dir Katariina Kemppainen.

Address: POB 1387, 00101 Helsinki.

Telephone: (9) 68131530; **Fax:** (9) 68131531; **Internet:** www.kios.fi; **e-mail:** kios@kios.fi.

Maj and Tor Nessling Foundation

Established by Maj and Tor Nessling in 1972 for the promotion of Finnish science and culture, especially in the field of environmental protection.

Activities: Operates nationally in the field of conservation and the environment, through awarding grants for scientific projects in all areas of environmental protection; also organizes symposia.

Geographical Area of Activity: Finland.

Finance: Grants disbursed €1,400,000 (2003).

Principal Staff: Financial Admin. Jarmo Hirvonen; Head of Research Dr Laura Höijer.

Address: Fredrikinkatu 20B, 16, 00120 Helsinki.

Telephone: (9) 4342550; **Fax:** (9) 43425555; **Internet:** www.nessling.fi; **e-mail:** toimisto@nessling.fi.

Paavo Nurmen Säätiö (Paavo Nurmi Foundation)

Established in 1968; aims to contribute to research into heart and vascular disease and to promote public welfare in Finland.

Activities: Provides funding to talented Finnish medical researchers for sabbatical research terms of between two and six months, for cardiovascular disease research. Also provides some support to Estonian cardiologists for visiting research tenures in Finland, and to Finnish scientists for visits to foreign research institutions. Awards the annual International Paavo Nurmi Foundation Award in recognition of an individual's outstanding work in the field of medical research. Also runs an annual symposia programme, and is a co-founding sponsor of the *Tiede 2000* (Science 2000) journal, which aims to make the latest research findings accessible to the public.

Geographical Area of Activity: Mainly Finland.

Restrictions: No grants for assistants or equipment.

Principal Staff: Man. Dir Vesa Manninen.

Address: Albertinkatu 21C, 16, 00120 Helsinki.

Internet: www.paavonurmensaatio.fi.

Paulon Säätiö (Paulo Foundation)

Founded in 1966 by Marja Paulo to support research in the fields of medicine and the economy, and to promote music and fine art.

Activities: Operates in the areas of the arts and humanities, economic affairs, medicine and health, and science and technology, nationally through research, grants to individuals and awarding prizes, and both nationally and internationally through awarding scholarships and fellowships.

Geographical Area of Activity: Finland.

Restrictions: Awards are made to Finns only.

Publications: *Why Finland is so Expensive.*

Finance: Grants disbursed €605,476 (1999–2000).

Trustees: Yrjö Palotie (Chair.); Aatto Prihti (Gen. Man.); Dr Jan Lindgren; Dr Matti Tikkanen.

Principal Staff: Yrjö Palotie.

Address: POB 90, 02231 Espoo.

Telephone: (9) 68102301; **Fax:** (9) 68102333; **Internet:** www.paulo.fi; **e-mail:** toimisto@paulo.fi.

Suomen Kulttuurirahasto (Finnish Cultural Foundation)

Founded in 1939 by Suomen Kulttuurirahaston Kannatusyhdistys r.y. (Association for the Finnish Cultural Foundation) to promote the development of cultural life in Finland.

Activities: The Foundation provides grants and scholarships for individuals, work groups and communities in the fields of arts and science. It operates primarily within Finland but also internationally through travel and research grants. Large-scale, long-term projects, especially relating to Finnish culture, which require major support are also encouraged. The Foundation's own cultural activities include annual events, and other special projects. The Mirjam Helin International Singing Competition, inaugurated in 1984, is held every fifth year. Its purpose is to support young, gifted singers. The Kirpilä Art Collection is a collection of Finnish art donated to the foundation by Dr Juhani Kirpilä. Seventeen Regional Funds have been established to support cultural life throughout the country.

Geographical Area of Activity: Primarily Finland; some international activity.

Publications: *Cultura* (series of publications); Annual Report; reports and brochures.

Finance: Total grants €19,635,658 (Sept. 2002).

Trustees: Kimmo Kontula (Chair.); Pentti Vartia (Vice-Chair.); K. Aho; I. Hanski; N. Jääskinen; H. Marttinen; H. Mäkelä; R. Nieminen; R. Nikula; A. Sallinen; J. Suominen.

Principal Staff: Sec.-Gen. Dr Paavo Hohti; Exec. Sec. Timo Arjas.

Address: Bulevardi 5A, POB 203, 00121 Helsinki.

Telephone: (9) 612810; **Fax:** (9) 640474; **Internet:** www.skr.fi; **e-mail:** info@skr.fi.

Svenska Kulturfonden (Foundation for Swedish Culture in Finland)

Founded in 1908 by the Svenska Folkpartiet to support educational institutions; associations, unions and institutions with cultural interests and purposes; individual scientific, literary and artistic activities; and other purposes serving Swedish culture in Finland.

Activities: Operates nationally in the fields of education, social studies, science and medicine, and the arts and humanities, through grants to institutions and individuals, conferences and courses. Maintains an art collection comprising works by contemporary Finno-Swedish artists and operates regional grant offices.

Geographical Area of Activity: Finland.

Restrictions: Support is given only to projects serving Swedish culture.

Publications: *Fonden i Fokus; 137 stiftelser, fonder & stödordningar; Pär Stenbäck 60*; annual and conference reports; catalogues.

Finance: Grants disbursed €6,727,517 (1999/2000).

Trustees: Pär Stenbäck (Chair.); G. Gayer, J. Olav (Vice-Chair.); U. Achrén; R. Bjurström; P. von Bonsdorff; N. Elfving; Susann Hartmann; A. Pråhl; L. Saxberg-Blomkvist; B. Stenman; B. Sundström; O. Witting.

Principal Staff: Dir Krister Ståhlberg; Grant Sec. Christina Fraser.

Address: Simonsgatan 8A, POB 439, 00101 Helsingfors.

Telephone: (9) 69307300; **Fax:** (9) 6949484; **Internet:** kulturfonden.fi; **e-mail:** kansliet@kulturfonden.fi.

Vaestoliitto—The Family Federation of Finland

Founded in February, 1941. Aims to raise awareness of population and family planning issues, promoting a balanced population in society, in order to improve the living conditions of families. A major shareholder of Familia Ltd, a condom importer.

Activities: Undertakes research, funds education programmes, campaigns to reform legislation, holds conferences, seminars and training, offers counselling, provides information and documentation and publishes a number of educational materials particularly on its focus areas of family, housing and population policy. Development projects are currently underway in India, Malawi, Mexico, Namibia and Nepal.

Geographical Area of Activity: Finland, Central and South America, Africa and Asia.

Publications: *Kotilääkäri* (health-care magazine); *Kanava* (periodical); publications on population issues; and the results of family and population studies.

Board of Trustees: Reino T. Hjerppe (Chair.).

Principal Staff: Man. Dir Helena Hiila; Head of Development Esko Ahonen.

Address: POB 849, 00101 Helsinki.

Telephone: (9) 228050; **Fax:** (9) 6121211; **Internet:** www.vaestoliitto.fi; **e-mail:** central.office@vaestoliitto.fi.

Wihurin Kansainvälisten Palkintojen Rahasto
(Wihuri Foundation for International Prizes)

Founded in 1953 by Antti Wihuri to promote and sustain the cultural and economic development of society by distributing international prizes, in particular the Wihuri–Sibelius Prize.

Trustees: A. Prihti (Chair.); M. Hurme (Vice-Chair.).

Principal Staff: Rep. Arto Mäenmaa.

Address: Arkadiankatu 21A 14, 00100 Helsinki.

Telephone: (9) 4542400; **Fax:** (9) 444590; **Internet:** www.wihurinrahasto.fi; **e-mail:** toimisto@wihurinrahasto.fi.

Jenny ja Antti Wihurin Rahasto (Jenny and Antti Wihuri Foundation)

Founded in 1942 by Jenny and Antti Wihuri to promote and sustain Finnish cultural and economic development.

Activities: Operates nationally in the fields of education, social welfare and studies, economic affairs, science and medicine, arts and humanities, law and other professions, through self-conducted programmes, research, grants to institutions and individuals, fellowships and scholarships, conferences and courses, publications and lectures.

Geographical Area of Activity: Finland.

Restrictions: Grants are available only to Finnish nationals.

Finance: Grants disbursed €6,800,000 (2002).

Trustees: A. Prihti (Chair.); M. Hurme (Vice-Chair.).

Principal Staff: Rep. Arto Mäenmaa.

Address: Arkadiankatu 21A 14, 00100 Helsinki.

Telephone: (9) 4542400; **Fax:** (9) 444590; **Internet:** www.wihurinrahasto.fi; **e-mail:** toimisto@wihurinrahasto.fi.

France

FOUNDATION CENTRES AND CO-ORDINATING BODIES

CIVITAS International

An international consortium inaugurated in 1995, comprising individuals, governmental and non-governmental organizations, and international organizations, promoting civic education, aiming to support education for citizenship in new and established democracies world-wide.

Activities: Operates a world-wide network to promote civic education, through computer networking and international exchange of educators; maintains the Civnet website for civic education practitioners, administrators, NGOs, etc., containing resources and other information on civic education and society.

Geographical Area of Activity: International.

Publications: *Civnet Journal* (6 a year).

Principal Staff: Exec. Dir Balazs Hidveghi.

Address: 8 rue des Ecrivains, 67000 Strasbourg.

Telephone: 3-88-24-71-00; **Fax:** 3-88-24-71-09; **Internet:** www.civnet.org/; **e-mail:** civitas@club-internet.

Fondation de France

Founded in 1969 with an initial endowment made by the Caisse des Dépôts et Consignations (Bank of Security Deposits) and 17 major French banks. The Foundation aims to encourage and develop the practice of making charitable donations, and is the only foundation in France empowered to support actions in all areas of general interest.

Activities: The Foundation operates in three main areas: financial contribution to projects carried out by organizations acting in the fields of social welfare, scientific and medical research, culture and the environment; assistance to individuals or companies in the creation of a foundation under the aegis of the Fondation de France; and the development of associations, through helping them to raise funds. In 2001 the Foundation had 680,000 donors, managed 531 individual foundations, and maintained seven regional delegations.

Geographical Area of Activity: France and Europe.

Publications: Annual Report; Newsletter; publications on social welfare, social work, philanthropy in France etc.

Finance: Total awards and scholarships €58,000,000 (2001).

Principal Staff: Chair. Bertrand Dufourcq; Man. Dir Francis Charhon; Vice-Pres. Olivier Chevrillon; Treas. Henri Moulard.

Address: 40 ave Hoche, 75008 Paris.

Telephone: 1-44-21-31-00; **Fax:** 1-44-21-31-01; **Internet:** www.fdf.org; **e-mail:** fondation@fdf.org.

Open Society Institute—Paris (Soros Foundations)

Established as the Open Society Institute's Paris branch, part of the Soros foundations network, which aims to foster political and cultural pluralism and reform economic structures in order to encourage private enterprise and a market economy.

Activities: Acts as a networking and resource centre to assist Soros foundations and affiliated organizations in Central and Eastern Europe in fostering cultural and educational exchange programmes with international donor organizations in Western European countries.

Geographical Area of Activity: Central and Eastern Europe.

Finance: Annual expenditure US $254,000 (2000).

Principal Staff: Exec. Dir Annette Laborey.

Address: 38 blvd Beaumarchais, 75011 Paris.

Telephone: 1-48-05-24-74; **Fax:** 1-40-21-65-41; **Internet:** www.soros.org; **e-mail:** sorosfr@worldnet.fr.

Réseau d'ONG Européennes sur l'Agro-alimentaire, le Commerce, l'Environnement et le Développement—RONGEAD (European NGOs on Agriculture, Food, Trade and Development)

Founded in 1983 to support professional and non-governmental development organizations in Europe and less-developed countries.

Activities: Acts as a co-ordinating body for European NGOs and NGOs and professional organizations in less-developed countries concerned with agriculture, food and trade issues in the developing world. Organizes an information exchange network, and education programmes in Europe, and runs training seminars for local groups in developing countries.

Geographical Area of Activity: Europe, Africa, Pacific region, Caribbean, North America.

Publications: *WTO and Developing Countries*.

Board of Trustees: Maurice Perroux (Pres.).

Principal Staff: Dir Joseph Rocher.

Address: 14 rue Antoine-Dumont, 69372 Lyon Cedex 08.

Telephone: 4-72-71-66-70; **Fax:** 4-78-69-86-96; **Internet:** www.rongead.org; **e-mail:** rongead@rongead.org.

FOUNDATIONS, TRUSTS AND NON-PROFIT ORGANIZATIONS

Académie Goncourt—Société des Gens de Lettres (Goncourt Academy—Goncourt Literary Society)

Founded in 1896 by a legacy of Edmond de Goncourt, to support literature, to give material assistance to a certain number of writers and to strengthen the links between them.

Activities: Awards the annual Prix Goncourt for the best prose work of the year published in French, as well as scholarships in different fields of literature. The Academy has 10 members. Since 1973 the Academy has aimed to encourage francophone literature throughout the world, and to support international cultural exchanges; it organizes conferences and lectures.

Geographical Area of Activity: France and francophone countries.

Principal Staff: Pres. Edmonde Charles-Roux; Sec.-Gen. Didier Decoin.

Address: c/o Drouant, place Gaillon, 75002 Paris.

Telephone: 1-45-20-27-21; **Internet:** www.academie-goncourt.fr.

Action contre la Faim (Action against Hunger)

Established in 1979 to combat hunger world-wide.

Activities: Operates emergency and post-emergency programmes to combat hunger; programmes include nutrition, health, water and food security, and agricultural development projects; sister organizations operate in Spain, the United Kingdom and the USA.

Geographical Area of Activity: Central and South America, Africa, Eastern Europe, Asia and the Far East.

Publications: Newsletter (monthly); *Géopolitique de la Faim; Alimentation en eau; La Faim dans le Monde; Souffles du Monde; La Malnutrition en Situation de Crise.*

Principal Staff: Pres. Benoit Miribel; Dir Gen. Jean-Christophe Rufin, Treas. Xavier Audéon.

Address: 4 rue Niepce, 75014 Paris.

Telephone: 1-43-35-88-88; **Fax:** 1-45-35-88-00; **Internet:** www.acf-fr.org; **e-mail:** info@acf.imaginet.fr.

Action d'Urgence Internationale—AUI (International Emergency Action)

Founded in 1977 with the aim of co-ordinating organizations and volunteers to provide aid during times of natural disaster.

Activities: Has provided emergency aid in numerous countries, including Algeria, Bangladesh, Colombia, Costa Rica, France, India, Italy, Nicaragua, the Philippines and Turkey. Organizes training courses and workshops in emergency medical care for volunteers who are then sent to disaster areas; researches into ways in which disasters may be anticipated and prepared for; holds conferences. There are member organizations in 15 countries.

Geographical Area of Activity: International.

Publications: *La Déferlante* (bulletin, three a year).

Principal Staff: Joint Pres. and Chair. Christian Herbette, Fréderique Bonneaud.

Address: Les Terraces de Montcalm, 1401 rue de Fontcouverte, 34070 Montpellier.

Telephone: 4-67-27-06-09; **Fax:** 4-67-27-03-59; **Internet:** www.aui-ong.org; **e-mail:** aui-ong@tiscali.fr.

Agence Internationale pour le Développement (Agency for International Development)

Founded in 1986 with the aim of helping developing countries to resolve their economic problems caused through increased industrialization. In 1998 formed the Federation of International Agencies for Development represented in 17 countries and including 165 NGO members.

Activities: Operates educational programmes with an emphasis on self-help; provides training for industrial work; promotes agricultural projects; works towards improving the quality of life of people in developing countries by improving sanitation conditions, children's services and humanitarian aid; conducts research; organizes seminars and symposia; operates a documentation centre and reference library. Holds General Consultative Status with the United Nations Economic and Social Council.

Geographical Area of Activity: International.

Publications: *Journal* (quarterly).

Finance: Annual budget approx. US $4,600,000.

Principal Staff: Pres. Abdelkbir El-Hakkaoui.

Address: 29 rue Traversiere, 75012 Paris.

Telephone: 1-40-19-91-51; **Fax:** 1-43-44-38-40; **Internet:** www.aide-federation.org; **e-mail:** international@aide-federation.org.

Agir Ici (Act Here)

Established to protect human rights, the environment, to fight poverty in countries of the South, and to support organizations working towards peace and disarmament.

Activities: Operates in the fields of the environment, human rights and international affairs (peace and disarmament), mainly through running public campaigns, with other French and international organizations, including promoting the writing of letters to political and economic decision-makers and lobbying for the reform of international financial institutions. Agir Ici had about 12,000 members in 2003.

Geographical Area of Activity: International.

Publications: Annual Report; brochures; country dossiers.

Address: 104 rue Oberkampf, 75011 Paris.

Telephone: 1-56-98-24-40; **Fax:** 1-56-98-24-09; **Internet:** www.agirici.org; **e-mail:** agirici@agririci.org.

Aide et Action

Established in 1981, by Pierre-Bernard Le Bas, to improve standards of education in Africa and India.

Activities: The organization supports the education of children currently in 12 less-developed countries, including Rwanda, Haiti, Togo, Senegal, Niger, Tanzania, Madagascar, Cambodia and India, through child sponsorship, building classrooms, training teachers, providing educational materials and equipment and materials for a mobile school, school canteens and gardens. Works in partnership with other organizations, including ActionAid (q.v.).

Geographical Area of Activity: Africa, India, South-East Asia and the Caribbean.

Publications: *Ecoliers du Monde* (quarterly).

Finance: Annual budget €18,000,000 (2002).

Board of Directors: Frederic Naquet (Pres.); Francoise Alcocer-Riboulet (Vice-Pres.); Monique Bremond (Treas.); Jacques Lemarechal (Sec.); Jean-Claude Bourrelier; Evelyne Delaistre; Jean Jourdan.

Principal Staff: Man. Dir Claire Calosci; African Programme Dir Youssouf Cissé; Volunteer Action Dir Jean-Charles Thélot.

Address: 53 blvd de Charonne, 75545 Paris Cedex 11.

Telephone: 1-55-25-70-00; **Fax:** 1-55-25-70-29; **Internet:** www.aide-et-action.org; **e-mail:** info@aide-et-action.org.

Alliance Israélite Universelle (Universal Jewish Alliance)

Founded in 1860 by Narcisse Leven, Charles Netter, Isidore Cahen, Eugène Manuel, Aristide Astruc and Jules Carvallo, to work for the emancipation and moral progress of Jewish people.

Activities: Operates internationally in the fields of education and religion through self-conducted programmes, publications and lectures. Maintains a network of schools in Belgium, Canada, France, Israel, Morocco and Spain, and a Hebrew teacher training college in Casablanca, Morocco, the Ecole Normale Hébraïque. The Alliance holds a Jewish library of more than 120,000 volumes and runs the Collège des études juives and the Nadir publishing house. Through the Consultative Council of Jewish Organizations, the Alliance contributes to the defence of international human rights.

Geographical Area of Activity: International.

Publications: *Les Cahiers de l'AIU; Les Cahiers du judaisme.*

Governing Board: Ady Steg (Pres.).

Principal Staff: Dir Jean-Jacques Wahl.

Address: 45 rue La Bruyère, 75009 Paris.

Telephone: 1-53-32-88-55; **Fax:** 1-48-74-51-33; **Internet:** www.aiu.org; **e-mail:** info@aiu.org.

ATD Quart-Monde (ATD Fourth World)

Founded by Father Joseph Wresinksi, as Aide à Toute Détresse (ATD) in 1957; aims to eliminate extreme poverty and exclusion all over the world, and is open to people of all religious or political convictions.

Activities: Operates in Europe, Africa, North and Central America and Asia in the fields of human rights and social development. Education and training programmes in the areas of nursery schools, family centres, literacy and basic skills training, regular Fourth World University gatherings and artistic and cultural programmes with children and young people are undertaken by members of ATD's Volunteer Corps. Raises awareness about the poverty affecting many of the world's population, carries out research into poverty in partnership with the people affected, and works to combat these problems. Holds consultative status with ECOSOC, UNICEF, ILO and the Council of Europe.

Geographical Area of Activity: Europe, Africa, North and Central America and Asia.

Publications: *Artisans of Democracy; The Human Face of Poverty; Talk With Us, Not At Us; This is How We Live: Listening to the Poorest Families;* and other publications.

Address: 107 ave du Général Leclerc, 95480 Pierrelaye.

Internet: www.atd-quartmonde.org; **e-mail:** information@atd-fourthworld.mvt.org.

Aviation Sans Frontières (Aviation Without Frontiers)

Established in 1980, by André Gréard, Gérald Similowski and Alain Yout, to make air transport available for humanitarian relief.

Activities: Operates in France and internationally, providing humanitarian relief through volunteer air services, transporting people in less-developed countries in need of medical aid, dispatching medical supplies and transporting medical personnel, offering emergency assistance following natural disasters, and assisting other NGOs in their activities; volunteers accompany children on flights to countries where they can be treated.

Geographical Area of Activity: France, Africa, South-East Asia and Central America.

Publications: Bulletin (quarterly, in French).

Finance: Funded by donations and membership fees. Assets 7,884,435,08 francs (2000).

Directors: J. Ritter (Pres.); A. Fournerat, J. Guerrier (Vice-Pres); G. Sévignac (Gen. Sec.); G. Pocheron (Treas.).

Address: Orly Freight 768, 94398 Orly Aérogares Cedex.

Telephone: 1-49-75-74-37; **Fax:** 1-49-75-74-33; **Internet:** www.asf-fr.org; **e-mail:** asfparis@asf-fr.org.

Centre d'Études, de Documentation, d'Information et d'Action Sociales—CÉDIAS—Musée Social (Centre for Social Studies, Documentation, Information and Action)

Founded in 1963 through the merger of the Office Central des Oeuvres de Bienfaisance and the Musée Social, which was founded in 1894.

Activities: Operates nationally in the field of education, and both nationally and internationally in the fields of social welfare and studies, economic affairs, law and other professions, through conferences, courses, publications and lectures organized and sponsored in France. Maintains a library containing documentation compiled in France and abroad on subjects in the social field.

Geographical Area of Activity: France.

Publications: *Revue Vie Sociale* (6 a year); *Les implicites de la politique familiale*; and other publications.

Administrative Council: Marc de Montalembert (Pres.); Edouard Secretan, Jean-Pierre Mallet (Vice-Pres.); Jacques Ladsous (Sec.-Gen.); Jacqueline Bonneau; Michel Chauvière; René Clouet; Philippe Godeau; Claude Meyer; Henri Pequignot; Monique Sassier; Antoine Savoye.

Principal Staff: Dir Jean-Yves Barreyre.

Address: 5 rue Las Cases, 75007 Paris.

Telephone: 1-45-51-66-10; **Fax:** 1-44-18-01-81; **Internet:** www.cedias.org; **e-mail:** administration.cedias@wanadoo.fr.

Centre Français de Droit Comparé (French Centre of Comparative Law)

Founded in 1951 to co-ordinate research and publication in the fields of international and comparative law within France; to co-ordinate libraries of comparative law and develop conformity of documentation in the field; to organize meetings on an international level; and to encourage exchange of scholars in the field.

Activities: Operates nationally and internationally in the field of international comparative law, through self-conducted programmes, research, conferences, courses, publications and lectures. Awards prizes annually for theses in comparative law.

Geographical Area of Activity: International.

Publications: *Revue Internationale de Droit Comparé* (4 a year); series of monographs.

Principal Staff: Pres. Prof. Jacques Robert; Sec.-Gen. Didier Lamèthe; Treas. André Delion.

Address: 28 rue Saint-Guillaume, 75007 Paris.

Telephone: 1-44-39-86-23; **Fax:** 1-44-39-86-28; **e-mail:** cfdc@legiscompare.com.

Centre International de Coopération pour le Développement Agricole—CICDA

Established in 1977 by Bertrand Naegelen, Jean-Marie Abbès and Jean-Marie Lechevallier to provide agricultural development aid.

Activities: Operates in the field of aid to less developed countries, through supporting agricultural development, in order to improve the quality of life of people living in rural areas of Bolivia, Brazil, Ecuador, Guatemala, Haiti, Morocco, Peru, Venezuela and Romania. Provides technical and financial support, the exchange of knowledge and information, and training for land-workers in these areas; and funds local development projects and publications focusing on local aid.

Geographical Area of Activity: Central and South America and the Caribbean, North Africa, and Eastern Europe.

Restrictions: Grants only to specific countries and agricultural organizations.

Publications: *Ruralter* (issues 1–18).

Finance: Funded by the European Union, the French Ministry of Foreign Affairs and various grants. Annual revenue and expenditure €2,000,000 (2001).

Principal Staff: Pres. Bertrand Naegelen; Dir Jean-Jacques Boutrou; Admin. and Finance Dir Elisabeth Muller.

Address: 45 bis, ave de la Belle Gabrielle, 94736 Nogent-sur-Marne Cedex.

Telephone: 1-43-94-72-01; **Fax:** 1-43-94-72-17; **Internet:** www.cicda.org; **e-mail:** cicda@cicda.org.

Centre International de Développement et de Recherche—CIDR (International Centre for Development and Research)

Established in 1982 to support less-developed countries.

Activities: Operates in Africa, including Burkina Faso, Cameroon and Mali, in the field of aid to less-developed countries, through providing assistance in areas such as agricultural development, health, micro-enterprise and food security. Raises awareness of development issues in France and abroad.

Geographical Area of Activity: Africa.

Publications: Annual Report.

Principal Staff: Contact: Renée Chao-Béroff.

Address: 17 rue de l'Hermitage, 60350 Autrèches.

Telephone: 3-44-42-71-40; **Fax:** 3-44-42-94-52; **e-mail:** cidr@compuserve.com.

Centre International de Recherche sur le Cancer—CIRC (International Agency for Research on Cancer—IARC)

Founded in 1965 as a self-governing body within the framework of the World Health Organization, to generate and disseminate information useful for the primary prevention of cancer, through both intra- and extra-mural activities.

Activities: Operates internationally in the field of medical research, through self-conducted programmes and collaboration with other agencies, as well as with national institutions and laboratories. The Agency has developed programmes that represent an integrated approach to the identification of causative factors in human cancer, and of individuals and population groups at different risks of developing cancer. Topics of research include: studies on geographical incidence and time trends; determination of environmental and occupational hazards; site-oriented studies; childhood cancer; nutrition and cancer; genetics and cancer; mechanisms of carcinogenesis; and host susceptibility in chemical carcinogenesis. Studies for the improvement of data collection and of research methods are also conducted. The Agency provides technical support in the form of computing services and statistical support, library and bibliographical services, banks of human biological material, and common laboratory services. Research training fellowships and a visiting scientist award are awarded annually, and training courses on cancer epidemiology are held in various countries.

Geographical Area of Activity: World-wide.

Publications: Biennial Report; *IARC Monographs on the Evaluation of Carcinogenic Risks to Humans; Directory of On-Going Research in Cancer Epidemiology; Cancer Incidence in Five Continents; IARC Scientific Publications* (symposia proceedings, manuals, monographs).

Finance: Regular budget US $18,000,000 (2003).

Governing Council: Membership is made up of representatives of each of the 16 Member States plus the Director-General of the World Health Organization.

Principal Staff: Dir Dr P. Kleihues; Communications Officer Dr N. Gaudin; Dir, Admin and Finance V. Hay.

Address: 150 cours Albert-Thomas, 69372 Lyon Cedex 08.

Telephone: 4-72-73-84-85; **Fax:** 4-72-73-85-75; **Internet:** www.iarc.fr; **e-mail:** gaudin@iarc.fr.

CIMADE—Service Oecuménique d'Entraide (Oceanic Service for Mutual Help)

Founded in 1939 by French Protestant youth movements under the presidency of the Rev. Marc Boegner for work among refugees and immigrants.

Activities: Supports work among refugees and migrant workers in France, with emphasis on the defence of human rights. CIMADE also attempts to raise public awareness of these groups in France and the rest of Europe. Internationally, the organization works in partnership with local organizations supporting projects in the fields of human rights, health and agriculture.

Geographical Area of Activity: Africa, the Middle East and Europe.

Publications: *Causes Communes* (journal, 6 a year); directory; special documents.

Finance: Annual budget €5,474,000.

Principal Staff: Pres. Jacques Stewart; Sec.-Gen. Jean-Marc Dupeux; Treas. Lionel Sautter.

Address: 176 rue de Grenelle, 75007 Paris.

Telephone: 1-44-18-60-50; **Fax:** 1-45-56-08-59; **Internet:** www.cimade.org; **e-mail:** direction@cimade.org.

Cité Internationale des Arts (International Centre for the Arts)

Founded in 1957 by Félix Brunau, Paul Leon and Eero de Snellman to gather the necessary funds for, and to ensure the construction and maintenance of, community buildings and installations at the Cité Internationale des Arts, as well as artists' studios and houses in the estate.

Activities: Operates internationally in the field of the arts, through the construction and management of studios which may be purchased by individuals or institutions of any nation, to enable an artist of their choice to reside at the Cité. Programmes are also carried out through the organization of concerts and exhibitions, and through the Association of Friends of the Cité Internationale des Arts.

Geographical Area of Activity: Mainly France.

Address: 18 rue de l'Hôtel de Ville, 75004 Paris.

Telephone: 1-42-78-71-72; **Internet:** www.citedesartsparis.net.

Cité Internationale Universitaire de Paris (International University Centre of Paris)

Founded in 1924 to provide accommodation for foreign students and professors.

Activities: The Cité forms part of the University of Paris and comprises at present 37 houses, accommodating some 6,000 students, professors and research workers of all nationalities. Cultural, sports and other communal activities are centralized in the Maison Internationale.

Geographical Area of Activity: France.

Address: 47B blvd Jourdan, 75014 Paris.

Telephone: 1-58-10-21-00; **Fax:** 1-45-80-39-38; **Internet:** www.ciup.fr.

Écoles Sans Frontières (Schools Without Frontiers)

Founded in 1980 to provide education to refugees in South-East Asia (Laos and Vietnam), and Albania.

Activities: Researches into the educational needs of refugees; finances training courses for teachers; organizes programmes in basic learning skills for refugees, in their own language where possible; and participates in resettlement projects. Volunteers participate in two-year programmes.

Geographical Area of Activity: South-East Asia and Albania.

Publications: Annual Report; educational books.

Finance: Annual budget approx. €611,572.

Principal Staff: Exec. Officers A. L. Jubert, N. Seywert.

Address: BP 466, 83514 La Seyne.

Telephone: 4-94-30-09-10; **Fax:** 4-94-30-10-25; **Internet:** perso.wanadoo.fr/ecolessansfrontieres; **e-mail:** esf.france@wanadoo.fr.

Emmaüs International/Emaús Internacional

Established internationally in 1971 (Emmaüs founded in 1949 by Abbé Pierre), an international movement promoting solidarity, combating the causes of exclusion and injustice.

Activities: Operates nationally and internationally in the areas of social welfare, development and conservation of the environment, assisting people with disabilities, those with addictions, ex-prisoners, refugees and other underprivileged people, through the creation of communities for marginalized people; promoting fair trade; developing networking between groups in less-developed countries; and supporting recycling activities. The international office acts as a liaison centre for member organizations world-wide.

Geographical Area of Activity: International.

Publications: *Emmaüs International Newsletter* (quarterly); *Tam–Tam* (quarterly).

Principal Staff: Pres. Renzo Fior; Deputy Pres. Koubi Koala; Sec.-Gen. Jean-Marie Viennet; Deputy Sec.-Gen. Ulla Hoyer; Treas. Alberto de Urquiza; Exec. Dir Alain Fontaine.

Address: 183 bis rue Vaillant Couturier, BP 91, 94143 Alforville Cedex.

Telephone: 1-48-93-29-50; **Fax:** 1-43-53-19-26; **Internet:** www.emmaus-international.org; **e-mail:** contact@emmaus-international.org.

Enfance et Partage (Children and Sharing)

Established in 1977 to protect children from neglect, and physical, psychological and sexual abuse.

Activities: Operates nationally (50% of its budget) and internationally (30% of its budget). Gives psychological support to child victims of physical, mental and sexual abuse in France through providing a telephone support line, legal support and psychotherapy; supports projects in less-developed countries in collaboration with other local and international NGOs: projects are currently in progress in Benin, Chile, Colombia, Madagascar, Mauritius, the Philippines and Togo; also provides emergency aid.

Geographical Area of Activity: France, Africa, South America and the Caribbean, and the Far East.

Restrictions: No public grants.

Publications: *Enfance et Partage* (quarterly).

Finance: Net assets 10,699,622 francs (1999); annual revenue 8,388,097 francs, expenditure 7,432,774 francs (1999).

Principal Staff: Pres. Jacqueline Darmigny; Vice-Pres. Micheline Zmirou; Treas. Annick Blevin; Dir Marie-Claude Vidal;.

Address: 2–4 Cité Ameublement, 75011 Paris.

Telephone: 1-55-25-65-65; **Fax:** 1-55-25-65-66; **Internet:** www.enfance-et-partage.org; **e-mail:** contacts@enfance-et-partage.org.

Enfants du Mekong (Children of the Mekong)

Established in Laos in 1958 by René Péchard to assist children and families in South-East Asia.

Activities: Operates in Cambodia, Laos, Nepal, the Philippines, Thailand, Tibet and Vietnam, as well as in France, constructing schools and medical centres, supporting individual children and their families, housing children from South-East Asia in France, supporting the French South-East Asian community, and issuing publications. Was awarded the French prix des Droits de l'Homme (human rights prize) in 1990.

Geographical Area of Activity: Cambodia, France, Laos, Nepal, the Philippines, Thailand, Tibet and Vietnam.

Publications: *Enfants du Fleuve* (series); *Revue Enfants du Mekong* (magazine).

Finance: Net assets €4,595,000 (2000); annual revenue €4,798,000, expenditure €4,746,000 (2000).

Council of Administration: François Foucart (Pres.); Alain Deblock (Vice-Pres.); Gérard Bruley des Varannes, Christine Lortholary Nguyen (Sec.-Gen.); Tristan de Bodman (Treas.); and 13 other members.

Principal Staff: Dir-Gen. Yves Meaudre.

Address: 5 rue de la Comète, 92600 Asnières.

Telephone: 1-47-91-00-84; **Fax:** 1-47-33-40-44; **Internet:** www.enfantsdumekong.com; **e-mail:** edmasn@enfantsdumekong.com.

Enfants Réfugiés du Monde—ERM

Established in 1981 to help refugee and displaced children in the developing world.

Activities: Provides aid to children in distress throughout the world, including providing food, shelter, health care, education and psychological support to those who have suffered trauma. Also runs training programmes for local personnel. Work focuses particularly on areas of Algeria, Bosnia, Cambodia, Gaza (Palestinian Autonomous Areas), Guatemala, Guinea, Lebanon, Kosovo, Rwanda and Sierra-Leone.

Geographical Area of Activity: Africa, the Middle East, South-Eastern Europe and Central America.

Publications: Newsletter (quarterly).

Finance: Total expenditure US $3,252,923 (1999).

Principal Staff: Pres. Phillipe Vals; Treas. Denis Wetzel; Sec.-Gen. Muriel Roque; Dir Nicole Dagnino.

Address: Cap Gaillard, 34 rue Gaston Lauriau, 93512 Montreuil.

Telephone: 1-48-59-60-29; **Fax:** 1-48-59-64-88; **Internet:** www.enfantsrefugiesdumonde.org; **e-mail:** erm@enfantsrefugiesdumonde.org.

Equilibre (Equilibrium)

Established in 1984 to support countries in the developing world.

Activities: Operates internationally in the field of aid to less-developed countries, through providing direct assistance to developing countries in the areas of agriculture, education, housing, micro-enterprise, health care and humanitarian aid. Also provides emergency relief.

Geographical Area of Activity: Africa and the Middle East.

Publications: Annual report; Newsletter (quarterly).

Principal Staff: Pres. Alain Michel.

Address: 23 allée du Mens, BP 1613, 69606 Villeurbanne (Lyon) Cedex.

Telephone: 3-20-38-05-80.

Fédération Internationale des Ligues des Droits de L'Homme—FIDH (International Federation of Human Rights)

Established in 1922, a non-profit NGO, to fight for international justice and defend human rights as contained in the Universal Declaration of Human Rights.

Activities: Operates internationally, representing 116 national human rights organizations, that are working in 90 countries to defend human rights. Organizes campaigns, lobbies internationally, co-ordinates a human rights network, provides information services, and works to protect people suffering from human rights abuses. Issues publications.

Geographical Area of Activity: International.

Publications: *La Lettre* (newsletter, 10 annually); *Mission Reports* (15 annually).

Finance: Annual revenue 11,248,000 francs, expenditure 10,871,000 francs (2000).

Principal Staff: Pres. Sidiki Kaba; Treas. Philippe Vallet.

Address: 17 passage de la Main d'Or, 75011 Paris.

Telephone: 1-43-55-25-18; **Fax:** 1-43-55-18-80; **Internet:** www.fidh.org; **e-mail:** fidh@fidh.org.

Fondation 30 Millions d'Amis (30 Million Friends Foundation)

Established in 1995 by Jean-Pierre Hutin to promote respect for and protection of animals.

Activities: Operates nationally and internationally to protect animals. Makes grants to centres for abandoned animals, provides food supplies and veterinary support for the treatment, vaccination and sterilization of animals. Campaigns against experimentation on animals, and for the protection of animals close to extinction. Runs an on-line animal adoption service.

Geographical Area of Activity: International.

Principal Staff: Pres. Reha Hutin.

Address: 40 cours Albert 1er, 75402 Paris Cedex 08.

Telephone: 1-56-59-04-44; **Fax:** 1-58-56-33-55; **Internet:** www.30millionsdamis.fr; **e-mail:** mabrouk@30millionsdamis.fr.

Fondation Agir Contre l'Exclusion—Fondation FACE (Campaign Against Exclusion Foundation)

Founded in 1993 on the initiative of Martine Aubry, by 13 French companies, including Casino, Club Méditerranée, Crédit Lyonnais, Renault and Péchiney, with the aim of mobilizing companies to develop, in collaboration with local authorities and local partners, campaigns against social exclusion.

Activities: The Foundation aims to diminish social exclusion in employment and local enterprise, through research and activities aimed locally and nationally. Enterprise centres in many different sectors, such as the environment, recreation, tourism, goods and services, aim to support the local community and rejuvenate training and employment facilities. In 2001 a total of 962 French companies were involved in the Foundation's activities.

Geographical Area of Activity: France.

Finance: Receives funding from a number of French companies. Assets approx. €7,662,451.

Governing Board: Antoine Guichard (Pres.); Marc Ladreit de Lacharriere, Frédéric Pascal (Vice-Pres.); Alain Minc (Treas.); Pierre de Saintignon.

Principal Staff: Dir Patrick Nedelec; Contact: Margaret Johnston-Clarke.

Address: 48 rue de la Roquette, 75011 Paris.

Telephone: 1-49-23-77-77; **Fax:** 1-42-23-77-94; **Internet:** www.fondationface.org; **e-mail:** secretariat@fondationface.org.

Fondation Air France

Established in 1993 by Air France and Servair for the education and training of disadvantaged children.

Activities: Operates in the field of education, nationally and internationally, through self-conducted programmes and grants to institutions. The Foundation's main focus is on children from underprivileged urban or rural areas, refugee children, and ill or disabled children.

Geographical Area of Activity: Mainly France.

Principal Staff: Chair. of Board Gérard Orizet; Gen. Sec. Marthe de la Taille Rivero.

Address: 1 ave du Maréchal Devaux, 91550 Paray-Vieille-Poste Cedex.

Telephone: 1-41-75-71-96; **Fax:** 1-41-75-71-97; **Internet:** www.airfrance.net; **e-mail:** mail.fondation@airfrance.fr.

Fondation Auchan pour la Jeunesse (Auchan Foundation for Youth)

Established in 1996 by the Auchan Group, one of the largest world-wide retailers, under the aegis of the Fondation de France (q.v.).

Activities: Supports projects oriented towards young people, in the fields of job creation, health and prevention, and community development. Priority is given to projects in close proximity to an Auchan hypermarket.

Geographical Area of Activity: France, particularly in areas of company operation.

Restrictions: Does not give money for sponsorship.

Principal Staff: Pres. Francis Cordelette; Vice-Pres. Marie-Hélène Boidin-Dubrule.

Address: 40 ave de Flandre, BP 137, 59964 Croix Cedex.

Telephone: 3-20-81-68-65; **Fax:** 3-20-81-69-32; **Internet:** www.auchan.com; **e-mail:** mfmairesse@auchan.fr.

Fondation de l'Avenir (Foundation for the Future)

Established in 1987 by the Mutualité Fonction Publique and the Association Française de Cautionnement Mutuel.

Activities: Operates nationally in the area of medicine and health, through supporting applied medical research into new surgical techniques, and training.

Geographical Area of Activity: France.

Publications: Newsletter (monthly).

Finance: Annual budget €5,200,000 (2001).

Scientific Council: Prof. Patrice Tran Ba Huy (Pres.); Jean Bachet (Sec.).

Principal Staff: Pres. Etienne Caniard.

Address: 28 rue Beaunier, 75014 Paris.

Telephone: 1-58-14-22-60; **Fax:** 1-58-14-22-70; **Internet:** www.fondationdelavenir.fr.

Fondation Brigitte Bardot (Brigitte Bardot Foundation)

Established in 1986 for the protection of wild and domestic animals world-wide.

Activities: Operates in France and world-wide in the area of conservation and the environment, promoting the defence of the rights of wild and domestic animals. Also runs a retirement home for animals in Normandy, France.

Geographical Area of Activity: International.

Publications: *Info Journal*.

Principal Staff: Pres. Brigitte Bardot.

Address: 45 rue Vineuse, 75116 Paris.

Telephone: 1-45-05-14-60; **Fax:** 1-45-05-14-80; **Internet:** www.fondationbrigittebardot.fr; **e-mail:** fbb@fondationbrigittebardot.fr.

Fondation Marcel Bleustein-Blanchet pour la Vocation (Marcel Bleustein-Blanchet Vocation Foundation)

Founded in 1960 by Marcel Bleustein-Blanchet to encourage young people to achieve their chosen vocation.

Activities: The Foundation gives financial and practical help to young people aged between 18 and 30 years: it awards 20 scholarships ('Bourses de la Vocation') annually to provide training for young French and European people in numerous branches of science, technology, medicine, the arts and sports. Two prizes, the Prix Littéraire de la Vocation and the Prix de Poésie, are awarded annually for literary work in the French language. 'Sister' foundations have been established in Belgium, Brazil, Israel, Spain and Switzerland.

Geographical Area of Activity: Europe.

Restrictions: Finance is not provided for pursuing religious or political vocations.

Principal Staff: Pres. Elisabeth Badinter.

Address: 104 rue de Rennes, 75006 Paris.

Telephone: 1-53-63-25-90; **Fax:** 1-42-22-16-66; **Internet:** http://pro.wanadoo.fr/fondationpourlavocation/.

Fondation BNP Paribas (BNP Paribas Foundation)

Established in 1984 to fund cultural and humanitarian projects, operating under the aegis of the Fondation de France (q.v.).

Activities: Operates in France and internationally, where BNP Paribas maintains offices, in the areas of medical research, culture, the arts and humanities and social welfare, through funding long-term and innovative projects, including art, book and museum exhibitions, dance and collaboration with recording companies, scholarships for students wishing to study law, finance or economics in France, supporting genetic medical research, as well as funding projects combating social exclusion.

Geographical Area of Activity: International.

Principal Staff: Pres. François Delbiesse; Sec.-Gen. Martine Tridde Mazloum.

Address: 3 rue d'Antin, 75002 Paris.

Telephone: 1-42-98-07-67; **Fax:** 1-42-98-14-11; **Internet:** www.bnpparibas.com.

Fondation Cartier pour l'Art Contemporain (Cartier Foundation for Contemporary Art)

Founded in 1984 by Alain-Dominique Perrin, to promote creative arts, and to establish direct dialogue between artists and the general public.

Activities: Commissions works of art to exhibit at the foundation's sites and abroad; collects and exhibits the works of young artists and stages exhibitions of its collection of contemporary art (maintains a collection of over 900 works of art by around 250 artists from France and world-wide); and commissions transitory or performance art for evening performances at the Foundation sites. The Foundation also organizes travelling exhibitions and promotes artistic exchange with foreign institutions, organizes conferences, and issues publications.

Geographical Area of Activity: Asia, South America, Europe and the USA.

Publications: Artists' books and exhibition catalogues.

Finance: Financed by the Cartier Group.

Principal Staff: Pres. Alain-Dominique Perrin; Dir Hervé Chandès.

Address: 261 blvd Raspail, 75014 Paris.

Telephone: 1-42-18-56-50; **Fax:** 1-42-18-56-52; **Internet:** www.fondation.cartier.fr; **e-mail:** herve.chandes@vendome.com.

Fondation Henri Cartier-Bresson (Henri Cartier-Bresson Foundation)

Established in early 2003 to promote photography in general as well as the work of Henri Cartier-Bresson.

Activities: The Foundation promotes the work of Henri Cartier-Bresson, through the establishment of a studio to house the photographer's works, negatives, books, films and designs, which is open to researchers. Every two years the Foundation awards the Henri Cartier-Bresson prize of €30,000, launched in June 2003. Also organizes exhibitions of Cartier-Bresson's work and the work of other photographers.

Finance: Budget approx. €381,000.

Principal Staff: Pres. Henri Cartier-Bresson; Dir Robert Delpire.

Address: 1 rue Thérèse, 75001 Paris.

Telephone: 1-47-03-61-00; **Internet:** www.henricartierbresson.org; **e-mail:** veronique@corporart.com.

Fondation de Coubertin (Coubertin Foundation)

Established as a foundation in 1973 for the further training of young craft workers, and for the conservation of and research into craft techniques.

Activities: Operates in the area of education and training, offering courses of 11 months for some 30 young craft workers annually, from France or abroad, between the ages of 20 and 25. Courses involve general courses and crafts such as joinery, decorative metal, fine-art foundry and stone masonry. Also organizes concerts open to the public, and seminars for professionals.

Geographical Area of Activity: International.

Address: BP 2, 78470 Saint-Rémy-lès-Chevreuse.

Telephone: 1-30-85-69-60; **Fax:** 1-30-85-69-99; **Internet:** www.fondation-coubertin.asso.fr; **e-mail:** info@fondation-coubertin.asso.fr.

Fondation Jean Dausset/CEPH—Centre d'Étude du Polymorphisme Humain (Centre for the Study of Human Polymorphism)

The Centre was founded in 1983 by Prof. Daniel Cohen and Prof. Jean Dausset to promote and conduct research into the human genome.

Activities: The Centre operates nationally and internationally in the fields of medicine and health, and science and technology, through self-conducted programmes, research and publications. It conducts genetic research and produced the first 'map' of the genetic constitution of human beings (genome map). Research is also carried out at its 'daughter' laboratory, Généthon, which is now an independent organization. The Centre maintains a database and the on-line Human BAC Library.

Publications: *Physical Map of the Human Genome*; scientific periodicals.

Finance: The Centre was founded using a US $10,000,000 bequest from a French art collector.

Board of Directors: The Board comprises the Founder Members, *de jure* Members, and Members elected by the Board according to their merit. Prof. Jean Dausset (Pres.); the French Ministers of Health, of the Interior and of Higher Education and Research; and a representative of the Paris Hospitals Social Welfare Department.

Address: 27 rue Juliette Dodu, 75010 Paris.

Telephone: 1-53-72-51-50; **Fax:** 1-53-72-51-28; **Internet:** www.cephb.fr; **e-mail:** webmaster@cephb.fr.

Fondation Simone et Cino del Duca (Simone and Cino del Duca Foundation)

Founded in 1975 by Simone del Duca to maintain, develop and improve the natural and cultural heritage, and to promote scientific research, especially biomedical research.

Activities: Operates internationally in the fields of science and medicine, and the arts and humanities, through making grants to organizations, awarding prizes and awarding a number of maintenance and travel grants for French research workers wishing to study abroad, and for foreign research workers to spend a period of time in a French laboratory. Grants are exclusively made to research workers whose scientific activity is in the following areas: the cardiovascular system (molecular and cellular biology, pathology, pharmacology and epidemiology), and the nervous system, behaviour and mental health (molecular and cellular biology, pathology, pharmacology and epidemiology), and are made to research workers provided that they have obtained a doctorate before applying for the grant. In the arts and humanities, the Foundation awards the Prix Mondial Cino del Duca and music, painting and sculpture prizes, makes two literary grants for published and unpublished authors, and organizes Medici conference weeks in Rome and conferences in Paris.

Geographical Area of Activity: International.

Publications: Report of operations.

Principal Staff: Pres. Simone del Duca.

Address: 10 rue Alfred-de-Vigny, 75008 Paris.

Telephone: 1-47-66-01-21; **Fax:** 1-46-22-45-02.

Fondation Eisai (Eisai Foundation)

Established in 2002 by the Eisai company to promote health.

Activities: Provides support to sick people and their families, through funding public awareness activities and health projects, organizing symposia to disseminate medical knowledge, and the creation of support centres. Also provides study scholarships to nurses and awards three annual prizes worth €6,000 each to projects organized by nurses or health-care workers, which aim to preserve the dignity of elderly people and increase their automomy.

Geographical Area of Activity: Mainly France.

Principal Staff: Pres. Dr Paul Cadre.

Address: 231 rue Saint Honoré, 75001 Paris.

Telephone: 1-47-67-00-05; **Fax:** 1-47-67-00-15; **Internet:** www.fondation-eisai.org; **e-mail:** contact@greenwich-corporate.com.

Fondation Electricité de France (France Electricity Foundation)

Established in 1987 to fund projects in the fields of the environment, culture, health, sport and solidarity.

Activities: Operates in France in the fields of the arts and humanities, scientific and medical research, and conservation and the environment, principally working in the areas of cultural heritage and conservation, and contemporary creative initiatives. Created an exhibition area, Espace EDF Electra, in Paris for exhibitions of contemporary art, concerts, conferences, etc. Collaborates with national institutions on cultural and environmental projects. Awards an annual medical research prize worth €45,000 and five post-doctoral research scholarships of €15,000 each. Assisted in the restoration of, and supports the cultural activities of, the Villa Medici in Rome. There are regional delegations throughout France.

Geographical Area of Activity: France, Europe, South America and China.

Restrictions: Individual artists are not supported.

Publications: Reports; catalogues; brochures.

Principal Staff: Pres. François Roussely.

Address: 9 Ave Percier, 75008 Paris.

Telephone: 1-40-42-63-48; **Fax:** 1-40-42-48-62; **e-mail:** joelle.cotten@edf.fr.

Fondation Énergies pour le Monde (Energy for the World Foundation)

Founded by Alain Liebard in 1990 to assist developing countries by providing energy sources which do not damage the environment.

Activities: The Foundation operates internationally in the field of aid to less-developed countries, through self-conducted programmes.

Geographical Area of Activity: International.

Publications: *Fondation Énergies pour le Monde Infos* (2 a year).

Trustee: Alain Liebard.

Address: 146 rue de l'Université, 75007 Paris.

Telephone: 1-44-18-00-80; **Fax:** 1-44-18-00-36; **Internet:** www.energies-renouvelables.org; **e-mail:** fondem@energies-renouvelables.org.

Fondation 'Entente Franco-Allemande' (Foundation for Franco-German Co-operation)

Established in 1981 to receive the funds offered by the German Government in settlement for the forced enrolment of French nationals in the German army during the Second World War and to distribute these funds to alleviate the social problems and uphold the human rights of these former soldiers, as well as to develop Franco-German co-operation through other projects.

Activities: Aims to develop Franco-German co-operation through funding projects in the fields of culture, science, sports, economics and social welfare.

Geographical Area of Activity: France and Germany.

Principal Staff: Pres. André Bord; Sec.-Gen. Jean Koening; Treas. Roger Koehren.

Address: 1 rue St-Léon, 67000 Strasbourg.

Telephone: 3-88-32-18-00; **Fax:** 3-88-22-48-14; **Internet:** www.fefa.fr; **e-mail:** info@fefa.fr.

Fondation d'Entreprise France Telecom (France Telecom Foundation)

Established in 1987 by France Telecom.

Activities: Operates in France. Supports music (particularly singing), through sponsoring training, concerts, and festivals for talented vocalists; finances specialized development and training for professional staff to care for people suffering from autism; and supports projects aimed at promoting socially relevant uses of the internet.

Geographical Area of Activity: France.

Finance: Budget €3,700,000 (2003).

Principal Staff: Sec.-Gen. Anne Pawloff; Finance and Development Odette Thoraval.

Address: 6 place d'Alleray, 75505 Paris Cedex 15.

Telephone: 1-44-44-89-63; **Fax:** 1-44-44-00-96; **Internet:** www.francetelecom.fr/fondation_v3/f_fondation.html; **e-mail:** la.fondation@francetelecom.com.

Fondation d'Entreprise Gaz de France (Gaz de France Foundation)

Founded in 1992 to pursue charitable works related to society, the environment and cultural heritage.

Activities: Operates nationally and internationally in the fields of the environment, cultural heritage and solidarity, especially relating to young people. Also supports relief projects, sporting activities, anti-literacy initiatives and employee volunteering.

Geographical Area of Activity: France and international, including Vietnam.

Finance: Funded solely by Gaz de France.

Officers and Directors: Pierre Gadonneix (Pres.); Jacques Maire (Dir. Gen.); Francine Delaval; Claude Detourne; Michel Francony; Jean-Louis Lefranc; Patrick Magd.

Principal Staff: Pres. Pierre Gadonneix; Sec.-Gen. Elisabeth Delorme.

Address: 37 rue du Général Foy, 75008 Paris.

Telephone: 1-47-54-28-02; **Fax:** 1-47-54-30-45; **Internet:** www.gazdefrance.com/institutionnels/mecenat/fondation.htm.

Fondation d'Entreprise TotalFinaElf pour la Biodiversité et la Mer (TotalFinaElf Corporate Foundation for Biodiversity and the Sea)

Founded in 1992 by TOTAL, an international oil and gas company.

Activities: Funds research, organizes campaigns, and provides support to further the preservation of marine biodiversity, particularly within the areas of islands, coral reefs and wetlands. The Foundation's actions include partnerships with Port-Cros National Park and Porquerolles Botanical Conservation Centre, WWF Indonesia, a worldwide long-term programme on coral reefs, and several others.

Geographical Area of Activity: International, especially in the countries in which the TotalFinaElf company is represented.

Publications: Press releases; leaflets; books; posters.

Principal Staff: Dir Christian Chavane; Gina Sardella-Sadiki.

Address: Tour Coupole, 2 place de la Coupole, 92078 Paris La Défense Cedex 47.

Telephone: 1-47-44-47-24; **Fax:** 1-47-44-25-32; **Internet:** www.totalfinaelf.com; **e-mail:** holding.foundation@totalfinaelf.com.

Fondation d'entreprise VINCI pour la Cité (VINCI Foundation for the City)

Established in May 2002 by the VINCI construction company to help disadvantaged people gain access to employment.

Activities: Grant programmes aim to help people who find themselves excluded gain access to employment, and to encourage citizens' initiatives aimed at sustainable development and quality of life. Priority is given to projects developing social responsibility, or helping the socially excluded get back to work.

Geographical Area of Activity: France and countries where the company operates.

Restrictions: Projects from a country other than France must be submitted to the foundation by a company employee.

Finance: Annual grant budget approx. €1,000,000.

Address: 1 cours Ferdinand de Lesseps, 92500 Rueil-Malmaison Cedex.

Telephone: 1-47-16-30-63; **Fax:** 1-47-16-49-45; **Internet:** www.groupe-vinci.com; **e-mail:** contact.fondation@vinci.com.

Fondation Européenne pour les Métiers du Patrimoine—FEMP (European Foundation for Heritage Skills)

Established in 1996 on the initiative of the Council of Europe to foster progress on a world-wide basis in cultural heritage conservation skills and their transmission; it continues the work of the Fondation Européenne Pro Venetia Viva (established in 1974) in the field of architectural heritage restoration, and promotes co-operation in this field between European countries.

Activities: Operates through promoting occupations which help improve the quality of life in its sphere of operation; development of in-service training programmes; dissemination of information; links and networking between professional partners; publicity; and seminars and conferences. Currently revising the Foundation's structure.

Geographical Area of Activity: Europe.

Publications: *European Directory of Training Centres in Heritage Skills and Crafts; Strategies for Vocational Training in Architectural Heritage Skills; Maintaining our heritage after 2000—Proceedings of the 2nd European Symposium of architectural heritage restoration firms organized by AEERPA;* activity reports, information leaflets, etc.

Governing Board: The Board comprises representatives of the Council of Europe, the European Parliament, the United Nations Educational, Scientific and Cultural Organization (UNESCO), and of cultural heritage organizations and businesses.

Principal Staff: Daniel Thérond.

Address: Palais de l'Europe, 67075 Strasbourg Cedex.

Telephone: 3-88-41-22-52; **Fax:** 3-88-41-27-55; **Internet:** culture.coe.fr/skills; **e-mail:** daniel.therond@coe.fr.

Fondation Européenne de la Science (European Science Foundation)

Founded in 1974, the Foundation assists its member organizations by bringing scientists together in its Scientific Programmes, Networks and European Research Conferences, and workshops, to work on topics of common concern; and through the joint study of issues of strategic importance in European science policy.

Activities: The scientific work sponsored by the Foundation includes basic research in natural and technical sciences, medical and bio-sciences, humanities and social sciences. The Foundation maintains close relations with other scientific institutions within and outside Europe. Through its activities, the Foundation adds value by co-operation and co-ordination across national frontiers and endeavours, offers expert scientific advice on strategic issues, and provides the European forum for fundamental science. The Foundation has 76 member organizations in 24 countries. Awards the annual European Latsis Prize, funded by the Latsis Foundation (q.v), made in recognition of an individual or organization's contribution to research in a particular scientific field. In 2004 will run a series of exploratory workshops.

Geographical Area of Activity: Europe.

Publications: Annual Report (in English and French); *ESF Communications* (2 a year); other specialized publications, studies and reports.

Finance: Assets €16,816,562 (2001); total budget €6,340,000 (2002).

Governing Board: Reinder van Duinen (Pres.); Max Kaase, Katherine Richardson Christensen (Vice-Pres); V. M. Schauinger-Horne (Sec.); and 29 others.

Principal Staff: Chief Exec. and Sec.-Gen. Prof. Enric Banda.

Address: 1 quai Lezay-Marnésia, 67080 Strasbourg.

Telephone: 3-88-76-71-25; **Fax:** 3-88-76-71-80; **Internet:** www.esf.org; **e-mail:** communications@esf.org.

Fondation Franco-Japonaise Sasakawa (Franco-Japanese Sasakawa Foundation)

Founded in 1990 by the Sasakawa Foundation (Japan, q.v.), to promote cultural awareness and harmony between France and Japan.

Activities: The Foundation operates in France and Japan in the fields of the arts and humanities, education, and science and technology, by awarding scholarships, research grants and travel grants in several areas, including education, the teaching of French and Japanese, translation and publication of works, art, scientific research, promoting exchanges of people and of knowledge, journalism, exhibitions, etc. The Foundation also organizes conferences, operates self-conducted programmes and issues publications. The Foundation in particular wishes to encourage projects dealing with contemporary rather than historical issues, and which favour the long-term development of Franco-Japanese relations.

Geographical Area of Activity: France and Japan.

Publications: *Cent Objets—Produits Artisanaux Traditionnels Japonais Commentés; Guide pour la promotion des objets d'artisanat traditionnel japonais;* cultural register of Japanese institutions located in France.

Finance: The Foundation received an initial grant of 132,000,000 francs from the Foundation for the Japanese Naval Construction Industry, and is financed by the Sasakawa Foundation.

Trustees: Shigeatsu Tominaga (Pres.); Maryse Aulagnon (Vice-Pres.); G.-C. Chazot (Treas.); D. Lallier (Sec.); P. Baudry; R. Hayama; J.-F. Jarrige; M. Mizutani; H. Nakamura; J.-B. Ouvrieu; L. Renaud; Y. Rousset-Rouard; Y. Sasakawa; M. Watanabe; K. Yoshiyuki.

Principal Staff: Chief Exec. Claire Gallian; Dir, Tokyo Office Akinori Seki.

Address: 27 rue du Cherche-Midi, 75006 Paris; (Japan Office) Nippon Foundation Bldg, 1-2-2 Akasaka, Minato-Ku, 107-0052 Tokyo.

Telephone: 1-44-39-30-40; (3) 6229-5448 (Tokyo); **Fax:** 1-44-39-30-45; (3) 6229-5449 (Tokyo); **Internet:** www.fond-fr-jap-sasakawa.org; **e-mail:** info@fond-fr-jap-sasakawa.org.

Fondation Fyssen (Fyssen Foundation)

Established in 1979 by A. H. Fyssen; aims to encourage all forms of scientific research into cognitive mechanisms, including thought and reasoning, that underly animal and human behavior, their biological and cultural bases, and phylogenetic and ontogenetic development.

Activities: Operates a research programme, awarding post-doctoral study grants and research grants to French scientists going abroad and to foreign scientists wishing to work in French research centres. Organizes symposia and publishes research results, and awards an annual scientific prize worth approximately €46,000.

Geographical Area of Activity: Mainly France.

Board of Directors: Mrs A. H. Fyssen (Pres.); Philippe Descola (Vice-Pres.); Stanislas Dehaerne; Robert A. Foley; Martin Giurfa; Colette Grinevald; Marc D. Hauser; Brigitte Kieffer; Jacques Mallet; Giacomo Rizzolatti; Tim Shallice; Sander van der Leeuw.

Address: 194 rue de Rivoli, 75001 Paris.

Telephone: 1-42-60-17-95; **Fax:** 1-42-60-17-95; **Internet:** www.fondation-fyssen.org; **e-mail:** info@fondation-fyssen.org.

Fondation Gan pour le Cinéma (Gan Film Foundation)

Established to safeguard the cinematographic heritage and promote the production of full-length feature films by new cinematographers.

Activities: Operates in France and internationally, including Hungary, Italy and Portugal, to promote cinema and the audiovisual arts through film restoration, supporting the work of new film-makers, offering financial assistance for the distribution of films, sponsoring French film festivals and awarding prizes. Also provides financial support to the Max Linder Panorama cinema in Paris.

Geographical Area of Activity: Mainly France.

Principal Staff: Pres. Jacques Giraud; Déléguée Générale Catherine Lecoq.

Address: 8–10 rue d'Astorg, 75008 Paris.

Telephone: 1-44-56-32-06; **Fax:** 1-44-56-86-39; **Internet:** www.fondation-gan.com; **e-mail:** contact@fondation-gan.com.

Fondation Hugot du Collège de France (Hugot Foundation of the Collège de France)

Founded in 1979 by the Collège de France to foster scientific and cultural exchange.

Activities: Operates internationally in the fields of science and medicine, the arts and humanities, religious studies, international relations and the conservation of natural resources, through grants to institutions, research, conferences and publications, and by arranging for scholars from abroad to teach at the Collège de France.

Geographical Area of Activity: International.

Governing Board: J. Bachelot; F. Bloch-Lainé; P. Boulez; P. Cahart; C. Cohen-Tannoudji; B. Frank; M. Fumaroli; P. Joliot; J. Narbonne; A. Ross; J. Thuillier.

Principal Staff: Pres. André Miquel; Vice-Pres. J. Thuillier; Sec. J. Bachelot; Treas. François Bloch-Lainé; Dir Jean-Pierre de Morant.

Address: 11 rue de l'Université, 75007 Paris.

Telephone: 1-42-96-04-22.

Fondation Nicolas Hulot pour la Nature et l'Homme (Foundation Nicolas Hulot for Nature and Humankind)

Established (as the Fondation Ushuaia) by Nicolas Hulot, to contribute to the discovery of nature and to the protection of the environment through exploration, research, education and communication. Recognized as an organization in the public interest in 1996.

Activities: Operates internationally in the areas of conservation and the environment and education, through offering grants to environmental projects of general interest, organizing clubs to develop small projects in schools, and publishing books and magazines to extend environmental knowledge.

Geographical Area of Activity: Belgium, France, Madagascar, Morocco, Romania, Senegal and Spain.

Publications: *Ma Planète* (magazine); Annual Report; and educational publications.

Finance: Receives funding from Electricité de France, L'Oréal and Monoprix: total revenue €2,385,000 (2000).

Principal Staff: Pres. Nicolas Hulot; Dir Cécile Ostria.

Address: 52 blvd Malesherbes, 75008 Paris.

Telephone: 1-44-90-83-00; **Fax:** 1-44-90-83-19; **Internet:** www.fondation-nicolas-hulot.org/index.php; **e-mail:** fnh@fnh.org.

Fondation Internationale pour la Sauvegarde de la Faune (International Foundation for the Conservation of Wildlife)

Founded in 1976, and known until 1990 as the Fondation Internationale pour la Sauvegarde du Gibier, to contribute throughout the world towards conservation of wildlife and of nature in all its forms and aspects, and to help to promote the rational and reasonable harvesting of national and international game populations in order to ensure their survival and their development for the benefit of humanity.

Activities: Operates internationally in the field of conservation of natural resources, through self-conducted programmes, research, grants to institutions and individuals, fellowships, scholarships, conferences, courses, publications and lectures. The Foundation co-operates in particular with the International Council for Game and Wildlife Conservation (CIC) and puts itself at the disposal of governments to study ways of improving legislation pertaining to hunting and wildlife conservation.

The Foundation has a 'sister' Foundation in Switzerland which shares the same title, President, Director and Treasurer, but has a different Board of Directors. In practice it is the French Foundation which decides on action, while the Swiss Foundation is mainly a financial body, trustee of the majority of the French body's funds. The following details refer to the French Foundation.

Geographical Area of Activity: International.

Publications: *African Wildlife: the Forgotten Resource; Proceedings of the International Symposium and Conference on Wildlife Management in Sub-Saharan Africa and Sustainable economic benefits and contribution towards rural development*; and numerous other reports and publications.

Finance: Annual budget approx. US $300,000.

Board of Directors: Members by right: The representative of the French Minister in charge of Hunting and Nature Conservation, the representative of the French Minister for Foreign Affairs, the President of the CIC and one of its Assistant Presidents; and 10 co-opted members.

Principal Staff: Founder and Pres. Prince Abdorreza of Iran; Dir Bertrand des Clers.

Address: 15 rue de Téhéran, 75008 Paris.

Telephone: 1-45-63-51-33; **Fax:** 1-45-63-32-94; **Internet:** www.wildlife-conservation.org; **e-mail:** igf@fondation-igf.fr.

Fondation La Poste

Established in 1995 and under the aegis of the Fondation de France (q.v.), principally to promote literature.

Activities: Operates nationally and in francophone countries in the area of the arts and culture, through financing festivals and literary prizes such as the Prix Wepler, promoting French songwriting through the Prix Timbres de Voix prize, and supporting publishing initiatives.

Geographical Area of Activity: France.

Principal Staff: Pres. Martin Vial; Delegate-Gen. Sylvie Pélissier.

Address: 4 quai du Point du Jour, 92777 Boulogne Billancourt.

Telephone: 1-41-41-62-07; **Fax:** 1-41-41-62-60; **Internet:** www.fondationlaposte.org.

Fondation Le Corbusier (Le Corbusier Foundation)

Founded in 1968 according to the wish of Charles Edouard Jeanneret, known as 'Le Corbusier', to maintain a museum in the Villa La Roche in Paris displaying his works, and to encourage research in the spirit defined by his own written and architectural work.

Activities: Operates internationally in the field of the arts and humanities. Maintains a permanent exhibition in the Villa La Roche of Le Corbusier's works: furniture, paintings and sculptures. Loans original works for exhibitions. Advises and supervises the preservation of buildings designed by Le Corbusier. Publishes an information bulletin. Maintains a library. Also awards research scholarships.

Address: Villa la Roche, 8–10 square du Docteur Blanche, 75016 Paris.

Telephone: 1-42-88-41-53; **Fax:** 1-42-88-33-17; **Internet:** www.fondationlecorbusier.asso.fr.

Fondation de Lourmarin Laurent-Vibert (Laurent-Vibert Foundation of Lourmarin)

Founded in 1927 by the Académie des Sciences, Agriculture, Arts et Belles Lettres d'Aix, according to the will of Robert Laurent-Vibert, with the aim of promoting literature and the arts.

Activities: The Foundation provides grants in the field of the arts and humanities, and invites annually six to eight artists and scholars of French and other nationalities to spend one month as guests at the Castle of Lourmarin. It conducts seminars on the national and international aspects of education, social welfare, the arts and conservation. Programmes are also carried out through lectures, concerts, plays and exhibitions, including the 'Musiques d'été à Lourmarin' music festival. More recently, the Foundation has widened its areas of interest to include the natural and social sciences, and collaborates in this field with the Académie des Sciences, Agriculture, Arts et Belles Lettres d'Aix.

Geographical Area of Activity: France.

Restrictions: Artists must be under 35.

Publications: Annual Report.

Principal Staff: Curator D. Antonelli; Man. J. Mead.

Address: Château de Lourmarin, BP 23, 84160 Lourmarin.

Telephone: 4-90-68-15-23; **Fax:** 4-90-68-25-19.

Fondation Marguerite et Aimé Maeght (Marguerite and Aimé Maeght Foundation)

Founded in 1964 by Marguerite and Aimé Maeght to acquire, preserve and exhibit contemporary art.

Activities: Operates nationally and internationally in the field of modern art, through exhibitions, permanent collections, conferences and publications. Presents exhibitions of contemporary art in its museum in Saint-Paul and exhibits its collections, including works by Braque, Giacometti, Kandinsky, Bonnard, Chagall, Calder, Miró, etc., abroad. Operates a library with documentation on various aspects of modern art, and a bookshop.

Geographical Area of Activity: Europe, the USA, Africa and Asia.

Publications: Catalogue and posters published to coincide with exhibitions.

Finance: Financed privately.

Trustees: A. Maeght (Chair.); J.-L. Prat (Vice-Chair.); M. David-Weill (Treas.); S. Balthazart-Maeght; E. Charles-Roux; H. Landais; I. Maeght; F. Voss; the Director of French Museums; the Director of Artistic Creation; the Préfet of Alpes-Maritimes.

Principal Staff: Dir Jean-Louis Prat.

Address: 06570 Saint-Paul.

Telephone: 4-93-32-81-63; **Fax:** 4-93-32-53-22; **e-mail:** contact@fondation-maeght.com.

Fondation MAIF (MAIF Foundation)

Established in 1989 by the Mutuelle Assurance des Instituteurs de France (mutual insurance company for primary school teachers) to promote technological improvements working towards an improved quality of life and an increase in safety.

Activities: Operates internationally in safety and risk prevention, promoting collaboration between local government, universities and research institutions, NGOs and industry, focusing on young people at risk and on traffic safety. Supports research, the establishment of a research institute and a database, offers prizes and research grants, issues publications and promotes conferences, meetings and the dissemination of information.

Geographical Area of Activity: International.

Finance: Endowment of approx. €11,500,000 francs; annual grants approx. €1,000,000.

Principal Staff: Pres. Charles Berthet; Sec.-Gen. Jacques Fournier; Dir Hubert Oliviero.

Address: Le Pavois, 50 ave Salvador Allende, 79000 Niort.

Telephone: 5-49-73-87-04; **Fax:** 5-49-73-87-03; **Internet:** www.fondation.maif.fr; **e-mail:** contact@fondation.maif.fr.

Fondation de la Maison de la Chimie (Chemistry Centre Foundation)

Founded in 1927 on the occasion of the centenary of the birth of Marcelin Berthelot to contribute to the advancement of chemical science in the widest sense and the development of its applications, by promoting exchanges among scholars, technicians and industrialists of all countries.

Activities: The Centre makes available its lecture rooms, technical facilities and professional staff to French, foreign and international organizations to enable them to expand their mutual relations. It accommodates permanently institutions operating in the field of chemistry and provides lodging facilities for participants in the meetings and conferences it sponsors. The Foundation co-operates with other institutions in arranging scientific, cultural, professional and educational events. Also makes a biennial award to recognise original work in chemistry of benefit to society, mankind or nature. The next award will be made in 2004 with a value of €30,000.

Geographical Area of Activity: France.

Board of Directors: Pierre Potier (Pres.); Arséne Schun (Vice-Pres); Jacques Hui (Gen. Sec.); Michel Poite (Treas.).

Address: 28 rue Saint Dominique, 75007 Paris.

Telephone: 1-40-62-27-00; **Fax:** 1-45-55-98-62; **Internet:** www.maisondelachimie.asso.fr; **e-mail:** x@maisondelachimie.asso.fr.

Fondation Méditerranéenne d'Études Stratégiques (Mediterranean Foundation for Strategic Studies)

Established in 1989 to promote strategic studies in all areas of Mediterranean affairs.

Activities: Operates in the areas of education, scientific research and information, organizing conferences, seminars and international meetings, conducting research, organizing training, and publishing and disseminating information.

Geographical Area of Activity: France.

Principal Staff: Pres. Jacques Lanxade; Vice-Pres. Roger Peiffer; Sec. Jean Charbonnier; Treas. and Sec.-Gen. Gérard Bennet.

Address: Place Georges Pompidou, 83000 Toulon; 21 place Joffre, 75007 Paris.

Telephone: 4-94-03-89-44 (Toulon); **Fax:** 4-94-03-89-45 (Toulon); **Internet:** www.fmes-france.org; **e-mail:** info@fmes-france.org.

Fondation Mérieux (Mérieux Foundation)

Founded in 1967 by Dr Charles Merieux to promote research and education in biology, immunology, epidemiology and individual and collective prevention.

Activities: Operates nationally and internationally in the fields of medical and veterinary research, education, social welfare and aid to less-developed countries, through self-conducted programmes of research, grants to institutions and individuals, scholarships to overseas candidates, conferences and publications. The Foundation is closely involved with the Institut pour le Développement de l'Epidémiologie Appliquée (Annecy), the Association pour la Médecine Préventive (in conjunction with the Pasteur Foundation), and Bioforce (a training programme for polyvalent health auxiliaries).

Geographical Area of Activity: International.

Principal Staff: Pres. Nicole de Beublain; Gen. Man. Prof. Marc Girard; CFO and Sec. Paul Caroly.

Address: 17 rue Bourgelat, 69002 Lyon.

Telephone: 4-72-40-79-79; **Fax:** 4-72-40-79-50; **Internet:** www.fond-merieux.org; **e-mail:** fondation.lyon@fondation-merieux.org.

Fondation Mondiale Recherche et Prévention SIDA (World Foundation for AIDS Research and Prevention)

Swiss foundation established in 1993 by Luc Montagnier and Federico Mayor, Director-General of UNESCO, to assist in the efforts to combat AIDS and to mobilize the private sector. The Foundation is also known as the Fondation mondiale pour la recherche contre le SIDA–World Foundation for AIDS Research and Prevention.

Activities: Operates internationally, in close co-operation with UNESCO, in the area of AIDS research and prevention, to promote global awareness and humanitarian concern; to develop research by opening four research centres in Europe, Africa, Asia and the USA; to help developing countries acquire indigenous capacities in building national AIDS programmes (including preventive education and assistance to AIDS orphans); and to promote networking among scientists and the twinning of universities within developing countries and between developed and developing countries.

Geographical Area of Activity: International.

Principal Staff: Pres. Prof. Luc Montagnier.

Address: c/o UNESCO, 1 rue Miollis, 75732 Paris 15.

Telephone: 1-45-68-38-41; **Fax:** 1-42-73-37-45.

Fondation Marc de Montalembert (Marc de Montalembert Foundation)

Established in 1994 in memory of Marc de Montalembert.

Activities: Aims to provide opportunities to young people from Mediterranean countries to experience other cultures, through scholarships in the fields of literature, architecture, music, photography and singing, and through the organization of discussion forums on themes relating to peace and tolerance amongst Mediterranean countries. Maintains a dialogue centre in Rhodes, Greece.

Geographical Area of Activity: Mediterranean countries.

Address: c/o Fondation de France, 40 ave Hoche, 75008 Paris.

Internet: www.fondationmdm.com.

Fondation Nationale pour l'Enseignement de la Gestion des Entreprises (French National Foundation for Management Education)

Founded in 1968 by the Conseil National du Patronat Français, the Assemblée Permanente des Chambres de Commerce et d'Industrie and the State to promote management education in France.

Activities: Operates both nationally and internationally in the field of management education, in five basic areas: the promotion of stronger ties between education and industry; the training and improvement of management teachers; the updating of the curricula of management training institutions; the development of management institutions; and the promotion of French management education abroad. Operates through research, grants both to institutions and individuals, scholarships, conferences, courses, seminars and publications.

Geographical Area of Activity: International.

Publications: Annual Report; newsletter (monthly); surveys on research and education in the field of management.

Finance: The Foundation is financed by French public authorities and businesses.

Board of Administration: Jean-Marie Descarpentries (Pres.); F. Andrieu; T. Audric; C. Barbaroux; J.-F. Bernardin; J.-P. Boisivon; E. d'Andre; R. Declerck; F. Delachaux; F. Demichel; B. Dufoug; J.-J. Dumont; H. de Carmoy; C. Gaymard; J.-P. Helfer; G. La Tour; J.-L. Levet; J. Maire; C. Michel; J.-M. Olivier; C. Rigodanzo; Y. Robin; J. Rojot; G. Sarkozy; T. Vielle; C. Vulliez.

Principal Staff: Sec.-Gen. Jean-Claude Cuzzi.

Address: 2 ave Hoche, 75008 Paris.

Telephone: 1-44-29-93-60; **Fax:** 1-47-54-05-99; **Internet:** www.fnege.fr; **e-mail:** info@fnege.fr.

Fondation Nationale des Sciences Politiques (National Foundation for Political Sciences)

Founded in 1945 by government ordinance to succeed the École Libre des Sciences Politiques (founded in 1872), in order to foster the progress and diffusion of the political, economic and social sciences in France and abroad.

Activities: Operates internationally in the fields of political, economic and social sciences, and international relations, through research, teaching, publications and documentation services. Research is conducted in the centres for study in the following areas: international relations, political life in France, economic activity, social affairs, contemporary European history, economic conditions, American studies, and social change. The Foundation's documentation services comprise a social science library of over 620,000 books and 6,000 periodicals, and compiling and keeping a documentation centre maintaining around 16,000 press-cuttings files since 1945. The Foundation also administers the Institut d'Études Politiques de Paris, assists the research and documentation activities of the Institutes of Political Studies at Grenoble and Bordeaux and owns Presses de Sciences Po.

Geographical Area of Activity: France.

Publications: *Revue française de science politique* (6 a year, jointly with the Association Française de Science Politique); *Critique Internationale* (quarterly); *Raisons Politique* (quarterly); *Revue économique* (6 a year); *Vingtième Siècle—Histoire* (quarterly); *Revue de l'OFCE* (quarterly); books and research monographs in the social sciences and history published by the Presses de Sciences Po.

Principal Staff: Pres. René Rémond; Dir Richard Descoings.

Address: 27 rue Saint-Guillaume, 75337 Paris Cedex 7.

Telephone: 1-45-49-50-50; **Fax:** 1-42-22-31-26; **Internet:** www.sciences-po.fr; **e-mail:** info@docum.sciences-po.fr.

Fondation Claude Pompidou (Claude Pompidou Foundation)

Established in 1970 at the instigation of Claude Pompidou to help children with disabilities, elderly people and people in hospital.

Activities: The Foundation supports projects helping children with disabilities, elderly people and people in hospital, as well as establishing residential homes and centres. Other current Foundation projects include an initiative to help elderly hospitalized people return home.

Geographical Area of Activity: France.

Council of Administration: Claude Pompidou (Pres.); Jacques Chirac (Vice-Pres.); Simone Veil (Sec.); Arthur Dehaine (Treas.).

Principal Staff: Dir Gen. Richard Hutin.

Address: 42 rue de Louvre, 75001 Paris.

Telephone: 1-40-13-75-00; **Fax:** 1-40-13-75-19; **Internet:** www.fondationclaudepompidou.asso.fr; **e-mail:** fondcp@club-internet.fr.

Fondation 'Pour la Science', Centre International de Synthèse (Foundation for International Scientific Co-ordination)

Founded in 1924 by Henri Berr to encourage liaison between different scientific disciplines, and to develop and co-ordinate research and contacts among experts and researchers.

Activities: The Centre holds international conferences for scientists of different disciplines, and issues scientific publications.

Publications: *Revue de Synthèse; Revue d'Histoire des Sciences; Semaines de Synthèse; L'Evolution de l'Humanité* (series).

Principal Staff: Dirs Michel Blay, Eric Brian; Sec.-Gen. Fabien Chareix; Treas. Jean-Marc Rohrbasser.

Address: 12 rue Colbert, 75002 Paris.

Telephone: 1-42-97-50-68; **Fax:** 1-42-97-46-46; **e-mail:** synthese@libertysurf.fr.

Fondation pour la Recherche Médicale (Foundation for Medical Research)

Founded in 1962 by Prof. Jean Hamburger, Prof. Jean Bernard and Dr C. Escoffier-Lambiotte, to promote all forms of scientific medical research, in particular research connected with the basic biological sciences related to medicine, and to co-ordinate these endeavours.

Activities: Operates exclusively in the field of medicine and the biological sciences on a national and international basis. Awards grants to both individuals and institutions especially in France, through grants to young researchers and to laboratories. Subsidizes study abroad and assists the purchase of scientific equipment. The Foundation also has its own publication *Recherche & Santé* mainly for its donors, organizes conferences, lectures and exhibitions, and maintains regional committees. Major annual awards include the Rosen Prize for Cancer Research, and a number of other prizes for research in molecular biology, endocrinology, immunology, infectiology, clinical investigation, neurobiology, nephrology and cancer. It also awards special prizes in the field of scientific communication.

Geographical Area of Activity: France.

Publications: Report of activities; *Recherche & Santé* (quarterly).

Principal Staff: Pres. Pierre Joly; Vice-Pres Jean Rosa, Jean-François Bach; Treas. Jean Farge.

Address: 54 rue de Varenne, 75335 Paris Cedex 07.

Telephone: 1-44-39-75-75; **Fax:** 1-44-39-75-99; **Internet:** www.frm.org; **e-mail:** info@frm.org.

Fondation pour la Recherche Stratégique (Foundation for Strategic Research)

Established by a number of French companies and by the merger of the Fondation pour les Etudes de Défense and the Centre de Recherche sur les Stratégies et les Technologies, to conduct politico-military research.

Activities: Conducts research into strategic issues, essentially in three areas: the politics of defence, technological and security issues, and the nature of crises and conflicts. Maintains a documentation centre and library.

Geographical Area of Activity: France.

Publications: Essays and occasional papers.

Administrative Council: B. Racine (Pres.); Gen. F. Arnauld; A. Delpuech; P. Humbert; H. Martre; D. Viollet; Gen. M. Waymel; and also representatives of several ministries and co-opted members.

Principal Staff: Dir François Heisbourg; Deputy Dir Yves Boyer; Sec.-Gen. L. Mille.

Address: 27 rue Damesme, 75013 Paris.

Telephone: 1-43-13-77-77; **Fax:** 1-43-13-77-78; **Internet:** www.frstrategie.org; **e-mail:** webmaster@frstrategie.org.

Fondation Ripaille (Ripaille Foundation)

Founded in 1976 by Mrs Harold Necker to promote the use of the Château de Ripaille, ancient residence of Duke Amédée VIII of Savoy, as a centre for study, meditation, work, training and cultural exchange in ecology, human and physical geography, and the conscientious development of resources and the environment, particularly in the most underprivileged areas and countries.

Activities: Lakes, inland waterways and coastlines are studied, as well as the problems of mountainous regions, with particular attention being paid to Lake Geneva. The centre organizes exchanges between the institutions and associations concerned at regional, national and international levels. It also organizes colloquia, seminars and congresses, exhibitions, tours and conferences; and holds cultural, artistic, historical or scientific events or meetings. The centre offers facilities for receptions.

Geographical Area of Activity: International.

Address: Château de Ripaille, 74200 Thonon-les-Bains.

Telephone: 4-50-26-64-44; **Fax:** 4-50-26-54-74; **Internet:** www.ripaille.fr/fondation.html; **e-mail:** fondation@ripaille.org.

Fondation Scelles (Scelles Foundation)

Established in 1993 by Jean Scelles to campaign against all forms of sexual exploitation and assist the victims of sexual violence.

Activities: Operates nationally and internationally in the field of human rights in three areas: collecting information for the Centre of International Research and Documentation on Sexual Exploitation database; giving grants to organizations assisting victims of sexual violence; and providing information to the public and the media on sexual exploitation through its publications.

Geographical Area of Activity: International.

Publications: *Info Scelles* (newsletter); Annual Report; and various publications.

Trustees: Philippe Scelles (Pres.); Anne-Marie Scelles (Vice-Pres.); Hubert de Roux (Sec.-Gen. and Treas.).

Principal Staff: Pres. Philippe Scelles.

Address: 14 rue Mondétour, 75001 Paris.

Telephone: 1-40-26-04-45; **Fax:** 1-40-26-04-58; **Internet:** www.fondationscelles.org; **e-mail:** fondationscelles@wanadoo.fr.

Fondation Schneider Electric pour l'Insertion des Jeunes (Schneider Electric Youth Opportunities Foundation)

Created by Schneider Electric SA in 1998, under the aegis of the Fondation de France, to help the development of young people.

Activities: In partnership with local NGOs, supports projects involving young people (under 30 years old) in the areas of culture, society, sport, the environment and creative enterprise. Helps young people to find employment by supporting Schneider Electric employees who wish to donate their time to training and imparting advice. Works internationally, helping orphans, improving health care access, providing education and training for under-achieving young people, rewards young entrepreneurs, supporting disabled children and working to eliminate violence against young people. Particularly focuses on projects in areas around Schneider Electric's sites, as well as operating international campaigns to promote the development of young people.

Geographical Area of Activity: International.

Address: 89 Ave Franklin Roosevelt, 92506 Rueil-Malmaison Cedex.

Telephone: 1-41-29-70-00; **Fax:** 1-41-29-71-00; **Internet:** www.foundation.schneider-electric.com; **e-mail:** fr-fondation@mail.schneider.fr.

Fondation Robert Schuman (Robert Schuman Foundation)

Established in 1992 to promote research into the history of European thought and ideals; European cultural co-operation; the world-wide dissemination of democratic, social and humanistic ideas and civic education; international co-operation; and humanitarian aid in Central and Eastern Europe.

Activities: Operates in France and internationally in the fields of the arts and humanities, international affairs, education and social welfare, through its four main programmes: University and cultural action; Relations with the Member States of the European Union; French–German relations (in particular collaborating with the Konrad-Adenauer-Stiftung and the ASKO Europa-Stiftung, q.q.v.); and Cultural and humanitarian aid in Central and Eastern Europe and the countries of the former USSR. The Foundation offers scholarships, promotes exchange programmes, provides financial and material support, organizes conferences on the European integration process and issues publications.

Geographical Area of Activity: Europe.

Publications: *Nouvelles Frontières de l'Europe; Le défi americain; Pour une politique culturelle européenne; La Fracture Numérique; La Lettre de la Fondation Robert Schuman* (weekly electronic newsletter); *Notes de la Fondation Robert Schuman; Observatoire des Elections en Europe* (electronic publication).

Governing Board: Jean Dominique Giuliani (Pres.).

Principal Staff: Dir Pascale Joannin.

Address: 29 blvd Raspail, 75007 Paris.

Telephone: 1-53-63-83-00; **Fax:** 1-53-63-83-01; **Internet:** www.robert-schuman.org; **e-mail:** info@robert-schuman.org.

Fondation René Seydoux pour le Monde Méditerranéen (René Seydoux Foundation for the Mediterranean World)

Founded in 1978 by Geneviève René Seydoux to promote and develop the links between the countries of the Mediterranean area in social, cultural and scientific fields.

Activities: The Foundation operates in the Mediterranean countries in the fields of culture, education and science, through self-conducted co-operation projects.

Geographical Area of Activity: European and Mediterranean countries.

Publications: *Répertoire méditerranéen des centres d'action, de recherche et de formation* (on-line newsletter).

Principal Staff: Pres. Jérôme Seydoux; Gen. Delegate Giovanna Tanzarella.

Address: 18 rue Séguier, 75006 Paris.

Telephone: 1-53-10-24-34; **Fax:** 1-53-10-87-12; **Internet:** www.rep-mediterra.org; **e-mail:** fondation-seydoux@fondation-seydoux.org.

Fondation Teilhard de Chardin (Teilhard de Chardin Foundation)

Founded in 1964 by Jeanne Mortier to preserve and disseminate the thought of Pierre Teilhard de Chardin (1881–1955) by the conservation and classification of his manuscripts and writings; the publication of his unpublished works; the defence of his thought against misinterpretation and of his texts against misuse; the collection of all documents and studies about him; the provision of facilities for the study of his works; the running of seminars, discussions and conferences; and the publication of accounts of these activities.

Activities: Operates internationally in those fields covered by the thought of Teilhard de Chardin, especially religion and science, philosophy and education, but also social welfare and studies, humanities and international relations, through the methods proposed in the aims of the Foundation. The Association des Amis de P. Teilhard de Chardin, under the Foundation, runs study centres in many countries throughout the world; these centres have their own meetings, publications, courses and lectures.

Geographical Area of Activity: International.

Publications: Annual Report; the complete works of Teilhard de Chardin (in progress); *Cahiers*.

Principal Staff: Pres. Henry de Lumley; Treas. Maurice Ernst.

Address: 38 rue Geoffroy-Saint-Hilaire, 75005 Paris.

Telephone: 1-43-31-18-55; **Fax:** 1-43-31-01-15; **Internet:** www.mnhn.fr/teilhard/fondass1.htm; **e-mail:** teilhard@mnhn.fr.

Fonds Européen pour la Jeunesse (European Youth Foundation)

Founded in 1972 by the Council of Europe to provide financial support to international youth activities undertaken by non-governmental national or international youth organizations and networks.

Activities: Funds youth meetings (category A), youth activities other than meetings (category B), administrative costs of international youth organizations and networks (category C) and pilot projects (category D). The Foundation has contributed financially towards activities connected with the European youth campaign against racism, xenophobia, anti-semitism and intolerance. A special Solidarity Fund for Youth Mobility has been created, a joint venture by the International Union of Railways and the Council of Europe, to assist such young people with the cost of rail travel when attending international activities.

Geographical Area of Activity: Europe.

Restrictions: No grants to individuals.

Finance: Finance provided by the Foundation's 43 member governments. Annual budget €2,800,000 (2002).

Programming Committee: Comprises representatives of member governments and international non-governmental youth organizations and national youth councils.

Principal Staff: Principal Admin. Jean-Claude Lazaro; Admin. Ita Mirianashuili.

Address: Directorate of Youth and Sport of the Council of Europe, 30 rue Pierre de Coubertin, 67000 Strasbourg.

Telephone: 3-88-41-20-19; **Fax:** 3-90-21-49-64; **Internet:** www.coe.int/youth; **e-mail:** eyf@coe.int.

Forum International de l'Innovation Sociale (International Forum for Social Innovation)

Founded in 1975 to promote social innovation and institutional transformation in private and public institutions.

Activities: Encourages meetings, studies and exchange of information, and the implementation of projects; disseminates information; organizes workshops and seminars; organizes international working conferences on institutional transformation; maintains an information centre on social innovation projects.

Geographical Area of Activity: International.

Publications: *FIIS-IFSI Annual Agenda*.

Principal Staff: Pres. Ghislaine Lambert-Foccroulle; Exec. Vice-Pres. David Gutmann; Sec.-Gen. Hervé Maillant; Treas. Anne Saniez.

Address: 60 rue de Bellechasse, 75007 Paris.

Telephone: 1-45-51-39-49; **Fax:** 1-45-51-39-42; **Internet:** www.continents.com/FIIS.htm; **e-mail:** ifsi.fiis@wanadoo.fr.

France Amérique Latine—FAL

Established in 1970 to support and provide aid to Central and South America.

Activities: Works to protect the cultural heritage of and support the people of Central and South America. Defends human rights by condemning violations of the rights of indigenous peoples and children within the region, and fighting discrimination regarding the image of the region throughout the rest of the world by holding conferences, debates, exhibitions and exchanges. Works to improve literacy and education, health care and sanitation, and provides emergency aid in Central and South America.

Geographical Area of Activity: France and Central and South America.

Publications: *FAL Magazine* (quarterly).

Principal Staff: Pres. Sophie Thono-Wesfreid.

Address: 37 blvd Saint Jacques, 75014 Paris.

Telephone: 1-45-88-20-00; **Fax:** 1-45-65-20-87; **Internet:** perso.club-internet.fr/vdedaj/fal; **e-mail:** falnationale@wanadoo.fr.

France-Libertés Fondation Danielle Mitterrand (Danielle Mitterrand France-Liberty Foundation)

Founded in 1981 by Danielle Mitterrand to improve living standards for the less affluent in society, and to protect their human rights.

Activities: Operates internationally in the fields of human rights, the environment, racial discrimination, apartheid, AIDS, poverty and hunger. The Foundation supports numerous projects including the construction of housing for 'street children' and orphans in Peru, providing humanitarian aid for landless people in Brazil and equipment for a clinic working to prevent deafness in children in Senegal; it works to combat the marginalization of the disabled in Mauritania, organizes an AIDS information campaign and provides disposable syringes in Africa, and runs several education programmes in Cambodia and Bangladesh.

Geographical Area of Activity: International.

Publications: Newsletter.

Principal Staff: Pres. Danielle Mitterrand; Sec.-Gen. Daniel Jacoby; Treas. Georges Abadie.

Address: 22 rue de Milan, 75009 Paris.

Telephone: 1-53-25-10-40; **Fax:** 1-48-74-01-26; **Internet:** www.france-libertes.fr; **e-mail:** contact@france-libertes.fr.

France Nature Environnement

Established in 1968 to co-ordinate environmental protection and conservation nationally and internationally; operates as a national federation of associations for the protection of nature and the environment.

Activities: Operates in France and internationally in the field of conservation and the environment, through the dissemination of information on the state of the environment in the areas of scientific research, the conservation of fauna and flora and the protection of biodiversity. Established national networks concerned with biodiversity, agriculture, forestry, water, industrial production cycles, power, waste, development, transport and health.

Geographical Area of Activity: International.

Publications: *Lettre du Hérisson.*

Principal Staff: Pres. Bernard Rousseau; Vice-Pres. Erwan Le Cornec, Christian Garnier, Marc William Millereau; Treas. Raymond Léost; Nat. Sec. Christophe Aubel, José Cambou.

Address: 5 rue Dupanloup, 45000 Orléans.

Telephone: 2-38-62-44-48; **Fax:** 2-38-52-11-57; **Internet:** www.fne.asso.fr; **e-mail:** secretariatorleans@fne-asso.fr.

French–American Foundation Comité Français

Founded in 1976 by Pierre Jouven to improve reciprocal understanding between France and the USA.

Activities: Operates in the fields of social studies and education, through self-conducted programmes, grants to individuals and scholarships; supports French students conducting research related to modern America.

Geographical Area of Activity: France and the USA.

Publications: Annual Report; Forums Proceedings.

Principal Staff: Pres. Michel Garcin; Vice-Pres. Patricia Moulin; Treas. Aymar de Lastours.

Address: 14 rue Delambre, 75014 Paris.

Telephone: 1-42-18-57-53; **Fax:** 1-42-18-57-54; **e-mail:** fafparis@aol.com.

Frères des Hommes International (Brothers to all Men International)

Founded in 1965 by Armand Marquiset to support development initiatives and education projects in developing countries, and increase awareness in developed countries of the problems faced by less-developed countries.

Activities: Supports local groups helping the underprivileged to have more control of their own development, and recruits European volunteers to work in Africa, Asia, and Southern and Central America; it conducts and supports research on development problems, issues publications, and attempts to increase public awareness of the less-developed countries, works to protect human rights, and provides humanitarian aid.

Geographical Area of Activity: Africa, Asia, and Central and South America.

Publications: *Info Terra* (monthly); *Témoignages et Dossiers* (quarterly); *Peuples en Marche* (monthly).

Finance: Annual budget approx. US $6,500,000.

Principal Staff: Dir Robert Fallay; Sec. Ginette Stivet.

Address: 9 rue de Savoie, 75006 Paris.

Telephone: 1-55-42-62-62; **Fax:** 1-43-29-99-77; **Internet:** www.france-fdh.org; **e-mail:** fdh@france.fdh.org.

Groupe Développement (Development Group)

Established in 1981.

Activities: Operates in the field of aid to less-developed countries. Promotes local action in developing countries, supporting social and rural development projects; facilitates information exchange between development organizations; campaigns for human rights and social justice for all, and against the sexual exploitation of women.

Geographical Area of Activity: Africa, Asia, the Middle East, and Central and South America.

Publications: *Transfaire* (newsletter); Annual Report.

Principal Staff: Sec.-Gen. Jean-François Dewitte.

Address: Bâtiment UTA 106, BP 07, 93350 Le Bourget Aéroport.

Telephone: 1-49-34-83-13; **Fax:** 1-49-34-83-10.

Handicap International

Founded in 1982 to aid the rehabilitation of physically disabled people in developing countries.

Activities: Operates internationally in 50 countries. Supports charitable programmes concerned with physically disabled people in less-developed countries; trains local people to adapt tools for appropriate use by disabled people, thus encouraging their integration into society; organizes workshops; maintains a library. Co-founder of the International Campaign to Ban Landmines.

Geographical Area of Activity: Europe, Africa, the Middle East, Central and East Asia, and Central and South America.

Publications: Newsletter (quarterly); technical publications; videos.

Finance: Resources €55,186,446 (2000).

Principal Staff: Pres. Jean-Noël Sersiron; Dir Ph. Chabasse, J. B. Richardier, C. Simonnot.

Address: 14 ave Berthelot, 69361 Lyon Cedex 07.

Telephone: 4-78-69-79-79; **Fax:** 4-78-69-79-94; **Internet:** www.handicap-international.org; **e-mail:** contact@handicap-international.org.

Inclusion International

Established in 1960 to support those with a mental disability, without regard to nationality, race or creed.

Activities: Operates internationally, promoting the provision of assistance to people with mental disabilities, and the interchange of experts and exchange of workers in the field; and supporting co-operation between organizations assisting the mentally disabled. Collaborates with the World Health Organization (WHO). The organization has 200 affiliated member organizations in 115 countries.

Geographical Area of Activity: World-wide.

Publications: *Inclusion* (newsletter); *Human Rights and Intellectual Disability; A Plain Speak on Disability and Human Rights* ; and other publications.

Trustees and Officers: Diane Richler (Pres.); Thérèse Kempeneers-Foulon (Sec.-Gen.); Fred Heddell (Treas.); Donald Wills (Immediate Past Pres.).

Address: c/o International Disability Centre, 13D chemin du Levant, 01210 Ferney-Voltaire.

Telephone: 4-50-40-01-97; **Fax:** 4-50-40-01-07; **Internet:** www.inclusion-international.org; **e-mail:** info@inclusion-international.org.

Institut Néerlandais (Netherlands Institute)

Founded in 1956 by Frits and Jacoba Lugt to develop cultural relations between France and the Netherlands.

Activities: Organizes exhibitions, lectures and concerts in order to present the culture of the Netherlands in France; study visits, language courses and exchanges are also arranged. Also mediates between French and Dutch cultural institutions and artists. The Institute has a library of some 40,000 books, mainly related to the arts.

Geographical Area of Activity: France and the Netherlands.

Trustees: The Government of the Netherlands and the Fondation Custodia (established by the founders to support the Institute).

Principal Staff: Dir Henk Pröpper; Deputy Dir Tanja Mensenkamp.

Address: 121 rue de Lille, 75007 Paris.

Telephone: 1-53-59-12-40; **Fax:** 1-45-56-00-77; **Internet:** www.institutneerlandais.com/; **e-mail:** info@institutneerlandais.com/.

Institut Océanographique—Fondation Albert 1er, Prince de Monaco (Oceanographic Institute—Albert 1st, Prince of Monaco Foundation)

Established in 1906 by Albert 1st, Prince of Monaco for the study and teaching of oceanographic science, and for knowledge of marine science to be transmitted to as many people as possible.

Activities: The Foundation comprises two institutions: the Institut Océanographique in Paris (also the headquarters of the Foundation), and the Musée Océanographique in Monaco. Supports exhibitions and maintains libraries at both centres.

Geographical Area of Activity: France and Monaco.

Publications: Books on marine science.

Principal Staff: Chair. Jean Chapon; Dir Lucien Laubier; Sec.-Gen. Claude Beauverger.

Address: 195 rue St-Jacques, 75005 Paris.

Telephone: 1-44-32-10-70; **Fax:** 1-40-51-73-16; **Internet:** www.oceano.org; **e-mail:** institut@oceano.org.

Institut Pasteur (Pasteur Institute)

Founded in 1886 by Louis Pasteur and incorporated as a foundation in 1887 in order to promote research into infectious and parasitic diseases, including their prevention and treatment, and into immunity from disease; to further the study of micro-organisms, including their role in natural processes, both normal and pathological, and the reactions they provoke; to further the study and teaching of all aspects of microbiology, as well as the training of scientific and technical staff in view of the growth of study into basic and applied microbiology; and to study all the theoretical and practical problems connected with microbiology and immunology or, more generally, with basic and applied biology.

Activities: Operates essentially in the field of microbiology and its related disciplines, through research, teaching, prevention and diagnosis of infectious and parasitic diseases. The Institute has a large library at its headquarters and operates through 21 branches throughout the world. The work of several of its laboratories has been recognized as of great importance by the World Health Organization and they have accordingly been granted the status of regional, national or international centres. The Institute has its own medical centre providing international vaccinations as well as specialized consultations (including allergies, tropical diseases and HIV).

Geographical Area of Activity: International.

Publications: Annual Report; *Research in Immunology* (10 a year); *Lettre de l'Institut Pasteur* (quarterly); *Annales de l'Institut Pasteur: Actualités* (quarterly); *Microbes and Infections* (15 a year); *Collections des Laboratoires de Références et d'expertise* (11-title series of technical publications).

Finance: The Research Centre is financed by donations, bequests, a grant from the State (since 1965) and profits from its manufacturing interests.

Governing Board: Philippe Rouvillois (Chair.).

Principal Staff: Pres. Philippe Kourilsky; Sec.-Gen. Véronique Wallon.

Address: 28 rue du Docteur Roux, 75015 Paris Cedex 15.

Telephone: 1-45-68-80-00; **Fax:** 1-43-68-81-86; **Internet:** www.pasteur.fr; **e-mail:** info@pasteur.fr.

Institut Pasteur de Lille (Pasteur Institute of Lille)

Founded in 1899 by the City of Lille for biological and medical research, training and analysis.

Activities: The four main areas are biological research (developing vaccinations against diseases caused by parasites, particularly tropical diseases; molecular oncology); public health, including providing information; training; and medical analysis and toxicology. Awards are available for French and non-French researchers.

Principal Staff: Dir Gen. André Capron.

Address: 1 rue du Professeur Calmette, BP 245, 59019 Lille Cedex.

Telephone: 3-20-87-78-00; **Fax:** 3-20-87-79-06; **Internet:** www.pasteur-lille.fr; **e-mail:** webmaster@pasteur-lille.fr.

International Association of Sanskrit Studies

Founded unofficially in 1973 at the International Congress of Orientalists, officially in 1977, by Dr V. Raghavan, Dr R. N. D. Dandekar, Dr L. Sternbach, Dr J. Filliozat and leading Sanskrit delegates from various countries to foster research and studies in the field of Sanskrit and Sanskrit-based literature, thought and culture; to exchange views on the subject; to hold annual world Sanskrit conferences; and to recommend aid for deserving projects.

Activities: Operates both nationally and internationally in the fields of the arts and humanities and religion, through research, conferences, courses, publications and lectures. Has members in Africa, Asia, Australia, North and South America and Europe.

Geographical Area of Activity: International.

Publications: Newsletter (periodic).

Principal Staff: Pres. Prof. R. K. Sharma; Sec.-Gen. Prof. John Brockington; Treas. Prof. Bruno Dagens.

Address: 52 rue du Cardinal Lemoine, 75005 Paris.

Telephone: 1-44-27-10-98.

International Fund for the Promotion of Culture

Established in 1974, an autonomous organization within UNESCO which became an operating body in 1993, to promote national cultures, artistic creation in all its forms and regional and international cultural co-operation. It is the only body within UNESCO which can be approached directly by individuals and organizations.

Activities: The Fund's main programme is Artists Across Frontiers, which supports young artists in all areas of the arts through offering bursaries to promote the international mobility of young artists, and for exchanges, scholarships, travel grants, international workshops and providing funding for disabled artists. Administers the UNESCO-Aschberg Bursaries for Artists programme in partnership with other public and private institutions. The Fund operates in collaboration with other international and national foundations. Since its establishment, the Fund has helped finance projects in 98 countries.

Geographical Area of Activity: International.

Restrictions: No grants for publications, meetings or fellowships.

Publications: Annual Report; *Réflexions* (annually); brochures, grants list, newsletter, etc.

Finance: Financed by an endowment of US $4,200,000, with an additional endowment of US $3,000,000 made in 1993, and contributions from governments, foundations, corporations, etc.

Board of Trustees: Bernard Faivre d'Arcier (Chair.); Felipe Massiani; HRH Princess Sarvath of Jordan; Marisa Berenson; Philippe Braunschweig; Ahmadou Kourouma; Arja Saijonmaa; Christopher Thomas.

Principal Staff: Dir Yudhishthir Raj Isar.

Address: 1 rue Miollis, 75732 Paris Cedex 15.

Telephone: 1-45-68-42-15; **Fax:** 1-45-66-50-62; **e-mail:** dir.ifpc@unesco.org.

International Union for Health Promotion and Education—IUHPE

Founded in 1951 as an independent global association of professionals and organizations committed to world-wide health promotion and education.

Activities: The Union aims to promote global health and contribute to the achievement of equity in health, through advocacy, professional development, networking, partnership building and strengthening capacity. The Union has members in more than 90 countries, and works through seven decentralized regional offices (in Africa, Europe, North America, Northern part of the Western Pacific, Southwest Pacific, and Central and South America and the Caribbean). It works closely with international organizations such as WHO, UNESCO and UNICEF to influence and facilitate the development of health promotion strategies and projects. It organizes a World Conference on Health Promotion and Health Education every three years, and also regional conferences, seminars and workshops. In 2001 launched the Global Forum on Health Promotion Dialogue.

Geographical Area of Activity: International.

Restrictions: This is not a grant-making organization.

Publications: *Promotion and Education* (quarterly, in English, French and Spanish); *Health Education Research* (official research journal of the IUHPE); electronic newsletter; conference reports, academic research and studies and information manuals.

Finance: Annual budget approx. €480,000.

Board of Directors: Maurice Mittelmark (Pres.).

Principal Staff: Exec. Dir Marie-Claude Lamarre; Communications and Development Man. Catherine Jones; Sec. Marie-Edmee Rakotomalala.

Address: 2 rue Auguste Comte, 92170 Vanves.

Telephone: 1-46-45-00-59; **Fax:** 1-46-45-00-45; **Internet:** www.iuhpe.org; **e-mail:** mclamarre@iuhpe.org.

Journalistes en Europe (Journalists in Europe Fund)

Founded in 1974 to increase and improve reporting on European affairs by helping journalists gain an increased understanding of Europe, including the European Union and its institutions.

Activities: Organizes three study and work experience programmes per academic year open to around 30 journalists of any nationality, dealing with various aspects of Europe, including the European Union, industry, the environment, culture and preparation for work as a foreign correspondent in Brussels.

Geographical Area of Activity: International.

Publications: *Europ Magazine* (quarterly, in English and French).

Finance: Annual budget 5,500,000 francs (1999/2000)).

Council: Stephen Somerville (Pres.); Francisco Pinto Balsemao (Vice-Pres.); Yves Agnès (Sec.); and 14 ordinary members.

Principal Staff: Dir Jacques Stoufflet; Sec. Ursula Sérafin.

Address: 4 rue du Faubourg Montmartre, 75009 Paris.

Telephone: 1-55-77-20-00; **Fax:** 1-48-24-40-02; **e-mail:** europmag@europmag.com.

Maison des Sciences de l'Homme (Social Sciences Centre)

Founded in 1957 to promote the study of human societies.

Activities: Operates internationally in the fields of the humanities and social sciences, through research, publications, exchange of scientific information and a library (of 90,000 volumes and 1,800 current periodicals) and documentation service.

Geographical Area of Activity: International.

Publications: *MSH Informations* (quarterly).

Finance: Financed through public and private donations.

Principal Staff: Sec.-Gen. Patrick Janicot; Dir M. Aymard; Sec. Marie-Françoise Balland.

Address: 54 blvd Raspail, 75270 Paris Cedex 06.

Telephone: 1-49-54-20-00; **Fax:** 1-49-54-21-33; **Internet:** www.msh-paris.fr.

Médecins du Monde Internationale (Doctors of the World International)

Established in 1980; aims to promote international solidarity through providing emergency health care and medical support internationally.

Activities: Operates in the field of medicine and health, sending voluntary doctors and other medical staff into areas of crisis and disaster to administer emergency aid and to provide necessary medical support. Also works to develop new approaches to health care in developing countries based on the principles of dignity and respect, works to improve standards and accessibility of public health facilities in less-developed regions, and promotes human rights and social justice.

Geographical Area of Activity: International.

Publications: *Médecins du Monde* (journal).

Finance: Annual budget €76,000,000 (2001).

International Delegation: Dr Bernard Granjou (Chair.); and representatives of the national members from Argentina, Belgium, Canada, Cyprus, France, Greece, Italy, Portugal, Spain, Sweden, Switzerland and the UK.

Principal Staff: Dir Int. Secretariat Alexandre Kamarotos.

Address: 62 rue Marcadet, 75018 Paris.

Telephone: 1-44-92-14-14; **Fax:** 1-44-92-14-55; **Internet:** www.medecinsdumonde.org; **e-mail:** international@medecinsdumonde.net.

Office International de l'Eau (International Office for Water)

Non-profit organization established in 1991 to promote improved water management throughout the world.

Activities: Operates internationally in the area of conservation and the environment. Has established a water data network for organizations and institutions involved in water resources managment and protection. Also holds international conferences, exhibitions and symposia and produces a number of water-related publications. In 2001 had 149 member organizations.

Geographical Area of Activity: International.

Publications: *Information d'Eaux* (monthly); *Network Newsletter* (quarterly); *International News* (annual).

Directors: J. Renard (Pres.); H. Torre, Y. Cheret, G. Delay (Hon. Pres.); C. Gaillard, B. Grange, G. Villalobos, A. Halder, M. Martinez, M. Maruenda, J. Puech, B. Saunier (Vice-Pres.); M.-M. Bourbigot, J. Thornton (Sec.); L. Blondeau, P. Hérisson (Treas.); and 24 others.

Address: 21 rue de Madrid, Paris, 75008.

Telephone: 1-44-90-88-60; **Fax:** 1-40-08-01-45; **Internet:** www.oieau.fr; **e-mail:** dg@oieau.fr.

Organisation Panafricaine de Lutte Contre le SIDA—OPALS (Pan-African Organization Against AIDS)

Founded in 1988 to provide an information service and training for medical practitioners and scientists involved in trying to prevent the spread of AIDS, and caring for AIDS patients.

Activities: Assists the establishment of mobile day-care centres for the provision of care and support in Africa; encourages the adaptation of European preventive campaigns to suit different ways of life in Africa; provides assistance for the training of specialists, including those involved in community development; organizes workshops; supports media prevention campaigns. Works in collaboration with other international organizations. There are members in 33 countries in Africa and Europe.

Geographical Area of Activity: Africa and Europe.

Publications: *OPALS Training Kit; SIDAFRIQUE* (quarterly).

Finance: The Foundation is financed by government grants, fundraising activities and from NGOs; annual budget approx. €152,500.

Principal Staff: Pres. Prof. Marc Gentilini.

Address: 15–21 rue de l'Ecole de Médecine, 75005 Paris.

Telephone: 1-43-26-30-86; **Fax:** 1-43-25-66-16; **e-mail:** opalsjav@ccr.jussiou.fr.

Partage avec les Enfants du Monde (Share with Third World Children)

Established in 1973 by Pierre Marchand to help orphans of the Vietnam war.

Activities: Operates nationally and internationally in the fields of aid to less-developed countries and social welfare, through assisting individual sponsors help children to access all that is vital for their development, i.e. food and shelter, care, clothing and education.

Geographical Area of Activity: Bangladesh, Benin, Brazil, Cambodia, Chile, Croatia, Ecuador, France, Haiti, Honduras, India, Thailand and Vietnam.

Finance: Annual budget approx. €9,147,000.

Address: 11 rue du Change, BP 70311, 60203 Compiègne.

Telephone: 3-44-20-92-92; **Fax:** 3-44-20-94-95; **Internet:** www.aranet.net/partage; **e-mail:** partage@wanadoo.fr.

Santé Sud (Southern Health)

Founded in 1986 to provide assistance to developing countries.

Activities: Operates in the field of assistance to less-developed countries, through long-term projects providing financial, technical and material aid, especially in the area of health care. Consists of 150 members who work as volunteers on the organization's projects. Works in co-operation with local grass-roots organizations in Africa, South America, the Middle East and Asia and has delegations in Mali and Tunisia.

Geographical Area of Activity: Africa, Asia, Central and South America and the Middle East.

Publications: *Santé Sud* (newsletter, quarterly).

Finance: Annual budget €1,200,000 (2002).

Principal Staff: Pres. Annick Wostyn; Dir Claude Isakov.

Address: 200 blvd National le Gyptis, 13003 Marseille.

Telephone: 4-91-95-63-45; **Fax:** 4-91-95-68-05; **Internet:** www.santesud.org; **e-mail:** santesud@wanadoo.fr.

Secours Catholique—Caritas de France (Catholic Assistance—Caritas France)

Founded in 1946 by Mgr Jean Rodhain as part of Caritas Internationalis (q.v.) with the aim of helping poor people throughout the world.

Activities: The organization provides aid to developing countries and operates its own programmes in the fields of education, human rights, health care and social welfare. It also provides grants to institutions and finances scholarships and fellowships. Also publishes annual statistical surveys of the extent of poverty in France.

Geographical Area of Activity: International.

Publications: *Messages* (monthly); *Le Sida en Question; Le France des sans ressources; L'Afrique des Grands Lacs; Le pétrole au Congo: pour qui coule l'or noir?* ; Annual Report.

Finance: Annual budget 551,229,146 francs (2000).

Principal Staff: Pres. Joël Thoraval; Sec.-Gen Jean Celier.

Address: 106 rue du Bac, 75341 Paris Cedex 07.

Telephone: 1-45-49-73-00; **Fax:** 1-45-49-94-50; **Internet:** www.secours-catholique.asso.fr; **e-mail:** info@secours-catholique.asso.fr.

Service d'Entraide et de Liaison—SEL

Christian aid organization founded in 1980 to help prevent suffering in the developing world.

Activities: Operates internationally in the field of aid to less-developed countries. Provides aid and assistance in developing countries, particularly to children. Supports development projects in the areas of education, health, nutrition, agriculture and other social concerns, and offers emergency relief to areas in crisis. Also maintains offices in Belgium and Switzerland.

Geographical Area of Activity: Africa, Asia, Central and South America, the Middle East, Croatia and Romania.

Principal Staff: Dir Patrick Guiborat.

Address: 9 rue de la Gare, 94234 Cachan.

Telephone: 1-45-65-83-03; **Fax:** 1-46-63-23-77; **Internet:** www.temanet.org/fr/ucpm/org/sel.html; **e-mail:** selfrance@hol.fr.

Solidarité (Solidarity)

Founded in 1980. Aims to reduce unemployment in rural areas and to improve the quality of life of people living in developing countries.

Activities: Promotes sustainable rural development in Africa, Central and South America and Asia. Supports local organizations financially, technically or physically in order to carry out development projects to encourage and enable rural people to become more independent. Creates small industries by using local resources; carries out research into suitable technologies; promotes improved medical and sanitary systems and environmental awareness. There is a particular focus on the development and empowerment of women and children, and tribal people's rights. Also disseminates information about the projects, runs training courses and liaises with local and international NGOs.

Geographical Area of Activity: Africa, Asia, Central and South America, and Europe.

Publications: *Solidarité* (magazine, quarterly); Annual Report.

Address: 52 rue du Château du Roi, BP 52, 81602 Gaillac Cedex.

Telephone: 5-63-41-10-14; **Fax:** 5-63-57-60-05; **Internet:** www.solidarite.asso.fr; **e-mail:** contact@solidarite.asso.fr.

Women's International Democratic Federation/Fédération Démocratique Internationale des Femmes

Founded in 1945 to prevent the recurrence of war and the resurgence of fascism for the sake of the wellbeing of women and children.

Activities: Defends the rights of women in every area of life, and in every region of the world. Works for equal rights in society and in the workplace, and for women's rights to adequate health care and education. Also promotes world peace and democracy, and campaigns against racial inequality and discrimination. Has members in 104 countries.

Geographical Area of Activity: International.

Principal Staff: Pres. Sylvie Jan; Vice-Pres. Mayada Abbassi.

Address: 25 rue du Charolais, 75012 Paris.

Telephone: 1-40-01-90-90; **Fax:** 1-40-01-92-70; **Internet:** www.fdif.eu.org; **e-mail:** fdif@fdif.eu.org.

World Heritage Fund

Established in 1972 by the Convention Concerning the Protection of the World Cultural and Natural Heritage to protect world cultural and natural heritage.

Activities: The Fund assists in identifying and preserving World Heritage sites through providing international assistance in five specific areas: preparatory assistance; promotion and education, technical co-operation; emergency assistance; and training.

Geographical Area of Activity: International.

Publications: *World Heritage Review* (bi-monthly magazine); *World Heritage Newsletter* (bi-monthly report).

Finance: The Fund receives its income essentially from compulsory contributions from states party to the Convention (amounting to 1% of their UNESCO dues) and from voluntary contributions. Approved budget US $3,995,000 (2003).

Governing Committee: 21 members elected for up to six year terms.

Principal Staff: Chair. Tamas Fejerdy.

Address: c/o World Heritage Centre, UNESCO, 7 place de Fontenoy, 75007 Paris.

Telephone: 1-45-68-15-71; **Fax:** 1-45-68-55-70; **Internet:** http://whc.unesco.org; **e-mail:** wh-info@unesco.org.

The Gambia

FOUNDATION CENTRE AND CO-ORDINATING BODY

Association of NGOs in The Gambia—TANGO

Activities: Co-ordinates activities of member organizations in order to ensure that resources are used efficiently to further social development in The Gambia. Works as an information forum and as a meeting place for NGOs to exchange information, knowledge and expertise. Also co-ordinates the National Poverty Alleviation Programme and works on voter education programmes to increase female participation in elections and to raise issues of agrarian concern.

Geographical Area of Activity: The Gambia.

Principal Staff: Dir Fatma Baldeh; M. Jeng.

Address: PMB 392, Serrekunda.

Telephone: 497771; **Fax:** 497772.

FOUNDATIONS, TRUSTS AND NON-PROFIT ORGANIZATIONS

Foundation for Research on Women's Health, Productivity and the Environment—BAFROW

Established in 1991 by nine individuals to assist in and contribute to the development of a conceptual framework regarding gender and development, and to facilitate dialogue on empowerment, focusing on major factors significant to the development and sustainability of women and female children.

Activities: Operates in the fields of conservation and the environment, economic affairs, education, and medicine and health, nationally through self-conducted programmes, conferences and training courses, and internationally through research. Projects include research into genital mutiliation, and a series of public education campaigns to end its practice, as well as the promotion of access to schooling for girls and research into the implications of polygamy for women. Works in association with other international organizations, including the American Jewish World Service (q.v.).

Geographical Area of Activity: Mainly The Gambia.

Publications: *Curriculum for Initiation Rites in Madinka, Fula and Jola; Needs Assessment Study for Skills Development for Circumcisers; Female Genital Mutilation (FGM).*

Governing Board: M. G. Bala-Gaye (Chair.); Veronic Wright (Vice-Chair.); Mariam Thomasi (Treas.); Fatou Waggeh (Sec.); Isatou Gaye; Alhaji Dawda Jallow; Altagi Luntang Jaiteh; Dr Tijan Senghore; Kaliba Senghore; Zoe Tembo.

Principal Staff: Dir Fatou Waggeh.

Address: 214 Tafsir Demba Mbye Rd, Tobacco Rd Estate, Banjul; POB 2854, Serrekunda.

Telephone: 225270; **Fax:** 223266; **e-mail:** bafrow@gamtel.gm.

Georgia

FOUNDATION CENTRES AND CO-ORDINATING BODIES

Centre for Training and Consultancy

Activities: Provides support to non-profit organizations in Georgia, for the institutional development of the not-for-profit sector. Offers training and consultancy services in institutional development, capacity-building and strategic planning. Promotes co-operation between Georgian NGOs and organizations from other Eastern and Western European countries. A regional partner of the Management for Development Foundation based in the Netherlands; maintains an office in Azerbaijan, with links to Armenia and Kyrgyzstan.

Geographical Area of Activity: Armenia, Azerbaijan, Georgia and Kyrgyzstan.

Principal Staff: Exec. Dir Matthias Valentin; Admin. Asst Marina Amzashvili.

Address: 30 Vazha-Pshavela Ave, Apt 7-8, 380077 Tbilisi.

Telephone: (32) 251982; **Fax:** (32) 325381; **Internet:** www.ctc.org.ge; **e-mail:** ctc@ctc.org.ge.

Horizonti, the Foundation for the Third Sector

Founded by Michael Clayton and Nino Saakashvili in 1997. Aims to support the development of a civil society in Georgia.

Activities: Assists in the development of foundations and similar organizations in Georgia by providing technical and financial assistance. Also offers grants, training and consulting and information. Operates five main programmes: Cross-Sectoral Partnership; Citizens Activation, Community Development and Constitutency Building; Organizational Development; Constituency Awareness Raising; and Sustainable Development Support.

Geographical Area of Activity: Caucasus, Georgia.

Restrictions: No grants to individuals; grants are for Georgian NGOs.

Publications: Annual Report; NGO databases; and publications on NGO organization and development (translated into Georgian).

Finance: Funded by the US Agency for International Aid (USAID) and by private donations.

Governing Board: Stephen Jones (Chair.); G. Bazgadze; L. Butkhuzi; G. Loladze; N. Saakashvili; M. Tsereteli.

Principal Staff: Dir Nino Saakashvili; Deputy Dir Nikoloz Oakley.

Address: 2 Dolidze Str., 6th Floor, 380015 Tbilisi.

Telephone: (32) 332816; **Fax:** (32) 987504; **Internet:** www.horizonti.org; **e-mail:** adm@horizonti.org.

FOUNDATIONS, TRUSTS AND NON-PROFIT ORGANIZATIONS

Caucasian Institute for Peace, Democracy and Development

Set up as an independent policy research organization.

Activities: The Institute's primary areas of research are regional security, state-building, democratization in the Caucasus, and the theory of nationalism and its fate in the post-Cold War context. Organizes round table discussions on issues concerning peace and democracy in Georgia; hosts an on-line discussion forum and services for journalists and researchers; and runs grants programmes in association with other organizations, including a competition to reward innovative work in the field of civic education.

Geographical Area of Activity: Georgia.

Publications: *CIPDD News; Ethnic-confessional Groups and Challenges to Civic Integration in Georgia; sazogadoeba da politika*; and other publications in Georgian.

Principal Staff: Dir Ghia Nodia.

Address: 1 M. Alexidze Str., 11th Floor, Tbilisi; POB 101, 380008 Tbilisi.

Internet: www.cipdd.org.

Open Society Georgia Foundation

Established in May 1994, an independent foundation, part of the Soros foundations network, which aims to foster political and cultural pluralism and reform economic structures in order to encourage private enterprise and a market economy.

Activities: Operates mainly in the fields of education, higher education, civil society, the arts and humanities, law, and information and the media, through supporting 26 national and regional programmes. Also supports other NGOs in Georgia, as well as regional projects in collaboration with the Soros foundations of Armenia and Azerbaijan.

Geographical Area of Activity: Georgia.

Publications: Annual Report.

Finance: Annual expenditure US $5,532,000 (2001).

Board of Directors: Lia Mukhashavria (Chair.); Levan Berzenishvili; Tamar Chikovani; Seit Devdariani; Keti Khutsishvili; David Usupashvili; Paata Zakareishvili;.

Principal Staff: Exec. Dir Michael Chackunashvili; Deputy Dir Nino Chinchaladze.

Address: 10 Chovelidze Str., 380008 Tbilisi.

Telephone: (32) 938999; **Fax:** (32) 291052; **Internet:** www.osgf.ge; **e-mail:** kartuli@osgf.ge.

Germany

FOUNDATION CENTRES AND CO-ORDINATING BODIES

Bundesverband Deutscher Stiftungen eV (Federal Association of German Foundations)

Founded in 1948 to represent the interests of German foundations.

Activities: Provides information about German foundations; publishes directories, books, reports, brochures and leaflets; organizes conferences, exhibitions and training for foundation staff. Maintains a database with over 12,000 entries for foundations and works internationally with similar national and international organizations.

Geographical Area of Activity: Germany.

Restrictions: Does not make grants.

Publications: *Verzeichnis Deutscher Stiftungen 2000; Schriftenreihen; Deutsches Stiftungswesen, Lebensbilder Deutscher Stiftungen; Ratgeber für Stifter; Die Verwaltung einer Stiftung; Tagungsberichte; Deutsche Stiftungen—Mitteilungen* (quarterly).

Governing Board: Dr Fritz Brickwedde (Chair.); Dr Ulrich Bopp (Vice-Chair.); Prof. Dr Rainer Hüttemann; Dr Heike Kahl; Karoline Krämer; Dr Wilheim Krull; Jürgen Regge.

Principal Staff: Man. Dir Dr C. Mecking.

Address: Alfried-Krupp-Haus, Binger Str. 40, 14197 Berlin.

Telephone: (30) 8979470; **Fax:** (30) 89794711; **Internet:** www.stiftungen.org; **e-mail:** bundesverband@stiftungen.org.

Maecenata Institut für Dritter-Sektor-Forschung (Maecenata Institute for Third-Sector Research)

Established in 1997 as an independent, non-profit-making institution to promote academic research, exchanges, documentation and information in the area of the third sector.

Activities: Operates in the field of research into the third sector, through collecting and publishing information on foundations and other third-sector organizations; maintaining a database on around 9,000 German foundations and trusts; carrying out research; organizing conferences; promoting research in the field through academic exchange; and developing an information centre.

Geographical Area of Activity: Germany, Europe and USA.

Publications: *Maecenata Actuell* (every 2 months); books, journals and electronic information.

Scientific Council: Prof. Dr Helmut Anheier; Prof. Dr Nikolaus Lobkowicz; Prof. Dr Christian Pfeiffer; Prof. Dr Robert Picht; Rupert Graf Strachwitz; Dr Markus Wanger; Prof. Dr Annette Zimmer.

Principal Staff: Dir Rupert Graf Strachwitz; Members Frank Adloff, Susanne Rindt, Sylvia Schmeikl, Dr Rainer Sprengel.

Address: Albrechtstr. 22, 10117 Berlin-Mitte.

Telephone: (30) 28387909; **Fax:** (30) 28387910; **Internet:** www.maecenata.de; **e-mail:** mi@maecenata.de.

Maecenata Management GmbH

Founded in 1989 by Count Rupert Strachwitz to provide management assistance to and for the third sector (non-governmental, non-profit-making institutions).

Activities: Operates in European Union and Eastern European countries, and in the USA, in the fields of the arts and humanities, conservation and the environment, economic and international affairs, education, and social welfare and social studies, through self-conducted programmes, research, conferences, training courses and publications. Maintains an office in Berlin.

Geographical Area of Activity: Germany, countries of the European Union, Central and Eastern Europe and the USA.

Restrictions: Does not make grants.

Publications: *Maecenata Stiftungsführer; Stiftungen-nutzen, führen und errichten: ein Handbuch; Kulturförderung, Mehr als Sponsoring; Der Zweite und der Dritte Sektor, Maecenata Aktuell; Maecenata Unternehmensführer.*

Finance: Holds 35 foundations in trust; total capital approx. €75,000,000.

Principal Staff: Dir Rupert Graf Strachwitz.

Address: Barer Str. 44, 80799 Munich.

Telephone: (89) 284452; **Fax:** (89) 283774; **Internet:** www.maecenata-management.de; **e-mail:** mm@maecenata-management.de.

Stifterverband für die Deutsche Wissenschaft eV (Donors' Association for the Promotion of Sciences and Humanities)

Founded in 1920 and re-established in 1949 by 61 national industrial and commercial organizations to support the sciences and humanities in research and teaching, as well as the rising scientific and technical generation; to undertake measures which might be helpful in bringing support to science and technology.

Activities: Operates nationally in the fields of education, the arts and humanities, and both nationally and internationally in the fields of science, medicine and international relations, through self-conducted programmes. The Association has around 3,000 members, comprising companies, associations and individuals making donations on an annual basis; administers more than 350 trusts and foundations (German Foundation Centre).

Geographical Area of Activity: Germany and international.

Publications: Annual Report; *Wirtschaft und Wissenschaft* (quarterly); *Materialien aus dem Stiftungszentrum; Materialien zur Wissenschaftsstatistik; Beiträge zu Statistiken über Forschung und Entwicklung; Schriftenreihe zum Stiftungswesen.*

Finance: Annual expenditure €110,400,000 (2001); 350 foundations in trust with a total capital of approx. €1,360,000,000 (2001).

Board of Trustees: There are up to 100 members on the Board.

Principal Staff: Pres. Dr Arend Oetker.

Address: Barkhovenallee 1, 45239 Essen.

Telephone: (201) 84010; **Fax:** (201) 8401459; **Internet:** www.stifterverband.de; **e-mail:** mail@stifterverband.de.

FOUNDATIONS, TRUSTS AND NON-PROFIT ORGANIZATIONS

Konrad-Adenauer-Stiftung eV (Konrad Adenauer Foundation)

Founded in 1964, emerging from the Society for Christian Democratic Education (founded in 1956), and named after the first Chancellor of the Federal Republic, Konrad Adenauer. The Foundation is guided by the same principles that inspired Adenauer's work.

Activities: Operates in the field of the humanities, development and international relations, through: granting scholarships to gifted individuals; organizing public events; and supporting projects in the field of international understanding (approximately 200 projects and programmes are organized in more than 100 countries). Offers political education and research for political projects; researches the history of Christian Democracy; supports and encourages European unification, operates a think-tank on domestic policy and the social market economy, international understanding and co-operation on development policy. Maintains two education centres and 21 education institutes.

Geographical Area of Activity: International.

Publications: Annual Report; *Die Frau in unserer Zeit* (quarterly); *Eichholz Brief* (quarterly); *Einblicke* (6 a year); *German Comments* (monthly); *KAS-Auslandsinformationen* (monthly).

Finance: Budget approx. DM200,000,000 (2001).

Governing Board: Prof. Günter Rinsche (Chair.); Wilhelm Staudacher (Sec.-Gen.); Dr Josef Thesing (Deputy Sec.-Gen.).

Address: Rathausallee 12, 53757 Sankt Augustin.

Telephone: (2241) 2460; **Fax:** (2241) 246591; **Internet:** www.kas.de; **e-mail:** zentrale@kas.de.

Aid to the Church in Need—Kirche-in-Not

Founded in 1947 by Fr Werenfried van Straaten to promote Christianity and support and provide pastoral relief to Catholics in need.

Activities: Operates in around 144 less-developed countries of Africa, Asia, Central and South America and the Caribbean, and Eastern Europe, through providing grants towards church-building and transport funds, for students, seminarians, novices and clergy, and in the area of the press, radio and religious literature; it also supports persecuted, oppressed and poor Catholics, Russian Orthodox, and refugees, regardless of religion. The organization's international office is located in Germany, and national offices operate in 16 countries in Europe, North and South America and Australia.

Geographical Area of Activity: International.

Publications: *Fifty Years of the Church in Need*; and other publications.

Finance: Annual budget approx. US $70,000,000.

Address: Bischof-Kindermann-Str. 23, 61462 Königstein.

Telephone: (6174) 2910; **Fax:** (6174) 3423; **Internet:** www.kirche-in-not.org/index.html; **e-mail:** int.zentrale-kin@kirche-in-not.org.

Allianz Kulturstiftung (Allianz Cultural Foundation)

Established in 2000 by Allianz AG (q.v.) for the promotion of culture, especially with regard to young people and European integration.

Activities: Operates in the area of culture, by making grants for activities including international festivals. Initiates its own projects as well as making grants in collaboration with cultural organizations for a range of cross-genre and cross-media projects, contemporary concepts and initiatives. The Foundation directs special attention to promoting futuristic, innovative projects that present new aspects and encourage international collaboration.

Geographical Area of Activity: Europe.

Restrictions: No grants to individuals.

Publications: Publications on foundations and philanthropy.

Finance: Initial capital approx €50,000,000.

Board of Trustees: Dr Robert Picht (Chair.).

Principal Staff: Foundation Cttee Chair. Dr Henning Schulte-Noelle; Foundation Cttee Vice-Chair. Dr Diethart Breipohl; Dir Dr Ludger Hunnekens.

Address: Maria-Theresia-Str. 4A, 81675 Munich-Bogenhausen.

Telephone: (89) 4107303; **Fax:** (89) 41073040; **Internet:** www.allianz-kulturstiftung.de; **e-mail:** kulturstiftung@allianz.de.

Allianz Umweltstiftung (Allianz Foundation for the Environment)

Established in 1990 by Allianz Versicherung to work towards ensuring a safe future.

Activities: Operates in Germany in the field of environmental conservation, focusing on the protection and development of the countryside, land planning and sustainable development. Supports innovative and inspirational projects. Sponsors the Benediktbeurer Talks, a forum for debating environmental protection issues.

Geographical Area of Activity: Germany.

Publications: *10 Jahre Allianz Umweltstiftung;* various project reports; video.

Finance: Assets approx. €51,000,000.

Principal Staff: Dr Lutz Spandau; Peter Wilde; Susanne Luberstetter; Nicole Steffen.

Address: Maria-Theresia-Str. 4A, 81675 Munich.

Telephone: (89) 4107336; **Fax:** (89) 41073370; **Internet:** www.allianz-umweltstiftung.de; **e-mail:** info@allianz-umweltstiftung.de.

ASKO Europa-Stiftung (ASKO Europe Foundation)

Established in 1990 by the ASKO Deutsche Kaufhaus AG company to promote academic research and education, especially in the area of European integration on a federal basis. In 1996, when ASKO Deutsche Kaufhaus AG merged with METRO AG, the Foundation became an independent entity.

Activities: Promotes study in the area of European integration. Special emphasis is given to Franco-German relations and their significance for the European integration process. As the Foundation is based in Saarbrücken, it is also strongly committed to the development of the European region spanning Saarlund—Lorraine—Luxembourg—Rhineland—Palatina—Walloni

Geographical Area of Activity: Europe.

Principal Staff: Chair. Arno Krause; Dir-Gen. Dr Michael Meimeth; Sec. Renate Preuth.

Address: Pestelstr. 2, 66119 Saarbrücken.

Telephone: (681) 926740; **Fax:** (681) 9267499; **Internet:** www.asko-europa-stiftung.de; **e-mail:** k.elbogen@saarnet.de.

Aventis Foundation

Established in 1996 by Hoechst AG, and formerly known as the Hoechst Foundation, for the promotion of international interdisciplinary projects in the areas of culture, society, business and science. In 1999 several other Hoechst foundations were integrated into its organizational structure.

Activities: Operates internationally, promoting interdisciplinary projects in areas such as the arts and humanities, science and technology, and economic and political affairs, through making grants to organizations. Special funds operate in the field of education, offering grants to gifted young people in need, and for scientific research.

Geographical Area of Activity: International.

Publications: Annual Report.

Finance: Annual grants expenditure approx. €2,500,000 (2000).

Board of Trustees: Jürgen Dormann (Chair.); Prof. Dr Uwe Bicker; Dr Frank L. Douglas; Jean-René Fourtou; Prof. Dr Jean-Marie Pierre Lehn; Pierre Messmer.

Principal Staff: Exec. Chair. Dr Friedmar Nusch.

Address: Industriepark Höchst, 65926 Frankfurt/Main.

Telephone: (69) 30582948; **Fax:** (69) 30523497; **Internet:** www.aventis-foundation.org.

Bellagio Forum for Sustainable Development

Founded in 1996 by a group of international donor organizations and initiated by the Fondazione San Paolo di Torino and the Rockefeller Foundation (qq.v.), to fund and provide expertise for activities that influence policy and thinking in the area of sustainable development.

Activities: The Forum's members provide funding and expertise for a wide range of activities that influence policy and thinking on sustainable development issues, as well as providing practical improvements towards environmental sustainability, within the broad categories of sustainable livelihoods, the media, policy and research. Initiatives include the Environmental Communications Award, launched in 2001; an annual environmental studies award at Oxford University in the UK; the Cooking Stove Project, a pilot initiative aiming to reduce the use of wood as fuel under way in Guatelama, India and the Philippines; a protection programme for the Mediterranean sea; and the development of a nature reserve in Lebanon. In 2003 the Forum had 28 member organizations based in Europe and the USA.

Geographical Area of Activity: International.

Board of Trustees: Hanns Michael Hölz (Chair.); Jan-Oluf Willums, Ulrich Witte (Deputy Chair.); Charles Buchanan (Treas.); Marianne Ginsburg; Mans Lönnruth; Rosemary Martin; Michele de Nevers; Jo Weir.

Principal Staff: Asst. Dir Jutta Richter.

Address: An der Bornau 2, Osnabrück 49090.

Telephone: (541) 9633490; **Fax:** (541) 9633491; **Internet:** www.bsfd.org; **e-mail:** info@bfsd.org.

Otto Benecke Stiftung eV (Otto Benecke Foundation)

Founded in 1965 by the Verband Deutscher Studentenschaften (Association of German Student Bodies) to provide assistance for refugee students and students from developing countries.

Activities: Operates internationally in the field of education, by providing a counselling and scholarship programme enabling students from less-developed countries (particularly refugees from Southern Africa) to study at universities, polytechnics and vocational schools in Germany and less-developed countries; it also runs a programme for training in manual and industrial occupations in African countries of asylum. International conferences are held, in collaboration with other organizations, on basic questions concerning the right to asylum.

Geographical Area of Activity: International.

Restrictions: Grants are made only to immigrants, refugees and asylum-seekers.

Publications: Conference reports; report of operations.

Trustees: Eberhard Diepgens (Chair.); Dr Lothar Theodor Lemper (Pres.); Klaus Laepple; Jonathan Grigoleit.

Principal Staff: Sec.-Gen. Hans-Günther Toetemeyer.

Address: Kennedyallee 105–107, 53175 Bonn.

Telephone: (228) 81630; **Fax:** (228) 8163300; **Internet:** www.obs-ev.de; **e-mail:** obs-ev@t-online.de.

Berghof Stiftung für Konfliktforschung GmbH (Berghof Foundation for Conflict Research)

Established in 1971 by Prof. Dr Georg Zundel to carry out research in peace-related conflict studies.

Activities: The Foundation acts as a research institute in all areas of conflict studies. It support action-oriented research into constructive conflict management and key issues in natural sciences and ethics. Also maintains the Berghof Center for Constructive Conflict Management in Berlin, Germany.

Geographical Area of Activity: Western, Central, Eastern and Southern Europe.

Restrictions: Grants restricted to Western, Southern, Central and Eastern Europe, for a three-year period of support only.

Publications: Specialist publications detailing the foundation's work.

Finance: Assets DM15,000,000 (1999); annual expenditure DM1,500,000 (1999).

Board of Trustees: Prof. Dr Horst Fischer (Chair.).

Principal Staff: Man. Dir Prof. Dr Georg Zundel; Dir Admin and Finance Management Renate Christaller.

Address: Altenstinstr. 48A, 14195 Berlin.

Telephone: (30) 84415433; **Fax:** (30) 84415499; **e-mail:** renate.christaller@berghof-center.org.

Bertelsmann Foundation (Bertelsmann Stiftung)

Founded in 1977 by Reinhard Mohn to support projects in education, economic and social issues, democracy and civil society, international co-operation and health.

Activities: Operates internationally in the following main areas: the annual Carl Bertelsmann Prize for innovative approaches to problem solving; Education, focusing on developing ideas for expanding the network within the education system; Economic and Social Issues, developing approaches toward a sustainable social market economy; Democracy and Civil Society, supporting citizen-oriented discussion and decision-making processes in communities and calls for public accountability and transparency; International Co-operation, dedicated to settling conflict through international change management for a peaceful balance of interests and constructive cultural co-existence; and Health, working towards a fundamental reform of the German health-care sector, also supporting the Academy of Manual Medicine, CKM Centre for Hospital Management, and the German Stroke Foundation; and Foundations, to assist in the improvement of the management, strategies and methods of foundations. In 2002, in conjunction with the C. S. Mott Foundation (q.v.), invested €1,000,000 over three years on an initiative aiming to facilitate the exchange of experience among community foundations from Europe, North America and Mexico.

Geographical Area of Activity: Germany, Europe and USA.

Restrictions: Operating foundation; no grants on application.

Publications: Annual Report; quarterly newsletters; publications related to projects undertaken.

Finance: The Foundation has a 68% (non-voting) shareholding in the media company, Bertelsmann AG. Annual expenditure €65,000,000 (2001).

Board of Management: Prof. Dr Heribert Meffert (Chair.); Gerd Schulte-Hillen (Vice-Chair.); Liz Mohn; Reinhard Mohn; Prof. Dr Werner Weidenfeld.

Principal Staff: Vice-Chair. Management Cttee Wolfgang Koeckstadt.

Address: Carl-Bertelsmann-Str. 256, Postfach 103, 33311 Gütersloh.

Telephone: (5241) 8170; **Fax:** (5241) 816677; **Internet:** www.bertelsmann-stiftung.de; **e-mail:** info@bertelsmann-stiftung.de.

BMW Stiftung Herbert Quandt (BMW Foundation Herbert Quandt)

Founded in June 1970 by BMW AG, on the 60th birthday of Herbert Quandt, to foster international dialogue.

Activities: The foundation seeks to foster national and international dialogue and mutual understanding between business, politics and society. Organizes a range of events bringing together leaders of industry and society, which aim to demonstrate the importance of co-operation between social institutions in order to ensure industrial nations have stable and successful economies. International events are often organized in co-operation with other organizations.

Geographical Area of Activity: International.

Restrictions: Unsolicited applications are not accepted: no scholarships or any other kind of financial support is provided.

Publications: Texts of lectures and conference documentation.

Finance: Annual expenditure DM4,000,000 (1999).

Trustees: Dr Horst Teltschik (Chair.).

Principal Staff: Exec. Dir Dr Kai M. Schellhorn.

Address: Hanauer Str. 46, 80788 Munich.

Telephone: (89) 38211630; **Fax:** (89) 38211636; **Internet:** www.bmwstiftunghq.com; **e-mail:** bmwstiftunghq@bmw.de.

Boehringer Ingelheim Fonds—Stiftung für Medizinische Grundlagenforschung (Foundation for Basic Research in Biomedicine)

Founded in January 1983 by the companies C. H. Boehringer Sohn and Boehringer Ingelheim International for the exclusive and direct promotion of basic research in biomedicine.

Activities: Operates nationally and internationally, through offering long-term scholarships and travel allowances to doctoral students, and organizing the International Titisee Conferences for established scientists.

Geographical Area of Activity: Europe (supports Europeans in Europe and overseas; scientists from overseas working in Europe).

Restrictions: No grants to scientific institutions; no grants for the payment of staff or for equipment or materials.

Publications: *B.I.F.F.—FUTURA* (quarterly).

Finance: Annual revenue and expenditure DM6,800,000 (2001).

Trustees: Dr Ingrid Ehses; Prof. Harald Goebell; Prof. Peter Herrlich; Prof. Herbert Jäckle; Prof. U. Benjamin Kaupp; Prof. Gert Riethmüller; Prof. Erwin F. Wagner.

Principal Staff: Man. Dir Dr Hermann Fröhlich; Public Relations Officer Dr Claudia Walther.

Address: Schlossmühle, Grabenstr. 46, 55262 Heidesheim.

Telephone: (6132) 89850; **Fax:** (6132) 898511; **Internet:** www.bifonds.de; **e-mail:** secretariat@bifonds.de.

Heinrich-Böll-Stiftung (Heinrich Böll Foundation)

Established in 1987 and associated with the German Green Party, to promote political education in the areas of ecology, solidarity, democracy, arms control and sexual equality; and to preserve the works and thoughts of the writer Heinrich Böll.

Activities: Operates nationally and internationally in the fields of the arts and humanities, conservation and the environment, international affairs, economic sustainability, and law and human rights; co-operates with NGOs working in 54 countries. Maintains 18 offices in Washington, DC, Brussels, the Czech Republic, India, Nigeria, Poland, Russia, and in Africa, the Middle East, South-East Asia and South America. Also founded the Feminist Institute and the Green Academy. Operates a fellowship study programme open to students and post-graduates in all fields and of all nationalities.

Geographical Area of Activity: International.

Publications: Annual Report.

Finance: Annual expenditure €35,785,000 (2002).

Board of Directors: Ralf Fücks; Barbara Unmüß; Dr Birgit Laubach.

Principal Staff: CEO Dr Burgit Laubach.

Address: Rosenthaler Str. 40–41, 10178 Berlin.

Telephone: (30) 285340; **Fax:** (30) 28534109; **Internet:** www.boell.de; **e-mail:** info@boell.de.

Robert Bosch Stiftung GmbH (Robert Bosch Foundation)

Founded in 1964 by the Bosch organization to embody the philanthropic and social endeavours of its founder, Robert Bosch (1861–1942).

Activities: The Foundation supports and promotes public health, especially in the institutions it runs: the Robert Bosch Hospital, Dr Margarete Fischer-Bosch Institute for Clinical Pharmacology and the Institute for the History of Medicine in Stuttgart; it also promotes international understanding (especially with France, the USA, Poland and the Czech Republic), social work, education, art and culture, the humanities, and social and natural sciences. It also defines project areas, develops innovative programmes, competitions and prizes, and supports promising pilot projects within these objectives.

Geographical Area of Activity: Europe and the USA.

Restrictions: Grants only given in defined areas of interest and for limited periods.

Finance: Net assets 92% of the common stock capital of Robert Bosch GmbH, amounting to €1,200,000,000; annual expenditure on funding and project activities €40,100,000 (2001).

Trustees: Dr Heiner Gutberlet (Chair); Dr Christof Bosch; Dr Hermann Eisele; Dr Hanna-Barbara Gerl-Falkowitz; Matthias Madelung; Dr Hubert Markl; Helga Solinger; Eberhard Stilz; Dr Reinhold Würth.

Principal Staff: CEO Dieter Berg.

Address: POB 10 06 28, 70005 Stuttgart.

Telephone: (711) 460840; **Fax:** (711) 460841094; **Internet:** www.bosch-stiftung.de; **e-mail:** info@bosch-stiftung.de.

Bundeskanzler-Willy-Brandt-Stiftung (Federal Chancellor Willy Brandt Foundation)

Established in 1994 by the German Bundestag to further the aims of the former Chancellor Willy Brandt. Aims to contribute to an understanding of the history of the 20th century, and of the development of the Federal Republic of Germany.

Activities: Promotes the ideals of Willy Brandt in the areas of the peace, freedom and unity of the German people; the safeguarding of democracy; and understanding and reconciliation between nations. Operates in the areas of the arts and humanities, education, international affairs, law and human rights, and social welfare, nationally and internationally, through self-conducted programmes, research, conferences, training courses and publications.

Geographical Area of Activity: International.

Restrictions: No grants. Conducts only its own projects.

Publications: *Schriftenreihe der Bundeskanzler-Willy-Brandt-Stiftung; Edition Willy Brandt—Berliner Ausgabe*; Annual Newsletter.

Finance: Annual expenditure €700,000 (2002).

Board of Governors: Dr Gerhard Groß (Chair); Prof. Dr Dieter Dowe; Prof. Dr Gregor Schöllgen.

Principal Staff: Exec. Dir Dr Wolfram Hoppenstedt.

Address: Rathaus Schöneberg, John-F.-Kennedy-Platz, 10825 Berlin.

Telephone: (30) 7877070; **Fax:** (30) 78770750; **Internet:** www.willy-brandt.de; **e-mail:** info@willy-brandt.de.

Brot für die Welt (Bread for the World)

Activities: Operates more than 700 self-help projects each year in around 80 developing countries, including countries of Central and South America, Africa and South-East Asia, in collaboration with partner organizations. Projects operate in the areas of education, advice and practical assistance, health and welfare, and emergency relief.

Geographical Area of Activity: Developing countries in Central and South America, Africa, South-East Asia and the Far East.

Finance: Total expenditure €67,457,340 (2001).

Address: Stafflenbergstr. 76, 70184 Stuttgart.

Telephone: (711) 21590; **Fax:** (711) 2159368; **Internet:** www.brot-fuer-die-welt.de; **e-mail:** bfdwinformation@brot-fuer-die-welt.org.

Sergiu Celibidache Stiftung (Sergiu Celibidache Foundation)

Founded in December 1999 by Serge Ioan and Joana Celebidachi.

Activities: The Foundation aims to promote the musical work of Sergiu Celibidiachi, through documentation, continuation and discussion of his music through seminars and publications. Activities include supporting young musicians, organizing master classes, discussions, and conducting courses and concerts. Organized the first Sergii Celibidachi Festival in October 2002 in Munich.

Geographical Area of Activity: Germany and international.

Board of Trustees: Serge Ioan Celebidachi (Pres.).

Principal Staff: Contact: Marc Hart.

Address: Ismaninger Str. 95, 81675 Munich.

Telephone: (89) 35062888; **Fax:** (89) 35062889; **Internet:** www.celibidache.com; **e-mail:** celibidachestiftung@web.de.

Gottlieb Daimler- und Karl Benz-Stiftung (Gottlieb Daimler and Karl Benz Foundation)

Founded by Daimler–Benz AG in 1986, to support research relating to the inter-relationships between human beings, the environment and technology.

Activities: The Foundation provides funds for research undertaken by groups working on special topics within the frame of defined research programmes; research activities are co-ordinated and the results published. The current topics deal with living in smart environments; the implications of ubiquitous computing; towards the qualification of the urban landscape; and group interaction in high-risk environments. Grants are also awarded to individuals for pre-doctoral research, to German nationals wishing to conduct research abroad, and to young foreign scientists carrying out research at German institutions.

Geographical Area of Activity: Germany and international, with an emphasis on Vietnam, the People's Republic of China and Cambodia.

Publications: *Bertha-Benz-Vorlesung* (annually); *Info* (2 a year); Report (every 2 years); progress reports.

Finance: Assets €37,500,000 (Dec. 2002); annual expenditure €2,500,000 (2002).

Trustees: Prof. Dr Werner Breitschwerdt; Prof. Dr Detler Ganten; Dr Manfred Gentz; Erich Klemm; Prof. Dr Bernd Rüthers; Prof. Dr Widmar Tanner; Dr Thomas Weber; Prof. Dr Ernst-Ludwig Winnacker; Prof. Dr Sigmar Wittig.

Principal Staff: Chair. Prof. Dr Gisbert Freiherr zu Putlitz; Member Board of Management Dr Diethard Schade; Man. Dir Dr Jörg Klein.

Address: Dr Carl-Benz-Platz 2, 68526 Ladenburg.

Telephone: (6203) 10920; **Fax:** (6203) 10925; **Internet:** www.daimler-benz-stiftung.de; **e-mail:** info@daimler-benz-stiftung.de.

Deutsche AIDS-Stiftung (German AIDS Foundation)

Established in 1996.

Activities: The Foundation's main areas of activity are: financial assistance for people with HIV and AIDS; improved care for those infected with HIV and AIDS; and promotion of any other measures which will assist in furthering the aims of the Foundation.

Geographical Area of Activity: Germany.

Finance: Assets DM35,000,000 (2001); annual expenditure DM3,400,000 (2000).

Principal Staff: Man. Dir Dr Ulrich Heide.

Address: Markt 26, 53111 Bonn.

Telephone: (228) 604690; **Fax:** (228) 6046999; **Internet:** www.aids-stiftung.de; **e-mail:** info@aids-stiftung.de.

Deutsche Bank Stiftung Alfred Herrhausen 'Hilfe zur Selbsthilfe' (Deutsche Bank Alfred Herrhausen 'Helping People to Help Themselves' Foundation)

Established in 1986 by Deutsche Bank AG.

Activities: Operates mostly in Germany in the areas of the humanities, economic affairs, and social welfare, aiming to help people towards self-help in social and humanitarian spheres, through self-conducted programmes, grants to individuals and grants for projects appropriate to the goals of the Foundation.

Geographical Area of Activity: Germany and Europe.

Publications: Annual Report (in German and English).

Finance: Annual expenditure €3,500,000 (2001).

Trustees: Dr Tessen von Heydebreck (Chair); Marc-Aurel von Dewitz; Friedhelm Herb; Hanns Michael Hölz; Alfredo Flores Pachón.

Principal Staff: Chief Exec. Christian J. Stronk; Man. Dir Jörg Eduard Krumsiek, Dr Peter A. Spitze, Christian Stronk.

Address: Barckhausstr. 1–3, 60262 Frankfurt.

Telephone: (69) 720911; **Fax:** (69) 91038836; **Internet:** www.deutsche-bank-stiftung.de; **e-mail:** office.dbstiftung@db.com.

Deutsche Bundesstiftung Umwelt (German Federal Foundation for the Environment)

Established in 1990 by the German Government for research, development and innovation in the field of the environment.

Activities: Encourages research, development and innovation in the field of environmentally- and health-friendly products, especially by small and medium-sized companies; promotes the exchange of information on the environment between the scientific and business communities; aims to safeguard national heritage from environmental damage. Also awards an annual environmental prize worth €500,000.

Geographical Area of Activity: Germany, with occasional grants to MEE states.

Restrictions: No grants to state-related organizations.

Publications: Newsletter; periodicals; and leaflets.

Finance: Assets €1,640,000,000; annual budget approx. €40,000,000.

Kuratorium: Prof. Dr Hans Tietmeyer (Chair.).

Principal Staff: Gen. Sec. Dr Fritz Brickwedde.

Address: An der Bornau 2, Postfach 1705, 49007 Osnabrück.

Telephone: (541) 96330; **Fax:** (541) 9633190; **Internet:** www.dbu.de; **e-mail:** zentrale@dbu.de.

Deutsche Gesellschaft für Auswärtige Politik—DGAP (German Council on Foreign Relations)

Founded in 1955 to examine problems of international relations, particularly with regard to European politics and economics; to promote research in these areas; to provide for documentation and to stimulate and deepen insight regarding problems of international relations.

Activities: Operates in the field of international relations, through research, conducted by the society's Research Institute, documentation, conferences and study groups, courses, publications and lectures; maintains a research library. Maintains a website on international relations.

Geographical Area of Activity: Germany.

Publications: *Jahrbuch Internationale Politik* (annually); *Internationale Politik* (monthly); *Internationale Politik (Transatlantic Edition)* (quarterly).

Principal Staff: Pres. Dr Hans-Dietrich Genscher; Exec. Vice-Pres. Leopold Bill von Bredow; Treas. Klaus Rettig; Dir Research Institute Prof. Dr Karl Kaiser.

Address: Rauchstr. 17–18, 10787 Berlin.

Telephone: (30) 2542310; **Fax:** (30) 25423116; **Internet:** www.dgap.org; **e-mail:** info@dgap.org.

Deutsche Krebshilfe eV (German Cancer Assistance)

Founded in September 1974 by Dr Mildred Scheel, Dr Helmut Geiger, D. Kühn, Bechtold Freiherr von Massenbach, F. L. Müller, Prof. Hermann Schardt, Heinz Schmidt and Martin Virchow to support the welfare of cancer patients, and to fight against cancer.

Activities: Operates in the fields of education, research and medicine and health, nationally through research and training courses, and nationally and internationally through self-conducted programmes and conferences. Makes grants to institutions to support research into cancer diagnosis, therapy, after-care and self-help, organizes and supports medical education projects, further education courses and information events. Also provides advice, help and financial support to people suffering from cancer. Administers the Dr. Mildred Scheel Stiftung für Krebforschung.

Geographical Area of Activity: International.

Publications: Booklets on cancer; videos; CD-ROM.

Finance: Annual expenditure approx. €71,500,000 (2000).

Board of Directors: Dr Dagmar Schipanski (Pres.); Dr H. Geiger (Vice-Pres.); K. Dörrie; Prof. Dr R. Fischer; Dr R. Grupp; W. Jacobs; F. C. Janssen; Dr G. Keding; Dr H.-J. Möhle; Dr A. Titzrath.

Principal Staff: Man. Achim Ebert, Victor Oehm.

Address: Thomas-Mann-Str. 40, Postfach 1467, 53111 Bonn.

Telephone: (228) 729900; **Fax:** (228) 7299011; **Internet:** www.krebshilfe.de; **e-mail:** deutsche@krebshilfe.de.

Deutsche Nationalstiftung (German National Trust)

Established in 1993 by former Chancellor Helmut Schmidt and a group of his friends, including Herman J. Abs, Gerd Bucerius, Kurt Körber and Michael Otto, to bring to the public consciousness the mutual relationship between science, art and literature, law, politics and commerce, and to influence the values of the nation with respect to domestic and international concerns so as to contribute to the common good; to promote and strengthen the process of German unity and promote German cultural identity within a European cultural mosaic; and to comment upon the pressing questions facing Germany at present and in the future.

Activities: Organizes annual meetings to consider urgent problems and discuss questions of national and European relevance; since its establishment the Foundation has had meetings on the following themes, among others: 'On the state of the nation' (1994), 'What do our neighbouring countries expect of the New Germany?' (1995), 'The why and the wherefore of German cultural policy abroad' (1996), 'Europe needs the East' (1998), 'Eighty years on from the Weimar Constitution. A look back at the culture of Weimar' (1999); 'European Union: National Self-interest. Germany and Europe on the threshold of the 21st century' (2000) and 'Democracy on the Test Bed' (2001). Bestows an annual National Prize of approximately €75,000; organizes forums; and publishes theses on various issues affecting Germany and Europe.

Geographical Area of Activity: Germany and European Union countries.

Publications: Annual Report; *Immigration to Germany and Europe—Problems and Consequences* (1995); *10 Theses on the Social and Economic Situation of Germany at the Threshold to the Twenty-First Century* (1996).

Finance: Assets €5,700,000 (2001).

Board of Management: Dr Klaus Asche; Prof. Dr Kurt Biedenkopf; Prof. Dr Reimar Lüst; Prof. Kurt Masur; Matthias Platzeck; Helmut Schmidt.

Principal Staff: Exec. Dir Dr Klaus Asche; Man. Dr Albrecht v. Kalnein.

Address: Feldbrunnenstr. 56, 20148 Hamburg.

Telephone: (40) 41336752; **Fax:** (40) 41336755; **Internet:** www.nationalstiftung.de; **e-mail:** grefer@nationalstiftung.de.

Deutsche Stiftung für internationale rechtliche Zusammenarbeit eV (German Foundation for International Legal Co-operation)

Established in 1992.

Activities: Offers advice in the field of law to countries of Central, Eastern and South Eastern Europe.

Geographical Area of Activity: Central, Eastern and South Eastern Europe.

Restrictions: No unsolicited applications for grants are accepted.

Finance: Funded by the German Federal government and the European Union.

Board of Trustees: Dr Franz Schoser (Chair.).

Principal Staff: Dir Matthias Weckerling; Deputy Dir Claus Vreden.

Address: Ubierstr. 92, 53173 Bonn.

Telephone: (228) 95550; **Fax:** (228) 9555100; **Internet:** www.irz.de; **e-mail:** info@irz.de.

Deutscher Akademischer Austauschdienst—DAAD (German Academic Exchange Service)

Founded in 1925, (re-founded in 1950), the DAAD is a joint organization of institutions of higher education which aims to promote academic exchanges between Germany and other countries.

Activities: Awards long- and short-term scholarships in all fields of study, to foreign students and young research workers, including 'sur place' scholarships tenable at some universities in developing countries, and to students from European countries for university summer vacation and language courses. Scholarships are also awarded to German students and research workers and are tenable in almost all countries of the world. The Foundation has bilateral agreements with German and foreign institutions and promotes student exchange in connection with specific research projects. Supports a programme of exchanges of university teachers for short-term teaching and research visits on a reciprocal basis. Through the Liaison Office for German University Personnel Abroad, requests are met from foreign universities for German academic teaching personnel. The Office supports them financially during their stay abroad and aids their subsequent reintegration in German academic life. A similar programme is administered for lecturers in German language and literature. Participates in an international trainee exchange programme for German and foreign students who are given the opportunity to receive practical training in industry, public services and research institutes. Short-term fellowships are awarded to foreign academics for study visits in Germany and a large number of study visits of groups of foreign academics and students to Germany are supported. Under the Artists-in-Berlin programme, a number of internationally known foreign artists are invited to Berlin every year for periods of six to 12 months. General questions of international academic and scientific relations, such as educational aid for less-developed countries, are also dealt with. DAAD maintains branch offices in Beijing, Cairo, Jakarta, London, Mexico City, Moscow, Nairobi, New Delhi, New York, Paris, Rio de Janeiro, Tokyo and Warsaw. In 1999 DAAD established the DAAD Foundation to acquire and administer capital donations for named scholarships.

Geographical Area of Activity: International.

advice to those involved in changing agricultural systems, and training for new academics; shares research findings through publications, conferences and international co-operation.

Geographical Area of Activity: Central and Eastern Europe.

Restrictions: Unsolicited applications are not accepted.

Principal Staff: Exec. Dir Prof. Klaus Frohberg.

Address: Theodor-Lieser-Str. 2, 06120 Halle/Saale.

Telephone: (345) 2928110; **Fax:** (345) 2928199; **e-mail:** frohberg@iamo.uni-halle.de.

INTEGRATA-Stiftung für Humane Nutzung der Informationstechnologie (INTEGRATA Foundation)

Founded in September 1999 by Prof. Dr Wolfgang Heilmann.

Activities: Aims to sponsor and implement research, and fund longer-term projects and academic institutions engaged in the pursuit of the humane use of information technology in the fields of work, education, health, art and culture, in particular in working and professional life.

Geographical Area of Activity: Germany.

Publications: *Thesis and Objectives on the Management of Tele-Processes*.

Address: Schleifmühleweg 70, 72070 Tübingen.

Telephone: (7071) 408698; **Fax:** (7071) 408699; **Internet:** www.integrata-stiftung.de; **e-mail:** info@integrata-stiftung.de.

International Environmental Foundation of the Kommunale Umwelt-AktioN U.A.N.

Established in March 2001 by the Kommunale Umwelt-AktioN U.A.N.

Activities: Promotes environmental protection activities in Germany and in other European countries, in particular the promotion of international waste water partnerships.

Geographical Area of Activity: Germany and Europe.

Restrictions: Grants only to communities which take part in international waste water partnerships.

Board of Trustees: Dr Wulf Haack (Chair.).

Principal Staff: Contact: Manfred Klein.

Address: Arnswaldtstr. 28, 30159 Hanover.

Telephone: (511) 3028562; **Fax:** (511) 3028556; **Internet:** www.intef-uan.de; **e-mail:** klein@nsgb.de.

International Society for Human Rights—ISHR

Established in 1972 to uphold the United Nations Universal Declaration of Human Rights; the organization operates independently of state institutions, religious bodies and politics.

Activities: Operates world-wide in the field of law and human rights. National sections operate in 24 countries, and the organization has 30,000 members. Projects include strengthening civil society in Central and Eastern Europe and the countries of the former USSR, promoting an International Criminal Court, and providing democracy and human rights training to the Ukranian military. ISHR holds consultative status with the Council of Europe.

Geographical Area of Activity: International.

Restrictions: No grants available directly, except through co-financed international projects.

Principal Staff: Pres. Alexander Frhr. von Bischoffshausen.

Address: Borsigallee 9, 60388 Frankfurt/Main.

Telephone: (69) 4201080; **Fax:** (69) 42010829; **Internet:** www.ishr.org; **e-mail:** is@ishr.org.

Internationale Bachakademie Stuttgart (Stuttgart International Bach Academy)

Established in 1981 by the Stuttgarter Konzertvereinigung eV for the development and management of a research and further education institute for German and foreign music researchers and musicians to carry out research into the theoretical and practical interpretation of the works of Johann Sebastian Bach.

Activities: Operates in the field of music through co-ordinating international research into Bach, and co-operating in the promotion of Bach's music. Organizes conferences and seminars, concerts and exhibitions both in Germany and abroad. Maintains a specialized library and documentation centre.

Geographical Area of Activity: International.

Restrictions: Unsolicited applications are not accepted.

Publications: Series of the Stuttgart International Bach Academy and Forum Bachakademie (both in German).

Finance: Assets €2,810,000 (2002); annual expenditure €7,160,000 (2002).

Principal Staff: Man. Dir Andreas Keller; Artistic Dir Prof. Dr h.c. Helmuth Rilling.

Address: Johann-Sebastian-Bach-Platz, 70178 Stuttgart.

Telephone: (711) 619210; **Fax:** (711) 6192123; **Internet:** www.bachakademie.de; **e-mail:** office@bachakademie.de.

Internationale Stiftung zur Förderung von Kultur und Zivilisation (International Foundation for Culture and Civilisation)

Established in 1995.

Activities: Supports cultural and humanitarian projects both in Germany and internationally, principally musical activities, including festivals, and partnerships with Amnesty International (q.v.).

Geographical Area of Activity: Germany and international.

Address: Germersheimer Str. 24, 81541 Munich.

Telephone: (89) 49001056; **Fax:** (89) 49001057; **Internet:** www.s-direktnet.de/homepages/juergen-hiller/page17.htm; **e-mail:** kulturstiftung-muenchensibig@t-online.de.

InWEnt—Internationale Weiterbildung und Entwicklung gemeinnützige GmbH (Capacity Building International)

Founded in 2002 through a merger of Carl Duisberg Gesellschaft e.V. and the Deutsche Stiftung für internationale Entwicklung (German Foundation for International Development), to promote international human resources development, advanced training and dialogue.

Activities: Promotes international human resources development, advanced training and dialogue, through structured long-term training programmes, practice-oriented training, conferences, seminars and workshops, policy dialogue and individual internships. Approximately 35,000 people participate in the Foundation's programmes each year.

Geographical Area of Activity: International.

Restrictions: Applications for grants are not accepted.

Publications: *Entwicklung und Zusammenarbeit* (monthly); *Development and Cooperation* (monthly); *Dialog* (quarterly journal); *Agriculture and Rural Development* (6 a year); catalogues; directories; Annual Report.

Finance: The Foundation is funded by the Federal Government, Länder governments, European Union and other multilateral bodies, and foundations.

Supervisory Board: Erich Stather (Chair.).

Principal Staff: Chief Exec. Dr Ulrich Popp; Man. Dir Dr Gudrun Kochendörfer-Lucius, Bernd Schleich.

Address: Zentrale Dokumentation, Tulpenfeld 5, 53113 Bonn.

Telephone: (228) 24345; **Fax:** (228) 2434766; **Internet:** www.dse.de; **e-mail:** dse@dse.de.

Japanisch–Deutsches Zentrum Berlin (Japanese–German Centre Berlin)

Founded in January 1985 by the City of Berlin to promote international co-operation, especially between Japan and Germany, in the fields of science and culture.

Activities: Organizes conferences, seminars and workshops in various fields of social and natural sciences, humanities and culture; and joint exhibitions and concerts of German and Japanese artists. Has its own language courses and introductory seminars. Manages the German side of the German–Japanese Forum, and co-ordinates several programmes for German–Japanese Youth Exchange. Maintains a library of over 9,000 volumes.

Geographical Area of Activity: The work of the Centre covers Germany and Japan, Europe, Asia and North America.

Restrictions: Unsolicited applications are not accepted.

Publications: *JDZB—Echo* (quarterly newsletter); directory of German–Japanese co-operation; three publication series of conference reports (occasional papers).

Finance: Annual expenditure approx. €2,300,000.

Address: Saargemünder Str. 2, 14195 Berlin.

Telephone: (30) 839070; **Fax:** (30) 83907220; **Internet:** www.jdzb.de; **e-mail:** jdzb@jdzb.de.

Körber-Stiftung (Körber Foundation)

Founded in 1959 by the industrialist Kurt A. Körber. The Foundation initiates, finances and runs its own projects within the broad areas of science and research, education, culture, care of the sick and elderly, and international understanding.

Activities: Operates the following programmes: the Bergedorf Round Table, which promotes open discourse between leading politicians, scientists, business people and publicists; the European Science Award; the German Students' Research Award; the German President's Award for Student Competition in German History; USable, the Transatlantic Idea Competition; German–Turkish relations; EUStory, the Programme on European History; Körber Clearing House, dealing with Russia and the Commonwealth of Independent States; the Körber European Science Award; Haus im Park Theatre; the International Opera Studio; the Boy Gobert Prize for young actors; and the School Drama Festival.

Geographical Area of Activity: Germany, the USA, Turkey, and Central and Eastern Europe.

Restrictions: The Foundation finances and runs its own projects; it does not make grants to individuals.

Publications: *Reflexion und Initiative* (report, 2 a year); information brochure.

Finance: Assets €533,000,000 (2002).

Board of Trustees: Ulrich Voswinckel (Chair.); Dr Sabine Bergmann-Pohl; Eberhard Reuther; Prof. Dr Dagmar Schipanski; Reinhard Stuth; Prof. Dr Fitz Vahrenholt.

Principal Staff: Chair. Christian Wriedt; Deputy Chair. Dr Klaus Wehmeier; Dr Wolf Schmidt.

Address: Kurt-A.-Körber-Chaussee 10, 21033 Hamburg.

Telephone: (40) 72502457; **Fax:** (40) 72503645; **Internet:** www.stiftung.koerber.de; **e-mail:** info@stiftung.koerber.de.

Else Kröner-Fresenius-Stiftung (Else Kröner-Fresenius Foundation)

Established in 1983 by Else Kröner to support scientific and medical research.

Activities: Operates in the fields of science and technology, and medicine and health, through making grants to research projects, especially innovative research in the areas of clinical research, nutritional medicine, dialysis and infections.

Restrictions: Basic research is not funded.

Finance: Annual expenditure DM5,600,000 (1999).

Administrative Board: H. Kröner (Chair.).

Principal Staff: Rudolf Herfurth.

Address: Oberusel, Postfach 1852, 61288 Bad Homburg.

Telephone: (6172) 89750; **Fax:** (6172) 897515.

Alfried Krupp von Bohlen und Halbach-Stiftung (Alfried Krupp von Bohlen und Halbach Foundation)

Founded in 1967 by Dr Alfried Krupp von Bohlen und Halbach for philanthropic aims of benefit to the community.

Activities: Operates nationally and internationally through support of projects in the fields of scientific research and teaching (including the fostering of young scientific talent), education, health services, sport, literature, music and the fine arts, through offering grants and fellowships (including an Internship Programme for students of Stanford University, CA, USA to train in Germany, and a China Studies Programme for German students to spend a year of study in the People's Republic of China). Awards an annual environmental prize.

Geographical Area of Activity: International.

Finance: Assets DM882,000,000 (Dec. 1999); annual expenditure DM47,800,000 (1999).

Governing Board: Prof. Dr B. Beitz (Chair.); Prof. Dr H. Leussink (Deputy Chair.); Prof. Dr D. Bergers; W. Clement; Dr G. Cromme; Prof. Dr R. Lüst; Prof. Dr P. Mikat; Dr F. Neuber; Dr K. O. Pöhl; Dr K. von Schenck.

Principal Staff: Pres. Prof. Dr B. Beitz; Deputy Members of the Board Dr T. Kempf, Dr R. Nentwig.

Address: Hügel 15, 45133 Essen; Postfach 230245, 45070 Essen.

Telephone: (201) 1881; **Fax:** (201) 412587; **Internet:** www.krupp-stiftung.de; **e-mail:** info@krupp-stiftung.de.

Karl Kübel Stiftung für Kind und Familie (Karl Kübel Foundation for Child and Family)

Founded in 1972 by Karl Kübel to support family-oriented programmes.

Activities: Operates nationally and internationally, mainly in German-speaking countries, Kosovo, India and the Philippines, through self-conducted programmes, grants to institutions, prizes, training courses, publications and the implementation of development projects. The Foundation's four main programmes are: the Karl Kübel Award and the support of family-centred self-help activities; family-centred housing projects; education through the Foundation's institutes in Germany and India; supporting development projects and training development personnel.

Geographical Area of Activity: International, mainly in German-speaking countries, Kosovo, India and the Philippines.

Board of Directors: Jörg Schmidt; Dr Claudia Warning.

Address: Darmstädter Str. 100, 64625 Bensheim; Postfach 1563, 64605 Bensheim.

Telephone: (6251) 70050; **Fax:** (6251) 700555; **Internet:** www.kkstiftung.de; **e-mail:** info@kkstiftung.de.

Kulturstiftung Haus Europa (House of Europe Cultural Foundation)

Founded in September 1990 by the Government of the German Democratic Republic (became an autonomous private foundation in 1992); it aims to promote the German effort for European understanding, European cultural networking, private initiative and funding for the arts and cultural affairs; to represent German interests in European cultural bodies; and to distribute European cultural information in Germany. The Foundation is managed by Maecenata Management GmbH (q.v.).

Activities: Promotes and manages cultural projects; holds conferences on international cultural matters; and issues publications.

Geographical Area of Activity: Europe.

Restrictions: Does not make grants.

Publications: Conference reports.

Finance: Financed by revenue from its capital, voluntary contributions and donations, European Union and regional and local government grants, business sponsorship, grants from other foundations, and the sale of publications. Annual expenditure DM70,000 (2000).

Advisory Board: Gabriele Muschter (Head); Dr Ingo Fessmann; Dr Albrecht Lempp; Prof. Dr Robert Picht; Prof. Dr Klaus Standke.

Principal Staff: Co-Chair. Rupert Graf Strachwitz, Bernhard Elias.

Address: c/o Maecenata Management GmbH, Barer Str. 44, 80799 Munich.

Telephone: (89) 284452; **Fax:** (89) 283774; **e-mail:** khe@maecenata-management.de.

Kulturstiftung der Länder (Cultural Foundation of the German Federal States)

Established in 1988 to promote and preserve national art and culture.

Activities: Operates nationally in the field of the arts, promoting and preserving cultural heritage of national importance.

Geographical Area of Activity: Germany and Eastern Europe.

Restrictions: Grants made only in Eastern Europe to art historians.

Publications: *Patrimonia* (series 1–250); *Sternstunden* (catalogue); fundraising brochures; Annual Report.

Finance: Annual expenditure €17,500,000 (2003).

Trustees: Dr Heribald Närger (Hon. Chair.); Dr Rolf Breuer (Chair.); Prof. Dr Jan Ph. Reemtsma, Prof. Dr h.c. Reinhold Würth (Vice-Chair.).

Principal Staff: Gen. Sec. Prof. Dr Karin V. Welck; Deputy Gen. Sec. Frank Däberitz; Dept Head Prof. Dr Joachim Fischer, Dr Britta Kaiser-Schuster.

Address: Lützowplatz 9, 10785 Berlin.

Telephone: (30) 8936350; **Fax:** (30) 8914251; **Internet:** www.kulturstiftung.de; **e-mail:** info@kulturstiftung.de.

Lateinamerika-Zentrum eV (Latin America Centre)

Established in 1961 by Prof. Hermann M. Görgen.

Activities: Operates in Central and South America, mainly in Brazil, supporting local organizations which develop projects to suit local needs; projects include schooling and training for disadvantaged children and young people, combating the abandonment of the countryside, promotion of women, basic health care, protection of the environment and the promotion and protection of indigenous peoples. Also publishes books on the politics of development and hosts exhibitions and workshops.

Geographical Area of Activity: Central and South America, with an emphasis on Brazil.

Restrictions: Operates in collaboration with local partner organizations. No grants to individuals.

Publications: *Tópicos* (German/Brazilian pamphlets); brochures concerning specific subjects.

Finance: Funding from Ministry of Co-operation and Development and the European Commission. Annual budget €1,200,000.

Board: Dr Helmut Hoffmann (Pres.); Astrid Prange, Dr Hans Thomas (Vice-Pres).

Principal Staff: One full-time and five part-time staff.

Address: Kaiserstr. 201, 53113 Bonn.

Telephone: (228) 210788; **Fax:** (228) 241658; **Internet:** www.lateinamerikazentrum.de; **e-mail:** laz@lateinamerikazentrum.de.

Rosa Luxemburg Stiftung—Gesellschaftsanalyse und Politische Bildung eV (Rosa Luxemburg Foundation—Business Analysis and Political Education)

Established in 1991 for the promotion of political education (associated with the PDS—Party of Democratic Socialism), knowledge and research, culture and the arts, and international understanding.

Activities: Operates in the fields of the arts and humanities, economic affairs, education, international affairs, and law and human rights, through promoting research; publications; awarding scholarships and the annual Rosa Luxemburg Prize; maintaining archives and a library with publications relevant to the work of the Foundation; and national and international projects, in particular in countries of Africa, Asia and Central and South America.

Geographical Area of Activity: International, in particular Africa, Asia and Central and South America.

Publications: *Utopie kreativ* (magazine).

Finance: Annual expenditure DM2,114,000 (1999).

Managing Board: Dr Lutz Brangsch; Prof. Dr Michael Brie; Dr Evelin Wittich.

Address: Franz-Mehring-Platz 1, 10243 Berlin.

Telephone: (30) 443100; **Fax:** (30) 44310222; **Internet:** www.rosalux.de; **e-mail:** info@rosaluxemburgstiftung.de.

Medical Women's International Association

Established in 1919, a non-profit-making, non-political, non-sectarian organization which aims to assist in the communication between female doctors world-wide, so as to encourage women into medicine, and to overcome gender related inequalities in the medical profession.

Activities: Operates in the field of medicine, encouraging women to enter the profession and to undertake postgraduate study, through regional and international scientific meetings and congresses, collaborating with the World Health Organization (WHO) and running local health and women's projects. Also sponsors a scholarship programme for postgraduate education, open to its members. There are national assocations in 43 countries, and individual members in a further 31 countries.

Geographical Area of Activity: International.

Publications: *Congress Report* (every 3 years); newsletter.

Principal Staff: Sec.-Gen. Dr Waltraud Diekhaus; Pres. Dr Shelley Ross; Treas. Dr Cajsa Rangnitt.

Address: Wilhelm-Brand Str. 3, 44141 Dortmund.

Telephone: (231) 9432771; **Fax:** (231) 9432773; **Internet:** www.mwia.net; **e-mail:** secretariat@mwia.net.

Medico International

Established in 1968 to send medical supplies to countries in need.

Activities: Operates world-wide, in particular in less-developed countries or in countries where emergency relief is necessary, in the field of medicine and health, offering medicines and medical equipment, medical personnel, ambulances and other equipment. Runs campaigns against landmines, and various projects in the areas of asylum, rehabilitation, AIDS, human rights and basic health care. Long-term projects have been instituted in Central and South America, North, Central and Southern Africa, the Middle and Far East, and Central Asia (Kurdistan).

Geographical Area of Activity: International.

Finance: Annual budget approx. €5,100,000.

Address: Obermainanlage 7, 60314 Frankfurt/Main.

Telephone: (69) 944380; **Fax:** (69) 436002; **Internet:** www.medico.de; **e-mail:** info@medico.de.

Messerschmitt Stiftung (Messerschmitt Foundation)

Established in 1976 by Prof. Willy Messerschmitt.

Activities: Operates in the fields of conservation of heritage, and science and technology; promotes science and research, especially in the area of aero- and space technology; also promotes the conservation of German art and cultural memorials both nationally and internationally. Owns several historically important Messerschmitt aircraft.

Geographical Area of Activity: Central Europe.

Finance: Annual expenditure DM8,000,000 (1999).

Trustees: Prof. Gero Madelung (Chair).

Principal Staff: Dr H. H. von Srbik.

Address: Pienzenauerstr. 17, 81679 Munich.

Telephone: (89) 981830; **Fax:** (89) 98290126.

Friedrich-Naumann-Stiftung (Friedrich Naumann Foundation)

Founded in 1958 by Dr Theodor Heuss (former President of the Federal Republic of Germany) with the objective of promoting a liberal foundation for political and civic education, improving the dialogue between Eastern and Western industrial countries, and developed and developing countries, and giving advisory and vocational assistance to developing countries.

Activities: Operates nationally and internationally, primarily in the field of civic education, but also in the areas of aid to less-developed countries, economic and international affairs, and law and human rights, through self-conducted programmes, research, scholarships and fellowships, prizes, conferences, training courses and publications. In developing countries assistance is given to co-operative associations, training institutes for journalism and organizations in the field of adult education. The Foundation has projects in around 45 countries and maintains offices in approximately 47 countries outside Germany.

Geographical Area of Activity: International.

Publications: Annual Report; *Liberal* (quarterly); publications on political and development issues.

Finance: Assets DM 75,000,000 (2000).

Board of Trustees: Walter Scheel (Hon. Chair.); Dr Jürgen Morlok (Chair.); Peter Menke-Glückert, Prof. Dr Karl-Hans Laermann (Vice-Chair.); and 26 others.

Principal Staff: Pres. Dr Omo Graf Lambedorff; Exec. Chair. Rolf Berndt; Treas. Dr Günter Storch.

Address: Alt-Nowawes 67, 14482 Potsdam.

Telephone: (331) 70190; **Fax:** (331) 7019188; **Internet:** www.fnst.de; **e-mail:** fnst@fnst.org.

Niedersächsische Sparkassenstiftung (Lower Saxony Savings Banks Foundation)

Established in 1984 by the Niedersächsischer Sparkassen und Giroverband savings bank.

Activities: Operates in the Federal State of Lower Saxony in the field of the arts, with an emphasis on fine art, music, conservation of monuments and museums. Supports projects carried out by other organizations, carries out its own activities, awards prizes and scholarships, and maintains an art collection.

Geographical Area of Activity: The Federal State of Lower Saxony, Germany.

Restrictions: Grants are made only to organizations in Lower Saxony.

Finance: Total assets approx. €22,000,000.

Principal Staff: Man. Dr Sabine Schormann; Deputy Man. Michael H. Schormann.

Address: Schiffgraben 6–8, 30519 Hannover.

Telephone: (511) 3603489; **Fax:** (511) 3603684; **Internet:** www.nsks.de; **e-mail:** sparkassenstiftung@nsgv.de.

Novartis-Stiftung für therapeutische Forschung in Nürnberg (Novartis Foundation for Therapeutical Research in Nuremberg)

Established in 1969 by Sandoz AG Nuremberg to further therapeutical research, and to carry out other research in the field of medicine.

Activities: Operates in the field of medical research, including awarding an annual prize in the field of pharmaceutical research.

Geographical Area of Activity: Germany.

Restrictions: Grants only made in specific areas.

Finance: Assets €12,000,000 (2002); annual expenditure €750,000 (2002).

Principal Staff: Contact: Almut Richter.

Address: Roon Str. 25, 90429 Nuremberg.

Telephone: (911) 27312342; **Fax:** (911) 27312056; **Internet:** www.novartispharma.de; **e-mail:** almut.richter@pharma.novartis.com.

Dr Werner Otto Stiftung

Founded in 1969 by Dr Werner Otto.

Activities: Funds medical research, principally in Hamburg, with an emphasis on research focused on children and young people. Awards a research prize every two years. Also operates the Werner Otto Institute, a paediatric centre established in 1974.

Geographical Area of Activity: Mainly Hamburg, Germany.

Board of Directors: Prof. Dr Heiner Greten; Prof. Dr Hartwig Huland; Prof. Dr Peter Ostendorf; Dr Michael Otto; Prof. Dr Werner Otto; Prof. Dr Peter Riedesser.

Principal Staff: Dir Dr Jürgen Bersuch.

Address: Heegbarg 30, 22391 Hamburg.

Telephone: (40) 60606111; **Fax:** (40) 60606570; **Internet:** www.werner-otto-stiftung.de; **e-mail:** info@werner-otto-stiftung.de.

Michael Otto Stiftung

Established in 1993 by Dr Michael Otto.

Activities: Principally supports environmental projects, with a focus on the prevention of pollution in seas, lakes and wetlands, and in conserving drinking water resources. Co-operates with other environmental organizations, as well as funding environmental education, including environmental professorships at the Botanical Institute of the Ernst Moritz Arndt University of Greifswald and the University of Hamburg.

Geographical Area of Activity: Mainly Germany.

Finance: Annual budget approx. €500,000.

Board of Directors: Dr Michael Otto (Chair.); Jochen Flasbarth; Detlev von Livonius; Prof. Dr Michael Succow; Carl Albrecht von Treuenfels; Prof. Dr Andreas Troge.

Principal Staff: Dir Dr Johannes Merck.

Address: Wandsbeker Str. 3–7, 22179 Hamburg.

Internet: www.michaelottostiftung.de/; **e-mail:** michaelottostiftung@otto.de.

Pesticides Action Network Europe—PAN Europe

Established in 1983 and facilitated by PAN Germany and Pesticide Action Network UK—PAN UK (q.v.); a network of European environmental NGOs promoting a sustainable alternative to the use of pesticides.

Activities: Operates in Europe in the area of conservation and the environment, promoting alternatives to the use of pesticides, through pesticide reduction programmes, lobbying, networking, publications and conferences.

Geographical Area of Activity: Europe.

Publications: *PAN Europe Monthly* (monthly e-mail newsletter).

Principal Staff: Co-ordinator Heike Schmitt.

Address: Nernstweg 32, 22765 Hamburg.

Telephone: (40) 39919100; **Fax:** (40) 3907520; **Internet:** www.pan-europe.net; **e-mail:** h.schmitt@pan-germany.org.

Max-Planck-Gesellschaft zur Förderung der Wissenschaften eV (Max Planck Society for the Advancement of Science)

Founded in 1948 to succeed the Kaiser-Wilhelm-Gesellschaft (founded 1911) with the object of promoting basic research in the sciences.

Activities: Operates nationally and internationally in the fields of science, medicine, social sciences and humanities, and law and other professions. Maintains international relations through self-conducted projects, research, conferences, prizes, publications and lectures. Basic research, particularly in the fields of biology, medicine, chemistry, physics and the intellectual sciences, is carried out in 80 institutes and research facilities belonging to the Society, with the aim of complementing research conducted at the universities.

Geographical Area of Activity: International.

Publications: Yearbook; information booklets.

Finance: Financed through public funds (84%). Annual budget approx. €1,253,000,000 (2002).

Principal Staff: Pres. Prof. Dr Peter Gruss; Sec.-Gen. Dr Barbara Bludau; Deputy Sec.-Gen. Dr Hardo Braun.

Address: Hofgartenstr. 8, 80539 Munich; Postfach 101062, 80084 Munich.

Telephone: (89) 21080; **Fax:** (89) 21081111; **Internet:** www.mpg.de; **e-mail:** user@mpg-gv.mpg.de.

Prix Jeunesse Foundation

Established in 1964 by the Government of Bavaria, the City of Munich, Bayerischer Rundfunk, Zweites Deutsches Fernsehen (ZDF) and the Bayerische Landeszentrale für Neue Medien to improve the quality of television world-wide for young people, to deepen understanding, to promote communication between nations and to increase programme exchange.

Activities: Operates internationally in the field of the media, especially children's and youth television, through research, scholarships and fellowships, awarding the Prix Jeunesse International Prizes for children's and youth television programmes, organizing Round Table conferences, training courses and issuing publications. Maintains a video library covering three decades of children's and youth television and organizes a bi-annual festival.

Publications: *WATCHwords* (on-line publication of the World Alliance of Television for Children).

Finance: The Foundation is financed by annual contributions from its founders.

Principal Staff: Sec.-Gen. Ursula von Zallinger; Man. Kirsten Schneid.

Address: c/o Bayerischer Rundfunk, Rundfunkplatz 1, 80300 Munich.

Telephone: (89) 59002058; **Fax:** (89) 59003053; **Internet:** www.prixjeunesse.de; **e-mail:** info@prixjeunesse.de.

Werner Reimers-Stiftung (Werner Reimers Foundation)

Founded in 1963 by Werner Reimers to contribute towards explaining the development of human society and its institutions, to analyze its present problems, to recognize tendencies of its further development and to open to it ways into the future.

Activities: Operates nationally and internationally in the fields of social welfare and studies, the physical and social sciences, medicine and the humanities. The interdisciplinary study groups organized by the Foundation form the focal point of its activities. The groups devote several years to the study of well-defined problems, meet regularly to exchange information and publish the results of their work. The meetings take place at the Foundation's conference centre and the Foundation provides travelling expenses and accommodation.

Restrictions: Does not award scholarships.

Publications: Report of operations.

Finance: Annual expenditure approx. €700,000.

Principal Staff: Prof. Dr Werner Knopp.

Address: Am Wingertsberg 4, 61348 Bad Homburg.

Telephone: (6172) 24058; **Fax:** (6172) 21408; **Internet:** www.reimers-stiftung.de; **e-mail:** irudolphe@suchprozesse.de.

Wilhelm Sander-Stiftung (Wilhelm Sander Foundation)

Founded in 1974 to support medical research.

Activities: Operates nationally and in Switzerland in the field of medicine and health, through sponsoring medical research and supporting the fight against ill health, especially cancer, by means of grants to institutions and individuals.

Geographical Area of Activity: Germany and Switzerland.

Publications: Report of operations and financial statement.

Finance: Annual grants expenditure €10,000,000 (2001).

Supervisory board: Dr h. c. Sogelter (Pres.).

Principal Staff: Chair. Dr J. Koppenhöfer; Ulrich Reuter.

Address: Goethestr. 74/IV, 80336 Munich.

Telephone: (89) 5441870; **Fax:** (89) 54418720; **Internet:** www.wilhelm-sander-stiftung.de; **e-mail:** w.sander-stiftung@t-online.de.

Save Our Future Umweltstiftung (Save Our Future Environmental Foundation)

Founded in 1989 by Jürgen Oppermann to create environmental awareness and encourage environmental protection.

Activities: Operates nationally and internationally in the field of environmental education and sustainability, mainly through projects in education for children, pre-school children and young people. Develops model projects like 'richtig leben', an Agenda 21 climate protection project for kindergartens, providing play activities for children as well as training for educators, as well as building up an internet-communication system for environmental education activities in Hamburg. Has also established the first two mobile environmental education vehicles as a model for China, in collaboration with Friends of Nature Beijing and the Shanghai Education Centre. Also organizes environmental round tables for young people in Germany, carried out a Sport and Environment campaign and established a Chair for water economy and water supply at the Technical University of Hamburg.

Geographical Area of Activity: International, mainly Germany and the People's Republic of China.

Restrictions: Only supports its own projects.

Publications: *Die Sonne und ihre Kinder* (children's publication); *Umweltschutz im Sportverein—Ein Praxisleitfaden* (video and brochures).

Board of Trustees: Jürgen Oppermann (Chair.); Sabine Kehrwieder (Deputy Chair.); Dr Jörg von Bargen; Peter Jessen.

Principal Staff: Man. Ralf Thielebein.

Address: Frauenthal 15, 20149 Hamburg.

Telephone: (40) 240600; **Fax:** (40) 240640; **Internet:** www.save-our-future.de; **e-mail:** info@save-our-future.de.

Eberhard-Schöck-Stiftung (Eberhard Schöck Foundation)

Established in 1992 by Eberhard Schöck to promote the building trade in the former communist countries of Central and Eastern Europe.

Activities: Operates internationally in Eastern and Central Europe in the areas of aid, economic affairs and education, through self-conducted programmes, grants, scholarships and fellowships, conferences, training courses and publications.

The Foundation runs practical programmes to train young building workers from the former communist countries of Europe to become self-employed builders in their own countries; it thus aims to contribute to stability and the principles of democracy and the market economy. It also runs practical programmes to train vocational teachers and managers of small- and medium-sized enterprises in the building trade. Since 1994, more than 250 craftsmen, executives and entrepreneurs from Central and Eastern Europe have participated in foundation programmes. Two prizes are offered by the Foundation: the Schöck Building Innovation Prize and the German Language Cultural Prize (in co-operation with the Dortmund Verein Deutsche Sprache).

Geographical Area of Activity: Central and Eastern Europe.

Restrictions: Grants are made only within the Foundation's own projects.

Publications: Annual Report; conference documentation; and commemorative publication.

Finance: Assets approx. DM21,000,000 (2000); annual revenue and expenditure DM770,000 (2000).

Board: Eberhard Schöck (Chair.); Dr J. D. Wickert (Deputy Chair.); Dr Christof Maisch.

Principal Staff: Man. Peter Möller.

Address: Vimbucher Str. 2, 76534 Baden-Baden; Postfach 110163, 76487 Baden-Baden.

Telephone: (7223) 967371; **Fax:** (7223) 967373; **Internet:** www.schoeck-stiftung.de; **e-mail:** stiftung@schoeck.de.

Ernst Schering Research Foundation

Founded in June 1991 by Schering AG to promote and honour outstanding research in the fields of biology, medicine and chemistry, to provide a bridge between academia and industry, and to promote dialogue between practitioners of basic and applied research.

Activities: Awards a number of prizes for outstanding research in the fields of biology, medicine and chemistry, including the Ernst Schering Prize, which is funded by the Schering Stiftung (q.v.), the Schoeller Junkmann Prize, the Walter Hohlweg Prize and the Avrion Mitchison Prize. Also awards fellowships internationally for postdoctoral students in biomedical research and medical chemistry who want to carry out research projects at renowned institutes in Germany and overseas; and sponsors lectures and workshops.

Geographical Area of Activity: Germany and international.

Board of Trustees: Prof. David T Baird; Prof. Piet Borst; Prof. John A Dormandy; Prof. Manfred Erhardt; Prof. Albin Eser; Dr Ursula F. Habenicht; Prof. Toni M Kutchan; Dr. Ursula Lachnit-Fixson; Prof. Jürgen Mittelstrass; Prof. Friedmund Neumann; Prof. Günter Stock; Prof. Björn Wallmark.

Principal Staff: Man. Dir Dr Monika Lessl.

Address: Friedrichstr. 81/82, 10117 Berlin.

Telephone: (30) 46812527; **Fax:** (30) 46818028; **Internet:** www.schering.de; **e-mail:** monika.lessl@schering.de.

Schering Stiftung

Established in 2002 by Schering AG to promote science and culture.

Activities: Active in the fields of scientific research, and culture and the arts. Funds various grant programmes carried out by the Ernst Schering Research Foundation (q.v.), including the Ernst Schering Prize and research fellowships, awards research grants of its own. In the field of culture and the arts, the Foundation makes grants in the fields of graphic arts, the performing arts, including dance, and music.

Geographical Area of Activity: Germany and international.

Council: Prof. Dr Jürgen Mittelstr. (Chair.); Dr Hubertus Erlen (Vice-Chair.); Prof. Dr Horst Bredekamp; Prof. Dr Manfred Erhardt; Prof. Dr Albin Eser; Prof. Dr Jutta Limbach; Prof. Dr Günter Stock.

Principal Staff: Dir Science Dr Monika Lessl; Dir Culture Ilona Muráti-Laebe.

Address: Friedrichstr. 81/82, 10117 Berlin.

Telephone: (30) 46812527; **Internet:** www.scheringstiftung.de/index-en.html; **e-mail:** info@scheringstiftung.de.

Heinz-Schwarzkopf-Stiftung Junges Europa (Heinz Schwarzkopf Foundation for European Youth)

Founded in 1971 to teach young people between the ages of 16 and 28 the fundamentals of the free social and economic systems and to promote contact and understanding between young people in Europe.

Activities: Operates in the European countries, including those of Eastern Europe, in the fields of international relations, culture, political and economic affairs, science and education, through international youth conferences and travel scholarships. Awards the annual Young European of the Year Prize, and promotes the European Youth Parliament.

Geographical Area of Activity: Western, Central and Eastern Europe.

Board of Trustees: Pauline Schwarzkopf (Chair.); André Schmitz-Schwarzkopf (Vice-Chair.); Dr Friedhelm Klaes; Dr Ekkehard Nümann; Inga Sorge.

Principal Staff: Man. Ilka Keuper.

Address: Sophienstr. 28–29, 10178 Berlin.

Telephone: (30) 28095146; **Fax:** (30) 28095150; **Internet:** www.heinz-schwarzkopf-stiftung.de; **e-mail:** info@heinz-schwarzkopf-stiftung.de.

Schweisfurth-Foundation

Founded in 1985 by Karl Ludwig Schweisfurth to promote an ecological culture: a new cultural approach towards the earth, plants, animals and people.

Activities: Has been operating nationally and internationally (mostly in Europe) in the fields of the environment, education, science and technology, and ecological agriculture, through self-conducted programmes, research, prizes, conferences and publications. It is currently undergoing a complete reorganization.

Geographical Area of Activity: Germany and Europe.

Restrictions: The Foundation runs its own projects—no funds or scholarships are given.

Publications: Project results; activity reports; brochures.

Finance: Annual expenditure DM2,200,000 (1999).

Trustees: Prof. Günter Altner; Hermann Graf Hatzfeldt; Dorothee Schweisfurth; Karl Ludwig Schweisfurth; Dr Antje Vollmer.

Principal Staff: Dr Franz-Theo Gottwald; Dr Manuel Schneider.

Address: Süedliches Schlossrondell 1, 80638 Munich.

Telephone: (89) 17959510; **Fax:** (89) 17959519; **Internet:** www.schweisfurth.de; **e-mail:** info@schweisfurth.de.

Hanns-Seidel-Stiftung eV (Hanns Seidel Foundation)

Founded in 1967 to promote the democratic and civic development of the German people on a Christian basis; to foster the academic sector; to foster international attitudes and understanding between peoples; and to promote the process of European unification.

Activities: The Foundation operates nationally in the fields of the arts and humanities and education; internationally it works in the fields of education, international affairs, health and social welfare, through promoting self-sufficiency and individual initiatives, and through scholarships, travel grants, conferences and publications.

Geographical Area of Activity: International.

Publications: *Hanns-Seidel-Stiftung Informationen;* Annual Report; Political Studies.

Finance: Financed by funds supplied by the German Government, the Government of the State of Bavaria, and by private donations. Annual expenditure DM76,000,000 (2000).

Principal Staff: Chair. Alfred Bayer; Man. Dir Manfred Baumgärtel.

Address: Lazarettstr. 33, 80636 Munich.

Telephone: (89) 12580; **Fax:** (89) 1258356; **Internet:** www.hss.de; **e-mail:** info@hss.de.

Sparkassen-Kulturstiftung Hessen-Thüringen (Hesse and Thuringia Savings Banks Cultural Foundation)

Established in 1989 by the Sparkassen- und Giroverband Hessen-Thüringen savings banks for the promotion of culture and the arts in the Federal States of Hesse and Thuringia.

Activities: Operates in Hesse and Thuringia in the fields of the arts and humanities, and conservation and the environment, through conservation of cultural heritage, research, and care for the environment; and in the fields of health and welfare, in particular with relation to young people, the aged, and public health care.

Geographical Area of Activity: Germany (Hesse and Thuringia).

Finance: Annual expenditure €1,3773,000 (2001).

Principal Staff: Man. Dr Thomas Wurzel.

Address: Alte Rothofstr. 9, 60313 Frankfurt/Main.

Telephone: (69) 2175511; **Fax:** (69) 2175499; **Internet:** www.sparkassen-finanzgruppe-ht.de.

Sparkassenstiftung für internationale Kooperation eV (Savings Bank Foundation for International Co-operation)

Established in 1992 for the promotion of economic and social development in less-developed countries and areas, in particular Central and Eastern Europe.

Activities: Operates internationally, especially in Central and Eastern Europe and Africa, in the fields of aid to less-developed countries establishing savings banks, through providing technical assistance in the fields of managerial infrastructure, human resource development, product development and information technology.

Geographical Area of Activity: International, especially Central and Eastern Europe and Africa.

Restrictions: Unsolicited applications for grants are not accepted.

Publications: Annual Report.

Principal Staff: Chair. Dr Holger Berndt; Man. Dir Dr Peter Langkamp.

Address: Buschstr. 32, 53113 Bonn.

Telephone: (228) 97030; **Fax:** (228) 9703613; **Internet:** www.sparkassenstiftung.de; **e-mail:** office@sbfic.de.

Axel Springer Stiftung (Axel Springer Foundation)

Founded in 1953 by Axel Springer to support scholarly and philanthropic activities within the country and abroad.

Activities: The Foundation supports all branches of learning through grants for research work, publications, conferences and courses of further education. Support is also given to persons in need as a result of sickness; for preventive health and fitness activities; for youth welfare; for refugees; for artistic events; and for the restoration of religious buildings. The Axel Springer Prize for Young Journalists is awarded annually in three categories (print, television and radio). The Foundation also encourages good relations between Germany and Israel by supporting youth exchange.

Geographical Area of Activity: Germany, Eastern Europe and Israel.

Restrictions: New projects are only occasionally supported.

Board of Directors: Ernst J. Cramer (Chair.).

Address: Axel-Springer-Str. 65, 10888 Berlin.

Telephone: (30) 25912203; **Fax:** (30) 2514526; **Internet:** www.asv.de.

Stiftung CAESAR (Centre of Advanced European Studies and Research)

Established in 1995 by the German Government and the Federal State of North-Rhine-Westphalia to support science and research.

Activities: Operates nationally and internationally in the fields of education, science and technology, through self-conducted programmes and training courses. Operates the CAESAR Centre (Centre of Advanced European Studies and Research). Current research priorities are: nano-technology/materials science; coupling of biological and electronic systems; and ergonomics in communications. Maintains a library.

Geographical Area of Activity: International.

Restrictions: No grants are made.

Publications: *Smart Materials; Proceedings of the First Caesarium* (1999); research materials and publications.

Finance: Net assets DM200,000,000 (2000); annual revenue and expenditure DM7,000,000 (2000).

Board of Trustees: Dr Wolf-Dieter Dudenhausen (Chair.); and 13 others.

Principal Staff: Admin. Dir Dr Hartwig Bechte; Scientific Dir Prof. Dr Karl-Heinz Hoffmann.

Address: Friedensplatz 16, 53111 Bonn.

Telephone: (228) 96560; **Fax:** (228) 9656111; **Internet:** www.caesar.de; **e-mail:** office@caesar.de.

Stiftung Deutsches Übersee-Institut (Foundation German Overseas Institute)

Founded in 1965 by the City of Hamburg for research and documentation on political, economic and social developments in overseas countries, especially in the countries of Africa, Asia, Central and South America, and the Near and Middle East.

Activities: Operates in the fields of aid to less-developed countries and development studies, conservation and the environment, economic affairs, education, and social welfare and social studies, nationally through self-conducted programmes, research and issuing publications, and nationally and internationally through conferences. Various institutes operate within the framework of the Foundation's research activities, such as the Deutsches Orient-Institut, the Institut für Asienkunde, the Institut für Iberoamerika-Kunde, the Institut für Afrika-Kunde and the Institut für Allgemeine Überseeforschung. Maintains an on-line bibliographical database on the social sciences, containing over 600,000 entries.

Restrictions: Applications for grants are not accepted.

Publications: Publishes 8 yearbooks, 9 research journals and about 50 monographs annually.

Finance: Finance provided by the Government of Germany (Ministry of Foreign Affairs), the Senate of Hamburg and various foundations.

Board of Directors: Dr Werner Draguhn (Chair.); Dr Klaus Bodemer; Prof Dr Cord Jakobeit; Prof. Dr Udo Steinbach.

Principal Staff: Exec. Dir Dr Werner Draguhn; Admin. Ingo Luplow.

Address: Neuer Jungfernstieg 21, 20354 Hamburg.

Telephone: (40) 42825593; **Fax:** (40) 42825547; **Internet:** www.duei.de; **e-mail:** duei@duei.de.

Stiftung Entwicklung und Frieden (Development and Peace Foundation)

Established in 1986 by the Federal States of North Rhine-Westphalia, Berlin, Brandenburg and Saxony on the initiative of Willy Brandt.

Activities: A cross-party, not-for-profit organization, which argues for a new political order in a world marked by globalization. The Foundation's work is based on three principles: global responsibility, cross-party and cross-cultural dialogue, and an interdisciplinary approach to understanding interdependencies. It carries out its work through conferences, including symposia, expert workshops and dialogues, and publications.

Geographical Area of Activity: Germany and international.

Restrictions: Does not make grants.

Publications: *Global Trends* (every 2 years); *Eine Welt* (series); *Policy Paper* (series, about 3 a year, in German and English); *SEF News* (3 a year, in German and English).

Finance: Annual expenditure approx. €650,000.

Executive Committee: Volker Kähne (Chair.); Dr Klaus Dieter Leister, Prof. Franz Nuscheler (Deputy Chair.).

Principal Staff: Dr Burkhard Könitzer.

Address: Gotenstr. 152, 53175 Bonn.

Telephone: (228) 95925; **Fax:** (228) 9592599; **Internet:** www.sef-bonn.org; **e-mail:** sef@sef-bonn.org.

Stiftung Europäisches Naturerbe—EURONATUR (European Nature Heritage Fund)

Established in 1987 by German environmental organizations for nature and environmental protection.

Activities: Operates in Europe, the Middle East, North Africa and the Philippines in the fields of conservation and the environment and enviromental policies, on an international level, through self-conducted programmes, grants to NGOs and individuals, conferences, training courses and issuing publications.

Geographical Area of Activity: Mainly Europe, the Middle East and North Africa and the Philippines.

Restrictions: Grants only for measures supporting self-conducted programmes.

Publications: *Euronatur* (quarterly journal); papers on scientific and environmental issues.

Finance: Assets €480,000 (2001); annual expenditure €2,492,000 (2001).

Trustees: Consists of five members.

Principal Staff: Man. Dir Gabriel Schwaderer.

Address: Konstanzer Str. 22, 78315 Radolfzell.

Telephone: (7732) 92720; **Fax:** (7732) 927222; **Internet:** www.euronatur.de; **e-mail:** info@euronatur.org.

Stiftung Internationale Jugendbibliothek (International Youth Library Foundation)

Established in 1996 by Christa Spangenberg to promote the education of children and youth (International Youth Library established in 1949 by Jella Lepman).

Activities: Operates in the fields of the arts and humanities, international affairs and education, nationally and internationally through self-conducted programmes and research, nationally through training courses and publications, and internationally through offering scholarships and fellowships. Seeks to give adults and educationalists an understanding of the significance of books for children and young people, through offering information to people and organizations involved in the preparation and distribution of children's literature; contributing to the further training of those involved; advising writers, illustrators, publishers, translators, etc.; co-operating with similar organizations in Germany and abroad; acquiring and distributing children's literature from Germany and abroad so as to extend international and inter-cultural understanding; and promoting research in the area of international literature for children, especially within the framework of the International Youth Library, which maintains a collection of approximately 500,000 volumes. Also offers study fellowships.

Geographical Area of Activity: International.

Restrictions: Applications for grants are not accepted; grants are made only to professionals working in the area of children's and youth literature.

Publications: *IJB Report* (2 a year); *The White Ravens* (annually); book and exhibition catalogues.

Finance: Sources of finance include the City of Munich, the Bavarian State Government, the Federal Ministry for Family and Youth and the Federal Ministry of Foreign Affairs. Annual expenditure DM3,030,000 (1999).

Principal Staff: Chair. Christa Spangenberg; Officer Dr Barbara Scharioth.

Address: Schloss Blutenburg, 81247 Munich.

Telephone: (89) 8912110; **Fax:** (89) 8117553; **Internet:** www.ijb.de; **e-mail:** bib@ijb.de.

Stiftung Jugend Forscht eV (Youth Research Foundation)

Founded in 1965 by Henri Nannen to promote competitions for young scientists under the age of 21 to encourage the research work of students, trainees and other young people.

Activities: Organizes competitions in Germany; also makes grants, and awards scholarships and fellowships.

Geographical Area of Activity: Europe and Germany.

Restrictions: Applications for grants are not accepted.

Publications: Commemorative volumes and brochures concerning the competitions; *Jugend forscht; Schüler experimentieren.*

Finance: Financed by the German Government, *Stern,* and companies. Annual expenditure approx. €900,000.

Trustee: Federal Ministry of Education and Research.

Principal Staff: Dr Uta Krautkrämer-Wagner.

Address: Baumwall 5, 20459 Hamburg.

Telephone: (40) 3747090; **Fax:** (40) 37470999; **Internet:** www.jugend-forscht.de; **e-mail:** info@jugend-forscht.de.

Stiftung fuer Kinder (Foundation for Children)

Established in 1986 to help children in less-developed countries learn and experience new forms of living together after their basic needs have been met, and to set an example of sharing in developed countries.

Activities: Operates in Germany, the Philippines and Romania, in the areas of development aid, education, law and human rights, and medicine and health, through research, grants to organizations and individuals, and issuing publications. Its main concern is to use its resources for the elimination of misery, to overcome social, economic, political and cultural domination and power structures through co-operation with project partners on a reciprocal basis. Maintains a database of more than 2,800 German children related foundations and associations.

Geographical Area of Activity: Europe and South East Asia (mainly Germany, Romania and the Philippines).

Restrictions: Grants are not normally made to individuals.

Publications: *Children—War and Persecution: Proceedings of the Congress, Hamburg, Sept. 26–29 1993; Migrating on the Edges: Migration Theory, Discussion and Philippine Case Study; Lesezeichen Philippinen: Insulare Streifzüge durch Geschichte, Politik, Gesellschaft, Wirtschaft und Kultur; Documents of the European Forum for Child Welfare; Focus Philippines* (journal); *CPP: Phoenix out of the ashes or in a downward current?; Ziel- oder Prozessorientierte Zusammenarbeit mit Projektpartnern im Süden?; Kinder und Jugendliche.*

Governing Board: Ekkehard Arnsperger (Chair.).

Address: Schwaighofstr. 14, 79100 Freiburg.

Telephone: (761) 71015; **Fax:** (761) 77306; **Internet:** www.stiftung-fuer-kinder.de; **e-mail:** stiftung.fuer.kinder@t-online.de.

Stiftung Kinder in Afrika (Children in Africa Foundation)

Founded in December 1984 by Horst W. Zillmer to grant aid and assistance to children in Africa.

Activities: Operates in Africa in the fields of education, and medicine and health, through grants to individuals and institutions. Projects since 1985 have taken place in Burkina Faso, Cameroon, Equatorial Guinea, Ghana, Kenya, Madagascar, Morocco, Mozambique, Namibia, South Africa, Sudan, Tanzania, Togo and Zambia.

Geographical Area of Activity: Africa (Burkina Faso, Cameroon, Equatorial Guinea, Ghana, Kenya, Madagascar, Morocco, Mozambique, Namibia, South Africa, Sudan, Tanzania, Togo and Zambia).

Board of Trustees: Klaus Dietzel; Andreas Graf Dönhoff; Horst W. Zillmer.

Principal Staff: Horst W. Zillmer.

Address: Holsteiner Str. 12c, 21465 Reinbek.

Telephone and Fax: (40) 7221105; **Internet:** www.kinder-in-afrika.de; **e-mail:** info@kinder-in-afrika.de.

Stiftung Lesen (Foundation for Reading)

Established in 1988 to promote reading.

Activities: Operates in the fields of the arts and humanities, and education for young people and adults, promoting the reading of books, newspapers and magazines; supporting a reading and oral culture; and supporting research into reading, communication and the media.

Restrictions: Applications for grants are not accepted.

Board of Trustees: Dr Georg Ruppelt (Chair.).

Principal Staff: Man. Prof. Dr Klaus Ring, Heinrich Kreibich.

Address: Fischtorplatz 23, 55116 Mainz.

Telephone: (6131) 288900; **Fax:** (6131) 230333; **Internet:** www.stiftunglesen.de; **e-mail:** mail@stiftunglesen.de.

Stiftung Ökologie & Landbau (Ecology and Agriculture Foundation)

Founded in 1962 by Karl Werner Kieffer to promote scientific research into the cultivation of agricultural produce with a view towards saving natural resources, preserving the ecological equilibrium and producing high-quality foodstuffs free of noxious substances.

Activities: Operates through the encouragement and support of the ecological schools of thought developing in agricultural science and practice; the co-ordination of exchange of knowledge and experience; support for active initiatives in training practice and science; and the organization of meetings and other events.

Publications: *Ökologie & Landbau; Ökologische Konzepte* (series); *SÖL-Sonderausgaben* (series); report on operations and activities.

Finance: Annual revenue and expenditure approx. €500,000.

Board of Trustees: Dagi Kieffer (Chair.); Dr Marion von Gienanth; Susanne Karim-Abadi; Johannes Kieffer; Dr Roman Lietha; Bernd Louisoder; Günther Strebel; Kurt Willenbacher.

Principal Staff: Dir Dr Ulrich Hampl, Peter Kieffer, Dr Uli Zerger.

Address: Weinstr. Süd 51, Postfach 1516, 67098 Bad Dürkheim.

Telephone: (6322) 989700; **Fax:** (6322) 989701; **Internet:** www.soel.de; **e-mail:** info@soel.de.

Stiftung Wasser für die Welt (Water for the World Foundation)

Established in 1986 to search for water in arid regions of the world.

Activities: Operates in the field of aid to less-developed countries, and science and technology, searching for water in arid regions, allocating water resources, irrigating agricultural land and supporting research projects. The Foundation currently runs one project only, in Nicaragua.

Geographical Area of Activity: Nicaragua.

Restrictions: One project only is running at present, in Nicaragua. Applications for grants are not accepted.

Principal Staff: Heribert Wirth.

Address: Ligastr. 6, 93049 Regensburg.

Telephone: (941) 37205; **Fax:** (941) 3782526.

Stiftung Weimarer Klassik und Kunstsammlungen (Weimar Classics Foundation)

Founded in October 1991 (becoming an independent foundation in 1994), the legal successor to the former non-independent National Research and Memorial Centre of Classical German Literature in Weimar, to preserve and expand the sites and collections of classical German literature in Weimar; to make them available to the public; to encourage the communication, research and dissemination of this cultural heritage; and to maintain the sites and collections of the former National Research and Memorial Centre, as well as the collections of 19th and 20th Century works. Formerly known as the Stiftung Weimarer Klassik, merged with the Kunstsammlungen zu Weimar on January 1st 2003.

Activities: Maintains the Goethe National Museum, the Schiller House, the Palace Museum, the Bauhaus Museum, the New Museum, Belvedere Palace, and 18 other literary museums, palaces and memorials, the Duchess Anna Amalia Library, the Goethe–Schiller Archives, five parks in and around Weimar, and several other properties. Carries out research, organizes exhibitions and events, issues numerous publications and holds conferences.

Geographical Area of Activity: Europe and USA.

Restrictions: Applications for grants are not accepted.

Publications: Publications on classical German literature; exhibition catalogues.

Finance: The Foundation is financed by the Federal Government, the State of Thuringia and the City of Weimar; annual expenditure €19,228,600 (2003).

Board of Trustees: The Board comprises 12 voting members.

Principal Staff: Pres. Hellmut Seemann.

Address: Burgplatz 4, 99423 Weimar; Postfach 2012, 99401 Weimar.

Telephone: (3643) 545100; **Fax:** (3643) 202174; **Internet:** www.swkk.de; **e-mail:** praesident@swkk.de.

Stiftung Weltethos (Global Ethic Foundation)

Established in 1995 by Count K. K. von der Groeben for intercultural and inter-religious research, education and encounter, for the dissemination of the idea of a global ethic, with the basic conviction that there can be no peace among nations without peace between religions, that there can be no peace among religions without dialogue between religions, and that there can be no dialogue between religions without research into the foundations of religions.

Activities: Operates nationally and internationally in the areas of the arts and humanities, education, international affairs, and human rights, through self-conducted programmes, research, grants to individuals and institutions, scholarships and fellowships, conferences, prizes, training courses and publications. A small research team engages in long-term work to further a global ethic, and the Foundation also supports wider initiatives and projects. The basis of the Foundation's programme is the Declaration toward a Global Ethic endorsed by the Parliament of the World's Religions in 1993 (i.e. a commitment to a culture of non-violence and respect for life, to a culture of solidarity and a just economic order, to a culture of tolerance and a life of truthfulness, and to a culture of equal rights and partnership between men and women).

Geographical Area of Activity: International.

Publications: *Global Responsibility: In Search of a New World Ethic; Yes to a Global Ethic; A Global Ethic for Global Politics and Economics; A Global Ethic and Global Responsibilities*; and other publications.

Board: Prof. Dr Hans Küng (Pres.); Prof. Dr Karl-Josef Kuschel (Vice-Pres.); Count K. K. von der Groeben; Dr Hans-Henning Pistor.

Principal Staff: Man. Dir Stephan Schlensog.

Address: Waldhäuser Str. 23, 72076 Tübingen.

Telephone: (7071) 62646; **Fax:** (7071) 610140; **Internet:** www.global-ethic.org; **e-mail:** office@global-ethic.org.

Stiftung West–Östliche Begegnungen (East–West Encounter Foundation)

Established in 1994 to promote contact between the peoples of Germany and the countries of the former USSR in order to promote friendship, international peace and understanding.

Activities: Operates in the areas of the arts and culture, education and international affairs, through projects of exchanges of information and of pupils, other young people and professionals.

Geographical Area of Activity: Germany and the countries of the former USSR.

Restrictions: Grants only to German institutions (e.g. registered NGOs, schools, institutes, etc.). No grants to individuals.

Publications: Activity report (3 a year).

Finance: Financed by an endowment consisting of the remaining assets of the former East German Society for German–Soviet Friendship; assets approx. €12,500,000; annual expenditure approx. €750,000.

Governing Board: Prof. Dr Harry Wünsche (Pres.).

Principal Staff: Chair. Dr Franz Hammerstein; Dir Cyrill Pech.

Address: Friedrichstr. 176–179, 10117 Berlin.

Telephone: (30) 2044840; **Fax:** (30) 20647646; **Internet:** www.stiftung-woeb.de; **e-mail:** secretariat@stiftung-woeb.de.

Stiftung Wissenschaft und Politik—Deutsches Institut für internationale Politik und Sicherheit (Foundation for Science and Politics—German Institute for International Affairs and Security)

Founded in 1962 with the aim of furthering scientific research into international affairs. The Foundation is publicly funded, but is politically independent. It maintains the Deutsches Institut für Internationale Politik und Sicherheit (German Institute for International Affairs and Security).

Activities: Initiates research into international affairs with the aim of assisting policy-makers; awards scholarships; organizes conferences and workshops; operates a number of research units, including EU Enlargement, European and Atlantic Security and Russian Federation and New Independent States; maintains a library of approximately 85,000 volumes and a computerized information system with more than 300,000 bibliographical references in international relations and area studies.

Geographical Area of Activity: Germany.

Restrictions: Applications for grants are not accepted.

Publications: *Internationale Politik und Sicherheit; Aktuelle Materialien zur Internationalen Politik;* special reports.

Finance: Annual expenditure €9,800,000 (2002).

Board of Trustees: Ulrich Hartmann (Pres.); Dr Frank-Walter Steinmeier, Prof. Dr Reimar Lüst (Deputy Pres.); and 18 others.

Principal Staff: Dir Dr Christoph Bertram; Deputy Dir Sr Stefan Mair, Dr Albrecht Zunker.

Address: Ludwigkirchplatz 3–4, 10719 Berlin.

Telephone: (30) 880070; **Fax:** (30) 88007100; **Internet:** www.swp-berlin.org; **e-mail:** swp@swp-berlin.org.

Stiftungsfonds Deutsche Bank zur Förderung der Wissenschaft in Forschung und Lehre (Deutsche Bank Endowment Fund for the Promotion of Science in Research and Teaching)

Established in 1970 by Deutsche Bank AG for the promotion of science and research.

Activities: Operates in the field of science and technology, mainly through funding programmes at universities and other institutions.

Finance: Assets approx. €5,000,000.

Address: c/o Stifterverband für die Deutsche Wissenschaft eV, Barkhovenallee 1, 45239 Essen.

Telephone: (201) 84010; **Fax:** (201) 8401301; **Internet:** www.stifterverband.de; **e-mail:** heinz-rudi@stifterverband.de.

Stipendienfonds Ruhrgas (Ruhrgas Scholarship Fund)

Established in 1984 by Ruhrgas AG to promote academic and scientific exchange between Germany and Norway.

Activities: Operates in Germany and Norway, offering a scientific scholarship programme for researchers in the fields of economy, history and law.

Geographical Area of Activity: Germany and Norway.

Restrictions: Grants made only to Norwegian students and scientists.

Finance: Assets approx. €1,500,000.

Address: c/o Stifterverband für die Deutsche Wissenschaft eV, Barkhovenallee 1, 45239 Essen; Postfach 164460, 45224 Essen.

Telephone: (201) 84010; **Fax:** (201) 8401301; **Internet:** www.ruhrgas.de; **e-mail:** k.e.johansen@arena.uio.no.

Studienstiftung des Deutschen Volkes eV (German National Scholarship Foundation)

Founded in 1948 to give grants and scholarships to particularly gifted German students and to aid them in their university studies.

Activities: Operates nationally in the fields of education, science and medicine, the arts and humanities, law and other professions, through grants to individuals, fellowships, scholarships, conferences and courses. Scholars may participate in summer schools arranged by the Foundation, be offered special research grants or receive special tuition at any German and many foreign universities. Also runs US programmes open solely to its scholarship recipients.

Geographical Area of Activity: Germany.

Publications: Annual report of operations and financial statement.

Finance: Annual expenditure DM51,252,000 (1999).

Principal Staff: Gen. Sec. Dr Gerhard Teufel.

Address: Ahrstr. 41, 53175 Bonn.

Telephone: (228) 820960; **Fax:** (228) 82096103; **Internet:** www.studienstiftung.de; **e-mail:** sdv@studienstiftung.bn.shuttle.de.

Südost-Institut—Stiftung für wissenschaftliche Südosteuropaforschung (South-East Institute—Foundation for Academic Research into South-East Europe)

Founded in 1930 by the German Government to carry out research into the history and politics of South-East Europe.

Activities: Operates nationally and internationally in the fields of the history and international affairs of South-East Europe, through research, conferences and publications.

Geographical Area of Activity: Europe.

Restrictions: No grants are made.

Publications: *Südost-Forschungen; Südosteuropäische Arbeiten; Südosteuropa; Untersuchungen zur Gegenwartskunde Südosteuropas; Südosteuropa Bibliographie.*

Finance: Annual expenditure €500,000 (2003).

Trustees: The Council of the Institute comprises 15 people.

Principal Staff: Dir Prof. Edgar Hösch.

Address: Güllstr. 7, 80336 Munich.

Telephone: (89) 7461330; **Fax:** (89) 74613333; **Internet:** www.suedost-institut.de; **e-mail:** soi.sekr@lrz.uni-muenchen.de.

Fritz Thyssen Stiftung (Fritz Thyssen Foundation)

Founded in 1959 by Amély Thyssen and her daughter, Anita Countess Zichy-Thyssen, to promote research and scholarship in universities and research institutes, particularly in Germany. Special consideration is given to the rising generation of scientists and scholars. Endowed with shares of the then Thyssen A.G, now ThyssenKrupp AG, from which it derives most of its income.

Activities: Supports particular research projects of limited duration, mainly in basic research in the humanities; international relations; state, economy and society; and medicine.

Geographical Area of Activity: Mostly Germany.

Publications: Annual Report.

Finance: Net assets €189,000,000 (Dec. 2001); annual expenditure €13,800,000 (2001).

Board of Trustees: Dr Klaus Liesen (Chair.); Dr Manfred Schneider (Vice-Chair.); Prof. Dr Wolfgang Frühwald; Prof. Dr Hubert Markl; Dr Arend Oetker; Alfred Freiherr von Oppenheim; Prof. Dr Horst Siebert.

Principal Staff: Exec. Dir Jürgen Chr. Regge.

Address: Am Römerturm 3, 50667 Cologne.

Telephone: (221) 2774960; **Fax:** (221) 27749629; **Internet:** www.fritz-thyssen-stiftung.de; **e-mail:** fts@fritz-thyssen-stiftung.de.

Alfred Toepfer Stiftung FVS (Alfred Toepfer Foundation FVS)

Founded in 1931 by Dr h.c. Alfred Toepfer to promote European unity and understanding between nations. The Foundation was formerly known as Stiftung FVS.

Activities: Operates in Europe in the fields of the arts, science, humanities, young people, European relations and the conservation of natural resources, through self-conducted programmes, grants to institutions and the awarding of prizes. Some 24 awards are made annually or every two years, for achievements in the field of European relations. The prizes are linked with academic scholarships or travel grants. Also operates an extensive scholarship programme for students from Central and Eastern Europe.

Geographical Area of Activity: Europe and Eastern Europe.

Publications: Annual Report.

Finance: Assets €100,165,487 (June 2002); annual expenditure €2,368,582 (July 2001–June 2002).

Board of Trustees: Jürgen Schrader (Pres.).

Executive Board: Birte Toepfer (Chair.); Ulrich-Christian Pallach.

Principal Staff: Man. Dir Andreas Holz.

Address: Georgsplatz 10, 20099 Hamburg.

Telephone: (40) 334020; **Fax:** (40) 335860; **Internet:** www.toepfer-fvs.de; **e-mail:** mail@toepfer-fvs.de.

Klaus Tschira Stiftung

Established by Dr Klaus Tschira, co-founder of SAP AG, in 1995.

Activities: Operates in the fields of promoting science and international scientific co-operation, with a current focus on information science and related fields and pure and applied research, as well as funding educational projects at universities. The Foundation spends 51% of its annual budget on its own projects, particularly the European Media Laboratory.

Geographical Area of Activity: International.

Restrictions: Grants not normally made to individuals.

Finance: Capital consists of approx. 11.5% of shares in SAP AG.

Board of Directors: Prof. Dr Siegfried Englert; Prof. Dr Haro Heuser; Gerhard Lindemann.

Principal Staff: Founder and Man. Dir Dr Klaus Tschira; Office Man. Beate Spiegel.

Address: Villa Bosch, Schloss-Wolfsbrunnenweg 33, 69118 Heidelberg.

Telephone: (6221) 533101; **Fax:** (6221) 533199; **Internet:** www.kts.villa-bosch.de; **e-mail:** beate.spiegel@kts.villa-bosch.de.

Kurt-Tucholsky-Stiftung (Kurt Tucholsky Foundation)

Founded 1969 by Mary Gerold-Tucholsky, to promote international communication and understanding.

Activities: Awards scholarships to German students to study abroad, and to foreign students to study in Germany for one year.

Geographical Area of Activity: International.

Principal Staff: Chair. Prof. Dr Fritz J. Raddatz.

Address: Moenckebergstr. 19, 20095 Hamburg.

Telephone: (40) 331819; **Fax:** (40) 30392000; **e-mail:** ktstiftung@aol.com.

Volkswagen Stiftung (Volkswagen Foundation)

Founded in 1961 by the Federal Republic of Germany and the State of Lower Saxony for the promotion of science, technology and the humanities in research and university teaching.

Activities: Operates nationally and internationally, through grants for specific purposes to academic and technical institutions engaged in research and teaching. The Foundation is free to support any area of science, as well as the humanities, but has limited its funding programme to a range of specific fields; special programmes operate for Central and Eastern Europe, Africa, Asia and Central and South America.

Geographical Area of Activity: International.

Restrictions: In the case of applications from abroad, co-operation with German research workers or scholars is usually essential.

Publications: Annual Report; *Crossing Borders* (information in English); *Impulse für die Wissenschaft*.

Finance: Assets DM3,900,000,000 (2000); annual grants expenditure DM190,000,000 (2000); total grants to date €2,800,000,000.

Board of Trustees: Th. Oppermann (Chair.); E. Bulmahn, Prof. Dr G. Neuweiler (Vice-Chair.); Prof. Dr K. J. Bade; Prof. Dr H. Bredekamp; Prof. Dr K. Brockhoff; Dr P. Hartz; Prof. Dr F. Hassauer; Prof. Dr B. Jockusch; Prof. Dr K. Kohse-Höinghaus; Prof. Dr G. Litfin; H. Putzhammer; Prof. Dr L. Schorn-Schütte; Prof. Dr W. Singer.

Principal Staff: Gen. Sec. Dr Wilhelm Krull.

Address: Kastanienallee 35, 30519 Hannover; Postfach 810509, 30505 Hannover.

Telephone: (511) 83810; **Fax:** (511) 8381344; **Internet:** www.volkswagenstiftung.de; **e-mail:** mail@volkswagenstiftung.de.

Dr Rainer Wild-Stiftung (Dr Rainer Wild Foundation for Healthy Nutrition)

Established in 1991 by Dr Rainer Wild, and accorded full legal status by the governing council of Karlsruhe in 1993, to organize actively, on an international basis, scientific research, public education, occupational training and scientific and cultural events aimed at advancing the area of healthy human nutrition.

Activities: Operates in industrialized societies in the fields of education, medicine and health, and science and technology in the area of nutrition, through research, scholarships and fellowships and awarding prizes. Awards the Dr Rainer Wild

Prize for outstanding accomplishments in the field of nutritional science; initiates research projects and provides financial support to young scientists from Germany and grants to students from abroad involved in research; and organizes scientific congresses and forums (including the Heidelberg Nutrition Forum) and cultural exhibitions.

Geographical Area of Activity: Germany and international.

Restrictions: No grants are made to individuals.

Publications: *Gesunde Ernährung; Internationaler Arbeitskreis für Kulturforschung des Essens Mitteilungen* (journal); *Healthy Nutrition*.

Finance: Assets €5,662,000 (Dec. 2001).

Trustees: Dr Fritz Kuhlmann; Susanne Langguth; Prof. Dr Barbara Methfessel; Prof. Dr Manfred Mueller; Prof. Dr Andrea Pfeifer; Dr Anna Maria Reichlmayr-Lais.

Board of Directors: Dr Hans-Joachim Arnold; Prof. Dr Rainer Wild; Prof. Dr Harald Schaumburg.

Principal Staff: CEO Frank Bronold; Head of Science Gesa Schönberger.

Address: In der Aue 4, 69118 Heidelberg.

Telephone: (6221) 89980; **Fax:** (6221) 899840; **Internet:** www.healthy-nutrition.org; **e-mail:** info@healthy-nutrition.org.

Yadigar Foundation

Established in 1993 to promote and support projects in the areas of education and social development.

Activities: Aims to promote and support projects in the areas of education and social development in the Central Asian republics of the former USSR, and in other developing countries in Africa and Asia. Since its establishment, the Foundation has provided financial and logistical support to public and private schools in Kyrgyzstan. Operates a scholarship programme for Central Asian students and scholars to study at higher education institutions in Germany as part of its aim of strengthening academic co-operation between Germany and Central Asia. Also organizes international conferences.

Geographical Area of Activity: Germany, Asia (with an emphasis on Central Asia) and Africa.

Principal Staff: Project Co-ordinator Rouslan Jali.

Address: Erasmusstr. 14, 40223 Düsseldorf.

Telephone: (211) 9337615; **Fax:** (211) 9337625; **e-mail:** rouslan@uni-bonn.de.

Carl-Zeiss-Stiftung (Carl-Zeiss Foundation)

Founded in 1889 by Dr Ernst Abbe with the following objectives: (i) to develop the precision technical industry, at the Optical Works and the Glass Works, Jena; to fulfil higher social obligations than individual owners could permanently guarantee towards all the employees in order to improve their situation with regard to their personal and economic rights; (ii) outside the works, to promote the general interests of the branches of precision technical industry as mentioned above, to participate in organizations and measures designed for the public good of the working population in Jena and its immediate neighbourhood; to promote study in natural and mathematical sciences in research as well as teaching. After the expropriation of the Carl-Zeiss-Stiftung in June 1948, the legal seat of the Foundation was transferred to the Federal Republic of Germany.

Activities: The Foundation's main interest is the operation of the two companies Carl Zeiss, Oberkochen and Schott Glaswerke, Mainz; as well as these commercial ventures the Foundation supports research in the field of science and technology. Operates through self-conducted programmes, research, conferences, courses, publications and lectures, and through grants to German institutions and individuals.

Geographical Area of Activity: Germany.

Restrictions: Religious or political institutions are not supported.

Publications: Annual report and financial statement.

Trustees: The Foundation is governed by a *Stiftungsverwaltung*, controlled by the Baden-Württemberg Ministry of Education and Research. There is a *Stiftungskommissar* who acts as an intermediary between the special board and the chief officers who form the Board of Management.

Address: Baden-Württemberg Ministry of Education, Research and the Arts, Königstr. 46, 70173 Stuttgart.

Internet: www.zeiss.de.

ZEIT Stiftung Ebelin und Gerd Bucerius (Ebelin and Gerd Bucerius Zeit Foundation)

Established in 1971 by Dr Gerd Bucerius for the promotion of science and scholarship, education and training, the arts and culture.

Activities: Operates in three areas: science and scholarships (including innovation in higher education, scholarship in the field of law, and research); education and training (including press and journalism and dialogue in society); and art and culture (including literature, art and museums, cultural heritage, and music and theatre), through research centres, scholarships and prizes. In 2000, the Foundation established the first private German law school, and in 2002, founded the Business Art Forum in Hamburg.

Geographical Area of Activity: Germany, Central, Eastern and Western Europe, Israel, Asia and USA.

Restrictions: The Foundation funds projects that it initiates itself.

Publications: Report (every 2 years); variety of brochures.

Finance: Annual revenue and expenditure approx. €27,800,000 (2002).

Board of Trustees: M. Lahnstein (Chair.); K. Asche; R. Herzog; G. D. von Holtzbrinck; M. Kohlhaüssen; S. Luther; H. Markl; J. Plog; H. Schmidt; K. Schmidt; T. Sommer; H. Voscherau; B. Wrede.

Principal Staff: Man. Dir Michael Göring.

Address: Feldbrünnenstr. 56, 20148 Hamburg.

Telephone: (40) 413366; **Fax:** (40) 41336700; **Internet:** www.zeit-stiftung.de; **e-mail:** zeit-stiftung@zeit-stiftung.de.

Ghana

FOUNDATIONS, TRUSTS AND NON-PROFIT ORGANIZATIONS

Bridge Foundation

Set up to support the development of disadvantaged children living in distressed non-formal urban settlements and rural communities.

Activities: Operates in the fields of social welfare and education for disadvantaged children, through the support of sports and literacy programmes, and vocational training initiatives. Runs a youth development resource centre for the promotion and channelling of the talents and energies of disadvantaged young people; also operates sports clubs and runs literacy programmes for out-of-school children, particularly homeless street children living in deprived urban areas.

Geographical Area of Activity: Ghana.

Board of Trustees: E. Ray Quarcoo (Founder and Pres.).

Principal Staff: Exec. Projects Co-ordinator Vincent C. D'Labouh.

Address: Planet House, 8 Third Ringway, Ringway Estates, POB 13463, Accra.

Telephone: (21) 229933; **Fax:** (21) 772391; **e-mail:** planet35@hotmail.com.

Greece

FOUNDATIONS, TRUSTS AND NON-PROFIT ORGANIZATIONS

Bodossaki Foundation

Founded in 1973 by Prodromos Bodossakis Athanassiadis to promote education, health care and the environment.

Activities: Operates nationally in the fields of conservation and the environment, education, and medicine and health, through self-conducted programmes, grants to institutions and individuals, scholarships and fellowships, and awarding prizes. Greek citizens are also eligible to apply for the Bodossaki Graduate Scholarships at Oxford University, United Kingdom (in science), London School of Economics, Hellenic Observatory, United Kingdom (in economics), and TUFTS University, Fletcher School of Law and Diplomacy, USA (in economics).

Geographical Area of Activity: Mainly Greece.

Publications: Information brochures.

Finance: Assets 17,700,000,000 drachmae (1999); annual revenue 1,000,000,000 drachmae, expenditure 800,000,000 drachmae (1999).

Trustees: Stamatis Mantzavinos (Pres.); Dimitris S. Vlastos (Sec.-Gen.); Georgios Bibilas; Ioannis Detsis; Georgios Kanellopoulos; Ioannis Kantzias; Alexandros Konstantinidis; Evangelos Perakis; Alexandros Tsekouras.

Principal Staff: Sec.-Gen. D. S. Vlastos.

Address: 20 Amalias Ave, 105 57 Athens.

Telephone: (1) 3248005; **Fax:** (1) 3237976; **Internet:** www.bodossaki-foundation.gr; **e-mail:** secr@bodossaki-foundation.gr.

The J. F. Costopoulos Foundation

Established in 1979 by Spyros and Eurydice Costopoulos, for the promotion of Greek culture and civilization both in Greece and internationally, through education, research and projects in art, archaeology and other relevant fields.

Activities: Operates in the fields of the arts and humanities, and education and research, through organizing and sponsoring exhibitions, and projects to support visual arts, museums, libraries, welfare societies and associations, churches, municipalities, conferences and publications, as well as theatre, dance, music and cinema.

Geographical Area of Activity: Europe; some activity in the USA.

Restrictions: Projects are mostly related to Greece and Greek culture, or to countries with active Greek communities. No scholarships are given to individuals for post-graduate studies.

Publications: Annual Report; exhibition brochures, catalogues and monographs.

Finance: Assets €77,067,988 drachmae (Dec. 2001); annual revenue and expenditure €5,008,391 (2001).

Trustees: Yannis S. Costopoulos (Chair.); A. S. Costopoulos (Vice-Chair.and Sec.); P. P. Costopoulos; C. Kerameus; D. P. Mantzounis.

Principal Staff: Curator Katerina Koskina; Accountant Athanassios Efthimiopoulos; Asst to the Curator Assimina Strongili.

Address: 40 Stadiou St, 105 64 Athens.

Telephone: (1) 3262730; **Fax:** (1) 3262731; **Internet:** www.costopoulosfoundation.org; **e-mail:** jfcfound@alpha.gr.

Foundation of the Hellenic World

Established in 1993 by Lazaros D. Efaimoglou and his family. Aims to raise awareness of the importance of Hellenic culture and history throughout the world.

Activities: Runs the cultural centre 'Hellenic Cosmos', which holds exhibitions, educational programmes and an internet café providing access to the Foundation's multimedia projects. Provides grants and scholarships for postgraduate and doctoral students to study in Greece or abroad (of which two are available for foreign students, with degrees in the humanities), and research funding for academics wishing to study aspects of Greek culture. Participates in a number of technological projects, a genealogy programme, made available to the public through cultural events, and produces publications, films and documentaries.

Geographical Area of Activity: Mainly Greece.

Trustees: Lazaros D. Efraimoglou (Pres.); Theodoros Papalexopoulos (Vice-Pres.); Ourania L. Efraimoglou (Sec.); Marina M. Efaimoglou (Treas.); Elias G. Klis; Marianna N. Tassi.

Principal Staff: Man. Dir Dimitris Efraimoglou.

Address: Poulopoulou 38, Athens 118 51.

Telephone: (1) 3422292; **Fax:** (1) 3422272; **Internet:** www.fhw.gr; **e-mail:** webmaster@fhw.gr.

Hellenic Foundation for European and Foreign Policy—ELIAMEP

Established in 1988 by Prof. Thanos Veremis and Prof. Theodore Couloumbis as an independent policy-oriented non-profit research institute.

Activities: Operates in South-Eastern Europe, the Black Sea region and the Eastern Mediterranean in the areas of economic and international affairs, through self-conducted programmes, research, scholarships and fellowships, conferences, training courses and publications.

Geographical Area of Activity: South-Eastern Europe, the Black Sea region and the Eastern Mediterranean.

Publications: *Southeast European Yearbook; Journal of South-East European and Black Sea Studies.*

Principal Staff: Pres. Prof. Loukas Tsoukalis; Dir Gen. Prof. Theodore Couloumbis.

Address: 4 Xenophontos St, 105 57 Athens.

Telephone: (2) 103315022; **Fax:** (2) 103642139; **Internet:** www.eliamep.gr; **e-mail:** eliamep@eliamep.gr.

Hellenic Society for Disabled Children

Founded in 1937 to prevent and treat physical disability in children.

Activities: Operates nationally in the fields of medicine, social welfare and education. Maintains eight centres in Greece, which provide rehabilitation for disabled children up to the age of 16 through physical, occupational and speech therapy and computer training. The centres also provide vocational training for people with disabilities aged between 15 and 28 years. Conferences and lectures are organized for medical staff to follow recent developments in their fields. Also extended to parents.

Geographical Area of Activity: Greece and Europe.

Restrictions: No grants outside Greece.

Publications: Report of operations and financial statement.

Finance: Annual revenue and expenditure approx. US $4,500,000.

Trustees: Mary Carella (Pres.); Antonios Markeziknis (Vice-Pres.); Ranya Kontoyannis (Sec.-Gen.); Alexios Giannopoulos (Treas.).

Principal Staff: Dir Zoe Daskalaki-Vassiliou.

Address: 16 Kononos St, 116 34 Athens.

Telephone: (1) 7212780; **Fax:** (1) 7228380; **Internet:** www.elepap.gr; **e-mail:** elepap@hol.gr.

Institute of International Social Affairs

Established in 1984, an international organization which aims to assist developing countries in Africa, Central and Eastern Europe and the countries of the former USSR.

Activities: Operates in Africa, Central and Eastern Europe and the countries of the former USSR to mitigate the effects of poverty, through research, and by providing support to developing countries in the areas of education, agriculture, health care, social development and humanitarian aid. Also raises awareness of these issues throughout the world, by disseminating information and holding conferences and seminars. Maintains an office in Belgrade.

Geographical Area of Activity: Africa, Central and Eastern Europe and the countries of the former USSR.

Finance: Annual budget approx. US $3,500,000.

Principal Staff: Pres. Nicholas Psarombas; Sec.-Gen. Dimitris Ghizelis; Gen. Man. Sophie Dima.

Address: 15 Faliruo, Athens.

Internet: http://psarobas.freeyellow.com/£intex1; **e-mail:** psarombas@hotmail.com.

The Kokkalis Foundation

Established in 1986 in honour of Socrates Kokkalis and his father Petros Kokkalis, to promote education, culture, medicine, sport and international co-operation.

Activities: Supports activities related to education, science, culture, sports and international co-operation, through grants, publications and research. Operates in Greece and internationally supporting health promotion activities, including a vaccination programme in Africa, peace promotion in the Balkan countries and the purchase of medical equipment. Also carries out research and publishes the results; awards scholarships, fellowships and internships; supports education programmes aimed at building a new South-Eastern Europe; has established the Kokkalis Program on South-Eastern and East-Central Europe at the John F. Kennedy School of Government, Harvard University; and hosts public forums and conferences and organizes lecture series.

Geographical Area of Activity: International, including Africa, the Balkans and Greece.

Publications: Research publications.

Board of Trustees: Socrates P. Kokkalis (Pres.); Niki A. Tzavella (Vice-Pres.); Petros S. Kokkalis (Treas.); Christos K. Halkias; Avgi P. Kokkali; Eleni S. Kokkali; Triphon I. Koutalidis.

Address: Premetis 3, Marousi 151 25, Athens.

Telephone: (1) 6105451; **Fax:** (1) 6105453; **Internet:** www.foundation.intranet.gr; **e-mail:** kf@kokkalisfoundation .org.

Lambrakis Research Foundation

Established in 1991 by Christos D. Lambrakis to promote the introduction of technological innovations in the Greek education system, the dissemination of Greek and European cultural heritage through the use of new technologies, and research into social and environmental issues and regional development within the framework of the European Union.

Activities: Operates in Greece and countries of the European Union in the areas of education, the arts and humanities, science and technology, and conservation of the environment, by undertaking studies, projects and awareness activities and addressing the increasing needs for human resources policies and human capital development, through self-conducted programmes, research, scholarships, conferences, training courses and publications (books, videos and CD-ROM multimedia publications on ancient and Byzantine history, astronomy, biology and chemistry). Offers Manolis Andronikos scholarships for archaeologists wishing to pursue postgraduate studies in archaeological computing.

Geographical Area of Activity: Europe.

Restrictions: Grants only to specific organizations.

Publications: *Teaching Greek as a Second (Foreign) Language; Teachers Training on ICT; ICT Policies in School Education, in Europe and the World*electronic multimedia publications; educational videos with accompanying printed material; conference proceedings.

Finance: Total income €5,763,685, expenditure €5,763,685 (2001).

Board of Directors: Christos D. Lambrakis (Pres.); Adamantios Pepelasis (Vice-Pres.); Leon B. Karapanayotis (Sec.); Stavros Psycharis (Treas.); and six others.

Principal Staff: Dir-Gen. Prof. Adamantios Pepelasis; Deputy Dir-Gen. Nikitas Kastis; Head, Educational Technology Dept George Tsakarisianos.

Address: 3 Paparigopoulou St, 105 61 Athens.

Telephone: (1) 3311848; **Fax:** (1) 3230668; **Internet:** www.lrf.gr; **e-mail:** lrf@lrf.gr.

A. G. Leventis Foundation

Established in 1979 to preserve the cultural heritage of Greece and Cyprus.

Activities: Operates in a number of areas in Cyprus and Greece as well as internationally, protecting and promoting the cultural heritage of Cyprus and Greece; working to preserve the environment; granting scholarships for postgraduate study abroad and at the University of Cyprus (particularly in the fields of education and science); financing publications; working in the field of social welfare; and funding agricultural and technical education in West Africa. Has branch foundations in Cyprus (the Anastasios G. Leventis Foundation), France and in Nigeria (q.q.v.).

Geographical Area of Activity: Cyprus, Greece and West Africa.

Publications: *The A. G. Leventis Collection: 19th and 20th Century Greek Paintings; The A. G. Leventis Foundation and the Cultural Heritage of Cyprus; Ancient Cypriot Art in Berlin;* numerous other publications.

Governing Board: A. P. Leventis (Chair.); Tassos Papadopoulos (Alternate Chair.); George David; Andreas Iacovides; Vassos Karageorghis; H. K. Leventis; Fotini Papadopoulos; Patroclos Stavrou; Theofilos Theofilou.

Address: 1 Vassileos Constantinou, 10674 Athens.

Telephone: (1) 729301518; **Fax:** (1) 7251951; **Internet:** www.leventisfoundation.org/.

Alexander S. Onassis Public Benefit Foundation

Established according to the will of the late Aristotle Onassis, as a public benefit foundation with numerous social and cultural activities.

Activities: The Foundation operates in the fields of education, medicine, social welfare, and the arts and humanities. Awards scholarships and research grants to Greeks and foreigners. Three international prizes are awarded every two years: for International Understanding and Social Achievement, for Culture (Letters, Arts and the Humanities) and for efforts to preserve the Environment; each prize carries a monetary award of US $250,000. The Onassis Cultural Competition Prizes for original music composition, for dance and choreography, and for writing an original script for a play, with first prizes of US $150,000, and second and third prizes of US $100,000 and US $75,000, respectively, for theatre, and prizes of US $100,000, US $75,000 and US $50,000 for dance, are awarded every three or four years. The Foundation also awards a 'Gold Medal' to heads of state in recognition of outstanding contributions to international understanding, has established the Athens Cultural Centre, the Onassis Cardiac Surgery Centre, a Centre for Hellenic Studies at the University of New York, and the Onassis Library for Hellenic and Roman Art, at the Metropolitan Museum of Art, New York.

Geographical Area of Activity: International.

Publications: Brochure, speeches.

Finance: The Foundation is the sole beneficiary of an endowment bequeathed to it by Aristotle Onassis.

Board of Directors: S. Papadimitriou (Pres.); P. Ioannides (Vice-Pres.); A. Zabelas (Vice-Pres. and Treas.); A. Papadimitriou (Gen. Sec.); Dr P. Marxer (Asst Sec.); G. Zabelas (Asst Sec.); Claire Agelidou; Helene Ahrweiler-Glykatzi; Archbishop Anastassios of Tirana and Albania; Michel Dologlou; Costas Grammenos; John Ioannidis; Paraskevas Ioannidis; Anthony Mantzavinos; Michael Sotirhos.

Principal Staff: Dir of Scholarships and Research and Dir of the Cultural Centre Marc Vlachos.

Address: 7 Eschinou St, 105 58 Athens; Heiligkreuz 6, Vaduz, Liechtenstein.

Telephone: (1) 3713000 (Athens); **Fax:** (1) 3713013 (Athens); **Internet:** www.onassis.gr; **e-mail:** pubrel@onassis.gr.

State Scholarships Foundation

Founded to grant scholarships to foreigners for postgraduate or post-doctoral studies in Greece.

Activities: The Foundation offers scholarships annually for postgraduate and post-doctoral studies in Greece to nationals of Africa, Central and South America, Asia, Australia, Central, Eastern and Western Europe, the USA and Canada, Japan, and to non-Greek nationals of Greek origin. Awards scholarships to teachers or researchers (foreigners or foreign nationals of Greek origin) working in Greek centres of studies abroad for further education in language, literature, philosophy, history and art. In 2002–03 the Foundation offered up to 60 scholarships for study in Greece for nationals (foreigners or of Greek origin) from Western Europe, Australia, Canada, Japan or the USA for post-doctoral study (three or four years); for post-doctoral research (six months to one year); for further education in Greek language, literature, philosophy, history and art for professors of Greek language in foreign universities (six months to one year); or for further study in fine arts (one to two years).

Geographical Area of Activity: International.

Principal Staff: Chief of Section M. Mikedaki-Drakaki.

Address: 14 Lyssicratous St, 105 58 Athens.

Telephone: (1) 3254385; **Fax:** (1) 3221863; **Internet:** www.iky.gr.

Swedish Institute at Athens

Founded in 1946 by King Gustaf VI Adolf and others to promote the study of the ancient culture of Greece and to stimulate and support cultural exchange between Sweden and Greece and to further education.

Activities: Operates internationally in the fields of the arts and humanities (mainly archaeology) and Greek–Swedish relations, through research, conferences, courses, publications and lectures.

Geographical Area of Activity: Greece.

Restrictions: Grants only to students at Swedish universities.

Publications: *Skrifter utgivna av Svenska institutet i Athen* (monographs); collections of articles in *Opuscula Atheniensia*.

Finance: Financed mainly by the Swedish Government.

Trustees: R. Alsing (Chair.); C.-G. Styrenius (Sec.).

Principal Staff: Dir Berit Wells; Asst Dir Arto Penttinen.

Address: Mitseon 9, 117 42 Athens.

Telephone: (210) 9232102; **Fax:** (210) 9220925; **Internet:** www.sia.gr; **e-mail:** swedinst@sia.gr.

Guatemala

FOUNDATION CENTRE AND CO-ORDINATING BODY

Consejo de Fundaciones Privadas de Guatemala (Council of Private Foundations of Guatemala)

Established in 1996, an association of foundations seeking to address the social needs of Guatemala.

Activities: The organization aims to co-ordinate and facilitate development projects; network with international organizations; promote the development of the non-profit sector and training within the sector; and develop initiatives between the government and civil society to research into finding solutions for social problems in Guatemala. Currently has 11 member organizations (corporate and private foundations and a research centre).

Geographical Area of Activity: Guatemala.

Principal Staff: Miguel Antonio Gaitán.

Address: Guatemala City.

FOUNDATIONS, TRUSTS AND NON-PROFIT ORGANIZATIONS

Fundación Esperanza de los Niños—ChildHope (Hope for the Children Foundation—ChildHope)

Founded in 1986 in Guatemala, to provide information about the problems of 'street children'—homeless young people living and working in the streets—and previously known as the Childhope International Foundation. Now a network of independent regional and national ChildHope (q.v.) groups operating in the United Kingdom and Europe, Asia and Central and South America.

Activities: Operates in the fields of human rights and social welfare, with the aim of upholding the Convention on the Rights of Children which was ratified by the Guatemalan Government in 1990. Operates programmes in the areas of mental health, children's rights, and research into various issues including child labour and violence against children.

Geographical Area of Activity: Guatemala.

Board of Trustees: Dr Carlos Cossich; Dr Carlos González Orellana; Tasso Hadjidodou; Ana Myrella Saadeh.

Principal Staff: Dir Dr Elizabeth Porras; Deputy Dir Lucas Ventura.

Address: 37 Calle Manzana X Lote 1C, 5-09, Villas Club El Dorado, Apdo Postal 992-A, Ciudad San Cristobal, Zona 8 de Mixco, Guatemala City.

Telephone: (2) 443-5321; **Fax:** (2) 205-9428; **e-mail:** childhope@guate.net.

Fundación Soros—Guatemala (Soros Foundation—Guatemala)

Established at the end of 1997; an independent foundation, part of the Soros foundations network.

Activities: Operates in the fields of civil society, economic reform, law and criminal justice, rural development and public administration. Supports the Guatemala Clarification Commission which was established to determine the extent and nature of human rights violations during the civil war. Other programmes are concerned with promoting improved relations between ethnic and linguistic groups. Also approved the establishment of justice, public policy and rural development institutes.

Geographical Area of Activity: Guatemala.

Finance: Annual expenditure US $3,651,000 (2001).

Board of Directors: Benjamín Son Turnil (Pres.); Eduardo González Castillo (Vice-Pres.); Rosario Pú Gómez (Treas.); Arnoldo Ortíz Moscoso (Sec.); Helen Mack Chang; Ricardo Stein Heinemann; Maria Caba Mateo; Raymundo Caz Tzub.

Principal Staff: Exec. Dir Ricardo Stein.

Address: Avda La Reforma 7-62, Zona 9, Edif. Aristos Reforma, Local 107, Guatemala City.

Telephone: (2) 360-2010; **Fax:** (2) 360-1999; **Internet:** www.soros.org/natfound/guatemala.cfm; **e-mail:** fsg@soros.org.gt.

Proyeto de Desarrollo Santiago—PRODESSA

Established in 1989 to promote development in rural communities in Guatemala and to help build a just and multicultural society.

Activities: Operates programmes in the fields of education, the environment and development, providing loans, grants and technical assistance.

Geographical Area of Activity: Guatemala.

Finance: Annual grants expenditure approx. US $1,000,000.

Principal Staff: Exec. Dir Oscar Azmitia.

Address: Km 15, Carretera Roosevelt, Zona 7, Mixco, Apdo Postal 13-B, 19103 Guatemala City.

Telephone: (2) 595-3911; **Fax:** (2) 595-3913; **Internet:** www.rds.org.gt/congcoop/prodessa; **e-mail:** prodessa@gold.guate.net.

Haiti

FOUNDATIONS, TRUSTS AND NON-PROFIT ORGANIZATIONS

Fondation Connaissance et Liberte (Haiti)—FOKAL

Established in 1995 to promote the development of open society in Haiti; an independent foundation, part of the Soros foundations network.

Activities: Operates in the fields of education, social, legal and health care reform. Operates programmes promoting debate, libraries, the Internet, early childhood education, local production and microcredit initiatives. Through the community library project the Foundation supports 30 community libraries, as well as providing training in library management, finance, book binding and computers, and literacy campaigns.

Principal Staff: Exec. Dir Michele D. Pierre-Louis.

Address: 7 rue des Marguerites, Turgeau, BP 2720, Port-au-Prince.

Telephone: 510-9814; **Fax:** 245-0008; **Internet:** www.soros.org/natfound/haiti; **e-mail:** mplfokal@hainet.net.

Honduras

FOUNDATIONS, TRUSTS AND NON-PROFIT ORGANIZATIONS

Fundación para la Inversión y Desarrollo de Exportaciones—FIDE (Foundation for Investment and Development of Exports)

Established in 1984 by R. Zablah, L. Bendeck and R. Medina Luna to promote investment in order to generate exports of non-traditional manufactured goods.

Activities: Operates in the areas of economic affairs nationally through training courses, and internationally through self-conducted programmes, conferences and publications. FIDE promotes sustainable development in Honduras through strengthening investment and export by seeking to improve the international competitiveness of the country and its business sector. Runs programmes in Europe and Asia, through representatives based in Italy and Taiwan.

Geographical Area of Activity: Honduras.

Publications: *Honduran Highlights; CIC Newsletter* (6 a year), Annual Report; Economic Report; promotional brochures.

Trustees: X. Arguello; L. Bendeck; E. Bográn; M. Bográn; J. Chávez; M. Contreras; A. Facussé; J. Kattan; R. Medina; V. Williams; R. Zablah.

Principal Staff: Exec. Pres. Norman García; Exec. Vice-Pres. Antonio Young.

Address: Condominio Lomas, 4th Floor, Col. Las Lomas del Guijarro, Tegucigalpa.

Telephone: 235-3471; **Fax:** 235-3484; **Internet:** www.hondurasinfo.hn; **e-mail:** cic@fidehonduras.com.

Hong Kong

FOUNDATIONS, TRUSTS AND NON-PROFIT ORGANIZATIONS

Asian Foundation for the Prevention of Blindness

Founded in 1981 by K. L. Stumpf, Dr Arthur Lim, Thomas Clydesdale, John Holmes, D. D. B. McLeod, Q. W. Lee and John Boyer, to investigate blindness and advance the science of ophthalmology.

Activities: The Foundation operates in South-East Asia, conducting and supporting research in ophthalmology, through grants to institutions and individuals; and assists in the training of all kinds of ophthalmic and multidisciplinary staff. The Foundation places special emphasis on cataract operations, the prevention of blindness and services which will benefit the blind directly. It also organizes conferences and co-operates with governmental and other organizations working for the prevention and cure of blindness.

Geographical Area of Activity: South-East Asia.

Principal Staff: Exec. Dir Grace Chan.

Address: 248 Nam Cheong St, Samshuipo, Kowloon.

Telephone: 2-7788332; **Fax:** 2-7881136; **e-mail:** genadmin@hksb.org.hk.

Croucher Foundation

Founded to promote education, learning and research in the areas of natural science, technology and medicine.

Activities: The Foundation operates a scholarship and fellowship scheme for individual applicants who wish to pursue doctoral or post-doctoral research in and outside Hong Kong. This scheme is limited to individual permanent residents of Hong Kong. The Foundation also makes grants to institutions: it offers senior research fellowships to universities in Hong Kong in order to promote research; contributes to international scientific conferences held in Hong Kong; supports advanced study institutes; funds international exchanges between scientific institutions in Hong Kong and other countries; and provides funds for a scheme to enable scientists in mainland China to undertake attachments at Hong Kong institutions.

Geographical Area of Activity: Hong Kong.

Restrictions: Individual scholarship scheme limited to permanent Hong Kong residents.

Trustees: Prof. Y. W. Kan (Chair.); I. R. A. MacCallum (Vice-Chair.); J. M. D. Cha; Prof. Sunney I. Chan; Prof. Y. K. Cheung; Prof. Timothy Cox; Dr Rayson Huang; Alice Lam; Hon. Justice Andrew Li; Prof. Kenneth Young.

Principal Staff: Dir Anthony Tsui.

Address: Rm 501, 9 Queen's Rd Central.

Telephone: 2-7366337; **Fax:** 2-7300742; **Internet:** www.croucher.org.hk; **e-mail:** info@croucher.org.hk.

Hungary

FOUNDATION CENTRE AND CO-ORDINATING BODY

Non-Profit Information and Training Centre (NIOK)

Established in 1993 by the Nonprofit Research Association to promote the development of civil society in Hungary.

Activities: Promotes the development of the third sector in Hungary, through the provision of capacity-building services to NGOs, and by supporting NGOs; maintains a library containing over 3,000 books, annual reports, newsletters and periodicals.

Geographical Area of Activity: Hungary.

Publications: *Citizen's Votes for Nonprofit Activities in Hungary; International Fund-Raising Techniques; Effective Management for Voluntary Organisations and Community Groups.*

Principal Staff: Dir Marianna Török.

Address: 1027 Budapest, Margit krt 58, I/4.

Telephone: (1) 201-9311; **Fax:** (1) 212-2374; **Internet:** www.niok.hu; **e-mail:** contact@niok.hu.

FOUNDATIONS, TRUSTS AND NON-PROFIT ORGANIZATIONS

Civic Education Project

Established in 1991, an international organization aiming to assist democratic reform through educational co-operation.

Activities: Operates in 20 countries of Central and Eastern Europe and the countries of the former USSR, through educational co-operation and collaboration between universities and institutions of tertiary education in the field of the social sciences (including economics, political science, law, journalism and media studies, international relations, etc.). Assists in the placement of visiting lecturers and scholars from the West, who spend one academic year in the region, and gives financial assistance to scholars from Eastern European countries who have trained in the West, but are returning to work in their home country. Maintains an office in Washington, DC.

Geographical Area of Activity: Central and Eastern Europe and the countries of the former USSR.

Publications: Conference proceedings; Discussion Series; Newsletter.

Finance: Financed by foundations, government grants and private contributions.

Board of Directors: Ann Clunan (Chair.); and 13 others.

Principal Staff: Pres. Donna Culpepper; Dir, Central and East European Programs Liana Ghent; Dir, Baltic and Eurasia Programs Jeffrey A. Meyers.

Address: 1051 Budapest, Szent Istvan ter 11/B.

Telephone: (1) 327-3219; **Fax:** (1) 327-3221; **Internet:** www.cep.org.hu; **e-mail:** cep@cepnet.hu.

EURATION Budapest—European Co-operation Foundation

Founded in 1990 by the Commercial and Credit Bank Ltd to promote Hungary's accession to the European Union and co-operation with neighbouring countries in Central Europe.

Activities: Operates in the fields of international affairs, science and education by funding research and organizing conferences.

Geographical Area of Activity: Europe.

Publications: *A Thousand Questions and a Thousand Answers on the EU; The European Community and Hungary in the mid-1990s; Europe-Pocket-Book; Hungary on the Road to the EU; Europe Today and Tomorrow* (4th edn); *European Small Encyclopaedia—Hungary and the European Union* (2nd edn); *Dialogue on Hungary's Accession to the European Union; Euration Report* (annually); conference reports.

Finance: Net assets 4,000,000 forint (2001).

Trustees: Dr Ervin Ernst (Pres.); Prof. Gabriella Izik Hedri (Exec. Dir); Imre Juhász; Prof. László J. Kiss; Dr Mátyás Loidl.

Principal Staff: Exec. Dir Prof. Gabriella Izik Hedri.

Address: 1051 Budapest, Vőrősmarty tér 2.

Telephone and Fax: (1) 318-2293; **e-mail:** euration@axelero.hu.

European Roma Rights Centre

Aims to raise awareness of human rights issues of the Roma (Gypsies).

Activities: Works internationally, providing legal support for Roma people in human rights cases, and carrying out research regarding the international human rights situation of Roma. Produces publications and legal findings, maintains a documentation centre of legal material and works as an advocate for Roma rights. Also offers scholarships to Roma students of law and public administration and internships to Roma people interested in human rights research and human rights law. Supported by Roma organizations and individuals. The organization was awarded the Netherlands Geuzen Medal of Honour in 2001 in recognition of its work promoting democracy and combating discrimination and racism.

Geographical Area of Activity: International.

Publications: *Roma Rights Quarterly* (newsletter, quarterly); *Roma in the Kosovo Crisis*; fact sheets; country reports; advocacy letters and press releases; legal submissions.

Directors: Prof. Bob Hepple (Chair.); Nicoleta Betu; Theo Van Boven; Deborah Harding; Karel Holomek; Jan Hrubala; Azbija Memedova; Rumyan Russinov; Joseph Schull.

Principal Staff: Exec. Dir Dimitrina Petrova.

Address: 1386 Budapest 62, POB 906/93.

Telephone: (1) 413-2200; **Fax:** (1) 413 2201; **Internet:** www.errc.org; **e-mail:** ccahm@errc.org.

Hungarian Foundation for Self-Reliance—Autonómia Foundation

Founded in 1990 to promote the development of civil society and the not-for-profit sector in Hungary.

Activities: Operates in three principal areas: Poverty and Ethnicity, providing loans and initiatives to assist Roma (Gypsy) people and others to become self-reliant; Environmental Sustainability, supporting projects involving Roma people; and Civil Society, assisting the development of non-profit organizations. Also awards an annual Tolerance Prize.

Geographical Area of Activity: Hungary.

Publications: Annual Report.

Finance: Financed mainly by European and Hungarian donors; total assets 230,477,000 forint (2000); total revenue 203,706,000 forint, total expenditure 190,688,000 forint (2000).

Board of Trustees: I. Boros; A. Csongor; Dr B. Daublebsky; Z. Endreffy; F. Karvalits; Dr E. Kállai.

Principal Staff: Exec. Dir Anna Csongor.

Address: 1137 Budapest, Pozsonyi út 14, II/9.

Telephone: (1) 237-6020; **Fax:** (1) 237-6029; **Internet:** www.autonomia.hu; **e-mail:** autonomia@autonomia.hu.

Hungarian Interchurch Aid

Established in 1991.

Activities: Provides international aid and emergency relief in Central and Eastern Europe and Africa; helps refugees and displaced people; supports programmes relating to social welfare issues in Hungary.

Geographical Area of Activity: Central and Eastern Europe, and Africa.

Publications: Annual Report.

Finance: Dir Rev. László Lehel.

Address: 1116 Budapest, Tomaj út. 4.

Telephone: (1) 208-4932; **Fax:** (1) 208-4934; **e-mail:** hia@ interchurch.hu.

National Foundation for Children and Youth

Founded in 1990 by the Government of Hungary to protect the rights of children in accordance with the Convention on the Rights of Children.

Activities: The Foundation organizes youth camps, youth exchange programmes, arts projects, cultural events and festival programmes; it also provides funding for scientific research work, children's hospitals and projects for physically disabled children. Also involved in developing curricula and training teachers.

Geographical Area of Activity: Mainly Hungary.

Principal Staff: Sec. Zsuzsa Nagy.

Address: 1145 Budapest, Amerikai út 96, POB 1399, Bp 62.

Telephone: (1) 252-4671; **Fax:** (1) 252-3537; **e-mail:** zsnapy@ ngyik.datanet.hu.

Open Society Institute—Budapest

Established in 1993 to develop and implement programmes in the areas of educational, legal, economic and social reform. The Institute is part of the Soros foundations network.

Activities: Together with its sister organization, the Open Society Institute in New York (q.v.), the Institute assists the Soros foundation network by creating network-wide programmes on common issues and by providing administrative, financial and technical support. The Institute also supports a variety of other initiatives throughout Central and Eastern Europe and the former USSR, with a strong emphasis on projects in the areas of the arts and humanities, education, human rights, ethnic and minority issues, civil society and women's issues. Administers a variety of programmes, including the Arts and Culture Network Program, Constitutional and Legal Policy Institute, East East Program, Education Support Program, Network Media Program, Information Program, International Policy Fellowships, Mental Disability Advocacy Program and the Roma Culture Initiative.

Geographical Area of Activity: Central and Eastern Europe.

Finance: Annual expenditure approx. US $17,606,000 (2000).

Advisory Board: George Soros (Chair.); Aryeh Neier (Pres.); Yehuda Elkana; Annette Laborey; William Newton-Smith; Wiktor Osiatynski; Istvan Rev; Cornelio Sommaruga.

Principal Staff: Exec. Dir Katalin E. Koncz.

Address: 1051 Budapest, Oktober 6 út 12.

Telephone: (1) 327-3100; **Fax:** (1) 327-3101; **Internet:** www.osi.hu; **e-mail:** info@osi.hu.

Soros Foundation—Hungary

Established in 1984, the first foundation in the Soros foundations network, it aims to support and initiate programmes to create and nurture the development of civil society, free expression and independent thought in the fields of culture, science, education and health care. It is an independent foundation, part of the Soros foundations network.

Activities: The Foundation operates mainly in the areas of education, information and the media, public health, the Roma (Gypsies) and ethnic minorities, civil society, the arts and culture, law and criminal justice, women's and youth programmes, and promoting accession to the European Union.

Geographical Area of Activity: Hungary.

Finance: Annual expenditure US $2,700,000 (2003).

Board of Directors: Gabor Halmei (Chair.); Gabor Bojar; Anna Csongor; Laszlo Halpern; Gabor Klaniczay; Boldizsar Nagy; Laszlo Jakab Orsos.

Principal Staff: Exec. Dir Anna Belia.

Address: 1023 Budapest, Bolyai út 14; H-1525 Budapest, Pf 34.

Telephone: (1) 315-0303; **Fax:** (1) 315-0201; **Internet:** www.soros.hu; **e-mail:** office@soros.hu.

Iceland

FOUNDATIONS, TRUSTS AND NON-PROFIT ORGANIZATIONS

West–Nordic Foundation

Founded in August 1986 as a result of an agreement signed by the Governments of Denmark, Finland, Iceland, Norway and Sweden, along with the autonomous Governments of the Faeroe Islands and Greenland, to provide funding for small- and medium-sized business enterprises in the Faeroe Islands, Greenland and Iceland; and to encourage industrial and technical co-operation between Nordic countries.

Activities: Makes loans to businesses in the Faeroe Islands and Greenland, financing new and existing fishing businesses, expanding the Greenland tourist industry as well as developing co-operative projects to include the participation of Icelandic businesses.

Geographical Area of Activity: The Faeroe Islands, Greenland and Iceland.

Finance: Annual contributions from the Governments of Denmark, the Faeroe Islands, Finland, Greenland, Iceland, Norway and Sweden. Assets 149,293,219 Danish kroner (2001); annual revenue 7,109,646 Danish kroner, expenditure 3,980,363 Danish kroner (2001).

Directors: Jørn Birk (Chair.); Sigurd Poulsen (Vice-Chair.); William Fries Møller; Carita Putkonen; Sturlaugur Porsteinsson; Bjørn Normann Hansen; Lars Engström.

Principal Staff: Man. Dir Sverri Hansen; Sec. Elva Olafsdottir.

Address: POB 8096, 128 Reykjavík.

Telephone: 530-2100; **Fax:** 530-2109; **Internet:** www.vestnorden.is; **e-mail:** elva@vestnorden.is.

India

FOUNDATION CENTRES AND CO-ORDINATING BODIES

Association of Voluntary Agencies for Rural Development

A network of organizations established in 1958 to strengthen voluntary action and capacity-building of Indian and Southern Asian NGOs.

Activities: Operates in India and Southern Asia in the fields of conservation and the environment, economic affairs, education, law and human rights, international affairs, medicine and health, science and technology, social welfare, and self-governance and empowerment of the disadvantaged, through research, conferences, workshops, seminars and projects (particularly in the areas of food security, women's empowerment and self-governance).

Geographical Area of Activity: India and Southern Asia.

Restrictions: Works in association with other NGOs; is not a funding agency.

Publications: *Voluntary Action* (every 2 months); planning studies.

Finance: Annual revenue and expenditure 550,000 Indian rupees.

Trustees: P. M. Tripathi (Pres.); Dr B. Mishra (Gen. Sec.); and 28 other members.

Principal Staff: Gen. Sec. Dr B. Mishra.

Address: 5 (FF) Institutional Area, D.D.U. Marg, New Delhi 110 002.

Telephone: (11) 23234690; **Fax:** (11) 23232501; **e-mail:** avard@del3.vsnl.net.in.

Centre for Advancement of Philanthropy—India

Founded in 1986 to provide philanthropic organizations with information, advice and assistance in the areas of law, taxation, investments, financial planning, management and resources.

Activities: Organizes training courses, seminars, conferences and workshops. Provides consultancy services; conducts research; publishes books and journals. Established the Bombay Community Public Trust in 1991 (which is now run independently).

Geographical Area of Activity: India.

Publications: *Management of Philanthropic Organizations; Enhancing Effectivess of Foundations; Profile 300*; and other publications.

Finance: Funded by grants from local foundations and companies and membership fees.

Directors: R. M. Lala (Chair.); R. R. Chaxi (Exec. Dir).

Principal Staff: Exec. Sec. Noshir H. Dadrawala.

Address: Mulla House, 4th Floor, 51 M.G. Rd, Flora Fountain, Mumbai 400 001.

Telephone: (22) 22846534; **Fax:** (22) 22675642; **Internet:** www.cozucare.org/cap/index.htm; **e-mail:** centphil@vsnl.com.

IndianNGOs.com Pvt Ltd

Social enterprise established to provide internet-based information on the social and development sector in India, to build the capacity of NGOs, donors, development professionals and students and to promote corporate social responsibility.

Activities: Provides internet-based information on the not-for-profit social and development sector in India, examples of good corporate giving practice internationally and in India, background information on issues facing NGOs and a searchable database of approximately 12,000 NGOs.

Geographical Area of Activity: India.

Principal Staff: Contact: Sanjay Bapat.

Address: Prasad, opposite Satyam Collections, Ghantali, Naupada, Thane 400 602.

Telephone: (22) 25348905; **Internet:** www.indianngos.com.

Sampradaan Indian Centre for Philanthropy

Founded in 1996 as a national support organization to promote the development of the non-profit sector, especially the philanthropy sector, in India.

Activities: A foundation centre aiming to foster co-operation between the state, corporations and civil society; encourage networking between donors and between donors and NGOs; and to carry out advocacy in support of philanthropy. Carries out its objectives through conducting conferences, seminars and workshops; carrying out research and providing documentation; conducting campaigns; offering advice and supporting the third sector; and maintaining a resource centre.

Geographical Area of Activity: India.

Restrictions: Does not give grants, nor does it collect funds for other organizations.

Publications: *Sampradaan* (newsletter, 6 a year); *Directory of Indian Donor Organisations; For God' Sake: Religious Charity and Social Development in India; Giving and Fund-Raising in India;* occasional papers, monographs, information leaflets and case studies.

Finance: Annual revenue 1,792,956 Indian rupees, expenditure 1,446,639 Indian rupees (2000).

Trustees: M. B. Athreya (Pres.); Rajiv Mehrotra; Dr C. V. Ramanan; K. K. Sachdev; Jyoti Sagar; Leela Samson; Pushpa Sundar; Shankar Vankateshwaran.

Principal Staff: Exec. Dir Pushpa Sundar.

Address: C-8/8704, Vasant Kunj, New Delhi 110 070.

Telephone: (11) 26899368; **Fax:** (11) 26121917; **Internet:** www.sampradaan.org; **e-mail:** icp@del2.vsnl.net.in.

FOUNDATIONS, TRUSTS AND NON-PROFIT ORGANIZATIONS

Afro-Asian Rural Development Organization—AARDO

Founded in Cairo in 1962 to restructure the economy of the rural populations of Africa and Asia, and to explore, collectively, opportunities for promoting welfare and eradicating malnutrition, disease, illiteracy and poverty among rural people in Africa and Asia. Formerly known as the Afro-Asian Rural Reconstruction Organization.

Activities: Conducts collaborative research on development issues; gives technical assistance for development projects and disseminates information; organizes international conferences and seminars; and awards over 100 individual training fellowships at nine institutes in India, China (Taiwan), Korea,

Japan, Malaysia and Egypt. Membership comprises 12 African and 14 Asian countries, and the Institute of Rural Development, Kenya.

Geographical Area of Activity: Africa and Asia.

Publications: *Afro-Asian Journal of Rural Development* (2 a year); *AARDO Newsletter* (2 a year, in Arabic and English); Annual Report; workshop and seminar reports.

Finance: Total revenue US $730,275, expenditure US $643,942 (2000).

Executive Committee: President; two Vice-Presidents; and members.

Principal Staff: Sec.-Gen. Dr Bahar Munip; Asst Sec.-Gen. Abdulla Yahia Adam.

Address: State Guest Houses Complex, Plot 2, Chanakypuri, New Delhi 110 021.

Telephone: (11) 26877783; **Fax:** (11) 24672045; **Internet:** www.aardo.org; **e-mail:** aardohq@nde.vsnl.net.in.

Ambuja Cements Foundation

Established in 1993 by Gujurat Ambuja Cements as an independent not-for-profit organization working in collaboration with local, national and international development agencies.

Activities: The Foundation manages human and natural resources for sustainable development, aiming to make people in India both productive and prosperous and to improve their quality of life, through technical and financial support, as well as serving as a catalyst for appropriate planning, implementation and post-implementation care. Operates in the areas of rural development, health, environmental awareness, empowerment of women, solutions to groundwater depletion, agricultural techniques, and wasteland development. Also provides disaster relief and long-term reconstruction support.

Geographical Area of Activity: India.

Address: c/o Gujurat Ambuja Cements, Tehsil Jaitaran Pali, 306709 Rajastan.

Telephone: (22) 22853044; **Fax:** (22) 22846270; **e-mail:** tushar@ambujamail.com.

Angaja Foundation

Founded in 1993 to help improve the lives of underprivileged people.

Activities: Works to protect children's rights focusing on: promoting creative non-formal education for children living in slum areas; increasing school admissions for children in need; improving government schools; providing health check-ups for children from slum areas; and health education for adult men and women and adolescents living in slum areas. Operates training and sensitization workshops for judges, public prosecutors of the lower courts, police, doctors, NGOs and the media on child rape, child sexual abuse, crimes against women and street children. Also runs a Child Sexual Abuse and Child Rape Programme which provides counselling, legal, financial and educational services.

Geographical Area of Activity: Delhi, India.

Restrictions: No grants made.

Publications: *Child Rape and Child Sexual Abuse—Sensitization for Lawyers, Police, Doctors and NGOs* (workshop report).

Finance: Funding from ActionAid (q.v.) and Siddartha's Intent. Annual revenue 3,000,000 Indian rupees, annual expenditure 2,000,000 Indian rupees.

Board of Trustees: Tarkeshwari (Pres.); Raka Sinha Bal (Gen. Sec.); Rajiv Bal (Treas.); Rahul Mane; Dr Jayunt Mitra.

Principal Staff: Gen. Sec. Raka Sinha Bal; Admin. and Accounts Officer C.V. Daniel.

Address: A-7, Amrit Nagar, Behind South Extention Part-I, New Delhi 110 003.

Telephone: (11) 224617414; **Fax:** (11) 224616717; **e-mail:** oop1133@bol.net.in.

Asian Development Research Institute

Established in 1991 by a group of social scientists in the eastern Indian state of Bihar.

Activities: The Institute is active in development and social science research, both in the Bihar region and internationally, particularly concentrating on promoting literacy development and education. Also active in the area of cultural regeneration, including documenting Bihar's folk art tradition. The Institute has established two financially independent research centres in Ranchi and New Delhi, and works in collaboration with foreign universities and development organizations. Also holds conferences and the annual ADRI Foundation Lecture.

Geographical Area of Activity: Mainly India.

Principal Staff: Admin. Sunita Lall.

Address: B.S.I.D.C. Colony, Opp. Boring Patliputra Rd, Patna 800 013.

Internet: www.adri-india.org.

Asian Institute for Rural Development

A national and regional NGO established in 1976 by Dr A. T. Ariyaratne, Dr K. C. Naik, M. V. Rajasekharan and others to undertake scientific research, training and field action in the area of rural development.

Activities: Operates in Asia and Africa in the fields of conservation and the environment, science and technology, and social welfare, through promoting networking among NGOs, running training programmes and field projects, carrying out research, working to develop public policy and issuing publications. Founding member of the Asian NGO Coalition for Agrarian Reform and Rural Development.

Geographical Area of Activity: Asia and Africa.

Restrictions: Does not make grants.

Publications: *AIRD News*.

Board of Trustees: Dr A. T. Ariyaratne (Patron); M. V. Rajasekharan (Chair.); N. Ariyaratne, Prof. G. Agarwal (Vice-Chair.); and 12 others, representing Bangladesh, India, Japan, Nepal, the Philippines, Sri Lanka and Canada.

Principal Staff: Project Co-ordinator Mr Madappa.

Address: No. 7/1, Ratnavilasa Rd, Basavangudi, Bangalore 560 004.

Telephone and Fax: (80) 26604091; **e-mail:** compu_land@hotmail.com.

Asian Youth Centre

Established in 1984 as a network of Asian youth NGOs.

Activities: Operates in the field of youth development, acting mainly as an information and discussion centre for organizations throughout Asia. Aims to raise global awareness of the problems of poverty in Asia, works towards social justice for all, and promotes volunteerism and the involvement of young people in development work. Also funds shelters, educational schemes and training centres to help underprivileged young people in India, including street children, and a child sponsorship programme.

Geographical Area of Activity: South-East Asia.

Publications: Annual Report.

Principal Staff: Dir V. Muthukumaran.

Address: L8, 26th Cross Anna Nagar East, Chennai 600 102.

Telephone: (44) 26451715; **Fax:** (44) 26263351; **Internet:** pcsadvt.com/ayc/index.htm; **e-mail:** arpudraj@giasmd01.vsnl.net.in.

The Bridge Foundation

Established in August 1984 by Dr Vinay Samuel to work with the economically disadvantaged in their struggle to attain economic security and social justice with dignity and self-worth.

Activities: Operates in Southern India in the field of micro-enterprise development, extending credit to people too poor to borrow from the traditional banking system, through self-conducted programmes and training courses. Loans are made to individuals and to groups from village communities wishing to acquire skills or equipment, and the Foundation offers training in basic accounting and group leadership. The Foundation is currently particularly interested in assisting marginalized women in rural areas, encouraging them to form self-help groups.

Geographical Area of Activity: Southern India.

Finance: Net assets 20,203,153 Indian rupees (1998/99).

Trustees: Dr Vinay Samuel; Jagadeesh Devadasan; David Lobo; Collin Timms.

Principal Staff: Gen. Man. E. Swaminathan.

Address: No 19, 3rd Cross, Hutchins Rd, St Thomas Town PO, Bangalore 560 084.

Telephone: (80) 25470146; **Fax:** (80) 25466485; **e-mail:** tbfindia@vsnl.com.

Chandana Art Foundation International

Established in 1999 by K. Venkatesh for the preservation and promotion of the art and cultural heritage of India, in particular aiming to foster an intellectual and artistic environment for children, women and disabled people and socially and economically disadvantaged people.

Activities: Promotes various forms of art, including traditional and folk art, puppetry, photography and tribal art, through research and documentation, education, exhibitions, workshops, scholarships, competitions, and cultural exchange programmes. Runs programmes for disabled people and for children.

Geographical Area of Activity: India, mainly Bangalore.

Principal Staff: Man. Trustee K. Venkatesh.

Address: No. 784, 10th Main, II Block, Srinivas Nagar, BSK I Stage, Bangalore 560 050, Karnataka.

Telephone: (80) 26524820; **Internet:** www.indev.nic.in/chandanaartfoundation; **e-mail:** cafivenkatesh@yahoo.com.

Chemtech Foundation

Activities: The Foundation organizes trade fairs, conferences and workshops focusing on environmental issues facing industry, and provides a marketing base for pollution-control companies. Sponsors visits of foreign delegations to India and of Indian delegations abroad. Has instituted the CHEM-TECH-CEW Awards to recognize individual, corporate and institutional initiative in scientific and economic achievement.

Geographical Area of Activity: India.

Advisory Board: Dr Ashok Ganguly (Chair.).

Principal Staff: Sec.-Gen. Tarun Hukku; Project Man. Hermant Shetty.

Address: 26 Maker Chambers VI, Nariman Point, Mumbai 400 021.

Telephone: (22) 2874758; **Fax:** (22) 2870525; **Internet:** www.chemtechworldexpo.com/CF/default.htm; **e-mail:** hermant_shetty@jasubhai.com.

Concern India Foundation

Established in 1991 to support development-oriented NGOs working for disadvantaged people.

Activities: Aims to provide disadvantaged people with opportunity, through funding and other support services to grassroots development NGOs working in the fields of education, health, community development and the environment. Also maintains five regional offices throughout India, and has representatives in Switzerland, the UK and the USA.

Geographical Area of Activity: India.

Publications: Annual Report.

Board of Trustees: A. B. K. Dubash (Chair.); Mohini Mubayi (Founder); Naheed H. Sorabjee; Laleh Ogle.

Principal Staff: Chief Exec. Kavita Shah.

Address: Ador House, 6 K. Dubash Marg, Mumbai 400 001.

Telephone: (22) 2029708; **Fax:** (22) 2043625; **Internet:** www.concernindia.org; **e-mail:** mumbai@concernindia.org.

Dignity, Education, Vision International—DEVI

Established in 1992 by Dr Sunita Gandhi, to promote education and development in India.

Activities: Provides education for the poor in India and encourages self-help through learning and development. Particular focus on empowering poor women from both rural and urban areas.

Geographical Area of Activity: India.

Principal Staff: Pres. Amitabh Chakrabarti.

Address: DEVI Sansthan, 12 Station Rd, Lucknow 207 123.

Telephone: (522) 228606; **Fax:** (522) 212888.

Disaster Mitigation Institute

NGO founded in 1993 by Ela Bhatt, Mihir Bhatt and Reema Nanavaty to mitigate the effects of natural disasters in India.

Activities: Together with partner organizations, the Institute runs a number of programmes concerned with disaster mitigation, including food security and nutrition support; drought relief and urban flood relief; urban risk reduction for vulnerable homes; and employment security. New initiatives include a community-based risk management training programme and a livelihood relief fund. Organizes conferences and produces a number of publications.

Geographical Area of Activity: India.

Publications: *Aafat Nivaran* (monthly journal); *Vipada Nivaran* (quarterly journal); Case Study Series; posters and brochures.

Trustees: M. R. Bhatt (Man. Trustee); E. R. Bhatt; A. Chatrapati; A. W. P. David; R. Jhabvala; A. Krishnaswami; A. Mishra; R. Nanavati; Sunita Narain.

Principal Staff: Tejalben R. Dave; M. R. Pancholi; D. Sinha.

Address: 411 Sakar Five Near Natraj Cinema, Ashram Rd, Ahmedabad 380 009.

Telephone: (79) 26583607; **Fax:** (79) 26582962; **Internet:** www.southasiadisasters.net; **e-mail:** dmi@icenet.net.

Environmental Protection Research Foundation

Founded in 1982 by Dr B. Subba Rao, Dr S. V. Ranade and Prof. J. M. Gadgil to promote research in the field of environmental engineering.

Activities: Operates in the fields of conservation and the environment. Helps companies, pollution control boards, local bodies and governmental agencies carry out effective implementation of pollution control programmes. Also runs development activities in agro-based industries, environmental degradation and watershed management.

Geographical Area of Activity: India.

Publications: *Souvenirs*; laboratory manuals.

Council of Managment: Dr B. Subba Rao (Pres.); Dr S. V. Ranade (Vice-Pres.); Prof. J. M. Gadgil (Man. Sec.); G. K. Dandekar; B. N. Kininge; T. Y. More; P. I. Parikh; Dr V. S. Shah; Dr R. M. Vora.

Principal Staff: Chief Development Officer Sushilkumar Bhandare.

Address: Arundhati, nr MSEB, Vishrambag, Sangli 416 415, Maharashtra.

Telephone: (233) 2300924; **Fax:** (233) 2301857; **Internet:** education.vsnl.com/eprf; **e-mail:** eprf@vsnl.com.

Foundation of Occupational Development—FOOD

Established in 1979 by Loyola Joseph and Ms Rajeswari S.

Activities: Operates in the areas of conservation and the environment, economic and international affairs, education, medicine and health, science and technology, and social welfare, nationally and internationally through research, and nationally through self-conducted programmes, prizes, conferences and training courses. The Foundation also provides low-cost housing, operates sanitation projects, a bulletin board service and acts as an internet service provider for NGOs. Works in partnership with local, national and international organizations.

Geographical Area of Activity: India.

Finance: Total assets 8,450,842 Indian rupees.

Principal Staff: Exec. Dir Loyola Joseph.

Address: Bharathiar Complex, C-Block, 1st Floor, 100 Feet Rd, Vadapalani, Chennai 600 026.

Telephone: (44) 24848201; **Fax:** (44) 24838826; **Internet:** www.xlweb.com/food; **e-mail:** food@xlweb.com.

Foundation for Revitalization of Local Health Traditions—FRLHT

Established in 1991.

Activities: Operates in the field of health and medicine by encouraging the use of traditional medicine as part of public health programmes. Promotes international co-operation in the understanding of traditional medicine and disseminates information on medicinal plants.

Geographical Area of Activity: India.

Restrictions: Research grants only.

Publications: *Amruth* (traditional health-care magazine, every 2 months).

Finance: Annual budget approx. US $1,140,625.

Board of Trustees: 23 members comprised of scientists, medical professionals, management and forestry workers.

Principal Staff: Dir Darshan Shankar.

Address: 50 MSH Layout, Anand Nagar, Bangalore 560 024.

Telephone: (80) 28565760; **Fax:** (80) 28565873; **Internet:** www.frlht-india.org; **e-mail:** darshan.shankar@frlht-india.org.

Rajiv Gandhi Foundation

Established in 1991 by Sonia Gandhi to promote the ideals of her late husband Rajiv Gandhi. The Foundation is independent of party or political affiliation and gives particular attention to providing enlarged opportunities to the underprivileged and deprived, and to promoting diversity and pluralism in human societies, the empowerment of women, the alleviation of poverty, and the regeneration of India's environment.

Activities: Operates mainly in the areas of natural resource management, libraries and education, health, welfare of the disabled, women and child development, applied science and technology in rural areas, and the promotion of grassroots democracy through local self-government. Its largest programmes include the establishment of village libraries throughout India; implementing schemes for rainwater harvesting and environmental regeneration in rural India through its own corps of volunteers; supporting the education of child victims of terrorism; projects for the economic and educational empowerment of women; and AIDS control and awareness campaigns. These are implemented through self-conducted programmes, grants to institutions, scholarships, research, conferences, and publications. The attached Rajiv Gandhi Institute for Contemporary Studies is a centre for interdisciplinary studies, including economic and legal reform, social issues and international relations; it also conducts seminars and workshops, and issues publications.

Geographical Area of Activity: India.

Publications: *Challenges of Globalization; Economic Reforms for the Poor; Salvaging the WTO's Future: Doha and Beyond.*

Finance: Funded by income from its corpus of approx. £4,400,000 and donor contributions for projects; total expenditure £490,600 (2001–2002).

Board of Trustees: Sonia Gandhi (Chair.); Manmohan Malhoutra (Sec.-Gen.); Dr M. S. Ahluwalia; Dr Y. K. Alagh; P. Chidambaram; Dr K. Choudhry; S. Dubey; R. Gandhi; Dr M. Giri; R. P. Goenka; Dr V. Krishnamurty; Dr S. Raha; Sir S. S. Ramphal; Dr M. Singh; Prof. M. S. Swaminathan; Priyanka Gandhi Vadra.

Principal Staff: Sec.-Gen. Manmohan Malhoutra; Dir, Rajiv Gandhi Institute for Contemporary Studies Prof. Bibek Debroy; Registrar S. S. Sharma.

Address: Jawahar Bhawan, Dr Rajendra Prasad Rd, New Delhi 110 001.

Telephone: (11) 23755117; **Fax:** (11) 23755119; **Internet:** www.rgfindia.com; **e-mail:** info@rgfindia.com.

Gandhi Peace Foundation

Founded in 1958 to promote the beliefs and practices of Mohandas Karamchand Gandhi.

Activities: The Foundation works towards helping people attain and maintain peaceful, happy and harmonious social relations, encourages the principles of truth and non-violence in national and international affairs, and promotes the teaching of the practices of Gandhi. Also active in environmental affairs, including forest preservation and support for environmental activists. Awards the annual Pranavanand Peace Award.

Geographical Area of Activity: India.

Publications: *Gandhi Marg* (quarterly in English, every 2 months in Hindi); several books.

Finance: Funded by the Gandhi Memorial Trust. Annual budget approx. 47,79,500 Indian rupees.

Principal Staff: Pres. Ravindra Varma.

Address: 221–223 Deen Dayal, Upadhyaya Marg, New Delhi 110 002.

Telephone: (11) 23237493; **Fax:** (11) 23236734.

Indian Council for Child Welfare

Established in 1952 to promote development services for children in India.

Activities: Promotes development services for children, particularly focusing on welfare and education. Runs educational programmes, childcare centres and creches for young children; operates childcare and education centres; disseminates information throughout India, enhancing awareness of children's needs; acts as an advocate for children's rights and benefits; funds training centres and organizes seminars, conferences and workshops on issues relating to child development. Maintains a library. There are 31 State or Union Territory Councils throughout India.

Geographical Area of Activity: India.

Address: 4 Deen Dayal Upadhayay Marg, New Delhi 110 002.

Telephone: (11) 23236616; **Fax:** (11) 23232427; **Internet:** www.iccw.org.

Indian Council for Cultural Relations

Founded in 1950 to establish and strengthen cultural relations between India and other countries.

Activities: Operates both nationally and internationally through the reciprocal development of studies in Indian and foreign universities; publications in English and other languages on different aspects of Indian culture; the exchange and presentation of cultural material with libraries and museums abroad; and the promotion of exchange visits of cultural delegations, scholars and artists. Organizes the Azad Memorial Lectures, international seminars, symposia and conferences; establishes chairs and centres of Indian studies abroad; looks after the welfare of foreign students in India; compiles select bibliographies and publishes books and journals in English, French, Spanish and Arabic. Also administers the Jawaharlal Nehru Award for international understanding, instituted by the Government of India in 1964. The Council has regional offices in Bangalore, Calcutta, Chandigarh, Chennai, Hyderabad, Lucknow, Mumbai and Trivandrum, and cultural centres in Almaty, Berlin, Cairo,

Colombo, Durban, Georgetown, Jakarta, Johannesburg, London, Moscow, Paramaribo, Port Louis, Port of Spain and Tashkent.

Geographical Area of Activity: International.

Publications: *Indian Horizons* (periodic, in English); *Africa Quarterly* (in English); *Thaqafat-ul-Hind* (quarterly, in Arabic); *Papeles de la India* (quarterly, in Spanish); *Rencontre avec l'Inde* (quarterly, in French); *Gagananchal* (quarterly, in Hindi).

Principal Staff: Pres. Shri Krishan Kant; Dir Gen. Shri Himachal Som.

Address: Azad Bhavan, Indraprastha Estate, New Delhi 110 002.

Telephone: (11) 23318303; **Fax:** (11) 23370732; **Internet:** www.members.tripod.com/~iccr/; **e-mail:** iccr@vsnl.com.

Indian Council for Research on International Economic Relations

Non-profit research organization established in August 1981.

Activities: Engages in policy-oriented research on issues related to India's national and international economic position. Current areas of research are trade, openness, industrial restructuring and competitiveness; financial liberalization and financial integration; macroeconomic management; World Trade Organization issues; and South Asia studies. Also runs training programmes and a public information programme to disseminate research findings in order to enhance general awareness of the issues involved.

Geographical Area of Activity: India.

Publications: Newsletter (2 a year); *India and Economic Cooperation in South Asia*; working papers; monographs.

Finance: Assets 128,885,058 Indian rupees (March 2000); annual revenue 20,044,677 rupees, expenditure 17,102,552 rupees (2000).

Board of Governors: I. G. Patel (Chair.); S. Acharya; M. Dubey; L. Gupte; J. Kathpalia; D. Khatkhate; U. S. Kotak; K. B. Lall; L. Mansingh; R. A. Mashelkar; N. R. N. Murthy; D. Nayyar; K. Parikh; S. A. Piramal; N. Ravi; N. K. Singh; T. N. Srinivasan; A. N. Varma.

Principal Staff: Chief Exec. Dr Arvind Virmani.

Address: Core 6-A, 4th Floor, Indian Habitat Centre, Lodi Rd, New Delhi 110 003.

Telephone: (11) 24645218; **Fax:** (11) 24620180; **Internet:** www.icrier.res.in; **e-mail:** info@icrier.res.in.

Indian Council of Social Science Research—ICSSR

Founded in 1969 by the Indian Government as an autonomous organization, to promote and co-ordinate research in social sciences.

Activities: The ICSSR funds research projects in social sciences proposed by scholars, and sponsors projects on its own initiative (e.g. research on the North-Eastern region of India, women's studies and entrepreneurship). It conducts surveys of research in the social sciences and publishes them periodically; awards research fellowships, contingency grants and grants for study and publications; gives financial support for conferences and seminars, and organizes or supports training courses in research methodology. It provides guidance and consultancy services in data-processing, and has a documentation centre which provides information support to social scientists. It collaborates in research and exchange programmes with a number of countries, and evaluates research proposals submitted by foreign nationals intending to undertake research in India. It part-finances 27 other research institutes throughout the country.

Geographical Area of Activity: India.

Publications: *ICSSR Journal of Abstracts and Reviews: Economics* (2 a year); *ICSSR Journal of Abstracts and Reviews: Geography* (2 a year); *ICSSR Journal of Abstracts and Reviews: Political Science* (2 a year); *ICSSR Newsletter* (quarterly); *ICSSR Research Abstracts Quarterly; Indian Psychological Abstracts and Reviews*(2 a year); *Indian Social Science Review;* NASSDOC research information series, ICSSR surveys of research; and various other publications.

Principal Staff: Chair. Dr V. R. Panchamukhi.

Address: Aruna Asaf Ali Marg, Jawahar Lal Nehru University Area, New Delhi 110 067.

Telephone: (11) 26179838; **Fax:** (11) 26179850; **Internet:** www.icssr.org; **e-mail:** info@icssr.org.

Indian Institute of Ecology and Environment

Activities: Operates in the fields of sustainable development, environmental protection, disaster mitigation, energy and resource management, the study of meteorological phenomena, population control and other environment and ecology related issues, through research, training, consultancy, and producing a number of publications on its findings. Particularly focuses on preparation for emergency disaster relief.

Geographical Area of Activity: India.

Publications: *International Encyclopaedia of Ecology and Environment; Encyclopaedia of International Environmental Laws; Concise Encyclopaedia of Indian Environment; Global Environmental Education: Visions of 2001; World Ecology and Environment Directory;* and other publications.

Address: A-15, Paryavaran Complex, Saket–IGNOU Rd, New Delhi 110 030.

Telephone: (11) 26865084; **Fax:** (11) 26967514; **Internet:** www.ecology.edu; **e-mail:** info@ecology.edu.

Indian National Trust for Art and Cultural Heritage—INTACH

Established in 1984 for the conservation of the Indian natural and man-made environment.

Activities: The Foundation supports the preservation of the cultural and natural heritage of India, including places of archaeological, historical, artistic and scientific value. It also promotes public awareness of cultural issues and preservation of Indian heritage and acts as a pressure group when necessary. Works through three divisions: Material Heritage; Architectural Heritage; and Natural Heritage. There are 140 Chapters in various states and territories of India. The INTACH (UK) Trust offers scholarships and funding for United Kingdom nationals to carry out research on India, and exchanges for young architects and planners in association with the Charles Wallace India Trust and the British Council (qq.v.).

Geographical Area of Activity: India and United Kingdom.

Publications: *Virasat* (quarterly newsletter).

Principal Staff: Chair. Capt. Amarinder Singh; Vice-Chair. S. K. Misra; Sec. Dr C. T. Misra.

Address: 71 Lodi Estate, New Delhi 1100 003.

Telephone: (11) 24631818; **Fax:** (11) 24611290; **Internet:** www.intach.net; **e-mail:** intach@del3.vsnl.net.in.

Inlaks Foundation

Founded in 1976 by Indoo Shivdasani to give education and medical assistance, mainly in India.

Activities: The Foundation's main activity is to award scholarships in any subject to exceptionally talented young Indians for study or research at any reputed university or institution, including the universitites of Oxford, Cambridge and London (United Kingdom), Harvard and Columbia (USA), and universities in Europe and elsewhere. It also assists young Indians through Take-Off Grants in India, which aim to develop individual talent, and offers Inlaks Fine Arts Awards to help artists under 35 years of age in India to develop their talent. Also funds and operates social and health projects. Maintains an office in London.

Geographical Area of Activity: International.

Restrictions: Candidates for scholarships abroad must have been accepted for a course before applying for a scholarship, and must be under 30 years of age.

Publications: Annual Report.

Board of Trustees: Lakshmi Shivdasani (Chair.); Ranjit Bhatia; Prof. Vir Chauhan; Dr Colin Lucas; Baron Andre di Pfyffer d'Altishofen; Dr Karlheinz Ritter; Narottan Sahgal; Countess Bina Sella di Monteluce; Count Nicolo Sella di Monteluce; Azad Shivdasani; Sonu Shivdasani.

Principal Staff: Sec. Tripti Dayal.

Address: St Stephen's College, University of Delhi, Delhi 110 007.

Telephone: (11) 27256539; **Internet:** www.inlaksfoundation .org; **e-mail:** inlaks@del2.vsnl.net.in.

International Foundation for Human Development—IFHD

Founded in 1993 to improve quality of life through development.

Activities: Promotes self-help, self-employment and long-term development programmes in collaboration with other national and international organizations. Works to improve education systems, and offers a number of scholarships and grants for students; promotes volunteerism and social justice; runs a documentation centre and library with reference to development studies and voluntary service. Runs conferences and workshops. Co-operates with NGOs in Asia and the Pacific, Africa and the Middle East.

Geographical Area of Activity: Asia, Africa and the Middle East.

Publications: *Asia Pacific Link*; Annual Report.

Address: Balaji Residency 106, 12-13–705/10/A&B, Gokul-nagar, Tarnaka, Hyderabad 500 017.

Fax: (40) 27154118; **Internet:** www.ifhd.org; **e-mail:** ifhd@ hd1.vsnl.net.in.

National Foundation for India

Activities: Established with the aid of the Ford Foundation, USA (q.v.). Operates in the fields of development studies, capacity building, and law and human rights in areas of North-East India. Main programme areas are Gender Equity and Justice, Public Affairs and Urban Governance, Regional Inbalances–Initiatives in the North East, and Development Communications. Awards media fellowships and makes grants in recognition of innovation in the field of social development.

Geographical Area of Activity: India.

Restrictions: No grants to groups and organizations affiliated to political or religious organizations.

Publications: *Status of the Girl Child in India; Accounta-blility and Decentralization in Urban Governance; Women's Empowerment: Role of Women's Universities and Women's Studies Centre; Assignment—Giving Voices to the Unheard*; and booklets.

Address: India Habitat Centre, Zone IV-A, Upper Ground Floor, Lodhi Rd, New Delhi 110 003.

Telephone: (11) 24648491; **Fax:** (11) 24641867; **Internet:** http://nfidel.tripod.com; **e-mail:** root@nfi.ren.nic.in.

National Institute for Sustainable Development

Founded in 1992 by Prakash Palande in order to improve conditions in villages in the Ahmednagar and Pune districts, India.

Activities: Works to improve the quality of life of mothers and children in under-developed areas of India, through community development, education and health care, working mainly for the upliftment of Bidi rollers and their children residing in the Ahmednagar district of India. Provides health-care services, awareness development, creche facilities, income generation, education and sponsorship programmes. In the Pune district, the Institute works to assist people affected by dam construction, through running programmes in land levelling, income generation, land development, health, hygiene and sanitation.

Geographical Area of Activity: Pune and Ahmednagar districts of Maharashtra State, India.

Restrictions: Does not make grants.

Finance: Supported by government and national and international funding organizations. Annual budget 3,000,000 Indian rupees.

Trustees: Prakash Palande (Pres.); Rajendra Kadam (Treas.), Dr Chandrashekhar Divekar (Sec.); K. K. Acharya; P. V. Adik; Dr Kihor Badhe; Gauri Gokhale.

Principal Staff: Admin. Officer Smirta Pawaz; Project Man. Yashwant Palghadmal.

Address: 'Sunder', HN 560, Survey No. 21/1, Sainikwadi, Wadgaonsheri, Pune 411 014.

Telephone: (20) 27033020; **Fax:** (20) 27031485; **e-mail:** nisd@pn2,vsnl,net,in.

Azim Premji Foundation

Established by Azim Premji, Chairman of the Wipro Corporation; aims to transform the lives of children in India through acting as a catalyst to universalize elementary education.

Activities: Aims to develop elementary education for all children in India, through funding training, development of the education system and innovative utilization of technology, creating models to promote oriented learning, building capacity through local planning processes, and effectively using research, academic, advocacy and communication tools to augment these efforts.

Geographical Area of Activity: India.

Board of Trustees: Chandra Sharad Behar; Nachiket Mor; Azim Premji; Yasmeen Premji; P. M. Singh; N. Vaghul.

Principal Staff: Chief Exec. Dilip Ranjekar; Dir Premji Yasmeen.

Address: 5 Papanna St, St Mark's Rd Cross, Bangalore 650 001.

Telephone: (80) 2272264; **Fax:** (80) 2291869; **Internet:** www.azimpremjifoundation.org; **e-mail:** info@ azimpremjifoundation.co.in.

C. P. Ramaswami Aiyar Foundation

Established in 1966 in remembrance of the work of statesman and educationalist Dr C. P. Ramaswami Aiyar.

Activities: Funds a number of projects and institutions to further Indian community development, including the C. P. Ramaswami Aiyar Institute of Indological Research, which carries out research, and holds seminars, courses and lectures on subjects relating to Indian culture and society; the C. P. Art Centre, an exhibition centre, which displays the work of Indian artists and holds workshops and demonstrations; and the Saraswathi Kendra Centre for Children, which provides aid for children suffering from behavioural and learning difficulties. Works in association with the Indian Government through the C. P. R. Environmental Education Centre, established in 1989 to promote environmental awareness, produce and disseminate basic educational and reference material on environment and to support environmental education projects.

Geographical Area of Activity: India.

Address: The Grove, 1 Eldams Rd, Chennai 600 018.

Telephone: (44) 24341778; **Fax:** (44) 24353176.

Ryan Foundation International

Founded in 1982 to promote the use of appropriate technologies in rural areas, and to provide safe water for those without it, through the use of renewable energy and minimal investment.

Activities: Organizes training programmes for government organizations and NGOs from all over the world, and income generating programmes for women in rural areas; disseminates information; conducts research; promotes community development organizations and co-operatives. The Foundation's main area of interest is a sea water distillation programme which uses solar energy and reflectors. It also conducts research into plants which grow well in sea water and looks at ways of exploiting their potential.

Geographical Area of Activity: International.

Publications: *Better Life Technologies for the Poor* (3 vols); *RYFO Handout; RYFO Income Generation Series; Drought Trees for Dry Villages; Water Management in Homes and Villages; How to Convert Sea Water into Drinking Water; Survival by Sea Water.*

Finance: Funded by founders' endowment, publication sales, membership fees, consultation fees and donations. Annual revenue 500,000 Indian rupees.

Principal Staff: Pres. Dr Felix Ryan; Exec. Dir Col J. Francis.

Address: 15 West Mada St, Srinagar Colony, Saidapet, Chennai 600 015.

Telephone: (44) 22351993; **Fax:** (44) 24910746; **e-mail:** felixryan@bify.com.

M. S. Swaminathan Research Foundation (Centre for Research on Sustainable Agricultural and Rural Development)

Founded in May 1988 by Dr M. S. Swaminathan, Prof. V. L. Chopra, Dr V. K. Ramachandran and Mina Swaminathan to support research and training in the application of modern science and technology, and to apply contemporary development experience to the problems of ecologically sustainable agricultural production and the distribution and consumption of agricultural commodities; to ensure a reasonable standard of living; and to secure the livelihood of poor people in rural areas.

Activities: Operates in the fields of rural development and science and technology through research, conferences, publications and training courses. The Foundation collaborates with individuals and other institutions to realize its aims and objectives. Programmes include the Every Child a Scientist project, Coastal Systems Research, Information Village Research Project, Farmers' Rights Information Service, and Eco-Technology and Eco-Jobs. Also operates four field centres across India.

Geographical Area of Activity: India.

Restrictions: Not a grant-making organization.

Publications: Annual Report; numerous books.

Finance: Net assets 296,436,759 Indian rupees (1999–2000); annual revenue 23,764,753 rupees, expenditure 12,411,508 (1999–2000).

Trustees: Dr M. S. Swaminathan (Chair.); Dr K. N. S. Nair (Vice-Chair.); Prof. V. L. Chopra; Anuradha Desai; Dr K. Kanungo; R. M. Lala; Dr V. K. Ramachandran; Mina Swaminathan; Dr Soumya Swaminathan; Dr Usha Barwale Zehr.

Address: 3rd Cross St, Taramani Institutional Area, Chennai 600 113.

Telephone: (44) 2541229; **Fax:** (44) 2541319; **Internet:** www.mssrf.org; **e-mail:** msswami@vsnl.net.

Lady Tata Memorial Trust

Founded in 1932 by Sir Dorabji Jamsetji Tata for the purpose of encouraging and advancing original research in medicine in its scientific aspect, in relation to the diseases of the blood, especially leukaemia, and related diseases.

Activities: Operates in the field of science and medicine: four-fifths of the Trust's annual income is allocated to international awards for study and research into leukaemia, with special reference to leukaemogenic viruses, the epidemiology, pathogenesis and immunology of leukaemia. One-fifth is allocated to Indian nationals working in India for scientific investigation into the alleviation of human suffering from the disease. International awards are made on the recommendation of a Scientific Advisory Committee, based in London.

Geographical Area of Activity: International.

Principal Staff: Sec. and Chief Accountant S. N. Batliwalla.

Address: Bombay House, 24 Homi Mody St, Fort, Mumbai 400 001.

Telephone: (22) 256657465; **Fax:** (22) 222826092; **Internet:** www.tata.co.in; **e-mail:** snbatliwalla@tata.com.

Sir Dorabji Tata Trust

Founded in 1932 by Sir Dorabji Jamsetji Tata for the relief of distress, the advancement of learning, especially research work in connection with medical and industrial problems; provision of scholarships in any branch of science or the arts; and to give aid to charitable institutions.

Activities: Operates nationally in the fields of social welfare and studies, science, medicine, and the arts and humanities. Projects are carried out through self-conducted programmes, research, grants to national institutions, grants to individuals, fellowships and scholarships. The Trust has established pioneering institutions in India, including the Tata Institute of Social Sciences (1936), the Tata Memorial Hospital (for cancer) (1941), the Tata Institute of Fundamental Research (1945, now known as the National Centre for Nuclear Science and Mathematics) and the National Centre for the Performing Arts (1966). In association with the United Nations, the Trust started the first Demographic Research Institute in 1956 (now the International Institute for Population Studies, Mumbai). The Foundation established the National Institute for Advanced Studies, Bangalore in 1988, the J. R. D. Tata Centre for Ecotechnology, Chennai in 1998 and the Sir Dorabji Tata Centre for Research in Tropical Diseases, Bangalore in 2000.

Geographical Area of Activity: India.

Restrictions: Although in the past it has responded to requests from abroad, the Trust's present policy (owing to exchange restrictions) is to limit its funding to projects within India.

Principal Staff: Dir R. M. Lala; Sec. and Chief Accountant S. N. Batliwalla.

Address: Bombay House, 24 Homi Mody St, Fort, Mumbai 400 001.

Telephone: (22) 2049131; **Fax:** (22) 2826092; **Internet:** www.tata.co.in; **e-mail:** snbatliwalla@tata.com.

Vanarai

Founded in 1986 by Mohan Dharia to promote use of natural resources and sustainable development throughout India.

Activities: The Trust implements sustainable development initiatives in villages in co-operation with villagers, schools, co-operatives, community leaders, etc. Villages taking part in Vanarai projects must adhere to certain conditions. Promotes the greening of rural and urban areas through tree-planting schemes run in co-operation with other organizations. Programmes include: training for farmers in integrated rural development, watershed management, new agricultural techniques, improved seeds, cattle breeding, nurseries, harvesting technologies, etc.; wasteland development, including lobbying local and central governments; empowerment of women and young people; sanitation and energy; and the Latur Project, which promotes integrated rural development in 21 villages in the Latur district, this project is implemented in conjunction with local and central governments and partially funded by the Sir Dorabji Tata Trust (q.v.).

Publications: *Vanarai* (magazine, monthly, in Marathi); booklets; videos; slides.

Trustees: Mohan Dharia (Pres.); Dr Vijay Bhatkar; Dr Ram Takwale; Girish Gandhi; Ravindra Dharia.

Principal Staff: Sec. Jimmy Rajadhyaksha; Project Co-ordinator Jaywant Deshmukh.

Address: 498 Aditya Residency, Parvati Mitra, Pune 411 009.

Telephone: (20) 24449351; **Fax:** (20) 24445299; **e-mail:** vanarai@ip.eth.net.

M. Venkatarangaiya Foundation

Established in 1981 in memory of Prof. Mamidipudi Venkatarangaiya; aims to empower women and abolish child labour.

Activities: The Foundation aims to abolish child labour through campaigning for a universal education system in India, enrolling children at school and providing support, and running summer camps and extra courses. Also works to empower women through action on issues such as livelihood and natural resource management. Maintains an office in the USA.

Geographical Area of Activity: India.

Finance: Man. Trustee M. Anandam.

Address: 28 Marredpalli West, 151 Country Club Dr., 4 Secunderabad, AP 500 026.

Telephone: (40) 27801320; **Fax:** (40) 27808808; **Internet:** www.mvfindia.org; **e-mail:** info@mvfindia.org.

World Teacher Trust

Founded in 1971 by Dr Ekkirala E. Krishnamacharya to promote health and hygiene; to establish and maintain hospitals and clinics; to distribute free medicines to the public; to promote homeopathic medicine; to establish and maintain educational institutions; and to organize seminars and conferences.

Activities: The Foundation promotes family life, human rights, social harmony, education, and health and welfare, and has members in Belgium, Denmark, Germany, Nigeria, Poland and Spain.

Geographical Area of Activity: Europe, and North and South America.

Restrictions: Does not support financial schemes, only those related to human values.

Publications: *My Light* (newsletter); Numerous books, articles, leaflets and pamphlets.

Trustees: Dr K. Parvatti (Hon. Chair.).

Principal Staff: Hon. Sec. B. Ramakrishna Raju.

Address: 14-38-2 Radhamadhavam, Muppidi Colony, Visakhapatham 530 002.

Telephone: (891) 2701531; **Fax:** (891) 2755834.

Indonesia

FOUNDATION CENTRE AND CO-ORDINATING BODY

International NGO Forum on Indonesian Development—INFID

Established in June 1985. Aims to give a voice to the concerns of the people represented by NGOs involved in Indonesia and to facilitate communication between NGOs inside and outside Indonesia.

Activities: Network of more than 100 NGOs from Indonesia, member countries of the Consultative Group for Indonesia and international organizations with a commitment to Indonesia. Works to alleviate poverty in Indonesia by addressing its root causes. Acts as an advocate for the creation and implementation of new policies relating to development aid, investment and trade to ensure that they are in the interests of the underprivileged and are based on principles of peace and justice. Also creates an environment in which democracy can develop and be strengthened, particularly placing an emphasis on human rights. Member organizations assemble twice a year, and the INFID Conference is held every two years. Maintains liaison offices in Belgium and Japan.

Geographical Area of Activity: Indonesia.

Publications: Publishes books, leaflets, booklets, fact sheets, etc. on issues related to INFID advocacy priorities.

Board Members: P. Armstrong; Z. A. Baso; R. Baswir; N. Choeldahono; M. Fidar; A. Flor; J. Isbister; A. Karyadi; S. Moniaga; A. Onorati; Y. Sakai; F. Santa Anna; F. Seymour; Z. K. Soesilo; D. Trisasongko.

Principal Staff: Exec. Sec. Binny Buchori.

Address: Jl. Mampang Prapatan XI No. 23, Jakarta 12790.

Telephone: (21) 7919 6721; **Fax:** (21) 7941 577; **Internet:** www.infid.be; **e-mail:** infid@nusa.or.id.

FOUNDATIONS, TRUSTS AND NON-PROFIT ORGANIZATIONS

Wahana Lingkungan Hidup Indonesia—WALHI/Friends of the Earth Indonesia (Indonesian Forum for the Environment)

Established in 1982 by a number of individuals to pursue justice, social equity, control of people over resources management, and fair governance.

Activities: Operates in Indonesia in the areas of conservation of natural resources, and civil and human rights, through advocacy, community empowerment, assisting community development and self-organization, and networking.

Geographical Area of Activity: Indonesia.

Restrictions: Grants made only to member organizations.

Publications: *Tanah Air* (magazine, every 3 months); *Simpul Jaringan* (magazine, monthly).

Finance: Net assets US $11,100; annual revenue US $759,455, expenditure US $674,940 (2001).

Trustees: Johnson Sotarduga Panjaitan (Chair.); Andreas Subiyono (Vice-Chair.); Wiwiek Awiati Trisnohandoko (Sec.); Alurcholis (Vice-Sec.); Aristan; Nico Andasputra; Effendi Panjaitan.

Principal Staff: Chair. Longgema Ginting.

Address: Jalan Tegal Parang Utara No. 14, Jakarta 12790.

Telephone: (21) 794 1672; **Fax:** (21) 794 1673; **Internet:** www.walhi.or.ik; **e-mail:** walhi@walhi.or.id.

Yayasan Dian Desa (Dian Desa Foundation)

Founded in 1972 to improve the welfare of rural communities by making use of effective and efficient technologies.

Activities: Aims to improve the welfare of rural communities in Indonesia, through acting as a catalyst, introducing new ideas, which are then implemented and popularized by village communities. Provides guidance, support and training to help people help themselves. Active in the fields of education and training, environmental conservation, public health and community development. Also supports the development of small businesses through the provision of micro-credit. Maintains branch offices in Kupang and Maumere.

Geographical Area of Activity: Indonesia.

Principal Staff: Exec. Dir Anton Soedjarwo.

Address: Jalan Kaliurang Km 7, POB 19, Yogyakarta.

Telephone: (27) 488 5247; **Fax:** (27) 488 5423; **e-mail:** anton@yoga.wasantara.net.id.

Yayasan Indonesia Sejahtera (Indonesian Prosperity Foundation)

Founded in 1974 to promote national self-reliance and sustainable development.

Activities: Operates through supporting development activities in Indonesia in the fields of education and training, institution building, community development and publications, and providing public information. Operates training courses, provides technical assistance to NGOs, carries out research and collaborates with other organizations. Also provides emergency and disaster relief.

Geographical Area of Activity: Indonesia.

Principal Staff: Exec. Dir Sunarti Teguh Santoso.

Address: JI. Tanjung No. 96, Solo 57145.

Telephone: (27) 172 3065; **Fax:** (27) 171 8506; **e-mail:** yissolo@indo.net.id.

Yayasan Indonesia untuk Kemajuan Desa—YASIKA (Indonesian Foundation for Rural Progress)

Founded in 1985 to reform socio-economic patterns of inequality to achieve a more equitable distribution of income and to develop initiatives in poor rural areas.

Activities: Operates in the areas of environmental conservation, community development and the development of small businesses, through grants and micro-credit loans. Also provides training and technical assistance to NGOs.

Geographical Area of Activity: Indonesia.

Principal Staff: Exec. Dir Surya Dharma.

Address: Jalan Airlangga No. 16 B, Medan 20112.

Telephone: (61) 453 5016; **Fax:** (21) 456 4794; **e-mail:** laras@indosat.net.id.

Yayasan Keanekaragaman Hayati Indonesia—KEHATI (Indonesia Biodiversity Foundation)

Founded in 1994 to promote biological diversity conservation and the sustainable use of natural resources, and to empower local communities.

Activities: Promotes biodiversity and the conservation of natural resources in local communities, through grants to projects in the fields of education and training, organizational development, environmental conservation, community development and research. Also runs training courses and workshops, publishes information for public use, lobbies government and provides technical assistance to NGOs. Also provides disaster relief.

Geographical Area of Activity: Indonesia.

Finance: Total endowment US $22,500,000.

Principal Staff: Exec. Dir Ismid Hadad.

Address: Patra Jasa Bld, 2nd Floor, Jalan Jend. Gatot Subroto Kav., 32–34, Jakarta 12950.

Telephone: (21) 522 8031; **Fax:** (21) 522 8033; **e-mail:** kehati@indo.net.id.

Iran

FOUNDATIONS, TRUSTS AND NON-PROFIT ORGANIZATIONS

Islamic Thought Foundation

Founded in 1984 to promote Islam internationally and to introduce Islamic teachings to all people of the world.

Activities: The Foundation operates in the fields of development studies, the arts and humanities, conservation, economic affairs, education, international affairs, human rights, medicine and health, science and technology, and social welfare.

Publications: *Echo of Islam; Mahjubah; Sauti ya Ummah; Message del'Islam; Al-Tahira-Ashra-Al-Wahda; Sakon Musulurci; ZamZam* (all monthly); and numerous books.

Principal Staff: Man. Dir Ali Akbar Ziaee.

Address: POB 14155-3899, Teheran.

Telephone: (21) 8744095; **Internet:** www.itf.org.ir; **e-mail:** itf@itf.org.ir.

Ireland

FOUNDATION CENTRE AND CO-ORDINATING BODY

DOCHAS—Irish Association of Non-Governmental Development Organizations

Established in 1993 as a co-ordinating body for NGOs in Ireland.

Activities: Promotes co-operation between development organizations in Ireland, to increase the efficiency and effectiveness of programmes carried out in less-developed countries. Disseminates information and research findings to its 24 members and promotes development education, as well as providing a forum for member agencies to meet together.

Geographical Area of Activity: Ireland.

Restrictions: Not a funding agency.

Publications: *DOCHAS Newletter* (monthly); Annual Report; and other publicatios.

Principal Staff: Dir Hans Zomer.

Address: 59 Deerpark Rd, Mount Merrion, Co. Dublin.

Telephone: (1) 2886141; **Fax:** (1) 2780571; **Internet:** www.dochas.ie; **e-mail:** anna@dochas.ie.

FOUNDATIONS, TRUSTS AND NON-PROFIT ORGANIZATIONS

Bóthar

Established in 1991 by a group of farmers, business people and community and church leaders under the chairmanship of the late T. J. Maher. Aims to help needy families to overcome hunger and malnutrition in a sustainable manner through the use of livestock in development aid.

Activities: Operates internationally in the field of aid to less-developed countries. Establishes livestock development projects for families in need, providing a sustainable solution to the problems of poverty and hunger. Each family receives a farm animal or animals, such as a dairy cow, a dairy goat, a flock of laying hens or three hives of bees, as well as the training and support necessary to establish a micro-farming enterprise. Nutrition is improved by the consumption of the resulting produce and income is generated by the sale of the surplus produce. Recipients pass on a gift of offspring similar to that which they receive to other families chosen by the community.

Geographical Area of Activity: Africa, Asia, Eastern Europe and the Middle East.

Finance: Funded by public subscription, grants from government agencies, NGOs and foundations.

Principal Staff: Gen. Sec. Peter Ireton; Global Projects Man. David Moloney, Dir, Donor Care Maureen Purcell.

Address: Old Clare St, Limerick.

Telephone: (61) 414142; **Fax:** (61) 315833; **Internet:** www.bothar.org; **e-mail:** bothar@eircom.net.

Concern Worldwide

Established in 1968; aims to eliminate poverty in developing countries.

Activities: Operates in the fields of development aid, emergency relief and advocacy and development education, working to alleviate the effects of severe poverty in the developing world, particularly in Africa and Asia. Projects involving volunteers include improving health care and sanitation, and providing clean water, food, shelter and education. Also works to eliminate poverty through advocacy, and funds development education on issues such as third-world debt, human rights, fair trade and refugees. Maintains offices in Belfast, Glasgow and London, and an affiliate organization in the USA.

Geographical Area of Activity: Africa, Asia, the Balkans, the Middle East, Central and South America and the Caribbean.

Publications: *Speak Out!* (newsletter, 3 a year); financial statement.

Finance: Total revenue €62,797,000, expenditure €58,262,000 (2001).

Principal Staff: Chief Exec. David Begg.

Address: 52–55 Lower Camden St, Dublin 2.

Telephone: (1) 4754162; **Fax:** (1) 4757362; **Internet:** www.concern.ie; **e-mail:** info@concern.ie.

European Foundation for the Improvement of Living and Working Conditions

Founded in 1975 by the Council of Ministers of the European Community (now the European Union—EU) to contribute to the formulation of policies which would improve living and working conditions in Member States.

Activities: Operates internationally (in the Member States of the EU) in the field of social welfare, by conducting research and publishing the results. The Foundation provides the EU with a scientific basis against which medium- and long-term policies for the improvement of social and work-related matters can be developed. In particular, the Foundation carries out research in the following areas: access to employment, work organization, health and safety at work, industrial relations, women and work, participation, social cohesion and integration, the role of public services, the elderly, and social aspects of the environment.

Geographical Area of Activity: Europe (Member States of the EU and candidate countries).

Restrictions: Does not make grants.

Publications: *Communiqué* (newsletter); research reports; information brochures and booklets; monographs.

Administrative Board: Comprises representatives of governments, trade unions and employers. There is also a Committee of Experts, composed of specialists from the Member States.

Principal Staff: Dir Raymond-Pierre Bodin.

Address: Wyattville Rd, Loughlinstown, Dublin 18.

Telephone: (1) 2043100; **Fax:** (1) 2826456; **Internet:** www.eurofound.eu.int; **e-mail:** postmaster@eurofound.eu.int.

GOAL

Founded in 1977 by Irish sports journalist John O'Shea and four of his friends, to relieve suffering in the developing world caused by war, disaster and catastrophe regardless of race, religion or nationality.

Activities: Operates in 19 countries of Africa, Asia, Central America and Eastern Europe, in the areas of aid to less-developed countries, nursery and primary education, medicine and health, and social welfare, through direct implementation of relief and development projects, and grants to missionary and indigenous organizations. Runs programmes that provide rehabilitation, emergency aid, housing, health care, clean water and education to those who need it, as well as a number of projects working with 'street' children around the world. It also runs training programmes for local people in less-developed countries, to help precipitate long-term improvements. Also maintains offices in the United Kingdom and the USA.

Geographical Area of Activity: Africa, Asia, Central America and Eastern Europe.

Publications: Newsletter.

Finance: Funded by a number of governments, United Nations agencies, NGOs and donations from the general public.

Trustees: Michael Spellman (Chair.); Jerry Sheehan (Sec.); Sean Dunne (Treas.); Conor Sparks; Brian McMahon.

Principal Staff: Chief Exec. John O'Shea; Asst Chief Exec. Michael Kiely.

Address: POB 19, Dunlaoghaire, Co. Dublin.

Telephone: (1) 2809779; **Fax:** (1) 2809215; **Internet:** www.goal.ie; **e-mail:** info@goal.ie.

Gorta—The Freedom from Hunger Council of Ireland

Established in 1965 by the Department of Agriculture; since 1979 the Department of Foreign Affairs has responsibility for the organization, which aims to eliminate world hunger, and to initiate and support long-term development programmes in less-developed countries world-wide.

Activities: Co-operates with local NGOs to support development projects in Africa, Asia and South America. Works to prevent famine through long-term projects encouraging self-sufficient community work that mitigates the effects of natural famine. Emphasizes the importance of local resources and trains local people so that they can manage their own projects. Raises funds through running charity shops throughout Ireland. Also hosts the annual World Food Day Conference.

Geographical Area of Activity: Africa, Asia and South America.

Address: 12 Herbert St, Dublin 2.

Telephone: (1) 6615522; **Fax:** (1) 6612627; **Internet:** www.gorta.ie; **e-mail:** admin@gorta.ie.

International Association for the Exchange of Students for Technical Experience—IAESTE

Founded in 1948 by James Newby to provide students at institutions of higher education with technical experience abroad relative to their studies in the broadest sense, and to promote international understanding and goodwill among the students of all nations.

Activities: Arranges the exchange of training places among its 82 member countries, mainly for students of engineering and technology, but also for students of agriculture, applied arts, commerce, languages and science, enabling them to spend between two and 18 months gaining experience abroad as trainees of industrial and other organizations.

Geographical Area of Activity: International.

Restrictions: Not a grant-making organization.

Publications: Annual Report; Activity Report.

Finance: Funded by member subscriptions.

Principal Staff: Gen. Sec. James Edward Reid.

Address: POB 6104, Swords, Co. Dublin.

Telephone: (1) 8402055; **Fax:** (1) 8402055; **Internet:** www.iaeste.org; **e-mail:** general.secretary@iaeste.org.

International Fund for Ireland

Founded in 1986 by the Governments of Ireland and the United Kingdom to promote dialogue and reconciliation between nationalists and unionists, and economic and social development.

Activities: Operates in Northern Ireland and the six border counties of the Republic of Ireland. Organizes programmes which promote economic development in towns and villages: the Community Regeneration and Improvement Special Programme (CRISP) for smaller, more rural areas; the Community Economic Regeneration Scheme (CERS) for larger urban areas; and the Border Towns and Villages Scheme, which operates in the Republic's border counties. Other programmes include: the Business Enterprise Programme, which promotes the development of local businesses through training schemes, marketing, business accommodation and revolving loan funds; the Rural Development Programme, which promotes the regeneration of disadvantaged rural areas; the Community Relations Programme, which supports projects and schemes to improve relations between communities in Northern Ireland and between Northern Ireland and the Republic; the Wider Horizons Programme, which promotes improved relations between communities in Northern Ireland through training and work experience schemes for young people abroad, and encouraging managers and young business people to take part in development programmes; the Key Programme, which works to develop the personal and entrepreneurial skills of young people while facilitating contact and dialogue; and the Interact Programme, which targets young people from disadvantaged areas and works to provide participants with an opportunity to improve their employability in an environment which promotes mutual understanding and reconciliation. Maintains an office in Belfast.

Geographical Area of Activity: Northern Ireland and the Republic of Ireland.

Finance: Total resources available to date approx. I£380,000,000.

Governing Board: W. T. McCarter (Chair.); M. E. Hanna; V. C. Haslett; H. Kirkpatrick; C. Lynch; E. Murtagh; L. Steele.

Principal Staff: Joint Dirs-Gen. Orla O'Hanrahan, Sandy Smith.

Address: POB 2000, Dublin 2.

Telephone: (1) 4780655; **Fax:** (1) 4751351; **Internet:** www.internationalfundforireland.com; **e-mail:** ciara .morgan@iveagh.irlgov.ie.

Ireland Funds

Ireland Funds support projects which advance the causes of peace, culture and charity in Northern and Southern Ireland.

Activities: Provides funding for projects working in the areas of peace and reconciliation, arts and culture, community development and education, and promoting relations between other countries of the world, and Ireland, both North and South. Funds raising money for the Ireland Funds operate in 11 countries: Australia, Canada, France, Germany, Ireland, Japan, Mexico, Monaco, New Zealand, the United Kingdom and the USA. Aims to raise US $100,000,000 by the end of December 2003.

Geographical Area of Activity: Ireland.

Restrictions: No grants to individuals; grants only to non-profit and charitable institutions; only projects within Northern and Southern Ireland are eligible for grants.

Publications: *Connections Magazine; FastFacts* (monthly magazine by fax).

Finance: Annual revenue approx. €16,900,000.

Principal Staff: Dir Kieran McLoughlin.

Address: 5 Foster Pl., Dublin 2.

Telephone: (1) 6627878; **Fax:** (1) 6627879; **Internet:** www.irlfunds.org; **e-mail:** info@irelandfunds.ie.

Irish Foundation for Co-operative Development

Founded by members of the board of Irish Co-operative

Organization Society Ltd to use the resources of the Irish agricultural co-operative movement to support the development of co-operatives in less-developed countries.

Activities: The Foundation operates in the field of aid to less-developed countries, through self-conducted programmes and grants to institutions.

Geographical Area of Activity: Mostly Africa.

Restrictions: The Foundation does not operate within the European Union (EU).

Finance: Financed by agricultural co-operatives in Ireland, the Irish Government and the EU.

Trustees: D. Boylan, James Brosnan; D. Cashman; Tom Corcoran; William Nagle; Michael O'Dwyer; John R. Tyrrell.

Principal Staff: Dir Martin Varley.

Address: 84 Merrion Sq., Dublin 2.

Telephone: (1) 6764783; **Fax:** (1) 6681784; **e-mail:** icos@iol.ie.

Irish Youth Foundation

Established in 1985 as an independent development trust to support projects and programmes making a positive difference in the lives of marginalized and socially excluded children and young people.

Activities: Operates in Ireland and the United Kingdom in the area of children and young people between the ages of five and 20, through research, grants to voluntary and community groups, and in partnership with statutory and state agencies. Supports projects tackling problems of poverty, unemployment, drugs, alcohol abuse, crime, violence and vandalism; AIDS preventative programmes which promote personal growth and development; and facilities and amenities for education and recreation. Promotes standards of excellence in service providers and in programmes, and seeks to identify, strengthen and expand existing programmes for Irish children and young people. There are Boards of Trustees in the UK and the USA, where the Foundation raises funds. Works in partnership with the International Youth Foundation (q.v.).

Geographical Area of Activity: Ireland and the United Kingdom.

Publications: Annual Report; various papers and studies on youth and children's sector issues.

Trustees (Ireland): Norma Smurfit (Pres.); Tony O'Reilly, Jr (Chair.); Ian Young (Fundraising); Tony Crooks (Research); Peter Murray (Devt); John Dunne; John F. Dunne; Evelyn Fitzpatrick; John F. Meagher; Rev. Paul Murphy; Tony Murphy; Nicola Harvey Neill; Redmond O'Donoghue.

Principal Staff: Exec. Dir Liam O'Dwyer.

Address: Glencullen House, Kylemore Rd, Ballyfermot, Dublin 10.

Telephone: (1) 6261090; **Fax:** (1) 6261072; **e-mail:** iryf@tinet.ie.

Refugee Trust

Founded in 1990 to assist refugees and displaced people.

Activities: Provides short- and long-term aid to refugees, including emergency relief for the improvement of living conditions; rehabilitation programmes, providing psychological treatment for those suffering the effects of trauma; and development and education projects. Works as an advocate for displaced people, lobbying for improved legislation throughout the world, and works to raise awareness of the world-wide refugee crisis.

Geographical Area of Activity: Africa and Central and South-Eastern Europe.

Principal Staff: Exec. Dir E. Norman Fitzgerald.

Address: 4, Dublin Rd, Stillorgan, Co. Dublin.

Telephone: (1) 2836678; **Fax:** (1) 2835155; **e-mail:** refugee-trust@club1.ie.

Royal Irish Academy

Founded in 1785 for the promotion of study in the sciences, humanities and social sciences.

Activities: Operates in the fields of the humanities, pure sciences and social sciences, through research programmes, a library, publications, conferences and a limited number of grants, mostly for exchange schemes with 'sister' bodies in Europe. The Academy is actively involved in the development of many academic and scientific disciplines in Ireland and provides international academic links including membership of the International Council of Scientific Unions and the European Science Foundation (q.v.).

Geographical Area of Activity: Ireland.

Publications: *Proceedings* (Mathematical and physical sciences; Biology and environmental sciences; Archaeology, Celtic studies, history, linguistics and literature); *Ériu* (annually: Irish philology and literature); *Irish Journal of Earth Sciences* (2 a year); *Irish Studies in International Affairs* (annually); conference proceedings (including *Biology Seminar Series* and *Microbiology Seminar Series*); books on Irish history, folklore and arts.

Finance: Awards range from €1,000 to €60,000.

Trustees: Dr M. E. F. Ryan (Pres.); Prof. M. J. Smith (Treas.); Prof. M. E. Daly (Sec.).

Principal Staff: Exec. Sec. Patrick Buckley.

Address: Academy House, 19 Dawson St, Dublin 2.

Telephone: (1) 6762570; **Fax:** (1) 6762346; **Internet:** www.ria.ie; **e-mail:** admin@ria.ie.

Self Help Development International

Founded in 1984, following the famine in Ethiopia, to provide long-term development assistance to less-developed countries in Africa.

Activities: Operates in the field of aid to less-developed countries, specifically in Africa (in Eritrea, Ethiopia, Kenya, Malawi and Uganda). Its programmes promote self-sufficiency, and the organization works to provide a long-term solution to poverty and its effects. Maintains field offices in Africa and projects are managed by local people. Works on programmes relating to agriculture and rural development, education and literacy, gender issues, food and famine prevention, emergency relief and refugees, and ecology and the environment.

Geographical Area of Activity: Africa.

Publications: Newsletter.

Principal Staff: Chief Exec. Michael Lambert.

Address: Main St, Hacketstown, Co. Carlow.

Telephone: (508) 71175; **Fax:** (508) 71292; **Internet:** www.selfhelpintl.ie; **e-mail:** info@selfhelpintl.ie.

Trócaire—Catholic Agency for World Development

Established in 1973 by the Catholic Bishops of Ireland to provide funding to developing countries in need, and to raise awareness in Ireland of development issues.

Activities: Operates internationally to relieve the suffering of people in need around the world, including those suffering the effects of poverty, conflict and oppression, through projects, grants, publications and conferences. Actively supports programmes in a number of areas including food security, education, health, human rights, community development of agriculture and microfinance. Funds emergency relief in man-made and natural disaster areas, engaging in food assistance, construction of new homes and providing emergency water, clothing and medical supplies. Also works to raise awareness within Ireland of development issues and problems suffered by people in other parts of the world.

Geographical Area of Activity: Africa, Asia, Central and South America and the Caribbean, the Balkans area and the Middle East.

Restrictions: No grants to individuals.

Publications: *Trócaire Development Review; Trócaire World; Campaigns Update*.

Finance: Assets I£8,479,287 (2000); annual revenue I£33,092,006, expenditure I£33,878,459 (2001).

Trustees: Archbishop Sean Brady (Chair.); Archbishop Dermot Clifford; Cardinal Desmond Connell; Bishop John Kirby; Bishop Donal Murray; Archbishop Michael Neary; Bishop Patrick Walsh.

Principal Staff: Dir Justin Kilcullen; Deputy Dir and Head of Communications and Education Eamonn Meehan.

Address: St Patrick's College, Maynooth, Co. Kildaire.

Telephone: (1) 2885385; **Fax:** (1) 2883577; **Internet:** www.trocaire.org; **e-mail:** info@trocaire.ie.

Women's Aid

Founded in 1974, Women's Aid is a feminist, service-based political and campaigning voluntary organization that aims to eliminate violence against women through effecting political, cultural and social change.

Activities: Provides information and support for women experiencing violence, including a national telephone helpline and support groups, and trains those who respond to women in cases of domestic violence. Operates development programmes at women's refuges in Dublin.

Geographical Area of Activity: Ireland.

Publications: *Making the Links* (1995); *Safety and Sanctions* (1999).

Finance: Funded by the Eastern Regional Health Authority. Assets I£11,958 (1999).

Trustees: M. Kelly (Chair.); N. Reilly (Vice-Chair.); R. McGuckian (Sec.); D. Charlton; E. N. Chleirigh; S. Duggan; M. Dunlop; M. Harris; J. Kennedy; M. Martin; T. O'Donnell; U. Regan.

Principal Staff: Dir Denise Charlton.

Address: Everton House, 47 Old Cabra Rd, Dublin 7.

Telephone: (1) 8684721; **Fax:** (1) 8684722; **Internet:** www.womensaid.ie; **e-mail:** info@womensaid.ie.

World Mercy Fund

Established in 1969 by Fr Thomas Rooney to fund health-care projects in Africa; has now expanded its operations internationally.

Activities: Works internationally to improve health-care facilities and support community development in less-developed countries, establishing clinics and hospitals and providing clean water and basic education. Provides funding to small community development projects. Branches of the Fund exist in Austria, Germany, Italy, Switzerland and the USA.

Geographical Area of Activity: International.

Publications: Regional reports.

Finance: Total income €8,036,000, expenditure €7,092,000 (June 2001).

Directors: Rev. Patrick Leonard (Pres.); Anthony Walsh (Vice-Pres.); M. Doyle; J. Kerry Keane; V. Keaveney; J. Keoghan; J. Lenehan; S. Purcell.

Principal Staff: Exec. Dir Joan Byrne.

Address: TRC House, Dundrum Rd, Dublin 14.

Telephone: (1) 2961360; **Fax:** (1) 2961368; **Internet:** www.worldmercyfund.ie; **e-mail:** info@worldmercyfund.ie.

Israel

FOUNDATIONS, TRUSTS AND NON-PROFIT ORGANIZATIONS

Lady Davis Fellowship Trust

Founded in 1973 in the name of the late Lady Davis of Montréal, Canada, to make the cultural heritage of ancient and modern Israel, and its achievements in development, state-building, scholarship, science and education, widely available and known to people from both technologically advanced and evolving societies; and to advance the interests of international scholarship and of higher education in Israel.

Activities: Operates through providing fellowships to visiting professors, post-doctoral researchers and doctoral students at the Hebrew University of Jerusalem and at the Technion—Israel Institute of Technology in Haifa. Since its establishment the Trust has supported more than 1,400 scholars, who have spent between three months and one year at these institutions. The fellowship programme is open to scholars of any age, from any region and in any field of study.

Geographical Area of Activity: International.

Publications: Report of operations.

Administrative Board: Chaired alternately by the President of the Hebrew University and the President of the Technion—Israel Institute of Technology, Haifa.

Principal Staff: Sec.-Gen. Harvey Lithwick; Exec. Sec. M. Mark Sopher.

Address: Hebrew University, Givat Ram, Jerusalem 91904.

Telephone: (2) 6512306; **Fax:** (2) 5663848; **Internet:** http://ldft.huji.ac.it; **e-mail:** ldft@vms.huji.ac.il.

Joseph S. and Caroline Gruss Life Monument Fund

Founded in 1968 by Joseph S. Gruss to assist ex-servicemen and -women upon completion of service in the Israeli defence force to integrate into civilian society.

Activities: Provides scholarships to ex-servicemen and -women from the Israeli defence force, as well as providing assistance to projects that further the personal development of ex-servicemen and -women in the fields of education and employment.

Geographical Area of Activity: Israel.

Finance: Receives interest from the Life Monument Fund.

Board of Trustees: Dr Y. Brick; Justice Dalia Dorner; Justice Eliyau Mazza; Prof. S. Shipiro; Justice Yaakuu Turkes.

Principal Staff: Exec. Dir Naomi Freund.

Address: 8 Hatzfirah St., POB 8052, Jerusalem 93102.

Telephone: (2) 5617176; **Fax:** (2) 5660549; **Internet:** www.gruss.org.il; **e-mail:** gruss@gruss.org.il.

Israel Institute of Applied Social Research

Founded in 1948 by Prof. Louis Guttman and others to plan and carry out research projects in the fields of social psychology, sociology, psychology and related disciplines; to supply government offices and other public and private institutions with research material and advice in the above areas in an attempt to direct and improve their operations; to co-operate with organizations in Israel and abroad which are engaged in these fields and in related fields; to raise the level of research in Israel in these areas and to maintain its professional standards.

Activities: The Institute carries out research projects initiated by its own staff and conducts research commissioned by government departments, public and academic institutions in Israel and abroad, and by private commercial and industrial organizations in a wide variety of theoretical and applied fields of social science. Projects include methodological and theoretical research; a continuing survey of social problem indicators; research on political attitudes, conflict resolution, demographic problems, the mass media, cultural activities, immigration and emigration, health and the quality of life; and market research. The Institute puts the use of its technical equipment and facilities at the disposal of other research organizations and provides advisory technical services.

Geographical Area of Activity: Israel.

Publications: Annual research report; occasional brochures in English, books, research papers and reports.

Address: Jerusalem.

Van Leer Jerusalem Institute

Founded in 1956 by the late Polly van Leer to serve as a centre for the study of issues related to society, culture and education, giving expression to the plurality of opinions in Israel.

Activities: Main areas of interest are research and practical work in education, social policy and Jewish–Arab coexistence; all projects are intended to generate lessons and implications of universal value, in addition to their impact on Israeli society. Through lectures, conferences and workshops (many at an international level), discussions are initiated on major social and cultural topics. The Institute also organizes active learning programmes in schools, various community-based activities and the production of videos.

Geographical Area of Activity: Israel.

Restrictions: The Institute does not make grants.

Publications: Books and journals.

Board of Trustees: Sir Zelman Cowen (Hon. Chair.); Ivar Samrén (Chair.); Dr Michael Anghel; Dr Rien van Gendt; Gideon Lahav; Dr Harry Leliveld; Prof. Gabriela Shalev; Dr Shimshon Shoshani.

Principal Staff: Dir Dr Shimshon Zelniker.

Address: POB 4070, Jerusalem 91040.

Telephone: (2) 5605222; **Fax:** (2) 5619293; **Internet:** www.vanleer.org.il; **e-mail:** vanleer@vanleer.org.il.

PEF Endowment Funds

Established in 1922 by Judge Louis D. Brandeis.

Activities: The Fund operates through making grants to organizations working in the fields of health and social services, immigrant absorption and public advocacy, as well as to religious organizations and educational and scientific institutions. Also operates a fundraising office in the USA.

Geographical Area of Activity: Mainly Israel.

Finance: Total assets US $75,832,720 (1998).

Principal Staff: Pres. Ben Frankel; Gen. Man. Judith Rubin.

Address: 1 Shimoni St, Jerusalem 92623.

Telephone: (2) 5631193.

Peres Center for Peace

Established in 1996 by Shimon Peres, to help make peace a

lasting reality in the Middle East; to advance Arab–Israeli co-operation through supporting projects in peace economics, education and social development; to advance peace throughout the Middle East through co-operation and presenting workable models of coexistence that increase mutual awareness and understanding; and to initiate academic research and teaching activities in the fields of diplomacy, negotiation and regional development.

Activities: Operates in the fields of international co-operation, through initiating and supporting projects in the areas of economics, agriculture, peace education and information technology. Maintains the Peres Institute for Diplomacy and Regional Co-operation and the Shimon Peres Archive.

Geographical Area of Activity: Middle East.

Publications: *Peace in Progress* (newsletter).

Governors: An international Board of Governors consists of senior statesmen, business leaders, architects of global public opinion and others. There is also an Advisory Board of experts and professionals.

Principal Staff: Pres. Uri Savir; Dir Gen. Dr Ron Pundak.

Address: 2 Ha'Shalom Rd, 4th Floor, Tel-Aviv 67892.

Telephone: (3) 5680680; **Fax:** (3) 5627265; **Internet:** www.peres-center.org; **e-mail:** info@peres-center.org.

Arthur Rubinstein International Music Society

Founded by Jan Jacob Bistritzky in 1980 in tribute to the artistry of Arthur Rubinstein (1887–1982) and to maintain his spiritual and artistic heritage in the art of the piano.

Activities: Organizes and finances the Arthur Rubinstein International Piano Master Competition (next competition scheduled for 2005); awards scholarships; runs music courses and master classes; organizes 'Hommage à Rubinstein' world-wide concert series, seminars, lectures, exhibitions, film shows and memorial festivals; and issues publications and recordings.

Geographical Area of Activity: International.

Principal Staff: Founder/Dir Jan Jacob Bistritzky.

Address: 12 Huberman St, Tel-Aviv 64075.

Telephone: (3) 6856684; **Fax:** (3) 6854924; **Internet:** www.arims.org.il; **e-mail:** competition@arims.org.il.

Henrietta Szold Institute—National Institute for Research in the Behavioural Sciences

Founded in 1941 by Henrietta Szold to undertake research in human behaviour, policy evaluation and experimentation, with special emphasis on children and youth.

Activities: Conducts research and experiments in the fields of education, psychometrics, sociology and psychology; operates an information retrieval centre for Israeli research in the social sciences; provides a measurement and evaluation service for the Israeli education system; organizes workshops and training courses; and maintains databases for researchers.

Geographical Area of Activity: Israel.

Publications: *Megamot* (quarterly); research reports.

Principal Staff: Dir Prof. Isaac Friedman.

Address: 9 Colombia St, Jerusalem 96583.

Telephone: (2) 6494444; **Fax:** (2) 6437698; **Internet:** www.szold.org.il; **e-mail:** szold@szold.org.il.

US–Israel Educational Foundation

Founded in 1956 to administer the Fulbright Program between the USA and Israel.

Activities: The Foundation enables outstanding Israeli and American scholars and students to pursue research, lectures and study at leading institutes of higher learning in the USA and Israel.

Geographical Area of Activity: Israel and the USA.

Restrictions: No grants to institutions or organizations.

Finance: Financed by the USA and Israeli governments. Annual budget approx. US $1,600,000.

Board of Trustees: Amb. Daniel C. Kurtzer (Hon. Chair.); William Cavness; Prof. Howard Cedar; Jonathan Friedland; Noah Gendler; Lawrence Gumbiner; Shlomo Herskovic; Dan Kyram; Richard LeBaron; Helen Motro; Prof. Yair Orgler; Michael Richard; Aharon Leshno Yaar.

Principal Staff: Exec. Dir Dr Neal Sherman.

Address: 1 Ben Yehuda St, POB 26160, Tel Aviv 61261.

Telephone: (3) 5172392; **Fax:** (3) 5162016; **Internet:** www.fulbright.org.il; **e-mail:** info@fulbright.org.il.

Italy

FOUNDATION CENTRE AND CO-ORDINATING BODY

Fondazione Giovanni Agnelli—Centro di Documentazione sulle Fondazioni (Giovanni Agnelli Foundation—Centre of Documentation on Foundations)

Non-profit research centre founded by Giovanni Agnelli in 1996 to gather information on Italian foundations.

Activities: Gathers and disseminates information relating to Italian foundations, monitoring their activities and working to improve their effectiveness and efficiency by identifying any resources needed, and noting trends and movements in the non-profit sector. Promotes foundations, and maintains a specialized library, an archive on Italian foundations and legal information on approximately 200 Italian foundations.

Geographical Area of Activity: Italy.

Publications: Newsletter (quarterly); Annual Report.

Address: Via Giacosa 38, 10125 Torino.

Telephone: (011) 6500500; **Fax:** (011) 6502777; **Internet:** www.fondazioni.it/info; **e-mail:** info@fondazioni.it.

FOUNDATIONS, TRUSTS AND NON-PROFIT ORGANIZATIONS

Accademia Musicale Chigiana (Chigiana Academy of Music)

Founded in 1932 by Count Guido Chigi Saracini to provide courses in advanced musical studies.

Activities: Operates internationally in the fields of education and the arts and humanities, through publications and courses, and scholarships and fellowships organized on an international basis.

Geographical Area of Activity: International.

Principal Staff: Artistic Dir Aldo Bennici.

Address: Via di Città 89, 53100 Siena.

Telephone: (0577) 22091; **Fax:** (0577) 288124; **Internet:** www.chigiana.it; **e-mail:** stampa@chigiana.it.

Association for the Study of the World Refugee Problem

Founded in 1951 (merged in October 1961 with the European Association for the Study of Refugee Problems) to promote, examine thoroughly and co-ordinate the scientific study of refugee problems in order to give competent organs throughout the world the scientific basis to solve these problems.

Activities: Operates internationally as an independent association in which scholars from all fields of knowledge co-operate with experts from national and international organizations to investigate refugee problems and to provide theoretical bases of possible solutions. The field of study has also been extended to the problems of migrant workers. The Association is a consultative body of the United Nations and the Council of Europe. National sections exist in most Western European countries and are connected by the International General Assembly; there are observers in many other countries. The scientific investigations are carried out by international committees of experts, each dealing with a particular aspect such as population and health, international refugees, cultural questions, legal questions, sociology, economic integration, housing and employment. Their findings are co-ordinated by the International Curatorium. The results of the Association's comparative research work are communicated to specialists from countries with refugee problems and also, often with recommendations, to governments and the appropriate organizations. Congresses are held annually in one of the member countries. The Association has members in 21 countries. The Secretariat-General is located in Italy, while the Head Office is situated in Vaduz, Liechtenstein.

Geographical Area of Activity: International.

Publications: *AWR Bulletin* (quarterly); reports are published regularly in four languages.

Finance: Annual budget approx. 45,000 Swiss francs.

Trustees: The Board of Trustees is composed of a President and Secretary elected by each national section. Franco Foschi (Pres.).

Principal Staff: Sec.-Gen. Aldo Clemente.

Address: Secretariat-General, Piazzale di Porta Pia 121, 00198 Rome.

Telephone: (06) 44250037; **Fax:** (06) 42744391.

Biblioteca dell'Accademia Nazionale dei Lincei e Corsiniana—Sezione Orientale (National Academy of the Lincei—Library, Oriental Section)

Founded in 1924 by Leone Caetani di Sermoneta, Prince of Teano, and formerly known as the Fondazione Leone Caetani, to promote knowledge of the ancient and contemporary Muslim world and Islamic culture, by means of conferences, lectures and publications.

Activities: Has organized a series of conferences on the Muslim world. Maintains a specialized library of 30,000 volumes, 350 manuscripts (Arabic, Persian and Ethiopian) and 350 periodicals on Arab-Islamic classical civilization, which constitutes the Oriental Section of the Biblioteca dell'Accademia Nazionale dei Lincei e Corsiniana.

Geographical Area of Activity: Italy.

Publications: *Fondazione Leone Caetani–Accademia Nazionale dei Lincei* (irregular).

Finance: Net assets €10,000.

Board of Directors: Prof. L. Petech (Pres.); G. Gnoli; G. Garbini; L. Ricci; R. Traini.

Principal Staff: Librarian Dr Valentina Sagaria Rossi.

Address: Via della Lungara 10, 00165 Rome.

Telephone: (06) 68027239; **Fax:** (06) 68027543; **Internet:** www.lincei.it; **e-mail:** biblioteca.sezor@lincei.it.

CENSIS—Fondazione Centro Studi Investimenti Sociali (Foundation Centre for the Study of Social Investment)

A research institute established in 1964, became a foundation in 1973. Aims to research all aspects of Italian society.

Activities: Operates in the fields of the arts and culture, economic affairs, social welfare, employment and the environment. Provides training and advice, and engages in research comissioned by exterior groups and institutions, including the European Union, chambers of commerce and private businesses. Publishes an annual report on the social situation in Italy.

Geographical Area of Activity: Italy and Europe.

Restrictions: No grants available.

Publications: Annual Report.

Finance: Funding from contracts. Annual budget US $5,000,000.

Directors: Giorgio Cigliana (Pres.); Giuseppe de Rita (Sec.-Gen.); Giuseppe Roma (Dir.).

Address: Piazza di Novella 2, 00199 Rome.

Telephone: (06) 860911; **Fax:** (06) 86211367; **Internet:** www.censis.it; **e-mail:** censis@censis.it.

Centro Studi e Formazione Sociale Fondazione Emanuela Zancan Onlus (Emanuela Zancan Onlus Foundation Centre for Social Studies and Training)

Founded in 1964 works in the field of research, in particular educational, social and health services.

Activities: Operates both nationally and internationally in the fields of education, health and social welfare and studies, through self-conducted programmes, research, conferences, publications and lectures. Works in collaboration with other institutions as well as with foreign experts.

Geographical Area of Activity: Italy and international.

Publications: *Studi Zancan* (journal, every two months).

Trustees: Dr G. Benvegnu Pasini (Pres.); Dr M. Diomede Canevini; S. Dugone; Dr M. Giordano; Giovanni Nervo; Prof. A. Palmonari; Prof. E. Rossi; Prof. I. de Sandre; Prof. G. Sarpellon.

Principal Staff: Scientific Dir Dr Tiziano Vecchiato.

Address: Via del Vescovado 66, 35141 Padua.

Telephone: (049) 663800; **Fax:** (049) 663013; **Internet:** www.fondazionezancan.it; **e-mail:** fz@fondazionezancan.it.

Compagnia di San Paolo

Established in 1563 as a brotherhood to help the poor and fight usury; now an independent grant-making foundation, aiming to foster civic, cultural and economic development.

Activities: Operates in the following areas in particular: scientific, economic and legal research; education; the arts and humanities; preservation of cultural heritage and activities, and of environmental assets; and health and welfare. The following permanent organizations also come under the remit of the Compagnia's institutional activities: the Istituto Superiore Mario Boella, which operates in the field of Information and Communication Technologies, in co-operation with Turin Polytechnic; the Consorzio Collegio Carlo Alberto, for setting up a Centre for Advanced Training in Finance and Economics, also in association with Turin University; the Ufficio Pio, which operates in co-operation with a strong network of volunteers and acts as a crisis centre for people most in need and gives training-as-you-study grants for the vocational training of socially at risk young people; and the Educatorio Duchessa Isabella, which during 2001 became the Fondazione per la Scuola (the Foundation for Schools) with the aim of becoming a centre for education able to support self-governing schools. Also maintains a searchable grants database.

Geographical Area of Activity: International.

Restrictions: Operates exclusively to the benefit of non-profit-making organizations. No grants are made to individuals.

Publications: Annual Report; Newsletter (3 a year); *Quaderni della Compagnia; Quaderni dell'Archivio Storico* (monograph series, in Italian).

Finance: Assets €4,800,000,000 (2000); grants disbursed €82,700,000 (2000).

Management Committee: Onorato Castellino (Chair.); Carlo Callieri, Giovanni Zanetti (Vice-Chair.); Lorenzo Caselli; Paolo Corradini; Mario Deaglio; Riccardo Roscelli.

Principal Staff: Sec.-Gen. Piero Gastaldo.

Address: Corso Vittorio Emanuele II 75, 10128 Turin.

Telephone: (011) 5596911; **Fax:** (011) 5596976; **Internet:** www.compagnia.torino.it; **e-mail:** info@compagnia.torino.it.

Cooperazione Internazionale—COOPI (International Co-operation)

An NGO established in 1965 by Fr Vincenzo Barbieri to contribute to the harmonious, integrated development of communities in less-developed countries, so that the ideals of equality and justice may be pursued through contact and collaboration between peoples.

Activities: Operates in the field of aid to less-developed countries, through projects concerning emergency aid, rehabilitation, reconstruction, and development intervention in various sectors, including health, sanitation, agriculture, training and education. Maintains an office in Brussels.

Geographical Area of Activity: Africa, Asia, Eastern Europe, the Mediterranean, the Middle East, and Central and South America.

Publications: Newsletter; *Un Volto per la Vita; Non Lasciamo Soli i Bambini della Sierra Leone; Ragazzi di Bucarest; Quel che resta del mondo; Piroga*.

Finance: Total assets €7,371,548 (2000); total revenue €1,632,019, total expenditure €1,605,544 (2000).

Executive Committee: Fr Vincenzo Barbieri (Pres. and Legal Rep.); Efrem Fumagalli; Olimpio Gasparotto; Davide Martina; Ennio Miccoli; Carla Ricci; Silvana Scandone; Paolo Tartaglia.

Principal Staff: Dir Michele Romano.

Address: Via De Lemene 50, 20151 Milan.

Telephone: (02) 3085057; **Fax:** (02) 33403570; **Internet:** www.coopi.org; **e-mail:** coopi@una.org.

EMERGENCY

Established in 1994 by Italian surgeon Gino Strada.

Activities: Provides medical and surgical care to the victims of war, through the provision of medical and technical personnel. Constructs and rehabilitates health clinics and hospitals, supports educational institutions and distributes medical and first aid supplies. Currently operates relief projects in Afghanistan, Cambodia, Iraq, Sierra Leone, and has supported humanitarian activities in Algeria, Chechnya, Eritrea and Rwanda.

Geographical Area of Activity: International.

Publications: *Activity Report 1994—2001*.

Finance: Annual expenditure €5,852,815 (2000).

Address: Via Bagutta 12, 20121 Milan.

Telephone: (2) 76001104; **Fax:** (2) 76003719; **Internet:** www.emergency.it; **e-mail:** info@emergency.it.

Ente Cassa di Risparmio di Firenze (Florence Savings Bank Foundation)

Founded in 1992 to promote social and economic development and to continue the tradition of Cassa di Risparmio di Firenze (a fund established in 1829 to encourage saving among poorer people and to promote socio-economic development through the distribution of banking profits).

Activities: The Foundation supports the arts and humanities, scientific research and technological innovation, medicine and health, social welfare and restoration projects, through self-conducted programmes and grants in Tuscany. Also administers three smaller foundations.

Geographical Area of Activity: Italy.

Publications: Newsletter.

Finance: Assets 1,254,404,710,059 lire (1999).

Board of Governors: Alberto Carmi (Pres.); Edoardo Speranza (Vice-Pres.); Vittorio Emanuele Rimbotti (Sec.-Gen.).

Principal Staff: Dir Antonio Gherdovich.

Address: Via Bufalini 6, 50122 Florence.

Telephone: (055) 2612214; **Fax:** (055) 2612756; **Internet:** www.entecarifirenze.it; **e-mail:** info@entecarifirenze.it.

Ente per gli Studi Monetari Bancari e Finanziari Luigi Einaudi (Luigi Einaudi Institute for Monetary, Banking and Financial Studies)

Founded in 1965 by the Bank of Italy and the Italian Banking Association to instruct and to interest young people in economics, particularly banking and finance.

Activities: Operates in the field of banking, through grants to individuals and groups of persons of any nationality for the study of banking and research into banking systems; awards scholarships for study in Italy and abroad. Results of research are published and circulated abroad.

Geographical Area of Activity: International.

Publications: *Quaderni di Ricerche* (research series); *Temi di Ricerca* (working papers); and other publications.

Finance: Net assets 6,599,156,980 lire (June 1999).

Board of Directors: I. Musu (Pres.); M. Sella (Vice-Pres.); F. Cesarini; P. Ciocca; R. Einaudi; P. Mottura; A. Pedone.

Principal Staff: Gen. Man. Florina Pierelli.

Address: Via Due Macelli 73, 00187 Rome.

Telephone: (06) 6790013; **Fax:** (06) 47924872; **Internet:** www.enteluigieinaudi.it; **e-mail:** einaudil@tin.it.

European Training Foundation

Established by the Council of Ministers of the European Community (now the European Union—EU) in 1990; began its activities in 1995.

Activities: The Foundation is an EU agency and part of the family of decentralised bodies. It is the EU's centre of expertise supporting vocational education and training reform in third countries (partner countries) within the context of the EU external relations programme. It also provides technical assistance to the European Commission for the implementation of the Tempus programme in the field of higher education. Provides expertise in the areas of human resources, vocational training reform policies, skills development for enterprises, management and entrepreneurial training, and active labour market policies. Supports the European Commission's project cycle and contributes to the development and design of country strategy papers and indicative and action programmes, including country analyses; sector analyses; analyses of needs and feasibility studies; training needs assessment methodologies; key indicators and benchmarking; impact assessment, evaluation and peer reviews; and examples of good practice.

Geographical Area of Activity: Central and Eastern Europe (future EU member states and Western Balkans), the republics of Central Asia (new independent states and Mongolia), Mediterranean partners of North Africa and the Middle East.

Restrictions: Not a training provider, nor a provider of financial assistance for individual students.

Principal Staff: Dir Peter de Rooji; Deputy Dir Ulrich Hillenkamp.

Address: Villa Gualino, Viale Settimio Severo 65, 10133 Turin.

Telephone: (011) 6302222; **Fax:** (011) 6302200; **Internet:** www.etf.eu.int; **e-mail:** info@etf.eu.int.

Fondation Emile Chanoux—Institut d'Etudes Fédéralistes et Régionalistes (Emile Chanoux Foundation—Institute for Federalist and Regionalist Studies)

Established in 1995, a university-level institute for the study and defence of federalism and regionalism, including linguistic minorities.

Activities: Operates in the fields of economic affairs, education, international affairs, law and human rights, and social welfare and social studies, through research, awarding prizes, grants to individuals, conferences, training courses and publications. The Foundation is in the process of creating a francophone university-level institution with courses organized in collaboration with French, Italian and Swiss universities, as well as a library.

Geographical Area of Activity: Europe.

Publications: *L'Ordre nouveau; Cahiers du fédéralisme.*

Finance: Annual revenue approx. €258,000.

Council of Administration: René Faval (Pres.); Ferdinand Kinsky (Vice-Pres.); Alexis Betemps; Franco Cometto; Frédéric Lepine; Arnaud Marc-Lipiansky; Hartmut Marhold; Mario Vietti; Simone Voyat.

Principal Staff: Dir Gen. Bernard Dorin.

Address: 4 rue A. Cretier, 11100 Aosta.

Telephone and Fax: (0165) 40777; **Internet:** www.fchanoux.org; **e-mail:** fondchanoux@fondchanoux.org.

Fondazione Giovanni Agnelli (Giovanni Agnelli Foundation)

Founded in 1966 on the 100th anniversary of Giovanni Agnelli's birth, by Fiat SpA and the Istituto Finanziario Industriale, to carry out research in social, cultural, political and economic problems in Italy and elsewhere.

Activities: The Foundation's broad areas of interest and current main programmes are: reform of the state and social pluralism in Italy, which studies and researches the reform of the state and the strengthening of civil society and social pluralism; new geo-economic framework, comprising three related programmes (the New Map of the World's Geo-economy, the Factors of Competition and Local Societies and the Economy and Territory in the Italian Geo-economy—these programmes examine the social and economic organization of Italy and issues relating to the world economy); and cultural universes and modernity, comprising three research programmes (Islam and Modernity, the Contemporary Arab World and the Pluralist Society in Italy and Europe). The Foundation also studies the history, culture and current conditions of populations of Italian origin in North and South America and Australia. The Senator Giovanni Agnelli International Prize for the Dialogue between Cultural Universes is awarded every two years.

Geographical Area of Activity: Italy.

Restrictions: Does not make grants.

Publications: *Altreitalie* (2 a year, in Italian and English); and numerous other publications.

Finance: Assets approx. €69,722,000.

Board of Directors: G. Agnelli (Chair.); U. Agnelli (Vice-Chair.); S. Agnelli; M. Agnelli Caracciolo di Castagneto; V. Chiusano; G. Gabetti; M. Pacini; A. Ronchey.

Principal Staff: Dir Marco Demarie.

Address: Via Giacosa 38, 10125 Turin.

Telephone: (011) 6500500; **Fax:** (011) 6502777; **Internet:** www.fondazione-agnelli.it; **e-mail:** staff@fga.it.

Fondazione Benetton Studi Ricerche (Benetton Foundation for Study and Research)

Founded in 1981, under present name since 1987, to promote study and research in the protection and promotion of the history of Veneto, the history of games and the development of landscapes.

Activities: Operates nationally and internationally in the areas of the arts and humanities, and conservation and the environment, through self-conducted programmes, research, prizes, conferences, training courses and publications. Research, experimentation and scientific field-work undertaken by the Foundation aims to develop initiatives to improve the knowledge, protection and promotion of the natural and built heritage. The Foundation's documentation centre contains a library, archives, and map and image collection.

Geographical Area of Activity: Mainly Europe.

Restrictions: Grants are not made to individuals, nor for sponsorship.

Publications: *Ludica* (annual review of games and sport); *Bollettino* (irregular); books on the foundation's research findings; annual booklet on Premio Internazionale Carlo Scarpa per il Giardino.

Finance: Annual expenditure €1,600,000 (2001).

Trustees: Luciano Benetton (Chair.); Gilberto Benetton (Vice-Chair.); Carlo Benetton; Giuliana Benetton; Carlo Bertelli; Tobia Scarpa.

Principal Staff: Dir Domenico Luciani.

Address: Via Cornarotta 7, 31100 Treviso.

Telephone: (0422) 5121; **Fax:** (0422) 579483; **Internet:** www.fbsr.it; **e-mail:** fbsr@fbsr.it.

Fondazione Ugo Bordoni (Ugo Bordoni Foundation)

Founded in 1952 by Cesare Albanese, Albino Antinori, Felice Calvanese, Antonio Carrelli, Romolo De Caterini, Andrea Ferrara-Toniolo, Alberto Fornò, Vittorio Gori, Ernesto Lensi, Algeri Marino, Enrico Medi, Michele Paris, Giuseppe Spataro and Scipione Treves, to facilitate and promote research and scientific studies applicable to the postal system, telecommunications and electronics; and to facilitate initiatives to further technical-scientific development in the same field.

Activities: Operates in the fields of electronics and communications, through research and publications, mainly in co-operation with the Istituto Superiore delle Comunicazioni e delle Tecnologie dell' Informazione (Advanced Institute for Communications and Information Technology). Collaborates with national and international bodies.

Geographical Area of Activity: Italy.

Publications: Report of operations; various scientific and technical publications.

Trustees: Bruno Amoroso (Chair.).

Principal Staff: Dir Francesco Fedi; Sec.-Gen. Giovanni Lanzara.

Address: Via B. Castiglione 59, 00142 Rome.

Telephone: (06) 54801; **Fax:** (06) 54804400; **Internet:** www.fub.it; **e-mail:** pressoffice@fub.it.

Fondazione Cariplo per le Iniziative e lo Studio sulla Multietnicità (Cariplo Foundation for Initiatives and Studies of Multi-ethnicity)

Established in 1993; aims to promote internationalism and multiculturalism, particularly within Europe.

Activities: Promotes study and research, especially in the field of immigration issues; holds seminars and produces publications promoting multi-ethnicity; funds training and owns a document archive consisting of national and international informative material.

Geographical Area of Activity: Mainly Europe.

Publications: *ISMU informa* (newsletter); *Multicultural Policies and Modes of Citizenship*.

Directors: Giuseppe Guzzetti (Pres.); Renato Ravasio (Sec.); Vincenzo Cesareo; Paolo Raineri; Carlo Vimercati.

Address: Foro Buonaparte 22, 20121 Milan.

Telephone: (02) 72023375; **Fax:** (02) 876042; **e-mail:** ismu@ismu.org.

Fondazione Cassa di Risparmio delle Provincie Lombarde—Fondazione Cariplo (Cariplo Foundation)

Founded in 1991 by the Cariplo Bank to promote the economic and cultural development of Italy.

Activities: Supports charity work in Italy in the areas of the arts and culture, health, the environment, education, scientific research, community foundations and social services. Particularly promotes the study of technology and the effect it can have on business and public administration systems. Makes grants to fund enterprise projects on this subject, and promotes its own programmes in co-operation with other institutions.

Geographical Area of Activity: Italy.

Restrictions: No grants to individuals.

Publications: *Documento Programmatico Pluriennale 2002–2006*; and other publications.

Finance: Assets 10,725,854,142,632 lire (1999); annual expenditure 417,512,957,838 lire (1999).

Directors: Giuseppe Guzzetti (Pres.); Carlo Sangalli, A. Scarselli (Vice-Pres.); R. Artoni; P. Morerio; F. Pierotti Cei; E. Riva; F. Scalvini; M. Spadacini.

Principal Staff: Sec.-Gen. Dr Renato Ravasio.

Address: Via Manin 23, 20121 Milan.

Telephone: (02) 62391; **Fax:** (02) 6239282; **Internet:** www.fondazionecariplo.it.

Fondazione Cesar (Cesar Foundation)

Founded in 1990 by UNIPOL Insurance Company.

Activities: Operates in the areas of social welfare, social economy and insurance, principally through carrying out research, studies and initiatives to support non-profit organizations and develop the welfare state, within both Italy and a European context.

Geographical Area of Activity: Italy.

Publications: *CesarInforma* (magazine, quarterly).

Principal Staff: Pres. Enea Mazzoli; Sec. Gen. Giancarlo Brunello.

Address: Via Galliera 26, 40121 Bologna.

Telephone: (051) 6437618; **Fax:** (051) 6437600; **Internet:** www.fondazionecesar.it; **e-mail:** info@fondazionecesar.it.

Fondazione Giorgio Cini (Giorgio Cini Foundation)

Founded in 1951 by Count Vittorio Cini in memory of his son Giorgio. The island of San Giorgio Maggiore, Venice, was entrusted to the Foundation for the purpose of restoring the area's historic buildings and supporting the development of social, cultural and artistic institutions in this area.

Activities: Operates through eight advanced-study institutes: the Institute for the History of Art; the Institute for the history of the Venetian State and Society; the Institute for Music; the Institute for Literature and Theatre; the Venice and the East Institute; the Venice and Europe Institute; the Intercultural Institute of Comparative Music Studies; and an institute devoted to the study and illustration of the works of Antonio Vivaldi. The Institutes each have their own director, possess a library, undertake research, organize study-encounters and seminars, and promote publications, concerts and artistic exhibitions. The Foundation works nationally and internationally organizing postgraduate courses, conferences and seminars on topics of historic, scientific, social or cultural interest.

Geographical Area of Activity: Italy.

Publications: Numerous publications.

Principal Staff: Chair. Prof A. Giovanni Bazoli; Vice-Pres. Marino Cortese, Francesco Valcanover; Sec.-Gen. Renzo Zorzi.

Address: Isola di San Giorgio Maggiore, 30124 Venice.

Telephone: (041) 5289900; **Fax:** (041) 5238540; **Internet:** www.cini.it; **e-mail:** fondacini@cini.it.

Fondazione Giordano Dell'Amore (Giordano Dell'Amore Foundation)

Founded in 1977 as the Finafrica Foundation by the Cassa di Risparmio delle Province Lombarde bank. Its purpose is to assist financial and credit institutions of transitional countries.

Activities: Offers training opportunities in Italy and provides technical assistance to banks and financial institutes in the beneficiary's home country (developing countries and countries of Eastern Europe); organizes international conferences; conducts research and issues publications.

Geographical Area of Activity: Europe, Africa, Asia, and Central and South America.

Publications: *Savings and Development* (quarterly review); studies on development issues, especially financial systems and intermediaries in developing and transitional economies.

Board of Directors: Mario Masini (Chair.); Giovanni Ancarini; Roberto Artoni; Maurizio Cavallari; Luca Galli; Arnaldo Mauri; Paolo Morerio; Paolo Raineri; Felice Tambussi.

Principal Staff: Scientific Sec. Dr Laura Vigano.

Address: Via L. Manara 15–17, 20122 Milan.

Telephone: (02) 5418441; **Fax:** (02) 55193005; **Internet:** www.fgda.org; **e-mail:** info@fgda.org.

Fondazione Guido Donegani (Guido Donegani Foundation)

Founded in 1951 by Ing. Guido Donegani to further the study of chemistry in Italy.

Activities: Operates internationally in the field of science. The Foundation awards study grants to Italian and foreign students and graduates in the field of chemistry, and has created special prizes for Italian scientists and technicians who have made an outstanding contribution towards the investigation or solution of problems in chemistry. It has also established courses of higher education and grants for research and experiment in the field of chemistry.

Geographical Area of Activity: Europe.

Publications: A series of publications regarding the activities of the Foundation, published by the Accademia Nazionale dei Lincei.

Finance: Source of finance is income from property and investments. Annual revenue approx. €77,000, expenditure approx. €72,000.

Principal Staff: Pres. Edoardo Vesentini; Vice-Pres. Marco Fortis; Alessandro Ballio; Sergio Carrá; Umberto Colombo; Gian Gualberto Volpi; Sec. Antonio Luigi Cocuzzi.

Address: Accademia Nazionale dei Lincei, Via della Lungara 10, 00165 Rome.

Telephone: (06) 6868223; **Fax:** (06) 6893616; **e-mail:** segreteria@lincei.it.

Fondazione Luigi Einaudi (Luigi Einaudi Foundation)

Founded in 1964 by the family of Luigi Einaudi, former President of Italy, with the help of local financial institutions and the Italian Government, to train young scholars in economics and political and historical studies, and to maintain a library in the social sciences open to all scholars.

Activities: Maintains the Luigi Einaudi Library which currently contains more than 200,000 volumes and 2,700 periodicals; awards fellowships and research grants, organizes seminars and conferences, and sponsors publications in the fields of economics, politics and history. Also operates internationally collaborating with the Collegio de México in Mexico and Cornell University in the USA; carrying out research into the effect of property on agricultural productivity in Europe and Central and South America; as well as developing projects dealing with regional integration, conflict resolution, comparative models of employment and social policy, and contemporary political thought.

Geographical Area of Activity: Mainly Italy.

Publications: *Annali della Fondazione Luigi Einaudi; Scrittori italiani di politica, economia e storia* (collection of classics); *Studi* (collection of monographs).

Finance: Endowment fund 2,200,000 lire (1999); annual revenue and expenditure 2,200,000 (1999).

Board of Administration: E. Filippi (Pres.); G. M. Bravo; F. Beraudo; T. Cozzi; A. D'Aroma; R. Einaudi; I. Massabò Ricci; M. Miano; G. Pichetto; W. Santagata; V. Zanone.

Principal Staff: Giovanni Prati.

Address: Palazzo d'Azeglio, Via Principe Amedeo 34, 10123 Turin.

Telephone: (011) 835656; **Fax:** (011) 8179093; **Internet:** www.fondazioneeinaudi.it; **e-mail:** informazioni@fondazioneeinaudi.it.

Fondazione ENI Enrico Mattei (Enrico Mattei ENI Foundation)

Founded in 1989 by the Ente Nazionale Idrocarburi (ENI) petrochemicals company, to undertake studies and research into economic, scientific and environmental problems through a multi-disciplinary approach and by fostering international research networks.

Activities: Operates internationally in three main programme areas: Sustainable Development; Political Economy; and the Firm and the Environment. Supports research projects, and offers research fellowships and scholarships for researchers from European Union countries. Maintains offices in Genoa, Turin, Venice and Rome.

Geographical Area of Activity: International.

Publications: Annual Report; Newsletter (quarterly); working papers.

Finance: Assets €28,526,593 (2001).

Board of Directors: G. Moscato (Pres.); G. Callera; S. Cao; C. Cuomo; C. Grande; V. Mincato; L. Patron; R. Poli; S. Russo; L. Sgubini; P. F. Tali.

Principal Staff: Exec. Dir Alessandro Lanza; Research Dir Prof. Carlo Carraro.

Address: Palazzo delle Stelline, Corso Magenta 63, 20123 Milan.

Telephone: (02) 52036934; **Fax:** (02) 52036946; **Internet:** www.feem.it; **e-mail:** letter@feem.it.

Fondazione Europa Occupazione: Impresa e Solidarieta (Europe Employment Foundation: Enterprise and Solidarity)

Founded in 1995 by the banking foundation, Fondazione Cassa di Risparmio di Roma, to promote social enterprise for the improvement of the welfare system.

Activities: Funds and supports social development enterprise projects by making grants, holding seminars and producing publications. Also works to better relations within Europe in order to increase the opportunities for co-ordinating employment policies in the non-profit sector.

Geographical Area of Activity: Italy.

Restrictions: Only makes grants within Italy.

Publications: Annual Report.

Finance: Net assets €19,768,409 (2001); annual expenditure €2,779,378 (2001).

Directors: Pablo Emilio Nistri (Pres.).

Address: Via Nazionale 39, 00184 Rome.

Telephone: (06) 476781; **Fax:** (06) 4741117; **Internet:** www.cosis.it; **e-mail:** info@cosis.it.

Fondazione Europea Dragan (Dragan European Foundation)

Founded in 1968 by Prof. Constantin Dragan to promote the spiritual unification of Europeans and a better understanding of the different cultures and histories of the countries of Europe, to develop a European culture and a European conscience, especially among young people.

Activities: Operates nationally and internationally in the fields of culture and history, science and technology, law and human rights, and health and medicine. Organizes campaigns and conferences, and issues publications to facilitate the development of a European cultural community. Maintains an office in Milan.

Geographical Area of Activity: Europe.

Publications: *Bulletin Européen* (monthly, in French and Italian); *Ponto-Baltica* (annual review of linguistics); *Rivista della Cooperazione Giuridica Internazionale* (quarterly review of law); conference reports and proceedings; information brochure.

Board of Directors: J. C. Dragan (Pres.); Veronica Gusa de Dragan (Vice-Pres.).

Address: Foro Triano 1a, Rome.

Telephone: (02) 58304816; **e-mail:** fed.stampa@librero.it.

Fondazione Giangiacomo Feltrinelli (Giangiacomo Feltrinelli Foundation)

Founded in 1949 by Giangiacomo Feltrinelli and Giuseppe del Bo to promote the study of history and the political, social and economic sciences.

Activities: The Foundation operates nationally and internationally in the fields of education, the humanities and international relations, by conducting research, holding conferences and publishing findings. Special attention is given to the history and development of socialism and of national and international labour movements. Maintains a library of 400,000 volumes and 20,000 periodicals.

Geographical Area of Activity: Italy.

Publications: *Annali; Quaderni.*

Board of Trustees: S. Veca (Pres.).

Address: Via Romagnosi 3, 20121 Milan.

Telephone: (02) 874175; **Fax:** (02) 86461855; **Internet:** www.feltrinelli.it; **e-mail:** fondfelt@mclink.it.

Fondazione Piera, Pietro e Giovanni Ferrero—ONLUS

Established in 1983 by Michele Ferrero for the welfare of pensioners of Ferrero companies, and to make grants for cultural activities and medical research.

Activities: Operates nationally, carrying out cultural activities in Alba, including conferences and publications; funding and organizing activities for Ferrero pensioners; and supporting medical research, especially in relation to the aged.

Geographical Area of Activity: Italy.

Publications: *Filodiretto* (magazine); and other publications.

Finance: Ferrero companies donate at least €516,000 annually; assets more than €2,750,000 (2002).

Board of Administration: Maria Franca Ferrero (Pres.); Gian Luigi Viglino (Vice-Pres.); Dott. Francesco Paolo Fulci; and others.

Principal Staff: Gen. Sec. Mario Strola.

Address: Strada di Mezzo 44, 12051 Alba.

Telephone: (0173) 295259; **Fax:** (0173) 363274; **Internet:** www.fondazioneferrero.it; **e-mail:** info@fondazioneferrero.it.

Fondazione per l'Istituto Svizzero di Roma (Foundation for the Swiss Institute of Rome)

Founded in 1949 to provide an opportunity for scholarly research or artistic activity for young Swiss in Rome; and to contribute to the development of intellectual relations between Switzerland and Italy.

Activities: Operates internationally in the field of the arts and humanities through conferences and courses.

Geographical Area of Activity: International.

Publications: *Bibliotheca Helvetica Romana,* vol. 10/4 (2000); *Bibliotheca Helvetica Romana,* vol. 27 (2000).

Governing Board: F. Pianca (Pres.); G. Caslani (Treas.).

Principal Staff: Dir Dott. Dieter Bachmann.

Address: Istituto Svizzero di Roma, Via Ludovisi 48, 00187 Rome.

Telephone: (06) 4814234; **Fax:** (06) 48904076; **e-mail:** info@istitutosvizzero.it.

Fondazione Ing. Carlo M. Lerici presso il Politecnico di Milano (Ing. Carlo M. Lerici Foundation at the Polytechnic of Milan)

Founded in 1947 by Carlo Maurilio Lerici to promote, develop and co-ordinate initiatives and activities concerned with archaeological prospecting both within Italy and abroad.

Activities: Carries out archaeological prospecting campaigns in Italy and abroad, including experimental surveys both independently and in collaboration with other institutions. Conducts research for the development of new instruments and of new methods of treatment, interpretation and representation of surveying results. Operates its own projects and holds conferences.

Geographical Area of Activity: Mainly Italy.

Restrictions: Does not make grants.

Publications: Occasional reports on specific research (limited circulation); *Prospezioni Archeologiche* (in Italian and English).

Governing Board: Prof. A. De Maio (Chair.); Dott. Mauro Cucarzi (Dir).

Address: Via Vittorio Veneto 108, 00187 Rome.

Telephone: (06) 4880083; **Fax:** (06) 4827085; **e-mail:** folerici@fon.it.

Fondazione Giovanni Lorenzini (Giovanni Lorenzini Medical Science Foundation)

Founded in 1969.

Activities: Operates internationally in the fields of biomedical education, social welfare and studies, science and medicine, particularly basic science and clinical applications, through programmes conducted on an international level, and conferences, lectures, courses, fellowships, scholarships and publications organized both nationally and internationally. A sister foundation, the Giovanni Lorenzini Medical Foundation, exists in Houston, TX, USA.

Geographical Area of Activity: International.

Publications: *Rassegna-Clinica Scientifica* (journal); abstracts and proceedings of the meetings organized by the Foundation.

Address: Via Andrea Appiani 7, 20121 Milan.

Telephone: (02) 29006267; **Fax:** (02) 29007018; **Internet:** www.lorenzinifoundation.org; **e-mail:** info@lorenzinifoundation.org.

Fondazione Medikinale International Parma

Established in 1983 to promote audio-visual media in biomedical sciences.

Activities: The foundation organizes the Prix Leonardo, a biennial international film festival of medicine, ecology, science and technology. It also maintains an archive of over 2,000 films and videos and promotes the creation and distribution of audio-visual material, particularly educational material, in science.

Geographical Area of Activity: International.

Publications: Reports.

Finance: Funded through public contributions, entry fees for the Prix Leonardo and sale of science videos.

Advisory Committee: Elio Giovati (Pres.); Alberto Rusconi (Vice-Pres.); Bruno Borchi; Prof. Angelo Franze; Federica Gardini; Maria Giovenzana; Giovanni Martinelli.

Principal Staff: Dir Karin Munck.

Address: Via Gramsci 14, c/o Università, 43100 Parma.

Telephone: (0521) 982031; **Fax:** (0521) 986975; **Internet:** www.prixleonardo.org; **e-mail:** info@prixleonardo.org.

Fondazione Nazionale Carlo Collodi (Carlo Collodi National Foundation)

Founded in 1952 for the diffusion of the works of Carlo Lorenzini (Collodi), particularly 'The Adventures of Pinocchio'; for the collection and exhibition of national and international publications regarding Carlo Collodi and his works; for the promotion of children's literature and establishment of a centre for the study of children's literature; and for the conservation and enlargement of the Monumental Park of Pinocchio in the village of Collodi.

Activities: Operates nationally through self-conducted programmes and grants to individuals, and both nationally and internationally through conferences, courses, publications and lectures. Maintains a library of works by Collodi, including translations; the Monumental Park of Pinocchio; and the International Study Centre for Young People's Literature. Awards the Rolando Anzilotti prize for a critical or historical monograph on children's or young people's literature.

Geographical Area of Activity: International.

Publications: *Quaderni della Fondazione Nazionale Carlo Collodi.*

Address: Villa Arcangeli, Via Pasquinelli 6, 51014 Collodi.

Internet: www.pinocchio.it/fondazione.htm.

Fondazione Adriano Olivetti (Adriano Olivetti Foundation)

Founded in 1962 by Maria Luisa Lizier Galardi, Dino Olivetti, Magda Olivetti Jaksic, Roberto Olivetti and Silvia Olivetti Marxer, to promote, develop and co-ordinate research on constitutional and federalist studies, the international organization of economic structures, city planning, local government, labour problems, the sociology of co-operation, cultural services and social work, and in general all studies aimed at increasing knowledge of the conditions upon which social progress depends.

Activities: Operates nationally and internationally, through self-conducted programmes, grants, research and publications, to improve the social and cultural basis of the community, through offering support in four main areas: Institutional and Public Policies; Processes of Economic and Social Development; Cultural and Social Policies; and Art, Architecture and Urban Studies.

Geographical Area of Activity: International.

Publications: *Esiste un Diritto di Ingerenza? L'Europa di fronte alla guerra; MoltepliCittà,* and numerous other publications.

Board of Directors: Mario Caglieris; Maria Luisa Lizier Galardi; Davide Olivetti; Erica Olivetti; Laura Olivetti; Lidia Olivetti; Gabriella Solaro Benaglia; Marco Vitale.

Principal Staff: Hon. Pres. Umberto Serafini; Pres. Laura Olivetti; Vice-Pres. Davide Olivetti; Sec.-Gen. Cinthia Bianconi.

Address: Via Guiseppe Zanardelli, 34, 00186 Rome.

Internet: www.fondazioneadrianolivetti.it; **e-mail:** fond .adrianolivetti@iol.it.

Fondazione Giulio Pastore (Giulio Pastore Foundation)

Founded in 1971 by the Associazioni Cristiane Lavoratori Italiani, Confederazione Italiana Sindacati dei Lavoratori, Democrazia Cristiana, Prof. Mario Romani, Prof. Vincenzo Saba, On. Vincenzo Scotti, Don Pierfranco Pastore and Idolo Marcone, to promote research and study concerning the problems of labour and the trade-union experience of workers, both as a single relevant discipline and in interdisciplinary terms; and to promote the diffusion and application of the results.

Activities: Operates in the fields of education, social welfare and studies, and economic affairs, nationally through self-conducted programmes, and both nationally and internationally through research, grants to individuals, fellowships, scholarships, conferences, courses, publications and lectures.

Geographical Area of Activity: International.

Publications: *Annali* (annual report of operations); *Lavoro e Sindacato* (6 a year).

Finance: Annual expenditure €400,000 (2002).

Directors: Michele Colasanto (Pres.).

Principal Staff: Sec.-Gen. Benedetto Cali.

Address: Via Collina 24, 00187 Rome.

Telephone: (06) 4817850; **Fax:** (06) 4815785; **Internet:** www.fondazionepastore.it; **e-mail:** fondazione.pastore@ tiscalinet.it.

Fondazione Alessio Pezcoller (Alessio Pezcoller Foundation)

Founded in 1980 by Prof. Alessio Pezcoller to promote biomedical research.

Activities: The Foundation operates nationally and internationally in the field of medicine and health, by awarding prizes: the AACR–Pezcoller International Award for Cancer Research, given annually to a scientist who has made a major scientific discovery in the field of cancer, and the FECS–Pezcoller Recognition for Contribution to Oncology, presented every two years to an individual for his or her unique contribution to oncology and for dedication of his or her professional life to research into cancer. The Foundation organizes an annual symposium promoting interaction between scientists working in basic oncological sciences, and a series of educational meetings for local medical doctors, which are held every two years.

Geographical Area of Activity: International.

Restrictions: No grants to individuals.

Publications: *The Pezcoller Foundation Journal* (2 a year).

Trustee: Guiseppe Bernardi.

Principal Staff: Sec. Giorgio Pederzolli; Editor, *The Pezcoller Foundation Journal* Dr Giuseppe Bernardi.

Address: Via Dordi 8, 38100 Trento.

Telephone: (0461) 980250; **Fax:** (0461) 980350; **Internet:** www.pezcoller.it; **e-mail:** pezcoller@pezcoller.it.

Fondazione Querini Stampalia (Querini Stampalia Foundation)

Founded in May 1869 by Count Giovanni Querini to support university studies in Venice and Padua, and to promote the diffusion of culture through library and museum services, and cultural activities, particularly in and around Venice.

Activities: Operates in the field of the arts and humanities, through seminars and conferences, training courses, concerts and publications. Maintains a library of 300,000 volumes and a museum.

Geographical Area of Activity: Italy.

Publications: Numerous historical and cultural publications.

Trustees: Prof. Emilio Rosini (Pres.).

Principal Staff: Dir Dr Giorgio Busetto.

Publications: Newsletter (quarterly); numerous publications on human rights issues.

Finance: Financed by Government and private funds.

Trustees: V. Abellan Honrubia; E. Altvater; A. Basso; P. Basso; L. Bimbi; L. Castellina; A. Cordova; J. de Souza Martins; L. Ferrajoli; F. Houtart; R. La Valle; E. Masina; P. Moggi; F. Rigaux; S. Senese; G. Tognoni.

Principal Staff: Pres. Elmar Altvater; Sec.-Gen. Linda Bimbi.

Address: Via della Dogana Vecchia 5, 00186 Rome.

Telephone: (06) 68801468; **Fax:** (06) 6877774; **Internet:** www.grisnet.it/filb; **e-mail:** filb@iol.it.

International Development Law Organization—IDLO

Founded in 1983 by L. Michael Hager, Gilles Blanchi and William Loris to improve the deployment of legal resources in the development process and the negotiating capability of developing countries.

Activities: IDLO trains development lawyers, mostly from developing countries. It provides practical training for mid-career legal advisers in government ministries, government organizations, banks, private companies and law firms. The Organization runs three programmes: a 10-week Development Lawyers' Course (DLC), two-week International Business Transactions (IBT) Seminars, the five-week Enterprise and Investment Lawyers' Course (EILC), and the three-week Public International Trade Law Course (PITLC)—all courses are conducted in English and French. The DLC focuses on development lawyer skills (advising, planning, negotiating, drafting, monitoring performance and resolving disputes) in the context of project financing, international contracting and foreign investment. IBT seminars address specialized legal topics related to economic development. The EILC is intended for lawyers who act as advisers in the economic reform process. In addition, IDLO organizes in-country training workshops upon special request. IDLO's members are the governments of 16 countries in Africa, Europe, Asia, Australasia and the USA.

Geographical Area of Activity: International.

Publications: Alumni Bulletin; Annual Report, Training Programme, and financial statements.

Finance: Governments, multilateral development organizations, foundations and private companies contribute towards IDLI's budget, programme and fellowship requirements. Total assets US $15,101,822 (2001); total income US $5,328,120, expenditure US $5,207,254 (2001).

Directors: James B. Hurlock (Chair.); Mohammed Y. Abdel-Aal, Attilio Massimo Iannucci (Vice-Chair.).

Principal Staff: Dir Gen. William T. Loris; Deputy Dir Gen. Gilles Blanchi, Pasquale Ferraro.

Address: Via di San Sebastianello 16, 00187 Rome.

Telephone: (06) 6979261; **Fax:** (06) 6781946; **Internet:** www.idlo.int; **e-mail:** idlo@idlo.int.

International Fund for Agricultural Development—IFAD

Founded in 1977, a specialized agency of the United Nations, to improve food production in developed countries and to assist developing countries in establishing productive farming methods and better standards of nutrition.

Activities: Finances agricultural development programmes through loans and grants; works to strengthen agricultural policies and institutions; supports projects which improve the living conditions and nutritional welfare of people in developing countries; provides information and advice for policy-makers; produces Evaluation Profiles on developing countries; maintains a library of about 20,000 volumes.

Geographical Area of Activity: Asia, Central and South America and the Caribbean, the Middle East and North Africa, and Sub-Saharan Africa.

Publications: *Governing Council Report* (annually, in Arabic, English, French and Spanish); *IFAD Annual Report* (in Arabic, English, French and Spanish); also publishes several books.

Finance: Total assets US $5,206,464,000 (2001).

Principal Staff: Pres. Lennart Båge.

Address: Via del Serafico 107, 00142 Rome.

Telephone: (06) 54591; **Fax:** (06) 5043463; **Internet:** www.ifad.org; **e-mail:** ifad@ifad.org.

Istituto Affari Internazionali—IAI (Institute of International Affairs)

Founded in 1965 by Altiero Spinelli to promote the study of international relations, in particular Europe's position in world affairs.

Activities: Promotes research, often in collaboration with research institutes of other countries, and belongs to a number of international networks of research centres. It organizes national and international conferences in international relations. The Institute's main fields of interest are: Italian integration and international competition; the evolution of European integration and European policy; new issues in the security and defence field; transition in Eastern Europe; international relations (particularly with the countries on the southern shore of the Mediterranean); and relations between Europe and Asia. It has an extensive library containing over 20,500 publications in book and periodical form, in the major European languages, on international relations, especially of a politico-cultural nature.

Geographical Area of Activity: Europe.

Publications: *The International Spectator* (quarterly English language review); *IAI Quaderni* (series, irregular); *Global FP* (journal); *L'Italia e la politica internazionale* (yearbook); numerous books and pamphlets, some in collaboration with other publishers.

Principal Staff: Pres. Stefano Silvestri; Vice-Pres. Roberto Aliboni, Paolo Guerrieri; Dir Gianni Bonvicini; Deputy Dir Ettore Greco.

Address: Via Angelo Brunetti 9, 00186 Rome.

Telephone: (06) 3224360; **Fax:** (06) 3224363; **Internet:** www.iai.it; **e-mail:** iai@iai.it.

Istituto Auxologico Italiano

Founded in 1963 as a scientific institute for biomedical research focusing on the treatment of diseases which undermine physical and psychological development. The scope of the Institute has broadened since, to encompass prevention, treatment and rehabilitation of endocrine, metabolic and cardiovascular diseases. In 1972 it was recognized by the Ministries of Health and for Universities and Scientific and Technological Research as a Scientific Institute for Research and Care.

Activities: Operates in the area of medicine and health, and in particular endocrinology and metabolism, cardiovascular disease and neuroscience. The Institute operates in three health-care centres: the Istituto Scientifico San Michele (Milan), the Istituto Scientifico San Luca (Milan) and the Istituto Scientifico San Giuseppe (Verbania); these centres care for approx. 165,000 patients each year. The diagnostic and clinical activities of the Institute are supported by the continuous research activity of several experimental laboratories.

Geographical Area of Activity: Mainly Italy.

Publications: Report of operations; *Acta Medica Auxologica* (scientific review).

Principal Staff: Pres. Giovanni Ancarani; Scientific Dir Prof. Alberto Zanchetti.

Address: Direzione Scientifica, Via Ariosto 13, 20145 Milan.

Telephone: (02) 582111; **Fax:** (02) 58211480; **Internet:** www.auxologico.it; **e-mail:** info@auxologico.it.

Istituto Carlo Cattaneo—Fondazione de Ricerca (Carlo Cattaneo Institute—Research Foundation)

Founded in 1965 by a group of academic scientific publishers, the foundation was granted foundation status in 1986. Aims to promote democratic values through the dissemination of research findings on politics and social science.

Activities: Conducts research, studies and activities relating to culture and education, particularly in the fields of social and political science. Spreads knowledge of Italian society, especially regarding its political system.

Geographical Area of Activity: Italy.

Publications: *Polis. Ricerche e studi su società e politica in Italia* (journal); *Politica in Italia* (annually); *Ricerche e studi dell-Istituto Cattaneo; Materiali di Ricerca dell'Istituto Cattaneo*.

Board of Trustees: Prof. Marco Cammelli; Prof. Raimondo Catanzaro; Prof. Renzo Costi; Prof. Umberto Paniccia; Prof. Francesca Zannotti.

Principal Staff: Pres. Prof. Raimondo Catanzaro; Dir Prof. Giancarlo Gasperdu.

Address: Via Santo Stefano 11, 40125 Bologna.

Telephone: (051) 239766; **Fax:** (051) 262959; **Internet:** www.cattaneo.org; **e-mail:** catt@cattaneo.org.

Istituto per la Cooperazione Economica Internazionale e i Problemi dello Sviluppo (Institute for International Economic Co-operation and Development)

Founded in 1966 to foster the development of Central and Eastern European countries and the Commonwealth of Independent States, through information, research, advice, technical assistance, etc., related to international economic co-operation, conflict resolution and development.

Activities: Carries out research and technical assistance programmes in co-operation with Italian ministries, the European Union, the International Bank for Reconstruction and Development (World Bank), United Nations agencies, the OECD and other international organizations and agencies.

Geographical Area of Activity: Italy, Eastern Europe and the republics of Central Asia.

Publications: Report of activities, documents, handbooks, guides, monographs, special series and conference proceedings.

Principal Staff: Pres. Dr Ing. Fausto Capalbo.

Address: Piazza Cola di Rienzo 68, 00192 Rome.

Telephone: (06) 3215095; **Fax:** (06) 3214690; **e-mail:** iceps@pelagus.it.

Istituto di Ricerche Farmacologiche Mario Negri (Mario Negri Institute of Pharmacological Research)

Founded in April 1961 by Mario Negri to promote technical and scientific research in pharmacology and in the biomedical sciences, in order to prevent and cure human and animal diseases.

Activities: Operates nationally and internationally in the fields of education, science and medicine, through self-conducted biomedical research programmes, research fellowships, scholarships, conferences, courses, publications and lectures. Research institutes are situated also in Ranica (Bergamo) and Santa Maria Imbaro (Chieti).

Geographical Area of Activity: International.

Publications: *Negri News* (monthly); *Research and Practice* (6 a year); scientific reports; books; journals; annual list of publications.

Finance: Net assets US $80,686,523 (2001); annual revenue $24,178,856, expenditure $20,747,119 (2001).

Trustees: P. Martelli (Pres.); F. Russo (Hon. Pres.); G. Di Benedetto; L. Berti; E. Decleva; A. Groppetti; F. Guasti; M. Russo; P. Sirtori.

Principal Staff: Dir Prof. Silvio Garattini; Admin. Maria Grazia Pezzoni.

Address: Via Eritrea 62, 20157 Milan.

Telephone: (02) 390141; **Fax:** (02) 3546277; **Internet:** www.marionegri.it; **e-mail:** mnegri@marionegri.it.

Istituto Luigi Sturzo (Luigi Sturzo Institute)

Founded in 1951 by a committee in honour of Luigi Sturzo, to promote the social sciences, in particular sociology, in Italy and abroad.

Activities: Operates in the fields of history and the social sciences, through research, conferences and discussions, scholarships and publications. Prizes are awarded to Italian and foreign scholars. Also maintains a library.

Publications: *Sociologia* (3 a year); scientific studies.

Principal Staff: Pres. Prof. Gabriele De Rosa; Sec.-Gen. Dott. Flavia Nardelli.

Address: Palazzo Baldassini, Via delle Coppelle 35, 00186 Rome.

Telephone: (06) 6840421; **Fax:** (06) 68404244; **Internet:** www.sturzo.it; **e-mail:** infopoint@sturzo.it.

Lama Gangchen World Peace Foundation

Founded in 1992 by TYS Lama Gangchen, to develop a culture of peace, through non-formal education and funding projects.

Activities: Works on international humanitarian projects and promotes world peace in the fields of the arts and humanities, conservation and the environment, non-formal education, and medicine and health, and provides aid to less-developed countries. Also operates cultural exchanges and promotes inter-religious dialogue.

Geographical Area of Activity: Europe, Asia and South America.

Restrictions: Grants only to specific organizations.

Publications: *Peace Times Quarterly*; books.

Principal Staff: CEO and UN Representative Isthar D. Adler.

Address: Via Marco Polo 13, 20124 Milan.

Telephone: (02) 29010263; **Fax:** (02) 6554711; **e-mail:** lamagangchen@compuserve.com.

Mani Tese (Outstretched Hands)

Founded in 1964 with the aim of awakening the Italian public to the problems of developing countries and financing development projects.

Activities: Operates self-conducted programmes, in conjunction with local partners in the areas of education, agriculture, infrastructure development, humanitarian aid and preventive health programmes, as well as organizing training courses in development studies; lobbies and campaigns on related issues, organizes conferences; maintains a reference library of 20,000 publications.

Geographical Area of Activity: Africa, Asia, and Central and South America.

Publications: *Mani Tese* (monthly newspaper); also publishes books, educational materials, audiovisual aids, pamphlets and brochures.

Finance: Financed by its local groups and members, the operation of two co-operatives, the European Commission, the Italian Ministry of Foreign Affairs and several city councils. Budget US $6,343,466,000 (1998).

Principal Staff: Dir Ugo Biggeri; Sec.-Gen. Sabina Sinicalchi.

Address: Piazza Gambara 7–9, 20143 Milan.

Telephone: (02) 4075165; **Fax:** (02) 4046890; **Internet:** www.manitese.it/manitese.htm; **e-mail:** info@manitese.it.

Society for International Development

Established in 1957, a global network of individuals and institutions concerned with development which is participative, pluralistic and sustainable.

Activities: The Society comprises approximately 3,000 individual members, 65 local chapters and 55 institutional members, as well as over 100 partner institutions from a variety of fields. Its purpose is to support development innovation at all levels; to encourage and facilitate the creation of a sense of community among individuals and organizations committed to social justice at local, national, regional and international levels; and to promote dialogue, understanding and co-operation for social and economic development that furthers the well-being of all peoples. Activities focus on five areas: sustainable livelihoods; democratic approaches to national governance; women's empowerment; international relations and global governance; and strengthening civil society in post-conflict situations. Projects are implemented at global, national and local level, and include networking and advocacy, cross-sectorial dialogues, research, publications and on-line debates.

Geographical Area of Activity: International.

Publications: Annual Report; *Development* (journal, quarterly); *Bridges* (newsletter, every 2 months); programme reports and other publications.

Principal Staff: Pres. Enrique Iglesias; Sec.-Gen. Roberto Savio; Man. Dir Stefano Prato.

Address: Via Panisperna 207, 00184 Rome.

Telephone: (06) 4872172; **Fax:** (06) 4872170; **Internet:** www.sidint.org; **e-mail:** info@sidint.org.

Svenska Institutet i Rom/Istituto Svedese di Studi Classici a Roma (Swedish Institute in Rome)

Founded in 1926 by Crown Prince Gustaf Adolf and others to further, within the framework of Swedish cultural activity, the knowledge of classical culture in the Mediterranean area; to act as a medium for Swedish humanistic research and education primarily in the field of classical antiquity and history of art and architecture.

Activities: Operates internationally in the fields of education and the arts and humanities, through research, fellowships, scholarships, conferences, courses, publications and lectures.

Geographical Area of Activity: International.

Publications: *Skrifter Utgivna av Svenska Instituet i Rom; Opuscula Romana; Svewromana.*

Address: Via Omero 14, Valle Giulia, 00197 Rome.

Telephone: (06) 3201596; **Fax:** (06) 3230265; **Internet:** www.svenska-institutet-rom.org; **e-mail:** srisv@vatlib.it.

Japan

FOUNDATION CENTRES AND CO-ORDINATING BODIES

JANIC—Japanese NGO Center for International Co-operation

A non-profit, non-partisan networking NGO established in 1987 to foster closer relations among Japanese NGOs working in international co-operation; to provide services for the development of NGOs; to encourage networking between domestic and international NGOs and related organizations; to encourage dialogue between NGOs and other sectors of society; to deepen Japanese public understanding of and support for the activities of NGOs; and to conduct research on NGOs and international co-operation.

Activities: Runs courses and training programmes; carries out research; hosts meetings; offers advisory services; conducts lobbying and networking activities aimed at Japanese government and business; promotes educational activities, including the 'Global Citizenship Education Caravan' held throughout Japan; and issues publications. Maintains a library and database on NGOs. In 2002 had 62 member organizations.

Geographical Area of Activity: Japan.

Restrictions: Does not make grants.

Publications: *Directory of Japanese NGOs Concerned with International Co-operation; NGO Correspondence: Global Citizens* (newsletter in Japanese, 10 a year); *Kokoro* (quarterly newsletter, in English); *Directory of Non-governmental Organizations in Japan 1994; Creating Together a New Partnership—NGO Support Schemes Contributing to People's Self-Reliance;* other publications on NGOs, conference and symposia reports.

Principal Staff: Chair. Yoshitaka Funato; Vice-Chair. Michiya Kumaoka, Takashi Shimosawa; Man. Dir Michio Ito.

Address: Saito Bldg, 5th Floor, 2-9-1 Kanda Nichiki-cho, Chiyoda-ku, Tokyo 101-0054.

Telephone: (3) 3294-5370; **Fax:** (3) 3294-5398; **Internet:** www.jca.apc.org/janic; **e-mail:** globalcitizen@janic.org.

Japan Foundation Center

Founded in November 1985 to disseminate information on foundations in Japan, provide assistance to member foundations, and publicize the role and activities of grant-making foundations.

Activities: The Center compiles and publishes information on the activities of grant-making foundations in Japan; conducts research and publishes the results; maintains a library of publications relating to Japanese and overseas foundations; and sponsors seminars, lectures and symposia.

Geographical Area of Activity: Japan.

Restrictions: No direct grant-making to individuals or organizations.

Publications: *JFC Views* (in Japanese); *Directory of Grantmaking Foundations* (in Japanese).

Principal Staff: Exec. Dir Seitaro Horiuchi.

Address: Believe Shinjuku 4F, 1-26-9 Shinjuku, Shinjuku-ku, Tokyo 160-0022.

Telephone: (3) 3350-1857; **Fax:** (3) 3350-1858; **Internet:** www.jfc.or.jp; **e-mail:** pref@jfc.or.jp.

FOUNDATIONS, TRUSTS AND NON-PROFIT ORGANIZATIONS

Asahi Beer Arts Foundation

Founded in 1989 by Asahi Breweries Ltd to contribute to the enhancement of Japanese culture by awarding grants for artistic and cultural activities including fine arts and music, and by extending financial support for international exchange in artistic and cultural activities.

Activities: Grants are made towards fine arts exhibitions in Japan, music concerts in Japan and in support of foreign students for scholarships, exhibitions and concerts.

Geographical Area of Activity: Japan.

Restrictions: Grants are only given for events held in Japan and scholarships to foreign students are only available to those studying in Japan.

Publications: *Guide to the Foundation; List of Scholarship Students*.

Finance: Funding provided by Asahi Breweries Ltd. Assets 734,000,000 yen (March 2000); annual revenue 300,000,000 yen, expenditure 195,000,000 yen (2000).

Board of Directors: Yuzo Seto (Chair. and Chair. of Asahi Breweries Ltd).

Address: Asahi Beer Azumabashi Bldg, 1-23-1 Azumabashi, Sumida-ku, Tokyo 130-8602.

Telephone: (3) 5608-5202; **Fax:** (3) 5608-5201; **Internet:** www.asahibeer.co.jp/culture/zaidan/geijutu/body_gei.htm.

Asahi Glass Foundation

Established in 1933 as the Asahi Foundation for Chemical Industry Promotion, by the Asahi Glass Company Ltd.; under current name since 1990. Supports research in scientific, technological and environmental areas.

Activities: Funds four research programmes aimed at contributing to solving the major issues facing mankind. Research grants are made in the fields of life sciences, information sciences, the environment, energy, humanity, and the global environment. The foundation also provides funding for overseas research at Chulalongkom University, Thailand and the Institute Technology Bandung, Indonesia.

Geographical Area of Activity: International.

Publications: *Questionnaire on Environmental Problems and the Survival of Humankind* (annually); *af News* (newsletter, 2 a year); Annual Report; research reports.

Finance: Total assets 11,869,817,943 yen (March 2002); total budget 650,000,000 yen (2002).

Board of Trustees: Shohei Inoue; Shinya Ishizu; Ryoichi Ito; Shigeru Ito; Mikio Kawaguchi; Yukiharu Kodama; Jiro Kondo; Akio Morishima; Shinroku Morohashi; Yasunori Nishijima; Kenzo Tanaka; Shoichiro Toyoda.

Principal Staff: Chair. and CEO Hiromichi Seya; Sr Exec. Kimihiko Sato.

Address: Foundation 2nd Floor, Science Plaza, 2nd Floor, 5-3, Yonbancho, Chiyoda-ku, Tokyo 102-0081.

Telephone: (3) 5275-0620; **Fax:** (3) 5275-0871; **Internet:** www.af-info.or.jp/index/index_e2.html; **e-mail:** post@af-info.or.jp.

Asia-Africa International Voluntary Foundation—AIV

Founded in 1989.

Activities: Operates in the fields of aid to less-developed countries, education, and medicine and health, through the provision of technical and financial assistance to encourage appropriate and sustainable development in less-developed countries. Promotes co-operation between Japan and developing countries.

Geographical Area of Activity: Asia and Africa.

Finance: Annual budget approx. US $159,000.

Principal Staff: Masuhisa Oka.

Address: 3 Tsubosaka Takatori-cho, Takaichi-gun, Nara 635-01.

Telephone: (744) 523172; **Fax:** (744) 523835.

Asia Crime Prevention Foundation

Founded in 1982 by Atsushi Nagashima with the purpose of promoting effective measures for the prevention of crime and the treatment of offenders in the Asian, Pacific, African and Central and South American regions.

Activities: Organizes lectures on crime prevention and the treatment of offenders; carries out research; provides grants to institutions and individuals for relevant study programmes. The Foundation has members in 93 countries, and has general consultative status with the United Nations. Maintains nine offices in Japan and international offices in Bangladesh, China, Fiji, India, Indonesia, Kenya, Republic of Korea, Malaysia, Mongolia, Nepal, Pakistan, the Philippines, the Solomon Islands, Sri Lanka, Thailand, Tonga and Uganda.

Geographical Area of Activity: International.

Publications: *ACPF Today;* newsletter.

Finance: The Foundation is financed by interest on capital, membership fees and donations from public and private sources. Net assets 100,000,000 yen (Dec. 1999).

Principal Staff: Chair. Minoru Shikita.

Address: Akasaka Belgo, Ste 1007, 3-11-14 Akasaka, Minato-ku, Tokyo 107-0052.

Telephone: (3) 3509-7732; **Fax:** (3) 3508-8870; **Internet:** www.acpf.org; **e-mail:** info@acpf.org.

Asia/Pacific Cultural Centre for UNESCO—ACCU

Founded in 1971 to promote mutual understanding and cultural co-operation among peoples in the Asia-Pacific region through the implementation of various programmes in the fields of culture, book development and literacy promotion.

Activities: Operates regionally in Asia and the Pacific in the fields of culture, book development and literacy, through joint programmes of UNESCO member states in the region for production of low-priced quality books for children, materials such as posters, booklets and videos for literates in rural areas, audiovisual materials; training of cultural and book personnel in the region; publications (see below); special programmes (annual photography contest and travelling exhibition, biennial Noma Concours for illustrators of children's picture books in developing countries; Asia/Pacific Programme for Regional Co-operation in Protection of Cultural Heritage and the International Exchange Programme for the Promotion of International Co-operation and Mutual Understanding); and maintenance of the ACCU Library, with emphasis on children's books and school textbooks from Asian countries, as well as UNESCO publications.

Geographical Area of Activity: Asia and the Pacific.

Restrictions: UNESCO member states in Asia-Pacific region.

Publications: *Asian/Pacific Book Development (ABD)* (quarterly); reference materials; meeting reports.

Finance: Annual revenue and expenditure 775,198,708 yen (March 2001).

Principal Staff: Pres. Kazuo Suzuki; Dir Gen. Muneharu Kusaba.

Address: 6 Fukuromachi, Shinjuku-ku, Tokyo 162-8484.

Telephone: (3) 3269-4435; **Fax:** (3) 3269-4510; **Internet:** www.accu.or.jp; **e-mail:** general@accu.or.jp.

Asian Community Trust

Founded in November 1979 to promote social and economic development in Asian communities, and mutual understanding between people in Japan and in neighbouring Asian countries, by assisting activities which contribute to development.

Activities: Provides financial assistance to institutions in South-East Asia for specific activities in rural development, education and youth development, health, environment and conservation, and the institutional development of NGOs; also administers a number of semi-independent trust funds. Operates two resource desks in Indonesia and the Philippines.

Geographical Area of Activity: South-East Asia.

Publications: *ACT Now* (2 a year); Annual Report.

Finance: Net assets 303,331,052 yen (1998); grant expenditure 7,980,000 yen (1999).

Trustees: Representatives of the following: Mitsui Trust and Banking Co., Ltd; Mitsubishi Trust and Banking Corpn; Sumitomo Trust and Banking Co., Ltd; Yasuda Trust and Banking Co., Ltd; Toyo Trust and Banking Co., Ltd; Chuo Trust and Banking Co., Ltd; Nippon Trust Bank, Ltd; Daiwa Bank, Ltd.

Principal Staff: Chair. Taroichi Yoshida; Exec. Sec. Toshihiro Menju.

Address: c/o Japan Center for International Exchange, 4-9-17 Minami Azabu, Minato-ku, Tokyo 106-0047.

Telephone: (3) 3446-7781; **Fax:** (3) 3443-7580; **Internet:** www.jcie.or.jp/act/index.html; **e-mail:** act@jcie.or.jp.

Asian Health Institute

An NGO established in 1980 by Dr Hiromi Kawahara to provide accessible and affordable health care for the poor throughout Asia.

Activities: Encourages the formation and maintenance of effective community health-care organizations through training. Courses funded by the Institute aim to enhance leadership skills so that more community-based health workers take the initiative to develop their own organizations, and work to combat curable diseases in less-developed parts of Asia.

Geographical Area of Activity: Asia.

Restrictions: No grants to individuals nor to organizations.

Publications: *Asian Health Institute* (newsletter, 3–4 a year).

Finance: Funded by membership fees and donations. Assets 460,000,000 yen (March 2000); annual revenue 260,000,000 yen, expenditure 116,800,000 yen (2000).

Directors: Dr Hiromi Kawahara (Chair) and others.

Principal Staff: Gen. Sec. Dr Hikaru Sato

Address: 987-30, Minamiyama, Komenoki-cho, Nisshin-Shi, Aichi 470-0111.

Telephone: (5617) 31950; **Fax:** (5617) 31990; **Internet:** www.jca.apc.org/ahi; **e-mail:** ahi@jca.apc.org.

Bridge Asia Japan

Established in 1993, as Indochina Co-operation Centre Japan, renamed in 1994, to undertake projects in Myanmar and Vietnam.

Activities: Operates in the areas of aid to less-developed countries, and conservation and the environment, in Myanmar and Vietnam, through self-conducted projects, especially to assist vulnerable people, including refugees, disabled people, and women and children. Projects include supporting education and school construction, water and sanitation, afforestation and training. Nationally, the organization supports exchanges and study tours, and issues publications. Maintains offices in Myanmar and Vietnam.

Geographical Area of Activity: Myanmar and Vietnam.

Publications: Newsletter and reports.

Finance: Annual revenue 115,832,038 yen, expenditure 107,148,923 yen (1998).

Principal Staff: Pres. Etsuko Nemoto; Sec.-Gen. Masahiro Araishi.

Address: 303 Shin-toshin Monsion, 3-48-21 Hon-machi, Shibuya-ku, Tokyo 151.

Telephone: (3) 3372-9777; **Fax:** (3) 5351-2395; **Internet:** www.jca.apc.org/baj.

Defense of Green Earth Foundation—DGEF

Founded in 1982 to promote the protection of the environment.

Activities: Supports projects to protect the environment, including afforestation projects, the protection of the Oze swamp, and attempts to reduce desertification; sponsors environmental research and surveys; aims to increase awareness of environmental issues.

Geographical Area of Activity: Japan.

Finance: Annual budget approx. US $620,175.

Principal Staff: Exec. Dir Katsuhiro Kotari.

Address: B1, Baji Chikusan-kaikan, 1-2, Kanda Surugadai, Chiyoda-ku, Tokyo 101-0062.

Telephone: (3) 3233-3376; **Fax:** (3) 3233-1248; **Internet:** www.ne.jp/asahi/defense/green/.

Global Environmental Action

Established in 1991 to promote sustainable development and help solve global environmental problems.

Activities: Operates internationally in the field of conservation and the environment, through organizing conferences and disseminating the results of conferences. Initiatives include an information resource for environmental NGOs in developing countries.

Geographical Area of Activity: International.

Principal Staff: Chair. Gaishi Hiraiwa; Exec. Dir Tsunemi Yasumoto.

Address: Tokyo Sakurada Bldg 304A, 1-1-3 Nishishinbashi, Minato-ku, Tokyo 105-0003.

Telephone: (3) 3503-7484; **Fax:** (3) 3503-6953; **Internet:** www.gea.or.jp; **e-mail:** gea@gea.or.jp.

Global Voluntary Service

Established in 1992 by Teiko Inabata to foster volunteer activity in developing nations, for the improvement of living conditions, expertise and for the protection of the environment.

Activities: Operates in less-developed countries, mainly Kenya, Peru and the Philippines, in the areas of rural and agricultural development, education, training, medical assistance, environmental protection and welfare for underprivileged women, through developmental education, medical missions, health programmes, vocational training, information provision, exchange of personnel, collaboration with other NGOs, exhibitions, study tours, work camps and seminars. Maintains an office in Tokyo, and overseas offices in Manila, Nairobi and Lima.

Geographical Area of Activity: Japan, and less-developed countries, in particular Kenya, Peru and the Philippines.

Publications: Annual Report; brochures and audiovisual materials.

Finance: Sources of finance are private and governmental agencies (60%), membership fees (20%) and fundraising activities (20%).

Trustees: Teiko Inabata (Chair.); Peter Baron; Seizo Inabata.

Principal Staff: Exec. Dir Seizo Inabata.

Address: 3-25-502 Funado-cho, Ashia City, Hyogo 659-0093.

Telephone: (797) 340078; **Fax:** (797) 341061; **Internet:** plaza15.mbn.or.jp/~gvs; **e-mail:** gvs@cc.mbn.or.jp.

The Hitachi Scholarship Foundation

Founded in 1984 by Hitachi Ltd (q.v.) and Kenichiro Komai, on the 75th anniversary of the company's establishment, to support the development of human resources in universities located in member states of the Association of South East Asian Nations (ASEAN) and contribute to advanced education, collaboration and co-operation among ASEAN universities and Japan; develop a human network among universities in ASEAN countries and Japan; and enhance cultural understanding and mutual relationship through networking between faculties in ASEAN countries and Japan.

Activities: Funds and supports study and research in Japan by promising young faculty members and graduate students from universities in Indonesia, Malaysia, the Philippines, Singapore and Thailand, as well as supporting activities promoting academic, educational and cultural interchanges between those countries and Japan. Awards grants, scholarships and fellowships.

Geographical Area of Activity: South-East Asia, including Indonesia, Malaysia, the Philippines, Singapore and Thailand.

Restrictions: Grants made to national university lecturers in five ASEAN countries only. No grants to individuals.

Finance: Hitachi Ltd donated the Foundation's endowment of approx. 2,100,000,000 yen. Net assets 3,000,000,000 yen; annual expenditure approx. 170,000,000 yen.

Board of Trustees: Appointed by Hitachi Ltd: Katsushige Mita (Chair.).

Principal Staff: Man. Dir T. Gomibuchi; Sec.-Gen. H. Sugai; Programme Officers M. Homma, Programme Officer M. Nunokami.

Address: 5-1, Marunouchi 1-chome, Chiyoda-ku, Tokyo 100-8220.

Telephone: (3) 3215-3761; **Fax:** (3) 3215-2449; **Internet:** www.hitachi.co.jp/int; **e-mail:** scholarship@hdq.hitachi.co.jp.

Honda Foundation

Founded in 1977 by Soichiro Honda to support the development of technology which is in harmony with the environment ('eco-technology').

Activities: Supports annual international symposia, seminars and workshops at which experts from all countries gather, in order to discuss scientific and technological problems inherent in modern civilization with a view to creating a better society. Awards the annual Honda Prize to an individual or organization, irrespective of nationality, for a distinguished achievement in 'eco-technology'.

Governing Board: Hiromori Kawashima (Pres.).

Principal Staff: Man. Dir Masaru Inoue.

Address: 1—1, 2-chome, Minami-Aoyama, Minato-ku, Tokyo 107-8556.

Telephone: (3) 3274-5125; **Fax:** (3) 3274-5103; **Internet:** www.soc.nii.ac.jp/hf/eng/profile/index.html; **e-mail:** xv6m-nkmr@asahi-net.or.jp.

Hoso-Bunka Foundation, Inc

Founded in 1974 by the Japan Broadcasting Corpn—NHK, to contribute to the advancement of broadcasting and the dissemination of culture through broadcasting.

Activities: The Foundation provides financial assistance for research in broadcasting technology; for the development of receiving equipment; for international co-operation in broadcasting; and for legal, socio-economic and cultural studies related to broadcasting. Awards the annual HBF Prizes for outstanding domestic television and radio programmes and broadcasting technology development.

Geographical Area of Activity: International.

Restrictions: Grants only to professional projects related to broadcasting culture.

Publications: *HBF* (annually, in Japanese); Annual Research Report (in Japanese); activity report (3 a year, in Japanese); activity report in English available on website.

Finance: Net assets 12,300,000,000 yen (April 2001); annual revenue 621,202,905 yen, expenditure 620,204,392 yen (2000–01).

Board of Directors: Ichiro Yoshikuni (Pres.); Noriyuki Musha (Gen. Man. Dir and Acting Exec. Sec.); Tadao Ishikawa; Ichiro Kato; Toshio Kawatake; Hiroshi Shiono; Yasuharu Suematsu.

Principal Staff: Acting Exec. Sec. Noriyuki Musha.

Address: Kyodo Bldg, 41-1 Udagawa-cho, Shibuya-ku, Tokyo 150-0042.

Telephone: (3) 3464-3131; **Fax:** (3) 3770-7239; **Internet:** www.hbf.or.jp; **e-mail:** inform@hbf.or.jp.

Institute of Developing Economies/Japan External Trade organization—IDE-JETRO

The Institute of Developing Economies was established in 1958 (reorganized in 1960 as a semi-governmental body) for basic and comprehensive research on economic and related affairs in developing countries, to contribute to the improvement of economic co-operation and trade relations between Japan and these countries. The Institute merged with the Japan External Trade Organization (JETRO) in July 1998. The new organization is an integral unit of the Japan External Trade Organization, a semi-governmental body under the supervision of the Ministry of International Trade and Industry.

Activities: The Institute operates in Asia, the Middle East, Africa, Eastern Europe, Central and South America and the Pacific and with various regional organizations. It conducts its own research projects on about 50 topics annually, covering various aspects of development, economic co-operation and statistical analysis; research is carried out by the Institute's own staff, with the co-operation of outside experts. It also runs a Joint Research Programme for joint studies with scholars in developing countries, and a Visiting Research Fellows Programme, under which foreign researchers or experts are invited to work at the Institute. Every year about 150 researchers are sent overseas for up to 30 days to conduct field surveys, and 34 research staff are sent abroad for two years. The Institute also collects and compiles statistical data, and maintains a library. Makes awards in recognition of outstanding publications. It holds international symposia, and conducts about 50 seminars and lectures a year in various parts of Japan, to inform the public on development issues.

Geographical Area of Activity: Asia, the Middle East, Africa, Eastern Europe, Central and South America and the Pacific.

Publications: *The Developing Economies* (quarterly, in English); *Ajia Keizai* (Asian Economies, monthly); *Ajiken warudo torendo* (Asian World Trends, monthly); *Middle East Studies Series; Joint Studies on Economlic Development Policies in ASEAN and Neighbouring Countries;* occasional papers, symposium proceedings, statistical data, bibliographies and research reports.

Finance: Annual budget 6,181,000,000 yen (March 2002).

Governing Body: The organization is an integral unit of JETRO, a semi-governmental body under the supervision of the Ministry of International Trade and Industry; I. Yamazawa (Exec. Vice-Pres. of JETRO and Pres. of IDE).

Principal Staff: Exec. Vice-Pres. of JETRO T. Nakata; T. Hayashi; M. Kagami.

Address: 3-2-2 Wakaba, Mihama-ku, Chiba-shi, Chiba 261-8545.

Telephone: (43) 299-9500; **Fax:** (43) 299-9724; **Internet:** www.ide.go.jp; **e-mail:** info@ide.go.jp.

The Institute of Energy Economics (Japan)

Founded in 1966 by the energy industry to conduct research and studies which will contribute towards the framing of Japan's energy policy and towards the business activities of the energy industries, through an extensive collection of information and data on the world energy situation and the energy policy in major countries, and through their objective and positive analysis.

Activities: Operates nationally and internationally in the fields of economic affairs and the conservation of natural resources, through self-conducted programmes, research, conferences, courses, publications and lectures. Current projects include a long-range forecast of the demand for energy in Japan; an analysis of the flow of the world's crude petroleum market and an evaluation of crude petroleum in the Japanese market; an analysis of structural change in the world's petroleum industry; recent trends in conservation from oil to coal; and evaluation of synthetic fuel. A number of researchers are sent abroad each year to obtain first-hand information on energy economy or to attend international conferences; several others are also sent to research institutes abroad under exchange programmes. Established the affiliated Oil Information Center in 1981 and the Asia Pacific Energy Resource Centre in 1996, both of which carry out research into energy related issues.

Publications: Report of operations and financial statement; *Energy Economy* (quarterly, in Japanese); *EDMC Energy-Trend* (monthly, in Japanese);.

Board of Directors: Yoshihiro Sakamoto (Pres.); Mitsuru Nitta (Sr Man. Dir); Kazuya Fujime; Masaharu Fujitomi; Kokichi Ito; Kensuke Kanekiyo; Tsutomu Toichi; Shunichiro Wakabayashi.

Principal Staff: Man. Dirs Kazuya Fujime, Dr Tsutomu Toichi.

Address: Inui Bldg, Kachidoki, 13-1, Kachidoki 1-Chome, Chuo-ku, Tokyo 104-0054.

Telephone: (3) 5547-0211; **Fax:** (3) 5547-0223; **Internet:** eneken.ieej.or.jp.

International Association of Traffic and Safety Sciences—IATSS (Honda-Fujisawa Commemorative Foundation)

Founded in 1974 by Soichiro Honda and Takeo Fujisawa with the purpose of contributing to better traffic management by studying problems, especially accidents, environmental pollution and the excessive consumption of energy.

Activities: Operates nationally and internationally in conducting research (for example projects on accident analysis; traffic signs; fuel economy; international comparative research on driver behaviour and opinions); collecting and applying data; sponsoring domestic and international conferences and meetings; publishing the results of research; and giving annual IATSS Dissertation, Literature and Achievement Awards to (respectively) the author of the best paper appearing in the *IATSS Review* , for outstanding literary works concerning the realization of an ideal mobile society, and the individual who has made the most useful contribution to traffic safety. The IATSS Forum promotes Japanese technologies to young people from the countries of South-East Asia.

Geographical Area of Activity: International.

Publications: *IATSS Forum News* (7 or 8 a year); *IATSS Research* (2 a year, in English); *IATSS Review* (3 a year); *White Paper on Traffic Safety* (annually, in English); *Statistics of Road Traffic Accidents in Japan* (annually, in English).

Address: 2-6-20, Chuo-ku, Tokyo 104-0028.

Telephone: (3) 3273-7884; **Fax:** (3) 3272-7054; **Internet:** www.soc.nii.ac.jp/iatss/english.

International Communications Foundation

Established in 1988 by Kokusai Denshin Denwa Co. Ltd (now KDD Corpn) to assist in the harmonious development of the world through the promotion of international communication.

Activities: Operates internationally in the area of communication, and science and technology, through supporting a range of projects relating to international telecommunications, including grants for research and conferences, social support and cultural activities, and educational programmes. Fellowships are also available for foreign students.

Geographical Area of Activity: International.

Finance: Endowment of 5,000,000,000 yen.

Principal Staff: Pres. Tohru Ohta.

Address: 2-3-1, Nishi-Shinjuku, Shinjuku-ku, Tokyo 163-0907.

Telephone: (3) 3347-7094; **Fax:** (3) 3347-6439; **Internet:** www.icf.or.jp; **e-mail:** info@icf.or.jp.

International Lake Environment Committee Foundation

Founded in 1987 by the Shiga Prefectural Government to promote the environmentally sound management of the world's lakes and reservoirs.

Activities: Operates nationally and internationally in the fields of aid to less-developed countries and conservation and the environment, through self-conducted programmes, research, conferences, training courses and publications. The Foundation's major activities include collecting and organizing data on the condition of lakes throughout the world; organizing training seminars on development issues and lake environment conservation in developing countries; promoting lake environment management; and providing support for the United Nations Environment Programme's International Environmental Technology Centre. Also maintains a database surveying the condition of the world's lakes and awards the annual Biwako Prize for Ecology.

Geographical Area of Activity: International.

Publications: *ILEC Newsletter* (three a year); *Lakes and Reservoirs: Research and Management* (quarterly journal); surveys and guidelines on lake management, and workshop reports.

Finance: Annual revenue and expenditure 165,000,000 yen (1999).

Board of Directors: Kei Yamazaki (Chair.); Prof. Tatuo Kira (Vice-Chair.); Hiroya Kotani; and 11 others.

Principal Staff: Dir Gen. Kei Yamazaki; Exec. Dir Hiroya Kotani.

Address: 1091 Oroshimo-cho, Kusatsu-shi, Shiga 525-0001.

Telephone: (775) 68-4567; **Fax:** (775) 68-4568; **Internet:** www.ilec.or.jp; **e-mail:** info@.ilec.or.jp.

International Medical Foundation of Japan

Founded in 1967 to promote co-operation in medicine with developing countries and to improve health planning in South-East Asian countries, and to contribute to the health needs of Japanese residents living abroad.

Activities: The Foundation organizes seminars, conferences and training courses, and generates and disseminates health- and medical-related information. Co-ordinates the Southeast Asian Medical Information Center (SEAMIC), which outside Japan operates in Brunei, Indonesia, Malaysia, the Philippines, Singapore, Thailand and Vietnam, promoting information exchange in the areas of infectious diseases, health statistics, medical information and nutrition improvement.

Geographical Area of Activity: Brunei, Indonesia, Japan, Malaysia, the Philippines, Singapore, Thailand and Vietnam.

Publications: *SEAMIC Newsletter* (quarterly); *SEAMIC Health Statistics* (annually).

Principal Staff: Pres. Toshio Yamazaki; Dir Gen. Dr Akio Tanaka; Exec. Dir Minoru Iida.

Address: Yaesu-Ichigaya Bldg, Ichigayatamachi 2-17, Shinjuku-ku, Tokyo 162-0843.

Telephone: (3) 3235-3012; **Fax:** (3) 3235-3017; **Internet:** www.seamic-imfj.or.jp; **e-mail:** miida@seamic-imfj.or.jp.

International Movement against All Forms of Discrimination and Racism—IMADR

Established in 1988 by the Burakumin in Japan, an NGO that seeks to eliminate all forms of discrimination world-wide, to promote international solidarity among minorites and to promote human rights.

Activities: Operates as a global network of minority groups and individuals. Seeks to eliminate racism and discrimination, to protect the rights of minority groups, support the development of indigenous people, and uphold the rights of migrants, through campaigns, disseminating information, lobbying, research, and providing training opportunities. Regional committees operate in Asia, North, Central and South America, and Europe. IMADR has consultative status with the United Nations Economic and Social Council (ECOSOC), and maintains an office in Geneva.

Geographical Area of Activity: International.

Restrictions: Grants only to specific organizations which are in partnership with IMADR.

Publications: *Connect* (quarterly newsletter) *Peoples for Human Rights* (annual journal); *ICERD: A Guide for NGOs*.

Board of Directors: Myriam Schreiber (Hon. Pres.); Nimalka Fernando (Pres.); Jacques Chevassus, Soon Man Rhim, Mario Jorge Yutzis (Vice-Pres.); and 12 others.

Principal Staff: Sec.-Gen. Kinhide Mushakoji.

Address: 3-5-11 Roppongi, Minato-ku, Tokyo 106-0032.

Telephone: (3) 3586-7447; **Fax:** (3) 3586-7462; **Internet:** www.imadr.org; **e-mail:** imadris@imadr.org.

Ishizaka Foundation

Founded in 1976 to further mutual understanding and friendship between Japan and other countries by cultural and educational interchange.

Activities: Provides scholarships for Japanese undergraduate and graduate students to study abroad, and for foreign students enrolled at Japanese universities. The Foundation also sponsors lectures and symposia which contribute to international cultural and educational interchange, and disseminates the proceedings.

Geographical Area of Activity: Brunei, Cambodia, Indonesia, Japan, Laos, Malaysia, Myanmar, Philippines, Singapore, Thailand and Vietnam.

Principal Staff: Chair. Takashi Imai.

Address: c/o Keidanren, 1-9-4 Otemachi, Chiyoda-ku, Tokyo 100-8188.

Telephone: (3) 3279-1411; **Fax:** (3) 5255-6233; **Internet:** www.keidanren.or.jp/japanese/profile/ishizaka/.

Iwatani Naoji Kinen Zaidan (Iwatani Naoji Foundation)

Founded in 1973 by Naoji Iwatani, President of Iwatani & Co., Ltd, to improve national welfare and promote international mutual understanding by providing assistance for research, development and international exchange in the fields of science and technology.

Activities: Operates nationally through providing grants for research and development projects in science and technology which will result in the improvement of the national welfare, and through giving recognition to those whose work in these fields will make a lasting contribution to Japan. The Foundation also provides aid for the promotion of international exchange of information in science and technology. It presents the Iwatani Naoji Memorial Prize each year for research into gas and energy; and the Iwatani International Scholarships, which are awarded to foreign students from East or South-East Asian countries, for postgraduate study in natural science and technology.

Geographical Area of Activity: Mainly Japan, some grants for East and South-East Asian students.

Publications: Annual Report; *Kenkyu Hokokusho* (report on the research results funded by the Foundation, annually, in Japanese).

Address: 712 TBR Bldg, 2-10-2 Nagata-cho, Chiyoda-ku, Tokyo 100-0014.

Telephone: (3) 3580-2251; **Fax:** (3) 3580-2700.

Japan Center for International Exchange

Founded in 1971 by Tadashi Yamamoto, to promote Japan's role in international affairs.

Activities: The Foundation operates internationally, specifically in the USA, Europe and the Asia-Pacific region. It sponsors exchange and study programmes, conducts comparative studies of public policy in Japan and the USA, organizes seminars and conferences, conducts research into all areas of policy development and international relations, examines relations between Japan and the Association of South-East Asian Nations (ASEAN), and encourages philanthropic works through the Asian Community Trust (q.v.). New initiatives include Global ThinkNet, the basis of the Center's research programmes, as well as administering a donor advised fund on behalf of Levi Strauss & Co.

Geographical Area of Activity: USA, Europe and the Asia-Pacific region.

Publications: *Asian Reflections on a New World after 9–11; A Gender Agenda: Asia–Europe Dialogue; JCIE Papers Series; Major Power Relations in Northeast Asia; Guidance for Governance; Asia Pacific Security Outlook; The Third Force: the Rise of Transnational Civil Society; Governance and Civil Society in a Global Age; New Perspectives on US–Japan Relations.*

Principal Staff: Pres. Tadashi Yamamoto.

Address: 4-9-17 Minami Azabu, Minato-ku, Tokyo 106-0047.

Telephone: (3) 3446-7781; **Fax:** (3) 3443-7580; **Internet:** www.jcie.or.jp; **e-mail:** admin@jcie.or.jp.

Japan Emergency NGOs—JEN

Established in 1994, a network of Japanese relief organizations operating internationally to give emergency relief.

Activities: Operates internationally in the fields of aid to less-developed countries and social welfare, especially in the area of disaster relief. Programmes currently operate in the countries of the former Yugoslavia (now Serbia and Montenegro), as well as Afghanistan, Chechnya, India, Mongolia and Pakistan.

Geographical Area of Activity: Afghanistan, Bosnia and Herzegovina, Chechnya, Croatia, India, Kosovo, Mongolia, Pakistan and Yugoslavia (Serbia and Montenegro).

Publications: Newsletter.

Finance: Annual budget approx. US $8,000,000.

Principal Staff: Pres. Mieko Osanai; Sec.-Gen. Keiko Kiyama.

Address: Mild Bldg, 4F, 2-26-5, Hyakunincho, Shinjuku-ku, Tokyo 169-0073.

Telephone: (3) 5332-9825-6; **Fax:** (3) 5332-9827; **Internet:** www.jen-npo.org; **e-mail:** info@jen-npo.org.

The Japan Foundation Centre for Global Partnership

Founded in 1972 to promote international cultural exchange and mutual understanding.

Activities: The Foundation works in a number of fields, but its three main programme areas are intellectual exchange programmes, regional and grass-roots programmes and fellowship programmes, focusing on Japanese studies, Japanese-language education, arts, publications, audio-visual media, sports and general culture.

Geographical Area of Activity: Japan and the USA.

Restrictions: No grants to individuals (except for the CGP Fellowship Programs); only supports projects from Japan or the USA.

Publications: Annual Report (in Japanese and English); *Kokusai Koryu Kikin News* (monthly, in Japanese).

Finance: Funded by investment income and other sources. Annual revenue US $18,013,877, expenditure US $15,640,130 (2000).

Advisory Committee: Hiroaki Fujii (Pres.); C. G. Campbell; K. Chino; T. S. Foley; R. P. Hearn; M. Iokibe; M. Meyerson; M. M. Mochizuki; T. Ogasawara; S. Ogata; K. Ohara; T. Shiina; J. E. Spero; A. Tanaka; E. Vogel.

Principal Staff: Exec. Dir Yoshihiko Wakumoto; Deputy Exec. Dir Kazuaki Kubo.

Address: Ark Mori Bldg 20F, 1-12-32 Akasaka, Minato-ku, Tokyo 107 6021.

Telephone: (3) 5562-3541; **Fax:** (3) 5562-3501; **Internet:** www.jpf.go.jp.

Japan International Volunteer Center

Established in 1980, originally to assist refugees from Indochina, now an international NGO supporting development.

Activities: Operates in seven countries of Asia, Africa and the Middle East (Cambodia, Palestinian Autonomous Areas, Ethiopia, Laos, South Africa, Thailand and Vietnam), as well as in Japan, in the fields of aid to less-developed countries, education and agricultural development, through projects in collaboration with local people; also involved in disaster relief operations in Africa and Asia.

Geographical Area of Activity: Asia, Africa and the Middle East.

Finance: Annual budget 356,000,000 yen (2000).

Principal Staff: Pres. Michiya Kumaoka; Sec.-Gen. Hiroshi Taniyama.

Address: 6F Maruko Bldg, 1-20-6 Higashi-Ueno, Taito-ku, Tokyo 110.

Telephone: (3) 3834-2388; **Fax:** (3) 3835-0519; **Internet:** www.jca.apc.org/jvc; **e-mail:** jvc@jca.apc.org.

Kajima Gakujitsu Shinko Zaidan (Kajima Foundation)

Founded in 1976 by Ume Kajima in memory of the late Morinosuke Kajima, to promote scientific research and international co-operation in science.

Activities: Research grants are awarded to candidates recommended by their university or learned society, in particular for science and technology. Finance is also provided for short-term (three months) and long-term (one year) studies overseas for Japanese researchers, and for visits by overseas researchers. The Foundation gives assistance to international scientific meetings held in Japan, and for co-operative research conducted by Japanese and foreign scholars.

Geographical Area of Activity: Mostly Japan.

Publications: Annual Report.

Address: 2-7 1-chome, Minato-ku, Tokyo 107.

Telephone: (3) 3404-3311; **Fax:** (3) 3474-1444; **Internet:** www.kajima.co.jp.

Kawakami Memorial Foundation

Founded in 1957 by Taizo Ishizaka, Hitoshi Ashida, Masamichi Yamagiwa, Teiichi Kawakita and others, to encourage scientific studies among young people.

Activities: Operates nationally in the fields of engineering, economic studies and law, through grants to individuals. The Foundation gives financial assistance for engineering and legal studies, holds an essay prize competition for economics and law, and awards scholarships to foreign students for study in Japan.

Geographical Area of Activity: Mainly Japan.

Publications: Report of operations and financial statement.

Address: Jouwa Yaesu Bldg, 2-4-1 Yaesu, Chuo-ku, Tokyo 104-0028.

Telephone: (3) 3275-1571.

Kokusai Kaihatsu Senta (International Development Center of Japan)

Founded in 1971 by Toshiwo Doko and Saburo Okita, to assist the advancement of the economic growth of developing countries by promoting Japanese development co-operation, and by contributing to the efforts of national and international organizations.

Activities: The Center organizes development training programmes (some of which are open to participants from developing nations) in, for example, development economics, project analysis, project leaders' training and language and cultural orientation. It conducts basic research on problems of economic development, and undertakes research and surveys commissioned by other organizations. It sponsors international conferences, accepts overseas research associates, and sends Japanese scholars (five or six a year) abroad for study connected with development problems.

Geographical Area of Activity: International.

Publications: Annual Report; *IDC Forum* (2 a year); regular series of working papers; occasional publications.

Finance: Total revenue 2,403,529,000 yen (2000).

Principal Staff: Chair. Saburo Kawai; Pres. Jinichiro Yabuta; Exec. Man. Dir Masaoki Takeuchi.

Address: Kyofuku Bldg 9-11, Tomioka 2-chome, Koto-ku, Tokyo 135-0047.

Telephone: (3) 3630-6911; **Fax:** (3) 3630-8120; **Internet:** www.idcj.or.jp/indexe.html.

Kokusai Koryu Kikin (The Japan Foundation)

Founded in 1972 to further international mutual understanding through the promotion of cultural exchange.

Activities: Operates internationally by offering fellowships to overseas scholars, enabling them to conduct research in Japan. Dissertation fellowships are offered to scholars in the social sciences and humanities, and professional fellowships to scholars engaged in studies on Japanese society and culture. Visiting professorships abroad are offered to Japanese professors, enabling them to teach in institutions overseas or to take part in research or conferences connected with Japan. Promotes Japanese language studies abroad and produces, collects and distributes materials which introduce Japanese culture abroad. Provides funding for cultural exhibitions and the performing arts, organizes lectures and seminars, and supports art-related and media exchanges (including Special Programs for Japan–Europe Cultural Exchange). The Japan Foundation Centre for Global Partnership was established in 1991 to promote relations between Japan and the USA through intellectual exchange and the promotion of mutual understanding. In 1995 the Japan Foundation Asia Center was established to achieve closer relations between Japan and other Asian countries through intellectual and cultural exchange and promoting an understanding of Asia among the Japanese people. The Foundation maintains overseas offices in Australasia, North, Central and South America, Asia, Africa and Europe, and Japanese Language Centres/Centres for Global Partnership in Australia, Brazil, Indonesia, Korea, Malaysia, Thailand, the United Kingdom and the USA; information may also be obtained from Japanese diplomatic missions.

Geographical Area of Activity: International.

Publications: Annual Report; *Japanese Book News* (quarterly); *Kokusai Koryu Kikin News* (monthly bulletin in Japanese); *CGP Newsletter* (quarterly); *Asia Center Newsletter* (quarterly); and other publications.

Finance: Annual budget 18,381,000,000 yen (2002).

Governing Board: Hiroaki Fujii (Pres.); Shinya Nagai (Sr Vice-Pres.); Kazuhito Tatebe, Sumio Wakamatsu, Sohei Yoshino (Exec. Vice-Pres).

Address: Ark Mori Bldg, 1-12-32 Akasaka, Minato-ku, Tokyo 107-6021.

Telephone: (3) 5562-3511; **Fax:** (3) 5562-3494; **Internet:** www.jpf.go.jp.

Maison Franco-Japonaise

Founded in 1924 by Paul Claudel and Eiichi Shibusawa for the collaboration and development of the French and Japanese cultures.

Activities: To achieve its objective, the Foundation conducts simultaneous studies of the French and Japanese cultures, organizes collections and exhibitions of study materials, meetings and conferences and publishes works relating to these studies. The Foundation operates research exchanges between France and Japan.

Geographical Area of Activity: France and Japan.

Publications: *Ebisu* (quarterly); *Nichifutsu Bunka; Dictionnaire historique du Japon; Hōbōgirin* (Encyclopaedia of Buddhism); scientific monographs on diverse subjects.

Finance: Activities are funded by private Japanese sources and by the French Ministry of Foreign Affairs.

Address: 3-9-25, Ebisu, Shibuya-ku, Tokyo 150-0013.

Telephone: (3) 5421-7641; **Fax:** (3) 5421-7651; **Internet:** www.mfj.gr.jp; **e-mail:** info@mfj.gr.jp.

The Matsumae International Foundation

Established in 1979 by Dr Shigeyoshi Matsumae to make a real contribution to permanent peace world-wide, by deepening the understanding of Japan, and establishing links with other countries through inviting to Japan young research workers of outstanding character, without regard to sex, race, religion, ideology or nationality.

Activities: Operates world-wide in the fields of medicine and health and science and technology, through offering grants to individuals, and scholarships and fellowships, tenable for three to six months and seven to twelve months. Applicants, who must apply from outside Japan, must be under the age of 40, and be post-doctoral researchers, or have a minimum of two years of research experience after the receipt of a Master's degree. Fields of study in the areas of natural science, engineering and medicine are prioritized.

Geographical Area of Activity: International.

Restrictions: Non-Japanese applicants must have a doctorate degree, be under the age of 40, not have been in Japan previously and have established professions or positions in their home country.

Publications: *Fellowship Announcement*; Newsletter.

Board of Directors: Dr Norio Matsumae (Chair.).

Address: 4-14-46 Kamiogi, Suginami-ku, Tokyo 167-0043.

Telephone: (3) 3301-7600; **Fax:** (3) 3301-7601; **Internet:** www.matsumae-if.org; **e-mail:** contact@matsumae-if.org.

Mitsubishi Ginko Kokusai Zaidan (Mitsubishi Bank Foundation)

Founded in 1981 by the Mitsubishi Bank, Tokyo, to deepen mutual understanding and promote cultural exchanges between Japan and the rest of the world and to promote world peace.

Activities: Provides grants for joint research in economic, social and cultural studies, and for exchanges of groups of people (usually aged between 18 and 39 years), and other activities. Funds conferences and seminars. Preference is given to programmes connected with Asia and the Pacific.

Geographical Area of Activity: Mostly the Asia-Pacific region.

Restrictions: Funding will only be considered if applied for through Japanese counterparts.

Board of Directors: Toshio Nakamura (Chair.); Masafumi Furuichi (Exec. Dir); and nine other members.

Address: 2-7-1 Marunouchi, Chiyoda-ku, Tokyo 100.

Telephone: (3) 3240-3317; **Fax:** (3) 3240-3367.

Moriya Foundation

Founded in March 1982 by Kimio Moriya to provide scholarships.

Activities: Offers scholarships to students from Asia enrolled in postgraduate courses in Japan. Certain universities are chosen each March, from which candidates are selected. Fields of study are limited to geography, history, education and related cultural sciences.

Geographical Area of Activity: Asia.

Finance: Total assets 319,305,000 yen (2002); annual revenue 12,052,000 yen, expenditure 11,634,000 yen (2002).

Principal Staff: Chair. Mutsuo Shirahama; Chief Sec. Norio Kato.

Address: c/o Teikoku Shoin Co., 3-29 Kanda Jimbo cho, Chiyoda-ku, Tokyo 101-0051.

Telephone: (3) 3263-7952; **Fax:** (3) 3262-7770; **Internet:** www.teikokushoin.co.jp; **e-mail:** somu@teikokushoin.co.jp.

Naito Foundation

Founded in 1969 by Toyoji Naito, to extend financial aid to researchers engaged in basic studies on the life sciences, particularly medical, biological, chemical and pharmaceutical studies for the prevention and treatment of human disease.

Activities: Operates nationally in the fields of education, science and medicine. Extends support to researchers in universities and public institutions, to Japanese researchers who wish to study abroad and to domestic research institutions. Sponsors educational visits to Japan by foreign research workers and supports the publication of reading materials in the life sciences. Arranges exhibitions for the promotion of studies and research in the life sciences, particularly pharmacy. Also awards prizes in recognition of outstanding contributions to the advancement of the life sciences.

Geographical Area of Activity: Mainly Japan.

Publications: Report of operations and financial statement; various books.

Finance: Net assets 1,742,240,147 yen (March 1999).

Trustees: Yuji Naito (Chair.).

Address: NKD Bldg, 42-6 Hongo 3, Bunkyo-ku, Tokyo 113-0033.

Telephone: (3) 3813-3005; **Fax:** (3) 3811-2917; **Internet:** www.naito-f.or.jp; **e-mail:** info@naito-f.or.jp.

Nihon Gakujutsu Shinko-kai (Japan Society for the Promotion of Science)

Founded in 1932 through an endowment granted by Emperor Showa, re-established in 1967 by the Japanese Government to contribute to the advancement of science.

Activities: Operates nationally through providing research fellowships and giving grants for joint research activities among Japanese scientists belonging to different institutions; promoting joint research by industrial concerns and universities; providing information services; publishing scientific works and producing films; and organizing lectures. The Society awards the International Prize for Biology annually to a person judged to have made outstanding scientific achievements in the field of biology. The Society operates internationally in providing research fellowships for overseas scientists, and grants to Japanese scientists for travel abroad; it supports international joint research projects, international research workshops and seminars. It also administers a number of bilateral programmes for scientific co-operation and exchange with various foreign academic institutions. Maintains overseas liaison offices in Egypt, France, Germany, Kenya, Sweden, the United Kingdom and the USA.

Geographical Area of Activity: International.

Publications: *Gakujutsu Geppo (Japanese Science Monthly)* (magazine); information resources; scientific publications.

Finance: About 99% of funds are provided by the Japanese Government, the rest by private sources. Annual budget approx. 115,900,000,000 yen (2002).

Governing Council: The 14 Council members, representing Japanese universities and other institutions, are appointed by the Minister of Education, Science and Culture.

Principal Staff: Pres. Hiroyuki Yoshikawa; Dir Gen. Motoyuki Ono.

Address: Yamato Bldg, 5-3-1 Kojimachi, Chiyoda-ku, Tokyo 102-8471.

Telephone: (3) 3263-1727; **Fax:** (3) 3263-1673; **Internet:** www.jsps.go.jp.

Nihon Keizai Chosa Kyogi-Kai (Japan Economic Research Institute)

Founded in 1962 to promote the overall development of Japan's economy and to contribute to interchange between nations in economic research and to the making of economic policy at industrial, national and international levels.

Activities: Operates both nationally and internationally in the fields of economic affairs and management, including urban and regional development, social infrastructure, energy, and industry, through research, international co-operation and dissemination of material. Economic research is carried out by research committees involving experts from industry, government agencies and the academic world. The resulting reports, as well as other up-to-date information on national and international economics, are distributed to members of the Institute and other organizations. Other activities include the organization of conferences, lectures and seminars, as well as playing an advisory role on private finance initiative (PFI) projects.

Geographical Area of Activity: International.

Finance: Derived from annual contributions by Japanese business corporations.

Governing Board: Yoh Kurosawa (Chair.); Hiroshi Kiyasu (Exec. Dir); Kosaku Inaba, Takashi Imai, Yotaro Kobayashi, Hiroyuki Yoshikawa (Representative Dirs).

Address: 3-3-4 Kandasurugadai, Chiyoda-ku, Tokyo 101-0062.

Telephone: (3) 5280-6105; **Fax:** (3) 5280-6106; **Internet:** www.jeri.or.jp; **e-mail:** info@jeri.or.jp.

Nihon Keizai Kenkyu Center (Japan Center for Economic Research)

Founded in 1963 to conduct studies and research on various problems of government finance, money and credit, economy, industry, management and other related subjects at home and abroad; and to promote mutual study and training of its members with the aim of contributing to the economic growth of Japan.

Activities: Conducts research on Japan's economy with particular emphasis on economic forecasting; organizes joint economic research; and undertakes research projects on a contractual basis. The Center sponsors economic study courses, seminars, lectures and symposia, and provides training for junior business people in advanced economics and research; it publishes the results of its research projects and operates a specialized library of 37,500 volumes, 861 periodicals and 1,280 statistics. At international level, the Center conducts joint research on specific problems with foreign institutions, organizes lectures and seminars for foreign economists, and sponsors an annual conference to which leading economists from both advanced and developing countries are invited. Study facilities are made available to a limited number of foreign researchers, particularly from Asia. There are approximately 370 institutional and 300 individual members.

Geographical Area of Activity: International.

Publications: Annual report and financial statement; *Bulletin* (fortnightly); *Economic Forecast Series* (quarterly, every 5 years, every 10 years); *International Conference Series.*

Trustees: The Center is governed by a Board of Directors mainly composed of leading economists from academic, business and governmental circles. There is a General Assembly and an Advisory Committee.

Principal Staff: Chair. Yutaka Kosai; Pres. Naohiro Yashiro.

Address: Nikkei Kayaba-cho Bldg, 2-6-1 Nihombashi-kayabacho, Chuo-ku, Tokyo 103-0025.

Telephone: (3) 3639-2801; **Fax:** (3) 3639-2839; **Internet:** www.jcer.or.jp; **e-mail:** jcernet@jcer.or.jp.

Nihon Kokusai Kyoiku Kyokai (Association of International Education, Japan)

Founded in 1957 by the Japanese Government as an independent foundation, to contribute to the development of education and science in Japan, and to promote international understanding and friendship.

Activities: Provides reception and follow-up programmes for foreign students who have been awarded Japanese Government scholarships, and awards Honors Scholarships for private students. It also conducts a scholarship programme for Japanese students participating in foreign student exchanges, sponsors seminars, and provides an information centre, as well as operating three international mutual exchange programmes between UNESCO Member States and Japan. Scholarships, of which around 1,950 were offered in 2002–03, offer a monthly stipend of 80,000 yen for up to 12 months, including travel expenses and a settling-in allowance.

Geographical Area of Activity: International.

Publications: Guides for students.

Finance: Annual budget 8,791,581,000 yen (2002).

Principal Staff: Chair. Youtaro Kobayashi; Pres. Kenji Tomioka.

Address: 4-5-29 Komaba, Meguro-ku, Tokyo 153-8503.

Telephone: (3) 5454-5211; **Fax:** (3) 5454-5231; **Internet:** www.aiej.or.jp; **e-mail:** ga@aiej.or.jp.

Nihon Kokusai Mondai Kenkyu-Sho (Japan Institute of International Affairs)

Founded in 1960 by Shigeru Yoshida, the late Prime Minister, as a national institution authorized by the Ministry of Foreign Affairs, to promote studies on international affairs and foreign policy; to encourage new thinking on major foreign policy issues; to give information on international affairs and foreign policy to its members; to promote wider public understanding of international affairs and foreign policy issues; and to provide a forum for discussion on these subjects and to exchange information with institutions abroad.

Activities: Operates in the field of international affairs mainly through research and publications, and through international conferences and seminars. Studies are conducted on the former USSR and East European countries (by the Center for Soviet Studies, established within the Institute in 1984), arms control and disarmament, international organizations, South-East Asia and the People's Republic of China. The Center for Asia-Pacific Studies, founded in 1987, conducts research relating to Japan's Asia-Pacific neighbours. Research at the Center for American Studies, set up in 1989, concentrates on US current affairs. In 1993 two centres were established: the European Studies Centre which conducts research on Western Europe and the Middle East, and the Global Issue Section which is responsible for research on human rights, nuclear proliferation, the United Nations and environmental issues. Maintains a library of 6,200 books and over 600 periodicals, and an on-line database of organizations working for conflict prevention in Asia-Pacific region.

Geographical Area of Activity: Japan.

Publications: *Kokusai Mondai* (International Affairs, monthly, in Japanese); *Rosia Kenkyu* (Russian Studies, 2 a year, in Japanese); *Japan Review of International Affairs* (2 a year, in English); *The JIIA Newsletter* (monthly, in Japanese).

Principal Staff: Chair. Gaishi Hiraiwa; Pres. Hisashi Owada.

Address: Kasumigaseki Bldg 11F, Kasumigaseki 3-2-5, 100-6011 Tokyo.

Telephone: (3) 3503-7263; **Fax:** (3) 3503-7186; **Internet:** www.jiia.or.jp; **e-mail:** info@jiia.or.jp.

Nihon Shinzo Zaidan (Japan Heart Foundation)

Founded in 1970 to contribute to the improvement of national welfare by providing financial aid for research on ailments of the heart and blood vessels, by educating the public about heart disease prevention, and by co-operating with counterpart organizations in foreign countries.

Activities: Operates nationally and in South-East Asia through providing grants to individuals, groups and research institutes engaged in research into heart and blood vessel diseases and providing finance for the publication of research findings; and internationally through maintaining contact and exchanging information with foreign institutions with similar interests.

Geographical Area of Activity: International, mainly Japan and South-East Asia.

Publications: *Kenko Heart* (monthly).

Finance: Research grants of up to 800,000 yen.

Principal Staff: Chair. Gaishi Hiraiwa; Vice-Chair. Tsuneaki Sugimoto; Pres. Takuji Shidachi; Sec.-Gen. Takao Muramatsu.

Address: 835A New Kokusai Bldg, 3-4-1 Marunouchi, Chiyoda-ku, Tokyo 100-0005.

Telephone: (3) 3201-0810; **Fax:** (3) 3213-3920; **Internet:** www.jhf.or.jp; **e-mail:** info@jhf.or.jp.

Nippon Foundation

Founded in 1962, as the Sasakawa Foundation, by Ryoichi Sasakawa, for general philanthropic purposes.

Activities: Operates nationally in supporting the development of shipbuilding technology, the prevention of marine disasters, and promotion of physical training and social welfare. The Foundation also gives international humanitarian assistance, particularly through the agencies of the United Nations, e.g. for programmes conducted by the World Health Organization (WHO), the UN High Commissioner for Refugees (UNHCR), the UN Children's Fund (UNICEF) and the UN Environment Programme (UNEP). It also supports the treatment of leprosy in a number of countries (through the Sasakawa Memorial Health Foundation); training in shipbuilding technology in developing countries; planning of ports, railway modernization and other transport improvements in developing countries; and activities aimed at strengthening links between Japan and the USA, the United Kingdom and Scandinavia. In Africa, the Foundation is conducting a project aimed at solving the food-shortage crisis through improved agricultural methods, and in Asia and Central and South America, it supports agricultural, crop-research and training programmes. The Foundation has also established various other national and international foundations.

Geographical Area of Activity: International.

Finance: Annual revenue approx. 54,000,000,000 yen.

Principal Staff: Chair. Ayako Sono; Pres. Yohei Sasakawa.

Address: Nippon Zaidan Bldg, 1-2-2 Asakawa, Minato-ku, Tokyo 107-8404.

Telephone: (3) 3502-2308; **Fax:** (3) 3502-2357; **Internet:** www.nippon-foundation.or.jp; **e-mail:** general@ps.nippon-foundation.or.jp.

Niwano Heiwa Zaidan (Niwano Peace Foundation)

Founded in 1978 to contribute to the realization of world peace and the enhancement of culture by promoting research and other activities, based on a religious spirit and serving the cause of peace.

Activities: Awards the Niwano Peace Prize annually to an individual or organization that is making a significant contribution to world peace through promoting inter-religious co-operation. The Foundation provides annual grants for research on aspects of ethics, religion and peace, conducts or commissions its own research on similar topics, and operates a Peace Research Institute. It sponsors lectures and symposia throughout Japan, and international exchanges for groups of young people. Recent initiatives include donations in support of international relief for Iraqi war victims.

Geographical Area of Activity: International.

Publications: *Dharma World* (6 a year); *A History of Japanese Religion*; and various other publications.

Finance: Total grants 432,580,000 yen (2002).

Principal Staff: Pres. Nichiko Niwano.

Address: Shamvilla Catherina, 5th Floor, 1-16-9 Shinjuku, Shinjuku-ku, Tokyo 160-0022.

Telephone: (3) 3226-4371; **Fax:** (3) 3226-1835; **Internet:** www.kosei-kai.or.jp; **e-mail:** info@rk-world.org.

OISCA International (Organization for Industrial, Spiritual and Cultural Advancement)

Established in 1961 by Dr Yonosuke Nakano to carry out development and reforestation projects in less-developed countries.

Activities: Operates internationally, with an emphasis on the Asia-Pacific region, in the areas of aid to less-developed countries, and conservation and the environment, through sending volunteers to assist indigenous organizations to carry out projects such as the planting of trees, the development of agriculture, and the Children's Forest Program. Co-operates with local NGOs and indigenous populations. Holds consultative status with the United Nations Economic and Social Committee (ECOSOC). Maintains four training centres in Japan. Affiliated organizations exist in more than 100 countries world-wide.

Geographical Area of Activity: The Asia-Pacific region.

Publications: Annual Report.

Principal Staff: Pres. Yoshiko Y. Nakano; Sec.-Gen. Yuichi Kobayashi.

Address: 6-12 Izumi 3-chome, Suginami-ku, Tokyo 168-0063.

Telephone: (3) 3322-5161; **Fax:** (3) 3324-7111; **Internet:** oisca.org; **e-mail:** overseas@oisca.org.

Peace Winds Japan

Established in 1996 to assist people internationally who are victims of political circumstances or natural disasters; a non-political, non-religious organization.

Activities: Operates internationally, assisting those in need in collaboration with local organizations, offering emergency relief, medical assistance, scholarships, social services, promoting equal rights for women, and supporting education, agriculture, and housing and sanitation. Projects operate in Indonesia, Mongolia, Sierra Leone, Timor Leste, and areas of Northern Iraq (Kurdistan), where the organization maintains branch offices, as well as in Afghanistan, the People's Republic of China, India, the Republic of Korea. Nationally, the organization promotes its work through symposia and lectures, and through fair trade activities.

Geographical Area of Activity: People's Republic of China, East Timor, Indonesia, Kosovo, Mongolia and areas of Northern Iraq (Kurdistan).

Publications: Annual Report; Newsletter.

Finance: Total income 762,826,742 yen, expenditure 626,661,355 yen (Jan. 2001).

Board of Trustees: Masaru Ishibashi (Pres.).

Principal Staff: Chief Exec. Kensuke Onishi.

Address: 2-11-5 Sakurashinmachi, Setagaya-ku, Tokyo.

Telephone: (3) 5451-5400; **Fax:** (3) 5451-5401; **Internet:** www.peace-winds.org; **e-mail:** meet@peace-winds.org.

The PHD Foundation—Peace, Health and Human Development Foundation

Established in 1981 by Dr Noboru Iwamura, the PHD Foundation aims to promote activities that would help bring about peace and health through human development among people in Asia and the South Pacific.

Activities: Works, by promoting the sharing of values, knowledge and skills, to improve the quality of life of those living in poverty in Asia and the South Pacific. Runs training programmes in Japan in order to provide long-term solutions for people suffering the effects of poverty, as well as follow-up programmes to consolidate technical and leadership skills. Also aims to build stonger links between the Japanese people and their less-wealthy neighbours.

Geographical Area of Activity: Asia and the South Pacific.

Publications: *Irebun Nepal* (study tour reports, 1983); *Kobe Hatsu Asia* (1986); *Asia No Kusanone Kokusaikoryu* (1993); and others.

Finance: Financed by membership fees, private contributions, income from publications sales, etc. Net assets 309,608,864 yen (March 2001); annual revenue and expenditure 62,678,656 yen (2001).

Trustees: Shizuo Imai (Chair.).

Principal Staff: Gen. Sec. Tatsuya Fujino (acting).

Address: 202 Motomach Urban Life, 5-4-3 Motomachi-dori, Chuo-ku, Kobe-shi, Hyogo 650-0022.

Telephone: (78) 351-4892; **Fax:** (78) 351-4867; **Internet:** www.kisweb.ne.jp/phd; **e-mail:** phd@mb1.kisweb.ne.jp.

Refugees International—Japan

Established in 1979 to assist in the restoration of the physical wellbeing and dignity of refugees throughout the world.

Activities: Operates internationally, offering emergency assistance, and carrying out projects in the fields of health and welfare, and education to aid refugees. Organizes annual fundraising exhibitions.

Geographical Area of Activity: International.

Publications: Newsletter (2 a year).

Finance: Annual expenditure on aid approx. 40,000,000 yen.

Address: c/o Showa Shell Sekiyu K.K. Ltd., 12F Daiba Frontier Bldg, 2-3-2 Daiba, Minato-ku, Tokyo 135-0091.

Telephone: (3) 5500-3093; **Fax:** (3) 5500-3094; **Internet:** www.d-plug.com/rijapan/.

Rohm Music Foundation

Established in 1991 for the promotion of music in Japan and throughout the world.

Activities: Operates in the field of the arts and humanities, through supporting young Japanese musicians, organizing international music exchange activities, offering grants for music research, awarding scholarships, disseminating information and carrying out research. Organizes the Kyoto International Music Students' Festival for the promotion of young musicians from around the world.

Geographical Area of Activity: Mostly Japan

Finance: Total income 226,053,000 yen, total expenditure 225,242,000 yen (March 2003).

Principal Staff: Chair. Ken Sato; Man. Dir Shoji Yokose.

Address: Nishi-Nakamizu-cho, Saiin, Ukyo-ku Kyoto 615-0044.

Telephone: (75) 311-7710; **Fax:** (75) 311-0089; **Internet:** www.rohm.com/rmf/index.html.

Rotary Yoneyama Memorial Foundation, Inc

Founded in 1956 (incorporated in 1967) by 21 Rotarians in Japan to contribute to the deepening of international understanding and goodwill by providing scholarships to foreigners (from countries where Rotary Clubs exist) who wish to study or engage in research at Japanese universities or research institutions.

Activities: Operates internationally in the field of education, through the allocation of fellowships and scholarships to students from outside Japan; applicants must be enrolled in a designated Japanese college or university in a full-time undergraduate or graduate capacity.

Geographical Area of Activity: International, where Rotary Clubs exist.

Publications: Report of operations and financial statement (in Japanese).

Trustees: The Foundation is governed by a Board of Trustees comprising 30 members; Nobuyuki Suenaga (Chair.).

Address: ABC Bldg 8F, 2-6-3 Shibakoen, Minato-ku, Tokyo 105.

Telephone: (3) 3435-1828; **Fax:** (3) 3578-8281; **Internet:** www.rotary-yoneyama.or.jp.

The Saison Foundation

Established in 1987 by Seiji Tsutsumi to carry out activities conducive to the stimulation of creativity among individuals or organizations engaged in art, especially contemporary Japanese theatre and dance, and to expedite international cultural exchanges.

Activities: Operates nationally and internationally in the field of the performing arts. The Foundation operates through two main grant programmes: the Domestic Grant Programmes, which support research, workshops, conferences, symposia and publications in the fields of contemporary Japanese theatre and dance, operate a scholarship programme for Japanese performing arts managers wishing to study arts administration overseas, and offer long-term grants to new and promising Japanese theatre and dance companies; and the International Grant Programmes, which support conferences, symposia and translation/publication projects aimed at communicating the essential aspects of contemporary Japanese theatre and dance to the international performing arts community, provide individual overseas fellowship grants for Japanese theatre and dance artists and specialists undertaking travel and research, fund international collaborative projects such as joint performances and workshops, and support overseas performances by Japanese performing artists and companies as well as performances in Japan by visiting foreign performing artists and companies. It also allows grantees to use its Morishita Studio in Tokyo.

Geographical Area of Activity: International.

Publications: Annual Report; *Viewpoint* (newsletter, quarterly).

Finance: Net assets 10,442,368,440 yen (2000); annual revenue 361,173,190 yen, expenditure 317,535,349 yen (2000).

Board of Directors: Seiji Tsutsumi (Chair.); Kazuo Kinumura (Vice-Chair.); Chuei Yagi (Man. Dir); Kunio Anzai; Shigeo Ikuno; Rokuro Ishikawa; Masao Katayama; Mikio Kawaguchi; Toshio Kawatake; Hiroshi Kida; Yotaro Kobayashi; Minoru Mori; Moriyuki Motono; Bun'ichiro Sano; Tomiji Yamazaki; there are also three Auditors and 31 Trustees.

Principal Staff: Sec.-Gen. and Dir Masao Katayama.

Address: 16-1, Ginza, 1-chome, Chuo-ku, Tokyo 104-0061.

Telephone: (3) 3535-5566; **Fax:** (3) 3535-5565; **Internet:** www.saison.or.jp; **e-mail:** foundation@saison.or.jp.

Sasakawa Peace Foundation

Established in 1986 by the Sasakawa Foundation (now the Nippon Foundation, q.v.), and the Japanese motorboat racing industry, to promote world peace and the development of international understanding through projects promoting international exchange and co-operation.

Activities: Operates internationally in the field of international affairs, through self-conducted programmes and grants to institutions. Four Area Funds (Sasakawa South-East Asia Co-operation Fund, Sasakawa Central Europe Fund, Sasakawa Japan-China Friendship Fund and Sasakawa Pacific Island Nations Fund) operate their own programmes and co-operate with international and local foundations and NGOs.

Geographical Area of Activity: International.

Restrictions: No grants made for theoretical academic research, operating expenditures, scholarships, fixed property, disaster relief, purchases of equipment, nor to individuals.

Publications: Annual Report; newsletter; brochure; operational guidelines for third mid-term programme.

Finance: Assets 75,656,795,000 yen (2001); annual expenditure 3,994,223,000 yen (2001).

Trustees: Setsuya Tabuchi (Chair.); Akira Iriyama (Pres.); Koji Imazu (Exec. Dir, Gen. Affairs) Akinori Seki (Exec. Dir, Programmes); and others.

Principal Staff: Communications Officer Yuko Nomura.

Address: Nippon Foundation Bldg, 4th Floor, 1-2-2, Akasaka, Minato-ku, Tokyo 107-8523.

Telephone: (3) 6229-5430; **Fax:** (3) 6229-5473; **Internet:** www.spf.org.jp; **e-mail:** spfpr@spf.or.jp.

Shakai Kogaku Kenkyu-Sho (Institute for Social Engineering, Inc)

Founded in 1969 with the purpose of seeking solutions to problems facing today's society, particularly in the field of economic and social development.

Activities: Operates nationally and internationally in conducting both independent and contractual research, to plan urban redevelopment, to design public policies for national and local development, and to forecast socio-economic and political trends. The Institute holds executive seminars, and provides information and consulting services for foreign business people and enterprises.

Geographical Area of Activity: Mostly Japan.

Principal Staff: Pres. and CEO Hideaki Tatebayashi; Principal and CEO Hitoshi Sakai.

Address: Grande Maison Moto-akasaka, 6th flr., 1-7-10, Moto-akasaka, Minato-ku, Tokyo 107-0051.

Telephone: (3) 3403-9051; **Fax:** (3) 3402-6540; **Internet:** www.shakoken.co.jp.

Philipp Franz von Siebold Stiftung (Philipp Franz von Siebold Foundation)

Founded in 1988 by the Ministry of Research and Technology of the Federal Republic of Germany, to study contemporary Japanese culture, economy and society, and the history of German–Japanese relations. The Foundation contains the German Institute for Japanese Studies, which promotes German–Japanese relations.

Activities: The Foundation operates nationally and internationally in the fields of arts and humanities, conservation, economic affairs, education, international affairs, law and human rights, medicine and health, science and technology, and social welfare and social studies, through research, programmes, conferences and publications. Also provides doctoral fellowships.

Geographical Area of Activity: Germany and Japan.

Publications: *Monographien aus dem Deutschen Institut für Japanstudien* (monograph series); *Japanstudien* (annually); *Bibliographische Arbeiten aus dem Deutschen Institut für Japanstudien* (series of bibliographical studies); *Miscellanea*; Annual Bulletin; newsletter (3 a year).

Trustees: Representatives of the Ministry of Education and Research, the Ministry of Foreign Affairs, the Minerva Society for Research, and the Alexander von Humboldt-Stiftung (all Germany).

Principal Staff: Chair. Wolf-Michael Catenhjausen.

Address: Nissei Kojimachi Bldg, 3-3-6 Kudan-Minami, Chiyoda-ku, Tokyo 102-0074.

Telephone: (3) 3222-5077; **Fax:** (3) 3222-5420; **Internet:** www.dijtokyo.org; **e-mail:** dijtokyo@dijtokyo.org.

Tokyu Foundation for Inbound Students

Established in 1975 by the Tokyu Corporation and other companies to promote international exchange, and, specifically, to promote communication between students and between students and the Japanese people, so as to foster the development of international goodwill between Japan and other countries in Asia and the Pacific, and to contribute to international co-operation and cultural exchange.

Activities: Operates through offering 24 scholarships a year to non-Japanese postgraduate students from the Asia-Pacific region to enable them to study in Japan. Scholarships are normally awarded for up to two years.

Geographical Area of Activity: Asia and Pacific areas.

Restrictions: Scholarships for doctoral degrees are available only to those under the age of 34; scholarships for master degrees are available only to those under the age of 29.

Finance: Net assets 2,155,170,570 yen (March 2001); annual revenue 112,154,394 yen, expenditure 117,562,273 yen (2001).

Board of Directors: Tetsu Goto (Chief Dir).

Principal Staff: Gen. Sec. Yasushi Teranaka.

Address: 1-21-6 Dogenzaka, Shibuya-ku, Tokyo 150.

Telephone: (3) 3461-0844; **Fax:** (3) 5458-1696; **e-mail:** tq.zaidan@246.ne.jp.

Toshiba International Foundation

Founded in 1989 by the Toshiba Corporation to promote international exchange activities and a better understanding of Japan.

Activities: Operates in the fields of the arts and humanities, education, international affairs and science and technology, through its own international programmes and the provision of grants to institutions. The Foundation also awards scholarships to overseas nationals to promote international understanding of Japan.

Geographical Area of Activity: International.

Publications: *Japan's Role in the 1990s; Proceedings of Toshiba International Foundation Symposium; TIFO News.*

Principal Staff: Chair. Fumio Sato; Vice-Chair. Shinji Fukukawa, Kenichi Kamiya; Man. Dir Shoichirou Amikura.

Address: 3rd Flr., Toshiba Bldg, 1-1 Shibaura 1-chome, Minato-ku, Tokyo 105-8001.

Telephone: (3) 3457-2733; **Fax:** (3) 3457-4389; **Internet:** www.toshiba.co.jp/about/tifo.

Toyota Zaidan (Toyota Foundation)

Founded in 1974 by Toyota Motor Corpn, to contribute towards the realization of a human-oriented society by providing grants for research and projects related to the human and natural environments, social welfare, education, culture and other fields.

Activities: Carries out projects in Japan and other countries, mainly in the developing world, that address topical issues in a variety of fields, including environmental sustainability, the improvement of social welfare, the advancement of education, the strengthening of civil society, and the preservation of cultural heritage. Provides research grants; grants to organizations addressing the foundation's priority areas; research and exchange programmes directed towards South-east Asia; and an independent programme allowing for support of initiatives that fall outside the foundation's priority areas. Also produces a comprehensive on-line grants database.

Geographical Area of Activity: Mainly Japan and developing countries.

Restrictions: In general, the Foundation does not approve grants for capital investment, plant or equipment; endowments; museum or library acquisitions; annual budgets of organizations or institutions, or of established programmes; propaganda or lobbying activities; religious activities; nor for unsponsored individuals.

Publications: *The Toyota Foundation Occasional Report* (2 a year); *The Toyota Foundation Report* (quarterly); annual report including financial statement; grants research reports; research briefings.

Finance: Total assets approx. 31,400,000,000 yen (1999).

Principal Staff: Chair. Tatsuro Toyoda; Pres. Shosaburo Kimura; Man. Dir Chimaki Kurokawa.

Address: Shinjuku Mitsui Bldg 37F, 2-1-1 Nishi Shinjuku, Shinjuku-ku, Tokyo 163-0437.

Telephone: (3) 3344-1701; **Fax:** (3) 3342-6911; **Internet:** www.toyotafound.or.jp; **e-mail:** admin@toyotafound.or.jp.

Jordan

FOUNDATIONS, TRUSTS AND NON-PROFIT ORGANIZATIONS

Noor Al Hussein Foundation

Established to initiate and support projects nationally and internationally in the fields of community development, education, culture, health and welfare (especially of children), women and business development.

Activities: Operates nationally, regionally and internationally in the above areas, through projects which promote self-help and participation in decision-making and project management. Funds community development programmes, including income generating micro-enterprises, largely through Foundation subsidiary The Jordan Micro Credit Company; child and family health projects, through its support of the Institute for Family Health and two SOS Villages; and Women and Enterprise Development projects, including its Jordan Design & Trade Center.

Geographical Area of Activity: Jordan.

Principal Staff: Chair. HM Queen Noor Al Hussein.

Address: POB 926687, Amman 11110.

Telephone: (6) 5606992; **Fax:** (6) 5606994; **Internet:** www.nhf.org.jo; **e-mail:** nhf@nic.net.jo.

Jordanian Hashemite Fund for Human Development—JOHUD

Established in 1977, an NGO dedicated to playing a role in advancing comprehensive and sustainable human development through the enhanced participation of Jordanian people.

Activities: Through its network of 50 community development centres, the Fund focuses on developing a model of integrated development activities, through support for projects working in a range of areas, including child development, family health and nutrition, education and awareness, leadership skills for women, young people, income generation, and enterprise development.

Geographical Area of Activity: Jordan.

Publications: *Humanity* (quarterly newsletter); JOHUD Brochure.

Principal Staff: Chair. HRH Princess Basma Bint Talal; Exec. Dir Farah Daghistani.

Address: POB 5118, Amman 11183.

Telephone: (962) 5825241; **Fax:** (6) 5827350; **Internet:** www.johud.org.jo; **e-mail:** exrd@nic.net.jo.

King Hussein Foundation

Established by Royal Decree in 1999 as a national and international NGO dedicated to the vision of the late King Hussein of Jordan.

Activities: Operates nationally and internationally in the fields of peace and democracy, education and leadership, the environment, and health.

Trustees: HM Queen Noor Al Hussein (Chair.); Prince Zeid Bin Shaker; Princess Wijdan Ali; and others.

Address: POB 608, Amman 11118.

Internet: www.noor.gov.jo/main/khf.htm; **e-mail:** k_h_f@hotmail.com.

Scientific Foundation of Hisham Adeeb Hijjawi

Established in 1981 by Hisham Hijjawi to support education in the field of technical and applied sciences.

Activities: Operates in Jordan and Palestinian Autonomous Areas in the field of education, and in particular in the area of research in technical and applied sciences at universities and colleges; also supports scientific conferences and workshops, funds the purchase of scientific equipment, and makes three awards annually for research projects in the applied sciences. The Foundation funds a technical university in the Palestinian Autonomous Areas.

Geographical Area of Activity: Jordan and Palestinian Autonomous Areas.

Trustees: Mohamed Al-Farra; Hassan A. Al Ebraheem; Mohamed Arafeh; Nizar Ali Araias; Abdul Aziz Sultan; Jamil A. Budeiri; Mohamed Hamdan; Munther Masri; Mohamed Milhem; Yousuf Abdel M'uti; Issam Naqib.

Principal Staff: Chair. Ayman Hijjawi; Herbert Batliner; Jaafar Hijjawi; Reem Hijjawi.

Address: POB 103, Amman 11810.

Telephone: (6) 5814257; **Fax:** (6) 5826861; **Internet:** www.sfohah.org; **e-mail:** hedblp@sfohah.org.

Abdul Hameed Shoman Foundation

A non-profit cultural institution established in 1978 by the Arab Bank PLC, to embody and perpetuate the legacy of the Bank's founder, the late Abdul Hameed Shoman, dedicated to the promotion of knowledge, research and development in the fields of science, and the arts and culture.

Activities: Awards annual prizes in 12 fields to young Arab researchers, whose work demonstrates exceptional scientific value. Also grants prizes, every two years to teachers of science in Jordanian prepatory and secondary schools, who can demonstrate original approaches to the teaching of science. It also awards prizes to Jordanian children who compete every year in different fields of knowledge. The Abdul Majeed Shoman International Award for Jerusalem was established in 1999 with a donation by Abdul Maheed Shoman, Chairman of the Board of Directors of the Arab Bank PLC and of the Foundation. It is awarded every two years in one of the folowing fields: historical studies, contemporary issues, creative literary works, and creative artistic works. In 1986 established the Qbdul Hameed Shoman Public Library; in 1987 established the Abdul Hameed Shoman Cultural Forum, which hosts the Monday Lectures, made by prominent Jordanian or Arab lecturers, and tackle important public issues, and the Dialogue of the Month, where prominent intellectuals present their viewpoints and opinions, as well as organizing seminars and workshops. In 1989, the Forum established the Cinematheque, which offers weekly screenings of modern and classical films. In 1999, established the Abdul Hameed Shoman Fund for the Support and Encouragement of Scientific Research, which funds research at Jordan universities.

Geographical Area of Activity: Jordan.

Publications: *Afaq Ilmyah* (Scientific Horizons, 6 a year); numerous works in Arabic and English.

Finance: Endowment based on 3% of net annual profits of the Arab Bank PLC.

Governing Board: Abdul Majeed Shoman (Chair.); Abdul Hameed Shoman (Deputy Chair.); Munib Rasheed Al-Masri; Dr Awadh Khulaifat; Haseeb Sabbagh; Thabit Al-Taher; Suzan Shoman.

Principal Staff: Dir Gen. Suzan Shoman; Dir, Scientific Research Support and the Prizes Abdul Rahman Al-Masri; Dir, Admin. and Finance Ahmad Yassin Rahhal.

Address: POB 940255, Amman 11194.

Telephone: (6) 5602155; **Fax:** (6) 5672541; **Internet:** www.shoman.org; **e-mail:** ashf@shoman.org.jo.

Kazakhstan

FOUNDATIONS, TRUSTS AND NON-PROFIT ORGANIZATIONS

Soros Foundation—Kazakhstan

Founded in September 1995 to promote open society; it is an independent foundation, part of the Soros foundations network, which aims to foster political and cultural pluralism and reform economic structures in order to encourage free enterprise and a market economy.

Activities: The Foundation operates in the fields of art and culture, education, economic affairs, medicine and health, law and criminal justice, media and information, youth and women's programmes and civil society. It provides support for innovative projects focused on reform of education at all levels, supports Kazakhstan's NGOs, libraries, archives and the independent mass media, economic and law reform projects, including policy-making, dissemination of information, and the national health-care system. Also awards travel grants to participants in international conferences and seminars.

Geographical Area of Activity: Kazakhstan.

Publications: Annual Report.

Finance: Annual expenditure US $4,142,000 (2001).

Board of Directors: Eugene Zhovtis (Chair.); Bulat Abilo; Irina Erofeeva; Auezhan Kodar; Asylbek Kozhahmetov; Victor Malinovsky; Rozlana Taukina.

Principal Staff: Exec. Dir Murat Mukhtarovich Auezov.

Address: 480091 Almaty, ul. Furmanova 117 kv. 20, POB 254.

Telephone: (3272) 503811; **Fax:** (3272) 503814; **Internet:** www.soros.kz; **e-mail:** sfk@soros.kz.

Kyrgyzstan

FOUNDATIONS, TRUSTS AND NON-PROFIT ORGANIZATIONS

Soros Foundation—Kyrgyzstan

Founded in September 1993 to promote open society; the Foundation is part of the Soros foundations network, which aims to foster the development of open societies around the world, particularly in the post-communist countries. The Soros Foundations help to build the infrastructure and institutions necessary for open societies by supporting a broad array of programmes in education, media and communications, human rights and humanitarian aid, science and medicine, arts and culture, economic restructuring and legal reform; the Foundation's specific mission is to promote the development of an open society in Kyrgyzstan.

Activities: The Foundation operates in the fields of civil society, legal reform, education, mass media, development of local governance, public health, economic reform, and other areas.

Geographical Area of Activity: Kyrgyzstan.

Publications: Annual Report; newsletters; quarterly bulletin; books.

Finance: Annual expenditure US $3,890,000 (2002).

Board of Directors: Mirgul Smanalieva (Chair.); Dmitry Kabak; Aktan Arym Kubat; Bolot Maripov; Shamaral Maychiyev; Vitaly Nishanov; Tolondu Toichubaev.

Principal Staff: Exec. Dir Medet Tiulegenov.

Address: Bishkek 720040, Logvinenko 55A.

Telephone: (312) 66-43-06; **Fax:** (312) 66-34-48; **Internet:** www.soros.kg; **e-mail:** office@soros.kg.

Latvia

FOUNDATION CENTRE AND CO-ORDINATING BODY

NVO Centrs (NGO Centre)

Founded in 1996 by WIBA Consult to promote the development of a democratic and pluralist society in Latvia through education and culture.

Activities: Operates nationally and internationally in the fields of the arts and humanities, and education, through promoting the not-for-profit sector in Latvia, gathering and disseminating information about civic society, human rights and democracy, organizing conferences, seminars and cultural projects, fundraising activities, maintaining a database of Latvian NGOs, and providing financial aid to NGOs and other organizations.

Geographical Area of Activity: Latvia.

Publications: Annual Report; *Directory of Latvian NGOs; NGOs News Report*.

Finance: Annual revenue €478,085, programme expenditure €346,255 (2001).

Governing Board: Jānis Baltač (Chair.); Andris Bērzinš; Andris Kreislers; Valdis Kudinš; Ole Lisborg; Jan Sand Sorensen; Vita Tērauda.

Principal Staff: Dir Kaija Gertnere-Ozola.

Address: 52/54–22, Lacplesa Str., Rīga 1011.

Telephone: 7283283; **Fax:** 7289227; **Internet:** www.ngo.org.lv; **e-mail:** info@ngo.org.lv.

FOUNDATIONS, TRUSTS AND NON-PROFIT ORGANIZATIONS

Latvia Children's Fund

Founded by the Latvian General Assembly in 1988 to protect children's rights.

Activities: The Fund operates programmes to support children's rights, to promote development, health and education, and support particularly talented children and family-oriented education. The Family programme aims to create new models of social protection for children lacking in parental care, through running Social Rehabilitation Centres and a Crisis Centre for 'street children' (homeless children). Associations of Latvians in the USA co-fund projects which give funds to needy families, and there are 26 international projects for the individual sponsorship of sick and needy children. The Development, Culture and Talent programme organizes competitions for talented new artists and musicians, as well as for school graduates who have made outstanding achievements in the humanities. Financial support is given to projects directed at the development of children's abilities. The Health programme organizes camps for disabled children, finances the modernization and development of children's medical institutions and the treatment of sick children, and gives support to children who are victims of abuse. The Orphan programme assists in the building of orphanages and offers study grants to orphans.

Geographical Area of Activity: Latvia.

Finance: The Fund has received grants from foundations and NGOs in Germany, Canada, the Netherlands, Norway, Sweden, the USA and other countries, as well as from local sponsors.

Principal Staff: Pres. Andris Berziņš.

Address: Brīvības gatve. 310-75, Rīga 1006.

Telephone: 7542072; **Fax:** 7541814; **Internet:** www.lbf.lv; **e-mail:** lbf@lbf.lv.

Soros Foundation—Latvia

Founded in June 1992 to promote the development of open society; the Foundation is part of the Soros foundations network, which aims to foster political and cultural pluralism and reform economic structures in order to encourage free enterprise and a market economy.

Activities: The Foundation funds a variety of projects in Latvia in its priority areas: education, criminal justice, civil society, health-care reform, legal reform and public policy. It also promotes scholarship exchanges.

Geographical Area of Activity: Latvia.

Publications: *Know Your Rights* (booklet).

Finance: Annual expenditure US $4,062,269 (2001).

Board of Directors: Sarmite Elerte (Chair.); Guntars Catlaks; Egils Levits; Janis Loze; Alla Petropavlovskaja; Talis Tisenkopfs; Andrejs Vasiljevs; Irina Vinnika.

Principal Staff: Exec. Dir Vita Tērauda.

Address: Alberta 13, Rīga 1010.

Telephone: 7039241; **Fax:** 7039242; **Internet:** www.sfl.lv; **e-mail:** sfl@sfl.lv.

Lebanon

FOUNDATIONS, TRUSTS AND NON-PROFIT ORGANIZATIONS

Fondation Arabe pour l'Image (Arab Image Foundation)

Established in 1996 to promote photography in North Africa and the Middle East.

Activities: Collects, preserves and promotes photographic material reflecting the culture and character of Arab countries of North Africa and the Middle East. Currently displays its collection in galleries, museums and in published monographs. Aims eventually to place the collection in an archive centre in Beirut, which will hold collections and exhibitions as a testament to Arab visual heritage. Also maintains an office in the USA.

Geographical Area of Activity: The Middle East and North Africa.

Restrictions: No grants to individuals.

Publications: *Histoires Intimes: 1900-1960; Portraits du Caire.*

Finance: Largely funded by Audi Bank (Lebanon) and private donors.

Trustees: Yto Barrada; Fouad Elkoury; Moukhtar Kocache; Walid Raad; Akram Zaatari; and others.

Principal Staff: Dir Zeina Arida.

Address: 8 rue Chukri Assaly, Achrafieh, Beirut.

Telephone and Fax: (1) 336820; **Internet:** www.fai.org.lb; **e-mail:** info@fai.org.lb.

Hariri Foundation

Founded in 1979 by Rafic Hariri as the Islamic Institute for Culture and Higher Education to promote education as a means of development for children and young people.

Activities: Operates in the fields of education and the arts and humanities, through language programmes designed to enable students to attend university, making loans to students, providing support for academic institutions affected by conflict in the Middle East, offering career guidance and support for educational organizations and programmes, and promoting Lebanese heritage through the renovation and care of old buildings and promoting relations with international organizations.

Geographical Area of Activity: The Middle East.

Publications: *Lebanon: Its History and Heritage; Lebanon at Present: Its Needs for Development*; and other research publications.

Principal Staff: Sabah Ariss.

Address: POB 48, Saida.

Telephone: (7) 7724740; **Fax:** (7) 7723221; **Internet:** www.hariri-foundation.org.lb; **e-mail:** hfb@cyberia.net.lb.

Institute for Palestine Studies, Publishing and Research Organization

Founded in 1963 by Najla Abou Izzedin, Maurice Gemayel, Said Himadeh, Burhan Dajani, Edmond Rabbath, Constantine Zurayk, Fuad Sarrouf, Nabih Amin Faris, Wadad Cortas and Walid Khalidi, to encourage research into all aspects of the Palestine problem.

Activities: Specializes in research into the history and development of Palestine, the Palestinian problem and the Arab–Israeli conflict, and possible ways of arriving at a peaceful resolution. The Institute publishes books, quarterly journals, documentaries, studies and opinion polls; conducts occasional seminars and makes grants; serves as a repository for documents, manuscripts, periodicals, books and other publications on Palestine and the Palestinian problem. Maintains offices in Beirut, Jerusalem, London, Nicosia, Paris, and Washington, D.C..

Geographical Area of Activity: The Middle East.

Publications: *Journal of Palestine Studies* (quarterly, in English); *Jerusalem Quarterly File* (in English); *Revue d'Etudes Palestiniennes* (quarterly, in French); *Majallat Al-dirasat al-Filistiniyah* (quarterly, in Arabic); *IPS Papers;* monographs.

Trustees: Hisham Nashabi (Chair.); Walid Khalidi (Exec. Sec.).

Principal Staff: Exec. Dir Philip Mattar.

Address: Nsouli-Verdun St, POB 11-7164, Beirut; (Cyprus) 13 Hera St, POB 5658, Nicosia, Cyprus; (USA) 3501 M St, NW, Washington, DC 20007, USA.

Telephone: (1) 804959 (Lebanon); 22756165 (Cyprus); (202) 342-3990 (USA); **Fax:** (1) 814193 (Lebanon); 22756324 (Cyprus); (202) 342-3927 (USA); **Internet:** www.palestine-studies.org; **e-mail:** ipsbrt@palestine-studies.org.

Liechtenstein

FOUNDATIONS, TRUSTS AND NON-PROFIT ORGANIZATIONS

International Health Care Foundation

International non-profit organization established by a group of dentists, in order to promote improved oral health care world-wide.

Activities: Operates internationally in the field of health care. Raises public awareness of the importance of dental health care; disseminates information and research results to dentists through lectures and conferences; carries out programmes to improve the quality of dental material and care in Europe and Asia; and offers accreditation to dental health-care products of benefit to patients. Operates in collaboration with international partner organizations in Europe and the Far East.

Geographical Area of Activity: Mainly Europe and Asia.

Publications: Newsletter.

Principal Staff: Hon. Sec. Dr Volker Scholz; Sec. Marina Schurte; Speakers Prof. Dr Andrea Mombelli, Prof. Denis O'Mullane.

Address: Austr. 24, POB 1246, 9490 Vaduz.

Telephone: 237 28 50; **Fax:** 237 28 51; **Internet:** www.ihcf.org; **e-mail:** info@ihcf.org.

Lithuania

FOUNDATION CENTRE AND CO-ORDINATING BODY

NGO Information and Support Centre

Founded by the Open Society Fund—Lithuania (q.v.) in 1995 to develop the NGO sector in Lithuania.

Activities: The Centre is jointly sponsored by the Open Society Fund—Lithuania and the United Nations Development Programme; it operates in the fields of information dissemination, consultancy, training and support for NGOs and their development. Promotes co-operation between NGOs and other institutions and provides information on the legal constitution of NGOs in Lithuania. Maintains an NGO database of funding sources and a library of over 1,000 publications.

Geographical Area of Activity: Lithuania.

Publications: *Partnership among NGOs and local governments; The Third Sector* (occasional newsletter); and other research publications.

Board of Directors: Girvydas Duoblys; Arunas Kucikas; Sarunas Liekis; Kristina Ona Polukordiene; Linas Sesickas; Violeta Toleikiene; Audrone Zubaviciene.

Principal Staff: Dir Vaidotas Ilgius.

Address: A. Jakšto 9-309 Str., 2001 Vilnius.

Telephone: (2) 126-045; **Fax:** (2) 618-782; **Internet:** www.nisc.lt; **e-mail:** info@nisc.lt.

FOUNDATIONS, TRUSTS AND NON-PROFIT ORGANIZATIONS

Lithuanian Children's Fund

Founded in 1988 to protect the interests of children in Lithuania.

Activities: Operates nationally, providing financial support to foster families, for housing and scholarships to gifted students. Also operates literacy and other educational programmes, as well as funding activities which aim to improve access to social, economic and health care services for Roma people.

Geographical Area of Activity: Lithuania.

Principal Staff: Pres. Juozas Nekrošius; Dir Romanas Burba.

Address: Zygimantu 6, Vilnius 2600.

Telephone: (2) 628-836; **Fax:** (2) 627-180.

Open Society Fund—Lithuania

Founded in October 1990 to promote the development of open society; it is part of the Soros foundations network, which aims to foster political and cultural pluralism and reform the economy so as to encourage free enterprise and a market economy.

Activities: The Fund operates programmes in the fields of education and higher education, civil society, the arts and culture, social welfare, law and criminal justice, publishing, public health and women's and youth programmes. The Fund has established several NGOs in Lithuania, including the Invisible College, the Foundation for Educational Change, Junior Achievement Lithuania, Lithuanian Journalism Centre, the Children Support Centre, the NGO Information and Support Centre (q.v.) and Soros International House.

Geographical Area of Activity: Lithuania.

Publications: Annual Report.

Finance: Annual expenditure US $3,828,000 (2001).

Board of Directors: Gintautas Bartkus (Chair.); Giedrius Dusevičius; Dalia Michelevičiute; Arunas Poviliunas; Dainius Puras; Sergejus Temčinas.

Principal Staff: Exec. Dir Diana Vilytė.

Address: Didžioji Str. 5, Vilnius 2001.

Telephone: (2) 685-511; **Fax:** (2) 685-512; **Internet:** www.osf.lt; **e-mail:** fondas@osf.lt.

Luxembourg

FOUNDATIONS, TRUSTS AND NON-PROFIT ORGANIZATIONS

Paul Finet Foundation

Founded in 1965 by the High Authority of the European Coal and Steel Community (now the European Commission of the European Union) to grant scholarships to the orphans of workers in the industries of the European Coal and Steel Community who have lost their lives as the result of accidents at work or occupational illness since 30 June 1965 (or since the date of their country's joining the Community, if later).

Activities: Operates in the Member States of the European Union (EU) in the field of education, through grants to individuals. Beneficiaries must be at least 14 years of age or already be following their normal course of studies. They must take courses of vocational training, general secondary education, or higher education in a university or establishment of university level. Grants are awarded annually and are renewable during the entire period of the education of the child concerned.

Geographical Area of Activity: Countries of the EU.

Finance: The Foundation is funded by an annual subsidy from the European Commission and by private donations.

Trustees: The Board comprises 22 members representing the European Commission, employers' organizations and trade union organizations.

Principal Staff: Chair. Anna Diamantopoulou.

Address: Bâtiment Jean Monnet, rue Alcide de Gasperi, 2920 Luxembourg.

Telephone: 4301-34341; **Fax:** 4301-34455; **Internet:** http://europa.eu.int/comm/secretariat_general/finet/index_en.htm; **e-mail:** sg-info@cec.eu.int.

Fondation Luxembourgeoise Raoul Follereau (Raoul Follereau Foundation)

Established in 1966 by Raoul Follereau to promote international solidarity, and to combat leprosy.

Activities: Operates in Africa, South America and the Far East in the fields of aid to less-developed countries, medicine and health, and social welfare. Its main aims are to combat leprosy and tuberculosis, and assist those who have been cured of these diseases, through projects. The Foundation is also involved in rural development projects, and with helping underprivileged children, through the Follereau-Children project. Also aims to increase awareness in Luxembourg of these issues. Operates in collaboration with other organizations, members of the International Federation of Anti Leprosy Associations.

Geographical Area of Activity: Africa, South America and the Far East.

Principal Staff: Pres. Jos Hilger; Vice-Pres. Marcel Thinnes; Sec.-Gen. Claudine Bruck.

Address: 151 ave du 10 Septembre, 2551 Luxembourg.

Telephone: 4466-061; **Fax:** 45-96-53; **Internet:** www.ffl.lu; **e-mail:** info@ffl.lu.

Third World Solidarity Action—ASTM (Action Solidarité Tiers Monde—ASTM)

Established in 1970 to support the political, economic and social emancipation of the people of the developing world and to address the global economic issues affecting this emancipation.

Activities: Works in partnership with indigenous organizations in the developing world, in the areas of education and sustainable development, concentrating on programmes in the areas of access to land, commercialisation of the agricultural production, micro-credit, health rights and women's rights. Also provides information on the cultures of the developing world, generates support for cultural activities and develops cultural exchanges between the developed and the developing world, initially through a pilot programme linking Luxembourg with Algeria, India and Senegal.

Geographical Area of Activity: Africa, Asia, Central and South America and the Middle East.

Publications: *Brennpunkt Drett Welt* (newsletter).

Principal Staff: Contact: Soraya Moket.

Address: 55 ave de la Liberté, 1931 Luxembourg.

Telephone: 400-42725; **Fax:** 400-42727; **Internet:** www.astm.lu; **e-mail:** astm@astm.lu.

Unity Foundation

A Baha'i funding agency.

Activities: Operates in the fields of sustainable development, education, and health care in less-developed countries, through grants, particularly aiming to raise the status of women, improve global health and hygiene, improve standards of literacy and promote peace. Lends financial support to projects in Africa, Asia and Central and South America, and has set up a non-profit publishing house and print shop in Zaire. Operates as co-financing partners with the Ministère des Affaires Etrangères of the Luxembourg government.

Geographical Area of Activity: Africa, Asia and Central and South America.

Principal Staff: Contact: Chantal Müller.

Address: 17 allée Léopold Goebel, 1635 Luxembourg.

Telephone and Fax: 25-26-20; **Internet:** www.unityfoundation.lu; **e-mail:** unityfoundation@pt.lu.

Macedonia

FOUNDATIONS, TRUSTS AND NON-PROFIT ORGANIZATIONS

Foundation Open Society Institute Macedonia—FOSIM

Founded in October 1992, and previously known as the Open Society Fund of Macedonia, to support the development of Macedonia as an independent and democratic state respectful of multi-ethnic cultural traditions, and to encourage the development of Western standards in the country; it is an independent foundation, part of the Soros foundations network.

Activities: The Institute operates in the fields of education, information and the media, publishing, Roma people and ethnic minorities, youth and women's programmes, public health, law and criminal justice, the arts and culture, civil society, and economic reform. Supported initiatives to assist refugees from Kosovo in 1999. The Institute finances directly and operates the following institutions in Macedonia: the Soros International House—Skopje, the Soros Centre for Contemporary Arts, the SOS Centre (which provides counselling to teenagers), the Civil Society Resource Centre and the Student Resource Centres.

Geographical Area of Activity: Macedonia.

Publications: Annual Report.

Finance: Annual expenditure US $5,997,000 (2001).

Trustees: Nikola Gelevski; Gjorgje Ivanov; Saso Klekovski; Slobodanka Markovska; Vladimir Milcin; Natalija Nikolovska; Nafi Saracini; Emilija Simoska.

Principal Staff: Exec. Dir Vladimir Milcin.

Address: Bul. Jane Sandanski 111, POB 378, 91000 Skopje.

Telephone: (92) 444488; **Fax:** (92) 444499; **Internet:** www.soros.org.mk; **e-mail:** osi@soros.org.mk.

Address: Santa Maria Formosa, Castello 5252, 30122 Venice.

Telephone: (041) 2711411; **Fax:** (041) 2711445; **Internet:** www.provincia.venezia.it/querini; **e-mail:** querini .stampalia@provincia.venezia.it.

Fondazione Ricci Onlus (Ricci Onlus Foundation)

Established in 1990 by Giovanni Mario Ricci, a non-profit corporation aiming to promote initiatives of a social and humanitarian nature, and to encourage the restoration and protection of the environmental, cultural and historical heritage of the middle and upper valley of the Serchio river.

Activities: Operates in Lucca province in the areas of the arts and humanities, and conservation and the environment, through self-conducted programmes, conferences and publications. Aims to acquire an art collection to exhibit to the public.

Geographical Area of Activity: Italy.

Publications: *Trent'anni di Poesie; Un Antico Comune nello Stato italiano; Barga fra storia e leggenda; La Rocca delle Verrucole; Giovan Battista Santini; I 'Selvaggi' della lucchesia*; exhibition catalogues; and other works.

Finance: Net assets US $1,500,000 (2000).

Board of Directors: Leonardo Mordini (Pres.); Cristiana Ricci (Vice-Pres.); Daniela Papi Mordini (Treas.); and 14 other members.

Principal Staff: Man. Dir Cristiana Ricci; Treas. Daniela Papi; Antonio Ricci.

Address: Via Roma 20, 55051 Barga, Lucca.

Telephone: (0583) 724357; **Fax:** (0583) 724921; **Internet:** www.fondazionericcionlus.it; **e-mail:** fondricci@iol.it.

Fondazione Rui (Rui Foundation)

Founded in 1959 by university teachers, professional workers and parents concerned with studying and resolving problems facing young people. The Foundation's activities are aimed at promoting the further training of university students and intellectuals, and promoting cultural activities for youth; awarding scholarships to Italian and foreign students, and acclimatizing the latter to the Italian way of life; and collaborating with national and international organizations to these ends.

Activities: Operates nationally in the field of the arts and humanities, and both nationally and internationally in the fields of education, social welfare and studies. Also active in the fields of international relations and aid to less-developed countries. Programmes are carried out internationally through self-conducted projects, and both nationally and internationally through research, fellowships and scholarships, conferences, courses, publications and lectures.

Geographical Area of Activity: Europe.

Publications: *Fondazione Rui* (magazine); *Universitas* (magazine); guides on higher education in Italy.

Principal Staff: Pres. Dott. Gianmario Roveraro; Dir Dott. Ing. Alfredo Razzano.

Address: Viale XXI Aprile 36, Rome.

Telephone: (06) 86321281; **Fax:** (06) 86322845; **Internet:** www.fondazionerui.it; **e-mail:** info@fondazionerui.it.

Fondazione di Studi di Storia dell'Arte 'Roberto Longhi' (Roberto Longhi Foundation for the Study of the History of Art)

Founded in 1971 by Prof. Roberto Longhi to promote and develop, with suitable scientific principles and critical severity, the study of the history of art among young Italian and foreign students.

Activities: Operates internationally in the field of the arts and humanities, through research and study courses. A number of grants, fellowships and prizes are available to both Italian and non-Italian students studying at the Foundation's own institute. The Foundation maintains a library of 35,000 art publications and 60,000 photographs of Italian art, and also a collection of pictures of some 200 important artists.

Geographical Area of Activity: International.

Trustees: M. Gregori (Pres.).

Address: Via Benedetto Fortini 30, 50125 Florence.

Telephone and Fax: (055) 6580794; **Internet:** www.iris .firenze.it/frl; **e-mail:** longhi@longhi.iris.firenze.it.

Fondo per l'Ambiente Italiano (Fund for the Italian Environment)

Founded in 1975 to increase awareness of environmental protection and the preservation of Italy's cultural heritage.

Activities: Operates nationally, acquiring historically, culturally or environmentally valuable sites and opening them to the public, and also running educational conferences and exhibitions.

Geographical Area of Activity: Italy.

Publications: Annual Report.

Board of Directors: Giulia Maria Crespi Mozzoni (Chair.); Andrea Emiliani, Federico Guasti, Vittorio Ripa di Meana (Vice-Chair.); Ezio Antonioni; Pier Fausto Bagatti Valsecchi; Giovanni Bazoli; Mila Brachetti Peretti; Luigi Colombo; Alberto Falck; Paola Gazzola Premoli; Giuseppe Notabartolo di Sciara; Alberto Ronchey; Lucio Rondelli; Francesco Valcanover; Lorenzo Vallarino Gancia; Guido Roberto Vitale; Paolo Viti.

Principal Staff: Sec.-Gen. Renato Bazzoni.

Address: Viale Coni Zugna 5, 20144 Milan.

Telephone: (02) 4676151; **Fax:** (02) 48193631; **Internet:** www.fondoambiente.it; **e-mail:** info@fondo-ambiente.it.

Institute for Scientific Interchange Foundation

Aims to provide an accessible scientific environment, while also funding research to perpetuate scientific discovery.

Activities: Operates internationally in the field of science and technology, through funding scientific programmes, and recruiting scientists to lecture and carry out research in order to encourage and support science. Proposals for research projects are considered by a Science Board within the Foundation, and carried out by research co-ordinators from more than 15 countries at the Institute's premises in Turin. Also administers European Union funded activities.

Geographical Area of Activity: International.

Trustees: Giorgio Ardito; Paola Bertella; Sergio Chiamparino; Daniele Ciravegna.

Principal Staff: Pres. Tullio Regge; Gen-Sec. Mario Rasetti; Dir Tiziana Bertoletti.

Address: Villa Gualino, Viale Settimio Severo 65, 10133 Turin.

Telephone: (011) 6603090; **Fax:** (011) 6600049; **Internet:** www.isi.it; **e-mail:** isi@isi36a.isi.it.

International Lelio Basso Foundation for the Rights and Liberation of Peoples

Founded in 1976 by Senator Lelio Basso to promote research into human rights issues in developing countries.

Activities: Operates in the fields of the environment, development studies and human rights. Promotes information exchange between politicians, academics and lawyers concerned with human rights issues; offers grants to individuals for research; operates training courses and workshops; and organizes seminars and conferences. In the 1990s the work of the Foundation concentrated on the environment and development, industrial hazards and human rights, and the rights of children, young people and refugees.

Geographical Area of Activity: International.

Malawi

FOUNDATIONS, TRUSTS AND NON-PROFIT ORGANIZATIONS

Tea Research Foundation (Central Africa)

Founded in 1966 to encourage research into Central African tea and coffee production, and tea and coffee production in other regions.

Activities: Finances and organizes research into all aspects of tea and coffee production in Central Africa, including economics, horticulture, biochemistry and conservation of natural resources; maintains research stations in Mimosa, Nsuwadzi and Thyolo; operates a tea factory for research and development purposes; has established a coffee research unit in Nsuwadzi; maintains a library.

Geographical Area of Activity: Southern Africa (Malawi, South Africa and Zimbabwe).

Publications: Annual Report; Newsletter (quarterly); *Tea Planter's Handbook; Coffee Manual for Malawi.*

Finance: Budget approx. US $1,300,000 (1999).

Board of Management: Prof. L. K. Mughogho (Chair.).

Principal Staff: Dir Dr A. M. Whittle.

Address: POB 51, Mulanje.

Telephone: 462277; **Fax:** 462209; **e-mail:** zeno.apostolides@bioagric.up.ac.za.

Malaysia

FOUNDATIONS, TRUSTS AND NON-PROFIT ORGANIZATIONS

Pesticide Action Network Asia and the Pacific—PAN Asia and the Pacific

Co-ordinating regional branch of PAN International, which aims to promote sustainable agricultural methods without the need for pesticides.

Activities: Co-ordinates agricultural programmes and projects in the Asia-Pacific region, particularly focusing on sustainable, pesticide-free farming methods, the empowerment of women and peasants in agriculture, and food security. This is done through disseminating information, campaigning, holding workshops and conferences, training and practical field work.

Geographical Area of Activity: The Asia-Pacific region.

Publications: *Pesticide Monitor* (newsletter, quarterly).

Governing Body: Sarojeni V. Rengam; Anwar Fazal; Irene Fernandez; Bishan Singh; Daisy Dharmaraj; Kim Jai Ok; Dr Romy Quijano; Koa Tasaka; Meriel Watts; Riza Tjahjadi.

Principal Staff: Exec. Dir Sarojeni V. Rengam.

Address: POB 1170, 10850 Penang.

Telephone: (4) 656-0381; **Fax:** (4) 657-7445; **Internet:** www.panap.net; **e-mail:** panap@panap.net.

Renong Group Scholarship Trust Fund—RGSTF

Esatbalished by the Renong Group in 1995 to promote education.

Activities: Provides scholarships to exceptional students in Malaysia to study overseas, specifically at universities in Australia, New Zealand, the UK and the USA, in the fields of business studies, engineering, information technology and computer science, and law.

Geographical Area of Activity: Malaysia.

Address: c/o Renong Berhad, MCOBA Bldg, 42 Jalan Syed Putra, 50460 Kuala Lumpur.

Telephone: (3) 2273-7277; **Fax:** (3) 2273-7244; **Internet:** www.renong.com.my/community/corp.htm; **e-mail:** rgstf@po.jaring.my.

Third World Network

Non-profit international network of organizations and individuals concerned with 'Third World' and development issues, and the relationship between the Northern and Southern hemispheres.

Activities: Carries out research on cultural, social, environmental and economic issues affecting less-developed countries and regions, and raises awareness of these issues by publishing a number of books and magazines. Also organizes seminars and represents the interests of developing countries at international conferences. Has offices in Ghana, India, Switzerland and Uruguay, and affiliated organizations in Africa, Asia, the Far East, and Central and South America.

Geographical Area of Activity: Africa, Asia, the Far East, and Central and South America.

Publications: *Third World Resurgence* (magazine, monthly); *Third World Economics* (magazine, fortnightly); *SUNS bulletin* (bulletin, daily); *TWN Features Service* (media service, 3 a week); other books on environment, technology, economics and trade issues.

Finance: Funded by magazine subscription fees.

Principal Staff: Dir Martin Khor.

Address: 121-S, Jalan Utama, 10450 Penang.

Telephone: (4) 226-6728; **Fax:** (4) 226-4505; **Internet:** www.twnside.org.sg; **e-mail:** twnet@po.jaring.my.

Women's Aid Organization

Established in 1982 to promote women's rights in Malaysia, originally through the provision of women's refuges.

Activities: Works as an advocate for women suffering domestic violence in Malaysia by monitoring the implementation of laws to protect them. Lends support to women suffering violence by helping them with legal advocacy, loans, and giving refuge to them and their children. Also raises awareness of the problem through research, conferences and disseminating information.

Geographical Area of Activity: Malaysia.

Principal Staff: Exec. Dir Ivy Josiah.

Address: POB 493, Jalan Sultan, 46760 Petaling Jaya, Selangor Darul Ehsan.

Telephone: (3) 7956-3488; **Fax:** (3) 7956-3237; **Internet:** www.wao.org.my; **e-mail:** wao@po.jaring.my.

The World Fish Center

Previously known as ICLARM, the Centre was conceived by the Rockefeller Foundation (q.v.) in 1973, and became a small programme of the University of Hawaii in 1975, and was incorporated in Manila in March 1977. It became a member of the Consultative Group on International Agriculture Research (CGIAR) in May 1992. Before it was known as ICLARM, the Centre was known as the International Centre for Living Aquatic Resources.

Activities: The World Fish Center is an autonomous, non-governmental, non-profit-making, international scientific and technical centre established to conduct, stimulate and accelerate research on all aspects of fisheries and other living aquatic resources. Main areas of research are: improving productivity, protecting the environment, improving policies, saving biodiversity and strengthening national programmes. The Centre operates through research, conferences, publications, scholarships and awarding prizes (the Naga Award is given annually to a nominated scientific paper or book by an author from a developing country in any area of fisheries science). Maintains project offices in nine countries (Bangladesh, Cameroon, Caribbean/Eastern Pacific, Egypt, Malawi, New Caledonia, the Philippines, the Solomon Islands and Vietnam) and is currently conducting research projects with collaborators in 50 countries and 39 regional and international organizations.

Geographical Area of Activity: International.

Publications: *NAGA* (quarterly); Operation Plan; Annual Reports; conference proceedings, reviews, studies, technical reports, education and software series.

Trustees: Prof. R. E. Kearney (Chair.); Linxiu Zhang (Vice-Chair.); D. H. Ahmad; Dr S. Ayyappan; Prof. T. Bjorndal; Dr

K. R. Christensen; Dr S. Garcia; J. Joshi; Dr Y. Hassan Khalil; Dr T. Nose; Dr A. Soegiarto; Dr M. J. Williams; Dr S. Williams.

Principal Staff: Dir Gen. Dr Meryl J. Williams; Deputy Dir Gen. Dr Paul S. Teng.

Address: Jalan Batu Maung, Batu Maung, Bayan Lepas, 11960 Penang; POB 500, 10670 Penang.

Telephone: (4) 626-1606; **Fax:** (4) 626-5530; **Internet:** www.worldfishcenter.org; **e-mail:** worldfishcentre@cgiar.org.

Malta

FOUNDATIONS, TRUSTS AND NON-PROFIT ORGANIZATIONS

Foundation for International Studies

Founded in 1986 by the Government of Malta to promote research and training in the fields of the arts, the environment, economic and international affairs, and law and human rights. The Foundation concerns itself largely with the Mediterranean region.

Activities: Organizes international conferences; operates its own international programmes and training courses. Initiatives include the Islands and Small States Institute, the International Environment Institute, the Future Generations Programme, and the Euro-Mediterranean Centre on Insular Coastal Dynamics.

Geographical Area of Activity: Europe, the Mediterranean region and the Middle East.

Restrictions: No grants to individuals.

Publications: *The Future of the Mediterranean; Med in the Law of the Sea; Journal of Mediterranean Studies.*

Finance: Funds from UNESCO, the European Union and the Council of Europe.

Board of Trustees: Rector of the University of Malta; Dir-Gen. UNESCO; Exec. Dir UNEP; and others.

Principal Staff: Dir Prof. Roger Ellul-Micallef (acting).

Address: Old University Bldg, St Paul's St, Valletta VLT 07.

Telephone: 21234121; **Fax:** 21230551; **Internet:** www.um.edu.mt/intoff/fis.html.

Malta Ecological Foundation

Founded in 1992 as the Malta Ecological Society to promote education on environmental issues and to study and protect the environment.

Activities: The Foundation organizes numerous environmental campaigns in Malta on land use, public transport, ecological tourism, human and animal rights, and smoking; organizes the Ecological Summit of Malta; conducts research; and provides consultancy services to national and local government, independent organizations, businesses and schools, as well as organizing the annual Ecological Generational Award.

Geographical Area of Activity: Malta.

Publications: *Making One World; The Caught Hedgehog; Ecological Stories; What You Can Do to Help the Environment; Rozina's Secret Cave; The Stakeholder* (newsletter); Annual Report; tourist leaflets.

Principal Staff: Dunstan Hamilton.

Address: POB 322, Valletta CMR 01.

Telephone: 21641486; **Fax:** 21338780; **Internet:** www.ecomalta.org; **e-mail:** eco@ecomalta.org.

Mexico

FOUNDATION CENTRE AND CO-ORDINATING BODY

Centro Mexicano para la Filantropía, AC (Mexican Centre for Philanthropy)

Founded in December 1988 to obtain and disseminate information on organizations and groups committed to philanthropic activities; to establish communications between philanthropic associations; and to promote relations with philanthropic organizations world-wide.

Activities: Operates through self-conducted programmes, research, conferences, training courses and publications to promote philanthropy.

Geographical Area of Activity: Mexico.

Publications: *Directorio de Instituciones Filantrópicas; Revista Filantropía.*

Board of Trustees: Maria Luisa Barrera de Serna; Jorge Aguilar Valenzuela; Mario Garciadiego Gonzalez Cos; Manuel Arango Arias.

Principal Staff: Pres. Jorge Villalobos Grzybowicz.

Address: Cerrada de Salvador Alvarado 7, Col. Escandón, CP 11800, México, DF.

Telephone: (55) 5277-61-11; **Fax:** (55) 5515-54-48; **Internet:** www.cemefi.org; **e-mail:** cemefi@cemefi.org.

FOUNDATIONS, TRUSTS AND NON-PROFIT ORGANIZATIONS

Centro Internacional de Mejoramiento de Maíz y Trigo—CIMMYT (International Maize and Wheat Improvement Centre)

Founded in 1966 by the Government of Mexico and the Rockefeller Foundation (q.v.), CIMMYT is an international, non-profit, agricultural research and training centre, working towards assisting the poor in developing countries through increasing the profitability, productivity and sustainability of maize and wheat farming systems.

Activities: Operates internationally through self-conducted programmes, research, fellowships, scholarships, conferences, courses, publications and lectures. Supports the development and distribution world-wide of higher-yielding maize and wheat with in-built genetic resistance to diseases and insects; the conservation and distribution of maize and wheat genetic resources; research on natural resource management in maize- and wheat-based cropping systems; documentation of new knowledge in the area of wheat and maize; development of more effective research methods; training; and technical consultation. Maintains regional offices in Afghanistan, Australia, Bangladesh, the People's Republic of China, Colombia, Costa Rica, Ethiopia, Georgia, Guatemala, India, Kazakhstan, Kenya, Malawi, Nepal, the Philippines, Syria, Turkey, Uruguay and Zimbabwe.

Geographical Area of Activity: International.

Publications: *CIMMYT Annual Report; World Wheat Overview and Outlook; World Maize Facts and Trends; Literature Update on Wheat, Barley and Triticale.*

Finance: Funding comes from overseas development assistance agencies.

Trustees: A. McCalla (Chair.); J. Holmberg (Vice-Chair.); R. Aveldaño; T. Colijn-Hooymans; N. Dun; R. Goodman; A. Gregson; A. Hirai; C. F. Jaramillo; K. M. Leisinger; J. Moncada de la Fuente; N. K. Olembo; M. Rai; T. G. Reeves; U. Tan-Kim-Yong; J. Usabiaga; J. Witcombe; Xin Zhiyong.

Principal Staff: Dir Gen. Masaru Iwanaga.

Address: Apdo 6-641, 06600 México, DF.

Telephone: (55) 5804-20-04; **Fax:** (55) 5804-75-58; **Internet:** www.cimmyt.org; **e-mail:** cimmyt@cgiar.org.

Consejo de Educación de Adultos de América Latina—CEAAL (Council for the Education of Adults in Latin America)

Established in 1982, an association of 210 organizations, aiming to improve adult literacy and advance social development throughout Central and South America and the Caribbean.

Activities: Operates in the field of education, consolidating the training and abilities of teaching staff in Central and South America and the Caribbean, promoting socio-cultural advancements in society, peace, human rights and democracy through education and raising adult literacy levels. Holds a General Assembly meeting every four years.

Geographical Area of Activity: Central and South America and the Caribbean.

Address: Toledo No. 46, Col. Juárez, 0660 México, DF.

Telephone: (55) 5533-17-55; **Fax:** (55) 5514-06-10; **Internet:** www.ceaal.org/index001.htm; **e-mail:** ceaal@laneta.apc.org.

Fundación Miguel Alemán AC (Miguel Alemán Foundation)

Founded in 1984 by Miguel Alemán Valdés to promote and support humanitarian activities, tourism development, health and ecological issues, and technological advances in agriculture.

Activities: The Foundation operates nationally in the fields of conservation and the environment, the arts and humanities, economic affairs, education, international affairs, medicine and health, science and technology, and social welfare, through self-conducted programmes, research, grants to institutions, prizes, conferences, training courses and publications.

Geographical Area of Activity: Mexico.

Publications: *Inform* (annually); several other publications.

Finance: Net assets approx. US $1,600,000.

Trustees: Miguel Alemán Velasco (Chair.); Beatriz Alemán de Girón (Treas.); Jorge Alemán Velasco (Speaker).

Principal Staff: Dir Fernando Castro y Castro; Managers: Guadalupe Pardo (Environment); Federico Chávez (Health); Alejandro de Antuñano (Humanities); Miguel Moto (Rural Devt); Elizabeth Sotomayor (Tourism).

Address: Ruben Darío 187, Col. Chapultepec Morales, 11570 México, DF.

Telephone: (55) 5250-65-76; **Fax:** (55) 5250-10-43; **Internet:** www.miguelaleman.org.mx; **e-mail:** fundaleman@mexis.com.

Fundación Mexico Unido (United Mexico Foundation)

Established in 1995 by group of young people who wanted to help promote the appreciation and development of authentic Mexican values and culture, and to promote human values.

Activities: Programmes operated by the Foundation include a 'telethon', which funds rehabilitation centres for children with disabilities, and Lazos, which provides financial support to schools and to poor children to ensure they receive an education.

Geographical Area of Activity: Mexico and South America.

Publications: *Friends of Teleton* (6 a year); publications promoting Mexican values and history.

Board of Trustees: Emilio Azcárraga; Gutierrez Cortina; Juan Diego; Javier Sordo Madaleno.

Principal Staff: Pres. Fernando Laseros; Dir Public Relations Jose Antonio Dorbecker; Dir Telethon Alejandro Puente.

Address: Copérnico 51, Col. Anzures, 11590 México, DF.

Telephone: (55) 5531-22-55; **Fax:** (55) 5531-14-98; **Internet:** www.mexicounido.org.mx.

Moldova

FOUNDATIONS, TRUSTS AND NON-PROFIT ORGANIZATIONS

Moldovan Charity and Health Fund

Founded in December 1988 by the Ministry of Health, the Ministry of Labour and Social Protection and the Federation of Independent Trade Unions, to provide humanitarian aid.

Activities: The Foundation operates in the fields of the arts and humanities, education, international affairs, law and human rights, medicine and health, and science and technology.

Geographical Area of Activity: Moldova.

Publications: *Charity; Pacea Civică.*

Finance: Funding is provided by the Government of Moldova.

Principal Staff: Dr Ion Cuzuioc.

Address: Chişinău 277012, Hânceşti Str. 1 c.303.

Telephone: (2) 72-96-89; **Fax:** (2) 73-53-22.

Soros Foundation—Moldova

Established in 1992 to promote the development of open society; it is part of the Soros foundations network, which aims to foster political and cultural pluralism and reform the economy so as to encourage free enterprise and a market economy.

Activities: The Foundation is currently developing and financing a range of projects in a variety of areas; the principal areas of concern are: education, through support for secondary schools, curriculum reform and grants for young people in higher education; independent media, through supporting independent and cultural publications by providing training and access to information; and civil society, promoting human rights and the rights of ethnic minorities, and providing grants for NGOs and access to information and training for NGO workers through the Contact centre for NGOs. Also works in the areas of rural development, law and criminal justice, youth, arts and culture, libraries and the internet, and funds national and international conferences.

Geographical Area of Activity: Moldova.

Finance: Annual expenditure US $4,606,000 (2001).

Board of Directors: Arcadie Barbarosie (Chair.); Raisa Botezatu; Andrei Cantemir; Vitalie Ciobanu; Alexandru Dorogan; Alexandru Muravschi; Andrei Popa.

Principal Staff: Exec. Dir Victor Ursu.

Address: Chişinău 277001, Bulgara Str. 32.

Telephone: (2) 27-00-31; **Fax:** (2) 27-05-07; **Internet:** www.soros.md; **e-mail:** foundation@soros.md.

Monaco

FOUNDATIONS, TRUSTS AND NON-PROFIT ORGANIZATIONS

Fondation Princesse Grace (Princess Grace Foundation)

Founded in 1964 to carry out general charitable activities.

Activities: Engaged in three on-going projects: the Boutiques du Rocher, which supports local craftspeople, the Classic Dance Academy, which funds training for talented young dancers, and the Irish Library. Also contributes to humanitarian projects related to children's health care, including some international work, and to cultural activities, providing scholarships to students of the arts. The Princess Grace Foundation—USA operates in the USA.

Geographical Area of Activity: Mainly Monaco and France.

Restrictions: No grants directly to students or children.

Finance: Total income €1,584,077, total expenditure €1,461,939 (2001).

Board of Trustees: HRH Princess of Hanover (Pres.); HSH Prince Albert of Monaco (Vice-Pres.); Jean-Claude Riey (Treas.); Lilliane Fautrier; Virginia Gallico; Luisita Albanese; Marie-Rose Lesluyes; Jean Pastorelli; Henry Rey.

Address: BP 520, 98015 Monte Carlo.

Telephone: 97-70-86-86; **Fax:** 97-70-79-99; **Internet:** www.fondation-psse-grace.mc; **e-mail:** fpg@fondation-psse-grace.mc.

Mongolia

FOUNDATIONS, TRUSTS AND NON-PROFIT ORGANIZATIONS

The Globe International

Founded in 1999 with the aim of supporting the development of Mongolian development and civil society.

Activities: Globe International aims to sustain Mongolian democracy and develop civil and humanitarian society primarily through support for the media, art and culture, within two main programmes; Media Development and Art and Culture Development, which include a focus on creating favourable social, legal and economic conditions for artists and journalists to work. Also seeks to broaden co-operation between Mongolia and the rest of the world through cultural exchanges.

Geographical Area of Activity: Mongolia.

Publications: Various handbooks, reports and articles.

Board: Khashkhuu Naranjargal (Pres.); Dolgor Chuluunbaatar; Khasbaatar Mergen; Bud Sum'Ya; Khorloo Tsevlee.

Principal Staff: Dir H. Naranjargal.

Address: Sukhbaatar dureg No. 8, City Cultural Palace, Tower A, 334 Ulaanbaatar.

Telephone: (11) 324764; **Fax:** (11) 324627; **Internet:** www.globeint.com; **e-mail:** globe@magicnet.mn.

Mongolian Foundation for Open Society

Established in 1996 to promote the development of open society in Mongolia. It is an independent foundation, part of the Soros foundations network.

Activities: Operates in the areas of education, information and the media, arts and culture, civil society, law and criminal justice, public health, economic development, women and youth. Also runs an extensive scholarship programme and an on-line grant database.

Geographical Area of Activity: Mongolia.

Publications: Annual Report.

Finance: Annual expenditure US $3,880,000 (2001).

Board of Directors: Luvsandendev Sumati (Chair.); Radnaa Burmaa; Ayurzana Enkh-Amgalan; Tuvdendorj Galbaatar; Jambalsuren Narantuya; Lhagvasuren Nomin.

Principal Staff: Exec. Dir Stephen D. Vance.

Address: Center for Science and Technological Information, 3rd floor, Baga Toiruu-49, Ulaanbaatar.

Telephone: (1) 313207; **Fax:** (1) 324857; **Internet:** www.soros.org.mn; **e-mail:** altantuya@soros.org.mn.

Morocco

FOUNDATIONS, TRUSTS AND NON-PROFIT ORGANIZATIONS

Fondation du Roi Abdul-Aziz Al Saoud pour les Etudes Islamiques et les Sciences Humaines (King Abdul-Aziz Al Saoud Foundation for Islamic Study and the Humanities)

Established in 1985 to offer library and database services to researchers working in the field of Islamic culture and in the humanities.

Activities: Maintains a research library of approximately 287,000 volumes and 1,992 periodicals, mainly in Arabic, English and French, but other languages are represented. The Foundation also maintains three databases: the Ibn Rushd database of more than 78,000 bibliographical references, with information on the Maghreb, Western European and West African Islamic communities; the Fahras database of approximately 58,000 references, with information covering the rest of the Arab world and general Islamic research; and the Mawsu'a database of over 241,000 entries containing bibliographical information on the human and social sciences, regarding their methodological and theoretical aspects. There is also a multimedia service. The Foundation also organizes, in collaboration with other research and documentation institutions, international conferences and seminars.

Geographical Area of Activity: Morocco.

Publications: *Etudes maghrébines.*

Address: BP 12585, Casablanca 20052; Blvd de la Corniche, Ain Diab, Anfa, Casablanca 20050.

Telephone: (2) 391027; **Fax:** (2) 391031; **Internet:** www.fondation.org.ma; **e-mail:** secretariat@fondation.org.ma.

Mozambique

FOUNDATIONS, TRUSTS AND NON-PROFIT ORGANIZATIONS

Foundation for Community Development/Fundação para o Desenvolvimento da Comunidade

Established in 1994 by Graça Machel, wife of Nelson Mandela and a former Minister of Education in Mozambique, to bring health care, education, economic development, access to technology and peace to the African continent.

Activities: The Foundation promotes economic development, health care and related programmes in disadvantaged communities in Mozambique and other parts of Africa, aiming to increase human and financial resources for development at the community level. Priority is given to education, health, water and training projects, which develop human potential, generate income, and put in place necessary infrastructure. The Foundation has financed the construction of hospitals and schools, and skills training, and has provided micro-credit funds. Also acts as an advocate in the areas of land tenure, promotes a landmine ban, supports education for girls and works in the areas of external debt and development issues.

Geographical Area of Activity: Mozambique and Africa.

Finance: In 1999 the Foundation received donations totalling US $12,500,000 from the Bill and Melinda Gates Foundation and the Craig and Susan McCaw Foundation (qq.v.).

Board of Trustees: Machel Graça (Chair.).

Principal Staff: Pres. Graça Machel; Exec. Dir Carlos Fumo.

Address: Av. Eduardo Mondlane 1160, CP 4206, Maputo.

Telephone: (1) 430430; **Fax:** (1) 422595; **e-mail:** fdc@zebra.uem.mz.

Namibia

FOUNDATIONS, TRUSTS AND NON-PROFIT ORGANIZATIONS

Desert Research Foundation of Namibia

Founded by Dr C. Koch in 1963 to promote ecological education and research training. Incorporates the Desert Ecological Research Unit.

Activities: The Foundation operates in the fields of conservation and the environment and education, through self-conducted programmes, ecological research in arid zones, international conferences, training courses and publications. Works in partnership with local communities to find solutions and finance to improve farming efficiency, manage natural resources and to disseminate information to local people.

Geographical Area of Activity: Southern Africa.

Publications: *Namib Bulletin; Desertification Newsletter*; and numerous other publications.

Finance: The Foundation is funded by grants, donations and a trust fund. Implements donor funds, annual budget approx N $10,000,000.

Trustees: E. Amkongo; N. Angula; C. Brain; G. Brückner; M. Mbumba; Z. Ngavirue; E. Pfeifer; H. Rumpf; M. K. Seely; P. Shiimi; K. Tjipangandjara.

Principal Staff: Exec. Dir Dr M. K. Seely.

Address: 7 Rossini St, POB 20232, Windhoek; POB 1592, Swakopmund.

Telephone: (61) 229855 (Windhoek); **Fax:** (61) 230172 (Windhoek); **Internet:** www.drfn.org; **e-mail:** drfn@drfn.org.na.

Rössing Foundation

Founded in 1978 by Rio Tinto Zinc, London (United Kingdom), and Rössing Uranium Ltd, Namibia, to promote education and research in Namibia.

Activities: Operates in the fields of education and social welfare and studies, through research, scholarships, training courses and conferences. The Foundation has four education centres at Khomasdal, Lüderitz, Ondangwa and Omaruru offering courses in needlework, textile design, vehicle maintenance, commercial practice, technical skills, office practice, typing, art, mathematics and English, and a Teachers' Programme. It maintains libraries at Katutura and the Khomasdal centre; promotes the study of science in high schools by supporting the Namibian Young Scientists National Exhibition held at the Khomasdal centre; awards local education bursaries for study in Namibian and South African institutions; organizes skills training workshops for the self-employed; and provides advice and help for women in rural areas to improve their craft design and make their products more marketable (it has arranged workshops, competitions and exhibitions). The agriculture programme has established 16 vegetable-growing centres throughout the country and provides equipment, seeds, advice and fertilizers, from its centre at Okombahe in the Damaraland area. The Foundation also offers training courses for subsistence and stock farmers, at the Brakwater Agricultural Training Centre near Windhoek, and horticultural courses at Okahandja training centre. The Okashana Centre in Ovamboland conducts seed and crop research, in conjunction with ICRISAT, Zimbabwe. The Shankara centre in the Kavango region was to be developed as a commercial crop production and agricultural research and experimentation centre. With help from IBIS, Denmark, the Young Farmers' Clubs were to be extended to cover more schools. The Foundation is supported by numerous national and international organizations.

Geographical Area of Activity: Southern Africa.

Finance: The Foundation has been funded almost entirely by Rössing Uranium Ltd. Total expenditure approx. N $18,000,000 (2000).

Trustees: J. S. Kirkpatrick (Chair.).

Principal Staff: Dir Len le Roux.

Address: Private Bag 13214, Windhoek.

Telephone: (61) 211721; **Fax:** (61) 211668; **Internet:** www.rf.org.na; **e-mail:** lleroux@rf.org.na.

Nepal

FOUNDATIONS, TRUSTS AND NON-PROFIT ORGANIZATIONS

Asia Pacific Mountain Network—APMN

Established in 1995, a network of organizations and individuals concerned with sustainable mountain development in the Asia-Pacific region.

Activities: Operates in the area of conservation and development in mountainous areas of Asia and the Pacific region, promoting the idea of a sustainable ecosystem in these areas. Disseminates information on this subject, encouraging information exchange amongst members; works on capacity-building, especially relating to technological advances and electronic communications; acts as an advocate for improved legislation in the field of sustainable mountain development; and supports the alleviation of poverty amongst mountain populations. New inititiatives include grassroots outreach activities targeting young people and the development of a subsidiary office in Central Asia. Operates a small grants programme.

Geographical Area of Activity: The Asia-Pacific region.

Publications: *APMN Bulletin* (2 a year); *Tough Terrain: Media Reports on Mountain Issues*.

Principal Staff: Admin. Ujol Sherchan.

Address: c/o ICIMOD, GPO Box 3226, Kathmandu.

Telephone: (1) 4525313; **Fax:** (1) 4522509; **Internet:** www.mtnforum.org/apmn; **e-mail:** apmn@mtnforum.org.

Himalayan Light Foundation

Founded to support the use of environmentally-friendly energy technology in order to improve the quality of life of people living in remote Himalayan communities.

Activities: Operates in the fields of conservation and the environment, education and social welfare, through self-conducted programmes, research and dissemination of information. The Foundation operates the Solar Sisters and Home Employment and Lighting Programme (HELP); it also provides solar lighting systems to remote monasteries (which, in turn, provide education for children and support for communities). The establishment of rural energy extension centres in rural areas also provides education and employment for local villagers.

Geographical Area of Activity: Nepal.

Address: POB 12191, Kathmandu.

Telephone: (1) 4425393; **Fax:** (1) 4412924; **Internet:** www.hlf.org.np; **e-mail:** info@hlf.mos.np.

INHURED International—International Institute for Human Rights, Environment and Development

Founded in 1991 to defend human rights in the Asia-Pacific region, particularly in Southern Asia.

Activities: Works to advance human rights and gender equality and to promote democracy in Asia, by strengthening existing human rights bodies; monitoring international institutions for signs of human and environmental rights abuses; observing elections; funding training; co-ordinating international conferences and workshops; and disseminating information. Offers internship and fellowship programmes for international and university students and scholars in the areas of human rights, environment, development and the democratization process. Also promotes environmental conservation.

Geographical Area of Activity: The Asia-Pacific region.

Finance: Funded by membership fees, donations, sale of publications and grants.

Principal Staff: Exec. Dir Gopal Krishna Siwakoti; Program Dir Anjana Shakya.

Address: GPO Box 4690, Kathmandu.

Telephone: (1) 4520054; **Fax:** (1) 4520042; **Internet:** www.inhured.org; **e-mail:** info@inhured.wlink.com.np.

Nepal Forward Foundation

Founded in 1996 to provide assistance in Nepal.

Activities: Operates in the fields of economic development, conservation and the environment, education and youth, and cultural preservation. Projects include installing solar panels in remote villages of Nepal in conjunction with the Himalayan Light Foundation (q.v.), promoting the export of organic tea from Nepal to Europe and the USA, and ecotourism initiatives. Also organizes cultural exchanges between Nepal and the USA, where it maintains an office.

Geographical Area of Activity: Nepal.

Principal Staff: Chair. Eric J. Durbani; Exec. Dir Kamal Z. El-Wattar.

Address: Murxana House, Lal Durbar, Durbar Marg, Kathmandu.

Telephone: (1) 426850; **Fax:** (1) 428844; **Internet:** www.nepalforward.org; **e-mail:** nepal.forward@ibm.netjane.kearns@nepalforward.org.

Netherlands

FOUNDATION CENTRE AND CO-ORDINATING BODY

Vereniging van Fondsen in Nederland (Association of Foundations in the Netherlands)

Established in 1988 the Association's membership is comprised of private foundations established in the Netherlands. Its aim is to promote the interests of its members and enable them to function effectively.

Activities: Promotes the interests of its member foundations and assists them to function in the most effective way by: providing information concerning foundations operating in the Netherlands; maintaining contact with public authorities, social organizations and the media; and providing advice on matters of management and donations policy. Also promotes the establishment of new foundations and the exchange of information between members. The Association has 180 members.

Geographical Area of Activity: Netherlands.

Publications: *Fondsenboek* (every 2 years); *Fondsendisk* (annually).

Finance: Financed by subscriptions from its members.

Governing Board: J. A. van de Ven (Chair.); H. J. A. Zwitser (Vice-Chair.); F. M. J. Luns (Treas.); C. G. C. Hooft Graafland; A. Offers; O. Regout; J. H. Scherphuis; M. A. van den Steenhoven-Key; H. J. C. de Vries.

Principal Staff: Dir D. J. M. van de Laarschot; Sec. V. L. A. M. Theewen.

Address: Jan van Nassaustraat 102, 2596 BW The Hague.

Telephone: (70) 326-27-53; **Fax:** (70) 326-22-29; **Internet:** www.verenigingvanfondsen.nl; **e-mail:** fin@xs4all.nl.

FOUNDATIONS, TRUSTS AND NON-PROFIT ORGANIZATIONS

The Canon Foundation in Europe

Founded in December 1987 by Canon Europa NV to facilitate mutual understanding and the development of scientific expertise, in particular between Europe and Japan.

Activities: The Foundation offers research fellowships and awards to individuals in all fields of interest, in order for Europeans to visit Japan, and to enable Japanese people to visit Europe.

Geographical Area of Activity: Europe and Japan.

Publications: Bulletin (annually).

Trustees: Dr W. R. van Gulik; P. Kers; H. Tsuruoka.

Principal Staff: Dir Corrie Siahaya-van Nierop.

Address: Rijnsburgerweg 3, 2334 BA Leiden.

Telephone: (71) 515-65-55; **Fax:** (71) 515-70-27; **Internet:** www.canonfoundation.org; **e-mail:** foundation@canon-europe.com.

Carnegie-Stichting, Watelerfonds (Carnegie Foundation, Wateler Fund)

Founded in 1927 by J. G. D. Wateler for the awarding of an annual peace prize.

Activities: Awards the Wateler Peace Prize each year to the person or institution having rendered the most valuable service in the cause of peace or having contributed to finding means of preventing war. The prize is given alternately to a person of Dutch and foreign nationality. In 2001, the prize was awarded to the UNHCR.

Geographical Area of Activity: International.

Trustees: The Board of Directors of the Carnegie Foundation.

Address: Carnegirplain 2, 2517 KJ The Hague.

Telephone: (70) 302-41-77; **Fax:** (70) 302-41-78; **Internet:** www.carnegie-stichting.nl; **e-mail:** info@carnegie-stichting.nl.

Co-operating Netherlands Foundations for Central and Eastern Europe

Established in 1991, a group of Netherlands foundations which work together to support local NGOs in nine countries of Central and Eastern Europe; the core foundations are the Foundation 'Oranje Fonds', the Foundation Het R. C. Maagdenhuis, the SKaN Foundation and the Foundation for Children's Welfare Stamps Netherlands; in addition, 35 foundations contribute to projects but do not co-ordinate them.

Activities: The Foundations operate in nine countries of Central and Eastern Europe, with the aim of easing the process of social transition. They work in the fields of human rights, health care and social welfare by making grants to local organizations and projects.

Geographical Area of Activity: Central and Eastern Europe (Bulgaria, Czech Republic, Croatia, Estonia, Latvia, Lithuania, Romania, Slovakia and West Ukraine).

Restrictions: Grants are made only to non-government-funded organizations and projects in Central and Eastern Europe.

Publications: Annual Report; quarterly journal.

Finance: Annual expenditure approx. €5,500,000.

Principal Staff: Co-ordinator Th. A. M. A. van der Ven.

Address: Postbus 156, 1200 AD Hilversum.

Telephone: (35) 624-96-51; **Fax:** (35) 624-61-32; **Internet:** www.cnfcee.nl; **e-mail:** info@cnfcee.nl.

Europa Nostra

Founded in 1963 as a pan-European Federation, for the protection of Europe's architectural and natural heritage.

Activities: Operates in Europe in the field of conservation, through research, conferences, publications and a conservation award scheme, of which photographic records are maintained. The federation makes recommendations to the Council of Europe and the European Union. Offers annual conservation awards (Europa Nostra Awards), Medals of Honour and an annual grant for the restoration of heritage in Europe. Maintains a small-scale Restoration Fund.

Geographical Area of Activity: Europe.

Publications: *Europa Nostra Review;* Annual Report; newsletter; bulletin; awards journal; all publications are in French and English.

Finance: Financed by sponsorship, membership subscriptions and support from European institutions. Annual budget approx. 700,000 Swiss francs.

Principal Staff: Pres. HRH the Prince Consort of Denmark; Exec. Pres. Otto van der Gablentz; Costa Carras, Catharina Collet (Vice-Pres.); Sec.-Gen. Sneška Quaedvlieg-Mihailović.

Address: Lange Voorhout 35, 2514 EC The Hague.

Telephone: (70) 302-40-50; **Fax:** (70) 361-78-65; **Internet:** www.europanostra.org; **e-mail:** office@europanostra.org.

European Cultural Foundation (Fondation Européenne de la Culture/Europese Culturele Stichting)

Founded in 1954 as an NGO, supported by private sources, to promote cross-cultural co-operation on a multilateral European level.

Activities: The Foundation initiates and manages its own programmes and projects, and gives grants to other bodies for European-level cultural activities. The Foundation emphasizes the importance of developing a pluralistic civil society in Europe by encouraging the linkage of cultural activity and social responsibility. The ECF acts as the central secretariat for two networks: a European network of independent associated institutes and centres for research and study in fields such as education, the media and the environment; and a network of National Committees based in 23 European countries. Current priorities for projects initiated and supported are: intercultural dialogue, funding projects which promote dialogue between different cultural groups in an innovative and action-oriented way; participation through the arts, funding initiatives supporting the use of art for confidence-building in individuals and communities; and strengthening the cultural sector, through funding initiatives creating new partnerships in the policy-making arena for arts or artistic activity funding. Within the context of EU enlargement, the Foundation is mobilizing its network and working on partnerships for cultural advocacy. It is making contributions to the current debate, organizing events and colloquiums, and raising public awareness through specific programmes.

Geographical Area of Activity: Europe.

Restrictions: ECF programmes are initiated, developed and run in partnership with other organizations. Grants are made only to non-profit organizations for a cultural co-operation project; grants are made only in Europe.

Publications: Annual Report (in English and French); *Beyond Borders Magazine* (2 a year).

Finance: Grants budget €600,000 (2003).

Trustees: HRH Princess Margriet of the Netherlands (Pres.); representatives from 18 European countries; and two representatives from the Council of Europe.

Principal Staff: Dir of Programmes and Grants Odile Chenal.

Address: Jan van Goyenkade 5, 1075 HN Amsterdam.

Telephone: (20) 676-02-22; **Fax:** (20) 675-22-31; **Internet:** www.eurocult.org; **e-mail:** eurocult@eurocult.org.

European Youth Forest Action—EYFA

Founded in 1986 as an activist network to encourage young people to work towards the prevention of environmental pollution and the decimation of forests.

Activities: The organization works in Europe in the field of conservation and the environment, through promoting sustainable ways of living and working, non-violent campaigns against ecologically and socially unsustainable systems, cultural activism and alternative media. Helps other organizations with their fundraising as well as providing financial services, including book-keeping assistance and the legal status to receive funds on behalf of other organizations.

Geographical Area of Activity: Europe.

Publications: *Green Pepper*.

Finance: Annual budget approx. €114,000.

Trustees: The Foundation is governed by an International Co-ordination Team whose membership changes annually.

Address: POB 94115, 1090 GC Amsterdam.

Telephone: (20) 665-77-43; **Fax:** (20) 692-87-57; **Internet:** www.eyfa.org; **e-mail:** eyfa@eyfa.org.

Eurotransplant International Foundation

Founded in 1967 with the aim of facilitating the exchange of human organs in order to save lives.

Activities: Supports co-operation between dialysis centres, tissue typing laboratories and transplant centres; aims to minimize the risks involved in organ transplants through tissue typing and matching; assists in the organization of organ transplants; works to achieve a high rate of utilization of donor organs; co-operates with similar organizations in Austria, Belgium, Germany, Luxembourg and Slovenia. The Foundation provides finance for programmes intended to improve the system whereby human organs may be transplanted. Maintains a databank of patients. There are members in five other countries.

Geographical Area of Activity: Europe.

Publications: Annual Report; *Eurotransplant Newsletter* (monthly).

Principal Staff: Pres. Prof. Dr Y. Vanrenterghem; Dir Dr Bernard Cohen; Dr Guido Persijn.

Address: POB 2304, 2301 CH Leiden.

Telephone: (71) 579-57-95; **Fax:** (71) 579-00-57; **Internet:** www.eurotransplant.nl.

De Faunabescherming

Founded in December 1975 to work toward scientific and ethical wildlife management.

Activities: Operates nationally in the field of conservation and wildlife management; organizes training courses and issues publications.

Geographical Area of Activity: Netherlands.

Publications: *Argus* (quarterly).

Principal Staff: R. Boeve; P. de Jong; J. Poeder.

Address: Amsteldijk Noord 135, 1183 TJ Amstelveen.

Telephone: (20) 641-07-98; **Fax:** (20) 647-37-00; **Internet:** www.faunabescherming.nl; **e-mail:** faunabescherming@wxs.nl.

FEMCONSULT (Consultants on Gender and Development)

Founded in 1985 as a non-profit organization, a multi-disciplinary group of professionals applying a gender perspective in programmes and projects in developing countries.

Activities: Offers technical expertise with a focus on gender-based constraints and opportunities for the development of programmes and projects aimed at the reduction of poverty. In particular, promotes the participation of women in development programmes; implements projects in developing countries focusing on women, in areas such as agriculture and rural development, human resources development, nutrition and food aid; small businesses; and public health. Also offers a range of consultancy services concerning development programmes and projects, including participatory planning; project identification and appraisal; pre-investment studies; project design, planning, management, monitoring and evaluation; institutional strengthening and training; social, poverty and gender assessment studies; and preparation of tender documents.

Geographical Area of Activity: International.

Publications: *FEMCONSULT* (newsletter, in English); *Project Report; Skills Bank* (2 a year, in Dutch and English); *Symposium Report*.

Principal Staff: Man. Dir Catharina M. G. van Heel.

Address: Nassauplein 26, 2585 EC The Hague.

Telephone: (70) 365-57-44; **Fax:** (70) 362-31-00; **Internet:** www.femconsult.nl; **e-mail:** gender@femconsult.nl.

FONDAD—Forum on Debt and Development

Activities: Engages in policy research relating to less-developed countries around the world, and the problems experienced by these areas, particularly regarding international financial issues. Acts as an international information network, and a forum for discussion for policy-makers and other groups working in the developing world. Also holds seminars and produces a number of publications.

Geographical Area of Activity: International.

Restrictions: No grants are available.

Publications: *New Challenges of Crisis Prevention: Addressing Economic Imbalances in the North and Boom-Bust Cycles in the South; Reforming the International Financial System; The Management of Global Financial Markets; Private Capital Flows to Africa: Perception and Reality;* and many other publications.

Principal Staff: Dir Jan Joost Teunissen.

Address: Noordeinde 107 A, 2514 GE The Hague.

Telephone: (70) 365-38-20; **Fax:** (70) 346-39-39; **Internet:** www.fondad.org; **e-mail:** info@fondad.org.

Friends of the Earth International/Les Amis de la Terre/Amigos de la Tierra

A federation of environmental organizations and groups active throughout the world.

Activities: Operates internationally in the area of the environment, by campaigning on issues such as genetically-modified crops, climate change, trade and sustainability, human rights, and natural resources. Also issues publications on sustainable use of the environment. The International Secretariat supports its member network, by raising funds, co-ordinating campaigns, organizing workshops, disseminating information and maintaining databases. There are member organizations in 68 countries world-wide, and 15 affiliated groups.

Geographical Area of Activity: International.

Publications: *Link;* electronic bulletins.

Principal Staff: Chair. Ricardo Navarro; Vice-Chair. Tony Juniper; Treas. Otto Sieber; Int. Co-ordinator Marijke Torfs.

Address: International Secretariat, POB 19199, 1000 GD Amsterdam.

Telephone: (20) 622-13-69; **Fax:** (20) 639-21-81; **Internet:** www.foei.org; **e-mail:** foei@foei.org.

Max Havelaar Foundation

Established in 1988 for fair and direct trade with small producers from developing countries.

Activities: Operates in developing countries in the areas of conservation and the environment, and international affairs. Promotes fair trade, co-operating with small-scale producers in developing countries, Dutch importers and consumers and maintains a register of producers and checks on importers to insure fair trade principles are adhered to.

Geographical Area of Activity: Africa, Asia, and Central and South America.

Publications: *Koffie met toekomst* (Coffee with a Future); *Meer dan heerlyk* (More than Delicious).

Finance: Financed through licence fees.

Principal Staff: Dir Hans Bolscher.

Address: Postbus 1252, 3500 BG Utrecht.

Telephone: (30) 233-70-70; **Fax:** (30) 233-29-92; **Internet:** www.maxhavelaar.nl; **e-mail:** maxhavelaar@maxhavelaar.nl.

Health Action International

Activities: An international network of over 150 health, consumer and development groups operating in more than 70 countries, working towards safe and effective medicine and health care which is accessible to all. Also carries out research and organizes training seminars and conferences, and campaigns for greater controls on the marketing of drugs.

Geographical Area of Activity: Africa, Asia and the Pacific, Europe, and North, Central and South America.

Publications: *HAI News* (global newsletter, 6 a year); *HAI-Lights* (regional newsletter for partners active in Europe and North America, 3 a year); reports; briefing papers.

Address: c/o HAI Europe, Jacob van Lennepkade 334-T, 1053 NJ Amsterdam.

Telephone: (20) 683-36-84; **Fax:** (20) 685-50-02; **Internet:** www.haiweb.org; **e-mail:** info@haiwab.org.

Alfred Heineken Fondsen Foundation

Established by Dr Alfred Heineken to award prizes in various fields.

Activities: The Foundation awards the Dr A. H. Heineken Prizes (known as the Amsterdam Prizes until 1994), and which were first awarded in 1988. Prizes are given in the areas of art, history, medicine and environmental sciences. The prize for art is open to artists living and working in the Netherlands; prizes for medicine, history and environmental sciences are open to candidates internationally.

Geographical Area of Activity: International.

Restrictions: The prize for art is open only to artists living and working in the Netherlands; prizes in the fields of medicine, history and environmental science are open internationally.

Trustees: The Board of Trustees comprises a president, a secretary and a treasurer.

Principal Staff: Chair. C. L. de Carvalho-Heineken.

Address: 2E Weteringplansoen 5, 1017 ZD Amsterdam.

Telephone: (20) 626-33-49; **Fax:** (20) 625-22-13; **Internet:** www.knaw.nl/heinekenprizes; **e-mail:** pentagon@pentagonbv.nl.

Dr H. P. Heineken Stichting (Dr H. P. Heineken Foundation)

Founded in 1963 by Heineken's Bierbrouwerij Maatschappij NV to promote science and culture.

Activities: Awards a prize amounting to approximately US $150,000 every two years to a person or team of any nationality, that has made an outstanding contribution in the fields of biochemistry or biophysics (including microbiology and the physiology of seed germination). The award is made on the basis of recommendations of a special commission of the Physics Department of the Royal Netherlands Academy of Sciences and Arts.

Geographical Area of Activity: International.

Trustees: The Board of Trustees comprises a president, a secretary, a treasurer and one other member.

Principal Staff: Chair. C. L. de Carvalho-Heineken.

Address: 2E Weteringplantsoen 5, 1017 ZD Amsterdam.

Telephone: (20) 626-33-49; **Fax:** (20) 625-22-13; **Internet:** www.knaw.nl/heinekenprizes; **e-mail:** pentagon@pentagonbv.nl.

Hollandsche Maatschappij der Wetenschappen (Dutch Society of Sciences)

Founded in 1752 by seven citizens of Haarlem for the promotion of science.

Activities: Operates nationally in the field of science through grants to institutions and individuals, conferences and courses, publications and lectures. Awards annual prizes and subsidies for research and publication of scientific work. The Society has 550 members.

Geographical Area of Activity: Netherlands.

Publications: Report of operations.

Trustees: The directors of the Society.

Principal Staff: Pres. Dr M. C. van Veen; Sec. Prof. Dr A. A. Verrijn Stuart (Natural Sciences), Prof. Dr D. M. Schenkeveld (Humanities and Social Sciences).

Address: Postbus 9698, 2300 LR Haarlem.

Telephone: (23) 532-17-73; **Fax:** (23) 536-27-13; **Internet:** www.hollmij.nl; **e-mail:** hollmij@wxs.nl.

Humanistisch Instituut voor Ontwikkelings Samenwerking—HIVOS (Humanistic Institute for Co-operation with Developing Countries)

Founded in 1968, a development organization working towards emancipation, democratization and the alleviation of poverty in developing countries.

Activities: Financial support is given to over 800 organizations in Africa, Asia and Central and South America, as well as to organizations in the Netherlands, with projects in the areas of economic self-reliance, arts and culture, human rights and AIDS, sustainable development and gender, and information and communication technology. Operates the North–South Plan, which issues loans, the HIVOS Culture Fund, which stimulates cultural diversity by giving financial support to the arts and culture in developing countries, and the ICT policy programme, which helps organizations in developing countries utilize the opportunities provided by information technology. The organization also provides information on development issues and promotes the interests of developing countries; and collaborates with related organizations. Manages the Fund for Sustainable Biodiversity Management, in association with the Stichting Novib (q.v.), launched in 2000. Maintains three regional offices in Costa Rica, India and Zimbabwe.

Geographical Area of Activity: Africa, Asia, Central and South America, South and Soouth East Europe, and the Netherlands.

Publications: Annual Review; *Hivos International* (newsletter).

Finance: Financed by the Dutch Government, the European Union and private donors and institutions. Total income €67,303,000, total expenditure €59,456,000 (2001).

Principal Staff: Chair. L. S. Groenman; Exec. Dir M. M. Monteiro.

Address: Raamweg 16, 2596 HL The Hague.

Telephone: (70) 376-55-00; **Fax:** (70) 362-46-00; **Internet:** www.hivos.nl; **e-mail:** hivos@hivos.nl.

Internationaal Instituut voor Sociale Geschiedenis (International Institute of Social History)

Founded in 1935 by Dr N. W. Posthumus and the Central Workers' Insurance Company, to preserve and make available for study material of importance for social history, especially in the field of socialism and the international labour movement.

Activities: Operates internationally in the field of social history, through the maintenance of a library and archives, and the publication of monographs, reviews and source material. Acquisitions include the archives of many socialist organizations and trade unions, and original documents, books, letters, pamphlets, posters, photographs, etc., relating to political events and leading Marxist, anarchist and socialist figures of the 19th and 20th centuries.

Geographical Area of Activity: International.

Publications: Annual Report; *International Review of Social History* (3 a year); *Sources for a History of the German and Austrian Working-class Movements* (series); *Studies in Social History* (series); *Contributions to the History of Labour and Society* (series); *Archives Michael Bakounine* (series); *Household Strategies for Survival, 1600–2000: Fission, Faction and Co-operation*; and various other publications.

Finance: The Institute is subsidized by an annual grant from the Netherlands Ministry of Education and Science, and by contributions from various institutions and organizations. Total expenditure approx. €6,000,000 (2001).

Governing Board: Eric de Ruitjer (Chair.).

Address: Cruquiusweg 31, 1019 AT Amsterdam.

Telephone: (20) 668-58-66; **Fax:** (20) 665-41-81; **Internet:** www.iisg.nl; **e-mail:** info@iisg.nl.

International Health Foundation

Founded in 1969, in Geneva, Switzerland, by AKZO group of companies to improve the health of people throughout the world.

Activities: Holds international conferences; encourages research into biomedicine; conducts research into specific problems, especially those concerned with ageing, contraception, menopause and mental health.

Restrictions: No grants to individuals.

Publications: *Female voice changes around and after the menopause; Contraceptive use and attitudes in Italy;* and other mainly women's health and mental health related publications.

Finance: Funded by the medical industry.

Board of Trustees: Prof. Jos Thijssen (Chair.); Prof. Tom Eskes (Sec.); Prof. Guy Goodwin; Prof. Elisabeth Johannisson; Prof. Paul Keller; Prof. Carlo LaVecchia.

Principal Staff: Dir Gen. Hugo Nieuwenhuyse; Sec. Nancy de Wit.

Address: Europalaan 506, 3526 KS Utrecht.

Telephone: (30) 287-90-90; **Fax:** (30) 287-90-91; **Internet:** www.ihf.nl; **e-mail:** info@ihf.nl.

Bernard van Leer Foundation

Founded in 1949 in Switzerland by Bernard van Leer to support humanitarian projects, and in particular to enhance opportunities for children who are hampered in their development by the social and economic circumstances in which they grow up, so that they are able to develop their innate potential. Funded by the Stichting Van Leer Foundation (q.v.), which until 2001 retained held shares in Huhtamaki Van Leer, originally Royal Packaging Industries Van Leer NV.

Activities: The Foundation aims to improve opportunities for vulnerable children aged up to 8, growing up in socially and economically difficult circumstances. The Foundation makes grants to support the development of culturally and contextually appropriate approaches to early childhood care and development; and shares knowledge and expertise in the area of early childhood development with the aim of informing and influencing policy and practice. Maintains a Resource Centre comprising documentation on early childhood, and materials on projects supported.

Geographical Area of Activity: Selected countries of Europe, Asia, Australasia, Africa, and North, Central and South America.

Restrictions: Unsolicited applications are rarely considered. No grants are made to individuals or for general organizational support. No study, research, or travel grants are offered. Grants must be for projects concerned with children aged 0–8 years.

Publications: *Early Childhood Matters* (bulletin, 3 a year); *Early Childhood Development: Practice and Reflections* (series); *Working Papers in Early Childhood Development* (series); *Espacio para la Infancia* (bulletin, 2 a year); Annual Report; and other publications.

Finance: Funding derived from the bequest of Bernard van Leer, which is managed by the Van Leer Group Foundation, Netherlands. Annual expenditure €19,400,000 (2001), including grants to outside organizations of €14,000,000.

Trustees: Trude Maas-de Brouwer (Chair.); Peter Bell; Joep Brentjens; Harry Leliveld; Amos Mar-Haim; Nancy Newcomb; Ivar Samrén.

Principal Staff: Exec. Dir Peter Laugham.

Address: Eisenhowerlaan 156, POB 82334, 2508 EH The Hague.

Telephone: (70) 331-22-00; **Fax:** (70) 350-23-73; **Internet:** www.bernardvanleer.org; **e-mail:** registry@bvleerf.nl.

MDF Training and Consultancy

Founded in October 1984 by Drs H. L. van Loo to provide

management training and consultancy for development projects. Formerly known as the Management Development Foundation.

Activities: Organizes training courses which cover all aspects of development projects, and aim to incorporate modern management theory with practical experience. Maintains branch offices in Sri Lanka, Belgium and Tanzania.

Geographical Area of Activity: International.

Board of Governors: P. F. A. Bakker; P. Engel; M. Monteiko.

Principal Staff: Chair., Board of Dirs Drs H. L. van Loo; Man. Dirs H. J. M. Snelder, Dr A. W. Rijneveld.

Address: Postbus 430, 6710 BK Ede.

Telephone: (318) 65-00-60; **Fax:** (318) 61-45-03; **Internet:** www.mdf.nl; **e-mail:** mdf@mdf.nl.

Milieukontakt Oost-Europa

Founded in 1988 to strengthen the environmental movement in Central and Eastern Europe and Central Asia.

Activities: The Foundation operates by giving direct financial support, training and advice to NGOs in these countries, particularly at a local level, and by encouraging partnerships between Eastern and Western environmental groups.

Geographical Area of Activity: Central and Eastern Europe, the countries of the former USSR and Central Asia.

Restrictions: The maximum grant size is US $4,000 and the maximum duration is one year.

Publications: Annual Report; magazine (3 a year) for Dutch contributors; fact sheets and other publications.

Finance: Net assets €185,832 (2001); annual revenue €1,372,097, expenditure €3,021,899 (2001).

Governing Board: Berend Jan van den Boomen (Chair.); Wim Combrink (Treas.); Carla Alma; Jan Dirx; Frans de Haas; Arie de Koning; Marijke Vos.

Principal Staff: Dir Jerphaas Donner.

Address: Postbus 18185, 1001 ZB Amsterdam.

Telephone: (20) 639-27-16; **Fax:** (20) 639-13-79; **Internet:** www.milieukontakt.nl; **e-mail:** info@milieukontakt.nl.

Nederlandsche Maatschappij voor Nijverheid en Handel (Netherlands Society for Industry and Trade)

Founded in 1777 by the Hollandsche Maatschappij der Wetenschappen (Netherlands Society of Sciences) for the furtherance of common welfare by promoting industry, commerce, transport and communications, mining, agriculture and fisheries in the Netherlands and its overseas possessions.

Activities: Operates nationally and internationally in the fields of social welfare and studies, economic affairs and the conservation of natural resources, through self-conducted programmes, conferences, publications and lectures. The Society comprises a number of local and regional departments which, although responsible to the head office, operate on an autonomous basis in their own region.

Geographical Area of Activity: Mainly the Netherlands and its overseas dependencies.

Publications: Annual Report; *Maatschappij Belangen* (monthly magazine).

Principal Staff: Dir H. G. M. Giezeman; Project Co-ordinator Annelies Weijschedé.

Address: Jan Van Nassaustraat 75, 2596 BP The Hague.

Telephone: (70) 314-19-40; **Fax:** (70) 324-75-15; **Internet:** www.nmnh.nl; **e-mail:** info@nmnh.nl.

Nederlandse Kankerbestrÿding—Koningin Wilhelmina Fonds (Dutch Cancer Society—Queen Wilhelmina Foundation)

Founded in 1949 to fight cancer.

Activities: Operates nationally in the field of cancer control, through subsidizing programmes at major specialized cancer hospitals, and providing grants for projects on fundamental, epidemiological, clinical and psychosocial cancer research, research on methods for cancer prevention, fellowships, scholarships, conferences, courses and publications. Promotes international scientific co-operation. The Foundation also runs a cancer information centre, a free telephone helpline, publishes information brochures for patients and the general public, and subsidizes national support groups for cancer patients. The Foundation is a member of the International Union against Cancer.

Geographical Area of Activity: Netherlands, its dependencies and former colonies.

Restrictions: There are limited funds for financial support of individual cancer patients.

Publications: Annual report and financial statement; *Current Cancer Research in the Netherlands* (annually); *Tydschrift Kanker* (with Nederlandse Vereniging voor Oncologie); *OverLeven* (quarterly magazine); progress reports and brochures.

Finance: Funded by people in the Netherlands. Assets 148,400,000 guilders (1999); annual revenue 123,100,000 guilders, expenditure 135,600,000 guilders (2000).

Governing Board: Dr M. Oosting (Pres.); Prof. Dr J. P. Vooijs (Vice-Pres.); M. Van der Struis (Treas.); H. W. Wefers Bettink (Sec.); T. H. Woltman.

Principal Staff: Gen. Man. Dr A. G. J. M. Hanselaar; G. Broekema; Dr G. Boerrigter; M. Halbesma; C. Honing; R. Kamphuis.

Address: POB 75508, 1070 AM Amsterdam.

Telephone: (20) 570-05-00; **Fax:** (20) 675-03-02; **Internet:** www.kankerbestrÿding.nl; **e-mail:** info@kankerbestryding.nl.

Netherlands Institute for Southern Africa—NiZA

Established in 1997 as a result of the merger of the Eduardo Mondlane Foundation, the Institute for Southern Africa and the Dutch Committee on Southern Africa. It is an independent NGO devoted to human rights, democracy and reconstruction in Southern Africa, and the dissemination of information on the region.

Activities: Operates in the Netherlands, Southern Africa and the European Union Member States. Preferred areas of activity are human rights, democracy, independent media and economic links between the Netherlands and Southern Africa, which the Institute supports through technical assistance and grants for small projects. Also organizes campaigns, conferences, debates and exchange programmes in order to stimulate the mutual contacts between Southern Africa and the Netherlands; and aims to influence Dutch and European policy towards Southern Africa through lobbying. Issues publications and disseminates information. Maintains a library and information and resource centre, which the Institute plans to make available through the internet.

Geographical Area of Activity: Netherlands, Southern Africa and European Union Member States.

Publications: *Zuidelijk Afrika* (quarterly); *MediaNews; NiZA Informatie* (quarterly magazine, in Dutch); Annual Report; conference reports and proceedings.

Finance: Total expenditure 5,520,556 guilders (2000).

Governing Board: Coen Stork (Pres.); Niels Feis (Treas.); Caroline van Dullemen; Marianne Heeremans; Ans Zwerver.

Principal Staff: Dir Peter Hermes.

Address: Prins Hendrikkade 33, POB 10707, 1001 ES Amsterdam.

Telephone: (20) 520-62-10; **Fax:** (20) 520-62-49; **Internet:** www.niza.nl; **e-mail:** niza@niza.nl.

Netherlands Organization for International Co-operation in Higher Education—NUFFIC (Nederlandse Organisatie voor Internationale Samenwerking in het Hoger Onderwijs)

Founded in 1952 by the Boards of Governors of all Netherlands universities to foster international co-operation in higher education and scientific research in the widest sense of the term, with special attention to those forms of international co-operation directed towards developing countries.

Activities: Operates both nationally and internationally in the field of education. NUFFIC's main activities include the following: co-ordinating and conducting programmes of co-operation and exchange that are sponsored by the Dutch Government and by the European Union; providing information about the programmes and about specific possibilities for studying in the Netherlands and in other countries; advising institutions and organizations on how qualifications earned by scholars in other countries should be evaluated; publicizing Dutch higher education in other countries; and providing foreign students with practical assistance.

Geographical Area of Activity: International.

Publications: Annual report and financial statement; *Study in the Netherlands* (annually, in English); *BISON Monitor of International Mobility in Education; The Netherlands Fellowships Programme; Scholarships for Study in the Netherlands Offered by the European Union.*

Finance: Annual revenue €12,679,000, expenditure €12,835,000 (2001).

Principal Staff: Dir Pieter van Dijk.

Address: Kortenaerkade 11, 2518 AX The Hague; POB 29777, 2502 LT The Hague.

Telephone: (70) 426-02-60; **Fax:** (70) 426-03-99; **Internet:** www.nuffic.nl; **e-mail:** nuffic@nuffic.nl.

Oranje Fonds

Founded in 1948 to support social welfare at home and, in exceptional cases, abroad. Formerly known as the Juliana Welzijn Fonds.

Activities: The Foundation operates in the fields of social services, community work and socio-cultural work, self-help groups, development programmes and experiments. Maintains an operational section which deals with projects abroad. Supports projects which are experimental and are aimed at improving existing ways and means, and which show an original approach or represent a new activity; makes grants to self-help groups and organizations.

Geographical Area of Activity: Netherlands.

Restrictions: No grants are made to individuals.

Publications: Annual Report; brochure.

Trustees: H. R. Okkens (Chair.); J. H. Scherphuis (Treas.); W. N. A. Verwoerd (Sec. and Man. Dir).

Principal Staff: Man. Dir W. N. A. Verwoerd.

Address: POB 90, 3980 CB Bunnik.

Telephone: (30) 656-45-24; **Fax:** (30) 656-22-04; **Internet:** www.oranjefonds.nl; **e-mail:** info@oranjefonds.nl.

PIOOM Foundation

Established in 1988.

Activities: Established as a non-partisan NGO to promote, support and conduct interdisciplinary research on the causes of human rights violations.

Geographical Area of Activity: International, with focus on Eastern Europe.

Publications: Newsletter; *World Conflict and Human Rights Map.*

Principal Staff: Research Dir Alex P. Schmid.

Address: c/o Leiden University, Wassenaarseweg 52, 2333 AK Leiden.

Telephone: (71) 527-38-48; **Fax:** (71) 527-37-88; **e-mail:** pioom@rulfss.leidenuni.nl.

Safe Internet Foundation

Founded in 1999 to promote a secure and responsible internet.

Activities: Acts as a forum for internet service organizations to encourage and promote systems and software so as to create a safe internet for everyone. Organizes conferences and activities.

Directors: Jan Baan (Chair.).

Principal Staff: Dir Ton Jansen.

Address: Zeestr. 80–82, 2518 The Hague.

Telephone: (70) 330-75-91; **Fax:** (70) 365-05-98; **Internet:** www.sif.nl.

SIW—Internationale Vrijwilligersprojekten (Foundation for International Voluntary Service)

Established in 1953, a youth exchange organization aiming to promote international contact, personal growth and voluntary service.

Activities: The Foundation operates world-wide, in the fields of the arts and humanities, conservation and the environment, and social welfare, through voluntary work. About 500 young Dutch people volunteer for work abroad annually, with projects operating in more than 50 countries. A number of projects operate in the Netherlands for overseas participants.

Geographical Area of Activity: International.

Restrictions: No direct applications from outside the Netherlands are accepted.

Finance: Financed through subsidies and an application fee.

Address: Willemstraat 7, 3511 RJ Utrecht.

Telephone: (30) 231-77-21; **Fax:** (30) 234-34-65; **Internet:** www.siw.nl; **e-mail:** info@siw.nl.

SOTA—Foundation for the Research of Turkestan, Azerbaijan, Crimea, Caucasus and Siberia

Established in 1991 by Mehmet Tutuncu as a centre of research and study into the Turkic peoples of the former USSR.

Activities: Carries out research and analysis relating to Turkey and the Central Asian countries of the former USSR, also organizes conferences and symposia. Promotes human rights and peace through democratic governance. Also aims to inform public opinion in Western Europe and the USA. Maintains an archive and library containing more than 4,000 books and periodicals, and more than 10,000 pamphlets and newspaper articles.

Geographical Area of Activity: Turkey and the republics of Central Asia.

Publications: *BITIG* (journal, quarterly); *Reform Movements and Revolution in Turkistan 1900–1924; Sefika Gaspirali and Turkic Women's Movement in Russia 1893–1920; Caucasus: War and Peace; Turkey: Ataturk's Legacy;* and numerous other books and publications.

Address: Postbus 9642, 2003 LP Haarlem.

Telephone and Fax: (23) 529-28-83; **Internet:** www.turkiye.net/sota/sotainfo.html; **e-mail:** sota@turkiye.net.

Stichting Agromisa (Agromisa Foundation)

Founded in 1934 with the purpose of improving the lives of people in developing countries through providing information on small-scale sustainable agriculture. The Foundation also aims to stimulate an awareness of development problems among the Dutch people.

Activities: Gives advice in the fields of nutrition, food processing, biogas, plant and animal husbandry, water and soil management, agricultural engineering, etc.; provides an internet database on natural resource management; runs projects in areas such as agro-biodiversity; organizes participation in local development for development workers; and maintains a library of books pertaining to small-scale agriculture.

Geographical Area of Activity: Africa, Asia, and Central and South America.

Restrictions: This is not a grant-making organization.

Publications: *Agrodok* (series of manuals on small-scale agriculture in English, French, Portuguese and Spanish); Newsletter (2 a year, versions in Dutch and English).

Finance: Funded by donations, subsidies, profits from sale of services and goods, etc.

Principal Staff: Chair. Dr J. J. Hardon; Dir M. Kuipers; Treas. R. van Weg.

Address: Postbus 41, 6700 AA Wageningen.

Telephone: (317) 41-22-17; **Fax:** (317) 41-91-78; **Internet:** www.agromisa.org; **e-mail:** agromisa@agromisa.org.

Stichting DOEN (DOEN Foundation—Sustainable Development and the Defence of Nature)

Founded in 1991 to deal with grant applications to the Special Payments Fund—FSP (which receives 35% of the net proceeds of the Dutch National Postcode Lottery). Since 1998, it has also been a beneficiary of the Sponsor Bingo Lottery, and has expanded its activities. The Foundation operates in the fields of nature and the environment, human rights, development co-operation, sport, welfare, art and culture.

Activities: The Foundation works to protect the environment and preserve nature; to support human rights organizations; and works on long-term programmes initiating sustainable change in developing countries, especially income-generating projects for marginalized groups and communities. Since 1998, Stichting DOEN has also actively supported sport, welfare, art and culture. DOEN operates directly in these areas as well as supporting other organizations in their work.

Geographical Area of Activity: International.

Restrictions: Grants made only to organizations.

Publications: Annual Report.

Finance: Annual grant expenditure approx. €16,336,000 (2001).

Governing Board: E. E. Bolhuis (Chair.); M. A. W. Külman; H. V. Latesleyn; S. M. Piët.

Principal Staff: Man. Dir M. Van den Hombergh.

Address: Postbus 75621, 1070 AP Amsterdam.

Telephone: (20) 573-73-33; **Fax:** (20) 573-73-70; **Internet:** www.doen.nl; **e-mail:** doen@doen.nl.

Stichting Europa Centrum (Europa Centrum Foundation)

Activities: The Foundation informs young people and schools about European integration.

Geographical Area of Activity: Europe.

Principal Staff: Dir Tessa Maas.

Address: Riouwstraat 137, 2585 HP The Hague.

Telephone: (70) 350-86-20; **Fax:** (70) 358-76-06; **Internet:** www.europacentrum.nl; **e-mail:** info@europacentrum.nl.

Stichting Fonds 1818 (1818 Fund Foundation)

Founded in 1990 by the VSB Bank, to provide financial support to social, cultural and educational projects.

Activities: The Foundation supports projects in the Hague, Netherlands and surrounding areas in the fields of the arts and culture, economic affairs, conservation and the environment, medicine and health, sport and recreation, animal welfare and social welfare.

Geographical Area of Activity: Principally the Hague, Netherlands.

Restrictions: No grants to individuals.

Publications: Annual Report; information brochure; quarterly magazine.

Principal Staff: Dir B. Polders.

Address: Riviervismarkt 4, 2513 AM The Hague; Postbus 895, 2501 CW The Hague.

Telephone: (70) 364-11-41; **Fax:** (70) 364-18-91; **Internet:** www.fonds1818.nl; **e-mail:** info@fonds1818.nl.

Stichting voor Fundamenteel Onderzoek der Materie—FOM (Foundation for Fundamental Research on Matter)

Founded in 1946 by Dr H. Bruining, Prof. Dr H. J. Clay, Prof. Dr H. A. Kramers, Prof. Dr J. M. W. Milatz, Dr H. J. Reinink and Prof. G. van der Leeuw, for the advancement of fundamental scientific research on matter in the Netherlands for the general interest, higher education, and industry.

Activities: Operates internationally in the field of physics through research, publications and lectures. The Foundation assists in the co-ordination of existing research projects and carries out its own work through research groups (of which there are 150). Research interests include: subatomic physics, nuclear physics, atomic physics and quantum electronics, molecular physics, condensed matter physics, thermonuclear research and plasma physics, applied and phenomenological physics and mathematical physics. In addition, research is carried out in six institutes which are financed completely or partly by FOM: the FOM Institute for Atomic and Molecular Physics, the FOM Institute for Plasma Physics, the Nuclear Accelerator Institute KVI, the FOM Institute for Subatomic Physics, the Dimes Institute for Submicron Physics and Technology and the FOM Institute for Condensed Matter. Maintains a reference library containing 2,400 volumes.

Geographical Area of Activity: Europe.

Restrictions: Grants only to researchers with a working address in the Netherlands.

Publications: *FOM-jaarboek* (in Dutch, annually); financial statement; proceedings.

Finance: Funded by Government, European Union, and industry and university contracts; annual budget approx €82,000,000.

Governing Board: Prof. Dr F. T. M. Nieuwstadt (Pres.); Prof. Dr E. J. Baerends; Prof. Dr F. A. Bais; Prof. Dr G. E. W. Bauer; Prof. Dr F. A. Berends; Dr K. Bulthuis; Prof. Dr R. P. Griessen; Dr H. A. Harding; Prof. Dr T. M. Klapwijk; Prof. Dr P. Kruit; Dr P. W. Kwant; Prof. Dr A. Lagendijk; Prof. Dr H. N. W. Lekkerkerker; Prof. Dr A. van Oosterom; Prof. Dr Th. J. A. Popma; Prof. Dr G. T. Robillard; Prof. Dr W. van Saarloos; Prof. Dr D. C. Schram; Prof. Dr R. R. Weynants; Prof. Dr L. van Wijngaarden; Prof. Dr B. Q. P. J. de Wit; Prof. Dr J. P. Woerdman.

Principal Staff: Dir Dr K. H. Chang.

Address: POB 3021, 3502 GA Utrecht.

Telephone: (30) 600-12-11; **Fax:** (30) 601-44-06; **Internet:** www.fom.nl; **e-mail:** info@fom.nl.

Stichting Gaudeamus (Gaudeamus Foundation)

Founded in 1945 by Walter Alfred Friedrich Maas for the purpose of assisting young composers and promoting contemporary music in general.

Activities: Operates internationally in the field of contemporary music, through the sponsoring of annual competitions and concert series; publication of information bulletins; and the maintaining of a library and record collection and documentation on composers and their works.

Geographical Area of Activity: International.

Publications: *Gaudeamus Information* (2 a year).

Trustees: Q. Bunschoten; J. de Heer; L. Leertouwer; A. van Nieuwkerk; R. Wolfensberger.

Principal Staff: Dir Henk Heuvelmans.

Address: Swammerdamstraat 38, 1091 RV Amsterdam.

Telephone: (20) 694-73-49; **Fax:** (20) 694-72-58; **Internet:** www.gaudeamus.nl; **e-mail:** info@gaudeamus.nl.

Stichting IKEA Foundation

Founded in 1982 by Ingvar Kamprad to promote architectural and interior design.

Activities: Supports innovation in furniture design, industrial design and landscaping. Awards the IKEA Grants and Scholarships and the IKEA Awards to institutions and companies which aim to improve working and living conditions, through projects in the fields of design, production, architecture, landscaping and the environment. The Foundation ceased its scholarship and grants programme in 1998 in order to create an international school for interior design, in co-operation with the University of Lund (Sweden). The school is now operational, and a limited number of scholarships are made available.

Geographical Area of Activity: International.

Finance: Receives grants and donations from foundations.

Board of Trustees:F. I. Kamprad (Chair.).

Principal Staff: Sec. L. D. G. Reeser Cuperus.

Address: POB 75505, 1070 AM Amsterdam.

Telephone: (20) 577-20-00; **Fax:** (20) 577-27-00.

Stichting Koningin Juliana Fonds (Queen Juliana Foundation)

Founded in 1948 to promote social welfare in the Netherlands (and, in exceptional cases, abroad).

Activities: Operates primarily nationally in the field of social work and community development, although some support is given to institutions outside the Netherlands. The activities of the Foundation cover social service, community work and socio-cultural work, the transitional area between social work and spiritual welfare, interest groups, self-help groups and projects for the unemployed. Assistance is also given for research and study in the field of social welfare.

Publications: Report of operations and financial statement.

Address: J. F. Kennedylaan 101, 3981 GB Bunnik; (postal) POB 90, 3980 GB Bunnik.

Telephone: (3405) 645-24; **Fax:** (3405) 622-04.

Stichting Liliane Fonds (Liliane Foundation)

Founded in March 1980 by Liliane Brekelmans to provide aid for disabled children in developing countries.

Activities: The Foundation operates in Africa, Asia and Central and South America; it offers grants to individuals in the field of medical and social rehabilitation.

Geographical Area of Activity: Africa, Asia, and Central and South America.

Publications: *Nieuwsbrief* (quarterly); *International Newsletter* (2 a year).

Finance: The Foundation is funded by donations.

Governing Board: G. Oostveen (Chair.); H. Van der Horst (Gen. Sec.); C. Bos (Treas.).

Principal Staff: Dir G. B. Dollevoet; Project Co-ordinator C. van den Broek; Co-ordinator, Fundraising L. Hoegen Dÿkhof; Co-ordinator, Gen. Affairs H. Cruts.

Address: Havensingel 26, 5211 TX 's-Hertogenbosch.

Telephone: (73) 518-94-20; **Fax:** (73) 518-94-21; **Internet:** www.lilianefonds.nl; **e-mail:** voorlichting@lilianefonds.nl.

Stichting Mondiaal Alternatief (Foundation for Ecological Development Alternatives)

Founded in 1974 to increase awareness of the dangers of pollution and deforestation, especially in developing countries.

Activities: Operates primarily in the fields of aid to less-developed countries and environmental conservation. The Foundation emphasizes the dependence of humans on the ecosystem; encourages respect for all life; lobbies governments on environmental issues; promotes ecologically-sound pest-control techniques, pesticide production and export; works to slow the rate of deforestation and encourages small communities to use alternative fuel sources; compiles statistics; maintains a reference library; and conducts international research programmes and conferences.

Geographical Area of Activity: International.

Publications: *Ecoscripts* (in English); brochures, research reports.

Trustees: Drs R. Gerrits; G. P. Hekska; A. Hoeksma; P. L. Th. A. Maréchal; I. Schade; Drs G. Snel.

Principal Staff: Contact: R. Gerrits.

Address: Korsholm 36, 2133 ER, Hoofddorp; Postbus 151, 2130 AD Hoofddorp.

Telephone: (23) 563-23-05; **Fax:** (23) 564-13-59.

Stichting NOVIB—Nederlandse Organisatie voor Internationale Ontwikkelingssamenwerking (NOVIB Foundation—Netherlands Organization for International Development Co-operation)

Founded in 1956 to promote sustainable development by supporting the efforts of poor people in developing countries. Also known as Oxfam Netherlands.

Activities: The Foundation has three main aims: to alleviate structural poverty through co-operating with partner organizations in Africa, Asia, Central and South America, and countries of the former USSR and Eastern Europe; to educate the Dutch about the non-Western world; and to support the interests of the poor in policy-making. The Foundation prioritizes projects in the fields of human rights, women's rights and the protection of the environment.

Geographical Area of Activity: Africa, Asia, Central and South America, Eastern Europe and the countries of the former USSR.

Publications: *Onze Wereld* (monthly magazine); *Novib News;* series of novels from developing countries.

Finance: Total income €138,452,000 (2001).

Governing Board: H. D. Tjeenk Willink.

Principal Staff: Dir Gen. M. Juan den Berg.

Address: Postbus 30919, 2500 GX The Hague.

Telephone: (70) 342-17-77; **Fax:** (70) 361-44-61; **Internet:** www.novib.nl; **e-mail:** info@novib.nl.

Stichting Praemium Erasmianum (Erasmus Prize Foundation)

Founded in 1958 by HRH Prince Bernhard of the Netherlands to award one or more monetary prizes, if possible annually, to individuals or institutions that have made a particularly important contribution to Europe in the cultural, social or socio-scientific sphere.

Activities: Operates internationally in the fields of education, social welfare and studies, the arts and humanities, law and other professions, through the awarding of the 'Erasmus Prize'. The prize amounts to €150,000.

Geographical Area of Activity: International.

Restrictions: No applications for grants are considered.

Publications: Report of prize-giving ceremony; series of publications in connection with the laureates.

Finance: Funded by private sources.

Governing Board: HRH Prince Bernhard of the Netherlands (Regent); Dr A. H. G. Rinnooy Kan (Chair.); and prominent Dutch personalities from cultural, social and economic circles.

Principal Staff: Dir Prof. Dr M. Sparreboom; Sec. Y. C. Goester.

Address: Jan van Goyenkade 5, 1075 HN Amsterdam.

Telephone: (20) 675-27-53; **Fax:** (20) 675-22-31; **Internet:** www.erasmusprijs.org; **e-mail:** spe@erasmusprijs.org.

Stichting Prins Bernhard Cultuurfonds (Prince Bernhard Cultural Foundation)

Established in London in 1940 to raise money to buy war material for the British and Dutch Governments. After the war it was decided to continue the fund to rebuild cultural life in the Netherlands and abroad.

Activities: Operates in the Netherlands, the Netherlands Antilles and Aruba. Emphasis is placed on self-generated activity, private initiative and non-professional work. The Foundation currently supports initiatives in the fields of the visual arts; dance; theatre; literature; music; conservation of historic buildings and monuments; research in the humanities; cultural education; and nature conservation. Promotes Dutch culture abroad, by providing financial support.

Geographical Area of Activity: Netherlands, Netherlands Antilles and Aruba.

Publications: Annual Report; newsletter.

Finance: The Foundation receives a share of the revenue of DeLotto and other national lotteries, income from its own collections, and from assets and gifts.

Executive Committee: L. C. Brinkman (Chair.); R. de Leeuw (Vice-Chair.); J. M. de Jong (Treas.).

Principal Staff: Dir Dr Adriana Esmeijer.

Address: POB 19750, 1000 GT Amsterdam.

Telephone: (20) 520-61-30; **Fax:** (20) 623-84-99; **Internet:** www.cultuurfonds.nl; **e-mail:** info@cultuurfonds.nl.

Stichting Reinwater (Clear Water Foundation)

Founded in September 1974 by D. M. J. Lasonder, E. de Bloeme and J. G. W. Bolomey to combat the pollution of European freshwater sources.

Activities: The Foundation operates nationally and internationally in the fields of environmental conservation, education, diffusing information and international affairs, through various self-conducted programmes, research and publications. It is concerned in particular with the water systems of the Rhine, Maas and Schelde rivers. Maintains a research and education ship.

Geographical Area of Activity: Netherlands, Belgium, France and Germany.

Publications: Books, reports and magazines on environmental issues.

Finance: Funding is provided by the Government of the Netherlands, the European Union, regional and local governments, and private bequests. Annual expenditure €472,000 (2001).

Trustees: P. Hordijk (Chair.); J. van den Akker; G. Geldof; J. R. Parsons; C. Ribbens; A. Wals.

Principal Staff: L. Absil; C. Bollaert; J. T. M. Houweling; W. Husslage; T. Lycklama; R. Pleune; T. Quax; A. ter Schure; R. Kuiper; K. van Drie.

Address: Vossiusstraat 20, 1071 AD Amsterdam.

Telephone: (20) 570-78-09; **Fax:** (20) 675-38-06; **Internet:** www.reinwater.nl; **e-mail:** info@reinwater.nl.

Stichting Triodos (Triodos Foundation)

Established in 1971 by Triodos Bank to provide financial support to initiatives which give impetus to social renewal.

Activities: Operates in the fields of aid to less-developed countries, the arts and humanities, conservation and the environment, education, and medicine and health, through grants to institutions. It operates mostly in the Netherlands. The Foundation is the Netherlands counterpart to the Triodos Foundations in the United Kingdom (q.v.) and Belgium.

Geographical Area of Activity: Mostly the Netherlands.

Board of Management: P. Blom; F. de Clerck.

Principal Staff: K. Jansen.

Address: Utrechtseweg 60, Postbus 55, 3700 AB Zeist.

Telephone: (30) 693-65-00; **Fax:** (30) 693-65-55; **e-mail:** triodos@triodos.nl.

Stichting Vluchteling (Netherlands Refugee Foundation)

Founded in 1976 (restructured 1982) by various churches and other groups in the Netherlands, to provide assistance for refugees outside the Netherlands.

Activities: Provides assistance to refugees through grants to various organizations active overseas, providing both emergency aid and long-term self-reliance projects; it has no field-workers of its own, but attempts to co-ordinate assistance and to inform the public of the plight of refugees.

Geographical Area of Activity: International.

Restrictions: No assistance provided to refugees in the Netherlands.

Publications: *Jaarverslag* (annual report).

Finance: Total grants expenditure 25,000,000 guilders (1999).

Governing Board: M. J. E. M. Jager (Chair.); A. Duÿser (Vice-Chair.); L. Donner-Voriskova; S. E. J. M. van Voorst tot Voorst.

Principal Staff: Dir A. Claassen.

Address: Stadhouderslaan 28, 2517 HZ The Hague.

Telephone: (70) 346-89-46; **Fax:** (70) 361-57-40; **Internet:** www.vluchteling.org; **e-mail:** info@vluchteling.org.

Technologiestichting—STW (Technology Foundation)

Founded in 1981 by Prof. W. A. Koumans and Dr C. le Pair, to promote research in technology. Formerly known as Stichting voor de Technische Wetenschappen.

Activities: Operates nationally in the field of applied science and engineering, through research, travel grants, lectures and publications. The Foundation subsidizes research projects at universities and technological institutes in the Netherlands: projects may be drawn from all technological fields, and are selected on the basis both of high scientific quality and of applicability in industry.

Geographical Area of Activity: Netherlands.

Publications: *Annual Utilization Report;* Annual Report; project reports and others.

Finance: Annual revenue and expenditure €46,000,000 (2001).

Principal Staff: Pres. Prof. Dr P. M. Dewilde; Dir Dr F. J. G. van de Linde.

Address: Van Vollenhovenlaan 661, 3527 JP Utrecht; Postbus 3021, 3502 GA Utrecht.

Telephone: (30) 600-12-11; **Fax:** (30) 601-44-08; **Internet:** www.stw.nl; **e-mail:** info@stw.nl.

Tilapia International Foundation

Founded in 1952 by J. D. F. Heine to encourage the breeding of the tilapia fish in order to relieve malnutrition in developing countries.

Activities: Organizes training programmes designed to educate people in the breeding of tilapia; provides financial assistance for the establishment of fish farms; disseminates information; active internationally.

Geographical Area of Activity: International.

Publications: Brochures.

Finance: Annual budget approx. €318,000.

Principal Staff: Founder and Hon. Chair. D. F. Heine; Chair. Dirk G. K. KamVice-Chair. J. Scholte Albers; Sec. Ben Heijne; Treas. Jan P. van Rossum.

Address: Postbus 2375, 3500 GJ Utrecht.

Telephone: (30) 294-87-00; **Fax:** (30) 293-68-10.

Eduard Van Beinum Stichting (Eduard Van Beinum Foundation)

Founded in 1960 by Phia Berghout for the stimulation of musical life in general and particularly the promotion of the artistic and social interests of musicians, all in the broadest sense.

Activities: Operates nationally and internationally in the arts; provides sums annually for commissions in the field of contemporary classical music, including operatic works.

Geographical Area of Activity: International.

Governing Board: F. A. W. Bannier (Pres.); Yvonne van Baarle (Sec.); A. G. Wiersma (Treas.); and two other members.

Principal Staff: Man. Aleida Hamel.

Address: POB 327, 1200 AH Hilversum.

Telephone: (35) 624-57-88; **Fax:** (35) 623-83-62; **e-mail:** a.h.hamel@chella.nl.

World Population Foundation

Established to work for the improvement of reproductive and sexual help in less-developed countries, in order that couples and individuals can make their own decisions on the number and spacing of offspring.

Activities: Operates in less-developed countries of South and South-East Asia, and East and Southern Africa, through supporting local NGOs and governmental organizations in the setting up and management of sexual and reproductive health projects. Provides information and training services. Also disseminates information and campaigns at national and international level and provides support to the Dutch Council on Youth and Population.

Geographical Area of Activity: Europe (especially the Netherlands), South and South-East Asia, and East and Southern Africa.

Finance: Annual turnover approx. €3,000,000.

Principal Staff: Chair. Dr Nicolaas Biegman; Dir Wouter A. Meijer.

Address: Ampèrestraat 10, 1221 GJ Hilversum.

Telephone: (35) 642-23-04; **Fax:** (35) 642-14-62; **Internet:** www.wpf.org; **e-mail:** office@wpf.org.

XminusY Solidarity Fund

Established in 1968; aims to promote self-determination and social change world-wide.

Activities: Provides financial support to small local groups in Africa, Asia, Central and South America and Eastern Europe, which would otherwise not be able to exist. Funded groups operate in the areas of human rights and social and political justice. The Fund also works in Western Europe as an advocate for these goals, and for international solidarity. Maximum grant awarded is approximately US $4,000.

Geographical Area of Activity: Africa, Asia, Central and South America, and Eastern and Western Europe.

Restrictions: Does not usually finance conferences, research projects, educational trips, travel expenses or general office expenses. No grants for children's projects, health programmes or projects that are income-generating.

Address: Wittenstr. 43–45, 1052 AL Amsterdam.

Telephone: (20) 627-96-61; **Fax:** (20) 622-82-29; **Internet:** www.xminy.nl; **e-mail:** xminy@xminy.nl.

Youth for Development and Co-operation

Established in Switzerland in 1947 as World Federalist Youth, a network of youth organizations.

Activities: Promotes communication between young people in the West, and those in developing countries. Works to strengthen opportunities for young people to participate in projects in the areas of sustainable development, human rights and the environment. Organizes international workshops, conferences, disseminates information and provides youth training.

Geographical Area of Activity: Europe, Africa, Central and South America, and Asia.

Principal Staff: Sec.-Gen Bas Auer.

Address: Overschiestr. 9, 1062 HN Amsterdam.

Telephone: (20) 614-25-10; **Fax:** (20) 617-55-45; **e-mail:** ydc@xs4all.nl.

Zero-Kap

Established as a foundation in 1988 by private individuals who set up a fund to advance interest-free loans to groups and organizations of the least-privileged in developing countries in order to develop income-generating activities.

Activities: Operates in the fields of income generation, education, health services, housing and infrastructure development, including the provision of water, electricity and roads.

Geographical Area of Activity: Asia, Africa, and Central and South America.

Restrictions: No grants to individuals.

Finance: Funded by private individuals or organizations who supply capital funding interest free for 10 years through the purchase of shares in units of €5,000 each.

Board of Trustees: Rens de Groot (Chair.); Jan Cornelissen (Treas.); Jan W. Henfling (Sec.).

Address: POB 274, 1400 AG Bussum.

Telephone: (35) 693-62-32; **Fax:** (35) 692-20-39; **Internet:** www.zero-kap.nl; **e-mail:** info@zero-kap.nl.

ZOA Vluchtelingenzorg (ZOA Refugee Care)

Founded in 1973 to provide assistance to people in need, as a sign of Christian compassion, through emergency relief, rehabilitation and reintegration programmes.

Activities: Operates in less-developed countries, co-operating with local organizations in areas such as primary health care; rural and agricultural development; water and sanitation; education and training; institutional and infrastructure development; emergency relief for returnees; humanitarian assistance; trauma counselling; and small enterprise development. Works in Afghanistan, Albania, Angola, Cambodia, Ethiopia, India, Laos, Rwanda, Sri Lanka, Sudan, Thailand and Uganda.

Geographical Area of Activity: Europe, Africa and Asia.

Publications: *ZOA News* (2 a year); *Humanitarian Assistance; Together with the Refugee*.

Finance: Total income €10,300,000 (2001).

Principal Staff: Exec. Dir D. J. Vermeer.

Address: POB 4130, 7320 AC Apeldoorn.

Telephone: (55) 366-33-39; **Fax:** (55) 366-87-99; **Internet:** www.zoaweb.org; **e-mail:** info@zoaweb.org.

Netherlands Antilles

FOUNDATIONS, TRUSTS AND NON-PROFIT ORGANIZATIONS

CARMABI Foundation

Established in 1955 as the Caribbean Marine Biological Institute; currently involved in applied marine natural resource research.

Activities: Operates in the area of conservation of the environment and research. Conducts marine biological research and conservation research (has established nature sanctuaries and parks in the Netherlands Antilles); provides advice to local government; and carries out an education programme for schoolchildren. Visiting scientists from the Netherlands and the USA carry out research.

Geographical Area of Activity: Netherlands Antilles.

Publications: Numerous scientific reports and publications.

Principal Staff: Dir Dr W. L. Bakhuis.

Address: POB 2090, Piscaderabaai z/n, Curaçao.

Telephone: (9) 462-42-42; **Fax:** (9) 462-76-80; **Internet:** www.curacao.com/carmabi; **e-mail:** carmabi@curacao.com.

New Zealand

FOUNDATION CENTRE AND CO-ORDINATING BODY

Philanthropy New Zealand

Established to facilitate effective grant-making.

Activities: Operates projects in the areas of taxation, research and education, through working with other organizations in the voluntary and not-for-profit sector, networking with Government departments, including lobbying for tax concessions for New Zealand foundations, supporting research, organizing seminars and conferences and issuing publications. Currently has 111 member organizations.

Geographical Area of Activity: The Asia-Pacific region.

Publications: Newsletter.

Finance: Financed by membership subscriptions. Assets $NZ30,700 (1999/2000); annual revenue $NZ62,814, expenditure $NZ63,505 (1999/2000).

Executive Committee: Judith Timpany (Chair.); Iain Hines (Deputy Chair.); and 10 others.

Principal Staff: Exec. Dir Robyn Scott.

Address: POB 1521, Wellington.

Telephone: (4) 499-4090; **Fax:** (4) 472-5367; **Internet:** www.philanthropy.org.nz; **e-mail:** info@philanthropy.org.nz.

FOUNDATIONS, TRUSTS AND NON-PROFIT ORGANIZATIONS

Cancer Society of New Zealand Inc

Founded in 1929 by the British Empire Cancer Campaign Society, for the alleviation, prevention and cure of cancer.

Activities: The Society supports cancer research through grants to institutions and individuals in New Zealand, and through travelling fellowships enabling New Zealand graduates to travel abroad for study; it holds conferences with international participation, and disseminates the results of research. Also provides information and support services to people affected by cancer.

Geographical Area of Activity: New Zealand.

Publications: *Research Report; Present State and Future Needs of Cancer Research in New Zealand.*

Address: POB 10847, Wellington.

Telephone: (4) 494-7270; **Fax:** (4) 494-7271; **Internet:** www.cancernz.org.nz; **e-mail:** admin@cancernz.org.nz.

Christian World Service

Established in 1945 to provide aid and fight injustice around the world.

Activities: Works in co-operation with partner organizations to carry out programmes in the areas of community development, education, leadership training, health care, refugee aid and income-generating activities for developing communities. Involved in campaigns for social justice (including the Jubilee 2000 campaign), and works in New Zealand to support the rights of Maori people. Also provides emergency relief for the victims of natural and man-made disasters. Currently working in Afghanistan, Kenya, Nicaragua and Sudan.

Geographical Area of Activity: International.

Restrictions: Does not encourage new applications for funding.

Address: POB 22-652, Christchurch.

Telephone: (3) 366-9274; **Fax:** (3) 365-2919; **Internet:** www.cws.org.nz; **e-mail:** cws@cws.org.nz.

Winston Churchill Memorial Trust

Founded in 1965 by Act of the New Zealand Parliament to give fellowships to New Zealand residents, for the advancement of any vocation carried out in New Zealand, or to the benefit in general of New Zealand.

Activities: Operates nationally in the fields of education, social welfare, economic affairs, science and medicine, the arts and humanities, and conservation of natural resources, and internationally in the field of international relations, through the award of up to 25 international fellowships each year. New Zealand residents may undertake an activity anywhere. Fellowships amount to as much as 80% of costs for short-term travel and activity followed by publication of a report within six months. Assistance is not renewable or extendable and is only available for travel outside New Zealand.

Geographical Area of Activity: New Zealand.

Restrictions: Fellowships are not granted for the gaining of academic or professional qualifications and are only available for travel outside New Zealand.

Publications: Annual report and financial statement; Fellows' reports; Bibliography reports.

Finance: Maximum individual grant disbursed $NZ10,000.

Trustees: A Trust Board of nine members, each appointed in rotation for a term of six years. Barry Dineen (Chair.); Sally Logan-Milne (Deputy Chair.).

Principal Staff: Co-ordinator Ingrid Kamstra.

Address: POB 805 Wellington.

Telephone: (4) 495-7256; **Fax:** (4) 495-9444; **Internet:** www.dia.govt.nz; **e-mail:** trusts@dia.govt.nz.

Family Planning Association of New Zealand, Inc

Founded in 1936 by Mrs S. L. Suckling and others to educate people about reproductive and sexual health and issues of sexuality.

Activities: Works to promote an informed and positive view of sexuality and to educate people in New Zealand and developing countries about sexual and reproductive health. Works as an advocate for these issues through the media, policy submissions and meetings; runs frequent information campaigns to raise public awareness; carries out training workshops and development of training materials; owns school-linked clinics and sexual and reproductive health centres, and has built relationships with other non-profit groups involved in health care. Aims in the future to concentrate particularly on improving the response to Maori people's sexual and reproductive health issues. Involved in schools, teaching comprehensive sexuality education, including some pre-school activities.

Geographical Area of Activity: New Zealand, South-East Asia and the Pacific region.

Publications: *Forum* (quarterly).

Finance: Funded by grants, government funding and donations.

National Council: Helen Eskett (Pres.).

Principal Staff: Exec. Dir Dr Gill Greer.

Address: POB 11515, Wellington.

Telephone: (4) 384-4349; **Fax:** (4) 382-8356; **Internet:** www.fpanz.org.nz; **e-mail:** anna.w@fpanz.org.nz.

Norman Kirk Memorial Trust

Founded in 1976 to promote the welfare and progress of the people of New Zealand and the South Pacific who have the ability to benefit from further education, study or training, but who need financial assistance in realizing their potential.

Activities: Within New Zealand, the Trust accepts direct applications from mature individuals who are either disadvantaged or disabled, and who are committed to taking advantage of education or training opportunities; or from mature applicants who are seeking a qualification or training that will enable them to take a fuller role in the community, as well as supporting organizations helping people achieve these aims. The Trust also funds a number of scholarships through other trusts focusing on education. Programme funding in the South Pacific region is made following the advice of other NGOs operating in the field; direct applications for these funds are not accepted.

Geographical Area of Activity: New Zealand and the South Pacific.

Restrictions: Does not consider direct applications from individuals or organizations based outside New Zealand. Grants to the South Pacific are allocated in co-operation with a partner agency working in the area.

Publications: Annual report of operations and financial statement.

Trustees: I. Johnstone (Chair.); Dr C. C. Aikman; T. Cleverley; Hon. M. Connelly; P. Kirk; H. Langford; J. G. O'Brien; D. Stevens; Hon. J. Sutton; Dr Peter Swain.

Principal Staff: Co-ordinator Stephanie Tyler-Wright.

Address: POB 805, Wellington.

Telephone: (4) 495-9326; **Fax:** (4) 495-9444; **Internet:** www.dia.govt.nz; **e-mail:** trusts@dia.govt.nz.

J. R. McKenzie Trust

Founded in 1940 by Sir John Robert McKenzie, to assist national organizations and local community groups in New Zealand.

Activities: The Trust supports those organizations working with people with special needs, especially children and young people, people 'at risk' or at significant social disadvantage. Focuses on social, health and developmental needs supporting project-related costs, training of paid and unpaid staff, equipment, publications, administration, salaries, volunteer expenses and organizational development. Also supports new and innovative approaches to social problems and organizations seeking to make their services more effective and empowering.

Geographical Area of Activity: New Zealand.

Restrictions: No grants are made to individuals, sports groups, schools and early childhood centres, out-of-school care programmes, rest homes and hospitals, environmental groups and religious and campaigning groups.

Finance: Grants approx. $NZ3,000,000 (Jan. 2003).

Trustees: Peter Holst (Chair.); six others and the Chairs of Rotary Committees of Auckland, Christchurch, Dunedin, Hamilton, Wellington and Auckland North.

Principal Staff: Exec. Dir Iain Hines.

Address: POB 10-006, The Terrace, Wellington.

Telephone: (4) 472-8876; **Fax:** (4) 472-5367; **Internet:** www.jrmckenzie.org.nz; **e-mail:** info@jrmckenzie.org.nz.

National Heart Foundation of New Zealand

Established in 1968, the Foundation is dedicated to the reduction of premature death and suffering from diseases of the heart and circulation.

Activities: The Foundation operates in the area of medicine and health, through research, providing grants for research projects, training fellowships for cardiology trainees to study overseas, senior fellowships and a Chair in Cardiovascular Studies; health promotion, through programmes to promote good health for all and reduce underlying causes of the disease; and medical care, to prevent people at high risk from developing heart and blood vessel disease and to improve the care and rehabilitation of people with heart disease. Operates around 20 branches throughout New Zealand.

Geographical Area of Activity: New Zealand.

Finance: Net assets $NZ8,538,000 (2001); annual revenue $NZ5,764,000, expenditure $NZ5,780,000 (2001).

Board of Trustees: F. Schaef (Chair.); S. Farquhar; H. Fear; B. Fraser; J. Napier; D. Nehua; Dr D. North; J. Nuthall; Prof. G. Nicholls; Prof. N. Sharpe; D. Strack; M. Taylor.

Principal Staff: Exec. Dir Tony Duncan; Medical Dir Dr Diana North.

Address: 9 Kalmia St, Ellerslie, POB 17160, Greenlane, Auckland 1130.

Telephone: (9) 571-9191; **Fax:** (9) 571-9190; **Internet:** www.nhf.org.nz; **e-mail:** info@nhf.org.nz.

New Zealand Association for International Relief, Rehabilitation and Development—CORSO

Founded in 1944 with the aim of working against poverty and injustice internationally; took over the New Zealand Freedom from Hunger Campaign in 1961; aims to fund long-term projects in the Pacific and South Asia working to improve the quality of life for those living in these areas.

Activities: CORSO is a volunteer organization run by a national co-ordinating group which represents regional committees. Its fundraising activities focus on a particular project; an annual appeal for funds finances the administration of the organization. Also organizes training courses and provides technical assistance to organizations. Occasionally holds public meetings on a specific project.

Geographical Area of Activity: Southern Asia and the Pacific region.

Publications: *Overview* (quarterly).

Finance: Funds are raised through regular donations and direct-mail appeals. Administration costs are covered by an annual appeal.

Address: 56 Victoria St, POB 9716, Wellington.

Telephone: (3) 477-3395; **Fax:** (3) 474-0736; **e-mail:** corso@earthlight.co.nz.

New Zealand Institute of International Affairs

Founded in 1934 to promote an understanding of international questions and problems particularly in so far as these may relate to New Zealand, the Commonwealth, and the countries of South-East Asia and the Pacific.

Activities: Operates internationally in the fields of economic affairs, law and other professions, international relations and aid to less-developed countries, through self-conducted programmes, research, conferences, publications and lectures.

Geographical Area of Activity: International.

Publications: *New Zealand International Review* (6 a year); pamphlet series; occasional papers and books.

Trustees: The Institute is governed by a National Council.

Principal Staff: Pres. Sir Kenneth Keith; Dir Brian Lynch.

Address: c/o Victoria University of Wellington, POB 600, Wellington.

Telephone: (4) 463-5356; **Fax:** (4) 473-1261; **e-mail:** nziia@vuw.ac.nz.

Pacific Development and Conservation Trust

Established in 1989 by the Government of New Zealand with funds from the French Government in recognition of the events surrounding the destruction of the Greenpeace ship the *Rainbow Warrior,* which was blown up and sunk in Auckland Harbour by French secret service agents.

Activities: Operates in New Zealand and the South Pacific through self-conducted programmes, research and grants; grants are available for groups to use for charitable purposes, to promote the enhancement and conservation of the environment, natural and historic resources and cultural heritage, and the peaceful, economic, physical and social development of the South Pacific and of its peoples, providing such development is consistent with sound conservation and resource management policies.

Geographical Area of Activity: New Zealand and the South Pacific.

Publications: Annual report and financial statements.

Trustees: The Trustee is the Secretary for Internal Affairs; there is also a Committee of Advisory Trustees. Rhys Richards (Chair.).

Principal Staff: Co-ordinator Michael Algar.

Address: POB 805, Wellington.

Telephone: (4) 495-9323; **Fax:** (4) 495-9444; **Internet:** www.dia.govt.nz; **e-mail:** trusts@dia.govt.nz.

Pacific Leprosy Foundation

Founded in 1939 to help people with leprosy.

Activities: Operates in the areas of medicine and health, and social welfare, working to eliminate leprosy as a threat to public health, through research and attention to sanitation and health issues, and providing medical and social assistance to those affected by leprosy.

Geographical Area of Activity: Australasia and the Pacific.

Publications: *Pacific Leprosy* (quarterly); Annual Report.

Principal Staff: Chair. Dr G. D. Watson.

Address: Private Bag 4730, Christchurch 8020.

Telephone: (3) 366-3685; **Fax:** (3) 366-7771; **e-mail:** pacleprosy@xtra.co.nz.

Peace and Disarmament Education Trust

Established in 1988 by the Government of New Zealand with funds from the French Government in recognition of the events surrounding the destruction of the Greenpeace ship the *Rainbow Warrior,* which was blown up and sunk in Auckland Harbour by French secret service agents.

Activities: Operates in New Zealand in the fields of education, international affairs, law and human rights, social studies and disarmament and arms control, through self-conducted programmes, research, grants to individuals and institutions, scholarships, conferences and training courses. The Trust aims to promote international peace, arms control and disarmament. It also offers scholarships for higher educational study in two categories: up to $NZ7,500 for a year's work towards a Master's thesis, and up to $10,500 each year for up to two years' work towards a Doctoral thesis.

Geographical Area of Activity: New Zealand.

Restrictions: Will not fund the purchase of land, buildings, furniture or fittings.

Publications: Annual Report; theses.

Finance: Established with a capital donation of $NZ1,500,000 from the French Government.

Trustees: The Trustee is the Secretary for Internal Affairs; there is also a Public Advisory Committee on Disarmament and Arms Control whose members are appointed for three years and who act as advisory trustees.

Principal Staff: Co-ordinator Ingrid Kamstra.

Address: Trust and Fellowships Office, Dept of Internal Affairs, POB 805, Wellington.

Telephone: (4) 495-7256; **Fax:** (4) 495-9444; **Internet:** www.dia.govt.nz; **e-mail:** trusts@dia.govt.nz.

Royal Forest and Bird Protection Society of New Zealand

Established in 1923.

Activities: Operates nationally in the field of nature conservation, protecting natural areas, and plants and animals native to New Zealand. Promotes sustainablity in farming and land management; works as an advocate for conservation by lobbying the Government on environmental issues; and supports the protection of Antarctica. Runs the Kiwi Conservation Club for young people.

Geographical Area of Activity: New Zealand and Antarctica.

Publications: *Forest and Bird Magazine* (quarterly).

Executive Committee: Gerry McSweeney (Pres.); Craig Potton (Vice-Pres.).

Principal Staff: Gen. Man. Lyn Bates; Conservation Man. Eric Pyle.

Address: 172 Taranaki St, POB 631, Wellington.

Telephone: (4) 385-7374; **Fax:** (4) 385-7573; **Internet:** www.forest-bird.org.nz; **e-mail:** office@wn.forest-bird.org.nz.

Sutherland Self Help Trust

Founded in 1942 with funds donated by A. F. H. Sutherland; the Trust's purpose is to help people in need through gifts to relevant charities and organizations in New Zealand.

Activities: Provides capital and training/equipment grants to institutions in New Zealand operating in the fields of education, science and technology, medicine and health, and social welfare. Particular focus on the care and advancement of physically disabled and disadvantaged children, community youth work, care of the sick and elderly people, and the alleviation of social problems, including alcohol and drug abuse and sexual abuse.

Geographical Area of Activity: New Zealand.

Restrictions: No grants to individuals, for administration costs, vehicles or overseas travel.

Principal Staff: Exec. Trustee G. J. Sutherland.

Address: 47–51 Rugby St, POB 193, Wellington.

Telephone: (4) 385-1563; **Fax:** (4) 384-9515.

Tindall Foundation

Established in 1995 by Stephen and Margaret Tindall with the aim of helping New Zealanders reach their full potential.

Activities: Active in five funding programme areas: family and social services; enterprise and employment; care of the environment; strengthening the third sector; and promoting philanthropy. Also operates a Young Entrepreneur Programme. A sizeable proportion of the Foundation's resources are allocated directly by appointed Fund Managers.

Geographical Area of Activity: New Zealand.

Publications: Annual Report.

Finance: Total assets $NZ489,877,062 (July 2002); total expenditure $NZ7,992,469 (2002).

Board of Trustees: John Avery; Keith Smith; Margaret Tindall; Stephen Tindall.

Principal Staff: Man. Trevor Gray.

Address: POB 33 181, Takapuna, North Shore City.

Telephone: (9) 488-0170; **Fax:** (9) 489-5327; **Internet:** www.tindall.org.nz; **e-mail:** ttf@tindall.org.nz.

The Todd Foundation

Established by the Todd family's corporate interests in 1972, for charitable purposes within New Zealand.

Activities: The General programme awards major grants within a theme. The current theme is youth, and grants are offered for substantial projects supporting children and young people. The Centenary programme funds two or three large grants each year for significant projects in conservation, environment, the arts, culture, education and health facilities. The Awards for Excellence are for postgraduate research projects within categories of science, technology, engineering, manufacturing, business and commerce. The Awards are administered through the New Zealand Universities' Vice-Chancellors' Committee.

Geographical Area of Activity: New Zealand.

Publications: Annual Report.

Finance: Grants disbursed $NZ834,000 (2002).

Trustees: A nominee each from the New Zealand Law Society, the New Zealand Council of Trade Unions, the New Zealand Manufacturers' Federation and the Federated Farmers of New Zealand; and others.

Principal Staff: Man. Shirley Day.

Address: Todd Bldg, Level 12, cnr Lambton Quay and Brandon St, POB 3142, Wellington.

Telephone: (4) 472-2970; **Fax:** (4) 473-4581.

Trade Aid

Established in 1972 to encourage sustainable development through fair trade.

Activities: Operates in 30 developing countries in the area of aid to less-developed countries and economic affairs, by promoting self-reliance through fair trade. Trade Aid imports products made by people from poor communities, offering a fair price for goods so as to provide a sustainable income. Also campaigns for a solution to the problem of 'third-world debt'.

Geographical Area of Activity: Africa, Asia and Australaisa, and Central and South America.

Publications: *Vital Magazine* (approx. 4 a year).

Principal Staff: Gen. Man. Geoff White.

Address: 174 Gayhurst Rd, POB 35-049, Christchurch.

Telephone: (3) 385-3535; **Fax:** (3) 385-3536; **Internet:** www.tradeaid.co.nz; **e-mail:** tradeaid@tradeaid.co.nz.

Volunteer Service Abroad—VSA

Established in 1962, a non-profit development agency.

Activities: Provides volunteers for local partner organizations in developing regions to assist local communities. Volunteers share knowledge and experience in a range of areas including health, education and training, community development, economic development, enterprise, conservation and agriculture.

Geographical Area of Activity: Africa, Asia and Australasia.

Publications: *Mosquito* (newsletter, quarterly); *New Zealand Abroad—The Story of VSA in Africa, Asia and the Pacific*; Annual Report; Application Pack.

Address: 8th Floor, 23 Molesworth St, Wellington; POB 12246, Wellington 1.

Telephone: (4) 472-5759; **Fax:** (4) 472-5052; **Internet:** www.vsa.org.nz; **e-mail:** vsa@vsa.org.nz.

Nicaragua

FOUNDATIONS, TRUSTS AND NON-PROFIT ORGANIZATIONS

Fundación Augusto César Sandino

Founded in 1980 by Fr Ernesto Cardenal, Silvia McEvans, Fr Uriel Molina and Dr Mariano Fiallos O. to support community and grass-roots self-help social and economic projects nationally.

Activities: The Foundation operates nationally in the fields of economic affairs, education, international affairs, medicine and health, and conservation and the environment, through self-conducted programmes, research, training courses and publications. Maintains a library and database and provides information services.

Geographical Area of Activity: Nicaragua.

Publications: *Con Vos* (3 a year, in English and Spanish).

Finance: Annual budget approx. C $2,000,000.

Principal Staff: Gen. Sec. Edwin Zablah.

Address: Apdo 2458, Zona Postal 5, Managua.

Telephone: (2) 774773; **Fax:** (2) 675670; **Internet:** www.facs.org.ni; **e-mail:** facs@facs.org.ni.

Nigeria

FOUNDATIONS, TRUSTS AND NON-PROFIT ORGANIZATIONS

African Refugees Foundation—AREF

Established in 1993 by Chief Segun Olusola to assist refugees in Africa.

Activities: Offers assistance to refugees and displaced people in Africa, as well as organizing workshops on peace initiatives and conflict mediation, seminars on conflict prevention and management, and working to develop policy for governments. Sister organizations exist in the United Kingdom and the USA. Has UN accreditation.

Geographical Area of Activity: Africa.

Board of Trustees: C. Amira; Chief Opral Benson; J. Elaiho; S. Dewale Solarin; Prof. Ekpo Eyo; Chief Newton Jibunoh; A. A. Ma'aji; Prof. G. O. Olusanya; A. Winfunke; Dr Z. Zawde; and representatives of international organizations.

Principal Staff: Founder and Pres. Chief Segun Olusola.

Address: Lagos State Old Secretariat, off Oba Akinjobi St, GRA Ikeja, POB 5051K, Lagos.

Telephone: (1) 2880246; **e-mail:** aref@mail.wangonet.org.

Institute of Human Rights and Humanitarian Law

A non-governmental, non-political, community-based human rights and education research network generating and sharing knowledge about law.

Activities: Operates in the field of human rights and humanitarian law, through education and training, advocacy, lobbying, dissemination of information, creating rural advice offices, research, and workshops, seminars and symposia. Maintains a Human Rights Documentation Centre.

Publications: *Human Rights Defender* (quarterly); *Christian to Christian Alert* (monthly newsletter); *Public Interest Law and Practice Journal* (monthly); Annual Report; and other publications.

International Advisory Board: Prof. Akin Oyebode (Chair.).

Principal Staff: Exec. Dir Anyakwee S. Nsirimovu.

Address: 2B Railway Close, D/Line, Humanity Complex, POB 2292, Port Harcourt, Rivers State.

Telephone and Fax: (84) 231716; **Internet:** www.kabissa.org/ihrhl; **e-mail:** ihrhl@ihrhl.org.

International Institute of Tropical Agriculture

Founded in 1967 by the Ford and Rockefeller Foundations (qq.v.) to contribute to the improvement of tropical farming techniques.

Activities: The Institute conducts research, at its own stations and in collaboration with institutions in other countries. The Resource and Crop Management Programme aims to develop methods of land use and cropping systems that will enable efficient, economical and sustained production of food crops for the humid and sub-humid tropics, with particular emphasis on the problems of small farmers: co-operating programmes have been established in Cameroon and Ghana. Crop improvement programmes aim to bring about genetic improvements and control pests: the Root and Tuber Improvement Programme covers cassava and yams, and includes co-operation with similar programmes in Cameroon and the Democratic Republic of the Congo (formerly Zaire); the Cereals Improvement Programme (maize and rice) involves co-operation with the West Africa Rice Development Association (Côte d'Ivoire), the International Rice Research Institute (Philippines), the International Maize and Wheat Improvement Centre in Mexico (q.v.) and African regional organizations; and the Grain Legume Improvement Programme (cowpeas and soybeans) is linked with projects in Brazil, Tanzania and Burkina Faso. The Institute's Genetic Resources Unit collects and stores germplasm for genetic research in collaboration with donors and recipients all over the world, and the Virology Unit studies virus diseases affecting crops. The Training Programme involves about 550 participants a year from African and other countries. Conferences and seminars are organized and the Institute also maintains a library and documentation centre.

Geographical Area of Activity: International.

Publications: Annual Report (in French and English); *IITA Research* (2 a year, in French and English); brochures, conference proceedings, technical papers, training manuals.

Principal Staff: Dir Gen. Dr Peter Hartmann.

Address: Oyo Rd, PMB 5320, Ibadan, Oyo State.

Telephone: (2) 2412626; **Fax:** (2) 2412221; **Internet:** www.iita.org; **e-mail:** iita@cgiar.org.

A. G. Leventis Foundation Nigeria

Established in 1988; a subsidiary foundation of the A. G. Leventis Foundation (q.v.) in Greece.

Activities: Active in the fields of education, the environment, health care and culture, although principal support has been given to training young farmers in modern agricultural methods, currently through the establishment of five schools in Ghana and Nigeria. The Foundation has also established an Environmental Resource Centre, in collaboration with the Nigerian Conservation Foundation, as well as developing an agro-forestry conservation programme, and donating equipment to technical colleges for vocational training of young Nigerians.

Geographical Area of Activity: Ghana and Nigeria.

Address: 8/10 Abibu Oki St, POB 26, General Post Office, Marina, Lagos.

Telephone: (1) 2660405; **Fax:** (1) 860574; **Internet:** www.leventisfoundation.org.

Nigerian Conservation Foundation

Established in 1980 by Chief S. L. Edu, and registered as a Charitable Trust in 1982. Its purpose is to conserve natural resources through conservation projects, environmental education and awareness and advocacy.

Activities: Pursues the conservation of nature and its resources with the aim of improving the quality of human life both in the present and future by: preserving the full range of Nigeria's bio-diversity which includes species, eco-systems and genetic diversity; promoting the sustainable use of natural resources for the benefit of the present and future generations; advocating actions that minimize pollution and wasteful utilization of renewable and non-renewable resources. Runs participatory community-based projects, conducts research, organizes workshops, seminars, conferences and various other training courses. NCF is an affiliate of the WWF—World Wide Fund for Nature (q.v.), and a partner-designate of Birdlife International (q.v.).

Geographical Area of Activity: Nigeria, West Africa.

Publications: *The Roan; NCF Matters; Tortoise Magazine; Expensive Rubbish; The Mid-Point; Art for Conservation; A Decade of NCF; Islam and Ecology; Christianity and Ecology; African Traditional Religion and Ecology; Environmental Education* (series of 11 vols); other publications and seminar proceedings.

Finance: Funded by donations, membership subscriptions and investment income. Net assets US $590,000 (1999); annual revenue US $160,000, expenditure US $180,000 (1999).

Governing Council and Trustees: Chief S. L. Edu (Life Pres.); Brigadier-Gen. Mobolaji Johnson (Chair.) Izoma P. C. Asiodu; Ambassador A. Alakija; Chief A. S. Guobadia; Alh. Abba Kyari; A. P. Leventis; Akintola Williams.

Principal Staff: Exec. Dir Dr Muhtari Aminu-Kano; Technical Programmes Dir Prof. Emmanuel Obot; Dir of Finance and Admin. Mr. David Anyanwoke; A. A. Mohammed.

Address: Km 19, Lagos-Epe Expressway, POB 74638, Victoria Island, Lagos.

Telephone: (1) 2642498; **Fax:** (1) 2642497; **Internet:** www.ncf-nigeria.org; **e-mail:** ncf@hyperia.com.

Nigerian Institute of International Affairs

Founded in 1961 as a private, non-governmental 'think-tank' in international affairs; the Institute was taken over by the Federal Government in 1971. However, while it has changed its status to that of a governmental institution, its character as an independent, non-political and non-profit-making organization remains unchanged. Its objectives are to encourage and facilitate the understanding of international affairs and of the circumstances, conditions and attitudes of foreign countries and their peoples; to provide and maintain means of information upon international questions and promote the study and investigation of international questions through conferences, lectures and discussions, and by the preparation and publication of books, records, reports, etc.; and to establish contacts with other organizations with similar objects. In order to achieve these objectives, the Institute is charged with promoting the scientific study of international politics, economics and jurisprudence, and providing facilities for the training of Nigerian diplomats and personnel, and those of other countries whose vocations relate to international affairs.

Activities: Operates through research, publications, lectures, conferences, seminars and the provision of library and documentation services.

Geographical Area of Activity: Nigeria.

Publications: *Nigerian Journal of International Affairs* (quarterly); *Nigeria: Bulletin on Foreign Affairs* (2 a year); *The Nigerian Forum* (monthly); occasional papers and books.

Principal Staff: Dir Gen. Prof. U. Joy Ogwu; Dir of Research Prof. B. E. Ate; Dir of Admin and Finance M. U. Osawemen; Dir of Library and Documentation Service Q. F. Coker.

Address: 13–15 Kofo Abayomi Rd, Victoria Island, POB 1727, Lagos.

Telephone: (1) 2615606/7; **Fax:** (1) 2611360; **e-mail:** dg@niianigeria.org.

Norway

FOUNDATIONS, TRUSTS AND NON-PROFIT ORGANIZATIONS

Janson Johan Helmich og Marcia Jansons Legat (Janson Johan Helmich and Marcia Jansons Foundation)

Activities: Operates in the field of education. Awards scholarships to Norwegian postgraduate students for advanced study abroad in any field, including doctoral or postgraduate study, and professional development.

Geographical Area of Activity: Norway.

Finance: 30 grants offered; maximum value of grant 75,000 kroner (1999).

Principal Staff: Reidun Haugen.

Address: Blommeseter Norderhov, 3512 Hönefoss.

Telephone: 32-13-54-65; **Fax:** 32-13-56-26; **Internet:** www.jansonlegat.no; **e-mail:** janlegat@online.no.

Sonja Henie–Niels Onstad Foundations, The Art Centre

Founded in 1968 by Sonja Henie and Niels Onstad to support and present international modern art in Norway.

Activities: Arranges exhibitions of modern and contemporary art; maintains a library and an art centre which houses a collection of modern and contemporary paintings; engages international artists for concerts and performances.

Geographical Area of Activity: Norway.

Publications: Catalogues.

Address: Kunstsentret, Sonja Heniesvei 31, 1311 Høvikodden.

Telephone: 67-80-48-80; **Fax:** 67-54-32-70.

International Peace Research Institute, Oslo—PRIO

Founded in 1959 by Johan Galtung, Ingrid Eide Galtung and Mari Holmboe Ruge (achieved independent status in 1966), to stimulate, organize and carry out scholarly research on the conditions necessary for peaceful relations between nations and other groups; to direct teaching and training in this sphere; to hold conferences and seminars; and to disseminate information on the results of its studies.

Activities: Carries out research on international issues related to military policy, disarmament, environmental security, ethnic conflict and conflict resolution, and disseminates results through publications, seminars and lectures. Offers a graduate course in peace research at the University of Oslo's International Summer School. Awards a limited number of student scholarships and guest scholarships (one to three months) for visiting researchers. As of 2003, PRIO hosts the Centre for the Study of Civil War.

Geographical Area of Activity: Norway.

Publications: Annual Report; *Journal of Peace Research* (bi-monthly journal); *Security Dialogue* (quarterly journal); books and reports.

Principal Staff: Information Dir Agnete Schjonsby.

Address: Fuglehauggta 11, 0260 Oslo.

Telephone: 22-54-77-00; **Fax:** 22-54-77-01; **Internet:** www.prio.no; **e-mail:** info@prio.no.

Skipsreder Anders Jahres Fond til Vitenskapens Fremme (Shipowner Anders Jahre's Foundation for the Promotion of Sciences)

Founded in 1953 by Anders Jahre to support research in medicine, law, chemistry and shipbuilding.

Activities: Grants are made to individuals and institutions, in particular to individuals at the University of Oslo and the Norwegian Institute of Advanced Technology. Awards two prizes for medicine to research workers in Scandinavia. Supports the Institute for Experimental Medical Research.

Geographical Area of Activity: Norway.

Trustees: The Rector of the University of Oslo (Chair.); five other members are nominated by the Faculties of Medicine and of Law, and the Norwegian Institute of Advanced Technology.

Address: UNIFOR, Management Foundation for Funds and Legacies at the University of Oslo, POB 1131, Blindern, 0317 Oslo.

Telephone and Fax 22-34-01-40; Internet: www.unifor.no /statutt_fond.asp?fond_id=69; **e-mail:** unifor@unifor.no.

Anders Jahres Humanitære Stiftelse

Established in 1966 by Anders Jahre; the Foundation is managed by UNIFOR at the University of Oslo.

Activities: Operates in the area of the arts and humanities, through the award of the Anders Jahre Prize for Culture, to promote Norwegian culture.

Board of Trustees: Øivin Fjeldstad (Chair.); Ellen Gjerpe Hansen; Herbjørn Hansson; Lars Roar Langslet; Sigurd Osberg.

Address: Postboks 440, Sentrum, 3201 Sandefjord.

Telephone: 33-46-02-90; **Fax:** 33-36-48-60; **Internet:** www.ajhs.no; **e-mail:** post@ajhs.no.

Chr. Michelsens Institutt—CMI (Chr. Michelsen Institute—CMI)

Established as Christian Michelsen in 1930; a private research foundation dedicated to studying the social sciences.

Activities: The Institute undertakes basic and applied research projects in the social sciences, in particular researching issues concerning development and human rights in Africa south of the Sahara, Asia and the Middle East. Research is carried out in all areas, including economics, anthropology, geography, history and political science. The Institute maintains an extensive library. Collaborates with similar organizations in Norway and in developing countries.

Geographical Area of Activity: Norway, Africa and South East Asia.

Publications: *CMI News; CMI Policy Brief*Annual Report; reports and working papers.

Finance: Grant from the Norwegian Ministry of Foreign Affairs; funds from commissioned research projects.

Principal Staff: Dir Dr Gunnar M. Sørbø; Deputy Dir Alf Morten Jerve.

Address: POB 6033, Postterminalen, 5892 Bergen; Fantoftvegen 38, 5036 Fantoft, Bergen.

Telephone: 55-57-40-00; **Fax:** 55-57-41-66; **Internet:** www.cmi.no; **e-mail:** cmi@cmi.no.

Minor Foundation for Major Challenges

Established in February 2000 by Peter Opsvik and members of his family.

Activities: The Foundation provides support to information projects that aim to limit human-created climate changes, through influencing public opinion and changing attitudes to these problems. Priority is given to projects run by Norwegian and foreign organizations which are innovative, experimental and untested, look likely to have the greatest impact, and would be difficult to realise without the Foundation's assistance.

Geographical Area of Activity: International.

Finance: Total grant expenditure approx. 1,500,000 krone (2001).

Board of Trustees: Ragnar Vik (Chair.); Sigmund Hågvar; Øyvind Ihlen; Tor Opsvik.

Address: c/o Advocate Ragnar Vik, POB 1397 Vika, 0114 Oslo.

Internet: www.minor-foundation.no; **e-mail:** info@minor-foundation.no.

Fridtjof Nansen Institute

Founded in May 1958 by the Norwegian Geographical Society to conduct applied social science research on international issues in the fields of resource management, the environment and energy.

Activities: The Institute operates internationally, in the fields of development studies, conservation and the environment, economic affairs and international affairs, through self-conducted programmes, collaboration with other research institutions nationally and internationally, conferences and publications. The Institute's research activities focus on European resource and environmental management; polar politics and law, Russia and Norway; climate politics; biodiversity; global governance; energy politics; and ocean politics.

Geographical Area of Activity: International.

Publications: *Yearbook of International Co-operation on Environment and Development (Green Globe Yearbook); Nansen News* (newsletter, 2 a year); books, reports and textbooks.

Finance: Funding is provided by governmental organizations and private companies.

Board of Directors: S. Ullring (Chair.); R. Andersen; F. Bull-Hansen; M. Greve; Inge Loønning; K. Midgaard; S. Rogne.

Principal Staff: Dir Arild Moe; Research Dir Olav Schram-Stokke.

Address: Fridtjof Nansens vei 17, Postboks 326, 1326 Lysaker.

Telephone: 67-11-19-00; **Fax:** 67-11-19-10; **Internet:** www.fni.no; **e-mail:** sentralbord@fni.no.

Norsk Utenrikspolitisk Institutt—NUPI (Norwegian Institute of International Affairs)

Founded in 1959 by the Stortinget (Parliament) to increase insight into questions concerning international relations by disseminating information, and to encourage the study of international problems of co-operation and the causes of international conflicts.

Activities: Operates nationally in the field of information and research, and both nationally and internationally in the fields of foreign affairs and international relations, through self-conducted programmes, research, conferences, courses, publications and lectures.

Geographical Area of Activity: Norway and the Russian Federation.

Publications: *Conference Proceedings; Internassional Politikk* (journal, four a year); *Forum for Development Studies* (journal, two a year); *NUPI-notat* (20–30 a year); *NUPI-rapport* (10–15 a year); and other articles, papers and books.

Principal Staff: Dir Sverre Lodgaard.

Address: Grønlandsleiret 25, POB 8159, 0033 Oslo Dep.

Telephone: 22-05-65-00; **Fax:** 22-17-70-15; **Internet:** www.nupi.no; **e-mail:** pub@nupi.no.

The Rafto Foundation

Established in 1986 to commemorate the life of Professor Thorolf Rafto.

Activities: The Foundation's principal activity is the annual award of the Rafto Prize, to encourage and honour individuals and organizations fighting for human rights, freedom and democracy around the world. Previous winners include the Romani People (1997), ECPAT (1998), Gennadij Grusjevoj (1999), Kim Dae-Jung (2000), Shirin Ebadi (2001), Sidi Mohammed Daddach (2002),.

Geographical Area of Activity: International.

Address: Rafto House, Menneskerettighetenes plass 1, 5007 Bergen.

Telephone: 55-21-09-50; **Fax:** 55-21-09-59; **Internet:** www.rafto.no; **e-mail:** secretariat@rafto.no.

Pakistan

FOUNDATION CENTRE AND CO-ORDINATING BODY

Pakistan Centre for Philanthropy

Membership organization serving grant-makers in Pakistan.

Activities: Provides a range of support services to foundations, philanthropists and corporate donors in Pakistan, as well as promoting the development of philanthropy.

Geographical Area of Activity: Pakistan.

Principal Staff: Exec. Dir Shahnaz Wazir Ali.

Address: c/o World Bank, 20 Shahrah-e-Jamhuriat, Ramna 5, Islamabad.

Telephone: (51) 22796416 ext. 407; **Fax:** (51) 2822396; **e-mail:** shahnazwa@hotmail.com.

FOUNDATIONS, TRUSTS AND NON-PROFIT ORGANIZATIONS

Hamdard Foundation Pakistan

Founded in 1964 to organize and supervise public charities; to bring about the advancement of learning and education, health and medical care, and emergency relief; to develop an indigenous or Eastern system of medicine and medical science; and to support general welfare and charitable purposes.

Activities: Supports the Institute of Health and Tibbi Research, the Society for the Promotion of Eastern Medicine, the College of Eastern Medicine and the Pakistan Tibbi Association; established the Madinat-al-Hikmat (City of Learning) in Karachi, comprising institutes for education, medicine, science, Islamic studies and comparative religion; also provides medical and health-care services in its clinics and dispensaries. Initiated the Shura Hamdard, a medico-scientific, educational and cultural service for the exchange of views on matters of national interest by leading intellectuals and business people. Grants are made to individuals and institutions for research and education, particularly in the fields of medicine and pharmacy, and for general charitable purposes. Awards fellowships and scholarships, publishes its own journals and other publications, and sponsors the publishing of books.

Geographical Area of Activity: Pakistan.

Publications: Report of operations and financial statement; *Hamdard-i-Sehat; Hamdard Naunehal; Akhbar-ut-Tibb; Hamdard Islamicus; Hamdard Medicus;* and books on health, medicine, religion, etc.

Finance: Annual revenue 70,815,783 rupees, expenditure 40,749,568 rupees (2000).

Trustees: Sadia Rashid (Pres.); Dr Navaid-ul-Zafar (Man. Dir); Mohammed Zaman Khan Achakzai; Dr M. Afzal; Dr Manzoor Ahmad; Prof. Dr Atta-ur-Rehman; Prof. Dr Lal Baha; Masood Ahmad Barakatee; L. A. D'Silva; Khalid M. Ishaque; Saleem Mehmud; Dr Fazal Mobin; Ehsan Rashid; M. D. Shami; Furqan Ahmad Shamsi; S. M. Zafar.

Address: Nazimabad No. 3, Karachi 74600.

Telephone: (21) 6616001; **Fax:** (21) 6611755; **e-mail:** hamdard@khi.paknet.com.pk.

Pakistan Institute of International Affairs

Founded in 1947 with the aim of promoting interest and research in international affairs in Pakistan.

Activities: Operates internationally through research, publications, seminars, lectures and conferences. The Institute has a specialized library with over 28,600 books and monographs. It assists the Institute's research staff, and helps Pakistani and foreign scholars in the field of international affairs and Pakistan foreign policy.

Geographical Area of Activity: South Asia.

Publications: *Pakistan Horizon* (quarterly).

Finance: Funded by government, publication sales, rental income and membership fees. Net assets US $184,553; annual revenue US $35,501, expenditure US $42,240 (2001).

Principal Staff: Chair. Fatehyab Ali Khan; Sec. Dr Qazi Shakil Ahmad; Research Officers Tehmina Mehmood, Naushin Wasi; Librarian Afsar Mehdi.

Address: Aiwan-e-Sadar Rd, POB 1447, Karachi 74200.

Telephone: (21) 5682891; **Fax:** (21) 5686069; **e-mail:** piia@cyber.net.pk.

Quaid-i-Azam Academy

Founded in 1976 by the Federal Government of Pakistan to undertake research on Quaid-i-Azam Mohammad Ali Jinnah (Founder of the Nation) and on the history of Pakistan.

Activities: Conducts and supports research on political, economic, social, religious and cultural aspects of the history of Pakistan; grants scholarships and professorships; sponsors and participates in lectures, conferences and seminars; awards seven prizes every three years to Pakistani or foreign scholars for work of academic merit on Quaid-i-Azam or on any aspects of modern Indo-Muslim history. The Academy maintains a library and collection of research materials and archives, and publishes the results of research.

Geographical Area of Activity: International.

Publications: Studies, translations and bibliographies.

Governing Board: Minister for Culture and Tourism (Chair.); and 21 other members.

Principal Staff: Dir Khwaja Razi Haides.

Address: 297 M. A. Jinnah Rd, Karachi 74800.

Telephone: (21) 9215234; **Fax:** (21) 9215236.

Zulekhabai V. M. Gany Rangoonwala Trust

Founded in 1967 by M. A. Rangoonwala to improve the life of indigent and deserving persons without any discrimination of caste, creed and colour, through the advancement of education and vocational training, the advancement of health and the prevention and relief of sickness, and through the care and comfort of the needy.

Activities: Operates nationally in the fields of education, social welfare, science and medicine, and the arts and humanities, and internationally in the fields of education, science and medicine, religion and the conservation of natural resources. Operates through self-conducted programmes, grants to institutions both at home and abroad, grants to individuals, fellowships, scholarships, conferences, courses, publications and lectures. Establishes, aids and maintains community centres, educational institutions, hospitals, dispensaries, maternity homes, nursing homes, clinics, sanatoria and medical research centres.

Geographical Area of Activity: International.

Publications: Report of operations and financial statement.

Principal Staff: Dir, Rangoonwala Centre Saeed A. B. Mirza.

Address: Rangoonwala Centre, Dhoraji Colony, Karachi 5.

Telephone: (21) 4938146; **Fax:** (21) 2310602.

Society for the Prevention and Cure of Blindness

Founded in 1960 by Haji Hasanally P. Ebrahim to work for the prevention of 'preventable' blindness and the cure of 'curable' blindness in Pakistan and elsewhere in the world; and, generally, to promote the cause, welfare, education, vocation, training, rehabilitation, employment, aftercare and recreation of blind and visually disabled persons.

Activities: Operates nationally and internationally in the fields of social welfare and medicine. Activities include providing ophthalmological services and facilities for the restoration and preservation of eyesight; the organizing and managing of permanent or temporary ophthalmological hospitals, including about 100 'Free Eye Camps' annually; collection of statistics and information about ophthalmological problems; and training teachers and social workers to examine children's eyesight. The Society runs an Eye Hospital in Karachi. It co-operates with similar organizations abroad through the exchange of information and publications, and the supply of corneas for grafting.

Geographical Area of Activity: International.

Publications: Annual report and financial statement; leaflets on eye problems and prevention of blindness.

Trustees: Haji Ali Akbar H. Ibrahim (Pres.).

Principal Staff: Sec.-Gen. Amir Ali L. Patel.

Address: Ground Floor, G-K 7/60, Bagh-e-Zehra St, Bagh-e-Zehra Complex, Kharader, Karachi.

Telephone: (21) 2205004; **Fax:** (21) 2311499.

Palestinian Autonomous Areas

FOUNDATIONS, TRUSTS AND NON-PROFIT ORGANIZATIONS

Research Center for Human and Social Development

Founded in 1994 by Dr Mohammad-Sufian Abu Nijaila, Dr Yousef S. Abu Maila, Dr Ehsan Khalil Al-Agha, Dr Mohammad Joma Abd El-Aziz and Dr Adnan M. Abu Nijela as a non-profit-making organization for the development of Palestinian society in the Gaza Strip, with an emphasis on women and young people, and on areas which support the peace process and contribute to political and social stability and prosperity.

Activities: The Center's objectives are to publicize the problems concerning Palestinian society; to carry out research projects dealing with the needs of Palestinian society; to advance the status of Palestinian women; to organize and conduct training courses and programmes in the areas of education, the development of society and welfare of local inhabitants; to set up a library in the humanities and social and economic development; to participate in mutual co-operation and understanding at local, regional and international level; to consolidate and create means of co-operation and co-ordination with scientific and other institutes and research centres nationally and internationally; and to prepare and conduct cultural studies and research projects, in addition to joint research projects which contribute to the construction of peace. The Center also organizes training courses and symposia, provides advisory services and issues publications.

Geographical Area of Activity: Palestinian Autonomous Areas.

Administrative and Supervisory Board: Dr Mohammad-Sufian Abu Nijaila (Chair.); Dr Yousef S. Abu Maila (Deputy Chair.); Dr Ehsan Khalil Al-Agha (Sec.); Dr Mohammad Joma Abd El-Aziz (Treas.); Dr Adnan M. Abu Nijela; Abeer Salah Abu-Ramadan; Dr Ayyoub M. El-Alem; Salma M. Hammad; Dr Sharif Kanaana; Dr M. M. Nairab; Malika Shukru Saqa.

Principal Staff: Chair. Dr Mohammad-Sufian Abu Nijaila.

Address: Zein Ed-deen Bldg, Thalatheeny St Remal, POB 1073, Gaza City.

Telephone: (7) 867903; **Fax:** (7) 864083; **e-mail:** rchsd@rannet.com.

Tamkeen

Set up in 2001, initially as a time-limited five-year programme, to increase the participation of civil society organizations in public discourse in the West Bank and Gaza..

Activities: Seeks to strengthen long-term democratic development and to encourage open and constructive dialogue on public issues in the Palestinian Autonomous Areas, through large and small grant awards and the provision of technical assistance to Palestinian NGOs which advocate on behalf of the community, and promote public discourse in areas such as civic education and youth leadership, advocacy for the disabled and human rights, rule of law, and transparency in government. Maintains a principal office on the West Bank, and two further satellite offices in Jerusalem and Nablus.

Geographical Area of Activity: Palestinian Autonomous Areas.

Finance: Initial funding of US $33,000,000 over five years from USAID; annual grants approx. US $5,000,000 (2001–02).

Address: Al-Sourani Bldg, 3rd Floor, behind Al-Kharmel School, Rimal, Gaza.

Telephone: (8) 2840170; **Fax:** (8) 2840070; **Internet:** www.tamkeen.org; **e-mail:** info@tamkeen.org.

Panama

FOUNDATIONS, TRUSTS AND NON-PROFIT ORGANIZATIONS

Fundación Dobbo Yala (Dobbo Yala Foundation)

Founded in 1990 to promote sustainable development for indigenous development and environmental conservation.

Activities: Provides administrative, technical and management support for environmental projects. Programmes include environmental education, training and extension of sustainable agriculture, socio-economic and environmental education, management of native forests projects, and training and support for indigenous micro-enterprises.

Geographical Area of Activity: Central America.

Publications: *El Valor del Ambiente en Los Kunas Desde una Perspectiva de Genero; Territorios Indigenas, Biodiversidad y Turismo*; and other publications.

Principal Staff: Exec. Dir Eligio Alvarado P.; Dir Finance Aurelio Chiari; Technical Dir Heraclio Herrera.

Address: Apdo 83-0308, Zona 3, Panamá.

Telephone: 265-1061; **Fax:** 265-4932; **Internet:** http://dobboyala.org; **e-mail:** dobbo@pty.com.

Paraguay

FOUNDATIONS, TRUSTS AND NON-PROFIT ORGANIZATIONS

Fundación Moisés Bertoni (Moisés Bertoni Foundation)

Established in 1988 to protect animals and plants in Paraguay.

Activities: The Foundation promotes the conservation of nature and biodiversity; management of protected areas; sustainable use of resources; and education and training in environmental management. Also runs eco-tourism projects in managed private game reserves.

Geographical Area of Activity: Paraguay.

Publications: *Plantas Comunes del Mbaracayo; Helechos del Mbaracayo; Maniteros de la Reserva de Mbaracayo; Plantas Medicinales de la Comunidad Guarani.*

Principal Staff: Exec. Dir Nancy Cardozo.

Address: Procer Carlos Arguello 208, Asunción.

Telephone: (21) 60-8740; **Fax:** (21) 60-8741; **Internet:** www.mbertoni.org.py; **e-mail:** mbertoni@mbertoni.org.py.

Peru

FOUNDATION CENTRE AND CO-ORDINATING BODY

Asociación Latinoamericana de Instituciones Financieras para el Desarrollo—ALIDE (Latin American Association of Development Financing Institutions)

Founded in 1968 to promote the participation of financial institutions in the social and economic progress of countries in Central and South America and the Caribbean.

Activities: The Association is made up of public and private development financing institutions; it encourages members to co-operate and contribute to the development and integration of Central and South American economies. The organization disseminates information; reports on investment projects; supports the collaboration of members on projects; organizes training projects and seminars; works to strengthen banking institutions in Central and South America; and maintains an information network, documentation centre and database. Also acts as an executive institution for projects and programmes being funded by international co-operation organizations and agencies.

Geographical Area of Activity: Central and South America and the Caribbean.

Restrictions: Only works with member organizations and institutions.

Publications: *ALIDE Bulletin* (6 a year, in English and Spanish); *Memoria de ALIDE* (annually); *Anales Asamblea General* (annually); Alide Noticias (monthly); *Directorio de Instituciones de Desarrollo* (every 2 years); numerous technical papers and publications.

Finance: Funded by grants from international organizations and foundations, and membership fees.

Principal Staff: Sec.-Gen. Rommel Acevedo.

Address: POB 3988, Lima 100.

Telephone: (1) 4422400; **Fax:** (1) 4428105; **Internet:** www.alide.org.pe; **e-mail:** mzamora@alide.org.pe.

FOUNDATIONS, TRUSTS AND NON-PROFIT ORGANIZATIONS

CEDRO—Centro de Información y Educación para la Prevención del Abuso de Drogas (Information and Education Centre for the Prevention of Drug Abuse)

Founded in 1986. Aims to raise awareness of drug abuse in Peru, and to help people afflicted by drug addiction.

Activities: Disseminates information about the impact of drug use, production and commercialization, and works to overcome problems in society that are drug-related. Funds community development projects in Peru, including working with 'street children' to overcome drug abuse through education and re-housing, where possible. Also provides vocational training and support, and funds research.

Geographical Area of Activity: Mainly Peru.

Publications: *Pscyhoactive Journal*.

Address: Roca y Bologna 271, San Antonio–Miraflores, Lima 18.

Telephone: (1) 4467046; **Fax:** (1) 4460751; **Internet:** ekeko2.rcp.net.pe/cedro; **e-mail:** postmaster@cedro.org.pe.

Pro Naturaleza—Fundación Peruana para la Conservación de la Naturaleza (Pro Nature—Peruvian Foundation for Nature Conservation)

Founded in 1984 by Cosapi SA to conserve natural communities and to promote sustainable conservation.

Activities: Supports the conservation of soils, water resources, flora, fauna and other renewable natural resources in Peru, and promotes the development of a conservation culture. Works in conjunction with the Tropical Rainforest Coalition.

Geographical Area of Activity: Peru.

Principal Staff: Exec. Dir Gustavo Suárez de Freitas C.

Address: Avda Nicolás Arriola 740, Lima 13.

Telephone: (1) 2113500; **Fax:** (1) 2248665; **Internet:** www.cosapi.com.pe/; **e-mail:** postmaster@cosapi.com.pe.

PROTERRA

Established in 1983, a non-profit organization and centre of investigation and promotion of environmental and development issues, which aims to improve the quality of life through achieving sustainable development.

Activities: Operates nationally and internationally, throughout Central and South America, in the fields of environmental policies and law, and sustainable development, through research, projects, training, publications, information dissemination, conferences, workshops, seminars and lobbying; co-operates with environmental workers and other national and international organizations; and supports projects in Peru and Central and South America, especially in the Andes and Amazonia regions. Participated in the drafting of the Peruvian Environment and Natural Resources Code. Maintains a library of books, magazines, documents, photographs, videos, etc. on the environment, and a databank of environmental legislation.

Geographical Area of Activity: Central and South America.

Publications: *Juridical Environmental Bulletin* (periodical); *The Awake of Pozuzo Magazine; Latin American Directory of Environmental Law* (1993); *Peruvian Environmental Directory* (1993); *Environment and Natural Resources Code* (1995, 2nd edn); books on environmental law and the environment.

Principal Staff: Exec. Dir Dr Walter Valdez Muñoz.

Address: Calle Madrid 166, Miraflores, Lima 18.

Telephone: (1) 2420238; **Fax:** (1) 2426363; **e-mail:** proterra@mail.cosapidata.pe.

Philippines

FOUNDATION CENTRES AND CO-ORDINATING BODIES

Asia Pacific Philanthropy Consortium—APPC

Established in 1994 as a network of grant-making organizations to support the emerging third sector in the Asia-Pacific region.

Activities: Assists foundations and corporate donors in the Asia-Pacific region, through technical support, training, research, information services, networking, exchanges and conferences. Currently developing a network of Internet-linked information centres in Asian societies, including Australia, China, Hong Kong, Korea, Japan, Philippines, Taiwan, and Thailand, with additional links being established in Bangladesh, India, Indonesia and Malaysia.

Geographical Area of Activity: Asia-Pacific region.

Publications: *Philanthropy and Law in Asia; Evolving Patterns of Asia Pacific Philanthropy; Emerging Civil Society in the Asia Pacific Community*.

Governing Council: Iftekhar Zaman (Chair.); Darwin Chen, Paiboon Wattanasirithan (Vice-Chair.).

Principal Staff: Exec. Dir Rory Tolentino; Program Officer Tina Pavia.

Address: Rooms 207–208, Centre for Social and Public Affairs, Social Development Complex, Atenoe de Manila University, Katipunan Rd, Quezon City.

Telephone: (2) 426-6001; **Fax:** (2) 426-1427; **Internet:** www.asianphilanthropy.org/appc/appc.html; **e-mail:** rftolentino@admu.edu.ph.

Asian NGO Coalition for Agrarian Reform and Rural Development—ANGOC

Founded in 1979 to encourage united action among Asian NGOs involved in rural development.

Activities: The Organization's four main fields of activity are: food security through sustainable agriculture (e.g. through the 200-Village Project); transforming financial institutions; developing the voluntary sector; and encouraging voluntary action. Member organizations operate in Bangladesh, India, Indonesia, Japan, Malaysia, Nepal, Pakistan, the Philippines and Sri Lanka.

Geographical Area of Activity: Asia and the Far East.

Publications: *Bank Watch;* numerous publications on NGOs in Asia.

Principal Staff: Exec. Dir Roel R. Ravanera.

Address: POB 3107, QCCPO 1103, Quezon City.

Telephone: (2) 433-7653; **Fax:** (2) 920-7434; **Internet:** www.philonline.com.ph/~angoc; **e-mail:** angoc@angoc.ngo.ph.

Association of Foundations

Founded in 1972 to foster broader public understanding of the nature of foundations as institutions in nation-building, to promote co-ordination and co-operation among member foundations with a view to the optimum use of available resources, to represent members whenever necessary, and to serve as a clearing house for information, establishing and maintaining a central file of foundation materials, and preparing and updating a directory of Philippine foundations.

Activities: Operates nationally through the dissemination of information, organization of conferences and workshops, liaison among members and between members and government agencies, maintenance of an information centre, and through various publications. Has approximately 135 member foundations and is one of six founding members of the Philippines Council for NGO Certification.

Geographical Area of Activity: Philippines.

Publications: Annual report and financial statement; *AF Brochure; Foundation Bulletin; Directory of Philippine Foundations; Donor Trends: A Resource Book of Development Assistance in the Philippines; Philippines NGOS: A Resource Book of Social Development NGOs*.

Directors: Judy Araneta Roxas (Chair.); Marissa Camacho Reyes (Pres.); Chuki Feria Miranda (Vice-Pres.); Lemia Liguaton Simbulan (Sec.); Rory Francisco Tolentino (Treas.).

Principal Staff: Exec. Dir Oman Q. Jiao.

Address: 9/F Rm 9001-A, Aurora Tower, Aurora Ave, Cubao, Quezon City.

Telephone: (2) 913-7231; **Fax:** (2) 911-9792; **Internet:** www.afphils.net; **e-mail:** afnational@edsamail.com.ph.

FOUNDATIONS, TRUSTS AND NON-PROFIT ORGANIZATIONS

Asian Women's Human Rights Council—AWHRC

Established in 1990 to foster solidarity amongst women's groups in the Asia region and to promote a feminist and critical perspective on human rights, including focusing on violence against women.

Activities: Pursues human rights for women in Asia through campaigns, lobbying, organizing workshops and conferences, networking, participating in regional and international meetings, conducting fact-finding missions, Women in Black protest actions, and organizing Courts of Women public hearings, as well as through issuing publications and producing and disseminating audio-visual material. AWHRC also maintains a regional office in Bangalore, India and the secretariat rotates between the Philippines and India every five years.

Geographical Area of Activity: Asia.

Publications: *Asia Womenews* (newsletter, 2 a year); *Quilt* (journal); *War and Crimes on Asian Women;* and other publications.

Finance: Funding from foundations and international funding agencies.

Council: Farida Akhter; Aruna Gnanadasan; Neelam Hussain; Wang Jiaxiang; Corinne Kumar; Ruth Manorama; Ita Nadia; Ibu Gedong Bagoes Oka; Eileen Pittaway; Meena Poudel; Nelia Sancho; Siriporn Skrobanek.

Principal Staff: Regional Co-ordinator Corinne Kumar.

Address: 1832 U.P., Bliss Diliman, Quezon City 1101.

Telephone and Fax: (2) 928-9437; e-mail: awhrc_manila@yahoo.com.

Ayala Foundation, Inc

Founded in 1961 by Col Joseph McMicking and his wife Mercedes Zobel to fund projects related to the arts, technology, social sciences and education. Formerly known as the Filipinas Foundation; now the socio-cultural development section of the Ayala Group of companies, one of the largest conglomerates in the Philippines.

Activities: Promotes and advances social development in the Philippines, including providing vocational training for disabled people, and funding environmental projects; technological development; funds cultural programmes, and runs the Ayala Museum. Also owns the Filipinas Heritage Library, the Center for Social Development and the Center of Excellence in Public Elementary Education.

Geographical Area of Activity: Philippines.

Publications: Annual Report.

Finance: Assets 408,952,462 Philippine pesos (1999); annual revenue 108,117,907 pesos, expenditure 119,124,932 pesos (1999).

Directors: Jaime Zobel de Ayala (Chair.); Jaime Augusto Zobel de Ayala, II, Fernando Zobel de Ayala (Vice-Chair.); Mercedita S. Nolledo (Sec.).

Principal Staff: Pres. Victoria P. Garchitorena; Exec. Dir Ma. Aurora F. Tolentino.

Address: 3rd Floor, Garden Square Bldg, cnr Legaspi St and Greenbelt Dr., Makati City.

Telephone: (2) 894-5620; **Fax:** (2) 813-4487; **Internet:** www.ayalafoundation.org; **e-mail:** info@ayalafoundation.org.

Center for the Development of Human Resources in Rural Asia—CENDHRRA

Founded in 1975 to promote the establishment of rural development projects for rural communities in Asia.

Activities: Organizes research into matters concerning rural development; operates training programmes and workshops in conjunction with NGOs; provides information to and encourages communication between those concerned with development projects; maintains a library of about 1,000 volumes.

Geographical Area of Activity: Asia.

Publications: *CENDHRRA Network News; CENDHRRA Development Memo* (10 a year); *Dialogue with Asia's Rural Man and Woman* (series); *CENDHRRA Directory of Development Partners; Solicitudo* (Development Information for Church Leaders); *Priests Forum for Development Newsletter*; monographs and occasional papers.

Trustees: Dr Antonio L. Ledesma (Pres.); Dr Angelita Y. Ledesma (Treas.); Evelyn T. Deles (Sec.); Dr Ngo-Huy Liem; Rafael C. Lopa; Stella Mendoza; Sandra Yu.

Address: POB 458, Greenhills Post Office, Metro Manila 1502.

Telephone: (2) 823-2928; **Fax:** (2) 823-7707; **e-mail:** cendhrra@info.com.ph.

ChildHope Asia Philippines

Established in 1986 in Guatemala, to provide information about the problems of 'street children'—homeless young people living and working in the streets—and previously known as the Childhope International Foundation. Now a network of independent regional and national ChildHope (q.v.) groups operating in the United Kingdom and Europe, Asia and Central and South America. ChildHope Asia Philippines was established in 1989.

Activities: Operates in Asia in the fields of human rights and social welfare, supporting and offering training to projects working with 'street children' in less-developed countries. Provides formal and informal education to street children, mobilizes local communiites against child prostitution, as well as running a drop-in centre for young street girls and girls who have been sexually abused.

Geographical Area of Activity: Asia.

Publications: Newsletter; research reports; directories.

Principal Staff: Regional Rep. Teresita Silva.

Address: 1210 Penafrancia St, Paco 1007, Manila.

Telephone: (2) 563-4647; **Fax:** (2) 563-2242; **Internet:** www.childhope.org.ph; **e-mail:** chap@childhope.org.ph.

Communication Foundation for Asia Media Apostolate

Founded in 1960 by Cornelio Lagerwey to encourage constructive use of the media for education and evangelical purposes, to improve the quality of work in the media industry.

Activities: Conducts seminars and workshops on media and communication, team-building, leadership training and other related programmes; produces videos and radio dramas; issues educational and catechetical publications.

Geographical Area of Activity: Asia.

Publications: *Barkada Magazine* (monthly); *Catholic Digest* (monthly); *Gospel Komiks* (6 a year); *Jesus* (5 a year); *Pambata* (monthly); civic education and catechetical material, manuals, songbooks.

Principal Staff: Pres. Fr Pedro C. Arguillas.

Address: 4427 Old Santa Mesa Rd, POB SM 434, Manila 1016.

Telephone: (2) 713-2981; **Fax:** (2) 713-2731; **Internet:** m-jpic.tripod.com/cfa-ma/; **e-mail:** cfamedia@mozcom.com.

Consuelo Foundation, Inc—CFI

The Foundation, formerly known as the Children and Youth Foundation of the Philippines, seeks to enhance the welfare and improve the prospects of disadvantaged Filipino children and young people, specifically those below 20 years of age, victims of abuse, 'street' children, children of indigenous people, out-of-school youth, child labourers, and those exposed to violence and armed conflict. Founded in 1993 through an affiliation agreement between two USA-based organizations, the Consuelo Foundation and the International Youth Foundation (q.v.). In 1995, it became a subsidiary of the Consuelo Foundation and now oversees children and youth programmes in the Philippines.

Activities: Together with around 90 community-based partner organizations, the Foundation works to give hope to young people, supporting programmes for community development, reproductive health, prevention of child sexual exploitation, and improvement of the lives of street children. It also manages a Resource Center and conducts the annual Consuelo Awards to recognise outstanding NGOs in the Philippines that have made a significant difference to the lives of disadvantaged Filipino children, women and families.

Geographical Area of Activity: Philippines.

Restrictions: Grants only made to partner organizations which must maintain excellent levels of organizational and service delivery standards.

Publications: *Building Bridges: The Development of a Leadership Training Program for Indigenous Youth; Looking After Filipino Children: A Compendium of Philippine Laws and Policies on Youth and Children; A Profile Report of Child and Women Abuse in the Province of Albay 1994–1999.*

Finance: Net assets US $1,377,889 (2001); annual revenue US $2,009,539, expenditure US $1,830,046 (2001).

Board of Trustees: Patti J. Lyons (Pres. and Chair.); Roy Joseph Rafols (Treas. and Sec.); Fe C. Arriola; Anne Marie G. Chanco; Alejandro A. Padilla; Felcitas C. Rixhon; Victor M. Taylor; Daniel Z. Urquico; Jeffrey N. Watanabe.

Principal Staff: Exec. Dir Felicitas C. Roxhon.

Address: 27/f Citibank Tower, Paseo de Roxas, Makati City.

Telephone: (2) 848-0601; **Fax:** (2) 848-0051; **Internet:** www.consuelo.org; **e-mail:** cfprogram@consuelo.org.

Cultural Center of the Philippines

Founded in 1966, the Center is mandated by Philippine Laws

to preserve, promote and enhance the Filipino people's cultural heritage, and to encourage the evolution of the national culture of the Philippines.

Activities: Operates as a national centre for the performing arts; encourages, conserves and disseminates Filipino creativity and artistic experience, through providing artistic programmes, services and facilities. Maintains a library.

Geographical Area of Activity: Philippines.

Publications: Union catalogues on dance, theatre and music, and various monographs.

Board of Trustees: B. N. Endriga (Pres.); P. D. Lagdameo (Chair.); R. Fernando (Co. Sec.); L. Alano-Cabili; D. G. Fernandez; V. L. Locsin; M. T. Mañosa; Fr B. Ma Perez; I. Ponce-Enrile Potenciano; P. C. Sison.

Address: Roxas Blvd, Cultural Center Complex, Pasay City, Metro Manila.

Telephone: (2) 832-1125; **Fax:** (2) 551-5960.

Haribon Foundation for the Conservation of Natural Resources, Inc

Established in 1972 by Alicia Busser, Dr Robert Kennedy and Pedro Gonzales to promote sustainable development for the Philippines, through community-based, socially equitable and scientifically-sound management of natural resources.

Activities: Operates nationally in the field of conservation and the environment, through self-conducted programmes, research, scholarships, conferences, training courses and community-based projects. Key programmes include the Marine Ecosystems Program, the Institutional Partnership Development Program and the Terrestial Ecosystems Program. Maintains links with local and international organizations.

Geographical Area of Activity: Philippines.

Trustees: Dr Reynaldo M. Lesaca (Pres.); Dr Angelina Glang (Vice-Pres.); Belen King (Treas.); Anabel Plantilla (Sec.); Carlos Caliwara; Divina Diokno; Ken Falco; Maximo T. Kalaw; Dr Liana McManus; Cristi Nozawa; Danny Ocampo.

Principal Staff: Exec. Dir Edgardo E. Tongson.

Address: 4F Fil Garcia Tower, 140 Kalayaan Ave, cnr Mayaman St, Diliman, Quezon City.

Telephone: (2) 920-7430; **Fax:** (2) 924-8976; **Internet:** www.haribon.org.ph; **e-mail:** info@haribon.org.ph.

Institute for Sustainable Rural Development Foundation

Founded in 1977 by Portia A. Nayve and Basil A. Rossi to support the research and development of an alternative lifestyle for sustainability.

Activities: The Foundation operates in the fields of conservation and the environment, education, medicine and health, and science and technology, through training courses and research. Runs a humane animal husbandry centre with a variety of poultry and other animals, which are used to stock similar units; various crop varieties are also grown.

Geographical Area of Activity: Philippines.

Publications: Several books and reports on development and alternative agriculture.

Principal Staff: Portia A. Nayve; Basil A. Rossi.

Address: Isarog Farms Palestina, Pili Camarines Sur, Bicol Bioregion.

International Institute of Rural Reconstruction

Established in 1960 to improve the quality of life of disadvantaged people living in developing countries of Asia, Africa, and Central and South America.

Activities: Operates internationally in the areas of aid to less-developed countries, and conservation and the environment, through projects promoting long-term sustainable development and self-sufficiency for people in poor communities. Programmes operate in the areas of education, the environment, development, health care and rural enterprise. In 1999 launched the Y. C. James Yen Citizens of the World Award to recognise individual commitment and accomplishment. Also trains local NGO and government leaders in order to increase efficiency in development work; and organizes international conferences.

Geographical Area of Activity: Africa, Asia, and Central and South America.

Publications: Produces a number of publications relating to sustainable development.

Board of Trustees: Michael S. Gerber (Chair.); J. Eugene Marans (Vice-Chair.); Pratima Kale (Pres.); Scott Killough (Vice-Pres.); James F. Kelly (Treas.); Jeffrey T. Olson (Sec.); Helena Z. Benitez; Jane K. Boorstein; Ping-sheng Yen Chin; J. Lin Compton; Joanne de Asis; James C. Diao; Anthony C. Gooch; Donald L. Holley; Pam S. Levin; Mary Racelis; G.N. Reddi; Francis M. Ssekandi; Washington SyCip.

Principal Staff: Pres. Pratima Kale.

Address: Y. C. James Yen Center, Silang, Cavite 4118.

Telephone: (46) 414-2417; **Fax:** (46) 414-4240; **Internet:** www.iirr.org; **e-mail:** information@iirr.org.

Ramon Magsaysay Award Foundation

Founded in 1957 by Belen H. Abreu, Paz Marquez Benitez, Jaime N. Ferrer, Jesus Magsaysay, Francisco Ortigas, Jr, Pedro Tuason and Leopoldo Uichanco, to honour the late Ramon Magsaysay, President of the Philippines, to perpetuate his memory and give concrete recognition and meaning to the ideals which characterized his life; to develop a systematic programme of annual awards to be known as the Ramon Magsaysay Award for persons in the Philippines and other Asian countries whose activities in different fields of service and endeavour best exemplify the life and ideals of Ramon Magsaysay.

Activities: Confers the Ramon Magsaysay Award: six annual awards of US $50,000 each are offered in the fields of government service; public service; community leadership; journalism, literature and creative communication arts; international understanding; and since 2001, emergency leadership. Also operates the Program for Asian Projects, to enable awardees to develop their projects and runs an essay writing competition. The Foundation maintains an Asian Library, housing an extensive collection of reference materials on contemporary Asia, as well as the Magsaysay Papers. Also organizes international seminars on issues affecting the Asian region, and offers film and slide presentations on the peoples and cultures of the region to secondary school pupils.

Geographical Area of Activity: Asia.

Restrictions: Grants are made only to people or institutions whose work is in Asia.

Publications: Newsletter.

Finance: Funded by the Rockefeller Brothers Fund (q.v.) from 1958 to 1968, the Foundation is now supported by the income from the Ramon Magsaysay Center, which it owns. The Rockefeller Brothers Fund grants approx. US $150,000 annually to support the awards.

Governing Board: Randolf S. David (Chair.).

Principal Staff: Pres. Carmencita T. Abella.

Address: Ramon Magsaysay Center, 1680 Roxas Blvd, Metro Manila.

Telephone: (2) 521-3166; **Fax:** (2) 521-8105; **Internet:** www.rmaf.org.ph; **e-mail:** rmaf@rmaf.org.ph.

Philippine–American Education Foundation

Founded in 1948 (as the United States Educational Foundation in the Philippines, present name 1969) by the Governments of the USA and the Republic of the Philippines to promote further mutual understanding by a wider exchange of knowledge and professional talents through educational contacts.

Activities: Operates both nationally and internationally in sponsoring research, educational conferences, lectures, seminars and scholarship and fellowship programmes, notably educational exchanges between students from the USA and the Philippines, the Philippine Fulbright Program for study in the USA, the Hubert H. Humphrey North–South Fellowship Program for professional candidates, and the East–West Center student degree awards providing financial assistance to students from the Philippines studying at the University of Hawaii. Also provides information and counselling services, and maintains an information resource library on American universities.

Geographical Area of Activity: North America and the Philippines.

Finance: Income is derived from the Governments of the USA and the Philippines, from private agencies and individuals.

Address: 3rd Floor, Accelerando Bldg, 395 Senator Gil J. Puyat Ave, Makati City 1200.

Telephone: (2) 812-0919; **Fax:** (2) 812-0822; **Internet:** www.paef.org.ph; **e-mail:** fulbright@paef.org.ph.

Press Foundation of Asia

Founded in 1968 by a group of Asian publishers and editors concerned about the failure of newspapers to relate fully to the needs and aspirations of the fast-developing Asian nations; the Foundation aims to improve editorial, production and management techniques, and to instil in journalists and publishers an awareness of their role and responsibilities.

Activities: The Foundation's training programme comprises intensive courses, seminars and workshops for journalists, dealing with coverage of different topics such as development economics, energy, science and the environment; it also provides training in new printing technology, design and marketing. The Foundation collaborates with national press institutions throughout the region, provides consultancy and information services, and operates a scheme whereby Western journalists are invited to participate in the Foundation's work and gain Asian experience. A databank is maintained and training manuals are published. Members are newspapers in 24 countries and territories of Asia and Australasia.

Geographical Area of Activity: Asia and Australasia.

Publications: *Environment Folio* (quarterly); *Asian Forum Newsletter; Asian Women and Children; PRESSASIA* (bulletin).

Finance: The Foundation was established with an endowment of US $600,000, and receives grants from other foundations, funds and newspapers, and donations.

Board of Directors: M. Nordin (Exec. Chair.); Tsuneo Watanabe (Vice-Chair.); M. Lubis (Chief Exec.); J. Mercado (Chief Operating Officer); K. Jasin; Kim Jin-Hyun; R. L. Locsin; Gengo Nakajima.

Principal Staff: Sec.-Gen. Khairul Bashar.

Address: 27 Tagbilaran St, Alabang Hills, Muntinlupa City, Metro Manila; POB 1843, Manila 1000, Metro Manila.

Telephone: (2) 523-3223; **Fax:** (2) 522-4365; **Internet:** www.pressfoundationofasia.com; **e-mail:** pfa@pressasia.org.

Tebtebba Foundation for Indigenous Peoples

Established in 1996; aims to resolve conflicts and promote sustainable development in indigenous communities.

Activities: Works internationally in the field of law and human rights, as an advocate to attain peace and social justice in indigenous territories around the world, and to promote indigenous rights. Provides training for indigenous leaders and acts as a consultant to indigenous organizations. Also disseminates information about issues affecting indigenous people, carries out research and holds conferences.

Geographical Area of Activity: International.

Address: 111 Upper Gen. Luna St, POB 1993, Baguio City 2600.

Telephone: (74) 443-9459; **Fax:** (74) 443-9459; **Internet:** www.skyinet.net/~tebtebba; **e-mail:** tebtebba@skyinet.net.

Villar Foundation Inc

Established by Manuel B. Villar, Jr and others in 1987 to initiate, undertake, support or otherwise foster educational, cultural, scientific, charitable and civic activities aimed at benefiting the Filipino people, in particular the poor and needy.

Activities: Operates financial assistance or incentive programmes for young people, aiming at skills development and livelihood assistance; socio-civic, cultural, educational, religious, scientific and technological projects for the social or economic amelioration of poor and needy Filipino people; social welfare and relief services for the poor; tree planting and other conservation programmes including historical preservation.

Geographical Area of Activity: Philippines.

Publications: Annual Report.

Principal Staff: Chair. Manuel B. Villar, Jr; Pres. Cynthia A. Villar; Treas. Jerry M. Navarrete; Exec. Dir Rhaegee B. Tamaña.

Address: C. Masibay St., BF Resort Village, Talon, Las Pinas City.

Telephone: (2) 872-3705; **Fax:** (2) 872-8540; **e-mail:** cvillar@surfshop.net.ph.

Poland

FOUNDATION CENTRES AND CO-ORDINATING BODIES

Academy for the Development of Philanthropy in Poland

Established in 1998; aims to support philanthropy in Poland and to promote its development and the long-term sustainability of Poland's third sector.

Activities: Promotes philanthropy in Poland and supports the development of the third sector, through a local grants programme, a grant programme for organizations promoting Polish–Jewish dialogue, a local youth fund, scholarships for young gifted people and participation in international philanthropy networks. Also operates the Benefactor of the Year competition, recognising corporate philanthropists in Poland.

Geographical Area of Activity: Poland.

Publications: *The White Book of Philanthropy—Coalition for Better Law.*

Address: ul. Poznańska 16 m. 7, 00-680 Warsaw.

Telephone: (22) 6220200; **Fax:** (22) 6220211; **Internet:** www.filantropia.org.pl; **e-mail:** arfp@filantropia.org.pl.

KLON/JAWOR

Established in 1990 as part of the Regardless of the Weather Foundation to provide access to information so as to promote the development of civil society; became independent in 2000.

Activities: Promotes the development of civil society through maintaining a database of Polish NGOs (JAWOR); conducting research, especially on the third sector in the European Union and local government and NGOs; supporting NGOs; issuing publications; promoting European networking; an internet programme; and generally assisting NGOs in their operations. Runs SPLOT, the Network of Information and Support Centers for NGOs.

Geographical Area of Activity: Poland.

Publications: *JAWOR; KLON; Citizen Information Center; Warsaw Information Guide for Senior; The Third Sector in the European Union; Know Your Rights* (series); and other publications on NGOs in Poland.

Address: ul. Szpitalna 5, lok. 5, 00-031 Warsaw.

Telephone: (22) 8289128; **Fax:** (22) 8289129; **Internet:** www.klon.org.pl; **e-mail:** klon@klon.org.pl.

FOUNDATIONS, TRUSTS AND NON-PROFIT ORGANIZATIONS

Barka Foundation

Founded in 1991 by Tomasz Sadowski, Maria Garwolińska and Barbara Sadowska to promote improved living and working conditions.

Activities: Operates in Poland, France, Germany and the Netherlands in the field of social welfare, through self-conducted programmes, scholarships, prizes, conferences, training courses and publications; assists the homeless through self-help projects throughout Poland; encourages co-operation and communication between NGOs. Operates four programmes in the fields of the community, social education, employment opportunity and housing. The Foundation also established the Poland-wide Confederation for Social Employment, which provides support to the long-term unemployed and homeless people.

Geographical Area of Activity: Poland, France, Germany and the Netherlands.

Publications: *Citizens' Initiatives of Greater Poland, Barka Bulletin.*

Finance: The Government of Poland provides 5% of the Foundation's funds.

Trustees: Tomasz Sadowski (Pres.); Krystyna Dorsz (Vice-Pres.).

Principal Staff: Teresa Belter.

Address: ul. Sw. Marcin 30/14, 61-806 Poznań.

Telephone and Fax: (61) 8532148; **Internet:** www.barka.org.pl; **e-mail:** barka@barka.org.pl.

Stefan Batory Foundation

Founded by George Soros in May 1988, to support the development of Polish society in the areas of science, culture, education, information and civil society, so as to strengthen democracy and free markets and encourage co-operation between the countries of Central and Eastern Europe. The Foundation is part of the Soros foundations network.

Activities: The Foundation supports the development of a democratic and open society. Through 15 programmes, the Foundation aims to foster civic attitudes and initiatives; increase co-operation between nations; advance educational development; and support cultural activity.

Geographical Area of Activity: Poland and Europe.

Restrictions: Grants only to organizations based in Poland.

Publications: Annual Report; *Stefan Batory Foundation Bulletin.*

Finance: Annual expenditure US $8,120,000 (2000).

Board of Directors: Aleksander Smolar (Chair.); T. Bogucka; N. Bolgert; G. Lindenberg; M. Nawrocki; J. Wygnanski; A. Ziabicki.

Principal Staff: Exec. Dir Anna Rozicka.

Address: ul. Sapiezzyńska 10A, 00-215 Warsaw.

Telephone: (22) 5360200; **Fax:** (22) 5360220; **Internet:** www.batory.org.pl; **e-mail:** batory@batory.org.pl.

Commercial Law Center Foundation

Established in December 1993 by the Polish Bar Association Foundation, Warsaw District Chamber of Legal Advisers and the Warsaw branch of the Polish Lawyers' Association, to inspire, support and organize co-operation among Polish legal practitioners; to collaborate with similar organizations abroad; and to offer facilities for learning Polish and foreign commercial law.

Activities: Operates nationally and internationally in the fields of economic affairs, education and law and human rights, through research, conferences and training courses. Maintains a computerized information centre for Polish lawyers and a library of books on USA and international law.

Board of Directors: A. Tynel (Chair.); J. Biejat; R. Malecki; I. Mirosz; S. Rymar; A. Staroń.

Principal Staff: Pres. Maciej Lach; Krystyna Sajna-Paliwoda; Pawel Swirski.

Address: al. Ujazdowskie 49, 00-536 Warsaw.

Telephone: (22) 6214412; **Fax:** (22) 6285685; **Internet:** www.prawo.org.pl; **e-mail:** info@prawo.org.pl.

Economic Foundation

Established in March 1990 by the National Commission (NSZZ) of Solidarność (Solidarity) to confront the problems of unemployment and education.

Activities: Organizes programmes in Poland in the fields of trade union education and economic affairs. Projects include establishing an international system of exhange for economic information, promoting small businesses, programmes to reduce unemployment, and social activities programmes. The Foundation holds conferences; organizes consultancy programmes, providing 'start-up' packs for people intending to start in business; and runs an occupational information centre for secondary-school students.

Geographical Area of Activity: Poland.

Publications: *Economics; Career Skills; Labour Code*; several publications of interest to the unemployed and people in business.

Principal Staff: Irena Muszkiewicz-Herok; Roman Schefke; Barbara Werner.

Address: ul. Olimpijska 2, 81-538 Gdynia.

Telephone: (58) 6222052; **Fax:** (58) 6225985; **Internet:** www.fungo.com.pl; **e-mail:** fungos@fungo.com.pl.

Foundation in Support of Local Democracy—FSLD

(Fundacja Rozwoju Demokracji Loaklnej)

Founded in September 1989 by Prof. Jerzy Regulski, Andrzej Celiński, Aleksander Paszyński, Walerian Pańko and Jerzy Stępień to promote civic self-government at local level.

Activities: Operates in the fields of education, and law and human rights, through self-conducted programmes, grants to institutions, conferences, training courses, publications, internet information systems and offering technical assistance. The Foundation's main activities are training and education programmes for local government officers, councillors, NGOs, community leaders and local business people; and consulting services in the technical areas of local government. Also involved in sharing the Polish experience in building democracy with other countries of Central, Eastern and Southern Europe and Kazakhstan.

Geographical Area of Activity: Poland, Central, Eastern and Southern Europe and Kazakhstan.

Publications: Publications on local government, legal and economic issues.

Finance: Finance is provided by national and foreign sponsors, the Foundation's own income and programmes; total assets €3,317,651 (2001); total income €140,993 (2001).

Supervisory Board: Prof. Jerzy Regulski (Chair.); Adam Kowalewski (Vice-Chair.); Iwo Byczewski; Janusz Kindler; Jan Król; Zbigniew Niemczycki; Grzegorz Nowakowski; Wieslaw Sikorski.

Principal Staff: Pres., Exec. Bd Krzysztof Lipski; Vice-Pres. Exec. Bd Barbara Imiolczyk, Irena Peszko.

Address: ul. Hauke-Bosaka 11, 01-540 Warsaw.

Telephone: (22) 8699200; **Fax:** (22) 8392285; **Internet:** www.frdl.org.pl; **e-mail:** biuro@frdl.org.pl.

France–Pologne pour l'Europe (France Poland for Europe)

Founded in 1990 as the Fondation de Pologne, the representative office of the Fondation de France (q.v.), registered as a Polish foundation in July 1996, to support the development of the non-profit sector in Poland, especially in the areas of education, social welfare, culture and local development; in 2003 re-launched as France–Pologne pour l'Europe.

Activities: The Foundation gives financial support through two main programmes, the Open School and the Organization of Leisure Time for Disadvantaged Children and Youth. Also awards prizes: the Andrzej Baczkowski Prize for individuals or institutions that have contributed to social dialogue in Poland, or to the implementation of social policy reforms; and the Baczko-Zakrzewski Prize for young architects, in particular those working in the field of public utility buildings. Currently designing new programmes.

Geographical Area of Activity: Poland.

Publications: Information brochure; newsletter (in Polish and French), grants list.

Finance: Financed by the Fondation de France, the French Caisse des Dépôts et Consignations (Bank of Security Deposits), French and Polish businesses, and private foundations and donors.

Executive Committee: Helena Góralska (Pres.); Pierre Giraudet (Hon. Pres.); Benedetta D'Aboville; Jacques de Chalendar; Anne Duruflé-Lozinski; Krzysztof Herbst; Maria Kotowska; Ryszard Praszkier; Patrick Rolland; Paweł Rozwadowski; Karol Sachs; Anne-Marie Seydoux.

Principal Staff: Dir Katarzyna Morawska; Magdalena Rodak; Teresa Zagrodzka.

Address: ul. L. Narbutta 27 m. 1,02-536 Warsaw.

Telephone: (22) 8810416; **Fax:** (22) 6463323; **Internet:** www.affp.org; **e-mail:** france-pologne-europe.wwa@affp.org.

Fundacja Bankowa im. Leopolda Kronenberga

(Leopold Kronenberg Foundation)

Established to mark the 125th anniversary of Bank Handlowy Warszawie SA to support general charitable work in Poland.

Activities: Operates in the areas of education, science, the arts and humanities, health care and social welfare, by supporting organizations and projects engaged in work in these areas. Also presents prizes for entrepreneurship.

Geographical Area of Activity: Poland.

Restrictions: Grants only to non-profit organizations in Poland.

Finance: Financed by the Bank Handlowy Warszawie SA.

Advisory Council: Prof. A. Rottermund (Chair.); Prof. H. Skarzyński (Vice-Chair.).

Principal Staff: Man. Dir Krzysztof Kaczmar.

Address: Traugutta 7/9, 00-950 Warsaw.

Telephone: (22) 8269051; **Fax:** (22) 6925095; **Internet:** www.kronenberg.org.pl; **e-mail:** poczta@kronenberg.org.pl.

Fundacja Biblioteka Ekologiczna (Ecological Library Foundation)

Founded in November 1988 by Jacek Purat.

Activities: The Foundation operates in the fields of conservation and the environment and economic affairs, through research, conferences, publications and a library. It distributes books; conducts research; organizes conferences; presents films; has established an ecological library; and organizes projects for the protection of endangered species in Poland.

Geographical Area of Activity: Poland.

Principal Staff: Pres. Jacek Purat; Jarosław Fiszer.

Address: ul. Kościuszki 79, 61-715 Poznań.

Telephone: (61) 521325; **Fax:** (61) 528276.

Fundacja Pogranicze (Borderland Foundation)

Established in 1990 to carry out cultural activities in Central and Eastern Europe.

Activities: Operates in the countries of Central and Eastern Europe in the fields of the arts and humanities, education, and law and human rights, through self-conducted programmes, conferences, training courses and publications. Maintains a library and an arts and cultural centre.

Geographical Area of Activity: Central and Eastern Europe.

Publications: *Krasnobruda* (quarterly, in Polish and English); also history books, literary criticism, poetry.

Finance: Annual budget approx. 400,000 new złotys.

Trustee: The Polish Ministry of Culture and Arts.

Principal Staff: Pres. Krzysztof Czyżewski.

Address: ul. Kościuszki 71, POB 36, 16-400 Suwalki.

Telephone and Fax: (87) 5650369; **Internet:** pogranicze .sejny.pl; **e-mail:** fundacja@pogranicze.sejny.pl.

Fundacja Trust for Civil Society in Central and Eastern Europe

Established in 2001, a consortium of grant-making organizations, including the Charles Stewart Mott Foundation, the Ford Foundation, the Open Society Institute, the German Marshall Fund of the United States and the Rockefeller Brothers Fund (qq.v.), formed to promote the development of civil society in Central and Eastern Europe.

Activities: Operates in seven countries of Central and Eastern Europe, promoting the development of indigenous third-sector organizations, through making grants to local intermediary non-profit organizations, for distribution to local NGOs.

Geographical Area of Activity: Bulgaria, the Czech Republic, Hungary, Poland, Romania, Slovakia and Slovenia.

Finance: Aims to have a fund of US $75,000,000 to be spent over 10 years.

Principal Staff: Exec. Dir Jacek Wojnarowski.

Address: ul. Solariego 1, 02-070 Warsaw.

Telephone: (22) 5768090; **Fax:** (22) 8259211; **e-mail:** trust@ trust.org.pl.

Institute for Private Enterprise and Democracy

Established in 1992 by the Polish Chamber of Commerce to carry out research into the Polish private sector and economic policy, and to support the development of the private sector.

Activities: Operates in Poland in the areas of economic affairs and social welfare, through research, conferences and the publication of policy and economic reports. Major projects include: a report on the state of the private sector in Poland; a study on the reform of the Polish tax system; business ethics and social responsibility; Polish women in private business; regional development and the promotion of entrepreneurship; legislative monitoring; and monitoring barriers to the development of small- and medium-sized enterprises and their financing in Poland. Supports the network of Chambers of Commerce in Poland.

Geographical Area of Activity: Poland.

Publications: *Influence of Justice on SME Development in Poland; Capital Investment Funding in Poland; Co-operation of NGOs with Local Self-Government; Economic Reform Today; Development of Entrepreneurship in Rural Areas; Sources of Inflation in Poland; Informal Labour Market; Dilemmas and Chances of Rural Development;* numerous other reports.

Principal Staff: Pres. and CEO Mieczysław Bąk; Vice-Pres. and Dir Int. Programs Prof. Tomasz Mroczkowski.

Address: ul. Trębacka 4, Rm 321, 00-074 Warsaw.

Telephone: (22) 8262596; **Fax:** (22) 8274673; **Internet:** www.iped.pl; **e-mail:** info@iped.pl.

Microfinance Centre for Central and Eastern Europe and the New Independent States

Established in 1997, a network of 70 microfinance organizations, to support such organizations in Central and Eastern Europe and the countries of the former USSR (New Independent States), in order to advance the economic development of these countries, improve employment, and alleviate poverty through microfinance.

Activities: Provides high quality training and technical assistance, impact assessments, conferences, workshops, seminars, and exchange visits, and organizes networking opportunities between policy and advocacy projects related to the microfinance legislative environment, through the undertaking of legal diagnostics and the centralization and dissemination of information.

Geographical Area of Activity: Central and Eastern Europe, and the New Independent States.

Publications: Newsletter.

Finance: Sources of finance are grants (including grants from the Ford Foundation, Open Society Institute q.q.v., and US Aid), training and conference fees. Net assets US $417,100 (2002); total revenue US $923,100, expenditure US $968,200 (2002).

Directors: Ken Vander Weele; Maria Nowak; Caroline Tsilikounas; Mariam Yesayan; Gert van Maanen; Tamar Lebanidze; Nejira Nalic.

Principal Staff: Exec. Dir Grzegorz Galusek; Dir, Training and Consulting John Guzowski; Research Co-ordinator Katarzyna Pawlak.

Address: ul. Koszykowa 60/62 m. 52, 00-673 Warsaw.

Telephone: (22) 6223465; **Fax:** (22) 6223485; **Internet:** www.mfc.org.pl; **e-mail:** microfinance@mfc.org.pl.

Polish–American Freedom Foundation

Established by the Polish–American Freedom Fund in the USA in 1999; began operating in Warsaw in 1999. Aims to support the development of civil society, democracy and a market economy in Poland.

Activities: Provides support to NGOs in Poland active in the areas of education, democracy and transformation, and operates a grant fund supporting local communities. Maintains an office in the USA.

Geographical Area of Activity: Poland.

Publications: Annual Report.

Finance: Total assets US $120,785,067 (Sept. 2001); total income US $4,262,241, total expenditure US $1,115,687 (2001).

Address: ul. Dobra 72, 00-312 Warsaw.

Telephone: (22) 8284373; **Fax:** (22) 8284372; **Internet:** www.pafw.pl; **e-mail:** paff@pafw.pl.

Polish–Czech–Slovak Solidarity Foundation

Established in 1990 by Jarosław Broda, Zbigniew Janas, Mirosław Jasiński and Mieczysław Piotrowski for the support of Polish–Czech–Slovak solidarity activities.

Activities: Operates in Central and Eastern Europe in the areas of aid to less-developed countries, the arts and humanities, education, independent media, international affairs, through self-conducted programmes, grants to institutions, conferences, training courses and publications.

Geographical Area of Activity: Central and Eastern Europe.

Trustees: Jarosław Szostakowski (Pres.); Julian Golak; Wojciech Król; Zbigniew Machej; Warcisław Martynowski; Zbigniew Niewiarowski.

Principal Staff: Katarzyna Krajewska.

Address: 5th Floor, ul. Flory 9, 00-586 Warsaw.

Telephone: (22) 481605; **Fax:** (22) 494978; **Internet:** free .ngo.pl/spczs; **e-mail:** spczs@free.ngo.pl.

Polish Environmental Partnership Foundation

Established in 1992 as a Programme Office of the German Marshall Fund of the United States (q.v.), present name and status since 1997, when it was registered as a foundation in Poland. It aims to promote and support non-profit organizations and communities which implement environmental projects, where these contribute to the development of democracy in Poland. Currently, the Partnership operates as part of the Environmental Partnership for Central Europe (EPCE, q.v.) consortium, which supports grass-roots environmental action in Central Europe. Sister foundations operate within the framework of the Consortium in the Czech Republic, Slovakia, Hungary and Romania.

Activities: Helps NGOs and local communities to solve environmental problems by supporting partnership action with the Government, businesses, universities and individuals. Provides direct financial support and technical assistance for community development. Maintains an Environmental Information Centre, disseminating information through weekly and monthly bulletins, providing a helpline for members and access to information resources.

Geographical Area of Activity: Central Europe.

Restrictions: Grants made only to NGOs registered in, and operating in, Poland.

Publications: Annual Report.

Finance: Financed by foundations; assistance programmes and businesses.

Trustees: J. Michalowski (Chair.); T. Borys; P. Czajkowski; M. Haliniak; E. Moczarska; J. Ozga; Tomás Ruzička; W. Sartorius; H. Wujek.

Principal Staff: Dir Rafal Serafin; Deputy Dir Krysztof Kwatera; Grants Officer Anna Woźniak.

Address: Bracka 6/6, 31-005 Kraków.

Telephone: (12) 4225088; **Fax:** (12) 4294725; **Internet:** www.epce.org.pl; **e-mail:** biuro@epce.org.pl.

Polska Fundacja Upowszechniania Nauki (Polish Foundation for Science Advancement)

Established in 1990 by the Polish Academy of Sciences, the Society for the Advancement of Sciences and Arts, the Society of the Polish Free University, the Scientific Publications Distribution Centre and the Polish Scientific Film Association. It is a leading non-profit organization working for the dissemination of Polish science in Poland and abroad, and for the diffusion of foreign science in Poland.

Activities: Operates nationally and internationally in the fields of education and science and technology, through conducting research and promoting public understanding of science; publishing books and producing films and audio-visual materials for teaching and study; organizing courses, seminars and competitions; supporting the activities of Polish institutions and scientific associations in Poland and abroad in the advancement of science; granting aid to foreign organizations seeking to promote knowledge in Poland of the scientific achievements of their respective countries. Three major achievements of the Foundation are Internet at Schools, a programme initiated by the President of the Polish Republic; the Post-Graduate Science Communication and Media Studies programme undertaken jointly with the Institute for Literary Research of the Polish Academy of Sciences; and establishing the Open Television University in Poland.

Geographical Area of Activity: Europe and USA.

Publications: Brochures and books.

Council: Prof. Witold Karczewski (Pres.); Prof. Kazimierz Frieske; Prof. Janusz Haman; Dr Mikołłaj Lipowski; Prof. Wacłław Strykowski; Prof. Saturnin Zawadzki.

Principal Staff: Prof. Janusz Haman; Dir Wojciech Wiśniewski.

Address: Pałac Kultury i Nauki, POB 27, 00-901 Warsaw.

Telephone: (22) 6209174; **Fax:** (22) 6209174; **Internet:** www.pan.pl/pfun; **e-mail:** pfun@pan.pl.

Pro Bono Foundation

Established in 1993 by a group of people connected with the pastoral services for the universities affiliated with the Rectory of St. Ann's Academic Church in Warsaw.

Activities: Supports NGOs in Poland active in the areas of charity, cultural and educational work, as well as funding Catholic organizations, the conservation of works of art and the promotion of the Catholic press. Funded projects include orphanages, symposia and scholarships, medical costs and community centres. The Foundation has also established an art gallery to promote the work of young artists.

Geographical Area of Activity: Poland.

Principal Staff: Pres. Bogdan Bartold.

Address: ul. Krakowskie Przedmiescie 68, 00-322 Warsaw.

Telephone: (22) 8283103; **Fax:** (22) 8453231; **Internet:** www.probono.art.pl; **e-mail:** galeria@probono.org.pl.

J&S Pro Bono Poloniae Foundation

Established by the J&S Group.

Activities: The Foundation makes donations to NGOs running programmes in the areas of education, culture and social communication.

Geographical Area of Activity: Poland.

Address: ul. Podchorązzch 83–4, 00-722 Warsaw.

Internet: www.jsprobono.pl; **e-mail:** fundacja@jsprobono.pl.

Stiftung für Deutsch–Polnische Zusammenarbeit (Foundation for German–Polish Co-operation)

Established in 1991 by the Governments of Poland and Germany to sponsor non-commercial projects of German–Polish interest.

Activities: Operates in Poland in the fields of the arts and humanities, conservation and the environment, education, international affairs, medicine and health, science and technology, and social welfare and social studies, through research, grants to institutions, scholarships and fellowships, conferences, training courses and publications.

Geographical Area of Activity: Germany and Poland.

Publications: Annual Report.

Finance: Total donations 1991–2001 approx. €250,000,000.

Address: ul. Zielna 37, 00-108 Warsaw.

Telephone and Fax: (22) 6253418; **Internet:** www.fwpn.org.pl; **e-mail:** fwpn@fwpn.org.pl.

Portugal

FOUNDATION CENTRE AND CO-ORDINATING BODY

Portuguese Foundation Centre

Established in 1993 by the Fundação Oriente (q.v.) in association with the Fundação Eng. António de Almeida and the Calouste Gulbenkian Foundation (qq.v.).

Activities: A membership organization of more than 80 foundations and trusts that operates to promote the interests of foundations in Portugal through co-operation and support.

Geographical Area of Activity: Portugal.

Principal Staff: Asst Custodia Marques.

Address: c/o Fundação Oriente, Rua do Salitre 62–66, 1269-065 Lisbon.

Telephone: (21) 3528280; **Fax:** (21) 3538285; **e-mail:** fundoriente@mail.telepac.pt.

FOUNDATIONS, TRUSTS AND NON-PROFIT ORGANIZATIONS

Fundação Eng. António de Almeida (Eng. António de Almeida Foundation)

Founded in 1969 at the bequest of Eng. António de Almeida to promote art, culture and education for all people, and with philanthropic aims.

Activities: The Foundation sponsors art exhibitions and musical recitals; makes grants to cultural institutions in Portugal and to Portuguese graduates for research work; awards the Prémio Eng. António de Almeida prize annually to students from six universities who have excelled in dedication to their studies; holds international conferences; and issues cultural publications. The Foundation also maintains a museum of art to exhibit items collected by the founder, which include furniture, textiles, porcelain, paintings, time-pieces and an important numismatic collection.

Geographical Area of Activity: Portugal.

Publications: Annual Report; periodical magazines in the spheres of literature, philosophy, ethnography and museums, and non-periodical magazines on art, culture and science.

Governing Board: Pres. Dr Fernando Aguiar-Branco.

Address: Rua Tenente Valadim 231–325, 4100-479 Porto.

Telephone: (22) 6067418; **Fax:** (22) 6004314; **Internet:** www.feaa.pt; **e-mail:** fundacao@feaa.pt.

Fundação Assistência Médica International (International Medical Assistance Foundation)

Established in October 1992 by Dr Fernando de la Vieter Nobre to provide medical and humanitarian aid world-wide.

Activities: Operates internationally in the fields of aid to less-developed countries, education, medicine and health, and social welfare, through self-conducted programmes, grants to institutions, conferences, training courses and publications. Awards the AMI Journalism Against Indifference prize.

Geographical Area of Activity: International.

Publications: *Ami Notícias* (quarterly).

Trustees: Dr Fernando de la Vieter Nobre (Pres.); Leonor Nobre (Vice-Pres.); Luisa Nemésio (Gen. Sec.).

Principal Staff: Pres. Dr Fernando de la Vieter Nobre.

Address: Patio Manuel Guerreiro, Rua José do Patrocínio 49, Marvila, 1949-008 Lisbon.

Telephone: (21) 8362100; **Fax:** (21) 8362199; **Internet:** www.fundacao-ami.org; **e-mail:** fundacao-ami@mail.telepac.pt.

Fundação da Casa de Mateus (Mateus House Foundation)

Established in 1970 by Francisco de Sousa Botelho de Albuquerque, Count of Mangualde, Vila Real and Melo to maintain the Casa de Mateus, study and publish its archives, and promote scientific, cultural and pedagogical activities.

Activities: The Foundation operates in the fields of the arts and humanities, including music, history and literature; and science. Part of the House is maintained as a museum. The Foundation awards the Prémio D. Diniz and the Prémio Morgado de Mateus in the field of literature. Courses in theatre, sculpture, drawing and painting are also held at the Foundation, as are exhibitions and seminars. The Foundation chairs the International Institute Casa de Mateus, established in 1986 by Portuguese public universities, academies and scientific institutes, which organizes meetings of national and foreign scientists. Has set up an artists' residence for artists from any country.

Geographical Area of Activity: Portugal.

Finance: Annual expenditure approx. 300,000,000 escudos.

Board of Directors: Fernando de Albuquerque (Chair. and Chief Exec.); Adriano Jordão (Musical Dir); Francisco de Albuquerque; Isabel de Albuquerque Taylor; Alain Demoustier; Vasco Graça Moura; Miguel Veiga.

Address: 5000-291 Vila Real.

Telephone: (259) 323121; **Fax:** (259) 326553; **e-mail:** casa.mateus@mail.telepac.pt.

Fundação Casa-Museu Mário Botas (Mário Botas House-Museum Foundation)

Established in 1984 by Mário Ferreira da Silva Botas to promote education, art, science and philanthropy nationally and internationally, and to promote the art of Mário Botas.

Activities: Awards scholarships and the Mário Botas Prize. Maintains an office in Lisbon.

Geographical Area of Activity: International.

Finance: Initial fund US $1,200,000.

Principal Staff: Chair. Dr Benigno José Mira Almeida Faria.

Address: Rua dos Barrancos, Apdo 171, 2450-901 Nazaré.

Telephone: (262) 560363.

Fundação Centro Cultural de Belém (Belém Cultural Centre Foundation)

Established in 1991 by the Government of Portugal and several Portuguese companies to promote culture and the arts, especially Portuguese culture. Formerly known as Fundação das Descobertas.

Activities: The Foundation's main aims are to manage the Belém Cultural Centre, run a permanent museum and a document centre, and facilitate exchanges with similar Portuguese and foreign institutions.

Geographical Area of Activity: Portugal.

Principal Staff: Pres. Prof. Frausto Da Silva; Dr Adelaide Rocha; Dr F. Hotta Veiga.

Address: Praça do Império, 1400 Lisbon.

Telephone: (21) 3612400; **Fax:** (21) 3612500; **Internet:** www.ccb.pt; **e-mail:** ccb@ccb.pt.

Fundação Cidade de Lisboa (City of Lisbon Foundation)

Founded in 1989.

Activities: Operates nationally and in Angola, Cape Verde, Mozambique and São Tomé and Príncipe, in the fields of aid to less-developed countries and education, through self-conducted programmes, grants to individuals and institutions, scholarships and prizes, and conferences.

Geographical Area of Activity: Portugal, Angola, Cape Verde, Mozambique and São Tomé and Príncipe.

Publications: Several books.

Trustees: Nuno Krus Abecasis; Eduardo Arantos Oliveira; João Correa Nunes; José Manuel Sousa; José Megre.

Principal Staff: Sec.-Gen. José Filipe Nogueira.

Address: Av. Miguel Bombarda 36, 9°F, 1050 Lisbon.

Telephone: (21) 7937329; **Fax:** (21) 7974022.

Fundação Dom Manuel II (Dom Manuel II Foundation)

Established in August 1966 by Dona Augusta Viktoria, Duchess of Bragança, widow of King Dom Manuel II of Portugal to help Portuguese emigrants.

Activities: Operates in the areas of aid to less-developed countries, conservation and the environment, education and social welfare, through self-conducted programmes, awarding prizes, and organizing conferences and training courses. Provides help in the areas of housing, integration of Portuguese emigrants into local communities, and education. Has established a subsidiary in Timor Leste, the Timorese Cultural Foundation, which operates a printing factory.

Geographical Area of Activity: Europe, Portuguese-speaking Africa, Timor Leste and Brazil.

Publications: *Futuro Real* (Bulletin).

Finance: Funded by donations and income from rented property.

Trustees: The Duke of Bragança (Pres.); Dr Augusto de Athayde; Dr Augusto de Amaral.

Principal Staff: Man. Nelson Figueiredo; Sec. Rosa Pratas.

Address: Rua Duques de Bragança 10, 1200-162 Lisbon.

Telephone: (21) 3423705; **Fax:** (21) 9242423; **Internet:** www.duke-of-braganza.com; **e-mail:** secretariado@casareal.co.pt.

Fundação Ricardo do Espírito Santo Silva (Ricardo do Espírito Santo Silva Foundation)

Founded in 1953 by Ricardo do Espírito Santo Silva to preserve the tradition of decorative arts and crafts, threatened by modern industrial development.

Activities: Maintains 18 workshops devoted to producing reproductions and to restoration in 21 traditional crafts, including cabinet-making, marquetry, decorative and enamel paintings, Arraiolos carpets, bookbinding, book decoration, chiselling, hand-made gold leaf, etc. Also runs workshops and restoration projects in Brazil, and collaborates with other organizations to form cultural associations and run exhibitions. The Foundation runs the Portuguese Museum-School for Decorative Arts, the College of Decorative Arts and the Arts and Crafts Institute.

Geographical Area of Activity: Portugal and Brazil.

Board of Directors: Dr Maria João Espírito Santo Bustorff Silva (Chair.).

Address: Largo das Portas do Sol 2, 1100 Lisbon.

Telephone: (21) 814600; **Fax:** (21) 814338; **Internet:** www.fress.pt; **e-mail:** geral@fress.pt.

Fundação Lusíada (Lusitanian Foundation)

Founded in 1986 by Abel de Lacerda Botelho.

Activities: Promotes Portuguese language and culture in Portuguese-speaking countries and countries with large Portuguese communities. Bestows awards in the fields of the arts and sciences, including providing funding to universities and medical institutions.

Geographical Area of Activity: Portugal and Portuguese-speaking countries world-wide.

Publications: *A Ideia de Portugal na Literatura Portuguesa dos Últimos Cem Anos; Espirituais Portugueses; Deus, of Mal e a Saudade; As Linhas Míticas do Pensamento Português; Teoria do Amor e da Morte; Verdade e Conjectura; A Nacionalidade Portuguesa de Cristovam Colombo; A Cidade Nova; De l'être du Portugal;* and others.

Principal Staff: Pres. Dr Abel de Lacerda Botelho.

Address: Largo do Mastro 34, RC, 1150 Lisbon.

Telephone: (21) 8851530; **Fax:** (21) 8851077; **e-mail:** fundacao.lusiada@net.pt.

Fundação Luso-Americana para o Desenvolvimento (Luso-American Development Foundation)

Founded in 1985 to promote co-operation between Portugal and the USA.

Activities: Operates in the fields of business, technology and science, education and culture. Provides funding for scholarships, internships, exchanges, conferences, publications, medical, scientific and technological research, business and trade development. The Foundation aims to implement projects in the following areas: research programmes and co-operation with American universities and other institutions; modernization of national and regional administration; environmental protection; cultural programmes; and co-operation with Portuguese-speaking African countries. Also maintains a documentation centre, housing around 5,000 items.

Geographical Area of Activity: Portugal and the USA.

Publications: Annual Report; brochures; newsletter; monographs.

Finance: An initial fund of US $38,000,000 was provided by the Government of Portugal; total grant expenditure 1,294,000,000 escudos (2001).

Board of Directors: Manuel Jacinto Nunes (Pres.); Manuel Soares Pinto Barbosa; Victor Manuel Ribeiro Constâncio; Jorge de Figueiredo Dias; António Franscico Barroso de Sousa Gomes; Vasco Navarro da Graça Moura; Edward Hutchinson Robbins; António Fernando Couto dos Santos; United States Ambassador to Portugal.

Principal Staff: Sec.-Gen. Fernando Durao.

Address: 21 Rua do Sacramento à Lapa, 1200-090 Lisbon.

Telephone: (21) 3935800; **Fax:** (21) 3963358; **Internet:** www.flad.pt; **e-mail:** fladport@flad.pt.

Fundação Oriente (Orient Foundation)

Established in 1988, a private institution which aims to encourage the maintenance and strengthening of historical and cultural ties between Portugal and Asia, particularly Macau, so as to bring the Macanese communities around the world into closer contact.

Activities: The Foundation carries out and supports cultural, educational, artistic and philanthropic activities. It awards funding to the following activities: exhibitions, cinema/video, theatre, music, dance, publications, conferences, festivals, health, philanthropic and social activities, and heritage recovery. Also provides support for Macau communities; conducts research; awards scholarships and prizes; and co-operates with other organizations. Established the Oriente Documentation and Information Centre which works to strengthen historical, cultural, scientific and artistic links between Portugal and countries and territories in the Far East. Operates primarily in Macau, but also in Portugal, the People's Republic of China, Timor Leste, Japan, Thailand, Malaysia, India and territories of the Far East which have cultural and historic links with Portugal, and where

Macanese communities exist. Also a founding member of the Portuguese Foundation Centre (q.v.), which was established in 1993.

Geographical Area of Activity: Europe and South-East Asia.

Publications: Annual Report; *Oriente* (quarterly); publications relating to historical and cultural relations between Portugal and Asia; newsletter.

Finance: Assets 57,786,283,000 escudos (2000); annual expenditure 5,181,227,000 escudos (2000).

Trustees: Prof. Dr J. J. Fraústo da Silva (Chair.).

Principal Staff: Pres. Dr Carlos Monjardino.

Address: Rua do Salitre 66–68, 1269-065 Lisbon.

Telephone: (21) 3585200; **Fax:** (21) 3527042; **Internet:** www.foriente.pt; **e-mail:** fundoriente@foriente.pt.

Fundação de Serralves (Serralves Foundation)

Established in 1989 as a partnership between the Government of Portugal and a group of companies and other institutions (now numbering 90) to promote contemporary art and to raise public awareness of environmental issues.

Activities: The Foundation operates nationally and internationally in the areas of the arts and humanities, and conservation and the environment, through self-conducted programmes, conferences, environmental education programmes and publications. It organizes environmental conferences, seminars on the management of urban green areas and open-air classes and nature clubs; and promotes the arts through sponsorship of art exhibitions, conferences, dance, music and video production. The Foundation established a Museum of Contemporary Art in Porto in 1998.

Geographical Area of Activity: International.

Publications: Information brochures, exhibition catalogues.

Governing Board: J. Vasco Marques Pinto (Chair.); V. Airão; B. Gomes; A. Gomes de Pinho; Fernando Guedes; A. B. Luís; J. Macedo Silva; A. C. Ribeiro de Sousa; A. Rocha Melo.

Principal Staff: Man. Dir Odete Patrício.

Address: Rua de Serralves 977–999, 4150 Porto.

Telephone: (22) 6180057; **Fax:** (22) 6173862; **Internet:** www.serralves.com.

Fundação Mário Soares (Mário Soares Foundation)

Founded in 1991 by Dr Mário Soares, the former President of Portugal.

Activities: Promotes and sponsors cultural, scientific and educational projects in the fields of political science, international relations and human rights. Awards the Mário Soares Foundation Prize annually, holds an archive and funds the João Soares Museum-House. Holds conferences and seminars in the areas of political science and contemporary history.

Geographical Area of Activity: Portugal.

Finance: Initial fund US $100,000,000.

Directors: Dr Mário Soares (Pres.); José Gomes Motta (Vice-Pres.).

Principal Staff: Sec.-Gen. Dr Carlos Barroso.

Address: Rua de S. Bento, 176, 1200-821 Lisbon.

Telephone: (21) 3964179; **Fax:** (21) 3964156; **Internet:** www.fundacao-mario-soares.pt; **e-mail:** fms@fmsoares.pt.

Fundação Arpad Szenes–Vieira da Silva (Arpad Szenes–Vieira da Silva Foundation)

Established in 1990 by the Portuguese Government, Lisbon Municipal Council, the Luso-American Development Foundation (q.v.), the Fundação Cidade de Lisboa (q.v.) and the Calouste Gulbenkian Foundation (q.v.) to promote and study the work of Arpad Szenes and Maria Helena Vieira da Silva.

Activities: Operates in the field of the arts and humanities, nationally through training courses, and nationally and internationally through research and conferences. The Foundation comprises a museum of the artists' works and works of other contemporary artists, and a study and documentation centre; it organizes exhibitions and conferences on modern art and cultural development, issues publications in the field of art criticism and 20th-century art history, and promotes exchanges with similar national and international institutions.

Geographical Area of Activity: Mainly Portugal and South America.

Publications: Catalogues of temporary exhibitions.

Finance: The Foundation is financed by the Ministry of Culture and other sponsors.

Trustees: Daniel Proença de Carvalho (Pres.); Bernardino Gomes; Jean-François Jaeger; João Corrêa Nunes; José Sommer Ribeiro; Pedro Tamen.

Principal Staff: Dir José Sommer Ribeiro; Deputy Dir Ivonne Felman Cunha Rego; Curator Marina Bairrão Ruivo.

Address: Praça das Amoreiras 58, 1250-020 Lisbon.

Telephone: (21) 3880044; **Fax:** (21) 3880039; **Internet:** www.fasvs.pt; **e-mail:** fasvs@fasvs.pt.

Calouste Gulbenkian Foundation

Founded in 1956 by Calouste Sarkis Gulbenkian as a perpetual foundation to operate in the general fields of charity, art, education and science, in Portugal and abroad.

Activities: In the field of charity, which includes preventive medicine as well as assistance to the sick, all aid is given in the form of support to public services, private institutions and individuals. The Foundation has helped to improve, extend or equip existing health and welfare institutions and has subsidized mass health campaigns against particular diseases, and the construction of nursing schools, hospitals, homes for the disabled, vacation camps and similar institutions. In the field of the arts, grants awarded for study in Portugal have been for architecture, painting, engraving, tiles, drama, cinema, restoration work, archaeology, ethnology, aesthetics and the history and criticism of art. The Calouste Gulbenkian Museum houses the founder's art collection. An Arts Library operates in the same building as the museum. The Modern Art Centre comprises Portuguese and foreign art collections, sculpture, drawings and prints. A collection of Portuguese and foreign sculptures is on permanent show in the Foundation gardens. The Foundation also promotes exhibitions, sponsors publications and meetings, and organizes courses and lectures. Its Music Department administers an orchestra, a ballet company and a choir, and supports and initiates various programmes. Activities in the field of education include grants for laboratory equipment, modernization of libraries, organization of research and study groups, specialized study abroad by teachers and lecturers at secondary schools and colleges, the allocation of scholarhips to students, publication of university manuals, and programmes in the field of education through art for children. The Science Department awards grants for scientific purposes to educational and other institutions. The Gulbenkian Science Institute in Oeira is involved in advanced teaching projects in the fields of medicine and biology, teacher training and the spreading of scientific knowledge in Portugal. International activities include the promotion of Portuguese culture, and the Foundation has a special interest in education, welfare and health in the Portuguese-speaking African countries and Timor Leste. It also seeks to benefit Armenian communities throughout the world. The Foundation maintains a branch in London and runs the Calouste Gulbenkian Cultural Centre in Paris.

Geographical Area of Activity: International.

Publications: Annual Report and Accounts; *Newsletter* (quarterly); *Colóquio/Letras* (periodical); Publications Plan.

Finance: Net assets €2,495,796,000 (2001); annual revenue €138,666,000, expenditure €131,750,000 (2001).

Board of Trustees: Dr Emílio Rui Vilar (Chair.); José Blanco; Mikhael Essayan; Eduardo Marçal Grilo; Eduardo Lourenço; Diogo Lucena; Isabel Mota; André Gonçalves Pereira; Artur Santos Silva.

Principal Staff: Carlos Baptosta da Silva (Sec. to the Bd.); Rui Esgaio (Chair. Office); Luis Pereira Leal (Music Dept.); Joao Castel-Branco Pereira (Museum); Jorge Molder (Modern Art Centre); Manuel Carmelo Rosa (Education and Scholarship Dept.); Manuel Rodrigues Gomes (Health and Human Development Dept.); Antonio Coutinho (Gulbenkian Science Institute); Alasdair Mackintosh (Finance and Investment Dept.); Paula Ridlmey (UK Branch—London); Francisco Bethencourt (Calouste Gulbenkian Cultural Centre—Paris).

Address: Av. de Berna 45A, 1067-001 Lisbon.

Telephone: (21) 7823000; **Fax:** (21) 7823025; **Internet:** www.gulbenkian.pt; **e-mail:** info@gulbenkian.pt.

Puerto Rico

FOUNDATIONS, TRUSTS AND NON-PROFIT ORGANIZATIONS

Puerto Rico Community Foundation

Established in 1985; aims to promote community development, funding and philanthropy, so as to improve the socio-economic development of Puerto Rico.

Activities: Operates nationally, through community development programmes in areas including the arts, business–community relations, and youth. More than 27% of its annual expenditure is directed towards youth programmes, including a programme to provide alternative education to adolescents who have dropped out of formal education and a university-based programme of youth volunteer service. Supports other non-profit organizations in Puerto Rico, promoting charitable work in order to solve social problems on the island. Also operates a regional Institute for the Development of Philanthropy (IDEFI), which provides training and technical assistance to philanthropic initiatives in other Caribbean countries.

Geographical Area of Activity: Puerto Rico.

Directors: Antonio Escudero Viera (Pres.); Alina Herrera (Treas.); William Lockwood (Sec.).

Principal Staff: Chief Exec. Dr Nelson I. Colón; Devt Dir Mary Ann Gabino.

Address: POB 70362, San Juan 00936-8362.

Telephone: 721-1037; **Fax:** 721-1673; **Internet:** www.fcpr.org; **e-mail:** webmaster@fcpr.org.

Romania

FOUNDATION CENTRE AND CO-ORDINATING BODY

CENTRAS—Assistance Centre for NGOs

Established in April 1995 to promote freedom of thought and creativity, education and free exchange of opinion and information based on democratic and humanitarian principles, through the development of Romania's non-profit sector.

Activities: Operates in the fields of NGO development, conservation and the environment, economic affairs, education, law and human rights, and social welfare, nationally through projects, research, conferences, training courses and publications, and internationally through projects and training courses.

Geographical Area of Activity: Romania.

Publications: *Attitudini* (magazine); *White Papers of the Romanian NGOs' Forum '98*.

Finance: Net assets US $78,700 (1999); annual revenue $174,500, expenditure $171,200 (1998).

Trustees: Dorin Tudoran (Pres.); Victor Babiuc; Adrian Ďdil; Juliana Geran-Pilon; S. Jecu; L. Petrescu; R. Soudriette; M. Stoica; A. Tasnadi; M. Toma.

Principal Staff: Exec. Dir Viorel Micescu.

Address: Nicolae Bakescu 25, 7th Floor, Apt 14, Bucharest 1.

Telephone: (21) 3100380/1; **Fax:** (21) 3100382; **e-mail:** centras@fx.ro.

FOUNDATIONS, TRUSTS AND NON-PROFIT ORGANIZATIONS

Black Sea University Foundation

Established in 1992 by 21 members of the Romanian scientific and cultural community, to develop better professional skills and increase knowledge through regional and international co-operation.

Activities: Operates internationally in the field of education, through training courses and workshops run by the Black Sea University, on topics in areas such as Peace Diplomacy, Ecology and Sea Resources, Economy and Management, Advanced and Applied Science, and Culture, Contemporary Problems and Future Studies. Courses are attended by scholars, professionals, government experts, etc. from around the world. The Foundation is currently co-operating with national and international institutions to establish a number of permanent research centres, including an International Centre on Negotiations for Conflict Resolution, an Applied Economy Centre, a Black Sea Study Centre, a Black Sea Zone Civilization Study Centre, a European Institute for Risk, Security and Communication Management, an International Institute for Environment and Development and the Black Sea University Network. It also collaborates with universities in other countries, and with international organizations.

Geographical Area of Activity: International.

Publications: *Letter from the Black Sea University* (newsletter, quarterly).

Trustees: Mircea Malitza (Pres.).

Principal Staff: Exec. Dir Virginia Mircea; Exec. Man. Lelioara Pena.

Address: Primăverii Blvd 50, Bucharest 1.

Telephone: (21) 2224118; **Fax:** (21) 2339125; **Internet:** www.bsufonline.org; **e-mail:** office@bsufonline.org.

Civil Society Development Foundation

Established in 1994 with funding from the European Union PHARE (Poland and Hungary Assistance for Economic Restructuring) programme.

Activities: Assists in the development of the non-profit sector in Romania. Runs the ACCES—Centre for NGO Development programme, which maintains a database of Romanian NGOs and a library; and training and research projects. Organizes public events aimed at improving the status of the non-profit sector in Romania.

Geographical Area of Activity: Romania.

Publications: Voluntar (weekly magazine for volunteers); Ghidul Finantatorilor (monthly grants guide); Directory of Civil Society in Romania (annual); and other publications.

Finance: Financed by the European Union PHARE programme.

Board of Directors: Dan Manoleli (Chair.).

Principal Staff: Exec. Dir Maria Sandor; Financial Dir Mariana Ciomartan.

Address: Splaiul Independenţei, No. 2K, 4th Floor, Sector 3, Bucharest.

Telephone: (21) 3100177; **Fax:** (21) 3100180; **Internet:** www.fdsc.ro; **e-mail:** fdsc@fdsc.ro.

Fondation Humanitas

Established in 1990 to promote humanitarian values and democracy; to provide a forum for international cultural dialogue; and to support socio-humanitarian causes.

Activities: The Foundation supports programmes which fight injustice; provides funding to students and researchers in the field of the humanities; organizes conferences and seminars; holds an archive of documents and historical information; and issues publications.

Publications: Newsletter; information brochure.

Principal Staff: Minhea Berindei.

Address: Piaţa Presei Libere 1, Sector 1, 79734 Bucharest.

Telephone: (21) 176575; **Fax:** (21) 181455.

Open Society Foundation—Romania—OSFR

Established in 1997, as the successor to the Soros Foundation for an Open Society, founded by George Soros in 1990, for the accomplishment of an open and pluralistic society, based on a stable and functioning democracy, with institutions that serve the individual. It is part of the Soros Foundations Network. Since 2000, it has created a network of 13 independent organizations, the Soros Open Network—SON, committed to supporting the reform process in the spirit of open society values.

Activities: Operates in fields connected to democracy, rule of law, child protection, European Union integration, and public policy. Through its network of organizations, OSFR supports economic development, health policies and services, rural assistance, cultural policies, education, legislative reform, community safety and mediation, regional co-operation, ethnic minorities and Roma issues, equal opportunities for women and men.

Geographical Area of Activity: Romania.

Saudi Arabia

FOUNDATIONS, TRUSTS AND NON-PROFIT ORGANIZATIONS

International Islamic Relief Organization

Established in 1978 to alleviate suffering world-wide.

Activities: Aids victims of natural disasters and war, and other displaced persons, on an international scale. Runs programmes to provide education, medical aid and social support; and sponsors projects and small businesses whose work contributes to the objectives of the Organization. Maintains more than 100 offices in Saudi Arabia and world-wide.

Geographical Area of Activity: International.

Principal Staff: Sec.-Gen. Dr Adnan Khaleel Pasha.

Address: POB 1285, Jeddah 21431.

Telephone: (2) 651-5411; **Fax:** (2) 651-8491; **e-mail:** enquiries@iiro.org.

King Faisal Foundation

Founded in 1975 to use the estate of the late King Faisal for charitable purposes.

Activities: Operates nationally and internationally in the fields of science and medicine, and the arts and humanities, chiefly by awarding the King Faisal International Prizes (for Arabic Literature, Islamic Studies, Service to Islam, Science and Medicine), with prizes totalling approx. US $1,000,000, and academic scholarships. The Foundation finances the King Faisal Centre for Research and Islamic Studies and the King Faisal School, a private university established in partnership with a US technology institute.

Geographical Area of Activity: International.

Restrictions: Nominations for King Faisal International Prize are not acceptable from political institutes.

Publications: *Al Faisal.*

Finance: Total assets approx. 1,441,000,000 Saudi riyal.

Trustees: All eight sons of King Faisal bin Abdulaziz.

Principal Staff: Dir Gen. HRH Prince Khalid Al-Faisal; Sec.-Gen. HH Prince Bandar bin Saud bin Khalid; Vice-Sec.-Gen. HE Yousef A. Al-Hamdan; Asst Sec.-Gen. Musaed A. Al-Said.

Address: King Fahed Rd, Olaya, POB 352, Riyadh 11411.

Telephone: (1) 465-2255; **Fax:** (1) 465-6524; **Internet:** www.kff.com; **e-mail:** info@kff.com.

Sultan Bin Abdulaziz Al-Saud Foundation

A private non-profit organization established by HRH Prince Sultan Bin Abdulaziz Al-Saud in 1995 to provide humanitarian, social and cultural services, and to empower Saudi Arabia to participate in the spread of knowledge through modern means of communication.

Activities: Operates in the fields of social welfare and education through four principal programmes: the City for Humanitarian Services, the Science and Technology Centre, the Programme for Medical and Educational Telecommunications (Medunet) and the Special Education Programme.

Geographical Area of Activity: Saudi Arabia.

Board of Trustees: HRH Prince Sultan Bin Abdulaziz Al-Saud (Chair.); HRH Prince Khaled Bin Sultan Bin Abdulaziz Al-Saud (Vice-Chair.); HRH Prince Faisal Bin Sultan Bin Abdulaziz Al-Saud (Sec.-Gen); and six other members.

Principal Staff: Sec.-Gen. HRH Prince Faisal Bin Sultan Bin Abdulaziz Al-Saud; Dir Gen. Rashid Aba Al-Khail.

Address: POB 64400, Riyadh 11536.

Telephone: (1) 482-7663; **Fax:** (1) 482-2617; **Internet:** www.sultanfoundation.org; **e-mail:** question@medu.net.

Senegal

FOUNDATION CENTRE AND CO-ORDINATING BODY

Forum for African Voluntary Development Organizations (FAVDO)

International association of approximately 450 African development organizations, which aims to provide mutual support and co-operation services, and to assist development organizations so as to aid the general development of people in Africa.

Activities: Operates in the field of aid to less-developed countries, through establishing links and communication networks between NGOs and governments and governmental organizations in Africa and internationally.

Geographical Area of Activity: Africa.

Address: Rue 4, Zone-B, BP 12093, Dakar.

Telephone: 825-55-47; **Fax:** 825-95-64; **e-mail:** mazide@sonatel.senet.net.

FOUNDATIONS, TRUSTS AND NON-PROFIT ORGANIZATIONS

Enda Tiers-Monde—Environnement et Développement du Tiers-Monde (Enda Third World—Environmental Development Action in the Third World)

Established in 1972 as an international associative organization active in combating poverty, and in the field of environmental development.

Activities: Operates in the fields of aid to less-developed countries and environmental development, through assisting local community organizations operating in areas such as cultural protection, urban economy, youth and energy. There are decentralized branches of the organization in Africa, South America and Asia, and representative offices in Europe.

Geographical Area of Activity: Africa, South America and the Caribbean, and Asia.

Publications: *Community Service An Alternative to Imprisonment: the Zimbabwean Experience; Moulding Citizens;* Reports.

Principal Staff: Pres. Cheikh Hamidou Kane; Exec. Sec. Jacques Bugnicourt.

Address: 4–5 rue Kléber, BP 3370, Dakar.

Telephone: 823-63-91; **Fax:** 823-51-57; **Internet:** www.enda.sn; **e-mail:** enda-dif@enda.sn.

Fondation des Organisations Rurales pour l'Agriculture et la Gestion Ecologique—FORAGE (Foundation of Rural Organizations for Agriculture and Economic Management)

Established in 1992 by Yancouba Tamba to support rural development.

Activities: Operates nationally in the areas of conservation and the environment and education, through research, grants and organizing training courses.

Trustees: M. Badji; S. Diémé; O. Badji; A. Manga; M. Manga; I. Niassy; A. Sané; L. Sané; I. Sonko.

Principal Staff: Chief Exec. Yancouba Tamba; Treas. Amadou Manga; Finance Co-ordinator Ansoumana Sané.

Address: BP 01, Marsassoum, Kolda.

Telephone: 95-31-46; **Fax:** 95-27-06; **e-mail:** sudinfo@telecomplus.sn.

Fondation Rurale pour l'Afrique de l'Ouest (West African Rural Foundation)

Established in 1993 to promote rural development.

Activities: Operates internationally, supporting community organizations working in the fields of rural development, the environment and human rights, through promoting research and collaboration between researchers in the area of agricultural and rural development research, providing training materials, offering technical and management advice, promoting links between organizations involved in rural development, and lobbying on behalf of rural organizations and individuals.

Geographical Area of Activity: West Africa.

Publications: *WARF Newsletter.*

Finance: Annual budget approx. US $1,500,000.

Principal Staff: Dir Fadel Diame.

Address: Rue 1 x D, Point E, Dakar.

Telephone: 824-14-00; **Fax:** 824-57-55; **e-mail:** fraocoor@metissacana.sn.

Fondation Léopold Sédar Senghor

Founded in 1975 by Léopold Sédar Senghor, former President of Senegal, to preserve national heritage and support training and research, especially in the areas of culture and international co-operation.

Activities: Operates nationally and internationally in the fields of the arts and humanities, education, law and human rights, and science and technology, through self-conducted programmes, research, grants, literary prizes, conferences, training courses and publications. Maintains offices in Brazil, France, the Ivory Coast, Switzerland and the USA.

Geographical Area of Activity: International.

Publications: *Ethiopiques* (2 a year); *Lettres Majeures* (bulletin).

Principal Staff: Pres. Basile Senghor.

Address: rues Alpha Hachamiyou Tall et René Ndiaye, BP 2035, 2035 Dakar.

Telephone and Fax: 821-53-55; **Internet:** www.refer.sn/flss/activ.htm; **e-mail:** senghorf@syfed.refer.sn.

Open Society Initiative for West Africa

Established in 2000; part of the global network of autonomous Soros foundations.

Activities: Provides funding to organizations working in the areas of human rights (including women's political and economic empowerment), democracy and governance, media and technology (including information and communications technologies), legal reform and transitional justice, and HIV/AIDS. Supports national projects and projects involving more than one country in West Africa. Maintains an office in Nigeria.

Geographical Area of Activity: West Africa.

Publications: Annual Report.

Finance: Annual grant distribution approx. US $10,000,000.

Board of Directors: Ellen Johnson Sirleaf (Chair.); Yassine Fall; Julius Ihonvbere; Alhaji Ahmed Joda; Fatimata Mbaye; Sudia Touré.

Principal Staff: Exec. Dir Kakuna Kerina; Senior Programme Officer Abdel-Fatau Musah.

Address: Immeuble EPI, Blvd du Sud X, rue des Ecrivans, Point E, Dakar.

Telephone: 869-10-24; **Fax:** 824-09-42; **Internet:** www.soros .org/osiwa; **e-mail:** osiwadakar@isowa.org.

Pan African Association for Literacy and Adult Education

Established to promote adult education and literacy in Africa. Originally known as the African Association for Literacy and Adult Education, which was founded in 1984 (combining the former African Adult Education Association and the Afrolit Society, both founded in 1968).

Activities: Promotes literacy and adult education, and aims to increase understanding of the concept of lifelong learning within Africa. Conducts studies on educational problems and literacy, holds conferences and disseminates information. Educators form networks to develop programmes concerned with such issues as literacy, women in adult education and development, environmental education, training of trainers, artists for development, participatory research, and university, adult and continuing education. Provides professional training to educators. Maintains a reference library and pool of expert educators to act as consultants.

Geographical Area of Activity: Africa.

Finance: Funded through membership fees and grants and donations from sister organizations.

Principal Staff: Co-ordinator of Steering Cttee Lamine Kane.

Address: rue 10, Bldg 306, BP 10358, Dakar.

Telephone: 824-44-13; **e-mail:** anafa@sentoo.sn.

Pesticide Action Network Africa—PAN Africa

Founded in 1996, PAN Africa works as one of the regional arms of PAN International. It aims to promote protection of the environment and pesticide-free sustainable agriculture, raise awareness of the problems and dangers related to pesticide use in agriculture, and work towards promoting an understanding of the issues surrounding the indiscriminate use of pesticides.

Activities: Works to disseminate information regarding the use of pesticides and their alternatives, through the publication of journals, leaflets and audiovisual material, and a Regional Documentation Centre. PAN Africa organizes workshops and training sessions, and has set up a databank on pesticides, sustainable agriculture and agro-ecology, and works to strengthen legislation in Africa regarding the use of toxic pesticides.

Geographical Area of Activity: Africa.

Publications: *Pesticides and Alternatives* (newsletter in French and English, 3 times a year).

Finance: Total revenue US $208,686, expenditure $193,284 (2000).

Steering Committee: Timothy Byakola; El Hadj Hanne; M. Appolinaire Etono Ngah; Patrice Okeli Obeli; Tiemoko S. Sangare; Mathieu Sawadogo; Dr Abou Thiam; Ngone War Toure; Dr Simplice Davo Vodouhe.

Principal Staff: Regional Co-ordinator Dr Abou Thiam; Programme Officer Henry René Diouf.

Address: BP 15938, Dakar-Fann, Dakar.

Telephone: 825-49-14; **Fax:** 825-14-43; **Internet:** www.pan-africa.sn; **e-mail:** panafrica@pan-africa.sn.

Serbia and Montenegro

FOUNDATIONS, TRUSTS AND NON-PROFIT ORGANIZATIONS

European Centre for Peace and Development —ECPD

Established in 1985 following an agreement between the United Nations University for Peace and the Government of Yugoslavia, to contribute to peace and development in Europe and to international co-operation in the transfer of knowledge.

Activities: Works towards finding solutions for acute and chronic problems of development and the quality of life in specific regions of Europe, particularly South-Eastern Europe, with an emphasis on countries in transition. Runs a series of inter-connected programmes: development of human resources; development of natural resources; economic development; scientific and technological development; social development; integrated development; development of international relations and co-operation; and management. Organizes and conducts postgraduate studies; research projects; international scientific meetings, conferences, symposia and seminars; provides consulting services; and publishes materials and papers relevant to its studies. Has been involved in science and research in numerous areas including environmental protection, modern and traditional medicine, banking, finance and international trade and the promotion of small and medium-sized enterprises. Runs its projects in co-operation with universities and institutions in host countries.

Geographical Area of Activity: International, with a current emphasis on South-Eastern Europe.

Publications: *Small Enterprises Management Today; Political Economy of Japanese and Asian Development; Clinical Immunology—Principles and Practices.*

Directors: Dr Pierre Marie Gallois (Pres., Council); Prof. Dr Shinichi Ichimura (Pres., Academic Council); Dr Norman Scott (Pres., Exec. Board).

Principal Staff: Exec. Dir Dr Negoslav P. Ostojic.

Address: 11000 Belgrade, Terazije 41.

Telephone: (11) 324-6041; **Fax:** (11) 324-0673; **e-mail:** ecpd@eunet.yu.

Foundation Open Society Institute—Representative Office Montenegro

An independent foundation, formerly the Podgorica office of the Fund for an Open Society—Yugoslavia (q.v.), established in 1999; part of the Soros foundations network, which aims to foster political and cultural pluralism and reform economic structures in order to encourage free enterprise and a market economy.

Activities: Operates in the areas of the arts and culture, education, information and the media, public health, civil society, Roma people, and women's and youth programmes. Support includes scholarships for students, funding for media campaigns and financing publications.

Geographical Area of Activity: Montenegro.

Finance: Annual expenditure US $2,083,000 (2001).

Board of Directors: Dragan Radonjic (Chair.); Borislav Banovic; Srdjan Darmanovic; Dzemalj Nikaj; Serbo Rastoder; Milka Takic.

Principal Staff: Exec. Dir Mirjana Popovic; Library Co-ordinator Biljana Maslovaric.

Address: 81000 Podgorica, Njegoseva 26.

Telephone: (81) 225066; **Fax:** (81) 225088; **e-mail:** montenegro@osim.cg.yu.

Fund for an Open Society—Serbia

Founded in June 1991. An independent foundation, part of the Soros foundations network, which aims to foster political and cultural pluralism and reform economic structures in order to encourage free enterprise and a market economy.

Activities: Operates in the fields of information and the independent media, education, economic reform, civil society, the arts and culture, science, law and criminal justice, public health, Roma and ethnic minorities, local government and public administration, and women's and youth programmes.

Geographical Area of Activity: Yugoslavia (now Serbia and Montenegro).

Publications: *Open News.*

Finance: Annual expenditure US $6,556,000 (2001).

Board of Directors: Sonja Licht (Pres.); Jovan Cirilov; Zagorka Golubovic; Milosav Milosavljevic; Radmila Nakarada; Milan Obradovic; Borka Pavicevic; Stanko Pihler; Lila Radonjic; Vlatko Rajkovic; Zoroslav Spevak; Nikola Tasic; Srbijanka Turajlic.

Principal Staff: Exec Dir. Ivan Vejvoda.

Address: 11000 Belgrade, Zmaj Jovina 34.

Telephone: (11) 302-5800; **Fax:** (11) 328-3602; **Internet:** www.fosyu.org; **e-mail:** office@fosyu.org.

Karić Foundation

Established in 1979 by the Karić family with the goal of helping others, and the promotion of Serbian national culture and tradition.

Activities: Operates in Serbia and Montenegro, Europe and the USA in the areas of the arts and humanities, education, international affairs, law and human rights, medicine and health, and social welfare, through awarding prizes (the Karić Brothers Awards), humanitarian projects, publishing, international co-operation and family development. Also maintains branches in Austria, Canada, Cyprus, UK and the USA.

Geographical Area of Activity: Serbia and Montenegro, Europe and the USA.

Publications: *Bulletin* (newsletter).

Finance: Assets DM4,000,000 (2000); annual revenue and expenditure DM3,500,000 (2000).

Board of Management: Milanka Karić (Pres.); Hafa Karić; Marijana Karić; Olivera Nedeljkovic; Slavica Karić.

Principal Staff: Dir Ljubinka Mitrović.

Address: 11070 Belgrade, Palmira Toljatija 3.

Telephone: (11) 600-356; **Fax:** (11) 609-752; **Internet:** www.karicfoundation.com; **e-mail:** karicfoundation@yahoo.com.

Kosova Foundation for Open Society

An independent foundation, formerly the Priština office of the Fund for an Open Society—Yugoslavia (q.v.), established in 1999; part of the Soros foundations network, which aims to foster political and cultural pluralism and reform economic structures in order to encourage free enterprise and a market economy.

Activities: Operates in the areas of humanitarian aid to refugees, as well as supporting small-scale projects in the fields of education, culture and the arts, information and the media, democratic institutions and human rights. Internationally the Foundation co-operates with the East–East programme, collaborating regionally on democracy programmes.

Geographical Area of Activity: Kosovo.

Finance: Annual expenditure (made by Open Society Institute—Macedonia on behalf of the Kosovo Foundation) US $2,595,000 (2001).

Board of Directors: Ekrem Beqiri (Chair.); Ibrahim Aslan; Agron Dida; Vjosa Dobruna; Flurim Gashi; Greta Kacinari; Nikibe Kelmendi; Shkelzen Maliqi;.

Principal Staff: Exec. Dir Luan Shllaku.

Address: 38000 Priština, Aktas II 38.

Telephone and Fax: (38) 549116; **e-mail:** info@kfos.org.

Slovakia

FOUNDATION CENTRES AND CO-ORDINATING BODIES

Greenway—Central and East European Network of Environmental Non-Governmental Organizations

Founded in 1985 by NGOs from Poland, Hungary and the former Czechoslovakia, to promote international co-operation in Central and Eastern Europe.

Activities: Greenway, which consists of 31 member organizations, operates throughout Central and Eastern Europe in the field of conservation and the environment, through self-conducted programmes, conferences, training courses and publications. Maintains an office for the Greenway Energy Working Group in Budapest.

Geographical Area of Activity: Central and Eastern Europe.

Publications: *Greenway Newsletter* (approx. 4 a year).

Finance: Funded by voluntary donations.

Trustees: Dubravka Bačun; Evgenij Kotsiubniak; Zviad Mukbahiani; Erzsebet Schmuck; Istvan Sidó.

Principal Staff: Int. Co-ordinator Elena Vartíková.

Address: POB 163, 814 99 Bratislava.

Telephone and Fax: (2) 5541-4674; **Internet:** www.fns.uniba.sk/zp/greenway; **e-mail:** greenway@isternet.sk.

Slovak Academic Information Agency–Service Center for the Third Sector—SAIA-SCTS

Established in 1990 to assist in the development of the education system and civil society in general.

Activities: Provides services for NGOs in Slovakia, including training and advisory services, a library on the third sector and an NGO database with approximately 3,000 entries. Also issues publications; organizes conferences and seminars; runs volunteer projects and grants the Heart on Palm volunteer awards; and collaborates regionally and internationally with other similar organizations on programmes. Its educational services include providing information, scholarship competitions, seminars and workshops for those wishing to study abroad. Maintains five branch offices throughout Slovakia.

Geographical Area of Activity: Slovakia.

Publications: *SAIA Bulletin; NonProfit* (monthly magazine); Annual Report; and other publications.

Finance: Total assets US $196,309 (2001); total income US $474,756, expenditure US $490,231 (2001).

Principal Staff: Exec. Dir Katarína Kostálová.

Address: Nám. slobody 23, 812 20 Bratislava 1.

Telephone: (2) 5441-1426; **Fax:** (2) 5441-1429; **Internet:** www.saia.sk; **e-mail:** saia@saia.sk.

Slovak Donors Forum

Established as an association of Slovak and foreign grant-making organizations to promote effective grant-making and support the third sector in Slovakia.

Activities: A group of NGOs and grant-making foundations that aims to provide support to third-sector organizations in Slovakia, through networking, communication and collaboration. Co-ordinates grant-making programmes, analyses the effects of legal and fiscal changes on non-profits and works to increase the development of philanthropy inside Slovakia. Currently drafting a code of ethics for foundations.

Geographical Area of Activity: Slovakia.

Principal Staff: Man. Zuzana Franova.

Address: c/o OSF–Bratislava, Bastova 5, 811 03 Bratislava.

Telephone: (7) 5441-7917; **Fax:** (2) 5441-8867; **Internet:** www.donorsforum.sk; **e-mail:** donorsforum@donorsforum.sk.

Slovak Humanitarian Council

Established in 1990 as the Czechoslovak Council for Humanitarian Co-operation—an independent non-governmental voluntary association of 169 organizations aiming to relieve human suffering which, after the split of Czechoslovakia into the Czech Republic and Slovakia, became the Czech Council for Humanitarian Co-operation (now the Council of Humanitarian Associations, q.v.) and the Slovak Humanitarian Council. The Council comprises numerous voluntary organizations and aims to promote the interests of the voluntary sector, and to provide humanitarian aid in collaboration with the state.

Activities: Supports the projects of its member organizations; offers advice on management and fund distribution; organizes training courses; disseminates information; provides consultancy services; and issues publications.

Geographical Area of Activity: Slovakia.

Publications: *Humanita* (newsletter, monthly); Annual Report.

Governing Board: Ivan Sykora (Pres.); Jaroslav Hinst (Vice-Pres.); Viktor Blaho; Peter Cekme; Jozef Dudás; Helena Jonásová; Iveta Liberková; Anna Slapková; Stefan Vancik.

Principal Staff: Dir Bohuslava Zániová.

Address: Ružová dolina 27, 821 09 Bratislava.

Telephone: (2) 5341-3970; **Fax:** (2) 5341-3655; **Internet:** www.shr.sk; **e-mail:** shr@changenet.sk.

FOUNDATIONS, TRUSTS AND NON-PROFIT ORGANIZATIONS

Children of Slovakia Foundation

Established in December 1995 by the International Youth Foundation (q.v.) to support the positive development of children and young people in Slovakia.

Activities: Operates in the fields of education and social welfare, specifically in the area of children and young people, through self-conducted programmes, grants to institutions and training courses.

Geographical Area of Activity: Slovakia.

Restrictions: Projects are limited to Slovakia.

Publications: Reports on the situation of children and young people in Slovakia.

Finance: Annual revenue approx. US $500,000.

Trustees: Dušan Antoš; Ján Badžoň; Pavol Dameš; Alena Heribanová; Daniel Hevier; Peter Kubik; Ján Šípoš; Zuzana Ťapáková; Filip Vagač.

Principal Staff: Exec. Dir Filip Vagač; Programme Dir Lucia Štasselová.

Address: Heydukova 3, 811 08 Bratislava.

Telephone: (2) 5263-6471; **Fax:** (2) 5263-6462; **Internet:** www.nds.sk; **e-mail:** nds@nds.sk.

Fund for the Development of the Carpathian Euroregion

Founded in 1994 by the Institute for East–West Studies, to support projects to improve the quality of life and the community in rural areas of the Carpathian mountains, through integrated community development.

Activities: The Fund operates in the Carpathian region, which encompasses areas of Hungary, Poland, Romania, Slovakia and Ukraine. It seeks to promote the development of civil society at local level; assist local NGOs in operating to the benefit of the community and the region; promote co-operation between countries in which the Carpathian region lies, and between NGOs and local government and other organizations; and promote citizen participation. The Fund runs two main programmes: the Capacity Building Programme and the Integrated Rural Community Development Programme. The foundation awards approximately 16% of grants to environmental projects. Maintains country offices in Hungary, Poland, Romania, Slovakia and Ukraine.

Geographical Area of Activity: The Carpathian region, bordering Hungary, Poland, Romania, Slovakia and Ukraine.

Board of Directors: Katarina Kostálová (Chair.); Christian Anghel; Sally Bowles; Stephen B. Heintz; Piotor Helsinki; Vasil Hudák; Mihály Kupa; Csaba Lörinezi; Bogdan Pankevich; George Penick; John Richardson; Tomás Sabol; Jan Szczucki; Viktor Vántus; Ana Vasilache.

Principal Staff: Exec. Dir. Sándor Köles.

Address: Hlavná 70, 04001 Košice.

Telephone: (55) 6221160; **Fax:** (55) 6221150; **Internet:** www.tuke.sk/ibis/fdce.html; **e-mail:** kysela@changenet.sk.

Green Perspective Foundation

Founded in April 1991 by Juraj Lukáč, Dagmar Balažová and Radoslav Potočný to support environmental protection, primarily focusing on protection and regeneration of natural forests within a philosophy of deep ecology.

Activities: The Foundation supports the activities of individuals, public initiatives and NGOs working in the above fields and education, through advisory, publishing, cultural, social and specific activities. The Foundation's main programmes include an annual award to the best forest protection activity open to applicants from the Czech Republic, Hungary, Poland and Slovakia, donations of books to rural libraries, financial help to students whose career goals are in accordance with the aims of the foundation, and a small grant initiative for forest protection activities.

Geographical Area of Activity: Czech Republic, Hungary, Poland and Slovakia.

Publications: Several books.

Finance: Net assets US $7,800 (2001).

Trustees: Juraj Lukáč; Vladimir Pirišik; Radoslav Potočný.

Principal Staff: Exec. Dir Mária Hudáková.

Address: 08213 Tulčík 27.

Telephone and Fax: (51) 778-9138; **Internet:** www.gpf.sk; **e-mail:** main@gpf.sk.

Jan Hus Educational Foundation

Founded in 1990 to support civil society and the development of higher education in the arts, humanities and law in the Czech Republic and Slovakia. Until 1993, the Foundation was a branch office of the Vzdělávací Nadace Jana Husa (q.v.). Since 1993, two sister organizations have been in operation, one in Slovakia and one in the Czech Republic.

Activities: Aims to contribute to the integration of Slovak civilization, science and arts into European culture. The Foundation's main project areas are to: support higher and continuing education, with a particular emphasis on the humanities, social sciences and civic–democratic education; initiate a fundamental transformation in the education system through the training and preparation of university teachers; and initiate and support permanent international academic co-operation.

Geographical Area of Activity: Slovakia and the Czech Republic.

Restrictions: Grants are made within Slovakia and the Czech Republic only.

Publications: Annual Report; *Velvet Philosophers.*

Finance: Net assets 10,257,898 koruny (Dec. 2000); annual revenue 7,610,075 koruny, expenditure 6,604,397 koruny (2000).

Board of Trustees: Dr Vladimír Jochmann (Chair.); Krístina Korená (Vice-Chair); Dr J. Balážová; Tomáš Holeček; Dr J. Jelínková; Dr E. Krák; Dr V. Krivý; J. Müller; Dr M. Petrusek; Dr M. Pospíšil; Dr P. Šuléř.

Principal Staff: Dir Jana Malovičová.

Address: Panenská 4, Box 313, 810 00 Bratislava.

Telephone: (2) 5443-2535; **Fax:** (2) 5443-2535; **Internet:** www.vnjh.sk; **e-mail:** vnjh@vnjh.sk.

Nadácia Pre Občiansku Spoločnost (Foundation for a Civil Society)

Established as the successor to the USA-based Foundation for a Civil Society's (q.v.) Bratislava office, to promote the development of the third sector in Slovakia.

Activities: The Foundation operates to develop civil society through education, culture and other community activities. It provides advice and funding for a wide range of projects. It also participates in environmental activities. Major programmes include the Slovak Visual Arts Prize.

Geographical Area of Activity: Slovakia.

Principal Staff: Pres. Wendy W. Luers.

Address: Grosslingova 4, 811 09 Bratislava.

Telephone: (2) 5296 2215; **Fax:** (2) 5024 4282; **Internet:** www.nos.sk; **e-mail:** nos@nos.sk.

Open Society Foundation—Bratislava

Founded in June 1992, an independent foundation, part of the Soros foundations network, which aims to support, develop, protect and strengthen democratic and liberal values of open society through the implementation of programmes and projects.

Activities: The Foundation's programme priorities include public administration, law and judiciary, Roma people, social integration, educational reform, education, children and young people, co-operation between European countries, library support, internet, publishing, public health, economic reform, arts and culture, media, criminal justice, women, civil society and European integration. Also operates as a partner within the NGO sector, at governmental and donor level, and with individuals in Slovakia, as well as with international partners.

Geographical Area of Activity: Slovakia.

Publications: Annual Report; *Manual for Foundations; Free Access to Information Law; Prevention of HIV Epidemics in CEE and NIS*; and other publications.

Finance: Annual expenditure US $3,493,557 (2001).

Board of Directors: Iveta Radicova (Chair.); Grigorij Meseznikov (Vice-Chair.); Jan Hrubala; Tomas Sabol; Katarina Vajdova; Maria Zelenakova.

Principal Staff: Exec. Dir Alena Pániková.

Address: Bastova 5, 811 03 Bratislava.

Telephone: (7) 5441-6913; **Fax:** (2) 5441-8867; **Internet:** www.osf.sk; **e-mail:** osf@osf.sk.

Pontis Foundation

Established in 1990 by the Foundation for a Civil Society in the USA (q.v.); aims to create a democratic Slovakia by bridging borders and engaging citizens.

Activities: Makes an annual award to companies in recognition of their corporate citizenship activities; develops international projects through its Institute for Civil Diplomacy; and operates a NGO Loan Programme. Also active in the fields of voter mobilization.

Geographical Area of Activity: Slovakia.

Board of Directors: Erben Pavol (Pres.); Ružička František; Alner Juraj; Katarína Mathernová; Peter Blaha; Peter Werner; Viktor Tekelhoff.

Principal Staff: Acting Dir Lenka Surotchak.

Address: Grösslingova 4, 811 09 Bratislava.

Telephone: (2) 5296-2215; **Fax:** (2) 5263-2362; **Internet:** www.pontisfoundation.sk; **e-mail:** pontis@pontisfoundatiopn.sk.

Slovenia

FOUNDATIONS, TRUSTS AND NON-PROFIT ORGANIZATIONS

Slovenian Science Foundation

Established in 1994 by the major Slovenian organizations for research, education, economy, finance and the media, and by the Ministry for Science and Technology, as an independent foundation for general scientific purposes and the development of science in Slovenia.

Activities: Operates in the fields of education, and science and technology, through basic and applied research, professional training and developing current and future research personnel, international scientific co-operation (including collaboration with the European Science Foundation, q.v. and other national science foundations), and a programme of public understanding of science and technology (including the annual Slovene Science Festival and the Slovene Park of Science and Technology project). The Foundation supports scientific training abroad through fellowships and scholarships, offers research grants, promotes scientific exchanges and joint research projects, organizes conferences and issues publications.

Geographical Area of Activity: Slovenia.

Publications: *Glasnik ustanove Slovenske znanstvene fundacije* (Slovenian Science Foundation Courier).

Trustees: Prof. Dr A. Umek (Pres.); Prof. Dr R. Bohinc; Prof. Dr V. Kaučič.

Principal Staff: Dir Dr Edvard Kobal.

Address: Štefanova ul. 15, 1000 Ljubljana.

Telephone: (1) 4263590; **Fax:** (1) 4263591; **Internet:** www.ustanova-szf.si; **e-mail:** info@ustanova-szf.si.

South Africa

FOUNDATION CENTRES AND CO-ORDINATING BODIES

CIVICUS—World Alliance for Citizen Participation

Established in 1993, an international alliance dedicated to strengthening citizen action and civil society world-wide, in particular in areas where participatory democracy, freedom of association of citizens and their funds for public benefit are threatened.

Activities: Operates world-wide in the areas of the arts and humanities, conservation and the environment, international affairs and social welfare, through self-conducted programmes, research, conferences and publications. Through its programmes and actions the organization seeks an increased understanding and promotion of the nature and contributions of civil society; a political, legal and fiscal environment that enables freedom and autonomy of association; innovative forms of funding and partnership in order to enhance the resource base of civil society organizations; the strengthening of the institutional, leadership, networking and advocacy capacities of the sector; and increased partnerships among business, government and civil society institutions. Holds a World Assembly every two years, and sponsors regional meetings. Current main focus is the CIVICUS Index on Civil Society project mapping the development of civil society worldwide.

Geographical Area of Activity: International.

Publications: *e-Civicus* (weekly bulletin); *Civil Society at the Millennium* (1999); *Promoting Corporate Citizenship: Opportunities for Business and Civil Society Engagement* (1999); *Sustaining Civil Society: Strategies for Resource Mobilization* (1997); *Legal Principles for Citizen Participation: Toward a Legal Framework for Civil Society Organizations* (1997); *Building Civil Society Worldwide: Strategies for Successful Communications* (1997); *The New Civic Atlas: Profiles of Civil Society in 60 Countries* (1997); *CIVICUS World* (6 a year); and others.

Board of Directors: Kenn Allen; Marcus Akuhata-Brown; Lesley Bulman; Stuart Etherington; Alan Fowler; Patrick Johnston; Amani Kandil; Elba Luna; Sara Hlupekile Longwe; Ezra Mbogori; Shantal Munro-Knight; Aruna Rao; Sadiqa Salahuddin.

Principal Staff: Sec.-Gen. and CEO Kumi Naidoo; Chief Operating Officer Jane Foster.

Address: 24 Pimm Cnr, Quinn St, Newtown, Johannesburg 2001.

Telephone: (11) 833-5959; **Fax:** (11) 833-7997; **Internet:** www.civicus.org; **e-mail:** info@civicus.org.

Southern African Grantmakers Association

Regional association of approximately 80 corporate and foundation grant-makers established in 1995.

Activities: Operates as a service organization, providing support for grant-makers in Southern Africa through workshops, publications, conferences and research, as well as lobbying to influence development policy and promoting philanthropy and grant-making.

Geographical Area of Activity: Southern Africa.

Restrictions: This is not a grant-making organization.

Publications: *Grantmaker; Corporate Social Investment Handbook 2000;* Annual Report; brochures.

Finance: Assets 4,256,680 rand (March 2000); annual revenue 2,108,071 rand, expenditure 2,335,720 rand (1999/2000).

Board of Trustees: Gail Campbell (Chair.); Cas Coovadia; Anne Emmett; Amelia Jones; Lulu Letlape; Joy Mills-Hackmann; Pam Richardson; Allan Wentzel.

Principal Staff: Exec. Dir Colleen Du Toit; Programme Man. Zaide Harneker.

Address: POB 31667, Braamfontein 2017.

Telephone: (11) 403-1610; **Fax:** (11) 403-1689; **Internet:** www.donors.org.za; **e-mail:** info@donors.org.za.

FOUNDATIONS, TRUSTS AND NON-PROFIT ORGANIZATIONS

Africa Foundation

Founded in 1992 to facilitate the empowerment and development of individuals, living in, or adjacent to, protected areas in Africa, by forging unique partnerships between conservation initiatives and local communities. Formerly known as the Rural Investment Trust, an independent arm of the South African based safari company, CC Africa.

Activities: Supports projects in the fields of education, health care and small business development. In the field of education, support includes building classrooms, pre-schools, laboratories and media centres and educational bursaries to community leaders; health-care activities include building medical clinics, AIDS prevention programmes, hosting educational workshops and providing family planning; and in the area of small business development, funding is given to promising entrepreneurs, supporting community centres and small businesses, and encouraging eco-tourism and community development initiatives. Projects are currently run in Botswana, Kenya, South Africa, Tanzania, Zanzibar and Zimbabwe. Also maintains an office in California, USA.

Geographical Area of Activity: Botswana, Kenya, South Africa, Tanzania, Zanzibar and Zimbabwe.

Address: POB 784826, Sandton 2146.

Telephone: (11) 809-4429; **Fax:** (11) 809-4345; **Internet:** www.africafoundation.org; **e-mail:** africafoundation@africafoundation.org.

Africa Institute of South Africa—AISA

Founded in 1960 by the South African Academy of Arts and Science and the University of South Africa, the Institute is the principal nationally-based centre for the study of African affairs, whose role is to inform South African society about trends and events in Africa.

Activities: The Institute collects, interprets and disseminates information and analyses on African, and especially Southern African, affairs. Information is disseminated through periodicals and other publications, commentary to the media, and through seminars, workshops and conferences. It conducts research, and maintains a specialized reference library of around 60,000 volumes and about 480 journals and a monitoring service. The Institute collaborates with other institutions and with researchers and academics in the field of African studies world-wide, and has co-operation agreements with centres of African studies abroad (including joint research projects). African studies seminar programmes are conducted. The Institute focuses primarily on the political, socio-economic, international and developmental issues facing Africa. While the geographical scope of its interest covers the entire continent, the Institute's main concern is with sub-Saharan Africa, and Southern Africa in particular.

Geographical Area of Activity: Africa.

Publications: Annual Report; *Inside AISA* (newsletter, 6 a year); *Africa Insight* (quarterly); *Africa at a Glance: Facts and Figures; Africa A–Z: Country Profiles; After September 11th: An African Perspective on USA Foreign Policy;* books; research papers, wall maps.

Finance: The Institute is funded through a state grant, corporate sponsorships and membership fees.

Principal Staff: Exec. Dir Dr Eddy Maloka; Chief Financial Officer Khehla Moloi.

Address: POB 630, Pretoria 0001; Nipilar House, cnr of Hamilton and Vermeulen Sts, Arcadia, Pretoria.

Telephone: (12) 328-6970; **Fax:** (12) 323-8153; **Internet:** www.ai.org.za; **e-mail:** ai@ai.org.za.

Endangered Wildlife Trust

Founded in October, 1973, a non-profit NGO that aims to conserve the diversity of species in Southern Africa. It is a fully-accredited NGO member of the IUCN—World Conservation Union (q.v.).

Activities: Founded to promote the conservation of biological diversity in Southern Africa; conducts research; organizes practical conservation campaigns; aims to raise public awareness of conservation and environmental issues; issues publications.

Geographical Area of Activity: Southern Africa.

Publications: *Vision* (annually); *EW* (magazine).

Trustees: Prof Robyn Stein (Chair.).

Principal Staff: Dir Dr Gerhard Verdoorn.

Address: Private Bag X11, Parkview 2122.

Telephone: (11) 486-1102; **Fax:** (11) 486-1506; **Internet:** www.ewt.org.za; **e-mail:** ewt@ewt.org.za.

Foundation for Education, Science and Technology—FEST

Established in 1955 to increase knowledge and understanding of the sciences.

Activities: The Foundation promotes education in mathematics, biology, geography and science and technology; promotes the study of Afrikaans and English in schools, and culture among the whole population; organizes the Annual National Youth Science Olympiad; disseminates information; holds annual conferences and seminars; sponsors competitions and awards; runs the Bureau for Scientific Publications, a science and technology museum, and resource centres.

Geographical Area of Activity: South Africa.

Publications: *Archimedes* (quarterly, in Afrikaans and English); *Easy Science; Science and Government Brief; Science and Parliament Report.*

Finance: Total assets 12,992,685 rand (2002); total income 16,135,365 rand, total expenditure 16,878,857 rand (2002).

Governing Council: Prof. Michael Kahn (Chair.); Prof. Mike Bruton; Cynthia Chishimba; Prof. Rosemary Falcon; Raymond Mabuza; Dr. Anastassios Pouris; Prof. Reckson Thakhathi.

Principal Staff: CEO Dr. Anastassios Pouris.

Address: Didacta Building, 211 Skinner St; POB 1758, Pretoria 0001.

Telephone: (12) 392-9300; **Fax:** (12) 320-7803; **Internet:** www.fest.org.za; **e-mail:** info@fest.org.za.

Gift of the Givers Foundation

Established in 1992; aims to to build bridges between peoples of different cultures and religions engendering goodwill, harmonious co-existence, tolerance and mutual respect.

Activities: Active nationally and internationally, through operating education, health-care and humanitarian programmes and providing support for a range of different projects, including bursaries for international study, HIV/AIDS workshops and anti-drug campaigns in South Africa. Outside of South Africa funding has also been made to projects in Afghanistan, Bosnia, Chechnya, Goma, India, Iran, Malawi, Mozambique, Palestinian Autonomous Areas, Rwanda, Somalia, Sudan and Turkey. In 2002 the Foundation launched the Millions for Africa Campaign.

Geographical Area of Activity: South Africa, Afghanistan, Bosnia, Chechnya, Goma, India, Iran, Malawi, Mozambique, Palestinian Autonomous Areas, Rwanda, Somalia, Sudan and Turkey.

Address: POB 8213, Cumberwood, Pietermaritzburg 3235.

Telephone: (33) 345-0163; **Fax:** (33) 394-3780; **Internet:** www.giftofthegivers.co.za; **e-mail:** info@giftofthegivers.co.za.

International Fundraising Consortium—INTERFUND

INTERFUND was founded in 1986 as a consortium of donors mainly based in Europe (and in particular Scandinavia) to help advance democracy through offering financial support for South African civil society organizations. In 1999, INTERFUND registered as a Section 21 South African company. Seeks to empower communities previously disadvantaged by the social and political injustices of apartheid. In doing so it aims to contribute to the building of a non-racial, non-sexist democracy, founded on strong civil society and respect for human rights.

Activities: INTERFUND's core operations are aimed at the creation of partnerships in advancing democracy, development, social and economic justice, and poverty alleviation, through mobilisation of financial, as well as non-financial, resources to support civil society initiatives aimed at the transformation of the power relationships within society and the eradication of poverty. Currently supports programmes in the following areas: poverty alleviation; HIV/AIDS; gender and women's development; human rights and democratisation; arts and culture; and environmental justice. In collaboration with the European Union, INTERFUND provides a capacity building resource for its project partners in order to optimise the manner in which core functions of the organizations are met. The Research and Information Department conducts research and information activities within the development sector and disseminates information to the private and corporate sectors, especially the development sector. Donor partners include Humanistisch Instituut voor Ontwikkelings Samenwerking—HIVOS (Netherlands, q.v.); IBIS; Norwegian Students' and Academics' International Assistance Fund (SAIH); Charles Stewart Mott Foundation (q.v.); European Union; African Harvest Management Company; and Joseph Rowntree Charitable Trust (q.v.).

Geographical Area of Activity: Southern Africa, particularly organizations operating in the provinces of KwaZulu Natal, Northern Province, Eastern Cape and Mpumalanga..

Restrictions: Grants are made only to specific non-governmental and community-based organizations in South Africa.

Publications: Annual Report; *Development Update* (quarterly journal); and occasional publications.

Principal Staff: Dir Alicia Pieterse.

Address: POB 32340, Braamfontein, Johannesburg 2017.

Telephone: (11) 403-2966; **Fax:** (11) 339-2740; **Internet:** www.interfund.org.za; **e-mail:** thina@itfd.co.za.

Nelson Mandela Children's Fund

Established by Nelson Mandela, who donated one-third of his salary for five years to start up the foundation.

Activities: The Foundation assists children in difficult social and economic circumstances. It aims to alleviate the plight of children, to fight exploitation and abuse, prevent homelessness, and provide education, counselling and care. The

Fund's main programmes operate in the areas of disability, education and development, leadership, and child welfare. In 2002 launched a joint initiative with The Diana, Princess of Wales Memorial Fund (q.v.) aiming to mitigate the impact of HIV/AIDS on children and support families coping with terminal illness and bereavement. Maintains offices in a number of countries world-wide, including Australia, France, the United Kingdom and the USA, with offices also opening in Germany, Italy and Japan. Also works in association with the independently registered Nelson Mandela Children's Fund (Canada) (q.v.).

Geographical Area of Activity: South Africa.

Finance: Total income 49,589,000 rand, grants disbursed 19,110,000 rand (2001).

Principal Staff: Founder and Chair. Nelson Mandela; CEO Sibongile Mkhabela.

Address: 33 Scott St, Waverly 2090; POB 797, Highlands North 2037.

Telephone: (11) 786-9140; **Fax:** (11) 786-9197; **Internet:** www.mandela-children.com; **e-mail:** info@nmcf.co.za.

Nelson Mandela Foundation

Established in 1999 by Nelson Mandela to develop infrastructure in the areas of democracy, education and health care.

Activities: Supports the development of democracy education and health care infrastructure in South Africa through encouraging the understanding and use of the democratic process by previously disenfranchized South Africans; financing the construction of new schools and equipping with new technology; and supporting primary health care projects across South Africa, particularly focusing on combating malaria, HIV/AIDS and tuberculosis, as well as providing family planning and access to fresh water.

Geographical Area of Activity: South Africa.

Finance: In 1999 the Foundation received donations totalling US $17,500,000 from the Bill and Melinda Gates Foundation (q.v.) and the Craig and Susan McCaw Foundation.

Principal Staff: Pres. Nelson Mandela; Chief Exec. John Samuel.

Address: Private Bag X70 000, Houghton 2041.

National Research Foundation—NRF

Established in April 1999 by the South African Government, replacing the former Foundation for Research Development, to support and promote research through funding, human resource development and the provision of the necessary research facilities in order to facilitate the creation of knowledge, innovation and development in all fields of science and technology, including indigenous knowledge, and thereby to contribute to the improvement of the quality of life of all the people of South Africa.

Activities: The Foundation offers research grants, scholarships and bursaries to researchers and students at the country's higher education institutions. All support programmes give high priority to the development of black and female researchers and building research capacity at previously disadvantaged institutions. The Foundation aims to focus on the development of skills and research related to South Africa's indigenous knowledge systems. Research and research skills are promoted across many disciplines; including natural sciences and engineering, agricultural and environmental sciences, health sciences, and social sciences and the humanities. Five national research facilities also offer opportunities for research, advanced training and international collaboration. The Foundation also promotes collaboration between disciplines and institutions through international agreements and exchange programme. Several research-related databases are maintained.

Geographical Area of Activity: South Africa.

Restrictions: Training of human resources through grants essential.

Publications: Annual Report; newsletter; research publications of national facilities.

Finance: Primary source of funding is an annual grant from the Government. Assets 547,737,000 rand (March 2002); total income 498,753,000 rand, total grants and bursaries 307,441,000 (2002).

Board of Directors: Prof. Daya Reddy (Chair.); Prof. Stef Coetzee; Bill Cooper; Prof. Carolyn Hamilton; Dr John Job; Dr Trevor Mdaka; Prof. Connie Mogale; Prof. Phuti Ngoepe; Maphumuzana Nxumalo; Bridgette Radebe; Prof. Herbert Vilakazi; Prof. Johan van Zyl.

Principal Staff: Pres. and CEO Dr Khotso Mokhele; Vice-Pres. Dr Gerhard von Gruenewaldt.

Address: POB 2600, Meiring Naudé Road Brummeria, Pretoria 0001.

Telephone: (12) 481-4000; **Fax:** (12) 349-1179; **Internet:** www.nrf.ac.za; **e-mail:** info@nrf.ac.za.

Open Society Foundation for South Africa

Founded in July 1993 to support the promotion and protection of human rights and open, democratic society. The Foundation is an independent foundation, part of the Soros foundations network.

Activities: The Foundation operates in the fields of civil society, education, law and criminal justice, public health, youth and women, democracy building, economic reform, and information and the media. Also runs a series of annual lectures.

Geographical Area of Activity: South Africa.

Publications: Annual Report.

Finance: Annual expenditure US $6,984,000 (2001).

Board of Directors: Fikile Bam; Azhar Cachalia; G. T. Ferreira; Bongani Majola; Nhlanhla Mjoli-Mncube; Murphy Morobe; Zyda Rylands; Michael Savage.

Principal Staff: Exec. Dir Zohra Dawood.

Address: POB 23161, Claremont 7735; 1st Floor, Colinton House, Fedsure Oval, 1 Oakdale Rd, Newlands 7700.

Telephone: (21) 683-3489; **Fax:** (21) 683-3550; **Internet:** www.osf.org.za; **e-mail:** admin@ct.osf.org.za.

Open Society Initiative for Southern Africa

Founded in 1997, an independent foundation, part of the Soros foundations network, to promote the development of an open society in Southern Africa.

Activities: Operates in countries of Southern Africa, supporting projects in the areas of education, human rights, democracy, health, media, economic affairs and business development. The Foundation is committed to developing funding strategies that encourage and develop self-reliance and effectiveness; provides start-up funds to projects which develop credible plans to sustain themselves; provides funds for projects with a life span of three years, donating approximately one-third of resources needed to operate projects.

Geographical Area of Activity: Southern Africa (Angola, Botswana, Lesotho, Malawi, Mozambique, Namibia, Swaziland, Zambia and Zimbabwe).

Finance: Annual expenditure US $6,108,000 (2001).

Trustees: Dr F. Van Zyl Slabbert (Chair.); Ottillie Abrahams; Maurice Attala; Obede Baloi; Oagile Dingake; Nokukhanya Gamedze; Thandi Henson; Puleng Letuka; Esther Mede.

Principal Staff: Exec. Dir Lucy Muyoyeta.

Address: Braamfontein Centre, 12th Floor, 23 Jorrisen St, Braamfontein 2017.

Telephone: (11) 403-3414; **Fax:** (11) 403-2708; **Internet:** www.soros.org/natfound/southern-africa; **e-mail:** osisainfo@osiafrica.org.

Rhino and Elephant Foundation

Established in 1988 for the protection of the rhinoceros and elephant from the threat of extinction in Southern Africa.

Activities: Provides funding for conservation and research projects, and practical support to wildlife management agencies; co-operates with other NGOs, government agencies and wildlife management organizations.

Geographical Area of Activity: Southern Africa.

Principal Staff: Chair. Clive Walker; Exec. Officer Heather Cowie.

Address: POB 381, Bedfordview 2008.

Telephone: (11) 453-7648; **Fax:** (11) 453-7649.

South African Institute of International Affairs

Founded in 1934 as an independent NGO, to perform a public educational role by promoting an understanding of international questions, especially South Africa's foreign relations.

Activities: Operates in the field of international relations, both nationally and internationally, with special emphasis on regional relations, conflict resolution, arms control and illegal economic migration. Activities include self-conducted programmes of research, Visiting Fellow programmes, fellowships and awards, study and discussion groups, lectures, public addresses, conferences, symposia and publications. Maintains a library and information service.

Geographical Area of Activity: South Africa.

Publications: *South African Yearbook of International Affairs* (annual); *South African Journal of International Affairs* (2 a year); occasional papers, special studies, reports and publications.

National Executive Council: F. Phaswana (Chair.); representatives of the Institute's branches: Cape Town, Witwatersrand, Pietermaritzburg, Durban, Pretoria and East London.

Principal Staff: Nat. Dir Dr Greg Mills.

Address: POB 31596, Braamfontein, Johannesburg 2017.

Telephone: (11) 339-2021; **Fax:** (11) 339-2154; **Internet:** www.wits.ac.za/saiia; **e-mail:** saiiagen@global.co.za.

South African Institute of Race Relations

Founded in 1929 to encourage peace, goodwill and practical co-operation between the various races in South Africa, and to promote a free and open society based on liberal democratic values.

Activities: The Institute conducts research on macro-economic, socio-economic, labour, constitutional and political trends, as well as on race relations in South Africa. Also administers a large bursary programme for students at universities and technikons, and provides a consultancy service.

Geographical Area of Activity: South Africa.

Publications: *South Africa Survey* (annually); *Frontiers of Freedom* (quarterly); *Fast Facts* (monthly); *Spotlight Series* (occasional).

Finance: Net assets 22,605,704 rand (1999); annual revenue 8,014,601 rand, expenditure 7,285,966 rand (1999).

Council: T. J. Sono (Pres.); Prof. L. Schlemmer, Dr M. M. A. Shezi, H. Suzman (Vice-Pres).

Principal Staff: Chief Exec. John Kane-Berman.

Address: POB 31044, Braamfontein, Johannesburg 2017.

Telephone: (11) 403-3600; **Fax:** (11) 403-3671; **Internet:** www.sairr.org.za; **e-mail:** sairr@sairr.org.za.

Helen Suzman Foundation

Established in 1995 to promote liberal democracy in South Africa and other Southern African countries.

Activities: Carries out research and surveys on political parties, elections and voter choice in Southern African countries; conducts training and empowerment programmes; and promotes networking between similar organizations in Southern Africa.

Geographical Area of Activity: Southern Africa.

Restrictions: Not a grant-making organization.

Publications: *Focus* (quarterly); *Can South Africa's democracy survive our history and political culture?; Political Opinion and the Crisis of Zimbabwe;* and other special reports.

Finance: Receives grants and donations.

Trustees: D. Band; C. Eglin; R. Erkens; R. Jafta; P. de Lille; N. Mathiane; T. Nolutshungu; R. Steyn; D. Unterhalter.

Principal Staff: Dir Lawrence Schlemmer.

Address: POB 1524, Parklands 2121.

Telephone: (11) 880-3352; **Fax:** (11) 880-1850; **Internet:** www.hsf.org.za; **e-mail:** hsfound@iafrica.com.

Desmond Tutu Educational Trust

Established in 1990 by Archbishop Desmond Tutu and Professor Jakes Gerwel, aiming to transform tertiary education in South Africa.

Activities: The Trust works to provide opportunities to historically disadvantaged students to develop knowledge and skills that are market orientated; contribute towards the restructuring of a non-racial education system; promote participation by black students in leadership programmes and develop the leadership capabilities of black students; reflect a curriculum responsive to the socio-economic needs of South Africa; facilitate dialogue, co-operation and institutional sharing amongst tertiary institutions; assist students to improve their academic and social performance; and facilitate involvement in community work. Operates through two main programmes: the Tertiary Education Linkages Programme (TELP), through which the Trust provides academic development services; and the Support to Tertiary Education Programmes (STEP) , through which it distributes grants. Also offers the Desmond Tutu Footprints of Legends Leadership Awards, including the Award for Promoting Social Justice and Equity.

Geographical Area of Activity: South Africa.

Address: POB 394, Kasselvlei 753.

Telephone: (21) 951-7544; **Fax:** (21) 951-7668; **Internet:** www.tututrust.org.za; **e-mail:** info@tututrust.org.za.

WWF South Africa

A national organization of the WWF—World Wide Fund for Nature (q.v.), until 1995 known as the Southern African Nature Foundation, which was established in 1968 by HRH Prince Bernhard of the Netherlands and Dr Anton Rupert, to assist in the protection and conservation for future generations of nature in all its forms; to educate the public in the interests of nature conservation; and to raise and distribute funds for urgent projects of nature conservation in Southern Africa.

Activities: Operates nationally in the field of conservation of natural resources to preserve genetic, species and ecosystem diversity; to promote sustainable use of resources; and to fight pollution. The organization has assisted in the creation or expansion of 11 national parks and 23 protected areas; funded or managed more than 1,000 conservation projects, including plant conservation programmes and projects to protect more than 70 species of animals; launched Conservation with People projects, which promote co-operative community-based conservation; promoted environmental education; and established six chairs and several research programmes in conservation, environmental education and wildlife management at South African universities.

Geographical Area of Activity: South Africa.

Restrictions: Funding is restricted to South African conservation activities which fall within WWF South Africa's strategic focus.

Publications: Annual Report; *Panda Bulletin* (3 a year).

Finance: Funded by membership fees, donations and sponsorship. Total assets 248,185,000 rand (2001–2001); annual revenue 43,888,000 rand, disbursements 29,859,000 rand (2001–2001).

Trustees: Dr Anton Rupert (Pres.); T. Vosloo (Chair.); Fred Phaswana (Vice-Chair.); and 130 others.

Principal Staff: CEO Dr Ian Macdonald.

Address: Private Bag X2, Die Boord, Stellenbosch 7613.

Telephone: (21) 888-2800; **Fax:** (21) 888-2888; **Internet:** www.panda.org.za; **e-mail:** wilhop@iafrica.com.

Spain

FOUNDATION CENTRES AND CO-ORDINATING BODIES

Agregación Nacional de Fundaciones para la Promoción de la Acción Social 'Luis Vives' (Luis Vives National Aggregation of Foundations for the Promotion of Social Action)

Founded in 1989 by the merger of 11 private foundations, now supervised by the Ministry of Social Affairs, to assist people with social problems, and to provide technical assistance and support to non-profit organizations in the area of social welfare and social services.

Activities: The organization provides technical support and consulting services to foundations active in the area of social services, especially with regard to management, programme design and evaluation. Also collaborates with such organizations in supporting projects in the field of social welfare. Promotes the development of new foundations and trusts. Offers grants for the participation of organizations in international forums and for international liaison, and promotes the international exchange of research in social welfare projects.

Geographical Area of Activity: Spain.

Publications: Annual Report; brochures.

Trustees: O. Alzaga Villaamil (Pres.).

Principal Staff: Dir Antonio Sánchez.

Address: Plaza de Oriente 7, bajo izquierda, 28013 Madrid.

Telephone: (91) 5400878; **Fax:** (91) 5419052; **Internet:** www.fundacionluisvives.org; **e-mail:** luisvives@fundacionluisvives.org.

Confederación Española de Fundaciones (Spanish Confederation of Foundations)

Established in 1995, an association of more than 470 non-profit foundations; in 2003 merged with the Centro de Fundaciones, to form a collective association of approximately 770 member foundations.

Activities: Provides a forum for foundations and represents their common interests; co-ordinates initiatives and resolves problems. Promotes co-operation between foundations nationally and internationally. Gives advice to foundations on a range of legal, fiscal, economic, financial and telecommunication issues; operates training courses, conferences and seminars; and maintains a database of foundations and other funding sources.

Geographical Area of Activity: Spain.

Publications: *BIS–Fundaciones* (fortnightly newsletter); *Tribuna de las Fundaciones* (monthly bulletin); monographs.

Principal Staff: Sec.-Gen. Miguel A. Cabra de Luna; Programme Co-ordinator Rosa Gallego Garcia.

Address: Velazquez 18, 2° izquierda, 28001 Madrid.

Telephone: (91) 5782585; **Fax:** (91) 5783623; **Internet:** www.fundaciones.org; **e-mail:** confederacion@fundaciones.org.

Fundación Empresa y Sociedad (Business and Society Foundation)

Established in 1995 to encourage Spanish and foreign companies working in Spain to improve their corporate community development. Part of the CSR Europe network.

Activities: Operates in the areas of research, debate and advice, promoting discussion on corporate community involvement in Spain. Carries out research on issues relevant to business, and acts as a source of information on community commitment, practice and experience. Links companies, NGOs and government agencies. Advises companies on corporate community involvement and establishing community involvement initiatives, and manages projects. Produces a database on community programmes and the voluntary sector. Awards the Premios Empresa y Sociedad in recognition of companies' community activities.

Geographical Area of Activity: Spain.

Publications: *Euroguía para Entidades sin Ánimo Lucro; La Estrategia Social de la Empresa*; Newsletter (fortnightly); Annual Report.

Finance: Total assets 106,992,130 pesetas (1999).

Trustees: Felipe Oriol Díaz de Bustamante (Chair.); Manuel Ramiro Regueira (Vice-Pres.); José Ignacio Olivares Zardosa (Gen. Sec.).

Principal Staff: Dir Francisco Abad.

Address: Goya 15, 2° derecha, 28001 Madrid.

Telephone: (91) 4358997; **Fax:** (91) 4353974; **Internet:** www.empresaysociedad.org; **e-mail:** fundacion@empresaysociedad.org.

Fundación Lealtad

Established in February 2001 to support the non-profit sector, particularly in the area of social action.

Activities: Aims to make the non-profit sector in Spain more effective and to help it attract donations, through research into the non-profit sector in Spain; disseminates the results through publications and reports.

Geographical Area of Activity: Spain.

Publications: Annual Report; *La Transparencia de la Solidaridad; Guia 1 de la Transparencia y Buenas Prácticas de las ONG* (two-part series).

Finance: Annual budget €386,867 (2001).

Principal Staff: Dir María Ortega.

Address: Plaza de la Lealtad 3, 4th planta, Madrid.

Telephone: (91) 7890100; **Fax:** (91) 7890120; **Internet:** www.fundacionlealtad.org.

FOUNDATIONS, TRUSTS AND NON-PROFIT ORGANIZATIONS

ANESVAD

Founded in 1968 by José Luis Gamarra Aranoa to undertake sanitary and social development projects in less-developed countries.

Activities: Operates nationally and internationally in the fields of aid to less-developed countries, education, law and human rights, and medicine and health, through self-conducted programmes, grants, conferences and publications. The organization has developed a wide range of projects including: the construction and maintenance of medical dispensaries and sanitariums; treatments to eradicate leprosy; distributing medicines; providing assistance to disabled ex-servicemen, refugees and immigrants; construction of community and training centres, water wells, dwellings, workshops and infrastructure; social integration programmes for single mothers; construction of orphanages and special assistance programmes for orphaned children; educational programmes providing professional training; construction of school buildings; scholarships; and literacy programmes. Supports projects in Africa, Asia, Central and South America, and Europe.

Geographical Area of Activity: Africa, Asia, Central and South America, and Europe.

Publications: Magazines, leaflets.

Finance: Annual revenue and expenditure 3,210,000,000 pesetas (2000).

Trustees: Angeles Ainzua; José Ignacio Castro; Jorge Fidalgo; José Luis Gamarra; Francisco Javier Ibarra; Andres Retolaza; José Luis Ruis de Ruiz; Jorge Sanz; José Miguel Sustacha.

Principal Staff: Pres. Jose Luis Gamarra; Dir Jose Ignacio Castro.

Address: Teofilo Guiard 2, 48011 Bilbao.

Telephone: (94) 4418008; **Fax:** (94) 4410739; **Internet:** www.anesvad.org; **e-mail:** anesvad@anesvad.org.

Centro de Investigación para la Paz—CIP (Centre for Peace Research)

Founded in 1984 by the Fundación Hogar del Empleado—FUHEM (q.v.), to conduct research in the areas of education, peace and ecology, and to publish its findings.

Activities: The Centre conducts research; disseminates information; organizes seminars and conferences; maintains a press and communications office, and a documentation centre containing around 5,000 publications, which is open to the public; organizes training courses for school teachers on educating for peace; and co-operates with international peace centres. In 1988 the Centre was awarded the 'Messengers of Peace' prize by the United Nations.

Geographical Area of Activity: Spain.

Publications: *Guerra y Paz en el comienzo del siglo XXI; De Nueva York a Kabul; La Situation del Mundo 2002; Políticas mundiales, tendencias peligrosas; Anuario sobre paz, militarización y conflictos; Papeles para la Paz; Colección de Economía Crítica* (series); *Ecología Política; CIP Reports on Peace and Ecology*; Annual Report; numerous books on peace studies and ecology.

Principal Staff: Chair. Enrique Benedicto Mamblona; Dir Mariano Aquirre.

Address: Calle Duque de Sesto 40, 28009 Madrid.

Telephone: (91) 4310280; **Fax:** (91) 5763271; **Internet:** www.cip.fuhem.es; **e-mail:** fuhem@fuhem.es.

Fundació Jaume Bofill (Jaume Bofill Foundation)

Founded in 1969 by Teresa Roca Formosa, Josep Maria Vilaseca Marcet and Frederico Bayer Ros, to encourage initiatives in the social sciences which seek to achieve a deeper understanding of society and to contribute in some tangible way towards its betterment. Merged with the Fundació Serveis de Cultura Popular in December 2000.

Activities: Promotes initiatives which work towards a better understanding of society and improving it by eliminating all forms of inequality and discrimination and extending culture and education to those who are socially deprived. Awards scholarships and individual research grants in sociology, political science, demography, city planning, etc.; makes grants to research teams and centres to further the development of research in these areas; supports meetings and discussions between social science researchers and co-operates with similar organizations, including those of international scope. Its activities come from the fields selected as a priority for sucessive four-year periods. The two priority fields for the period 2001–05 are education and citizenship.

Geographical Area of Activity: Catalonia.

Publications: Newsletter (quarterly, in Catalan); books containing research projects of major contemporary relevance (also in Catalan).

Finance: Annual expenditure 239,700,148 pesetas (2000).

Trustees: T. Roca (Pres.); Joan Majó (Vice-Pres.); N. Castanyer (Sec.); X. Aragay; M. Casals; A. Castiñeira; J. Cornet; A. Ramon; I. Tubella; J. A. Vicens.

Principal Staff: Dir J. Sánchez; Grants Officer T. Climent.

Address: Provença 324, 08037 Barcelona.

Telephone: (93) 4588700; **Fax:** (93) 4588708; **Internet:** www.fbofill.org; **e-mail:** fbofill@fbofill.org.

Fundació CIDOB (CIDOB Foundation)

Established in 1973 to study and carry out research in the area of international relations and international co-operation.

Activities: Operates in the areas of development studies, education and international affairs, through self-conducted programmes, research, conferences, training courses and publications. Fields of interest are international politics, strategic studies, development and co-operation, intercultural relations, migrations and population and development, with a geographical focus on the Arab world, Asia, sub-Saharan Africa, Central and South America, Central and Eastern Europe, countries of the former USSR, and the Mediterranean region. Also maintains a documentation centre.

Geographical Area of Activity: Spain.

Publications: *Anuario Internacional; Afers Internationals; Annual Report;* monographs and special reports.

Finance: Annual revenue approx. 200,000,000 pesetas.

Principal Staff: Dir Josep Ribera; Man. Dir Francesca Munt; Asst. Dir Anna Borrull, Carmen Claudín; Pres. Narcís Serra.

Address: Elisabets 12, 08001 Barcelona.

Telephone: (93) 3026495; **Fax:** (93) 3022118; **Internet:** www.cidob.org; **e-mail:** cidob@cidob.org.

Fundació 'La Caixa' ('La Caixa' Foundation)

Established in 1991, following the merger of the Fundació Caixa de Pensions and the Fundació Caixa de Barcelona.

Activities: Administers the funds that the Caja de Ahorros y Pensiones de Barcelona allots to its social welfare programme. Aims to respond to social needs not met by other institutions, in the fields of culture, education, science, and social aid and health-care initiatives, both through its own programmes and programmes in conjunction with other organizations, both in Spain and in countries where La Caixa savings bank operates. The Foundation owns two science museums, a school of nursing and art galleries (the Foundation maintains a collection of contemporary art).

Geographical Area of Activity: Spain and international, in countries where La Caixa operates.

Publications: *Estrella* (6 a year); Annual Report; brochures.

Finance: Funded by the Caixa d'Estalvis i Pensions de Barcelona; annual budget €169,000,000 (2002).

Board of Trustees: Josep Vilarasau (Chair.); Alejandro Plasencia (Vice-Chair.).

Principal Staff: Sec.-Gen. Luis Reverter; Dir Gen. Luis Monreal; Deputy Dir Gen. Antoni Aliana, Aurora Sanz.

Address: Avda Diagonal 621–629, 08028 Barcelona.

Telephone: (93) 4046000; **Fax:** (93) 4046116; **Internet:** www.fundacio.lacaixa.es; **e-mail:** info.fundacio@lacaixa.es.

Fundación de los Agentes Comerciales de España (Foundation of Spanish Commercial Agents)

Established in 1989 for cultural and social purposes.

Activities: Operates in the areas of economic affairs, education, international affairs and social welfare, nationally and internationally through self-conducted programmes and conferences, and nationally through grants to individuals and institutions, prizes and publications. Maintains a database.

Geographical Area of Activity: International.

Publications: *La Gaceta del Agente Comercial* (journal, 6 a year).

Principal Staff: Pres. José Luis Vazquez Dequint; Montserrat Trill.

Address: Goya 55, 5°, 28001 Madrid.

Telephone: (91) 4363666; **Fax:** (91) 5770084; **Internet:** www.cgac.es; **e-mail:** fundacion@cgac.es.

Fundación Isaac Albéniz (Isaac Albéniz Foundation)

Established in November 1986 by Federico Sopeña, Paloma O'Shea, Elena G. Botín, J. L. Martínez Marauri, Pedro Robles and Luis Revenga to support the arts and humanities and education.

Activities: Operates in the areas of the arts and humanities and education, through self-conducted programmes, research, scholarships and fellowships, publications and training courses. Principal activities are the Concurso Internacional de Piano de Santander Paloma O'Shea, supporting a music school, maintaining an archive and documentation centre and funding a music academy in Santander.

Geographical Area of Activity: Spain.

Publications: *Rubinstein y España; Albénez; Imágenes de la Música Iberoamericana; Imágenes de Isaac Albéniz.*

Principal Staff: Pres. Paloma O'Shea; Vice-Pres. Vicente Ferrer, Enrique Franco.

Address: Barquillo 6, 4° derecha, 28004 Madrid.

Telephone: (91) 5230419; **Fax:** (91) 5329661; **Internet:** www.fundacionalbeniz.com; **e-mail:** fundacion@albeniz.com.

Fundación Alzheimer España (Alzheimer Foundation of Spain)

Founded in 1991 to inform, assess, support and train families and carers of those suffering from Alzheimer's Disease, to increase the possibilities of early diagnosis and to disseminate information about the disease.

Activities: Operates in the fields of medicine and health and social welfare and social studies, through training courses, consultancy, publications and international conferences. A founding member of Alzheimer Europe.

Geographical Area of Activity: Spain.

Publications: *Vivir con la enfermedad de Alzheimer; Vivencias Familiares;* Proceedings of the European Conference on Alzheimer's Disease and Public Health; Bulletin (quarterly).

Governing Board: Micheline Selmes (Chair.); Prof. Juan José López-Ibor (Vice-Chair.); Dr Adolfo Toledano (Treas.); Dr Jacques Selmes (Gen. Sec.); Antonio López Puertas; Luis Felipe Ramos Llano.

Principal Staff: Social Worker Diana Gonzalez Paez; Carmen Rodriguez Seizo.

Address: Calle Pedro Muguruza 1, 6c, 28036 Madrid.

Telephone: (91) 3431165; **Fax:** (91) 3595950; **Internet:** www.alzheimer.rediris.es; **e-mail:** alzheuro@yahoo.es.

Fundación Carlos de Amberes (Carlos de Amberes Foundation)

Established in 1594 by Carlos de Amberes, a Flemish merchant living in Madrid, to support pilgrims from the then Spanish Low Countries. In 1988 the Foundation adapted its aims from acts of charity to cultural activities, aiming to build a united Europe.

Activities: Operates in the field of the arts and humanities, acting as a cultural link between Spain, Belgium, Luxembourg, France and the Netherlands, through organizing exhibitions, courses, seminars, conferences and music concerts, held at the Foundation's headquarters. Maintains a library specializing in European Union issues.

Geographical Area of Activity: Spain.

Publications: Annual Report; exhibition catalogues.

Executive Commitee: Miguel A. Aguilar (Pres.); Daniel de Busturia (Sec.).

Principal Staff: Dir Catherine Geens.

Address: Claudio Coello 99, 28006 Madrid.

Telephone: (91) 4352201; **Fax:** (91) 5781092; **Internet:** www.fcamberes.org; **e-mail:** fca@fcaamberes.org.

Fundación Ramón Areces (Ramón Areces Foundation)

Founded in March 1976 by Ramón Areces Rodríguez to support scientific and technical research.

Activities: The Foundation co-operates with other organizations interested in the promotion and preservation of Spanish culture and scientific research. Awards research grants for scientific and technical projects, and scholarships to universities and research centres abroad. The cultural programme includes lectures, symposia, conferences and inter-university courses.

Geographical Area of Activity: Spain.

Finance: Annual expenditure approx. US $11,000,000.

Trustees: Isidoro Alvarez (Pres.); César Alvarez; José A. Alvarez; J. Hermoso; Florencio Lasaga; Carlos Martínez Echavarría; Juan Manuel de Mingo; Jorge Pont; José R. Tamargo.

Principal Staff: Sec.-Gen. Juan González-Palomino.

Address: Vitruvio 5, 28006 Madrid.

Telephone: (91) 5158982; **Fax:** (91) 5645243; **Internet:** www.fundacionareces.es.

Fundación Banco Bilbao Vizcaya Argentaria—Fundación BBVA (Bilbao Vizcaya Argentaria Bank Foundation)

Founded in 1988 to create conditions which support discussion on the problems and challenges faced by society. Merged with the Fundación Argentaria in 2000.

Activities: Operates internationally, principally in Europe, in the fields of economic and international affairs, law, and science and technology, through programmes, research, symposia, conferences, publications and summer courses. Collaborates in its areas of interest with other groups and organizations. It has established several programmes, including a series of international symposia and projects on such topics as finance, genetic therapy, visions of Europe, Ibero-American law and culture; the Permanent Brains Trusts, to analyze and evaluate forms of innovations in specific areas; and Documenta, the Foundation's information and publications centre.

Geographical Area of Activity: Spain, Europe, the USA, and Central and South America.

Restrictions: Does not make grants.

Publications: Working papers; Annual Report; Newsletter; books.

Finance: Total assets €81,145,695 (2001); total expenditure €10,193,165 (2001).

Board of Patrons: Francisco Gonzalez Rodríguez (Pres.); Ramón Bustamante y de la Mora; Jesús María Caínzos Fernández; José Maldonado Ramos; Gregorio Marañón y Bertrán de Lis; Marcelino Oreja Aguirre; Rafael Pardo Avellaneda.

Principal Staff: Man. Dir Rafael Pardo Avellaneda.

Address: Gran Vía 12, 2°, 48001 Bilbao.

Telephone: (94) 4875252; **Fax:** (94) 4244621; **Internet:** www.fbbva.es; **e-mail:** informacion@fbbva.es.

Fundación Pedro Barrié de la Maza, Conde de Fenosa (Pedro Barrié de la Maza, Count of Fenosa Foundation)

Founded in 1966 by Pedro Barrié de la Maza, Conde de Fenosa, to promote research in the sciences and in the field of arts and letters; to support deserving Spanish students; to promote the industrialization and prosperity of Spain in general and the Galician region in particular; and to support charitable, educational and social institutions, with priority to those in the Galician region.

Activities: Operates mainly in the Galician region in the fields of education, social welfare and studies, science, medicine and the arts and humanities, through self-conducted programmes, research, grants to individuals and institutions, conferences, courses and publications. The Foundation awards scholarships, prizes and research grants, and has financed the construction and equipment of technical schools and cultural and social institutions. Established the Galician Institute of Economic Studies in 1994.

Geographical Area of Activity: Spain (Galicia).

Publications: *Diccionario de Diccionarios; Yemen. En la tierra de la Reina de Saba; Reconstrucción del Coro Pétreo del Maestro Mateo.*

Finance: Total assets approx. €600,000,000.

Trustees: Carmela Arias y Díaz de Rábago (Pres.); José Maria Aria Mosquera, Joaquín Arias y Díaz de Rábago (Vice-Pres.); and 14 others.

Principal Staff: Gen. Sec. Vicente Arias Mosquera.

Address: Cantón Grande 9, 15003 A Coruña.

Telephone: (981) 221525; **Fax:** (981) 224448; **Internet:** www.fbarrie.org; **e-mail:** public@fbarrie.org.

Fundación Bios para la Conservación de la Naturaleza (Bios Foundation for Nature Conservation)

Founded in May 1989 by Carlos Segovia, Jesús Vozmediano and Anastasio Senra to support the study and conservation of nature and the environment.

Activities: The Foundation operates nationally and internationally in the field of conservation and the environment, through self-conducted programmes, research, training courses and publications.

Geographical Area of Activity: International.

Publications: *Anastasio Senra Ornithological Station Bulletin.*

Trustees: Carlos Segovia (Pres.).

Principal Staff: Dir, Biological Reserve of Puerto Moral Dr Enrique E. Alés; Dir, Anastasio Senra Ornithological Station Antonio J. de Andrés.

Address: Avda Manuel Siurot 3, Edif. San Leandro 6-2, 41013 Seville.

Telephone: (95) 4615697; **Fax:** (95) 4214251; **e-mail:** fbios@bme.es.

Fundación Marcelino Botín (Marcelino Botín Foundation)

Established in 1964 by Marcelino Botín to satisfy any cultural, intellectual and welfare requirement.

Activities: Operates in the fields of science and technology, social sciences, arts and creativity, heritage and social development, through grants, awarding prizes (such as the Manuel Valcárcel International Piano Composition Competition with a first prize of €9,000) and organizing conferences, training courses, concerts and exhibitions.

Geographical Area of Activity: Europe.

Publications: Library includes section on Cantabria in historical documents, art, environment and sustainable development.

Finance: Annual expenditure €11,000,000 (2003).

Trustees: Emilio Botín Ríos (Pres.).

Principal Staff: Dir Rafael Benjumea Cabeza de Vaca.

Address: Pedrueca 1, 39003 Santander.

Telephone: (942) 226072; **Fax:** (942) 360494; **Internet:** www.fundacionmbotin.org; **e-mail:** direccion@fundacionmbotin.org.

Fundación Caja de Madrid (Caja de Madrid Foundation)

Established in 1990 by the Caja de Madrid savings bank to operate in the fields of the arts and humanities.

Activities: Operates mainly in Spain in the fields of the arts and humanities, social welfare and conservation, through various programmes, grants for research, scholarships, bursaries and travel grants. The Music Programme promotes music through concerts, operatic productions and television programmes; the Madrid Programme seeks to inform on the history and culture of Madrid through publications; the Programme for the Elderly awards prizes for works on ageing, and funds residential homes and care for the elderly in rural areas; and the Third Sector Programme assists in the development of new foundations and non-profit organizations, and funds the training of staff. The Foundation has established a care home for children with AIDS. The Foundation is also currently funding the restoration of a monastery at Sijena. It works in collaboration with other public and private sector organizations.

Geographical Area of Activity: Spain.

Publications: Annual Report; *Música y Educación* (quarterly); books and brochures.

Principal Staff: Pres. Miguel Blesa de la Parra.

Address: Plaza de San Martin 1, 28013 Madrid.

Telephone: (90) 2246810; **Fax:** (91) 3792020; **Internet:** www.fundacioncajamadrid.org/; **e-mail:** consultasfundacion@cajamadrid.es.

Fundación Cánovas del Castillo (Cánovas del Castillo Foundation)

Established in 1980.

Activities: Organizes training programmes, conferences, exhibitions and other activities; promotes research on social and cultural subjects; produces various publications.

Geographical Area of Activity: Spain.

Publications: Newsletter; and other publications.

Principal Staff: Pres. Carlos Robles Piquer; Gen. Sec. Francisco Sanabria Martín.

Address: Calle Marqués de la Enseñada 14, 28004 Madrid.

Telephone: (91) 3195904; **Fax:** (91) 3198258; **Internet:** www.canovas.org; **e-mail:** canovas@intelideas.com.

Fundación Eduardo Capa (Eduardo Capa Foundation)

Established in December 1998 by Eduardo Capa Sacristán and Julia Sanz Vaca to house the Eduardo Capa sculpture collection.

Activities: Operates in the areas of the arts and humanities, and education, through self-conducted programmes, conferences, training courses and publications; also holds a summer university of sculpture and organizes temporary sculpture exhibitions.

Geographical Area of Activity: Spain.

Publications: Cataloges of temporary exhibitions.

Finance: Financed by local government; annual revenue and expenditure 250,000,000 pesetas (2000).

Trustees: Eduardo Capa Sacristán (Founder-Pres.); Luis Diaz Alperi (Pres.); Manuel Tarancón Fandós (First Vice-Pres.).

Principal Staff: Dir Fernando Capa Sanz; Man. José Garcia Gomez; Museum Dir Aurora Martín Nájera.

Address: Apdo de Correos 5030, 3080 Alicante.

Telephone: (96) 5152969; **Fax:** (96) 5268505; **Internet:** www.fundacioncapa.net; **e-mail:** fundacioncapa@telefonica.net.

Fundación Científica de la Asociación Española Contra el Cáncer (Scientific Foundation of the Spanish Anti-Cancer Association)

Established in 1971 to combat cancer.

Activities: Conducts basic research in cancer prevention; awards grants to institutions and individuals, including fellowships for studies in oncology in Spain and abroad; compiles epidemiological statistics, disseminates information, and participates in international conferences.

Geographical Area of Activity: Mainly Spain.

Publications: *Estadística* (annually); information and monographs.

Principal Staff: Pres. Cecilia Plañiol Lacalle; Sec.-Gen. Miguel Serván García.

Address: Amador de los Ríos 6, 28010 Madrid.

Telephone: (91) 3194138; **Fax:** (91) 3190966; **Internet:** www.aecc.es/fundacion/index.html; **e-mail:** information@aecc.es.

Fundación CODESPA—Futuro en Marcha (Co-operation for the Promotion and Development of Welfare Activities)

Established in 1985 to promote the economic and social development of the countries of Central and South America and the Mediterranean.

Activities: Operates nationally and internationally, in Central and South America, North Africa, the Middle East and the Philippines, in the fields of aid to less-developed countries, economic affairs, education and social welfare, through awarding grants to institutions, conferences, training courses and issuing publications. Maintains offices in Peru, Venezuela and Honduras.

Geographical Area of Activity: Central and South America, North Africa, the Middle East, the Philippines and Spain.

Publications: *CODESPA Foundation Bulletin.*

Finance: Assets 1,684,607,000 pesetas (2000).

Executive Committee: C. O'Shea Artiñano; J. Segurado García; R. Cabello de Alba y Gracia; M. R. Llamas Madurga; J. Benjumea Puigcerver; A. Rodríguez Rodo; I. Estape de Rojas; A. César Betran Sanz.

Principal Staff: Pres. Laureano López Rodó; Dir Javier Segurado Garcia.

Address: Rafael Bergamín 12 bajo, 28043 Madrid.

Telephone: (91) 7444240; **Fax:** (91) 5102100; **Internet:** www.codespa.org; **e-mail:** codespa@ibm.net.

Fundación Rafael del Pino (Rafael del Pino Foundation)

Aims to contribute towards the improvement of the knowledge of the future leaders of Spain, to promote private initiative and the fostering of the free market and free enterprise principles.

Activities: Operates in the fields of training, providing scholarships to Spanish and Spanish–American students, funding research programmes, funding management training for NGOs and organizing seminars; lectures and meetings, including the Free Enterprise Forum; Spanish cultural heritage, including lectures and conferences and grants to projects aiming to protect and develop Spain's cultural heritage; and a series of awards and prizes, recognising Spanish literature, dissertations in the fields of economy, law, business, politics, international relations, mass media and education, and initiatives aiming to eliminate inefficient regulations or foster competition within the goods and services markets.

Geographical Area of Activity: Spain.

Principal Staff: Pres. and Founder Rafael del Pino y Moreno; Vice-Pres. María del Pino y Calvo-Sotelo; Dir Amadeo Petitbò Juan.

Address: Rafael Calvo 39, 28010 Madrid.

Telephone: (91) 3968600; **Fax:** (91) 3968619; **Internet:** www.fundacionrafaeldelpino.es; **e-mail:** 600f@fundacionrafaeldelpino.es.

Fundación Desarrollo Sostenido—FUNDESO (Foundation for Sustainable Development)

Established in December 1995 by Rafael Guardans Cambó to promote socio-economic programmes in developing countries.

Activities: Operates nationally and internationally, especially in Central and South America, in the areas of aid to less-developed countries, education and social welfare, through self-conducted programmes, scholarships and fellowships, and conferences. Maintains nine regional offices in Spain.

Geographical Area of Activity: International, with an emphasis on Central and South America.

Finance: Total project expenditure €5,256,550 (2000–2001).

Principal Staff: Pres. Alfonso Quereda Hurtado; Gen. Dir Rafael Guardans Cambó.

Address: Gran Vía 16, 4° izquierda, 28013 Madrid.

Telephone: (91) 7014704; **Fax:** (91) 7014701; **Internet:** www.fundeso.org; **e-mail:** fundeso@fundeso.org.

Fundación Empresa-Universidad de Zaragoza (University of Zaragoza Business Foundation)

Founded in 1982 by the Universidad y Cámara de Comercio e Industria de Zaragoza to promote business research and training.

Activities: Operates nationally and internationally, in the fields of aid to less-developed countries, arts and humanities, conservation and the environment, economic affairs, education, international affairs, law and human rights, medicine and health, science and technology, and social welfare and social studies, through research, grants to individuals, scholarships and fellowships, prizes, conferences and training courses.

Geographical Area of Activity: International, with an emphasis on Europe, and Central and South America.

Publications: Newsletter.

Finance: Assets 261,938,387 pesetas (1998); annual revenue 586,395,111 pesetas, expenditure 567,456,900 pesetas (1998).

Principal Staff: Pres. Javier Rico Gambarte; Vice-Pres. Felipe Pétriz Calvo; Dir Gen. Juan Antonio Ramón Gómez.

Address: Fernando el Católico 2, 50005 Zaragoza.

Telephone: (976) 351508; **Fax:** (976) 558549; **Internet:** www.feuz.es; **e-mail:** feuz@globalmail.net.

Fundación Entorno, Empresa y Medio Ambiente (Environmental Business Foundation)

Established in 1995, as Fundación Teneo para la Mejora del Medio Ambiente y la Conservación de la Naturaleza, with the support of 16 companies, to advise businesses on environmental matters.

Activities: Operates in Spain and in Central and South American countries in three main programme areas: information and training; research and education; and nature conservation. Organizes training programmes, workshops, conferences and seminars; supports research into environmental issues; and offers scholarships for environmental research carried out abroad. Maintains an on-line corporate database.

Geographical Area of Activity: Spain, and Central and South America.

Publications: *Environmental Magazine;* conference reports and technical publications.

Finance: Assets €3,000,000 (1998/99); annual expenditure €2,400,000 (1999).

Trustees: Javier Salas Collantes (Chair.); Miguel Cuenca Valdivia (Vice-Chair.); Alvaro Muñoz López (Gen. Sec.); Cristina García-Orcoyen Tormo; Miguel Delibes Castro; Enrique Fuentes Quintana; Angel Martin Municio.

Principal Staff: Dir Cristina García-Orcoyen Tormo.

Address: Calle Padilla 17, Atico, 28006 Madrid.

Telephone: (91) 5756394; **Fax:** (91) 5757713; **Internet:** www.fundacion-entorno.org; **e-mail:** administrador@fundacion-entorno.org.

Fundación Fondo de las Cajas de Ahorros Confederadas para la Investigación Económica y Social (Foundation for Economic and Social Research)

Founded in 1968 by the Confederación Española de Cajas de Ahorros to study all scientific matters related to savings and savings banks; its research has been extended to include economics and financial systems, fiscal and taxation law, contemporary history and statistics, with special emphasis on their relation to the field of savings, and to similar European institutions.

Activities: Maintains close links with economic ministries and financial centres, and over 3,000 research projects have been completed. The Foundation has an extensive library specializing in the above subjects, a publishing fund which has produced over 300 titles and a small grants fund for sustainable development projects in Spain.

Geographical Area of Activity: Spain.

Publications: *Papeles de Economía Española; Perspectivas del Sistema Financiero; Cuadernos de Información Económica; Documentos de Trabajo* (periodicals).

Principal Staff: Hon. Pres. Enrique Fuentes Quintana; Pres. Manuel Pizarro Moreno; Vice-Pres. Juan R. Quintás Seoane; Dir Gen. Victorio Valle.

Address: Juan Hurtado de Mendoza 19, 28036 Madrid.

Telephone: (91) 3504400; **Fax:** (91) 3508040; **Internet:** www.funcas.ceca.es; **e-mail:** suscrip@funcas.ceca.es.

Fundación Hogar del Empleado—FUHEM (Workers' Centre Foundation)

Founded in 1966 (existed as an association since 1949), to promote the welfare of workers and their families.

Activities: The Foundation operates through editing magazines and other publications; creating educational and professional centres; organizing courses and conferences for professionals; and other activites directed at fostering employment and social participation, promoting tolerance, respect for human rights, peace, issues of co-operation for development, and humanitarian assistance initiatives. It owns seven schools, and established the Centro de Investigación para la Paz (q.v.) in 1984, which carries out research in the fields of international relations, environmental issues and economics.

Geographical Area of Activity: Spain.

Publications: *Papeles de cuestiones internacionales; Ecología política; La situación del mundo (World Watch Institute Report); Anuario CIP; Observatorio de conflictors; Guias didacticas de educación para el desarrollo; Colección de Economía Critica* (2 a year).

Board of Trustees: Enrique Bendicto Mamblona (Pres.); Francisco Montiel Lara (Sec.); Adolfo Nuñez Astray (Treas.); J. A. Garde Roca; J. Echeverria-Torres Tovar; E. Parajua Gallego.

Address: Calle Duque de Sesto 40, 28009 Madrid.

Telephone: (91) 4310280; **Fax:** (91) 5763271; **Internet:** www.fuhem.es; **e-mail:** fuhem@fuhem.es.

Fundación Intervida (Intervida Foundation)

Established in 1995 to assist vulnerable children and their families in the developing world.

Activities: Works in the area of capacity building, education and development in less-developed countries, focusing on children in need and their families. Currently working in Bangladesh, Bolivia, El Salvador, Guatemala, India, Mali and Peru, where it also maintains offices.

Geographical Area of Activity: South-East Asia and Central and South America.

Publications: *Contigo* (newsletter); and other publications.

Finance: Annual revenue and expenditure 7,963,092,000 pesetas (1999).

Address: Pujades 77–79, 4°, 08005 Barcelona.

Telephone: (93) 3001101; **Fax:** (93) 096868; **Internet:** www.intervida.org; **e-mail:** intervida@intervida.org.

Fundación para la Investigación Agraria de la Provincia de Almería—FIAPA (Foundation for Agricultural Research in the Province of Almería)

Established in 1988 to operate in the field of teaching, financing and promotion of research and development.

Activities: Operates in the Almería region of Spain, North Africa and South America in the field of science and technology, and specifically agricultural research, through research, grants, scholarships and fellowships, conferences, training courses and issuing publications. Also acts as an information and co-ordination centre for the development of the agricultural economy.

Geographical Area of Activity: Spain (Almería), North Africa and South America.

Publications: Numerous agricultural publications; books; and research reports.

Board of Patrons: The Board comprises a number of organizations including the Ministry of Agriculture and Fisheries of the Andalusian Government, provincial and city councils, businesses, and the Universities of Almería and Málaga. Its Chair. is the Minister of Agriculture and Fisheries of the Andalusian Government.

Principal Staff: Man. Dir Isabel M. Cuadrado Gómez.

Address: Carretera de la playa s/n, La Cañada de San Urbano, 04120 Almería.

Telephone: (950) 291981; **Fax:** (950) 290092; **Internet:** www.fiapa.es; **e-mail:** fiapa@fiapa.es.

Fundación Yannick y Ben Jakober

Established in 1993 by Yannick Vu, Ben Jakober and Georges Coulon Karlweis for the preservation and restoration of natural heritage and also the promotion of the arts in general, and painting and sculpture in particular, through the exhibition of works, supporting the circulation and knowledge of the arts and artistic interchange.

Activities: Operates nationally and internationally in the field of the arts, through self-conducted programmes, conferences, publications and art exhibitions.

Geographical Area of Activity: Mainly Spain.

Restrictions: No grants available.

Publications: *Piccoli Principi Nella Grande Pittura Europea; Domenico Gnoli; Ben Jakober; Yannick Vu.*

Trustees: Ben Jakober; Georges Coulon Karlweis; Yannick Vu; Supervising body: Conselleria de Cultura, Govern de les Illes Balears.

Principal Staff: Pres. Yannick Vu; Sec. Ben Jakober; Admin. Officer. Xanthe Jeffries; Public Relations Officer Isabel Palou; Technical Supervisor Edgar da Cunha.

Address: Finca Sa Bassa Blanca, Camino del Col Baix, Malpas, 07400 Alcudia, Mallorca.

Telephone: (971) 546915; **Fax:** (971) 897163; **Internet:** www.fundacionjakober.arrakis.es; **e-mail:** fuybjako@arrakis.es.

Fundación Laboral Sonsoles Ballvé Lantero (Sonsoles Ballvé Lantero Labour Foundation)

Established in 1974 by José Luis Ballvé and Eulalia Lantero for the protection of mentally and physically disabled children, and for the protection of pensioners and workers of Campofrío Alimentación, and to support their children's education in the arts, humanities, science, technology and social welfare by offering scholarships, courses and seminars.

Activities: Operates nationally and internationally in the fields of social welfare, training, education, the arts and humanities and recreational activities.

Geographical Area of Activity: Europe.

Publications: *ECOS* (monthly); Annual Report.

Finance: Assets €3,005,000 (2001); annual revenue and expenditure €300,000 (2001).

Board of Trustees: Eulalia Lantero (Pres.); Pedro Ballvé; and 10 others.

Principal Staff: Exec. Dir Manuel Ortega Porras.

Address: Calle Fundación Sonsoles Ballvé 2, 1°, 09007 Burgos.

Telephone: (947) 283103; **Fax:** (947) 283136; **e-mail:** fundacion.sonsolesballve@cf.campofrio.es.

Fundación MAPFRE (MAPFRE Foundation)

Founded in 1975 by the MAPFRE insurance company, to promote safety at work, on the road, and in the home.

Activities: Operates in Europe and Central and South America. Its main activities are in the following areas: safety at work; industrial hygiene; ergonomics; the prevention of environmental pollution; road safety; fire prevention; product safety; consumer protection; and civilian defence. Provides a number of scholarships for professionals from Eastern Europe, including scholarships for postgraduate study and to attend safety courses, awards research grants, and promotes the dissemination of technical and scientific knowledge through publications.

Geographical Area of Activity: Spain, Portugal and Central and South America.

Publications: *MAPFRE Seguridad*; books; brochures.

Finance: The Foundation is funded by Grupo Empresarial MAPFRE. Total assets €12,212,692 (2000); total expenditure €3,942,639 (2000).

Principal Staff: Pres. Carlos Alvarez Jiménez; Sec. Alberto Mauzauo Martos; Dir Gen. José Angel Fernando Pablo.

Address: Carretera de Pozuelo a Majadahonda s/n, 28220 Majadahonda, Madrid.

Telephone: (91) 6265507; **Fax:** (91) 5812142; **Internet:** www.mapfre.com/pe/pmapfre/es/e10/e100000.shtml; **e-mail:** informacion.fundacio@MAPFRE.com.

Fundación MAPFRE Estudios (MAPFRE Foundation for Studies)

Established in 1975 by MAPFRE Mutualidad for the promotion and development of educational and research activities related to the world of insurance, risk, safety, finance, business administration and European law.

Activities: Operates through courses, seminars and international meetings; diffusion of publications and magazines; and financial assistance for research studies and projects. Has collaboration agreements with public and private institutions working in its chosen fields, including educational programmes in the fields of insurance, safety, finance, business administration and studies on Central and South America.

Geographical Area of Activity: Europe, USA, and Central and South America.

Publications: *Revista Gerencia de Riesgos; Instrucciones Técnicas de Seguridad Integral;* books and documents.

Board of Trustees: Filomeno Mira Candel (Pres.); Julio Castelo Matrán (Vice-Pres.); Miguel Ángel Martínez Martínez (Dir Gen.); Alberto Manzano Martos (Sec.-Gen.); Alvaro Armada; Julio Caubín Hernández; Carlos Álvarez Jiménez; Francisco Martínez García; Antonio Guardiola Lozano; José Manuel Martínez Martínez; Miguel Marquéz; Ignacio Medina.

Address: Monte del Pilar, s/n, 28023 El Plantío, Madrid.

Telephone: (91) 5812008; **Fax:** (91) 3076642; **Internet:** www.mapfre.com/estudios; **e-mail:** promocion.fme@MAPFRE .com.

Fundación MAPFRE Medicina (MAPFRE Foundation for Medicine)

Established in 1975 by MAPFRE Mutualidad to promote health and scientific investigation.

Activities: Operates nationally and internationally in the fields of education, medicine and health, science and technology, and social welfare, through self-conducted programmes, research, grants to individuals and institutions, scholarships and fellowships, prizes, conferences, training courses and issuing publications. Affiliate organizations operate in Argentina, Brazil, Mexico, Portugal and Venezuela.

Geographical Area of Activity: International.

Publications: *Revistas MAPFRE Medicina; Revistas MAPFRE Investigación Cardiovascular*; other publications.

Finance: Annual revenue and expenditure approx. 2,000,000 pesetas.

Address: Carretera de Pozuelo a Majadahonda s/n, 28220 Majadahonda, Madrid.

Telephone: (91) 6265704; **Fax:** (91) 6265825; **Internet:** www.mapfremedicina.es; **e-mail:** infofmm@mapfremedicina .es.

Fundación Mar Océano (Ocean Sea Foundation)

Established in 1959 to promote knowledge of Spain's historic figures and their actions; to maintain and promote historic monuments; to research the history of the Spanish army; to promote Spanish heritage world-wide; and to assist in the commemoration of historic events in countries with which Spain has had links.

Activities: Operates internationally, in countries with which Spain has had historic links, in the field of the arts and humanities, through programmes of research and commemoration, and conferences. Does not make grants for political, religious or commercial projects.

Geographical Area of Activity: International.

Trustees: Pascual Barberán (Pres.); F. Gutierrez de Luna (Vice-Pres.); M. J. Molina (Sec.); C. Romero Morellón (Treas.); F. Agullo Soler; I. Alegre; P. Barberán Molina; M. Muriel.

Address: Alcalde Sainz de Baranda 53, 28009 Madrid.

Telephone: (91) 5735227; **Fax:** (91) 4096880; **e-mail:** barberán@retemail.es.

Fundación Juan March (Juan March Foundation)

Founded in 1955 by Juan March Ordinas to stimulate studies of direct relevance and utility to Spanish scientific and cultural life; and to assist social institutions.

Activities: The Foundation's headquarters in Madrid serve as a cultural centre. The Foundation organizes science courses and workshops, awards prizes, and makes grants for fellowships and group research programmes in the fields of scientific and technical research. The Centre for International Meetings on Biology, established in 1991 within the Juan March Institute for Study and Research, promotes collaboration between Spanish and foreign scientists working in the field of biology. A Centre for Advanced Study in the Social Sciences opened in 1987, within the Juan March Institute, to promote and conduct research, and offer postgraduate courses. Cultural activities include the organization of art exhibitions, music concerts, lectures, film projections, etc. The Programme for Cultural Advancement in Spanish Provinces operates with central, regional and local governments. Grants are made to institutions devoted to social welfare. The Foundation awards scholarships to artists and researchers in the visual arts undertaking work nationally and abroad. Maintains a library, research and documentation centre, including a specialized collection in Spanish Contemporary Theatre and Music.

Geographical Area of Activity: International.

Publications: *Anales* (annual report); *Boletín Informativo* (monthly); *SABER/Leer* (monthly); literary criticism, Spanish literary thought, monographs, etc.

Finance: Annual expenditure approx. 1,200,000,000 pesetas.

Trustees: J. March Delgado (Pres.); C. March Delgado (Vice-Pres.); J. Gomá Lanzón (Sec.); L. March Delgado; E. Piñel López; J. Prohens Mas; A. Lafita Pardo; A. Rodríguez Robles; P. Vallbona.

Principal Staff: Exec. Dir José Luis Yuste Grijalba.

Address: Castelló 77, 28006 Madrid.

Telephone: (91) 4354240; **Fax:** (91) 5763420; **Internet:** www.march.es; **e-mail:** webmaster@march.mail.es.

Fundación Ana Mata Manzanedo (Ana Mata Manzanedo Foundation)

Established in 1977 by Ana Mata Manzanedo to provide assistance to those in need.

Activities: Operates mostly in Spain, particularly in the Burgos area, in the areas of education, social welfare and conservation of historic heritage, through grants to institutions and individuals, and through providing scholarships and fellowships.

Geographical Area of Activity: Mostly Spain.

Finance: Net assets 290,472,140 pesetas (1998); annual revenue 18,038,488, expenditure 16,548,384 (1998).

Trustees: Moises Arroyo Alcalde (Pres.); Fernando Dancausa Treviño (Vice-Pres.); José Antonio Mata González; Luis Mata Urraca; Pilar Salazar Martinez.

Principal Staff: Sec. Gustavo Adolfo Burgos Peña.

Address: Calle Vitoria 10, 6°, 09004 Burgos.

Telephone: (947) 206716; **e-mail:** famama@teleline.es.

Fundación Mujeres (Foundation for Women)

Established in June 1994 by 20 women to support women's participation in political and social affairs, to promote women in business and education and to promote co-operation between women in Spain and those in developing countries.

Activities: Operates nationally and internationally in the areas of aid to less-developed countries, international affairs, social welfare and social studies, with an emphasis on promoting equal opportunities between men and women and preventing violence against women. The Foundation operates through self-conducted programmes, research, conferences, training courses and publications.

Geographical Area of Activity: International.

Publications: *Fundación Mujeres Bulletin* (3 a year); *Innova; Women In;* educational materials.

Finance: Net assets 625,300 pesetas (1998); annual revenue 405,782,106 pesetas, expenditure 390,040,709 pesetas (1999).

Trustees: Carlota Bustelo García del Real; Teresa Gallego Mendez; Paloma Gascón Vera; Marta Continente Gonzalo; Virtudes Monteserín Rodríguez; Isabel Serrano Sánchez; Florentina Alarcón Hita; Lucía Ruano Rodríguez; Elena Valenciano Marínez-Orozco; Nuria Arévalo Casado; Teresa Nueva España; Purificación Gutiérrez López; Purificación Causapié Lopesino; Beatríz Jiménez de Parga Maseda; Estrella Rodriguez Pardo; Isabel Martinez Lozano.

Principal Staff: Dir Celia Gómez González.

Address: Raimundo Lulio 1, 28010 Madrid.

Telephone: (91) 5912420; **Internet:** www.fundacionmujeres.es; **e-mail:** mujeres@fundacionmujeres.es.

Fundación ONCE (ONCE Foundation—Spanish National Organization for the Blind—Foundation)

Founded in 1988 by ONCE, the Spanish National Organization for the Blind, the Foundation aims to assist people with disabilities and their integration in society.

Activities: Operates primarily in Spain in the fields of medicine and health, and social welfare; co-operates with government agencies to help the disabled; organizes the Spanish national lottery, tickets for which are sold by blind people and disabled people; makes grants and low-interest loans for employment creation, education, rehabilitation, training and to assist in the breaking down of communication and social barriers; and promotes sports for its role in the personal and social development of people with disabilities. Maintains an online information resource.

Geographical Area of Activity: Mainly Spain.

Publications: Annual Report; information brochures; books concerning disability and social issues.

Finance: Receives a percentage of revenue from the lottery tickets sold by ONCE, equivalent to 20% of ONCE's operating revenue. Assets 34,706,206,000 pesetas (2000); annual revenue 12,716,603,000 pesetas, expenditure 12,892,763,000 pesetas (2000).

Trustees: HRH Princess Margarita de Borbón (Pres. of Honour); José María Arroyo Zarzosa (Pres.); Francisco Morata Andreu; Maria Teresa Mogín Barquín; Paulino Azúa Berra, Rafael de Lorenzo García, Luis J. Cañón Reguera, Mario García Sánchez (Vice-Pres.); Fernando Jáuregui Campuzano; Santiago Galván Domínguez; Teresa Lasala Fernández; Emiliano Martín García; Manuel Antón Gómez; Fernando Mendía González; Angeles Cozar Gutiérrez; Juan Manuel Barco Iruretagoyena; Ernesto Uría Izco; Teresa Palahí Juan; José Ballesteros López; José María Ibáñez Martínez Losa; Juan Enrique González Martínez; Vicente Ruíz Martínez; Alberto Arbide Mendizabal; Alberto Galerón de Miguel; Rafael González Millán; Eugenio Ferradas Moledo; Matías Sainz Ocejo; Aurelia Millán Pérez; Miguel Carballeda Piñeiro; Mario Loreto Sanz Robles; Ana Osaba Saenz; Martín Ortega Sánchez; Luisa Escribano Toledo; Andrés Ramos Vázquez; Jorge Iniguez Villanueva.

Principal Staff: Man. Dir José Manuel Pichel Jallas; Adjunct Man. Dir Rafael González Millán; Dir Accessibility Miguel Pereyra Etcheverría; Dir Co-operation Jorge Antonio Piñeiro; Dir Social Relations Miguel Angel Cabra de Luna; Dir Sports Miguel Sagarra Gadea.

Address: Calle Sebastián Herrera 15, 5°, 28012 Madrid.

Telephone: (91) 5068918; **Fax:** (91) 5393487; **Internet:** www.once.es; **e-mail:** sio@once.es.

Fundación Amancio Ortega

Founded in July 2001 by Amancio Ortega to promote all types of activities in the fields of culture, education, research and science.

Activities: The Foundation has chosen the field of science as its initial area for support, making grants to self-managing projects by not-for-profit organizations, in particular prioritizing support of pilot projects oriented towards the modernization of civil society theory and practice.

Geographical Area of Activity: International, but at present Galicia, Spain.

Board of Trustees: Amancio Ortega Gaona (Chair.); Jose Castellanos Rios; Juan Manuel Urgoitz Lopez de Ocana; Carlos Espinosa de Los Monteros; Jose Arnau Sierra; Antonio Abril Abadin.

Principal Staff: Gen. Man. Felipe Gomez-Pallete.

Address: Avda Diputacion, Sabon, Arteixo, 15142 A Coruna.

Telephone: (981) 185596; **Fax:** (981) 185595; **Internet:** www.faortega.org; **e-mail:** general@faortega.org.

Fundación José Ortega y Gasset (José Ortega y Gasset Foundation)

Established in December 1978 as a private, non-profit-making academic research institute, to further the cultural legacy of the philosopher and essayist José Ortega y Gasset (1883–1955).

Activities: Operates in the fields of the humanities and social sciences, through research and study activities, including postgraduate and doctoral research projects, seminars, lectures, exhibitions, and cultural and scientific meetings that cover unlimited topics. Emphasis is placed on subjects covering Iberia, Europe and Central and South America. The Foundation runs an International Programme of Spanish Language, Latin American and European Studies at its centre in Toledo, providing study opportunities for undergraduate and graduate students, as well as the annual Young Hispanic Leaders Program providing young US citizens of Hispanic origin with the opportunity to familiarize themselves with Spain's political, economic, social and cultural environment. It has links with universities in the United Kingdom, USA, Argentina, Colombia, Puerto Rico and Israel. Maintains the private library and archives of José Ortega y Gasset.

Geographical Area of Activity: Spain.

Publications: *Revista de Occidente* (monthly).

Governing Board: HM King Juan Carlos I (Hon. Chair.); Antonio Garriges Walker (Chair.); Soledad Ortega Spottorno (Founder); José Varela Ortega (Vice-Chair.); Francisco Prados de la Escosura (Gen. Dir); Jesús Sánchez Lambás (Gen. Sec.).

Principal Staff: Pres. Antonio Garriges Walker.

Address: Fortuny 53, 28010 Madrid.

Telephone: (91) 3084007; **Fax:** (91) 3084007.

Fundación Paz y Solidaridad (Peace and Solidarity Foundation)

Founded in 1989 to support education and sustainable development projects in less-developed countries.

Activities: Works in Central and South America, the Mediterranean region and the Middle East, through carrying out research into globalization, and supporting education and sustainable development programmes in co-operation with local organizations. Also seeks to raise awareness of development issues in Spain through conferences, symposia and exhibitions, as well as disseminating information through a series of publications.

Geographical Area of Activity: Central and South America, the Mediterranean region and the Middle East.

Publications: Annual Report; education and development publications.

Finance: Annual budget 232,500,000 pesetas (1999).

Principal Staff: Pres. Javier Doz; Vice-Pres. Laureano Cuerdo; Dir Gracia Santos; Treas. Andrés Gómez; Sec. Ramon Baeza.

Address: Fernandez de la Hoz 12, 28010 Madrid.

Telephone: (91) 3083648; **Fax:** (91) 3194933; **Internet:** www.ccoo.es/pazysolidaridad/index.htm; **e-mail:** fps@fps.ccoo .es.

Fundación Principe de Asturias (Prince of Asturias Foundation)

Established in 1980; aims to support projects in the Asturias region.

Activities: Distributes the annual Prince of Asturias Awards, rewarding scientific, technical, cultural, social and humanitarian work done by individuals and organizations. Also awards scientific and Spanish language scholarships, and a range of other initiatives, including assisting in the development of the Moscow Virtuosi orchestra. Founding member of the Asturian Bear Foundation.

Geographical Area of Activity: Mainly Asturias region of Spain, but also international.

Board of Trustees: José Ramón Álvarez Rendueles (Pres.).

Address: General Yague, 2, 33004 Oviedo.

Internet: www.fpa.es.

Fundación Promi (Promi Foundation)

Founded in 1998, aims to uphold the rights of mentally disabled people.

Activities: Works to improve the quality of life of mentally disabled people throughout Europe, through projects, conferences and training programmes, concentrating on integration in work and society, and the rehabilitation of people with mental disabilities. Promotes and helps NGOs and other organizations with similar aims and lends its support to businesses employing people with mental disabilities. Maintains two research and information centres.

Geographical Area of Activity: Europe.

Publications: *Deficiencia, Enfermedad Mental y Senilidad: Mecanismos Legales de Protección*; and numerous other publications relating to disability.

Finance: Assets €8,640,276 (Dec. 1999); annual revenue €142,145, expenditure €252,124 (1999).

Principal Staff: Pres. Juán Peréz Marin; Sec. José María de la Paz Calatrava.

Address: Avda Fuente de las Piedras, s/n, 14940 Cabra (Córdoba).

Telephone: (95) 7520112; **Fax:** (95) 7521207; **Internet:** www.promi.es; **e-mail:** fundación@promi.es.

Fundación Fernando Rielo (Fernando Rielo Foundation)

Founded in 1981 by Fernando Rielo, Spanish poet and philosopher, to promote understanding between different cultures and traditions.

Activities: The Foundation operates internationally, organizing conferences, seminars and concerts, and poetry, music, education and philosophy courses. Awards prizes, scholarships and grants to foster cultural activity, and in particular literature, including the annual Fernando Rielo World Mystical Poetry Prize. Maintains close ties with foundations and universities abroad, including establishing the Fernando Rielo Chair in Spanish Literature and Thought at the University of the Philippines, and operates exchange programmes with foreign universities for Spanish university teachers. The Foundation has 31 delegations world-wide.

Geographical Area of Activity: International.

Publications: *Equivalencias/Equivalences* (3 a year, in English and Spanish); several poetry collections and books on philosophy and education.

Address: Jorge Juan 82, No 1°, 28009 Madrid.

Telephone: (91) 5754091; **Fax:** (91) 4352351; **Internet:** www.rielo.com; **e-mail:** fundacion@rielo.com.

Fundación María Francisca de Roviralta (María Francisca de Roviralta Foundation)

Established in 1959 by José María Roviralta and Manuel Roviralta for general charitable purposes.

Activities: Operates internationally in the fields of aid to less-developed countries, the arts and humanities, conservation and the environment, education, law and human rights, medicine and health, science and technology, and social welfare, through making grants to institutions. Four programmes are run by the Foundation: social assistance; health care and medical research; scientific research; and culture and arts.

Geographical Area of Activity: International.

Publications: Annual Report.

Finance: Annual expenditure €3,000,000 (1999).

Trustees: Gerardo Salvador (Pres.); Andreas Graf; Javier Serra López-Chicheri; Augusto Testor Permanyer; Pilar Anadón Trigo.

Principal Staff: Pres. Gerardo Salvador; First Vice-Pres. and Sec. Augusto Testor; Second Vice-Pres. Pilar Anadón.

Address: 20–24 Tuset, 08006 Barcelona.

Telephone: (93) 2177700; **Fax:** (93) 2178221; **Internet:** www.roviralta.org; **e-mail:** fundacion@roviralta.org.

Fundación Santa María (Santa María Foundation)

Founded in 1977 by a religious order to provide the disadvantaged in society with access to education and culture, and to promote the development of pedagogic sciences and specialist training for teaching staff.

Activities: The Foundation operates programmes in four main areas. The Special Programmes aim to integrate marginalized groups at a social and cultural level; provide training for volunteers working in prisons; promote women; organize occupational workshops; and provide financial support for the construction of libraries, houses, etc. The Literature Programme organizes competitions for teenagers and children to stimulate artistic and literary creativity. The Social Research Programmes provide a platform for discussing the problems facing society from a Christian perspective. The Pedagogical Programmes organize training courses for teachers; provide research grants to centres whose interests are similar to those of the Foundation; and operate the Foundation's prize programme.

Geographical Area of Activity: Europe and South America.

Restrictions: Grants only to people who work or study in Spain.

Publications: Annual Report; brochures; grants list; monographs.

Finance: The Foundation is funded by annual contributions from Ediciones S.M. Assets €3,100,000 (2002).

Trustees: J. Anso; C. Díaz Chomón; J. María Elvira; E. Fernandez Moscoso; P. González-Blasco; R. González Gallarza; F. Lejarza; J. A. Ortega Díaz- Ambrona; Ignacio Zabala.

Principal Staff: Dir José Joaquin Cerezo; Marta Arias; Paula Benito Baltasar; José Maria González Ochoa; Lucia Rodriguez; Marta Cereceda de Vicente.

Address: Calle General Moscardó 3, 2°, 28020 Madrid.

Telephone: (91) 5359600; **Fax:** (91) 5359601; **Internet:** www.fundacionsantamaria.org; **e-mail:** fsm@fundacionsantamaria.org.

Fundación Santillana (Santillana Foundation)

Founded in July 1979 to promote co-operation in education, the media and culture.

Activities: The Foundation supports experimental educational projects; conducts conferences and studies on educational policies; organizes cultural exhibitions; publishes educational materials; and conducts projects on the mass media. Operates nationally and in Central and South America, and co-operates with organizations in other European countries.

Geographical Area of Activity: Spain, and Central and South America.

Publications: Catalogues; conference and symposia proceedings and results.

Finance: Annual expenditure more than 100,000,000 pesetas.

Trustees: Jesús de Polanco (Pres.); Francisco Pérez González, Ricardo Diez-Hochleitner (Exec. Vice-Pres).

Principal Staff: Sec. José Luis López de la Cuesta.

Address: Torre de Don Borja, 39330 Santillana del Mar.

Telephone: (94) 2818203; **Fax:** (94) 2818374; **Internet:** www.fundacionsantillana.org; **e-mail:** gonzalezinfundacion@santillana.es.

Fundación Juanelo Turriano (Juanelo Turriano Foundation)

Established in 1987 by José Antonio García-Diego.

Activities: Dedicated to the historical study of science and technology, in the manner deemed to be most beneficial to society. The Foundation's major project is the partial reconstruction of the Artificio de Toledo built by Juanelo Turriano in 1569. Also makes study grants, awards fellowships and organizes exhibitions.

Publications: *The Twenty One Books of Engineering and Machinery of Juanelo Turriano*; and other publications.

Finance: Annual budget €190,000.

Trustees: Begoña García-Diego y Ortiz (Pres.); Bernardo Revuelta García (Vice-Pres.); María de las Nieves Vázquez Menéndez (Sec.); José María Aguirre González; Javier Goicolea Zala; Ignacio González Tascón; Antonio Quijada Lesmes; Francisco Vigueras González.

Principal Staff: Man. Dir Javier Goicolea Zala.

Address: Prim 5, 28004 Madrid.

Telephone: (91) 5313005; **Fax:** (91) 5313003; **Internet:** w3.mecanica.upm.es/juanelo.html; **e-mail:** fundacion@juaneloturriano.com.

Fundación Universidad-Empresa (University Industry Foundation)

Founded in 1973 by the Universities of Madrid and the Chamber of Commerce and Industry, to promote co-operation between the universities and industries of Madrid.

Activities: The Foundation carries out joint university–industry research activities; organizes postgraduate seminars, training programmes, short courses and Masters Degree programmes; develops undergraduate internships in Spain and other European Union countries for Spanish students, and postgraduate internships in Spain for Spanish postgraduates; and carries out activities in the fields of environmental co-operation, military electronics, telework and e-business.

Geographical Area of Activity: Europe.

Publications: Quarterly bulletin; periodicals; books dealing with university–industry relations.

Finance: Annual expenditure approx. 900,000,000 pesetas.

Board of Governors: Fernando Fernández-Tapias Román; (Pres.); Angel Gabilondo Pujol, José Ramón Busto Saiz (Vice-Pres.); José María Osorio Sánchez (Treas.); Alberto Durán Ruiz de Huidobro (Sec.).

Principal Staff: Dir Fernand Martínez Gómez.

Address: Carretera Ponzano 69–71, 9°, 19, 28003 Madrid.

Telephone: (91) 3990906; **Fax:** (91) 3992178; **Internet:** www.fue.es; **e-mail:** redfue@redfue.es.

Institut Europen de la Mediterrània—IEMED (European Institute of the Mediterranean)

Consortium supported by the Government of Catalonia, the Spanish Ministry of Foreign Affairs and Barcelona City Council, formed from the Catalan Institute of the Mediterranean, founded in 1989.

Activities: Promotes research, debate and diffusion activities which enable IEMED to discuss the main issues on the Mediterranean agenda; it acts as a platform for initiatives, servicing co-operative projects in countries from the South and East of the Mediterranean. Also operates as a cultural centre for the promotion of mutual understanding and dialogue, through art, science and culture.

Geographical Area of Activity: The Mediterranean region.

Publications: *IEMED.info* (newsletter); *Quaderns de la Mediterrània* (journal, two a year); brochures; books.

Principal Staff: Pres. Jordi Pujol; Vice-Pres. Ana Palacio; Dir Andreu Claret; Joan Clos; Josep A. Duran.

Address: Calle Girona 20–22, 5A planta, 08010 Barcelona.

Telephone: (93) 2449850; **Fax:** (93) 2470165; **Internet:** www.iemed.org; **e-mail:** info@iemed.org.

Instituto Europeo de Salud y Bienestar Social (European Institute for Health and Social Welfare)

Founded to encourage social health and environmental preservation through multiple co-operation.

Activities: The foundation focuses on environmental protection, health and safety at work, health management and social protocol. It also organizes conferences and seminars, maintains a documentation centre, and supports research into the environment and social issues.

Geographical Area of Activity: Europe.

Publications: Jose Antonio de Urbina (Pres.); Manuel Peña (Gen. Sec.); Sonia Fernandez-Duran (Dir.).

Obligaciones del empresario en prevención; Calidad en la asistencia sanitaria; and other publications.

Principal Staff: Gen. Sec. Manuel Peña.

Address: Joanquín Costa 16, El Viso, 28002 Madrid.

Telephone: (91) 4118090; **Fax:** (91) 4118080; **Internet:** www.ie-es.com; **e-mail:** secretaria@ie.es.com.

Paz y Cooperación (Peace and Co-operation)

Founded in 1982 by Joaquin Antuña with the aim of promoting disarmament, sustainable development in developing countries and human rights world-wide.

Activities: Organizes and manages co-operative projects in 20 countries around the world, which operate in the fields of human rights, co-operative development, children and young people, women and development, micro-credit, education, health, agriculture and the environment, and integral development with local communities and authorities. Also funds the International Peace and Co-operation School Award, an annual event that promotes education for peace and global solidarity.

Geographical Area of Activity: International, with an emphasis on Central and South America, Palestinian Autonomous Areas, Equatorial Guinea, India, South Africa and Mauritania.

Publications: *Education and Solidarity; Another Mankind: Third Millennium* (weekly television debate show on issues including the peace culture, non-violence and solidarity).

Governing Board: Joaquin Antuña (Pres.); Maria del Pino Monzón (Vice-Pres.); Belén Alvaró (Sec.); Blanca Gómez de Segura (Public Relations Dir).

Principal Staff: Project Man. Almudena Briones; Assts to Pres. Virginia Marriott, Ana Campuzano.

Address: Calle Melendez Valdes 68, 28015 Madrid.

Telephone: (91) 5496156; **Fax:** (91) 5435282; **Internet:** www.peaceandcooperation.org; **e-mail:** pazycoop@eurosur.org.

Sabera Foundation

Created in 1999 by Spanish pop singer and songwriter Nacho Cano to support development projects in India, with a particular emphasis on women.

Activities: The Foundation works towards the social transformation of women in India, through support for integration and education projects, the creation of safe shelter, health-care, nutrition and self-employment/micro-finance programmes. Also launched a branch in the USA in 2002.

Geographical Area of Activity: India.

Publications: Bulletin (monthly).

Finance: Funded through private donations and sponsorship.

Principal Staff: Press Officer José Domingo.

Telephone: (91) 4116730; **Internet:** www.saberafoundation.org.

Sri Lanka

FOUNDATIONS, TRUSTS AND NON-PROFIT ORGANIZATIONS

Agromart Foundation

Established in 1982 to train individuals in rural areas to be entrepreneurs and to empower them to participate in the socio-economic and political process.

Activities: Works in the areas of agriculture, small industry group training, providing micro-credit and transfer of technologies and skills. Focus is on empowering women in rural areas to acquire the skills necessary for their chosen field of self-employment; developing entrepreneurship in rural areas, especially amongst women; facilitating access to credit for agriculture and industry and promoting rural savings and self-help groups for non-bank funding through Agromart Production Societies; and promoting environmental awareness amongst rural entrepreneurs. Operates seven regional offices in Sri Lanka.

Geographical Area of Activity: Sri Lanka.

Publications: *Agro News* (quarterly journal); *Poverty to Prosperity—Success Stories of Entrepreneurs;* Annual Report.

Board of Trustees: Beulah Moonesinghe (Chair.); C. Goonetilleke (Treas.); A. C. B. Pethiyagoda (Sec.); R. M. Pillai (Asst Sec.); P. Gunasekera; S. W. Kiriarachchi; Nimala De Mel; L. Perera; K. Weeratunga.

Address: 38 Iswari Road, Colombo 6.

Telephone: (1) 366803; **Fax:** (1) 366804; **Internet:** www.agromart.com; **e-mail:** agromart@slt.lk.

International Water Management Institute

Founded in 1984, and formerly known as the International Irrigation Management Institute, to improve water resources management and irrigated agriculture in developing countries, through research.

Activities: The Institute's activities include research on water resources management and irrigated agriculture related to the design and management of irrigation systems, environment and health, performance assessment, and policy and institutions; organizes workshops and conferences. Carries out research through regional offices in India, Pakistan, South Africa and Thailand, maintains staff in China, Ghana, Kenya, Nepal, Senegal and Uzbekistan and is currently working in 20 countries across Asia and Africa.

Geographical Area of Activity: Africa and Asia.

Publications: *IIMI Review;* research, project and annual reports; discussion papers; workshop and conference proceedings.

Finance: Annual budget approx. US $10,600,000.

Principal Staff: Acting Dir Sarath Abayawardena.

Address: POB 2075, Colombo.

Telephone: (1) 787404; **Fax:** (1) 786854; **Internet:** www.cgiar.org/iwmi; **e-mail:** iwmi@cgiar.org.

Regional Centre for Strategic Studies

Established in 1993 as an NGO to carry out collaborative research on international issues relating to Southern Asia, and to network and interact with similar organizations.

Activities: Operates in the field of international affairs, through carrying out research into issues relating to Southern Asia, including regional security, conflict and co-operation. Promotes communication exchange between organizations and individuals; organizes seminars and workshops; promotes research; and disseminates information through its publications. Also distributes the Kodikara Awards to scholars from Bangladesh, Bhutan, India, Maldives, Nepal, Pakistan and Sri Lanka, and the Mahbub ul Haq Research Awards for Non-Traditional Security Issues in South Asia, sponsorsing collaborative research projects in the fields of governance in plural societies and security, environment and security, globalisation and security, and conflict resolution.

Geographical Area of Activity: Southern Asia.

Publications: Books; policy studies; monographs; newsletter.

Finance: Funded through grants from donor organizations.

Board of Directors: Dr R. A. Ariyaratne; Dr Lorna Devarajah; Dilip Kodikara; Dr Tressie Leitan; Dr Vernon L. B. Mendis; Gamini Weerakoon.

Principal Staff: Exec. Dir Prof. Sridhar K. Khatri.

Address: 2 Elibank Rd, Colombo 5.

Telephone: (1) 599734; **Fax:** (1) 599993; **Internet:** www.rcss.org; **e-mail:** rcss@sri.lanka.net.

A. M. M. Sahabdeen Trust Foundation

Founded in 1991 by Dr A. M. M Sahabdeen to advance knowledge, social development and to promote inter-cultural and international understanding through awards to outstanding scientists, scholars and community leaders.

Activities: Operates in the fields of education and social development by awarding educational scholarships, particularly to students in need. Makes grants to organizations in a variety of educational and social welfare fields including hostels, libraries, educational institutions, rehabilitation and refugee centres. In 1991 the Foundation established the Sri Lankan International Awards to honour scholars and scientists in the Asian Region, and others who have made outstanding contributions to human progress in the fields of International Understanding, Science, Literature and Human Development. In 1998 the Foundation established the Mohamed Sahabdeen Institute for Advanced Studies and Research at Pahamune in the Kurunegala District.

Geographical Area of Activity: Europe, South East Asia and USA.

Publications: *The Sufi Doctrine in Tamil Literature; Iraivanum Pirapanyanum; God and the Universe; The Circle of Lives.*

Finance: Net assets 14,900,000 rupees (2001–2002); income 2,100,000 rupees, expenditure 1,100,000 rupees (2002).

Board of Trustees: Dr A. M. M. Sahabdeen (Chair.); Dr Hilali Noordeen; Samiya Noordeen; M. R. Sahabdeen; S. R. Sahabdeen; A. M. M. Zubair.

Principal Staff: Chair. Dr A. M. M. Sahabdeen; Dir M. Rizvan Sahabdeen; Sec. A. M. M. Zubair.

Address: 30/12 Bagatelle Road, Colombo 3.

Telephone: (1) 502447; **Fax:** (1) 505081; **e-mail:** sifani@eureka.lk.

Worldview International Foundation

Founded in Sri Lanka in 1979 to promote communication in development programmes and the transfer of information between countries.

Activities: The Foundation supports programmes which enhance communication skills; works towards a better understanding in industrialized countries of the development process in developing countries; supports the use of appropriate technologies; promotes international understanding and co-operation; and uses audio-visual media to promote human resources development through the process of 'development communication'. The Foundation has members in 52 countries world-wide, and maintains a network of Media Centres and the Worldview Global Media group of companies.

Geographical Area of Activity: Africa, Asia, the Far East and Australasia, and North, Central and South America.

Publications: *WIF News Bulletin* (quarterly); Annual Report.

Finance: Annual budget approx. US $3,500,000.

Central Council: Ismail Serageldin (Pres.).

Principal Staff: Sec.-Gen. Arne Fjørtoft.

Address: 713 D. P. Wijesingha Mawatha, Pelawatta, Battaramulla.

Telephone: (74) 419100; **Fax:** (74) 419200; **Internet:** www.wifoundation.org; **e-mail:** wif@wifoundation.org.

Sweden

FOUNDATION CENTRE AND CO-ORDINATING BODY

The Hague Club

Established in 1971, the Club is an informal association of individuals. Its purpose is to facilitate discussion and co-operation between Chief Executives of important foundations in Europe and prominent persons involved with foundations.

Activities: Membership of the Club is restricted to the Chief Executives of selected foundations in Europe (and one foundation from Israel), and so-called Corresponding Members from different parts of the world. The members convene once a year, while the day-to-day affairs are conducted by a Steering Committee elected for a period of two years. The members of the Club are the Chief Executives of Fundação Calouste Gulbenkian, Fondation Roi Baudouin, Bernard van Leer Foundation, European Cultural Foundation, Ramón Areces Fundación, Nuffield Foundation, Juliana Welzijn Fonds, Finnish Cultural Foundation, Fritz Thyssen Stiftung, Bodossaki Foundation, Jenny and Antti Wihuri Foundation, Volkswagen Stiftung, Leverhulme Trust, Nestlé Foundation, Bank of Sweden Tercentenary Foundation, Robert Bosch Stiftung GmbH, Novartis Foundation, Egmont Fonden, Knut och Alice Wallenberg Stiftelse, Fondazione Adriano Olivetti, Fundación Juan March (qq.v.) and the Velux Foundation. The Corresponding Members are the Chief Executives of Consiglio Italiano per le Scienze Sociali, Italy, the Council on Foundations, USA (q.v.), Fundacão Roberto Marinho, Brazil (q.v.), Japan Center for International Exchange, Japan (q.v.), The Myer Foundation, Australia (q.v.), and the Central European University, Hungary.

Geographical Area of Activity: Mainly Europe.

Restrictions: Does not make grants.

Address: c/o The Bank of Sweden Tercentenary Foundation, POB 5675, 11486 Stockholm.

Telephone: (7) 631 05 66; **Fax:** (7) 323 48 77.

FOUNDATIONS, TRUSTS AND NON-PROFIT ORGANIZATIONS

Folke Bernadottes Minnesfond (Folke Bernadotte's Memorial Foundation)

Founded in 1948 by the Swedish Relief Committee for Europe, in memory of Count Folke Bernadotte, to promote understanding between nations, particularly through enabling young persons to become acquainted with the culture, ideals and social conditions of other countries, and to bring aid to those in need. To the extent that organizations commemorating Count Folke Bernadotte, and having largely similar aims, are formed in other countries, the Foundation seeks to co-ordinate the activities of these organizations.

Activities: Offers scholarships to people living in Sweden, and under the age of 35, who want to travel outside Scandinavia in order to experience other cultural conditions. Some kind of exchange must be included, and the social aspect is important. Scholarships are also given to those taking part in camps and volunteering.

Geographical Area of Activity: International.

Restrictions: No scholarships for study.

Address: POB 24009, 104 50 Stockholm.

Telephone: (8) 662 25 05; **Internet:** www.come.to/folke.bernadotte.minne.

Cancerfonden (Swedish Cancer Society)

Founded in 1951 to support, organize and co-ordinate cancer research that is primarily concerned with basic medical and scientific research tasks; to promote the development of new research and treatment methods in cancer cases and to lend support to other measures in the interest of cancer patients; and to support educational activities concerned with the aims and means of cancer research and with the prevention, symptoms and treatment of cancer diseases.

Activities: Awards grants to individuals of any nationality to carry out cancer research, or research in a related science, including biochemistry, cell biology, pathology, virology, immunology, etc. Awards for Swedish researchers are tenable in countries outside Sweden; foreign recipients must carry out their research in Sweden. The Society also disseminates information on cancer for public education purposes.

Geographical Area of Activity: Sweden.

Restrictions: No grants to individuals.

Publications: Annual Report; *Rädda Livet* (6 a year).

Principal Staff: Pres. Ingemar Eliasson; Sec.-Gen. Ursula Tengelin; Dir of Communications Johan af Donner.

Address: David Bagares gata 5, 101 55 Stockholm.

Telephone: (8) 677 10 00; **Fax:** (8) 20 71 04; **Internet:** www.cancerfonden.se; **e-mail:** info@cancerfonden.se.

Anna-Greta och Holger Crafoords Fond (Anna-Greta and Holger Crafoords Foundation)

Founded in 1980 by Anna-Greta and Holger Crafoord through a donation to the Royal Swedish Academy of Sciences, to promote basic scientific research nationally and internationally.

Activities: Operates in the fields of mathematics and astronomy, geosciences, biosciences (with particular emphasis on ecology), and medicine (rheumatoid arthritis). The Foundation provides grants to individuals and institutions in Sweden for scientific research and awards the Nobel Prizes in Physics and Chemistry totalling 9,000,000 kronor each.

Geographical Area of Activity: International.

Principal Staff: Sec.-Gen. Prof. Erling Norrby.

Address: Lilla Frescativägen 4a, POB 50005, 104 05 Stockholm.

Telephone: (8) 673 95 00; **Fax:** (8) 15 56 70; **Internet:** www.kva.se; **e-mail:** info@kva.se.

Diakonia

An NGO-supporting organization established in 1966 to promote equality for all people.

Activities: Operates in South-East Asia, Central and South America, Africa and the Middle East in the areas of aid to less-developed countries, conservation and the environment, international affairs, and law and human rights, through making grants to organizations.

Geographical Area of Activity: South-East Asia, Central and South America, Africa and the Middle East.

Restrictions: Grants are not made to individuals, nor are they given to organizations in Europe or in the countries of the former USSR.

Finance: Eighty per cent of the budget comes from the Swedish Government, the rest from private donors. Annual expenditure 200,000,000 kronor (1999).

Trustees: Bertis Svensson (Chair.); Gunnel Andreasson (First Vice-Chair.); Bernt-Olof Carlsson (Second Vice-Chair.).

Principal Staff: Dir Bo Forsberg; Financial Man. Krister Adolfsson; Chief of Staff Gunilla Melsted.

Address: Starrbäcksgatan 11, 172 99 Sundbyberg.

Telephone: (8) 453 69 00; **Fax:** (8) 453 69 29; **Internet:** www.diakonia.se; **e-mail:** diakonia@diakonia.se.

Eden Foundation

Established in 1985, to preserve the variety of plant species available, to promote biodiversity and campaign against the artificial creation of plants.

Activities: Operates in the field of conservation and the environment, and aid to less-developed countries. Runs a research project in Niger on the impact of desertification, and carries out direct seeding tests, through giving seed to local farmers.

Geographical Area of Activity: Niger.

Address: Skreav 45B, 311 72 Falkenberg.

Internet: www.eden-foundation.org; **e-mail:** webmaster@eden-foundation.org.

Ekhagastiftelsen (Ekhaga Foundation)

Founded in 1944 by Gösta Videgård, engineer, to support research into agricultural production without the use of poisons and artificial means; and into the production of natural foods and medical methods based on the capacity of human beings to cure themselves.

Activities: Operates nationally and internationally in the fields of science and medicine, through grants to Scandinavian institutions and individuals, and the provision of fellowships and scholarships.

Geographical Area of Activity: Sweden and Europe.

Finance: Grants approx. 10,000,000 kronor (2001).

Address: Kungsgatan 18, 111 35 Stockholm.

Telephone: (8) 22 30 01; **Fax:** (8) 21 83 76; **Internet:** www.ekhagastiftelsen.se; **e-mail:** info@ekhagastiftelsen.se.

Föreningen Svenska Atheninstitutets Vänner (Association of the Friends of the Swedish Institute at Athens)

Founded in 1976 by Anders Sundberg and 13 others with the aim of supporting the Swedish Institute at Athens (q.v.) and promoting cultural contacts between Sweden and Greece.

Activities: Provides grants to institutions and individuals, and awards prizes and scholarships within Scandinavia; organizes conferences and training courses.

Geographical Area of Activity: Scandinavia.

Publications: *Hellenika* (quarterly).

Governing Board: Prof. Inge Jonsson (Chair.); Anders Sundberg (Sec.); Per Eric Mattsson (Treas.).

Principal Staff: Man. Dir and Sec. Anders Sundberg.

Address: POB 14124, 104 41 Stockholm.

Telephone and Fax: (8) 663 21 02.

Handikapporganisationernas Internationella Biståndsstiftelse (Swedish Organization of Disabled Persons—International Aid Association)

Founded in 1981 to support development aid programmes for disabled people, and to promote the establishment of programmes for the disabled in developing countries.

Geographical Area of Activity: International.

Publications: *Handling* (2 a year).

Principal Staff: Sec.-Gen. Barbro Carlsson; Methods Development Tiina Nummi-Soedergren.

Address: Magnus Ladulåsgatan 63 IV, POB 4060, 102 61 Stockholm.

Telephone: (8) 462 33 61; **Fax:** (8) 714 59 22; **e-mail:** tiini@shie.se.

Hjärt-Lungfonden (Swedish Heart Lung Foundation)

Founded in 1904 by a number of prominent citizens, physicians and laymen with the royal family as patrons, to combat by every available means tuberculosis and heart and chest diseases in Sweden. Also known as the Svenska Nationalföreningen mot Hjärt-och Lungsjukdomar (Swedish National Heart and Lung Disease Association).

Activities: Operates nationally in the field of social welfare and studies, and both nationally and internationally in the fields of science and medicine, through research, self-conducted programmes, grants to institutions and individuals, publications and lectures. Also awards scholarships and fellowships to persons of Swedish and other nationalities, and organizes conferences and courses with national as well as international membership.

Geographical Area of Activity: Mainly Sweden.

Publications: Report of operations and financial statement; quarterly review; information brochures on heart and lung diseases.

Governing Board: G. Boman; Marianne Lundin; Princess Christina Fru Magnuson; L. Rydén; P. Sjöstrand; B.-E. Skoogh.

Principal Staff: Sec.-Gen. and CEO K. Hallerby.

Address: Riddargatan 18, 114 51 Stockholm.

Telephone: (8) 566 242 00; **Fax:** (8) 566 242 29; **Internet:** www.hjart-lungfonden.se; **e-mail:** info@hjart-lungfonden.se.

Institut Mittag-Leffler (Mittag-Leffler Foundation of the Royal Swedish Academy of Science)

Founded in 1916 by Gösta Mittag-Leffler and Signe Lindfors Mittag-Leffler to promote pure mathematics in Sweden and Scandinavia with international co-operation; previously known as the Mittag-Leffler Foundation of the Royal Swedish Academy of Science.

Activities: Conducts research in pure mathematics; awards grants and scholarships open to researchers who have recently obtained a doctorate, and to advanced graduate students researching within the topic of the year.

Geographical Area of Activity: International.

Restrictions: Grants restricted to the annual theme.

Publications: *Acta Mathematica; Arkiv för matematik.*

Governing Board: Christer Kiselman (Chair.).

Principal Staff: Dir K.-O. Widman.

Address: Auravägen 17, 182 60 Djursholm.

Telephone: (8) 622 05 60; **Fax:** (8) 622 05 89; **Internet:** www.ml.kva.se; **e-mail:** koskull@ml.kva.se.

International Foundation for Science

Founded in 1972 by the national academies or research councils of 12 countries, to encourage scientific work in developing countries.

Activities: Provides young scientists and technologists of outstanding merit from developing countries with financial and other support in their work; the researchers must carry out the work in their own country, and research is restricted to biological and agricultural sciences, and the chemistry of natural resources. The sharing of scientific information between researchers and advisers is encouraged by regional meetings and visits to project sites. As of 2002 there were 135 member organizations (scientific academies, research councils and national and international organizations) in 90 countries.

Geographical Area of Activity: International.

Publications: Report of operations and financial statement; electronic newsletter; Annual Report.

Finance: Core contributions to the budget come from Australia, Denmark, France, Germany, the Netherlands, Norway, Sweden, Switzerland and the USA; restricted contributions are made by several other countries. Annual budget approx. US $5,000,000 (2001).

Board of Trustees: Bruno Messerli (Chair.); Pierre Roger (Vice-Chair.).

Principal Staff: Dir Dr Michael Ståhl.

Address: Grev Turegatan 19, 114 38 Stockholm.

Telephone: (8) 545 818 00; **Fax:** (8) 545 818 01; **Internet:** www.ifs.se; **e-mail:** info@ifs.se.

Konstnärsnämnden (The Arts Grants Committee)

Founded in 1976 to administer state grants in the arts. Incorporates IASPIS, the International Artists' Studio Programme in Sweden.

Activities: The Foundation operates nationally and internationally in the area of the arts; it awards grants to individuals in all areas of the arts with the exception of literature.

Geographical Area of Activity: International.

Restrictions: Grants open to Swedish residents and artists working in Sweden, and occasionally outside of Sweden.

Finance: Funded by the Swedish Government; annual revenue and expenditure 140,000,000 kronor (2002).

Trustees: The Committee is governed by a Board appointed by the Government of Sweden.

Principal Staff: Gunilla Fredholm; Lars Olof Gustafson; Nils Johansson; Dir of IASPIS Sara Arrhenius.

Address: Box 1610, 111 86 Stockholm.

Telephone: (8) 402 35 70; **Fax:** (8) 402 35 90; **Internet:** www.konstnarsnamnden.se; **e-mail:** info@konstnarsnamnden.

Konung Gustaf V:s 90-Årsfond (King Gustaf V 90th Birthday Foundation)

Founded in 1949 by the Swedish people in honour of King Gustaf's 90th birthday, to support voluntary youth activities.

Activities: Awards grants to Swedish youth organizations for their international exchange programmes and international conferences on voluntary activities for young people.

Geographical Area of Activity: Sweden.

Restrictions: No grants to individuals.

Publications: *Möten med mening, 1999; För Europa; förening, 2001.*

Board of Trustees: Gunnar Brodin (Pres.).

Principal Staff: Gen. Sec. Lennart Elbe.

Address: Kungl Slottet, 111 30 Stockholm.

Telephone and Fax: (8) 108 433; **Internet:** www.gv90.a.se.

Kulturfonder for Sverige och Finland (Swedish and Finnish Cultural Foundation)

Activities: Grants are provided for a broad range of activities which aim to increase contact and understanding between the people of Sweden and Finland, especially in the fields of culture, the environment and industry. Also works to promote the Finnish language in Sweden.

Geographical Area of Activity: Sweden and Finland.

Finance: Mats Jönsson; Raili Rajavuori.

Address: Föreningen Norden, Box 12707, 112 94 Stockholm.

Telephone: (8) 654 19 90.

Kvinna Till Kvinna Foundation

Founded in 1993 in response to the war in the Balkans and the atrocities committed on women; aims to support women in conflict situations.

Activities: Supports a range of projects targeting women living in conflict or post-conflict areas, in the Balkans and Israel/Palestinian Autonomous Areas, in a range of areas, including campaigning for gender sensitivity in international peace accords, reproductive health information and health care, promoting dialogue, training for empowerment and employment, addressing domestic violence, legal advice, and other issues, including sex-trafficking, which arise in conflict and post-conflict situations. Also seeks to build networks amongst women's groups. Maintains eight field offices in Albania, Bosnia-Herzegovina, Croatia, Georgia, Israel/Palestinian Autonomous Areas, Kosovo, Macedonia and Serbia.

Geographical Area of Activity: Albania, Bosnia-Herzegovina, Croatia, Georgia, Israel/Palestinian Autonomous Areas, Kosovo, Macedonia and Serbia.

Finance: Bulk of funding from the Swedish International Development Agency; total budget 32,000,000 kronor (2001).

Principal Staff: Contact: Kerstin Greback.

Address: Kristinebergs Slottsväg 8, 112 52 Stockholm.

Telephone: (87) 02 98 20; **Fax:** (86) 43 23 60; **Internet:** www.iktk.se; **e-mail:** info@iktk.se.

Nobelstiftelsen (Nobel Foundation)

Founded in 1900 in accordance with the will of Alfred Nobel to award annual prizes to those who, during the preceding year, are judged to have conferred the greatest benefit on mankind in each of the following fields: physics, chemistry, physiology or medicine, literature and peace.

Activities: Operates internationally in the fields of science and medicine, literature and peace promotion, through the prizes to individuals, a peace prize to institutions or individuals, conferences and publications. Prize-winners are chosen by the Royal Academy of Sciences, Stockholm (Physics, Chemistry), the Nobel Assembly at the Karolinska Institutet, Stockholm (Physiology or Medicine), the Swedish Academy, Stockholm (Literature) and the Norwegian Nobel Committee (Peace). In 1968 the Central Bank of Sweden instituted an Alfred Nobel Memorial Prize in Economic Sciences of the same value as the Nobel Prize.

Geographical Area of Activity: International.

Publications: Annual report and financial statement; *Les Prix Nobel; Nobel Lectures.*

Board of Directors: Prof. B. Samuelsson (Chair.); M. Storch (Deputy Chair.); M. Sohlman (Exec. Dir); G. Berge; H. Engdahl; Prof. E. Norrby; J. Wallenberg.

Principal Staff: Exec. Dir Michael Sohlman.

Address: Sturegatan 14, POB 5232, 102 45 Stockholm.

Telephone: (8) 663 09 20; **Fax:** (8) 660 38 47; **Internet:** www.nobel.se.

Nordiska Afrikainstitutets Resestipendiefond (Nordic Africa Institute Travel Fund)

Founded in 1962 to provide funds for researchers associated with universities and other research institutions in the Nordic countries (Denmark, Finland, Iceland, Norway and Sweden) to conduct fieldwork in Africa.

Activities: Provides travel grants for those preparing and conducting research projects concerned with development issues in Africa, and emphasis is placed on the social sciences and closely related fields.

Geographical Area of Activity: The Nordic countries (Denmark, Finland, Iceland, Norway and Sweden) and Africa.

Restrictions: Grants only to researchers associated with institutions in the Nordic countries.

Finance: Annual budget 1,000,000 kronor (2000).

Principal Staff: Programme Officer Ingrid Andersson.

Address: c/o Nordiska Afrikainstitutets Program- och Forskningsråd, POB 1703, 751 47 Uppsala.

Telephone: (18) 56 22 00; **Fax:** (18) 56 22 90; **Internet:** www.nai.uu.se; **e-mail:** nai@nai.uu.se.

Erik Philip-Sörensens Stiftelse (Erik Philip-Sörensens Foundation)

Founded in 1976 to promote research into genetic science and the humanities.

Activities: In the field of genetic science, research grants are made to individuals or groups regardless of the institute where they choose to operate. Both basic research and specialized research are supported. Grants in the field of the humanities are awarded on the recommendation of Lund University.

Geographical Area of Activity: Sweden.

Restrictions: The Foundation does not give grants for research work outside Sweden; only accepts applications from Swedish universities.

Address: c/o Mannerheimer Swartling Advokatbyrå, Box 4291, 203 14 Malmö.

Telephone: (40) 25 08 00; **Fax:** (40) 25 08 01; **Internet:** www.epss.m.se/.

Reumatikerförbundet (The Swedish Rheumatism Association)

Founded in 1945 by the Swedish Confederation of Trade Unions, the Co-operative Union and Wholesale Society, the Federation of Swedish Farmers' Associations, the Federation of Swedish Trade Unions, and different associations of workers in social welfare, to combat rheumatic diseases in Sweden.

Activities: Operates nationally running a hospital for rheumatic patients; enables information to be exchanged among members and others interested; makes grants for research in rheumatology, and participates in international conferences.

Geographical Area of Activity: Sweden.

Publications: *Reumatikertidningen* (periodical); annual report and financial statement.

Finance: Research grants disbursed US $1,800,000 (2000).

Address: Alströmergatan 39, Box 12851, 112 98 Stockholm.

Telephone: (8) 692 58 00; **Fax:** (8) 650 64 15; **Internet:** www.reumatikerforbundet.org; **e-mail:** info@reumatikerforbundel.org.

Right Livelihood Awards Foundation

Established in 1980 by Jakob von Uexkull to administer the Right Livelihood Awards.

Activities: Administers the Right Livellihood Awards, known as the 'alternative Nobels', to four individuals each year, in recognition of individuals who develop practical solutions to challenges to society, including air and water pollution, the danger of nuclear war, the abuse of human rights and the destitution of the poor.

Geographical Area of Activity: International.

Publications: *Cornerstones* (newsletter, 2 a year); brochures; bibliographies of prize winners; and publications by prize winners.

Finance: Makes four annual awards of US $200,000 each.

Address: POB 15072, 104 65 Stockholm.

Telephone: (8) 702 03 40; **Fax:** (8) 702 03 38; **Internet:** www.rightlivelihood.se; **e-mail:** info@rightlivelihood.se.

Star of Hope International

Established as an aid organization to assist in long-term development, and give assistance after disasters.

Activities: Operates internationally in the fields of aid to less-developed countries, through assisting local organizations in areas of greatest need, and particularly through helping children. Maintains offices in Argentina, Brazil, China, Colombia, Finland, Ghana, Haiti, Kenya, Latvia, Norway, Philippines, Romania, Russia, Rwanda, Trinidad, Ukraine and the USA.

Geographical Area of Activity: International.

Publications: Newsletter.

Principal Staff: Contact: Lennart Eriksson.

Address: Remersholmes gata 6, 117 40 Stockholm.

Telephone: (8) 658 11 90; **Fax:** (8) 791 90 17; **Internet:** www.starofhope.org; **e-mail:** info@starofhope.org.

Stiftelsen Blanceflor Boncompagni-Ludovisi, född Bildt (Blanceflor Boncompagni-Ludovisi, née Bildt Foundation)

Founded in 1955 to promote educational visits abroad for Swedish and Italian citizens.

Activities: Grants are provided to individuals under the age of 35 for study in scientific fields (for example, chemistry, physics, medicine, dentistry and engineering) where study abroad is seen to be of specific value. Grants are awarded for higher education (at university or the equivalent) to those not eligible for state or community grants. The preferred host countries are Canada, Germany, Italy, Japan, Sweden, Switzerland, the United Kingdom and the USA.

Geographical Area of Activity: International.

Restrictions: No grants to groups or associations, nor for undergraduate study. Grants are made for study in certain disciplines only.

Finance: Annual grants approx 6,200,000 kronor.

Principal Staff: Treas. Dag Wersén.

Address: Grev Turegatan 9A, 114 46 Stockholm.

Telephone: (8) 678 01 65; **Fax:** (8) 678 36 00; **Internet:** www.blanceflor.home.se.

Stiftelsen Globträdet (The Globetree Foundation)

Founded in November 1982 by Kajsa B. Dahlström and Ben van Bronckhorst to support the education of children, with particular emphasis on the environment with an international perspective.

Activities: The Foundation operates nationally and internationally in the fields of aid to less-developed countries, the arts and humanities, conservation and the environment, education, and medicine and health; it operates self-conducted programmes, organizes training courses, conferences and research programmes, offers grants to individuals, and awards scholarships and fellowships.

Geographical Area of Activity: International.

Publications: *Meeting in the Globetree;* books and teaching aids.

Principal Staff: Chair. Kajsa B. Dahström; Vice-Chair. Sam H. Samuelsson; Treas. Eva Nilsson.

Address: Föreningen Globträdet, Bergsgatan 2 (3tr), 112 23 Stockholm.

Telephone: (8) 652 35 26; **Fax:** (8) 652 21 77; **Internet:** www.globetree.org.

Stiftelsen Dag Hammarskjölds Minnesfond (Dag Hammarskjöld Foundation)

Established in 1962 in memory of the second Secretary-General of the United Nations to organize seminars, conferences, consultations and workshops on the social, political, economic and cultural issues facing developing countries and to publish and disseminate the results.

Activities: Operates internationally to carry out its aims.

Geographical Area of Activity: International.

Restrictions: The Foundation is an operating and not a grant-making foundation; its work programmes are carried out under its own auspices.

Publications: *Development Dialogue* (2 a year); manuals and reports based on seminars and conferences.

Trustees: Lars Anell (Chair.); Sheila S. Coronel; Elinor Hammarskjöld; Dr Göran Hydén; Dr Lydia P. Makhubu; Dr Mary Robinson; Dr Bo Sundqvist.

Principal Staff: Exec. Dir Olle Nordberg; Asst Dir Niclas Hällström.

Address: Övre Slottsgatan 2, 753 10 Uppsala.

Telephone: (18) 10 27 72; **Fax:** (18) 12 20 72; **Internet:** www.dhf.uu.se; **e-mail:** secretariat@dhf.uu.se.

Stiftelsen för Miljöstrategisk Forskning (Swedish Foundation for Strategic Environmental Research)

Founded in 1994 to encourage research, especially in the field of the environment.

Activities: The foundation supports environmental research programmes in the area of sustainable development, and promotes co-operation between universities, industry and international centres of research.

Geographical Area of Activity: International.

Finance: Total assets 4,700,000,000 (Dec. 2000); annual research budget approx. 250,000,000 kronor (2001).

Address: Gamla Brogatan 36–38, 111 20 Stockholm.

Telephone: (8) 791 10 20; **Fax:** (8) 791 10 29; **Internet:** www.mistra.org; **e-mail:** mail@mistra.org.

Stiftelsen Riksbankens Jubileumsfond (The Bank of Sweden Tercentenary Foundation)

Established in 1962 by the Bank of Sweden to commemorate the bank's tercentenary, and to support scientific research particularly in the humanities and social sciences.

Activities: Aims to support research in the humanities and social sciences, through awards, donations and scholarships. Programmes include the Bank of Sweden Donation, targeting research in the humanities, social sciences, theology and law; the Nils-Eric Svensson Fund which promotes educational exchanges between young researchers in Sweden and the rest of Europe; and the Humanities and Social Sciences Donation, which particularly supports multidisciplinary and co-operative research efforts. Internationally, the Foundation funds a Swedish–German Research Awards for Scientific Co-operation programme in conjunction with the Alexander von Humboldt Stiftung, and is one of a number of foundations funding the Budapest Collegium research centre.

Geographical Area of Activity: Sweden and international.

Restrictions: No grants to undergraduate students nor to doctoral students working individually.

Publications: Annual report and financial statement; conference reports.

Finance: Assets 10,000,000,000 kronor (2000); grants expenditure 500,000,000 kronor (2000).

Trustees: Prof. E. Österberg (Chair.); Sonia Karlsson (Vice-Chair.); Prof. Rune Åberg; Per Bill; Johan Bygge; Berndt Ekholm; Prof. Christer Jönsson; Lars-Erik Klangby; Lennart Kollmats; Prof. Mats Larsson; Lars Lilja; Majléne Westerlund Panke.

Principal Staff: Dir Dr Dan Brändström.

Address: POB 5675, 114 86 Stockholm.

Telephone: (8) 506 264 00; **Fax:** (8) 506 264 30; **Internet:** www.rj.se; **e-mail:** rj@rj.se.

Stockholm Environment Institute

Founded in 1989 by the Swedish Parliament to unite scientific research and policy development, particularly in the areas of environment and development.

Activities: The Institute has four main centres, in Stockholm, Tallinn, Boston (USA) and York (United Kingdom). Research is carried out in five main programme areas: Sustainable Development; Atmospheric Environments; Climate and Energy Resources; Water Resources; and Risk and Vulnerability. Maintains regional offices in Belgium and Thailand, and work is carried out in more than 20 countries world-wide.

Geographical Area of Activity: International.

Publications: Newsletters; fact sheets.

Board: Lars Anell (Chair.); M. Brown; C. Fussler; Prof. C. Holling; A. Jansson; E. S. Lindgren; Sunita Nurain; Dr Y. Sokona; Dr M. Tabucanon.

Principal Staff: Exec. Dir Roger Kasperson.

Address: Lilla Nygaten 1, POB 2142, 103 14 Stockholm.

Telephone: (8) 412 14 00; **Fax:** (8) 723 03 48; **Internet:** www.sei.se; **e-mail:** postmaster@sei.se.

Stockholm International Peace Research Institute—SIPRI

Founded in 1966 by the Swedish Parliament to conduct scientific research on questions which are important for international peace and security with the intention of contributing to the understanding of the conditions for peaceful solutions of international conflicts and for creating a stable peace.

Activities: Operates internationally in the field of international affairs, through research, publications and symposia. SIPRI's research programme centres around the following projects: weapons control and disarmament documentation survey; weapons transfers; building a co-operative security system in and for Europe; chemical and biological warfare and weapons control; study of armed conflicts and their prevention; export controls; integrating fact databases in the field of international relations and security; military expenditure and weapons production; and military technology and international security. Maintains databases on international relations and military issues.

Geographical Area of Activity: International.

Publications: *SIPRI Yearbook;* research reports and books.

Finance: Government grant 26,053,000 kronor (2003).

Governing Board: Rolf Ekeus (Chair., Sweden); Alyson J. K. Bailes (Dir); Dr W. van Eekelen (Netherlands); Dr N. Elaraby (Egypt); Sir M. Goulding (United Kingdom); Prof. H. Haftendorn (Germany); Dr C. Kelleher (USA); Prof. R. Sutherland (Canada); Dr Alexei G. Arbatov (Russia).

Principal Staff: Dir Alyson J. K. Bailes.

Address: Signalistgatan 9, 169 70 Solna.

Telephone: (8) 655 97 00; **Fax:** (8) 655 97 33; **Internet:** www.sipri.org; **e-mail:** sipri@sipri.org.

Sverige–Amerika Stiftelsen (Sweden–America Foundation)

Founded in 1919 by representatives of private business and industry, with the aim of developing understanding between Sweden and the USA and Canada by promoting the exchange of scientific, cultural and practical experiences between the countries.

Activities: Provides awards and scholarships to Swedish nationals for advanced study and research in the USA or Canada. Supports a trainee programme for Swedes in the USA, and a counselling service for prospective students, with a reference library of US and Canadian university catalogues.

Geographical Area of Activity: Sweden, the USA and Canada.

Publications: Annual Report.

Address: Grev Turegatan 14, POB 5280, 102 46 Stockholm.

Telephone: (8) 611 46 11; **Fax:** (8) 611 40 04; **Internet:** www.sweamfo.se; **e-mail:** info@sweamfo.se.

Sweden–Japan Foundation

Founded in 1971 with the purpose of increasing understanding between the people of Sweden and Japan.

Activities: Operates in the fields of research and development, industry, science, commerce and culture, through the provision of scholarships for undergraduate students, organizing courses, seminars and study trips, and the publication of relevant documentation. The Foundation encourages cultural exchange and co-operation between the two countries.

Geographical Area of Activity: Sweden and Japan.

Publications: *Japan-Nytt* (monthly newsletter); papers.

Address: Grev Turegatan 14, 114 46 Stockholm.

Telephone: (8) 611 68 73; **Fax:** (8) 611 73 44; **Internet:** www.swejap.a.se; **e-mail:** info@swejap.a.se.

The Swedish NGO Foundation for Human Rights

Established in 1991 for the promotion of human rights in less-developed countries, supplementing the activities of its member organizations, the Church of Sweden, Diakonia (q.v.), the Swedish Red Cross and Swedish Save the Children.

Activities: Operates in less-developed countries in Africa, Asia, and Central and South America and the Caribbean in the field of human rights, including providing information; monitoring human rights; providing legal aid, education and training; campaigning; carrying out research; and networking. Also aims to inform and educate on human rights in Sweden, through publications, seminars and information for use in schools.

Geographical Area of Activity: Africa, Asia, Central and South America and the Caribbean, and Sweden.

Restrictions: Grants are not made to individuals or to international organizations, nor for development work or health care, unless this is in the context of human rights.

Publications: Newsletter; Biennial Report.

Finance: Financed by its founding organizations and the Swedish International Development Co-operation Agency. Total income 14,775,000 kronor, expenditure 14,367,000 kronor (2000).

Board of Directors: Bo Forsberg; Eva Geidenmark; Malin Greenhill; Hilda Lind; Sia Åkermark.

Principal Staff: Sec.-Gen. Anita Klum.

Address: Drottinggatan 101, 113 60 Stockholm.

Telephone: (8) 54 54 9970; **Fax:** (8) 30 30 31; **Internet:** www.humanrights.se; **e-mail:** info@humanrights.se.

Swedish Research Centre in Cyprus

Founded in 1974 by Paul Åström and Gunnar Michelson to promote Swedish research in the humanities in Cyprus, especially in the field of archaeology, and to promote scientific and cultural relations between Sweden and Cyprus.

Activities: Operates in Cyprus in the fields of archaeology, and the arts and humanities in general, through research.

Geographical Area of Activity: Cyprus and Sweden.

Trustees: Prof. Paul Åström (Chair.); Ulla Öbrink (Sec.).

Principal Staff: Treas. Gunnar Michelson.

Address: c/o Astrom, William Gibsons väg 11, 433 76 Jonsered.

Telephone: (31) 795 66 00; **Fax:** (31) 795 67 10; **e-mail:** paul.astrom@swipmet.se.

Taiga Rescue Network—TRN

Established in 1992 to give a voice to those wanting to see sensitive development in the boreal region, through the linking and publicizing of local campaigns on behalf of the boreal forests and peoples. Almost 200 organizations participate in the network, which is the only international network of NGOs, indigenous peoples and individuals working to defend the world's boreal forests.

Activities: Operates internationally in the field of forest conservation. Projects include forest mapping, supporting the rights of indigenous peoples, youth activities, monitoring of trade flows, international forest policy, forest certification and combating illegal logging activities in Russian forests. TRN's International Co-ordination Centre is located in Jokkmokk, Sweden. Maintains a Russian Co-ordination Centre in Moscow and a West European Co-ordinator in Amsterdam. The affiliated Boreal Forest Network operates in Canada.

Geographical Area of Activity: Europe, North America and Russia.

Restrictions: Grants only to participating organizations to finance joint projects.

Publications: *Taiga News;* reports; fact sheets; brochures.

Finance: Receives grants from participating organizations, private foundations, governmental institutions and the European Union. Income €240,876, expenditure €252,700 (2000).

Board: The International Reference Group consists of 30 representatives from participant organizations in North America, Europe and Russia.

Principal Staff: Int. Co-ordinator Elisa Peter; Information Co-ordinator Ola Larsson; Russian Co-ordinator Dima Aksenov; Western Europe Co-ordinator Arjan Alkema.

Address: POB 116, 96223 Jokkmokk.

Telephone: (971) 170 39; **Fax:** (971) 120 57; **Internet:** www.taigarescue.org; **e-mail:** info@taigarescue.org.

Transnationella Stiftelsen för Freds- och Framtidsforskning—TFF (Transnational Foundation for Peace and Future Research)

Founded in 1986 by Christina Spännar and Jan Øberg, to promote conflict mitigation, peace research and education, in order to improve conflict understanding and promote alternative security and global development based on non-violent politics and economics.

Activities: The Foundation has established the following programmes: world images and peace thinking; European orders of peace and co-operation; reconciliation and forgiveness; Gandhi's relevance in the contemporary world; economy, ecology and ethics; conflict mitigation—theory and practice in the former Yugoslavia (now Serbia and Montenegro), the Commonwealth of Independent States and Burundi; demilitarization and sustainable development; and the United Nations in the emerging world order.

Geographical Area of Activity: International.

Restrictions: Not a grant-making organization.

Publications: *TFF Newsletter* (annually); *TFF Statements*; Annual Report; books, research reports, occasional papers and TFF press information.

Finance: Donations, research grants and book sales.

Principal Staff: Dir Jan Øberg.

Address: Vegagatan 25, 224 57 Lund.

Telephone: (46) 14 59 09; **Fax:** (46) 14 45 12; **Internet:** www.transnational.org; **e-mail:** comments@transnational.org.

Knut och Alice Wallenbergs Stiftelse (Knut and Alice Wallenberg Foundation)

Founded in 1917 by Knut Agathon Wallenberg and Alice O. Wallenberg to promote research and education of value to Sweden.

Activities: Operates primarily nationally in the fields of education, medicine, the natural sciences and the arts and humanities, through grants to institutions, particularly for heavy equipment and laboratories.

Geographical Area of Activity: Sweden.

Restrictions: Grants are not made to individuals, with the exception of scholarship programmes established by or supported by the Foundation. Only Swedish applications are considered.

Finance: Grants budget €66,150,000 (1999).

Principal Staff: Dr Prof. Erna Möller.

Address: POB 16066, 103 22 Stockholm.

Telephone: (8) 545 017 80; **Internet:** http://wallenberg.org/kaw; **e-mail:** kaw@kaw.se.

Dr Marcus Wallenbergs Stiftelse för Utbildning i Internationellt Industriellt Företagande (Dr Marcus Wallenberg Foundation for Further Education in International Industry)

Founded in 1982 with the aim of providing financial assistance for education in industry and business.

Activities: The Foundation awards grants to Swedish citizens for study abroad. Grants are also made to educational institutions.

Geographical Area of Activity: Sweden.

Principal Staff: Chair. Peter Wallenberg; Exec. Officer Ulla Rasch-Anderson.

Address: POB 160 66, 103 22 Stockholm.

Internet: http://wallenberg.org.

Wenner-Gren Foundation for Scientific Research

Founded in 1955 by Dr Axel Wenner-Gren to promote international co-operation in scientific research in Sweden; and to organize symposia and conferences in the sciences.

Activities: Maintains a building which serves as a residence for foreign researchers and their families, and a venue for international symposia organized by the Foundation. Awards post-doctoral fellowships to Swedes for training abroad and to foreign scientists in Sweden. Books are also published.

Geographical Area of Activity: International.

Principal Staff: Head Scientific Secretariat Bertil Daneholt; Head Admin. Inger Franzén.

Address: Sveavägen 166, 113 46 Stockholm.

Telephone: (8) 736 98 00; **Fax:** (8) 31 86 32; **Internet:** www.wenner-grenstift.a.se/.

Switzerland

FOUNDATION CENTRES AND CO-ORDINATING BODIES

Association of Grantmaking Foundations in Switzerland (Verein der Vergabestiftungen in der Schweiz)

Created in May 2001 under the initiative of 11 of Switzerland's biggest foundations.

Activities: Represents its member foundations in Switzerland, promoting transparency, offering technical experience and expertise, presenting a platform for the exchange of experience between foundations, and encouraging the development of new foundations. In 2003 there were 19 member organizations.

Geographical Area of Activity: Switzerland.

Administrative Council: Dr Benno Schubiger (Pres.); Dr Philipp Egger; Christian Felber; Dr Jacques Kaegi; Annabel von Klenck; Dr Roger Schmid.

Principal Staff: Sec.-Gen. Linda Zurkinden-Erismann.

Address: Bundesgasse 16, Postfach 7426, 3001 Berne.

Telephone: (31) 3104241; **Fax:** (31) 3112152; **Internet:** www.swissfoundations.ch; **e-mail:** info@swissfoundations.ch.

International Council of Voluntary Agencies—ICVA

Founded in 1962 ICVA functions as an advocacy network adding value to the work of the NGOs that form its membership. It aims to facilitate a successful partnership between NGOs and international agencies and to act as a catalyst and a tool for the accurate, timely and effective exchange of information, concerns and issues among member NGOs, international humanitarian agencies and governments working towards common objectives. These objectives include the alleviation of human suffering in disaster areas, protection and promotion of human rights, the strengthening of civil society and democracy, the promotion of equality and the sustenance of human development.

Activities: ICVA facilitates access and NGO input to the Standing and Executive Committees of the United Nations High Commissioner for Refugees (UNHCR). In addition, ICVA supports the partnership between UNHCR and NGOs through the Partnership in Action (PARinAC) programme. This process has introduced new structures and mechanisms for co-operation at regional and national levels. The organization also identifies areas where partnerships could be further strengthened. ICVA has acted as a global focal point since the beginning of the PARinAC process in the early 1990s and has recently developed a PARinAC website (www.icva.ch/parinac). As one of the three NGO networks on the United Nations Inter-Agency Standing Committee, ICVA facilitates dialogue between NGOs and the main international body for humanitarian co-ordination. ICVA is also actively involved in the Sphere Project. In 2003 ICVA had over 70 member agencies and observers.

Geographical Area of Activity: International.

Restrictions: This is not a grant-making agency.

Publications: *Talk Back* (newsletter, available on website and via e-mail); Annual Report; Activity Reports.

Finance: Total assets 246,502 Swiss francs (2001); annual revenue 1,031,244 Swiss francs, expenditure 1,032,223 Swiss francs (2001).

Executive Committee: Composed of 11 representatives of member agencies.

Principal Staff: Co-ordinator Ed Schenkenberg van Mierop.

Address: 48 chemin du Grand-Montfleury, 1290 Versoix.

Telephone: (22) 9509600; **Fax:** (22) 9509609; **Internet:** www.icva.ch; **e-mail:** secretariat@icva.ch.

Interphil—International Standing Conference on Philanthropy

Founded in 1969 by CAF (the Charities Aid Foundation, q.v.), the European Cultural Foundation (q.v.), Fomento de entitades beneficias and Stifterverband für die deutsche Wissenschaft (q.v.) to promote the principles and the practices of philanthropy; it is a voluntary, non-governmental, non-profit association working for the good of the community.

Activities: The Conference works internationally towards the advancement of the non-profit sector, in the fields of education, research, the arts, conservation and social welfare and social studies, through self-conducted programmes, prizes, conferences, lectures, advisory services and publications. Interphil is committed to the strengthening of civil society in Central and Eastern Europe, as well as in other parts of the world.

Geographical Area of Activity: International.

Restrictions: No grants are made to individuals.

Publications: *Philanthropy International*; conference reports.

Finance: Funded through membership contributions.

Board of Directors: Countess Anne Sforza (Pres.); Rena Sha'shua-Hasson, Colin Graham (Vice-Pres); Cyril Ritchie (Exec. Dir and Treas.); Nina Belyaeva; Milena Smit; Engin Ural.

Principal Staff: Exec. Dir Cyril Ritchie.

Address: CIC Case 20, 1211 Geneva 20.

Telephone: (22) 7336717; **Fax:** (22) 7347082.

Swiss Coalition of Development Organisations

Established in 1971 to pursue development projects common to the five member organizations; Swissaid (q.v.), the Catholic Lenten Fund, Bread for All, Swiss Interchurch Aid, Helvetas (q.v.) and Caritas (q.v.).

Activities: The Swiss Coalition focuses on development policy, acting as an advocate within Switzerland for disadvantaged social classes in the South. It works through a combination of lobbying, public relations works and grass-roots mobilization in activities designed to be politically effective.

Geographical Area of Activity: International.

Restrictions: No grants available.

Publications: *Swiss Coalition News* (quarterly newsletter in English); *Global+* (quarterly newsletter in French and German); other magazines, documents and papers.

Finance: Funded by member organizations; annual budget US $3,200,000.

Directors of member organizations.

Principal Staff: Dir Peter Niggli.

Address: Monbijoustr. 31, Postfach 6735, 3001 Berne.

Telephone: (31) 3909330; **Fax:** (31) 3909331; **Internet:** www.swisscoalition.ch; **e-mail:** mail@swisscoalition.ch.

FOUNDATIONS, TRUSTS AND NON-PROFIT ORGANIZATIONS

Abegg-Stiftung Riggisberg

Founded by Werner Abegg for the collection and restoration of ancient woven fabrics dating up to the 18th century; the collection and display of works of minor arts, sculptures and paintings from the Near East, Byzantium, the European Middle Ages and the Renaissance and Baroque periods; the education of textile restorers; research in the fields of textiles and minor arts.

Activities: The Foundation supports textile restoration projects and students of textile restoration, through creating and running a degree course in textile art at the University of Applied Science, Berne. Maintains a library and a museum. Promotes scientific exchange in textile art by founding a research institute, organizing conferences and issuing publications.

Geographical Area of Activity: Switzerland.

Publications: Collection catalogues and other specialist publications.

Principal Staff: Dir Dr Regula Schorta.

Address: Werner Abegg-Str. 67, 3132 Riggisberg.

Telephone: (31) 8081201; **Fax:** (31) 8081200; **Internet:** www.abegg-stiftung.ch; **e-mail:** info@abegg-stiftung.ch.

Aga Khan Development Network

A group of eight development organizations operating in the fields of health, culture, education and economic development.

Activities: Operates in the fields of economic development, education, health and welfare, culture and NGO development, mainly in Asia and Africa. The Network consists of the Aga Khan Foundation and the Aga Khan Trust for Culture (qq.v.), Aga Khan Education Services, Aga Khan Fund for Economic Development, Aga Khan Health Services, Aga Khan Planning and Building Services, Aga Khan University and University of Central Asia.

Geographical Area of Activity: Mainly Asia and Africa.

Restrictions: No grants to individuals or for research; grants made in specific countries or regions only; no grants for construction.

Publications: Annual Report; various publications by individual network members.

Finance: Funded by individual agencies.

Board of Trustees: His Highness the Aga Khan (Chair.).

Address: 1–3 ave de la Paix, POB 2369, 1211 Geneva 2.

Telephone: (22) 9097200; **Fax:** (22) 9097291; **Internet:** www.akdn.org.

Aga Khan Foundation (Fondation Aga Khan)

Founded in 1967 by His Highness Prince Karim Aga Khan to promote new and effective solutions to certain well-defined problems that impede social development in developing countries.

Activities: The Foundation operates nationally and internationally in the fields of health, education, rural development and NGO enhancement and related concerns, including community participation, women and the environment, through grants to institutions, fellowships and scholarships, and publications. Prefers to fund innovative solutions to generic problems. With few exceptions, the Foundation provides funding for programmes in countries where it has branch offices and local professional staff to monitor implementation. Travel and study awards are made only to sponsored staff directly involved in programme implementation. The Foundation has branches in Afghanistan, Bangladesh, India, Kenya, Kyrgyz Republic, Mozambique, Pakistan, Syria, Tajikistan, Tanzania and Uganda, and affiliates in Canada, Portugal, the United Kingdom and the USA.

Geographical Area of Activity: Afghanistan, Bangladesh, Canada, India, Kenya, Kyrgyz Republic, Mozambique, Pakistan, Portugal, Syria, Tajikistan, Tanzania, Uganda, UK and USA.

Restrictions: No grants to individuals or for research; grants made in specific countries or regions only; no grants for construction.

Publications: Annual Report; numerous reports and evaluations.

Finance: The Foundation is financed by the Aga Khan, public donations and grants from development agencies; annual budget US $103,000,000 (2002).

Board of Directors: His Highness Prince Karim Aga Khan (Chair.); Prince Amyn Aga Khan; Maître André Ardoin; Guillaume de Spoelberch.

Principal Staff: Gen. Man. Thomas G. Kessinger; Finance Man. Christopher Beck.

Address: 1–3 ave de la Paix, POB 2369, 1211 Geneva 2.

Telephone: (22) 9097200; **Fax:** (22) 9097291; **Internet:** www.akdn.org; **e-mail:** akf@akdn.ch.

Aga Khan Trust for Culture

Founded by His Highness Prince Karim Aga Khan in June 1988, to promote a deeper understanding of the role of the built environment in society, and the development of Muslim societies.

Activities: The main activities of the Trust focus on architecture and its importance in cultural and social development; it supports enterprises which it expects to become self-sustaining in time. The Trust supports the Aga Khan Program for Islamic Architecture at Harvard University and Massachusetts Institute of Technology (MIT), USA, and the Historic Cities Support Program; operates a Music Initiative in Central Asia; offers the Aga Khan Award for Architecture; and maintains a documentation centre.

Geographical Area of Activity: International, in countries where Muslims have a significant presence, with an emphasis on Asia and Africa.

Publications: The Trust publishes international and regional seminar proceedings, and monographs; Annual Report.

Finance: Funds are provided by private donations and international development organizations.

Trustees: His Highness Prince Karim Aga Khan; Prince Amyn Aga Khan; Maître André Ardoin; Guillaume de Spoelberch.

Principal Staff: Stefano Bianca; Nicholas Bulloch; Tom G. Kessinger; Suha Özkan.

Address: Aga Khan Development Network, 1–3 ave de la Paix, POB 2049, 1211 Geneva 2.

Telephone: (22) 909-7200; **Fax:** (22) 909-7292; **Internet:** www.akdn.org; **e-mail:** aktc@akdn.ch.

Alp Action—Fondation de Bellerive

Founded in 1990 as the International Corporate Fund for the Environment under the auspices of the Bellerive Foundation (q.v.), Alp Action aims to contribute to the preservation of the natural and cultural heritage of the Alps.

Activities: Operates in the region of the Alps, in the fields of conservation and the environment, through self-conducted programmes and grants to institutions. The organization supports projects which contribute to the preservation of flora, fauna, rivers and mountain lakes, encourage traditional agriculture and crafts and rehabilitate historic sites. Projects are selected by Alp Action on the basis of their beneficial long-term impact. Disseminates information, raises public awareness and develops educational materials.

Geographical Area of Activity: The Alps region of Europe.

Restrictions: Grants only for projects in the Alps.

Council: Catherine Aleya Aga Khan; Jean Bernard Ducrest; Charles Poncet; Nicolas Sursock.

Principal Staff: Dir Susanna Trucchia.

Address: 4 rue Munier Romilly, 1206 Geneva.

Telephone: (22) 7043512; **Fax:** (22) 7043501; **Internet:** www.cyberalps.com; **e-mail:** alpaction@bellevue.org.

Avina Stiftung (Avina Foundation)

Founded by Stephen Schmidheiny in 1994 to build partnerships with the corporate sector and the leaders of civil society to promote sustainable development in Central and South America and parts of Europe.

Activities: Funds activities that promote relations between civil society and private sector leaders, principally change-oriented projects in the fields of formal and non-formal education and training, citizen participation and grassroots social involvement, eco-efficiency and effective management of natural resources, economic and community development, and corporate social responsibility. Active in 12 countries across Europe and Central and South America: Argentina, Bolivia, Brazil, Chile, Ecuador, Peru, Paraguay, Portugal, Spain, Uruguay, the USA and Venezuela, where the Foundation also maintains offices.

Geographical Area of Activity: Europe, and Central and South America.

Finance: Total grant expenditure US $43,900,000 (2001).

Administrative Council: Stephen Schmidheiny (Pres. and Founder); Brizio Biondi-Morra; German Castellanos; Peter Cleaves; Roberto Codas; Raul Gauto.

Principal Staff: Exec. Dir Peter Cleaves.

Address: POB 1474, 8640 Hurden.

Telephone: (55) 4151111; **Fax:** (55) 4151150; **Internet:** www.avina.net; **e-mail:** foundation@avina.net.

Bellerive Foundation

Founded in 1977 by Prince Sadruddin Aga Khan to foster the protection of the environment, conservation of natural resources and nature, and respect for all life.

Activities: The Foundation operates internationally in five main programme areas: Energy for Survival, operating conservation projects; Bellerive Conferences; Respect for Life, providing a holistic approach to conservation; Alp Action (q.v.); and Youth Empowerment, through the organization of youth parliaments. Develops links with organizations pursuing similar objectives.

Geographical Area of Activity: International.

Restrictions: Operates its own programmes, and does not usually fund the work of any other organizations or individuals.

Publications: *Earth Focus* (magazine for youth, quarterly); numerous books and publications.

Finance: Annual budget approx. 2,000,000 Swiss francs.

Principal Staff: Dir Gen. Nazir Sunderij; Dir, External Relations Barry Gilbert-Miguet.

Address: POB 3006, 1211 Geneva 3.

Telephone: (22) 7043500; **Fax:** (22) 7043501; **Internet:** www.bellerive.org; **e-mail:** fondation@bellerive.org.

Bertarelli Foundation

Founded in 1998 by Ernesto Bertarelli and Dona Bertarelli-Späth to increase general understanding of infertility and to improve the quality and availability of reproductive health care.

Activities: Works to achieve its mission through supporting projects, funding research, awarding grants, producing publications and organizing conferences. Also provides a number of information resources, including a reproductive health internet site for the general public, a resource service for journalists and a number of documentaries on reproductive health and infertility treatment, sponsored by the Foundation. Awards the annual Bertarelli Foundation Award in Reproductive Health. As of April 2003 the Foundation was reviewing its grant policy.

Geographical Area of Activity: International.

Restrictions: Grants only to individuals and organizations working in a non-profit environment, especially those exploring the social implications of infertility.

Publications: *Bertarelli Foundation Brochure; Bertarelli Infertility Study: International; Bertarelli Infertility Study: Australia.*

Finance: Funded by the Bertarelli family, and through fundraising. Annual revenue and expenditure US $1,000,000 (2000).

Directors: Dona Bertarelli-Späth (Chair.); Dr Lars Hamberger (Vice-Chair.); J. Koechlin (Sec.); Dr E. Y. Adashi; Ernesto Bertarelli; J. D. Carr; D. M. Germand; Dr D. M. de Kretser; Dr D. Rosenthal; Dr Z. Rosenwaks; Dr A. van Steirteghem.

Principal Staff: Exec. Dir Jerome Koechlin.

Address: 118 rue du Rhône, 1204 Geneva.

Telephone: (22) 8405175; **Fax:** (22) 8405186; **Internet:** www.bertarelli.edu; **e-mail:** secretary@bertarelli.edu.

Sophie und Karl Binding Stiftung (Sophie and Karl Binding Foundation)

Founded by Sophie and Karl Binding in 1963.

Activities: Provides financial support and technical assistance to projects operating in the fields of social welfare, the environment, education and the arts and culture. Awards the annual Prix Binding pour la Forêt; provides holiday accommodation for disabled children and their families; funds educational scholarships; and supports cultural exchanges between different ethnic groups in Switzerland.

Geographical Area of Activity: Switzerland.

Restrictions: Grants for Swiss-based organizations only.

Advisory Council: Bernhard Christ (Pres.); Carl Binding (Vice-Pres.); Andreas Adank; Heinz Rätz.

Principal Staff: Sec.-Gen. Benno Schubiger.

Address: Rennweg 50, 4020 Basel.

Telephone: (61) 3171239; **Fax:** (61) 3131200; **Internet:** www.binding-stiftung.ch/flash.html; **e-mail:** contact@binding-stiftung.ch.

Ludwig Borchardt Stiftung (Ludwig Borchardt Foundation)

Founded in 1931 by Ludwig Borchardt and Emily Borchardt-Cohen, to promote architectural research in Ancient Egypt; to maintain the Swiss Institute for Architectural and Archaeological Research of Ancient Egypt in Cairo; and to assist similar institutes as well as researchers. Originally known as the Borchardt-Cohen'sche Stiftung.

Activities: Supports the Institute's excavations and research in Egypt, which are partly undertaken in collaboration with other archeological institutes in Egypt.

Geographical Area of Activity: Egypt.

Publications: *Beiträge zur Aegyptischen Bauforschung und Altertumskunde* (Contributions on Ancient Egyptian Architecture and Archaeology); reports and articles.

Finance: Funded through privately held assets of the Foundation.

Trustees: Dr Hans Konrad Peyer (Chair.); Prof. Dr Charles Bonnet; Dr Gerhard Haeny; Dr Horst Jaritz.

Principal Staff: Dir Dr Horst Jaritz; Deputy Dir Cornelius von Pilgrim.

Address: Pestalozzistr. 2, Postfach 1126, 8201 Schaffhausen.

Telephone: (52) 6300620; **Fax:** (52) 6256240; **e-mail:** info@peyerlaw.ch.

CBM International—Christian Blind Mission International (Christoffel Blindenmission)

Founded in 1908 as a Christian charitable service, now an international network of associated organizations, and the umbrella organization for Christoffel Blindenmission and Christian Blind Mission, working for the prevention and curing of blindness, and for services for blind and other disabled people throughout the world.

Activities: The organization operates in more than 100 countries world-wide in the fields of medicine, health education, vocational education and medical research, through the provision of financial assistance for church and voluntary organizations in developing countries, and through the establishment of eye hospitals and educational and medical centres. Works alongside the WHO in the Eradication of Avoidable Blindness by the Year 2020 campaign, and concentrates on cataract operations, combating river blindness (onchocerciasis), trachoma and childhood blindness. In 2000 more than 10.8 million patients with ophthalmological complaints were examined and treated. Maintains a number of regional offices, which assist local project partners. Associated organizations exist in Australia, Austria, Belgium, Canada, Germany, Italy, New Zealand, the United Kingdom and the USA.

Geographical Area of Activity: International.

Finance: International Project Budget €39,300,000 (1999).

Board: Dr Peter Bosshard (Chair.); Reinhold Behr; Christian Garms; Jürgen Gotthardt; John Jeffries; David McComiskey; Dr Urban Pachlatko; Hans B. Petersen.

Principal Staff: Dir of Overseas Services Christian Garms.

Address: Seestr. 160, Postfach 104, 8027 Zürich.

Telephone: (1) 2022124; **Fax:** (1) 2012055; **Internet:** www.cbmi.org; **e-mail:** cbmizurich@cbmi.org.

Centre Européen de la Culture (European Cultural Centre)

Founded in 1950 by Denis de Rougemont and Salvador de Madariaga to contribute to the unification of Europe by encouraging cultural pursuits.

Activities: Conducts training programmes for young people through its Euroateliers programme. Previously the Centre housed a number of other cultural events, workshops and festivals, but in 2001 these activities were curtailed. Members of the Centre are national and international cultural institutions established by the Centre, and other individuals and organizations..

Geographical Area of Activity: Europe.

Publications: *Newsletter* (periodic, in English, French and German); *Temps Européens*; various books.

Finance: Annual budget approx. 800,000 Swiss francs.

Principal Staff: Exec. Pres. Jean-Fred Bourquin; Gen. Sec. Claus Hassig.

Address: Villa Moynier, 120B rue de Lausanne, 1202 Geneva.

Telephone: (22) 7322803; **Fax:** (22) 7384012; **Internet:** www.europeans.ch; **e-mail:** cecge@vtx.ch.

The Cogito Foundation

Established to promote dialogue between the natural and social sciences.

Activities: Aims to bridge the gap between science and technology and the humanities and social sciences, through funding for research projects and their dissemination through conferences and publications, and scholarships and fellowships for graduate researchers from Switzerland wishing to study at a foreign institution.

Geographical Area of Activity: Switzerland.

Foundation Council: Simon Aegerter (Pres.); Irene Aegerter (Vice-Pres.); Christof Aegerter; Urs R. Behnisch; Hans Weder; Rüdiger Wehner.

Address: Schwyzerstr. 62d, 8832 Wollerau.

Telephone: (1) 7877676; **Fax:** (1) 7877677; **Internet:** www.cogitofoundation.ch; **e-mail:** info@cogitofoundation.ch.

Defence for Children International

Independent NGO, founded in 1979 to provide practical help to children internationally, and to promote and protect the rights of the child.

Activities: Works in the field of children's human rights, promoting issues involving children that are inadequately documented. Initiates world-wide action in response to abuses of children's human rights, and generally seeks to improve children's rights internationally, taking up specific cases regarding violations of human rights. Publishes information about children's rights, and monitors the implementation of laws that should protect children. There are 60 Sections and Associate Members world-wide.

Geographical Area of Activity: International.

Address: 1 rue de Varembé, CP 88, 1211 Geneva 20.

Telephone: (22) 7340558; **Fax:** (22) 7401145; **Internet:** www.defence-for-children.org; **e-mail:** dci-hq@pingnet.ch.

Earthwatch

Founded in 1973 by the United Nations Environment Programme (UNEP). In 1994 the organization became the responsibility of all relevant United Nations agencies.

Activities: Earthwatch co-ordinates the work of the United Nations agencies working in the area of the human environment, in order to provide information on sustainable development, the state of the environment and environmental change to governments, industry and other organizations.

Geographical Area of Activity: International.

Publications: *Earth Views* (3 a year).

Principal Staff: Co-ordinator Arthur Dahl.

Address: UN System-wide Earthwatch Co-ordination, UNEP, International Environment House, 11–13 chemin des Anémones, Châtelaine, 1219 Geneva.

Telephone: (22) 9178207; **Fax:** (22) 7973471; **Internet:** www.earthwatch.unep.net; **e-mail:** earthwatch@grid.unep.ch.

European Foundation for the Advancement of Medicine

Established to promote the amelioration of health care in Europe.

Activities: Operates in Europe in the field of medicine and health, through promoting further education in areas such as molecular medicine, health economics, biology and chemistry; exchange of information within medicine and law; the implementation of disease control campaigns; and collaboration nationally and internationally in the fields of public health and applied research. The Foundation carries out research, organizes conferences and workshops, makes grants for postgraduate study, awards prizes, and issues publications.

Geographical Area of Activity: Europe.

Principal Staff: Pres. Curt Engelhorn; Vice-Pres. François Schiltz.

Address: Steinengraben 28, 4051 Basle.

Telephone: (61) 2069100; **Fax:** (61) 2069109.

The Evian Group

Founded in 1995 by the late Katsuo Seiki, founding executive director of the Tokyo-based Global Industrial and Social Progress Research Institute (GISPRI) and Jean-Pierre Lehmann, Professor of International Political Economy at IMD (International Institute for Management Development).

Activities: Holds annual meetings aimed at increasing contact between Asia and Europe, to consolidate business relations between them and thereby increase their contribution to the World Trade Organization (WTO). Also operates regional meetings, runs the Brains Trust 'think tank' and aims to support the next generation of leaders through the Young Evian programme.

Geographical Area of Activity: Asia and Europe.

Publications: *Policy Briefs*; web-based newsletter.

Principal Staff: Exec. Dir Jean-Pierre Lehmann; Deputy Dir Marc Laperrouza.

Address: c/o International Institute for Management Development, POB 915, 1001 Lausanne.

Internet: www.eviangroup.org; **e-mail:** info@eviangroup.org.

Focus on Hope—Nana Mouskouri Foundation

Established by Nana Mouskouri.

Activities: Set up to support cultural and arts projects, particularly in the areas of cinema and music, to provide advice and financial help to young artists, and to award cultural prizes incuding the Nana Mouskouri Foundation Prix 'Focus Hope'. Also sponsors exhibitions and cultural events, including a travelling exhibition on the Parthenon Marbles.

Geographical Area of Activity: International.

Address: c/o BfB Gestion, 26 rue de la Corraterie, 1204 Geneva.

Fondation pour le Développement de la Psychothérapie Médicale (Foundation for the Development of Medical Psychotherapy)

Founded in 1982 with the aim of promoting the development of medical psychotherapy.

Activities: Finances and organizes activities aiming to help people who are mentally ill; particularly interested in supporting projects involving group therapy; awards prizes; holds conferences and seminars.

Principal Staff: Pres. Dr E. de Perrot; Sec. Dr D. Peter.

Address: CITB, Hôpital Nestlé, Chuv, 1011 Lausanne.

Telephone: (21) 314 1930.

Fondation Hindemith (Hindemith Foundation)

Founded in 1968 in execution of the will of Johanna-Gertrud Hindemith, widow of the composer Paul Hindemith, to maintain his musical and literary heritage; to encourage interest and research in the field of music, in particular contemporary music, and to disseminate the results of this research.

Activities: Operates internationally in the field of music, through self-conducted programmes, research, publications, courses, lectures and concerts. Maintains a course centre, the Hindemith Music Center Blonay, near Vevey, Switzerland; and a centre of archives, documentation and publication, the Hindemith-Institut Frankfurt, Germany.

Geographical Area of Activity: International.

Restrictions: No grants to outside organizations currently available.

Publications: *Hindemith General Original Edition; Les Annales Hindemith; Hindemith-Forum.*

Trustees: Dr A. Eckhardt (Pres.); M. F. Margot (Exec. Vice-Pres.); Dr A. Briner; Prof. H. D. Resch; M. A. Schober.

Principal Staff: Dir, Hindemith Music Center Blonay M. S. Dähler; Dir, Hindemith-Institut Frankfurt Prof. Dr G. Schubert.

Address: 41 champs Belluit, 1807 Blonay.

Telephone: (21) 9430528; **Fax:** (21) 9430529; **Internet:** www.hindemith.org.

Fondation Internationale Pénale et Pénitentiaire—FIPP (International Penal and Penitentiary Foundation)

Founded in 1951 as successor to the Commission Internationale Pénale et Pénitentiaire.

Activities: Promotes studies in the field of crime prevention and treatment of offenders, especially by scientific research, publications and teaching. The IPPF has members (a maximum of three) from the following countries: Argentina, Austria, Belgium, Chile, Denmark, Egypt, Finland, France, Germany, Hungary, Ireland, Italy, Japan, Luxembourg, the Netherlands, New Zealand, Norway, Poland, Portugal, Spain, Sweden, Switzerland, the United Kingdom and the USA; and corresponding members from Australia, Brazil, Canada, Cape Verde, Greece, India and the Russian Federation.

Geographical Area of Activity: International.

Publications: Report of operations; reports of sessions and meetings (in French and English).

Trustees: The Foundation is governed by an Executive Committee and a Council; Jorge de Figueiredo Dias (Pres.); Jean Pradel, Minoru Shikita (Vice-Pres).

Principal Staff: Sec.-Gen. Dr Konrad Hobe; Treas. Pierre-Henri Bolle.

Address: Berne, Switzerland; c/o Dr Konrad Hobe, Ministerialrat, Bundesministerium der Justiz, Aussenstelle Berlin, 10104 Berlin, Germany.

Telephone: (30) 2025-9226 (Germany); **Fax:** (30) 2025-9525 (Germany).

Fondation Latsis Internationale (Latsis Foundation)

Activities: Operates in the field of science and technology. The Fondation Européenne de la Science (q.v.) awards the annual European Latsis Prize, funded by the Foundation, which is made in recognition of an individual under the age of 40 or organization's contribution to research in a particular scientific field.

Geographical Area of Activity: Europe.

Address: 3–5 chemin des Tuileries, 1293 Bellevue, Geneva.

Fondation Charles Léopold Mayer pour le Progrès de l'Homme (Foundation for the Progress of Humanity)

Founded in 1982 by Charles Léopold Mayer (1880–1971) to fund projects which would contribute to the progress of humanity.

Activities: The Foundation focuses on seven main areas: the promotion of peace; an end to exclusion; the future of the earth and its ecological systems; science, technology and society; peasant farming and modernization; promotion and exchange between cultures; and state and society. Set up a grants programme for young people with French newspaper *Le Monde*. Approximately two-thirds of the annual budget is allocated to grants and the remaining third spent on Foundation-initiated programmes.

Geographical Area of Activity: International.

Restrictions: Currently does not accept unsolicted individual applications for scholarships, fellowships or travel grants.

Publications: Numerous books and brochures.

Finance: Annual budget 10,000,000 Swiss francs.

Trustees: F. Astier (Pres.); R. George (Vice-Pres.); P. Calame (Pes. Management Board); Jean-Paul Astier; B. Hervieu; S. Humberset; J. Poulet-Mathis; D. Talmant; J. Tarradellas.

Principal Staff: Dir Gen. Pierre Calame.

Address: 9 chemin de Longeraie, 1006 Lausanne.

Telephone: (21) 3425010; **Fax:** (21) 3425011; **Internet:** www.fph.ch; **e-mail:** lausanne@fph.ch.

Fondation Jean Monnet pour l'Europe (Jean Monnet Foundation for Europe)

Founded in 1978 to contribute to the construction of a united Europe in accordance with the aspirations of Jean Monnet.

Activities: Maintains archives, conducts research and holds international conferences on topics related to European political and economic unity; publishes the results of research. Also awards the Jean Monnet Medal and operates the European School competition; in 2003 held in Liechtenstein and Switzerland.

Geographical Area of Activity: Europe.

Restrictions: No grants to individuals.

Publications: *Cahiers rouges* (series); books on European topics.

Finance: Funded through public sources.

Principal Staff: Pres. Prof. Henri Rieben.

Address: Ferme de Dorigny, 1015 Lausanne.

Telephone: (21) 6922090; **Fax:** (21) 6922095; **Internet:** www.jean-monnet.ch; **e-mail:** francoise.nicod@fjme.unil.ch.

Fondation Nestlé pour l'étude des problèmes de l'alimentation dans le monde (Nestlé Foundation for the Study of the Problems of Nutrition in the World)

Founded in 1967 by Nestlé Alimentana SA, Vevey, to further the improvement of nutrition, particularly in those areas of the world suffering from malnutrition, by encouraging basic and applied research directly connected with human nutrition.

Activities: Operates internationally by developing and sponsoring nutrition-related research projects, awarding research grants to individuals and institutions, awarding scholarships for postgraduate studies in nutrition to candidates from selected African nutrition units, organizing scientific conferences, and publishing and disseminating scientific literature.

Geographical Area of Activity: Low- and lower–middle-income countries.

Publications: Annual Report; scientific publications.

Finance: Net assets 54,000,000 Swiss francs (2000); annual revenue and expenditure 3,500,000 Swiss francs (2000).

Trustees: Prof. E. Jéquier (Pres.); Prof. J. P. Flatt; Prof. M. Gebre-Medhin; Prof. J. Hautvast; Dr R. G. Whitehead.

Principal Staff: Dir Dr P. Suter.

Address: 4 place de la Gare, POB 581, 1001 Lausanne.

Telephone: (21) 3203351; **Fax:** (21) 3203392; **Internet:** www.nestlefoundation.org; **e-mail:** nestle.foundation@vtxnet.ch.

Fondation Simón I. Patiño (Simón I. Patiño Foundation)

Set up in 1959 in memory of the Bolivian industrialist, Simón I. Patiño, by his heirs. Its principal objective is to create and develop for South America and in particular Bolivia, research and application programmes in the spheres of education, culture, research, health, nutrition, hygiene, agriculture and ecology.

Activities: Operates internationally in the fields of education, culture, research, health, nutrition, hygiene, agriculture and ecology, through self-conducted programmes and publications, conducted at a number of operational centres. The Albina R. de Patiño Paediatric Centre, in Cochabamba, provides medical care, and carries out training and research; it also runs a nutritional centre for malnourished children. The Simón I. Patiño Pedagogical and Cultural Centre, also in Cochabamba, offers literacy programmes through a network of village-based libraries, a central library and cultural events. In Pairumani, the Foundation conducts agricultural research at its Phytoecogenetic Research Centre, and at its Seed Centre, and applied programmes at the Pairumani Model Farm. In Santa Cruz and Concepción, the Foundation develops applied agro-biological programmes aimed at sustainable agricultural and environmental development, at the Centre for Applied Ecology. A cultural centre is managed in La Paz, which also hosts the Documentation Centre for Latin-American Arts and Literature. Internationally, in particular in Switzerland, the Foundation provides university scholarships for high-potential Bolivian students, who will return to help in Bolivian development. It is also active in the field of arts and culture, through organizing visual arts exhibitions and musical events and offering scholarships for young artists. The Foundation's publishing house publishes books on philosophy and Latin American culture, poetry and literature.

Geographical Area of Activity: Central and South America (with an emphasis on Bolivia), Europe.

Restrictions: Principally establishes and maintains its own programmes.

Publications: *Bolivia Ecológica* (monthly); *Revista Boliviana de Ecología y Conservación Ambiental* (quarterly); Annual Report; other publications.

Governing Board: Ernst Schneider (Pres.); Jaime Ortiz-Patiño (Vice-Pres.); Raoul Lenz (Sec.); N. du Chastel; John Dubouchet; Jean-Pierre Imhoos; Helmut Maucher; Cristina Patiño.

Principal Staff: Exec. Dir G. de Sartiges.

Address: 8 rue Giovanni-Gambini, CP 182, 1211 Geneva 25.

Telephone: (22) 3470211; **Fax:** (22) 7891829; **e-mail:** fondpatino@econophone.ch.

Fondation Denis de Rougemont pour l'Europe

Founded in 1987; named after Denis de Rougemont, the founder of the Centre Européen de la Culture (European Cultural Centre, q.v.).

Activities: Promotes the unification of Europe and an awareness of cultural solidarity among Europeans, mainly through publications. Awards the Denis de Rougemont Prize annually to a person or organization contributing to the advancement of European unity.

Geographical Area of Activity: Europe.

Publications: *Denis de Rougemont et l'Europe des Régions*; *Denis de Rougemont: Introduction à sa vie et son œuvre*.

Finance: Annual budget approx. 200,000 Swiss francs.

Principal Staff: Pres. Claude Haegi; Vice-Pres Eric Gabus, Jean-Claude Veillon.

Address: 12 rue de l'Arquebuse, 1204 Geneva.

Telephone: (22) 8071715; **Fax:** (22) 8071718; **Internet:** www.fondationderougemont.org; **e-mail:** contact@fondationderougemont.org.

Fondation Charles Veillon

Established in 1972 to promote dialogues in which opinion, experience and philosophy can be linked together.

Activities: Operates in the fields of international relations and culture, through promoting dialogue covering European culture, philosophy, federalism and interdisciplinary studies; and offering the Prix Européen de l'Essai Charles Veillon for an essay dealing with contemporary society.

Geographical Area of Activity: Europe.

Address: Lausanne.

Internet: www.culturactif.ch/fondations/fondationcharlesveillon1.htm.

Fondation Franz Weber (Franz Weber Foundation)

Founded in 1975 by Franz Weber.

Activities: Operates in the field of conservation and the environment. Promotes the protection of nature and wildlife and defence of animal rights. Runs a series of national and international campaigns fighting the destruction of natural habitats and campaigning for the rights of indigenous species. Campaigns to obtain legal status for animals.

Geographical Area of Activity: International.

Publications: *Journal Franz Weber.*

Finance: Funded by contributions, donation and legacies. Annual expenditure approx. 2,000,000 Swiss francs.

Address: Case Postale, 1820 Montreux 1.

Telephone: (21) 964-4284; **Fax:** (21) 964-5736; **Internet:** www.ffw.ch; **e-mail:** ffw@ffw.ch.

Fondation Hans Wilsdorf—Montres Rolex (Hans Wilsdorf Foundation)

Established in 1945 and the sole owner of the share capital of Montres Rolex SA.

Activities: The Foundation funds projects and organizations in the fields of social welfare, arts and culture, and scientific and medical research.

Geographical Area of Activity: Mainly Switzerland.

Finance: Total assets approx. €9,000,000,000.

Principal Staff: Pres. Pierre Mottu; Sec.-Gen. Serge Bednarczyk.

Address: CP 3245, 1211 Geneva 3.

Telephone: (22) 7373000; **Fax:** (22) 7002956; **Internet:** www.rolex.com; **e-mail:** fhw@swissonline.ch.

Foundation AMURT (Switzerland)

Founded in 1985, part of an international network of AMURT organizations, originally founded in India, which work in the fields of relief and development, aiming to help the populations of developing countries regardless of race, religion or nationality.

Activities: AMURT provides direct help to developing countries around the world, running long-term development co-operation projects in over 80 countries responding to educational, medical and social needs in order to improve the quality of life for many people, as well as special programmes focusing on the needs of women and children. The Foundation also operates disaster relief projects, providing immediate aid for the victims of war, famine and natural disasters. Projects are currently in progress in Africa, Asia, South-Eastern Europe, Central and South America and the Caribbean, and the Middle East and North Africa.

Geographical Area of Activity: Africa, Asia, South-Eastern Europe, Central and South America and the Caribbean, and the Middle East and North Africa.

Restrictions: Not a grant-making organization.

Finance: Annual revenue and expenditure 2,252,305 Swiss francs (1999).

Principal Staff: Programme Dir. Bhola Sah.

Address: Seestr. 23, 8610 Uster.

Telephone: (43) 3990681; **Fax:** (43) 3990685; **Internet:** www.amurt.org; **e-mail:** info@amurt.org.

Foundation for Development and Partnership in Africa

Founded in 1963 by Hans and Hedwig Meyer-Schneeberger to support agricultural self-help projects in Africa.

Activities: Operates in Zimbabwe, Tanzania and South Africa, providing grants to agricultural co-operatives and other self-help projects, especially women's groups. Provides funding for local development NGOs.

Geographical Area of Activity: South Africa, Tanzania and Zimbabwe.

Restrictions: No grants to individuals.

Publications: *FEPA—Mitteilungsblatt* (bi-annual publication).

Finance: Annual revenue and expenditure approx. 120,000 Swiss francs.

Trustees: A. Enderli; M. Gerber; U. Haller; A. Keller; A. Rieder; L. Staehelin; S. Zurbuchen.

Principal Staff: Barbara Müller.

Address: Postfach 151, 4005 Basle.

Telephone: (61) 681-8084; **Fax:** (61) 691-7516; **e-mail:** bemueller@bluewin.ch.

Foundation for Environmental Conservation

Founded in 1975 by the International Union for Conservation of Nature and Natural Resources—IUCN (now the World Conservation Union, q.v.), the World Wildlife Fund—WWF (now the WWF—World Wide Fund for Nature, q.v.) and the late Prof. Dr Nicholas Polunin, to undertake, in co-operation with appropriate individuals, organizations and other groups, all possible activities to maintain the biosphere and further environmental conservation.

Activities: The Foundation promotes studies of environmental change and ecosystems; issues publications; organizes conferences (notably the International Conferences on Environmental Future), lectures (including the Baer-Huxley Memorial Lectures) and specialist workshops; awards prizes for achievement in environmental conservation; and supports such initiatives as the World Campaign for the Biosphere, Biospheric Day and Biospheric Club.

Geographical Area of Activity: International.

Publications: Reports of operations; proceedings of the International Conferences on Environmental Future; *Environmental Conservation* (quarterly journal); *Environmental Challenge; World Who is Who and Does What in Environment and Conservation.*

Governing Board: The Board includes representatives from the World Conservation Union and the WWF, and others; Pres. and CEO Dr Nicholas Vladimir Polunin.

Principal Staff: Environmental Conservation Officer Lynn Curne.

Address: 7 chemin Taverney, 1218 Grand-Saconnex, Geneva.

Telephone: (22) 7982383; **Fax:** (22) 7982344.

Anne Frank-Fonds (Anne Frank Fund)

Founded in 1963 by Otto H. Frank, father of Anne Frank, to promote charitable, social and cultural activities and tolerance in the spirit of Anne Frank and to protect the literary heritage and rights of the author.

Activities: Operates in the fields of the arts and humanities and social welfare, through awarding the Anne Frank Literary Award (worth 20,000 Swiss francs); providing medicines to ageing winners of Israel's Yad Vashem award for 'righteous gentiles' through the Anne Frank Medical Fund for the Righteous, founded in 1987; sponsoring the Anne Frank-Shoah Library which specializes in the Nazi Holocaust period; providing finance for exchange visits and meetings of young Israelis, Germans and Arabs; providing support to Israeli and Palestinian peace organizations; supporting educational projects; and other related organizations and projects. Also makes grants to the Anne Frank Museum in Amsterdam and financed a professorship in ethics at the University of Basel.

Geographical Area of Activity: International.

Finance: Total grants 570,000 Swiss francs (2001).

Principal Staff: Pres. Dr V. C. Frank-Steiner; Sec. C. Demenga.

Address: Steinengraben 18, 4051 Basel.

Telephone: (61) 2741174; **Fax:** (61) 2741175; **Internet:** www.annefrank.ch; **e-mail:** info@annefrank.ch.

Fritz Gerber Stiftung für begabte junge Menschen (Fritz Gerber Foundation for Gifted Young People)

Established by Fritz Gerber in March 1999 to assist talented young people.

Activities: Offers grants to young gifted people between the ages of 10 and 25, in need of financial assistance in order to develop a specific talent. Grants are made in areas outside formal education, including sport, and the arts and culture.

Geographical Area of Activity: Switzerland.

Finance: A donation of €12,400,000 from Fritz Gerber to establish the Foundation; annual grants approx. 3,500,000 Swiss francs (2002).

Principal Staff: Pres. Fritz Gerber.

Address: Kirchgasse 38, 8024 Zürich.

Telephone: (1) 2605383; **Fax:** (1) 2546035; **Internet:** www.fritz-gerber-stiftung.ch; **e-mail:** lanffer@bluewin.ch.

Global Harmony Foundation

Established in 1989 by B. Affolter, R. Boschi, N. Dajani and C. Pfluger to promote sustainable development for under-privileged people, charitable work and conservation of the environment.

Activities: Operates in the fields of aid to less-developed countries, conservation and the environment and education, through self-conducted programmes, conferences, training courses and publications. The Foundation's programmes aim to foster greater self-reliance and self-esteem using traditional practices and with regard for local cultural frameworks. Areas of interest include pre-schooling, nutritional and health-care; improvement of nutrition, health and hygiene; education of women; and facilitation of the development of schools, institutions and communities.

Geographical Area of Activity: Programmes operate in Brazil, Costa Rica, Dominican Republic, India and Mexico.

Publications: Training booklets and documents.

Finance: Annual budget approx. 1,500,000 Swiss francs.

Trustees: Sir Peter Ustinov (Hon. Pres.); N. Dajani (Chair. and Chief Technical Adviser); B. Affolter; P. O. Essig; C. Mustad; C. Pfluger; G. Rossi.

Principal Staff: Sec.-Gen; B. Affolter.

Address: World Trade Centre, 2 ave Gratta-Paille, POB 433, 1000 Lausanne 30.

Telephone: (21) 6411088; **Fax:** (21) 6411089; **Internet:** www.global-harmony.org; **e-mail:** admin@global-harmony .org.

Helvetas, Association Suisse pour la Coopération Internationale (Helvetas, Swiss Association for International Co-operation)

Founded in 1955 to support international development programmes.

Activities: Operates internationally in the form of aid to less-developed countries, through self-conducted programmes, financial support for NGOs and grants to institutions. Aid is provided at present to Asia (Bhutan, Kyrgyzstan, Laos, Malaysia, Nepal, the Philippines, Sri Lanka and Vietnam), Africa (Benin, Cameroon, Lesotho, Mali, Mozambique, Tanzania and Togo) and Central and South America and the Caribbean (Colombia, Dominican Republic, Guatemala, Haiti and Paraguay). Assistance is given for agriculture, civil and mechanical engineering, technical training, community development, small-scale industries, vocational training, forestry, rural drinking-water supplies and construction of secondary roads and bridges. The Association works to reduce the economic dependency of less-developed countries and promotes fair trade practices. Projects, most of which are co-financed by the Swiss Federal Government, are carried out by Swiss technical staff in close collaboration with the governments of the countries involved, or by locally active non-governmental groups. The Association also conducts an information campaign in Switzerland about the problems of developing countries, through conferences, publications and lectures.

Geographical Area of Activity: Africa, Asia, and Central and South America and the Caribbean.

Publications: Annual Report and financial statement; *Partnerschaft* (quarterly bulletin, in German and French).

Trustees: The Association is governed by a Central Committee composed of 16 members; Peter H. Arbenz (Pres.); Rosemary Lausselet (Vice-Pres.).

Principal Staff: Sec.-Gen. E. Werner Külling.

Address: St Moritzstr. 15, 8042 Zürich.

Telephone: (1) 3686500; **Fax:** (1) 3686580; **Internet:** www.helvetas.ch; **e-mail:** info@helvetas.ch.

Hilfswerk der Evangelischen Kirchen Schweiz—HEKS (Swiss Interchurch Aid)

Founded in 1946 to contribute to the reconciliation and reconstruction of Europe in co-operation with the Protestant churches of the respective partner countries.

Activities: Organizes projects in developing countries in the fields of education, agricultural development and human rights; supports emergency aid; assists refugees both in developing countries and in Switzerland; awards scholarships; and operates social programmes in Switzerland. Supports projects in Africa, Asia, Central and South America and Europe. Promotes co-operation in Western and Eastern Europe; makes financial contributions to church centres; and provides disaster relief in conjunction with other organizations.

Geographical Area of Activity: Europe, Asia, Africa, and Central and South America.

Restrictions: Grants are made primarily to local organizations.

Publications: Annual Report (in French and German); *HEKS-Magazin HANDELN* (quarterly); *Terre Nouvelle* (5 a year).

Finance: Annual budget approx 74,000,000 Swiss francs.

Principal Staff: Gen. Sec. Franz Schüle.

Address: Stampfenbachstr. 123, POB 332, 8035 Zürich.

Telephone: (1) 3616600; **Fax:** (1) 3617827; **Internet:** www.heks.ch; **e-mail:** info@hekseper.ch.

Helmut Horten Stiftung (Helmut Horten Foundation)

Founded by Helmut Horten to support health-care research and related initiatives.

Activities: The Foundation provides support to the health-care system both in Switzerland and internationally, through financial contributions to medical research facilities, hospitals, and other health care institutions, as well as to individuals who are in need of medical care. Preference is given to funding large-scale research projects, particularly where the foundation is the sole funder. Significant initiatives funded by the Foundation include the Horten Center for Applied Research and Science and the Institute for Research in Biomedicine in Bellinzona, Switzerland. Scholarships are also occasionally awarded.

Geographical Area of Activity: Mainly Switzerland.

Board of Trustees: Dr Georges A. Streichenberg (Pres.); August von Finck; Heidi Horten; Dr Hellmuth Reichel; Alberto Togni.

Principal Staff: Gen. Man. Giacomo Muzzarelli.

Address: World Trade Center, 6982 Agno/Lugano.

Telephone: (91) 6102280; **Fax:** (91) 6001212; **Internet:** www.helmut-horten-stiftung.ch/; **e-mail:** info@ helmut-horten-stiftung.org.

Institut Suisse de Recherche Expérimentale sur le Cancer (Swiss Institute for Experimental Cancer Research)

Founded in 1964 by G. Candardjis, J.-L. de Coulon, H. Isliker, P. Mercier, A. de Muralt, A. Sauter, P. Schumacher, R. Stadler and F. Zumstein to conduct experimental research on cancer.

Activities: Operates both nationally and internationally in the fields of education, science and medicine, through research, scholarships, conferences and courses.

Geographical Area of Activity: International.

Publications: Bi-annual Report.

Trustees: G. Muller (Pres.); J. M. Tissot (Man. Dir) M. Aguet (Dir); Prof. A. Aguzzi (Chair., Scientific Bd); Dr J. Deka; Dr L. Kühn; G. Muller; Dr Y. J. Paternot; E. Thomke.

Principal Staff: Dir M. Aguet.

Address: 155 chemin des Boveresses, 1066 Epalinges/Lausanne.

Telephone: (21) 6925858; **Fax:** (21) 6526933; **Internet:** www.isrec.ch; **e-mail:** relations.publiques@isrec.unil.ch.

Institut Universitaire de Hautes Études Internationales (Graduate Institute of International Studies)

Founded in 1927 by Prof. W. Rappard and Prof. P. Mantoux to carry out teaching and research devoted to the scientific study of contemporary international relations; and to contribute to the advancement of international fellowship through the impartial observation and objective analysis of ideas and events.

Activities: Operates internationally, as a teaching and research institution, in the fields of history of international relations, international economics, international law, and political science. The Institute's curriculum enables students of any nationality to qualify for the Diploma and Doctor's degrees in international relations, both conferred by the University of Geneva, and a Certificate in international relations, conferred by the Institute. Scholarships are available only to students of the Institute. Maintains a library which owns the printed documents of the League of Nations and serves as a depository of the publications of the United Nations.

Geographical Area of Activity: International.

Trustees: The Head of the Department of Education of the Canton of Geneva; the Head of the Federal Department of Foreign Affairs; the Rector of the University of Geneva; J. P. Roth; K. Schwab; R. Simmen; J. Somavia; C. Sommaruga.

Address: 132 rue de Lausanne, CP 36, 1211 Geneva 21.

Telephone: (22) 9085700; **Fax:** (22) 9085710; **Internet:** http://heiwww.unige.ch.

International Baccalaureate Organization—IBO

Founded in 1968 to promote international secondary education and administer an international examination giving access to higher education in all countries, and to undertake educational research in relation to this objective, as well as for other educational purposes.

Activities: Offers the Primary Years Programme for children between the ages of three and 11, the Middle Years Programme for those aged between 11 and 16 years, and the Diploma Programme for students aged between 16 and 19 years.

Geographical Area of Activity: International.

Restrictions: Funds are used exclusively for curriculum development and examination administration. No grants are awarded.

Publications: Annual Review; *IB World; Statistical Bulletin;* curriculum support materials.

Finance: Annual budget approx. US $15,000,000.

Trustees: The Organization is governed by a Council which determines general policy.

Principal Staff: Dir Gen. George Walker; Deputy Dir Gen. Ian Hill.

Address: 15 route des Morillons, 1218 Grand-Saconnex, Geneva.

Telephone: (22) 7917740; **Fax:** (22) 7910277; **Internet:** www.ibo.org; **e-mail:** ibhq@ibo.org.

International Council on Alcohol and Addictions—ICAA

Founded in 1907 to reduce and prevent the harmful effects of the use of alcohol and other drugs.

Activities: Conducts training programmes for health professionals on drug and alcohol problems, with particular reference to basic health care, socio-cultural and other relevant factors, and studies methods of prevention, treatment and rehabilitation. The International Congress on Alcohol, Drugs and other Dependencies is held every three or four years, and other international conferences, symposia and study groups are also organized. The Council works with the WHO and other international, regional and national bodies: there are member organizations and individual members in 90 countries. Maintains a library of approximately 6,000 volumes on drug dependence, approximately 12,000 pamphlets, reprints, etc., and 120 periodicals. Regional offices are maintained in Argentina, Azerbaijan and Egypt.

Geographical Area of Activity: International.

Publications: *ICAA News* (quarterly); *Book of Abstracts* (annual) *Report of Plenary Sessions* (annual).

Principal Staff: Pres. I. Al-Awaji; Exec. Dir Dr Jörg Spieldenner.

Address: CP 189, 1001 Lausanne.

Telephone: (21) 3209865; **Fax:** (21) 3209817; **Internet:** www.icaa.ch; **e-mail:** secretariat@icaa.ch.

International Council on Human Rights Policy—ICHRP

Established in 1998 in order to carry out research into the practical applicability of human rights policy, to conduct practical policy research into dilemmas and problems that face organizations working in the field of human rights.

Activities: Co-ordinates research, publishes research reports and recommendations. Sets up seminars, conferences and workshops. Carries out policy research designed to protect and promote human rights internationally.

Geographical Area of Activity: International.

Restrictions: No grants to individuals. All revenue goes to Council research.

Publications: *Ends and Means: Human Rights Approaches to Armed Groups; Local Perspectives: Foreign Aid to the Justice Sector; The Persistence and Mutation of Racism; Performance and Legitimacy: National Human Rights Institutions; Hard Cases; Bringing Human Rights Violators to Justice Abroad—A Guide to Universal Jurisdiction; Taking Duties Seriously: Individual Duties in International Human Rights Law—A Commentary; Racial and Economic Exclusion—Policy Implications.*

Finance: Annual expenditure 1,620,000 Swiss francs (2000).

Exec. Board: T. Hammarberg (Chair.); H. Jilani (Vice-Chair.); L. T. van Boven (Treas.); C. Bunch; A. Imam; W. Kälin.

Principal Staff: Exec. Dir Robert Archer; Finance Dir Anouchiravan Rousta.

Address: 48 chemin du Grand-Montfleury, CP 147, 1290 Versoix.

Telephone: (22) 7753300; **Fax:** (22) 7753303; **Internet:** www.ichrp.org; **e-mail:** ichrp@international-council.org.

International Institute for the Rights of the Child

Founded in 1995 by Dr Bernard Comby and Jean Zermatten for the promotion of children's law at an international level.

Activities: Operates in the field of law and human rights, specifically for children. Holds international seminars, provides training both nationally and internationally, publishes a number of books on the subject of children's rights in the law and has set up an interactive website.

Geographical Area of Activity: International.

Restrictions: Grants only available to those who attend annual seminar in October.

Publications: Newsletter; five books on children's law.

Finance: Funded by the Swiss Confederation and by individual companies.

Trustees: Dr. Bernard Comby (Pres.); Jean Zermatten (Dir).

Principal Staff: Asst to the Dir Paola Riva; Co-ordinator Alexandra Prince.

Address: c/o Institut Universitaire Kurt Bösch, CP 4176, 1950 Sion 4.

Telephone: (27) 2057300; **Fax:** (27) 2057302; **Internet:** www.childsrights.org; **e-mail:** ide@iukb.ch.

International Red Cross and Red Crescent Movement

The International Red Cross and Red Crescent Movement is composed of the National Red Cross and Red Crescent Societies, the International Committee of the Red Cross (ICRC), founded in 1863 to help wounded soldiers on the battlefield, and the International Federation of Red Cross and Red Crescent Societies (the Federation), founded in 1919 (as the League of Red Cross and Red Crescent Societies) to promote humanitarian activities in peacetime.

Activities: The ICRC is an impartial, neutral and independent organization whose exclusively humanitarian mission is to protect the lives and dignity of victims of war and internal violence, and to provide them with assistance. It directs and co-ordinates the international relief activities conducted by the Movement in situations of conflict. It also endeavours to prevent suffering by promoting and strengthening humanitarian law and universal humanitarian principles.

The Federation comprises 176 National Red Cross and Red Crescent Societies; it acts as a permanent body for liaison, co-ordination and study, advising members on the development of their services to the community. It also organizes international emergency relief operations for the victims of natural disasters, and co-ordinates relief preparedness programmes.

Geographical Area of Activity: International.

Publications: ICRC: *International Review of the Red Cross* (quarterly); *Red Cross Red Crescent* (quarterly Movement magazine produced jointly with the Federation); *Forum* (annual); Annual Report. Federation: *Annual Review; Handbook of the International Red Cross and Red Crescent Movement* (with the ICRC); *Red Cross, Red Crescent* (quarterly, in English, French and Spanish); *Weekly News; World Disasters Report* (annually); newsletters, guides and manuals.

Finance: ICRC budget approx. 915,600,000 Swiss francs (2002).

The Assembly is the supreme governing body of the ICRC, overseeing all its activities. It formulates policy, defines general objectives and institutional strategy, and approves the budget and accounts. Composed of members of the ICRC, it is collegial in character, and its President and Vice-Presidents are the President and Vice-Presidents of the ICRC.

ICRC Council: Jakob Kellenberger (Pres.); Ernst Brugger; Jacques Forster; Liselotte Kraus-Gurny; Jakob Nüesch.

Federation General Assembly: Astrid N. Heiberg (Pres.).

Federation Secretariat: Sec.-Gen. Didier Cherpitel.

Address: ICRC: 19 ave de la Paix, 1202 Geneva.

Telephone: ICRC: (22) 7346001; Federation: (22) 7304222; **Fax:** ICRC: (22) 7332057; Federation: (22) 7330395; **Internet:** www.icrc.org; **e-mail:** press.gva@icrc.org.

International Service for Human Rights—ISHR

Established in 1984 to provide information and training to defenders of human rights world-wide.

Activities: Operates world-wide in the field of law and human rights, through offering studies and reports, training in international procedures relating to the protection of human rights, advisory services, information and support, and upholding human rights. Offers fellowships of two to six months for experienced defenders of human rights to work at the secretariat, and internships for self-funded students or graduates. Runs an annual training course in Geneva for human rights defenders from all regions.

Geographical Area of Activity: International.

Restrictions: Not a grant-making organization; does not campaign on individual cases.

Publications: *Human Rights Monitor* (quarterly); *HR–Dossiers–DH; Manuals; HR-Documentation-DH* (series).

Executive Council: C. Flinterman (Pres.); A. Clapham; M.-J. Cocher; M. Forst; G. Gallón; D. Hayward; B. Lindnaes; R. Nair; L. Picard; B. Ras-Work; V. Scheffers.

Principal Staff: Dir Morris Tidball-Binz; Dir Information Marianne Berndtsson; Dir Training Franziska Surber.

Address: 1 rue de Varembé, CP 16, 1211 Geneva 20.

Telephone: (22) 7335123; **Fax:** (22) 7330826; **Internet:** www.ishr.ch.

International Union Against Cancer—UICC

Founded in 1933 as a world federation of non-governmental agencies and organizations which combat cancer.

Activities: Together with its members and collaborating organizations, the Union conducts activities throughout the world promoting collaboration between cancer organizations, among cancer investigators, physicians and allied health professionals and experts. Work focuses on four priority areas: building and enhancing cancer control capacity; tobacco control; population-based cancer prevention and control; and transfer of cancer knowledge and dissemination. Research and information programmes covering: tumour biology; epidemiology and prevention; treatment and rehabilitation; detection and diagnosis; professional education; campaigns and public education; patient support; international collaborative activities; tobacco and cancer. It organizes international conferences, study groups and courses, and administers the following fellowships: UICC International Cancer Technology Transfer Fellowships; Yamagiwa-Yoshida Memorial International Cancer Study Grants; American Cancer Society UICC International Fellowships for Beginning Investigators; AstraZeneca and Novartis UICC Translational Cancer Research Fellowship; UICC Trish Greene International Oncology Nursing Fellowships; UICC Asia-Pacific Cancer Society Training Grants; and UICC Latin America COPES Education and Training Fellowships. The Union manages GLOBALink, a computer communications system.

Geographical Area of Activity: International.

Publications: *UICC International Directory of Cancer Institutes and Organizations* (electronic); *International Journal of Cancer and Predictive Oncology* (30 a year); *UICC News* (quarterly); *Annual Report*; *International Calendar of Meetings on Cancer* (2 a year); manuals (most publications are available electronically).

Finance: Income from membership dues, national subscriptions, grants and donations. Annual budget approx. US $5,000,000.

Council: Dr J. Seffrin (Pres.); Dr L. J. Denis (Treas.).

Address: 3 rue du Conseil-Général, 1205 Geneva.

Telephone: (22) 8091811; **Fax:** (22) 8091810; **Internet:** www.uicc.org; **e-mail:** info@uicc.org.

Internationale Stiftung Hochalpine Forschungsstationen Jungfraujoch und Gornergrat (International Foundation of the High-Alpine Research Stations Jungfraujoch and Gornergrat)

Founded in 1930 by representatives of scientific institutions in Belgium, Germany, Austria, France, the United Kingdom and Switzerland, to promote high-altitude research. Italy is also a member of the Foundation.

Activities: Supports the research station and Sphinx observatory on the Jungfraujoch, and the two astronomical observatories, Gornergrat South and Gornergrat North. Research is undertaken in the fields of physiology, physics, environment, astronomy and astrophysics.

Geographical Area of Activity: International.

Publications: Annual Report.

Trustees: H. Debrunner (Chair.); and two representatives from each of the founding organizations.

Principal Staff: Dir H. Debrunner.

Address: Sidlerstr. 5, 3012 Berne.

Telephone: (31) 6314051; **Fax:** (31) 6314405.

Internationale Stiftung Preis E. Balzan-Fonds

(International E. Balzan Prize Foundation-Fund)

Founded in 1956 by Angela Lina Balzan to honour the memory of her father Eugenio Balzan, a famous Italian journalist, who died in 1953. The foundation acts jointly through two foundations, one under Swiss law and the other under Italian law. The International E. Balzan Prize Foundation-Fund manages Eugenio Balzan's estate and the International E. Balzan Prize Foundation-Prize awards the Balzan Prizes.

Activities: Four prizes are awarded annually: two within the humanities, and two within the sciences on subjects chosen each year. The prizes are worth 1,000,000 Swiss francs each and one-half of this amount must be reserved by the winner to research projects preferably involving young scholars and scientists. In 2002 prizes were to be awarded in the areas of sociology, history of the humanities, developmental biology and geology. In addition, a Prize for Humanity, Peace and Brotherhood among Peoples is awarded at intervals of not less than three years. The General Prize Committee, responsible for the selection of the candidates, is made up of 18–20 European academics and scientists. The candidates are submitted by universities and learned societies from all over the world, following an invitation by the Chairman of the Balzan General Prize Committee to Presidents of Academies and Universities, and other simiar institutions, to submit nominations for the awards.

Geographical Area of Activity: International.

Restrictions: Personal applications not accepted.

Publications: *Premi Balzan* (published each February with information on the winners and the foundation, in English, French, German and Italian).

Finance: In 2000 the value of the peace prize was 2,000,000 Swiss francs; four prizes annually for other categories are valued at 1,000,000 Swiss francs each.

Board (International Foundation Fund): L. Bürkler-Giussani (Chair.); A. Casanova; M. C. Dietrich; C. Fontana; C. Guazzaroni; P.-D. Klingenberg; A. Kowner.

Board (International Foundation Prize): B. Bottai (Chair.); C. Fontana (Vice-Chair.); A. Casanova; V. Mathieu; G. Rumi; S. Salvemini.

Address: Piazetta Umberto Giordano 4, 20122 Milan, Italy.

Telephone: (02) 76002212 (Milan); **Fax:** (02) 76009457 (Milan); **Internet:** www.balzan.it; **e-mail:** balzan@balzan.it.

IUCN—World Conservation Union/UICN—Union mondiale pour la nature/UICN—Unión Mundial para la Naturaleza

Founded in 1948 as an independent international organization of states, government agencies and NGOs working in partnership to promote the management and conservation of the world's living resources.

Activities: The IUCN's objectives are to influence, encourage and assist societies throughout the world to conserve the integrity and diversity of nature and to ensure that any use of natural resources is equitable and ecologically sustainable. The organization provides a neutral forum for government and NGO members to discuss conservation issues and plan action. It builds partnerships between governments and environmental organizations so as to develop conservation strategies, test new ideas through field projects, or build local and regional capacity. Assists countries in the preparation of national Conservation Strategies, and supervises and supports field projects. Operations are increasingly decentralized and are carried out through an expanding network of regional and country offices, located principally in developing countries. The IUCN has regional and country offices worldwide. There are 74 member countries, and over 980 of NGO, governmental agency, affiliate and individual members, spread across 140 countries.

Geographical Area of Activity: International.

Publications: *World Conservation* (quarterly); *The Red Book: the Extinction Crisis Face to Face; Transboundary Protected Areas for Peace and Co-operation; the Relationship Between Nature Conservation, Biodiversity and Organic Agriculture*; Annual Report; and other specialist publications.

Finance: Total donations received 81,132,895 Swiss francs, total expenditure 88,950,000 Swiss francs (2001).

Governing Board: Yolanda Kakabadse Navarro (Pres.) and a council comprising 36 members.

Principal Staff: Dir Gen. Achim Steiner.

Address: 28 rue Mauverney, 1196 Gland.

Telephone: (22) 9990001; **Fax:** (22) 9990002; **Internet:** www.iucn.org; **e-mail:** mail@iucn.ch.

Jacobs Foundation

Established in 1988 by Klaus J. Jacobs with the aim of empowering youth.

Activities: Operates nationally and internationally in the fields of secondary education and developmental psychology, to help young people reach their full potential, through grants to individuals and organizations, projects and conferences.

Geographical Area of Activity: International.

Restrictions: No support is given for endowments, regular operating budgets, or to religious organizations.

Publications: Annual Report.

Finance: Assets 110,000,000 Swiss francs (Sept. 2000); annual revenue 1,130,000 Swiss francs, expenditure 4,800,000 Swiss francs (1999–2000).

Board of Directors: Klaus J. Jacobs (Chair.); Paul B. Baltes; Flavio Cotti; Johann Christian Jacobs; Sir Michael Rutter; Marta Tienda; Heinrich Ursprung.

Principal Staff: Dir Gen. Theo E. Brenner; Admin. Asst Judith Kressig.

Address: Seefeldquai 17, 8034 Zürich.

Telephone: (1) 3886123; **Fax:** (1) 3886137; **Internet:** www.jacobsfoundation.org; **e-mail:** jf@jacobsfoundation.org.

C. G. Jung-Institut Zürich (C. G. Jung Institute Zurich)

A training institute, founded in 1948 by Prof. C. G. Jung, C. A. Meier, K. Binswanger, L. Frey-Rohn and J. Jacobi, for education and research in its primary field: analytical psychology.

Activities: Operates internationally in the fields of analytical psychology, education, science and medicine, through research, courses and contacts with others interested in psychology and the publication of scientific works.

Geographical Area of Activity: International.

Finance: Funded by tuition fees and donations.

Trustees: Dr Brigitte Spillmann-Jenny (Pres.).

Principal Staff: Dir of Studies Ursula Weiss.

Address: Hornweg 28, 8700 Küsnacht.

Telephone: (1) 9141040; **Fax:** (1) 9141050; **Internet:** www.jung.edu; **e-mail:** info@junginstitut.ch.

Kosova Foundation for Economic Reconstruction and Development

Established in 1999 to establish and supervise reconstruction projects in the Kosovo region of Yugoslavia.

Activities: The Foundation supports projects aimed at strengthening the economic development of Kosovo, including partnership projects that are developed and implemented jointly between foreign institutions and Kosova organizations. Support is given to projects aiming to transfer skills to Kosovo that will strengthen the capacity of indigenous organizations to become self-sustainable, while simultaneously promoting strong relationships between these organizations and their foreign counterparts. Maintains additional offices in Lugano, Switzerland, the United Kingdom and the USA.

Geographical Area of Activity: Kosovo.

Finance: Funding from ethnic Albanians world-wide.

Principal Staff: Chair. Ajim Gjinali.

Address: Via Serafino Balestra 18, 6900 Lugano.

Limmat-Stiftung (Limmat Foundation)

Founded in 1972 by Dr Arthur Wiederkehr, to promote initiatives for the common good in Switzerland and abroad, especially by offering the necessary organizational infrastructure.

Activities: Operates nationally and internationally in the fields of education, medicine, agriculture, computer science, advancement of the poor (especially women) and vocational training. Programmes are instruction-orientated and encourage self-help. 'Special Patronage' projects are organized to realize specific undertakings according to the wishes of individual donors. The Foundation operates a Project Centre in Zürich.

Geographical Area of Activity: International.

Publications: Annual Report; *Familie und Erziehung* (Family and Education, bulletin); *Changing Mentalities—Vocational Training and Development Co-operation.*

Finance: Total assets 22,782,900 Swiss francs (Dec. 2001); total income and expenditure 807,800 Swiss francs (2001).

Governing Board: H. G. Rhonheimer (Pres.); F. Geinoz (Exec. Dir and Gen. Man.); Dr M. Durrer; Dr F. Faller; Prof. U. Farri; Dr C. George; M. Juon; Dr H. Thomas; Dr F. Tschui.

Address: Rosenbühlstr. 32, 8044 Zürich.

Telephone: (1) 2522838; **Fax:** (1) 2522877; **Internet:** www.limmat.org; **e-mail:** limmat@limmat.org.

The Lutheran World Federation

Founded in 1947 to serve Lutheran churches as an instrument for mission, service, communication and study. In 2002 the Federation comprised 133 member churches in 73 countries, representing about 95% of the world's Lutheran Christians.

Activities: Operates internationally in the fields of communication and education, social welfare, human rights, religion and ecumenical relations, and aid to less-developed countries. The Federation offers annual study awards (mainly at graduate level) in theology and other disciplines, and vocational courses for members of Lutheran churches throughout the world. It also organizes programmes of research in different cultures, conferences and seminars. Maintains a Peace Fund, supporting the human rights ministries of member churches with training, financial and other assistance. Projects include assisting churches in developing countries with various communication projects, and developing theological education in Africa and Central and South America. The Federation has two international news services, and publishes studies and specialized publications on development issues. Maintains projects and programmes in 70 countries.

Geographical Area of Activity: International.

Publications: *Lutheran World Information/Lutherische Welt-Information* (fortnightly news bulletins); *LWF Today/LWB Heute* (annually); *LWF Documentation/LWB Dokumentation; LWF Studies/LWB-Studien; LWF Educator; LWF Women; LWF Youth; Development Education Forum*; working papers.

Finance: Annual budget approx. US $100,000,000.

Trustees: The Board of Trustees comprises the President, Treasurer, five Vice-Presidents and the Chairpersons of the five Programme Committees.

Principal Staff: Pres. Rt Rev. Dr Christian Krause (Germany); Gen. Sec. Rev. Dr Ishmael Noko (Zimbabwe).

Address: 150 route de Ferney, POB 2100, 1211 Geneva 2.

Telephone: (22) 7916111; **Fax:** (22) 7916630; **Internet:** www.lutheranworld.org; **e-mail:** info@lutheranworld.org.

Media Action International

Established in 1998 by journalists; aims to use mass media for humanitarian purposes in conflict and crisis situations. It also seeks to combat poverty, illiteracy and disease, through promoting unbiased information-giving in all areas, and the use of the media for peace-building and development.

Activities: Operates internationally, with the aim of promoting objective media coverage, and the use of the media to aid in peace-building and development. Works with the United Nations and other aid agencies and donors. Projects include the provision of information through the media in countries stricken by natural disasters or conflict, the promotion of editorially-independent journalism, training of journalists and other professionals, and the production of books relating to media use.

Geographical Area of Activity: Africa, Asia and Europe.

Restrictions: No grants to individuals; seeks working partnerships with other non-profits.

Publications: *Essential Field Guides to Humanitarian and Conflict Zones; Radio and HIV/AIDS: Making a Difference, a guide for radio practitioners, health workers and donors; Lifeline Media, Reaching Populations in Crisis; The Afghanistan Monitor.*

Finance: Operational budget 500,000 to 1,500,000 Swiss francs.

Board of Trustees: *Charles Adams; Laurence Déonna; Bridget Dommen; Edward Girardet; Loretta Hieber; Alain Modoux; Henry Muller; Stephen Somerville.*

Principal Staff: Dir Ed Girardet; Communication Edouard Markiewicz; Admin. Marilu D'Onorio.

Address: 42 rue de Lausanne, 1201 Geneva.

Telephone: (22) 9500750; **Fax:** (22) 9500752; **Internet:** www.mediaaction.org; **e-mail:** info@mediaaction.org.

Novartis Foundation for Gerontology

Established by Novartis AG (q.v.) to promote healthy ageing; previously known as the Sandoz Foundation for Gerontological Research, set up in 1986.

Activities: Works in the fields of public health education in the area of medicine of ageing, principally through its website, which offers information to older people on health issues and is also aimed at health-care professionals. Maintains a database of drugs, and offers information on alternative medicine and an Ask the Doctor facility on its website.

Geographical Area of Activity: International.

Restrictions: Grants only for specific internet programmes.

Publications: *HealthandAge.com Newsalert* (on-line newsletter, every 2 weeks); *Travel Health Newsletter* (newsletter, every 2 weeks); *Positive Ageing Newsletter* (monthly newsletter); and other publications.

Board of Trustess: Prof. H. B. Stähelin (Pres.); C. Studer (Vice-Pres.); Prof. G. Andrews; Y. Hasler; Prof. E. G. Lakatta; Prof. J. P. Michel.

Principal Staff: Exec. Dir Yvonne Hasler.

Address: Lichtstr., 4002 Basle.

Telephone: (61) 3247421; **Fax:** (61) 3244294; **Internet:** www.healthandage.com; **e-mail:** yvonne.hasler@group.novartis.com.

Novartis Foundation for Sustainable Development

Established by the Novartis AG, with the aim of improving the quality of life of poor people in less-developed countries.

Activities: The foundation's recent focus has been on supporting projects within the areas of access to basic health-care, leprosy and health, and social development. Projects are run in numerous developing countries in the South, including Brazil, China, Mali, Nepal, Palestinian territories, Sri Lanka, Tanzania. In the area of health-care, support has been given to a pilot scheme developing an integrated health-care programme, including upgrading medical facilities and providing training, setting up a micro-health insurance organization, and running awareness campaigns on improving nutrition, hygiene and health. Projects to combat leprosy include a campaign to provide free drug treatment to all leprosy patients, improving access to diagnosis and treatment, and operating rehabilitation programmes. Social development projects currently focus on village development, psycho-socio support for AIDS victims, support for self-help groups, youth training centres and women empowerment projects.

Geographical Area of Activity: International, particularly countries of the South, including Brazil, China, Mali, Nepal, Palestinian territories, Sri Lanka, Tanzania.

Restrictions: No unsolicited applications normally accepted.

Board of Trustees: Prof. Dr Klaus Leisinger (Pres. and Exec. Dir); Urs Bärlocher; Alexandre F. Jetzer; Jean-Marie Lehn; Dr Andreas Seiter.

Principal Staff: Exec. Dir Prof. Dr Klaus Leisinger.

Address: WRO-1002.11.59 POB, 4002 Basle.

Telephone: (61) 6977200; **Fax:** (61) 6977104; **Internet:** www.foundation.novartis.com; **e-mail:** novartis.foundation@group.novartis.com.

Parthenon Trust

Established in 1995 for general charitable purposes.

Activities: The Trust's primary interests are humanitarian assistance (including longer-term development in the developing world), medical research, treatment and care and assistance to the disadvantaged. Particular emphasis is on helping children in need, refugees and famine victims.

Geographical Area of Activity: International.

Restrictions: Grants are not made to individuals.

Finance: Expenditure £12,221,003 (2001).

Board of Trustees: Y. G. Whittaker (Chair.); Dr J. M. Darmady; Prof. C. N. Hales.

Principal Staff: Sec. John E. Whittaker.

Address: Saint-Nicholas 9, 2000 Neuchatel.

Telephone: (32) 7248130; **Fax:** (32) 7248131.

Pestalozzi Children's Village Foundation

Founded in 1947 to assist children in need, and to further the educational welfare of youth in all parts of the world.

Activities: Operates internationally in the fields of aid to less-developed countries and education, through grants for relief programmes, in particular those to assist children in need, and for education and vocational training. Runs the Pestalozzi Children's Village in Trogen, Sitzerland. Its educational programmes operate in Bangladesh, Cambodia, El Salvador, Ethiopia, Haiti, India and Peru; also sponsors educational institutions for children in Romania.

Publications: Annual report and financial statement.

Principal Staff: Sec. Thomas Mächler; Pres. Ulrich Gut.

Address: Hallwylstr. 72, 8004 Zürich.

Telephone: (1) 2983434; **Fax:** (1) 2983435.

Pro Helvetia (Arts Council of Switzerland)

Founded in 1939 to promote the arts.

Activities: The Foundation promotes creative cultural activities and cultural works relating to Switzerland nationally and internationally.

Geographical Area of Activity: International.

Publications: *Passages* (Swiss cultural magazine published bi-annually); brochures; information sheets.

Trustees: The Board of Trustees comprises 25 specialists from all fields of the arts.

Principal Staff: Dir Pius Knüsel.

Address: Hirschengraben 22, 8024 Zürich.

Telephone: (1) 2677171; **Fax:** (1) 2677106; **Internet:** www.pro-helvetia.ch; **e-mail:** info@pro-helvetia.ch.

Pro Juventute

Established in 1912 by Dr Carl Horber.

Activities: Works to protect and improve the quality of life for children and adolescents in the family and in society as a whole. Operates in the areas of education, human rights, health care and social welfare. Funds projects, makes grants to individuals, organizes conferences and produces a number of publications.

Geographical Area of Activity: Switzerland.

Finance: Funded by donations and the sale of stamps, cards and other products.

Principal Staff: Pres. Christine Beerli; CEO Brigitte Zünd.

Address: Seehofstr. 15, 8032 Zürich.

Telephone: (1) 2567777; **Fax:** (1) 2567778; **Internet:** www.projuventute.ch; **e-mail:** info@projuventute.ch.

Ramsay Foundation

Set up to support educational and arts and cultural activities.

Activities: Aims to further and enhance education, through support for pedagogy, training and post-training initiatives, as well as through funding for art and cultural activities, both in Switzerland and overseas. Outside of Switzerland grants have been made to projects in Africa, Brazil, Bulgaria, Croatia, Germany, India, Israel, Russia, the United Kingdom and Ukraine.

Geographical Area of Activity: Switzerland and international, including Africa, Brazil, Bulgaria, Croatia, Germany, India, Israel, Russia, the United Kingdom and Ukraine.

Finance: Annual grants expenditure 161,749 Swiss francs (2001).

Board of Trustees: Clara Bodenmann-Ritter (Pres.); Donald Vollen (Vice-Pres.).

Address: Freie Str. 89, 4051 Basel.

Telephone: (61) 2709040; **Fax:** (61) 2709059; **Internet:** www.ramsayfoundation.ch; **e-mail:** info@ramsayfoundation.ch.

Gerbert Rüf Stiftung (Gerbert Rüf Foundation)

Established by Heinrich Gerbert in 1997.

Activities: Supports scientific research projects at educational institutions related to innovation and the transfer of information, as well as funding teaching initiatives.

Geographical Area of Activity: Mainly Switzerland.

Publications: Governing Council: Dr Theodor Fässler (Pres.); Prof. Dr Peter Forstmoser (Vice-Pres.); Prof. Dr Philipp U. Heitz; Prof. Dr Piero Martinoli; Prof. Dr Verena Meyer; Prof. Dr Hans Heinrich Schmid; Prof. Dr Carl August Zehnder.

Finance: Annual income approx. 10,000,000 Swiss francs.

Principal Staff: Gen. Man. Dr Philipp Egger.

Address: Bäumleingasse 22, 4051 Basel.

Telephone: (61) 2708822; **Fax:** (61) 2708823; **Internet:** www.grstiftung.ch; **e-mail:** info@grstiftung.ch.

Roche Research Foundation for Scientific Exchange and Biomedical Collaboration

Established in 1971, on the 75th anniversary of the Roche Group (q.v.), to promote scientific research in the field of biomedicine.

Activities: The Foundation awards Roche Research Foundation Fellowships to Swiss nationals engaged in experimental biomedical research in Switzerland or abroad, or to non-Swiss biomedical researchers who wish to work in Switzerland. An MBA Fellowship Programme for Medical and Science Graduates was initiated in 1997, to assist Swiss residents, or employees of a Roche Group company, who must be graduates in medicine or science. Support is given through Swiss educational and health-care institutions as well as to researchers and clinicians based abroad for study at Swiss institutions, or for research by Swiss nationals abroad.

Geographical Area of Activity: Mainly Switzerland.

Principal Staff: Pres. Beat Gähwiler; Vice-Pres. Susanne Suter; Sec.-Gen. Prof. Klaus Müller.

Address: c/o F. Hoffmann-La Roche Ltd, Bldg 9218,08, 4070 Basle.

Telephone: (61) 6885227; **Fax:** (61) 6881460; **Internet:** www.research-foundation.org; **e-mail:** research.foundation@roche.com.

Rroma Foundation

Established to support the Roma in Central and Eastern Europe; the Foundation was part of the Soros network of foundations, but is now a fully independent foundation.

Activities: Supports programmes in the fields of the culture, education, community development, and human rights, including the training of Roma as teachers, journalists and human rights advisers, support for schools and summer schools, grants for publishing projects, offering scholarships, supporting bilingual journals and newspapers, grants for arts projects, and providing legal advice and assistance; promotes liaison between majority populations and the Roma minority; established a Roma Social Bureau in Bulgaria, which offers advice on civil rights issues, and planned to establish a similar bureau in Ukraine. Currently providing support to Roma refugees in Switzerland.

Geographical Area of Activity: Mainly Central and Eastern Europe.

Publications: Background reports.

Board of Trustees: Cristina I. Kruck (Chair.).

Principal Staff: Exec. Dir Dr Stephane Laederich.

Address: Forchstr. 353, 8008 Zürich.

Telephone: (1) 3836326; **Fax:** (1) 3836302; **Internet:** www.rroma.org/rroma_foundation/rroma-foundation.html; **e-mail:** sl@rroma.org.

Sandoz Fondation de Famille (Sandoz Family Foundation)

Established in 1964 by Marcel Edouard Sandoz, the son of the founder of Sandoz SA of Basle (now Novartis SA), to hold the Sandoz family's company shareholding.

Activities: Seeks to encourage entrepreneurial commitment through its commercial shareholdings, as well as encouraging creativity and private initiative. In 1982 it established the Fondation Edouard et Maurice Sandoz (FEMS), which awards the annual FEMS Prize to support artistic development, as well as supporting a range of cultural events and organizations. In 1999 the Foundation launched a programme funding science professorships at Swiss universities.

Geographical Area of Activity: Mainly Switzerland.

Board of Directors: Pierre Landolt (Pres.); Victor Bischoff; Gabriel Prêtre; Olivier Verrey.

Address: Sandoz Family Offce SA, 85 ave Gen. Guisan, 1009 Pully.

Telephone: (21) 72113136; **Internet:** www.sandozfoundation.ch; **e-mail:** info@sandozfamilyoffice.ch.

Schwab Foundation for Social Entrepreneurship

Established in 1998 by Hilde and Klaus Schwab, founder of the World Economic Forum (q.v.); aims to identify, recognize and disseminate initiatives in social entrepreneurship that have significantly improved people's lives and have the potential to be adapted to other settings.

Activities: Promotes social entrepreneurship and the exchange of information through a series of initiatives, including GEXSI (Global Exchange for Social Investment), a platform for social investors to find worthwhile projects to fund; awards for Schwab Social Entrepeneurs, followed by annual summits; and various meetings and conferences. Also maintains an on-line database of social entrepreneurs worldwide.

Geographical Area of Activity: International.

Board of Trustees: Klaus Schwab (Pres. and co-Founder) Hilde Schwab (co-Founder); Paulo Cuelho; Guy Fontanet; Quincy Jones; Zanele Mbeki; Sadako Ogata; Adolf Ogi; Lord David Puttnam; Muhammad Yunus.

Principal Staff: Man. Dir Dr Pamela Hartigan.

Address: 91–93 route de la Capite, 1223 Cologny/Geneva.

Internet: www.schwabfound.org.

Schweizerisch-Liechtensteinische Stiftung für archäologische Forschungen im Ausland—SLFA

(Swiss-Liechtenstein Foundation for Archaeological Research Abroad—SLFA)

Established in 1986 with the personal participation of HSH Prince Hans-Adam II of Liechtenstein to assist developing countries to preserve their national heritage and to contribute to international solidarity in the field of archaeological research.

Activities: Carries out research in the areas of archaeological, ethnographical and cultural research in developing countries, including Bhutan, Ecuador, Jordan, Mali and Peru, in collaboration with local research organizations and universities.

Geographical Area of Activity: International.

Restrictions: Only supports its own research.

Publications: Annual Report; research publications.

Finance: Funding from Prince Hans-Adam II of Liechtenstein, private sponsors and the Swiss state. Annual budget 2,287,430 Swiss francs (2000).

Board of Directors: Pres. Dr Hans Heinrich Coninx; Vice-Pres. Danielle Ritter; Vice-Pres. Dr Egmond Frommelt.

Principal Staff: Gen.-Sec. Dr Eberhard Fischer; Admin. Claudia Zürcher.

Address: Generalsekretariat, c/o Rietberg Museum, Gablerstr. 15, 8002 Zürich.

Telephone: (1) 2017669; **Fax:** (1) 2010548; **Internet:** www.slsa.ch/www.slsa.li; **e-mail:** slsa@smile.ch.

Schweizerische Akademie der Medizinischen Wissenschaften (Swiss Academy of Medical Sciences)

Founded in 1943 to promote medical research in Switzerland and research carried out by the Swiss in other countries; to promote medico-scientific co-operation in Switzerland; to issue ethical guidelines for the medical profession; and to award prizes for medical scholars.

Activities: Supports advanced medical research; awards a limited number of grants and scholarships for research; patronizes symposia on various medical topics; awards several prizes, including the Bing Prize and the Ott Prize; organizes scientific meetings; and produces medico-scientific publications. Support restricted to Switzerland.

Geographical Area of Activity: Switzerland.

Publications: Annual Report (in French and German); *Ethical Guidelines for Physicians*; *SAMW Bulletin* (quarterly, in German and French); various information brochures.

Finance: Annual budget approx. 2,000,000 Swiss francs.

Principal Staff: Pres. Prof. W. Stauffacher.

Address: Petersplatz 13, 4051 Basle.

Telephone: (61) 2699030; **Fax:** (61) 2699039; **Internet:** www.samw.ch; **e-mail:** mail@samw.ch.

Schweizerische Stiftung für Alpine Forschungen (Swiss Foundation for Alpine Research)

Founded in 1939 to organize, finance and equip expeditions to mountains outside Europe and to the Arctic and Antarctic regions; and for Alpine research.

Activities: Operates internationally in the fields of science, mountaineering and alpine safety—high altitude medicine, glaciology, geology, avalanches, ecological deterioration of high altitude regions, etc., through self-conducted programmes and research, carried out both at home and abroad, and through publications and topographical maps. The Foundation's website operates as a resource on alpine research.

Geographical Area of Activity: International.

Publications: Annual Report; Newsletter.

Principal Staff: Pres. Jürg Marmet; Sec. Dr F. H. Schwarzenbach.

Address: Binzstr. 23, 8045 Zürich.

Telephone: (1) 4610147; **Fax:** (1) 4610711; **Internet:** www.alpineresearch.ch; **e-mail:** alpineresearch@access.ch.

Schweizerischer Nationalfonds zur Förderung der wissenschaftlichen Forschung/Fonds National Suisse de la Recherche Scientifique (Swiss National Science Foundation)

Founded in 1952 by the Schweizerische Naturforschende Gesellschaft, the Akademie der Medizinischen Wissenschaften, the Schweizerische Geisteswissenschaftliche Gesellschaft, the Schweizerischer Juristenverein and the Schweizerische Gesellschaft für Statistik und Volkswirtschaft, to grant financial support to basic research in all scientific disciplines, at Swiss universities and other scientific institutions.

Activities: Operates both nationally and internationally in the fields of education, science and medicine, the arts and humanities, law and other professions, through grants to individuals and institutions, research, fellowships, scholarships, conferences, courses, publications and lectures. To be eligible for a research grant, candidates must be resident in Switzerland (regardless of citizenship); candidates for fellowships must be resident in Switzerland or have Swiss or Liechtenstein nationality. The Foundation is responsible for several national research programmes and implements the National Centres of Competence in Research (NCCR). Maintains a database of funded projects, containing approximately 3,500 entries.

Geographical Area of Activity: Mainly Switzerland.

Publications: Annual Report; *Facts and Figures; List of Publication Grants; Fellowship Programmes at a Glance; Horizonte / Horizons* (quarterly); *SNFinfo*.

Finance: Total grants 377,300,000 Swiss francs (2001).

Governing Board: Dr Fritz Schiesser (Pres., Council of the Foundation); Prof. Heidi Diggelmann (Pres., Research Council).

Principal Staff: Dir Dr Hans Peter Hertig; Deputy Dir Annalise Eggimann; Vice-Dir Dr Jean-Bernard Weber.

Address: Wildhainweg 20, 3001 Berne.

Telephone: (31) 3082222; **Fax:** (31) 3082265; **Internet:** www.snf.ch; **e-mail:** pri@snf.ch.

Secours Dentaire International (International Dental Rescue)

Founded in 1981 to support co-operation and development in medical dentistry in less-developed countries.

Activities: Operates in Africa and the Caribbean in the field of dentistry. Teaches and trains staff for dental clinics; provides technical skills and trains school teachers. Maintains clinics in Benin, Burkina Faso, Cameroon, the Congo, Gabon, Haiti, Madagascar, Tanzania and Zimbabwe.

Geographical Area of Activity: Africa and Haiti.

Restrictions: No grants to individuals.

Publications: Some specialist publications.

Finance: Funded by donations.

Board of Trustees: Dr Ingrid Jent (Pres.); Quentin Voellinger (Vice-Pres.).

Address: Hochwacht, 9552 Bronschhofen.

Telephone: (71) 9115557; **Internet:** www.secoursdentaire.ch; **e-mail:** j.jent@vtx.ch.

Serono Foundation for the Advancement of Medical Science

Established by Serono, the Swiss pharmaceuticals company.

Activities: The Foundation aims to promote scientific activity which furthers human health and welfare, through supporting scientific workshops and meetings and funding postgraduate fellowships. Funding is provided for annual postdoctoral fellowships. The Foundation publishes proceedings from its series of workshops and meetings.

Geographical Area of Activity: International.

Restrictions: No grants to commercial organizations.

Publications: Proceedings from Foundation workshops.

Finance: Annual budget US $800,000.

Board of Directors: E. Borden; A. Eshkol; A. Galazka; G. E. Griffin; H. S. Jacobs; J. C. Martinou; R. Stanhope; M. Vannini.

Principal Staff: Sec. Renée Beaudry.

Address: 12 chemin des Aulx, 1228 Plan-les-Ouates, Geneva.

Telephone: (22) 7069368; **Fax:** (22) 7069398; **Internet:** www.serono-foundation.org; **e-mail:** renee.beaudry@serono.com.

Stiftung Kinderdorf Pestalozzi (Pestalozzi Children's Village Foundation)

Founded in 1946 by Walter Robert Corti to provide help for children in need and distress, and to be a place of meeting and co-operation, a centre of mutual understanding beyond all national, religious and linguistic barriers.

Activities: Operates in Central America, East Africa, Asia and South Eastern Europe in the programme fields of access to education and inter-cultural living together; addressing the needs of disadvantaged children and young people. All programmes and projects are partner-based with the Foundation not operating and implementing projects directly, but co-operating with local structures (government and non-goverment organizations). Currently the Foundation is running co-operation projects in Cambodia, Ethiopia, El Salvador, Guatemala, Honduras, India, Myanmar, Romania and Serbia. The Foundation also operates a village providing a home for children and adolescents, who live in family-like groups and have access to general and vocational training and education in a range of schools and colleges. The village also serves as a facility for exchange projects, bringing together approximately 100 children and young people each year from around the world for inter-cultural activities.

Geographical Area of Activity: Africa, Asia, Central America, South-Eastern Europe and Switzerland.

Restrictions: Project proposals which are outside the Foundation's range of activities and supported countries will not be considered.

Publications: Annual Report (available in English, French and German); other publications.

Trustees: The Foundation is governed by a Council of 25 members; Brigitta M. Gadient (Pres.); Raeto Conrad (Vice-Pres.); Mario Frick (Treas.).

Principal Staff: CEO Markus Mader.

Address: Haus Grund, 9043 Trogen.

Telephone: (71) 3437373; **Fax:** (71) 3437330; **Internet:** www.pestalozzi.ch; **e-mail:** info@pestalozzi.ch.

Stiftung 'Leben für Alle' (Foundation 'Life for All')

Established in 1989, an NGO formed to help alleviate suffering.

Activities: Operates in Africa, Asia, Eastern Europe and South America in the fields of aid to less-developed countries, education and social welfare, primarily for children and women, through direct help to those suffering, disaster relief, running children's homes and schools, and providing medical care. 'Sister' organizations have been established in Germany, India and the USA.

Geographical Area of Activity: Africa, Asia, Eastern Europe and South America.

Restrictions: Grants are made directly to projects, no grants are made to individuals.

Finance: Annual revenue 1,659,490 Swiss francs, expenditure 1,663,399 Swiss francs (1999).

Principal Staff: Pres. Dr M. A. Kämpfen; Programme Dir Bhola Sah.

Address: Beckenhofstr. 1, Postfach 6771, 8023 Zürich.

Telephone: (1) 8260218; **Fax:** (1) 8260377; **Internet:** www.life-for-all.org; **e-mail:** info@life-for-all.org.

Stiftung Szondi Institut: Lehr- und Forschungs-Institut für Allgemeine Tiefenpsychologie und Speziell für Schicksalspsychologie (Szondi Institute Foundation)

Founded in 1969 by Dr Leopold Szondi to promote in-depth research in psychology.

Activities: Conducts research on the influence of heredity and environment on neuroses, psychoses and criminality, and on psychological tests, in particular the Szondi test. The Institute trains future psychotherapists and collaborates with researchers from other countries.

Principal Staff: Sec. Jacqueline Aerne.

Address: Krähbühlstr. 30, 8044 Zürich.

Telephone: (1) 2524655; **Fax:** (1) 2529188; **Internet:** www.szondi.ch; **e-mail:** info@szondi.ch.

Stiftung Vivamos Mejor (Vivamos Mejor Foundation)

Established in 1981 to aid social groups in Central and South America.

Activities: The Foundation supplies information and technical assistance in the fields of education, health, housing and community development, while incorporating local labour and funds in order to promote self-sufficiency and the use of local resources.

Geographical Area of Activity: Central and South America.

Restrictions: Grants only to own projects.

Publications: Annual Report; *Intercambio*.

Finance: Annual budget approx. 2,500,000–3,000,000 Swiss francs.

Trustees: Peter Tschopp (Pres.); Pierre Gygi (Delegate).

Principal Staff: Man. Dir Jürg Meichle; Asst Man. Lorenz Jungi.

Address: Spitalackerstr. 61, POB 478, 3000 Berne 25.

Telephone: (31) 3313929; **Fax:** (31) 3320309; **Internet:** www.vivamosmejor.ch; **e-mail:** info@vivamosmejor.ch.

Swiss Insurance Training Centre/Centro Suizo de Formación Aseguradora/Schweizerisches Zentrum für Versicherungsschulung

Founded in 1960 by the Swiss Reinsurance Company to promote the training of insurance specialists from all parts of the world, including developing countries; to establish and maintain a training centre for that purpose.

Activities: Operates internationally in the fields of education and economic affairs. Provides seminars and workshops in general insurance and life insurance and insurance management training, supplemented by bespoke courses for insurance companies and markets.

Geographical Area of Activity: International.

Publications: *Review* (twice-yearly publication for alumni).

Governing Board: Dr W. Ackermann; Dr W. Anderson; B. Berli; M. Liès; Dr H. Lüthy.

Principal Staff: Principal Hermann Hefti; Man. Training and Development Carlos Arocha.

Address: Seestr. 133, 8002 Zürich.

Telephone: (1) 2852050; **Fax:** (1) 2852051; **Internet:** www.sitc.ch; **e-mail:** sitc@swissre.com.

Swiss Solidarity Foundation

The Foundation was proposed in 1997 by the Swiss Government (its establishment would have to be ratified formally through a referendum) in response to criticism of the role it played during and after the Second World War. It was to promote solidarity nationally and internationally, focusing on the future; however, its future establishment was, in 2003, unclear.

Activities: The Foundation was to support projects in Switzerland and abroad in the areas of alleviation of poverty, the prevention of violence, and the creation of effective social structures.

Geographical Area of Activity: International.

Restrictions: No grants to individuals.

Finance: The Foundation was to be given the equivalent value of 500 metric tons of gold by the Swiss Federal Government.

Address: c/o Federal Dept of Finance, Bundesgasse 3, 3003 Berne.

Telephone: (31) 3232034; **Fax:** (31) 3227549; **e-mail:** info@gs-efd.admin.ch.

SWISSAID Foundation

Established to work towards a peaceful world, free from violence, war, poverty and hunger.

Activities: Operates in collaboration with local partner organizations in Africa (Chad, Guinea-Bissau, Niger and Tanzania), Asia (India and Myanmar) and Central and South America (Colombia, Ecuador and Nicaragua) to assist in sustainable development. Maintains offices in 10 countries.

Geographical Area of Activity: Africa, Asia, and Central and South America.

Publications: *SWISSAID Spiegel/Le Monde* (quarterly, in German and French).

Principal Staff: Chief Exec. Caroline Morel.

Address: Jubilaeumstr. 60, Postfach, 3000 Berne 6.

Telephone: (31) 3505353; **Fax:** (31) 3512783; **Internet:** www.swissaid.ch; **e-mail:** postmaster@swissaid.ch.

Swisscontact—Swiss Foundation for Technical Co-operation

Founded in 1959 by the Swiss private sector and Swiss universities to promote technical assistance in Asia, Africa and Central and South America and Eastern Europe.

Activities: Conducts its own projects in Asia, Africa, Central and South America, and Eastern Europe, with the collaboration of local organizations and by providing expert volunteers to offer technical support and assistance. Programmes include the organization of professional training centres in the technical field as well as the promotion of small-scale enterprises and ecology in Asia (India, Indonesia, Nepal and the Philippines, Sri Lanka and Vietnam), Africa (Benin, Burkina Faso, Kenya and Mali), Central and South America (Bolivia, Colombia, Ecuador, El Salvador and Peru), and Eastern Europe (Albania and the Russian Federation).

Geographical Area of Activity: Asia, Africa, Central and South America, and Eastern Europe.

Restrictions: No grants to individuals.

Publications: Annual Report (in English, German and Spanish).

Finance: Annual revenue 33,300,000 Swiss francs, expenditure 33,300,000 francs (2001).

Trustees: The Board of Trustees is composed of 38 members. There is an Executive Committee composed of 11 members.

Principal Staff: Pres., Exec. Cttee Dr Hans Peter Ming; Exec. Dir. Dr Urs Egger; Deputy Exec. Dir Peter Lutz.

Address: Döltschiweg 39, POB, 8055 Zürich.

Telephone: (1) 4541717; **Fax:** (1) 4541797; **Internet:** www.swisscontact.org; **e-mail:** sc@swisscontact.ch.

Terre des Hommes Foundation

Founded in 1960 by Edmond Kaiser to support children in distress.

Activities: Provides short-term and long-term direct help to children in need without racial or religious prejudices. Conducts projects in more than 30 countries all over the world in the following priority intervention areas: health, social work and children's rights. All projects have an emphasis on the protection and support of children in need. Also provides emergency humanitarian aid. It operates through self-conducted programmes and grants to institutions and individuals. Also maintains offices in Belgium, Canada, Denmark, France, Germany, Italy, Luxembourg and Syria.

Geographical Area of Activity: Over 30 countries in Europe, Central and South America, Africa and Asia.

Publications: Annual Report; *Triebfeder / L'Obstiné* (newsletter, quarterly); general brochure; country information sheets; various publications on child trafficking, juvenile justice and street children.

Finance: Funded by private donations; and institutional funds from the Swiss Government, European Union and USAID. Annual revenue and expenditure approx. 32,000,000 Swiss francs (2001).

Trustees: The Foundation is governed by a council elected by the general assembly which is representative of the 52 volunteer groups.

Principal Staff: Sec.-Gen. Peter Brey; Dir Programmes I Philippe Buchs; Dir Programmes II Ignacio Packer.

Address: En Budron C8, 1052 Le Mont-sur-Lausanne.

Telephone: (21) 6546666; **Fax:** (21) 6546677; **Internet:** www.tdh.ch; **e-mail:** info@tdh.org.

Tibet-Institut Rikon (Tibetan Monastic Institute in Rikon)

Founded in 1967 by Henri Kuhn-Ziegler and Jacques Kuhn to take care of the spiritual and religious needs of the Tibetans living in exile in Switzerland; to serve immediate teaching purposes by enabling Tibetan scholars and learned priests to teach their young compatriots and to convey to them the values of their ancient culture, as well as enabling Tibetan scholars and priests to learn German and other Western languages in order to become informed about the Western way of living and thinking; to serve as a meeting-place of Tibetan and Western cultures.

Activities: Operates internationally in the fields of education, social welfare and studies, science and medicine, and the arts and humanities, through research carried out both in Switzerland and in co-operation with European and American institutions, and conferences, courses, publications and lectures. Research is undertaken in the fields of history of religion, literature, cultural anthropology, linguistics, medicine and related disciplines. Courses are held on Tibetan religion, history, script and language, and basic instruction is given in the techniques of meditation. Formal opinions and reports on Tibetan affairs are prepared by the monks. Maintains a library with a Western and Tibetan section, and film and photograph archives.

Geographical Area of Activity: International.

Publications: Annual report and financial statement; *Opuscula Tibetana* (series of publications).

Governing Board: Jacques Kuhn (Chair.); Mathilde Kuhn (Hon. Pres.); Peter Grieder (Curator); Kalsang Chokteng; Hans-Heinrich Kuhn; Chungdak Dawa Koren; Dr Peter Lindegger; Dr Kaspar Schiller; Roland Steffan; Lodro Tulku.

Address: Wildbergstr. 26, 8486 Rikon/Zürich.

Telephone: (52) 351729; **Internet:** www.tibet-institut.ch.

Vision Africa

A missionary organization, founded in 1949 as the Swiss Branch of the Sudan United Mission (SUM), itself founded in 1904, to carry out missionary activities and charitable projects.

Activities: Operates in the fields of development and evangelism in Africa, working closely with African evangelical churches in Cameroon, Chad and Niger. It runs programmes that work to improve standards in health care, education and agriculture, as well as doing missionary work and constructing churches.

Geographical Area of Activity: Africa.

Restrictions: Grants only to specific organizations.

Publications: *Via-Info* (every 2 months, in French and German); videos and leaflets.

Finance: Financed by evangelical churches and individuals in Europe. Annual revenue 1,569,530 Swiss francs, expenditure 1,543,850 Swiss francs (1999).

Principal Staff: Dir Hansjürg Labèr.

Address: Moosbrunnenstr. 5, Postfach 73, 8426 Lufingen.

Telephone: (1) 8136171; **Fax:** (1) 8136141; **Internet:** www.visionafrica.ch; **e-mail:** zentrale@visionafrica.ch.

Volkart Stiftung (Volkart Foundation)

Founded in 1951 on the 100th anniversary of the Volkart Group.

Activities: Supports selected ideas, projects and organizations in the fields of sustainability, civil society, ecology, education, health, youth, and the arts and culture, through grants to organizations based in Brazil, India, Portugal and Switzerland.

Geographical Area of Activity: Brazil, India, Portugal and Switzerland.

Address: Volkart Haus, POB 343, 8401 Winterthur.

Telephone: (52) 2686868; **Fax:** (52) 2686889; **Internet:** www.volkart.ch; **e-mail:** info@volkartfoundation.com.

Welfare Association

Established in 1983 in Geneva to support Palestinian society in sustainable development. Registered under the name Welfare Association, it is also known in the region by its Arabic name, Ta'awoun, which means co-operation.

Activities: Supports sustainable development initiatives in the Palestinian Autonomous Areas, in the period up until the end of 2003 concentrating on vertical development, through support for high-impact projects. Operates within three core programmes: Institution Building, Human Resource Development, and Culture and Identity, as well as running special programmes in Lebanon, for the revitalization of the Old City of Jerusalem and the PNGO project, to assist NGOs in delivering services to poor and marginalized sectors of the community. Future support is likely to be given to Information Technology projects and the Palestinian Remembrance Museum.

Geographical Area of Activity: Palestinian Autonomous areas.

Publications: *Tanmiya* (neswletter, in Arabic and English); other publications.

Finance: Total assets approx. US $36,000,000; contributions between 1983–2000 totalled over US $100 million.

Board of Trustees: Abdul Majeed Shoman (Chair.);.

Address: POB 6269, 1211 Geneva 6.

Internet: www.welfareassociation.org.

Women's World Summit Foundation/Fondation Sommet Mondial des Femmes

Founded in March 1991 by Elly Pradervand after the Children's Summit to support the implementation of the United Nations Development Goals to inform, educate, train, empower and communicate, especially in relation to women and children.

Activities: Operates in the fields of human rights, communication and fundraising, advocacy, monitoring and lobbying, and co-operation with other organizations; maintains a resource centre of information on women's and children's issues. The Foundation promotes the implementation of the Conventions on Women's and Children's Rights and participates in United Nations NGO working groups; organizes annual award panels for the Prize for Women's Creativity in Rural Life; convenes the annual World Rural Women's Day (15th October), the World Day for Prevention of Child Abuse (19th November), Walk Your Talk initiatives and training workshops for Circles of Compassion.

Geographical Area of Activity: International.

Publications: *Empowering Women and Children* (newsletter).

Board of Directors: Filomin Chioma Steady (Pres.); Elly Pradervand (Exec. Dir); Munira N. A. Al-Nahed; Saïda Benhabyles; Ela Bhatt; Asha Kambon; Wu Quing; Gulzar Samji.

Principal Staff: Exec. Dir and Founder Elly Pradervand.

Address: POB 2001, 1211 Geneva 1.

Telephone: (22) 7386619; **Fax:** (22) 7388248; **Internet:** www.woman.ch; **e-mail:** wwsf@vtxnet.ch.

World Alliance of YMCAs—Young Men's Christian Associations

Founded in 1844 by George Williams and centred on the Christian faith, the organization works for the physical, emotional and spiritual welfare of women and men of all faiths and of none.

Activities: The YMCA runs programmes world-wide in the areas of youth, emergency aid, peace-building, gender and globalization. It operates internationally through 14,000 local associations in 122 countries. There are about 45,000,000 members world-wide. The national associations of countries form the World Alliance, which holds consultative status with the United Nations.

Geographical Area of Activity: Africa, Asia, Europe, Americas, Pacific and the Middle East.

Restrictions: Does not make grants.

Publications: *YMCA World; World Week of Prayer;* Directory; Secretary General's Report; Executive Committee Minutes.

Executive Committee: Caesar Molehatsi (Pres.); Alice Pederseh (Deputy Pres.); Dorothy de Sing (Treas.).

Principal Staff: Sec.-Gen. Bartholomew Shaha.

Address: 12 clos Belmont, 1208 Geneva.

Telephone: (22) 8495100; **Fax:** (22) 8495110; **Internet:** www.ymca.int; **e-mail:** office@ymca.int.

World Economic Forum

Founded in 1971 by Prof. Klaus M. Schwab to contribute to the growth of world-wide prosperity through economic co-operation and the promotion of enterprise. Supervised by the Swiss Federal Council, with consultative status with the United Nations.

Activities: Encourages the direct exchange of information between world leaders in business, politics and the academic sphere, to promote world-wide prosperity, particularly through engaging its corporate members in global citizenship. The organization holds an annual meeting, the World Business Summit, in Davos, Switzerland, and arranges Industry Summits and conferences geared to the requirements of the specific needs of individual countries or regions. The Project Trustees '21' seeks to improve the state of the world in the transition from the 20th to the 21st century, through networking of global decision-makers, creating task forces comprising people from all sections of humanity.

Geographical Area of Activity: International.

Publications: *Global Competitiveness Report* (annually, in collaboration with the International Monetary Fund—IMF); *World Link* (magazine, 6 a year).

Finance: Assets approx. 3,500,000 Swiss francs.

Principal Staff: Pres. Prof. Klaus M. Schwab; Man. Dir José-Maria Figueres-Olsen, Donna Redel, Frédéric Sicre.

Address: 91–93 route de la Capite, 1223 Cologny.

Telephone: (22) 869-1212; **Fax:** (22) 786-2744; **Internet:** www.weforum.org/; **e-mail:** contact@weforum.org.

World Scout Foundation

Founded in 1969 to support the 28,000,000 participants in the world scout movement.

Activities: Finances scouting activities; provides support to the World Organization of the Scout Movement.

Geographical Area of Activity: International.

Publications: *UPDATE* (magazine); Annual Report.

Finance: Total assets approx. 50,000,000 Swiss francs.

Principal Staff: Exec. Sec. Doreen Taillens.

Address: POB 241, 1211 Geneva 4.

Telephone: (22) 7051010; **Fax:** (22) 7051020; **Internet:** www.scout.org; **e-mail:** worldbureau@world.scout.org.

Worlddidac Foundation

Established in 1984 by Worlddidac—the World Association of Publishers, Manufacturers and Distributors of Educational Materials.

Activities: Awards the Worlddidac Award, presented to the manufacturers of the best educational materials, in order to promote creativity and innovation in the production of educational materials.

Geographical Area of Activity: International.

Publications: *Worlddidac Award Booklet.*

Board of Trustees: David C. Macey (Pres.); Beat Jost; Susanne Klopfenstein; Paul Perjes.

Address: Bollwerk 21, POB 8866, 3001 Berne.

Telephone: (31) 3117682; **Fax:** (31) 3121744; **Internet:** www.worlddidac.org/award; **e-mail:** info@worlddidac.org.

WWF International (World Wide Fund for Nature)

Founded in 1961 by Sir Peter Scott and others, to promote the conservation of natural resources and the diversity of species and ecosystems world-wide; originally known as the World Wildlife Fund.

Activities: WWF confronts world-wide environmental problems through a combination of practical projects, research, lobbying, education and public awareness. To date the organization has carried out more than 11,000 projects in 130 countries. WWF International consists of a global network of 27 national organizations, five associate organizations and 21 Programme Offices. Awards scholarships through the Prins Bernhard Scholarship Fund.

Geographical Area of Activity: World-wide.

Publications: *WWF News* (quarterly); *Living Planet Report* (periodically updated); *Wildlife of India* (CD ROM).

Finance: Total assets US $39,263,000 (2002); annual operating income US $63,029,000, annual expenditure US $63,239,000 (2002).

Trustees: Chief Emeka Anyaoku (Pres.); Sara Morrison (Vice-Pres.); André Hoffmann (Hon. Treas.); Dr Zainal Adlin; Teymour Alireza; Prof. George Benneh; Michael de Pencier; Marco Frey; Ernesto de Garilao; Jamshyd Godrej; Gustav Harmer; Quincy Hunsicker; HM Queen Noor of Jordan; William Reilly; Daniel Richard; Dr Rauno Väisänen; Carl-Albrecht von Treuenfels; Christopher Ward; Hans Wijers.

Principal Staff: Dir Gen. Claude Martin; Deputy Dir Gen. Christian Kornevall; Programme Dir Dr Chris Hails.

Address: Ave du Mont-Blanc, 1196 Gland.

Telephone: (22) 3649111; **Fax:** (22) 3645358; **Internet:** www.panda.org.

Zuger Kulturstiftung Landis und Gyr (Landis and Gyr Zug Cultural Foundation)

Established in 1971 by the Gyr family to promote and develop activities in the fields of science, culture and social affairs.

Activities: Operates in the fields of the arts and humanities, through offering 6–12-month scholarships in fine arts, literature, performing arts and culture criticism, linked to accommodation in Berlin, Bucharest, Budapest, London or Zug. Makes grants to the Collegium Budapest and New Europe College, Bucharest, and for arts projects in Switzerland which promote modern art.

Geographical Area of Activity: Europe.

Finance: Annual expenditure approx. 2,000,000 Swiss francs.

Trustees: Dr Hugo Bütler (Chair.); Prof. Dr Iso Camartin (Vice-Chair.); Dr Ursula Brunner; Heinz Hertach; Prof. Dr Peter von Matt; Elisabeth Mijnssen; Oskar K. Ronner; Ulrich Straub.

Principal Staff: Dir Hanna Widrig.

Address: Dammstr. 16, POB 4858, 6304 Zug.

Telephone: (41) 7242312; **Fax:** (41) 7245383.

Taiwan

FOUNDATION CENTRE AND CO-ORDINATING BODY

Taiwan Philanthropy Information Center

Established in 1999 by the Himalaya Foundation (q.v.) as a centre of information on the non-profit sector in Taiwan.

Activities: Informs on the non-profit sector in Taiwan and elsewhere by maintaining a database of not-for-profit organizations operating in Taiwan and a library on philanthropy and the third sector.

Geographical Area of Activity: Taiwan.

Address: c/o Himalaya Foundation, 167 Fu Hsing North Rd, 9F-1, Taipei 105.

Telephone: (2) 2544-8282; **Fax:** (2) 2718-5850; **Internet:** www.npo.org.tw.

FOUNDATIONS, TRUSTS AND NON-PROFIT ORGANIZATIONS

921 Foundation

Founded in 1999.

Activities: Active in the field of disaster relief and rehabilitation, particularly following earthquakes, through assistance and counselling to children and young people who have lost their families, providing rescue teams to prepare equipment and train personnel, and investigating, researching and planning rebuilding programmes.

Geographical Area of Activity: Taiwan.

Finance: Assets NT $5,174,338,000 (2000).

Principal Staff: Chair. Nita Ing; Contact: Yi-Ju Liou.

Address: 156 Chang Chuen Rd, 6F, Taipei.

Telephone: (2) 2561-7921; **Fax:** (2) 2521-7378; **Internet:** www.921fund.org.tw; **e-mail:** sos@921fund.org.tw.

Advantech Foundation

Founded in 1997 by Advantech Corporation.

Activities: Provides support to educational research both in Taiwan and overseas, aiming to put the results into practice at individual, social and corporate level to improve people's standard of living.

Geographical Area of Activity: Taiwan and international.

Finance: Total expenditure NT $21,742,656 (1999).

Principal Staff: Chair. K. C. Liu; Contact: Lina Chou.

Address: 1 Alley 20, Lane 26, Rueiguang Rd, Taipei.

Telephone: (2) 2792-7818; **Fax:** (2) 2794-7302; **Internet:** www.tic100.org.tw; **e-mail:** lina.chou@advantech.com.tw.

Asian Vegetable Research and Development Center

Founded in 1971 to encourage research and development of vegetable farming in the tropics and sub-tropics; and to help improve nutrition, health, employment and income in developing countries.

Activities: Organizes training programmes for specialists; finances research into vegetable development; maintains a large vegetable 'gene-bank'; holds workshops, seminars and conferences; operates regional programmes on vegetable research and development networks; runs an information service; maintains an information database and a library of about 25,000 books. There are two regional facilities, in Thailand and Tanzania, and regional networks serving Southern Asia, South-Eastern Asia and Southern Africa.

Geographical Area of Activity: International, in developing countries.

Publications: *Centerpoint* (newsletter); annual progress report; seminar proceedings; technical bulletins.

Finance: Annual budget US $9,086,000 (2002).

Principal Staff: Dir Gen. Dr Thomas A. Lumpkin.

Address: POB 42, Shanhua 741.

Telephone: (6) 583-7801; **Fax:** (6) 583-0009; **Internet:** www.avrdc.org.tw; **e-mail:** avrdcbox@netra.avrdc.org.tw.

Chia Hsin Foundation

Founded in 1963 by Dr Ming-yu Chang and Ming-chong Oung, Chairman of the Board of Directors and Managing Director respectively of the Chia Hsin Cement Corporation, for the promotion of culture in Taiwan.

Activities: Operates nationally in the fields of the arts and humanities, social studies, science and medicine, law and education, through research projects, courses, conferences, lectures, publications, fellowships and scholarships, and grants to both individuals and institutions. Grants the Chia Hsin Technology Award, the Distingushed Contribution Award, the Chia Hsin Prize for Journalism and the Chia Hsin Athletics Award. Also facilitates and finances study abroad for a limited number of students, and provides universities with free copies of Master of Arts and doctoral theses.

Geographical Area of Activity: Taiwan.

Publications: Report of operations.

Finance: Assets approx. NT $53,387,042.

Board of Directors: Jen-Shieng Yian (Chair.).

Address: 96 Chung Shan Rd, N, Section 2, Taipei 10449.

Telephone: (2) 2523-1461; **Fax:** (2) 2511-4002; **Internet:** www.chcgroup.com.tw/eng/business_subsidiary_foundation.htm; **e-mail:** ch_found@chcgroup.com.tw.

Chiang Ching-Kuo Foundation for International Scholarly Exchange—CCK Foundation

Founded in 1989 by the Government of Taiwan and the private sector to promote Chinese studies and scholarly exchange.

Activities: Operates internationally in the fields of the arts and humanities, economic affairs, education, international affairs, law and human rights, medicine and health, and social welfare and social studies, through research, grants to institutions and individuals, and awarding scholarships and fellowships. Programmes cover the American Region (including North, Central and South America), the Asian/Pacific Region, the European Region and the Republic of China. Maintains an office in the USA and the Chiang Ching-kuo International Sinological Center at Charles University in the Czech Republic.

Geographical Area of Activity: International.

Publications: Annual Report; newsletter (quarterly); *Building for the Future: the First Decade*.

Finance: Assets US $89,588,141 (2000); annual revenue $5,167,724, expenditure $4,062,029 (2000).

Board of Directors: Yih-yuan Li (Chair.); Morris Chang; Fredrick F. Chien; Hungdah Chiu; Cho-Yun Hsu; Douglas Hsu; Ying-Mao Kao; Ambrose King; Chen-Fu Koo; Wei-Fan

Kuo; Lawrence Lau; Huan Li; Chan Lien; Ts'ui-jung Lui; Kao-Wen Mao; James C. Y. Soong; Robert Tsao; Ovid J. L. Tzeng; Yueh-sheng Weng; Shyi-kun Yu; Yin-shih Yu.

Principal Staff: Chair. Yih-Yuan Li ; Pres. Yun-Han Chu.

Address: 13F, 65 Tun-Hwa South Rd, Section 2, Taipei 106.

Telephone: (2) 2704-5333; **Fax:** (2) 2701-6762; **Internet:** www.cckf.org; **e-mail:** cckf@ms1.hinet.net.

Himalaya Foundation

Established in 1990; a corporate foundation which aims to enable capable people of Chinese ancestry to develop their talents and participate broadly in the world community.

Activities: Operates in the fields of the arts and culture, Chinese studies, economic affairs and civil society, through research, grants, exchanges, publications and involvement in international philanthropic associations. Also involved in the development of civil society and the third sector, setting up the Taiwan Philanthropy Information Center (q.v.) that informs on the non-profit sector in Taiwan and elsewhere by maintaining a database of foundations in the country and a library on philanthropy and the third sector. The Foundation has established the NPO Development Center for not-for-profit organization IT capacity building and the NPO book website providing publications relating to the third sector or published by not-for-profit organizations.

Geographical Area of Activity: Taiwan, Asia and USA.

Restrictions: Prefers to fund projects that have tangible and far-reaching benefits for society.

Publications: *Directory of Foundations in Taiwan; Handbook on Good Practices for Laws Relating to Non-Governmental Organizations* (Chinese translation); series of books on the non-profit sector.

Finance: Net assets $1,300,000 (2000); annual revenue $1,500,000, expenditure $1,500,000 (2001).

Board of Trustees: Harold H. C. Han (Chair.).

Principal Staff: Exec. Dir S. Gong; Asst Exec. Dir Andy Kao.

Address: 167 Fu Hsing North Rd, 9F-1, Taipei 105.

Telephone: (2) 2544-8282; **Fax:** (2) 2718-5850; **Internet:** www.himalaya.org.tw; **e-mail:** hmfdtion@ms24.hinet.net.

Pacific Cultural Foundation

Founded in 1974 to promote international cultural exchange.

Activities: Provides grants for foreign students to research Chinese culture; organizes courses, lectures, exhibitions and concerts; arranges cultural exchanges; maintains a library; and awards prizes. The Foundation was responsible for the setting up of the Center for Chinese Culture and Art Studies. Awards the Publication Grant in Chinese Studies to support the publication of research by foreign students on contemporary Chinese problems, and research and writing grants in Chinese studies to foreign students conducting research on contemporary Chinese problems.

Geographical Area of Activity: International.

Publications: Annual Report; newsletter; conference proceedings.

Finance: Total endowment NT $58,000,000 (2000); total expenditure NT $33,246,582 (2000).

Board of Trustees: Huan Lee (Chair.).

Principal Staff: Exec. Dir Yu-Sheng Chang.

Address: 38 Chungking South Rd, Section 3, Taipei.

Telephone: (2) 2337-7155; **Fax:** (2) 2337-7167; **Internet:** www.pwf.org.tw; **e-mail:** pwf@pwf.org.tw.

Syin-Lu Social Welfare Foundation

Founded in 1987.

Activities: Works through campaigning for the rights of physically and mentally disabled people to ensure their entitlement to social benefits; funds education, rehabilitation, housing, leisure and counselling services for physically and mentally disabled people; trains professionals to mobilize community services on behalf of people with disabilities; and publishes relevant information.

Geographical Area of Activity: Taiwan.

Finance: Total expenditure NT $108,057,800.

Principal Staff: Chair. Ching-I Tsung; Exec. Dir Mei-Ling Chen.

Address: 364 Chilin Rd, 4F, Taipei.

Telephone: (2) 2592-9778; **Fax:** (2) 2592-8514; **Internet:** www.syinlu.org.tw; **e-mail:** syinlu@syinlu.org.tw.

Tajikistan

FOUNDATIONS, TRUSTS AND NON-PROFIT ORGANIZATIONS

Open Society Institute Assistance Foundation—Tajikistan

Founded in 1996 to promote the development of open society in Tajikistan. An independent foundation, part of the Soros foundations network, which aims to foster political and cultural pluralism and reform economic structures in order to encourage free enterprise and a market economy.

Activities: Operates principally in the fields of educational and electoral reform, human rights and legal reform, regional co-operation, information and the media, and arts and culture.

Geographical Area of Activity: Tajikistan.

Finance: Annual expenditure US $1,778,000 (2001).

Board of Directors: Oinhol Bobonazarova (Chair.); Mamadsho Ilolov; Nur Tabarov; Yevgenya Narzullaeva.

Principal Staff: Exec. Dir Zuhra Halimova.

Address: 65 Tolstoy St, 734003 Dushanbe.

Telephone: (372) 21-19-58; **Fax:** (372) 51-01-42; **e-mail:** zuhra.halimov@osi.tajik.net.

Tanzania

FOUNDATIONS, TRUSTS AND NON-PROFIT ORGANIZATIONS

Mwalimu Nyerere Foundation

Established in 1996 as a permanent tribute to Mwalimu Julius Nyerere, the country's first President; it is an independent body not linked to any political party, and its aim is to promote 'peace, unity and people-centred development in Africa'.

Activities: Seeks to carry out its aims through: encouraging and organizing dialogues within Africa, among and between governments, people, NGOs and local institutions; co-operating with other similar institutions within and outside Africa; collecting, analysing and disseminating information; and establishing a specialist library. Operates three programmes, the African Unity Programme, Institutional Capacity Building, and Justice for All. Also aims to promote the study of the principles adopted and practised by Mwalimu Julius Nyerere, through collecting, analysing and cataloguing documents, letters, reports, etc. concerning him, and to make available to the public all such information. The Foundation took a leading role in facilitating Burundi peace talks in 1999. Maintains a Documentation Research Centre.

Geographical Area of Activity: Africa.

Publications: *The Work of the Mwalimu Nyerere Foundation* (Swahili version); *Africa Today and Tomorrow* (collection of speeches by Mwalimu Julius Nyerere).

Finance: Annual revenue US $2,457,180 (2001).

Trustees: Al Noor Kassum (Interim Chair.); Joseph Butiku (Sec. and Exec. Dir); Dr Nikolaos Georgulas; Kate Kamba; Maria J. Kamm; Hashim Mbita; N. E. Mkono; Gertrude Mongella; Haroub Othman; Dr Salim A. Salim; Jotham Tumwesigy; J. S. Warioba.

Principal Staff: Exec. Dir Joseph W. Butikin.

Address: 6 Sokoine Dr., POB 71000, Dar es Salaam.

Telephone: (22) 2118354; **Fax:** (22) 2119216; **Internet:** www.nyererefoundation.or.tz; **e-mail:** mnf-tanzania@raha.com.

Thailand

FOUNDATION CENTRE AND CO-ORDINATING BODY

Center for Philanthropy and Civil Society

Established in 1997 under the National Institute of Development Administration, for the support of the third sector.

Activities: Aims to encourage the development of philanthropy and the third sector in Thailand, through carrying out reseach; maintaining databases; training and advisory services; lobbying; co-ordinating the activities and programmes of third-sector organizations; and educational programmes. Maintains an information centre.

Geographical Area of Activity: Thailand.

Executive Board: Dr J. Vichit-Vadakan (Chair.); Dr N. Wedchayanon (Dir); Dr C. Bhakdibutr; Dr K. Chintakananda; P. Khanobdee; R. Krabuanrat; T. Nakasuwan; Dr A. Sirivedhin; C. Suetrong; Dr S. Thananan; A. Watcharasin.

Address: National Institute of Development Administration, Seri Thai Rd, Klongchan Bangkapi, Bangkok 10240.

Telephone: (2) 377-7206; **Fax:** (2) 374-7399; **e-mail:** juree@nida.nida.ac.th.

FOUNDATIONS, TRUSTS AND NON-PROFIT ORGANIZATIONS

Asian Institute of Technology

Founded in 1959 as the SEATO Graduate School of Engineering, the Institute became fully independent under its present title in 1967. It aims to help meet the growing need for advanced engineering education in Asia.

Activities: Provides advanced (postgraduate) education in engineering, science and allied fields, through academic programmes leading to higher degrees, through research by students, faculty and research staff directed towards the solution of technological problems relevant to Asia, and through special programmes, including conferences, seminars and short courses. The Institute provides scholarships and grants to assist well-qualified students from the region. The Institute comprises four schools: the School of Advanced Technologies, School of Civil Engineering, School of Environment, Resources and Development and School of Management; there are also a number of Academic Centres. Maintains databases.

Geographical Area of Activity: Asia.

Publications: *Annual Report on Research and Activities; AIT Review* (3 a year); Annual Report.

Trustees: Dr Thanat Khoman (Chair. Emer.); Anand Panayarachun (Chair.); Prof. Hans van Ginkel, Jan Axel Nordlander (Vice-Chair.) and 30 others.

Principal Staff: Pres. Prof. Jean-Louis Armand.

Address: POB 4, Klong Luang, Pathumthani 12120.

Telephone: (2) 516-0110; **Fax:** (2) 516-2126; **Internet:** www.ait.ac.th; **e-mail:** webteam@ait.ac.th.

Children's Foundation

Founded in 1979 to support the welfare of children in Thailand.

Activities: The prime focus of the Foundation is the welfare of children in Thailand. Activities are within three programme areas: Educational and Cultural Institute Programmes, including support for village schools and projects helping homeless children; Children's Welfare and Education Institute, meeting basic needs of children; and the Children's Institute, developing knowledge in the community. Promotes physical and mental development of children, co-ordinates educational activities, provides scholarships and works in partnership with other NGOs. Also provides humanitarian relief and supports environmental preservation activities.

Geographical Area of Activity: Thailand.

Restrictions: Projects must be practical, transparent and simple enough to be monitored and evaluated.

Finance: Annual income approx. 40,000,000 Baht.

Principal Staff: Pres. Sophon Supapong.

Address: 95/24 Moo 6, Soi Kiatruammit, Puttamonthon 4 Rd, Kratoomlom, Sampran, Nakornpratom 73220.

Telephone: (2) 814-1481; **Fax:** (2) 814-0369; **e-mail:** childthai@bangkok.com.

Ecpat International

Established in 1991, initially as a three-year project, to combat child prostitution in Asian countries.

Activities: Carries out local, national and international activities aimed at protecting children in every part of the world, including the whole range of issues revolving around the commercial sexual exploitation of children. Organizes conferences, operates an information and resource centre, carries out research and develops models of prevention and disseminates information. The Ecpat Network comprises 71 independent groups in 62 different countries across Asia, Central, South and North America, Eastern and Western Europe, the Middle East, North Africa, and the Pacific.

Geographical Area of Activity: Asia, Central, South and North America, Eastern and Western Europe, the Middle East, North Africa, and the Pacific.

Publications: Annual Report.

Board: Josephine de Linde (Chair.).

Principal Staff: Exec. Dir Carmen Madrinan.

Address: 328 Phaya Thai Rd, Bangkok 10400.

Telephone: (2) 215-3388; **Fax:** (2) 215-8272; **Internet:** www.ecpat.net/; **e-mail:** info@ecpat.net.

Empower Foundation

Founded in 1994.

Activities: Active within two main programme areas: women and prostitution, and AIDS prevention and problem solving. Carries out educational activities in the fields of legal rights, social benefits and AIDS prevention; grants scholarships; and provides medical fees and emergency funds for prostitutes. Also provides leadership training.

Geographical Area of Activity: Thailand.

Restrictions: Applications from domestic organizations for projects seeking to combat prostitution are rarely approved.

Publications: *Life Leading.*

Finance: Annual revenue approx. 800,000 Baht.

Principal Staff: Sec.-Gen. Chantawipa Apisuk.

Address: 9–12 Soi Phiphat, Silom Rd, Bangkok 10500.

Telephone: (2) 236-9272; **Fax:** (2) 236-9272; **e-mail:** empower@mozart.inet.co.th.

Foundation for Agricultural and Rural Development

Founded in 1980 to help poor rural people achieve a better quality of life.

Activities: Works to create opportunities for poor people in the rural areas of North-East Thailand by operating leadership training programmes; organizes seminars and consultation activities for marginalized groups; provides technical assistance to NGOs to strengthen the community; and acts as a community resource centre providing information for NGOs and community organizations in Thailand and overseas (Cambodia, Philippines and Vietnam). Also awards grants to individuals suffering from AIDS and scholarships to school children.

Geographical Area of Activity: Mainly Thailand.

Finance: Total assets 7,245,551 Baht (2000).

Principal Staff: Dir Wanchai Juliasukon.

Address: 108/725-727 Soi Jangwattana 4, Jangwattana Rd, Bangkhen, Anusawaree, Bangkok 10220.

Telephone: (2) 970-0180; **Fax:** (2) 970-0812; **e-mail:** farm@a-net.net.th.

Foundation for Women

Founded in 1984 to support women's development, help women and children victimized by violence, and to promote and support women's rights and equality.

Activities: Provides grants to projects promoting women's rights and equality, and to organizations helping marginalized women, particularly in the North and North-East of Thailand. Also provides training for women and young people in the areas of violence against young people, women and their rights; provides technical assistance and temporary accommodation to women who have experienced violence; and carries out research and data collection activities on various kinds of problems affecting women, including female trafficking, as well as disseminating this information to government and private organizations.

Geographical Area of Activity: Thailand.

Publications: Newsletter.

Finance: Annual income approx. 3,000,000 Baht.

Principal Staff: Dir Dr Chalermsri Tammaboot.

Address: 35/267 Soi Charan, Sanitwong 62, Charan, Sanitwong Rd, Bang Yikan, Bang Plad, Bangkok 10700.

Telephone: (2) 433-5149; **Fax:** (2) 434-6774; **e-mail:** ssw@mozart.inet.co.th.

Dr Sem Foundation

Established in 1995 to help children and families affected by AIDS.

Activities: Provides education and training to children from AIDS-infected families, develops public information campaigns, trains teachers, teaches sanitation methods, as well as preventing and seeking solutions to problems such as drug abuse, homelessness amongst children, hunger and child prostitution. Operates a scholarship scheme. Also educates children in agricultural skills and introduces children to traditional Thai cultural values. Part of the Foundation's giving is co-ordinated through temples in Thailand.

Geographical Area of Activity: Thailand.

Finance: Total assets 7,245,551 Baht.

Principal Staff: Dir Chuchawal Pringpuangkeo.

Address: 255/164 Ban Lormnum, Moo 2, Tambon Nongpuang, Salapee Chiengmai 50140.

Telephone: (5) 342-3862; **Fax:** (5) 343-8017; **Internet:** www.cmnet.co.th/drsem; **e-mail:** semenx@chingagmai.anet.net.th.

Seub Nakhasathien Foundation

Founded in 1990 to promote the environment.

Activities: Operates in the field of conservation of forest and natural resources through providing youth training programmes, teacher training programmes, exhibitions on environmental issues, and campaigning on environmental and conservation issues.

Geographical Area of Activity: Thailand.

Publications: *Seub Journal*; leaflets; and strategy reports.

Finance: Annual revenue approx. 3,000,000 Baht.

Principal Staff: Man. Nittaya Wongsawat.

Address: 50 Kasetsart Alumni, Association Tower, Pahonyotin Rd, Ladyao, Chatuchag, Bangkok 10900.

Telephone: (2) 561-2469; **Fax:** (2) 561-2470; **Internet:** www.seub.or.th; **e-mail:** seub@internetksc.th.com.

Siam Society

Founded in 1904 to investigate and encourage the arts and sciences in relation to Thailand and its neighbouring countries.

Activities: Operates internationally in the fields of education, economic affairs, the arts and humanities, religion, international relations and the conservation of natural resources, through self-conducted programmes, research, grants to institutions and individuals, fellowships, scholarships, conferences, courses, publications and lectures. Maintains a library.

Geographical Area of Activity: South-East Asia.

Publications: *Journal of the Siam Society* (2 a year); *Natural History Bulletin* (2 a year); books; monographs; report of operations and financial statement.

Principal Staff: Pres. Bilaibhan Sampatisiri.

Address: 131 Asoke Rd, Sukhumvit 21, Bangkok 10110.

Telephone: (2) 661-6470; **Fax:** (2) 258-3491; **Internet:** www.siam-society.org; **e-mail:** info@siam-society.org.

Thai–Rath Newspaper Foundation

Originally founded in 1979 and approved as a public charity organization in 1999.

Activities: Oversees and supports 101 Thai–Rath Witthaya Schools, provides humanitarian relief and awards the Kampon Wacharapon prize for an outstanding journalistic thesis. Also carries out research, including research into the development of arithmetic studies for primary school children, as well as providing training to teachers.

Geographical Area of Activity: Thailand.

Finance: Total endowment approx. 25,000,000 Baht.

Principal Staff: Chair. Khun Ying Praneetsilp Vacharaphol.

Address: 1 Viphavadirangsit Rd, Bangkok 10900.

Telephone: (2) 272-1030; **Fax:** (2) 272-1754; **Internet:** www.thairath.co.th/foundation/mainE.html.

TISCO Foundation

Founded by the Tisco Group in 1982.

Activities: Provides support for social and economic development activities, through the award of scholarships, medical funding for patients in need, and grants for employment activities by poor people. Also provides humanitarian relief.

Geographical Area of Activity: Thailand.

Finance: Annual income approx. 10,000,000 Baht, total grants 7,500,000 (2001).

Principal Staff: Man. Pattira Wattanawarangkul.

Address: 48/11 Tisco Tower, 5th Floor, Sathorn Rd, Bangrak, Bangkok 10500.

Telephone: (2) 638-0555; **Fax:** (2) 638-0554; **Internet:** www.tiscogroup.com/tcabout_7.htm; **e-mail:** foundation@tisco.co.th.

Toyota Thailand Foundation

Established by the Toyota Company in Thailand in 1992.

Activities: Active in the fields of education, social welfare and community development in Thailand, through funding NGOs and training schemes. Projects include an initiative to encourage children to eat more green vegetables, provision of scholarships in engineering at the Institute of Traffic and Transport Engineering at Chulalongkorn University, support for orphans whose parents have died from AIDS and a programme to empower young women.

Geographical Area of Activity: Thailand.

Finance: Total assets approx. 250,000,000 Baht.

Principal Staff: Pres. Police Gen. Pao Sarasin.

Address: 186/1 Moo 1, Old Railway Rd, Sumrongtai, Prapadang, Samutprakarn.

Telephone: (2) 386-1590; **Fax:** (2) 384-7350; **Internet:** www.toyota.co.th/eng/contribution/foundation.asp; **e-mail:** tff@toyota.co.th.

Trinidad and Tobago

FOUNDATIONS, TRUSTS AND NON-PROFIT ORGANIZATIONS

Trinidad and Tobago Institute of International Affairs

Founded in 1964 by Dr George E. Dhanny for the study of international affairs.

Activities: The work of the Institute includes studies on North–South economic relations, and participation in international conferences. It co-operates with similar institutes abroad, particularly in the acquisition of publications for the library. Recent research interests and activities include: World Trade Organization (WTO) negotiations, New Lomé arrangements, free trade areas of the Americas negotiations, the United Nations system, and funding of UN peace-keeping forces.

Geographical Area of Activity: The Caribbean, Central and South America, Europe, the USA, South-East Asia and the Far East.

Publications: *Perspectives* (annually).

Finance: The work of the Institute is financed from membership fees and donations.

Principal Staff: Founder/Exec. Dir Dr George E. Dhanny.

Address: 105 Woodford St, Newtown, Port of Spain, Trinidad.

Telephone: 628-7623; **Fax:** 628-7623.

Turkey

FOUNDATION CENTRES AND CO-ORDINATING BODIES

Iktisadi Kalkinma Vakfi (Economic Development Foundation)

Founded in 1965 by the Istanbul Chamber of Commerce and the Istanbul Chamber of Industry, to contribute to Turkey's economic and social development.

Activities: Operates in the fields of economic affairs and international relations, by conducting or supervising research on Turkey's relations with economic groupings in the world, particularly the European Union (EU); and by formulating and expressing (in collaboration with other appropriate institutions) the point of view of the Turkish private sector on Turkish–EU relations. The Foundation also organizes conferences, seminars and courses with the aim of informing public opinion and training administrative staff in relevant skills. Maintains a library which is the depository library of EU publications in Turkey and a representative office in Brussels.

Geographical Area of Activity: Turkey.

Publications: Research reports; bulletin (every 4 months); magazine (every 2 months).

Principal Staff: Sec.-Gen. Dr Şebnem Karauçak; Research Man. Leyla Tunç Yeltin; Project and Publication Man. Aykin Alagöz; Senior Researcher Handan Soğuk.

Address: Rumeli Caddesi 85–87, 80220 Osmanbey, Istanbul.

Telephone: (212) 2307367; **Fax:** (212) 2477587; **Internet:** www.ikv.org.tr; **e-mail:** ikv@ikv.org.tr.

Third Sector Foundation of Turkey—TÜSEV

Established in 1993 to promote the development of the third sector in Turkey.

Activities: Operates as a foundation centre, to promote the development of philanthropy and civil society in Turkey. Facilitates grants for research projects, promotes giving and the establishment of foundations by individuals and companies, lobbies on behalf of the voluntary sector and represents the Turkish voluntary sector at international conferences and networks.

Geographical Area of Activity: Turkey.

Publications: *Turkish Foundations During the Republican Period. Directory of Member Foundations and Associations of the Third Sector Foundation of Turkey*; Annual Report; newsletter; financial statements; periodicals; monographs; and information brochures.

Principal Staff: Pres. Dr Üstün Ergüder; Vice-Pres. Namik Ceylanoglu.

Address: Bankalar Caddesi Minerva Han 2, Kat 5, 80020 Karakoy/Istanbul.

Telephone: (212) 2438309; **Fax:** (212) 2438305; **Internet:** www.tusev.org.tr/; **e-mail:** info@tusev.org.tr.

FOUNDATIONS, TRUSTS AND NON-PROFIT ORGANIZATIONS

Anatolian Development Foundation

Established in 1981 to promote sustainable rural development in the region of Anatolia (which covers areas in Turkey and Iraq); and to provide emergency aid, development and rehabilitation assistance to disaster-stricken and poor areas of Turkey, as well as Bosnia and Herzegovina, Kosovo and Macedonia.

Activities: Operates through education programmes in the fields of economic affairs, education, international affairs, law and human rights, and social welfare, to increase awareness of development and refugee issues; supports projects in the areas of agriculture, animal husbandry, health care and sanitation, education and training; and offers emergency relief to refugees and to those affected by natural disasters. Works through self-conducted programmes, and grants and fellowships. Offers humanitarian assistance to Bosnia and Herzegovina, Kosovo and Macedonia.

Geographical Area of Activity: Anatolia (areas of Turkey and Iraq), and South-Eastern Europe.

Publications: Annual Reports.

Finance: Net assets US $1,000,000 (2001).

Trustees: Dr Ahmet Akyürek; B. Akyürek; E. Kay; H. Özcan; S. Zeyrek.

Principal Staff: Pres. Dr Ahmet Akyürek.

Address: Atatürk Bulvari No 121/181, Bakanliklar, 06640 Ankara.

Telephone: (312) 4182668; **Fax:** (312) 4176728; **Internet:** www.akv.org.tr; **e-mail:** akv@marketweb.net.tr.

Arkadaş

Activities: An independent non-profit organization dedicated to environment and development issues such as wildlife, afforestation, developing countries, human rights, peace and disarmament; takes part in campaigns, lobbying and public awareness-raising; organizes seminars and conferences, training courses and field projects.

Geographical Area of Activity: International.

Principal Staff: Sec.-Gen. Yaşar Öztürk; Chair. Ümit Öztürk.

Address: İlhan Akgün Caddesi 12/C, 33960 Sílífke.

Telephone and Fax: (324) 7143726; **e-mail:** greenscreen@gn.apc.org.

Beyaz Nokta Vakfi (White Point Foundation)

Established in 1994 by Ishak Alaton, Faruk Ekina, Yohsel Domanic, Mimin Erlunt and Ibrahim Kocabaş to promote problem-solving in society.

Activities: Operates throughout Turkey in the field of education, through self-conducted programmes, research, prizes, conferences, training courses and publications. Projects include non-formal education for children unable to remain in the education system, a civic education project, a campaign to encourage responsible car driving and donations of science equipment to develop children's interest in science education.

Geographical Area of Activity: Turkey.

Restrictions: Grants to foundation members only.

Finance: Assets US $15,000 (2000); annual revenue $100,000, expenditure $90,000 (2001).

Trustees: M. Tinaz Titiz (Chair.); Dr Cemil Çahmakli (Vice-Chair.); Azmi Macun; Kamil Tanriverdi; Erol Aydin.

Principal Staff: Gen. Man. Güler Yüksel.

Address: Sair Nedim Sokak No 2/9 Bade Apt, 06690 Çankaya-Ankara.

Telephone: (312) 4414870; **Fax:** (312) 4415399; **Internet:** www.beyaznokta.org; **e-mail:** bnv@beyaznokta.org.tr.

Economic and Social History Foundation of Turkey

Established in 1991 by 264 members of the scientific and cultural community to create an archival and library collection of sources relating to the economic and cultural heritage of Turkey, and to promote historical study.

Activities: Operates in the area of history and the preservation of historical heritage, and the development of NGOs, nationally and internationally, through self-conducted programmes, research, conferences and publications. Co-operates with similar national and international organizations. Maintains an information and documentation centre, a liaison office in Ankara and an on-line database of Turkish NGOs.

Geographical Area of Activity: Turkey.

Publications: Books, magazines, journals and newsletters.

Board of Directors: S. Aksoy; A. S. Baban; A. Bartu; H. Bulutoğlu; Y. Gülöksüz; Ş Pamuk; O. Silier; Ö. Taner; İ. Tekeli; M. Tunçay; B. Ünal.

Principal Staff: Sec.-Gen. Orhan Silier.

Address: Val. Konaği C. Samsun, Apt No 57, 80200 Istanbul.

Telephone: (212) 2332161; **Fax:** (212) 2343290; **Internet:** www.tarihvakfi.org.tr; **e-mail:** tarihvakfi@tarihvakfi.org.tr.

Çevre Koruma ve Ambalaj Atiklari Degerlendirme Vakfi (Environment Protection and Packaging Waste Recovery and Recycling Trust)

Established in 1991 by a number of national and multinational companies to promote and organize economically efficient and environmentally friendly packaging, waste recovery and recycling based on the principle of co-responsibility.

Activities: Operates in the field of conservation and the environment, through research and training courses, and organizing national and international conferences.

Publications: Dönùsün (bulletin); Annual Report.

Finance: Total assets approx. US $400,000.

Principal Staff: Chair. Okyar Yaryalar; Sec.-Gen. Erol Metin.

Address: Cenap Şahabettin Sok, No. 94, Koşuyolu Kadiköy/Istanbul.

Telephone: (216) 4287890; **Fax:** (216) 4287895; **Internet:** www.cevko.org.tr; **e-mail:** cevko@cevko.org.tr.

Hisar Education Foundation

Established in December 1970 by a number of individuals to contribute to the implementation of advanced education systems in Turkey and to provide institutions of all levels with funds for grants, scholarships and equipment.

Activities: Operates nationally in the field of education, through self-conducted programmes, scholarships and fellowships, conferences, training courses and publications. As well as making educational grants to various schools, the Foundation runs its own primary school.

Geographical Area of Activity: Turkey.

Publications: *Educating Young Children.*

Finance: Net assets US $3,464,000 (1998).

Board of Directors: Feyyaz Berker (Pres.); Hüsnü Özyeğin (Vice-Pres.); Halis Komili (Sec.-Gen.); Oğuz Dağdelen; Oya Eczacibaşi; Muharrem Kayhan; Nihal Pulat.

Principal Staff: Gen. Co-ordinator Vedat Urul.

Address: Lale Sok., Bizimtepe Tesisleri 10/1 Kuruçeşme, 80820 Beşiktaş.

Telephone: (212) 2577009; **Fax:** (212) 2573000; **e-mail:** hisar1@hev.org.

The Human Resource Development Foundation—HRDF

Founded in 1988 by a number of people, to improve the quality of life of those living in Turkey, Azerbaijan and Kazakhstan; to contribute to social development; and to strengthen human resources in these areas.

Activities: Operates in Turkey, Azerbaijan and Kazakhstan in the fields of education, health care (including family planning), human rights and social welfare. The Foundation implements programmes including field projects, training and surveys which are supported by donor organizations.

Geographical Area of Activity: Turkey, Azerbaijan and Kazakhstan.

Publications: A number of publications (books, bulletins, leaflets, newsletters and training manuals) in Turkish on reproductive health and sex education; some manuals are available in Azeri and Russian.

Finance: Annual revenue US $491,000, expenditure $491,000 (2001).

Trustees: Dr Türkiz Gökgöl; Turgut Tokus; Prof. Dr Olcay Neyzi; Hasip Buldanlioglu; Prof. Dr Aysen Bulut; Nuray Fincancioglu; Demet Güral.

Principal Staff: Exec. Dir Dr Demet Güral.

Address: Yenicarsi Caddesi 54, Beyoglu 80050 Istanbul.

Telephone: (212) 2931605; **Fax:** (212) 2931009; **e-mail:** ikgv@ikgv.org.

Human Rights Foundation of Turkey

Founded in 1990 to provide medical treatment and rehabilitation for survivors of torture and to document human rights violations in Turkey.

Activities: Operates nationally and internationally in the fields of law and human rights, and medicine and health, through self-conducted programmes, research, conferences, training courses and publications.

Publications: *Human Rights in Turkey* (monthly reports); and special reports.

Finance: Funding is provided by the United Nations, European Union and the Red Cross (q.v.).

Trustees: Yavuz Önen (Pres.); Selim Öker (Sec.-Gen.); and seven others.

Address: Menekse 2 Şokak 16/5, 06640 Kızılay, Ankara.

Telephone: (312) 4177180; **Fax:** (312) 4254552; **Internet:** www.tihv.org.tr; **e-mail:** tihv@tr-neth.

IHH Humanitarian Relief Foundation

Established in 1995 by Bülent Yildirim and Mehmet Köse to support any person victimized by conflict or disaster.

Activities: Operates in the areas of aid to less-developed countries, education, law and human rights, medicine and health, and social welfare, by making grants to individuals, offering scholarships, carrying out emergency relief, and defending human rights.

Geographical Area of Activity: South-Eastern Europe, Central Asia, the Middle East, Africa and the Far East.

Publications: Annual Report; booklets.

Trustees: Mehmet Köse; Hüseyin Oruç; Murat Yaş; Ahmet Kaskin; Murat Yilmaz; Osman Atalay; Sedat Beyhan.

Address: Büyük Karaman Caddesi Taylasan sokak, No 3, 34230 Fatih/Istanbul.

Telephone: (212) 6312965; **Fax:** (212) 6217051; **Internet:** www.ihh.org.tr; **e-mail:** info@ihh.org.tr.

International Blue Crescent

Established in 1999 to provide humanitarian relief in Turkey and world-wide to alleviate human suffering caused by war, hunger, natural disasters, environmental problems and disease.

Activities: Operates humanitarian relief programmes in Central and South-Eastern Europe, Central Asia, the Middle

East and Africa, including the provision of food, medical supplies, educational materials and clothing; redevelopment projects in disaster areas; and infrastructure projects.

Geographical Area of Activity: International.

Principal Staff: Pres. Recep Üker; Vice-Pres. Muzaffer Baca.

Address: Bostanci Cami St, Cesur Apt 11/3, 81110 Bostanci, Istanbul.

Telephone: (216) 4646881; **Fax:** (216) 3615745; **Internet:** www.bluecrescent.net; **e-mail:** ibc@bluecrescent.net.

Turkish Family Health and Planning Foundation

Established in 1985 by Vehbi Koç to increase the quality and accessibility of reproductive health-care information and services for women in Turkey.

Activities: Operates nationally in the fields of women's and children's health care, reproductive health and family planning, and the enhancement of women's status in society. Publishes information, holds conferences and engages in projects in order to carry out its mission.

Geographical Area of Activity: Turkey.

Finance: Assets US $1,350,000 (1999); annual revenue and expenditure $650,000 (1999).

Directors: Feyyaz Berker; Prof. Dr Baran Tuncer; Bülent Eczacibaş; Prof. Dr Selçuk Erez; Şinasi Ertan; Necati İkizoğlu; Dr Nuran Kandemir; Erdoğan Karakoyunlu; Suna Kiraç; H. Ayduk Koray; Hüsnü M. Özyeğin.

Principal Staff: Exec. Dir Yaşar Yaşer.

Address: Güzel Konutlar Sitesi, A Blok D:3–4, Ulus Mahallesi, 80600 Etiler, Istanbul.

Telephone: (212) 2577941; **Fax:** (212) 2577943; **Internet:** www.tapv.org.tr; **e-mail:** info@tapv.org.tr.

Turkish Foundation for combatting Soil Erosion, for Reforestation and the Protection of Natural Habitats

Established in 1992 to draw attention to soil erosion, land degradation and their associated effects.

Activities: Operates in Turkey through supporting projects such as education programmes, local conservation and development, rural development and land rehabilitation, as well as lobbying for sustainable policies and collaborating with similar NGOs and government agencies.

Geographical Area of Activity: Turkey.

Publications: Annual report.

Finance: Financed by membership subscriptions; annual budget approx. US $2,000,000.

Board of Directors: Nihat Gökyigit (Chair.); Hayrettin Karaca (Chair. Board of Trustees); Ümit Y. Gürses (Gen. Dir).

Principal Staff: Gen. Dir Ümit Y. Gürses.

Address: PK 213 Levent, 80620 Istanbul.

Telephone: (212) 2837816; **Fax:** (212) 2811132; **Internet:** www.tema.org.tr; **e-mail:** tema@tema.org.tr.

Türkiye Çevre Vakfi (Environment Foundation of Turkey)

Founded in 1978 by Dr Cevdet Aykan, Serbülent Bingöl, Muslih Fer, Ertuğrul Soysal, Prof. Dr Necmi Sönmez, Engin Ural and Altan Zeki Ünver, to establish a documentation centre on the environmental problems of Turkey and of other countries; to prepare and release articles and programmes for the mass media; to sponsor, carry out and publish research on environmental issues; to co-operate with institutions in other countries dealing with environmental problems; and to play an advocacy role in promoting the quality of the environment.

Activities: Operates in the field of conservation and the environment, through research, organizing national and international conferences and seminars, publications, environmental advice, promoting public awareness of environmental issues, and co-operation with the media and with international organizations. Maintains a library. Grants scholarships to Turkish university students studying in Turkey.

Geographical Area of Activity: Central Asia and the Black Sea region.

Restrictions: Grants made only to specific NGOs working in Central Asia and the Black Sea region.

Publications: Newsletter (quarterly, in Turkish); books on the environment.

Finance: Net assets approx. US $650,000 (2002); expenditure approx. $340,000 (2002).

Trustees: Turgut Tokuş (Chair.); Engin Ural (Sec.-Gen.); Dr Cemil Özgül; Ali Padir; Prof. Dr Yüksel Öztan.

Principal Staff: Sec.-Gen. Engin Ural.

Address: Tunali Hilmi Caddesi 50/20, 06660 Ankara.

Telephone: (312) 4255508; **Fax:** (312) 4185118; **Internet:** www.cevre.org; **e-mail:** cevre@cevre.org.

Türkiye Kalkinma Vakfi (Development Foundation of Turkey)

Founded in 1969 to alleviate poverty and improve the quality of life among resource-poor rural families, through small-scale agricultural investment projects and agricultural vocational training.

Activities: The Foundation develops and manages a wide range of agricultural development programmes in five regions of rural Turkey. Two of its programmes, bee-keeping development and broiler production, have become national programmes. Others include dairy farming, introduction of fodder crops, work with fruit and vegetables, sericulture improvement, development of small-scale irrigation schemes, introduction of better-yielding varieties of wheat, combating internal and external parasites in sheep, and assistance to rural communities in cheese production. The Foundation manages centres for training young women in rug-weaving, and assists with the marketing of the rugs. Many of the projects involve supervision of credits provided by the Agricultural Bank to participating farmers. The Foundation maintains regional offices.

Geographical Area of Activity: Eastern and South-Eastern Turkey.

Publications: *TKV Bulletin* (monthly); *Mellifera* (annually); books and reports on specific areas of activity.

Finance: Funds are derived from the Turkish Government, institutions and individuals in Turkey, Europe and the USA, bilateral technical assistance programmes with Germany and Switzerland, and loans from national and international agencies.

Board of Trustees: Altan Ünver (Chair.).

Principal Staff: Gen. Man. Önder Topaç.

Address: Kirkpinar Sokak 20/6, 06540 Çankaya, Ankara.

Telephone: (312) 4404500; **Fax:** (312) 4404232; **Internet:** www.tkv-dft.org; **e-mail:** tkvinfo@ktg.com.tr.

Umut Foundation

Established in 1993 to promote conflict resolution and peace.

Activities: The Foundation operates in Europe (especially South-Eastern Europe), the Middle East and Turkey, promoting peaceful conflict resolution, helping young people develop strong leadership skills, promoting the rule of law and co-operating with similar NGOs.

Geographical Area of Activity: Turkey, South-Eastern Europe and the Middle East.

Publications: *Who's Who in Europe in the Science and Art of Peace and Reconciliation; Terror and Struggle Against Organised Crime*; Monographs.

Board of Directors: Nazire Dedeman (Pres.); Fikeet Ilkiz; Özben Önal; Sibel Savoci; Prof. Dr Ilter Turan.

Principal Staff: Co-ordinator Tanzer Gezer.

Address: Yildizposta Caddesi 52, Esentepe, 80700 Istanbul.

Telephone: (212) 2757600; **Fax:** (212) 2886675; **Internet:** www.umut.org.tr; **e-mail:** vakif@umut.org.tr.

Vehbi Koç Vakfi (Vehbi Koç Foundation)

Founded in 1969 by Vehbi Koç, and supported by Koç Holding SA (q.v.), for the allocation of financial support in education, medicine, culture and related areas.

Activities: Operates nationally in the fields of education, social welfare, science, arts and culture, and medicine and health, through research, conferences, courses, seminars, lectures, awards, scholarships and travel grants. Provides grants for social welfare, buildings and medical equipment for hospitals in Turkey. Supports public museums, including the Sadberk Hanim Müzesi, which exhibits collections in the fields of ethnography, archaeology and artistic cultural traditions; the Rahim H. Koç Museum, the first Turkish museum to be devoted to the history of technology and industry; and the Suna-Inan Kiraç Research Institute on Mediterranean Civilisations, which researches archaeology and indigenous cultures. Also funds the building of schools, established the Koç University, as well as funding the Vehbi Koç Professorship of Turkish Studies at Harvard University's Faculty of Arts and Sciences. In 1990 the Tofaş Fiat Fund was created in conjunction with the Turkey Fiat Group to provide scholarships to students in Italy and Turkey, to support conservation work and to sponsor bilingual (Italian and Turkish) art publications.

Geographical Area of Activity: Mainly Turkey and Western Europe.

Finance: Receives donations from Koç group companies. Total assets €229,373,015 (2001); total expenditure €44,425,017 (2001).

Board of Trustees: Semahat Arsel (Chair.); Rahmi M. Koç (Vice-Chair.); Aydin Bolak (Vice-Chair.); Evren Artam; Temel Atay; Prof. Dr Mahmut Birsel; Prof. Dr Üstün Ergüder; Sevgi Gönül; Suna Kiraç; Ersin Özince.

Principal Staff: Gen. Sec. Inal Avci; Gen. Man. Erdal Yidirim.

Address: Nakkaptepe, Azizbey Sokak No. 1, Kuzguncuk, 81207 Istanbul.

Telephone: (216) 5310000; **Fax:** (216) 5310099; **Internet:** www.vkv.org.tr; **e-mail:** info@vkv.org.tr.

Ukraine

FOUNDATION CENTRES AND CO-ORDINATING BODIES

GURT Resource Centre for NGO Development

Established to promote the development of civil society in Ukraine.

Activities: Aims to assist in the infrastructural development of the third sector in Ukraine, through providing information and support, including technical support, maintaining databases, organizing training workshops, advisory services, and publishing. New initiatives include a Ukrainian NGO training centre, a Black Sea Regional NGO Conference and the development of a volunteer centre. In 2002 launched a lobbying programme supported by the Westminster Foundation for Democracy (q.v.), aiming to increase participation of NGOs in local policy and decision-making processes, enhance social partnership practices in civil society, and raise the level of NGOs' transparency and accountability.

Geographical Area of Activity: Ukraine.

Publications: *Nova Hromada* (magazine); *How to Establish NGOs in Ukraine; The Third Sector in Ukraine and Organizations that Promote its Development; Using Media in Lobbying and Marketing Campaigns*; database of Ukrainian NGOs.

Principal Staff: Dir Bohdan Maslych.

Address: 01025 Kiev, POB 126.

Telephone: (44) 552-1052; **Fax:** (44) 551-6339; **Internet:** www.gurt.org.ua; **e-mail:** info@gurt.org.ua.

Innovation and Development Centre—IDC

Established in 1996.

Activities: Operates as an information centre on the development of the third sector in Ukraine, through issuing publications and the operation of an e-mail service, Ukrainian NGO Net. Publications give information on grants offered by international and local organizations, events and other publications concerning NGOs, foundations and charities operating in Ukraine. Also provides support to local organizations. Priority programmes include Kindness and Respect; Kids of Chernobyl; Natural Disaster Relief; and Domestic Violence Prevention.

Geographical Area of Activity: Ukraine.

Publications: *Third Sector* (weekly, in Ukrainian); *Crossroads* (every 2 months, in Ukrainian); *Account of non-profit organizations* (every 2 months, in Ukranian); various books on non-profit management.

Finance: Receives donations from individuals and corporations; total grants US$740,000 (2002).

Board of Trustees: Mink Mullay (Chair.); Andriy Haidamashko; Oleksander Sydozenko.

Principal Staff: Dir Oleksander Sydozenko.

Address: 01023 Kiev, Esplanadna St 28, Office 6.

Telephone and Fax: (44) 248-7239; **Internet:** www.idc.org.ua; **e-mail:** idc@idc.org.ua.

FOUNDATIONS, TRUSTS AND NON-PROFIT ORGANIZATIONS

Dr F. P. Haaz Social Assistance Foundation

Established in 1987 in memory of Dr F. P. Haaz to provide assistance to elderly and disabled people and all those in need of social assistance.

Activities: Involved in helping the development of legal reforms in Ukraine in support of elderly people, people with disabilities and others in need. Has also established the Mother Marie Mercy Center, the Janush Corchak Rehabilitation Institute for Children with Mental Handicaps, the Alexander Men Philanthropical College, the Humanist Youth Charity Society and the Socio-psychological Assistance Center.

Geographical Area of Activity: Ukraine.

Publications: *Charter of Odessa; Comments on the Constitution of Ukraine; A Legal Weapon for Ukrainian Civil Society;* other reports.

Finance: Annual revenue 300,000 hrivnas (2000), expenditure 385,000 hrivnas (2000).

Principal Staff: Pres. A. G. Muchnik; Vice-Pres L. G. Bogomolova, G. B. Tsyrfa.

Address: 650023 Odesa, 68 Pushkinskaya St.

Telephone: (482) 22-67-46; **Fax:** (482) 34-62-08; **Internet:** haaz.com.od.ua; **e-mail:** fsp@eurocom.od.ua.

Information Society of Ukraine Fund

Set up to promote the development and support of the Ukrainian nation's intellectual potential.

Activities: Operates in co-operation with NGOs, state institutions and private companies in the areas of IT (information technology) education, IT business and society development. The Fund acts as a consultant to NGOs as well as providing technical and material support. Projects include Internet Education for Teachers, training teachers in the use of information technology; an on-line experts' council; and Computers for Schools, which aims to provide schools throughout Ukraine with new and used computers.

Geographical Area of Activity: Ukraine.

Principal Staff: Pres. Andrey Koloduke; Exec. Dir Evgeni Drobkov.

Address: 04053 Kiev, 83A Melnykova St.

Telephone: (44) 213-3352; **Internet:** www.isu.org.ua; **e-mail:** isu@isu.org.ua.

International Renaissance Foundation (Ukraine)

Founded in March 1990 to support the transformation of Ukraine into a free, pluralistic and independent state, tolerant of diversity, and based on the rule of law and a free market system, integrated into the modern world. The Foundation is an independent Foundation, part of the Soros foundations network.

Activities: Operates, with an emphasis on education, civil society, culture, information and the media and youth, in the fields of the arts and humanities, conservation and the environment, economic affairs, education, law and human rights, medicine and health, science and technology, and social welfare, through self-conducted programmes, scholarships and fellowships, conferences and training courses, grants to individuals and institutions, and issuing publications.

Geographical Area of Activity: Ukraine.

Finance: Annual expenditure US $6,544,000 (2001).

Board of Directors: Hryhoriy Nemyria (Chair.); Roman Zyvarych; Mridula Ghosh; Aleksander Pakhaver; Mykola Knyazhytsky.

Principal Staff: Exec. Dir Yevhen Bystrysky.

Address: 04053 Kiev, 46 Artema vul.

Telephone: (44) 461-9709; **Fax:** (44) 216-7629; **Internet:** www.irf.kiev.ua; **e-mail:** irf@irf.kiev.ua.

United Kingdom

FOUNDATION CENTRES AND CO-ORDINATING BODIES

Allavida—Alliances for Voluntary Initiatives and Development

Allavida aims to provide the resources—funding, skills and information—that people and organizations working for the development of their communities need in order to achieve their own objectives. It was formed in 2001 by the merger of Charity Know How and Alliance magazine, both of which were formerly part of CAF—Charities Aid Foundation (q.v.). Charity Know How, in the period 1991–2001, made some 2,500 grants towards increasing the skills, knowledge and experience of NGOs and community organizations throughout Central and Eastern Europe and the countries of the former USSR.

Activities: Allavida has closed its main grants programme (incorporating the general, partnership development and global grants programmes) and was to conduct a consultation exercise in 2003 to decide on future grant-making activity. It is likely that future grant programmes will operate in the regions where Allavida currently runs longer-term programmes, including Bosnia, Croatia, Kenya, Romania and Serbia.

Geographical Area of Activity: Probably South-East Europe, East Africa, Russia and Central Asia.

Restrictions: Currently no grants available.

Publications: *Alliance* (quarterly journal); *Corporate Community Involvement: Philanthropy or Self-interest?;* Country Reports; Annual Report; Guidelines for Applicants; Leaflet; Application Form.

Finance: Funded by a variety of trusts and foundations. Grants disbursed £49,000 (2001–02).

Principal Staff: Dir Andrew Kingman.

Address: 55 Bondway, London SW8 1SJ.

Telephone: (20) 7735-8006; **Fax:** (20) 7735-7608; **Internet:** www.allavida.org; **e-mail:** enquiries@allavida.org.

Association of Charitable Foundations

Formed in September 1989 to support the work of charitable grant-making trusts and foundations. The Association aims to improve the understanding of trusts and foundations among grant-seekers and the general public; to promote communication and co-operation between trusts, foundations and funders; to encourage philanthropy and the development of new grant-making foundations; and to influence policy-making.

Activities: The Association is a membership organization, in which full voting membership is open to any charitable organization based in the United Kingdom whose principal function is grant-making, supported by income from property or another assured source (except for grants from government or other grant-making trusts). Associate membership is open to other grant-makers. In 2002 there were over 300 members. The Association's activities include lobbying for public policy and legislation affecting grant-making charities; conducting seminars and conferences; liaising with government departments concerned with grant-making and with other organizations of the voluntary sector; assisting individuals and corporations planning to set up new foundations; and research. Member foundations convene interest groups on areas such as the arts, education, the environment, housing, international funding and Northern Ireland. Current initiatives include the Association's Philanthropy UK project, co-funded by the Esmée Fairbairn Foundation, the Gatsby Charitable Foundation and the Lloyds TSB Foundation for England and Wales (qq.v.). The Association also maintains contacts with a variety of relevant bodies in the USA, Europe, Australia and elsewhere, and with WINGS and the European Foundation Centre (qq.v.).

Geographical Area of Activity: United Kingdom.

Restrictions: Does not make grants, nor does it give individual advice to grant-seeking organizations or individuals.

Publications: *Trust and Foundation News* (quarterly); *Good Grant-Making—a practical guide* (1993); *Fairness in Funding: an equal opportunities guide for grant-makers* (1995); *Monitoring and Evaluation: a practical guide for grant-making trusts* (1998) *Voluntary Sector Infrastructure—the issues for grant-making trusts* (1999); and several other publications.

Finance: Net assets £57,865 (Dec. 2000); annual revenue £520,899, expenditure £524,622 (2000).

Principal Staff: Chair. Shirley Turner; Chief Exec. Nigel Siederer; Deputy Chief Exec. Bernie Morgan; Treas. David Green.

Address: 2 Plough Yard, Shoreditch High St, London EC2A 3LP.

Telephone: (20) 7422-8600; **Fax:** (20) 7422-8606; **Internet:** www.acf.org.uk; **e-mail:** acf@acf.org.uk.

Association of Medical Research Charities

Founded in 1972 to promote medical research in the United Kingdom.

Activities: Represents the interests of its members; promotes medical research and the advancement of charities conducting medical research; and encourages co-operation between member charities. Maintains an on-line medical research funding guide. The Association currently has 110 member charities.

Geographical Area of Activity: United Kingdom.

Publications: *The Association of Medical Research Charities Handbook.*

Executive Council: Dame Bridget Ogilvie (Chair.); Pamela Goldberg (Vice-Chair.); James Brook Turner (Hon. Treas.); F. Keith Cowey; Rick Fuller; Dr Richard Harvey; Dr Trevor A Hince; Fergus Logan; Betty McBride; Delyth Morgan; Simon Moore; Dr John Toy.

Principal Staff: Chief Exec. Diana Garnham.

Address: 61 Gray's Inn Rd, London WC1X 8TL.

Telephone: (20) 7269-8820; **Fax:** (20) 7269-8821; **Internet:** www.amrc.org.uk; **e-mail:** info@amrc.org.uk.

CAF—Charities Aid Foundation

Established in its original form in 1924 as part of the National Council of Social Service; launched as an independent foundation in 1974, under a Declaration of Trust between the NCSS (now the National Council for Voluntary Organisations, q.v.) and the Trustees of the Foundation; aims to increase the resources available to the voluntary sector.

Activities: Operates the CharityCard Account scheme for private and corporate donors, giving them greater flexibility when donating tax-effectively. Also manages Give As You

Earn, the payroll deduction scheme, and a comprehensive information service offering data on all areas of charitable activities. These services are used by about 350,000 individuals and 6,000 companies. Services offered to charities include banking, investment and administration designed to meet the specific needs of charities. Publishes research findings and statistics concerning the voluntary sector. Organizes annual conferences on matters of current concern to charities and voluntary organizations. All CAF surpluses are distributed in grants, throughout the voluntary sector. CAF maintains a number of overseas offices.

Geographical Area of Activity: United Kingdom, Europe, Southern, East and West Africa, the USA, India and Australia.

Restrictions: No grants to indivduals.

Publications: *Dimensions of the Voluntary Sector*; and numerous other publications on the non-profit sector.

Finance: Funds under CAF management £1,200,000,000 (Jan. 2001).

Trustees: Sir Brian Jenkins (Chair.); B. Buse; Ian D. R. Campbell; Sir Tim Chessells; Lord Dahrendorf; Sylvia Denman; Stuart Etherington; Kenneth G. Faircloth; Roger Lyons; Ian Macgregor; Rt Rev. A. W. Morgan; Dr J. Martin Owen; Prof. Naomi Sargant; Lady Tumim.

Principal Staff: Chief Exec. Stephen Ainger.

Address: Kings Hill, West Malling ME19 4TA.

Telephone: (1732) 520000; **Fax:** (1732) 520001; **Internet:** www.cafonline.org; **e-mail:** enquiries@cafonline.org.

Charities Advisory Trust

Founded in 1979 to promote the effective use of resources by charities and to advise on charity trading.

Activities: Operates in the above areas and also runs CARD AID, Museum Stores and a hotel in India, from which all profits go to charitable and environmental projects in India, as well as hosting training courses for UK NGO professionals in development policy. Also makes small grants of up to £200 to projects within the UK and internationally in a variety of areas including homelessness, cancer research and relief, physical and learning disabilities, peace and reconciliation, work with refugees, and museums and the arts.

Geographical Area of Activity: Mainly United Kingdom and India.

Restrictions: No grants to individuals, large fundraising organizations or to missionary charities.

Publications: *The Charity Shops Handbook; Charities, Trading and the Law; Trading by Charities: a Statistical Analysis.*

Address: Radius Works, Back Lane, London NW3 1HL.

Telephone: (20) 7794-9835; **Fax:** (20) 7431-3739; **Internet:** www.charitiesadvisorytrust.co.uk; **e-mail:** people@charitiesadvisorytrust.co.uk.

Community Foundation Network

Set up in 1991 as the support organization for United Kingdom community foundations and formerly known as the Association of Community Trusts and Foundations.

Activities: Works to promote the concept of community foundations (as organizations that encourage philanthropy, identify local needs and make grants), to stimulate their growth and development, and provide information and practical support. The grant programme managed by the Network and delivered by community foundations currently concentrates on isolation and access, aspirations and experiences, economic disadvantage, and children's voices.

Geographical Area of Activity: United Kingdom.

Restrictions: Members (community foundations) make grants to voluntary and community groups within their own areas. Network grants only available to community foundations.

Publications: *Changing the Future: community foundations and grant-making;* Newsletter (quarterly); Annual Review; manuals; information sheets; publications list.

Finance: Total grant budget for Network supported grant programme approx. £18,000,000 (2002–03).

Trustees: George Hepburn (Chair.); Sir John Weston (Pres.).

Principal Staff: Operations Man. Allan Brown; Asst Dir Network Services Clare Brooks; Asst Dir Development Karen Summer.

Address: Swallow House, 11 Northdown St, London N1 9BN.

Telephone: (20) 7713-9326; **Fax:** (20) 7713-9327; **Internet:** www.communityfoundations.org.uk; **e-mail:** network@communityfoundations.org.uk.

Disasters Emergency Committee

Established in 1963 to provide support for relief sector charities in the United Kingdom dealing with the effects of major overseas disasters.

Activities: Operates through providing an accredited national forum for fundraising and a focal point for public response, facilitating co-operation, co-ordination and communication, and ensuring that funds are used effectively and properly. The Committee has a Rapid Response Network of partners which provide free facilities as and when required, comprising television and radio, the banking sector, Consignia (formerly the Post Office), regional and national telephone companies, and a range of organizations in the corporate sector. The aid agencies which meet the Committee's membership criteria are Actionaid (q.v.), CAFOD, CARE International, Christian Aid, Concern Universal, MERLIN, Oxfam, Save the Children, Tearfund, British Red Cross Society and World Vision (qq.v.), and Help the Aged.

Geographical Area of Activity: International.

Publications: *DEC Policy Handbook; Annual Review 2002.*

Finance: The Committee is funded by voluntary donations and grants from its member agencies. Total assets £9,290,961 (March 2002); total income £7,172,211, expenditure £16,013,302 (2002).

Board of Trustees : David Glencross (Chair.); the Chief Executives of all member agencies; and up to four independent trustees.

Principal Staff: Chief Exec. Brendan Gormley; Appeals Man. Patricia Sanders.

Address: 15 Warren Mews, London W1T 6AZ.

Telephone: (20) 7387-0200; **Fax:** (20) 7387-2050; **Internet:** www.dec.org.uk; **e-mail:** info@dec.org.uk.

International NGO Training and Research Centre—INTRAC

Founded to provide specialist training, research and consultancy services to organizations involved in international development and relief.

Activities: The Centre promotes improved organizational and management capacity for NGOs, carries out research and conducts analyses of global NGO trends, and supports the development of the NGO sector. Institutional development programmes operate in Central Asia and Malawi. The Linking Programme promotes relationships between NGOs and NGO support organizations; partners in the Linking Programme work in Kazakhstan, Malawi, South Africa, Colombia, Kenya, Krygyzstan, Pakistan and India. Also works with local support organizations in Central and Eastern Europe.

Geographical Area of Activity: Central Asia, countries of the former USSR, Malawi and Central and Eastern Europe.

Restrictions: Does not make grants.

Publications: *ONTRAC* (newsletter, 3 a year); Annual Report; publications on issues affecting NGOs in development; occasional paper series; resource materials.

Finance: Total income £1,227,166, total expenditure £1,157,599 (March 2002).

Board of Trustees: Jonathan Benthall (Chair.); Anne Coles (Vice-Chair.); James Rowland (Treas.); Derek Roebuck (Co. Sec.).

Principal Staff: Exec. Dir Brian Pratt; Dir of Finance Peter Howlett; Dir of Training and Capacity Building Brenda Lipson.

Address: POB 563, Oxford OX2 6RZ.

Telephone: (1865) 201851; **Fax:** (1865) 201852; **Internet:** www.intrac.org; **e-mail:** info@intrac.org.

National Council for Voluntary Organisations—NCVO

Founded in 1919 as the National Council of Social Service to promote the systematic organization of voluntary social work, both nationally and locally. It is an independent charity, which acts as a resource centre for voluntary organizations and protects the interests and independence of voluntary organizations.

Activities: NCVO promotes the cause of the voluntary sector, working to increase its effectiveness, identify unmet needs and encourage initiatives to meet them. It represents over 1,700 national organizations, comprising large charities and also small organizations involved in all areas of voluntary and social action. It also has links with other voluntary bodies and groups, government departments, local authorities, the European Union and the business sector. NCVO provides advice, consultancy and support for trustees and staff of voluntary organizations on a range of issues, to help organizations work more effectively. It also provides information and advice, holds conferences and seminars, and publishes books, reports and a monthly magazine.

Geographical Area of Activity: United Kingdom.

Publications: Annual Report; *Voluntary Sector* (monthly); *Voluntary Agencies Directory* (annually); departmental productions; NCVO Publications is the publishing imprint of NCVO and publishes a range of books on issues affecting the voluntary sector.

Governing Board: Lord Plant of Highfield (Pres.); Winifred Tumim (Chair.).

Principal Staff: Chief Exec. Stuart Etherington; Head of Publications Maria Kane.

Address: Regent's Wharf, 8 All Saints St, London N1 9RL.

Telephone: (20) 7713-6161; **Fax:** (20) 7713-6300; **Internet:** www.ncvo-vol.org.uk; **e-mail:** ncvo@ncvo-vol.org.uk.

FOUNDATIONS, TRUSTS AND NON-PROFIT ORGANIZATIONS

1990 Trust

Established to promote good race relations nationally.

Activities: Operates in the United Kingdom and Europe, aiming to improve social and economic development for people of Asian, Caribbean and African origin, and to highlight policies which enhance or adversely affect good race relations. Provides training and consultancy services on a range of race-related issues, carries out research and policy work, and supports community interaction through conference support and convening meetings. Also provides an electronic resource through its web pages, which aims to be the most extensive electronic repository of information on issues that affect the lives of African, Asian, and Caribbean communities in Europe and the world.

Geographical Area of Activity: Europe.

Publications: *Black to Black* (newsletter, quarterly); *Forward* (report, every 3 years).

Principal Staff: Chair. Rita Patel; Chandra Pamar.

Address: Suite 12, Winchester House, 9 Cranmer Rd, London SW9 6EJ.

Telephone: (20) 7582-1990; **Fax:** (870) 1277657; **Internet:** www.blink.org.uk; **e-mail:** blink1990@blink.org.uk.

ActionAid

Founded in 1972 by Cecil Jackson Cole, ActionAid works in partnership with poor people to eradicate poverty by overcoming the injustice and inequity that cause it.

Activities: Works directly with poor communities and through local partner organizations in 40 countries of Africa, Asia, Central and South America and the Caribbean to improve access to food, water, education, health care, shelter and a livelihood. These programmes are designed to address the underlying causes of poverty by helping poor people to recognize, promote and secure their basic rights. It runs three major international campaigns: food, education and HIV/AIDS. There are regional offices in Guatemala, India, Thailand and Zimbabwe, and offices in Washington, DC and Brussels. ActionAid UK and its sister organizations in France, Greece, Ireland, Italy and Spain form the ActionAid Alliance.

Geographical Area of Activity: Africa, Asia, Central and South America and the Caribbean.

Restrictions: Grants only to approved partner organizations.

Publications: *Common Cause* (twice yearly supporters' magazine); Annual Report and accounts; educational and campaigning resources; training packages; and a range of videos and other publications.

Finance: Annual revenue £68,100,000 expenditure £71,900,000 (2001).

Trustees: Ken Burnett (Chair); Dawn Airey; Mary Kaphweleza Bandy; Richard Blackburn; Robert Chambers; Gonzalo Crespi de Valldaura; Anna Feuchtwang; Candido Gryzbowski; Prof. Barbara Harriss-White; Noerine Kaleeba; David Lammy; Janie Ligon; Peter Moore; Dr Roshi Naidoo; M. Ramaswami.

Principal Staff: Chief Exec. Salil Shetty; Dir of Finance Nigel Saxby-Soffe.

Address: Hamlyn House, Macdonald Rd, London N19 5PG.

Telephone: (20) 7561-7561; **Fax:** (20) 7272-0899; **Internet:** www.actionaid.org; **e-mail:** mail@actionaid.org.uk.

The Sylvia Adams Charitable Trust

Established in 1995 to make grants to charities working to alleviate poverty and disease, in particular among children, and to support charities working with the homeless, projects in developing countries, health education and hospitals.

Activities: Provides start-up, time-limited and matched funding for specific projects. Fifty per cent of grants are made to United Kingdom charities, and 50% to organizations working overseas, particularly in Africa, South America and the Indian subcontinent.

Geographical Area of Activity: United Kingdom, and Africa, Southern Asia and South America.

Restrictions: No grants are made to individuals.

Finance: Annual revenue £812,976, expenditure £940,986 (March 2001).

Principal Staff: Dir Kate Baldwin.

Address: Sylvia Adams House, 24 The Common, Hatfield, AL10 0NB.

Telephone: (1707) 259-259; **Fax:** (1707) 259-268; **e-mail:** kate.baldwin@virgin.net.

Afghanaid

Established in 1981 to provide humanitarian relief to Afghans in hardship and distress, and to assist with the rehabilitation and development of Afghanistan.

Activities: Operates in Afghanistan through major infrastructure work such as building and maintaining roads and bridges; macro-irrigation structures; and sustainable community development projects, including agriculture, microfinance, income generation, health education for women, animal health, and women's resource centres.

Geographical Area of Activity: Afghanistan.

Restrictions: Currently funding its own projects only.

Publications: Annual Report; regular newsletters.

Finance: Annual revenue £2,322,802, expenditure £1,943,416 (March 2001).

Trustees: Alastair Pitcairn (Chair.); Elizabeth Winter (Vice-Chair.); Ian Anderson; Barbara Bubb; Jonathan Goodhand; David Page; Tigger Stack.

Principal Staff: Man. Dir Brian Smith; UK Dir and Co. Sec. Fraser Mackay.

Address: 16 Mortimer St, 2nd Floor, London W1N 7RD.

Telephone: (20) 7255-3355; **Fax:** (20) 7255-3344; **Internet:** www.afghanaid.org.uk; **e-mail:** info@afghanaid.org.uk.

Africa Educational Trust

Founded in 1958 by Sir Alexander Carr-Saunders, K. E. Robinson, K. Kirkwood, P. J. A. Calvocoressi, R. A. Oliver, G. M. Scott and C. Legum, to support education in and outside Africa, for persons who, in the opinion of the trustees, are wholly or partly of African descent, and to advise on educational immigration and welfare provisions for African students.

Activities: Offers individual scholarships for study in the United Kingdom or Ireland to students and refugees from Africa. Students are selected in consultation with liberation movements, and there is an emphasis on technical and developmental studies. Scholarships include the Michael Scott Fund which is used to provide books and other teaching materials to schools and libraries in South Africa, Namibia, Rwanda and Somalia; the B. W. Andrzejewski Fund which makes awards of £2,000 to promote language, literature and broadcasting in Western Africa; the Rex Collings Fund which also makes awards of approx. £2,000 to encourage publishing and literacy in Africa; and the Kenneth Kirkwood Fund which provides fees and emergency payments for African students at undergraduate and postgraduate level. The Trust also partly finances study for refugees in the United Kingdom.

Geographical Area of Activity: Africa, United Kingdom and Ireland.

Publications: Annual Report; *The Situation of AET Sponsored Namibians After their Return Home*.

Finance: Annual revenue £944,1914, expenditure £571,181 (Aug. 2001).

Governing Board: Prof. I. Lewis (Chair.); T. Connor (Hon. Treas.); B. Andrzejewski; Dr C. Beer; R. Desai; Prof. D. Hayward; C. Hill; J. Kellock; P. S. Tomlinson; Dr C. Trelfgarne.

Principal Staff: Exec. Officer J. Landymore.

Address: Africa Centre Ltd, 38 King St, London WC2E 8JS.

Telephone: (20) 7240-0726; **e-mail:** aet@cwcom.net.

Aga Khan Foundation (United Kingdom)

Established in 1973 to promote social development in developing countries of Asia and Africa by funding health, education and rural development programmes, without regard to race, religion or background. An affiliate of the Aga Khan Foundation in Switzerland (q.v.).

Activities: Channels funds to support organizations and programmes principally in less-developed countries in Asia and Africa, and also in Canada, Portugal, Tajikistan, Switzerland, the United Kingdom and the USA. The Foundation is involved in conservation and the environment, education, medicine and health, and social welfare, through grants to institutions, promoting community self-help projects, scholarships and fellowships, conferences and publications. It operates programmes to aid child development and education, especially by improving the quality of formal education and early childhood education; family health and nutrition through community-oriented health development; and rural development through income-generation and the management of renewable resources. Promotes skills development, training and technical exchanges internationally.

Geographical Area of Activity: International.

Restrictions: The Foundation does not solicit applications for funding, nor will it respond positively to any such requests.

Publications: Project briefings, information sheets on Foundation activities, and evaluation reports on Foundation-supported projects.

Finance: Annual revenue £9,877,779, expenditure £8,757,694 (2000).

Board of Directors: His Highness Prince Karim Aga Khan (Chair.); Prince Amyn Aga Khan; Maître André Ardoin; Guillaume de Spoelberch.

AKF UK National Committee: Dr Azim Lakhani (Chair.); Abdul Bhanji (Vice-Chair.); Nasim Devji; Habib Motani; Ferid Nanji; Guy Stringer; Lady Maureen Thomas; Shafik Sachedina (*ex-officio*).

Principal Staff: Chief Exec. Aly-Raza Nazerali.

Address: 3 Cromwell Gardens, London SW7 2HB.

Telephone: (20) 7591-6812; **e-mail:** unit@akf.org.

Agency for Co-operation and Research in Development—ACORD

Established in 1976 to alleviate poverty world-wide and to protect human rights.

Activities: Operates in 18 countries in Africa in the fields of aid and social welfare, through grants and research into long-term development. Currently running programmes around four core themes: conflict, gender, livelihoods and HIV/AIDS within a global programme for promoting social activism.

Geographical Area of Activity: Africa.

Publications: Annual Report.

Finance: Annual revenue £7,891,000 (2000).

Trustees: Molly Kane (Chair.); Maggie Pankhurst (Hon. Treas.); Moussa Ba; Nigel Cross; Ivan Godfreid; Marie Goretti Nyirarukundo.

Principal Staff: Exec. Dir David Waller; Programme Dir Bonaventure Watana; Dir Finance Golam Morshed.

Address: Dean Bradley House, 52 Horseferry Rd, London SW1P 2AF.

Telephone: (20) 7227-8600; **Fax:** (20) 7799-1868; **Internet:** www.acord.org.uk; **e-mail:** florencek@acord.org.uk.

Al Fayed Charitable Foundation

The Foundation was established in 1987 for general charitable purposes.

Activities: Operates nationally. The Foundation was to receive the proceeds (estimated at £7,000,000) from Mohamed Al Fayed's sale of his collection of royal memorabilia from the Paris home of Edward, Duke of York and his wife, the former Mrs Simpson.

Geographical Area of Activity: United Kingdom.

Finance: Annual revenue £628,943, expenditure £635,252 (2001).

Trustees: Mohamed Al Fayed; A. Fayed; S. Fayed.

Principal Staff: Belinda White.

Address: c/o 5th Floor, Harrods Ltd, 87–135 Brompton Rd, Knightsbridge, London SW1X 7XL.

Telephone: (20) 7730-1234; **e-mail:** bjwhite_acf@compuserve.com.

Alchemy Foundation

Founded as the Starlight Foundation in 1985 by Richard and Annabel Stilgoe, to support mental and physical health care of the elderly and children, and to assist in famine relief.

Activities: Operates world-wide in the fields of aid and development, arts and humanities, conservation and the environment, education, medicine and health, science and technology, and social welfare. It promotes self-conducted programmes and research, and bestows grants on individuals and institutions. It aims in particular to aid people (especially children) suffering from mental or physical illness or disability, and people suffering from the effects of famine.

Geographical Area of Activity: International.

Finance: Annual revenue £587,500, expenditure £513,913 (April 2002).

Trustees: A. Armitage; A. Murison; Esther Rantzen; Rev. D. Reeves; Annabel Stilgoe; Holly Stilgoe; Jack Stilgoe; Dr Jemima Stilgoe; Joe Stilgoe; Richard Stilgoe; Rufus Stilgoe.

Principal Staff: Richard Stilgoe; Annabel Stilgoe.

Address: Trevereux Manor, Limpsfield Chart, Oxted RH8 0TL.

Telephone: (1883) 730600; **Fax:** (1883) 730800.

All Saints Educational Trust

Founded in 1979 to promote the training of teachers and research and development in education.

Activities: The trust aims to promote higher and further education through: making awards to those undertaking teacher training and to teachers who wish to gain further qualifications; providing teaching aids, libraries and other resources; promoting research, particularly in home economics and religious studies.

Restrictions: United Kingdom and European Union applicants only; courses must lead to degrees awarded by United Kingdom institutions.

Finance: Net assets £8,670,000 (2001–02); total revenue £414,000, expenditure £572,000 (2001–02).

Trustees: The Bishop of London (Chair.).

Principal Staff: Clerk R. C. Poulton.

Address: St Katharine Cree Church, 86 Leadenhall St, London EC3A 3DH.

Telephone: (20) 7283-4485; **Fax:** (20) 7621-9758; **Internet:** www.aset.org.uk; **e-mail:** enquiries@aset.org.uk.

Allied Domecq Trust

Founded in 1982, as the Allied-Lyons Trust, for general charitable purposes.

Activities: Supports national and international charitable organizations operating in the fields of the arts, education and the environment. Awards one-off grants or recurrent grants for up to four years.

Geographical Area of Activity: International.

Finance: Annual revenue approx. £650,000.

Trustees: W. E. Mason (Chair.); A. J. Hales; A. S. Pratt.

Principal Staff: C. Burns.

Address: 24 Portland Place, London W1N 4BB.

Telephone: (20) 7323-9000; **Fax:** (20) 7323-1742.

Amnesty International

Founded in 1961 by Peter Benenson and others to secure throughout the world the provisions of the Universal Declaration of Human Rights (1948) and other internationally recognized human rights instruments.

Activities: Operates internationally in the field of human rights. The organization works against the imprisonment, detention or other physical restrictions imposed on any person by reason of their political, religious or conscientiously held beliefs or by reason of their ethnic origin, gender, colour, language, national or social origin, economic status, birth or other status, provided that he or she has not used or advocated violence ('prisoners of conscience'), as well as working against the detention of any political prisoner without fair trial or any trial procedures that do not conform to internationally recognized norms; the death penalty, and the torture or other cruel, inhuman or degrading treatment or punishment of prisoners, whether or not they have used or advocated violence; and the extrajudicial execution of persons whether or not detained, and 'disappearances', whether or not the persons affected have used or advocated violence. Also seeks to co-operate with other not-for-profit organizations, the United Nations and regional inter-governmental organizations; ensure control of international military, security and police relations, to prevent human rights abuses; and organizes human rights education and awareness raising programmes. Amnesty International has 56 national sections and more than 1,000,000 members and subscribers in 162 countries and territories. It has more than 7,800 volunteer groups world-wide.

Geographical Area of Activity: International.

Publications: *Amnesty International Report* (annually); *The Wire* (10 a year); reports and briefing papers.

Finance: Annual budget £20,940,000 (2001/02).

International Executive Committee: The International Executive Committee comprises a Chair. and eight other members.

Principal Staff: Sec.-Gen. Irene Khan.

Address: International Secretariat, Peter Benenson House, 1 Easton St, London WC1X 0DW.

Telephone: (20) 7413-5500; **Fax:** (20) 7956-1157; **Internet:** www.amnesty.org; **e-mail:** amnestyis@amnesty.org.

Ancient India and Iran Trust—AIIT

Established in July 1978 by Prof. Sir Harold Bailey, Prof. Joan van Lohuizen, Dr Raymond Allchin and Dr Bridget Allchin; aims to promote public and academic interest in the early cultures and languages of the Indo-Iranian world.

Activities: Promotes public and academic interest in the early cultures and languages of the Indo-Iranian world, through maintaining a library open to the public, running courses and lectures, and organizing regular symposia and seminars on related subjects.

Geographical Area of Activity: Central and South Asia.

Restrictions: Small research grants only to researchers in the regions covered when funds permit.

Publications: *The Crossroads of Asia:Transformation in Image and Symbol; Living Traditions: Studies in the Ethnoarchaeology of South Asia; Ghandharan Art in Context: East–West Exchanges at the Crossroads of Asia; South Asian Archaeology,* 1995 (conference proceedings).

Finance: Funded by interest from capital endowment, donations and grants from foundations.

Board of Trustees: Dr Bridget Allchin; Dr Raymond Allchin; Sir Nicholas Barrington; Nigel Chancellor; Dr Robin A. E. Coningham; Dr Almut Hintze; Neil Kreitman; Prof. Nicholas Sims-Williams; Dr Giles Tilotson.

Principal Staff: Custodian James Cormick; Sec. Jose John; Librarian Wieslaw Mical.

Address: Brooklands House, 23 Brooklands Ave, Cambridge CB2 2BG.

Telephone: (1223) 356841; **Fax:** (1223) 361125; **Internet:** www.indiran.co.uk; **e-mail:** indiran@aol.com.

Anglo-German Foundation for the Study of Industrial Society

Established in 1973 by inter-governmental agreement between the Federal Republic of Germany and the United Kingdom, and incorporated by Royal Charter, to promote the study of modern industrial society and foster contacts between industrial, economic and social policy-makers in the two countries.

Activities: Finances selected research projects and meetings of practical value to both countries, mainly on the living and working environment, economic, social and industrial policies, and business management; the projects are usually Anglo-German comparisons, carried out jointly. It is particularly interested in research concerning the effects on German and British industrial society of global economic change, unemployment and public spending. Organizes conferences and meetings.

Geographical Area of Activity: United Kingdom and Germany.

Restrictions: Does not award scholarships.

Publications: Annual Report; information leaflet; publications list; reports listing results of research projects.

Finance: Financed by contributions from both Governments, plus investment income. Annual grant expenditure approx. £500,000.

Trustees: Bryan Rigby (Chair.); Prof. Dr C.-C. von Weizsäcker (Vice-Chair.); Simon Broadbent; Lord Croham; John Edmonds; Prof. Robert Leicht; Dr Erika Mezger; Dr Anita Pfaff; Dr Jürgen Ruhfus; Dr Andrew Sentance; Peter van Siemens; Prof. D. Wedderburn.

Principal Staff: Dir Keith Dobson; Deputy Dir Dr Ray Cunningham.

Address: 34 Belgrave Sq., London SW1X 8DZ.

Telephone: (20) 7823-1123; **Fax:** (20) 7823-2324; **Internet:** www.agf.org.uk; **e-mail:** info@agf.org.uk.

Anglo-Jewish Association

Founded in 1871 by Jacob Waley, Dr A. Benisch, Sir Francis Goldsmid, Sir George Jessel and Sir David Salomons to promote the education of Jews and of other persons in Jewish matters, to advance the Jewish religion, and to relieve poverty, especially among Jews.

Activities: Operates in the field of education. The Association administers the income from a number of educational trusts; and arranges lectures and other events to promote understanding of Jewish ethical and communal issues.

Geographical Area of Activity: International.

Principal Staff: Gen. Sec. Cynthia Steuer.

Address: Suite 5, 107 Gloucester Place, London W1U 6BY.

Telephone: (20) 7486-5055; **Fax:** (20) 7486-5155; **Internet:** www.anglojewish.co.uk; **e-mail:** info@anglojewish.co.uk.

Anti-Slavery International

Founded in 1839 (known as the Anti-Slavery Society for the Protection of Human Rights until 1990); aims to eradicate slavery and forced labour in all their forms.

Activities: The organization seeks to attain its aims through: research and the publication of information about all forms of slavery throughout the world; generating greater awareness of such abuses; campaigning nationally and internationally; and working with local partners to help the victims of human rights injustices. The organization has consultative status with the UN Economic and Social Council, and has members world-wide. Launched the annual Anti-Slavery Award in 1991.

Geographical Area of Activity: International.

Restrictions: Does not make grants.

Publications: *Anti-Slavery Reporter* (newsletter, quarterly); various other publications on issues including bonded, forced and child labour; annual report and accounts.

Finance: Sources of finance include trusts and foundations, the public, European Union and Government funding, etc. Annual revenue £720,067, expenditure £706,021 (2000/01).

Executive Committee: R. Norton (Chair.); J. Gaselee (Vice-Chair.); P. Buxton (Treas.).

Principal Staff: Dir Mary Cunneen.

Address: Thomas Clarkson House, The Stableyard, Broomgrove Rd, London SW9 9TL.

Telephone: (20) 7501-8920; **Fax:** (20) 7738-4110; **Internet:** www.antislavery.org; **e-mail:** info@antislavery.org.

The Arab–British Chamber Charitable Foundation

Founded in 1980 by the Joint Arab–British Chamber of Commerce for the advancement of science and education for needy young people and adults from Arab states, with particular emphasis on fields of relevance to Arab countries, for example industry, commerce, technology and the professions.

Activities: Awards scholarships and makes grants to Arab students for postgraduate study in the United Kingdom; makes donations to charities working on health and education projects in the Arab world.

Geographical Area of Activity: United Kingdom and the Middle East.

Finance: Receives 12.5% of the net annual profits of the Joint Arab–British Chamber of Commerce. Annual revenue £109,166, grants disbursed £92,069 (June 2002).

Trustees: Rt Hon. Lord Denman; Dr S. N. Jaroudi; Sir John Wilton; Dr A. B. Zahlan.

Principal Staff: Sec. H. de Las Casas.

Address: Longmead, Benhall Green, Benhall, Saxmundham IP17 1HU.

Telephone: (1728) 603359; **Fax:** (1728) 603359; **e-mail:** abccf@abcc.org.uk.

Arthritis Research Campaign

Founded in 1936 to promote research into the causes and cure of arthritis and associated rheumatic diseases; formerly known as the Arthritis and Rheumatism Council for Research in Great Britain and the Commonwealth.

Activities: Operates primarily in the United Kingdom in the field of science and medicine, through research grants to individuals and institutions for medical research. Produces a range of education booklets for patients and reports for medical professionals. Organizes meetings, arranges university appointments and awards travelling and other research fellowships.

Geographical Area of Activity: Mainly United Kingdom.

Publications: *Arthritis Today* (magazine, 4 a year); Annual Report and financial statement; series of booklets on rheumatic disease.

Finance: Expenditure on medical research in the United Kingdom £21,000,000 (2000).

Executive and Finance Committee: Prof. Roger Sturrock (Chair.).

Principal Staff: Chief Exec. F. Logan.

Address: Copeman House, St Mary's Court, St Mary's Gate, Chesterfield S41 7TD.

Telephone: (1246) 558033; **Fax:** (1246) 558007; **Internet:** www.arc.org.uk; **e-mail:** info@arc.org.uk.

Arts Council of England

The national strategic policy body for the arts in England.

Activities: Operates in England in the area of the arts. Distributes both National Lottery and Government funds to artists and arts organizations (see also Lottery Arts Fund for England, Scotland, Wales and Northern Ireland). Funding programmes seek to support the highest artistic achievements and to make these available to as many people as possible; to encourage new work and new audiences; to bring challenging art to all sectors of the community; and to celebrate the diversity of cultures contributing to artistic life in England. Operates in partnership with Regional Arts Offices, which are responsible for funding and development of the arts in their areas. Currently working on the £40,000,000 Creative Partnerships initiative, which will develop long-term partnerships between schools, cultural and creative organizations and artists; Decibel, a project funding culturally diverse projects and Artsmark, a national arts award for schools.

Geographical Area of Activity: England.

Publications: Annual Review.

Finance: Receives a grant-in-aid from the Government: £335,00,000 (2003/04); also responsible for distributing a portion of the National Lottery money for the arts.

Principal Staff: Chair. Gerry Robinson; Chief Exec. Peter Hewitt.

Address: 14 Great Peter St, London SW1P 3NQ.

Telephone: (20) 7973-6517; **Internet:** www.artscouncil.org.uk; **e-mail:** enquiries@artscouncil.org.uk.

Ashden Charitable Trust

Established in 1990 for general charitable purposes. One of the Sainsbury Family Charitable Trusts, which share a common administration.

Activities: Operates nationally and internationally (mainly in Africa) in the field of conservation and the environment, and nationally in the areas of homelessness, urban rejuvenation, emergency aid, and community arts.

Geographical Area of Activity: United Kingdom and Africa.

Restrictions: No grants are made to individuals.

Publications: Annual Report.

Finance: Total assets £21,636,131 (April 2002); annual revenue £1,891,631, expenditure £996,185 (2002).

Trustees: S. Butler-Sloss; R. Butler-Sloss; J. S. Portrait.

Principal Staff: Dir Michael Pattison; Financial Dir P. Spokes.

Address: Allington House, 1st Floor, 150 Victoria St, London SW1E 5AE.

Telephone: (20) 7410-0330; **e-mail:** sfct@sfct.org.uk.

Association for International Cancer Research

Independent cancer research charity, which supports fundamental research into the causes, prevention and treatment of cancer.

Activities: Operates world-wide, offering research grants in the area of medicine and health, especially for international collaborative projects, recently-qualified researchers, and work in under-funded areas of cancer research. Currently supporting 200 projects world-wide.

Geographical Area of Activity: International.

Publications: Newsletter.

Finance: Financed by donations, covenants, legacies and direct mail fundraising; total research grants approx. £7,000,000 (2000).

Board of Directors: J. F. Matthews (Chair.); Sir John McMillan; J. Ogilvy; Prof. D. B. Thomas; M. Thomson; Prof. C. R. Wolf.

Principal Staff: Chief Exec. Derek Napier.

Address: Madras House, South St, St Andrews KY16 9EH.

Telephone: (1334) 477910; **Fax:** (1334) 478667; **Internet:** www.aicr.org.uk; **e-mail:** jane.wilson@aicr.org.uk.

Andrew Balint Charitable Trust

Founded in 1977 for general charitable purposes.

Activities: Operates nationally and internationally. Awards grants to organizations, usually registered charities operating in the fields of education, medicine and health, and social welfare.

Geographical Area of Activity: International.

Finance: Annual revenue £275,174, expenditure £230,469 (April 2002).

Trustees: A. Balint; Mrs A. Balint; Dr G. Balint-Kurti.

Principal Staff: J. K. Oliver.

Address: 4–6 Canfield Pl., Suite A, London NW6 3BT.

Telephone: (20) 7624-2098; **Fax:** (20) 7624-2076.

George Balint Charitable Trust

Founded in 1973 to provide funds for general charitable purposes.

Activities: The Trust awards grants to recognized charities, nationally and internationally.

Geographical Area of Activity: International.

Restrictions: No grants are made to individuals.

Finance: Annual revenue £305,476, expenditure £480,565 (April 2002).

Trustees: George Balint, Dr Andrew Balint; G. Rothschild; Mrs Balint-Farkers.

Principal Staff: Admin. J. K. Olver.

Address: 4–6 Canfield Pl., Suite A, London NW6 3BT.

Telephone: (20) 7624-2098; **Fax:** (20) 7624-2076.

Paul Balint Charitable Trust

Founded in 1977 to provide funds for general charitable purposes.

Activities: The Trust operates in the fields of medicine and health, education and social welfare, through grants to registered charities nationally and internationally.

Geographical Area of Activity: International.

Finance: Annual revenue £234,196, annual expenditure £247,810 (April 2002).

Trustees: Dr A. Balint; M. G. Balint; P. A. Balint; Dr G. Balint-Kurti.

Principal Staff: Correspondent Dr Andrew Balint.

Address: 4–6 Canfield Place, Suite A, London NW6 3BT.

Telephone: (20) 7624-2098.

Baring Foundation

Founded in 1969 for general charitable purposes.

Activities: International grants are given to United Kingdom-registered organizations working to improve the capacity of NGOs and community-based organizations in Central and South America and sub-Saharan Africa. Recent funding themes include addressing the problems arising from migration and displacement of people.

Geographical Area of Activity: Sub-Saharan Africa, and Central and South America.

Restrictions: No grants to individials. Applicant organizations must be registered in the United Kingdom.

Publications: Annual Report; *Computers in Grant-Making: a practical guide for funders; Lending Money; Voluntary Sector Infrastructure; Merging Interests*.

Finance: Total grants disbursed approx. £3,000,000 (2002).

Trustees: N. H. Baring (Chair.); T. A. Baring; R. D. Broadly; M. Findlay; J. A. Lewis-Jones; A. D. Loehnis; J. Peers; Christopher Steane; Sir Crispin Tickell.

Principal Staff: Dir Toby Johns.

Address: 60 London Wall, London EC2M 5TQ.

Telephone: (20) 7767-1348; **Fax:** (20) 7767-7121; **Internet:** www.baringfoundation.org.uk; **e-mail:** baring.foundation@uk.ing.com.

Barnardo's

Established in 1871 to help children, young people and their families in the United Kingdom.

Activities: Provides guidance, support and care to young people and their families, including counselling for abused children, support for families with a disabled child, family centres, fostering and adoption schemes, help for homeless young people, schools and shared houses for those leaving care, support for children and families with HIV and AIDS, and research and lobbying activities. Maintains regional offices throughout the United Kingdom.

Geographical Area of Activity: United Kingdom.

Publications: *What Works?* (series); *Counting the Cost of Child Poverty; Joined-Up Youth Research, Policy and Practice: A New Agenda for Change?*; and numerous other publications.

Finance: Financed through Barnardo's shops, fundraising, trusts and foundations, campaigns, etc. Annual revenue £143,500,000, expenditure £154,900,000 (2001/02).

Trustees: Dr D. E. Barnardo (Chair.).

Principal Staff: Pres. Cherie Blair; Chief Exec. R. Singleton.

Address: Tanners Lane, Barkingside, Ilford IG6 1QG.

Telephone: (20) 8550-8822; **Fax:** (20) 8551-6870; **Internet:** www.barnardos.com; **e-mail:** webmistress@barnardos.org .uk.

BBC Children in Need Appeal

Charity established in 1980 (in its present form) by the BBC (British Broadcasting Corporation) to make a positive difference to the lives of disadvantaged children.

Activities: Operates nationally by distributing grants to registered charities and voluntary and community groups for projects that will improve the lives of children who are disadvantaged, including those experiencing poverty or deprivation, suffering from illness, abuse or neglect, with mental or physical disabilities, and children with behavioural and psychological disorders.

Geographical Area of Activity: United Kingdom.

Restrictions: Grants to groups supporting disadvantaged children and young people under the age of 18 living in the United Kingdom. No grants are made to individuals or businesses.

Publications: Annual Report; supporter pack.

Finance: Net assets £13,076,908 (2001); grants expenditure £25,219,523 (2001–02).

Trustees: Yogesh Chauhan; Tim Cook; Will Day; Lorraine Heggessey; Diane Louise Jordan; Michelle Kershaw; Neena Mahal; Simon Milner; Liz Rylatt; Sir Robert Smith; Terry Wogan; Steve Wood.

Principal Staff: Dir Martina Milburn.

Address: POB 76, London W3 6FS.

Telephone: (20) 8576-7788; **Fax:** (20) 8576-8887; **Internet:** www.bbc.co.uk/pudsey; **e-mail:** pudsey@bbc.co.uk.

BBC World Service Trust

Founded in November 1992 by the BBC (British Broadcasting Corporation) as the BBC Marshall Plan of the Mind Trust, present name since 1999. The Trust aims to utilize the skills and services of the media to act as a catalyst for change.

Activities: The Trust operates in the following areas: promoting health, through a leprosy programme in India, a trachoma programme in Tanzania, and Sexwise, a sexual health education programme, operating world-wide; developing civil society, through the Independent Radio for Russia programme, training projects to develop reporting skills in Nigeria, Indonesia, Croatia, Ukraine, the Russian Federation, Serbia and Montenegro, Tajikistan and Zimbabwe, and Bridging the Gap, an initiative to promote the role of NGOs in Romania; building an independent media, through the establishment of schools of journalism in Romania, Serbia and Montenegro and the Russian Federation, and providing tailor-made media training in more than 30 countries world-wide; working to eradicate poverty through a broadcast project for Mongolian youth; developing a communications strategy in Zambia; working with UNHCR to give children a voice in the media, particularly those living in war zones; a programme developed with UNICEF, looking at children's rights world-wide; a radio series discussing issues facing Arab youth; a programme uncovering trafficking in Eastern European women; a series of humanitarian programmes for Iraqi people, and other human rights programmes, including projects aimed at raising awareness of what human rights mean at individual and country level. The Trust aims to work in partnership with local organizations and people to create sustainable services for communities.

Geographical Area of Activity: Africa, Asia, Central and South-Eastern Europe, the Middle East and countries of the former USSR.

Restrictions: Does not make grants to organizations.

Publications: Newsletter; Annual Report; fact-sheets and work-books to accompany programmes broadcast.

Finance: Grant of £4,000,000 from the United Kingdom Government's Know-How Fund, other monies raised from European Union TACIS and PHARE programmes, and foundations, charities and business. Annual revenue £4,600,000, expenditure £4,500,000 (March 2001).

Trustees: Nigel Chapman (Chair.).

Principal Staff: Contact: Melanie Lowndes.

Address: POB 76, Strand, London WC2B 4PH.

Telephone: (20) 7557-2462; **Fax:** (20) 7379-1622; **Internet:** www.bbc.co.uk/worldservice/trust; **e-mail:** wstrust@bbc.co .uk.

Beaverbrook Foundation

Founded in 1974 by Lord Beaverbrook for general charitable purposes. The Foundation's activities are restricted to New Brunswick and Nova Scotia in Canada, and the United Kingdom.

Activities: Provides funds to charities and maintains an art gallery.

Geographical Area of Activity: Canada (New Brunswick and Nova Scotia) and the United Kingdom.

Restrictions: Grants are not made to individuals.

Publications: Annual accounts.

Finance: Total income £428,752, total expenditure £682,911 (Sept. 2002).

Trustees: Lord Beaverbrook (Chair.); Lady Aitken (Deputy Chair.); Hon. M. Aitken; T. M. Aitken; Lady Beaverbrook; J. E. A. Kidd; Laura Levi.

Principal Staff: Gen. Sec. and Admin. J. S. Ford.

Address: 11 Old Queen St, London SW1H 9JA.

Telephone: (20) 7222-7474; **Fax:** (20) 7222-2189; **Internet:** www.beaverbrookfoundation.org.uk.

Beit Memorial Fellowships for Medical Research

Founded in 1909 by Sir Otto Beit to promote the advancement by research of medicine and the allied sciences in their relation to medicine.

Activities: Approximately five fellowships are awarded every two years to post-doctorates who hold a degree from a university in the United Kingdom or Commonwealth, irrespective of nationality. Candidates must generally be under 35 years of age. Fellowships are usually held for three years, to carry out medical research in the United Kingdom or Ireland.

Geographical Area of Activity: United Kingdom and the Commonwealth.

Finance: Total income £353,259, total expenditure £372,820 (Sept. 2001).

Trustees: Sir Jeremy Morse (Chair.); Prof. Sir C. Chantler; N. Gold; Prof. E. R. Huehns; Prof. Sir Stanley Peart; W. Waldegrave.

Principal Staff: Admin. Sec. M. Goble.

Address: c/o Institute of Molecular Medicine, John Radcliffe Hospital, Headington OX3 9DS.

Telephone: (1865) 222679; **Fax:** (1865) 222600; **e-mail:** beit .fellowships@hammer.imm.ox.ac.uk.

Beit Trust

Founded in 1906 by Alfred Beit for charitable purposes of an educational or public nature which will best promote the welfare of the inhabitants of Zimbabwe, Zambia and Malawi.

Activities: Works in Zimbabwe, Zambia and Malawi in the fields of education and health and welfare, usually in the form of building grants. Operates a secondary school bursary scheme and also a Postgraduate Fellowships scheme for students from Zimbabwe, Zambia and Malawi at universities in the United Kingdom, Ireland and South Africa.

Geographical Area of Activity: Malawi, Zambia and Zimbabwe.

Restrictions: Applications should normally be submitted through the Trust's office in Africa.

Publications: Annual Report.

Finance: Net assets £62,763,782 (2001); annual revenue £2,081,933, expenditure £2,917,577 (2001).

Trustees: Sir Alan Munro (Chair.); R. A. C. Byatt; C. J. Driver; Dame Maeve Fort; Sir Cosmo Haskard; R. P. Lander; Prof. J. G. G. Ledingham.

Principal Staff: Sec. Brig. C. L. G. Henshaw; Representative in Africa T. M. Johnson.

Address: Beit House, Grove Rd, Woking GU21 5JB; POB 76, Chisipite, Harare, Zimbabwe.

Telephone: (1483) 772575; **Fax:** (1483) 725833; **e-mail:** beit.trust@clara.co.uk.

Benesco Charity Limited

Founded in 1970 to advance medical research and education.

Activities: Provides funds to registered charities to support medical research, education and welfare.

Restrictions: Does not award grants to individuals.

Publications: Annual Report.

Finance: Annual revenue £3,678,500, expenditure £3,768,692 (April 2002).

Trustees: Lord Wolfson of Sunningdale (Chair.); J. Ragol-Levy; H. Prevezer.

Address: 129 Battenhall Rd, Worcester WR5 2BU.

BibleLands

Founded in 1854 as the Turkish Missions Aid Society; also formerly known as the Bible Lands Society; its original aim was to support existing Christian missions in the lands of the Bible; currently it works in partnership with local Christians in the lands of the Bible who show the compassion of Jesus as they tend, treat and teach the young and the needy.

Activities: Focuses on the welfare of children, young people and others in need, with an emphasis on health and education. BibleLands has a special concern for children, education, vocational training (including nurses), special needs, medical care, social care and the support and care of refugees.

Geographical Area of Activity: Middle East.

Restrictions: No grants are made to individuals.

Publications: *The Star in the East* (2 a year).

Finance: Assets £7,640,000 (2001); annual revenue and grants expenditure £3,300,000 (2002).

Council of Trustees: Rev. Douglas Dennis (Pres.); Dr Cyril Young (Chair.); Hugh Boulter (Vice-Chair.); Kenneth Mills (Hon. Treas.); Jane Bisson; Rev. Daniel Burton; Rev. Michael Cleaves; Rev. Anthony Crowe; Tim Izzett; Joanna Robertson; John Wells; Rev. Ralph Wilkins; Rev. John Woodger; Felicity Young.

Principal Staff: Dir Nigel Edward-Few; Head of Finance Revd. Nick Plant; Head of Overseas Programmes Mo Burnley.

Address: POB 50, High Wycombe HP15 7QU.

Telephone: (1494) 897950; **Fax:** (1494) 897951; **Internet:** www.biblelands.org.uk; **e-mail:** info@biblelands.org.uk.

Biotechnology and Biological Sciences Research Council—BBSRC

The BBSRC was established in 1994, one of the organizations formed by the splitting up of the Science and Engineering Research Council (SERC). The SERC was replaced by the BBSRC, the Engineering and Physical Sciences Research Council (EPSRC—q.v.) and the Particle Physics and Astronomy Research Council (PPARC—q.v.).

Activities: Promotes research in the fields of biotechnology and the biological sciences. Supports research both nationally and internationally.

Geographical Area of Activity: United Kingdom and international.

Finance: Financed by the United Kingdom Government.

Address: Polaris House, North Star Ave, Swindon SN2 1UH.

Telephone: (1793) 413200; **Fax:** (1793) 413201; **Internet:** www.bbsrc.ac.uk.

BirdLife International

Founded in 1922 as the International Council for Bird Preservation, renamed BirdLife International in 1993; a world-wide partnership of organizations working for the diversity of all life through the conservation of birds and their habitats.

Activities: Operates internationally in the field of conservation, through programmes (for example bird surveys and studies; conservation programmes for particular species or areas and for the sustainable use of natural resources; public education campaigns; and provision of expert advice to governments on bird conservation issues); support for local societies and their projects; international conferences; conservation expeditions; compiling and disseminating information, including a computer databank, international data books and other publications. There are over 300 member organizations and regional offices in Belgium, Ecuador, Indonesia, Jordan, and the Netherlands. Maintains a reference library of 4,000 volumes..

Geographical Area of Activity: International.

Publications: *Bird Red Data Book; Bird Conservation International* (quarterly); BirdLife Conservation Series; Annual Report; newsletter; technical publications; study reports; surveys; conference proceedings.

Finance: Annual revenue £4,230,632, expenditure £4,628,223 (2000). Network annual world-wide budget US $263,333,892 (2000).

Principal Staff: Chair. Dr Gerard A. Bertrand; Treas. A. P. Leventis; Dir Dr Michael Rands.

Address: Wellbrook Court, Girton Rd, Cambridge CB3 0NA.

Telephone: (1223) 277318; **Fax:** (1223) 277200; **Internet:** www.birdlife.org.uk; **e-mail:** birdlife@birdlife.org.uk.

The Body Shop Foundation

Established in 1989 to provide a means of gathering together funds raised by directors, employees, national and international franchisees and friends of The Body Shop in order to allocate these to social, human and environmental welfare.

Activities: The Foundation operates nationally and internationally in the fields of human and civil rights, and animal and environmental protection.

Geographical Area of Activity: International.

Restrictions: Does not accept unsolicited applications for funding.

Finance: Annual revenue £1,355,731, grants disbursed £734,749 (2001).

Trustees: Bill Hughes; Jo Martin; Annalisa Nicolova-Cinque; Anita Roddick; Gordon Roddick; Peter Youngs.

Principal Staff: Grants Officer D. Osborne.

Address: Watersmead, Littlehampton BN17 6LS.

Telephone: (1903) 731500; **Fax:** (1903) 844202; **Internet:** www.the-body-shop.com; **e-mail:** thebodyshopfoundation@the-body-shop.com.

Book Aid International

Founded as the Ranfurly Library by Hermione, Countess of Ranfurly, in 1954; present name adopted in 1994. Book Aid

International's vision is of a world in which everyone enjoys access to the information they need, and every country has a lively book trade that reflects local values and culture. It works in partnership with organizations in developing countries to support local initiatives in literacy, education and publishing.

Activities: Provides over 750,000 selected books and journals each year to support learning and skills development in over 40 developing countries around the world. Responds to requests from organizations that urgently need up-to-date information resources. Its partners include library networks, schools, universities, vocational colleges and hospitals.

Geographical Area of Activity: International, primarily sub-Saharan Africa, the Caribbean and South-East Asia.

Publications: *Interchange* (newsletter).

Finance: Annual revenue £4,145,341, annual expenditure £4,275,638 (2001).

Council: Tim Rix (Chair.).

Principal Staff: Dir Sara Harrity; Deputy Dir David Membrey.

Address: 39–41 Coldharbour Lane, London SE5 9NR.

Telephone: (20) 7733-3577; **Fax:** (20) 7978-8006; **Internet:** www.bookaid.org; **e-mail:** info@bookaid.org.

Born Free Foundation

Founded by Bill Travers and Virginia McKenna to co-ordinate and develop effective campaigns to prevent animal suffering, protect endangered species and their habitats, and keep wildlife in the wild.

Activities: The Foundation's programmes include Zoo Check, to monitor conditions of wildlife in zoos, safari parks and circuses, with the aim of preventing the abuse of captive animals; ELEFRIENDS Elephant Protection Group, aiming to combat poachers and end trade in ivory; Big Cat Campaign, to rescue big cats in captivity and protect those in the wild; Wolf Campaign, to save Ethiopian wolves from extinction and provide information on the species; Dolphin Campaign, to bring about an end to the practice of holding dolphins and whales captive in marine parks, and to protect orca in the wild; Primate Campaign, to protect orphaned and abused baby chimpanzees at a sanctuary in Uganda, and to protect primates in the wild; and UK Wildlife Campaign, which supports conservation and animal rescue centres, and raises awareness of the plight of wildlife in the United Kingdom.

Geographical Area of Activity: International.

Finance: Annual revenue £1,865,011, expenditure £1,667,725 (March 2001).

Principal Staff: CEO Will Travers.

Address: 3 Grove House, Foundry Lane, Horsham RH13 5PL.

Telephone: (1403) 240170; **Fax:** (1403) 327838; **Internet:** www.bornfree.org.uk; **e-mail:** info@bornfree.org.uk.

Bridge House Estates Trust Fund

The Trust can trace its origins back as far as 1097 when a special tax was raised to help repair the wooden London Bridge. The Fund increased through administration of property assets both in the City of London and in the surrounding countryside. It built Blackfriars Bridge and Tower Bridge, and purchased Southwark Bridge; maintaining bridges in the City of London is still the main purpose of the Fund, although a Charitable Scheme was set up in 1995.

Activities: The Charitable Scheme enables the Trust Fund to apply its surplus money for the benefit of Greater London. Any year's income which is above that required to support the City bridges the Fund maintains may be applied towards charitable aims to benefit Greater London and its inhabitants. The Fund concentrates its distribution of grants in five main areas: transport and access for older and disabled people; environmental conservation; support for children and young people; assistance to older people so that they can carry on living within the community; and the provision of technical assistance to voluntary organizations. In exceptional cases the Trust may fund outside these priority areas. Also operates a small grants scheme.

Geographical Area of Activity: United Kingdom (Greater London).

Restrictions: Grants are made in Greater London only. They are not made to individuals, statutory bodies, political parties, for medical or academic research, to churches or religious bodies for religious purposes or maintenance of religious buildings, nor to educational establishments.

Publications: Annual Report; Guidelines for Applicants.

Finance: Assets £598,216,000 (March 2001); annual revenue £34,455,000, grants disbursed £15,724,000 (2001).

Grants Committee: Patrick Roney (Chair); William Fraser (Deputy Chair.); Richard Agutter; Wilfred Archibald; John Barker; John Bird; Michael Cassidy; Jonathan Charkham; Antony Eskenzi; John Holland; Joyce Nash; Barbara Newman; Richard Scriven; Sir Alan Traill.

Principal Staff: Chief Grants Officer Clare Thomas; Deputy Chief Grants Officer Sara Llewellin.

Address: Corporation of London, POB 270, Guildhall, London EC2P 2EJ.

Telephone: (20) 7332-3710; **Fax:** (20) 7332-3720; **Internet:** www.bridgehousegrants.org.uk; **e-mail:** bridgehousetrust@corpoflondon.gov.uk.

Britain–Nepal Medical Trust

Founded in 1967 by Dr J. Cunningham to assist the people of Nepal to improve their health.

Activities: Operates in Nepal in the field of health and community development through self-conducted programmes, research and training courses.

Geographical Area of Activity: Nepal.

Restrictions: Funds currently restricted to the Trust's own work.

Publications: Annual Report.

Finance: Annual revenue £624,422, expenditure £685,638 (2001).

Trustees: Dr I. A. Baker (Chair.); Dr I. A. Campbell; Dr I. Harper; Dr G. Holdsworth; J. Mecaskey; Dr K. Ovreberg; Dr N. Padfield; Dr D. Patterson; Dr J. Payne; P. Saunders; Dr S. Sinclair; T. Tamang; P. Wilson.

Principal Staff: Trust Co-ordinator J. Banez-Ockelford; Co. Sec. and Admin. A. G. Peck.

Address: Export House, 130 Vale Rd, Tonbridge TN9 1SP.

Telephone: (1732) 360284; **Fax:** (1732) 363876; **e-mail:** bnmtuk@compuserve.com.

British Academy

Established in 1902 to promote the study of the humanities and social sciences.

Activities: The United Kingdom national academy for the humanities and social sciences. Operates nationally and internationally in the fields of academic research in the humanities and social sciences. Provides grants to British-based scholars for a wide range of personal research projects, for conference attendance, and for international collaboration. Supports research posts (post-doctoral and senior level) and a series of scholarly projects. Also funds a number of British institutes abroad and in the United Kingdom. Publishes monographs or serial publications relating to various aspects of the social sciences. Organizes and publishes papers from lectures, conferences and symposia. Maintains links with international partners (academies and research councils) and supports international scholarly collaboration. Member of international organizations including the European Science Foundation (q.v.), ALLEA and the Union Académique Internationale.

Geographical Area of Activity: International.

Restrictions: In most cases, awards offered only for post-doctoral research in the humanities and social sciences undertaken by scholars normally resident in the United Kingdom.

Publications: Monographs and other scholarly publications; Annual Proceedings; Biannual Review.

Finance: Sources of finance: mainly British Government departments; some private foundations and private funds. Net assets £9,559,367 (March 2001); annual revenue £35,135,803, expenditure £34,746,899 (2000–01).

Principal Staff: Pres. Lord Runciman; Vice-Pres. Prof. J. S. Morrill, Prof. K. I. B. Spärck Jones; Treas. J. S. Flemming; Sec. P. W. H. Brown.

Address: 10 Carlton House Terrace, London SW1Y 5AH.

Telephone: (20) 7969-5200; **Fax:** (20) 7969-5300; **Internet:** www.britac.ac.uk; **e-mail:** secretary@britac.ac.uk.

The British Council

Established to promote educational and cultural relations between the United Kingdom and other countries world-wide.

Activities: Operates internationally through cultural, educational, English language and information programmes. Maintains 227 offices and teaching centres in 109 countries world-wide.

Geographical Area of Activity: International.

Publications: Numerous publications in the fields of English language, education and the arts.

Finance: Financed by a grant-in-aid from the Government, and revenues from its teaching and examination activities. Total income £571,000,000 (2003–04).

Board of Trustees: Baroness Helena Kennedy (Chair.); Sir Tim Lankester (Deputy Chair.); Catherine Eva; Charles Grant; Sir Michael Jay; Jude Kelly; Gerard Lemos; Prof. Lord May of Oxford; Heather Rabbatts; Sir Robert Smith.

Principal Staff: Dir Gen. David Green.

Address: 10 Spring Gardens, London SW1A 2BN.

Telephone: (161) 957-7755; **Fax:** (161) 957-7762; **Internet:** www.britishcouncil.org; **e-mail:** general.enquiries@britcoun.org.

British Heart Foundation

Founded in 1961 by Lord Evans and a group of eminent colleagues, the British Heart Foundation is the leading British medical research charity working in the field of cardiovascular disease.

Activities: The Foundation funds medical research into the causes, prevention, diagnosis and treatment of heart disease. It provides support and information to sufferers and their families, through British Heart Foundation nurses, rehabilitation programmes and support groups. The Foundation educates the public and health professionals about heart disease prevention and treatment. It promotes training in emergency life-support skills for the public and health professionals, and provides equipment to hospitals and other health providers. In 2000–01 the Foundation spent £67,000,000 on research, education and patient care.

Geographical Area of Activity: United Kingdom.

Publications: Leaflets and videos for members of the public, patients and their families, schools, hospitals and doctors' surgeries.

Finance: Total assets £200,314,000 (March 2002); annual revenue £64,725,000, total charitable expenditure £67,482,000 (2002).

Trustees: Prof. Sir Keith Peters (Chair.); and 29 other members.

Principal Staff: Dir Gen. Maj.-Gen. Leslie Busk; Sec. and Finance Dir John Edwards; Medical Dir Prof. Sir Charles George.

Address: 14 Fitzhardinge St, London W1H 4DH.

Telephone: (20) 7935-0185; **Fax:** (20) 7486-5820; **Internet:** www.bhf.org.uk.

British Institute of Archaeology at Ankara

Founded in 1948 to support British research in the archaeology and associated subjects (geography, art history, history, literature) of Turkey and the surrounding regions.

Activities: Acts as a centre for research in Turkish archaeology and ancillary subjects. A number of research and travel grants and a post-doctoral research fellowship are offered each year for British Commonwealth citizens who are students of archaeology or related fields. Also makes travel grants and administers an annual fieldwork award sponsored by the Society for the Promotion of Hellenic Studies. The Institute also organizes lectures in the United Kingdom, and publishes the results of research.

Geographical Area of Activity: United Kingdom and Turkey.

Publications: *Anatolian Studies; Anatolian Archaeology;* monograph series.

Finance: Annual revenue £379,000, grants disbursed £120,000 (2000).

Principal Staff: Chair. Sir Timothy Daunt; Sec. Dr Stuart Campbell; Treas. Dr Nicholas Milner.

Address: 10 Carlton House Terrace, London SW1Y 5AH; İngiliz Arkeoloji Enstitüsü, Tahran Caddesi 24, Kavaklidere, 06700 Ankara, Turkey.

Telephone: (20) 7969-5204; **Fax:** (20) 7969-5401; **Internet:** britac3.britac.ac.uk/institutes/ankara; **e-mail:** biaa@britac.ac.uk.

British Institute of International and Comparative Law

Founded in 1958 to provide an international centre for the study of the practical application to current problems of public international law, private international law, European Community (now European Union) law and comparative law.

Activities: The Institute organizes lectures, seminars and conferences, and publishes books and periodicals in its fields of interest. It also operates the Commonwealth Legal Advisory Service, a scheme promoting the exchange of ideas, advice and assistance between Commonwealth governments.

Geographical Area of Activity: International.

Publications: *International and Comparative Law Quarterly; Bulletin of Legal Developments* (fortnightly); and monographs.

Council of Management: Rt Hon. Lord Bingham of Cornhill (Chair.); and 47 members.

Principal Staff: Chair. Exec. Committee Michael Hutchings; Dir Dr Mads Andenas; Dir of Studies M. Anderson.

Address: Charles Clore House, 17 Russell Sq., London WC1B 5JP.

Telephone: (20) 7862-5151; **Fax:** (20) 7862-5152; **Internet:** www.biicl.org; **e-mail:** info@biicl.org.

British Red Cross Society

The British Red Cross, founded in 1870 by Royal Charter and part of the International Red Cross movement (q.v.), has some 80,000 volunteers, working in its 70 branches throughout the United Kingdom. They provide emergency services and skilled care for those in need and crisis both in their local community and overseas.

Activities: In the United Kingdom, operates through local branches and centres to provide a full range of services in the community which include: medical loans, home from hospital, therapeutic care, emergency response, fire-victim support, domiciliary care, First Aid duties and First Aid training. Funds are raised to enable the British Red Cross to send aid in the form of money, materials or personnel, to disaster-stricken areas of the world.

Geographical Area of Activity: International.

Restrictions: No grants are made to individuals.

Publications: Annual Report and Review.

Finance: Annual revenue £160,849,000, expenditure £131,668,000 (2001).

Trustees: John McClure (Chair.); C. Dixon-Carter, Sir Alan Munro, Michael Walsh (Vice-Chair.).

Principal Staff: Dir Gen. Sam Younger.

Address: 9 Grosvenor Crescent, London SW1X 7EJ.

Telephone: (20) 7235-5454; **Fax:** (20) 7245-6315; **Internet:** www.redcross.org.uk; **e-mail:** information@redcross.org.uk.

Burden Trust

Founded in 1913 for charitable purposes in the fields of medical research and hospitals, schools and training institutions, care of and homes for the aged, necessitous persons and children, with a bias towards the Anglican Church.

Activities: Operates internationally, disbursing grants in the above areas.

Geographical Area of Activity: International.

Finance: Annual revenue £169,780, grants disbursed £189,500 (2002).

Trustees: Dr M. G. Barker (Chair.); R. E. J. Bernays (Deputy Chair.); M. C. Baker; Rt Rev. George Cassidy; A. C. Miles; Prof. G. M. Stirrat; M. C. Tosh.

Principal Staff: Hon. Sec. M. C. Tosh.

Address: Little Clandon, The Street, West Clandon, Guildford GU4 7ST.

Telephone: (1483) 222561; **Fax:** (1483) 224187.

CAB International

Established as the Imperial Agricultural Bureaux in 1913, became an international non-profit organization with a new constitution in 1985; aims to disseminate scientific knowledge in order to promote sustainable development and human welfare.

Activities: Operates in three principal areas: information for development, providing access to information for people in less-developed countries; bioscience, carrying out research into biodiversity, pest management and environmental issues; and publishing books on applied life sciences, journals and information in electronic forms. Maintains research offices in Kenya, Malaysia, the People's Republic of China, and Trinidad, and marketing offices in the United Kingdom and the USA.

Geographical Area of Activity: International.

Publications: *CAB International Report on Activities 2000–2002*; Annual Review.

Principal Staff: Dir Gen. Dr Denis Blight.

Address: Nosworthy Way, Wallingford OX10 8DE.

Telephone: (1491) 832111; **Fax:** (1491) 833508; **Internet:** www.cabi.org; **e-mail:** corporate@cabi.org.

Edward Cadbury Charitable Trust, Inc

Founded in 1945 for general charitable purposes.

Activities: Supports small or new organizations and projects involved with the voluntary sector in the West Midlands (especially in the fields of education and Christian mission), the ecumenical movement and inter-faith relations.

Geographical Area of Activity: United Kingdom (West Midlands).

Restrictions: Grants are made to registered charities only: grants are not made to students nor to individuals.

Finance: Annual revenue £718,529, expenditure £924,459 (April 2002).

Trustees: C. E. Gillett (Chair.); N. R. Cadbury; C. R. Gillett; A. S. Littleboy; C. S. Littleboy.

Principal Staff: Correspondent and Trust Man. S. Anderson.

Address: College Walk, Selly Oak, Birmingham B29 6SL.

Telephone: (121) 472-1838; **Fax:** (121) 472-7013.

William Adlington Cadbury Charitable Trust

Founded in 1923 to provide funds for general charitable purposes, with preference given to the West Midlands.

Activities: The Trust's main funding areas are: the West Midlands, the rest of the United Kingdom, as well as cross-community projects between Northern Ireland and the Republic of Ireland, and national charities working overseas (Africa). It operates in the fields of the Society of Friends and other religious organizations, social welfare, health and medicine, conservation of the environment, and education, through grants to registered charities.

Geographical Area of Activity: United Kingdom and Africa.

Restrictions: Grants only to charities registered in the United Kingdom; no funding for individuals. International grants currently to organizations known to the Trust.

Publications: Annual Report; grant policy and guidelines.

Finance: Annual revenue £506,377, expenditure £644,086 (March 2002).

Trustees: Sophy J. Blandy; Brandon Cadbury; Rupert A. Cadbury; Katherine M. Van Hagen Cadbury; J. C. Penny; C. Margaret Salmon; Sarah Stafford; W. James B. Taylor; A. D. M. Thomas.

Principal Staff: Sec. C. M. Stober.

Address: 2 College Walk, Birmingham B29 6LQ.

Telephone: (121) 472-1464; **Internet:** www.wa-cadbury.org.uk; **e-mail:** info@wa-cadbury.org.uk.

CAFOD—Catholic Fund for Overseas Development

Established in 1962 as the official organization of the Roman Catholic Bishops' Conference of England and Wales, through which the Catholic Church in those countries shares its resources with sister churches and other partners throughout the world in order to work with them to combat poverty, hunger, ignorance, disease and suffering.

Activities: Funds projects in more than 80 developing countries in Africa, Central and South America and the Caribbean, Asia, the Pacific and the Middle East; and helps the needy and refugees in Central and Eastern Europe. The main work is in the funding of development projects in food production; preventive health; vocational training; community development; non-formal education; and block grants made to Church development agencies. Specialized fields include emergency aid and relief funds for refugees, and projects concerned with AIDS. Grants are occasionally made for medicines and equipment together with student grants. Grants are also made to volunteer programmes through recognized agencies. Campaigns are conducted in the United Kingdom to raise awareness of the causes of poverty and injustice world-wide. CAFOD also co-funds with the United Kingdom Overseas Development Administration and the European Union.

Geographical Area of Activity: International.

Restrictions: Projects involving heavy construction costs are not undertaken, nor are funds provided for primary or secondary education.

Publications: Annual Review; *The CAFOD Journal; LINK; FRIDAY.*

Finance: Grants from benefactors including the United Kingdom Government, the European Union, and Comic Relief, the Millennium Commission and the Community Fund (formerly the National Lottery Charities Board, qq.v.). Total income £26,000,000 (2001/02).

Trustees: Rt Rev. John Crowley (Chair.); Most Rev. Patrick Kelly, Archbishop of Liverpool; Peter Langan; Mildred Nevile.

Principal Staff: Dir Julian Filochowski.

Address: Romero Close, Stockwell Rd, London SW9 9TY.

Telephone: (20) 7733-7900; **Fax:** (20) 7274-9630; **Internet:** www.cafod.org.uk; **e-mail:** hqcafod@cafod.org.uk.

Cambridge Commonwealth Trust

Established in 1982 by the University of Cambridge under the Chairmanship of His Royal Highness The Prince of Wales to provide financial assistance for outstanding students from overseas who, without help, would be unable to take up their places at Cambridge University.

Activities: Awards scholarships to students from Commonwealth countries and Myanmar and Sudan who wish to study at the University of Cambridge. Preference is given to students from developing countries. The Trust works in collaboration with the Cambridge Overseas Trust, the Cambridge European Trust (qq.v.) and other agencies.

Geographical Area of Activity: International.

Address: POB 252, Cambridge CB2 1TZ.

Telephone: (1223) 327308; **Fax:** (1223) 313138.

Cambridge European Trust

Established in 1995 by the University of Cambridge to provide part-cost financial assistance to help outstanding students from countries of the European Union (other than the United Kingdom) to take up their places at Cambridge University.

Activities: Awards annual scholarships to students from countries of the European Union (outside the United Kingdom). Works in collaboration with the Cambridge Commonwealth Trust and the Cambridge Overseas Trust (qq.v.).

Geographical Area of Activity: European Union countries.

Principal Staff: Chair. HRH Duke of Edinburgh.

Address: POB 252, Cambridge CB2 1TZ.

Telephone: (1223) 327308; **Fax:** (1223) 313138.

Cambridge Overseas Trust

Established in 1982, formerly the Chancellor's Fund, by the University of Cambridge under the Chairmanship of His Royal Highness The Prince of Wales to provide financial assistance for outstanding students from overseas who, without help, would be unable to take up their places at Cambridge University.

Activities: Awards scholarships annually to enable graduates who are citizens or permanent residents of countries outside the Commonwealth to study at the University of Cambridge. The Trust works in collaboration with the Cambridge Commonwealth Trust, Cambridge European Trust (qq.v.) and other agencies.

Geographical Area of Activity: International.

Address: POB 252, Cambridge CB2 1TZ.

Telephone: (1223) 327308; **Fax:** (1223) 313138.

Camelot Foundation

Founded in 1996 for general charitable purposes.

Activities: Operates nationally in the areas of health and welfare, especially disadvantaged and disabled people and refugees, through offering grants. Works through two main programmes, the Transforming Lives Programme and the Strategic Change Programme, with additional support through the Annual Leadership Awards Programme and the Annual Policy Forum.

Geographical Area of Activity: United Kingdom.

Restrictions: No grants are made to individuals.

Finance: Annual revenue £1,047,687, expenditure £611,320 (March 2002).

Trustees: Caroline Pickering (Chair.) David Bryan (Vice-Chair.); John Graham; Frances Hasler; Robert McGowan; Dot Renshaw; Anne Spackman; Dianne Thompson; Neil Wragg.

Principal Staff: Dir Susan Elizabeth.

Address: University House, 11–13 Lower Grosvenor Place, London SW1W 0EX.

Telephone: (20) 7828-6085; **Fax:** (20) 7937-0574; **Internet:** www.camelotfoundation.org.uk; **e-mail:** info@camelotfoundation.org.uk.

Cancer Research UK

Established in 2002, as a result of the merger of the Cancer Research Campaign and the Imperial Cancer Research Fund, to investigate all matters connected with or bearing on the causes, prevention, treatment and cure of cancer.

Activities: Supports and undertakes a comprehensive programme of research in institutes, hospitals, universities and medical schools throughout Britain and Northern Ireland. Works in anti-cancer drug development and to ensure cancer sufferers receive new treatments as quickly as possible; carries out research into the psychological impact of cancer and improving communication between doctor and patient; provides a wide range of authoritative cancer information publications and guidelines for general practitioners; and promotes cancer prevention through education and research. Also trains cancer scientists and doctors.

Geographical Area of Activity: United Kingdom.

Publications: Annual Report; scientific report; brochures; leaflets; factsheets; accounts.

Finance: Combined research expenditure of Imperial Cancer Research Fund and Cancer Research Campaign approx. £132,000,000 (2001–02).

Council: Representatives of the Royal College of Physicians of London, Royal College of Surgeons of England, Royal Society, Royal Veterinary College, Medical Research Council; fund governors and members appointed to represent particular branches of science; Rt Hon. Baroness Hayman (Chair.).

Principal Staff: Dir Gen. Dr Paul Nurse; Dir of Laboratory Research Dr Richard Treisman.

Address: POB 123, Lincoln's Inn Fields, London WC2A 3PX.

Telephone: (20) 7242-0200; **Fax:** (20) 7269-3100; **Internet:** www.cancerresearchuk.org.

CARE—Christian Action Research and Education

Founded in1983 to promote Christian standards, particularly in family life and education.

Activities: Operates a national Homes programme and Pregnancy Counselling Centres throughout the United Kingdom, and carries out research and education work. Maintains an office in Brussels to carry out networking, research and communication work and provide information briefings to members of the European Parliament. Also campaigns on an international level.

Geographical Area of Activity: United Kingdom and Europe.

Restrictions: Not a grant-making organization.

Publications: *CARE* (magazine, 3 a year); and numerous other publications.

Address: 53 Romney St, London SW1P 3RF.

Telephone: (20) 7233-0455; **Fax:** (20) 7233-0983; **Internet:** www.care.org.uk.

Carnegie Trust for the Universities of Scotland

Founded in 1901 to promote the development of Scottish universities.

Activities: Provides grants to Scottish undergraduates to help with university fees and to staff and graduates of Scottish universities to fund study and research. Also makes a number of larger grants to projects of interest to Scottish universities as a whole.

Geographical Area of Activity: Scotland.

Finance: Assets £41,848,282 (2002); annual revenue £1,827,811, grants disbursed £1,512,872 (2002).

Trustees: Sir L. Robertson (Chair.); E. Brown; Lady Balfour of Burleigh; Rev. R. Buchanan-Smith; Lord Cameron of Lochbroom; David Edward; Earl of Elgin; C. A. MacLeod; T. B. Hunter; Eileen Mackay; Lord Wilson of Tillyorn; and 15 *ex officio* members.

Principal Staff: Sec. and Treas. Sir John Arbuthnott.

Address: Cameron House, Abbey Park Pl., Dunfermline KY12 7PZ.

Telephone: (1383) 622148; **Fax:** (1383) 622149; **Internet:** www.carnegie-trust.org; **e-mail:** jgray@carnegie-trust.org.

Carnegie United Kingdom Trust

Founded in 1913 by Andrew Carnegie for the improvement of the well-being of the masses of the people of Great Britain and Ireland, by such means as are embraced within the meaning of the word 'charitable' according to Scottish or English law, and which are best fitted from age to age for securing these purposes, remembering that new needs are constantly arising as the masses advance.

Activities: Operates within the United Kingdom and the Republic of Ireland. Policies for the period 2001–06 are: Rural Community Development, village initiatives that help local communities help themselves; Village Halls, to encourage the broader use of village halls as centres of services for the community, e.g. as healthy living centres, post offices, surgeries, shops, resource centres, computer centres etc; Creativity and Imagination, to enhance the capacity of creative and imaginative groups of people to benefit others; and Young People, to encourage active participation of youth, particularly in public policy decision-making, and increase the role and responsibility of young people in education, health, the community, etc.

Geographical Area of Activity: United Kingdom and Ireland.

Restrictions: Grants are not given to individuals and are only made to voluntary organizations registered (recognized in Scotland) as charitable.

Publications: Annual Report; *Policy Guidelines*.

Finance: Assets £33,431,424 (2001); annual revenue £1,730,851, grants disbursed £1,144,700 (2001).

Trustees: William Thomson (Chair.); David Stobie (Vice-Chair.); George Atkinson; Urmila Banerjee; Linda Brown; Sir Neil Cossons; Dr David Fraser; Lady Anthony Hamilton; Jeremy Holmes; Joy Kinna; Janet Lewis-Jones; L. Linaker; Rosie Millard; Anthony Pender; Sandy Saddler; Dr David Smith; C. Roy Woodrow.

Principal Staff: Chief Exec. C. John Naylor.

Address: Comley Park House, Dunfermline KY12 7EJ.

Telephone: (1383) 721445; **Fax:** (1383) 620682; **Internet:** www.carnegieuktrust.org.uk.

Sir Ernest Cassel Educational Trust

Founded in 1919 by Sir Ernest Cassel to promote adult education by voluntary bodies, and the higher education of women.

Activities: Awards Mountbatten Memorial Grants to Commonwealth students experiencing hardship in their final year of higher education. Overseas research grants are made to junior teaching staff in British faculties for the study of foreign languages, literature and civilization, and administered by the British Academy (q.v.). Also makes grants to adult education institutions in the United Kingdom.

Geographical Area of Activity: United Kingdom.

Trustees: Countess Mountbatten of Burma (Chair.).

Principal Staff: Sec. David Constable.

Address: 199 West Malvern Rd, Malvern WR14 4BB.

Telephone: (1684) 572437.

Charity Islamic Trust Elrahma

Established in 1993 to assist the needy in the Muslim community in the United Kingdom and internationally.

Activities: Operates in the fields of social welfare, education and religion nationally and internationally, through grants for the building of schools, mosques and institutions for orphans, and for the relief of poverty.

Geographical Area of Activity: International.

Finance: Annual revenue £1,671,845, expenditure £1,752,227 (2001).

Principal Staff: Contact: M. Zamir.

Address: 3 The Ave, London NW6 7YG.

Telephone: (20) 8459-3244; **Fax:** (20) 8451-7993.

Leonard Cheshire International

Founded in the United Kingdom in 1948 by Group Capt. Leonard Cheshire, the organization has undertaken international work since 1955. LCI's mission is to work with disabled people throughout the world by providing the environment necessary for each individual's physical, mental and spiritual wellbeing.

Activities: Provides support and guidance to more than 250 locally-run programmes for disabled people and their families, in 57 countries outside the United Kingdom; programmes include rehabilitation centres, skills training centres, community-based support services and residential homes. The organization also advises local communities on obtaining grants for new developments.

Geographical Area of Activity: International.

Restrictions: Grants only to Leonard Cheshire Services.

Publications: *Compass* (quarterly); Annual Report.

Principal Staff: Chair. Richard Thomas; Int. Dir Rupert Ridge.

Address: 30 Millbank, London SW1P 4QD.

Telephone: (20) 7802-8224; **Fax:** (20) 7802-8275; **Internet:** www.lcint.org; **e-mail:** international@london.leonard-cheshire.org.uk.

ChildHope

Established in 1990, ChildHope is dedicated to improving the lives and defending the rights of 'street children'—homeless young people living and working in the streets. It is linked to independent ChildHope (q.v.) organizations in Brazil and the Philippines.

Activities: Operates in the fields of human rights and social welfare, through financial support and providing training for projects helping children, in particular 'street children' in developing countries. Currently supports street children projects in Bangladesh, Bulgaria, Brazil, Ethiopia, Kenya, Macedonia, Nepal, Peru, Romania and Tanzania. ChildHope acts as a capacity building consultant throughout Central and Eastern Europe. Also operates a library and information service.

Geographical Area of Activity: Asia, Africa, Central and Eastern Europe, and Central and South America.

Publications: Annual Report; *Street Children—Resource Sheets for Project Management*; Newsletter.

Finance: The Foundation receives funding from the United Kingdom Government, the European Union, various foundations, trusts and charities, individual supporters and members of the public. Annual revenue £661,814, expenditure £771,710 (2001).

Trustees: Kathy Lavidge (Chair.); Kay Stevens (Hon. Treas.); Jackie Bell; Rodney Buse; Andrew Carrick; Mike Hadfield; Sandra Scott.

Principal Staff: Exec. Dir Geoffrey Cordell.

Address: Lector Court, 151 Farringdon Rd, London EC1 3AF.

Telephone: (20) 7833-0868; **Fax:** (20) 7833-2500; **Internet:** www.childhopeuk.org; **e-mail:** chuk@gn.apc.org.

Children's Aid Direct

A charitable organization established to aid children in need world-wide.

Activities: Aims to assist children affected by conflict, natural disasters or poverty in less-developed countries, through providing shelter, health care, food, education and advice. Works in collaboration with local communities. Carries out information and education activities in the United Kingdom, to inform people about the lives of children with whom the organization works.

Geographical Area of Activity: International.

Finance: Annual revenue £6,958,000, expenditure £8,470,000 (Sept. 2001).

Principal Staff: Exec. Dir. Nick Thompson.

Address: Crown House, 6–8 Crown St, Reading RG1 2SE.

Telephone: (118) 958-4000; **Fax:** (118) 958-1230; **e-mail:** enquiries@cad.tele2.co.uk.

Childwick Trust

Founded in 1985, the Trust operates in six main areas: to assist old people in need; charities connected with horse breeding or racing; Jewish charities in the United Kingdom; charities involved in education and assistance for people who have worked in the mining industry in South Africa; and charities benefiting disabled people in the United Kingdom.

Activities: The Trust operates nationally and internationally in the above areas.

Geographical Area of Activity: United Kingdom and South Africa.

Restrictions: No grants to individuals and grants are made to United Kingdom-based organizations only.

Finance: Annual revenue £2,526,068, expenditure £2,385,000 (April 2002).

Trustees: J. D. Wood (Chair.); A. R. G. Cane; S. Frost; Hon. C. A. S. Grimston; P. G. Glossop;.

Principal Staff: Trust Sec. Karen Groom.

Address: 9 The Green, Childwick Bury, St Albans AL3 6JJ.

Telephone: (1727) 812486; **Fax:** (1727) 844666.

Christian Aid

Founded by the British Council of Churches to finance practical programmes of aid, development and relief among the world's neediest people, including refugees and disaster victims; and to deepen understanding of poverty by carrying out educational work in the United Kingdom.

Activities: Operates mainly in developing countries, through regional and local organizations in the fields of relief, resettlement, development (in areas including agriculture, health, urban welfare and water resources) and education. Some funds are granted to community, race relations and development education projects in the United Kingdom.

Geographical Area of Activity: International.

Publications: Annual Report; Audited Accounts; quarterly list of grants; *Christian Aid News;* catalogue of current publications and resources list.

Finance: Assets £24,700,000 (2002); annual revenue £50,000,000, grants disbursed £54,300,000 (2002).

Trustees: The Board of Trustees is appointed by the British and Irish Churches.

Principal Staff: Dir Daleep Mukarji.

Address: 35 Lower Marsh, London SE1 7RT.

Telephone: (20) 7620-4444; **Fax:** (20) 7620-0719; **Internet:** www.christian-aid.org.uk; **e-mail:** info@christian-aid.org.

Winston Churchill Memorial Trust

Founded in 1965 to provide travelling fellowships to promote understanding of overseas countries, and the acquisition of knowledge to make participants more effective in their work and their community upon their return.

Activities: About 100 fellowships are awarded annually to British citizens of any age, for an average stay overseas of eight weeks, so that they can learn more about their trade or profession, or about other countries.

Publications: Newsletter (2 a year); explanatory leaflets.

Finance: Total grants approx. £530,000 (2003).

Board of Trustees: Winston S. Churchill (Chair.); and 11 others.

Principal Staff: Office Man. S. Matthews.

Address: 15 Queen's Gate Terrace, London SW7 5PR.

Telephone: (20) 7584-9315; **Fax:** (20) 7581-0410; **Internet:** www.wcmt.org.uk; **e-mail:** office@wcmt.org.uk.

Citizenship Foundation

Founded in 1989 to promote improved understanding of citizenship, political, social and legal systems, and participation in community and voluntary projects. The Foundation had as its predecessor the Law in Education Project, established in 1984 to develop teaching materials which introduce students to the notions of responsibilities and rights, and the role of law in democratic society.

Activities: Operates a wide range of programmes in the fields of the law and human rights, and education. Currently working in Australia, Brazil, Mexico, Kosovo, Russia and Turkey.

Geographical Area of Activity: International.

Publications: *Passport to Life;* Annual Report; educational resources and publications.

Finance: Total assets £203,952 (2001) total income £812,253, total expenditure £791,930 (2001).

Principal Staff: Chief Exec. Tony Breslin.

Address: Ferroners House, Shaftesbury Pl., Aldersgate St, London EC2Y 8AA.

Telephone: (20) 7367-0500; **Fax:** (20) 7367-0501; **Internet:** www.citfou.org.uk; **e-mail:** info@citfou.org.uk.

City Parochial Foundation

Founded in 1891 for general charitable purposes in the Metropolitan Police District of London and the City of London.

Activities: Operates within all London Boroughs and the City of London; main priority areas are combating social isolation, and working to alleviate discrimination, isolation and violence. Grants are made to organizations working in these areas.

Geographical Area of Activity: London Boroughs and City of London.

Restrictions: No grants are made to individuals, nor for community business initiatives, medical research or equipment, trips abroad, one-off events, major capital appeals, the direct replacement of public funds, publications or endowment appeals.

Publications: *Capital Youth; Financial Fitness; London Prisons Link*; Annual Report; Grant Guidelines; Grants Review.

Finance: Total grants disbursed £1,120,570 (2002).

Principal Staff: Chair. Prof. Gerald Manners; Clerk Bharat Mehta.

Address: 6 Middle St, London EC1A 7PH.

Telephone: (20) 7606-6145; **Fax:** (20) 7600-1866; **Internet:** www.cityparochial.org.uk; **e-mail:** info@cityparochial.org.uk.

Clore Duffield Foundation

Founded in 1964, as the Clore Foundation, to provide financial assistance for general charitable purposes. Money is donated at the discretion of the trustees.

Activities: Donations are made to registered charities usually in the United Kingdom, with a particular focus on supporting children, young people and society's most vulnerable individuals, principally in the fields of museum and gallery education, art and design education, performing arts education, health, social welfare and disability. Operates a main grants programme, with grants ranging between £10,000 and £2,500,000, a small grants programme for museum and gallery education, an Artworks Programme making awards for high-quality art teaching and funding art research, and the Clore Cultural Leadership Programme, promoting the leadership and management of cultural organizations in the United Kingdom, which was to be launched in September 2003.

Geographical Area of Activity: Mainly United Kingdom.

Publications: Annual Report and Accounts.

Finance: Total income £2,621,196, total expenditure £6,008,093 (2001).

Trustees: Vivien L. Duffield (Chair.); C. Deletra; D. T. D. Harrel; Sir J. Stevens; M. Trask; Sir M. Weinberg.

Principal Staff: Exec. Dir Sally Bacon.

Address: Unit 3, Chelsea Manor Studios, Flood St, London SW3 5SR.

Telephone: (20) 7351-6061; **Internet:** www.cloreduffield.org.uk; **e-mail:** cloreduffield@aol.com.

Colt Foundation

Established in 1978; promotes research into social, medical and environmental problems created by commerce and industry, and supports the publication of the results of such research.

Activities: Finances research projects, especially concerning occupational health, carried out at universities and research establishments in the United Kingdom. The Foundation also supports research scientists, awarding grants to PhD and MSc students whose subjects are relevant to occupational and environmental medicine. Projects include: ELEGI—Edinburgh Lung and Environment Group Initiative; The Institute of Occupational Health: Sickness Absence in the NHS (National Health Service); Medical Research Council Environmental Epidemiology Unit, Southampton; Department of Physiology, University of Bristol; Silsoe Research Institute; National Heart and Lung Institute with the Royal Brompton Hospital; research on particle toxicology at Napier University, Edinburgh; the Arthritis Research Campaign Unit of Chronic Disease Epidemiology, University of Manchester; and the Centre for Occupational and Environmental Health, University of Manchester.

Geographical Area of Activity: United Kingdom.

Restrictions: Grants are not made to individuals, to projects outside the United Kingdom, nor to the general funds of charities.

Publications: Annual Report.

Finance: Assets £11,297,047 (2001); annual revenue £352,442, grants disbursed £502,449 (2001).

Trustees: T. J. Ault; Prof. D. Coggon; C. M. Gilchrist; N. Lebus; P. Lebus; W. McD. Morison; A. O'Hea; J. O'Hea; P. O'Hea.

Principal Staff: Dir Jackie Douglas.

Address: New Lane, Havant PO9 2LY.

Telephone: (23) 9249-1400; **Fax:** (23) 9249-1363; **Internet:** www.coltfoundation.org.uk; **e-mail:** jackie.douglas@uk.coltgroup.com.

Comic Relief

Established in 1984, as Charity Projects, to provide aid for disadvantaged people in the United Kingdom and Africa.

Activities: Operates in the United Kingdom and internationally, principally in Africa (one-third of grants are made in the United Kingdom, and two-thirds in Africa, although a new International Grants programme has been established to make grants internationally). Grants programmes in the United Kingdom and in Africa focus on social welfare, giving grants to small organizations. International projects are run to support children, including those affected by conflict and orphans. The organization runs the Red Nose Day fundraising campaign every two years and in Summer 2002 launched the Sport Relief fundraiser.

Geographical Area of Activity: International (mainly Africa and the United Kingdom).

Publications: Annual report and accounts; information leaflet.

Finance: Money raised for Red Nose Day £61,000,140 (2001).

Trustees: Sir Tim Bell (Pres.); P. Bennett-Jones (Chair.); R. Curtis (Vice-Chair.); C. Howes (Sec.); M. Harris (Treas.); E. Freud; L. Henry; M. Letts; L. Newman; N. Varma; B. Adoloyo Fayemi; C. Lloyd; M. Freud; E. Nicoli.

Principal Staff: CEO K. Cahill; Grants Dir L. Firth; Business Dir M. Ager; Marketing Dir A. Horton-Mastin.

Address: 89 Albert Embankment, 5th Floor, London SE1 7TP.

Telephone: (20) 7820-5555; **Fax:** (20) 7820-5500; **Internet:** www.comicrelief.com; **e-mail:** red@comicrelief.org.uk.

CommonWeal

Founded in 1972, and formerly known as Scottish Churches Action for World Development, to unite Scottish churches in support of world development.

Activities: Concerned with tackling questions of poverty, injustice and conflict in the world, through encouraging exchange of views, and action in Scotland and in partnership with people overseas, working for just, peaceful structures, relationships and processes; finding strategies for empowerment and disarmament; and taking part in inter-faith and cross-cultural dialogue. Organizes workshops and conferences; provides resource material, advice and information; and co-operates with other agencies in development and environmental work.

Geographical Area of Activity: International.

Restrictions: CommonWeal is not a funding agency.

Publications: Educational materials.

Principal Staff: Exec. Sec. Chris Booth.

Address: J. B. Priestley Library, University of Bradford, Richmond Rd, Bradford BD7 1DP.

Telephone: (1274) 233404.

Commonwealth Foundation

An inter-governmental organization originally founded in 1965 to support the work of the non-governmental sector within the Commonwealth, in particular the strengthening of civil society, sustainable development and poverty eradication, and to facilitate pan-Commonwealth and inter-country connections between people, their associations and communities at all levels.

Activities: The Foundation supports programmes in four areas: Civil Society, including developing citizen input into making society better; Professional Exchange, supporting the work of over 30 Commonwealth Professional Associations; Arts and Culture including the Commonwealth Writers Prize; and the annual Commonwealth Understanding Fellowship Scheme. *Ad-hoc* responsive grants are also available in these four areas. Priority is given to projects incorporating the following values: respect for diversity and human dignity and opposition to all forms of discrimination; adherence to democracy, the rule of law, good governance, freedom of expression and the protection of human rights; the elimination of poverty and the promotion of people-centred development and progressive removal of the wide disparities in living standards among Commonwealth member countries; and international peace and security, the rule of international law and opposition to terrorism. Also hosts an on-line discussion forum.

Geographical Area of Activity: Commonwealth countries.

Finance: Funded by Commonwealth governments.

Principal Staff: Chair. Graça Machel; Dir Colin Ball; Deputy Dir Rudo Chitiga; Programme Officer Nicole Brown, Andrew Firmin, Seth Lartey.

Address: Marlborough House, Pall Mall, London SW1Y 5HX.

Telephone: (20) 7930-3783; **Fax:** (20) 7839-8157; **Internet:** www.commonwealthfoundation.com.

Commonwealth Relations Trust

Founded in 1937 to promote a common understanding between, and unity of ideals in, the countries of the Commonwealth.

Activities: The Trust funds the Commonwealth Programme jointly with the Nuffield Foundation (q.v.). The Programme's aim is to support the development of service provision or policy-making in developing Commonwealth countries, and to promote links between the United Kingdom and these countries. It does this by funding activities which develop the expertise and experience of practitioners and policy-makers. The Trust is particularly interested in projects in the fields of education, law, mental health, child welfare, older people and their families, working in Eastern and Southern African Commonwealth countries.

Geographical Area of Activity: United Kingdom and the Commonwealth.

Restrictions: Grants are made to non-profit organizations based in the United Kingdom. No grants are made to individuals.

Finance: Commonwealth Programme offers four grants of up to £250,000 each (2002).

Trustees: Baroness O'Neill (Chair.); A. B. Atkinson; Dr P. Doyle; Dame Brenda Hale; Prof. Sir Robert May; Prof. Sir Michael Rutter; Anne Sofer.

Principal Staff: Dir Anthony Tomei.

Address: 28 Bedford Sq., London WC1B 3EG.

Telephone: (20) 7631-0566; **Fax:** (20) 7323-4877; **Internet:** www.nuffieldfoundation.org; **e-mail:** atomei@nuffieldfoundation.org.

Community Foundation for Northern Ireland

Founded in 1979 to support voluntary and community projects in Northern Ireland; until 2003 known as the Northern Ireland Voluntary Trust.

Activities: The Foundation's main emphasis is on community empowerment and social justice, supporting projects which deal with social problems in urban and rural areas: young people, women's groups, unemployed people, community care, the arts, education, welfare rights and inter-community activity. Also maintains an office in Derry.

Geographical Area of Activity: Northern Ireland.

Publications: Annual report and accounts; *Infonotes* (publication series); *In Brief* (report series).

Finance: Assets £7,576,284 (2001); total grants £3,440,000 (2002).

Trustees: M. Black (Chair.); V. Anderson; M. Armstrong; M. Blood; M. Conway; B. Devine; S. Douglas; Dr M. Fitzduff; J. Flynn; Dr N. Kearney; P. McDonagh; M. Mills; A. Paisley.

Principal Staff: Dir Avila Kilmurray.

Address: Community House, Citylink Business Park, Albert St, Belfast BT12 4HQ.

Telephone: (28) 9024-5927; **Fax:** (28) 9032-9839; **Internet:** www.nivt.org; **e-mail:** info@nivt.org.

Community Fund

Founded in 1994, as the National Lottery Charities Board, to help meet the needs of the most disadvantaged in society and improve the quality of life of the community. Name changed in April 2001.

Activities: Operates nationally and internationally through capital grants and revenue funding. The principal grants programmes are: main grants (funding projects that help people or communities overcome problems that stop them from playing a full part in economic, social and community activities); grants for projects up to £60,000; international grants (for NGOs based in the United Kingdom to work in collaboration with NGOs abroad in the area of development education and addressing the causes of poverty and inequality); research grants (for social and medical research, in particular in the areas of young and old people, minority ethnic groups and people with learning disabilities); small grants; and Awards for All (for small groups involved in areas such as sports, heritage and the arts, and community and voluntary activities).

Geographical Area of Activity: Throughout the United Kingdom, and also international.

Restrictions: Only funds United Kingdom charities, and international charities and voluntary groups that are based in the United Kingdom.

Finance: Revenue comes from the Board's share of 28% of the profits derived from the United Kingdom's National Lottery; grants total £375,000,000 (2000/01).

Trustees: Lady Diana Brittan (Chair.); Dame Valerie Strachan (Deputy Chair.); the Chair. of the England, Wales, Scotland, Northern Ireland and United Kingdom Cttees; and others.

Principal Staff: Chief Exec. Richard Buxton.

Address: St Vincent House, 16 Suffolk St, London SW1Y 4NL.

Telephone: (20) 7747-5300; **Fax:** (20) 7747-5347; **Internet:** www.community-fund.org.uk; **e-mail:** enquiries@community-fund.org.uk.

Concern Universal

Founded in 1976 to provide aid to less-developed countries.

Activities: Promotes development and improved living conditions in less-developed countries, particularly among refugees, victims of war, people with AIDS and their children.

Geographical Area of Activity: Sub-Saharan Africa, Central and South America and Asia.

Restrictions: Does not make grants.

Finance: Annual revenue £4,071,619, grants disbursed £4,253,653 (2002).

Governing Council: D. McLeish (Chair.); Friedenstern Howard (Vice-Chair.); Rachel Shirley (Hon. Sec.); Bishop Donald Arden; Dan Bishop; Michael Lloyd; Joan McGee; Michael Powner.

Principal Staff: Exec. Dir Dr Ian Williams; Deputy Exec. Dir Gerry Carthy.

Address: 21 King St, Hereford HR4 9BX.

Telephone: (1432) 355111; **Fax:** (1432) 355086; **e-mail:** cu.uk@concern-universal.org.

Conservation Foundation

Founded in 1982 by Prof. David Bellamy and David Shreeve to provide a means for interested parties—governments, corporations, institutions, organizations and associations—to collaborate on environmental causes in which common ground can be found.

Activities: The Foundation works nationally and internationally in the fields of conservation and the environment, working with commercial and environmental organizations to create award schemes, research and information programmes, conferences, educational materials, multimedia presentations and publications. Supports ethno-medical research by young scientists in rainforests, and local conservation projects in the United Kingdom and Europe. Organized a conference for European and Russian NGOs as part of its London Initiative on the Russian Environment.

Geographical Area of Activity: International.

Publications: *Network 21* (environmental news service); *Parish Pump* (newsletter).

Council: John Senior (Chair.); Prof. David Bellamy (Pres.); George Arthur; Dr Biddy Baxter; John Curtis; William Moloney; David Shreeve.

Principal Staff: Exec. Dir David Shreeve.

Address: 1 Kensington Gore, London SW7 2AR.

Telephone: (20) 7591-3111; **Fax:** (20) 7591-3110; **Internet:** www.conservationfoundation.co.uk; **e-mail:** info@conservationfoundation.co.uk.

Dr M. Aylwin Cotton Foundation

Established in 1971 by the late Dr Mary Aylwin Cotton to promote the advancement of education and learning by furthering the study of the archaeology, architecture, history, language and art of cultures related to the Mediterranean area.

Activities: Offers Cotton Foundation Fellowship awards to academic researchers, Publication Grants towards the costs of publishing academic research, and other awards for studies in the archaeology, history, language and art of the Mediterranean. All awards, fellowships and grants are open to men and women of all nationalities.

Geographical Area of Activity: International.

Trustees: Albany Trustee Co Ltd; David Ridgway.

Principal Staff: Anne McMillan.

Address: Pollet House, POB 232, St Peter Port, Guernsey GY1 4LA.

Telephone: (1481) 724136; **Fax:** (1481) 710478; **Internet:** www.cotton-foundation.org; **e-mail:** info@cotton-foundation.org.

Marie Curie Cancer Care

Founded in 1948 by T. B. Robinson and four others, to provide in-patient and community care for cancer patients. Previously known as the Marie Curie Memorial Foundation, Marie Curie Cancer Care is dedicated to the care of people affected by cancer and the enhancement of their quality of life, through its caring services, cancer research and education.

Activities: Operates Marie Curie hospices throughout the United Kingdom. Provides a network of Marie Curie Nurses across the United Kingdom, giving practical nursing care at home to people with cancer, free of charge. The Foundation also has its own Marie Curie Research Institute at Oxted in Surrey, and runs education and training courses for health professionals involved in cancer care. Maintains an office in Scotland.

Geographical Area of Activity: United Kingdom.

Publications: Annual report and accounts; other leaflets and brochures.

Finance: Annual revenue £71,969,000, expenditure £66,643,000 (2001/02).

Trustees: Governed by a Council; Sir Nicholas Fenn (Chair.).

Principal Staff: Chief Exec. Trevor Lake.

Address: Camelford House, 87–89 Albert Embankment, London SE1 7TP.

Telephone: (20) 7599-7777; **Fax:** (20) 7599-7788; **Internet:** www.mariecurie.org.uk; **e-mail:** info@mariecurie.org.uk.

Marie Curie Research Institute

Established, as part of Marie Curie Cancer Care (q.v.), to apply the latest advances in research to the development of new methods for the prevention, early detection and improved treatment of cancer.

Activities: Offers graduate studentships, postgraduate and post-doctoral fellowships, and clinical research training fellowships at the Institute. Collaborates internationally in its research, and holds international meetings.

Restrictions: Only research within the Institute, or for collaborative programmes, is supported.

Publications: Numerous research publications.

Principal Staff: Dir Dr P. O'Hare.

Address: The Chart, Oxted RH8 0TL.

Telephone: (1883) 722306; **Fax:** (1883) 714375; **Internet:** www.mcri.ac.uk; **e-mail:** g.currie@mcri.ac.uk.

Cystic Fibrosis Trust

Founded in 1964 to finance medical and scientific research aimed at understanding, treating and curing cystic fibrosis and ensuring that people with cystic fibrosis receive the best possible care and support in all aspects of their lives.

Activities: The Trust's principal objectives are to fund research to find a cure for cystic fibrosis and to improve symptom control; ensure appropriate clinical care for those with cystic fibrosis; and to support those affected by cystic fibrosis by providing information, support and where appropriate, financial assistance.

Geographical Area of Activity: Mainly United Kingdom.

Publications: Report of operations and financial statement; *CF Today* (5 a year); *CF Talk; Focus on Fundraising;* extensive booklet series.

Finance: Net assets £2,619,000 (2002); annual revenue £6,829,000, expenditure £7,219,000 (2002).

Trustees: Tony Angel; Duncan Bluck; Sir Peter Cresswell; Sir Robert Johnson; Peter Levy; Dr James Littlewood.

Principal Staff: Chief Exec. Rosie Barnes.

Address: 11 London Rd, Bromley BR1 1BY.

Telephone: (20) 8464-7211; **Fax:** (20) 8313-0472; **Internet:** www.cftrust.org.uk; **e-mail:** enquiries@cftrust.org.uk.

Roald Dahl Foundation

Founded in 1991 to support charitable work in haematology, neurology and literacy.

Activities: Provides funding in the United Kingdom only, in the areas of haematology, neurology and literacy. Its haematology and neurology funding is specifically for young people under 25 years suffering from blood disorders (excluding cancer), epilepsy and head injury, and funds are given for specialist paediatric nursing, with an emphasis on community care; residential and day-care centres for young people; medical equipment which allows patients to be cared for at home; and young people with the above-mentioned medical conditions, suffering financial hardship. The Foundation's Literacy programme funds specific literacy work to improve poor literacy skills among children and young people, and their families, in out of school clubs and centres for young people aged between 16 and 25, and computer/technological and other assistance to enable children and young people who are visually impaired or head injured to access the written word. The Foundation is also involved with the nationally sponsored Readathon reading event. The Foundation aims to help organizations to whom funds are not readily available, i.e. small or new organizations.

Geographical Area of Activity: United Kingdom.

Restrictions: Grants are made in the United Kingdom only to organizations with charitable status. Grant applications are not considered for general appeals from large, established charities; for research (in any field); nor for school or tertiary education fees.

Finance: Assets £1,414,969 (2002).

Trustees: F. Dahl; M. A. F. Goodwin; R. E Hills.

Principal Staff: Deputy Dir Linda Lazenby.

Address: 92 High St, Great Missenden HP16 0AN.

Telephone: (1494) 890465; **Fax:** (1494) 890459; **Internet:** www.roalddahlfoundation.org.

Daiwa Anglo-Japanese Foundation

Founded in 1988 by Yoshitoki Chino, then Chairman of Daiwa Securities Ltd. The organization aims to enhance the understanding between the peoples of the United Kingdom and Japan in the field of culture; to enable British and

Japanese academics and students to further their education by travel; and to make grants to educational or research charities in the United Kingdom and Japan.

Activities: The Foundation's programme consists of three elements: Daiwa Scholarships, of which seven or more are awarded annually to British graduates aged 20 and over, in subjects other than Japanese, to enable them to study Japanese for 20 months in Japan; general grants, about 100 of which are made annually to institutions and individuals in the United Kingdom and Japan for Japanese studies, professional and academic visits and exchanges, and cultural activities; and Daiwa Foundation Japan House in London, where activities include seminars, exhibitions, concerts, lectures as well as providing a centre for the encouragement of non-governmental and non-commercial relations between the United Kingdom and Japan. Small grants are available to individuals and institutions; foundation awards of between £10,000 and £25,000 are available for institutionally-based applicants supporting collaboration between Japanese and United Kingdom partners, and Daiwa Adrian Prizes of approximately £50,000 are awarded every three years in recognition of significant scientific collaboration between British and Japanese research teams. Maintains a reference library and information centre. In 2000 a partnership between the Foundation and the Arts and Humanities Research Board was instituted, offering two fellowships in the creative and performing arts..

Geographical Area of Activity: United Kingdom and Japan.

Restrictions: Grants are made for United Kingdom–Japanese exchange only.

Finance: Assets £38,071,572 (2000–01); annual revenue £1,333,363, total expenditure £1,501,737 (2001–02).

Trustees: Sir David Wright (Chair. and Joint Man. Trustee); Y. Chino (Vice-Chair.); N. P. Clegg (Joint Man. Trustee); Lady Adrian; Prof. Sir Alec Broers; Lord Carrington; H. Fujii; T. Kusuda; Lord Roll of Ipsden.

Principal Staff: Dir Gen. Marie Conte-Helm.

Address: Daiwa Foundation Japan House, 13–14 Cornwall Terrace, London NW1 4QP.

Telephone: (20) 7486-4348; **Fax:** (20) 7486-2914; **Internet:** www.daiwa-foundation.org.uk; **e-mail:** office@dajf.org.uk.

David Davies Memorial Institute of International Studies

Founded in 1954 as a memorial to Lord Davies to advance and promote the development of the study of international relations in the political, economic, legal, social, educational, conservational and other fields; to carry out research into current problems in international relations, and to make the results of such research and study available for the benefit of the members of the Institute, other organizations with similar objects and the public at large, and, in particular, to publish and disseminate information on such problems.

Activities: Operates in the field of international relations, through study groups, its Journal and an Annual Memorial Lecture.

Geographical Area of Activity: United Kingdom.

Publications: *International Relations* (3 a year); occasional papers; books arising from work of study groups.

Finance: Total income £149,144, total expenditure £101,442 (Sept. 2001).

Principal Staff: Pres. Lord Healey of Riddlesden; Chair. Sir John Boyd; Dir Peter Unwin.

Address: 300 Kew Green, Richmond TW9 3BH.

Telephone and Fax: (20) 8940-8037; **e-mail:** munwin@ddmi.org.uk.

Miriam Dean Refugee Trust Fund

Founded in 1964 to provide aid to victims of war or other disasters.

Activities: Awards grants to charitable organizations abroad, particularly in Tanzania and India.

Geographical Area of Activity: India and Tanzania.

Finance: Annual revenue £118,546, expenditure £123,663 (2001).

Trustees: J. Budd; H. Capon; T. Dorey; V. Dorey; G. Livermore.

Principal Staff: Brian Tims.

Address: St Peters Vicarage, High St, Shipton Bellinger, Tidworth SP9 7UF.

Telephone: (1980) 842244; **e-mail:** trustees@miriamdean.fsnet.co.uk.

Delius Trust

Founded in 1935 according to the will of Jelka Delius to promote the music of Frederick Delius by providing financial aid for performances and recordings and by publishing a collected edition of his works.

Activities: Operates nationally and internationally in the field of the arts and humanities, through providing grants to individuals and institutions towards the cost of performances and to finance recordings.

Publications: *The Collected Edition of the works of Frederick Delius*; several other books on the life and works of Frederick Delius.

Finance: Total income £127,680, total expenditure £108,541 (2001).

Trustees: David Lloyd-Jones (Chair.); Helen Faulkner; Martin Williams.

Principal Staff: Sec. Marjorie Dickinson.

Address: 16 Ogle St, London W1P 8JB.

Telephone: (20) 7436-4816; **Fax:** (20) 7637-4307; **Internet:** www.delius.org.uk/g_trust.htm; **e-mail:** deliustrust@mbf.org.uk.

Diabetes UK

Founded in 1934, and previously known as the British Diabetic Association, to fund research into the prevention, treatment and cure of diabetes; to provide information and support to people living with diabetes.

Activities: Funds and initiates research into the causes and treatment of diabetes (about 38% of expenditures); provides advice and information to people with diabetes, and to health-care professionals; campaigns against discrimination and promotes improved services for people with diabetes.

Geographical Area of Activity: United Kingdom.

Publications: Annual report and accounts; *Diabetes Update* (quarterly journal); *Balance* (bi-monthly magazine); publications and leaflets.

Finance: Annual research budget approx. £5,200,000 (2001).

Board of Trustees: Sir Michael Hirst (Chair.).

Principal Staff: Chief Exec. Paul Streets.

Address: 10 Parkway, London NW1 7AA.

Telephone: (20) 7424-1000; **Fax:** (20) 7424-1001; **Internet:** www.diabetes.org.uk; **e-mail:** info@diabetes.org.uk.

Diageo Foundation

Established in 1998 by Diageo PLC, which includes the brands Guinness and Burger King, with a commitment to contribute 1% of Diageo's world-wide trading profit, less interest, to the community; aims to act as a primary funding and support organization for social investment programmes and charitable giving.

Activities: Operates internationally, principally where Diageo PLC businesses operate, through the following main programmes: Local Citizens; Alcohol Education; Global Brands; Our People (i.e. employee involvement); Skills for Life; and Water of Life. Works in collaboration with community charitable groups.

Geographical Area of Activity: International.

Restrictions: Does not fund individuals, medical charities, religious or political organizations, or animal welfare charities.

Finance: Total income £2,121,545, total expenditure £1,126,447 (June 2002).

Principal Staff: Admin. Julie Hodsden.

Address: Henrietta House, 8 Henrietta Pl., London W1G 0NP.

Telephone: (20) 7927-5368; **Fax:** (20) 7927-4637; **Internet:** www.diageo.com/ad/citizenship/community/dia_found .html?352; **e-mail:** diageofoundation@diageo.com.

Diana, Princess of Wales Memorial Fund

Established in 1997 in memory of Diana, Princess of Wales (1961–97) by donations from the public and revenue from commemorative goods, including the sale of a music single by Elton John.

Activities: In March 1998 it was announced that the Fund would award grants of £1,000,000 to each of the six charities formally supported by Diana, Princess of Wales (the English National Ballet, Leprosy Mission (q.v.), National AIDS Trust, Centrepoint, The Hospital for Sick Children—Great Ormond Street and Royal Marsden Hospital). Grants of £1,000,000 were also awarded to the Osteopathic Centre for Children, Leonard Cheshire—Park House and the Elton John Aids Foundation (q.v.). The Fund also provided grants to numerous charities operating in the areas of the arts, education, care of children, young people and families, health, homelessness and to organizations which help the victims of landmines. Nationally, the Fund's programme for 2002 focused on Transition to Adulthood and Independence, funding projects for young people between the ages of 12 and 25, working with prisoners' families, young refugees and asylum seekers. Internationally, from 2002, the Foundation supported practical and advocacy projects assisting communities affected by landmines and other explosive remnants of war.

Geographical Area of Activity: International.

Finance: Annual revenue £5,740,000, grants disbursed £9,852,000 (2001).

Trustees: Lady Sarah McCorquodale (Pres.); Anthony Julius (Vice-Pres.); Andrew Hind (Treas.); Tahera Aanchanwan; Lord Bhatia; Douglas Board; Rt Hon. Earl Cairns; Michael Gibbins; Jenny McAleese; Roger Singleton; Christopher Spence; Caroline Whitfield.

Principal Staff: Chief Exec. Andrew Purkis.

Address: County Hall, Westminster Bridge Rd, London SE1 7PB.

Telephone: (20) 7902-5500; **Fax:** (20) 7902-5511; **Internet:** www.theworkcontinues.org; **e-mail:** info@memfund.org.uk.

Ditchley Foundation

Founded in 1958 by Sir David Wills to promote, carry out or advance any charitable objects, and in particular any branches or aspects of education likely to be for the common benefit of British subjects and citizens of the USA.

Activities: Exclusively supports in-house activities; maintains Ditchley Park as a conference centre and supports the Ditchley conference programme. Facilities are available to other bodies on a fee-paying basis. Organizes invitation-only conferences on topics of international concern to the British and American peoples, with the participation of other nationalities, particularly from Member States of the European Union. American and Canadian Ditchley Foundations exist with similar aims, and to assist in the work of the United Kingdom Ditchley Foundation.

Restrictions: No grants to individuals or groups unless at Ditchley.

Publications: Annual report and financial statement; newsletters and conference reports.

Council of Management: John Major (Chair.).

Principal Staff: Dir Sir Nigel Broomfield.

Address: Ditchley Park, Enstone, Chipping Norton OX7 4ER.

Telephone: (1608) 677346; **Fax:** (1608) 677399; **Internet:** www.ditchley.co.uk; **e-mail:** info@ditchley.co.uk.

Dulverton Trust

Founded in 1949 by the first Lord Dulverton for general charitable purposes at the discretion of the Trustees.

Activities: Operates nationally and to a lesser extent in East Africa and Southern Africa in the fields of youth and education, conservation, general welfare, religion, industrial relations, peace and security.

Geographical Area of Activity: United Kingdom, East Africa and Southern Africa.

Restrictions: No grants in area of medicine and health, nor to organizations based in Greater London or Northern Ireland, nor to museums, arts organizations, expeditions, schools, colleges or universities. Grants only made to registered charities and never to individuals.

Finance: Assets £102,000,000 (2000).

Trustees: Col D. V. Fanshawe (Chair.); Lord Carrington; Lord Dulverton; The Earl of Gowrie; Sir John Kemp-Welch; Sir Malcolm Rifkind; Dr Catherine Wills; C. A. H. Wills; Hon. Robert Wills.

Principal Staff: Dir Sir Robert Corbett; Deputy Dir Col C. P. R. Bates.

Address: 5 St James's Pl., London SW1A 1NP.

Telephone: (20) 7629-9121; **Fax:** (20) 7495-6201; **e-mail:** trust@dulverton.org.

Earth and Space Foundation

Founded in 1994 by Dr Charles Cockell to fund expeditions and field work that bring the space exploration and environmental communities together.

Activities: The Foundation funds expeditions and field-work with awards that further the vision of 'the earth as an oasis, cared for by a space-faring civilization'. Awards are made annually and recent projects include meteorite analysis in Australia and mapping of coral reefs in Madagascar.

Geographical Area of Activity: International.

Restrictions: Grants available for field work and expeditions.

Finance: Income from grants and private donations.

Board of Directors: Dr Charles Cockell (Chair.); Dr Dale Stokes; Dr Donald White.

Address: POB 46, Cambridge CB1 3UW.

Internet: www.earthandspace.org; **e-mail:** info@ earthandspace.org.

John Ellerman Foundation

Formed in 1992 by the merger of the New Moorgate Trust Fund and the Moorgate Trust Fund, for general charitable purposes.

Activities: Works in the United Kingdom and, to a limited extent, in Southern Africa. Grants given are based on merit and worthiness, and are made in particular to areas such as medical research and medical care, social welfare and disability, the arts and the environment.

Geographical Area of Activity: Currently United Kingdom only.

Restrictions: Grants are not made to individuals, nor for education; only supports organizations with an office in the United Kingdom.

Finance: Assets £109,229,000 (March 2001); annual revenue £4,898,000, grants disbursed £4,116,750 (2001).

Trustees: P. C. Pratt (Chair.); A. Boschi; Dr J. H. Hemming; D. D. Martin-Jenkins; D. Parry; Surgeon Vice-Admiral A. Revell; B. Scott.

Principal Staff: Dir Dr Christopher P. Hanvey.

Address: Aria House, 23 Craven St, London WC2N 5NS.

Telephone: (20) 7930-8566; **Fax:** (20) 7839-3654; **Internet:** ncvo-vol.org.uk/jef.html; **e-mail:** postmaster@ellerman.prestel.co.uk.

Engineering and Physical Sciences Research Council—EPSRC

The EPSRC was established in 1994, one of the organizations formed by the splitting up of the Science and Engineering Research Council (SERC). The SERC was replaced by the EPSRC, the Particle Physics and Astronomy Research Council (PPARC—q.v.) and the Biotechnology and Biological Sciences Research Council (BBSRC—q.v.).

Activities: Aims to promote and support high-quality basic, strategic and applied research, and related postgraduate training in engineering and the physical sciences (chemistry, physics and mathematics). It places special emphasis on meeting the needs of the users of its research and training outputs, in order to enhance the United Kingdom's industrial competitiveness and quality of life.

Geographical Area of Activity: United Kingdom.

Restrictions: Grants only to universities.

Publications: *Newsline;* and other publications.

Finance: Funded by the Government; annual expenditure £478,000,000 (2001–02).

Principal Staff: Chief Exec. Prof. John O'Reilly.

Address: Polaris House, North Star Ave, Swindon SN2 1ET.

Telephone: (1793) 444000; **Internet:** www.epsrc.ac.uk; **e-mail:** infoline@essrc.ac.uknh.

English-Speaking Union of the Commonwealth

Founded in 1918 by Sir Evelyn Wrench to promote the mutual advancement of the education of the English-speaking peoples of the world.

Activities: Operates internationally through groups in over 40 countries in the fields of education, the arts and humanities, science, environment, and international affairs, through self-conducted programmes and conferences. Provides scholarships and fellowships for British graduates and teachers to pursue research at US universities and institutions, for study trips to the USA, and awards for British graduates or holders of professional qualifications to work on projects in developing countries.

Geographical Area of Activity: International.

Publications: Annual Report; *Concord* (magazine, 2 a year); *ESU Newsletter* (6 a year).

Finance: Annual revenue £1,762,001, expenditure £1,505,665 (April 2002).

Trustees: HRH Prince Philip, Duke of Edinburgh (Pres.); Lord Watson of Richmond (Chair.); Rt Hon. the Lord Hunt of Wirral, Lady Appleyard (Deputy Chair.).

Principal Staff: Dir Gen. Valerie Mitchell; Financial Controller Ronald Dellal.

Address: Dartmouth House, 37 Charles St, London W1J 5ED.

Telephone: (20) 7529-1550; **Fax:** (20) 7495-6108; **Internet:** www.esu.org; **e-mail:** esu@esu.org.

European Association for Cancer Research

Founded in 1968 to advance cancer research by facilitating communication between scientists.

Activities: Operates internationally (mainly in Europe) in the field of medicine and science, by organizing conferences, sponsoring research, awarding fellowships and issuing publications. There are about 2,000 members in 50 countries both within and outside Europe.

Geographical Area of Activity: International (mainly Europe).

Publications: *EACR Newsletter* (2 a year); *European Journal of Cancer* (monthly).

Principal Staff: Sec.-Gen. Prof. Helga M. Ögmundsdóttir; Contact: P. Saunders.

Address: Cancer Research Laboratories, Pharmacy School, Nottingham NG7 2RD.

Telephone: (115) 951-5114; **Fax:** (115) 951-5115; **Internet:** www.eacr.org; **e-mail:** paul.saunders@nottingham.ac.uk.

The Eveson Charitable Trust

Founded in 1994 according to the will of Violet Eveson for general charitable purposes.

Activities: Provides grants to organizations working in Herefordshire, Worcestershire and the West Midlands, including Birmingham and Coventry, in the fields of the physically or mentally disabled, hospitals and hospices, the elderly, blind and deaf people, children, the homeless and medical research.

Geographical Area of Activity: United Kingdom (Herefordshire, Worcestershire and the West Midlands).

Restrictions: Grants are made only in Herefordshire, Worcestershire and the West Midlands; no grants for indivduals.

Finance: Total assets £64,575,635 (April 2002); annual revenue £2,169,021, grants disbursed £2,015,884 (2002).

Trustees: Bruce R. Maughfling (Chair.); J. Martin Davies; Rt Rev. John Oliver, David P. Pearson; Bill Wiggin.

Principal Staff: Admin. Alex D. Gay.

Address: 45 Park Rd, Gloucester GL1 1LP.

Telephone: (1452) 501352; **Fax:** (1452) 302195.

Esmée Fairbairn Foundation

Founded in 1961, as the Esmée Fairbairn Charitable Trust (name changed in 2001).

Activities: Money is distributed to charities in the United Kingdom at the discretion of the trustees, with emphasis placed on prevention and self-help. There are four priority areas of interest: social development; the arts and heritage; education; and the environment. In 2001 the Foundation launched Rethinking Crime and Punishment, a major three-year initiative funding projects to increase public understanding of and involvement in the criminal justice system.

Geographical Area of Activity: United Kingdom.

Restrictions: Guidelines must be obtained from the Foundation office before an application is submitted.

Publications: Application guidelines.

Finance: Grants disbursed approx. £26,000,000 (2003).

Trustees: J. S. Fairbairn (Chair.); C. J. M. Hardie (Vice-Chair. and Treas.); Sir Antony Acland; A. G. Down; F. Fairbairn; M. Lane Fox; R. Kent; K. Lampard; Baroness Linklater; Lord Rees-Mogg; W. Sieghart.

Principal Staff: Dir Margaret Hyde; Deputy Dir Kathryn Sykes.

Address: 11 Park Pl., London SW1A 1LP.

Telephone: (20) 7297-4700; **Fax:** (20) 7297-4701; **Internet:** www.esmeefairbairn.org.uk; **e-mail:** info@esmeefairbairn.org.uk.

Federal Trust for Education and Research

Founded in 1945 under the auspices of William Beveridge to explore, through research and education, the suitability of federal solutions to problems of governance at national, continental and global level.

Activities: Involved in carrying out and promoting research, nationally and internationally, in the fields of international citizenship, constitutional developments, good governance at European and global level, European Union (EU) enlargement and various aspects of EU policy, through self-conducted programmes, conferences and publications. The Trust currently conducts research into the issue of devolution in the United Kingdom, democracy and stakeholder participation in the United Kingdom, the United Kingdom's relationship with the countries of the European Union, European Union policy, the role of international organizations such as the International Monetary Fund, the United Nations, and the World Trade Organization in developing global governance.

Publications: *European Futures; The Euro Debate; Treaty of Nice Explained;* newsletter; books; reports.

Trustees: John Pinder (Chair.); Sir Donald Maitland (Pres.).

Principal Staff: Dir Brendan Donnelly.

Address: 7 Graphite Square, Vauxhall Walk, London SE11 5EE.

Telephone: (20) 7735-4000; **Fax:** (20) 7735-8000; **Internet:** www.fedtrust.co.uk; **e-mail:** governance@fedtrust.co.uk.

Feed the Minds

Founded by Lord Coggan in 1964 to support the development of Christian literature programmes in less-developed countries.

Activities: The organization supports local publishers of all denominations to produce, distribute and broadcast materials needed by the communities they serve. Operates the Feed the Minds Scholarship Fund to enable local publishers to train staff to professional standards, and writers' workshops to help young authors to develop their writing skills.

Geographical Area of Activity: International.

Restrictions: No grants are made to individuals or for building projects.

Publications: *Theological Book Review; Feed the Minds News.*

Finance: Annual revenue £636,276, expenditure £633,248 (March 2002).

Trustees: J. Clark (Chair.); Pres. Dr Pauline Webb (Pres.); C. Bayne (Treas.); Rev. Canon J. Lowe.

Principal Staff: Admin. Jackie Marsh.

Address: 1 Marylebone Rd, London NW1 4AQ.

Telephone: (8451) 212102; **Fax:** (20) 7643-0388; **Internet:** www.feedtheminds.org; **e-mail:** info@feedtheminds.org.

Finnish Institute in London Trust

Founded in 1990, the purpose of the Trust is to finance and administer the Finnish Institute in London and thus to foster good relations between Finland and the United Kingdom.

Activities: Promotes exchanges in the fields of the humanities and performing arts, social and natural sciences, and technology, through the provision of grants for education and training and providing information on Finnish activities and resources. Maintains a library of approximately 2,000 volumes in English and Finnish.

Principal Staff: Dir Timo Valjakka.

Address: Finnish Institute, 35–36 Eagle St, London WC1R 4AJ.

Telephone: (20) 7404-3309; **Fax:** (20) 7404-8893; **Internet:** www.finnish-institute.org.uk; **e-mail:** info@finnish-institute.org.uk.

Focus Humanitarian Assistance Europe Foundation

Established by the Ismaili Muslim community in Europe and North America; a network of agencies providing emergency humanitarian assistance in less-developed countries. The organization is an affiliate of the Aga Khan foundations network (q.v.).

Activities: Operates in less-developed countries of Africa, and Central and Southern Asia, providing humanitarian assistance to areas stricken by natural disasters or by conflict. Sister organizations operate in Canada, Pakistan and the USA. Maintains liaison offices in Afghanistan, France, Portugal, the Russian Federation and Tajikistan.

Geographical Area of Activity: Africa, and Central and Southern Asia.

Finance: Annual revenue £7,722,560, expenditure £8,222,189 (2001).

Principal Staff: Contact: Ghulam Panjwani.

Address: 205–209 Addiscombe Rd, Croydon CR0 6SP.

Telephone: (20) 8654-6131; **Fax:** (20) 8655-1649; **e-mail:** focuseurope@focushumanitarian-europe.org.

Foundation for International Environmental Law and Development—FIELD

Founded in 1989 by James Cameron and Philippe Sands to contribute to the progressive development of international law, including the law of the European Union for the protection of the environment and the attainment of sustainable development.

Activities: Operates world-wide in the area of law in relation to conservation and the environment, through self-conducted programmes, research and conferences. Specialist programme areas are: international law and sustainable development; climate change and energy; trade, environment and sustainable development; and biodiversity and marine resources. These operate in conjunction with work and research into biodiversity, forests, and the establishment and implementation of national environmental legislation. The Foundation offers advisory services on international and European Union environmental issues; carries out research, teaches specialist postgraduate courses for students from developed and developing countries; offers placements to students and lawyers in its London office; and issues publications.

Geographical Area of Activity: International.

Publications: Series of books on International Law and Sustainable Development; books on international and European Union environmental law, and environmental issues.

Finance: Assets £30,000 (Nov. 2000).

Trustees: Madeleine Colvin; Robin Griffith; Alan Jenkins; Janet Maughan.

Principal Staff: Dir Antony Gross.

Address: 52–53 Russell Sq., London WC1B 4HP.

Telephone: (20) 7637-7950; **Fax:** (20) 7637-7951; **Internet:** www.field.org.uk; **e-mail:** field@field.org.uk.

Foundation for Sport and the Arts

Founded in 1991 by Littlewoods, Vernons and Zetters football pools companies to promote greater participation in, and enjoyment of, sport and the arts.

Activities: Operates nationally in the field of the arts and sports. Seeks to enhance the quality of life of the community in general, through funding in the areas of sport and the arts at every level. Its main objective is to help increase participation in, and enjoyment of, sport and the arts by the whole community. Grants range from £50 to £75,000.

Geographical Area of Activity: United Kingdom (excluding the Isle of Man and the Channel Islands).

Restrictions: Potential applicants are requested to telephone to ask for current guidelines. No grants are made for horse-racing or professional association football.

Finance: Financed by subscriptions from Littlewoods and Vernons football pools.

Trustees: Sir Tim Rice (Chair.); Lord Brabazon of Tara (Deputy Chair.); Nicholas Allott; Lord Attenborough; Dame Janet Baker; Rt Hon. Sir Christopher Chataway; Lord Faulkner; Lord Grantchester; Clive Lloyd; Steve Roberts; Gary Speakman.

Principal Staff: Sec. to the Trustees Grattan Endicott; Admin. Rylda Blake; Finance Officer Peter Higgins.

Address: POB 20, Liverpool L13 1HB.

Telephone: (151) 259-5505; **Fax:** (151) 230-0664.

Foundation for the Study of Infant Deaths

Founded in 1971 by Mrs J. Hunter-Gray to raise funds for research into sudden infant death syndrome ('cot death'); to support bereaved parents; and to act as an information centre.

Activities: Operates in England, Wales and Northern Ireland in the fields of medicine and health, and social welfare and studies, through self-conducted programmes, research, grants to institutions and individuals, conferences, training courses and publications. The Foundation supports research programmes in various areas concerning the sudden and unexplained death of infants, including epidemiology, immunology, pathology, statistics and infection. Research grants relevant to sudden infant death syndrome (SIDS) are offered to researchers in the United Kingdom.

Geographical Area of Activity: England, Wales and Northern Ireland.

Publications: Newsletter (2 a year); numerous leaflets.

Finance: Net assets £1,174,000 (2000); annual revenue £1,064,000, expenditure £1,276,000 (2000).

Council of Trustees: Colin Baker (Chair.); the Countess of Limerick (Vice-Chair.); and 29 others.

Principal Staff: Dir Joyce Epstein.

Address: Artillery House, 11–19 Artillery Row, London SW1P 1RT.

Telephone: (870) 787-0885; **Fax:** (870) 787-0725; **Internet:** www.sids.org.uk/fsid; **e-mail:** fsid@sids.org.uk.

Foundation for Women's Health Research and Development—FORWARD

Founded by Efua Dorkenoo in 1983 to promote improved reproductive health among African women and their children, and education to counter traditional practices which are prejudicial to the health of women and children.

Activities: The primary objective of the Foundation since 1985 has been to campaign for the elimination of female genital mutilation (FGM), through sponsoring local health and education programmes, supporting community self-help groups, facilitating the development of co-ordinated policies on the issue within local authorities in the United Kingdom, disseminating information to professionals and students working on the issue, and providing training for professionals, including health workers, to provide better services to affected women.

Geographical Area of Activity: United Kingdom and Africa, in particular Nigeria, Ghana and Kenya.

Restrictions: Not a grant-making organization.

Publications: *Child Protection and Female Genital Mutilation; Holistic Care for Women: a Practical Guide for Midwives; Female Genital Mutilation: Proposals for Change; Out of Sight, Out of Mind; Another Form of Physical Abuse: prevention of female genital mutilation in the United Kingdom* (video); on-line newsletter and other publications.

Finance: Financed through grants from foundations and charities, and by the United Kingdom Department of Health.

Principal Staff: Chair. Naana Otoo-Oyertey; Dir Adwoa Kluvitse.

Address: 50 Eastbourne Terrace, 6th Floor, London W2 6LX.

Telephone: (20) 7725-2606; **Fax:** (20) 7725-2796; **Internet:** www.forwarduk.org.uk; **e-mail:** forward@forwarduk.org.uk.

Anne Frank Trust UK

Founded in 1991 to advance public education in the United Kingdom in the principles of racial and religious tolerance and democracy.

Activities: Organizes travelling exhibitions, and produces and distributes educational resources.

Geographical Area of Activity: United Kingdom.

Restrictions: Does not make grants.

Publications: *Moral Courage—Who's Got It?* (2002) (training pack and video for schools); *Anne Frank Declaration—Guidelines for Teaching Human Rights, Citizenship and Democracy* (2000); *The Web of Insights* (1998, training pack for youth leaders); other training manuals and resources for schools.

Finance: Annual revenue £249,793, expenditure £222,650 (2000).

Board of Trustees: Jack Morris (Chair.); George Gyte; Tom Jupp; Imran Khan; Dr Gillian Klein; Robin Richardson; Eva Schloss; Rabbi David Soetendap.

Principal Staff: Exec. Dir Gillian Walnes; Senior Admin. Laurie Burnley-Myers; Admin. Joanne Hoffman.

Address: POB 11880, London N6 4LN.

Telephone: (20) 8340-9077; **Fax:** (20) 8340-9088; **Internet:** www.annefrank.org.uk; **e-mail:** afet@afet.org.uk.

Gaia Foundation

Founded in 1985, as the Gaia Foundation to Spread Knowledge of the New Whole Earth Consciousness, beginning its work in the Amazon region.

Activities: Collaborates with projects in Europe, Central and South America, Africa and Asia to protect biodiversity and promote sustainable living. Co-ordinates information and seeks to create links between communities, individuals and organizations in the North and communities in the South, and to encourage financial collaboration in projects in developing countries.

Geographical Area of Activity: Europe, Central and South America, Africa and Asia.

Restrictions: Does not make grants to individuals.

Publications: *Cool Tobacco, Sweet Coca; Biopiracy—The Plunder of Nature and Knowledge; Indigenous Peoples of Colombia and the Law; The Forest Within; The Movement for Collective Intellectual Rights; Raiding the Future: Patent Truths or Patent Lies*; briefings; papers.

Finance: Annual revenue £1,082,378, expenditure £1,126,318 (June 2001).

Principal Staff: Dir Liz Hosken.

Address: 18 Well Walk, London NW3 1LD.

Telephone: (20) 7435-5000; **Fax:** (20) 7431-0551; **Internet:** www.thegaiafoundation.org; **e-mail:** gaia@gaianet.org.

Gatsby Charitable Foundation

Founded in 1967 to provide funds for general charitable purposes. One of the Sainsbury Family Charitable Trusts, which share a common administration.

Activities: The Foundation gives grants for work in the following areas: aid to less-developed countries (Africa), economic and social research, mental health, plant science, technical education, cognitive neuroscience, disadvantaged children and young people, social development, and the arts. The Foundation also funds the Sainsbury Centre for Mental Health. Local trusts, directed by local trustees, have been established in Cameroon, Kenya, Tanzania and Uganda to fund development projects.

Geographical Area of Activity: United Kingdom and Africa.

Restrictions: Unsolicited applications are not normally considered for funding. Grants are not normally made to individuals.

Publications: *Gatsby Papers; Technology Transfer: Report on Six Pilot Projects*; Annual Report.

Finance: Net assets £461,772,000 (April 2002); annual revenue £35,189,000, expenditure £38,399,000 (April 2002).

Trustees: A. T. Cahn; J. S. Portrait; C. T. S. Stone.

Principal Staff: Dir Michael Pattison; Finance Dir P. Spokes.

Address: Allington House, 1st Floor, 150 Victoria St, London SW1E 5AE.

Telephone: (20) 7410-0330; **Fax:** (20) 7410-0332; **Internet:** www.gatsby.org.uk; **e-mail:** contact@gatsby.org.uk.

J. Paul Getty Jr General Charitable Trust

Founded in 1985 to support general charitable purposes in areas of deprivation in the United Kingdom.

Activities: Involved in projects assisting the homeless, offenders and ex-offenders, the mentally ill, drug and alcohol addicts, community groups, self-help groups, and projects working with young people and ethnic minorities. Some support may also be given to conservation projects.

Geographical Area of Activity: United Kingdom.

Restrictions: Financial assistance is provided only to registered charities, not individuals. Charities already widely supported are unlikely to be considered. Preference is given to projects outside the South-East of the United Kingdom; no funds are offered outside the United Kingdom.

Finance: Annual revenue £1,575,697, grants disbursed £1,323,230 (2000).

Trustees: Christopher Gibbs; James Ramsden; Vanni Treves.

Principal Staff: Admin. Bridget O'Brien Twohig.

Address: 1 Park Sq. West, London NW1 4LJ.

Telephone: (20) 7486-1859.

The Glass-House Trust

Established in 1993 (as the Alex Sainsbury Charitable Trust), to work in the areas of parenting, family welfare and child development. One of the Sainsbury Family Charitable Trusts, which share a common administration.

Activities: Operates in the above areas through making grants to United Kingdom organizations working nationally and internationally. It also supports projects in the areas of child-care and family support, education and research/policy development.

Geographical Area of Activity: International.

Finance: Total assets £12,901,278 (April 2002); annual income £595,101, expenditure £659,928 (2002).

Trustees: J. S. Portrait; A. J. Sainsbury; J. M. Sainsbury; T. J. Sainsbury.

Principal Staff: Dir Michael Pattison.

Address: Allington House, 1st Floor, 150 Victoria St, London SW1E 5AE.

Telephone: (20) 7410-0330; **e-mail:** sfct@sfct.org.uk.

Glencore Foundation for Education and Welfare

Founded in 1994 for general charitable purposes.

Activities: Awards grants nationally and internationally at the discretion of the trustees, with a particular focus on Jewish education and welfare in Israel and internationally.

Geographical Area of Activity: International, particularly Israel.

Restrictions: Grants are not made to individuals.

Finance: Annual revenue £1,781,301, expenditure £1,781,084 (2001).

Trustees: J. Boxer; D. Dreyfuss; M. D. Paisner; J. G. Pattullo; L. M. Weiss.

Principal Staff: Contact: Colin Smith.

Address: c/o Glencore UK Ltd, 50 Berkeley St, London W1J 8HD.

Telephone: (20) 7629-3800; **Fax:** (20) 7499-5555.

Goodenough College

The College was founded in 1930 to improve international tolerance and understanding amongst people on the brink of their careers by providing a forum in which they could interact.

Activities: The College provides residential and educational facilities for 640 postgraduate students. It runs an extensive programme of conferences, lectures, debates and concerts, open to members and the general public.

Geographical Area of Activity: International.

Finance: Independently funded.

Board of Trustees: Sir Christopher Wates (Chair.).

Principal Staff: Dir Major-Gen. Tim Toyne-Sewell.

Address: Mecklenburgh Sq., London WC1N 2AN.

Telephone: (20) 7837-8888; **Fax:** (20) 7833-5829; **Internet:** www.goodenough.ac.uk; **e-mail:** director@goodenough.ac.uk.

Great Britain–Sasakawa Foundation

Founded in 1984 for the advancement of the education of the citizens of the United Kingdom and Japan in each other's institutions, culture, language, history, science and industry.

Activities: Operates principally in the United Kingdom and Japan, especially favouring projects involving reciprocal action between the two countries. Special awards include the Biennial Sasakawa Prize for Translation, for the translation of Japanese literature into English, and the Great Britain Sasakawa Foundation Cup, for outstanding contributions towards the teaching of Japanese.

Geographical Area of Activity: Mainly United Kingdom and Japan.

Restrictions: Grants are only made to citizens of either the United Kingdom or Japan, but consideration may be given to projects dealing with matters concerning the two countries from national and multinational organizations elsewhere.

Publications: Annual report and accounts; and brochures.

Finance: Annual revenue £766,019, total expenditure £650,778 (2001).

Trustees: (UK) Prof. Peter Mathias (Chair.); Earl of St Andrews; Baroness Brigstocke; Jeremy Brown; Michael French; Baroness Park of Monmouth; (Japan) Kazuo Chiba; Akira Iriyama; Prof. Harumi Kimura; Yohei Sasakawa; Prof. Shoichi Watanabe.

Principal Staff: Chief Exec. Peter Hand.

Address: Dilke House, 1 Malet St, London WC1E 7JN; Nippon Foundation, Bldg 4F, Akasaka, Minato-ku, Tokyo 107-0052 Japan.

Telephone: (20) 7436-9042 (London); (3) 6229-5465 (Tokyo); **Fax:** (3) 6229-5467 (Tokyo); **Internet:** www.gbsf.org.uk; **e-mail:** gbsf@gbsf.org.uk.

HALO Trust

Established in 1989; specializes in the removal of the debris of war, particularily mine clearance.

Activities: Operates in countries of Africa, South-East and Central Asia, and the Caucasus, through training local teams of managers, mine clearers, mechanics, medical staff, technicians and drivers. The Trust also uses teams of Mine Awareness trainers.

Geographical Area of Activity: Africa, South-East and Central Asia, and the Caucasus.

Restrictions: No grants are disbursed.

Finance: The Trust is financed by donations from private individuals, charities and foundations, and national governments. Annual revenue £10,369,429, expenditure £11,457,452 (March 2002).

Trustees: A. Blyth; A. Grinling; A. Robathan; G. Willoughby.

Principal Staff: Dir G. Willoughby.

Address: Gilchristland, Closeburn, Thornhill DG3 5HN.

Fax: (1848) 331122; **Internet:** www.halotrust.org; **e-mail:** mail@halotrust.org.

Hamlet Trust

Founded in 1989 by Dr Peter Barham for the development of self-help initiatives for people with long-term mental health problems in Central and Eastern Europe and Central Asia.

Activities: Operates in the field of medicine, health and community development, through providing a training programme and a grant-making programme. Runs the

Programme for the New Europe to research and develop partnerships with mental health projects in the region. Collaborates with its network organizations in 15 countries including Albania, Armenia, Bosnia and Herzegovina, Estonia, Georgia, Romania, Slovenia and Ukraine. Produces publications and training materials to support and co-ordinate self-help initiatives for the long-term mentally ill, and promotes the exchange of information. Also operates a small grants programme for members of its network.

Geographical Area of Activity: Central and Eastern Europe and Central Asia.

Publications: *Out Loud* (journal, quarterly); Annual Report; *Toolkits*.

Finance: Total assets £113,552 (2001); annual revenue £523,301, expenditure £548,263 (2001).

Trustees: Ray Rowden (Chair.); Paul Craig (Chair. Small Grant Cttee); Peter Marshall (Treas.); Susann Hill; Rachel Jenkins; Kris Kingsland; Vyvyan Kinross; Edith Morgan; Joanna Morrison; Andrew Wetherell.

Principal Staff: Dir Jo Lucas.

Address: Norvin House, 45–55 Commercial St, London E1 6BD.

Telephone: (20) 7247-8666; **Fax:** (20) 7247-1984; **Internet:** www.hamlet-trust.org.uk; **e-mail:** office@hamlet-trust.demon.co.uk.

Paul Hamlyn Foundation

Founded in 1987 (incorporating an earlier Paul Hamlyn Foundation, founded in 1972) to contribute to developments in the areas of the arts, education, and overseas projects in India.

Activities: Operates in the United Kingdom and India in the above fields. The Foundation operates the following programmes: Increasing Access to the Arts; the Arts in Education; a Foundation Award for Artists; education, particularly the effects of inequality, disadvantage, exclusion and truancy; access to books and reading projects for young people in public care; a small grants scheme to support local initiatives; and development schemes, promoting NGOs, and schemes for disadvantaged children in India. The Foundation received a £200,000,000 bequest from its founder, Paul Hamlyn, who died in August 2001.

Geographical Area of Activity: United Kingdom and India.

Restrictions: Funding from the Foundation is normally for one year only. The Foundation does not make grants for general appeals or endowments; capital projects; buying, maintaining or refurbishing property or equipment; individuals, except where the Foundation has established a special scheme; education projects concerned with particular issues; large national charities; organizations which do not have charitable purposes.

Publications: Annual Report; guidance notes.

Finance: Grants disbursed £3,200,000 (2000–01).

Trustees: M. Fitzgerald; Lord Gavron; J. Hamlyn; M. Hamlyn; S. Mitchell.

Principal Staff: Dir Patricia Lankester; Finance Dir Barry Gillions; Admin. Faye Williams.

Address: 18 Queen Anne's Gate, London SW1H 9AA.

Telephone: (20) 7227-3500; **Fax:** (20) 7222-0601; **Internet:** www.phf.org.uk; **e-mail:** information@phf.org.uk.

HDRA—The Organic Organisation

Founded in 1958 by Lawrence Hills to research and promote organic gardening, farming and food; known as the Henry Doubleday Research Association until November 1999.

Activities: Operates in the fields of conservation and the environment and education, through self-conducted programmes nationally and internationally, research, conferences and training courses. The Association runs organic gardens, an education and conference centre, and a consultancy department on organic waste disposal and organic garden design. It collaborates with other organic research centres and groups in the United Kingdom and overseas, and conducts forestry research. Also maintains a Heritage Seed Library and trades through Organic Enterprises Ltd and was due to open the Vegetable Kingdom visitor centre in 2003.

Geographical Area of Activity: International.

Publications: *The Organic Way* (quarterly); numerous other books, booklets, scientific papers and leaflets.

Finance: Annual revenue £2,097,652, expenditure £2,079,416 (2001).

Management Council: Rt Hon. Earl Kitchener (Pres.); Gerald Pearson (Vice-Pres.); Dr Bill Blyth (Chair.); Dr Bill Bourne (Vice-Chair.); David Allan; Richard Bearman; Dr Sally Bucknall; Wendy Ellicock; Dr Anthony Garrett; Roger Keys; Jon Lucas; Anthony Harbour; Dr Bob Askins; John Petrie; Kate Pinder; Julia Scott; Caroline Ungoed-Thomas.

Principal Staff: Chief Exec. and Sec. Alan Gear; Exec. Dir Jackie Gear.

Address: Ryton Organic Gardens, Ryton on Dunsmore, Coventry CV8 3LG.

Telephone: (24) 7630-3517; **Fax:** (24) 7663-9229; **Internet:** www.hdra.org.uk; **e-mail:** enquiry@hdra.org.uk.

Headley Trust

Founded in 1973 for general charitable purposes. One of the Sainsbury Family Charitable Trusts, which share a common administration.

Activities: Operates nationally and internationally in a variety of fields, including arts and the environment (nationally and abroad), medicine and health, aid to less-developed countries, education and social welfare.

Geographical Area of Activity: International.

Restrictions: Unsolicited applications are not normally accepted. Grants are not normally made to individuals.

Finance: Total income £3,345,000, total expenditure £3,717,000 (2001).

Trustees: J. R. Benson; J. S. Portrait; Lady S. Sainsbury; Rt Hon. Sir T. Sainsbury; T. J. Sainsbury.

Principal Staff: Dir Michael Pattison.

Address: Allington House, 1st Floor, 150 Victoria St, London SW1E 5AE.

Telephone: (20) 7410-0330; **e-mail:** sfct@sfct.org.uk.

HelpAge International

Founded in 1983 by Help the Aged (Canada), HelpAge India, HelpAge Kenya, Help the Aged (United Kingdom) and Pro Vida Colombia; a global network of non-profit-making organizations helping people over the age of 60, enabling members to support each other and share skills and experience.

Activities: Provides expertise and grants to organizations serving the needs of older people in 70 developing countries, assisting them to help the most disadvantaged to lead independent lives. Promotes a positive image of old people world-wide, assisting them to achieve their full potential. Works in advocacy, training and research, dissemination of information, international fundraising, disaster relief, refugee resettlement and rehabilitation. Develops and supports programmes designed to meet the financial, material, medical and social needs of older people world-wide. Maintains regional offices in Belgium, Bolivia, Jamaica, Kenya and Thailand.

Geographical Area of Activity: International.

Restrictions: Grants only to older people and those working with them. Mainly funds own projects.

Publications: *Ageways* (quarterly, in English and Spanish); *Ageing and Development Newsletter* (in English and Spanish); *The Ageing and Development Report: Poverty, Independence and the World's Older People; Better Nutrition for Older People: Assessment and Action; Adding Health to Years: a* *basic guidebook on older people's health; Older People in Eastern and Central Europe: the price of transition to a market economy; Learning to Listen: counselling skills for helpers of older people; Independence for life; Gender Briefings; Nothing about us without us: Older people and decision-making in East and Central Europe; Older people in disasters and humanitarian crises: Guidelines for best practice;* Annual Review; leaflets in English, Spanish and Portuguese.

Finance: Annual revenue £11,398,000, expenditure £11,526,000 (2000).

Governing Board: Hon. Flora Macdonald (Chair.); Dr Mary Ann Tsao (Vice-Chair.).

Principal Staff: Chief Exec. Todd Petersen; Deputy Chief Exec. and Dir of Devt Mark Gorman; Dir of Programmes Adam Platt.

Address: York House, First Floor, 207–221 Pentonville Rd, London N1 9UZ.

Telephone: (20) 7278-7778; **Fax:** (20) 7843-1840; **Internet:** www.helpage.org; **e-mail:** hai@helpage.org.

Heritage Lottery Fund

Using money raised by the National Lottery, the Heritage Lottery Fund aims to improve the quality of life by safeguarding and enhancing the heritage of buildings, objects and the man-made and natural environment, which have been important in the formation of the character and identity of the United Kingdom, assisting people to enjoy their heritage and allowing them to hand it on to future generations.

Activities: The Fund makes grants to support a wide range of projects involving the local, regional and natural heritage of the United Kingdom, helping groups and organizations of all sizes with projects that aim to conserve and enhance the country's diverse heritage, encourage more people to be involved in their heritage and make sure that everyone can learn about, have access to and enjoy their heritage. Projects supported range from those involving countryside and parks, industrial, transport and maritime history, to records such as local-history archives, spoken-history records, historic buildings and museum and gallery collections.

Geographical Area of Activity: United Kingdom.

Publications: *HLF News; Strategic Plan;* Annual Report; Application Pack.

Finance: Revenue comes from the Fund's share of 28% of the profits derived from the United Kingdom National Lottery. Total capital and revenue grants since the Fund's establishment £2,100,000 (as at April 2002).

Trustees: Liz Forgan (Chair.); and 14 others.

Principal Staff: Dir Anthea Case.

Address: Heritage Lottery Fund, 7 Holbein Pl., London SW1W 8NR.

Telephone: (20) 7591-6000; **Fax:** (20) 7591-6001; **Internet:** www.hlf.org.uk; **e-mail:** enquire@hlf.org.uk.

Terrence Higgins Trust

The Terrence Higgins Trust was established in 1982 to reduce the spread of HIV and to promote good sexual health; to provide services and support for those affected to improve their quality of life and to campaign for greater public understanding of HIV and AIDS.

Activities: Works nationally providing advice, information and support to people affected by AIDS and HIV infection, including a telephone helpline, counselling services, legal advice, practical support, a hardship fund and the publication of many resources which are of service to a number of organizations and individuals.

Geographical Area of Activity: United Kingdom.

Restrictions: Grants only made from an emergency hardship fund.

Publications: Numerous publications on HIV and AIDS issues.

Finance: Annual revenue £11,129,000, expenditure £8,225,000 (March 2001).

Management Board: Prof. Ian Weller (Chair.); John Bedford; Dr Ade Fakoya; Janet Grant; Julian Groves; Karin Pappenheim; Paul Theobold; Simon Urquhart; Dave Wakefield.

Principal Staff: Chief Exec. Nicholas Partridge.

Address: 52–54 Gray's Inn Rd, London WC1X 8JU.

Telephone: (20) 7831-0330; **Fax:** (20) 7242-0121; **Internet:** www.tht.org.uk; **e-mail:** info@tht.org.uk.

Hilden Charitable Fund

Founded in 1963 for general charitable purposes.

Activities: Principally involved in race relations, minorities, juvenile delinquency and penal affairs, homelessness and developing countries (through United Kingdom charities).

Geographical Area of Activity: United Kingdom and developing countries.

Restrictions: No grants are made to individuals.

Trustees: M. G. Duncan; A. M. A. Rampton; D. S. Rampton; G. J. S. Rampton; H. M. C. Rampton; M. B. H. Rampton; C. H. Rodeck; E. K. Rodeck; C. Younger.

Principal Staff: Sec. Rodney Hedley.

Address: 34 North End Rd, London W14 0SH.

Telephone: (20) 7603-1525.

Jane Hodge Foundation

Founded in 1962 to provide funds for the advancement of medical research and medical and surgical science, education and religion.

Activities: Provides grants to registered charities throughout the world, with particular emphasis on those supporting research into cancer, diseases affecting children, polio and tuberculosis.

Geographical Area of Activity: International.

Restrictions: Grants only to exempt or registered charities.

Publications: Annual Memorial Lecture.

Finance: Annual revenue £1,210,761, grants disbursed £1,434,510 (Oct. 2001).

Trustees: M. Cason; I. H. Davies; J. Harrison; Sir J. Hodge; Lady Moira Hodge; R. J. Hodge; T. Hodge; D. L. Jones.

Principal Staff: Sec. M. Cason.

Address: Ty Gwyn, Lisvane Rd, Lisvane, Cardiff CF14 0SG.

Telephone: (29) 20766521.

Homeless International

Founded in 1989 for the relief of poverty.

Activities: Operates internationally supporting community-led housing and infrastructure related development, through grants to organizations, working in collaboration with local partners on long-term development. Also provides advisory and financial services, carries out research, and gives specialist technical assistance. A £350,000 fund guarantees loans made by overseas banks to community-led projects in India and South America.

Geographical Area of Activity: Africa, Asia, and Central and South America.

Publications: Annual Report; guidelines.

Finance: Annual revenue £1,464,000, expenditure £985,013 (March 2001).

Principal Staff: Chair. Bill Payne.

Address: Queens House, 16 Queens Rd, Coventry CV1 3DF.

Telephone: (24) 7663-2802; **Fax:** (24) 7663-2911; **Internet:** www.homeless-international.org; **e-mail:** hello@homeless-international.org.

A. S. Hornby Educational Trust

Founded for the advancement of the English language, and its teaching and learning as a foreign language.

Activities: Provides scholarships and grants for foreign teachers to study teaching English as a foreign language in the United Kingdom. Awards include the English Speaking Union Summer School Bursary and British Council Summer School Scholarships. Works in collaboration with the British Council (q.v.).

Geographical Area of Activity: International.

Restrictions: Grants are made through the British Council; there are no direct grants.

Finance: Annual revenue £481,693, expenditure £314,235 (March 2001).

Trustees: Since 1978 the Trustees have been appointed by the British Council.

Principal Staff: Contact: P. C. Collier.

Address: Crays Pond House, Crays Pond, Reading RG8 7QG.

Telephone: (1491) 680318.

John Innes Foundation

Founded in 1910 by John Innes for the provision and maintenance of an institute for research into the growth of plants and related subjects.

Activities: The Foundation provides grants to students for the advancement of education in agriculture, horticulture and biotechnology. It also provides land and buildings for research and supports a library containing material on the history of genetics and containing rare botanical books.

Finance: Annual revenue £614,972, expenditure £652,366 (March 2002).

Trustees: Peter Innes; Prof. C. J. Leaver; J. F. Oldfield; Lord Selborne.

Address: Colney Lane, Norwich NR4 7UH.

Telephone: (1603) 450222; **Fax:** (1603) 450045; **Internet:** www.jic.bbsrc.ac.uk.

Interights—International Centre for the Legal Protection of Human Rights

Established in 1982 to support and promote the development of legal protection for human rights and freedoms world-wide through the effective use of international and comparative human rights law.

Activities: The Centre works in Africa, Commonwealth states of the Caribbean, Central and Eastern Europe and Southern Asia, providing technical advice and assistance to strengthen capacity and develop jurisprudence in each region and internationally. Programmes are developed in consultation with lawyers, judges, NGOs and others and generally combine casework, education and training, institutional development and provision of resources. The Centre also offers representation before regional and international tribunals; conducts workshops and seminars on the techniques associated with the use and interpretation of human rights law; publishes materials to ensure the dissemination of developments in human rights law; and maintains a specialized public library on international and comparative human rights law.

Geographical Area of Activity: International.

Publications: *INTERIGHTS Bulletin* (quarterly journal); *Commonwealth Human Rights Law Digest* (journal, 3 a year); and other reports and publications.

Finance: Annual revenue £1,058,838, expenditure £989,474 (March 2002).

Board of Trustees: Lord Lester of Herne Hill (Pres.); Laura Cox (Chair.); Jeremy McBride (Vice-Chair.); and others.

Principal Staff: Contact: John Musgrave.

Address: 33 Islington High St, London N1 9LH.

Telephone: (20) 7278-3230; **Fax:** (20) 7278-4334; **Internet:** www.interights.org; **e-mail:** ir@interights.org.

Intermediate Technology Development Group—ITDG

Founded in 1966 by Fritz Schumacher and his associates to promote the use of appropriate technologies, particularly in developing countries.

Activities: Operates in the fields of poverty reduction and technology, energy, transport, food production, agri-processing, manufacuring enterprise, small-scale mining, shelter provision and disaster reduction. Within the United Kingdom, the Group acts as a consulting body with national education authorities advising on education for sustainable development, and focusing on design and technology in the curriculum. The Group's Sustainable Technology Education Project (STEP), and its Development@IT education materials are used by students and teachers as classroom resources.

Geographical Area of Activity: Southern and East Africa, South-East Asia, and Central and South America.

Publications: Annual Reports (international and by region); numerous other publications.

Finance: Annual income £14,100,000, expenditure £13,700,000 (2001–02).

Address: Schumacher Centre, Barton Hall, Bourton on Dunsmore, Rugby CV23 9QZ.

Telephone: (1926) 634400; **Fax:** (1926) 634401; **Internet:** www.itdg.org; **e-mail:** itdg@itdg.org.uk.

International Alert

Founded in 1985 by Martin Ennals and other human rights advocates, to promote peaceful conflict resolution.

Activities: Operates primarily in Africa (the Great Lakes region and West Africa), Eurasia, Sri Lanka and Colombia, working with organizations and individuals to facilitate dialogue and the development of peace initiatives in societies in conflict, to develop and enhance local capacities through funding and training, to examine the causes of conflict and to promote greater international awareness of conflict, conflict resolution and peace-building.

Geographical Area of Activity: International, but particularly Africa (Great Lakes region and West Africa), Eurasia, Colombia and Sri Lanka.

Publications: Annual Report; briefings; conference papers; newsletters; resource packs; research reports and other publications (all available to download from the website).

Board of Trustees: Leah Levin (Chair.); Philip Deer, Dame Pauline Neville-Jones (Vice-Chair.); Tahir Maher (Hon. Treas.); Count Claes Cronstedt; Dr Francis Deng; Dr Marianne Heiberg; Kamal Hossain; Ambassador Ould-Abdallah; Lt. Gen Arnold Quainoo; John Tirman; Wigberto Tanada; Henny Van der Graaf.

Principal Staff: Sec.-Gen. Dr Kevin Clements.

Address: 346 Clapham Rd, London SW9 0AP.

Telephone: (20) 7627-6800; **Fax:** (20) 7627-6900; **Internet:** www.international-alert.org; **e-mail:** general@international-alert.org.

International Health Exchange

Established in 1981, aims to bring about improvements to the health of people in developing countries.

Activities: Operates in the fields of medicine and health, and social welfare, through providing skilled, mostly European, health workers in all areas of health services (e.g. doctors, midwives, health visitors, physiotherapists, nutritionists and nurses skilled in fields such as nutrition, mother and child health, communicable disease control and health promotion) to organizations in less-developed countries; provides information on jobs and health issues; assists in the recruitment of health workers for less-developed countries; provides training workshops, advice and information services to health workers; and encourages health workers to seek work in less-developed countries.

Geographical Area of Activity: International.

Publications: *The Health Exchange Magazine* (6 a year); *Health Exchange Magazine Job Supplement* (5 a year); Annual Report; handbooks, reports and guides.

Finance: Total income £270,442, total expenditure £323,565 (Sept. 2001).

Board of Trustees: Barbara Krypers (Chair.).

Principal Staff: Dir Ivan Scott.

Address: First Floor, 134 Lower Marsh, London SE1 7AE.

Telephone: (20) 7620-3333; **Fax:** (20) 7620-2277; **Internet:** www.ihe.org.uk; **e-mail:** info@ihe.org.uk.

International Institute for Environment and Development

Founded in 1971 as the International Institute for Environmental Affairs in the USA, the Institute promotes sustainable world development through research, policy studies, networking and information dissemination.

Activities: The Institute aims to address issues of global significance such as mining, the paper industry and food systems through transforming decision-making at all levels: local, national and international. Maintains offices in Edinburgh, Dakar (Senegal), and an affiliate organization, IIED-América Latina, in Buenos Aires (Argentina).

Geographical Area of Activity: Primarily Africa, Asia, and Central and South America.

Publications: Annual Report; numerous publications.

Finance: Annual revenue £8,756,571, expenditure £8,306,638 (2001–02).

Trustees: Jan Pronk (Chair.); Derek F. Osborn (Vice-Chair.); L. Bethlehem; S. Cairncross; A. Hardoy; A. Hasan; Prof. I. Kikula; J. Marton-Lèfevre; Y. Renard; N. Roling; D. Runnalls; P. Sands; M. Sarin; Y. Sokona; D. Suratgar; J. F. Taylor; J. Warford.

Principal Staff: Exec. Dir Nigel Cross.

Address: 3 Endsleigh St, London WC1H 0DD.

Telephone: (20) 7388-2117; **Fax:** (20) 7388-2826; **Internet:** www.iied.org; **e-mail:** mailbox@iied.org.

The International Institute for Strategic Studies

Founded in 1958, its objective, amended in 1992, is to promote on a non-party basis the study and discussion of, and the exchange of information upon, military strategy, weapons control, regional security and conflict resolution.

Activities: Operates in the field of international affairs by providing an independent centre for research, debate and the dissemination of information. Most research is carried out by a team of Research Fellows and Research Associates and funded by various foundations. Most research is in three interrelated areas: the changing nature of international security; national and regional security; and arms control and demilitarization. The Institute, which is a membership organization, holds several conferences a year, including a major annual conference for members, and an annual memorial lecture (given by an important international figure) in memory of the first Director, Alastair Buchan, and discussion meetings and seminars. Maintains a library and information centre.

Publications: *The Military Balance* (annually); *Strategic Survey* (annually); *Survival* (quarterly); *Survival* (quarterly); *Adelphi Papers* (monographs, 8–10 a year); *World Directory of Strategic Study Centres* (occasional); *Strategic Comments* (10 a year).

Finance: Net assets £11,000,000 (October 2000); annual budget approx. £4,000,000 (2002).

Principal Staff: Dir Dr John Chipman.

Address: Arundel House, 13–15 Arundel St, Temple Pl., London WC2R 3DX.

Telephone: (20) 7379-7676; **Fax:** (20) 7836-3108; **Internet:** www.iiss.org; **e-mail:** iiss@iiss.org.

International Lifeboat Federation

Founded in 1924 to co-ordinate the activities of national non-government and government lifeboat organizations.

Activities: Provides technical assistance to countries exploring how to start a marine search and rescue service to meet the International Maritime Organisation (IMO) World Maritime Search and Rescue Regional Plan, through operating training programmes, search and rescue services, medical care, communications and finance; finances research into lifeboat design; and promotes exchange of information. Maintains a reference library.

Geographical Area of Activity: International.

Publications: *Conference Report* (every 4 years); ILF Newsletter (twice yearly).

Principal Staff: Gerry Keeling; Lorraine Peterson; Ian Ventham.

Address: c/o Royal National Lifeboat Institution, West Quay Rd, Poole BH15 1HZ.

Telephone: (1202) 663446; **Fax:** (1202) 663399; **Internet:** www.lifeboats.org; **e-mail:** sec@lifeboats.org.

International Planned Parenthood Federation—IPPF

Founded in 1952, the IPPF is a Federation of autonomous family planning associations. It has member associations in over 150 countries, and works in more than 180 countries world-wide. It is the world's largest voluntary organization working in sexual and reproductive health, choice and rights. It promotes and defends the rights of women and men, including young people, to decide freely the number and spacing of their children, and the right to the highest possible level of sexual and reproductive health.

Activities: Initiates and supports the promotion of sexual and reproductive health world-wide, including family planning. Highlights these and related issues, including human rights, HIV/AIDS, gender, young people, refugees, violence against women, and poverty, to the media, governmental organizations, NGOs and the general public. Works to mobilize financial resources to fund programmes and materials, and provides training on issues relating to population, development and sexual and reproductive rights, and young people. The International Medical Panel of the IPPF, comprising leading medical experts, provides guidelines and statements on current medical and scientific thinking and the best practices. The IPPF offers contraceptive services and equipment, ranging from clinical and office equipment to vehicles, for member associations and other public health bodies. A Youth Working Group exists to ensure programmes are accessible to young people and to promote young people's rights.

Geographical Area of Activity: Europe, Asia (South and South-East), Oceania, Africa, the Middle East, the USA, and Central and South America.

Restrictions: Only funds member family planning associations.

Publications: *Newsletter for Donors* (quarterly); *Family Planning Handbook for Health Professionals; IPPF Directory of Hormonal Contraceptives* (on-line publication); *IPPF Medical Bulletin* (6 a year, in English, French and Spanish); *News, News, News* (on-line publication); *Mezzo* (in English, French and Spanish); *Press* (2 a year, in English, French and Spanish); *Voice* (in English, French and Spanish); books, factsheets, audiovisual materials and cassettes.

Finance: Contributions to IPPF's budget come from private citizens, foundations and governments. Total assets US $41,814,000 (2001); total income US $80,256,000, expenditure US $83,646,000 (2001).

Principal Staff: Dir Gen. Dr Steven Sinding.

Address: Regent's College, Inner Circle, Regent's Park, London NW1 4NS.

Telephone: (20) 7487-7900; **Fax:** (20) 7487-7950; **Internet:** www.ippf.org; **e-mail:** info@ippf.org.

International Refugee Trust

Founded to help refugees overseas, the Trust provides funding for small projects.

Activities: Operates in the fields of medicine and health, education and training, and social welfare, through projects run by local people aimed at encouraging independence. Projects include a mobile clinic for Sudanese refugees; a secondary school for refugees in Uganda; programmes in Sudan, including a health clinic for mothers, young children and the elderly, and provision of care and education for displaced children; a medical care project in Jordan for refugee mothers and babies from Iraq; aid for refugees returning to Rwanda, where funds have been used to provide food, medical care, building materials, seeds and agricultural equipment; and food and medical aid for Myanma refugees on the Thai-Myanmar border.

Geographical Area of Activity: Africa, Asia and the Middle East.

Publications: Newsletter; Annual Report.

Finance: Total income £262,939, total expenditure £203,769 (March 2002).

Principal Staff: Contact: Francesca Roberts.

Address: POB 31452, London W4 4JG.

Telephone: (20) 8994-9120; **Fax:** (20) 8742-0315; **Internet:** www.irt.org.uk; **e-mail:** info@irt.org.uk.

International Save the Children Alliance

Established as the international arm of Save the Children (q.v.) to promote a world view that 'respects and values each child; listens to and learns from children; and where all children have hope and opportunity'. Twenty-nine organizations world-wide are members of the Alliance.

Activities: Operates internationally through its 29 member organizations in more than 120 countries, promoting children's rights, assisting children involved in war or natural disasters, and delivering immediate and lasting improvements to children's lives world-wide. Promotes the International Convention on the Rights of the Child. Maintains a regional office in Brussels.

Geographical Area of Activity: International.

Publications: *Children's Rights: A Second Chance;* reports and other publications.

Principal Staff: Chief Exec. Burkhard Gnärig.

Address: 275–281 King St, London W6 9LZ.

Telephone: (20) 8748-2554; **Fax:** (20) 8237-8000; **Internet:** www.savethechildren.net; **e-mail:** info@save-children-alliance.org.

International Tree Foundation

Formerly known as Men of the Trees; aims to sustain and enhance the environment through the planting and protection of trees.

Activities: Plants trees world-wide to increase land fertility; particularly active in desert areas and tropical rain forests. Supports sustainable projects in developing countries and operates the ITF Youth Awards Competition to enable volunteers to visit tree planting projects overseas.

Geographical Area of Activity: International.

Finance: Total income £227,442, total expenditure £146,873 (Sept. 2001).

Principal Staff: Chair. P. Rapson; Vice-Chair. F. E. Auty.

Address: Sandy Lane, Crawley Down RH10 4HS.

Telephone: (1342) 712536; **Fax:** (1342) 718282; **Internet:** www.internationaltreefoundation.org; **e-mail:** info@internationaltreefoundation.org.

International Voluntary Service

Founded in 1934 by Pierre Ceresole and Jean Inebnit as the British branch of Service Civil International (q.v.), to provide opportunities for men and women, young and old, irrespective of their race, nationality, creed or politics, to join together in giving useful voluntary service to the community in a spirit of friendship and international understanding.

Activities: Operates nationally and internationally through the provision of volunteers for community service and project exchanges with about 40 countries, throughout Eastern and Western Europe and North America.

Geographical Area of Activity: Europe and North America.

Restrictions: This is not a grant-making organization.

Publications: Annual Report; international work-camp listing.

Finance: Annual budget approx. £140,000.

Governing Board: National Committee of seven members.

Principal Staff: Chair. Sheila Hawkins; Treas. Robin Mackie.

Address: 7 Upper Bow, Edinburgh EH1 2JN.

Telephone: (131) 226-6722; **Fax:** (131) 226-6723; **Internet:** www.ivsgbn.demon.co.uk; **e-mail:** ivs@ivsgbscot.demon.co.uk.

Iran Heritage Foundation

Set up in 1995 by David Khalili to preserve and promote the history, language and culture of Iran.

Activities: Operates predominantly by funding publications; fellowships; exhibitions; conferences and seminars; scholarships, internships and travel awards; film, theatre and the performing arts; books for libraries; and lectures. Grants made include funding for Iranian studies fellowships and Persian language teaching; publication of journals, textbooks, research, catalogues and manuscripts devoted to the history, language and culture of Iran; restoration of late 19th and early 20th century Iranian films; and funding for film festivals, research and theatre productions.

Geographical Area of Activity: Mainly United Kingdom, although some awards internationally.

Board of Directors: Vahid Alaghband, Sedigheh Rastegar (Co-Chair.); Manouchehr Azmoudeh; Farhad Hakimzadeh; Zinat Irvani; Dr Nasser D. Khalili; Hashem Khosrovani; Eskandar Maleki; Ali Sarikhani; Dr Ali Sattraipour.

Principal Staff: Man. Dir Farhad Hakimzadeh; Sec. and Treas. Bagher Baradar.

Address: 4 Stanhope Gate, London W1K 1AH.

Telephone: (20) 7493-4766; **Fax:** (20) 7499-9293; **Internet:** www.iranheritage.org; **e-mail:** info@iranheritage.org.

J. N. F. Charitable Trust

Founded in 1939 for the relief of poverty in the territory of the State of Israel and such other purposes in the prescribed region as are charitable according to the law of England, especially such purposes as in the opinion of the Trust are directly or indirectly beneficial to persons who are of Jewish religion, race or origin.

Activities: Operates in Israel and other regions of the Middle East in the field of social welfare.

Geographical Area of Activity: Israel and the Middle East.

Restrictions: No grants are made to individuals.

Publications: Financial statement; associated publishers, the JNF Publishing Company, publishes a variety of titles.

Principal Staff: Co. Sec. H. Bratt.

Address: 58–70 Edgware Way, Edgware HA8 8GQ.

Telephone: (20) 8421-7600; **Fax:** (20) 8905-4299; **e-mail:** info@jnf.co.uk.

Japan Foundation Endowment Committee—JFEC

Founded in 1974 by the University Grants Committee (UGC) to administer an endowment made by the Japanese government through the Japan Foundation (q.v.) for the promotion of Japanese studies within universities in the United Kingdom.

Activities: JFEC's current remit is to provide small grants to support academic research in Japanese studies by staff and doctoral research students in higher education institutions in the United Kingdom, covering research on any aspect of Japan within the humanities and social sciences (including comparative studies where Japan is a major element). Applications are considered for funding for fieldwork in Japan, the purchase of research materials and other forms of research support, limited periods of language training and the partial support of doctoral students.

Geographical Area of Activity: United Kingdom.

Restrictions: Applications must be made by staff of United Kingdom higher education institutions; applications may not be made directly by students. Funding is not available for coursework or Masters dissertations.

Publications: Annual Report.

Finance: Grants disbursed approx. £60,000 per year.

Trustees: Dr R. J. Goodman (Chair.).

Principal Staff: Sec. Dr P. J. Hayward.

Address: University of Sheffield, Corporate Planning Office, Sheffield S10 2TN.

Telephone: (114) 222-9205; **Fax:** (114) 276-8496; **Internet:** www.shef.ac.uk/uni/cpo/jfec; **e-mail:** jfec@sheffield.ac.uk.

JCA Charitable Foundation

Founded in 1891 as the Jewish Colonization Association by Baron Maurice de Hirsch, to assist Jews in need, particularly in those countries where they were oppressed.

Activities: Provides funds to organizations involved in assisting Jewish refugees; finances agricultural institutions and research in Israel, and international school networks for Jewish students; encourages the formation of Jewish groups within institutions throughout the world.

Geographical Area of Activity: International.

Restrictions: Does not make grants to individuals; nor does it usually accept applications from bodies not currently linked to the Foundation.

Publications: Annual Report; *Centenary Brochure*.

Finance: Annual revenue £1,087,000, grants disbursed £2,027,000 (2001).

Address: Victoria Palace Theatre, Allington St, London SW1E 5EA.

Telephone: (20) 7828-0600; **Fax:** (20) 7828-6882; **e-mail:** jcafoundation@aol.com.

Jephcott Charitable Trust

Founded in 1965 for general charitable purposes.

Activities: Main current areas of interest are projects in developing countries to improve quality of life, especially in the fields of population control, education, health and the environment. Grants are mainly given to charities involved in smaller projects.

Geographical Area of Activity: International.

Restrictions: No grants are made to large national organizations, nor to those concerned with education or alleviating poverty in the United Kingdom.

Trustees: M. Jephcott (Chair.); J. Bunnell; P. Davis; K. Morgan; A. T. North; C. Thomas; H. Wolley.

Principal Staff: Sec. Meg Harris.

Address: Cotley, Streatham Rise, Exeter EX4 4PE.

Jerusalem Trust

Founded in 1982 for the advancement of Christian religion; the advancement of Christian education and learning; and for the benefit of charitable purposes or charitable institutions determined by the trustees. One of the Sainsbury Family Charitable Trusts, which share a common administration.

Activities: Operates nationally and internationally in the areas of Christian evangelism and relief work overseas; Christian media; Christian education; Christian art; Christian evangelism and social responsibility work in the United Kingdom.

Geographical Area of Activity: International.

Restrictions: Unsolicited applications are unlikely to be successful. No grants are made to individuals.

Finance: Net assets £72,445,000 (2001); annual revenue £3,046,000, expenditure £3,307,000 (2001).

Trustees: V. E. Hartley Booth; Rev. Canon G. Bridger; Lady S. Sainsbury; Rt Hon. Sir T. Sainsbury; D. Wainman.

Principal Staff: Dir Michael Pattison.

Address: Allington House, 1st Floor, 150 Victoria St, London SW1E 5AE.

Telephone: (20) 7410-0330; **e-mail:** sfct@sfct.org.uk.

Jewish Philanthropic Association for Israel and the Middle East

Founded in 1968 to assist the needy, the mentally and physically disabled, the wounded and the old; protect children from cruelty and suffering; aid necessitous immigrants; and promote education.

Activities: Operates in Israel and territories of the Middle East in the above areas.

Geographical Area of Activity: Israel and the Middle East.

Finance: Annual income £2,076,223, total expenditure £2,117,634 (Sept. 2001).

Trustees: Sir Trevor Chinn; M. Paisner; R. Preston.

Principal Staff: Chief Exec. Jonathan Kestenbaum.

Address: Balfour House, 741 High Rd, Finchley, London N12 0BQ.

Telephone: (20) 8446-1477; **Fax:** (20) 8446-1180; **e-mail:** central@ujia.co.uk.

Elton John Aids Foundation

Founded in 1993 and operating in the United Kingdom and the USA to promote research into and to advance public awareness of AIDS, and to alleviate the financial need of AIDS sufferers.

Activities: Supports AIDS charities and sufferers nationally and internationally. Works in 27 countries world-wide promoting the establishment of local agencies to provide help in a manner appropriate to the district and country, and funds programmes to train doctors, nurses and volunteers in primary healthcare so that help can be given locally. Nationally the Foundation works with the Government and the voluntary sector to develop a national strategy; funds complementary services; donates to the National Hardship Fund for people with HIV/AIDS; works with hospitals and treatment centres on improving in-patient food; and supports and funds an HIV/AIDS Brain Impairment facility at the Mildmay Mission Hospital. Maintains an office in Los Angeles, CA, USA.

Geographical Area of Activity: International.

Publications: Newsletter (quarterly).

Finance: Total income £2,447,258, total expenditure £2,768,674 (2001).

Trustees: Elton John (Chair.).

Principal Staff: Exec. Dir (UK) Robert Key.

Address: 1 Blythe Rd, London W14 0HQ.

Telephone: (20) 7603-9996; **Fax:** (20) 7348-4848; **Internet:** www.ejaf.org/ejafuk/ejafuk.html; **e-mail:** admin@ejafuk.com.

J. E. Joseph Charitable Fund

Founded in 1946 by J. E. Joseph for the relief of poverty and the advancement of education, particularly among Sephardic communities.

Activities: Operates nationally and internationally in the fields of education and social welfare, by making grants to institutions and individuals.

Geographical Area of Activity: United Kingdom, and the Middle and Far East.

Restrictions: Grants are limited to certain restricted communities in the United Kingdom and the Middle and Far East.

Finance: Annual revenue £122,657, expenditure £113,567 (April 2002).

Principal Staff: Contact: R. J. Leon.

Address: 6 Lyon Meade, Stanmore HA7 1JA.

Telephone: (20) 8952-3818; **Fax:** (20) 7289-8780.

JPMorgan Fleming Educational Trust

Founded in 1974 to promote education in the United Kingdom.

Activities: The Trust supports schools, tertiary-level educational establishments, museums and research bodies; projects which provide education and training to young people with special needs, and to those in inner-city and rural areas and to ethnic minorities; arts education projects; and new methods of advancing education. Also provides scholarships and bursaries to organizations for education fees and maintenance.

Geographical Area of Activity: United Kingdom.

Restrictions: No grants are given to individuals. Grants are made exclusively in the United Kingdom.

Finance: Annual revenue £679,000; total expenditure £866,000 (2001).

Trustees: JPMorgan Fleming Marketing Ltd.

Principal Staff: Dir Duncan Grant.

Address: 10 Aldermanbury, London EC2V 7RF.

Telephone: (20) 7325-8771; **Fax:** (20) 7325-8195; **e-mail:** duncan.grant@jpmorganfleming.com.

JPMorgan Fleming Foundation

Founded in 1985 for general charitable purposes, particularly in the field of education.

Activities: Funds recognized charitable organizations in the United Kingdom working with children and young people in the areas of education and training, education for those with special needs, education in the arts, and other charitable purposes.

Geographical Area of Activity: United Kingdom.

Restrictions: Grants are not awarded directly to individuals, and international activities are limited.

Finance: Total income £349,000, total expenditure £323,000 (2001).

Trustees: JPMorgan Fleming Marketing Ltd.

Principal Staff: Dir Duncan Grant.

Address: 10 Aldermanbury, London EC2V 7RF.

Telephone: (20) 7325-1308; **e-mail:** duncan.grant@jpmorganfleming.com.

Just World Partners

Founded as the UK Foundation for the South Pacific in 1981 by Canon Rex Davis for the advancement of education and the relief of poverty in the islands and territories of the South Pacific. Present name since 2000.

Activities: Operates in the South Pacific and South-East Asia by providing technical and management support to a range of projects, and by helping partner organizations access funding support. The Foundation supports income generating projects in northern Vietnam, Vanuatu and Fiji; poverty reduction projects in northern Vanuatu, Vietnam and West Papua New Guinea; environment projects in Kiribati, Solomon Islands, Vanuatu, Fiji and Tonga, conflict resolution projects in Papua New Guinea and Fiji; and health projects in northern Vietnam, northern Philippines, Papua New Guinea, Vanuatu, Fiji and Kiribati.

Geographical Area of Activity: South Pacific and South-East Asia.

Finance: The Foundation's funds come from a variety of sources, including the Department for International Development, the European Commission of the European Union, the States of Jersey and Guernsey and other trusts and charities.

Address: 4A Newmills Rd, Dalkeith EH22 1DU.

Telephone: (131) 663-7428; **Fax:** (131) 663-7433; **Internet:** www.justworld.org.uk; **e-mail:** jw@justworld.org.uk.

Ian Karten Charitable Trust

Founded in 1980 to promote education.

Activities: Provides scholarships to British and Israeli students for undergraduate and postgraduate study at universities and tertiary-level institutions. Provides funding to charities in the United Kingdom and Israel for the establishment of technological training centres for adults with disabilities.

Geographical Area of Activity: United Kingdom and Israel.

Restrictions: No grants are made to individuals.

Finance: Total revenue £352,888, total expenditure £563,449 (Sept. 2002).

Trustees: Ian H. Karten (Chair.); Ellen Frankel; M. E. Karten; T. M. Simon.

Principal Staff: Hon. Admin. Ian H. Karten (no paid staff, services outsourced).

Address: The Mill House, Newark Lane, Ripley GU23 6DP.

Telephone: (1483) 225020; **Fax:** (1483) 222420; **e-mail:** tim.simon@timsim.com.

Karuna Trust/Aid for India

Established in 1980 for the relief of poverty through educational, medical and skills projects, particularly in India.

Activities: Operates in India in the fields of aid to less-developed countries, education, and medicine and health, through self-conducted programmes and grants; also issues publications.

Geographical Area of Activity: India.

Restrictions: No grants are made to individuals; grants made to registered charities only.

Publications: Annual Report.

Finance: Annual revenue £971,414, expenditure £796,098 (2001).

Trustees: Dr W. Stones (Chair.); Hilary Blakiston; Dr Keith Downer; Iain Robertson; Simon Turnbull; David Zukas.

Principal Staff: Dir Peter Joseph; Treas. Patrick Francis.

Address: 72 Holloway Rd, London N7 8JG.

Telephone: (20) 7700-3434; **Fax:** (20) 7700-3535; **Internet:** www.karuna.org; **e-mail:** info@karuna.org.

Kennedy Memorial Trust

Founded in 1966 from the proceeds of a National Memorial Appeal launched by the Lord Mayor of London following the death of President Kennedy, to enable graduates from the United Kingdom to spend one year studying at one of the faculties of Harvard University or the Massachusetts Institute of Technology.

Activities: Operates in the field of education, through granting about 12 scholarships annually tenable by United Kingdom citizens ordinarily resident in the United Kingdom, and wholly or mainly educated there. Scholarships are tenable in all areas of the arts, science, social science and political studies.

Geographical Area of Activity: United Kingdom.

Restrictions: Fellowships to United Kingdom citizens only.

Finance: Awards for 2002 are tuition fees, travel costs and a stipend of US $18,000.

Trustees: Trustees appointed by the Prime Minister.

Principal Staff: Sec. Anna Mason.

Address: 3 Birdcage Walk, Westminster, London SW1H 9JJ.

Telephone: (20) 7222-1151; **Fax:** (20) 7222-7189; **Internet:** www.kentrust.demon.co.uk.

King George's Fund for Sailors

Founded in 1917 by HM King George V to raise funds to support Marine Benevolent and Welfare Institutions throughout the United Kingdom and the Commonwealth. Granted a Royal Charter in 1920.

Activities: Operates both nationally and internationally in the field of social welfare, through grants to institutions. The Fund aids societies which support past and present Officers and Ratings of the Royal Navy, the Merchant Navy and Fishing Fleets, and their dependants; and also those which support training for a career at sea.

Geographical Area of Activity: United Kingdom and Commonwealth countries.

Restrictions: No grants to individuals.

Publications: *Flagship* (newsletter, twice yearly); *Nautical Welfare Guide* (every 2–3 years); annual report and accounts.

Finance: Annual revenue £3,081,000, grants disbursed £2,387,000 (2001).

General Council Admiral Sir Brian Brown (Chair.); Capt. D. C. Glass (Deputy Chair.); S. K. Knowles (Hon. Sec.); T. Brenton, QC (Hon. Counsel).

Principal Staff: Dir Gen. Commander B. W. Bryant.

Address: 8 Hatherley St, London SW1P 2YY.

Telephone: (20) 7932-0000; **Fax:** (20) 7932-0095; **Internet:** www.kgfs.org.uk; **e-mail:** seafarers@kgfs.org.uk.

King's Fund

Founded in 1897 (as King Edward's Hospital Fund for London) by King Edward VII, then Prince of Wales, originally for the support, benefit and extension of the hospitals of London, now interpreted broadly to include all the health services in Greater London.

Activities: Supports the health of Londoners through policy analysis, service development and education. The Fund operates in seven main areas: health and social care; health-care policy; primary care; public health; leadership development; rehabilitation; and health systems. Activities include giving grants to innovative health projects in London, running leadership courses for National Health Service (NHS) managers, and producing frequent publications on key policy issues. Also provides conference and library facilities. Also distributes King's Fund Millennium Awards, funded by the Millennium Commission (q.v.).

Geographical Area of Activity: United Kingdom (London).

Publications: Annual Report; guidelines for applicants; reports.

Finance: Net assets £140,726,000 (Dec. 2001); annual revenue £8,426,000, expenditure £12,732,000 (2001).

Trustees: Sir Graham Hart (Chair.).

Principal Staff: Chief Exec. Rabbi Julia Neuberger.

Address: 11–13 Cavendish Sq., London W1G 0AN.

Telephone: (20) 7307-2400; **Fax:** (20) 7307-2801; **Internet:** www.kingsfund.org.uk; **e-mail:** injg@kehf.org.uk.

Ernest Kleinwort Charitable Trust

Founded in 1963 for general charitable purposes.

Activities: The Trust principally operates internationally in the fields of wildlife, environmental conservation and family planning, and nationally in the fields of the disabled, medical research, elderly and youth welfare.

Geographical Area of Activity: International.

Restrictions: Preference is given to charities operating in Sussex.

Finance: Annual revenue £1,276,330, expenditure £1,598,215 (March 2002).

Trustees: R. M. Ewing; Lady Madeline Kleinwort; M. R. Kleinwort; Sir Richard Kleinwort; Kleinwort Benson Trustees Ltd; Earl of Limerick; Sir Christopher Lever; S. M. Robertson.

Principal Staff: Sec. S. P. I. Dawes.

Address: POB 191, 10 Fenchurch St, London EC3M 3LB.

Telephone: (20) 7475 6246; **Fax:** (20) 7475-5558.

Frank Knox Fellowships

Founded in 1949 by Mrs Frank Knox to enable graduates from the United Kingdom to spend one year studying at one of the faculties of Harvard University.

Activities: Operates in the field of education, through fellowships, available only to citizens of the United Kingdom normally resident in the United Kingdom.

Geographical Area of Activity: United Kingdom.

Restrictions: Fellowships only to United Kingdom citizens.

Finance: Awards for 2002 are tuition costs and a stipend of US $18,000.

Trustees: The President and Fellows of Harvard University.

Principal Staff: Sec. Anna Mason.

Address: 3 Birdcage Walk, Westminster, London SW1H 9JJ.

Telephone: (20) 7222-1151; **Fax:** (20) 7222-7189; **Internet:** www.franknox.harvard.edu.

Kreitman Foundation

Founded in 1970 for general charitable purposes.

Activities: Operates nationally and internationally, mainly funding practical projects in the fields of medicine, research, education and the arts.

Geographical Area of Activity: International.

Restrictions: Awards grants to registered charities only.

Finance: Annual income £996,843, total expenditure £582,838 (April 2002).

Trustees: E. A. Charles; H. Kreitman; S. I. Kreitman.

Principal Staff: Henry Charles.

Address: Devonshire House, 1 Devonshire St, London W1W 5DR.

Telephone: (20) 7304-2000; **Fax:** (20) 7304-2020.

Heinz and Anna Kroch Foundation

Founded in 1962 by Falk Heinz Kroch and Anna Kroch to further medical research, and relieve individuals suffering severe poverty and financial hardship who have ongoing medical problems.

Activities: Operates in the United Kingdom and Ireland. The Foundation's main concern is the assistance of individuals who suffer severe poverty and financial hardship. Applications must come through the social services or another recognized agency.

Geographical Area of Activity: United Kingdom and Ireland.

Restrictions: No grants for holidays and education projects.

Finance: Annual revenue £143,888, expenditure £132,706 (April 2001).

Trustees: M. Cottam; H. J. Kroch; A. C. Kroch; D. Lang; C. T. Richardson; J. Seagrim.

Principal Staff: Admin. H. Astle.

Address: POB 5, Bentham, Lancaster LA2 7XA.

Telephone: (1524) 263001; **Fax:** (1524) 263001; **e-mail:** hakf50@hotmail.com.

Kulika Charitable Trust

Founded in 1981 for general charitable purposes.

Activities: Operates in the fields of education, sustainable agriculture and development in East Africa, mainly in Uganda. Currently concentrating on providing scholarships, runs a training and awareness programme in sustainable agriculture, supporting poverty alleviation and development projects and funding environment and conservation projects. Operates in Uganda through the Kulika Charitable Trust (Uganda).

Geographical Area of Activity: East Africa, mainly Uganda.

Finance: Assets £4,887,297 (2000); annual revenue £381,852, expenditure £709,683 (Aug. 2001).

Trustees: A. J. F. C. M. van Amelsvoort; D. J. Burnstone; P. A. M. Brenninkmeyer; T. A. Brenninkmeyer; S. Errington; Dr C. P. Peacock; M. M. E. Wentworth-Stanley; Langersal Ltd.

Principal Staff: A. Jones.

Address: 4 The Mount, Guildford GU2 4YN.

Telephone: (1483) 563567; **Fax:** (1483) 562505; **Internet:** www.kulika.org; **e-mail:** info@kulika.org.

Maurice and Hilda Laing Charitable Trust

Established in 1996 as the Hilda Laing Charitable Trust.

Activities: The Trust supports organizations promoting Christianity throughout the world, through funding religious education as well as funding projects working to combat poverty and support people with physical and mental disabilities.

Geographical Area of Activity: International.

Restrictions: No grants to individuals.

Finance: Annual revenue £1,901,702, expenditure £1,368,065 (2000).

Board of Trustees: Robert Harley; Sir Euan Harper; Peter Harper; Lady Hilda Laing; Sir Maurice Laing; Donald Parr.

Principal Staff: Admin. Elizabeth Harley.

Address: 33 Bunns Lane, London NW7 2DX.

Telephone: (20) 8238-8890; **Fax:** (20) 8238-8897.

Kirby Laing Foundation

Founded in 1972 for general charitable purposes.

Activities: Operates nationally and internationally, making donations to registered charities. Most donations overseas are channelled through United Kingdom registered charities. Grants are co-ordinated with the Beatrice and J. W. Laing Trusts, and with the Maurice Laing Foundation (qq.v.).

Geographical Area of Activity: International (through United Kingdom-based charities).

Restrictions: No grants to individuals.

Finance: Annual revenue £1,671,533, expenditure £1,251,102 (2000).

Trustees: D. E. Laing; Sir Kirby Laing; Lady Laing; S. Webley.

Principal Staff: Admin. E. A. Harley.

Address: 33 Bunns Lane, London NW7 2DX.

Telephone: (20) 8238-8890; **Fax:** (20) 8238-8897.

Maurice Laing Foundation

Founded in 1972 for general charitable purposes.

Activities: Operates nationally and internationally, making grants to registered charities, with special emphasis on environmental, medical, educational and religious projects. Most donations overseas are channelled through United Kingdom registered charities. Donations are co-ordinated with the Beatrice and J. W. Laing Trusts, and the Kirby Laing Foundation (qq.v.).

Geographical Area of Activity: International (through United Kingdom-based charities).

Restrictions: No grants to individuals.

Finance: Annual revenue £3,530,146, expenditure £3,526,421 (2000).

Trustees: D. Edwards; A. Gavazzi; P. J. Harper; J. H. Laing; Sir Maurice Laing; T. D. Parr.

Principal Staff: Admin. E. A. Harley.

Address: 33 Bunns Lane, London NW7 2DX.

Telephone: (20) 8238-8890; **Fax:** (20) 8238-8897.

Beatrice Laing Trust

Founded in 1952 for the relief of poverty, and for the advancement of the evangelical faith internationally.

Activities: Grants are made to charities working in deprived sections of the community in the United Kingdom, to missionary societies and, less frequently, to individuals working in the field of missions, in the United Kingdom and abroad. Most donations overseas are channelled through United Kingdom registered charities. The Trust co-ordinates donations with the J. W. Laing Trust and the Kirby Laing and Maurice Laing Foundations (qq.v.).

Geographical Area of Activity: Mainly United Kingdom.

Restrictions: No grants to individuals.

Finance: Annual revenue £1,173,278, expenditure £940,528 (April 2000).

Trustees: Paula Blacker; Charlie Laing; Sir Maurice Laing; Sir Martin Laing; D. E. Laing; C. M. Laing; J. H. Laing.

Principal Staff: Admin. E. A. Harley.

Address: 33 Bunns Lane, London NW7 2DX.

Telephone: (20) 8238-8890; **Fax:** (20) 8238-8897.

Allen Lane Foundation

Founded in 1966 by Sir Allen Lane to support general charitable purposes.

Activities: The Foundation funds a variety of projects in the United Kingdom and has a limited programme in the Republic of Ireland. Current priorities include refugees and asylum seekers; black and ethnic minority communities; elderly people; those experiencing mental health problems; those experiencing violence or abuse; offenders and former offenders; and travellers. Priority is given to projects which will make a long-term difference to the problems addressed. Grants in the Republic of Ireland are made only for work in penal affairs.

Geographical Area of Activity: Mainly United Kingdom and the Republic of Ireland.

Restrictions: No grants are made to individuals.

Finance: Net assets £14,800,000 (2002); annual revenue £468,000, expenditure £638,000 (2002).

Trustees: Guy Dehn; John Hughes; Clare Murpurgo; Christine Teale; Zoë Teale; Juliet Walker; Jane Walsh.

Principal Staff: Exec. Sec. Heather Swailes.

Address: 90 The Mount, York YO24 4AR.

Telephone: (1904) 613223; **Fax:** (1904) 613133; **Internet:** www.allenlane.demon.co.uk; **e-mail:** enquiries@allenlane.demon.co.uk.

Law Society Charity

Established to offer support in the field of law and justice nationally and internationally.

Activities: Operates in the United Kingdom and abroad in the field of law, offering grants to organizations furthering law and justice, including support for legal education, the welfare of members of the profession and the promotion of human rights.

Geographical Area of Activity: International, but mainly England and Wales.

Restrictions: Grants are usually made only to United Kingdom organizations.

Finance: Total income £2,492,473, grants disbursed £1,984,280 (April 2002).

Trustees: N. Dodds (Chair.); A. Caplen; H. Davies; S. Gadhia; C. Glasser; M. Howells; D. Malhotra; M. Mathews; D. Merkel; F. Smith; R. Venables.

Principal Staff: Company Sec. B. Bilimoria.

Address: 113 Chancery Lane, London WC2A 1PL.

Telephone: (20) 7320-5755.

League for the Exchange of Commonwealth Teachers

Founded in 1901 by Elizabeth Ord Marshall to promote friendly and educational intercourse among the countries of the Commonwealth, mainly through the exchange of teachers.

Activities: Operates nationally and internationally in the field of education by organizing one-year exchanges between teachers in the United Kingdom and in Commonwealth countries. Approximately 400 grants are offered annually. A separate programme promotes the exchange of teachers between different parts of the United Kingdom.

Geographical Area of Activity: United Kingdom and the Commonwealth.

Publications: Annual Report and handbooks.

Finance: The League receives grants from the United Kingdom Government for certain categories of expenditure (cost of living and travel grants for teachers; and administration grants).

Board of Governors: Mike Nichol (Chair.); Martin Hesketh (Hon. Treas.); and 12 others.

Principal Staff: Dir Anna Tomlinson.

Address: 7 Lion Yard, Treamdoc Rd, London SW4 7NQ.

Telephone: (870) 770-2636; **Fax:** (870) 770-2637; **Internet:** www.lect.org.uk; **e-mail:** info@lect.org.uk.

Bernard van Leer Foundation UK Trust

Founded in 1972 to further the education of disadvantaged children aged up to seven.

Activities: Operates internationally in the field of education, through its support for institutions providing education facilities and opportunities for disadvantaged children.

Geographical Area of Activity: International.

Restrictions: No grants are made to individuals.

Publications: Newsletter.

Finance: Annual revenue £297,564, expenditure £46,127 (2000).

Trustee: The Royal Bank of Scotland PLC.

Principal Staff: Dir of Trust Dept Don Henderson.

Address: c/o Royal Bank of Scotland PLC, Private Trust and Estate Services, Capital House, 2 Festival Sq., Edinburgh EH3 9SU.

Telephone: (131) 523-2658; **Fax:** (131) 228-9889.

Leprosy Mission International

Christian charity established in 1874 by Wellesley Bailey to provide ministry to people affected by leprosy world-wide.

Activities: Works in co-operation with national governments and with other organizations to improve the quality of life of people suffering from leprosy, by lending support through ministry, raising awareness of leprosy in all areas, removing stigma attached to the disease, and reducing discrimination for victims. Runs centres to provide suitable medication and carry out surgery, engages in research into leprosy and its treatment, and provides socio-economic assistance to patients in developing countries.

Geographical Area of Activity: Africa, and Southern and South-East Asia.

Publications: *Partners Magazine; Ask Prayer Guide*; Annual Review; Annual Report and financial statements.

Principal Staff: Gen. Dir Trevor Durston; Admin. Joyce Missing.

Address: 80 Windmill Rd, Brentford TW8 0QH.

Telephone: (20) 8326-6767; **Fax:** (20) 8326-6777; **Internet:** www.leprosymission.org; **e-mail:** s&d@tlmint.org.

Leukaemia Research Fund

Founded in 1960 to encourage, promote and assist research into the leukaemias, Hodgkin's disease and other lymphomas, myeloma and related conditions.

Activities: The Fund is devoted to fighting leukaemia and related blood diseases on a carefully co-ordinated national scale, through research and training doctors in specialist leukaemia care. Finances clinical fellowships and research projects at hospitals and university medical centres throughout the country, and conducts a major research development programme consisting of specialized centres focusing on key areas of fundamental research; operates a patient information programme. The Fund's programme of international involvement aims to ensure that the benefits of research nationally and internationally are available for the benefit of leukaemia patients; it supports a programme of lectures, meetings and workshops including a one-day annual International Research Symposium.

Geographical Area of Activity: United Kingdom.

Restrictions: Grants for research only.

Publications: Annual review; newsletters; patient information booklets.

Finance: Annual expenditure on research approx. £20,000,000.

Executive Committee: The Earl Cadogan (Chair.); J. A. C. Barrington (Vice-Chair.); K. S. Carmichael (Hon. Treas.); P. Bassett; G. Brocklebank; P. Burrell; A. Dart; R. Delderfield; Z. Floyd; P. C. Hart; D. Hensby; J. Hodgson; K. Lomas; Dr G. McDonald; M. Naddell; D. Payne; H. Potter; C. Sharp; B. Swain; V. Todd.

Principal Staff: CEO Douglas Osborne; Scientific Dir Dr David Grant.

Address: 43 Great Ormond St, London WC1N 3JJ.

Telephone: (20) 7405-0101; **Fax:** (20) 7405-3139; **Internet:** www.lrf.org.uk; **e-mail:** info@lrf.org.uk.

Leverhulme Trust

Founded in 1925 under the provisions of the will of the first Viscount Leverhulme to provide scholarships for research and education.

Activities: Grants are made to institutions and charitable organizations in the United Kingdom and abroad for specific research projects, for educational innovations and under Trust-approved schemes of academic interchange between the United Kingdom and other countries. A number of smaller individual awards of research fellowships and grants, emeritus fellowships and studentships for study abroad are made under annually publicized schemes. Also provides grants to support artists' residencies. Grants to institutions are made by the Trustees, meeting quarterly; awards to individuals are made annually on the recommendation of the Trust's Research Awards Advisory Committee.

Geographical Area of Activity: United Kingdom and Europe.

Restrictions: Does not give support in the areas of medicine or social policy. Grants for endowments, buildings, equipment or general funds are excluded.

Publications: Brochure on policies and procedures; newsletter (quarterly); Annual Report.

Finance: The Trust's shareholding, originally in Lever Brothers, now mainly in Unilever PLC. Grant and research expenditure £25,200,000 (2001).

Trustees: Sir Michael Angus (Chair.); Dr J. W. Anderson; A. C. Butler; A. S. Ganguly; Sir Michael Perry; N. W. A. Fitzgerald.

Principal Staff: Dir Prof. Richard Brook; Deputy Dir Alison Cooper.

Address: 1 Pemberton Row, London EC4A 3BG.

Telephone: (20) 7822-5220; **Fax:** (20) 7822-5084; **Internet:** www.leverhulme.org.uk; **e-mail:** enquiries@leverhulme.org.uk.

Levy Foundation

Founded in 1965 for general charitable purposes; formerly known as the Joseph Levy Charitable Foundation.

Activities: Operates mainly in the areas of medicine and health and children and young people.

Restrictions: No grants are made to individuals.

Trustees: N. W. Benson; J. Jason; S. Krendel; N. F. Levy; P. L. Levy.

Principal Staff: Dir Sue Nyfield.

Address: 6 Camden High St, London NW1 0JH.

Telephone: (20) 7333-8111; **Internet:** www.levyfoundation.org.uk; **e-mail:** webmaster@levyfoundation.org.uk.

Linbury Trust

Founded in 1973 for general charitable purposes. One of the Sainsbury Family Charitable Trusts, which share a common administration.

Activities: Operates nationally and internationally in the fields of aid to less-developed countries, the arts and humanities, conservation and the environment, education, medicine and health (in particular the aged and research into Chronic Fatigue Syndrome), and social welfare.

Geographical Area of Activity: International.

Restrictions: No grants are made directly to individuals.

Finance: Net assets £181,726,000 (April 2002); annual revenue £7,216,000, expenditure £5,878,000 (2002).

Trustees: Lord Sainsbury of Preston Candover; Lady S. Sainsbury; J. S. Portrait.

Principal Staff: Michael Pattison.

Address: Allington House, 1st Floor, 150 Victoria St, London SW1E 5AE.

Telephone: (20) 7410-0330; **e-mail:** sfct@sfct.org.uk.

Living Water Charitable Trust

Formally incorporated in 1991 by Jane Shields to support and initiate projects to educate and empower the community to improve the quality of life for all.

Activities: Operates nationally and internationally in the fields of education and conservation and the environment, through self-conducted programmes, grants to institutions and conferences. Supports projects to protect and improve the environment and create learning opportunities, in particular in developing countries. Developed Beo, an environmental board game.

Geographical Area of Activity: Central and Eastern Europe, including the Baltic states and the Russian Federation, South and Central America, Africa, the Far East and Australasia.

Publications: Annual Report.

Finance: Profits made from the sale of the Beo board game are covenanted to the Trust by Beo Ltd.

Board of Trustees: Jane Shields.

Address: 5 Holyrood Rd, Edinburgh EH8 8AE.

Telephone: (131) 558-3313; **Fax:** (131) 558-1550; **Internet:** www.livingwater.org.uk/lwct1.html; **e-mail:** lwct@zetnet.co.uk.

Lloyd Foundation

Founded in 1972 to enable children of British citizens where the family are living by necessity overseas to obtain a British education.

Activities: Awards grants to enable the children of British citizens where the family are living by necessity abroad to attend the nearest English-language school; when there is no alternative, the Foundation assists with boarding fees in the United Kingdom.

Geographical Area of Activity: World-wide.

Publications: Financial statement.

Finance: Net assets £2,171,649 (2002); grants £90,460 (2002).

Board of Trustees: B. W. Howes (Chair.); J. H. Caesar (Vice-Chair.); S. Chambers; C. A. G. Golding; S. J. Green; D. T. E. Marjoram; A. M. S. Pont; M. A. J. Swinley; J. Watt.

Principal Staff: Sec. M. E. Keyte.

Address: Fairway, Round Oak View, Tillington, Hereford HR4 8EQ.

Telephone and Fax: (1432) 760409.

Lloyds TSB Foundation for England and Wales

Established in 1986 to alleviate community and social need.

Activities: Operates in England and Wales in the area of social welfare. The Foundation makes grants to organizations that work in the area of social welfare, and supports and works in partnership with organizations helping people, especially those who are disadvantaged or disabled, play a fuller role in their communities. It runs two grant-making programmes: the Community Programme and the Collaborative Programme. Within the Community Programme grants for local, regional and national projects and pilot projects are available. Funds are allocated to two main areas: Social and Community Needs, including advice services, community relations, community services, cultural enrichment, disabled people and promotion of health; and Education and Training, including lifelong learning, literacy skills, pre-school education, life skills and skills training for disabled and disadvantaged people. Approximately one-half of all grants are allocated within special interest areas, which for 2000–02 were family support, challenging disadvantage and discrimination and promoting effectiveness in the voluntary sector. Lloyds TSB Foundations also operate in Northern Ireland, Scotland and the Channel Islands.

Geographical Area of Activity: England and Wales.

Restrictions: Restrictions include: grants to recognized charities only, no grants to individuals, no grants for overseas travel and no loans or business finance.

Finance: Total expenditure £25,787,013 (2001).

Trustees: Joanna Foster (Chair.); Prof. Murray Stewart (Deputy Chair.); Rev. Rachel Benson; Virginia Burton; Ann Curno; Dr Pauleen Lane; John Penny; Howard Phillips; Linda Quinn; Gareth Roberts; Karamjit Singh; Colin Webb.

Principal Staff: Dir Gen. Kathleen Duncan.

Address: POB 140, St Mary's Court, 20 St Mary at Hill, London EC3R 8NA; Black Horse House, Phoenix Way, Swansea Enterprise Park, Swansea SA7 9EQ.

Telephone: (20) 7204-5276 (London); **Fax:** (20) 7204-5275 (London); **Internet:** www.lloydstsbfoundations.org.uk; **e-mail:** guidelines@lloydstsbfoundations.org.uk.

Ludwig Institute for Cancer Research

The Institute aims to carry out research into cancer.

Activities: Research into cancer is undertaken by staff financed by and working within the Institute in conjunction with medical centres and hospitals. The Institute works in collaboration with University College London, Imperial College of Science and Medicine, London, Cancer Research UK (q.v., formed by the merger of Cancer Research Campaign and Imperial Cancer Research Fund), Medical Research Council, and with overseas branches.

Geographical Area of Activity: United Kingdom.

Restrictions: No research grants or endowments are awarded.

Finance: Expenditure on medical research £7,000,000 (2000–01).

Scientific Committee: Dr L. J. Old (Chair.); Prof. A. Munro Neville (Sec.); Sir Walter Bodmer; Dr D. Fearon; Dr G. Klein; Dr H. zur Hausen; Dr S. Hellman; Dr A. Pardee; Dr Lucy Shapiro; Dr P. Sharp.

Address: Horatio House, 77–85 Fulham Palace Rd, 5th Floor South, London W6 8JC.

Telephone: (20) 8735-9240; **Fax:** (20) 8741-4990; **Internet:** www.licr.org.

Lyndhurst Settlement

Founded in 1968 for general charitable purposes, in particular those dealing with social problems, civil liberties and the protection of the environment.

Activities: Supports charities seeking to prevent as well as ameliorate poverty. Its main concerns include social problems; civil liberties, particularly in relation to prisoners; minority rights in the United Kingdom and abroad; and environmental issues, including the discouragement of population growth.

Geographical Area of Activity: Mainly United Kingdom.

Restrictions: Grants are not made to individuals, nor to medical or religious charities. Grants are normally only made to charities registered in the United Kingdom.

Finance: Total expenditure £193,573 (April 2002).

Trustees: Michael Isaacs; Kenneth Plummer; Anthony Skyrme.

Address: 15–19 Cavendish Pl., 2nd Floor, London W1G 0DD.

The Mackintosh Foundation

Founded in 1988 by Sir Cameron Mackintosh, for general charitable purposes.

Activities: Operates in the fields of the arts and humanities (in particular the performing arts), education and medicine and health. Provides funding through grants to institutions and individuals.

Geographical Area of Activity: United Kingdom and the USA.

Restrictions: No grants for politics or religion.

Publications: Information sheet.

Finance: Net assets £11,779,318 (2002); annual revenue £945,523, expenditure £898,064 (2002).

Trustees: D. Michael Rose (Co. Sec.); Nicholas Allott; Alain Boublil; Martin McCallum; Sir Cameron Mackintosh; Nicholas Mackintosh; Patricia Macnaughton.

Principal Staff: Appeals Dir Nicholas Mackintosh.

Address: 1 Bedford Sq., London WC1B 3RB.

Telephone: (20) 7637-8866; **Fax:** (20) 7436-2683.

Macmillan Cancer Relief

Founded in 1911 by Douglas Macmillan for the purpose of engaging in any activities which may lessen the suffering of cancer patients, including the protection and preservation of the health of their families and carers.

Activities: Operates training courses for doctors and nurses in the care of patients, particularly pain control; funds specialist Macmillan nurses and doctors; provides care in the home and through special units within hospitals; provides cash grants to patients in need, grants and scholarships for relevant study, and academic appointments; provides a telephone helpline; and funds certain charities in the United Kingdom which offer support and information to cancer sufferers.

Geographical Area of Activity: United Kingdom and Ireland.

Restrictions: Activities are restricted to the United Kingdom and Ireland (where funds are provided for patient support only).

Publications: *Macmillan News* (quarterly); Annual Review; booklets.

Finance: Total income approx. £70,000,000, direct charitable expenditure approx. £43,000,000 (2001).

Board of Management: Richard Hambro (Chair.); Johnathan Asquith (Treas.); Sir Christopher Benson; James Dundas; Sir Christopher France; Prof. Geoffrey Hanks; the Duchess of Kent; David Male; Anthony Simonds-Gooding; Prof. Jenifer Wilson-Barnett.

Address: 89 Albert Embankment, London SE1 7UQ.

Telephone: (20) 7840-7840; **Internet:** www.macmillan.org .uk; **e-mail:** info@macmillan.org.uk.

Maxco Trust

Founded in 1970 to promote donations to Christian causes.

Activities: Operates internationally. Distributes income and capital as requested by donors and assists in the maximizing of donations by helping donors to take full advantage of tax concessions. Manages trusts on behalf of donors, promoting gifts to Christian charitable organizations including churches, missionary societies and bible colleges.

Geographical Area of Activity: International.

Restrictions: Does not accept applications for grants.

Publications: Booklet.

Finance: Total assets £21,877,122 (2000); total income £1,792,289, expenditure £1,695,277 (2000).

Trustees: P. A. Lovegrove (Chair.); M. D. Birchall; M. J. Cansdale; W. R. Frampton; Col P. C. Harvey; R. L. Simpson; N. W. H. Sylvester.

Principal Staff: Dir P. B. Cockburn.

Address: 57 Beacon Way, Rickmansworth WD3 7PB.

Telephone: (1923) 350221; **Internet:** www.maxco.btinternet .co.uk; **e-mail:** maxco@btinternet.com.

Mayfair Charities Ltd

Founded in 1968 for the benefit of charitable organizations promoting orthodox Judaism.

Activities: Grants are made to charities nationally and internationally for educational and religious purposes in Israel, the United Kingdom and the USA.

Geographical Area of Activity: United Kingdom, Israel and the USA.

Finance: Annual revenue £4,957,000, expenditure £3,749,000 (March 2000).

Principal Staff: Dir B. S. E. Freshwater.

Address: 158–162 Shaftesbury Ave., London WC2H 8HR.

Telephone: (20) 7836-1555; **Fax:** (20) 7379-6365.

Medical Foundation for the Care of Victims of Torture

Established in 1986 by Helen Bamber to provide medical and psychological care to victims of torture and their families, and to raise public awareness of torture.

Activities: Operates in the United Kingdom, aiming to provide survivors of torture with medical treatment, practical assistance and psychotherapeutic support, document evidence of torture, provide training for health professionals working with torture survivors, educate the public and decision-makers about torture and its consequences, and ensure that the United Kingdom offers support to asylum-seekers and refugees. Some overseas projects are also run by the Foundation.

Geographical Area of Activity: United Kingdom.

Restrictions: Services are for the victims of torture and organized violence.

Publications: Reports.

Finance: Financed mostly by individual supporters. Annual revenue £5,266,000, expenditure £4,674,000 (2001).

Trustees: Rex Bloomstein; Simon Erskine; Roy van Gelder; Elizabeth Gordon; Gill Gorell Barnes; Stan Newman; David Walburn.

Principal Staff: Dir Malcolm Smart.

Address: 96–98 Grafton Rd, London NW5 3EJ.

Telephone: (20) 7813-7777; **Fax:** (20) 7813-0011; **Internet:** www.torturecare.org.uk; **e-mail:** info@torturecare.org.uk.

MENCAP—Royal Society for Mentally Handicapped Children and Adults

Founded to campaign for equal rights for people with learning difficulties.

Activities: Campaigns locally, nationally and in Europe to highlight learning disability issues; provides residential, education and employment services, leisure opportunities, and support and advice for those with learning disabilites and their families and carers. The Society's leisure division, Gateway, supports 700 clubs and projects throughout the United Kingdom, which provide sport, music, dance and drama facilities. Projects supported by MENCAP include: Open University K503 Working as Equal People/Leonardo da Vinci Vocational Training Programme; The Video Journalism in Europe Project; ADAPT Flexible Learning Systems; NOW Women in Social Enterprises Project.

Geographical Area of Activity: Mainly England, Wales and Northern Ireland.

Publications: *Viewpoint* (newspaper); variety of campaign reports.

Principal Staff: Pres. Lord Rix; Chair. Brian Baldock; Chief Exec. Fred Heddell.

Address: 123 Golden Lane, London EC1Y 0RT.

Telephone: (20) 7454-0454; **Fax:** (20) 7608-3254; **Internet:** www.mencap.org.uk; **e-mail:** info@mencap.org.uk.

Mental Health Foundation

Founded in 1949, the Foundation's purpose is to support research into learning disabilities and mental health problems. The Foundation incorporates the Foundation for People with Learning Disabilities.

Activities: The Foundation awards grants and fellowships for research into the causes and the treatment of mental disorders. Research must be undertaken in the United Kingdom. Funds are also provided for community and self-help projects, and the education of the public to increase awareness of the problems of those suffering mental health problems and those with learning disabilities.

Geographical Area of Activity: United Kingdom.

Publications: *Fundamental facts: all the latest facts and figures on mental illness; Bright futures: promoting children and young people's mental health; Building expectations: opportunities and services for people with a learning disability*; information booklets; research and policy briefings.

Finance: Annual revenue £3,648,477, expenditure £3,625,730 (2000).

Trustees: Christopher Martin (UK Chair.); Lord Dalhousie (Chair., Scotland).

Principal Staff: Chief Exec. Dr Andrew McCulloch.

Address: 7th Floor, 83 Victoria St, London SW1H OHW.

Telephone: (20) 7802-0300; **Fax:** (20) 7802-0301; **Internet:** www.mentalhealth.org.uk; **e-mail:** mhf@mhf.org.uk.

Mercers' Charitable Foundation

Founded in 1983 by the Worshipful Company of Mercers (City of London) to make grants for charitable purposes according to English law.

Activities: Operates nationally in the field of the arts, conservation, education, the advancement of religion, medicine and social welfare. The Foundation makes grants to education, heritage, arts, medical and social welfare projects. The co-administered Mercers' Educational Trust Fund provides grants to individuals for educational purposes, whilst welfare projects are funded by the Whittington Charity and the Earl of Northampton's Charity.

Geographical Area of Activity: United Kingdom.

Restrictions: No grants are made to individuals.

Trustees: The Mercers' Company.

Principal Staff: Grants Man. H. W. Truelove.

Address: Mercers' Hall, Ironmonger Lane, London EC2V 8HE.

Telephone: (20) 7726-4991; **Fax:** (20) 7600-1158; **Internet:** www.mercers.co.uk; **e-mail:** mail@mercers.co.uk.

Mercury Phoenix Trust

Established in memory of Freddie Mercury, principal singer of the pop group Queen, by the remaining members of the group and the group's manager, to assist people with AIDS and HIV world-wide.

Activities: Operates world-wide in the areas of medicine and health, and social welfare, through making grants to relieve the poverty and distress of people with HIV and AIDS, and to increase awareness of AIDS. Has funded projects in collaboration with the World Health Organization (WHO), and projects in various African countries, India and Nepal.

Geographical Area of Activity: International.

Finance: Annual revenue £211,105, expenditure £197,843 (March 2002).

Trustees: M. Austin; H. J. Beach; B. H. May; R. M. Taylor.

Principal Staff: Admin. Peter Chant.

Address: The Mill, Mill Lane, Cookham SL6 9QT.

Telephone: (1628) 527874; **Fax:** (1628) 520347.

MERLIN—Medical Emergency Relief International

A charity established in 1993 by Merlin Board Ltd to provide health care in areas in crisis around the world.

Activities: Operates mostly in Africa, South-East Asia and the countries of the former USSR in the areas of aid to less-developed countries, and medicine and health, through international programmes and projects, including projects in emergency medical relief, health education and infrastructure, and strategic development. Projects are currently active in Afghanistan, Democratic Republic of the Congo, Georgia, Kenya, Liberia, Russia, Sierra Leone and Tajikstan. Assists the World Health Organization (WHO) to implement the Roll Back Malaria campaign, and promotes cost-effective treatment for tuberculosis, improved access to primary health care, and training for health professionals. A member of the Disaster Emergencies Committee (q.v.).

Geographical Area of Activity: Africa, South-East Asia and the countries of the former USSR.

Restrictions: This is not a grant-making organization.

Publications: Annual Report.

Finance: Financed by donors. Annual revenue £6,496,097, expenditure £6,704,877 (2000).

Principal Staff: Chief Exec. Warren Lancaster; Head of Devt Lena Young; Head of Finance Adrian Harper; Sr Health Adviser Linda Doull.

Address: 5–13 Trinity St, Borough, London SE1 1DB.

Telephone: (20) 7378-4888; **Fax:** (20) 7378-4899; **Internet:** www.merlin.org.uk; **e-mail:** hq@merlin.org.uk.

Millennium Commission

Founded in 1993 under the National Lottery Act, to help communities celebrate the end of the second millennium and the begining of the third.

Activities: The Commission was established to operate through four main programme areas, Millennium Projects, Millennium People, Millennium Festival, and Millennium

Dome, based on five main themes, encouraging environmental sustainability, promoting science and technology, revitalising our cities, investing in education, and supporting our communities. Initiatives were put forward by communities and represented the largest ever non-governmental investment in the social and community infrastructure throughout the United Kingdom. Grants are made within the five themes of: Building; Breathing; Uniting; Exploring; and Learning.

Geographical Area of Activity: United Kingdom.

Publications: Newsletter (quarterly); Annual Report and accounts.

Finance: Revenue comes from the Commission's share of 28% of the profits derived from the United Kingdom's National Lottery.

Commissioners: Tessa Jowell (Chair.).

Address: Portland House, Stag Pl., London SW1E 5EZ.

Telephone: (20) 7880-2001; **Fax:** (20) 7880-2000; **Internet:** www.millennium.gov.uk; **e-mail:** info@millennium.gov.uk.

Mines Advisory Group

Founded to improve living conditions for those living in areas affected by mines and unexploded ordnance.

Activities: Promotes landmine clearance and awareness of unexploded ordnance, through collecting and analyzing information on incidents and providing advice to local communities on safe practice. Provides training and employment to local communities, and clears land which can be returned to productive use.

Geographical Area of Activity: Angola, Azerbaijan, Cambodia, Chad, Eritrea, Iran, Iraq, Kosovo, Laos, Lebanon, Mauritania, Somalia, Sri Lanka, Sudan, Thailand, Uganda and Vietnam.

Publications: Country reports.

Address: 47 Newton St, Manchester M1 1FT.

Telephone: (161) 236-4311; **Fax:** (161) 236-6244; **Internet:** www.mag.org.uk; **e-mail:** maguk@mag.org.uk.

Minority Rights Group International

Established to support the rights of ethnic, religious and linguistic minority groups world-wide.

Activities: Carries out research and publishes reports on minorities world-wide; lobbies the United Nations, international organizations and governments on behalf of the rights of minority groups; networks with similar organizations internationally; and educates on the rights of minority groups. Main programmes operate in Europe and Central Asia, Asia and the Pacific, and Africa and the Middle East. There are also specific programmes for Roma people and inter-regional programmes. Maintains a co-ordination office in Budapest.

Geographical Area of Activity: International.

Publications: *Outsider* (newsletter); *World Directory of Minorities;* reports; training manuals; workshops reports.

Finance: Total assets £837,214 (Dec. 2001); total income £1,686,693, total expenditure £1,716,408 (2001).

Council Members: Maja Daruwala (Chair.); Wim Jacobs (Treas.).

Address: 379 Brixton Rd, London SW9 7DE.

Telephone: (20) 7978-9498; **Fax:** (20) 7738-6265; **Internet:** www.minorityrights.org; **e-mail:** minority.rights@mrgmail.org.

The Mission to Seafarers

Founded in 1856 as a voluntary society within the Anglican Church, and originally known as the Missions to Seamen, to care for the welfare of seafarers of all nationalities and religions.

Activities: Operates through a network of chaplains, staff and volunteers who visit seafarers on their ships and offer support in times of distress, spiritual support and help for those with problems; provides social and recreational centres in more than 100 major ports; has links with parish clergy to provide support for seafarers' families.

Geographical Area of Activity: International.

Publications: *The Sea* (newspaper, every 2 months); *Flying Angel news* (quarterly newspaper).

Finance: Assets £26,990,000 (2001); annual revenue £5,035,000, expenditure £4,804,000 (2001).

Council: David Newbigging (Chair.); Michael Everard (Vice-Chair.); J. W. Hickman (Treas.); and 30 others.

Principal Staff: Sec.-Gen. Rev. Canon Bill Christianson.

Address: St Michael Paternoster Royal, College Hill, London EC4R 2RL.

Telephone: (20) 7248-5202; **Fax:** (20) 7248-4761; **Internet:** www.missiontoseafarers.org; **e-mail:** general@missiontoseafarers.org.

Monument Trust

Founded in 1965 for general charitable purposes. One of the Sainsbury Family Charitable Trusts, which share a common administration.

Activities: Operates nationally in the fields of the arts, the environment, health and community care, AIDS and social development.

Geographical Area of Activity: United Kingdom.

Restrictions: Unsolicited applications are unlikely to be successful. No grants are made directly to individuals.

Finance: Net assets £116,810,000 (April 2002); total income £4,316,000, annual expenditure £3,393,000 (2002).

Trustees: S. Grimshaw; R. H. Gurney; L. Heathcoat-Amory; Sir Anthony Tennant.

Principal Staff: Dir Michael Pattison.

Address: Allington House, 1st Floor, 150 Victoria St, London SW1E 5AE.

Telephone: (20) 7410-0330; **e-mail:** sfct@sfct.org.uk.

The Henry Moore Foundation

Founded in 1977 by Henry Moore for the education of the public in the appreciation of the fine arts and the works of Henry Moore in particular.

Activities: Operates nationally and internationally through self-conducted programmes, and nationally through research, grants to institutions, scholarships and fellowships, and through publications.

Geographical Area of Activity: International.

Restrictions: No grants are made to individuals.

Publications: *Henry Moore Bibliography* (5 vols); *Henry Moore: Complete Sculpture* (6 vols); *Henry Moore: Complete Drawings*; other publications on Henry Moore, and on the works of other artists.

Finance: Net assets £89,389,254 (March 2002); annual revenue £2,324,420, expenditure £4,609,887 (March 2002).

Trustees: Sir Ewen Fergusson (Chair.); P. J. Gaynor (Vice-Chair.); Sir Alan Bowness; Marianne Brouwer; Dr Andrew Causey; Joanna Drew; Sir Ernest Hall; Margaret McLeod; Lord Rayne; Sir Rex Richards; Henry Wrong.

Principal Staff: Dir Timothy Llewellyn; Admin. Charles M. Joint.

Address: Dane Tree House, Perry Green, Much Hadham SG10 6EE.

Telephone: (1279) 843333; **Fax:** (1279) 843647; **Internet:** www.henry-moore-fdn.co.uk; **e-mail:** info@henry-moore-fdn.co.uk.

John Moores Foundation

Founded in 1964 to provide funding for general charitable purposes.

Activities: Awards grants to voluntary organizations in Northern Ireland and on Merseyside working in the following areas: women's groups; ethnic minorities; education in race, gender or disability awareness; advice on welfare rights; second chance learning; and community work. On Merseyside, the Foundation also awards grants to voluntary organizations, providing support services for carers, services for homeless and unemployed people, and childcare services.

Geographical Area of Activity: United Kingdom (Northern Ireland and Merseyside).

Restrictions: No grants to individuals; grants to organizations only awarded on Merseyside and in Northern Ireland.

Publications: *Applying for a Grant* (leaflet).

Finance: Grants disbursed £677,921 (2001–02).

Trustees: P. Bassey; M. McAleese; B. Moores; J. Moores.

Principal Staff: Grants Dir Tara Parveen.

Address: Gostins Bldg, 7th Floor, 32–36 Hanover St, Liverpool L1 4LN.

Telephone: (151) 707-6077; **Fax:** (151) 707-6066; **Internet:** www.jmf.org.uk; **e-mail:** jmf@dial.pipex.com.

Multiple Sclerosis Society of Great Britain and Northern Ireland

Founded in 1953 by Sir Richard Cave, to promote research into the cause and cure of multiple sclerosis, and to provide a welfare and support service for people with multiple sclerosis and their friends, families and carers.

Activities: Conducts and supports research within the United Kingdom and gives grants to institutions and individuals (including researchers from the Commonwealth); holds international conferences, disseminates information and runs a specialist helpline.

Geographical Area of Activity: United Kingdom.

Publications: *MS Matters; MS Worldwide* (twice yearly newsletter); Annual Report; information booklets.

Finance: Annual revenue £21,400,000, expenditure £24,600,000 including annual research expenditure approx. £2,000,000 (2000).

Principal Staff: Chief Exec. Mike O'Donovan.

Address: 372 Edgeware Rd, Staples Corner, London NW2 6ND.

Telephone: (20) 8438-0700; **Fax:** (20) 8438-0701; **Internet:** www.mssociety.org.uk; **e-mail:** info@mssociety.org.uk.

Gilbert Murray Trust

Founded in 1956 to promote the study of ancient Greek literature and thought, and the propagation of Hellenic culture; to promote, with the help of travelling fellowships, scholarships, grants or other means, the study of the purpose and work of the United Nations.

Activities: Operates internationally in the fields of international relations and Hellenic culture, through grants to institutions and organizations, and grants to individuals. The Trust has two committees: the Classical Committee, which awards annual grants for travel to Greece, and the International Committee, which offers awards of £250 to students under 25 years, who are or have been students at a university or similar institution in the United Kingdom, to travel abroad to study international affairs.

Geographical Area of Activity: International.

Publications: Annual Report.

Finance: Annual revenue £7,351, expenditure £5,405 (April 2002).

Trustees: Prof. E. W. Handley (Chair.); D. E. R. Faulkner (Hon. Treas.); Prof. J. P. Barron; Mary Bull; Prof. C. Carey; Prof. P. E. Easterling; Dr P. H. Lyon; N. S. Marsh; Prof. Peter Parsons; R. A. Sims; Dr O. Taplin; Dr M. B. Trapp.

Principal Staff: Contact: David Faulkner.

Address: 99 Blacketts Wood Drive, Chorleywood, Rickmansworth WD3 5BS.

Telephone: (20) 7862-8700; **Fax:** (1923) 447814; **e-mail:** david.faulkner@cim.ox.ac.uk.

Muscular Dystrophy Group of Great Britain and Northern Ireland

Founded in 1961 by Frederick Nattrass, John Walton and Joseph Patrick to fund medical research into muscular dystrophy and allied diseases, and to offer support to those affected and to their families.

Activities: Finances research by means of grants to individuals and United Kingdom institutions, and organizes conferences. Member of the Founding Board of the European Neuromuscular Centre, and collaborates with and promotes the exchange of information between similar associations in other countries. Provides a range of information to people living with Muscular Dystrophy.

Geographical Area of Activity: United Kingdom.

Publications: *Annual Research Review; Target MD* (quarterly magazine); fact sheets.

Finance: Annual revenue £6,377,000, expenditure £5,462,000 (2001).

Trustees: Prof. M. Bobrow (Chair.); J. A. Patrick (Vice-Pres. and Vice-Chair.); and 22 others.

Principal Staff: Chief Exec. Christine Cryne.

Address: 7–11 Prescott Pl., London SW4 6BS.

Telephone: (20) 7720-8055; **Fax:** (20) 7498-0670; **Internet:** www.muscular-dystrophy.org.

Music Sound Foundation

Established in 1997 to promote the teaching of music.

Activities: Operates in the United Kingdom in the areas of primary, secondary and tertiary education in the field of music, through making grants to schools, to music students to pay for instruments, and to music teachers for training.

Geographical Area of Activity: United Kingdom.

Restrictions: Does not currently fund community projects or music therapy.

Publications: Annual Review.

Finance: Assets £6,900,000 (March 2000); annual revenue £405,000, expenditure £428,000 (2000).

Board of Trustees: Eric Nicoli (Chair.).

Principal Staff: Admin. Janie Orr.

Address: 4 Tenterden St, Hanover Sq., London W1A 2AY.

Telephone: (20) 7355-4848; **Fax:** (20) 7495-1424.

Muslim Aid

Established in 1985 to alleviate poverty.

Activities: Distributes grants through partner organizations in the fields of emergency relief, health care, education, water conservation, skills training, orphan care and shelter.

Geographical Area of Activity: Africa, Asia, Europe and South America.

Restrictions: Aid distributed through partner organizations only.

Publications: Newsletter (annual); Annual Review.

Finance: Receives donations from individuals and organizations in the United Kingdom and overseas.

Board of Trustees: Iqbal A. K. M. Sacranie (Chair.); Chowdhury Mueen-Uddin (Vice-Chair.); Farooq Murad (Sec.); Mehboob Kantharia (Treas.); A. K. M. Abdussalam; Dr Manazir Ahsan; Dr Kadhel Al-Rawi; Ahmed von Denffer; M. H. Faruqi. Dr Suhaib Hasan; Dr Abdul Majid Katme; Zahid Pervez; Dr Tariq Yusuf Rajbee; Ghulam Sarwar; S. M. T. Wasti.

Principal Staff: Co-ordinator E. Mohamed; Asst Co-ordinator M. Kroessin; Asst to Head of Donations Dept Z. Kasmani.

Address: POB 3, London N1 7UB.

Telephone: (20) 7387-7171; **Fax:** (20) 7387-7474; **Internet:** www.muslimaid.org; **e-mail:** info@muslimaid.org.

National Art Collections Fund—The Art Fund

Founded in 1903 to foster the visual arts and to help public museums, galleries and historic houses to acquire works of art.

Activities: Operates in the United Kingdom in the arts, through grants or bequests to regional and national institutions for the acquisition of works of art of national and historical importance. Campaigns on behalf of museums and galleries, particularly on issues such as free admission to national collections and funding for acquisitions, as well as promoting art to a wider audience.

Geographical Area of Activity: United Kingdom.

Publications: *Review* (annually); *Art Quarterly*.

Finance: Assets £37,450,000 (2000); total income £9,786,000, expenditure £5,802,000 (2000).

Executive Committee: Prof. Brian Allen (Chair.), R. Hambro (Treas.); and 16 others.

Principal Staff: Dir David Barrie.

Address: Millais House, 7 Cromwell Pl., London SW7 2JN.

Telephone: (20) 7225-8400; **Fax:** (20) 7225-4848; **Internet:** www.artfund100.org; **e-mail:** info@nacf.org.

National Asthma Campaign

Founded in 1990 by the Asthma Research Council, the Asthma Society and Friends of the Asthma Research Council; dedicated to conquering asthma. Funds research, offers help and advice and campaigns for a better deal for people with asthma.

Activities: Provides funds for grants for research to United Kingdom institutions; operates the Asthma Helpline for people with asthma; runs activity holidays for children.

Geographical Area of Activity: United Kingdom.

Publications: Information booklets, posters, factsheets, videos and other publications.

Finance: Expenditure on medical research £2,945,000 (2000–01).

Trustees: Sir Stuart Burgess; Andrew Gairdner; Tom Garrett; Prof. Duncan Geddes; Dr Chris Griffiths; John Griffiths; Christopher McLaren; Dr Martyn Partridge; Prof. John Price; Howard Ridley; Dr Rebecca Rosen; Brian Schirn; Dr Madge Vickers; Trisha Weller.

Principal Staff: Chief Exec. Donna Covey.

Address: Providence House, Providence Place, London N1 0NT.

Telephone: (20) 7226-2260; **Fax:** (20) 7704-0740; **Internet:** www.asthma.org.uk.

National Endowment for Science, Technology and the Arts—NESTA

Established in July 1998 under the National Lottery Act 1998, which committed £200,000,000 of National Lottery money to this national endowment, whose purpose is to support talented individuals in science, technology and the arts.

Activities: Operates nationally in the fields of the arts and humanities, conservation and the environment, education, and science and technology, through three main programme areas: fellowships to assist exceptional individuals in pursuing their ideas and fulfilling their potential; invention and innovation, helping the development of ideas which could be used for commercial and social benefit; and education, promoting creativity. Aims to make seed grants which will act as a catalyst to develop projects and individuals' potential.

Geographical Area of Activity: United Kingdom.

Restrictions: Grants are restricted to the United Kingdom.

Publications: Annual Report; *Looking Ahead—NESTA's Strategy 2000–2003*.

Finance: Net assets £250,000,000 (Feb. 2003); annual revenue approx. £24,400,000 (2003).

Trustees: Lord Puttnam of Queensgate (Chair.); Daniel Alexander; Dr Yvonne Barnett; Paul Daniel; Prof. Sir Christopher Evans; Sue Hunter; Prof. Janice Kirkpatrick; Baroness McIntosh of Hudnall; François Matarasso; Dr Bridget Ogilvie; Derek Wanless.

Principal Staff: Chief Exec. Jeremy Newton; Deputy Chief Exec. Janet Morrison.

Address: Fishmongers' Chambers, 110 Upper Thames St, London EC4R 3TW.

Telephone: (20) 7645-9500; **Fax:** (20) 7645-9501; **Internet:** www.nesta.org.uk; **e-mail:** nesta@nesta.org.uk.

National Foundation for Educational Research in England and Wales

Founded in 1946; an independent educational research body which aims to gather, analyze and disseminate research-based information in order to improve education and training.

Activities: The organization undertakes research on behalf of its members: the English and Welsh local authorities, professional associations and external sponsors in all areas of education, from pre-school and primary to further and higher education. Provides evaluation services on the impact of various education and training programmes at local and national levels. Develops and researches tests of all types, including those for the National Curriculum. Maintains a full range of support services including library, information service, in-house publishing unit, computing and statistics, and survey administration. Also works internationally in co-operation with overseas partner organizations.

Geographical Area of Activity: United Kingdom (England and Wales).

Publications: Research findings; *NFER News* (twice yearly newsletter); *Annual Survey of Trends in Education*.

Finance: Annual revenue £22,675,000, expenditure £9,653,000 (March 2001).

Trustees: Lord Preston (Chair.); N. Harrison (Vice-Chair.); R. D. C. Bunker (Hon. Treas.); and 25 others.

Principal Staff: Dir Gen. Dr S. Hegarty.

Address: The Mere, Upton Park, Slough SL1 2DQ.

Telephone: (1753) 574123; **Fax:** (1753) 691632; **Internet:** www.nfer.ac.uk; **e-mail:** enquiries@nfer.ac.uk.

National Society for the Prevention of Cruelty to Children—NSPCC

Founded in 1889 by Rev. Benjamin Waugh to provide protection for children and to draw public and Government attention to their plight.

Activities: The Society works to prevent children suffering harm as a result of cruelty, to protect children at risk of harm and to help children who have suffered cruelty. In 1999 the FULL STOP Campaign was launched, comprising five action programmes: Protecting the Child; the Child in the Family; the Child in School; the Child in the Community; and the Child in Society. Operates the Child Protection Helpline, a free telephone service, child protection units throughout the United Kingdom, prevention programmes in local communities, the NSPCC National Child Protection Training Centre training and consultancy service for child welfare professionals; and also conducts research into child abuse and trends, produces literature to inform the general public, and campaigns on behalf of children.

Geographical Area of Activity: United Kingdom.

Publications: Annual Report; Annual Review; *Get Ready* (parenting magazine); and numerous other specialist publications.

Finance: More than 85% of the Society's income is provided by donors and supporters; net assets £60,375,000 (March 2002); annual revenue £90,584,000, expenditure £83,435,000 (2002).

Board of Trustees: John Norton (Chair.); Hon. Mrs Birkbeck (Vice-Chair.); Lady Moyra Campbell (Deputy Vice-Chair.); Adrian Burn (Treas.); and others.

Principal Staff: Dir and Chief Exec. Mary Marsh; Dir of Appeals and Deputy Chief Exec. Giles Pegram; Chief Operating Officer David Prescott.

Address: National Centre, 42 Curtain Rd, London EC2A 3NH.

Telephone: (20) 7825-2500; **Fax:** (20) 7825-2525; **Internet:** www.nspcc.org.uk; **e-mail:** infounit@nspcc.org.uk.

The National Trust for Places of Historic Interest or Natural Beauty

Founded in 1895 to support the preservation of historic buildings or sites of natural beauty in England, Wales and Northern Ireland.

Activities: Maintains historically or architecturally important buildings, as well as parks, gardens, coast and countryside to which it may provide public access; also conducts educational programmes. The Trust has 3,000,000 members.

Geographical Area of Activity: England, Wales and Northern Ireland.

Restrictions: Does not normally make grants.

Publications: Magazine (3 a year); *National Trust Handbook for Members and Visitors* (annually); *Information for Visitors with Disabilities* (annually); over 70 further publications promoting the work of the Trust.

Finance: Annual expenditure approx. £180,000,000.

Principal Staff: Chair. Sir William Proby; Dir Gen. Fiona Reynolds.

Address: Rowan, Kembrey Park, Swindon SN2 6UG.

Telephone: (870) 458-4000; **Fax:** (20) 8466-6824; **Internet:** www.nationaltrust.org.uk; **e-mail:** enquiries@ntrust.org.uk.

NCH

Founded in 1869, and formerly known as NCH Action for Children, to provide help for children and young people suffering as a result of poverty, disability, abuse, neglect and social exclusion.

Activities: Operates nationally, through campaigning for policy changes to benefit children and young people. Operates in the following areas: ending child poverty and social exclusion; providing safeguards for children and young people at risk of abuse; promoting education and health; preventing youth crime and homelessness; improving the quality of life for children in care; foster care; family centres and residential homes; mediation services; and ensuring safe use of the internet for children. Runs short break projects, residential centres and community centres. Maintains offices in Wales and Scotland.

Geographical Area of Activity: United Kingdom.

Principal Staff: Chair. Gordon Edington; Vice-Chair. Robin Wendt; Treas. Dr Keith Aldred; Chief Exec. Deryck Mead.

Address: 85 Highbury Park, London N5 1UD.

Telephone: (20) 7704-7000; **Fax:** (20) 7226-2537; **Internet:** www.nch.org.uk.

Airey Neave Trust

Founded in 1979 in memory of Airey Neave, by Sir John Tilney, and the late Baroness Airey of Abingdon and Lord McAlpine of Moffat, for the furtherance of research into personal freedom under the law, and for financial help for the educational needs of refugees.

Activities: Funds research projects into all aspects of individual freedom under the law, of which approximately one-half are related to terrorism. Gives direct help to refugees by contributing towards their postgraduate fees so that they can qualify or re-qualify in their trades or professions.

Geographical Area of Activity: United Kingdom.

Restrictions: Grants to individuals are made to refugees and to Fellows attached to law faculties only.

Publications: *Children Enslaved; The Victims of Terrorism; The International Covenant on Civil and Political Rights and the UK; Study of the Operation and Impact of the Council of Europe Committee for the Prevention of Torture; Political Violence and Commercial Victims; The Position of Refugees in British and European Law and Practice; Terrorist Use of Weapons of Mass Destruction.*

Finance: Annual expenditure £50,360 (2001–02).

Trustees: Dame Veronica Sutherland (Chair.); Lord Goodhart; Hon. Sir William McAlpine; Sir Nigel Mobbs; Hon. Patrick Neave; Lord Sutherland of Houndwood; Hugh Tilney; Prof. Paul Wilkinson.

Principal Staff: Pres. Rt Hon. Lord Mayhew of Twysden; Sec. and Admin. Hannah Scott.

Address: POB 36800, 40 Bernard St, London WC1N 1WJ.

Telephone: (20) 7833-4440; **e-mail:** hanth.c@aol.com.

New Economics Foundation

Established in 1996 as a research organization ('think tank') aiming to develop practical and enterprising solutions to the social, environmental and economic challenges facing the local, regional, national and global economies.

Activities: Carries out research and policy work, principally focusing on participative democracy, local economic renewal, local works and reshaping the global economy. Involved in the development of the LETS alternative currency schemes, as well as developing community time banks, and introducing benchmark surveys on ethical consumption and corporate performance. The Foundation was also involved in forming the Institute for Social and Ethical Accountability.

Geographical Area of Activity: United Kingdom.

Publications: *NEF Newsletter; Plugging the Leaks; The Competitive Inner City; Taking Flight: the Rapid Growth of Ethical Consumerism*; numerous other publications and research reports.

Finance: Assets £722,506 (June 2001); annual revenue £1,937,249, expenditure £1,617,187 (2001).

Board of Trustees: Sue Gillie (Chair.).

Principal Staff: Exec. Dir Ed Mayo; Deputy Dir Andrea Westall.

Address: Cinnamon House, 6–8 Cole St, London SE1 4YK.

Telephone: (20) 7407-7447; **Fax:** (20) 7407-6473; **Internet:** www.neweconomics.org; **e-mail:** info@neweconomics.org.

New Opportunities Fund—NOF

The Fund was established under the National Lotteries Act 1998, and is responsible for distributing National Lottery grants throughout the United Kingdom for health, education and environmental initiatives.

Activities: The Fund works with other organizations, including other Lottery distributors, to support sustainable projects in the United Kingdom that improve the quality of life for individuals and communities, promote social inclusion, encourage community involvement and complement and enhance relevant national, regional and local strategies and programmes. Operates in the fields of health, education and the environment. Current grant programmes include: Healthy Living Centres; Living with Cancer; Community Access to Lifelong Learning; Out of School Hours Learning; Out of School Hours Childcare; Activities for Young People; ICT (information and communication technology) Training for Teachers, School Librarians and Public Librarians; the Digitization of Learning and Community Materials; Green Spaces and Sustainable Communities; and contribution to the joint Lottery distributor programme Awards for All. Maintains a searchable on-line database of grants awarded.

Geographical Area of Activity: United Kingdom.

Publications: *Initiative* (newsletter).

Finance: Revenue comes from the Fund's share of 28% of the profits derived from the United Kingdom's National Lottery.

Trustees: Baroness Jill Pitkeathley (Chair); Prof. Eric Bolton (Deputy Chair.); Jill Barrow; David Campbell; David Carrington; Tom Davies; Prof. Breidge Gadd; Prof. Sian Griffiths; Polly Hudson; Dugald Mackie; Prof. Allan Patmore; Barbara Stephens; Geoff Thompson.

Address: 1 Plough Place, London EC4A 1DE.

Telephone: (20) 7211-1800; **Fax:** (20) 7211-1750; **Internet:** www.nof.org.uk; **e-mail:** general.enquiries@nof.org.uk.

Northern Rock Foundation

Established in 1997 by the former Northern Rock Building Society, to support disadvantaged people in the North-East of England, especially in Northumberland, Tyne and Wear, Durham and Teesside.

Activities: Operates in the North-East of England and Cumbria to combat disadvantage, through making grants in the areas of disability, young and old people, small organizations, penal reform, rural and urban regeneration, the arts (including literary awards), combating discrimination against homosexuals, and living in the North-East.

Geographical Area of Activity: North-East of England (Northumberland, Tyne and Wear, Durham and Teesside), and Cumbria.

Restrictions: Operates primarily in the North-East of England, although applications from the North of England and Scotland are also considered. Grants are made to registered charities only, which have an office or representation in the North-East of England. No grants for medical research, hospitals, animal welfare, promotion of religion, vehicles or endowment funds.

Publications: *Rock Reports* (newsletter).

Finance: Total expenditure £11,509,978 (2001).

Trustees: P. R. M. Harbottle (Chair.); Sir David Chapman; D. Faulkner; L. P. Finn; Lord Howick of Glendale; C. Jobe; F. Nicholson; Lady Russell; J. Shipley; J. Ward.

Principal Staff: Dir Fiona Ellis.

Address: 21 Lansdowne Terrace, Gosforth, Newcastle upon Tyne NE3 1HP.

Telephone: (191) 284-8412; **Fax:** (191) 284-8413; **Internet:** www.nr-foundation.org.uk; **e-mail:** generaloffice@nr-foundation.org.uk.

Novartis Foundation

The Novartis Foundation was established in 1997 as the direct successor to the Ciba Foundation, following the creation of the Novartis company (which resulted from the merger of the Ciba and Sandoz pharmaceutical companies). The Ciba Foundation was created in 1947 to advance and promote research in medicine, chemistry, biology and allied subjects.

Activities: Operates internationally in the fields of chemistry, medicine and the biological sciences through its own programmes. Almost 7,000 scientific meetings have been held at the Foundation, including international multidisciplinary symposia, study groups, lectures and discussions. Over 400 scientific books arising from these meetings have been published. Accommodation is provided for scientists visiting London. Runs a bursary scheme for young scientists to attend Novartis Foundation symposia and afterwards spend up to three months working with one of the other participants.

Geographical Area of Activity: International.

Restrictions: No direct research funding; grants are made only in relation to its own symposium programme.

Publications: Eight Symposium volumes per year; Annual Report; electronic bulletin (every 3 months).

Finance: Charitable expenditure £1,300,000 (2001).

Trustees: Prof. Sir Keith Peters; Prof. Sir David Weatherall; Lord Mustill; Prof. Richard Perham; Prof. Sir Michael Rutter.

Principal Staff: Dir Dr Derek Chadwick; Deputy Dir Dr Gregory Bock; Asst Dir Zarir Suntook (Finance and Admin.).

Address: 41 Portland Pl., London W1B 1BN.

Telephone: (20) 7636-9456; **Fax:** (20) 7436-2840; **Internet:** www.novartisfound.org.uk; **e-mail:** dchadwick@novartisfound.org.uk.

Nuffield Foundation

Founded in 1943 by Lord Nuffield for the advancement of social well-being, particularly through scientific research; for the care of the aged; and for the advancement of education.

Activities: Grants are awarded to institutions in the United Kingdom. Major grants are for experimental or development projects in education or social welfare. Small grants and fellowships in science and social science are also offered under research grant schemes, which are open to members of universities and other research institutions. Support is occasionally given to projects which are conducted in-house, including the Nuffield Council on Bioethics, the Nuffield Curriculum Project and the Nuffield Languages Programme. Fellowships and other awards are available to citizens of the United Kingdom. Sponsors the Commonwealth Programme in conjunction with the Commonwealth Relations Trust (q.v.) and administers the Elizabeth Nuffield Educational Fund, which makes grants to women studying to improve their employment prospects.

Geographical Area of Activity: United Kingdom and Commonwealth countries of Eastern and Southern Africa.

Restrictions: No grants to individuals.

Publications: Annual Report; guide for applicants.

Finance: Annual revenue £8,103,955, expenditure £7,483,377 (2001).

Trustees: Baroness O'Neill (Chair.); Sir Tony Atkinson; Dr P. Doyle; Lord May; Prof. G. Richardson; Prof. Sir Michael Rutter; A. Sofer.

Principal Staff: Dir Anthony Tomei.

Address: 28 Bedford Sq., London WC1B 3EG.

Telephone: (20) 7631-0566; **Fax:** (20) 7323-4877; **Internet:** www.nuffieldfoundation.org; **e-mail:** atomei@nuffieldfoundation.org.

Officers' Association

Founded in 1919 by Admiral of the Fleet Earl Beatty, Field Marshal Earl Haig and Air Marshal Sir Hugh Montagu Trenchard, for the relief of financial distress among male or female ex-officers of HM Naval, Military or Air Forces, their widows and dependants, and to assist such persons in such ways as are legally charitable.

Activities: Operates both in the United Kingdom and abroad in the field of social welfare, through grants to individuals; providing advice on finding accommodation in homes for the elderly; the running of a home for the elderly and an estate for disabled ex-officers; and through a Resettlement and Employment Department.

Geographical Area of Activity: International.

Publications: Report of operations and financial statement.

Finance: Net assets £8,294,000 (Oct. 2001).

Principal Staff: Chair. Lt-Col. R. Nunneley; Gen. Sec. Maj. Gen. A. I. Ramsey; Dir of Employment Col H. Sandars; Head of Benevolence S. A. Hewitt; and a Council of about 100 members.

Address: 48 Pall Mall, London SW1Y 5JY.

Telephone: (20) 7930-0125; **Fax:** (20) 7930-9053; **Internet:** www.officersassociation.org.uk; **e-mail:** postmaster@oaed.org.uk.

OneWorld International Foundation

Founded in 1999 to promote sustainable use of resources and the protection of human rights and democratic structures, through operating as an on-line media gateway without regard to geographic or linguistic barriers.

Activities: The Foundation operates a network of 11 OneWorld Centres (in Austria, Canada, Costa Rica, Finland, India, Italy, the Netherlands, Spain, the United Kingdom, the USA and Zambia) dedicated to the promotion of human rights and sustainable development; the OneWorld network aims to utilize the potential of the internet to achieve its objectives. OneWorld International Ltd, a not-for-profit company, carries out the day-to-day support and co-ordination of the network; the company also undertakes production contracts for like-minded organizations.

Geographical Area of Activity: Austria, Central and South America, Finland, India, Italy, the Netherlands, Spain, the USA and Zambia.

Trustees: Pranlal Sheth (Chair.); Jertta Blomstedt; James Deane; Rutger Engelhardt; Angel Font; Larry Kirkman; Charika Marasinghe; Dipuo Mvelase; Fr Gabriele Pipinato.

Principal Staff: Dir Anuradha Vittachi; Governance Man. Miles Litvinoff.

Address: 89 Albert Embankment, 17th Floor, London SE1 7TP.

Telephone: (20) 7735-2100; **Fax:** (20) 7840-0798; **Internet:** www.oneworld.net; **e-mail:** foundation@oneworld.net.

Oppenheimer Charitable Trust

Founded in 1961 by the Diamond Trading Company (Pty) Ltd, to make donations to registered charitable institutions in the United Kingdom. Following a reappraisal of its objects in 1971, the Trust now aims to channel the finances available into national and international organizations contributing towards the well-being of the local people in areas where companies of the De Beers group operate.

Activities: Operates in the fields of science and medicine, the arts and humanities, aid to less-developed countries and social welfare, particularly in relation to young people and the aged, in areas where companies of the De Beers group are active.

Geographical Area of Activity: International, although mainly United Kingdom.

Restrictions: Grants only to specific organizations.

Finance: Annual income £57,800, grants disbursed £54,629 (Oct. 2000).

Trustees: Sir Christopher Collet; M. J. M. Farmiloe; G. I. Watson.

Principal Staff: Sec. Nicholas Stacey.

Address: 17 Charterhouse St, London EC1N 6RA.

Telephone: (20) 7404-4444; **Fax:** (20) 7430-8640.

Opportunity International UK

Founded as Opportunity Trust in 1992 to empower people and communities in developing countries, and to overcome poverty and secure sustainable improvement in the quality of life in these countries.

Activities: Operates in the fields of aid to less-developed countries, economic affairs and education, through self-conducted programmes, research, grants to institutions and publications. Works through 60 partner organizations world-wide, providing small business loans to those without access to the formal banking sector. In 2002 made loans worth £81,700,000 to organizations in 25 different countries.

Geographical Area of Activity: International.

Publications: Annual Report; newsletter (quarterly).

Finance: Assets £300,000 (2000); annual revenue and expenditure £5,100,000 (2001).

Trustees: Colin Webster (Chair.).

Principal Staff: Dir Neil Cuthbert.

Address: Angel Court, 81 St Clements, Oxford OX4 1AW.

Telephone: (1865) 725304; **Fax:** (1865) 295161; **Internet:** www.opportunity.org.uk; **e-mail:** info@opportunity.org.uk.

Overseas Development Institute—ODI

Founded in 1960 as an independent non-governmental centre for development research and a forum for discussion of the problems facing developing countries.

Activities: Operates nationally and internationally in the fields of economic affairs, development policy and social studies, through research, publications and the ODI Fellowship Scheme. The Institute's main research and policy programmes are: Poverty and Public Policy Group (which includes the Centre for Aid and Public Expenditure); International Economic Development Group; Humanitarian Policy Group; Rural Policy and Environment Group; and Forest Policy and Environment Group. Manages three international networks of practitioners, policy-makers and researchers: the Agricultural Research and Extension Network; the Rural Development Forestry Network; and the Humanitarian Practice Network. Also hosts the Secretariat of the Active Learning Network on Accountability and Performance in Humanitarian Assistance. Maintains a reference library and information centre.

Geographical Area of Activity: International.

Publications: Annual Report; *Briefing Papers; Development Policy Review* (quarterly); *Disasters* (quarterly); *Natural Resources Perspectives;* books and pamphlets.

Council: Baroness Jay (Chair.).

Principal Staff: Dir Simon Maxwell; Sec. Allen Brown.

Address: 111 Westminster Bridge Rd, London SE1 7JD.

Telephone: (20) 7922-0300; **Fax:** (20) 7922-0399; **Internet:** www.odi.org.uki; **e-mail:** odi@odi.org.uk.

Oxfam

Founded in 1942, as the Oxford Committee for Famine Relief, to relieve poverty, distress and suffering in any part of the world. Now, Oxfam works with poor people regardless of race or religion in their struggle against hunger, disease, exploitation and poverty world-wide, through relief, development, research and public education.

Activities: Assistance is given in the form of financial grants to a wide variety of agencies working in the field. Provides relief in emergencies, but is also concerned with long-term sustainable development. Runs educational and campaigning programmes to raise public awareness of the nature and causes of poverty. Campaigning is in three main areas. Oxfam's Trade Campaign, Make Trade Fair, calls for world trade rules to be changed, to end poverty for millions of people. The Education Campaign calls on governments and institutions to make education for all a reality. The Cut Conflict Campaign calls on governments to recognise their responsibilities and take action on the small arms trade, refugee rights, war crimes and landmines. In 2001–02, 88% of total income was made available for Oxfam's primary objectives.

Geographical Area of Activity: International.

Publications: Annual review; report and accounts; *The Campaigner* (quarterly); *Oxfam News* (quarterly); general and technical publications; educational and audio-visual materials.

Finance: Funds are raised through volunteer-run shops, local and national fundraising events, and a wide range of donation schemes. Total revenue £189,400,000, charitable expenditure £114,900,000 (2001/02).

Council of Management: Rosemary Thorpe (Chair.); Jeremy Swift (Vice-Chair.); David Kingsmill (Hon. Treas.); and nine others.

Principal Staff: Dir Barbara Stocking.

Address: 274 Banbury Rd, Oxford OX2 7DZ.

Telephone: (1865) 311311; **Fax:** (1865) 312417; **Internet:** www.oxfam.org.uk.

Oxfam International

Established in 1995 as a confederation of 12 autonomous NGOs (in Australia, Belgium, Canada—Ontario and Québec,

Germany, Hong Kong, Ireland, the Netherlands, New Zealand, Spain, the United Kingdom and the USA), which aim to combat poverty and injustice.

Activities: Member NGOs operate in the field of aid to less-developed countries, both through long-term development projects and through providing emergency relief, working in collaboration with local partners in more than 100 countries world-wide. Projects include campaigning to reduce countries' debt and for universal primary education, in accordance with Oxfam's aim to promote five fundamental rights: sustainable livelihood, life and security, to be heard, basic social services and an identity. Established a Washington Advocacy Office in 1995, to lobby the International Bank for Reconstruction and Development (World Bank), the International Monetary Fund and the United Nations on behalf of member NGOs.

Geographical Area of Activity: International.

Restrictions: Makes grants through affiliate organizations.

Publications: *Towards Global Equity.*

Finance: Total assets US $349,358 (2001); annual revenue $1,611,614, expenditure $1,517,607 (2001).

Principal Staff: Chair. Ian Anderson; Exec. Dir Jeremy Hobbs.

Address: 266 Banbury Rd, Suite 20, Oxford OX2 7DL.

Telephone: (1865) 313639; **Fax:** (1865) 313770; **Internet:** www.oxfam.org; **e-mail:** information@oxfaminternational .org.

Particle Physics and Astronomy Research Council—PPARC

The PPARC was established in 1994, one of the organizations formed by the splitting up of the Science and Engineering Research Council (SERC). The SERC was replaced by the PPARC, the Engineering and Physical Sciences Research Council (EPSRC—q.v.) and the Biotechnology and Biological Sciences Research Council (BBSRC—q.v.).

Activities: The PPARC is the United Kingdom's strategic science investment agency, which funds research, research infrastructure, training, education, and public understanding activities in four areas of science: particle physics, astronomy, cosmology and space science. It provides research grants and studentships to scientists in British universities, and funds the United Kingdom's membership of international bodies such as the European Laboratory for Particle Physics, CERN, the European Space Agency and the European Southern Observatory (ESO). It also funds the United Kingdom telescopes located overseas in Hawaii, Australia and Chile, as well as the Astronomy Technology Centre at the Royal Observatory in Edinburgh and the MERLIN/VLBI National Facility. The Public Understanding of Science and Technology Awards Scheme provides funding to small local projects and to national initiatives aimed at improving public understanding of the PPARC's areas of science.

Geographical Area of Activity: United Kingdom; funding for telescopes in Australia, Chile and Hawaii.

Publications: *Frontiers; At the Edge of Knowledge; Astronews;* Annual Report.

Finance: Funded by the United Kingdom Government. Total assets £70,014,000 (March 2001); total income £212,884,000, expenditure £220,850,000 (2001).

Principal Staff: Chair. Peter Warry; Chief Exec. Prof. Ian Halliday; Sec. Glenys Short.

Address: Polaris House, North Star Ave, Swindon SN2 1ET.

Telephone: (1793) 442000; **Fax:** (1793) 442002; **Internet:** www.pparc.ac.uk; **e-mail:** webmaster@pparc.ac.uk.

Peace Brigades International

Founded in 1981 to promote non-violent peace-keeping and human rights.

Activities: The organization's main programme areas are protective international accompaniment, whereby those threatened with violence are accompanied by a Peace Brigades International volunteer in order to deter death squads and other violent groups; peace education, which teaches non-violent methods of resolving conflicts; and documenting conflicts and peace initiatives in order to promote the global non-violent movement. The organization has worked in South-Eastern Europe, and is currently working in the Far East and Central America. Country groups and regional offices are located in Australia, Austria, Belgium, Canada, France, Germany, India, Italy, the Netherlands, New Zealand, Norway, Spain, Sweden, Switzerland and the USA.

Geographical Area of Activity: International.

Restrictions: No funding is given to groups or individuals.

Publications: *PBI Project Bulletin; Emergency Response Network Alerts;* country reports.

Finance: Assets £492,760 (Dec. 2001); annual revenue £1,809,601, expenditure £1,369,730 (2001).

Address: Unit 5, 89–93 Fonthill Rd, London N4 3HT.

Telephone: (20) 7561-9141; **Fax:** (20) 7281-3181; **Internet:** www.peacebrigades.org; **e-mail:** info@peacebrigades.org.

Penal Reform International

Established in 1989 to promote the development of international agreements in the areas of prisons and law enforcement, including the abolition of the death penalty, reduction in the prison population, and the promotion of social integration rather than custodial sentences.

Activities: The organization has members in more than 80 countries world-wide, and carries out regional programmes in Africa, Central and South America and the Caribbean, Central and Eastern Europe and the republics of Central Asia, Southern Asia, and the Middle East and North Africa, in collaboration with NGOs and individuals. These programmes include providing expertise, training and advisory services; organizing conferences; and lobbying. The organization has consultative status with the United Nations and the Council of Europe. The headquarters are in London, and there are offices in Kathmandu, Paris, Moscow, San José (Costa Rica), Washington, DC and Bucharest, and sub-regional offices in Burundi, Georgia, Kazakhstan, Malawi and Rwanda.

Geographical Area of Activity: International.

Publications: Reports; newsletters; manuals and policy documents.

Principal Staff: Exec. Dir Paul English; Admin. Dir Catherine Leonard.

Address: The Bon Marché Centre, Unit 450, 241–251 Ferndale Rd, Brixton, London SW9 8BJ.

Telephone: (20) 7924-9575; **Fax:** (20) 7924-9697; **Internet:** www.penalreform.org; **e-mail:** headofsecretariat@pri.org.uk.

Pesticide Action Network UK—PAN UK

An NGO, founded in 1987, and part of PAN International, to promote healthy food, sustainable agriculture and a safe environment without using hazardous pesticides.

Activities: Supports projects with partner organizations in developing countries, researching related issues and undertaking policy advocacy. Provides information through publishing briefings, books and journals.

Geographical Area of Activity: International.

Restrictions: Not a grant-making organization.

Publications: *Pesticides News; Current Research Monitor*; Annual Report.

Finance: Total income £668,891, total expenditure £666,915 (2001).

Principal Staff: Dir Barbara Dinham.

Address: Eurolink Centre, 49 Effra Rd, London, SW2 1BZ.

Telephone: (20) 7274-8895; **Fax:** (20) 7274-9084; **Internet:** www.pan-uk.org; **e-mail:** admin@pan-uk.org.

Pilgrim Trust

Founded in 1930 by Edward Stephen Harkness for such charitable purposes within Great Britain and Northern Ireland as the trustees may from time to time determine.

Activities: Operates nationally in the fields of social welfare, the arts, and the conservation of the national heritage, through grants to charities.

Geographical Area of Activity: United Kingdom.

Restrictions: No grants to individuals or non-United Kingdom organizations.

Publications: Annual report and financial statement; guidelines.

Finance: Assets £51,550,609 (2001); annual revenue £1,656,292, grants disbursed £2,041,415 (2001).

Trustees: M. Moore (Chair.); Nicolas Barker; Rt Hon. Lord Bingham; Sir Richard Carew-Pole; Lord Cobbold; Lady Jay; Neil MacGregor; Dame Ruth Runciman; E. Turton.

Address: Cowley House, 9 Little College St, London SW1P 3XH.

Telephone: (20) 7222-4723; **Fax:** (20) 7976-0461.

PLAN International

Established in 1937 by John Langdon-Davies and Eric Muggeridge; aims to create child-focused development programmes to aid communities world-wide.

Activities: Operates internationally in less-developed countries, through child sponsorship, in order to assist in community development. PLAN operates programmes in five priority areas: health, education, habitat, livelihood, and building relationships. Health programmes include: safe motherhood and child survival, early childhood care and development, reproductive health and HIV/AIDS; education programmes include: access to quality education, out of school education, and adult literacy and vocational skills; habitat programmes include: land and housing tenure, sanitation, and managing natural resources; livelihood programmes include: improved agricultural production, credit and financial services, and vocational training; and building relationships programmes aim to ensure that children and their communities play a leading part in all development projects, and promote the relationships between sponsors and their sponsored children. Sister organizations operate in 15 other countries.

Geographical Area of Activity: Africa, Asia, and Central and South America and the Caribbean.

Finance: Financed by individual sponsors of children, the Department for International Development, the European Commission of the European Union, donations from foundations, etc. Annual revenue £24,361,641, expenditure on programmes £23,710,990 (2002).

Governing Board: Baroness Gardner of Parkes; J. Boateng; J. L. F. Buist; N. A. Chalmers; J. Clare; S. A. Dobson; A. Grant; D. C. Morley; A. J. Sutherland; D. N. Tarsh.

Principal Staff: Chief Exec. Marie Staunton; Co. Sec. John Pinchard; Programme Funding Man. Craig Stein.

Address: 5–6 Underhill St, London NW1 7HS.

Telephone: (20) 7482-9777; **Fax:** (20) 7482-9778; **Internet:** www.plan-international.org/uk; **e-mail:** mail@plan-international.org.uk.

Plunkett Foundation

Founded in 1919 by Sir Horace Curzon Plunkett to promote and disseminate information regarding the principles of co-operative business systems. The Foundation's work is supported by members in the United Kingdom and overseas.

Activities: Undertakes training courses, consultancy projects and research studies on co-operative development and management in the United Kingdom and in developing countries. Assists rural communities to establish and run enterprises that provide essential services. Organizes study programmes for organizations and individuals. Maintains a library of over 20,000 books, pamphlets, reports and periodicals on co-operation world-wide, with plans to make the collection available on-line.

Geographical Area of Activity: International.

Publications: Annual Report; *The Journal of Co-operative Studies; Directory and Statistics of Agricultural Co-operatives and Farmer Controlled Businesses in the UK; Rural Connections* (quarterly newsletter); and other publications.

Finance: The Foundation's international work is supported by partners and agencies including the British Overseas Development Agency, the Government's Know-How Fund, the European Commission of the European Union, the International Bank for Reconstruction and Development (World Bank) and the United Nations. Annual revenue £300,384, expenditure £303,257 (2000).

Board of Trustees: David Button (Chair.).

Principal Staff: Chief Exec. Richard Moreton.

Address: 23 Hanborough Business Park, Long Hanborough OX29 8SG.

Telephone: (1993) 883636; **Fax:** (1993) 883576; **Internet:** www.plunkett.co.uk; **e-mail:** info@plunkett.co.uk.

Polden-Puckham Charitable Foundation

Founded in 1990 for general charitable purposes.

Activities: Operates in the United Kingdom in the areas of promoting the peaceful resolution of conflicts and resolving the underlying causes; ecology and the environment; and human rights, particularly where it is related to peace, ecological issues and policy changes relating to women's issues. Grants normally fall into three categories: Peace and Security; Economic Sustainability; and Other Areas, and are generally in the range of £3,000–£4,000. The Foundation is linked with the Society of Friends (Quakers).

Geographical Area of Activity: Mostly United Kingdom.

Restrictions: Does not respond to applications outside its field of interest. Only makes grants to overseas organizations with which it is already in contact. No grants for individuals, travel bursaries, overseas study, academic research, capital projects, community projects, international aid/development organizations or general appeals.

Publications: Annual Report and accounts.

Finance: Annual revenue £393,765, expenditure £393,765 (April 2002).

Trustees: C. M. Carolan; C. F. Freeman; D. B. Gillett; H. J. Gillett; J. Gordon; H. Swailes; A. Wilson.

Principal Staff: Sec. M. Bevis Gillett.

Address: BM PPCF, London WC1N 3XX.

Internet: www.polden-puckham.org.uk.

Policy Studies Institute—PSI

Founded in 1978 (formerly known as Political and Economic Planning—PEP, founded in 1931) as an independent research organization, undertaking studies of social, economic and cultural policy.

Activities: Operates nationally and internationally, carrying out research in the fields of the arts and humanities, education, training, economic affairs, and social and political studies, examining selected problems. Research areas are: arts and culture, communications, criminal justice, disability, education and training, employment, ethnic minorities, evaluation, family life, health, household budgets, income and wealth, industrial relations, information, the legal system, local and regional studies, new technology, policing, social care, social security, women and young people. The Institute publishes the results of its research. In 1998 the Institute became a wholly-owned subsidiary of the University of Westminster.

Geographical Area of Activity: International.

Publications: Research Papers; Annual Report; *Policy Studies* (quarterly journal); *Cultural Trends* (quarterly journal); and numerous other publications.

Council: Sir Leonard Peach (Chair.); Sir Richard O'Brien (Pres.); and 20 others.

Principal Staff: Dir Jim Skea; Sr Research Admin. Raj Chitnavis.

Address: 100 Park Village East, London NW1 3SR.

Telephone: (20) 7468-0468; **Fax:** (20) 7388-0914; **Internet:** www.psi.org.uk; **e-mail:** website@psi.org.uk.

Population Concern

The organization was established originally as the international branch of the Family Planning Association of the United Kingdom. It became fully independent in 1991.

Activities: Operates internationally in partnership with local organizations in about 20 countries, providing sexual and reproductive health services, including family planning. The organization also provides technical assistance and assists in the building of capacity of partner organizations. In the United Kingdom, Population Concern aims to improve understanding of how reproductive choice, rights and responsibilites contribute to population stabilization and the advancement of human development by alleviating poverty, distress, ill health and environmental degradation. Funding is provided by the European Union, the Department for International Development and private trusts and foundations.

Geographical Area of Activity: International.

Publications: Annual Review; *Young People: Sexual and Reproductive Health* (booklet); *Partnerships in Action*.

Finance: Annual revenue £2,391,683, expenditure £2,773,707 (March 2002).

Trustees: Dilys Cossey (Chair.); Anthony Browne; Josy Eldred; John Higginbotham; Timothy Maxwell; Alastair Service; Hazelo Slavin; Peter Styles.

Principal Staff: Chief Exec. Ros Davies.

Address: Studio 325, Highgate Studios, 53–79 Highgate Rd, London NW5 1TL.

Telephone: (870) 7702476; **Fax:** (20) 7267-6788; **Internet:** www.populationconcern.org.uk; **e-mail:** info@populationconcern.org.uk.

Porter Foundation

Founded in 1970 by Sir Leslie Porter and Dame Shirley Porter to support projects in the fields of education, culture, conservation and the environment, and health and welfare.

Activities: Operates in the United Kingdom and Israel in the fields of the arts, conservation and the environment, education and medicine, through grants to institutions.

Geographical Area of Activity: United Kingdom and Israel.

Finance: Annual revenue £1,191,151, expenditure £975,570 (April 2002).

Trustees: David Brecher; Sir Leslie Porter; Dame Shirley Porter; Steven Porter.

Principal Staff: Exec. Dir Paul Williams.

Address: POB 229, Winchester SO23 7WF.

Telephone: (1962) 849684; **Fax:** (1962) 863903; **e-mail:** theporterfoundation@btinternet.com.

PPP Foundation

Established to improve standards in the provision of health care; to advance knowledge, skills and services in health care and public health; and to enhance the contributions of health-care practitioners to the quality of life of all the community; formerly known as the PPP Healthcare Medical Trust.

Activities: The Trust funds medical research and its practical application, as well as providing grants to charities and other organizations to support the education and training of people involved in the provision, management and administration of health care; the relief of sickness and disability and the relief of the aged, and public health initiatives. In 2002 four new programme areas were agreed: supporting the development of leadership in all its forms amongst health-care professionals; capacity building in the institutions concerned with the education, training, development and life-long learning of health-care professionals; encouraging health service improvement and redesign initiatives and supporting the uptake of innovation and the spread of good practice; and supporting health improvement in the developing world.

Geographical Area of Activity: United Kingdom; and designated areas of Africa and Asia as part of specific grant programmes.

Restrictions: No grants for capital building.

Publications: Annual report and accounts.

Finance: Net assets £537,286,000 (2002); grant budget approx. £17,000,000 (2002).

Trustees: Sir David Carter (Chair.); L. Banks; Prof. Y. Carter; Michael B. Sayer; Dr E. Vallance; and others.

Principal Staff: Chief Exec. Stephen Thornton.

Address: 13 Cavendish Sq., London W1G 0PQ.

Telephone: (20) 7307-2622; **Fax:** (20) 7307-2623; **Internet:** www.pppfoundation.org.uk; **e-mail:** info@pppfoundation.org.uk.

The Prince's Trust

The Prince's Trust was founded in 1976 by HRH The Prince of Wales to enable young people, in particular the most disadvantaged, to develop themselves and serve the community. Incorporates the Royal Jubilee Trusts comprising the Queen's Silver Jubilee Trust (founded in 1977) and King George's Jubilee Trust (founded in 1936); and has merged with The Prince's Youth Business Trust, The Prince's Trust for the Welsh Environment and The Prince's Trust Volunteers.

Activities: Operates in the United Kingdom, the Commonwealth, and Eastern and Western Europe to further the development of young people aged 14–30, through grants to organizations, groups and individuals, training courses and publications. Particular emphasis is placed on projects to aid the community, education, training and employment programmes, and helping young offenders and the homeless. Runs a business start-up programme for young people, the Prince's Trust Volunteers programmes, a European programme, a community grant initiative and a programme for young care leavers.

Geographical Area of Activity: United Kingdom, the Commonwealth, and Eastern and Western Europe.

Publications: Annual Report; *Trust* (magazine); *Update* (volunteers' newsletter); *Business* (magazine, quarterly); *Europe—A Manual, Partners in Europe;* Study Support Resources Pack; *A Place for Success* (Study Support Centre's Report); *Changing Inside* (Young Offenders Report).

Finance: Total assets £28,596,000 (March 2002); total income £46,489,000, total expenditure £46,097,000 (2002).

Principal Staff: Pres. HRH The Prince of Wales; Chair. Sir William Castell; Chief Exec. Tom Shebbeare.

Address: 18 Park Sq. East, London NW1 4LH.

Telephone: (20) 7543-1234; **Fax:** (20) 7543-1200; **Internet:** www.princes-trust.org.uk; **e-mail:** info@princes-trust.org.uk.

Project Trust

Founded in 1967 to promote a broader education for young people through volunteer work-experience schemes abroad, and for general charitable purposes.

Activities: Sends European school leavers overseas to take part in voluntary work, usually in developing countries.

Geographical Area of Activity: South and Central America, Africa, the Middle East, and South and East Asia.

Restrictions: Not a grant-making organization.

Publications: *Project Post* (newsletter, quarterly); Annual Report.

Trustees: P. L. H. Bristol; I. G. Fallon; Hon. P. H. Lewis.

Principal Staff: Dir Lavinia Bristol; Assistant Dir John Fraser.

Address: The Hebridean Centre, Isle of Coll, Argyll PA78 6TE.

Telephone: (187) 923-0444; **Fax:** (187) 923-0357; **Internet:** www.projecttrust.org.uk; **e-mail:** info@projecttrust.org.uk.

A. M. Qattan Foundation

Founded in 1993 by Abdul Mohsen Al-Qattan to advance education, cultural development and awareness; to preserve the cultural values and heritage and enrich the social fabric of Palestinian communities world-wide.

Activities: Operates in the Middle East in the fields of education, culture, science and the promotion of the NGO sector.

Geographical Area of Activity: Middle East (Palestinian communities).

Publications: *Flowers of Palestine; Young Artist of the Year Award* (catalogue); research reports; and numerous other publications.

Finance: Privately funded by A. M. Al-Qattan.

Trustees: Abdul Mohsen Al-Qattan; Hani Al-Qattan; Leila Al-Qattan; Omar Al-Qattan.

Principal Staff: Admin. Man. Julia Helou.

Address: 5 Princes Gate, Kensington Rd, London SW7 1QJ.

Telephone: (20) 7581-8774; **Fax:** (20) 7581-0741; **Internet:** www.qattanfoundation.org; **e-mail:** amqf@lineone.net.

Rank Foundation

Founded in 1953 by Lord and Lady Rank to promote the Christian religion, education and general charitable purposes in the United Kingdom and overseas.

Activities: Provides funds to organizations working in the promotion of Christianity (funds in this area are committed to an associated charity, the Foundation for Christian Communication Ltd). Also makes grants in the areas of education, in particular grants to needy pupils at independent schools (upon application from their headteacher), and educational programmes for young offenders; youth; and other charitable projects, including the elderly and the disabled.

Geographical Area of Activity: Mostly United Kingdom.

Restrictions: No grants are made to individuals.

Publications: Annual Report.

Finance: Total assets £187,360,000 (2001); annual revenue £7,523,000, grants disbursed £6,512,000 (2001).

Trustees: F. A. Packard (Chair.); M. D. Abrahams; Earl St Aldwyn; J. A Cave; A. E. Cowen; M. E. T. Davies; L. G. Fox; J. R. Newton; D. R. Peppiatt; V. A. L. Powell; Dr M. J. Scurr; Lord Shuttleworth; D. R. W. Silk.

Principal Staff: Finance Dir and Company Sec. John Cowling.

Address: POB 2862, Whitnash, Leamington Spa CV31 2YH.

Telephone: (1926) 744550; **Fax:** (1926) 882209; **Internet:** www.rankfoundation.com; **e-mail:** john.cowling@rankfoundation.com.

The Ruben and Elisabeth Rausing Trust

Established in 1995 by Dr Sigrid Rausing.

Activities: The Trust's funding is divided between four programme areas: human rights, supporting women, social and economic regeneration, and the environment. Support emphasizes the promotion and protection of human rights, gender equality, self-reliance and sustainability, including research on the impact of aid on gender issues, and hands-on conservation projects, including groups focusing on issues such as dam building, pesticides and toxic waste.

Geographical Area of Activity: Mainly but not exclusively Europe and the United Kingdom; USA work is often international.

Restrictions: No grants to individuals; does not generally accept unsolicted applications.

Publications: Annual Report.

Finance: Net assets £95,500,000 (Dec. 2001); total revenue £52,700,000, expenditure £9,400,000 (2001).

Board of Trustees: Robert Bernstein; Joshua Mailman; Lisbet Rausing; Sigrid Rausing.

Principal Staff: Dir Jo Andrews; Asst to Dir Clare Deane.

Address: 39 Sloane St, London SW1X 9LP.

Telephone: (20) 7235-9560; **Fax:** (20) 7235-9580; **e-mail:** rer@articnet.com.

Rayne Foundation

Founded in 1962 by Lord Rayne for general charitable purposes.

Activities: Operates nationally and (for certain specific projects) internationally, in the fields of the arts, education, medicine and social welfare, especially the welfare of young people and the elderly, through grants to registered charities only.

Geographical Area of Activity: Mostly United Kingdom.

Finance: Annual revenue £1,951,021, expenditure £1,598,127 (Nov. 2001).

Trustees: Lord Rayne (Chair.); Lord Bridges; Sir Claus Moser; Lady Rayne; R. A. Rayne; Prof. Dame Margaret Turner-Warwick.

Principal Staff: Contact: Robert Dufton.

Address: Carlton House, 33 Robert Adam St, London W1U 3HR.

Telephone: (20) 7935-3555; **Fax:** (20) 7935-3737; **e-mail:** rdufton@lms-plc.com.

Reuters Foundation

Founded in 1982 by Reuters, the international news and information organization, to aid the media in developing countries, and to narrow the gap in information technology between developed and developing countries.

Activities: Organizes training courses for practising journalists from developing countries and Eastern Europe in subjects including international and business news-writing and international television journalism. Reuter Foundation Fellowships are offered to journalists of all nationalities for study at the University of Oxford and at Stanford University, USA. The Foundation is also involved in educational and community projects, health care, environmental issues and the arts in communities where Reuters has offices. Operates AlertNet, an internet service aimed at providing news, field reports and forums to the international disaster relief community: www.alertnet.org, and AIDfund, a programme which provides funding to aid organizations dealing with large-scale natural disasters. Also makes annual awards marking journalistic achievement in the areas of environmental news reporting and news graphics.

Geographical Area of Activity: International.

Restrictions: Does not support political or religious causes, extremist or militant causes, sport events (unless fundraising for eligible causes), or animal causes (unless part of a broader environmental scheme). Does not consider unsoliticited requests for support, unless from Reuters staff.

Publications: *Reuterslink* (2 a year).

Finance: Annual revenue £3,962,245, expenditure £3,946,997 (2000).

Board of Trustees: David Ure (Chair.); Geert Linnebank; Maureen Marlowe; Sir Crispin Tickell; Geoffrey Weetman; Devin Wenig.

Principal Staff: Dir Rosemary Martin.

Address: 85 Fleet St, London EC4P 4AJ.

Telephone: (20) 7542-7015; **Fax:** (20) 7542-8599; **Internet:** www.foundation.reuters.com; **e-mail:** foundation@reuters.com.

Rhodes Trust

Founded in 1902 by Cecil John Rhodes, for educational and general purposes.

Activities: The Trust operates internationally in the field of education, by awarding 90 Rhodes Scholarships annually for overseas graduates (mainly from the Commonwealth and the USA) to study at the University of Oxford. Applicants must be between the ages of 19 and 25 (those applying from Kenya must be under the age of 27). Scholarships cover tuition fees, a maintenance allowance and travel costs.

Geographical Area of Activity: International.

Board of Trustees: Prof. Sir Richard Southwood (Chair.).

Principal Staff: Warden Dr John S. Rowett; Sec. to the Warden Sue Taylor.

Address: Rhodes House, South Parks Rd, Oxford OX1 3RG.

Telephone: (1865) 270902; **Fax:** (1865) 270914; **Internet:** www.rhodeshouse.ox.ac.uk; **e-mail:** admin@rhodeshouse.ox.ac.uk.

Rowan Charitable Trust

Founded in 1964 to promote humanitarian causes.

Activities: Operates nationally and internationally (in Africa, Asia and the Pacific, Central and South America, and the Middle East) in the fields of aid to less-developed countries, development studies, conservation and the environment, economic affairs, human rights, medicine and health, and social welfare, through grants to registered charities, self-conducted programmes, research, training courses and publications.

Geographical Area of Activity: Africa, Asia and the Pacific, Central and South America, and the Middle East.

Finance: Annual revenue £314,898, expenditure £536,788 (Oct. 2001).

Trustees: C. R. Jones; H. Russell.

Address: c/o PricewaterhouseCoopers, 9 Greyfriars Rd, Reading RG1 1JG.

Telephone: (118) 959-7111; **Fax:** (118) 960-7706.

Joseph Rowntree Charitable Trust

Founded in 1904 by Joseph Rowntree, who placed particular emphasis on justice, equal opportunity and the unique value of each individual.

Activities: Operates by making grants, mainly in the United Kingdom and Southern Africa, supporting work on peaceful resolution of international and other conflicts; racial justice; democratic process; corporate responsibility; intercommunity issues in Northern Ireland and Southern Africa; and work connected with the Religious Society of Friends (Quakers).

Geographical Area of Activity: United Kingdom, Republic of Ireland, Europe and Southern Africa.

Restrictions: No grants for large established charities; general appeals; local work (except in Northern Ireland or parts of Yorkshire); building, buying or repairing buildings; providing care for elderly people, children, people with learning difficulties, people with physical disabilities, or people using mental health services; work in mainstream education, including schools and academic or medical research; work on housing and homelessness; travel or adventure projects; business development or job creation; paying off debts; work which the Trust believes should be funded by the State; educational bursaries; work outside the United Kingdom, Ireland and South Africa; and the arts.

Publications: Information leaflets, triennial reports.

Finance: Assets £149,862,785 (2001); annual revenue £3,938,138, grants disbursed £3,959,669 (2001).

Trustees: A. D. S. Gunn (Chair.); T. Allport; M. Bryan; P. Coltman; C. Davis; J. Guest; R. McCarthy; M. McNaughton; B. Meeson; E. Miles; R. Morton; V. Shend'ge; D. T. Shutt; P. Stark.

Principal Staff: Sec. S. Pittam; Deputy Sec. J. R. Prager; Asst Sec. N. Perks.

Address: The Garden House, Water End, York YO30 6WQ.

Telephone: (1904) 627810; **Fax:** (1904) 651990; **Internet:** www.jrct.org.uk; **e-mail:** jrct@jrct.org.uk.

Joseph Rowntree Foundation

Founded in 1904 by Joseph Rowntree, and formerly known as the Joseph Rowntree Memorial Trust, to seek out the causes of social problems, and, by better understanding them, help improve policy and practice development in the United Kingdom.

Activities: Funds research and development projects in the fields of housing, social care and social policy, concentrating on building communities, new housing developments, developing care services and neighbourhood renewal. Initiatives include supporting action in rural areas, work on fathers and parenting, tackling racial harassment, misuse of drugs and young carers. The Foundation runs the Joseph Rowntree Housing Trust (a registered housing association), a number of residential care homes, and the United Kingdom's first continuing care retirement community.

Geographical Area of Activity: United Kingdom.

Restrictions: No grants to individuals.

Publications: *Search* (2 a year); *Findings* (research summaries, about 90 a year); Annual Report; and about 80 research reports a year.

Finance: Net assets £218,500,000 (2001); grants disbursed £6,600,000 (2001).

Trustees: Kenneth Dixon (Chair.); Sir William Utting (Deputy-Chair.); Dame Margaret Booth; Dame Ann Bowtell; Catherine Graham-Harrison; Susan V. Hartshorne; Robert Maxwell; Nigel Naish; Debby Ounsted.

Principal Staff: Dir Lord Best.

Address: The Homestead, 40 Water End, York YO30 6WP.

Telephone: (1904) 629241; **Fax:** (1904) 620072; **Internet:** www.jrf.org.uk.

Joseph Rowntree Reform Trust Ltd (including the JRSST Charitable Trust)

Founded in 1904 by Joseph Rowntree to promote political reform, constitutional change and social justice.

Activities: Operates in the field of politics, propagandist activities, and 'pressure groups', through self-conducted programmes and through grants to organizations and individuals.

Note: Although the Joseph Rowntree Reform Trust is not charitable in law, its subsidiary, the JRSST Charitable Trust, makes charitable grants for purposes closely related to those of the Joseph Rowntree Reform Trust.

Geographical Area of Activity: Mainly United Kingdom.

Restrictions: Does not provide funding for research.

Finance: Grants disbursed approx. £750,000 (2000).

Directors: Archy Kirkwood (Chair.); Christine Day; Christopher Greenfield; Pam Giddy; Diana Scott; Lord David Shutt of Greetland; Prof. Lord Trevor Smith of Clifton.

Principal Staff: Sec. Tina Walker.

Address: The Garden House, Water End, York YO30 6WQ.

Telephone: (1904) 625744; **Fax:** (1904) 651502; **Internet:** www.jrrt.org.uk; **e-mail:** info@jrrt.org.uk.

Royal Aeronautical Society

Founded in 1866 for the general advancement of aeronautical art, science and engineering, the Royal Aeronautical Society is the global forum for the entire aerospace community.

Activities: Awards scholarships for study and research in aeronautics by citizens of the United Kingdom and the Commonwealth, in approved United Kingdom or foreign establishments; issues professional qualifications and medals; maintains a library and ensures the highest professional standards in all aerospace disciplines. It also plays a key role in influencing opinion on aviation matters.

Geographical Area of Activity: International.

Publications: *The Aeronautical Journal; Aerospace International; The Aerospace Professional* (all monthly).

Finance: Annual revenue £2,669,120, expenditure £2,549,625 (2001).

Principal Staff: Dir Keith Mans.

Address: 4 Hamilton Pl., London W1J 7BQ.

Telephone: (20) 7670-4300; **Fax:** (20) 7499-6230; **Internet:** aerosociety.com.

Royal Air Force Benevolent Fund

Founded in 1919 by Lord Trenchard for the relief of distress experienced by anyone who has entered productive service in the Royal Air Force, or any of its associated Forces, as well as their immediate dependants. The Fund also maintains the RAF Memorial on the Victoria Embankment, London.

Activities: Operates internationally in the fields of social welfare, through grants and loans to eligible individuals. The Fund owns homes in Sussex and Aberdeenshire, offering long-term residential, and short-term respite care, as well as jointly owning homes in Northumberland, Avon, Lancashire and Powys. It also manages the Royal Air Force Benevolent Fund Housing Trust.

Geographical Area of Activity: United Kingdom.

Publications: Report of operations and financial statement.

Finance: Annual charitable expenditure approx. £15,000,000.

Council: Sir Richard George (Chair.); and 20 Trustees.

Principal Staff: Air Chief Marshal Sir David Cousins.

Address: 67 Portland Pl., London W1B 1AR.

Telephone: (20) 7580-8343; **Fax:** (20) 7636-7005; **Internet:** www.rafbf.org.uk; **e-mail:** info@rafbf.co.uk.

Royal Anthropological Institute of Great Britain and Ireland

Founded in 1871 by the merger of the Ethnological Society and the Anthropological Society, to encourage the study of the 'Science of Man'.

Activities: Operates nationally and internationally in anthropology, through publications, conferences and lectures, the provision of library facilities for research, the promotion of anthropological film, and grants and scholarships to individual researchers from trust funds. It also manages a photographic archive, and raises funds. Awards several international prizes, such as the Curl Essay Prize, the Wellcome Medal for Medical Anthropology, the Lucy Mair Medal for Applied Anthropology, and the J.B. Donne Essay Prize in the Anthropology of Art.

Geographical Area of Activity: International.

Restrictions: Grants and scholarships are open only to those replying to published advertisements.

Publications: Report of operations and financial statement; *Journal of the Royal Anthropological Institute* (quarterly journal, incorporating *Man*); *Anthropology Today* (6 a year); *Anthropological Index Online* (internet service).

Finance: Assets approx. £939,000.

Council: Prof. Wendy James (Pres.); Prof. Julian Thomas (Vice-Pres.); Prof. John Davis; Dr Robert Foley); and others.

Principal Staff: Dir Hilary Callan.

Address: 50 Fitzroy St, London W1T 5BT.

Telephone: (20) 7387-0455; **Fax:** (20) 7388-8817; **Internet:** www.therai.org.uk; **e-mail:** admin@therai.org.uk.

Royal Asiatic Society of Great Britain and Ireland

Founded in 1823 by Henry Thomas Colebrooke to promote the study of Asia.

Activities: Main activities are publishing journals and books, managing library and collection, organizing lectures, seminars and exhibitions, and operating a fellowship programme.

Geographical Area of Activity: Asia.

Publications: *Journal of the Royal Asiatic Society* (3 a year); books; monographs.

Council of Management: Prof. A. J. Stockwell (Pres.).

Principal Staff: Dir Rachel Ward; Sec. A. P. Thomas.

Address: 60 Queen's Gardens, London W2 3AF.

Telephone: (20) 7724-4741; **Fax:** (20) 7706-4008; **Internet:** www.royalasiaticsociety.org; **e-mail:** info@royalasiaticsociety.org.

Royal British Legion

Founded in 1921 by Field Marshal Earl Haig, to promote the welfare of ex-service people and their dependants.

Activities: The Legion provides assistance to those serving, or who have served in the armed forces and to their dependants. Assists disabled and needy ex-service men and women, and their dependants, by running residential homes, providing sheltered employment and special housing, proving entitlement to pensions and assisting individual cases of hardship, advising on small businesses and providing resettlement training; it also arranges visits to war graves abroad. There are over 3,000 branches in the United Kingdom and more than 50 overseas.

Geographical Area of Activity: International.

Publications: Annual report and accounts; *Legion* (magazine); leaflets, fact sheets.

Finance: Annual expenditure approx. £40,000,000 (2002).

Principal Staff: Pres. Lt Gen. Sir Roderick Cordy-Simpson; Chair. I. P. Cannell; Gen. Treas. J. A. Tedder; Sec.-Gen. Ian Townsend.

Address: 48 Pall Mall, London SW1Y 5JY.

Telephone: (20) 7973-7200; **Fax:** (20) 7973-7399; **Internet:** www.britishlegion.org.uk; **e-mail:** info@britishlegion.org.uk.

Royal Commission for the Exhibition of 1851

Founded in 1850 to enquire into the promotion of the Great Exhibition; supplementary charter in 1851, to apply the surplus funds of the Exhibition to increase the means of industrial education and extend the influence of science and art upon productive industry.

Activities: Operates in the fields of the physical and biological sciences, pure and applied, and engineering and industrial design, principally through postgraduate research awards and fellowships. Some other special awards are made.

Publications: Annual Report; *Record of Award Holders in Science, Engineering and the Arts, 1891–2000*.

Finance: Net assets £39,113,099 (Dec. 2000); annual revenue £1,134,143, expenditure £1,375,585 (Dec. 2001).

Board of Management: Sir Alan Rudge (Chair.); W. L. Banks; A. Baxter; J. Dyson; Sir Robert Honeycombe; I. Macgregor; K. M. H. Mortimer; Lord Linley; Sir John Meurig Thomas; Dr C. L. Vaughan; Prof. D. Wallace; Prof. A. Windle.

Principal Staff: Pres. HRH Prince Philip, Duke of Edinburgh; Sec. J. P. W. Middleton.

Address: Sherfield Bldg, Imperial College, London SW7 2AZ.

Telephone: (20) 7594-8790; **Fax:** (20) 7594-8794; **Internet:** www.royalcommission1851.org.uk; **e-mail:** royalcom1851@imperial.ac.uk.

Royal Commonwealth Society

Founded in 1868 (present name 1956); its aim is to promote the increase and spread of knowledge with respect to the people and countries of the Commonwealth.

Activities: Operates internationally in the fields of development studies, international affairs and education by holding conferences and other meetings, lectures and a major Commonwealth essay competition; maintains a library of 500,000 items on the Commonwealth (situated at the University of Cambridge Library), suitable for researchers and general readers; provides residential and conference facilities. There are over 10,000 members world-wide, and branches, representatives and affiliated organizations in 35 countries.

Geographical Area of Activity: International.

Restrictions: Not a grant-making organization.

Publications: Annual Report; newsletters, reports on conferences and seminars.

Principal Staff: Pres. Chief E. C. Anyaoku; Chair. Central Council Sir Michael McWilliam; Dir Gen. Stuart Mole.

Address: 18 Northumberland Ave, London WC2N 5BJ.

Telephone: (20) 7930-6730; **Fax:** (20) 7930-9705; **Internet:** www.rcsint.org; **e-mail:** info@rcsint.org.

Royal Geographical Society (with The Institute of British Geographers)

Founded in 1830 by Sir John Barrow and others for the advancement of geographical science and the improvement and diffusion of geographical knowledge.

Activities: The Society aims to stimulate the awareness and enjoyment of geography at all levels, for all people, both in the United Kingdom and world-wide. It supports more than 20 research groups; promotes geography within the British education system; produces scholarly publications; provides training in scientific field techniques; assists personal development in young people through expeditions; presents a popular national lecture series; and provides advice and information through its large map collection, library and picture library.

Geographical Area of Activity: International.

Publications: *The Geographical Journal; The Geographical Magazine; Area; Transactions.*

Finance: Total grants approx. £200,000 (2002).

Trustees: Prof. R. Cooke (Pres.); Earl of Selborne (Immediate Past Pres.); Prof. R Hudson, A. Millett, Prof. D. Thomas (Vice-Pres); D. Lyon (Hon. Treas.); Prof. A. Werritty (Vice-Pres., Chair. Annual Conference); Prof. A. Church, Dr M. Firth (Hon. Secs); and 15 ordinary members.

Principal Staff: Dir and Sec. Dr Rita Gardner.

Address: 1 Kensington Gore, London SW7 2AR.

Telephone: (20) 7591-3000; **Fax:** (20) 7591-3001; **Internet:** www.rgs.org; **e-mail:** info@rgs.org.

Royal Institute of International Affairs—RIIA

Founded in 1919 to encourage and facilitate the scientific study of international questions. The Institute is precluded by its charter from expressing opinions of its own.

Activities: Operates as an independent centre for the study of international political and economic affairs, through self-conducted programmes of research, discussion, exposition and publication, designed to serve an informed public in general and the Institute's 3,000 members in particular. The Institute maintains a library and information service, and runs an active programme of meetings for its members. Its research programme includes work on Europe, the countries of the former USSR, Japan and East Asia, the Middle East, international economic relations, international security questions and international energy and environmental issues. All research is directed towards publication; meetings, seminars and conferences related to research are organized at home and abroad.

Geographical Area of Activity: International.

Restrictions: The Institute is exclusively an operating body, and does not give grants.

Publications: *The World Today* (monthly); *International Affairs* (quarterly); *Chatham House Papers;* RIIA Discussion Papers; and various books.

Principal Staff: Dir Victor Bulmer-Thomas.

Address: Chatham House, 10 St James's Sq., London SW1Y 4LE.

Telephone: (20) 7957-5700; **Fax:** (20) 7957-5710; **Internet:** www.riia.org; **e-mail:** contact@riia.org.

Royal National Institute of the Blind—RNIB

Founded in 1868, the purpose of the Institute is to provide advice, information and services to enable blind and partially-sighted people to take charge of their own lives; and to challenge the underlying causes of blindness by helping to prevent, cure or alleviate it.

Activities: The Institute provides information, support and advice to people with sight problems, through access to braille, large print, 'talking' books, computer training and seeking innovative and imaginative solutions to everyday challenges, as well as campaigning to change society's attitudes, actions and assumptions, so that people with sight problems can enjoy the same rights, freedoms and responsibilities as fully sighted people. Also funds pioneering research into the prevention and treatment of eye disease and promotes eye health by running public health awareness campaigns.

Geographical Area of Activity: United Kingdom.

Publications: Annual Report; Braille, large-print and 'talking' books; videos; magazines; leaflets.

Finance: Annual revenue £88,219,000, expenditure £84,474,000 (2001/02).

Executive Council: Colin M. Low (Chair.); Kevin Carey (Vice-Chair.).

Principal Staff: Dir Gen. Prof. Ian Bruce.

Address: 105 Judd St, London WC1H 9NE.

Telephone: (20) 7388-1266; **Fax:** (20) 7388-2034; **Internet:** www.rnib.org.uk; **e-mail:** helpline@rnib.org.uk.

Royal National Lifeboat Institution—RNLI

Founded in 1824 by Sir William Hilary to save lives at sea.

Activities: Provides volunteer lifeboat services in the United Kingdom and Ireland, through 224 lifeboat stations.

Geographical Area of Activity: United Kingdom and Ireland.

Restrictions: Does not make grants.

Publications: Annual Review; fact sheets.

Finance: Funded by public donations; annual revenue £127,895,000, expenditure £103,995,000 (2001).

Trustees: HRH the Duke of Kent (Pres.); Peter C. Nicholson (Chair.); Sir John James (Deputy Chair.); Iain R. Bryce (Treas.); and others.

Principal Staff: Chief Exec. Andrew Freemantle.

Address: West Quay Rd, Poole BH15 1HZ.

Telephone: (1202) 663-000; **Fax:** (1202) 663-167; **Internet:** www.rnli.org.uk; **e-mail:** info@lifeboats.org.uk.

Royal Over-Seas League

Founded in 1910 by Sir Evelyn Wrench to promote friendship and understanding; it is a self-funding, non-profit-making organization that operates under a Royal Charter, and is pledged to work for the service of others, the good of the Commonwealth, and humanity in general.

Activities: The League has over 22,000 members world-wide. It encourages the arts, in particular among the young people of the Commonwealth, through staging an Annual Music Competition, an Annual Open Exhibition and a Literary Lecture programme. Also commissions works of art and musical compositions, and awards scholarships to artists and musicians for travel and study overseas. In 1995 the League initiated joint welfare projects including travelling eye camps in Sri Lanka, and projects in Nambia which support school bursaries and resource materials for bushmen and farm children.

Geographical Area of Activity: International.

Publications: *Overseas* (quarterly journal).

Principal Staff: Dir Gen. Robert F. Newell.

Address: Over-Seas House, Park Pl., St James's St, London SW1A 1LR.

Telephone: (20) 7408-0214; **Fax:** (20) 7499-6738; **Internet:** www.rosl.org.uk; **e-mail:** info@rosl.org.uk.

Royal Society

Founded in 1660 to promote natural knowledge; granted a Royal Charter by King Charles II in 1662.

Activities: Operates both nationally and internationally in the fields of education, natural and applied science (including mathematics, engineering and medicine), international scientific relations and the conservation of natural resources, through self-conducted programmes, research, grants to institutions and individuals, fellowships and scholarships, conferences, publications and lectures. The Society provides an independent source of advice on scientific matters, notably to the British Government.

Geographical Area of Activity: International.

Publications: *Proceedings: Mathematical, Physical and Engineering Sciences; Proceedings: Biological Sciences; Philosophical Transactions: Mathematical, Physical and Engineering Sciences; Philosophical Transactions: Biological Sciences; Notes and Records of the Royal Society; Biographical Memoirs; Year Book of the Royal Society.*

Finance: Annual expenditure approx. £22,000,000.

Council: Consists of 21 annually-elected Fellows; Lord May of Oxford (Pres.).

Principal Staff: Exec. Sec. Stephen Cox.

Address: 6–9 Carlton House Terrace, London SW1Y 5AG.

Telephone: (20) 7839-5561; **Fax:** (20) 7930-2170; **Internet:** www.royalsoc.ac.uk; **e-mail:** webmanager@royalsoc.ac.uk.

Royal Society for the encouragement of Arts, Manufactures and Commerce—RSA

Founded in 1754 by William Shipley for the encouragement of the arts, manufactures and commerce.

Activities: Operates nationally and internationally in the arts, manufacturing and commerce, design, education and the environment; it seeks to promote change and growth in those areas of society through its forum for discussion and its programme of projects and awards. There are about 22,000 members, including individuals in 70 countries.

Geographical Area of Activity: International.

Restrictions: Not a grant-making organization.

Publications: *RSA Journal* (every 2 months); other reports and publications.

Finance: Budget approx. £5,000,000.

Governing Board: HRH Prince Philip, Duke of Edinburgh (Pres.); Neil Cross (Chair.).

Principal Staff: Dir Penny Egan; Finance Dir Bernard Kelly.

Address: 8 John Adam St, London WC2N 6EZ.

Telephone: (20) 7930-5115; **Fax:** (20) 7839-5805; **Internet:** www.thersa.org; **e-mail:** general@rsa.org.uk.

The Royal Society of Medicine

Founded in 1805 to promote the interests of medical science using its neutrality to encourage co-operation in medicine and provide education through conferences, publications and a library.

Activities: Operates nationally and internationally in medicine and science, through self-conducted programmes, conferences, publications, and the award of research fellowships, chiefly for British physicians, in some cases tenable abroad.

Publications: *The Evolution of Orthopaedic Surgery; The Patient's Internet Handbook; The History of the Royal Society of Medicine; Journal of the RSM; Tropical Doctor; AIDS and Hepatitis Digest; International Journal of STD and AIDS; Journal of Medical Biography; Journal of Telemedicine and Telecare; Annals of Clinical Biochemistry; Clinical Risk; Handbook of Practice Management; Health Information on the Internet; Health Services Management Research; Journal of Health Services Research and Policy; Journal of Integrated Care Pathways; Journal of Laryngology and Otology.*

Finance: Net assets £24,008,131 (2001).

Governing Council: Sir Barry Jackson (Pres.).

Principal Staff: Exec. Dir Dr Anne Grocock; Dir of Finance David Laughton.

Address: 1 Wimpole St, London W1G 0AE.

Telephone: (20) 7290-2900; **Fax:** (20) 7290-2909; **Internet:** www.rsm.ac.uk; **e-mail:** webmaster@rsm.ac.uk.

Royal Society for the Prevention of Cruelty to Animals—RSPCA

Founded as the Society for the Prevention of Cruelty to Animals in 1824, present name since 1840. Promotes animal welfare.

Activities: The Society encourages responsible pet care; supports animal welfare projects; operates a telephone 'cruelty hotline'; carries out campaigning work, including opposition to fox-hunting and the use of animals for cosmetics testing, calling for a reduction in and the regulation of the importation of primates to United Kingdom research laboratories, and regulations covering welfare of animals transported for slaughter; and educates in schools and through its network of education professionals. Also carries out scientific and technical research on all aspects of farm, wild, laboratory and companion animal welfare.

Geographical Area of Activity: England and Wales, with some international activity.

Publications: *Science Review; Animal Life; Animal Action*; Annual Review.

Finance: Net assets £144,797,000 (2001); total income £69,933,000, expenditure £70,449,000 (2001).

Governing Council: Michael Tomlinson (Chair.); Lewis Page (Vice-Chair.); Ian McIlveen (Treas.); Alan Anyon (Deputy Treas.); and 20 Council members.

Principal Staff: Dir Gen. Jackie Ballard.

Address: Wilberforce Way, Southwater, Horsham RH13 9RS.

Telephone: (870) 010-1181; **Fax:** (870) 7530-284; **Internet:** www.rspca.org.uk.

Royal Society for the Protection of Birds—RSPB

Founded as the Society for the Protection of Birds in 1891, became the Royal Society for the Protection of Birds 1904, to protect the great crested grebe. The Society now promotes the conservation of birds and wildlife throughout the United Kingdom and world-wide.

Activities: The Society works to protect and re-create habitats for endangered birds and wildlife. It acquires land and manages many nature reserves; campaigns for better protection and management of wildlife sites not in conservation ownership; works in partnership with conservation organizations, including BirdLife International (q.v.), in Europe and Africa; and aims to develop awareness of conservation issues through education, and to influence education in agriculture, planning and other key professions. Programmes include birds and biodiversity, biodiversity and sustainability, and collaboration with local communities on issues of national importance. Also seeks to influence national and international government policy.

Geographical Area of Activity: United Kingdom, Europe, Africa, Asia and Middle East.

Finance: Total income £63,193,000, total charitable expenditure £41,031,000 (March 2002).

Address: The Lodge, Sandy SG19 2DL.

Telephone: (1767) 680551; **Internet:** www.rspb.org.uk.

Rufford Foundation

Founded by J. H. Laing in 1982 for general charitable purposes.

Activities: The Foundation has a special interest in conservation, the environment and sustainable development in developing countries, however, projects in the fields of medicine and health care, and social welfare (particularly those related to HIV/AIDS) are also supported.

Geographical Area of Activity: International.

Restrictions: Grants to registered charities only, no grants to individuals. No funding for building or construction projects.

Finance: Total assets approx. £63,000,000 (April 2002); annual revenue £2,500,000, grant expenditure £2,200,000 (2002).

Board of Trustees: C. R. F. Barbour; A. Gavazzi; A. J. Johnson; J. H. Laing; V. Lees; K. W. Scott; M. I. T. Smailes.

Principal Staff: Officer Terry Kenny.

Address: Babmaes House, 5th Floor, 2 Babmaes St, London SW1Y 6RF.

Telephone: (20) 7925-2582; **Internet:** www.rufford.org; **e-mail:** kenny@rufford.org.

Bertrand Russell Peace Foundation

Founded in 1963 by Bertrand Russell to campaign for international disarmament, peace and social justice.

Activities: Organizes campaigns for peace and disarmament and for political prisoners; and the European Peace and Human Rights Conference.

Geographical Area of Activity: Europe.

Publications: *The Spokesman* (quarterly); books and pamphlets.

Trustees: Ken Coates (Chair.); Michael Barratt Brown; Ken Fleet; Regan Scott.

Principal Staff: Dir and Sec. Ken Fleet; Publications Officer Tony Simpson.

Address: Russell House, Bulwell Lane, Nottingham NG6 0BT.

Telephone: (115) 978-4504; **Fax:** (115) 942-0433; **Internet:** www.spokesmanbooks.com; **e-mail:** elfeuro@compuserve.com.

Karim Rida Said Foundation

Founded in 1982 to alleviate poverty and suffering amongst children and young people in the Middle East.

Activities: Operates in the fields of health, education, disability and children at risk, through grants to institutions working with poor and diasdvantaged children and young people, particularly in the fields of disability, health and education. Awards scholarships to students from the Middle East for postgraduate study in the United Kingdom. Grants are usually made to experienced NGOs in Iraq, Jordan, Lebanon, Palestinian Autonomous Areas and Syria. Supports cultural activities in the United Kingdom which promote a better understanding of Arab culture, largely through sponsorship of the British Museum's Arab World Education Programme.

Geographical Area of Activity: Middle East (in particular Jordan, Lebanon, Palestinian Autonomous Areas, Syria and Iraq) and the United Kingdom.

Publications: *KRSF News* (newsletter).

Finance: Annual revenue £1,172,991, expenditure £1,401,463 (August 2001).

Trustees: Wafic Said (Chair.); Ghayth Armanazi; Dr Peter Clark; Sirine Idilby; Lord Powell of Bayswater; Rosemary Said.

Principal Staff: Dir Catherine Roe; Admin. Ita Gallagher.

Address: 4 Bloomsbury Pl., 2nd Floor, London WC1A 2QA.

Telephone: (20) 7691-2772; **Fax:** (20) 7691-2780; **Internet:** www.krsf.org; **e-mail:** director@krsf.org.

St John Ambulance

A foundation of the Order of St John which traces its roots back to the 11th century Crusades. The St John Ambulance Association was founded in the United Kingdom in 1877 to provide care for the sick and organize classes in first aid.

Activities: Provides first aid and care training to almost 500,000 people every year in the United Kingdom. Care programmes include: primary health care for the homeless; training courses for those working with the homeless; conferences to promote healthy lifestyles, aimed at young people; care courses; care handbook; young carers support groups; young carers resource pack. Operates first aid courses for young people through co-operation with schools; develops new courses and course materials to meet the needs of communities and customers; provides first aid cover at sporting and entertainment events, at national and local levels. The organization is supported by more than 47,000 volunteer workers, more than half of whom are under the age of 18 years. Internationally, St John Ambulance has diversified its activities in order to meet the needs of different communities, in addition to first aid, it provides dental and opthalmic care, relief and disaster planning, primary health care, operates youth programmes, and in some cases provides the statutory ambulance service. There are members in 42 countries world-wide. Maintains a reference library.

Geographical Area of Activity: International.

Publications: Annual Report.

Finance: Funded entirely by donations from major corporate donors and members of the public; total income £48,916,473, total expenditure £45,469,117 (Dec. 2001).

Principal Staff: Chief Exec. Lewis Martin.

Address: 27 St John's Lane, London EC1M 4BU.

Telephone: (8700) 104950; **Fax:** (8700) 104065; **Internet:** www.sja.org.uk.

The Salvation Army

Founded in 1865 by William Booth for the advancement of the Christian religion as promulgated in the religious doctrines which are professed, believed and taught by the Army and, pursuant thereto, the advancement of education, the relief of poverty and other charitable objects beneficial to society or the community of mankind as a whole. A quasi-military command structure was introduced in 1878. The organization operates in 107 countries.

Activities: Promotes the advancement of the Christian religion. Also organizes specific projects around the world, including emergency housing, feeding and clothing; medical and educational work; agricultural training and social welfare programmes.

Geographical Area of Activity: International.

Publications: *The Salvation Army Year Book; All the World* (quarterly); *Words of Life* (annual review).

Finance: Total income £109,200,000, total expenditure £87,410,000 (March 2002).

Trustees: The Salvation Army International Trustee Co.

Principal Staff: Gen. John Gowans; Chief of Staff Commr John Larsson.

Address: 101 Queen Victoria St, London EC4P 4EP.

Telephone: (20) 7332-0101; **Fax:** (20) 7236-4981; **Internet:** www.salvationarmy.org.

Sargent Cancer Care for Children

Founded in 1968 as the Malcolm Sargent Cancer Fund for Children, to promote the care of those under the age of 21 who suffer from cancer, leukaemia or Hodgkin's disease in the United Kingdom.

Activities: The organization aims to support all young people with cancer and their families, through counselling, financial help and practical care. Grants are made to assist with travel expenses to and from hospital, fuel bills, clothing, etc., and two holiday homes are run in Scotland and Ireland. Youth programmes include computer projects, support groups and recreational activities.

Geographical Area of Activity: United Kingdom.

Restrictions: Applications must be made through a hospital social worker.

Publications: Annual Report; *Upbeat* (supporter magazine); *Sargent Youth Newsletter*.

Finance: Annual income approx. £8,000,000, total expenditure £9,906,000 (2000/01).

Trustees: John Pendower (Chair.); P. N. Gerrard; T. Holley; D. Knowles; Gordon Morrison; Prof. Tony Oakhill; Sir A. H. Smith; Dr Diana Tait.

Principal Staff: Acting Chief Exec. Siun Cranny.

Address: Griffin House, 161 Hammersmith Rd, London W6 8SG.

Telephone: (20) 8752-2800; **Fax:** (20) 8752-2806; **Internet:** www.sargent.org; **e-mail:** care@sargent.org.

Save the Children

Established in 1919 to assist disadvantaged and vulnerable children world-wide; has a commitment to the rights of children, as now enshrined in the United Nations Convention on the Rights of the Child.

Activities: Runs programmes nationally and internationally to help children in the areas of social protection, welfare and inclusion, education, health, food security and nutrition, HIV/AIDS and children, and work. Supports projects in around 70 countries. Provides emergency relief as well as long-term development and prevention work. Collaborates in its work with local, national and international organizations, and governments.

Geographical Area of Activity: International.

Restrictions: No grants to individuals; works in partnership with other NGOs, governments and local, national and international organizations.

Publications: Annual Report; financial accounts; and subject-specific publications.

Finance: Assets £44,219,000 (2001–02); annual revenue £110,800,000, expenditure £116,600,000 (2001–02).

Trustees: Barry Clarke (Chair.); Victoria Hardman (Deputy Chair.); Robert Willott (Hon. Treas.); Mark Baker; Terry Bamford; Frances D'Souza; Barrie Hudson; Sue Jagelman; Jonathan Katz; Joy Kearney; Judy Marris; Barbara Mitchelmore; Su Sayer; Colin Smith; James Strachan; Louise Terry.

Principal Staff: Dir Gen. Mike Aaronson; Dir of Programmes Ken Caldwell.

Address: 17 Grove Lane, London SE5 8RD.

Telephone: (20) 7703-5400; **Fax:** (20) 7703-2278; **Internet:** www.savethechildren.org.uk; **e-mail:** enquiries@scfuk.org.uk.

Scope

Founded in 1952 by I. D. Dawson-Shepherd, E. Hodgson, A. Moira and Jean Garwood, for the care, welfare, treatment, education and training of children and adults who have cerebral palsy. Formerly known as the Spastics Society.

Activities: Aims to ensure that all people with cerebral palsy and related disabilities, their families and carers, have access to properly resourced services which meet their needs; services in England and Wales include creating education and employment opportunities, support for families and carers, research, information and advice services, support for self-help groups, campaigning and other activities. Maintains the Cerebral Palsy Helpline (telephone) which gives information, advice and counselling. Local teams and field workers operate, and there are more than 280 affiliated local groups. Holds an annual conference and exhibition.

Geographical Area of Activity: United Kingdom.

Publications: Annual report and financial statement; *Disability Now* (monthly); *Campaign News and other Campaigns;* research and public policy reports; other information literature. Supports the medical and scientific publications house, the Mac Keith Press, which publishes the journal *Development Medicine and Child Neurology*.

Finance: Total assets £35,633,000 (2001–02); annual revenue £93,171,000, expenditure £89,935,000 (2002).

Executive Council: G. McCarthy (Chair.); P. J. Clery, S. Collington (Vice-Chair.); L. Unwin (Treas.); D. Bloomfield; C. Davies; A. Drane; D. Hayes; J. Hildreth; S. Hughes; I. Jones; J. Kelly; L. Marsh; A. Nicholas; P. Roper; A. Townsend; J. Yeats.

Principal Staff: Pres. the Duke of Westminster; Chief Exec. Richard Brewster; Sec. to the Board Sue Bell.

Address: Head Office: 6 Market Rd, London N7 9PW; Enquiries: Cerebral Palsy Helpline, POB 833, Milton Keynes MK12 5NY.

Telephone: (808) 800-3333; **Fax:** (1908) 321051; **Internet:** www.scope.org.uk; **e-mail:** cphelpline@scope.org.uk.

Shell Foundation

Established by the Royal Dutch/Shell Group in June 2000 to support initiatives world-wide in the area of sustainable development.

Activities: Operates world-wide in the field of conservation and the environment, mainly through its Sustainable Energy Programme, but also through two further programmes, the Sustainable Communities and the Promoting Youth Enterprise Programmes, all of which offer grants for projects carried out by non-profit-making groups or organizations.

Geographical Area of Activity: International.

Publications: *Fuel for Thought* (quarterly newsletter).

Finance: Budget US $30,000,000 (2000–03).

Trustees: Mark Moody-Stuart (Chair.); Prof. José Goldemberg; Sir John Houghton; Jyoti Munsiff; Harry Roels; Pieter Winsemius.

Principal Staff: Dir Tim Hollins; Deputy Dir Kurt Hoffman.

Address: Shell Centre, London SE1 7NA.

Telephone: (20) 7934-2727; **Fax:** (20) 7934-7348; **Internet:** www.shellfoundation.org; **e-mail:** info@shellfoundation.org.

Shelter—National Campaign for Homeless People

Founded to improve the quality of life of homeless people and those with inadequate housing.

Activities: The organization supports homeless people through the following programmes: Shelterline, a free national telephone helpline, which provides advice and information; Housing Aid Centres at 59 locations, which provide information, advice and advocacy; Homeless to Home Projects, which aim to resettle homeless families; the Street Homelessness Project, which works with local authorities and voluntary organizations to help reduce the number of people sleeping in the street; the National Homelessness Advice Service; and the Homework Project, which aims to prevent homelessness through educating children and providing educational materials to schools. In addition to these programme areas, Shelter runs Shelter Training, works with politicians at all levels on housing and welfare issues, and is closely involved with initiatives dealing with social exclusion.

Geographical Area of Activity: United Kingdom.

Publications: *Roof* (newsletter, every 2 months); Annual Report; various publications on housing-related subjects.

Finance: Total assets £7,829,000 (March 2002); annual revenue £30,035,000, expenditure £30,622,000 (2002).

Board of Trustees: Prof. Peter Robson (Chair.).

Principal Staff: Dir Chris Holmes; Sec. Henny Baxter.

Address: 88 Old St, London EC1V 9HU.

Telephone: (20) 7505-4699; **Fax:** (20) 7505-2030; **Internet:** www.shelter.org.uk.

Sight Savers International—Royal Commonwealth Society for the Blind

Founded in 1950 to prevent and cure blindness and promote the welfare, education and employment of blind people in developing countries.

Activities: Operates in over 25 developing countries in the field of blindness prevention and cure. Works in co-operation with the World Health Organization and major international NGOs. Projects are designed and delivered with the assistance of local and regional organizations and national agencies in order to bring services to the maximum number of people.

Geographical Area of Activity: Africa, Southern Asia, the Caribbean and India.

Publications: Annual report and accounts; *Sight Savers News; Try to See it My Way;* and a variety of leaflets describing the Society's work.

Trustees: The Society is governed by a council of 18 members; HRH Princess Alexandra (Pres.); Sir John Coles (Chair.).

Principal Staff: Exec. Dir Richard Porter.

Address: Grosvenor Hall, Bolnore Rd, Haywards Heath RH16 4BX.

Telephone: (1444) 446600; **Fax:** (1444) 446688; **Internet:** www.sightsavers.org; **e-mail:** info@sightsaversint.org.

The Henry Smith Charity

Established in 1628 for the relief of the poor kindred of Henry Smith, the relief and maintenance of Godly preachers, and limited charitable purposes.

Activities: Operates in the United Kingdom (with local programmes in certain United Kingdom counties), in the areas of medicine and health, and social welfare, through making grants for projects in the fields of hospitals, hospices, young people, the elderly, disabled people, counselling and family advice, homelessness, drugs and alcohol, community service, general welfare and medical research.

Geographical Area of Activity: United Kingdom.

Restrictions: Grants are not made to individuals, except for the relief of the poor kindred of Henry Smith and clergy of the Church of England; grants are made to charitable organizations only, and no grants are made for purposes outside the charity's objectives. Grants are usually made to small charities, not to other grant-making organizations.

Publications: Annual Report.

Finance: Annual revenue £24,351,000, expenditure £25,735,000 (2001).

Trustees: J. Sheffield (Chair.); A. Allen; D. Barran; Lord Egremont; Lady Euston; Lord Gage; M. Gallyer; C. Godman-Law; J. Hambro; Lord Hamilton of Dalzell; T. Holland-Martin; Sir J. James; G. Lee-Steere; M. Lowther; T. Millington-Drake; M. Newton; R. Norman; P. Smallridge; P. Urquhart.

Principal Staff: Dir R. Hopgood; Grants Admin. V. Graham.

Address: 5 Chancery Lane, Clifford's Inn, London EC4A 1BU.

Telephone: (20) 7320-6884; **Fax:** (20) 7320-3842; **Internet:** www.henrysmithcharity.org.uk.

Sobell Foundation

Founded in 1977 for general charitable purposes.

Activities: The Foundation operates in the fields of medicine and health, and social welfare, through supporting projects which benefit children, the elderly, the poor, the ill and the disabled. Supports Jewish charities in the United Kingdom and Israel, and non-Jewish charities mainly in the United Kingdom.

Geographical Area of Activity: United Kingdom and Israel.

Finance: Annual revenue £2,626,474, expenditure £4,061,929 (April 2002).

Principal Staff: Contact: Penelope Jane Newton.

Address: POB 2137, Shepton Mallet BA4 6YA.

Telephone: (1749) 813387; **Fax:** (1749) 813136; **Internet:** www.sobellfoundation.org.uk; **e-mail:** enquiries@sobellfoundation.org.uk.

Soroptimist International

An NGO established in 1921 to strive for human rights and advance the status of women.

Activities: The organization is an international NGO with more than 93,000 female members in 122 countries worldwide. Operates internationally in the areas of aid to less-developed countries, the arts and humanities, conservation and the environment, economic affairs, education, international affairs, law and human rights, and medicine and health, through projects, grants and seminars. The organization consists of four federations: the Americas, Europe, Great Britain and Ireland, and the South-West Pacific.

Geographical Area of Activity: International.

Publications: *The International Soroptimist;* federation magazines.

Finance: Annual membership dues.

Trustees: 12 voting members (three representatives from the four Federations that make up the organization); plus four officers.

Principal Staff: Int. Pres. Irmeli Torssonen; Exec. Officer Janet Bilton.

Address: 87 Glisson Rd, Cambridge CB1 2HG.

Telephone: (1223) 311833; **Fax:** (1223) 467951; **Internet:** www.sorop.org; **e-mail:** sorophq@dial.pipex.com.

Spinal Research

Established to fund research nationally and internationally with the aim of ending permanent paralysis caused by spinal cord injury.

Activities: Operates nationally and internationally in the field of medical research into spinal cord injury, through funding laboratories in its research network.

Geographical Area of Activity: International.

Publications: Newsletters; Annual Review; research updates.

Principal Staff: Chief Exec. J. Miall; Dir of Devt P. Banyard; Head of Research J. Cavanagh.

Address: Bramley Business Centre, Station Rd, Bramley, Guildford GU5 0AZ.

Telephone: (1483) 898786; **Fax:** (1483) 898763; **Internet:** www.spinal-research.org; **e-mail:** info@spinal-research.org.

Sport England Lottery Fund

Began operations in January 1995. The English Sports Council is responsible for the Fund.

Activities: The Fund operates three main programmes: More People, More Places and More Medals. The More People programme targets young people, ensuring they have the opportunity to pursue sporting activity, as well as promoting the delivery of sporting opportunities and services at a local level. Under the other two programmes the Fund aims to provide the best possible sporting facilities as well as increasing the likelihood of sporting success and ensuring sporting opportunity to people who might be socially excluded. As a lottery distributor the Fund has distributed over £1,000,000,000. Other designated United Kingdom Lottery sports distributors in Scotland, Wales and Northern Ireland have the same function and purpose as the Sport England Lottery Fund, but operate in different ways and run different programmes. These organizations are: UK Sport (previously the UK Sports Council), 40 Bernard St, London WC1N 1ST; SportScotland (previously the Scottish Sports Council), Caledonia House, South Gyle, Edinburgh EH12 9DQ; Sports Council for Wales, the Welsh Institute of Sport, Sophia Gdns, Cardiff CF11 9SW; Sports Council of Northern Ireland, House of Sport, Upper Malone Rd, Belfast BT9 5LA.

Geographical Area of Activity: United Kingdom.

Restrictions: Will normally fund a maximum of 65% of the total project cost. Each funding programme has specific criteria for grant-making.

Finance: Sport receives a 16.6% share of 28% of the profits derived from the United Kingdom National Lottery; the Sport England Lottery Fund receives approx. 75.6% of this share for distribution in England (the rest is split, according to population, between the other United Kingdom sports councils, with 9.2% going to UK Sport); annual revenue approx. £224,281,000 (2000–01).

Principal Staff: Chair. Patrick Carter; Vice-Chair. Tessa Sanderson; Acting Vice-Chair. Brigid Simmonds; Chief Exec. David Moffett; Dir, Sport England Lottery Fund David Carpenter.

Address: 16 Upper Woburn Place, London WC1H 0QP.

Telephone: (20) 7273-1500; **Fax:** (20) 7383-5740; **Internet:** www.sportengland.org; **e-mail:** info@sportengland.org.

Staples Trust

One of the Sainsbury Family Charitable Trusts, which share a common administration.

Activities: Operates principally in the areas of aid to less-developed countries (mostly in East and Southern Africa, South and South-East Asia and South America), conservation and the environment, and women's issues.

Geographical Area of Activity: International.

Restrictions: No grants are made to individuals, and unsolicited applications are rarely successful.

Finance: Net assets £13,637,744 (April 2002); annual revenue £566,253, expenditure £566,406 (2002).

Trustees: P. Frankopan; J. S. Portrait; Jessica Sainsbury; A. J. Sainsbury; T. J. Sainsbury.

Principal Staff: Dir Michael Pattison.

Address: Allington House, 1st Floor, 150 Victoria St, London SW1E 5AE.

Telephone: (20) 7410-0330; **e-mail:** sfct@sfct.org.uk.

Stewards Company Limited

Founded in 1922 for general charitable purposes.

Activities: Provides grants to religious charitable organizations throughout the world, particularly those involved in missionary work. Grants are co-ordinated with the Beatrice Laing Trust (q.v.).

Geographical Area of Activity: International.

Finance: Assets £106,785,739 (2002); grants disbursed £6,531,694 (2002).

Trustees: Stewards Co. Ltd.

Principal Staff: Sec. B. J. Chapman.

Address: POB 133, Bath BA1 2YU.

Telephone: (1225) 427-236; **Fax:** (1225) 427-278.

Sir Halley Stewart Trust

Established in 1924 by Sir Halley Stewart to promote and support new experimental research in the medical, social, educational and religious fields, in order to help prevent human suffering through supporting innovative or pioneering projects.

Activities: Operates nationally and internationally through research and development grants. Approximately 44% of the Trust's grants are awarded to research workers for medical research, in particular in the areas of problems of the elderly, preventing disability in children and researching tropical diseases. The remaining 56% is awarded to social, educational and religious projects, especially small innovative projects, projects dealing with the ethical and social issues associated with the medical research projects supported, projects dealing with cultural and racial divides, projects to help people move beyond disadvantage, and exploring spiritual needs.

Geographical Area of Activity: United Kingdom and West/South Africa.

Restrictions: Only postal applications are accepted.

Publications: *Notes for those seeking grants* (five yearly report).

Finance: Assets £22,496,000 (March 2001); grants disbursed £1,006,000 (2002).

Trustees: Lord Stewartby (Pres.); Prof. John Lennard-Jones (Chair.); George Russell (Hon. Treas.); B. Allpress; Dr A. C. Berry; Michael Ross Collins; Rev. Dr L. Griffiths; Prof. C. Hallett; William P. Kirkman; Prof. Phyllida Parsloe; Dr Duncan Stewart; Prof. P. Whitfield; Prof. G. Wilcock; Prof. J. Wyatt.

Principal Staff: Admin. Sue West.

Address: 22 Earith Rd, Willingham CB4 5LS.

Telephone and Fax: (1954) 260707; **Internet:** www.sirhalleystewart.org.

Marie Stopes International

Founded as the Mothers' Clinic in 1921, by Marie Stopes. The organization's mission is to support the right to have children by choice, not by chance, through the provision of information and services.

Activities: The organization lobbies governments and international organizations in order to influence policy and allocation of resources in the areas of family-planning services and reproductive health care. Provides information, and family-planning and health-care services in 38 countries world-wide, working in collaboration with local organizations. Each programme is managed and run by a local team, and meets the specific needs of the country.

Geographical Area of Activity: Afghanistan, Albania, Angola, Australia, Austria, Bangladesh, Bolivia, Cambodia, People's Republic of China, Colombia, Ethiopia, Fiji, Honduras, India, Kenya, Madagascar, Malawi, Mexico, Mongolia, Mozambique, Myanmar, Namibia, Nicaragua, Nepal, Pakistan, Peru, Philippines, Romania, Sierra Leone, South Africa, Sri Lanka, Tanzania, Uganda, United Kingdom, Vietnam, Yemen, Zimbabwe.

Publications: *First People* (newsletter); *Handbook on European Community Support;* Annual Report; and other publications.

Principal Staff: Chief Exec. Dr Tim Black; Deputy Chief Exec. Helen Axby; Dir of External Relations Patricia Hindmarsh.

Address: 153 Cleveland St, London W1T 6QW.

Telephone: (20) 7574-7400; **Fax:** (20) 7574-7417; **Internet:** www.mariestopes.org.uk; **e-mail:** services@stopes.org.uk.

The Strathspey Charitable Trust

Founded in 1990 by Giles Baker to provide aid to people disadvantaged by poverty, principally in Asia, Africa and South America.

Activities: Supports organizations principally in Asia, Africa and South America through provision of medical aid, famine relief and micro-finance to support the development of small businesses and access to safe drinking water.

Geographical Area of Activity: Asia, Africa and South America.

Finance: Financed by family donations and loans; net assets £455,938 (April 2002); annual expenditure approx. £80,000 (2002).

Board of Trusees: John Alcock; Giles Baker; Peter Rose.

Address: 29 Admiral Parker Drive, Shenstone, Lichfield WS14 0NS.

Internet: www.strathspeycharitabletrust.org.uk.

The Stroke Association

Established in 1899 as the National Association for the Prevention of Tuberculosis, it became The Stroke Association in 1992; its purpose is to provide practical support to people who have had strokes, and their families; and to increase awareness of stroke in society.

Activities: Operates in England and Wales; provides community services; maintains a central information service and a network of regional information centres; offers support to families, and to those suffering from dysphasia; provides welfare grants; makes grants for stroke research.

Geographical Area of Activity: England and Wales.

Publications: *Stroke News* (quarterly); leaflets and booklets.

Finance: Assets £9,174,000 (2001); annual revenue £12,266,000, total charitable expenditure £12,696,000 (2001).

Council: Lord Skelmersdale (Chair.); and 19 others.

Principal Staff: Chief Exec. Margaret Goose.

Address: Stroke House, Whitecross St, London EC1Y 8JJ.

Telephone: (20) 7556-0300; **Fax:** (20) 7490-2686; **Internet:** www.stroke.org.uk; **e-mail:** stroke@stroke.org.uk.

The Bernard Sunley Charitable Foundation

Founded in 1960 to provide funds for general charitable purposes world-wide.

Activities: Provides financial assistance to charitable projects in the United Kingdom and overseas in areas including education, the arts and humanities, wildlife and the environment, hospitals and medical research, churches and chapels, community aid, youth clubs and training, and provision for the elderly.

Geographical Area of Activity: International.

Restrictions: No grants are made to individuals.

Publications: Annual Report.

Finance: Annual income £2,466,000, annual expenditure £2,866,000 (March 2002).

Trustees: Sir Donald Gosling; Bella Sunley; John B. Sunley; Joan Tice.

Principal Staff: Dir Dr Brian Martin.

Address: 20 Berkeley Sq., London W13 6LH.

Telephone: (20) 7408-2198; **Fax:** (20) 7499-5859.

Survival International

Founded in 1969, a world-wide organization supporting the rights of tribal peoples to decide their own future, and to protect their lives, lands and human rights.

Activities: The organization runs campaigns to attract international support for indigenous peoples under threat; provides information and educational materials; and supports health and educational projects which benefit indigenous peoples; it has members in more than 90 countries.

Geographical Area of Activity: International.

Publications: *Urgent Action Bulletin* (6 a year); *Tribale* (catalogue); Annual Report; colour reports.

Principal Staff: Dir Gen. Stephen Corry.

Address: 6 Charterhouse Bldgs, London EC1M 7ET.

Telephone: (20) 7687-8700; **Fax:** (20) 7687-8701; **Internet:** www.survival-international.org; **e-mail:** info@survival-international.org.

Tearfund

Founded in 1968 by the Evangelical Alliance to serve churches in the United Kingdom and Ireland; a relief and development agency within the World Evangelical Fellowship, working for the relief of poverty, suffering and distress among peoples of the world.

Activities: Operates internationally in supplying aid to less-developed countries, by making grants to institutions and by directly supporting approximately 250 personnel overseas; it also runs an educational programme, comprising work with churches and young people in the United Kingdom and Ireland, to extend their understanding of and responsibility for Christian mission.

Geographical Area of Activity: Asia, Africa, Central Europe and Latin America.

Restrictions: No grants to individuals; grants made to specific church-based organizations.

Publications: *Tear Times*.

Finance: Net assets £15,924,000 (2001); annual revenue £32,632,000, expenditure £33,150,000 (2001).

Board of Directors: D. White (Chair.); M. Buttrick (Treas.); E. Cathcart; Rev. S. Finamore; A. Hickford; K. Hurst; A. de Leyser; Rev. I. Prior; Rev. J. Smith; M. Smith; S. Tillett; Prof. A. Tomkins.

Principal Staff: Gen. Dir D. Balfour; Deputy Dir A. G. Fairbairn.

Address: 100 Church Rd, Teddington TW11 8QE.

Telephone: (20) 8977-9144; **Fax:** (20) 8943-3594; **Internet:** www.tearfund.org; **e-mail:** enquiry@tearfund.org.

Television Trust for the Environment—TVE

Founded in 1984 by Central Independent Television, WWF (World Wide Fund for Nature, q.v.) and the United Nations Environment Programme, to advance the education of the public world-wide by the dissemination of information on the environment and resources of the world, using electronic communications.

Activities: TVE is editorially independent and functions as both producer and distributor, encouraging film-makers to make new programmes and promoting the distribution of finished films. Since 1985 TVE has produced and co-produced around 1,000 films on environment, development, human rights and health issues. It distributes programmes either free or on a subsidized basis to television stations in developing countries, has set up a distribution system to schools and colleges, runs environmental education projects, and has undertaken a feasibility study for a clearing-house to improve the distribution of environmental programmes. Also maintains offices in Beijing, Calcutta, Colombo, Seoul and Tokyo.

Geographical Area of Activity: International.

Publications: *Moving Pictures Bulletin (International)* (back issues only); *Moving Pictures 6* (on-line database).

Trustees: Ivan Hattingh (Chair.); Anita Anand; Tore Brevik; Anthony Brough; Richard Burge; Adrian Cowell; Richard Creasey; Morten Giersing; Halle Jorn Hansen; Carol Haslam; Roger James; Mehr Kahn; Mai Masri; Robert Phillis; Margo Picken; Robert San George; Vic Sutton; Erna Witoelar.

Address: Prince Albert Rd, London NW1 4RZ.

Telephone: (20) 7586-5526; **Fax:** (20) 7586-4866; **Internet:** www.tve.org; **e-mail:** tve-uk@tve.org.uk.

Thomson Foundation

Founded in 1962 by Roy Thomson (later Lord Thomson of Fleet), to provide training facilities for journalism and television in developing countries.

Activities: Practical training is given in the United Kingdom for media management and senior journalists, and specialized training in television production and engineering by arrangement; training teams are provided to help overseas media and media institutions to raise professional standards.

More recently, the emphasis has been upon providing experienced trainers to supply in-country training. The Foundation works in collaboration with UNESCO and other organizations to provide training advisory services to developing countries, and consultants may be seconded to overseas institutions.

Geographical Area of Activity: International.

Publications: Training manuals for journalism, television engineering video tapes.

Finance: Total income £1,847,000, expenditure £2,008,000 (2001).

Principal Staff: Chair. David Cole; Dir Gareth Price.

Address: 37 Park Pl., Cardiff CF10 3BB.

Telephone: (29) 2035-3060; **Fax:** (29) 2035-3061; **Internet:** www.thomsonfoundation.co.uk; **e-mail:** enquiries@thomfound.co.uk.

Sir Jules Thorn Charitable Trust

Founded in 1964 for the benefit of the medical profession and general charitable purposes.

Activities: The Trust's primary objective is the funding of medical research in the United Kingdom, through grants to medical institutions. Certain funds are available for general charitable purposes. In 2001 the Trust launched the Sir Jules Thorn Award for Biomedical Research, awarding £993,138 over five years to a gene therapy research project. Also makes an annual Special Project award of £500,000 linked to an annually selected theme.

Geographical Area of Activity: United Kingdom.

Restrictions: Grants are not made to individuals, nor to applicants from countries other than the United Kingdom.

Finance: Annual revenue £3,715,31, expenditure £3,460,617 (2001).

Principal Staff: Dir David Richings.

Address: 24 Manchester Sq., London W1U 3TH.

Telephone: (20) 7487-5851; **Fax:** (20) 7224-3976; **Internet:** www.julesthorntrust.org.uk; **e-mail:** julesthorntrust@compuserve.com.

Trans-Antarctic Association

Founded in 1962 by the Committee of Management of the Trans-Antarctic Expedition, to further research in subjects relating to the Antarctic.

Activities: Makes annual awards to individuals for research and exploration in the Antarctic regions, publication of results, cost of travel to Antarctica, or attendance at international meetings concerned with Antarctic science.

Restrictions: Awards are made to citizens of the United Kingdom, Australia, New Zealand and South Africa only.

Finance: Assets approx. £278,221; annual awards approx. £15,000.

Committee of Management: J. R. Heap (Chair.); Dr D. J. Cantrell (Grants Sec.); Dr P. D. Clarkson; H. H. Atkinson; W. G. Lowe; Dr J. Paren.

Address: c/o British Antarctic Survey, High Cross, Madingley Rd, Cambridge CB3 0ET.

Telephone: (1223) 221429; **Fax:** (1223) 362616; **Internet:** www.antarctica.ac.uk/corporate/heritage/taa.html; **e-mail:** mlcu@bas.ac.uk.

Triodos Foundation

Established in 1995 by Triodos Bank for the general support of charitable activities.

Activities: Operates nationally and internationally in all areas, through grants to institutions, including micro-finance initiatives. Supports charitable needs identified through the work of the Triodos Bank. It is the United Kingdom counterpart to Stichting Triodos, Netherlands (q.v.) and to the Triodos Foundation in Belgium.

Geographical Area of Activity: International.

Finance: Total income £57,252, total expenditure £39,532 (2001).

Trustees: P. Blom; G. Saunders.

Principal Staff: Admin. R. Tutin.

Address: Brunel House, 11 The Promenade, Bristol BS8 3NN.

Telephone: (117) 973-9339; **Fax:** (117) 973-9303; **Internet:** www.triodos.co.uk; **e-mail:** mail@triodos.co.uk.

Trusthouse Charitable Foundation

Established in 1997 following the takeover of the Forte company by Granada (and superseding the non-charitable but grant-distributing Council of Forte, established in 1904 to promote temperance), for general charitable purposes.

Activities: The Council of Forte made grants mainly to medical projects and for the support of former members of the armed forces. Applications are now considered from all charitable causes.

Geographical Area of Activity: United Kingdom.

Restrictions: The Foundation will not normally support the following: small local charities; applications from individuals; foreign charities (although applications are considered from organizations which are based in the United Kingdom and are operating overseas).

Finance: Annual income £1,727,329, total expenditure £2,578,722 (June 2002).

Principal Staff: Contact: W. D. Brogden.

Address: S. G. Hambros Trust Co. Ltd., SG House, 41 Tower Hill, London EC3N 4SG.

Telephone: (20) 7597-3000; **Fax:** (20) 7702-9263.

Tudor Trust

Founded in 1955 for general charitable purposes, principally social welfare in disadvantaged areas of the United Kingdom.

Activities: Primarily supports charitable activity within the United Kingdom in the field of social welfare, especially organizations working to help people who are drug and alcohol abusers, elderly (especially mentally infirm and/or very frail), homeless, mentally ill, offenders, families under pressure, or young people in danger of becoming alienated. Also supports practical projects from organizations working directly in under-resourced areas with high levels of social disadvantage. Funds projects serving communities in both urban and rural areas, with a current focus on projects addressing rural isolation, or disadvantaged young people, families and older people.

Geographical Area of Activity: United Kingdom.

Restrictions: Applications for funding from outside the United Kingdom are not accepted. No grants are made to individuals, and demand for funding greatly exceeds the available finance. Currently unlikely to fund projects dealing with physical illness, learning or physical disabilities. No applications accepted by either fax or e-mail.

Finance: Grants disbursed £22,634,000 (March 2002).

Trustees: Grove Charity Management Ltd.

Principal Staff: Dir Christopher J. M. Graves.

Address: 7 Ladbroke Grove, London W11 3BD.

Telephone: (20) 7727-8522; **Fax:** (20) 7221-8522; **Internet:** www.tudortrust.org.uk; **e-mail:** general@tudortrust.org.

Twenty-Ninth May 1961 Charity

Founded anonymously on 29 May 1961 for general charitable purposes.

Activities: Operates nationally in the fields of education, social welfare, science and medicine, and the arts and humanities, through grants to institutions.

Geographical Area of Activity: United Kingdom.

Restrictions: Grants are not made to individuals.

Finance: Annual revenue £3,178,414, distributions to charities £3,405,580 (April 2002).

Trustees: J. H. Cattell; A. Mead; V. E. Treves; P. Varney.

Address: MacFarlanes Solicitors, 10 Norwich St, London EC4A 1BD.

Telephone: (20) 7831-9222.

UNA Trust

Founded in 1968 for the relief of distress, poverty and disease; the provision of education, recreation and other forms of leisure-time activity for children, young people and adults, with the objective of improving their conditions of life; the provision of assistance to the needy, homeless and ill in times of natural catastrophe; the provision of further education for young men and women, and the provision of facilities to enable them to perform voluntary service in education, relief, rescue and social service throughout the world; to support generally within its powers the efforts of the United Nations or any other world body to relieve world poverty, hunger or distress; and to promote the study of international problems and institutions with a view to assisting such relief.

Activities: Operates nationally and internationally in the fields of education and international relations, through self-conducted programmes. UNA volunteers work in Africa, the Middle East and Central and South America, helping communities to achieve greater control over their own resources.

Geographical Area of Activity: International.

Restrictions: By decision of the Trustees, the funds are used almost exclusively to assist the educational work of the United Nations Association and the work of UNA International Service (UNAIS).

Finance: Income approx. £250,000.

Principal Staff: Deputy Dir and Sec. P. Dyson.

Address: 3 Whitehall Ct, London SW1A 2EL.

Telephone: (20) 7930-2931; **Fax:** (20) 7930-5893; **Internet:** www.una-uk.org; **e-mail:** pdyson@una-uk.org.

United Society for Christian Literature

Founded in 1799 (incorporated 1899) to disseminate the Christian message through the use of the printed word, and thus to serve the Churches at home and abroad.

Activities: Operates internationally in the fields of religion and education, by making grants to institutions for the production and dissemination of Christian literature in developing countries and Eastern Europe, principally through Feed the Minds (q.v., founded in 1964 to raise funds for literature and communication programmes in developing countries) and Eurolit (for similar programmes in Eastern Europe).

Geographical Area of Activity: International.

Restrictions: No grants are made to individuals.

Publications: Report of operations and financial statement.

Finance: Annual revenue £334,662, expenditure £238,259 (March 2002).

Committee: Dr P. Webb (Pres.); J. Clark (Chair.); F. Shaw (Hon. Sec.); J. C. Bayne (Treas.); A. Brink; Rev. B. Brown; Rev. Dr Peter Doble; Hugh de B. Lawson Johnston; Prof. J. Lieu; Rev. Canon J. B. Lowe; Fr F. Makambwe; Rev. J. Sutton; Rev. J. Yates.

Principal Staff: Gen. Sec. Dr Alwyn Marriage.

Address: 1 Marylebone Rd, London NW1 4AQ.

Fax: (20) 7643-0388.

United Society for the Propagation of the Gospel

Founded in 1701 by Dr Thomas Bray, DD, as the Society for the Propagation of the Gospel (SPG), it merged with the Universities' Mission to Central Africa (founded in 1857) in 1968. It exists to help churches work together to fulfil the mission of bringing the message of God to all parts of the world.

Activities: Committed to the idea of partnership and acting as servant to the World Church in its one mission, the Society awards financial grants, funds sabbatical programmes, bursary awards for international local schemes and Youth Community Programmes. The Society also organizes the movement of church personnel between countries, sponsoring British people (medical practitioners, priests, teachers, accountants, etc.) abroad and people from other countries to spend time in Britain or elsewhere. The Society also works in the United Kingdom and Ireland, where its work is mainly in education, engaging in mission education and training, and providing resources for mission services.

Geographical Area of Activity: International.

Publications: *Yearbook* (annually); quarterly newsletter; educational, promotional and prayer material.

Finance: Assets £47,000,000 (2000); annual revenue £6,572,208, total expenditure £8,819,067 (2001).

Governors: Rev. D. J. Tuck (Chair.); E. Powell (Vice-Chair.); Judge Aglionby; J. Arden; D. Clutterbuck; G. Gordon-Carter; Roger Hurd; Rev. A. Moses; W. Peters; Rev. Canon G. Smith; Rev. Canon I. G. Smith-Cameron; D. Yates.

Principal Staff: Gen.-Sec. Bishop Mano Rumalshah.

Address: Partnership House, 157 Waterloo Rd, London SE1 8XA.

Telephone: (20) 7928-8681; **Fax:** (20) 7928-2371; **Internet:** www.uspg.org.uk; **e-mail:** enquiries@uspg.org.uk.

Van Neste Foundation

Founded in 1959 for general charitable purposes.

Activities: Operates nationally and internationally, especially in developing countries and Eastern Europe, in the areas of assisting the disabled and the elderly, and the promotion of religion, the community and the family.

Geographical Area of Activity: International.

Finance: Total income £214,407, total expenditure £173,712 (April 2002).

Trustees: M. T. M. Appleby (Chair.).

Principal Staff: Sec. F. J. F. Lyons.

Address: 15 Alexandra Rd, Clifton, Bristol BS8 2DD.

Telephone: (117) 973-5167.

Victoria League for Commonwealth Friendship

Founded in 1901 to promote friendship and understanding among the peoples of the Commonwealth.

Activities: The League runs a hostel in London, provides student accommodation, and organizes trips and events for United Kingdom and Commonwealth members and guests in the United Kingdom. It established and supports, in co-operation with the British Council and the Foreign and Commonwealth Office, HOST (Hosting for Overseas Students), which organizes weekends with British families for young overseas visitors. The League operates autonomously in Australia, New Zealand, Papua New Guinea, Scotland, South Africa and Zimbabwe; there are affiliated organizations in Canada, the USA and Bermuda.

Geographical Area of Activity: International.

Publications: Report of operations and financial statement.

Finance: Total income £280,692, total expenditure £271,576 (2001).

Principal Staff: Chair. L. Colin Webber; Gen. Sec. John Allan.

Address: Victoria League House, 55 Leinster Sq., London W2 4PW.

Telephone: (20) 7243-2633; **Fax:** (20) 7229-2994.

VSO

Founded in 1958 and formerly known as Voluntary Service Overseas, to help developing nations solve their economic, technical and educational problems. Operates as an international development agency that promotes volunteering to fight global poverty and disadvantage, bringing people together to share skills, creativity and learning to build a fairer world.

Activities: VSO works to achieve specific goals in education, HIV and AIDS, disability, health and social well-being, secure livelihoods and participation and governance. The organization adopts three approaches in its work; empowerment, partnership and commitment to training, through a range of approaches, including international volunteering, networking and alliance-building, awareness-raising and advocacy.

Geographical Area of Activity: Africa, the Caribbean, Eastern Europe, South and South-East Asia, and the Pacific,.

Restrictions: Does not make grants.

Publications: Annual report and review; education and development publications for development practitioners; advocacy papers; working papers.

Finance: Annual revenue £29,873,000, expenditure £32,179,000 (2001).

Trustees: Baroness Diana Warwick of Undercliffe (Chair); Frank Almond; Simon Burrall; Tony Dogbe; James Lawrie; Penny Maylin; Janet Moore; Prof. Peter Mortimore; Jean Penders; Hugh Richardson; Prof. Bhupinder Sandhu; Shirley Seward; Kathy Sykes; Sir John Vereker.

Principal Staff: Chief Exec. Mark Goldring; Campaign Information Officer Anna Thomas.

Address: 317 Putney Bridge Rd, London SW15 2PN.

Telephone: (20) 8780-7200; **Fax:** (20) 8780-7300; **Internet:** www.vso.org.uk; **e-mail:** enquiry@vso.org.uk.

Charles Wallace India Trust

Founded in 1978 to provide funds to enable citizens of India to undertake study or research, or to gain professional experience in the United Kingdom.

Activities: The Trust normally provides grants in the areas of the performing and visual arts, Indian artistic and cultural heritage, and the humanities.

Geographical Area of Activity: India.

Restrictions: Grants only made to Indian citizens normally resident and domiciled in that country between the ages of 24 and 48.

Publications: Annual Report.

Finance: Assets £6,737,945 (2000); annual revenue £210,087, grants disbursed £299,432 (April 2002).

Trustees: Prof. Judith M. Brown; C. E. Lampert; C. Perchard.

Principal Staff: Dr Frank Taylor.

Address: 9 Shaftesbury Rd, Richmond TW9 2TD.

Telephone: (20) 8940-9295.

War on Want

Founded in 1951 by Harold Wilson and Victor Gollancz to campaign against world poverty.

Activities: Operates nationally and internationally in the fields of aid to less-developed countries and development studies, through grants to institutions, and organizing training courses and conferences. Current campaigns include: promoting workers and human rights in Colombia and Guatemala; supporting a referendum on the future of Western Sahara; promoting the rights of children and refugees in Palestinian Autonomous Areas; campaigning for the introduction of Tobin—a small tax on foreign currency exchanges, the revenue from which would go to support international development. Also operates projects in South Africa and Tanzania, India, Bangladesh, Indonesia, Cuba, Haiti, Brazil, Netherlands and the United Kingdom.

Geographical Area of Activity: Africa, Asia, and Central and South America.

Restrictions: No unsolicted applications accepted.

Publications: *Upfront* (magazine): *confront* (bulletin).

Finance: Total project expenditure £581,412 (2000–01).

Principal Staff: Chief Exec. Louise Richards.

Address: Fenner Brockway House, 37–39 Great Guildford St, London SE1 0ES.

Telephone: (20) 7620-1111; **Fax:** (20) 7261-9291; **Internet:** www.waronwant.org; **e-mail:** mailroom@waronwant.org.

WaterAid

Founded in 1981 by the workers and organizations of the United Kingdom water industry to promote access to safe water and sanitation for all people.

Activities: Works through partner organizations in developing countries in Africa and Asia to raise the quality of life for people through improved domestic water supply, sanitation and associated hygiene practices. Projects are organized to minimize the risk of failure, WaterAid involves the village/community in all stages of construction and maintenance, thereby encouraging a sense of community ownership and responsibility, and provides a training programme which includes information on maintenance of necessary equipment. WaterAid also uses its experience, research and good practice to influence governments and other international organizations and feed into wider development policies.

Geographical Area of Activity: Africa and Southern Asia.

Restrictions: Grants only to specific (partner) organizations.

Publications: *Oasis* (twice yearly journal).

Finance: Total assets £4,646,727 (March 2002); annual revenue £11,032,964, expenditure £10,378,034 (2002).

Governing Board: The organization is governed by a Council elected from its members. Membership comprises the privatized water companies and most of the other water undertakings in England and Wales; the water companies of Scotland and Northern Ireland; the major trades unions associated with the industry; the Water Research Centre (WRC); the Chartered Institution of Water and Environmental Management (CIWEM); and the Institution of Water Officers (IWO).

Principal Staff: Dir Ravi Narayanan.

Address: Prince Consort House, 27–29 Albert Embankment, London SE1 7UB.

Telephone: (20) 7793-4500; **Fax:** (20) 7793-4545; **Internet:** www.wateraid.org.uk; **e-mail:** information@wateraid.org.uk.

Waterside Trust

Established to support Christian causes in the United Kingdom and world-wide, aiming to deliver a strategic and cost-effective programme of philanthropic giving to improve the lives of disadvantaged people.

Activities: Operates nationally and internationally in the above area, through making grants to organizations which provide Christian formation and pastoral care, offer educational and recreational activities for disadvantaged young people and young offenders; provide care and support for the elderly and deprived families; and funding organizations involved in community development. Ethics and Church management and finance are also areas of interest.

Geographical Area of Activity: International.

Restrictions: No grants are made to individuals.

Finance: Annual revenue £1,689,239 (2001).

Trustee: Irvine Bay Trustee Co.

Principal Staff: Robert Clark.

Address: 56 Palmerston Pl., Edinburgh EH12 5AY.

Telephone: (131) 225-6366; **Fax:** (131) 220-1041.

Wates Foundation

Founded in 1966 by Norman E. Wates, Ronald W. Wates and Allan C. Wates mainly for improvement of the quality of life, particularly in the urban community.

Activities: The Foundation awards a wide selection of grants in the fields of education, social welfare, science, health and the arts and humanities. The Foundation's particular interest is the physical and spiritual well-being of young people, notably the problems of youth unemployment, alcohol and drug abuse, young offenders and young people at risk. It offers opportunities for self-fulfilment through education, recreation and voluntary work within the community.

Geographical Area of Activity: Mostly United Kingdom.

Restrictions: Grants are not made to individuals, and recipients must have charitable status. Only a small proportion of the funds available is allocated to United Kingdom charities for projects overseas.

Finance: Annual revenue £1,634,782, grants disbursed £1,600,000 (2000–01).

Trustees: Jane Wates (Chair.).

Principal Staff: Dir Brian Wheelwright.

Address: 1260 London Rd, London SW16 4EG.

Telephone: (20) 8764-5000; **Fax:** (20) 8679-1541; **e-mail:** director@watesfoundation.org.uk.

WellBeing

Established in 1964 to support research concerned with better health of women and babies; formerly known as Birthright.

Activities: The organization is the fundraising arm of the Royal College of Obstetricians and Gynaecologists and is the only national charity in the United Kingdom that funds research in to all types of women's gynaecological health and that of their newborn babies. Awards grants and training fellowships in three main areas: pregnancy, birth and care of newborns; women's gynaecological cancers; and quality of life issues.

Geographical Area of Activity: United Kingdom and the Republic of Ireland.

Finance: Total grants £616,000 (2002).

Trustees: Sir Victor Blank (Chair.).

Principal Staff: Dir Jane Arnell.

Address: 27 Sussex Pl., Regent's Park, London NW1 4SP.

Telephone: (20) 7772-6400; **Fax:** (20) 7724-7725; **Internet:** www.wellbeing.org.uk; **e-mail:** wellbeing@rcog.org.uk.

Wellcome Trust

Founded in 1936 by the will of the late Sir Henry Wellcome to support clinical and basic scientific research into human and veterinary medicine.

Activities: Supports research in all branches of clinical medicine (except cancer research) and basic biomedical sciences, through the provision of clinical and non-clinical research fellowships and postgraduate studentships, and programme, travel, project, refurbishment and equipment grants. Special interests include support of research into tropical medicine, population issues and the history of medicine. Special initiative funding includes the Joint Infrastructure Fund, University Challenge Fund, functional genomics, pathogen genome sequencing, United Kingdom Population Biomedical Collections and the Cardiovascular Initiative; the Trust is currently providing a significant contribution to the Human Genome Project.

Geographical Area of Activity: International.

Publications: *Grants Handbook 2000; Wellcome News* (quarterly magazine); *Planning for the Future: the Wellcome Trust 2000–2005;* Annual Report and Accounts; grants information booklet.

Finance: Assets £15,000,000,000 (1999/2000); annual income £332,000,000, annual expenditure £544,000,000 (2000/01).

Board of Governors: Sir Dominic Cadbury (Chair.); Prof. Sir Michael Rutter (Deputy Chair.); Prof. Julian Jack; Prof. Adrian Bird; Prof. Martin Bobrow; Prof. Christopher Edwards; Alastair Ross Goobey; Prof. Jean Thomas; Prof. Mark Walport; Edward Walker-Arnott.

Principal Staff: Dir Prof. Mark Walport.

Address: 183 Euston Rd, London NW1 2BE.

Telephone: (20) 7611-8888; **Fax:** (20) 7611-8545; **Internet:** www.wellcome.ac.uk; **e-mail:** contact@wellcome.ac.uk.

Westminster Foundation for Democracy

Founded in April 1992 by Royal Prerogative to strengthen pluralist democratic development overseas. The three main political parties in the United Kingdom are represented on the Governing Board, which also includes a representative of the smaller parties and non-party representatives.

Activities: Works internationally by giving grants to institutions including human rights groups, trades unions, parliaments and other representative institutions, election administration groups, the independent media, women's groups and other NGOs involved in political development. It funds initiatives which will make a tangible and practical contribution to pluralist democratic institutions overseas.

Geographical Area of Activity: Priority areas are Central and Eastern Europe, the countries of the former USSR and English-speaking countries of Africa. Some grants are made in Asia and the Middle East.

Restrictions: No grants are made to projects in the United Kingdom; nor are grants made to schools, businesses, research, nor for conferences.

Finance: Receives funding from the United Kingdom Government's Foreign and Commonwealth Office; annual revenue £4,155,000 (2000/01), expenditure approx. £4,077,000 (2000/01).

Trustees: Michael Gapes (Chair.); Nik Gowing, Michael Moore (Vice-Chair.); Michael Aaronson; Georgina Ashworth; Frances D'Souza; Nicola Duckworth; Mary Kaldor; Patrick Smith; Caroline Spelman; Richard Spring; Gisela Stuart; Michael Trend.

Principal Staff: Chief Exec. David Spelman; Programme Dir, Africa and the Rest of the World Dr Elizabeth Marsh; Programme Dir, Eastern Europe Jadranka Foster; Co.-Sec. and Dir of Finance Valerie Blackwell.

Address: 125 Pall Mall, London SW1Y 5EA.

Telephone: (20) 7930-0480; **Fax:** (20) 7930-0449; **Internet:** www.wfd.org; **e-mail:** wfd@wfd.org.

Garfield Weston Foundation

Founded in 1958 for general charitable purposes.

Activities: Grants are made for the support of activities in the areas of religion, conservation and the environment, education, the arts, medicine and health, and welfare, community and youth.

Geographical Area of Activity: Primarily United Kingdom, with limited funding available overseas.

Restrictions: Grants are made to registered charities only (with the exception of applications from churches). No grants are made for animal welfare projects.

Publications: Annual Report.

Finance: Annual expenditure £33,272,000 (April 2002).

Trustees: Guy Weston (Chair.).

Principal Staff: Admin. Fiona M. Hare.

Address: Weston Centre, Bowater House, 68 Knightsbridge, London SW1X 7LQ.

Telephone: (20) 7589-6363; **Fax:** (20) 7584-5921; **e-mail:** ffoster@wittington-investments.co.uk.

Whitley Animal Protection Trust

Founded in 1964 to promote research into the protection of animals.

Activities: Supports research and development initiatives into animal welfare and protection, nationally and internationally.

Geographical Area of Activity: International.

Finance: Annual revenue £358,854, expenditure £301,812 (2001).

Trustees: E. Whitley; E. J. Whitley; J. Whitley; P. A. Whitley.

Principal Staff: Sec. M. T. Gwynne.

Address: R. Gwynne and Sons, Edgbaston House, Walker St, Wellington, Telford TF1 1HF.

Telephone: (1952) 641651; **Fax:** (1952) 247441.

Harold Hyam Wingate Foundation

Founded in 1960 by Harold Hyam Wingate, the principal objective being the general advancement of Jewish and other charitable purposes.

Activities: The Foundation's main interests lie in supporting Jewish organizations and in the fields of medical research and health care, the performing arts and education, the latter particularly where relevant to problems associated to social exclusion. Grants are made to established charitable organizations, to established and new projects of study and research, and to establish and endow scholarships, fellowships, professional chairs, prizes and awards. The Wingate Scholarships were established in 1988 to help individuals undertake projects in almost any field, excluding fine art; they are open to individuals over 24 years of age who are citizens of the United Kingdom, the Commonwealth or Israel and are living in the British Isles, and are awarded as a result of an annual competition. In 2001 46 Wingate Scholarships were awarded averaging £7,000 each. Capital projects are also considered on a selective basis.

Geographical Area of Activity: International; scholarships for citizens of the United Kingdom, Commonwealth countries, Ireland, Israel and European Union Member States.

Finance: Total Foundation grants £400,000 (2002); annual scholarships approx. £350,000.

Trustees: J. Drori; Anthony John Wingate; Prof. David Wingate; Jonathan Wingate; Roger Wingate.

Principal Staff: Admin., Foundation Karen Marshall; Admin., Scholarships Faith Clark.

Address: 20–22 Stukeley St, 2nd Floor, London WC2B 5LR.

Internet: www.wingate.org.uk; **e-mail:** clark@wingate.org .uk.

The Wolfson Family Charitable Trust

Founded in 1958, and formerly known as the Edith and Isaac Wolfson Charitable Trust, for the advancement of medical and surgical science, to promote religion, and for general charitable purposes.

Activities: Operates through grants to institutions, in the United Kingdom and Israel in the above areas.

Geographical Area of Activity: United Kingdom and Israel.

Publications: Biennial Report.

Finance: Assets £38,505,000 (2002); annual revenue £2,716,000, grants disbursed £6,997,000 (2002).

Trustees: Lord Wolfson of Marylebone (Chair.); Sir Eric Ash; Sir Martin Gilbert; Prof. B. Jay; M. Paisner; Sir Bernard Rix; Hon Janet Wolfson de Botton; Lady Wolfson; Hon. Laura Wolfson Townsley.

Principal Staff: Sec. Dr Victoria Harrison.

Address: 8 Queen Anne St, London W1G 9LD.

Telephone: (20) 7323-5730; **Fax:** (20) 7323-3241.

The Wolfson Foundation

Founded in 1955 for the support of scientific and medical research and higher education.

Activities: Operates throughout the United Kingdom, the Commonwealth and Israel in the fields of education, science and medicine, through grants to institutions. Grants are awarded towards the promotion of scientific and medical research. The support of excellence in universities is a priority.

Geographical Area of Activity: United Kingdom, the Commonwealth and Israel.

Publications: Annual Report.

Finance: Net assets £635,134,000 (2002); annual revenue £37,278,000, grants disbursed £34,619,000 (2002).

Trustees: Lord Wolfson of Marylebone (Chair.); Prof. Sir Eric Ash; Lord McColl; Lord Quinton; Lord Quirk; Sir Derek Roberts; Lord Turnberg; Prof. Sir David Weatherall; Lady Wolfson; Hon. Janet Wolfson de Botton; Hon. Laura Wolfson Townsley.

Principal Staff: Exec. Sec. Dr Victoria Harrison.

Address: 8 Queen Anne St, London W1G 9LD.

Telephone: (20) 7323-5730; **Fax:** (20) 7323-3241.

World Education Fellowship

Founded in 1921 by Beatrice Ensor as the New Education Fellowship; became the World Education Fellowship in 1966. The original aim of the Fellowship was to encourage progressive methods in learning and teaching among members of the teaching profession and parents.

Activities: Operates internationally in the field of education, through self-conducted programmes, research, conferences, courses, publications and lectures. The Foundation studies the impact of modern methods and technical advances on education, devises study courses and conferences for the promotion of world understanding, and assists teachers in the solution of day-to-day classroom problems. The Fellowship is represented in Australia, Belgium, Egypt, Germany, India, Italy, Japan, the Republic of Korea, Nepal, the Netherlands, Pakistan, South America, Sri Lanka and the USA.

Geographical Area of Activity: International.

Restrictions: No funds available for grants, scholarships, research or other projects.

Publications: *New Era in Education* (journal) and sectional publications.

Principal Staff: Gen. Sec. Guadalupe G. de Turner.

Address: 54 Fox Lane, London N13 4AL.

Telephone: (20) 8245-4561; **Fax:** (20) 8245-4561; **e-mail:** gde-turner@bigwig.net.

World Land Trust

Established in 1990.

Activities: Concerned with conservation initiatives, including land purchase and management of threatened areas. Involved in fundraising and public awareness campaigns. Involved in international conservation projects in Belize, Brazil, Ecuador, Turks and Caicos Islands and Patagonia (Argentina).

Geographical Area of Activity: Central and South America and the Caribbean.

Restrictions: No grants to individuals. All funds go directly to WLT projects.

Publications: *WLT News* (twice a year).

Finance: Individual, corporate and trust donations.

Trustees: Dr G. A. Bertrand; Gil S. Child; Jane Krish; Adrian Penrose; Prof. Renton Righelato.

Principal Staff: Chief Exec. John A. Burton.

Address: Blyth House, 3 Bridge St, Halesworth IP19 8AB.

Telephone: (1986) 874422; **Fax:** (1986) 874425; **Internet:** www.worldlandtrust.org; **e-mail:** worldlandtrust@btinternet .com.

World in Need

Founded by C. Jackson-Cole in 1965 to alleviate suffering and advance Christianity.

Activities: Operates nationally and internationally in the fields of aid to less-developed countries, economic affairs, education, social welfare and social studies through investing in social entrepreneurs world-wide. Recently established the BasicNeeds project in mental health and development, and Street (UK) to support micro-enterprise development. Previously helped establish organizations such as ActionAid (q.v.), Help the Aged, Opportunity International UK (q.v.) and ACET (AIDS Care Education and Training).

Geographical Area of Activity: International.

Restrictions: Start-up or growth funding for new social ventures.

Finance: Total income £422,634, total expenditure £348,179 (March 2002).

Trustees: Roger Young (Chair.).

Principal Staff: Dir R. A. John.

Address: 103 High St, Oxford OX1 4BW.

Telephone: (1865) 249111; **Internet:** www.world-in-need .org.uk; **e-mail:** contact@world-in-need.org.uk.

World Society for the Protection of Animals

Founded in January 1981 by the merger of the International Society for the Protection of Animals and the World Federation for the Protection of Animals. Its aim is to promote effective means for the protection of animals, for the prevention of cruelty to and the relief from suffering and exploitation of animals.

Activities: Operates internationally, with over 400 member animal welfare societies in more than 90 countries, in the field of protection of animals and conservation of their environment, and in related areas of education, international relations and international law, through self-conducted programmes, education campaigns, research, conferences and courses, publications and lectures.

Geographical Area of Activity: International.

Publications: *Animals International*; Annual Report.

Finance: Annual revenue £5,444,000, expenditure £4,913,000 (2001).

Trustees: The Society is governed by an international board of 35 members.

Principal Staff: Dir Gen. Peter Davies.

Address: 89 Albert Embankment, London SE1 7TP.

Telephone: (20) 7587-5000; **Fax:** (20) 7793-0208; **Internet:** www.wspa.org.uk; **e-mail:** wspa@wspa.org.uk.

Young Men's Christian Association—YMCA

Founded in 1844 by George Williams and centred on the Christian faith, it works for the physical, emotional and spiritual welfare of women and men of all faiths and of none.

Activities: The YMCA works with young people, particularly in times of need, and with the world community. Its programmes include training, particularly for those with special needs; providing safe, secure, affordable housing; counselling drug abusers and victims of abuse; running education courses; children's day camps; outdoor adventure activities; leadership training courses; Christian music and drama groups; and many other sport, recreational and community activities. The YMCA's development agency, Y Care International, works in developing countries by channelling financial support through local YMCAs for projects developed in, and with, their local communities. The YMCA is an international movement with more than 30 million members and volunteers working in over 123 countries world-wide.

Geographical Area of Activity: International.

Publications: Annual review and summary accounts; *Y Care International's Annual Review;* booklets and educational material.

Finance: Total assets £11,949,000 (March 2002); total income £34,735,000, expenditure £33,153,000 (2002).

Trustees: Peter Posner (Chair.).

Principal Staff: Nat. Sec. E. Thomas.

Address: 640 Forest Rd, London E17 3DZ.

Telephone: (20) 8520-5599; **Fax:** (20) 8509-3190; **Internet:** www.ymca.org.uk; **e-mail:** enquiries@ymca.co.uk.

Zochonis Charitable Trust

Founded in 1977 to provide funds for general charitable purposes.

Activities: Operates nationally and internationally in the fields of education, social welfare and the arts and humanities.

Geographical Area of Activity: International.

Restrictions: Awards grants to registered charities only.

Finance: Annual revenue £1,147,913, expenditure £1,129,078 (April 2001).

Trustees: R. B. James; A. Whittaker; J. B. Zochonis.

Address: Deloitte & Touche, 201 Deansgate, POB 500, Manchester M60 2AT.

Telephone: (161) 455-8380; **Fax:** (161) 829-3803.

Zurich Community Trust

Founded in 1973, and formerly known as the Allied Dunbar Charitable Trust, for general charitable purposes and to help the most disadvantaged in the community move from dependence to independence locally, nationally and in developing countries.

Activities: The Foundation operates nationally and in developing countries in the fields of law and human rights, and medicine and health. Current programmes include: the India Programme, combining funding and management development opportunities; the five-year Inclusion Programme, which is providing £1,000,000 to help socially-excluded people help themselves; the six-year Dementia Programme, involving £2,000,000 in funding for 14 projects; and the Older People programme, making grants of £1,500,000 over three years to tackle the issues facing older people. Incorporates Zurich Cares, a staff volunteering and payroll giving programme, and the Zurich Advice Network Foundation, supported by over 5,000 members of the company's franchise network, and currently involved in the £2,000,000 Kids 2 Care 4 funding programme.

Geographical Area of Activity: International.

Restrictions: No grants to individuals, for research, animal welfare, emergency or disaster appeals, nor to political, religious or mainstream educational institutions (unless directly benefiting people with disabilities).

Finance: Zurich Financial Services donates a percentage of pre-tax United Kingdom profits to the Trust, and funds raised by company employees. Grants £2,500,000 (2000).

Principal Staff: Chair. Chris Gillies; Dir of Community Affairs Chris Staples.

Address: POB 1288, Swindon SN1 1FL.

Telephone: (1793) 511227; **Fax:** (1793) 506982; **Internet:** www.zurich.org.uk; **e-mail:** communityaffairs@uk.zurich .com.

United States of America

FOUNDATION CENTRES AND CO-ORDINATING BODIES

Advocacy Institute

Established to assist people to influence and change public policy world-wide.

Activities: Operates in more than 48 countries in the field of human rights, in areas including improving public health, fighting poverty, working towards sustainable development, protecting the environment and promoting gender equality. The Institute promotes political and social justice for all and strengthens world-wide movements working towards these goals. Its work also includes advocacy skills development, developing and analysing new strategies, and international networking of advocates. The Institute is linked with a number of NGOs dealing with critical human rights problems all over the world. The Advocacy Institute Fellows Program aims to strengthen the ability of social change leaders world-wide, whilst the Leadership for a Changing World program is a national award scheme run in conjunction with the Ford Foundation (q.v.) and the Robert F. Wagner School of Public Service, New York University.

Geographical Area of Activity: International.

Publications: *Advocacy for Social Justice: A Global Action and Reflection Guide; Justice Begins at Home: Strengthening Social Justice Advocacy in the US; Become a Leader for Social Justice;* Annual Report; resource guides; and other publications.

Directors: D. Cohen, M. Pertschuk (Co-Chair.); K. D. Sheekey (Pres. and Chief Exec.); R. D. Paisner (Treas.); Linda Tarr-Whelan (Sec.).

Address: 1629 K St, NW, Suite 200, Washington, DC 20006-1629.

Telephone: (202) 777-7575; **Fax:** (202) 777-7577; **Internet:** www.advocacy.org; **e-mail:** info@advocacy.org.

Civil Society International—CSI

Established as a private non-partisan information organization, aiming to publish materials from voluntary and non-profit organizations in the USA and distribute them world-wide and assist in the creation of partnerships between US organizations and organizations in the countries of the former USSR.

Activities: Aims to promote co-operation between NGOs in the USA and the West, and similar organizations in the countries of the former USSR. Runs information-based projects relating to the third sector, including maintaining a website containing over 2,000 documents with information regarding developments in the countries of the former USSR, news of grant and conference announcements and research on civil society in the USA and abroad; providing advisory and training services on effective use of the internet for non-profit charitable organizations; and publicizing reform efforts made by the countries of the former USSR and groups in the USA, which are working towards social change and improvements in living conditions.

Geographical Area of Activity: Former USSR, USA, Asia, Africa and the Middle East.

Restrictions: Does not make grants.

Publications: *CivilSoc* (e-mail list); *Internet Resources for Eurasia* (2001); *The Post-Soviet Handbook* (1999); *Civil Society in Central Asia* (1999).

Finance: Receives donations from foundations and individuals, and funding from sales of publications.

Board of Directors: Ronald S. Bernis; Richard Greene; Bob Ness; Maryann Ness; Vladimir Raskin; Daniel Waugh.

Principal Staff: Dir Holt Ruffin.

Address: 2929 NE Blakeley St, Seattle, WA 98105.

Telephone: (206) 523-4755; **Fax:** (206) 523-1974; **Internet:** www.civilsoc.org; **e-mail:** csi@civilsoc.org.

Council on Foundations, Inc

Founded in 1949 and incorporated in 1957 as a publicly-supported charitable organization.

Activities: The Council's members (more than 1,300 grant-makers) include independent, community- and company-sponsored foundations and corporate contributors; regional associations of grant-makers are also affiliated with the Council and work closely with it in providing information and services. The Council provides a variety of technical and advisory services to guide its members on matters ranging from legal and tax issues to investment management, programme development and grant-making principles and practices. It maintains regular liaison with other parts of the philanthropic sector, including the Foundation Center (q.v.), through direct communication and participation in conferences and 'umbrella' organizations. The Council conducts an annual conference and other meetings throughout the year to assist its members in their grant-making activities; and sponsors research and educational programmes. Awards offered include the Wilmer Shields and Distinguished Grantmaker Awards.

Geographical Area of Activity: USA.

Publications: Annual Report; *Council Columns; Foundation News and Commentary Magazine; The Magazine of Philanthropy; Principles and Practices for Effective Grantmaking*; and numerous other publications.

Finance: Assets $15,574,289 (2000); annual revenue $18,158,824, expenditure $15,336,988 (2000).

Board of Directors: M. Mountcastle (Chair.); E. D. Carson, L. Wallin Ziegenbein (Vice-Chair.); G. Yates (Treas.); P. Spivey (Sec.); G. Yates (Treas.); Dorothy S. Ridings (*ex officio*); Susan Berresford; Diana Campoamor; Sanford R. Cardin; Timothy J. McClimon; Anne Rhodes; and others.

Principal Staff: Pres. and CEO Dorothy S. Ridings.

Address: 1828 L St, NW, Suite 300, Washington, DC 20036.

Telephone: (202) 466-6512; **Fax:** (202) 785-3925; **Internet:** www.cof.org; **e-mail:** webmaster@cof.org.

Foundation Center

Chartered in 1956 by the Board of Regents of the University of the State of New York for the gathering, analysis and dissemination of information about the philanthropic foundations, in the public interest.

Activities: Operates as an information resource on US foundations. The Center includes in its libraries information about foundations and the grants they award, as well as published information about the foundation field in all its aspects, including historical records and supporting references in related fields. The New York and Washington, DC, libraries have comprehensive national collections of source materials on foundations and their grant-making activities. They include current primary public records, and the standard reference works and services, as well as books, reports, guides and other publications relating to philanthropy at large, including information on foundations in other countries. The New York library also collects historical materials, archives and supporting references in related fields. The Cleveland and San Francisco libraries offer extensive regional information on foundation funding and access to full national data.The Center co-ordinates a regional library network in over 200 locations in the USA, information is also available on-line through DIALOG. The Foundation also maintains an office in Atlanta, GA.

Geographical Area of Activity: USA.

Restrictions: The Center does not direct applications for funds to particular foundations, nor does it arrange introductions to foundation officials or assist persons seeking positions in foundations..

Publications: Annual report and financial statement; *The Foundation Directory; Philanthropy News Digest; RFP Bulletin; FC Stats; The Foundation Grants Index* (quarterly and annually); *Guide to US Foundations, Their Trustees, Officers, and Donors; The Foundation 1000; Foundation Fundamentals; Foundation Giving; The Foundation Grants Index Quarterly; Foundation Grants to Individuals; Grant Guides; Guide to Proposal Writing; National Directory of Corporate Giving; Corporate Foundation Profiles; FC Search* (database on CD-ROM); numerous books, studies and directories on aspects of philanthropy.

Finance: Assets $18,366,070 (Dec. 2001); annual revenue $14,187,746, expenditure $13,971,401 (2001).

Board of Trustees: Barry D. Gaberman (Chair.); Sara L. Engelhardt (Pres.).

Address: 79 Fifth Ave, New York, NY 10003-3076.

Telephone: (212) 620-4230; **Fax:** (212) 691-1828; **Internet:** www.fdncenter.org.

Independent Sector

Founded in 1980, a national coalition of foundations, non-profit organizations and corporations which aims to strengthen philanthropy and citizen action in the USA.

Activities: Acts as a forum for member organizations, as a source of information and as a mediator between the grant-making and grant-seeking communities. Also works to encourage volunteer work and community action in society. Supports and engages in non-profit initiatives in areas such as public policy, research and communications.

Geographical Area of Activity: USA.

Publications: *The New Nonprofit Almanac IN BRIEF: Facts and Figures on the Independent Sector; Outcome Measurement in Nonprofit Organizations: Current Practices and Recommendations; What You Should Know About Nonprofits; Facts and Finding Series* (series of research reports); numerous reports, papers and other publications.

Finance: Funded by membership dues, grants and other contributions. Total assets $12,127,336 (2000); annual revenue $6,877,714, expenditure $7,604,444 (2000).

Directors: John R. Seffrin (Chair.); Herman Art Taylor (Vice-Chair.); Marilda Gandara (Treas.); Christopher Gates (Sec.) and 30 board members.

Principal Staff: Interim Pres. and CEO Peter Shiras.

Address: 1200 18th St, NW, Suite 200, Washington, DC 20036.

Telephone: (202) 467-6100; **Fax:** (202) 467-6101; **Internet:** www.independentsector.org; **e-mail:** info@independentsector.org.

InterAction—American Council for Voluntary International Action

Formed in 1984 by the merger of the American Council of Voluntary Agencies for Foreign Service and Private Agencies Collaborating Together, InterAction is a coalition of more than 160 US private and voluntary organizations dedicated to international humanitarian issues. Its main purpose is to enhance the effectiveness and professional capacities of its members while fostering partnership, collaboration and leadership within the voluntary organization community.

Activities: Member organizations' activities include disaster relief, refugee protection, assistance and resettlement, sustainable development, public policy and educating the American public on global development issues.

Geographical Area of Activity: USA.

Publications: *Monday Developments* (every 2 weeks); *InterAction Member Profiles* (every 2 years); newsletters, media guides.

Finance: Member organizations pay membership dues; government grants and private funding.

Directors: The Board of Directors comprises one representative from each member agency. An Executive Committee is elected by the Board.

Principal Staff: Pres. and CEO M. McClymont.

Address: 1717 Massachusetts Ave, NW, Suite 701, Washington, DC 20036.

Telephone: (202) 667-8227; **Fax:** (202) 667-8236; **Internet:** www.interaction.org; **e-mail:** ia@interaction.org.

International Society for Third-Sector Research—ISTR

Founded in March 1992, ISTR is a major international association promoting research and education in the fields of civil society, philanthropy and the non-profit sector. Committed to building a global community of scholars and interested others dedicated to the creation, discussion and advancement of knowledge relating to the third sector and its impact on human and global well-being and development internationally. The Society's mission is to promote the development of high-quality research and education internationally on third sector-related issues, theories and policies; and to enhance the dissemination and application of knowledge about the third sector as widely as possible throughout the world. ISTR strives to broaden the participation of researchers in all parts of the world and in all disciplines, with special emphasis given to expand the number of third sector researchers in developing nations and Central and Eastern Europe.

Activities: Members come from 84 countries. Holds conferences every two years to promote the exchange of ideas and research findings in the voluntary sector, and promotes discussion and co-operation between researchers and scholars. ISTR has established a number of regional research networks: African Research Network, Asia/Pacific Research Network, European Research Network and Latin America and the Caribbean Research Network.

Geographical Area of Activity: International.

Publications: *Inside ISTR* (quarterly newsletter); *ISTR Report*; *Voluntas;* membership directory (on-line).

Directors: Alan Fowler (Pres.); Masayuki Deguchi (Pres. Elect); Kathleen D. McCarthy (Sec.); Freda Donoghue (Treas.); Rosa Maria Fischer; Dorothy K. Gordon; Adam Habib; Lev I. Jakobson; Lalit Kumar; Jean-Louis Laville; Jenny Onyx; Paul Opoku-Mensah; Marilyn Taylor; Soledad Teixidó; Andrés A. Thompson; Virginia A. Hodgkinson, Sandra J. Newman, Rupert Taylor (*ex officio*).

Principal Staff: Exec. Dir Margery B. Daniels; Prog. Asst Donna L. Jakuta.

Address: 559 Wyman Park Bldg, 3400 N. Charles St, Baltimore, MD 21218-2688.

Telephone: (410) 516-4678; **Fax:** (410) 516-4870; **Internet:** www.istr.org; **e-mail:** istr@jhu.edu.

National Network of Grantmakers

A network of organizations and individuals involved in funding social and economic justice, founded in 1980.

Activities: The Network has 400 members; promotes mutual support amongst members, and democracy and openness in grant-making; organizes conferences. Provides services to both funders and grant-seekers.

Geographical Area of Activity: USA.

Board of Directors: D. Edwards; D. Feeney; M. Fine; E. Gurzinsky; C. Lipat; I. Malavé; R. McKay; B. Meyer; J. Palmer; S. Ramirez; C. Renfro; J. Vaughn; M. Warsh; R. Williams; J. Wilson.

Principal Staff: Interim Dir Nicole Trombley; Dir Special Projects Julio C. Dantas.

Address: 150 Court St, 2nd Floor, Brooklyn, NY 11210.

Fax: (718) 923-1400; **Internet:** www.nng.org; **e-mail:** nng@nng.org.

Synergos—The Synergos Institute

Established in 1986; aims to develop effective, sustainable and locally-based solutions to poverty in Africa, Asia and Central and South America.

Activities: In partnership with other groups, Synergos aims to strengthen the capacity of civil society in less-developed countries, through its projects, Global Philanthropy and Foundation Building, Bridging Leadership and Global Philanthropists Circle, which assist grass-roots grant-making organizations to develop their skills and effectiveness in order to provide long-term solutions and sustainable development.

Geographical Area of Activity: Africa, Asia, and Central and South America.

Publications: *Foundation Building Sourcebook: A Practitioner's Guide Based upon Experience from Africa, Asia and Latin America*; case studies; conference reports; and other publications.

Finance: Funded by private foundations, international agencies, corporations and individual donations.

Directors: Peggy Dulany (Chair.); S. Bruce Shearer (Pres.); Wanda Engel Aduan; Etienne Allard; Valentin von Arnim; Lance Dublin; Juliette Gimon; Dorian S. Goldman; Nadine B. Hack; Brian Henderson; H. Peter Karoff; Maria E. Lagomasino; Cornelio Marchan; Marcus Augusto de Moraes; Sithembiso Nyoni; Richard D. Parsons; Kim Samuel-Johnson; Adele S. Simmons; James Sligar; Michael W. Sonnenfeldt; Sarah Spencer.

Principal Staff: Pres. S. Bruce Schearer.

Address: 9 East 69th St, New York, NY 10021.

Telephone: (212) 517-4900; **Fax:** (212) 517-4815; **Internet:** www.synergos.org; **e-mail:** synergos@synergos.org.

Woodrow Wilson National Fellowship Foundation

Founded in 1945.

Activities: Awards fellowships for research in the humanities and social sciences. Thirty-five Charlotte W. Newcombe Doctoral Dissertation Fellowships are awarded annually for research in areas of religious or ethical values in all fields (open to scholars enrolled in doctoral programmes in the humanities at a US university); 15 research grants in women's studies are awarded annually to doctoral candidates at US universities; 80 one-year-long Andrew W. Mellon Fellowships in Humanistic Studies are awarded to doctoral candidates.

Trustees: Nancy Weiss Malkiel (Chair.); Frank W. Wadsworth, John C. Wilcox (Vice-Chair.); Gilbert Casellas; John S. Chamberlin; James R. Connor; Elizabeth A. Duffy; Eleanor Thomas Elliott; Charles E. Fiero; Juliet J. Goodfriend; Frederick L. A. Grauer; J. Roderick Heller, III; Carleton A. Holstrom; N. Gerry House; Shirley A. Jackson; Nancy L. Lane; Richard A. Levao; William Lilley, III; Howard A. Paster; Edward Joseph Perkins; Lee Etta Powell; Dennis R. Reigle; Sharon P. Robinson; James M. Rosser; Louis A. Simpson; Catharine R. Stimpson; Marvin J. Suomi; John Sweetland; Robert Weisbuch; Stephen A. Weiswasser; Michael R. Winston.

Principal Staff: Pres. Robert Weisbuch; Exec. Vice-Pres. John Cross.

Address: CN5281, Princeton, NJ 08543-5281.

Telephone: (609) 452-7007; **Fax:** (609) 452-0066; **Internet:** www.woodrow.org/mellon; **e-mail:** webmaster@woodrow.org.

FOUNDATIONS, TRUSTS AND NON-PROFIT ORGANIZATIONS

AAFRC Trust for Philanthropy

Founded in 1985 by the American Association of Fund-Raising Counsel.

Activities: Aims to increase public awareness and understanding of philanthropy through conducting programmes; funds and commissions research into philanthropy and promotes projects set up by other similar organizations. Develops and conducts college courses on philanthropy in conjunction with the American Association of Colleges; and sponsors the John Grenzebach awards for outstanding research in the field. Co-ordinates Giving USA, an annual analysis of all sources of philanthropic funding in the USA.

Geographical Area of Activity: USA.

Publications: *Giving USA* (annually); *Giving USA Update* (irregular); report and newsletter.

Principal Staff: Chair. Leo. P. Arnoult; Vice-Chair. Hank Goldstein; Treas. Richard T. Jolly; Sec. Del Martin.

Address: 10293 North Meridian St, Suite 175, Indianapolis, IN 46290.

Telephone: (317) 816-1613; **Fax:** (317) 816-1633; **Internet:** www.aafrc.org; **e-mail:** info@aafrc.org.

Abundant Life Seed Foundation

Activities: Non-profit organization dedicated to the preservation of biodiversity through the propagation and distribution of open-pollinated 'heirloom' and rare seeds. Operates the World Seed Fund, which donates seeds world-wide, and education programmes. Hosts two discussion forums on general gardening and rare seeds.

Geographical Area of Activity: International.

Publications: *Newsletter* (3 a year); Annual Catalogue; publications relating to areas of interest.

Principal Staff: Crystie Kisler; Matthew Dillion; Jim Pivarnik.

Address: POB 772, Port Townsend, WA 98368.

Telephone: (360) 385-5660; **Fax:** (360) 385-7455; **Internet:** www.abundantlifeseed.org; **e-mail:** abundant@olypen.com.

ACCION International

Founded in 1961, an independent agency aiming to assist local organizations reaching small businesses in urban and rural areas of North, Central and South America and sub-Saharan Africa.

Activities: Advises on issues affecting small businesses; assists in employment and financial projects, small business development and micro-credit loan programmes; and provides management assistance for development agencies. Maintains a small reference library and publishes a monthly e-mail newsletter. In 2001 launched the Citi-ACCION Outstanding Microentrepreneur Prize with Citigroup and the Citigroup Foundation (q.v.).

Geographical Area of Activity: North, Central and South America, sub-Saharan Africa.

Restrictions: Does not lend to, nor fund, individuals directly.

Publications: *Ventures* (newsletter); *ACCION International Publications* (annual); Annual Report; and other leaflets, manuals, discussion papers and publications on microfinance.

Finance: Annual revenue $12,285,774 (2001); total expenditure $10,615,316 (2001).

Principal Staff: Pres. and CEO María Otero.

Address: 56 Roland St, Suite 300, Boston, MA 02129.

Telephone: (617) 625-7080; **Fax:** (617) 625-7020; **Internet:** www.accion.org.

ACDI/VOCA

Established in 1997 by the merger of Agricultural Co-operative Development International (ACDI) and Volunteers in Overseas Co-operative Assistance (VOCA), as a development organization with the aim of promoting the liberalization of markets and democratic principles, alongside environmentally sound use of natural resources.

Activities: Aims to provide farmers with the necessary resources to succeed in the world economy. It does this through programmes that lend the technical expertise and experience of consultants to farmers and businesses in developing countries, enabling them to make use of the economic opportunities that are afforded to them, as well as creating international co-operative partnerships. The organization works on many long-term projects as well as short-term volunteer assignments; supports local environment groups; helps develop member-controlled businesses and associations; encourages sustainable agricultural methods; and works towards the protection of national parks and reserves. Members include agribusinesses and farm credit banks. Maintains offices in more than 35 countries.

Geographical Area of Activity: International.

Publications: *World Report* (quarterly newsletter); *1999: Building on Global Success; 1998: A History of Accomplishments, a Vision of the Future*; Annual Report.

Board of Directors: David Graves (Chair.).

Principal Staff: Pres. M. W. Deegan; Exec. Vice-Pres. D.R. Crane, Jr.

Address: 50 F St, NW, Suite 1100, Washington, DC 20001.

Telephone: (202) 383-4961; **Fax:** (202) 783-7204; **Internet:** www.acdivoca.org.

Acumen Fund

Founded in October 2002 with seed money from the Rockefeller Foundation (q.v.), the Cisco Systems Foundation and a group of individual investors.

Activities: Aims to accelerate global change, through the adoption of a venture capital model. Innovative projects with high potential to solve social and economic problems are supported through the provision of financial and technical assistance. Programmes include Health Technology Changing Lives, supporting innovative methods of accessing health care for underserved groups in society in Africa and South Asia; Economic and Civic Enterprise, targeted at supporting entrepreneurs in Egypt and Pakistan.

Geographical Area of Activity: International.

Publications: Newsletter (quarterly).

Board of Directors: Catherine S. Muther (Chair.); Margo Alexander; Stuart Davidson; Angela Glover Blackwell; Roberta R. Katz; Jacqueline Novagratz.

Principal Staff: Chief Exec. Jacqueline Novogratz.

Address: 74 Trinity Place, 9th Floor, New York, NY 10006.

Telephone: (212) 566-8821; **Fax:** (212) 566-8817; **Internet:** www.acumenfund.org; **e-mail:** postmaster@acumenfund.org.

Adventist Development and Relief Agency International—ADRA

Formed in 1956 by the Seventh-day Adventist Church as an independent humanitarian agency, to provide disaster relief and individual and community development without prejudice, to those in need, regardless of age, political or religious affiliation or ethnicity.

Activities: An independent NGO, ADRA works in disaster areas and parts of the developing world, providing aid and support. Its development programmes help to improve education, health care, food supplies and economic and social well-being for people in more than 125 countries and territories, helping to achieve sustainable change and long-term humanitarian solutions.

Geographical Area of Activity: International.

Publications: *ADRA Works* (quarterly newsletter); *ADRA's World* (weekly 30-minute television programme).

Finance: Assets $15,852,144 (2001); annual revenue $69,002,341, expenditure $64,599,362 (2001).

Principal Staff: Pres. Charles Sandfur; Exec. Vice-Pres. Mario H. Ochoa; Senior Vice-Pres. Byron Scheuneman.

Address: 12501 Old Columbia Pike, Silver Spring, MD 20904.

Telephone: (301) 680-6380; **Fax:** (301) 680-6370; **Internet:** www.adra.org; **e-mail:** 104100.140@compuserve.com.

AED—Academy for Educational Development

Established in 1961 with the aim of solving social problems in the USA and world-wide.

Activities: Operates nationally and internationally in 130 countries world-wide in the areas of energy conservation and the environment, health, social welfare, democracy building, education and youth development, through research, training and education, technical assistance, and running programmes and projects. Sponsors conferences. Maintains offices in New York and Nashville, TN, and field offices in 49 countries.

Geographical Area of Activity: World-wide.

Finance: Annual budget approx. US $135,000,000.

Principal Staff: Pres. and CEO Stephen F. Moseley; Chair. Edward W. Russell.

Address: 1825 Connecticut Ave, NW, Washington, DC 20009-5721.

Telephone: (202) 884-8000; **Fax:** (202) 884-8400; **Internet:** www.aed.org; **e-mail:** communications@aed.org.

Africa–America Institute

Founded in 1953 to help further development in Africa, improve African–American understanding and inform Americans about Africa.

Activities: Engages in educational training, development assistance and informational activities. Programmes include: Africa Policy Information Center; African Graduate Fellowship; African Training for Leadership and Advanced Skills (ATLAS); Development Training; International Visitors Program for Short-Term African Visitors; Services to US Corporations; and Southern African Refugee Training. Sponsors African–American Conferences, media workshops and regional conferences and seminars. Maintains a branch office in Washington, DC, and offices in Benin, Burkina Faso, Ghana, Guinea, Madagascar, Mali, Mozambique, Namibia, Nigeria, Senegal, and South Africa.

Geographical Area of Activity: Southern Africa and the USA.

Publications: *Alert; Iroko; Contact: Africa 2002;* Annual Report; also conference reports, art exhibit catalogues, bulletins and educational materials.

Finance: Annual budget approx. $15,000,000.

Principal Staff: Chair. Kofi Appenteng; Pres. Mora McLean.

Address: Chanin Bldg, 380 Lexington Ave, New York, NY 10168-4298.

Telephone: (212) 949-5666; **Fax:** (212) 682-6174; **Internet:** www.aaionline.org; **e-mail:** aainy@aaionline.org.

African Christian Relief, Inc

A Christian relief organization established to provide short-term aid to victims of disaster and civil war; it is now concentrating on more long-term solutions to those in need in both Africa and the USA.

Activities: Provides families in Africa and the USA with food, water, clothing and medical supplies when needed; also runs self-sufficiency programmes to enable the poor to help themselves. Provides aid in times of emergency and disaster, but also concentrates on long-term projects, including developing farming projects and building hospitals in Africa, as well as supporting local projects in the USA, especially concentrating on countering 'gang' culture through mentoring, recreation and outreach programmes. It also offers the opportunity to sponsor children.

Geographical Area of Activity: Africa and the USA.

Address: 7941 East Lakeside Parkway, Suite 109, Tucson, AZ 85730.

Telephone: (520) 722-8447; **Fax:** (520) 298-1404; **Internet:** www.ibs-net.com/acr/index.htm; **e-mail:** acr@ibs-net.com.

African Development Foundation

Established by the US Congress in 1980 as an independent agency, to provide economic assistance to grass-roots communities in Africa.

Activities: Operates in Africa through providing economic development assistance and capacity-building resources in the areas of: agricultural production; micro- and small enterprises; micro-credit; education and training; natural resource management and conservation; travel grants; research; institutional strengthening; and educational outreach, through publications and electronic media. Currently funds projects in Benin, Botswana, Cameroon, Cape Verde, Ghana, Guinea, Lesotho, Mali, Namibia, Niger, Nigeria, Senegal, Tanzania, Uganda and Zimbabwe.

Geographical Area of Activity: Sub-Saharan Africa (specifically Benin, Botswana, Cameroon, Cape Verde, Ghana, Guinea, Lesotho, Mali, Namibia, Niger, Senegal, Tanzania, Uganda and Zimbabwe).

Restrictions: Grants only in those sub-Saharan African countries where the Foundation is active; grants only to registered African NGOs and community-based organizations.

Publications: *Participatory Development: ADF—Funded Projects;* issue papers; project briefs; reports.

Finance: Annual appropriation from US Government $14,400,000 (2000).

Board of Directors: Ernest G. Green (Chair.); Willie Grace Campbell (Vice-Chair.); Nathaniel Fields (Pres.); Claude Allen.

Principal Staff: Pres. Nathaniel Fields.

Address: 1400 Eye St, NW, 10th Floor, Washington, DC 20005-2248.

Telephone: (202) 673-3916; **Fax:** (202) 673-3810; **Internet:** www.adf.gov; **e-mail:** zdft@africaonline.co.za.

African Development Institute

A public policy research institute set up in 1995 to promote the human and material development of Africa.

Activities: The Institute works to promote alternative development strategies through three strategies: problem-oriented research, empowering education, and advocacy of self-reliant and endogenous development policies. Has special consultative status with the Economic and Social Council of the United Nations.

Geographical Area of Activity: Africa.

Publications: *Sankofa* (quarterly newsletter).

Principal Staff: Exec. Dir Kwame Akonor; Pres. Enock Mensah.

Address: POB 1644, New York, NY 10185.

Fax: (201) 461-3871; **Internet:** www.africainstitute.com; **e-mail:** ca498@freenet.buffalo.edu.

African Wildlife Foundation

Founded in 1961 as the African Wildlife Leadership Foundation, adopting its present name in 1982; the Foundation promotes wildlife management and conservation in Africa.

Activities: Operates in the field of conservation and the environment. Maintains field offices in Kenya, Rwanda, South Africa, Tanzania, Uganda and Zimbabwe, and also works in the Democratic Republic of Congo, Mozambique and Zambia collaborating with numerous agencies on environmental conservation projects. Programmes include AWF Heartlands, making land economically and environmentally viable; Conservation Service Centers, offering expertise in business planning, law, entrepreneurship and community economic development; and the Critical Species project, sponsoring research into endangered species in Africa. The Foundation also awards Charlotte Conservation Fellowships to African conservation professionals engaged in post-graduate research.

Geographical Area of Activity: Democratic Republic of Congo, Kenya, Mozambique, Rwanda, South Africa, Tanzania, Uganda, Zambia and Zimbabwe.

Publications: Annual Report.

Finance: Funding from individuals, government and multilateral agencies, foundations and corporations. Total assets $7,546,920 (June 2002); annual revenue $9,309,000, expenditure $9,393,821 (2002).

Trustees: Lelia S. Green (Chair.).

Principal Staff: Pres. and CEO Patrick J. Bergin; Vice-Pres. Programs Helen W. Gichohi.

Address: 1400 16th St, NW, Suite 120, Washington, DC 20036.

Telephone: (202) 939-3333; **Fax:** (202) 939-3332; **Internet:** www.awf.org; **e-mail:** africanwildlife@awf.org.

Africare

Founded in 1971, originally in response to severe droughts in West Africa, now aiming to help families and communities in every major region of Africa.

Activities: Has field offices in 27 countries in Africa, operating development and self-help programmes in the areas of food and nutrition, water, the environment and health. Constructs wells and irrigation systems to produce fresh water, and works on food production and security as well as private-sector development. Africare also provides emergency aid for the victims of natural crises like drought, as well as those brought about by warfare. Currently concerned with the AIDS crisis in Africa, particularly focusing on the plight of AIDS orphans and child sufferers of the disease.

Geographical Area of Activity: Africa.

Publications: *Africare* (on-line newsletter); Annual Report.

Finance: Total assets $59,784,984 (June 2001); annual revenue $35,801,998, expenditure $35,761,264 (2001).

Directors: Nelson R. Mandela (Hon. Chair.); Maria Walker (Hon. Vice-Chair.); George A. Dalley (Chair.); Rev. Yvonne Seon (Vice-Chair.); Clyde B. Richardson (Treas.); Joseph C. Kennedy (Sec.).

Principal Staff: Pres. Julius E. Coles.

Address: Africare House, 440 R St, NW, Washington, DC 20001.

Telephone: (202) 462-3614; **Fax:** (202) 387-1034; **Internet:** www.africare.org; **e-mail:** africare@africare.org.

Afrilife International

Set up to help developing countries and emerging democracies primarily in Africa achieve economic and social well-being. A member of the Lifeline Africa Foundation network.

Activities: Works in programmes in the fields of humanitarian assistance; health education; and health policy research; obtaining and distributing medical supplies, provides staff and volunteers to transfer medical techniques and technology to doctors and medical staff in the host country and provides a forum for discussion of domestic and international health-care policies and issues. Maintains international offices in Kenya, Liberia, Nigeria and Uganda.

Geographical Area of Activity: International, particularly Africa.

Trustees and Officers: Godson Offaro (Chair.); Christian C. Elias (Pres. and CEO); Keche Ogbole (Sec. and Treas.).

Address: 4110 18th St, POB 55280, Washington, DC 20040.

Telephone: (301) 918-9600; **Fax:** (301) 270-6081; **Internet:** www.afrilife.org; **e-mail:** godson@afrilife.org.

Daniele Agostino Foundation

Founded in 1992 by Flavia Robinson to promote the well-being of Mayan women and children.

Activities: Aims to promote the well-being of Mayan women and children through grants to support projects active in the fields of education, health, women's co-operatives and photography.

Geographical Area of Activity: Mainly Mexico and Guatemala.

Restrictions: No grants to individuals.

Finance: Annual expenditure approx. $1,000,000.

Trustees: Flavia Robinson (Pres.); Marshall Robinson (Vice-Pres.); Lorna Opatow (Treas.); Peter de Janosi.

Address: 870 United Nations Plaza, No. 53C, New York, NY 10017.

Fax: (212) 752-1668; **Internet:** www.dafound.org; **e-mail:** da .found@verizon.netkl.

The Ahmanson Foundation

Founded in 1952 by Howard F. Ahmanson, Dorothy G. Sullivan and others for general charitable services.

Activities: Operates mainly in southern California, with emphasis on Los Angeles, in the fields of education, arts and culture, medicine and health, and science and welfare. Types of support include programme support, capital, research, endowment and scholarships.

Geographical Area of Activity: USA (primarily Southern California).

Restrictions: No grants are made to individuals. Grants are made only to organizations that are tax-exempt.

Publications: Annual Report.

Finance: Assets $785,613,000 (2001); grants disbursed $46,574,905 (2000).

Officers and Trustees: Robert H. Ahmanson (Pres.); Leonard E. Walcott (Vice-Pres. and Man. Dir); William H. Ahmanson (Vice-Pres.); Karen A. Hoffman (Sec.); Kristen K. O'Connor (Treas.); William Howard Ahmanson, Jr; Daniel N. Belin; Lloyd E. Cotsen; Robert M. DeKruif; Robert F. Erburu.

Principal Staff: Man. Dir Leonard E. Walcott.

Address: 9215 Wilshire Blvd, Beverly Hills, CA 09210.

Telephone: (310) 278-0770; **e-mail:** koconnor@ theahmansonfoundation.org.

Alavi Foundation

Founded in 1973, and formerly known as the Mostazafan Foundation of New York, with religious, philanthropic and educational aims.

Activities: Operates its own programmes emphasizing research into the Islamic religion; publishes and distributes educational and religious material. Contributes to educational centres and Sunday schools for the teaching of Middle Eastern languages and of the Islamic religion and culture.

Publications: *Fundamentals of Islamic Teachings; A Glance at the Life of Prophet Mohammed.*

Finance: Total assets $82,555,915 (2001); total grants $994,868 (2001).

Officers and Directors: Mohammad Geramian (Pres.); Alireza Ebrahimi (Sec.); Abbas Mirakhor (Treas.); Hoshang Ahmadi; Mehdi Hodjat; Mohammad Pirayandeh.

Address: 500 Fifth Ave, 39th Floor, New York, NY 10110-0397.

Telephone: (212) 944-8333; **Fax:** (212) 921-0325.

Alcoa Foundation

Founded in 1952 by the Aluminum Company of America (Alcoa) to improve the quality of life for people in communities where Alcoa plants or offices are located, and for the public at large.

Activities: Operates nationally and internationally (in countries where Alcoa operates) in the fields of education, the arts, conservation and sustainability, medicine and health, and social welfare. Grants are given to educational institutions for equipment, improvement of facilities, and the provision of fellowships and scholarships. The Foundation also makes grants for cultural events and to health and welfare organizations, hospitals and medical centres, civic and community organizations, and youth organizations. Funds are also available for disaster relief.

Geographical Area of Activity: International.

Restrictions: No grants are made to individuals, other than through the Sons and Daughters Scholarship programme for the children of Alcoa employees, and only certified charitable organizations are considered.

Publications: Annual Report.

Finance: Total assets US $409,678,168 (Dec. 2001); total grants US $21,326,190 (2001).

Officers and Directors: Kathleen W. Buechel (Pres. and Treas.); Grace A. Smith (Sec. and Asst Treas.); R. E. Belda; E. J. Edwards; B. S. Jeremiah; R. B. Kelson; W. E. Leahey, Jr; R. C. Nascimento; G. J. Pizzey; R. F. Slagle.

Principal Staff: Sr Programme Officer Kimberly Hamilton.

Address: Alcoa Corporate Center, 201 Isabella St, Pittsburgh, PA 15212-5858.

Telephone: (412) 553-2348; **Fax:** (412) 553-4532; **Internet:** www.alcoa.com/global/en/community/foundation.asp; **e-mail:** alcoa.foundation@alcoa.com.

George I. Alden Trust

Founded in 1912 by George I. Alden for the promotion of education in schools, colleges or other educational institutes, with a preference for industrial, vocational or professional education; for the promotion of work carried out by the Young Men's Christian Association in Massachusetts; and for the benefit of the Worcester Trade Schools and the Worcester Polytechnic Institute.

Activities: Involved in the fields of higher and vocational education in the USA, through funding, research, conferences, scholarships and endowment funds.

Geographical Area of Activity: USA.

Publications: Annual Report; information brochure.

Finance: Assets $177,000,000 (Dec. 2000); grants disbursed $8,000,000 (2000).

Officers and Trustees: Susan B. Woodbury (Chair.); Warner S. Fletcher (Sec.); Harry G. Bayliss (Treas.).

Address: 370 Main St, 12th Floor, Worcester, MA 01608.

Telephone: (508) 757-9243.

Alliance for International Educational and Cultural Exchange

Formed by a group of US international exchange organizations to create and promote public policies that facilitate international cultural exchanges between the USA and other countries around the world, so as to improve cultural understanding between people of different nations.

Activities: Supports the interests of international exchange organizations in the USA, through advocacy, information services and networking. Also organizes a programme of government relations activities, and provides a place where the issues and concerns of leaders of international exchange groups can be discussed and addressed. It endeavours to inform the public about the importance of the role of international exchange globally, nationally and in terms of individuals.

Geographical Area of Activity: USA.

Publications: *The Policy Monitor* (quarterly journal); *News News News* (bulletin); *Action Alerts; International Exchange Locator: a Resource Directory for Educational and Cultural Exchange* (2000 edition).

Directors: K. Keith (Chair.); M. Assefa (Vice-Chair.); T. Linney (Treas.).

Principal Staff: Exec. Dir M. McCarry; Asst Dir and Sr Policy Specialist J. M. Taiber.

Address: 1776 Massachusetts Ave, NW, Suite 620, Washington, DC 20036-1912.

Telephone: (202) 293-6141; **Fax:** (202) 293-6144; **Internet:** www.alliance-exchange.org; **e-mail:** info@alliance-exchange .org.

Jenifer Altman Foundation

Founded in 1991 by Jenifer Altman.

Activities: Makes grants within the fields of environmental health and mind–body health, primarily supporting work on the impact of endocrine disrupting chemicals and other foetal contaminants on human health and on biodiversity. Also administers the Mitchell Kapor Foundation (q.v.).

Geographical Area of Activity: Europe, Central and South America, Asia and the USA.

Restrictions: No grants to individuals.

Publications: Biennial Report (available on-line); grants list; programme policy statement; application guidelines.

Finance: Assets $20,211,986 (June 2001); grants disbursed $1,163,028 (2001).

Officers and Directors: Michael Lerner (Pres.); Thomas Silk (Sec.); Albert Wells (Treas.); Anne Bartley; Catherine Porter.

Principal Staff: Exec. Dir Marni Rosen.

Address: POB 29209, San Francisco, CA 94129.

Telephone: (415) 561-2182; **Fax:** (415) 561-6480; **Internet:** www.jaf.org; **e-mail:** info@jaf.org.

American Association of University Women Educational Foundation—AAUW

Founded in 1959 by the American Association of University Women to encourage, among the members of the AAUW and the community, the continuation of education beyond college; to enable women scholars to carry on advanced research, study and creative work; to engage in and promote studies and research in education; to provide for the diffusion of knowledge obtained thereby and to foster intellectual and educational growth; to encourage standards of excellence in public school education and in higher education; and to co-operate with other organizations whose purposes and activities are similar.

Activities: Operates nationally and internationally in the field of education. Provides dissertation fellowships for women of the USA; career development grants to graduates wishing to re-enter the workforce, advance or change their careers; community action grants for individual women, AAUW branches and local community-based non-profits for innovative programmes or non-degree research projects promoting equality and education for women and girls; Eleanor Roosevelt teacher fellowships promoting professional development opportunities for women teachers; grants for improving girls' learning opportunities; and selected professions fellowships for women in the USA studying designated degree programmes where participation by women is traditionally low. International Fellowships are awarded for graduate and postgraduate study to women who are not US citizens or permanent residents for study in any country other than their own (these awards are jointly sponsored by the International Federation of University Women). Also makes several prestigious national awards recognizing excellence in achievement and the AAUW Legal Advocacy Fund supports women fighting sex discrimination cases in higher education.

Geographical Area of Activity: International.

Restrictions: Grants only to women.

Publications: Report of operations and financial statement.

Finance: Grants $3,500,000 (2001); international fellowships ranging from $18,000 to $50,000.

Principal Staff: Pres. Mary Ellen Smyth; Dir Nancy Eynon Lark.

Address: 1111 16th St, NW, Washington, DC 20036.

Telephone: (202) 785-7777; **Fax:** (202) 872-1425; **Internet:** www.aauw.org; **e-mail:** foundation@aauw.org.

American Council of Learned Societies—ACLS

Founded in 1919 (incorporated in 1924) for the advancement of humanistic studies in all fields of learning and the maintenance and strengthening of relations among the national societies devoted to such studies.

Activities: The Council comprises 64 American scholarly organizations concerned with the humanities and related social sciences. ACLS Fellowships are offered to US citizens or permanent residents to carry out post-doctoral research in the humanities.

Geographical Area of Activity: International.

Publications: Annual Report; Occasional Paper series; newsletter; and other titles.

Finance: Assets $73,406,517 (Sept. 2001); annual revenue $12,992,160, annual expenditure $12,413,357 (2001).

Officers and Directors: Patricia Meyer Spacks (Chair.); Marshall Cohen (Vice-Chair.); Francis Oakley (Interim Pres.); Fedwa Malti-Douglas (Sec.); Charlotte Kuh (Treas.); and 10 others.

Address: 228 East 45th St, New York, NY 10017-3398.

Telephone: (212) 697-1505; **Fax:** (212) 949-8058; **Internet:** www.acls.org; **e-mail:** grants@acls.org.

American Councils for International Education—ACTR/ACCELS

Originally founded in 1974, as the American Council of Teachers of Russian (ACTR), a non-profit organization working in the fields of education, training and consulting. It became the American Councils for International Education in 1998 and incorporates ACTR and ACCELS (American Council for Collaboration in Education and Language Study). Its aims are to advance the development of teaching materials, training and research in the fields of Russian and English languages, and to strengthen communication between different communities of academics and scholars in language, literature and area studies in the USA and the countries of Eastern Europe, Russia and Central Asia; and to further educational reform through building institutions, training and education, and technical assistance.

Activities: Operates in the field of education, funding academic exchanges, professional training, institution building, research, materials development, technical assistance and consultation. Currently, ACTR is the professional association which focuses on educational, research and training programmes for citizens of the USA, while ACCELS deals with exchanges, training and technical assistance programmes in Eastern Europe, Russia and Central Asia. ACCELS runs over 40 educational programmes in the countries of the former USSR.

Geographical Area of Activity: USA and countries of the former USSR.

Restrictions: Not a grant-maker in its own right, administers government funding.

Publications: Annual Report, specialist videos, papers, journals and books in fields of interest.

Finance: Programmes funded by the US Department of Education, Library of Congress, Governments of Kazakhstan, Kyrgyzstan, Russia and Uzbekistan, the Open Society Institute (OSI, q.v.), and others; total expenditure $43,406,471 (June 2001).

Trustees: Dr R. D. Brecht (Chair.); J. F. Collins; Dr D. E. Davidson; H. M. Fulbright; Dr B.D. Gaines; L. T. Kurlander; P. Merrill; R. Morningstar; E. S. Muskie, Jr; Robert Rose; Dr R. Sagdeev.

Address: 1776 Massachusetts Ave, NW, Suite 700, Washington, DC 20036.

Telephone: (202) 833-7522; **Fax:** (202) 833-7523; **Internet:** www.actr.org; **e-mail:** general@actr.org.

American Express Foundation

Founded in 1954 by the American Express Company and its subsidiaries for charitable purposes in the areas of community service, education and employment, cultural programmes, historic preservation and economic independence.

Activities: Supports projects world-wide within the themes of community service, cultural heritage and economic independence. Projects supported include those involved with the arts and humanities, education, historic conservation, community welfare, minorities, AIDS, drug abuse, child development and welfare, and the disabled. Involved in efforts to create partnerships between public and private organizations, especially in the fields of education, employment and training programmes; and programmes to promote understanding of the world's cultural diversity and heritage. The Foundation aims to promote the development of the tourism industry through its Academies of Travel and Tourism in the USA and its international Travel and Tourism Programme, currently operating in Brazil, Canada, Hong Kong, Hungary, Ireland, Mexico, Russia, South Africa and the United Kingdom.

Geographical Area of Activity: International.

Restrictions: Grants only made to non-profit organizations.

Publications: *Philanthropy at American Express Report*.

Finance: Total assets US $337,567 (2001); total giving US $18,884,619 (2001).

Trustees: Kenneth I. Chenault; Harvey Golub; Jonathan Linen; Thomas Schick; Mary Beth Salerno.

Principal Staff: Pres. Mary Beth Salerno; Sec. and Vice-Pres., International Programmes Cornelia W. Higginson; Dir Terry Savage; Mary Ellen Craig; Priscilla Li; Anna Mariella; Glenda Noel-Doyle; Anne Wickham; Angela Woods.

Address: 200 Vesey St, 48th Floor, New York, NY 10285-4804.

Telephone: (212) 640-5661; **Fax:** (212) 693-1033; **Internet:** www.americanexpress.com/corp/philanthropy.

American Foundation for AIDS Research—amfAR

Founded in 1985 by the merger of the AIDS Medical Foundation and the National AIDS Research Foundation to prevent HIV infection and the death and disease associated with HIV/AIDS and to protect the human rights of all people threatened by HIV/AIDS.

Activities: Raises funds to provide grants and awards to support AIDS research, AIDS prevention and treatment education, and the advocacy of sound AIDS-related public policy. Awards grants to non-profit institutions for basic biomedical and clinical research in fields related to HIV/AIDS and for post-doctoral investigators to study at other institutions.

Geographical Area of Activity: International.

Restrictions: Grants only to non-profit organizations.

Publications: *HIV/AIDS Treatment Directory* (2 a year); *The amfAR Newsletter* (quarterly); Annual Report; reports and brochures.

Finance: Funded through donations from individuals, businesses and foundations. Net assets $18,151,319 (2000–2001); annual revenue $21,522,895, expenditure $19,728,700 (2001).

Directors: M. Krim (Founding Co-Chair. and Chair. of the Board); E. Taylor (Founding Int. Chair.); K. Cole, P. J. Matson (Vice-Chair.); W. Sheft (Treas.); W. D. Zabel (Sec.).

Principal Staff: CEO J. Radwin; Vice-Pres. Communications D. Hernan; Vice-Pres. Clinical Research and Prevention Programmes K. R. Frost; Grants Admin. K. Cozad.

Address: 120 Wall St, 13th Floor, New York, NY 10005-3902.

Telephone: (212) 806-1600; **Fax:** (212) 806-1601; **Internet:** www.amfar.org; **e-mail:** grants@amfar.org.

American Foundation for the Blind, Inc

Founded in 1921 to support visually-impaired people and to educate the general public about blindness.

Activities: Provides educational, vocational, advisory and social services, and publications (including 'talking books') related to blindness; awards a number of scholarships for undergraduate and graduate visually-impaired and blind students, including the Delta Gamma Foundation Florence Margaret Harvey Memorial Scholarship and the Rudolph Dillman Memorial Scholarship for students in the field of rehabilitation or education of blind or visually impaired people, the Gladys C. Anderson Memorial Scholarship and the R. L. Gillette Scholarship for female students studying religious music, classical music or literature, the Karen D. Carsel Memorial Scholarship and the Ferdinand Torres AFB Scholarship for full-time students in economic need, and the Paul W. Ruckes Scholarship for students pursuing a degree in engineering or in computer, physical or life sciences. Also distributes Helen Keller Achievement Awards promoting achievement of individuals who act as role models or improve the quality of life of individuals with visual impairment.

Geographical Area of Activity: USA.

Publications: *Access World: Technology for Consumers with Visual Impairment* (every 2 months); *AFB Directory of Services for Blind and Visually Impaired Persons in the US and Canada; Journal of Visual Impairment and Blindness* (10 a year); *Long Cane News* (2 a year).

Principal Staff: Pres. and Exec. Dir Carl R. Augusto; Exec. Vice-Pres. Walter L. Decker.

Address: 11 Penn Plaza, Suite 300, New York, NY 10001.

Telephone: (212) 502-7600; **Fax:** (212) 502-7777; **Internet:** www.afb.org; **e-mail:** afbinfo@afb.net.

American Foundation for Pharmaceutical Education—AFPE

Founded to provide support for graduate study of pharmaceutical science.

Activities: Funds research and offers grants, fellowships and scholarships in the field of pharmaceutical sciences, particularly pharmaceutics, pharmacology, manufacturing pharmacy, pharmaco-economics and medicinal chemistry. In 2000 the Foundation awarded 17 Gateway Undergraduate Research Scholarships, three First Year Graduate Scholarships, 74 AFPE Pre-Doctoral Fellowships, three Clinical Pharmacy Fellowships in the Biomedical Research Sciences and 15 New Investigators Program for Pharmacy Faculty Grants.

Geographical Area of Activity: USA.

Restrictions: Grants are usually only open to those studying in the USA.

Finance: Total scholarships and grants $794,000 (2000–2001).

Board of Directors: Ernest Mario (Chair.); Frederick W. Telling (Vice-Chair.); Lonnie Hollingsworth (Treas.).

Principal Staff: Pres. Robert M. Bachman; Grants Man. R. M. Probst.

Address: 1 Church St, Suite 202, Rockville, MD 20850-4158.

Telephone: (301) 738-2160; **Fax:** (301) 738-2161; **Internet:** www.afpenet.org; **e-mail:** afpe@worldnet.att.net.

American Friends Service Committee—AFSC

Founded in 1917, AFSC is a Quaker organization which aims to overcome poverty, injustice and strife in the world through practical aid and non-violent means. The work is based on the belief in the good of every person, regardless of race or religion.

Activities: Operates in Africa, Asia, Central and South America and the Caribbean, Eastern Europe, the Middle East and the USA, in the areas of peace-building, conflict resolution, demilitarization, community development, economic and social justice, and supporting youth. It aims to address the root causes of poverty, injustice and conflict, working for relief both through immediate aid and long-term development projects.

Geographical Area of Activity: Africa, Asia, Central and South America and the Caribbean, Eastern Europe, the Middle East and the USA.

Publications: *A Joyful Shout; The Maquiladora Reader: Cross-Border Organizing Since NAFTA; Peacework; AFSC Resource Catalogue; Quaker Service Bulletin* (2 a year for a $10 donation); *Youth & Militarism; Quiet Helpers—Quaker Service in Postwar Germany; Still Pulling Strings: US Military Policy in Latin America and the Caribbean Post-war;* periodicals, regional newsletters, article downloads, booklets, training manuals and videos.

Finance: Assets $210,199,000 (Sept. 2000); annual revenue $38,699,000, expenditure $38,339,000 (2000).

Clerks: Paul Lacey (Presiding Clerk); Phil Lord, John Munson, Susan Waltz (Asst Clerk); James Fletcher (Treas.).

Principal Staff: Gen. Sec. Mary Ellen McNish.

Address: 1501 Cherry St, Philadelphia, PA 19102.

Telephone: (215) 241-7000; **Fax:** (215) 241-7282; **Internet:** www.afsc.org; **e-mail:** afscinfo@afsc.org.

American Health Assistance Foundation

Founded in 1973 to support medical research on age-related and degenerative diseases.

Activities: Offers funding for study in the field of major health issues affecting Americans. Makes grants for research into Alzheimer's Disease, Macular Degeneration, Glaucoma and heart disease and stroke. Also operates a free help line and the Alzheimer's Family Relief Program.

Geographical Area of Activity: International.

Publications: Annual Report; booklets, newsletters and publications in the fields of Alzheimer's Disease, Macular Degeneration, Glaucoma, heart disease and stroke.

Finance: Grants disbursed approx. $2,724,000 (2000).

Directors: E. H. Michaels (Pres.); C. Raymond (Vice-Pres.); E. R. Kuykendall (Treas.); P.J. Feliciano (Sec.); L. Nunez; B. K. Regan; J. Rice.

Principal Staff: Dir of Research Grants Dr Kevin Ryder.

Address: 22512 Gateway Center Drive, Clarksburg, MD 20871.

Telephone: (301) 948-3244; **Fax:** (301) 258-9454; **Internet:** www.ahaf.org; **e-mail:** grants@ahaf.org.

American Heart Association, Inc

Founded in 1948 with the aim of preventing premature strokes and cardiovascular disease.

Activities: The Association awards fellowships for US undergraduate research, and grants-in-aid to support research in the fields of cardiovascular disease and stroke. International Research Fellowships enable researchers who are US citizens or permanent residents to study in foreign institutions, or foreign citizens to study at US institutions. The Association also bestows awards aimed at encouraging clinically trained physicians to pursue careers in cardiovascular and stroke research, as well as supporting stroke survivors and their families.

Geographical Area of Activity: International.

Restrictions: No grants to individuals working at private companies, nor to organizations receiving funding from a different source.

Publications: *Stroke Connection* (bi-monthly magazine).

Finance: Net assets $551,628,586 (June 2002); income $532,404,018, expenditure $531,850,401 (2002).

Directors: J. Walter Sinclair (Chair.); Lynn A Smaha (Pres.); William J. Bryant (Chair.-Elect); Rose Marie Robertson (Pres.-Elect); Richard P. Southworth (Sec. and Treas.); and 36 others.

Principal Staff: CEO M. Cass Wheeler.

Address: National Center, 7272 Greenville Ave, Dallas, TX 75231.

Telephone: (301) 223-2307; **Internet:** www.americanheart.org; **e-mail:** ncrp@amhrt.org.

American Historical Association

Founded in 1884 for the promotion of historical studies, the collection and preservation of historical manuscripts, and the dissemination of historical research.

Activities: Operates mainly nationally in the field of education and historical studies, by supporting research, awarding two major fellowships and a variety of prizes for work on various aspects of history, and issuing publications.

Geographical Area of Activity: USA.

Restrictions: Research grants only made to AHA members.

Publications: *American Historical Review; Perspectives* (newsletter); *Directory of History Departments and Organizations in the United States and Canada* ; Annual Report; essays, studies, doctoral dissertations, details of grants and fellowships for historians.

Finance: Fellowships total approx. $30,000.

Directors: James M. McPherson (Pres.); Jonathan Spence (Pres.-Elect); Lynn Hunt (Past Pres.); William A. Weber (Vice-Pres., Teaching); William J. Cronon (Vice-Pres., Profession); Roy Rosenzweig (Vice-Pres., Research); Myrna Ivonne Wallace Fuentes; Victoria A. Harden; Maureen Murphy Nutting; David Harris Sacks; Stefan A. Tanaka; Quintard Taylor, Jr).

Principal Staff: Exec. Dir Anita A. Jones; Controller Randy Norrell.

Address: 400 A St, SE, Washington, DC 20003-3889.

Telephone: (202) 544-2422; **Fax:** (202) 544-8307; **Internet:** www.theaha.org; **e-mail:** aha@theaha.com.

American Institute of Pakistan Studies

Founded in 1973 by Dr Hafeez Malik, it aims to promote scholarly exchange between the USA and Pakistan and to support research on issues relevant to Pakistan.

Activities: Offers pre-doctoral and post-doctoral research fellowships to scholars who are US citizens and are engaged in research on Pakistan, in all fields of the humanities and social sciences. Also administers lectureships and organizes academic conferences.

Geographical Area of Activity: USA.

Restrictions: Grants only made to US citizens.

Publications: *Pakistan Studies News* (newsletter).

Directors: Brian Spooner (Pres.); Wilma Heston (Treas.); Robert LaPorte (Sec.).

Address: Dept. of Anthropology, University of Pennsylvania, Philadelphia, PA 19104.

Telephone: (215) 898-5207; **Fax:** (215) 898-7462; **Internet:** jsis.artsci.washington.edu/programs/soasia/AIPS/aipshome.htm; **e-mail:** brian@pardis.sas.upenn.edu.

American Jewish Joint Distribution Committee—JDC

Founded in 1914 to distribute funds raised by the Orthodox Central Committee for the Relief of Jews, the American Jewish Relief Committee and the People's Relief Committee; the organization aims to provide aid to Jews in need in a non-partisan and non-political way, in every continent outside North America.

Activities: JDC represents the American Jewish community overseas and works by funding programmes of relief, rescue and reconstruction in a number of countries. It works to ensure that all elderly survivors of the Holocaust are able to live out their lives in dignity; revives and strengthens Jewish communities; and endeavours to help social service concerns in Israel. Shelter, food and health care are provided for those who need it, especially in areas struck by natural disasters and famine, and JDC has sought to rescue many people from areas of conflict, including Jews, Muslims and Christians from Sarajevo during the crisis in the former Yugoslavia (now Serbia and Montenegro). In Israel the current focus is on supporting disadvantaged, abused and neglected children and young people, planning and co-ordinating social services for elderly people and helping the absorption of Jewish immigrants from Ethiopia and the Caucasus and developing self-sufficiency through employment programmes. There are special non-sectarian programmes which aid non-Jews in distress as an expression of the Jewish belief in their responsibility to relieve suffering wherever it exists.

Geographical Area of Activity: International.

Address: POB 321, 847A Second Ave, New York, NY 10017.

Telephone: (212) 885-0852; **Internet:** www.jdc.org; **e-mail:** idp@jdc.org.

American Leprosy Foundation—The Leonard Wood Memorial

Founded by Major General Leonard Wood in 1928, as the Leonard Wood Memorial for the Eradication of Leprosy. The name American Leprosy Foundation was added in 1941. Aims to conduct, maintain and support research and clinical studies working towards the eradication of Hanson's Disease (leprosy).

Activities: Although its administrative offices are in the USA, the Leonard Wood Memorial research centre is based in the Philippines. It carries out clinical and laboratory-based research on treatments, drugs and vaccinations to treat leprosy, tuberculosis and other infectious and non-infectious diseases. The centre consists of three major branches: the Clinical Research Branch, the Skin Clinic and Epidemiology Branch, and the Laboratory Branch.

Restrictions: Not a grant-making organization.

Publications: Numerous specialist publications.

Principal Staff: Asst Dir Roland V. Cellona.

Address: 11600 Nebel St, Suite 210, Rockville, MD 20852.

Telephone: (301) 984-1336; **Fax:** (301) 770-0580; **Internet:** users.erols.com/lwm-alf; **e-mail:** lwm-alf@erols.com.

American Near East Refugee Aid—ANERA

Established in 1968, ANERA works towards improving the lives of the people of the Middle East by reducing poverty and suffering. It aims to address long-term issues relating to Palestinian and Lebanese people, as well as providing emergency aid in time of war.

Activities: ANERA works in various fields in the Middle East, providing humanitarian aid and relief and partial funding to community, micro-credit and environmental services; working with local organizations to improve community services and health care; providing education for all; aiming to increase employment; providing sustainable agricultural solutions; developing infrastructure; and advancing information technology resources.

Geographical Area of Activity: Palestinian Autonomous Areas, Jordan, Lebanon, Israel.

Publications: Annual Report; quarterly newsletter.

Finance: Assets $1,973,987 (2000); annual revenue $7,264,734, expenditure $7,092,496 (1999–2000).

Directors: Peter Gubser (Pres.); Philip Davies and Nina Dodge (Vice-Chair.).

Address: 1522 K St, NW, Suite 202, Washington, DC 20005-1270.

Telephone: (202) 347-2558; **Fax:** (202) 682-1637; **Internet:** www.anera.org; **e-mail:** anera@anera.org.

American Philosophical Society

Founded in 1743 by Benjamin Franklin.

Activities: The Society promotes scholarly research in the sciences and humanities through grants and fellowships. Awards, about 100 of which are made each year, are open to US citizens and to foreign nationals for research in the USA. Other special grants made for research are: Franklin Research Grants, Daland Fellowships in Clinical Investigation, Phillips Grants for Native American Research, Sabbatical Fellowships for the Humanities and Social Sciences; and Library Resident Research Fellowships. The Society holds two annual conferences or symposia and has a library of 180,000 volumes and 5.5 million manuscripts, specializing in the history of science.

Geographical Area of Activity: USA.

Restrictions: Institutions are not eligible to apply. Grants available to residents of the USA or to US citizens abroad. Foreign nationals whose research may only be carried out in the USA may apply. No support is given to pre-doctoral study or research.

Publications: *Proceedings* (quarterly); *Transactions* (bi-monthly monograph series); *Mendel Newsletter* (annual publication); Memoirs; Year Book; News (2 a year).

Finance: Grants disbursed approx. $400,000 annually.

Address: 104 South Fifth St, Philadelphia, PA 19106-3387.

Telephone: (215) 440-3400; **Internet:** www.amphilsoc.org; **e-mail:** eroach@amphilsoc.org.

American Refugee Committee—ARC

Established in 1978 by Neal Ball; a non-profit non-sectarian organization that aims to improve the quality of life of refugees, asylum-seekers and displaced persons, and to enable them to rebuild their lives with dignity and purpose.

Activities: ARC sends medical teams and other specialists to refugee camps in a number of countries, to provide adequate health-care and humanitarian assistance. It runs programmes to improve water and sanitation in refugee camps, teaches shelter repair and construction, gives resettlement advice and assistance, offers micro-credit and vocational training, provides psycho-social services, looks after primary health-care concerns and works towards enabling refugees to return home. Works in collaboration with other international organizations, such as the United Nations High Commissioner for Refugees (UNHCR).

Geographical Area of Activity: International.

Finance: Receives private donations from foundations, corporations and individuals. Assets $3,778,059 (2001); annual expenditure $28,192,527 (2001).

Directors: Mary Tjosvold (Chair.); C. D. Winslow (Recent Past Chair.); S. Cairns, M. J. Howett, Jr (Vice-Chair.); H. Cleveland (Sec.); G. J. Skovholdt (Treas.).

Principal Staff: Pres. Hugh Q. Parmer; Vice-Pres. Joe Bock; Dir, Human Resources Colleen Striegel; Dir, Finance Moses Nyangau; Dir, Int. Operations Huy Pham; Dir, Development Karen Frederickson; Special Asst to the Pres., Planning, Policy and Evaluation Karen Johnson Elshazly.

Address: 430 Oak Grove St, Suite 204, Minneapolis, MN 55403.

Telephone: (612) 872-7060; **Fax:** (612) 607-6499; **Internet:** www.archq.org; **e-mail:** archq@archq.org.

American–Scandinavian Foundation

Founded in 1910 by Niels Poulson to promote international understanding through educational and cultural exchange between the USA and Denmark, Finland, Iceland, Norway and Sweden.

Activities: Awards fellowships and grants, arranges trainee placements and cultural programmes, and issues publications. It makes several awards, including an annual Translation Prize and the triennial Birgit Nilsson Prize.

Geographical Area of Activity: USA and Scandinavia.

Publications: *Scandinavian Review* (3 a year); *The Longboat* (newsletter) *Scan* (quarterly newsletter); *Directory of Fellows;* Annual Report.

Finance: Annual grants approx. £500,000.

Executive Trustees: Kristjan T. Ragnarsson (Chair.); and approx. 100 others.

Principal Staff: Pres. Edward P. Gallagher; Exec. Vice-Pres. Lynn Carter.

Address: Scandinavia House, 58 Park Ave, New York 10016-3007.

Telephone: (212) 879-9779; **Fax:** (212) 686-1157; **Internet:** www.amscan.org; **e-mail:** asf@amscan.org.

American Schools of Oriental Research—ASOR

Founded in 1900 by the Society of Biblical Literature, the Archaeological Institute of America and the American Oriental Society, to support research into the peoples and cultures of the Near East.

Activities: Operates internationally in the fields of education and the humanities by conducting and supporting research into Middle Eastern culture, from earliest times to the present day, especially through archaeological, anthropological and historical projects; runs research institutes in the Near East (the W. F. Albright Institute of Archaeological Research, Jerusalem, the American Center of Oriental Research, Amman and the Cyprus American Archaeological Research Institute, Nicosia); awards research fellowships and publishes the results of research.

Geographical Area of Activity: USA and the Middle East.

Publications: *Bulletin of the American Schools of Oriental Research; ASOR Newsletter; Near Eastern Archaeology; Journal of Cuneiform Studies.*

Trustees: Sidnie White Crawford; Ernest Frerichs; Timothy Harrison; Oystein La Bianca; Oded Borowski; Douglas Clark; Eric Cline; Larry Herr; Martha Joukowsky; P. Kyle McCarter; P. E. MacAllister; Jodi Magness; Eric Meyers; Martin Meyerson; Beth Nakhai; Kevin O'Connell; Martha Risser; Austin Ritters Pach; Jim Poss; Richard Scheuer; Brian Schmidt; Joe Seger; Lydie Shufro; Gough Thompson.

Principal Staff: Chair. P.E. MacAllister; Pres. L. T. Geraty; Sec. J. Strange.

Address: 656 Beacon St, 5th Floor, Boston, MA 02215.

Telephone: (617) 353-6570; **Fax:** (617) 353-6575; **Internet:** www.asor.org; **e-mail:** asor@bu.edu.

AmeriCares Foundation, Inc

Initiated by Robert C. Macauley in 1975, and officially founded in 1982; a private non-profit organization which aims to provide emergency relief and humanitarian assistance internationally, regardless of religion, race or political affiliation.

Activities: Provides victims of famine, war and natural disasters internationally with emergency relief supplies, including medicines, nutritional items, clean water, shelter and clothing. Countries receiving support in 2002 included Democratic Republic of the Congo, Rwanda, Afghanistan and Madagascar. It also operates nationally, supporting long-term health-care and outreach programmes, and has established Camp AmeriKids for children in the USA with life-threatening illnesses.

Geographical Area of Activity: International.

Publications: *AmeriCares World* (quarterly newsletter); Annual Report; financial statements.

Finance: Total assets $51,473,200 (June 2002); annual support of donations and goods worth $414,930,875, expenditure $426,120,702 (2002).

Principal Staff: Founder and Chair. Robert C. Macauley.

Address: 161 Cherry St, New Canaan, CT 06840.

Telephone: (203) 972-5500; **Fax:** (203) 966-6028; **Internet:** www.americares.org; **e-mail:** info@americares.org.

America's Development Foundation—ADF

Founded in 1980, ADF is a private non-profit organization which aims to help the development of democracy throughout the world.

Activities: Operates internationally in 30 countries, across Eastern Europe, Russia, the Middle East, Central America and the Caribbean, and Africa. Provides training, assistance and grants to NGOs in order to strengthen democracy and democratic institutions, promote the development of civil society, and support fundamental human rights. Provides legal aid and advocacy services.

Geographical Area of Activity: International.

Principal Staff: Pres. Michael D. Miller; Vice-Pres. Finance Jay Rios; Vice-Pres. Program Operations Karen K. Diop.

Address: 101 North Union St, Suite 200, Alexandria, Virginia, 22314.

Telephone: (703) 836-2717; **Fax:** (703) 836-3379; **Internet:** www.adfusa.org; **e-mail:** adf@adfusa.org.

Amerind Foundation, Inc

Founded in 1937 by William Shirley Fulton to promote anthropological studies of the native peoples of America, the preservation and conservation of their material culture and the development of related educational programmes.

Activities: Organizes anthropological field research, collections study, seminars and visiting scholar programmes, and co-operates with organizations and individuals engaged in similar work. Maintains an anthropological research facility, archaeological, ethnographic and fine arts museum complex, archaeological site files, photographic collections and a library.

Geographical Area of Activity: USA, Mexico and northern areas of South America.

Restrictions: Grants are made only for advanced seminars and internships.

Publications: *Amerind New World Studies Series*; and other publications.

Finance: Funded through endowment, donations and income earned.

Governing Board: W. D. Fulton (Pres.); P. L. Formo; M. Fulton; G. J. Gumerman; M. W. Hard; P. Johnson; J. W. Moore; L. Schiever.

Principal Staff: Dir Dr John A. Ware.

Address: 2100 N. Amerind Rd, POB 400, Dragoon, AZ 85609.

Telephone: (520) 586-3666; **Fax:** (520) 586-4679; **Internet:** www.amerind.org; **e-mail:** amerind@amerind.org.

AMIDEAST—America–Mideast Educational and Training Services, Inc.

International NGO founded in 1951 by Dorothy Thompson to strengthen mutual understanding and co-operation between Americans and peoples of the Middle East and North Africa.

Activities: Operates in the fields of education, educational exchange and training, through projects funded by the US and foreign governments, individuals and foundations. Organizes conferences, engages in institution-building, short- and long-term English language training, exchange programmes and scholarship management. Maintains a network of field offices in the Middle East and North Africa.

Geographical Area of Activity: USA, the Middle East and North Africa.

Restrictions: Not a grant-making organization.

Publications: *The Advising Quarterly*; and educational resources.

Finance: Assets $9,069,823 (2001); annual revenue $29,864,200, expenditure $25,641,622 (2001).

Directors: Dr Mary Gray (Chair.).

Principal Staff: CEO and Pres. Amb. William A. Rugh; Sr Vice-Pres., Programmes Diana L. Kamal; Sr Vice-Pres., Finance William J. Benz.

Address: 1730 M St, NW, Suite 1100, Washington, DC 20036-4505.

Telephone: (202) 776-9600; **Fax:** (202) 776-7000; **Internet:** www.amideast.org; **e-mail:** inquiries@amideast.org.

Ananda Marga Universal Relief Team—AMURT

Founded in India in 1965, AMURT works towards improving the quality of life of the poor and underprivileged and offering long-term solutions to break the poverty cycle; it aims to provide opportunities for everyone regardless of race, religion, sex or social status. It also provides emergency supplies for victims of natural and man-made disasters.

Activities: Works towards mitigating the effects of poverty and developing local solutions in more than 40 countries world-wide in the fields of education, health, micro-enterprise and community development. AMURT field officers are based in the area for which they work, helping to provide both short- and long-term solutions to poverty-related problems and assistance for disaster victims. A sister organization, AMURTEL, established in 1975, concentrates on the problems affecting women and children.

Geographical Area of Activity: Asia, Africa, Europe and the Americas.

Principal Staff: Exec. Dir Clark Forden; Prog. Dir Peter Sage.

Address: 7627 16th St, NW, Washington, DC 20012.

Telephone: (202) 829-8676; **Fax:** (202) 829-0462; **Internet:** www.amurt.net; **e-mail:** amurtglobal@amurt.net.

Annenberg Foundation

Founded in 1989 by Walter H. Annenberg, who died in 2002, for general charitable purposes.

Activities: Operates mainly in the fields of education, especially early childhood and pre-collegiate education and cultural programmes, primarily in the USA.

Geographical Area of Activity: Primarily USA.

Restrictions: Unsolicited requests from organizations outside the USA are not accepted; no grants are made to individuals; no grants for scholarships or book publications.

Publications: Application Guidelines.

Finance: Assets $2,755,835,168 (June 2000); annual expenditure $133,487,973 (2000).

Officers and Trustees: Leonore A. Annenberg (Pres. and Chair.); Wallis Annenberg (Vice-Pres.); Gail C. Levin (Sec.); Charles Weingarten; Gregory Weingarten; Lauren Weingarten Bon.

Principal Staff: Exec. Dir Dr Gail C. Levin.

Address: St Davids Center, 150 Radnor-Chester Rd, Ste A-200, St Davids, PA 19087.

Telephone: (610) 341-9066; **Internet:** www.annenbergfoundation.org; **e-mail:** info@whannenberg.org.

Anti-Defamation League of B'nai B'rith—ADL

Founded in 1913, to counter the defamation of Jewish people; aims to identify and combat anti-semitic and bigoted sentiments, and promote democratic ideals and civil rights for all.

Activities: Operates internationally through carrying out research on and monitoring anti-semitic and racist groups all over the world, and disseminating information. Also serves as a resource for governments, media and the public, runs courses educating people about the Holocaust and related issues, and works towards safeguarding religious liberty in the world. Carries out an annual audit of anti-semitic incidents. Also supports peace talks in the Middle East. Maintains offices throughout the USA, and in Israel, Austria (for Central and Eastern Europe) and the Russian Federation. Established the Dore Schary Awards in 1982 in honour of ADL's former chairman, which are made to student film and video productions dealing with the themes of hatred, bigotry, racism, anti-semitism, prejudice or discrimination and diversity.

Geographical Area of Activity: International.

Restrictions: Only runs one award scheme, otherwise no grants are made.

Finance: Dore Schary Awards total $4,000 annually.

Address: 823 United Nations Plaza, New York, NY 10017.

Internet: www.adl.org; **e-mail:** webmaster@adl.org.

Arca Foundation

Founded in 1952 by Nancy S. Reynolds to promote the well-being of humanity throughout the world.

Activities: Addresses both international and domestic issues. Seeks to influence public policy, especially economic and political issues in the USA. Supports projects in Central and South America and the Caribbean which promote a foreign policy based on respect for human rights, national sovereignty and international law. Currently focusing on US policy towards Cuba, reform of political party funding, education, fighting deterioration in conditions for working people, capital punishment, and the need for strong coalitions to create equality for all individuals in society.

Geographical Area of Activity: USA, and Central and South America and the Caribbean.

Restrictions: Does not extend grants to direct social services or research fellowships. No grants made to individuals, groups outside the USA, scholarship funds or scholarly research, government programmes, nor to capital projects/endowments.

Publications: Annual Report.

Finance: Assets $67,676,327 (Dec. 2001); annual revenue $1,890,372, expenditure $3,060,917 (2001).

Officers and Directors: Smith W. Bagley (Pres.); Nancy R. Bagley, Ellsworth Culver (Vice-Pres); Mary E. King (Sec.); Eric Sklar (Treas.); Nicole L. Bagley; Mike Lux; Janet Shenk; Margery A. Tabankin.

Principal Staff: Exec. Dir D. F. Edwards; Programme Assoc. B. Roberts; Admin. C. Gamerman; Admin. Asst. N. Prichard.

Address: 1308 19th St, NW, Washington, DC 20036.

Telephone: (202) 822-9193; **Fax:** (202) 785-1446; **Internet:** www.arcafoundation.org; **e-mail:** grants@arcafoundation.org.

Arthritis Foundation

Founded in 1948 to improve lives through leadership in the prevention, control and cure of arthritis and related diseases.

Activities: Operates nationally in the fields of education, science and medicine, through self-conducted programmes, research, grants to institutions and individuals, fellowships, scholarships, conferences, courses, publications and lectures. Five key areas of work are: increasing funding to arthritis-related research; building awareness; empowering health actions, through involving everyone in healthy behaviour; influencing national health policy; and exploring all possible research angles. Awards the Russell L. Cecil Arthritis Medical Journalism Awards, the Arthritis Investigator Award and the Segal Clinical Scientist Grants for Osteoarthritis Biomarkers. Has made awards totalling over $244,000,000 since it was founded.

Geographical Area of Activity: USA.

Publications: *Arthritis Today* (every 2 months); Annual Report; and numerous publications on the care and treatment of arthritis.

Finance: Total assets $191,282,448 (2001); total revenue $132,669,290, total expenditure $140,047,232 (2001).

Board of Trustees: Carol L. Climas (Chair); Leigh F. Callahan (Senior Vice-Chair); Robert F. Meenan (Sec.); Pattye T. Moore (Treas.); Edith H. Nixon, Laura Robbins, Michael J. Stewart, Norine M. Walker, Ronald G. Wilson (Vice-Chair.).

Principal Staff: Pres. and CEO Tina J. Mantella.

Address: 1330 West Peachtree St, Atlanta, GA 30309.

Telephone: (404) 872-7100; **Fax:** (404) 877-3170; **Internet:** www.arthritis.org; **e-mail:** researchhelp@arthritis.org.

Asia Foundation

Established in 1954, the Foundation is a private, non-profit NGO dedicated to advancing the mutual interests of the USA and the Asia-Pacific region.

Activities: Operates in four main areas: governance, law and civil society; economic reform and development; women's political participation; and international relations, through collaboration with partner organizations from the public and private sectors to support institutional development, exchanges and dialogue, technical assistance, research and policy engagement. The Foundation maintains a network of 14 offices throughout Asia, as well as an office in Washington, DC. In 2001 launched the Give2Asia fundraising initiative.

Geographical Area of Activity: USA and the Asia-Pacific region.

Publications: Annual Report; *Asian Perspectives Series; Program Profiles;* Project List.

Finance: Assets $33,705,000 (2002); total revenue $68,146,000, expenditure $61,166,000 (2002).

Officers and Directors: William P. Fuller (Pres.); William L. Ball, III (Chair.); Michael H. Armacost (Vice-Chair.); Gordon Hein (Vice-Pres., Programmes); Peter S. Slawson (Treas.); Susan J. Pharr (Sec.).

Principal Staff: Pres. William P. Fuller; Vice-Pres. and Dir Nancy Yuan.

Address: 465 California St, 14th Floor, San Francisco, CA 94104.

Telephone: (415) 982-4640; **Fax:** (415) 392-8863; **Internet:** www.asiafoundation.org; **e-mail:** info@asiafound.org.

Asia Society

Founded in 1956, by John D. Rockefeller, III, the Asia Society is a non-profit, non-political organization which aims to promote understanding between Asia and the USA and to improve communications and relations between the USA and Pacific-Asia.

Activities: Sponsors programmes and conferences throughout both the USA and Asia to spread awareness of issues affecting Asia. The programmes cover contemporary affairs, corporate issues, cultural matters and education, and the Asia Society funds conferences dealing with politics, economics and policies regarding relations between Asia and the USA.

Geographical Area of Activity: USA, South-East Asia and Australia.

Publications: Publishes books, reports and catalogues that cover arts and culture, politics and society, and education.

Finance: Funding from individuals, institutions and foundations.

Board of Trustees: Richard C. Holbrooke (Chair.); Ronnie C. Chan (Vice-Chair.); Henry Cornell (Treas.); Susan E. Lynch (Sec.).

Principal Staff: Pres. N. Platt; Exec. Vice-Pres. and Dir of Museum and Cultural Programmes Vishakha N. Desai.

Address: 725 Park Ave, New York, NY 10021.

Telephone: (212) 288-6400; **Fax:** (212) 517-8315; **Internet:** www.asiasociety.org; **e-mail:** info@asiasociety.org.

Asian Cultural Council

Founded in 1963 by John D. Rockefeller, III, and originally known as the JDR 3rd Program, it has been formally affiliated to the Rockefeller Brothers Fund (q.v.) since 1991. It was established to support cultural exchange in the visual and performing arts between the USA and Asia. The Asian Cultural Council received some initial support for administrative expenses from the JDR 3rd Fund, but has to raise funds for grant programmes from other foundations, government agencies, corporations and individuals.

Activities: The emphasis of the grant programme of the Council is on providing individual fellowship awards to artists, scholars, students and specialists in the visual and performing arts for research, travel, study and creative work involving cultural exchange between Asia and the USA. A limited number of grants is also made to arts organizations and educational institutions for specific projects of Asian American cultural exchange. As funds are limited, priority consideration is currently given to individuals in East and South-East Asia seeking grant assistance for research, travel, study, training or creative activity in the USA. The geographic purview of the Council comprises those countries of Asia extending from Pakistan eastwards to Japan. Has additional offices in Taiwan, Hong Kong and Japan.

Geographical Area of Activity: Mainly Asia.

Restrictions: No grants to individuals for lecture programmes, personal exhibitions, individual performance tours, undergraduate studies, nor for activities by individuals within their home countries. No grants to organizations for publications, film and video productions, capital campaigns or general programme or administrative costs.

Publications: Annual Report; information brochure.

Finance: Receives donations from foundations, companies and individuals.

Officers and Trustees: E. J. McCormack (Chair.); R. S. Lanier (Pres.); R. A. Phillips, Jr (Vice-Pres. and Sec.); I. Shapiro (Treas.); R. M. Bliss; C. G. Campbell; K. H. C. Fung; J. Natori; A. M. O'Neill; R. S. Pirie; D. Rockefeller, Jr; S. C. Rockefeller; M. I. Sovern; S. Tsutsumi.

Principal Staff: Dir Ralph Samuelson.

Address: 437 Madison Ave, 37th Floor, New York, NY 10022-7001.

Telephone: (212) 812-4300; **Fax:** (212) 812-4299; **Internet:** www.asianculturalcouncil.org; **e-mail:** acc@accny.org.

Aspen Institute

Founded in 1950 as a global forum for world leaders and policy-makers to discuss issues affecting the human condition.

Activities: Runs a series of Seminar Programs and Policy Programs aimed at encouraging corporate leaders to act responsibly and providing the forum for debates on domestic and international issues ranging from the growth of micro-enterprises to the control of nuclear weapons. Operates internationally through a network of partner organizations in Europe and Asia.

Geographical Area of Activity: International.

Restrictions: Not a grant-making organization.

Publications: *Aspen Peaks* .

Finance: Total assets $82,151,714 (2001); annual revenue $37,154,925, expenditure $40,134,503 (2001).

Board of Trustees: William E. Mayer (Chair.); Elmer W. Johnson (Pres.); Henry E. Catto, Lester Crown (Vice-Chair.); Linda M. Lentz (Sec.).

Address: 1000 North 3rd St, Aspen, CO 81611.

Telephone: (970) 925-7010; **Fax:** (970) 925-4188; **Internet:** www.aspeninst.org; **e-mail:** info@aspeninstitute.org.

Association for Progressive Communications—APC

(La Asociación para el Progreso de las Comunicaciones)

An internet network established in 1990 by a group of seven computer networks from around the world in order to promote and facilitate the use of information and communications technologies by groups and individuals working in the areas of human rights, environmental protection and peace, in order to use the internet to further the development of civil society.

Activities: APC operates in various areas: the promotion of non-commercial internet space for NGOs; network development, aiding existing communication service providers to expand; women, promoting gender-aware web design and use; improving networking capabilities in Africa; information dissemination; and special projects, including the APC Betinho Prize of $7,500 awarded to groups or NGOs in any country that have used information and communication technology significantly and successfully in development work. APC has member internet networks world-wide and the directorate is based in South Africa.

Geographical Area of Activity: International.

Publications: *APCNews* (monthly newsletter); numerous other publications.

Principal Staff: Chair. S. Hackenthal; Vice-Chair. M. Sigillito; Sec. J. Casasbuenas; Treas. K. Banks.

Address: Presidio Bldg 1012, Torney Ave, POB 29904, San Francisco, CA 94129.

Telephone: (416) 516-8138; **Fax:** (416) 516-0131; **Internet:** www.apc.org; **e-mail:** apcadmin@apc.org.

Atkinson Foundation

Founded in 1939 by George H. Atkinson and Mildred M. Atkinson for general charitable purposes.

Activities: Priority areas of interest are: tax-exempt, not-for-profit organizations, mainly in San Mateo County, California, working in the areas of the disadvantaged, the homeless, child welfare, family planning, the disabled, education, welfare and AIDS; and international development, technical assistance, population and health education projects in Mexico, Central America and the Caribbean.

Geographical Area of Activity: USA, and Central and South America and the Caribbean.

Restrictions: The Foundation does not give directly to individuals, nor does it finance research and grants are only made to US 501c3 tax-exempt organizations.

Publications: Annual Report.

Finance: Assets $15,711,379 (2002); grants expenditure $624,500 (2002).

Officers and Directors: Duane E. Atkinson (Pres.); Ray N. Atkinson, Thomas J. Henderson (Vice-Pres); James C. Ingwersen (Sec.); John E. Herrell (Treas.); Elizabeth H. Curtis (Admin.); Linda L. Lanier.

Principal Staff: Admin. Elizabeth H. Curtis.

Address: 1100 Grundy Lane, Suite 140, San Bruno, CA 94066-3030.

Telephone and Fax: (650) 876-0222.

AT&T Foundation

Founded in 1984 by AT&T Corp. (q.v.) as a philanthropic organization dedicated to the support of education, arts and culture and civic and community services nationally and internationally.

Activities: Operates in the fields of education, arts and culture, and civic and community service, and provides 25% of its budget to a local grants initiative, operated by local offices supporting communities in their area. Within the field of education, support is given to projects focusing on the use of technology to enhance teaching and learning, and promoting family involvement in education, providing professional development opportunities for educators and promoting lifelong learning and community collaboration. Civic and community service programme grants are given to health services for those in need, diversity in the workplace, environmental projects, national US organizations conducting public policy research, and projects enhancing the effectiveness of the voluntary sector. The arts and culture programme assists the production and creation of new artistic work, brings the work of women artists and artists of diverse cultures to a wider public, and mobilizes new technologies to promote artistic innovation and increase access to the arts. Local grants are given within areas where the company operates or has a significant presence.

Geographical Area of Activity: International, including Argentina, Australia, Brazil, Canada, Chile, China, Colombia, Denmark, France, Germany, Hong Kong, Japan, Mexico, Netherlands, New Zealand, Peru, Puerto Rico, South Africa, Spain, Sweden, Taiwan, the United Kingdom and the USA.

Restrictions: No support for individuals; campaigning or political organizations; endowments or memorials; construction or renovation projects; sports teams or sports-related activities or competitions; fundraising events; or advertising. Rarely responds to unsolicited requests for support.

Publications: Biennial Report.

Finance: Assets $48,824,236 (2001); charitable expenditure $44,196,080 (2001).

Officers and Trustees: Richard J. Martin (Chair.); Esther Silver-Parker (Pres.); Robert E. Angelica (Treas.); Adele Ambrose; Harold W. Burlingame; David P. Condit; Regina Egea; Curt Fields; David Grain; Timothy J. McClimon; Vivian Nero; Barbara Peda; Rob Stoddard; Steve Van Dorselaer.

Principal Staff: Exec. Dir Timothy J. McClimon; Operation Dir and Sec. Vivian Nero; Vice-Pres. Marilyn Reznick; Vice-Pres. Suzanne Sato; Vice-Pres. Mitzi Vaimberg.

Address: 32 Ave of the Americas, 24th Floor, New York, NY 10013.

Telephone: (212) 387-4801; **Fax:** (212) 387-4882; **Internet:** www.att.com/foundation; **e-mail:** Mcclimon@att.com.

Ayala Foundation USA

Established in 2000 to build links between Filipino communities in the USA and the Philippines. Linked to the Ayala Foundation in the Philippines (q.v.).

Activities: Assists the development of philanthropic giving for the Philippines in partnership with individuals and organizations/networks of Filipinos in the USA. Aims to increase awareness of socio-economic issues affecting poverty, hunger, illiteracy, environmental degradation and homelessness. Raises funds to support projects in the Philippines including assistance to poor communities; education, technological and business skills development to help economically disadvantaged young people and adults to find employment; and enhancing cultural, historical and environmental conservation awareness through communication, publication and governance.

Geographical Area of Activity: USA and the Philippines.

Restrictions: Grants are made in the Philippines to non-profit organizations engaged in social development.

Finance: Assets $78,577 (2002); annual expenditure $192,573 (2002).

Principal Staff: Exec. Dir Myrna Roberta H. Araneta.

Address: 255 Shoreline Dr., Suite 128, Redwood City, CA 94065.

Telephone: (650) 598-3126; **Fax:** (650) 508-8988; **Internet:** www.ayalafdnusa.org; **e-mail:** info@ayalafoundation.org.

Francis Bacon Foundation, Inc

Founded in 1938 by Walter Conrad Arensberg and Louise Stevens Arensberg to conduct and promote research in history, philosophy, science and literature, with special reference to the life and works of Francis Bacon, and his influence on his own and succeeding times; to make grants to colleges and universities; and to create and operate a library for those purposes.

Activities: Operates in the fields of education and the arts and humanities, nationally through self-conducted programmes, grants to institutions, particularly in southern California, conferences and courses, and both nationally and internationally through publications and lectures. Awards

Visiting Professorships and Lectureships in the Humanities to smaller colleges and universities to enable them to attract outstanding scholars. Maintains a library.

Geographical Area of Activity: USA.

Publications: Annual Report.

Finance: Assets $3,899,268 (2001); grants disbursed $158,300 (2001).

Trustees: Elizabeth S. Wrigley (Pres.); John Niven (Vice-Pres.); Emrys J. Ross (Sec. and Treas.); Henry J. Gibbons; Jack T. Ryburn.

Principal Staff: Contact Corene Pindroh.

Address: 100E Corson St, Suite 200, Pasadena, CA 91103-3841.

Telephone: (626) 795-5894; **Fax:** (626) 795-1015.

François-Xavier Bagnoud US Foundation (Fondation François-Xavier Bagnoud)

Established by Countess Albina du Boisrouvray, her family and friends, in memory of her son, François-Xavier Bagnoud.

Activities: Operates internationally in the areas of health and welfare, science and technology, and education. The Foundation established the François-Xavier Bagnoud Center for Health and Human Rights at Harvard University School of Public Health in 1992; it has funded a Chair in Aerospace Engineering at the University of Michigan College of Engineering; and awards the $250,000 François-Xavier Bagnoud Aerospace Prize. Through the Association François-Xavier Bagnoud, which it finances with donations of approximately $5,000,000 annually, the Foundation supports homes for sick, abandoned and/or HIV-infected young children in the USA, Brazil, Colombia, India, Thailand and Uganda, and projects for the welfare of orphaned children in Rwanda.

Geographical Area of Activity: International.

Restrictions: Grants are made only to pre-selected organizations, and no grants are made to individuals.

Finance: Total assets $593,739 (2000); total grants $569,983 (2000).

Principal Staff: Exec. Dir Donald Casey.

Address: 350 Madison Ave, 16th Floor, New York, NY 10017-3700.

Telephone: (212) 849-8112; **Fax:** (212) 849-8113; **Internet:** www.fxbfoundation.org/about.htm; **e-mail:** info@fxb.org.

Baltic–American Partnership Fund—BAPF

Established in 1998 by the United States Agency for International Development (USAID) and the Open Society Institute (q.v.) to support the continued development of democratic institutions and market economies in the Baltic states by improving the sense of civic ownership and increasing individual capacity to participate effectively in political and economic decision-making.

Activities: Sub-grantees were selected to implement the Fund's programmes: the Open Estonia Foundation, the Soros Foundation–Latvia and the Open Society Fund Lithuania (q.q.v.), for their long-term track records in civil society development and the promotion of positive social change. Each foundation has established a Baltic–American Partnership Program—BAPP, advised by a local expert council, and managed by a local programme officer. Based upon the Fund's overall strategy, set by its board and in dialogue with the Open Society Foundation boards, the BAPP local councils and staff develop the annual programme plans for their countries. Funds of $15,000,000 were to be used over a ten-year period to support projects in collaboration with other donors. Support is provided for the institutional development of non-profit organizations and for initiatives strengthening the legal and regulatory framework in which non-profit organizations function.

Geographical Area of Activity: Baltic countries (Estonia, Latvia and Lithuania).

Publications: Annual Report.

Finance: Start-up fund of $15,000,000 (USAID and the Open Society Institute each contributed $7,500,000 over a ten year period).

Directors: Juris Padegs (Chair.); Stephen J. Del Rosso, Jr; Deborah A. Harding; Robert A. Kushen; William S. Moody; Lawrence P. Taylor; Jane M. Wales; Michaela L. Walsh.

Principal Staff: Exec. Dir Rebecca Tolson.

Address: 925 Ninth Ave, New York, NY 10019.

Telephone: (212) 548-0319; **Fax:** 9212) 547-6901; **Internet:** www.bapf.org; **e-mail:** bapf@bapf.org.

Bank of America Foundation

Founded in 1998 by the Bank of America Corpn, to fund private, non-profit, tax-exempt organizations providing services to communities nationally and internationally in areas where the company operates.

Activities: Support is given through grants, investments and loans within three main areas: providing educational opportunites; building inclusive communities and promoting cultural outreach, including economic development and environmental awareness; and arts and culture. A Volunteer Grants Program supports non-profit organizations where company associates volunteer their time; education grants are made to a variety of learning, educator development and literacy projects; and the Joe Martin Scholarship Program offers financial assistance to students who are dependants of company employees.

Geographical Area of Activity: USA and areas where the Bank of America Corpn operates.

Publications: Programme policy statement.

Finance: Total assets US $2,212,307 (2000); total giving US $85,755,841 (2000).

Officers and Trustees: Kenneth D. Lewis (Chair. and CEO); Lynn E. Drury (Pres. and Exec. Dir); James S. Wagele (Vice-Pres.); Sandra Cohen (Sec.); John Fatheree (Treas.); Judy Tufo (Financial Officer); Kathleen Burke; David Coulter; William Goodyear; Raymond McKee; Michael O'Neill.

Principal Staff: CEO Kenneth D. Lewis; Dir., Admin. Mike Sweeney.

Address: 100 North Tryon St, Charlotte, NC 28255-0001.

Telephone: (888) 488-9802; **Internet:** www.bankofamerica .com/foundation.

Baptist World Aid

Established to work in the field of international relief and development. It is a division of the Baptist World Alliance.

Activities: Operates, without regard to race or religion, in famine, disaster and refugee relief work. Funds long-term development programmes in the areas of training in self-sufficiency, agriculture, health and education in developing countries. It also offers fellowship assistance to Baptists across the world.

Geographical Area of Activity: International.

Finance: Funded by individuals and member churches.

Principal Staff: Dir Paul Montacute.

Address: 405 North Washington St, Falls Church, VA 22046.

Telephone: (703) 790-8980; **Fax:** (703) 893-5160; **Internet:** www.bwanet.org; **e-mail:** bwa@bwanet.org.

Beldon Fund

Established to promote the protection of the environment in the USA.

Activities: Operates nationally in the area of conservation and the environment, through making grants to non-profit organizations. The Fund's three major programmes concentrate on Human Health and the Environment, focusing on New Advocates, Human Exposure to Toxic Chemicals and Environmental Justice; Corporate Campaigns, seeking to combat corporate efforts to block the development of a national consensus on the environment; and the Key States programme, organizing a consensus on environmental protection to put to policy makers. A separate fund exists for discretionary grants outside these areas, as well as a dedicated fund, now known as the Belvedere Fund, which is held by the Rockefeller Family Fund.

Geographical Area of Activity: USA.

Restrictions: Does not make grants to individuals, nor for scholarships.

Finance: Total assets $87,613,861 (Dec. 2001); total grants $11,574,645 (2001).

Board of Directors: John Hunting (Pres., Chair., Treas.); Roger Milliken, Jr (Vice-Chair.); Holly Schadler (Sec., Gen. Counsel); Patricia Bauman; Ann Fowler Wallace; Wade Greene; Gene Karpinski; Lael Stegall.

Principal Staff: Exec. Dir Bill Roberts; Chief Operating Officer Azade Ardali; Man. Javier Sanchez; Office Man. Angie Velez; Grants Man. Holeri Faruolo.

Address: 99 Madison Ave, 8th Floor, (Cross St 29th St), New York, NY 10016.

Telephone: (212) 616-5600; **Fax:** (212) 616-5656; **Internet:** www.beldon.org; **e-mail:** info@beldon.org.

Benton Foundation

Founded in 1981, following the principles of William Benton relating to the use of communications to benefit society and help solve social problems.

Activities: The Foundation works in three areas in order to achieve its objectives: it defines and advocates public policies which recognize new media's capacity for working in the public interest; helps NGOs use the media and communications technologies to best provide information for the public; and works to create internet-based 'knowledge networks' which are accessible sources of information for non-profit action groups, journalists and educators. Established the Richard M. Neustadt Center for Communications in the Public Interest.

Publications: *Technology Literacy Benchmarks for Non-profit Organizations; Benton Foundation 20 Year Report; Youth Activism and Global Engagement; Networking for Better Care: Health Care in the Information Age; Native Networking: Telecommunications and Information Technology in Indian Country; Losing Ground Bit by Bit: Low-Income Communities in the Information Age; Effective Language for Discussing Early Childhood Education and Policy; Universal Service: A Historical Perspective and Policies for the 21st Century;* and others.

Finance: Funded by an endowment, and by other foundations and trusts. Total assets $15,019,043 (2001).

Directors: Charles Benton (Chair.); Worth Bruntjen (Treas.); Henry Rivera (Gen. Counsel); Marjorie C. Benton; Shelley Benton; Elizabeth Daley; Terry Goddard; Harold A. Richman; Terry T. Saario; Jorge R. Schement; Leonard Schrager; Andrea L. Taylor.

Principal Staff: Pres. Andrea L. Taylor; Exec. Vice-Pres. Karen Menichelli.

Address: 1625 K St, NW, 11th Floor, Washington, DC 20006.

Telephone: (202) 638-5770; **Fax:** (202) 638-5771; **Internet:** www.benton.org; **e-mail:** benton@benton.org.

Better World Fund

Established in 1997 along with its sister organization, the United Nations Foundation (q.v.), following a gift of $1,000,000,000 to the United Nations by R. E. (Ted) Turner; the Fund aims to promote the United Nations through supporting projects designed to inform the public world-wide about the organization's economic, social, environmental and humanitarian work.

Activities: Conducts and finances projects such as the Better World Campaign, aimed at educating the public about the work and role of the United Nations in addressing global issues, and building public support for the organization, in particular highlighting the UN's work to strengthen international security through global co-operation. In conjunction with the United Nations Foundation, the Fund sponsors the daily *UN Wire* news summary on United Nations and global affairs.

Geographical Area of Activity: International.

Publications: Campaign fact sheets.

Address: 1225 Connecticut Ave, NW, 4th Floor, Washington, DC 20036-1868.

Telephone: (202) 462-4900; **Fax:** (202) 462-2686; **Internet:** www.betterworldfund.org.

Blue Moon Fund

Founded in 1944 by W. Alton Jones to promote environmental conservation and world peace.

Activities: The Foundation provides grants to organizations concerned with the protection of environmental resources from pollution, animal and plant conservation, and the prevention of nuclear war. In 2002 the Foundation began a restructuring process, whereby the endowment of the Foundation was to be distributed among three new foundations, the aims and grant application guidelines for which were, in May 2002, being developed. Commitments to existing grantees of the Foundation were to be honoured.

Geographical Area of Activity: International.

Restrictions: No grants are made to individuals, for building construction, endowment funds, basic research, scholarships, fellowships, international exchanges or conferences.

Publications: Annual Report.

Finance: Assets $426,534,443 (1999).

Officers and Trustees: Patricia Jones Edgerton (Pres.); Bradford W. Edgerton (Vice-Pres.); Diane Edgerton Miller (Vice-Pres.); James R. Cameron (Sec.); William A. Edgerton (Treas.); Bernard F. Curry; James S. Bennett; Scott McVay.

Principal Staff: Dir J. P. Myers.

Address: 232 East High St, Charlotteville, VA 22902.

Telephone: (804) 295-2134; **Fax:** (804) 295-1648; **Internet:** www.wajones.org; **e-mail:** grants@wajones.org.

BP Foundation, Inc

Founded in 1952 by Amoco Corporation for charitable, educational and general purposes; formerly known as the BP Amoco Foundation, Inc.

Activities: Concentrates support on projects with Amoco employee involvement and humanitarian aid following natural disasters in areas of the world in which Amoco Corporation and its subsidiaries have commercial activities.

Geographical Area of Activity: International.

Restrictions: Grants only for areas in which Amoco Corporation have commercial activities. Amoco will not accept unsolicited applications for grants.

Publications: Annual Report.

Finance: Assets $75,646,774 (2001); grants expenditure $38,840,397 (2001).

Officers and Directors: George S. Spindler (Chair.); Paula Banks (Pres.); Annie Smith (Sec.); John S. Ruey (Treas.); J. E. Boyajian; J. L. Carl; Inge Freitheim; M. P. Johnson; R. L. McNeel; D. F. Work.

Principal Staff: Sec. Catherine M. Baker.

Address: 200 East Randolph Dr., Chicago, IL 60601.

Telephone: (312) 856-6306; **Fax:** (312) 616-0826; **Internet:** www.bpamoco.com; **e-mail:** foundation@bpamoco.com.

Lynde and Harry Bradley Foundation, Inc

Founded in 1942 as the Allen-Bradley Foundation, Inc to support local and national initiatives. Present name adopted in 1985.

Activities: The Foundation operates locally in the fields of the arts, education, medicine and health care, social welfare and public policy. Support is given to US organizations involved in research into national and international public policy, and grants are made to institutes of higher education on a national level, especially in the field of the arts and humanities. Promotes citizenship and civil society.

Geographical Area of Activity: USA.

Publications: Annual Report; Schedule of Grants; *Fifteen Years of Giving* (report).

Finance: Assets $579,739,000 (2001); annual grants disbursed $35,304,281 (2001).

Officers and Directors: A. M. Taylor (Chair.); T. L. Rhodes (Vice-Chair.); W. J. Roper (Sec.); R. N. Berkopec (Treas.); D. P. Schmidt (Exec. Vice-Pres.); R. Coleman; T. Considine; M. Grebe; J. Clayburn La Force; I. Andrew Rader; Brother Bob Smith; D. V. Uihlein, Jr.

Address: POB 510860, Milwaukee, WI 53203-0153.

Telephone: (414) 291-9915; **Fax:** (414) 291-9991; **Internet:** www.bradleyfdn.org.

Bridge to Asia Foundation

Founded in 1987 by Jeffrey Smith to aid the modernization of education in China and other countries.

Activities: The Foundation helps libraries at universities and research institutes upgrade their collections, through donations of books, journals and other materials in Canada, China, Vietnam and other countries.

Geographical Area of Activity: Canada, China, South-East Asia, South Asia and USA.

Finance: Annual budget $350,000 (2002).

Trustees: Geraldine Kunstadter (Chair.); Jeff Smith (Pres.); Newton Liu (Vice-Pres.); Richard Gossett; Victoria Johnson; Prof. Tunney Lee; Prof. Kathleen Price; Deborah Yang.

Principal Staff: Pres. Jeff Smith; Vice-Pres. Newton Liu.

Address: 665 Grant Ave, San Francisco, CA 94108-2430.

Telephone: (415) 678-2990; **Fax:** (415) 678-2996; **Internet:** www.bridge.org; **e-mail:** asianet@bridge.org.

Bristol-Myers Squibb Foundation

Established to fund and support projects that enhance and extend human lives around the world.

Activities: Supports a broad range of initiatives which deal with important health and social matters around the world, including women's health education and biomedical research. Support includes research grants and donations of medical supplies and pharmaceutical products. One of the foundation's largest projects is a programme to address the HIV/AIDS problem in Southern and Western African countries, funding research, training, education and community outreach work in order to reduce the impact the epidemic has had in these countries.

Geographical Area of Activity: International.

Restrictions: Does not award grants to individuals; political, social, fraternal or veterans' organizations; religious or sectarian organizations unless engaged in action significantly beneficial to the community; organizations in receipt of funds from United Way; endowments; advertising; conferences, videos or events.

Finance: Funded by the Bristol-Myers Squibb Company. Total assets $26,867,580 (Dec. 2000); total giving $15,836,964 (2000).

Directors: Peter R. Dolan (Chair.); John L. Damonti; John L. McGoldrick; John L. Skule.

Address: 345 Park Ave, 43rd Flr., New York, NY 10154-0037.

Telephone: (212) 546-4000; **Internet:** www.bms.com/aboutbms/founda.

British Schools and Universities Foundation

Founded in 1961 to promote closer relations between the USA and the British Commonwealth, through educational assistance.

Activities: A charitable foundation, which makes grants to educational institutions in the United Kingdom and the British Commonwealth, and supports reciprocal Anglo-American education.

Geographical Area of Activity: United Kingdom, the British Commonwealth and the USA.

Publications: Annual Report.

Finance: Grants and awards in the range of $200,000–$2,700,000 per year.

Board of Directors: A. Scott Bushey (Chair.); David Lipson (Pres.); Paul DeF. Hicks, Jr (Vice-Pres. Investments and Asst Treas.); Daniel O'Day, Jr. (Vice-Pres Scholarships); John Tepper Marlin (Treas.); Patrick M. Russell (Sec.); Rosalind Candlin Benedict; Michael A. Findlay; Nina Freedman; Albert H. Gordon; Fletcher Hodges, III; Mary Ellen O'Brien; John E. Stiller; Leonard Vickers; Robert P. Wessely; Charles S. Whitman, III; Denis B. Woodfield.

Address: 575 Madison Ave, Suite 1006, New York, NY 10022-2511; White Walls, 12 Pilgrims Way, Guildford GU4 8AB, United Kingdom.

Telephone: (212) 662-5576; **Internet:** www.bsuf.org; **e-mail:** bsuf@mcimail.com.

Brookings Institution

Founded in 1927 by Robert S. Brookings and others to conduct and foster research, education, training and publication on public policy issues in the broad fields of economics, government administration, foreign policy and the social sciences.

Activities: Conducts policy-oriented research through an Economic Studies programme, which investigates issues in international economics, economic growth and stability, industrial organization and regulation, labour economics, public finance, social economics and urban economics; a Governmental Studies programme on political institutions, regulation and economic policy, and social policy; and a Foreign Policy Studies programme concerned with national security policy, international economic policy, energy and regional studies. The Institution also conducts educational conferences on public policy issues for leaders in government, business and the professions. Research fellowships tenable at the Institution are awarded to support policy-oriented predoctoral research in economics, government, foreign policy and national security policy.

Geographical Area of Activity: USA.

Publications: *Brookings Papers on Economic Activity* (2 a year); *Brookings Review* (quarterly); Annual Report; books.

Trustees: The Institution is governed by a Board of Trustees consisting of 35 members.

Address: 1775 Massachusetts Ave, NW, Washington, DC 20036-2188.

Telephone: (202) 797-6000; **Fax:** (202) 797-6004; **Internet:** www.brook.edu; **e-mail:** webmaster@brookings.edu.

Brother's Brother Foundation

Founded in 1958 by Dr Robert Hingson, to distribute donated educational, medical, agricultural and humanitarian aid to those in need internationally.

Activities: Distributes donated aid shipments, including agricultural, educational and humanitarian resources to those in need, whether because of war, or natural or man-made disasters, and regardless of race, religion or political affiliation.

Geographical Area of Activity: International.

Publications: Newsletter.

Finance: Value of relief help $170,000,000 (2002).

Principal Staff: Chair. Tim Romps; Vice-Chair. Carolyn Winschel; Sec. Austin Henry; Treas. Joe Senko; Pres. Luke L. Hingson.

Address: 1200 Galveston Ave, Pittsburgh, PA 15233-1604.

Telephone: (412) 237-2324; **Internet:** www.brothersbrother.org; **e-mail:** mail@brothersbrother.org.

Pearl S. Buck International

Established by the writer Pearl S. Buck, an international development and humanitarian organization dedicated to helping children.

Activities: Works to improve the quality of life and available opportunities for children who suffer discrimination owing to the circumstances of their birth, by promoting tolerance and human rights, mitigating the effects of injustices suffered by children, and supporting many related programmes around the world, with a particular emphasis on projects working in Asia. Also runs child sponsorship and adoption programmes.

Geographical Area of Activity: International, with an emphasis on Asia.

Address: POB 181, 520 Dublin Road, Perkasie, PA 18944.

Telephone: (215) 249-0100; **Internet:** www.pearl-s-buck.org.

Burroughs Wellcome Fund

Founded in 1955 by the Burroughs Wellcome Co., USA, as a private non-profit foundation to advance medical science by supporting research and other scientific and educational activities.

Activities: The Fund has two primary goals, to help outstanding scientists early in their career, and to advance fields in the basic medical sciences that are undervalued or in need of particular encouragement. The Fund makes grants primarily to institutions within the USA and Canada for research in the basic biomedical sciences through competitive award programmes, which comprise five main categories—career development of scientists, emerging infectious diseases, translational research, interfaces in science and science education. Most grants are made on a competitive basis, however grants are also made to non-profit organizations conducting activities to improve the general environment for science.

Geographical Area of Activity: USA and Canada.

Restrictions: No grants are made to individuals.

Publications: Annual Report; *FOCUS* (newsletter); programme brochures; special reports.

Finance: Assets $580,000,000 (Aug. 2002); annual expenditure $31,472,533 (2002).

Board of Directors: Dr Gail Cassell (Chair.); Mary Ellen Avery; Stephen D. Corman: Dr Marye Anne Fox; Dr Henry G. Friesen; Dr Phil Gold; Albert J. Hudspeth; David M. Kipnis; I. George Miller; Dr Mary-Lou Pardue; Dr Jerome Strauss; Dr Judith Swain; Philip R. Tracy; Dr Jean D. Wilson.

Principal Staff: Pres. Dr Enriqueta C. Bond; Vice-Pres. Finance S. Schoedler; Communications Dir Mirinda J. Kossoff.

Address: POB 13901, Research Triangle Park, NC 27709-3901.

Telephone: (919) 991-5100; **Fax:** (919) 991-5160; **Internet:** www.bwfund.org; **e-mail:** info@bwfund.org.

Bush Foundation

Founded in 1953 by Mr and Mrs Archibald Granville Bush to encourage and promote charitable, scientific, literary and educational efforts.

Activities: Operates predominantly on a regional basis, especially in Minnesota, North Dakota and South Dakota, with broad interests in education, human services and health, the arts and humanities, medicine and the development of leadership. Awards fellowships to individuals and grants to institutions. Operates the Bush Leadership Fellows Program, the Bush Fellowships for Artists, and the Bush Medical Fellow Program. Also supports projects across the USA, making grants to historically black private colleges and tribally controlled colleges.

Geographical Area of Activity: USA (mainly Minnesota, North Dakota and South Dakota).

Publications: Annual Report; proposal guidelines; application requirements.

Finance: Assets $836,335,488 (Nov. 2000); annual grants expenditure $44,852,609 (2000).

Officers and Directors: Ann Wynia (Chair.); Frank B. Wilderson, Jr (First Vice-Chair.); C. Angus Wurtele (Second Vice-Chair); Anita M. Pampusch (Pres.); Merlin E. Dewing (Sec.); Connie Thompson (Chief Financial Officer); Ivy S. Bernhardson (Treas.); Sharon Sayles Belton; Shirley M. Clark; Thomas E. Holloran; Richard D. McFarland; Diana E. Murphy; William P. Pierskalla; Kennon V. Rothchild; Gordon M. Sprenger; Kathryn H. Turnheim; W. Richard West, Jr.

Principal Staff: Pres. Anita M. Pampusch; Grants Man. Kelly M. Kleppe.

Address: 332 Minnesota St, East 900, St Paul, MN 55101.

Telephone: (651) 227-0891; **Fax:** (651) 297-6485; **Internet:** www.bushfoundation.org; **e-mail:** info@bushfoundation.org.

J. Homer Butler Foundation

Founded in 1961 with donations from the late Mabel A. Tod to assist projects that care for sick people, especially leprosy patients.

Activities: Funds projects helping seriously ill people, with a particular emphasis on the relief of leprosy sufferers.

Geographical Area of Activity: Central and South America, Africa, Asia (the Philippines, India).

Restrictions: No grants to individuals.

Finance: Total assets $4,700,000 (Nov. 2002); annual grants $170,000 (2002).

Principal Staff: Pres. Henry J. Zenorini; Grants Admin. Dorothy Montalto.

Address: POB 1841, Old Chelsea St, New York, NY 10011.

Telephone: (718) 356-9293; **Fax:** (718) 442-5088.

Bydale Foundation

Founded in 1965 by James P. Warburg to support various charitable purposes.

Activities: The Foundation operates in the fields of international understanding, economics, higher education, the environment, the arts, law and civil rights, and social welfare, through grants to organizations for research, conferences and projects.

Restrictions: No grants made to individuals.

Finance: Assets $13,581,815 (2001); total grants $748,250 (2001).

Officers and Directors: Joan M. Warburg (Pres.); Milton D. Solomon (Vice-Pres. and Sec.); Frank J. Kick (Treas.); Sarah W. Bliumis; James P. Warburg, Jr; Jennifer Warburg; Philip N. Warburg.

Principal Staff: Vice-Pres. Milton D. Solomon.

Address: 11 Martine Ave, White Plains, NY 10606.

Telephone: (914) 683-3519.

The Camargo Foundation

Founded in 1967 by Jerome Hill to promote the arts and education related to French and Francophone studies.

Activities: Awards Camargo Fellowships to visual artists, creative writers and composers, and to scholars engaged in French cultural and Francophone Studies. Grants are residential, and a $3,500 stipend is provided for each Fellow. Co-sponsors classical music concerts and an annual festival of literature. Maintains premises in Cassis, France for residential fellowships.

Geographical Area of Activity: Cassis, France.

Restrictions: Finance is only available for residential grants.

Publications: Bulletin (published on-line).

Board of Trustees: Ann ffolliott; Cynthia A. Gehrig; Michèle Moss Guehenno; Mari Hill Harpur; Cheryl Hooper; Paul C. Sheeline; George White.

Principal Staff: Exec. Dir Michael J. Pretina.

Address: 125 Park Square Court, 400 Sibley St, Saint Paul, MN 55101-1928.

Telephone: (202) 302-7303; **Internet:** www.camargofoundation.org; **e-mail:** camargo@jeromefdn.org.

Iris and B. Gerald Cantor Foundation

Founded in 1978 by B. Gerald Cantor, Iris Cantor and others to support the arts, international cultural life and medical research.

Activities: Operates mainly in the areas of the arts and humanities, especially fine arts, museums, medicine and health, and higher education. Supports the exhibition and study of the works of Rodin and has donated more than 450 Rodin sculptures to art institutions throughout the world. The Foundation has contributed to the reconstruction of part of the Metropolitan Museum of Art in New York, the art museum at Stanford University, the Brooklyn Museum, and the Los Angeles County Museum of Art. In the field of medical research, the Foundation has a particular focus on funding research into the early diagnosis and treatment of breast cancer. The Foundation has also established two Iris Cantor Women's Network Centers, in Los Angeles and New York.

Geographical Area of Activity: USA.

Restrictions: No grants are made to individuals, and the Foundation contributes only to pre-selected organizations.

Finance: Funded by the Cantor family.

Board of Directors: Iris Cantor (Chair. and Pres.); Joel Rothstein (Treas.); Randi Aitken; Suzanne Fisher; Michele Geller; Monica G. Muhart; Judith Sobol.

Principal Staff: Exec. Dir Judith Sobol.

Address: POB 811, Beverly Hills, CA 90213.

Telephone: (310) 277-4600; **Fax:** (310) 277-0232; **Internet:** www.cantorfoundation.org; **e-mail:** jsobol@ibgcf.org.

Carnegie Corporation of New York

Founded in 1911 by Andrew Carnegie to promote the advancement and diffusion of knowledge and understanding among the peoples of the USA, Russia and of certain countries that are, or have been, members of the British Commonwealth.

Activities: Current areas of interest are education; international peace and security; international development; and strengthening US democracy. Also operates a Carnegie Corporation Scholars Program, supporting research by outstanding young scholars, as well as a Special Opportunities Fund for projects falling outside the main areas of interest. Support is directed towards the development of children and youth, childhood health and development, educational achievement, science education and the reform of education; the development of human resources in less-developed countries; and co-operative security and the avoidance of conflict between nations. Grant programmes support: science-based analyses of the ways in which the risk of nuclear war can be diminished; projects linking educational reform to social and economic changes; research into the prevention of problems for children and young teenagers such as school failure, school-age pregnancy, childhood injury and substance abuse; and efforts to improve maternal and infant health in English-speaking countries of Africa and to strengthen indigenous scientific capacity to solve development problems. Most grants are made to organizations in the USA, but support is also given overseas with a current focus on Commonwealth Africa. Projects involving both Russian and American participants are also funded. Supports conferences and seminars, exchange programmes and publications.

Geographical Area of Activity: USA and countries that are, or have been, members of the British Commonwealth, and Russia.

Restrictions: No grants to individual schools.

Publications: Annual Report; *New Directions for Carnegie Corporation of New York; Carnegie Quarterly;* Programme Guidelines; grants list; general information pamphlet.

Finance: Assets $1,600,000,000 (Sept. 2002); grants budget approx. $60,000,000 (2002–2003).

Board of Trustees: Helene L. Kaplan (Chair.); Martin L. Liebowitz (Vice-Chair.); Vartan Gregorian (Pres.); Bruce Alberts; Geoffrey T. Boisi; James B. Hunt; William McDonough; Sam Nunn; Olara A. Otunnu; William A. Owens; Thomas R. Pickering; Ruth J. Simmons; Raymond W. Smith; Marta Tienda.

Principal Staff: Pres. Vartan Gregorian; Vice-Pres. Neil Grabois, Susan Robinson King, Edward Sermier, D. Ellen Shuman.

Address: 437 Madison Ave, New York, NY 10022.

Telephone: (212) 371-3200; **Fax:** (212) 754-4073; **Internet:** www.carnegie.org.

Carnegie Endowment for International Peace

Private non-profit organization dedicated to advancing co-operation between nations and promoting active international engagement by the United States. Founded in 1910 by Andrew Carnegie, its work is non-partisan, and works to achieve practical results.

Activities: The Carnegie Endowment conducts research, publishes information, holds meetings, and occasionally creates new institutions and international networks. Activities operate in three main fields: the Global Policy Program, the China Program and the Russian and Eurasian Program. The interests of Endowment associates are international, and concentrate on relations between governments, businesses, international organizations and civil society, focusing on the economic, political and technological forces driving global change. Through the Carnegie Moscow Center, founded in 1992, the Endowment helps to develop a tradition of public policy analysis in the states of the former USSR, and to improve relations between Russia and the United States. The Endowment publishes *Foreign Policy*, one of the world's leading magazines about international politics and economics which reaches readers in more than 120 countries.

Geographical Area of Activity: USA and the Russian Federation.

Restrictions: Not a grant-making organization.

Publications: *Foreign Policy* (6 a year); *Funding Virtue: Civil Society Aid and Democracy Promotion; The Third Force: the Rise of Transnational Civil Society;* monographs, books, working papers, reports and other publications on international relations and foreign policy.

Finance: Key sources of funding are the endowment and grants.

Trustees: William H. Donaldson (Chair.); Gregory B. Craig (Vice-Chair.); and 21 others.

Principal Staff: Pres. Jessica T. Mathews.

Address: 1779 Massachusetts Ave, NW, Washington, DC 20036-2103.

Telephone: (202) 483-7600; **Fax:** (202) 483-1840; **Internet:** www.ceip.org; **e-mail:** info@ceip.org.

Carnegie Hero Fund Commission

Founded in 1904 by Andrew Carnegie to recognize, with the award of medals and sums of money, heroism voluntarily performed by civilians in the USA and Canada, in saving, or attempting to save, the lives of others at extraordinary risk to the life of the rescuer.

Activities: Operates in the USA and Canada in the field of social welfare, through grants to individuals, including scholarship assistance and continuing aid to those disabled in their attempts to save others, and grants to the dependants of those who died in such attempts. National Carnegie Hero Fund Foundations were established in 1908 in the United Kingdom, 1909 in France and 1911 in Belgium, Denmark,

Italy, the Netherlands, Norway, Sweden and Switzerland. These foundations also award medals and diplomas to individuals in those countries who have risked or lost their lives, as well as cash grants.

Geographical Area of Activity: USA and Canada.

Restrictions: Act of herosim must have occurred in the USA or Canada and the Commission must be notified within two years.

Publications: Annual Report; leaflets.

Finance: Assets $30,250,351 (Dec. 2001); grants expenditure $723,307 (2001).

Officers and Trustees: Robert W. Off (Pres.); Priscilla J. McCrady (Vice-Pres.); W. F. Rutkowski (Exec. Dir and Sec.); J. M. Walton (Treas.); S. R. Brand; E. B. Buchanan; A. H. Burchfield, III; B. R. Fisher, Jr; E. H. Genter; T. J. Hilliard, Jr; D. M. Hillman; M. J. Laskow; P. F. Mathieson; C. R. McCrady; P. J. McCrady; A. M. McGuinn; F. B. Robinson; A. M. Scully, Jr; W. P. Snyder, III; W. F. Toerge; S. P. Veeder; J. M. Walton; T. L. Wentling, Jr; A. W. Wishart, Jr.

Principal Staff: Exec. Dir Walter F. Rutkowski.

Address: 425 Sixth Ave, Suite 1640, Pittsburgh, PA 15219-1823.

Telephone: (412) 281-1302; **Fax:** (412) 281-5751; **Internet:** www.carnegiehero.org; **e-mail:** carnegiehero@carnegiehero.org.

Carthage Foundation

Founded in 1964 by Richard M. Scaife for general charitable purposes; shares administrative offices with the Sarah Scaife Foundation and the Scaife Family Foundation (qq.v.).

Activities: Operates mainly in the area of public policy research, especially in the fields of international affairs, government, the law and public policy, through grants for conferences, seminars and other purposes.

Geographical Area of Activity: USA.

Restrictions: No grants are made to individuals.

Publications: Annual Report.

Finance: Assets $23,611,584 (2001); total grants $2,115,000 (2001).

Officers and Trustees: Richard M. Scaife (Chair.); R. Daniel McMichael (Sec.); Michael W. Gleba (Treas.); Alexis J. Konkol (Asst Sec.); Roger W. Robinson, Jr (Asst Treas.).

Address: 1 Oxford Center, 301 Grant St, Suite 3900, Pittsburgh, PA 15219-6401.

Telephone: (412) 392-2900; **Internet:** www.scaife.com.

Center for Citizen Initiatives—CCI

Founded in 1983, CCI works to support democracy in post-communist Russia, to encourage economic reform and to provide aid to disadvantaged people in the Russian Federation.

Activities: Funds a number of volunteer programmes in the Russian Federation, including a Productivity Enhancement Program (PEP), providing US-based management training for Russian entrepreneurs; the Next-Steps Program addressing public corruption in the Russian Federation; encouraging business enterprise by supporting training in initiatives for self-employment; the Schultz Fund, promoting the development of philanthropy; a programme providing Russian orphans with marketable employment skills; and creating business management schools. Operates seven partner offices in the Russian Federation.

Geographical Area of Activity: Russian Federation.

Publications: *PEP Brochure 2000; PEP Profiles 2000;* brochures; newsletter (quarterly).

Board of Directors: Arlie Schardt (Chair.); Suzanne Campbell; Don Chapman; Patricia Dowden; Anthony Garrett; Nancy GlaserLily Golden; Eric Hart; George M. Ingram; Francis Macy; James Sorenson; Sharon Tennison; Neil R. G. Young.

Principal Staff: Pres. Sharon Tennison.

Address: POB 29912, San Francisco, CA 94129.

Telephone: (415) 561-7777; **Fax:** (415) 561-7778; **Internet:** www.ccisf.org; **e-mail:** info@ccisf.org.

Center for Communications, Health and the Environment—CECHE

Private, non-profit institution founded in 1990. Aims to assist under-served communities in the USA, Central and Eastern Europe and developing countries.

Activities: Operates in Bulgaria, the Czech Republic, Hungary, India, Poland, Romania, the Russian Federation, Ukraine and the countries of the former Yugoslavia (now Serbia and Montenegro), supporting programmes that improve life styles and reduce health risks, and counteract the harmful effects of pollution. Main programme areas, which focus on the use of mass media and information technology, are the development of the private voluntary sector; community and school-based projects; environment and public health programmes; public education; and professional training in the media and health.

Geographical Area of Activity: Central and Eastern Europe (Bulgaria, the Czech Republic, Hungary, Poland, Romania, the Russian Federation, Ukraine and the countries of the former Yugoslavia, now Serbia and Montenegro), India and the USA.

Restrictions: Grants only to non-profit organizations.

Publications: *Global Health and Environmental Bulletin; Monitor* (on-line and print periodical); fact sheets; project reports; Annual Report.

Finance: Funding from foundations, international organizations and local government. Net assets $900,000 (2001); annual revenue and expenditure $1,000,000 (2001).

Directors: Dr Sushma Palmer (Chair.); Amb. Mark Palmer (Vice-Chair.); Dr C. Wayne Callaway; Dr Leonard Silverstein.

Address: 4437 Reservoir Rd, NW, Washington, DC 20007.

Telephone: (202) 965-5990; **Fax:** (202) 965-5996; **Internet:** www.ceche.org; **e-mail:** ceche@igc.org.

Center for Cultural and Technical Interchange between East and West—East–West Center

Founded in 1960 by the US Congress with a mandate 'to promote better relations and understanding between the United States and the nations of Asia and Pacific through co-operative study, training and research'; the Center is a public, non-profit national and international research and education institution.

Activities: The Center receives most of its financial support from the US Congress, but there are also contributions from Asian and Pacific governments, as well as from private agencies and corporations. Its staff regularly co-operate in study, research and training with research fellows, graduates and professionals in business and government in the areas of economic change, international co-operation, national economic development strategies, energy policy, politics and security, environmental issues, behaviour and health and Pacific islands development. Its facilities include administrative and research offices, three residential halls and an international conference centre equipped for simultaneous translation.

Geographical Area of Activity: South-East, East and Southern Asia, the Pacific and the USA.

Restrictions: Grants only for degree and non-degree scholarships, workshop participants and visiting fellowships.

Publications: Annual Report; Issues Papers; research findings; papers; *International Production Networks in Asia: Rivalry or Riches?; Regional Dynamics and Future US Policy; Population Aging Raises Questions for Policymakers; AsiaPacific Issues; Asia-Pacific Population and Policy; East–West Center Observer* (quarterly newsletter); Annual Report; special reports; working papers; research findings; conference proceedings; and staff contributions in external publications.

Finance: Receives funding from US Government, foundations, Asian and Pacific governments. Net assets $1,718,793 (Sept. 2001); annual revenue $227,069, expenditure $347,545 (2001).

Board of Directors: George R. Ariyoshi (Chair.); Edison H. Miyawaki (Vice-Chair.); Joan M. Bickson; Mark Fukunaga; John N. Hawkins; Lawrence M. Johnson; Daniel B. T. Lau; Peter C. Lewis; Gerald M. Pang; G. Markus Polivka; Ihakara Puketapu; Jean E. Rolles; Joichi Saito; Puongpun Sananikone; Oswald K. Stender; Ratan Tata; Gulab Watumull; R. J. Zlatoper.

Principal Staff: Pres. Charles E. Morrison; Treas. Ricky Kubota.

Address: 1601 East–West Rd, Honolulu, HI 96848-1601.

Telephone: (808) 944-7111; **Fax:** (808) 944-7376; **Internet:** www.eastwestcenter.org; **e-mail:** ewcinfo@eastwestcenter.org.

Center for International Health and Cooperation

Founded in 1991 by a group of physicians to promote healing and peace in countries affected by conflict, ethnic violence or natural disaster.

Activities: Operates in the area of humanitarian education internationally, through funding multi-disciplinary professional training for humanitarian workers; organizing conferences and symposia bringing together field workers and policy makers, dealing with international problems, such as land-mines; runs a programme in the Horn of Africa, which has been involved in relief and rehabilitation projects, including CIHC–Jaipur foot amputee projects in Nicaragua and Somalia; as well as funding field operations in Albania, East Timor (now Timor Leste), Indonesia, Kosovo, Macedonia, Palestine and in the former Yugoslavia (now Serbia and Montenegro). Maintains offices in Geneva, London and Dublin.

Geographical Area of Activity: Africa, Asia, Europe, the Middle East and the USA.

Directors: K.M. Cahill, M.D (Pres. and Dir); B. Boutros-Ghali; F. M. Deng; J. Eliasson; A. A. Farah; Lady Hamlyn; P. Hansen; E. O'Brien; J. O'Hare; Lord D. Owen; P. Tarnoff.

Principal Staff: Brendan Cahill; Larry Hollingworth; Michael Veuthey.

Address: 850 Fifth Ave, New York, NY 10021.

Telephone: (212) 636-6294; **Fax:** (212) 636-7863; **Internet:** www.cihc.org; **e-mail:** mail@cihc.org.

Center for Victims of Torture—CVT

Founded in 1985, CVT works locally, nationally and internationally to heal the wounds of government-sponsored torture on individuals, their families and their communities, and to stop torture world-wide.

Activities: Provides direct care for victims of torture and their families in the USA and West Africa; carries out research into the long-term effects of torture and how to care for torture victims effectively; runs training programmes for health-care, education and social work professionals in the USA and abroad; and works towards the elimination of torture through research, public policy initiatives and education campaigns in collaboration with other human rights and civic organizations.

Geographical Area of Activity: USA and West Africa.

Publications: Annual Report; *Storycloth* (newsletter); training materials for social workers, physicians, health workers and educators.

Finance: Total assets $1,643,233 (2000); annual revenue $3,343,154, expenditure $3,259,155 (2000).

Directors: V. Kudrle (Chair.); N. J. Feldman (Vice-Chair.).

Principal Staff: Exec. Dir D. A. Johnson; Deputy Dir R. B. Rendler; Chief Financial Officer K. Wetherby.

Address: 717 East River Rd, Minneapolis, MN 55455.

Telephone: (612) 436-4800; **Fax:** (612) 436-2600; **Internet:** www.cvt.org; **e-mail:** sxenos@cvt.org.

Centre for Development and Population Activities—CEDPA

Founded in 1975, a non-profit international organization which aims to help and empower women at all levels of society and to involve them in development work.

Activities: Operates internationally in 40 countries in collaboration with partner NGOs and networks, in the areas of gender equality and developing the role of women in society, through linking reproductive health care with women's empowerment; improving facilities and capabilities of development centres and networks; increasing women's involvement in policy-making; and promoting youth involvement in development agendas.

Geographical Area of Activity: International.

Publications: *Advocacy: Building Skills for NGO Leaders; Gender and Development; Gender, Reproductive Health, and Advocacy; Strategic Planning: An Inquiry Approach; Social Mobilization for Reproductive Health; Choose a Future! Issues and Options for Adolescent Boys; Integrating STDs and AIDS Services into Family Planning; Choose a Future! Issues and Options for Adolescent Girls; CEDPA Network* (quarterly newsletter); *Promoting Women in Development Reports-in-Brief;* newsletter (quarterly); booklets; Annual Report.

Finance: Total assets $3,928,059 (2001); annual revenue $28,411,648, expenditure $24,483,589 (2001).

Board of Directors: Peggy Curlin (Pres.); Linda M. Fuselier (Chair.); Mary P. Quin (Vice-Chair.); Esther B. Hewlett (Sec.); Alicia S. Ritchie (Treas.); and 17 others.

Principal Staff: Pres. Peggy Curlin; Senior Vice-Pres. Programs Taly Valenzuela; Vice-Pres. External Relations Julie H. Crudele; Vice-Pres. Finance and Admin. Patricia D. Shannon.

Address: 1400 16th St, NW, Suite 100, Washington, DC 20036.

Telephone: (202) 667-1142; **Fax:** (202) 332-4496; **Internet:** www.cedpa.org; **e-mail:** cmail@cedpa.org.

The Century Foundation

Founded in 1919 by Edward A. Filene for research on major economic, political and social institutions and issues. Formerly known as the Twentieth Century Fund, Inc.

Activities: Research is conducted nationally and internationally in the fields of communications, international affairs and economic development, and on major political, economic and social institutions. Main programme areas are the Ageing of America, Economic Inequality, Media and Society, American Foreign Policy, US Politics and Policy, and the Economy. Research results are published in book form. Awards the Leonard Silk Journalism Fellowship to an established journalist producing a book on what the Foundation considers an important contemporary issue.

Geographical Area of Activity: International.

Restrictions: Not a grant-making foundation.

Publications: Annual Report; newsletter; studies and paperback series, books.

Finance: Assets $64,761,960 (June 2001); total grants $55,000 (2001).

Trustees: Alan Brinkley (Chair.); Richard C. Leone (Pres.); and 24 others.

Principal Staff: Contact: Jason Renker.

Address: 41 East 70th St, New York, NY 10021.

Telephone: (212) 535-4441; **Fax:** (212) 535-7534; **Internet:** www.tcf.org.

The J. P. Morgan Chase Foundation (J. P. Morgan Chase Foundation)

Established in 1956 as the Manufacturers Hanover Foundation, becoming the Chemical Bank Foundation in 1993. Merged with the J. P. Morgan Charitable Trust, following the merger of J. P. Morgan and Chase Manhattan Bank in 2000.

Activities: Operates in the fields of the arts and humanities, community development, education and youth (especially early childhood and youth). Grants are mainly given in the New York City area and parts of New York state where the Chemical Bank operates, but also internationally through US-based non-profit organizations.

Geographical Area of Activity: USA and international.

Restrictions: No grants are made to individuals.

Publications: Annual Report.

Finance: Total assets $137,439,675 (Dec. 2000); annual grants expenditure $44,656,800 (2000). Total combined contributions of company and foundation $74,112,936 (2001).

Principal Staff: Pres. Michael Feller; Sec. and Treas. Steven W. Gelston.

Address: 1 Chase Manhattan Plaza, 5th Floor, New York, NY 10081.

Telephone: (212) 552-1112; **Internet:** www.jpmorganchase .com/grants.

Chatlos Foundation, Inc

Founded in 1953 by William F. Chatlos.

Activities: The Foundation operates nationally and internationally, providing funding in the fields of bible colleges and seminaries (amounting to 33 per cent of funding), religious causes (30 per cent of funding), medicine and health, liberal arts colleges (principally private colleges) and social welfare.

Geographical Area of Activity: Mainly USA.

Restrictions: Only non-profit organizations which are tax exempt for US federal income tax purposes may apply. No grants directly to international organizations, individuals, to individual churches, secondary schools, arts or medical research organizations.

Publications: Information brochure; application guidelines.

Finance: Assets $114,373,200 (Dec. 2000).

Board of Directors: Kathryn A. Randle (Chair.); William J. Chatlos (Pres. and Treas.); Joy E. D'Arata (Vice-Pres.); Carol J. Chatlos (Sec.); Esther Kemsey; Charles O. Morgan, Jr; Michele C. Roach.

Address: POB 915048, Longwood, FL 32791-5048.

Telephone: (407) 862-5077; **Internet:** www.chatlos.org.

The Chicago Community Trust

Founded in 1915 for such charitable purposes as will best make for the mental, moral, intellectual and physical improvement, assistance and relief of the inhabitants of the County of Cook, State of Illinois.

Activities: Operates mainly in Greater Chicago in the fields of education, health, basic human needs, the arts and humanities, and community development, through grants for both general operating support and specific programmes..

Geographical Area of Activity: USA (Chicago, IL).

Restrictions: No grants are made to individuals.

Publications: Annual Report; *Trust News* (three a year); grant guidelines; financial statement.

Finance: Assets $1,290,757,893 (2000); total revenue $49,531,648, expenditure $44,320,321 (2000).

Executive Committee: James J. Glasser (Chair.); Virginia Ojeda; P. Beidler; H. Morgan Bilandic; A. Cepeda; M. Field; Sue Ling Gin; M. Koldyke; M. Laing; H. Livingston; J. Nichols; Q. Primo.

Principal Staff: Pres. and CEO Donald M. Stewart; Chief Financial Officer Carol Crenshaw.

Address: 111 East Wacker Dr., Suite 1400, Chicago, IL 60601.

Telephone: (312) 616-8000; **Fax:** (312) 616-7955; **Internet:** www.cct.org; **e-mail:** info@cct.org.

Children of the Americas—COTA

Established by Dr William and Judy Schwank as a national network of volunteers who provide free medical care to children world-wide, and especially in Guatemala.

Activities: Operates in the fields of medicine and health, and social welfare. Medical teams travel to Guatemala regularly to provide medical treatment. Children are also referred to the organization's medical team in Kentucky from throughout the world. Has established an orphanage and a surgical centre in Guatemala. Also provides educational services and scholarships in Mexico and Central America.

Geographical Area of Activity: International (especially the USA, Mexico and Guatemala).

Publications: *One Child* (newsletter); Annual Report.

Finance: Total revenue $595,556, expenditure $581,680 (2000).

Address: 3109 Wild Dove Lane, Mariposa, CA 95338.

Telephone: (209) 966-6605; **Internet:** www .americaschildren.org; **e-mail:** allkids@americaschildren.org.

Children International

Established in 1936, Children International is a non-profit humanitarian organization which aims to help children around the world to overcome the effects of poverty in order to become healthy, well-educated, self-sustaining and integrated members of society.

Activities: Runs programmes in Chile, Colombia, the Dominican Republic, Ecuador, Guatemala, Honduras, India, Nepal, the Philippines and the USA for the benefit of children, providing the opportunity for people to support children in the developing world through a sponsorship programme. Sponsor contributions are used to assist children particularly in the fields of health and education, as well as buying basic provisions such as food and clothing. Also operates children and family assistance programmes in the West Bank/Jerusalem area, Kenya, Uganda and Zambia.

Geographical Area of Activity: Chile, Colombia, the Dominican Republic, Ecuador, Guatemala, Honduras, India, Kenya, Nepal, Palestinian Autonomous Areas, the Philippines, Uganda, USA and Zambia.

Publications: *Children International* (newsletter); Annual Report.

Finance: Total assets $29,638,3964 (Sept. 2002); annual revenue $80,643,015, expenditure $79,171,437 (2002).

Board of Directors: Cheryl Bevel; James R. Cook; A. Max Fiskin; Joan Horan; Charles Maahs; Fred Mitchell; Dean Oskvig;.

Principal Staff: Pres. and CEO James R. Cook.

Address: POB 219055, Kansas City, MO 64121.

Telephone: (816) 942-2000; **Internet:** www.children.org; **e-mail:** children@children.org.

Children's Wish Foundation International

Founded in 1985 by Linda Dozoretz, the Foundation aims to fulfil the wishes of terminally-ill children who are not expected to reach the age of eighteen.

Activities: Regardless of religion, race or economic status, the Foundation provides children who have been diagnosed as being terminally ill with an experience, following their own personal wish, to enjoy with their family. Also runs a programme which donates entertainment and educational supplies and provides children's entertainers for hospitals; and supports summer camps for young people with terminal illnesses.

Geographical Area of Activity: International.

Executive Board: Ed Carmichel; Roger Christian; Linda Dozoretz; Ed Evans; Keith Gregg; Arthur Stein.

Principal Staff: Pres. and CEO Arthur Stein; Exec. Dir Linda Dozoretz; Vice-Pres. Operations and Communications Christy Andrews.

Address: POB 28785, Atlanta, GA 30358.

Telephone: (770) 393-9474; **Fax:** (770) 393-0683; **Internet:** www.childrenswish.org; **e-mail:** contact@childrenswish.org.

China Medical Board of New York, Inc

Founded in 1928 by the Rockefeller Foundation (q.v.) to provide financial support to the Peking Union Medical College and similar institutions in the Far East.

Activities: The Board assists health profession educational institutions to enhance educational and research activities in medicine, nursing and public health. Grants are made to designated national medical, nursing and public health educational institutions in Hong Kong, Indonesia, Republic of Korea, Malaysia, the Philippines, Singapore, China (Taiwan), Laos, Myanmar, Thailand and the People's Republic of China (including Tibet).

Geographical Area of Activity: Far East (Hong Kong, Indonesia, Republic of Korea, Malaysia, the Philippines, Singapore, China—Taiwan, Laos, Myanmar, Thailand and the People's Republic of China—including Tibet).

Restrictions: Grants are not ordinarily given for the direct provision of health services, to individuals, for buildings nor to professional and scientific organizations.

Publications: Annual Report.

Finance: Assets $219,061,921 (June 2000).

Board of Trustees: Dwight H. Perkins (Chair.); Roy Schwarz (Pres.); Mary Brown Bullock; Jordan J. Cohen; Don Eugene Detmer; Michael A. Duffy; Thomas S. Inui; Tom G. Kessinger; Peter Robbins; Roy Schwarz; Gloria H. Spivak.

Address: 750 Third Ave, 23rd Floor, New York, NY 10017.

Telephone: (212) 682-8000; **Fax:** (212) 949-8726; **Internet:** www.iime.org/cmb.htm; **e-mail:** 75460.452@compuserve.com.

Christian Children's Fund—CCF

Founded in 1938 by a Presbyterian minister; aims to assist children world-wide.

Activities: Operates in the USA and in over 30 less-developed countries, including South Eastern Europe, through child sponsorship, grants and contributions aiming to provide long-term solutions to help combat poverty, in order that children can grow up safely, healthy and educated. Through a number of programmes, funded by sponsors, donors, foundations and grant organizations, the Fund provides better access to health care, immunization, clean water, better nutrition, clothing, educational assistance and training for children in need, regardless of race, religion or gender. CCF also provides emergency assistance/relief, micro-enterprise activities for parents and assistance to AIDS orphans.

Geographical Area of Activity: Africa, Asia, South America, the Caribbean, South-Eastern Europe and the USA.

Restrictions: No grants to individuals.

Publications: *Giving Children a Chance and a Future* (annual report); *When AIDS Hits Home* (special report).

Finance: Assets $36,208,159 (2002); annual revenue $132,743,158, expenditure $135,445,114 (2002).

Directors: E. T. DeJarnette, Jr (Chair.); Ann C. Crouter, William E. Leahey (Vice-Chair.); Lewis T. Booker (Sec.); Steven A. Markel (Treas.); and others.

Principal Staff: Pres. John F. Schultz; Vice-Pres. International Cheri W. Dahl; Vice-Pres. Marketing and Sponsor Services Betty J. Forbes; Vice-Pres. International Programmes Michelle J. Poulton; Vice-Pres. Finance and Operations Charles W. Tysinger.

Address: 2821 Emerywood Parkway, POB 26484, Richmond, VA 23261.

Telephone: (800) 776-6767; **Internet:** www.christianchildrensfund.org.

Winston Churchill Foundation of the United States

Activities: Offers no fewer than 11 scholarships annually for postgraduate work in engineering, mathematics and science at Churchill College, University of Cambridge, United Kingdom; candidates must be US citizens aged between 19 and 26 years, holding a bachelor's degree from a US college or university and enrolled at one of the 74 US institutions participating in the programme.

Finance: The average value of each award is $27,000 (including travel and living allowances). Assets $11,730,935 (1999); annual revenue $1,477,223, expenditure $511,838 (1999).

Board of Trustees: John L. Loeb, Jr (Pres.); Patrick A. Gerschel (Treas.); Wendell Fenton (Sec.); HRH The Duke of Edinburgh Hon. Trustee); William L. Bernhard; Sir John Boyd; Deborah L. Brice; Sir Alec N. Broers; Winston S. Churchill; Lady Margaret Colville; Kristina P. Davison; Mario J. Gabelli; Colin Goddard; Sir William Hawthorne; Ross Perot, Jr; Bruno L. Schroder; Lady Soames.

Principal Staff: Exec. Dir Harold Epstein.

Address: POB 1240, Gracie Station, New York, NY 10028.

Telephone: (212) 879-3480.

Citigroup Foundation

Established to improve the quality of life of children, families and communities world-wide, through supporting organizations contributing to education and economic and community development and quality of life.

Activities: Operates world-wide in the areas of education and community development, with a small amount of funding for arts education, and health and welfare. In the area of education, the Foundation operates through funding projects in early childhood, technology for the classroom, higher education for minority groups and women, and financial literacy. In community development, it supports organizations funding affordable housing, small business loans in the USA, micro-credit in less-developed countries and welfare-to-work initiatives.

Geographical Area of Activity: International.

Restrictions: Grants are not made to individuals, to political causes, religious organizations, nor for fundraising events; prospective grantees are usually approached by the Foundation: unsolicited applications are less likely to succeed.

Finance: Total assets $193,865,626 (Dec. 2001); total giving $50,733,278 (2001).

Board of Directors: Sanford I. Weill (Chair.); Charles O. Prince; Charles V. Raymond.

Principal Staff: CEO and Pres. Charles V. Raymond.

Address: 850 Third Ave, 13th Floor, New York, NY 10022.

Telephone: (212) 793-8451; **Fax:** (212) 793-5944; **Internet:** www.citibank.com/citigroup/corporate/foundation/index.htm; **e-mail:** citygroupfoundation@citigroup.com.

Liz Claiborne and Art Ortenberg Foundation

Founded in 1984 by Arthur Ortenberg and Elizabeth Claiborne Ortenberg to foster natural resource and wildlife conservation and protection.

Activities: The Foundation's main programmes are: the mitigation of conflict between the land and the resource needs of local communities and the preservation of biological diversity; the implementation of scientific, technical and practical conservation of biological diversity in rural landscapes outside of parks and reserves; and the implementation of relevant, field-based, scientific, technical and practical training programmes for local people. These programmes operate in the Rocky Mountain region of the USA and in developing countries in Africa, Central and South America and Asia.

Geographical Area of Activity: USA (Rocky Mountains), Africa, Asia, and Central and South America.

Publications: Information brochure.

Finance: Assets $43,428,370 (Dec. 2001); annual expenditure $1,867,149 (2001).

Trustees: Robert Dewar; Elizabeth Claiborne Ortenberg; Arthur Ortenberg; Mary Pearl; David Quammen; Alison Richard; David Western.

Principal Staff: Dir James Murtaugh; Dir Jeffrey T. Olson.

Address: 650 Fifth Ave, 15th Floor, New York, NY 10019.

Telephone: (212) 333-2536; **Fax:** (212) 956-3531; **e-mail:** lcaof@fcc.net.

Edna McConnell Clark Foundation

Incorporated in New York in 1950 and in Delaware in 1969, the two organizations merged in 1974. The Foundation's aim is to improve conditions for persons who are poorly or unfairly served by the established institutions of society.

Activities: Operates nationally in the field of social welfare and internationally in the field of tropical disease research only, particularly in sub-Saharan Africa. The Foundation's grant-making focuses on four distinct programmes: improving the efficacy of social welfare services in protecting children from abuse or neglect; providing funding for specific communities in New York City where poor housing and under-investment increase the risk of family homelessness; implementing reforms in middle schools in urban areas in order to improve the education offered to disadvantaged students in grades six to nine; and attempting to control or reduce the two major causes of infectious blindness in the developing world, onchocerciasis and trachoma. Programmes include the Tropical Disease Research Program, the Program for New York Neighbourhoods, the Program for Children, the Program for Student Achievement, and the Program for Youth Development. The Foundation also maintains a small Special Projects fund to respond to important or interesting projects that relate to its basic mission, but fall outside the specific programme areas. In 1999 launched the International Trachoma Initiative in conjunction with Pfizer Inc.

Geographical Area of Activity: Mainly USA, but occasionally runs international programmes.

Restrictions: Grants are not made to individuals, nor for scholarship or capital purposes.

Publications: *Grants and News* (quarterly newsletter); Annual Report; Grant Guidelines; information brochure; programme specific publications.

Finance: Assets $712,816,913 (Sept. 2000); grants disbursed $43,565,802 (2000).

Officers and Trustees: Edward C. Schmults (Chair.); Michael A. Bailin; Patricia C. Barron; H. Lawrence Clark; James McConnell Clark, Jr; John M. Emery; Theodore A. McKee; James E. Preston; Mary E. Procter; Ruth A. Wooden; James McConnell Clark, Hays Clark (Emer.).

Principal Staff: Pres. Michael A. Bailin; Vice-Pres. Nancy Roob.

Address: 250 Park Ave, Suite 900, New York, NY 10017.

Telephone: (212) 551-9100; **Fax:** (212) 986-4558; **Internet:** www.emcf.org; **e-mail:** info@emcf.org.

Clean Water Fund

Established in 1978, it aims to help people campaign for clean, safe water, clean air and protection from pollution everywhere.

Activities: Involved in training, research and education intended to ensure safe drinking water and clean seas. Promotes safe solid waste management, control of workplace and community toxic hazards, conservation of natural resources and protects public health and environmental safety.

Geographical Area of Activity: USA only.

Restrictions: No large grants available.

Principal Staff: David R. Zwick.

Address: 4455 Connecticut Ave, NW, Suite A300-16, Washington, DC 20008-2328.

Telephone: (202) 895-0432; **Fax:** (202) 895-0438; **Internet:** www.cleanwaterfund.org; **e-mail:** cwf@cleanwater.org.

Cleveland Foundation

Founded in 1914 by Frederick Goff to provide the means through which individuals can contribute most effectively to philanthropies in the Cleveland area and to provide leadership in dealing with community problems.

Activities: Operates principally for the benefit of citizens of the Greater Cleveland community with broad purposes in the fields of health, social services, education, civic affairs, economic development, the environment, and arts and culture, through scholarships and grants; grants are made primarily to tax-exempt private agencies, and in some cases to governmental agencies. Also administers the annual Anisfield-Wolf Book Awards, presented to books which address the issue of racism or expand appreciation of human diversity.

Geographical Area of Activity: USA (Cleveland, OH).

Restrictions: No grants for religious purposes, and not normally for endowments, membership drives, fundraising projects, travel, publications and videos.

Publications: Annual Report; newsletter; application guidelines; financial statement; information brochure; information for donors, attorneys and financial planners.

Finance: Assets $1,499,767,419 (2001); total expenditure $62,276,948 (2001).

Trustees and Distribution Committee: Cathy Monroe Lewis (Chair.); John Sherwin, Jr (Vice-Chair.); James E. Bennett; Tana N. Carney; Doris A. Evans; Benson P. Lee; Alex Machaskee; Rev. Dr Otis Moss, Jr; Charles A. Ratner; Jerry Sue Thornton; Jacqueline F. Woods.

Principal Staff: Pres., Exec. Dir Steven A. Minter; Exec. Vice-Pres. Susan L. Eagan; Chief of Staff Leslie A. Dunford.

Address: 1422 Euclid Ave, Suite 1300, Cleveland, OH 44115-2001.

Telephone: (216) 861-3810; **Fax:** (216) 589-2039; **Internet:** www.clevelandfoundation.org; **e-mail:** asktcf@clevefdn.org.

Co-operative Housing Foundation—CHF International

Founded in 1952 as the Foundation for Co-operative Housing; an international development organization which believes that safe, affordable housing is the foundation upon which families can build a livelihood, a healthy community and a peaceful, democratic society.

Activities: Operates internationally, and has worked in around 100 countries since its inception, in the area of housing and community development. Offers technical expertise in communities, habitat and finance, and serves as a catalyst for sustainable positive change in low- and moderate-income communities world-wide, helping to improve housing, economic circumstances and environments. Works in partnership with other organizations to develop systems, policies and practices that increase access to affordable housing, community services and finance.

Geographical Area of Activity: International.

Restrictions: No grants to individuals; grants are only given to project-specific local organizations.

Publications: *Strengthening a Market-Orientated Housing Delivery System through NGOs; Hurricane-Resistant Home improvement Program Toolkit; Building a Better World* (annual international programme report); newsletter (quarterly); factsheets; bulletins.

Principal Staff: Pres. and CEO Michael E. Doyle; Communications Heather L. Bowen; Exec. Support Officer Karina L. Jackson.

Address: 8601 Georgia Ave, Suite 800, Silver Spring, MD 20910-3440.

Telephone: (301) 587-4700; **Fax:** (301) 587-7315; **Internet:** www.chfhq.org; **e-mail:** kjackson@chfhq.org.

Coca-Cola Foundation

Founded in 1984 by the Coca-Cola Co. to improve the quality of life in the community and support education.

Activities: Supports all aspects of elementary, secondary and adult education (including health, minorities, arts, mathematics and college preparation) through campaigns, scholarships and fellowships, special projects, endowment funds, etc., to public and private institutions, as well as projects fostering cultural understanding.

Geographical Area of Activity: International.

Restrictions: No grants are made to individuals.

Publications: Annual Report.

Finance: Total assets $59,075,032 (Dec. 2001); grants disbursed $12,091,774 (2001).

Officers and Directors: I. Saunders Jones (Chair.); D. R. Greene (Pres.); J. W. Jones (Sec.); J. E. Chestnut (Treas.); John Alm; R. M. Beale; R. B. Kirkman; R. P. Wilkinson; C. L. Curtis; R. W. Donaldson; J. H. Downs.

Address: 1 Coca-Cola Plaza, NW, Atlanta, GA 30301.

Telephone: (404) 676-2568; **Fax:** (404) 676-8804; **Internet:** www2.coca-cola.com/citizenship/foundation_coke.html.

Jane Coffin Childs Memorial Fund for Medical Research

Founded in 1937 by Alice S. Coffin and Starling W. Childs to further research into the causes, origins and treatment of cancer.

Activities: Operates both nationally and internationally in the field of cancer research, through post-doctoral fellowships; US citizens may hold fellowships in any country, foreigners must study in the USA.

Geographical Area of Activity: International.

Publications: Report of operations and financial statement.

Finance: Net assets $39,630,840 (June 2001).

Trustees: Board of Managers of 11 members; R. S. Childs (Chair.); Board of Scientific Advisers of 12 members; Dr Joan A. Steitz (Chair. and Dir).

Principal Staff: Admin. Dir Elizabeth M. Ford.

Address: POB 3333, New Haven, CT 06510.

Telephone: (203) 785-4612; **Fax:** (203) 785-3301; **Internet:** www.jccfund.org; **e-mail:** info@jccfund.org.

Commonwealth Fund

Founded in 1918 by Anna M. Harkness and others to enhance the common good.

Activities: Major programme areas supported are as follows: to improve health insurance coverage and access to medical care; to improve the quality of health-care services; to promote ways for elderly Americans to participate more fully in community life; to develop the capacities of children and young people; and to improve the health of minorities. Also supports related projects in these areas. Promotes innovative health-care policy and practice in the USA and abroad. The Fund operates internationally in the field of education, through the Harkness Fellowships Program, which provides health policy fellowships to potential leaders from Australia, New Zealand and the United Kingdom for study and research in the USA. It also makes grants to enhance the quality of life in New York City.

Geographical Area of Activity: International.

Publications: Annual Report; grants list; *Commonwealth Fund Quarterly* (newsletter).

Finance: Assets $550,680,215 (June 2001); expenditure $15,349,829 (2001).

Officers and Directors: Charles A. Sanders (Chair.); Karen Davis (Pres.); Stephen C. Schoenbaum (Sr Vice-Pres.); Helene L. Kaplan (Vice-Chair.); John E. Craig, Jr (Exec. Vice-Pres. and Treas.); Lewis W. Bernard; William R. Brody; Frank A. Daniels, Jr; Karen Davis; Jane E. Henney; Lawrence S. Huntington; Walter E. Massey; Robert M. O'Neill; Robert C. Pozen; James R. Tallon, Jr; Samuel O. Thier.

Principal Staff: Dir, Grants Man. Andrea C. Landes.

Address: Harkness House, 1 East 75th St, New York, NY 10021-2692.

Telephone: (212) 606-3844; **Fax:** (212) 606-3500; **Internet:** www.cmwf.org; **e-mail:** cmwf@cmwf.org.

Compton Foundation, Inc

Founded in 1973 as the successor to the Compton Trust by members of the Compton family, to address community, national and international concerns in the areas of peace and world order, population and the environment.

Activities: Operates both nationally and internationally in the fields of peace and world order, family planning, the environment, equal educational opportunity, community welfare and social justice, and culture and the arts.

Geographical Area of Activity: Central America and sub-Saharan Africa.

Restrictions: The Foundation does not make grants to individuals.

Publications: Report (every 2 years); information brochure.

Finance: Total assets $85,673,417 (2001); total expenditure $10,902,064 (2001).

Officers and Directors: James R. Compton (Pres.); Ann C. Stephens (Vice-Pres. and Sec.); Gloria Duffy (Treas.); Randolph O. Compton; W. Danforth Compton; Richard Morrison; David Orr; Lee Etta Powell; Carol Wall.

Principal Staff: Exec. Dir Edith Eddy; Programme Officer for the Environment Suzanne Michell; Sr Grants Man. Charlotte Johnson.

Address: 535 Middlefield Rd, Suite 160, Menlo Park, CA 94025.

Telephone: (650) 328-0101; **Fax:** (650) 328-0171; **Internet:** www.comptonfoundation.org; **e-mail:** info@comptonfoundation.org.

Conservation International

Founded in 1987 for conservation and environmental purposes.

Activities: Active in 33 countries; collaborates with governments and other organizations to promote sustained biological diversity and ecosystems and prevent species extinction, along with basic economic and social requirements. Conducts programmes in Central and South America, Africa, Asia and the Pacific; carries out research; promotes educational projects and ecotourism; researches and markets rain forest products; and assists in the formulation of policy. Grants are made to individuals and to local not-for-profit organizations in all countries or regions which are hot spots or wilderness areas.

Geographical Area of Activity: International.

Publications: *Conservation Frontlines* (newsletter); The Rain Forest Imperative: A Ten-Year Strategy to Save Earth's Most Threatened Ecosystems.

Principal Staff: Chair. and CEO Peter Seligmann; Pres. Russell A. Mittermeier; Chair. Emer. Charles J. Hedlund; Chair., Exec. Cttee Gordon E. Moore; Vice-Chair. Meredith A. Brokaw, Harrison Ford, Lewis W. Coleman, E. O. Wilson.

Address: 1919 M St, NW, Suite 600, Washington, DC 20036.

Telephone: (202) 912-1000; **Fax:** (202) 912-1040; **Internet:** www.conservation.org.

Consultative Group on International Agricultural Research—CGIAR

Founded in 1971 by the International Bank for Reconstruction and Development (World Bank) and other United Nations agencies, to improve the quantity and quality of food in developing countries and eradicate poverty.

Activities: Comprises a network of 16 autonomous international agricultural research centres and organizations in Central and South America, Asia, Africa, the Middle East, Europe and the USA. There are about 55 donor members (governmental and multilateral agencies, and private foundations) providing long-term financial support for agricultural research, as well as the governments of 30 countries. A Technical Advisory Committee of scientists monitors the research programmes, which focus on increasing productivity, protecting the environment, saving biodiversity, improving policies and strengthening national research.

Geographical Area of Activity: International.

Publications: *CGIAR News*; Annual Report; study papers; research documents; and other publications.

Finance: Annual budget approx. $345,000,000 (2000).

Principal Staff: Chair. Ian Johnson; Exec. Sec. Francisco Reifschneider.

Address: The World Bank, MSN G6–601, 1818 H St, NW, Washington, DC 20433.

Telephone: (202) 473-8951; **Fax:** (202) 473-8110; **Internet:** www.cgiar.org; **e-mail:** cgiar@cgiar.org.

Cottonwood Foundation

Established in 1992 to promote empowerment, cultural diversity and to protect the environment.

Activities: Supports grassroots organizations in the USA and internationally which empower people to meet their basic needs, promotes cultural diversity, including the survival of an endangered or threatened culture, and protect the environment.

Geographical Area of Activity: International.

Restrictions: No funding for political or religious organizations, governmental agencies, for-profit businesses, individuals or universities.

Publications: Annual Report; Newsletter; on-line bulletin.

Finance: Total grants approx. US $40,000.

Board of Directors: Jeff Washburne (Chair.); Craig Miller (Vice-Chair.); Suzanne Wisnieewski (Treas.); Sonia Blesic (Sec.); Paul Moss (Exec. Dir); Valerie Aas; Kristin Bothun; David Fawcett; Karen Grabau; Jan Lucke; Paul Schmiechen.

Principal Staff: Exec. Dir Paul Moss.

Address: Box 10803, White Bear Lake, MN55110.

Telephone: (651) 426-8797; **Fax:** (651) 426-0320; **Internet:** www.cottonwoodfdn.org; **e-mail:** cottonwood@igc.org.

Council on International Educational Exchange

Founded in 1947 by organizations active in the field of international education and student travel, in order to improve understanding and co-operation between countries and to help re-establish student exchange after the Second World War.

Activities: The Council represents educational institutions in developing educational exchange policy, provides consultation services and evaluation of exchange programmes, and acts as a clearing-house for information. It organizes conferences and seminars, and administers Study Abroad Programs in Argentina, Australia, Belgium, Chile, the People's Republic of China, Costa Rica, Cuba, the Czech Republic, the Dominican Republic, France, Ghana, Hungary, India, Italy, Japan, Jordan, Mexico, the Netherlands, Poland, Republic of Ireland, Romania, Russian Federation, Senegal, South Africa, Spain, Taiwan, Thailand, Turkey and Vietnam. Its Council Travel Services, offering support to students working abroad, was sold to USIT World in 2001.

Geographical Area of Activity: International.

Publications: *Journal of Studies in International Education* (bi-annual); *Council–ISP News* (monthly newsletter); *Update* (monthly); *Work, Study, Travel Abroad: The Whole World Handbook; Volunteer! The Comprehensive Guide to Voluntary Service in the US and Abroad; Going Places; The High School Student's Guide to Study, Travel and Adventure Abroad; Basic Facts on Study Abroad; Where to Stay USA and Smart Vacations: The Traveler's Guide to Learning Adventures Abroad.*

Finance: Annual budget approx. $275,000,000.

Principal Staff: Pres. and Chief Exec. Stevan Trooboff.

Address: 633 Third Ave, New York, NY 10017-6706.

Fax: (212) 822-2779; **Internet:** www.ciee.org.

Council for International Exchange of Scholars

Founded in 1947, in order to assist the US Government in administering the Fulbright Scholar Program.

Activities: Aims to increase mutual understanding between the people of the USA and those of other nations; to strengthen the ties which unite the USA with other nations; and promote international co-operation for educational and cultural advancement. Awards about 800 Fulbright Scholar Awards for research and lecturing abroad annually, open to US citizens holding a doctorate or comparable professional qualification, along with university or college teaching experience, for research or teaching in any discipline, in over 140 countries world-wide. Open also to nationals of those same 140 countries to conduct research or lecture within the USA.

Geographical Area of Activity: International.

Publications: *Fulbright Online Awards Catalog; Fulbright Scholar Program: Grants for Faculty and Professionals.*

Finance: Funded by the US Dept of State, Bureau of Educational and Cultural Affairs.

Principal Staff: Exec. Dir Patti McGill Peterson; Deputy Exec. Dir Ellen Barclay.

Address: 3007 Tilden St, NW, Suite 5-L, Washington, DC 20008-3009.

Telephone: (202) 686-4000; **Fax:** (202) 362-3442; **Internet:** www.iie.org/cies; **e-mail:** cieswebmaster@cies.iie.org.

Counterpart

Founded in 1965 by Elizabeth Silverstein, and formerly known as the Foundation for the Peoples of the South Pacific, to manage humanitarian and development programmes world-wide which benefit local NGOs, charities, organizations which promote civil society, foreign demobilized military dependants and veterans.

Activities: Operates internationally, in more than 60 countries, including the countries of the former USSR, South-East Asia and the South Pacific, in the fields of aid and humanitarian assistance to less-developed countries, conservation and the environment, civil society, enterprise development, health and child survival, food security, human rights and energy, through self-conducted programmes, research, grants to institutions, conferences and training courses. Affiliated to organizations in numerous countries, including Australia, Belgium, Canada, the Caribbean, Germany and the United Kingdom. Maintains a number of international offices.

Geographical Area of Activity: International.

Publications: Annual Report; newsletters.

Finance: Assets $3,756,688 (2001); annual revenue $19,128,515 (2001).

Trustees: Elizabeth Silverstein (Hon. Chair. and Founder); Stanley W. Hosie (Chair.); Lelei Lelaulu (Pres. and Chief Exec.); Bryant George (Sec.); Sally Brumbaugh; Perry Eaton; Charles Eddy; Eva Haller; Paul G. Irwin; John A. Hoyt; Eamon M. Kelly; Barbara Pyle; Mark Silverstein; Lekha Singh; David M. Sloan.

Principal Staff: Pres. and CEO Lelei Lelaulu.

Address: 1200 18th St, NW, Suite 1100, Washington, DC 20036.

Telephone: (202) 296-9676; **Fax:** (202) 296-9679; **Internet:** www.counterpart.org; **e-mail:** info@counterpart.org.

Covenant Foundation

Established in 1990, by the Crown Family Foundation in partnership with the Jewish Education Service of North

America. Aims to build on strengths within the field of Jewish education in North America, and thus perpetuate the identity and cultural heritage of Jewish people.

Activities: Operates in the field of Jewish education in the USA and Canada. Supports innovative programmes in Jewish schools and institutions, and bestows the Covenant Jewish Educators' Award to outstanding Jewish educators.

Geographical Area of Activity: USA and Canada.

Restrictions: No funding for endowments, building funds or tuition fees.

Publications: *Ten Year Report: 1999/2000* (available on-line).

Finance: Annual grants approx. $1,200,000.

Directors: S. Ain; H. W. Appelman; S. Crown; Dr A. Eisen; E. N. Evans; A. L. Goldman; Dr B. D. Katz; M. Lainer; B. G. Manilow; M. Minow; Dr S. B. Nasatir; Dr J. Reimer; Dr J. S. Woocher.

Principal Staff: Exec. Dir Dr Judith Ginsberg.

Address: 1270 Ave of the Americas, Suite 304, New York, NY 10020-1700.

Telephone: (212) 245-3500; **Fax:** (212) 245-0619; **Internet:** www.covenantfn.org; **e-mail:** info@covenantfn.org.

Creating Hope International

Founded in 1982; aims to help victims of war, political unrest and natural disasters through grass-roots programmes so that they can rebuild their lives for a better future.

Activities: Provides technical and financial assistance to raise the level of education, health and economy throughout parts of the world where people, particularly women and children, are underprivileged, poor, oppressed or generally in need. Fosters world-wide interest in these causes in order to increase funding for those who lack basic health-care, educational and training opportunities. Currently concentrates on assisting women and children in Afghanistan, founding the Afghan Institute of Learning in 1995.

Geographical Area of Activity: International.

Directors: Toc Dunlop (Pres. and Exec. Dir); Sakena Yacoobi (Vice-Pres. and Dir of Operations); Betsy Amin-Arsa; Dr Parwin Borouman; Annette Vitale-Salajanu; Dr Janet Yamamoto.

Principal Staff: Pres. and Exec. Dir Toc Dunlop; Vice-Pres. and Dir, Operations Sakena Yacoobi.

Address: POB 1058, Dearborn, MI 48121.

Telephone: (313) 271-6213; **Fax:** (313) 565-8515; **Internet:** www.creatinghope.org; **e-mail:** sakena@creatinghope.org.

Arie and Ida Crown Memorial

Founded in 1947 by members of the Crown family for general charitable purposes.

Activities: Operates primarily in the metropolitan Chicago area, with emphasis on Jewish welfare funds in the fields of social welfare, education, the arts and humanities, health care, community development, inner cities, youth, the elderly and the disabled.

Geographical Area of Activity: USA (Chicago area) and Israel.

Restrictions: No grants are made to individuals; no unsolicited applications accepted.

Officers and Directors: Susan Crown (Pres.); Lester Crown (Vice-Pres. and Treas.); Arie Steven Crown; James Schine Crown; Rickie Crown; William Crown; Charles Goodman; Barbara Goodman Manilow; Sara Crown Star; Arnold Weber.

Principal Staff: Programme Officer Jennifer Collins.

Address: 222 North LaSalle St, Suite 2000, Chicago, IL 60601.

Telephone: (312) 236-6300.

The Crudem Foundation

Charitable foundation established in 1994 by Dr T. J. Dubuque, Jr to support missionary activities in Haiti.

Activities: Operates in the field of medicine and health, specifically providing support to a mission hospital in Milot, northern Haiti.

Geographical Area of Activity: Haiti.

Restrictions: Supports only Project Crudem in Haiti.

Finance: Total assets $341,377 (2001); total revenue $448,422 (2001).

Trustees: David G. Butler; Hope E. Carter; Theodore J. Dubuque, Jr; Thomas G. Flynn; Maurice H. Hartigan, II; Peter J. Kelly; Charlotte Kiesel; Thomas O'Toole; Susan M. Reese; Howard G. Seitz; Thomas L. Sheer; Virginia V. Weldon.

Principal Staff: Pres. Dr T. J. Dubuque; Sec. Joan M. Rask.

Address: 9043 Ladue Rd, St Louis, MO 63124-1901.

Telephone: (314) 994-7030; **Fax:** (314) 432-3567; **e-mail:** crudemdub@aol.com.

Barbara Delano Foundation, Inc

Founded in 1986 in New York as the Barbara Gauntlett Foundation, Inc. Offers support for endangered species and the protection of the environment.

Activities: Focuses funding on wildlife habitat and species protection and makes grants ranging from $1,000 to $250,000, to projects in developing countries. Grants support anti-poaching efforts, land purchases for conservation, enhancement of wildlife/people interaction and the reduction of consumption of rare wildlife through educational activities and regulatory reform. Priority is given to small grass-roots organizations with low overheads and innovative conservation programmes. Currently concentrating on the protection of the following animals: bears, elephants, exotic birds, apes, large cats, marine mammals, marine turtles, rhinos and sharks.

Geographical Area of Activity: International.

Finance: Assets $39,558,107 (2000); total grants approx. $7,658,255 (2000).

Officers and Directors: Suwanna B. Gauntlett (Pres.); Christopher C. Angell (Sec.); Charles C. Goodfellow, III (Treas.); Jerome A. Manning; Neal P. Myerberg.

Principal Staff: Programme Dir Peter D. Knights; Programme Asst Becky Zug.

Address: 450 Pacific Ave, Suite 201, San Francisco, CA 94133.

Telephone: (415) 834-1758; **Fax:** (415) 834-1759; **Internet:** www.bdfoundation.org; **e-mail:** bdfoundation@usa.net.

Charles Delmar Foundation

Founded in 1957 by Charles Delmar for general charitable purposes, to be undertaken mainly in the Washington area and in Puerto Rico and Central and South America.

Activities: Operates both nationally and internationally in the fields of education and social welfare, with emphasis on inter-American studies, higher education, literacy, the arts, hospitals, and youth and child welfare agencies.

Geographical Area of Activity: USA, India, and Central and South America.

Restrictions: No grants are made to individuals.

Finance: Assets $9,333,917 (Dec. 2001); grants expenditure $583,250 (2001).

Officers and Trustees: Mareen D. Hughes (Pres.); R. Bruce Hughes (Sec.-Treas.).

Address: 5203 Leesburg Pike, Falls Church, VA 22041.

Arthur S. DeMoss Foundation

Founded in 1955 as the National Liberty Foundation of Valley

Forge Inc to provide support for Christian agency and Church programmes in the USA and abroad, mainly in developing countries.

Activities: Offers financial support to set up and run Christian evangelical programmes in the USA and in developing countries; operates a fund matching programme.

Geographical Area of Activity: International.

Finance: Total assets $444,341,972 (2001); expenditure $36,078,266 (2001).

Officers and Directors: Nancy S. DeMoss (Chair. and CEO); Robert G. DeMoss (Pres., Sec. and Treas.); Charlotte A. DeMoss; Nancy L. DeMoss.

Address: 777 South Flagler Dr., Suite 1600, West Palm Beach, FL 33401.

Telephone: (561) 804-9011.

Deutsche Bank Americas Foundation

Established to carry out Deutsche Bank's philanthropic aims in the USA, Canada, and Central and South America.

Activities: Operates throughout the Americas in the areas of community development, education, the environment and the arts and culture, through grants to local organizations with which the Foundation works in partnership.

Geographical Area of Activity: USA, Central and South America, and Canada.

Publications: Annual Report; Guidelines; *Community Focus* (newsletter).

Finance: Total assets $3,854,263 (Dec. 2000); total giving $12,056,444 (2000).

Principal Staff: Pres. Gary Hattem; Vice-Pres. Robyn Ince.

Address: 31 W. 52nd St., New York, NY 10019.

Telephone: (646) 324-2909; **Fax:** (646) 324-2901; **Internet:** www.db.com/community; **e-mail:** gary.s.hattem@db.com.

Development Gateway Foundation

Established, in partnership with the International Bank for Reconstruction and Development (World Bank), to reduce poverty and support sustainable development through the use of information and communication technologies.

Activities: Aims to address the lack of digital technology in less-developed countries and reduce poverty, through funding information and communication technology initiatives at local, national, regional and global levels, particularly focusing on projects that bring access, applications and technology to people in the greatest need. Planned to establish a network of research and training centres in less-developed countries; activities were to include identifying the products best suited for developing access to the internet. The Foundation's central programme is the Development Gateway portal, sharing knowledge, tools and resources for development practitioners. It includes a searchable database on development projects; economic data and statistics for more than 150 countries; practical tools for procurement, government and learning through the internet; research papers; and policy statements.

Geographical Area of Activity: International.

Finance: Annual expenditure approx. $50,000,000.

Board of Directors: Mamphela Ramphele (Chair.); K. Y. Amoako; Yuzo Harada; Michael Hofmann; Akbar Khawaja; Former Pres. Alpha Oumar Konaré; Mark Malloch Brown; Wond Wossin Mesfin; Mohamed Muhsin; Romain Murenzi; Mary O'Kane; Jerry Rao; Alan Rossi; Lucio Stanca; Chander Mohan Vasudev; James D. Wolfensohn; Jun-Cheol Yang; Jean-Paul Zens; Guangyao Zhu.

Principal Staff: Pres. Mamphela Ramphele; CEO John MacArthur.

Address: 815 Connecticut Ave, NW, Suite 620, Washington, DC 20006.

Internet: www.developmentgateway.org/node/118859/en/index; **e-mail:** info@dgfoundation.org.

Cleveland H. Dodge Foundation, Inc

Founded in 1917 by Cleveland H. Dodge to promote the well-being of mankind throughout the world.

Activities: Makes grants to selected international organizations active in the Middle East, to selected national agencies in the USA, and to organizations based in New York City. Grants in the USA are mainly for education, youth programmes, child welfare and cultural programmes.

Geographical Area of Activity: USA and the Middle East.

Restrictions: No grants are made to individuals.

Publications: Annual Report; programme policy statement.

Finance: Total assets $54,642,155 (2000); total grants $2,815,716 (2000).

Officers and Directors: Cleveland E. Dodge, Jr (Pres.); William Dodge Rueckert (Vice-Pres.); Gilbert Kerlin (Sec.); Phyllis M. Criscuoli (Treas. and Exec. Dir); Bayard Dodge; David S. Dodge; Robert Garrett; Sally Dodge Mole; Bayard D. Rea; Ingrid R. Warren; Mary Rea Weidlein.

Principal Staff: Exec. Dir Phyllis M. Criscuoli.

Address: 670 West 247th St, Bronx, NY 10471.

Telephone: (718) 543-1221; **Fax:** (718) 543-0737.

William H. Donner Foundation, Inc

Founded in 1961 with funds originally donated by William Donner, the Foundation supports programmes concerned with US–Canadian affairs, international relations, education and public policy.

Activities: Operates nationally, through funding programmes to support the growth of undergraduate and graduate studies programmes in Canadian affairs at US universities; and to support experimental grants in fields such as education and public affairs.

Geographical Area of Activity: USA.

Restrictions: No grants are made to individuals.

Publications: Annual Report.

Finance: Assets $135,032,057 (Oct. 2001); grants disbursed $10,909,100 (2001).

Officers and Trustees: Curtin Winson, Jr (Pres.); Robert Donner, Jr (Vice-Pres. and Asst Treas.); Joseph W. Donner, Jr (Sec.); Deborah Donner (Treas.); and 12 others.

Principal Staff: Special Advisers William T. Alpert, James V. Capua.

Address: 60 East 42nd St, Suite 1651, New York, NY 10165.

Telephone: (212) 949-0404; **Fax:** (212) 949-6022; **Internet:** www.donner.org; **e-mail:** dfeeney@donner.org.

Camille and Henry Dreyfus Foundation, Inc

Founded in 1946 by Camille E. Dreyfus to advance the sciences of chemistry, biochemistry, chemical engineering and related sciences as a means of improving human relations and circumstances throughout the world.

Activities: Assists academic institutions in fostering fundamental research and in training students for graduate study for the doctoral degree in chemistry. Other qualifying organizations, such as research institutes with similar goals, are also eligible for grant consideration. Sponsors the New Faculty Awards Program, Post-doctoral Program in Environmental Chemistry, the Dreyfus Teacher–Scholar Awards Program, the Scholar/Fellow Program for Undergraduate Institutions, the Special Grant Program in the Chemical Sciences, the Dreyfus Faculty Start-Up Grant Program for undergraduate institutions and the Senior Scientist Mentor Initiative. Also sponsors the ACS Awards administered by the American Chemical Society: the ACS Award for Encouraging Women into Careers in the Chemical Sciences and the ACS Award for Encouraging Disadvantaged Students into Careers in the Chemical Sciences.

Geographical Area of Activity: USA.

Restrictions: Grants are not made to individuals.

Publications: Annual Report; programme brochures.

Finance: Assets $120,713,650 (Dec. 2001); grants expenditure $6,444,117 (2001).

Officers and Directors: Dorothy Dinsmoor (Pres.); John R. H. Blum (Vice-Pres.); Edward A. Reilly (Sec.); Henry C. Walter (Treas.); Marye Anne Fox; Joshua Lederberg; H. Marshall Schwarz; Harry H. Wasserman.

Principal Staff: Exec. Dir Mark J. Cardillo; Assoc. Dir Gerald L. Brandenstein.

Address: 555 Madison Ave, 20th Floor, New York, NY 10022.

Telephone: (212) 753-1760; **Internet:** www.dreyfus.org; **e-mail:** admin@dreyfus.org.

Dreyfus Health Foundation

Founded in 1965 as the Dreyfus Medical Foundation; it is a division of The Rogosin Institute, an independent, non-profit institution for scientific and medical research, treatment and education, which is affiliated with Cornell University Medical College and New York Presbyterian Hospital; the Foundation aims for better health world-wide through the optimization of the use of available resources.

Activities: Operates in Africa, Asia, Central and Eastern Europe, South America, Central America and the Caribbean, the Middle East and North America, supporting innovative scientific and health projects through its own programmes and through funding special projects. The Foundation operates through the following programmes: Problem-solving for Better Health, which aims to improve health at local level and promote international exchange of ideas; and Communications for Better Health, disseminating information through the internet and CD-ROMs.

Geographical Area of Activity: Africa, Asia, Central and Eastern Europe, North, Central and South America, the Caribbean and the Middle East.

Publications: Newsletter; health database; special publications.

Trustees: Trustees of the Rogosin Institute: Paul Seidenberg (Vice-Chair.); Albert L. Rubin (Pres.); Kurt H. Stenzel (Vice-Pres.); Barry H. Smith (Sr. Vice-Pres.); Charlotte M. Ford; Soloman J. Freedman; Bruce R. Gordon; Dana W. Hiscock; Ralph R. Hochberg; Arthur S. Hoffman; Leon M. Jaroff; Arthur A. Klein; Stephen S. Mills; Mark J. Mundy; Robert R. Riggio; Charles Rizzo; Henry S. Stefens; Paul E. Taylor, Jr; Arnold H. Tracy; Seymour H. Wigod.

Principal Staff: Dir Barry H. Smith; Dir of Operations Corley E. Smith.

Address: 205 East 64th St, Suite 404, New York, NY 10021.

Telephone: (212) 750-5075; **Fax:** (212) 371-2776; **Internet:** www.dhfglobal.org; **e-mail:** postmaster@dhfglobal.org.

Duke Endowment

Founded in 1924 by James B. Duke to provide in some measure for the physical, mental and spiritual needs of mankind.

Activities: Provides assistance to non-profit hospitals and child-care institutions in North and South Carolina; to rural United Methodist Churches and retired ministers in North Carolina; and to Davidson College, and Duke, Furman and Johnson C. Smith Universities.

Geographical Area of Activity: USA (North and South Carolina).

Restrictions: No awards are made outside the states of North and South Carolina.

Publications: *Issues* (newsletter); Annual Report; reports on foundation programmes.

Finance: Total assets approx. $2,100,000,000 (2002); grants disbursed $116,554,909 (2002).

Principal Staff: Pres. Elizabeth H. Locke; Vice-Pres. Eugene W. Cochrane, Jr.

Address: 100 North Tryon St, Suite 3500, Charlotte, NC 28202-4012.

Telephone: (704) 376-0291; **Fax:** (704) 376-9336; **Internet:** www.dukeendowment.org; **e-mail:** info@tde.org.

Dumbarton Oaks

Founded in 1940 by Mr and Mrs Robert Woods Bliss to promote research and study in the areas of Byzantine, Pre-Columbian and landscape architecture studies.

Activities: The Dumbarton Oaks Research Library and Collection houses important research and study collections in the above three fields. It offers residential summer fellowships, as well as one-year junior and post-doctoral fellowships. Dumbarton Oaks also makes grants to assist scholarly projects in the three fields with which it is concerned, and organizes conferences and symposia on Byzantine, Pre-Columbian and landscape architecture studies.

Restrictions: Grants are limited to applicants holding a doctorate or the equivalent for research purposes or to fund a suitable project.

Publications: Numerous studies, texts, catalogues and conference proceedings.

Trustees for Harvard University: Laurence H. Summers (Pres.); D. Ronald Daniel (Treas.); Hanna Holborn Gray; Conrad K. Harper; James R. Houghton; Robert E. Rubin.

Principal Staff: Dir Edward L. Keenan.

Address: 1703 32nd St, NW, Washington, DC 20007.

Telephone: (202) 339-6410; **Fax:** (202) 339-6419; **Internet:** www.doaks.org; **e-mail:** dumbartonoaks@doaks.org.

Earhart Foundation

Founded in 1929 by Harry Boyd Earhart to support education and research.

Activities: The Foundation awards fellowships and grants for graduate study and research in the fields of history, economics, political science and international affairs. Grants are made to individuals and institutions.

Geographical Area of Activity: USA.

Restrictions: Not for general operating support, endowment or building programmes.

Publications: Annual Report.

Finance: Assets $84,121,972 (2001); grants disbursed $5,488,920 (2001).

Officers and Trustees: David B. Kennedy (Pres.); Dennis L. Bark (Chair.); Earl I. Heenan, Jr (Vice-Chair.); Antony T. Sullivan (Sec. and Dir of Programmes); Edward H. Sichler, III (Treas.); Thomas J. Bray; Ann K. Irish; Paul W. McCracken; John H. Moore; Robert L. Queller; Richard A. Ware.

Address: 2200 Green Rd, Suite H, Ann Arbor, MI 48105.

Telephone: (313) 761-8592.

Earth Island Institute

Established in 1982 by David Brower to develop conservation and environment projects.

Activities: Operates in the field of conservation, preservation and restoration of the environment, by promoting citizen action and incubating a diverse group of global projects. Provides mentoring, training and support for over 40 projects doing work in more than 25 countries including Borneo, Russia, Taiwan and the USA. Supported projects include Aral Sea Environmental Alliance; Baikal Watch; Bay Area Wilderness Training; the International Marine Mammal Project; Global Services Corps; SAVE International; the Tibetan Plateau Project; West Africa Rainforest Network; and the Yggdrasil Institute.

Geographical Area of Activity: International.

Publications: *Earth Island Journal;* Annual Report.

Finance: Assets $6,983,623 (2001); annual revenue $5,405,538, expenditure $5,088,433 (2001).

Principal Staff: Exec. Dir John A. Knox; Exec. Dir David Phillips; Grants Man. Jodi Levin.

Address: 300 Broadway, Suite 28, San Francisco, CA 94133-3312.

Telephone: (415) 788-3666; **Fax:** (415) 788-7324; **Internet:** www.earthisland.org; **e-mail:** earthisland@earthisland.org.

Earthrights International

Founded in 1994, by Ka Hsaw Wa, Katie Redford and Tyler Giannini to defend human rights and protect the environment.

Activities: Operates in South-East Asia in the fields of human rights and the environment. The organization investigates and exposes human rights and environmental abuses; increases accountability of governments and trans-national corporations which undertake development projects in the region; protects individuals and communities working to protect the environment; publishes materials for human-rights workers and environmental activists; and provides education and training at grass-roots level, including running the Earthrights Schools training activists in South-East Asia and the Amazon region. Maintains an office in Thailand; however, the organization's permanent offices are located in the USA, which enables it to use the legal system and media, and to communicate with the United Nations in New York and with other NGOs with similar aims.

Geographical Area of Activity: South-East Asia and USA.

Publications: *Valued Less Than a Milk Tin: Discrimination Against Ethnic Minorities in Burma by the Ruling Military Regime* (2001) *Total Denial Continues* (2000); *Earth Rights: Linking the Quests for Human Rights and the Environment; Destructive Engagement* (1999); *Total Denial* (1996); *Human Rights and the Environment* (1997); and *School for Rape* (1998).

Finance: Funded by private foundations and individuals. Annual revenue and expenditure approx. $750,000 (2000).

Officers and Trustees: Oronto Douglas; Ka Hsaw Wa; David Hunter; Ouyporn Khunkaew; Marian Manilov; Neil A. F. Popovic; Michael Rauenhaus; Katharine J. Redford; Tom Van Dyck.

Principal Staff: Co-Founder and Co-Dir Tyler Giannini, Ka Hsaw Wa, Katharine Redford.

Address: 1612 K St, NW, Suite 401, Washington, DC 20006.

Telephone: (202) 466-5188; **Fax:** (202) 466-5189; **Internet:** www.earthrights.org; **e-mail:** infousa@earthrights.org.

Earthtrust

Established in 1976 by Don White.

Activities: Conservation organization dedicated to the preservation of wildlife and the natural environment. Organizes international campaigns against whaling and damage to dolphin stocks through the use of drift nets. Other initiatives include the Endangered Wildlife Initiative, Saving Whales and the Sea Turtle Protection Project. The organization is also involved in research and environmental education.

Geographical Area of Activity: International.

Principal Staff: Pres. and Chief Exec. Don White.

Address: 1118 Maunawili Rd, Kailua, HI 96734.

Telephone: (808) 261-5339; **Fax:** (815) 333-1158; **Internet:** www.earthtrust.org; **e-mail:** sue@flipperfund.com.

Easter Island Foundation

Established in 1989 to promote the conservation and protection of the cultural heritage of Easter Island and other Polynesian islands.

Activities: Promotes archaeological research. Encourages the local economy of Easter Island. Provides scholarships to academically promising Easter Island students for further education. Created the William Mulloy Library, on Easter Island. Issues publications and sponsors conferences.

Geographical Area of Activity: Easter Island and Polynesia.

Publications: *Rapa Nui Journal;* series of books about Easter Island and other Polynesian islands.

Principal Staff: Pres. Christopher Stephenson.

Address: POB 6774, Los Osos, CA 93412.

Telephone: (805) 528-8558; **Fax:** (805) 534-9301; **Internet:** www.islandheritage.org; **e-mail:** rapanuibooks@att.net.

eBay Foundation

Founded in 1998; aims to promote and support philanthropy and to build a strong national community. Operates as a donor-advised fund administered by the Community Foundation Silicon Valley.

Activities: Makes grants to a range of national non-profit organizations that provide help and training to those who seek new skills, especially in the area of new technology. Operates a Community Grants Program, a Global/National Grants Program and an Employee Gift Matching Program.

Geographical Area of Activity: USA.

Restrictions: No grants are made to individuals.

Address: c/o Community Foundation Silicon Valley, 60 South Market St, Suite 1000, San Jose, CA 95113.

Internet: pages.ebay.com/community/aboutebay/foundation/grantprogram.html; **e-mail:** ebayfdn@cfsv.org.

ECOLOGIA—Ecologists Linked for Organizing Grassroots Initiatives and Action

Founded in 1989, aiming to provide technical advice and assistance in ecological matters to grass-roots groups in Eastern Europe, Central Asia and the USA.

Activities: Operates in the field of conservation and the environment by working with local environmental groups in the countries of the former USSR and Eastern Europe, providing training, information and technical assistance. Promotes the development of democratic and informed decision-making skills within environmental matters. Maintains offices in Lithuania, Tajikistan and the Russian Federation. Established the Virtual Foundation (q.v.) where it is involved in co-operative projects with other non-profit organizations. The Baltic Mini-Grant Program funds small-scale community and environmental projects developed by Estonian, Latvian and Lithuanian non-profit organizations to meet local needs.

Geographical Area of Activity: Eastern Europe and the republics of Central Asia, the Far East, Central and South America and Africa.

Restrictions: No grants to independent organizations nor to individuals except from the Baltic Mini-Grants Program.

Board of Directors: Randy Kritkausky (Pres.); Carolyn Schmidt (Sec.); Ed Shoener (Treas.); Dr Aleg Cherp; Dr Rachel Golden; Paul Soler-Sala.

Principal Staff: Pres. and Exec. Dir R. Kritkausky; C. Gauthier; L. Kritkausky; S. Mack; C. Schmidt; E. Shoener.

Address: POB 268, 4 Mill St, Middlebury, VT 05753.

Telephone: (802) 388-8075; **Fax:** (802) 388-8069; **Internet:** www.ecologia.org; **e-mail:** ecologia@ecologia.org.

Albert Einstein Institution

Founded in 1983 to promote the strategic use and study of non-violence as a means of achieving effective results in international conflicts and struggles.

Activities: Promotes the use of non-violent solutions to conflicts throughout the world. The Institute also advances the study of non-violence as a means of defending democratic freedoms and institutions, examining the past use of non-violent action and dedicating itself to finding how peace, freedom and justice can be achieved without the need for violence and war. It communicates the results of its research to the general public through the media, conferences and its own publications as well as running a policy and outreach programme advising groups involved in conflict about the potential effectiveness of non-violent action, through courses, workshops, consultations and dissemination of written materials.

Geographical Area of Activity: International.

Publications: Monographs and handouts; papers, reports and publications on non-violent action.

Directors: H. McFerson (Chair.); E. Defeis; C. Goering; S. Marks; G. Sharp.

Principal Staff: Pres. G. Sharp; Special Asst H. Merriman; Officer Man. & Translations Co-ordinator J. Raqib.

Address: 427 Newbury St, Boston, MA 02115-1801.

Telephone: (617) 247-4882; **Fax:** (617) 247-4035; **Internet:** www.aeinstein.org; **e-mail:** einstein@igc.org.

Elie Wiesel Foundation for Humanity

Founded in 1986 by Elie Wiesel, winner of the Nobel Peace Prize, for the promotion of human rights and peace worldwide.

Activities: Seeks to promote human rights and peace through the creation of a new forum for the discussion of the ethical and moral issues confronting the world. Holds international conferences. Established a Humanitarian Award, and the Elie Wiesel Prize in Ethics (an essay competition). Operates also in Israel, in the area of education.

Geographical Area of Activity: USA and Israel.

Restrictions: No grants made.

Publications: Conference reports.

Principal Staff: Pres. Elie Wiesel; Vice-Pres. Marion Wiesel, Arnold Thaler.

Address: 529 Fifth Ave, Suite 1802, New York, NY 10017.

Telephone: (212) 490-7777; **Fax:** (212) 490-6006; **Internet:** www.eliewieselfoundation.org; **e-mail:** info@eliewieselfoundation.org.

EngenderHealth

Established in 1943 as a non-profit organization which aims to improve reproductive health services around the world and make them safe, reliable and available to everyone; known as AVSC International until March 2001.

Activities: Works in over 30 countries in the area of health, improving family planning and reproductive health care, working with governments, health institutions and clinic staff to develop services where none currently exist, and improving care in already existing facilities. This is done through technical assistance and training; running training seminars and providing on-site help for health-care workers on safe medical techniques; management and supervision; research on family planning issues and attitudes; and through publications which make technical reference material and information accessible to those working in the area of reproductive health. The organization is also involved in women's general health care, including HIV/AIDS issues and maternity services.

Geographical Area of Activity: International.

Publications: *EngenderHealth Update* (quarterly on-line newsletter); *EngenderHealth Working Papers* (on-line); *Client-Education Materials; Counselling, Informed Choice, and Informed Consent; Medical and Surgical Guidelines; Service Management / Quality of Care; About EngenderHealth* (all print publications).

Finance: Annual revenue $32,500,000, total expenditure $29,900,000 (2000–2001).

Board of Directors: Lyman B. Brainerd, Jr (Chair.).

Principal Staff: Pres. Dr Amy E. Pollack.

Address: 440 Ninth Ave, 2nd Floor, New York, NY 10001.

Telephone: (212) 561-8000; **Fax:** (212) 561-8067; **Internet:** www.engenderhealth.org; **e-mail:** info@engenderhealth.org.

Enterprise Development International

Established in 1985, aiming to provide a long-term solution to poverty through micro-enterprise in developing countries and the USA.

Activities: Operates in the field of international development through partner organizations, by providing small loans, business training and on-going encouragement and support to those with the desire to start or expand small businesses in the developing world, in order to enable families to afford better nutrition, housing, health care and education for themselves. Also runs the Enterprise Fund for Women, working through local faith-based organizations in India, Mexico, Nicaragua, the Philippines and Romania.

Geographical Area of Activity: International.

Publications: *The Enterprising Times* (quarterly newsletter).

Finance: Total assets $716,514 (1999); income $1,218,320, total expenditure $1,249,532 (1999).

Board of Directors: Stephen Rosenburgh (Chair.); Charles W. Seale (Vice-Chair.); C. W. Gardner (Treas.); Colby May (Sec.); and 21 others.

Principal Staff: Pres. and CEO Juan Benitez.

Address: 10395 Democracy Lane, Fairfax, VA 22030.

Telephone: (703) 277-3360; **Fax:** (703) 277-3348; **e-mail:** enterprise@endpoverty.com.

EnterpriseWorks Worldwide

Non-profit organization, formerly known as Appropriate Technology International, that aims to provide economic opportunity for all as a long-term solution to poverty in the developing world.

Activities: Operates in the field of economic development in more than 60 countries in Africa, Asia, and Central and South America, supporting small businesses in order to increase the earning power, income and quality of life of the world's 2,000,000,000 small producers, with the aim of breaking the poverty cycle and enabling the underprivileged to provide their families with a better quality of life. EnterpriseWorks focuses on producers in the areas of small-scale irrigation, energy, oilseeds and staple foods, treecrops, dairy and other livestock, and natural products.

Geographical Area of Activity: Africa and Asia.

Directors: Hon. Robin L. Beard; Nancy Bearg; Ann Beaudry; Ela Bhatt; Murray Brauman; Williams W. Burrington; Ambassador Francis Cook; John M. Kamya; Hon. Andrew Maguire; Hon. James P. Moody; Hon. Donald M. Payne; Iqbal Quadir; Irene Rosenberg Wurtzel.

Principal Staff: Pres. and CEO Nancy Bearg.

Address: 1828 L St, NW, Suite 1000, Washington, DC 20036.

Telephone: (202) 293-4600; **Fax:** (202) 293-4598; **Internet:** www.enterpriseworks.org; **e-mail:** info@enterpriseworks.org.

Environmental Partnership for Central Europe

Founded in 1991 by the Charles Stewart Mott Foundation (q.v.), the German Marshall Fund of the United States (q.v.), the Moriah Fund, the Rockefeller Brothers Fund (q.v.), the Sasakawa Peace Foundation of Japan (q.v.), and two anonymous donors. The Partnership is administered by the German Marshall Fund. It is a consortium of five foundations located in the Czech Republic, Hungary, Poland, Romania and Slovakia focusing on community-based environmental projects.

Activities: The consortium operates in the field of conservation of the environment in Central and Eastern Europe, and especially in the Czech Republic, Hungary, Poland, Romania and Slovakia. Focus is on citizen participation, through community-based projects. Maintains regional offices in the Czech Republic, Hungary, Poland and Slovakia.

Geographical Area of Activity: Central and Eastern Europe.

Publications: Report; *A Decade of Nurturing the Grassroots—the Environmental Partnership for Central Europe (EPCE) 1991-2000; Caring for the Land*.

Principal Staff: US Project Dir Irmgard Hunt.

Address: 11 Dupont Circle, NW, Suite 210, Washington, DC 20036.

Telephone: (202) 588-9018; **Fax:** (202) 462-8097; **e-mail:** 006155568@mcimail.com.

Epilepsy Foundation

Founded in 1968 by merger of the Epilepsy Foundation (founded in 1954) and the Epilepsy Association of America (founded in 1965) as the national, voluntary health organization for the prevention and cure of seizure disorders, the alleviation of their effects, and improvement of the quality of life for people who have these disorders.

Activities: Operates mainly nationally in the field of medicine and health; conducts and supports research, awards fellowships for research and exchange of expertise (including the Fritz E. Dreyfuss International Travel Program); supports training programmes for sufferers from epilepsy; holds conferences; and disseminates information through its publications.

Geographical Area of Activity: Mainly USA.

Publications: Annual Report; *Between Us* (quarterly); *Epilepsy USA* (bi-monthly and on-line newsletter); *Kids News* (quarterly); brochures and specialist publications.

Board of Trustees: Linda K. Warner (Chair.); Martha J. Morrell (Immediate Past Chair.); William E. Braunlich (Senior Vice-Chair.); Tony Coelho (Vice-Chair.); A. G. Newmyer, III (Treas.); George Thomas Beall (Sec.).

Principal Staff: Pres. and Chief Exec. Eric R. Hargis.

Address: 4351 Garden City Dr., Landover, MD 20785-7223.

Telephone and Fax: (301) 459-3700; **Internet:** www.efa.org.

Esperança, Inc (Hope)

Founded in 1970 to support the work of Fr Luke Tupper. The organization aims to provide adequate health care for children around the world.

Activities: Operates in the field of medicine and health in developing countries, working to improve health care, particularly focusing on reducing child mortality. Maintains a clinic in Brazil, and currently runs projects in Belize, Bolivia, Mexico, Nicaragua, Peru and the USA, including training doctors and nurses so as to improve the quality of health services, informing mothers on disease-prevention methods, and funding health education.

Geographical Area of Activity: USA, Central and South America and West Africa.

Directors: Rob Church (Chair.); Jim Wentworth (Sec. and Chair.-Elect); Tom Harris (Treas.); and 15 directors.

Principal Staff: Pres. and CEO Raul Espericueta.

Address: 1911 West Earll Dr., Phoenix, AZ 85015.

Telephone: (602) 252-7772; **Fax:** (602) 340-9197; **Internet:** www.esperanca.org; **e-mail:** info@esperanca.org.

Etruscan Foundation

Founded in 1958 to support the work of students and scholars interested in classical archaeology, especially the history of ancient Etruscan civilization, and the preservation of the natural and cultural heritage of Tuscany, ancient land of the Etruscans.

Activities: The Foundation sponsors excavations and an annual lecture on Etruscan and Italic archaeology; organizes seminars on art history, history and medicine, and educational programmes on architectural preservation, classical archaeology and medieval archaeology; organizes field training courses in classical archaeology; funds internships and fellowships; and maintains a library of 600 volumes and a museum.

Geographical Area of Activity: USA and Italy.

Publications: *Etruscan Studies*.

Board of Trustees: Robert Dorit (Pres.); Michael Goldberg (Vice-Pres.); Richard Olken (Sec.); Elizabeth Bracher (Treas.); Peter Cinelli; Kenneth M. Davies; Kenneth Katz; Erik Nielsen; Marco Nobili; Federica Piccolomini; Vittorio Re; Francesca Stratton.

Principal Staff: Admin. Gwen Dwyer.

Address: c/o Grants Management Associates, 77 Summer St, 8th Floor, Boston, MA 02110-1006.

Telephone: (617) 426-7172; **Fax:** (617) 426-5441; **Internet:** www.etruscanfoundation.org; **e-mail:** office@etruscanfoundation.org.

Eurasia Foundation

Founded in 1993 with funds from the US Agency for International Development (USAID) to promote the advancement of democratic institutions and private enterprise in the countries of the former USSR.

Activities: Supports private sector and democratic institution development through the distribution of grants, and through collaborating on specific programmes with other interested institutions and individuals. Grants are made to support innovative projects within the following areas: private enterprise development; public administration and policy; and civil society. Projects supported include a small business lending programme, an economics education and research consortium and an initiative towards independent media. The Foundation maintains offices in the Russian Federation, Armenia, Azerbaijan, Georgia, Kazakhstan, Kyrgyz Republic, Ukraine and Uzbekistan. The Foundation awards approximately 1,000 grants, totalling approximately $20,000,000 annually through its field offices. Around 40 partnership projects annually are supported, with grants of $100,000, on average.

Geographical Area of Activity: Eastern Europe and republics of Central Asia (countries of the former USSR).

Restrictions: Grants only to organizations and individuals in mandate and geographical area.

Publications: Annual Report; information brochure; application guidelines; newsletter.

Finance: Annual budget $25,000,000.

Officers and Trustees: Sarah C. Carey (Chair.); B. Frenzel (Vice-Chair.); Amb. Edward Djerejian; E. Dyson; A. Guff; G. Helland; F. Ingriselli; T. Kemp; S. King; K. Klose; Hon. E. Lawson; T. Pickering; and 10 others.

Principal Staff: Pres. Charles William Maynes.

Address: 1350 Connecticut Ave, NW, Suite 1000, Washington, DC 20036.

Telephone: (202) 234-7370; **Fax:** (202) 234-7377; **Internet:** www.eurasia.org; **e-mail:** eurasia@eurasia.org.

Family Care International

Established in 1986 to promote sexual and reproductive health and rights in developing countries, particularly regarding the safety of pregnancy and childbirth.

Activities: Works in Anglophone and Francophone Africa, Asia (Laos), and Central and South America and the Caribbean, in partnership with NGOs, governments and international agencies on a number of programmes relating to urgent women's health issues. These include maternal health, adolescent sexual and reproductive health, family planning, unsafe abortion and violence against women. There is a particular focus on safe motherhood (pregnancy and childbirth), providing support and adequate health care for expectant mothers and providing a woman-centred approach to reproductive health. The organization provides direct technical assistance to partner organizations in more than 24 countries world-wide, information and advocacy services, and training materials. Maintains offices in Bolivia, Burkina Faso, Colombia, Ecuador, Kenya, Mexico, Nigeria and Tanzania.

Geographical Area of Activity: Anglophone and Francophone Africa, Asia (Laos), and Central and South America and the Caribbean.

Restrictions: No grants available.

Publications: Produces a number of publications including guidelines, training materials and other information regarding reproductive and sexual health and rights issues.

Address: 588 Broadway, Suite 503, New York, NY 10012.

Telephone: (212) 941-5300; **Fax:** (212) 941-5563; **Internet:** www.familycareintl.org; **e-mail:** info@familycareintl.org.

Family Health International

Established in 1971; aims to improve reproductive and family health care in developing countries.

Activities: Operates in the USA and more than 60 less-developed countries in the field of family planning and reproductive health, through research, health service support, fellowships, and training and information programmes. Works to improve the accessibility and safety of reproductive health-care services and family-planning methods in order to improve the quality of life of families in developing parts of the world. Also runs programmes focusing on the prevention of HIV/AIDS and other sexually-transmitted diseases, and the care of sufferers of such diseases. Maintains local offices in 30 countries.

Geographical Area of Activity: International.

Publications: More than 2,000 full-text materials are available on-line in English, French and Spanish, including periodicals, working papers, reports and training materials.

Principal Staff: CEO Albert J. Siemens; Pres. Willard Cates Jr.

Address: POB 13950, Research Triangle Park, Durham, NC 27709.

Telephone: (919) 544-7040; **Fax:** (919) 544-7261; **Internet:** www.fhi.org; **e-mail:** services@fhi.org.

Feed the Children, Inc

Founded in 1979, Feed the Children is a Christian non-profit charitable organization that aims to provide support and aid to children, families and people in need all over the world.

Activities: Works in the USA and internationally in four main fields: food supply; sustainable development; medical care; and emergency relief. Distributes food, and provides medical assistance and educational opportunities to children in 96 countries, and supports orphanages, schools and other charities and NGOs financially. Sends medical teams and supplies to developing regions, and promotes self-sustaining development for families, so as to provide a long-term solution to poverty and hunger.

Geographical Area of Activity: International.

Finance: Total revenue $553,397,898, total expenditure $579,068,632 (2002).

Principal Staff: Pres. Larry Jones.

Address: POB 36, Oklahoma City, OK 73101-0036.

Telephone: (405) 942-0228; **Fax:** (405) 945-4177; **Internet:** www.christianity.com/feedthechildren; **e-mail:** ftc@feedthechildren.org.

Feed My People Children's Charity

A charitable organization which aims to improve children's chances of survival throughout the world.

Activities: Operates, especially in developing countries, in a number of fields relating to child survival and the improvement of their quality of life. Programmes include child survival projects; promoting breastfeeding of infants; provision of immunization for women and children; providing education, food, clothing and medical help to children of pre-school and school age; medical services, including operating health clinics, and supplies to children living in disadvantaged communities; emergency food and medical assistance; and training in basic health care and nutrition for parents. Also runs a micro-enterprise scheme and sustainable gardening projects to improve family life.

Geographical Area of Activity: International.

Address: 11052 North 24th Ave, Phoenix, AZ 85029.

Telephone: (602) 678-3285; **Fax:** (602) 678-3288; **e-mail:** dsaacct@earthlink.net.

FINCA International, Inc

Founded in 1984 to support the economic and human development of families trapped in severe poverty, to enable them to create their own jobs, raise household incomes and improve their standard of living. This is done through a global network of locally managed, self-supporting institutions.

Activities: Supports economic self-sufficiency in less-developed countries, through the creation of sustainable development projects, including village banks to provide loans of between $50 and $1,000 to individuals and to initiate savings programmes. Operates in North, Central and South America, Africa and in certain Central Asian countries of the former USSR. New programmes were planned to begin in South Africa and Kosovo.

Geographical Area of Activity: North, Central and South America, Africa and the former USSR.

Publications: *Village Banknotes* (quarterly).

Finance: Assets $36,671,482 (Aug. 2001); annual revenue $32,573,164, expenditure $26,231,596 (2001).

Board of Directors: Robert W. Hatch (Chair.); Richard M. Williamson (Treas.); Rupert W. Scofield (Sec.); Carlos Camacho; JoAnn Field; John K. Hatch; Harold D. Jastram; José Maria Mendez; Agrinna Mussa; Hans Niehorster; Franz Orschel; James Semakadde; Rita E. Spillman.

Principal Staff: Exec. Dir Rupert W. Scofield.

Address: 1101 14th St, NW, 11th Floor, Washington, DC 20005.

Telephone: (202) 682-1510; **Fax:** (202) 682-1535; **Internet:** www.villagebanking.org; **e-mail:** finca@villagebanking.org.

Firefly Children's Network

Established to address the underlying issues of neglect of Russian children abandoned due to disabilities.

Activities: Aims to help children with disabilities in Russian orphanages, through the provision of information to individuals, non-government and government organizations to help the development of effective programmes and the even distribution of humanitarian aid within the Russian Federation, including the development of an on-line resource centre; conferencing facilities for professionals to share information and expertise; and the development of children's rehabilitation centres.

Geographical Area of Activity: Russian Federation.

Board of Directors: Jonathan Baker; Julie Baker; Diana England; Steve Hull; Dr John Phillips; Derek van Bever.

Principal Staff: Exec. Dir Nicole Whitmarsh.

Address: POB 21582, Washington, DC 20009.

Telephone: (202) 232-5706; **Fax:** (202) 232-5708; **Internet:** www.fireflykids.org; **e-mail:** nwhitmarsh@fireflykids.org.

First Peoples Worldwide

Established by the First Nations Development Institute to work as an advocate for indigenous rights world-wide.

Activities: Operates world-wide in the field of human rights for indigenous peoples. Works to help sustain the land and culture of indigenous peoples in a number of ways, including encouraging and enabling indigenous peoples to take an active role in issues concerning the environment, the economy and the legal system; providing technical and financial support for culturally-appropriate development programmes; advocating self-governance; building and maintaining a database containing information on indigenous land rights and self-governance; and operating a fellowship programme for community leaders. It has been engaged in direct work in Southern Africa and Australia, and is currently operating projects in South America.

Geographical Area of Activity: Africa, Australia, and South America.

Principal Staff: Exec. Dir Rebecca Adamson.

Address: 11917 Main St, Stores Bldg, Fredericksburg, VA 22408.

Telephone: (540) 371-5615; **Fax:** (540) 371-3505; **Internet:** www.firstpeoples.org; **e-mail:** infofpw@firstnations.org.

Flight Safety Foundation

Founded in 1945 by R. Crane, H. DeHaven and J. Morrison to promote and foster improvements in international conditions of air safety.

Activities: Publishes, and distributes to members, bulletins on aviation safety and accident prevention. Conducts specialized research and carries out flight safety analyses for operators. Organizes annual business air safety seminars and annual awards. Has a membership of 640 organizations, individuals, companies, etc. from more than 150 countries. Maintains a library of approximately 1,000 volumes.

Geographical Area of Activity: International.

Publications: *Annual Index; Accident Prevention* (monthly); *Airport Operations* (6 a year); *Aviation Mechanics Bulletin* (6 a year); *Cabin Crew Safety* (6 a year); *Flight Safety Digest* (monthly); *Helicopter Safety* (6 a year); *Human Factors and Aviation Medicine* (6 a year); seminar and workshop proceedings, special reports, technical manuals and studies, membership directory; Annual Report.

Finance: Annual budget approx. $2,500,000.

Trustees: The Foundation is governed by a Board of Governors composed of 35 members, one-third of whom retire each year; Stuart Matthews (Pres.).

Address: 601 Madison St, Suite 300, Alexandria, VA 22314-1756.

Telephone: (703) 739-6700; **Fax:** (703) 739-6708; **Internet:** www.flightsafety.org.

Food for the Hungry

Founded in the USA in 1971 as a Christian organization with the purpose of relieving poverty world-wide.

Activities: Operates programmes in the fields of health care, community development, nutrition and emergency relief; provides an information and education service; organizes seminars and workshops; provides training for farmers; promotes child sponsorship; gives financial assistance to other development organizations.

Geographical Area of Activity: International.

Publications: *Feeding the Hungry* (newsletter).

Finance: Financed by the United Nations, governments, national organizations, private foundations and donations. Annual budget approx. US $50,000,000.

Principal Staff: Pres. Tetsunao Yamamori.

Address: 7729 East Greenway Rd, Scottsdale, AZ 85260.

Telephone: (480) 998-3100; **Internet:** www.fh.org; **e-mail:** hunger@fh.org.

Food for the Poor, Inc

Established in 1982 by Robin Mahfood, an NGO that seeks to link the Church in developed countries with that in less-developed areas, in order to help the poor.

Activities: Works internationally to support the poor in developing countries. Has links with 12,000 primarily religious and indigenous NGOs world-wide, and works with them to raise funding and develop projects to improve conditions in Central and South America and the Caribbean, especially in the areas of food supplies, education, health care and social welfare.

Geographical Area of Activity: Central and South America and the Caribbean.

Restrictions: Operates only in Central and South American and Caribbean countries.

Publications: Annual Report; newsletters.

Finance: Funded by donations from the public, businesses and foundations. Total expenditure $351,446,951 (2002).

Directors: R. G. Mahfood (Chair. and CEO); Most Rev. P. Boyle (Vice-Pres.); Rev. G. Bennett; G. Bonina; Rev. L. Frade; F. Issa; P. T. Kennedy; T. Lorden; R. Maingot; A. J. Pereira; D. Price; Rev. G. Ramkissoon.

Principal Staff: Chief Financial Officer M. Pierre-Chavannes.

Address: 550 SW 12th Ave, Dept 9662, Deerfield Beach, FL 33442-3110.

Telephone: (954) 427-2222; **Fax:** (954) 570-7654; **Internet:** www.foodforthepoor.org.

Ford Foundation

Founded in 1936 by Henry Ford and his son Edsel B. Ford, the Foundation is a resource for innovative people and institutions world-wide, aiming to strengthen democratic values, reduce poverty and injustice, promote international co-operation and advance human achievement.

Activities: Grants are made primarily to institutions within the Foundation's three programme areas: Asset Building and Community Development, which brings together four previously separate programmes: Urban Poverty, Rural Poverty and Resources, Reproductive Health and Population, and Program-Related Investments; Peace and Social Justice, which comprises two units, Human Rights and International Co-operation, and Governance and Civil Society; and Education, Media, Arts and Culture (EMAC), which also comprises two units: Education, Knowledge and Religion, and Media, Arts and Culture. The Foundation has field offices in Brazil, Chile, the People's Republic of China, Egypt, India, Indonesia, Philippines, Mexico, Namibia, Nigeria, the Russian Federation, South Africa and Vietnam. Support is given for conferences and seminars, general purposes, matching funds, publications, research, programme-related investments, seed money, special projects, technical assistance, endowment funds, fellowships and individual grants.

Geographical Area of Activity: International.

Restrictions: Support not given for personal needs, religious activities or building construction.

Publications: Annual Report; *Report* (quarterly); *Current Interests* (every 2 years).

Finance: Assets $10,814,696,000 (Sept. 2001); total grants $829,190,310 (2001).

Trustees: Paul A. Allaire (Chair.); Alain J. P. Belda; Susan V. Berresford; Anke A. Ehrhardt; Kathryn S. Fuller; Wilmot G. James; Yolanda Kakabadse; David T. Kearns; Wilma P. Mankiller; Richard Moe; Yolanda T. Moses; Luis G. Nogales; Deval L. Patrick; Ratan N. Tata; Carl B. Weisbrod; W. Richard West.

Principal Staff: Pres. Susan V. Berresford; Exec. Vice-Pres. And Sec. Barroon M. Tenny; Senior Vice-Pres. Barry D. Gaberman; Vice-Pres. Alison Bernstein, Melvin Oliver; Bradford Smith; Linda B. Strumpf, Alexander Wilde; Treas. Nicholas M. Gabriel; Assoc. Ge. Counsel Nancy P. Feller.

Address: 320 East 43rd St, New York, NY 10017.

Telephone: (212) 573-5000; **Fax:** (212) 351-3677; **Internet:** www.fordfound.org; **e-mail:** office-secretary@fordfoundation.org.

Forefront

Established to cultivate a world-wide respect for human rights by strengthening human rights organizations throughout the world; formerly the Center for Sustainable Human Rights Action.

Activities: Operates internationally in the field of human rights. Provides training resources, technical assistance and information through publications, thereby seeking to provide solutions and strategies for long-term effectiveness for human rights institutions and organizations world-wide. Also runs campaigns.

Geographical Area of Activity: International.

Publications: *Human Rights Institution-Building Handbook Series;* Regional Studies; Programme Reports.

Board of Directors: Martin Dunn (Chair.); Angela Brown, Stacey Kabat, Miguel Angel de los Santos (Vice-Chair.); Mimi Doretti (Sec.); Samuel Kofi Woods (Treas.).

Principal Staff: Dir Lesley Carson.

Address: 333 7th Ave, 13th Floor, New York, NY 10001-5004.

Telephone: (212) 845-5200; **Internet:** www.forefrontleaders .org; **e-mail:** forefront@forefrontleaders.org.

Foreign Policy Association

Founded in 1918 to educate Americans about international events and issues and to encourage them to participate in the foreign policy process.

Activities: Seeks to educate Americans about international issues, principally through its Great Decisions programme, which consists of an annual impartial briefing of eight key foreign policy issues, discussed by groups, and at seminars and public forums aimed at both students and adults. Also publishes books, leaflets and produces other educational online resources.

Geographical Area of Activity: International.

Restrictions: Not a grant-making organization.

Publications: *Global Views; FPA Today; Great Decisions Online; Global Jobs; Foreign Policy Alert* (on-line newsletters); *Great Decisions* (annual programme guide).

Board of Directors: Mary L. Belknap (Vice-Chair.); Noel V. Lateef (Pres.); John E. Merrow (Treas.); James M. Walsh (Sec.); and 47 others.

Address: 470 Park Ave South, New York, NY 10016.

Telephone: (212) 481-8100; **Fax:** (212) 481-9275; **Internet:** www.fpa.org; **e-mail:** kfaulkner@fpa.org.

Foundation for a Civil Society

Founded in 1984, reorganized in 1990, to act as a co-ordinating body to promote civil society, democracy and market economy. Formerly known as the Foundation for a Civil Society (Charter 77 Foundation–New York).

Activities: The Foundation has two main functions: to act as a catalyst, initiating and supporting projects; and to act as facilitator, connecting funding sources with institutions and individuals wishing to establish programmes and projects. The Foundation has an extensive network of high-level contacts in the USA and other parts of the world. The major programmes of the Foundation include the New Slovakia initiative designed to ensure that the new governments in the Slovak Republic move smoothly toward European integration. The Foundation's offices in the Czech Republic and Slovakia became independent NGOs known as Nadace VIA and Nadácia Pre Občiansku Spoločnost (qq.v.), respectively.

Geographical Area of Activity: International, with an emphasis on Central and Eastern Europe.

Finance: Total assets $257,195 (1999); income $1,094,063 (1999).

Trustees: Bernard Aidinoff (Chair.); Wendy W. Luers (Pres.); and 14 others.

Address: POB 2235, New York, NY 10021.

Telephone: (212) 717-9778; **Fax:** (212) 717-5255; **Internet:** www.fcsny.org; **e-mail:** megan@fcsny.org.

Foundation for Deep Ecology

Established in 1990. Concerned with the environment, conservation and protection of biodiversity and wilderness, ecological agriculture and the environmental impact of economic globalization and the technological systems that serve it.

Activities: The Foundation focuses on fundamental ecological issues in three areas: Biodiversity and Wilderness, including protection of forests, aquatic ecosystems and other habitats, wildlands philanthropy (i.e. buying land to save it), wilderness recovery (supporting the design and implementation of large-scale wilderness recovery networks), funding for activists campaigning for full protection of species and ecosystems, and funding efforts to eliminate resource extraction on public lands; Ecological Agriculture, including support for alternative models of agriculture that support biodiversity, local self-reliance and healthy agrarian communities, support for efforts to combat industrialization of agriculture, and support for efforts to link conservationists with farmers and activists in order to integrate habitat preservation and restoration with diverse farming practices; and Education, including campaigns to educate the public about and to resist the growth of the new macro-economic trends and the technological systems that drive these trends (e.g. international free-trade agreements), and providing aid to groups working towards viable local economic systems (for example community-building, local currencies and defining new technological and economic systems). From 2003 the Foundation is to increase its focus on wildlands philanthropy, meaning there will be a reduction in available grants in the remaining grant programmes.

Geographical Area of Activity: USA, Canada and South America (primarily Chile and Argentina). Grants to some groups in the United Kingdom, Spain and the Netherlands.

Restrictions: No new grant proposals accepted.

Publications: Guidelines.

Finance: Net assets $170,604,000 (June 2000); annual expenditure $13,019,300 (2000).

Officers and Directors: Douglas R. Tompkins (Pres.); Quincey Tompkins Imhoff, Kristine McDivitt Tompkins (Vice-Pres.); Debra B. Ryker (Sec./Treas.).

Principal Staff: Grants Admin. Elizabeth Unwin; Programme Dir Jerry Mander; Biodiversity and Wilderness Programme Officer John Davis; Ecological Agriculture Programme Officer Melanie Adcock.

Address: 1062 Fort Cronkhite, Sausalito, CA 94965.

Telephone: (415) 229-9339; **Fax:** (415) 229-9340; **Internet:** www.deepecology.org; **e-mail:** info@deepecology.org.

Foundation for Latin American Anthropological Research

Founded in 1969 by Dr Nicholas M. Hellmuth to engage in academic research in the fields of archaeology, art history and tropical flora and fauna.

Activities: Operates in the fields of the arts and humanities, with respect to ancient cultures of Central America, especially in the areas of archaeology, ethno-history, ethnography and the history of sports, conservation and the environment, and education, through self-conducted programmes, conferences and training courses, and field trips to Central America. Most research is carried out in Mexico, Guatemala, Honduras and Belize, but the Foundation also carries out studies of Mesoamerican art in museums world-wide. Maintains libraries in Austria and Guatemala and a photographic archive.

Geographical Area of Activity: Mainly Mexico and Central America.

Publications: Books on archaeology, pre-Columbian art, ancient architecture and sports in Pre-Hispanic America.

Finance: Annual revenue and expenditure approx. $150,000.

Principal Staff: Dir Dr Nicholas M. Hellmuth.

Address: Brevard Community College, 1519 Clear Lake Rd, Cocoa, FL 32922.

Telephone: (407) 632-1111; **Fax:** (407) 633-4565; **Internet:** www.maya-art-books.org/html/flaar.html; **e-mail:** flaarmaya@yahoo.com.

Foundation for Middle East Peace

Founded in 1979 by Merle Thorpe, Jr to assist in an understanding of Israeli–Palestinian problems, including the identification of US interests, and to contribute to a just and peaceful resolution.

Activities: Carries out research into Middle East peace, and supports elements in the Arab and Jewish communities which are working towards peace between Israelis and Palestinians.

Geographical Area of Activity: Israel and Palestinian Autonomous Areas.

Restrictions: No grants are made to individuals, grants are made only to organizations and projects that contribute to Israeli–Palestinian peace.

Publications: *The West Bank: Hostage of History; Prescription for Conflict: Israel's West Bank Settlement Policy; Error and Betrayal in Lebanon; Facing the PLO Question; A Policy for the Moment of Truth; No Trumpets, No Drums; Report on Israeli Settlement in the Occupied Territories* (6 times a year); settlement reports.

Finance: Funded by endowment and annual income.

Trustees: Peter M. Castleman (Chair.); Stephen Hartwell (Treas.); Calvin H. Cobb, Jr.; James J. Cromwell; Richard S. T. Marsh; Richard Murphy; Prof. William Quandt; Sally S. Thorpe.

Principal Staff: Pres. Philip C. Wilcox Jr; Editor Geoffrey Aronson.

Address: 1761 N. St, NW, Washington, DC 20036.

Telephone: (202) 835-3650; **Fax:** (202) 835-3651; **Internet:** www.fmep.org; **e-mail:** info@fmep.org.

Foundation for Russian American Economic Cooperation

Established in 1989, the Foundation for Russian American Cooperation to foster expanded economic ties between Russia and the United States, with a special focus on building bridges between the Russian Far East and the United States West Coast.

Activities: The Foundation works through building bilateral and multilateral relationships and serving as a hub through which grassroots organizations, the private sector, regional officials and federal decision-makers are interconnected. The Foundation's activities reflect the contemporary realities of USA—Russia relations in a range of areas including small and medium enterprise development, nuclear cities, customs reform, sustainable development, legislative reform, good governance, law enforcement, public health and non-profit capacity building.

Geographical Area of Activity: USA and the Russian Federation (with an emphasis on the Russian Far East).

Publications: *Fast Fax* (monthly newsletter); *News Digest* (weekly Russia report).

Directors: T. Allison; P. Buzytsky; C. Chase; S. Crabtree; S. Crown; J. Cullen; B. Davis; Z. Degtjar; R. Devereaux; B. Dugan; M. Evans; B. Forbush; J. Fuller; N. Gordon; T. Kennedy; E. Luttrell; R. Munro; M. Niles; J. Platt; J. Schmidt; G. Tarleton; J. Thornton; T. Tierney; B. Walsh.

Principal Staff: Pres. Carol Vipperman; Business Man. Maryann Ness.

Address: 2601 Fourth Ave, Suite 310, Seattle, WA 98121.

Telephone: (206) 443-1935; **Fax:** (206) 443-0954; **Internet:** www.fraec.org; **e-mail:** fraec@fraec.org.

Francis Families Foundation

Founded in 1989 as a result of the merger of the Parker B. Francis Foundation and the Parker B. Francis, III Foundation. The Foundation's purpose is to fund medical fellowships in pulmonary medicine and anaesthesiology and to support principal educational and cultural institutions within the Greater Kansas City metropolitan area.

Activities: Awards fellowships to citizens of the USA or Canada (or to foreign nationals intending to take up permanent residence in the USA or Canada) for post-doctoral research related to pulmonary disease. Also supports child and youth development programmes from pre-school care through to higher education and cultural programmes in the Greater Kansas City metropolitan area.

Geographical Area of Activity: North America.

Publications: Annual Report.

Finance: Assets $117,192,433 (Dec. 2001); grants disbursed $5,164,805 (2001).

Executive Committee: Ann F. Barhoum; David V. Francis; J. Scott Francis; Susan F. Neves; and 6 other members.

Principal Staff: Exec. Dir Jerry Kitzi.

Address: 800 West 47th St, Suite 717, Kansas City, MO 64112.

Telephone: (816) 531-0077; **Internet:** www.francisfoundation.org; **e-mail:** webmaster@francisfoundation.org.

Franciscans International

Established in 1989.

Activities: Works in collaboration with other NGOs, the United Nations and Franciscans around the world on global issues, especially relating to peace-making and concern for the poor, including projects on religious intolerance, human rights, migration and development in Africa. Also runs an internship programme. Aims to represent the poor at the United Nations. Maintains offices in Geneva and Nairobi.

Geographical Area of Activity: International.

Publications: *FI Newsletter* (quarterly).

Principal Staff: Exec. Dir Agostinho Diekmann; Dir, New York Florence Deacon; Dir, Geneva John Quigley; Exec. Sec., Geneva Alessandra Aula.

Address: 211 East 43rd St, Rm 1100, 11th Floor, New York, NY 10017-4707.

Telephone: (212) 490-4624; **Fax:** (866) 283-0134; **Internet:** www.franciscansinternational.org; **e-mail:** franintl@franciscansinternational.org.

The Freedom Forum

Non-partisan, international foundation established in 1991 under the direction of Allen H. Neuharth, as the successor to a foundation started in 1935 by newspaper publisher Frank E. Gannett. It is dedicated to free press, free speech and free spirit for all people.

Activities: An operating foundation, which focuses on four main priorities: the Newseum, First Amendment issues, newsroom diversity and world press freedom. The Newseum is an independent affiliate, funded by the Freedom Forum, an interactive museum of news, based in Arlington. The Foundation also funds the First Amendment Center, another independent affiliate, with offices at Vanderbilt University in Nashville, TN, New York City and Arlington, which works to preserve and protect First Amendment freedoms through information and education. The Center serves as a forum for the study and exploration of free-expression issues, including freedom of speech, of the press and of religion, the right to assemble and to petition the government. Makes several annual awards in recognition of quality journalism and to promote freedom of speech. The Foundation has operating offices in Buenos Aires, Hong Kong, Johannesburg, London and Cocoa Beach, FL, but operates principally in the USA.

Geographical Area of Activity: Mainly USA.

Restrictions: This is an operating foundation, which does not accept unsolicited requests for funding.

Publications: Annual Report; information brochures; conference and seminar reports; video and audio tapes of programmes.

Finance: Funded by income from an endowment of diversified assets.

Directors: Charles L. Overby (Chair. and CEO); Peter S. Prichard (Pres.); Kenneth A. Paulson (Sr Vice-Pres. and Exec. Dir, First Amendment Center); Joe Urschel (Sr Vice-Pres. and

Exec. Dir, Newseum); Christine Wells (Sr Vice-Pres., International Initiatives); Mary Kay Blake (Sr Vice-Pres., Partnerships and Initiatives); Constance Aguayo (Vice-Pres., Human Resources); Nicole F. Mandeville (Sr Vice-Pres. Finance and Treas.); Pamela Galloway-Tabb (Vice-Pres., Gen. Services); Jack Hurley (Vice-Pres., Broadcasting); Max Page (Vice-Pres. and Deputy Dir, Nuseum); Roderick Sandeen (Vice-Pres., Admin.).

Principal Staff: Chief Exec. Charles L. Overby.

Address: 1101 Wilson Blvd, Arlington, VA 22209.

Telephone: (703) 528-0800; **Fax:** (703) 284-3770; **Internet:** www.freedomforum.org; **e-mail:** news@freedomforum.org.

Freedom from Hunger

Founded in 1946 to eliminate the causes of chronic hunger through development and self-help projects in partnership with local organizations.

Activities: Promotes innovative and sustainable self-help solutions to fight against chronic hunger and poverty in 12 countries of Africa, Asia, and Central and South America and the Caribbean. The Credit with Education programme seeks to empower women in developing countries through small cash loans and health, family planning and nutrition education, working with local partner organizations and designed to enable women to identify and combat the root causes of chronic hunger. As of 2003 more than 150,000 women were participating in the programme.

Geographical Area of Activity: Africa, Asia, and Central and South America and the Caribbean.

Publications: Annual Report; Briefing Sheets; newsletter.

Finance: Annual budget approx. $5,000,000.

Directors: Weldon H. Wasson (Chair.); Marcia Griffiths (Vice-Chair.); Sheila C. Cheston (Sec.); Charles V. Moore (Treas.); Edwin T. Baldridge; Alfred C. Bartholomew; Melissa Brown; David L. Chatfield; Jacqueline A. Corcoran; and 12 others.

Principal Staff: Pres. Dr Christopher Dunford; Senior Vice-Pres. Ellen Vor der Bruegge.

Address: 1644 DaVinci Court, Davis, CA 95616.

Telephone: (888) 708-2555; **Fax:** (530) 758-6241; **Internet:** www.freefromhunger.org; **e-mail:** info@freefromhunger.org.

Freeman Foundation

Founded in 1978 in Vermont for the promotion of international understanding and farmland preservation.

Activities: Concerned with protecting the environment and conserving natural resources, as well as international studies. Promotes a greater understanding and appreciation of oriental cultures, histories and economies in the USA, as well as a greater understanding of American culture, institutions and people in the countries of the Far East. Projects supported by the Foundation must contribute to and enhance the development of a vibrant, international free enterprise system. Offers general support, programme development and funds. Runs an exchange programme.

Geographical Area of Activity: International.

Restrictions: No grants are made to individuals.

Finance: Total assets $1,619,093,718 (2001); total grants $86,714,475 (2001).

Trustees: Houghton Freeman; George C. Snell; Morgan Guaranty Trust Co. of New York.

Principal Staff: Contact: Elizabeth Wong.

Address: 1211 Ave of the Americas, 38th Floor, New York, NY 10036.

Telephone: (212) 789-5734; **e-mail:** wong_elizabeth@jpmorgan.com.

French–American Foundation

Founded in 1976 to strengthen relations between the USA and France.

Activities: Promotes opportunities for professionals of the USA and France to discuss problems concerning both countries, and to stimulate change through mutual co-operation. Assists in the exchange of specialists, study tours, conferences, lectures, internships and fellowships, and special studies. Also operates a French office.

Geographical Area of Activity: USA and France.

Restrictions: No grants available.

Publications: Annual Report; project reports.

Board of Directors: Michael E. Patterson (Chair.); Anastassios Fondaras (Vice-Chair.); Anthony A. Smith (Pres.); and 45 others.

Principal Staff: Pres. Anthony A. Smith.

Address: 509 Madison Ave, Suite 310, New York, NY 10022.

Telephone: (212) 829-8800; **Fax:** (212) 829-8810; **Internet:** www.frenchamerican.org.

Freshwater Foundation

Activities: Operates in the field of conservation and the environment, encouraging the protection of freshwater resources through educational programmes, resource management, demonstration projects and research. Established the Gray Freshwater Biological Institute at the University of Minnesota.

Geographical Area of Activity: International.

Finance: Total assets $2,370,639 (2001); total revenue $699,471 (2001).

Principal Staff: Pres. and CEO Lance Yohe.

Address: 2500 Shadywood Rd, Navarre, MN 55331.

Telephone: (612) 449-0092; **Fax:** (612) 449-0592.

Alfred Friendly Foundation

Founded by the late Alfred Friendly in 1983 to promote a free press, and co-operation between the press and other institutions in the USA and abroad.

Activities: Provides work experience in the USA for foreign journalists through a fellowship programme. Applications are accepted from journalists from Eastern Europe and less-developed countries with an emerging free press.

Geographical Area of Activity: International.

Restrictions: Each applicant must have an excellent command of English, at least three years' experience as a print journalist, a demonstrated commitment to journalism in his or her home country, and be currently employed as a journalist.

Publications: Newsletter.

Finance: Total grants $251,547 (June 2001).

Directors: Kenneth F. Bunting; Milton Coleman; Alfred Friendly, Jr; Jean Friendly; Jonathan Friendly; Nicholas Friendly; Lucinda F. Murphy; David Nalle; James M. Naughton; Geneva Overholser; Robert J. Rosenthal; Madelyn A. Ross; John M. Sirek; Ellen Soeteber; Susan Talalay; Howard A. Tyner; Peter S. Young.

Principal Staff: Pres. and Treas. Jean U. Friendly; Vice-Pres Lucinda F. Murphy, John G. Murphy; Sec. Alfred Friendly, Jr; Exec. Dir John Sirek.

Address: 2000 L St, NW, Suite 200, Washington, DC 20036-4997.

Telephone: (202) 416-1691; **Fax:** (202) 416-1695; **Internet:** www.pressfellowships.org; **e-mail:** afpf@aol.com.

Bill and Melinda Gates Foundation

Established in 1994, by William (Bill) Gates and Melinda Gates, to help improve the lives of people world-wide through health and learning; the Gates Learning Foundation (founded in 1997 as the successor to the Microsoft/American Library Association) and the William H. Gates Foundation (founded in 1994) were integrated into the Bill and Melinda Gates Foundation in 1999.

Activities: The Foundation integrates the operations of the Gates Learning Foundation, which operated in the USA, and the William H. Gates Foundation, which operated both nationally and internationally. Works in the areas of medicine and health, education and community welfare, through three main projects: Global Health (especially projects in the areas of vaccine-preventable diseases, reproductive and child health, and conditions associated with poverty, including a $100,000,000 donation over ten years to the Global Fund for AIDS and Health and the $1,000,000 Gates Award for Global Health administered by the Global Health Council—q.v.); Learning (projects include providing libraries with internet access and technology training; education, e.g. the Gates Millennium Scholars programme to assist talented minority students to pursue higher education studies; and public access to information); and Community Giving in the Pacific North-West (Washington, Oregon and Idaho), especially in the areas of vulnerable children and lifelong learning. Some Special Projects are financed—this programme is pro-active and does not accept applications. The Foundation established a scholarship programme in 2000, setting up the Gates Cambridge Trust, endowed with $210,000,000, to enable gifted graduate students from any country outside the United Kingdom to study at the University of Cambridge. In 2002 the Foundation announced that more than $40,000,000 was to be used to establish a network of small schools in the USA offering college courses; and in 2003 launched the Grand Challenges in Global Health initiative, in partnership with the National Institutes of Health (NIH), with a grant of $200,000,000.

Geographical Area of Activity: International.

Finance: Total assets $32,751,466,000 (2001); annual expenditure $1,146,958,000 (2001).

Executive Committee: William H. Gates, Sr CEO and Co-Chair.); Patty Stonesifer (Pres.and Co-Chair.); Richard Akeroyd; William H. Foeges; Allan Golston; Terrence Meersman; Dr Gordon W. Perkin; Tom Vander Ark.

Principal Staff: Exec. Dir, Global Health Program Dr R. D. Klausner.

Address: POB 23350, Seattle, WA 98102.

Telephone: (206) 709-3140; **Fax:** (206) 709-3180; **Internet:** www.gatesfoundation.org; www.gates.scholarships.cam.ac .uk; **e-mail:** info@gatesfoundation.org.

GE Fund

Founded in 1952 as the General Electric Foundation for the support of education in the USA. Adopted present name in 1994, as a result of the merger of the General Electric Foundation and the General Electric Foundation, Inc.

Activities: The Foundation provides financial assistance to institutions for general education; graduate research and teaching; minority group education; physical science, engineering, computer science, mathematics, industrial management and business administration education; selected public schools; and arts and cultural centres. Grants are also awarded to other US organizations, including those concerned with international understanding and culture. Grants are made internationally to support higher education institutions and government-run schools and community organizations working to improve access to education for disadvantaged people, raise educational achievement and to test innovative solutions or implementing best practice that can be replicated.

Geographical Area of Activity: International.

Restrictions: Unlikely to make grants to unsolicited projects.

Publications: Annual Report.

Finance: Total assets $18,827,392 (2001); grants approx. $40,701,47 (2001).

Directors: William J. Conaty (Chair.); Pamela Daley; Benjamin W. Heineman, Jr; Joyce Hergenhan; Henry A. Hubschman; Steven Kerr; Keith Sherin; Lloyd G. Trotter.

Principal Staff: Pres. Joyce Hergenhan; Sec. Gisele N. Hill; Treas. Michael J. Cosgrove; Comptroller Christopher King.

Address: 3135 Easton Turnpike, Fairfield, CT 06828.

Telephone: (203) 373-3216; **Fax:** (203) 373-3029; **Internet:** www.ge.com/fund; **e-mail:** gefund@corporate.ge.com.

General Service Foundation

Founded in 1946 by Clifton R. Musser and Margaret Kulp Musser.

Activities: Makes grants to charitable organizations that operate in the following fields: International Peace, particularly in Central America, Mexico and the Caribbean; Reproductive Health and Rights in the USA and Mexico; and Resources, in particular water resources, in the USA, west of Mississippi.

Geographical Area of Activity: North and Central America and the Caribbean.

Restrictions: Grants are not made to individuals, for annual campaigns, capital expenditures or relief.

Finance: Assets $75,643,248 (2000); grants disbursed $4,450,869 (2000).

Officers and Directors: R. W. Musser (Pres.); M. J. Musser (Vice-Pres. and Treas.); M. L. Estrin (Vice-Pres.); R. Halby (Sec.); W. L. Boyd; N. Brew; C. Clements; B. De Buys; W. Dominick; R. L. Estrin; Marlene Fried; P. Halby; R. Halby; S. Halby; M. M. Lloyd; W. T. Snidow; A. Werbach.

Principal Staff: Pres. R. W. Musser.

Address: 557 North Mill St, Suite 201, Aspen, CO 81611.

Telephone: (970) 920-6834; **Fax:** (970) 920-4578; **Internet:** www.generalservice.org; **e-mail:** info@generalservice.org.

German Marshall Fund of the United States—GMF

Created in 1972 by a gift from the German people as a permanent memorial to the Marshall Plan. The Fund is an American institution that promotes understanding and co-operation between the USA and Europe in the spirit of the post-war Marshall Plan.

Activities: The Fund's grant-making promotes the study of international and domestic policies, supports comparative research and debate on key issues, and assists policy and opinion leaders' understanding of these issues. Makes grants in the following areas: foreign policy; economics; the environment; civic participation and democratization; and immigration and integration. Projects must address issues important to European countries, and the USA, and they must involve people or institutions on both sides of the Atlantic. GMF has a particular interest in leadership development. Programmes that involve political, media and other professionals who have a strong interest in trans-atlantic relations and leadership potential will be given special attention. Projects normally include the transfer of experience and innovations, preferably involving practitioners and policy-makers. In 2003 launched the Balkan Trust for Democracy, in a funding partnership with USAID and the Charles Stewart Mott Foundation (q.v.). Also maintains offices in Berlin, Bratislava, Brussels and Paris.

Geographical Area of Activity: USA and Europe.

Publications: Annual Report; *Worldviews 2002 Survey*.

Finance: Assets $207,238,005 (May 2002); annual revenue $18,889,853, annual expenditure $30,833,218 (2002).

Trustees: Guido Goldman, Marc Leland (Co-Chair.); Jeffrey A. Goldstein; Lee Hamilton; David Ignatius; Robert M. Kimmitt; Scott Klug; Mara Liasson; Thomas Presby; Richard Roberts; John A. Ross; Steven G. Rothmeier; Barbara Shailor; Amity Shlaes; Jenone Walker; Vin Weber; Suzanne H. Woolsey.

Principal Staff: Pres. C. Kennedy; Dir of Programmes P. Henderson; Dir, Berlin Office Heike MacKerron; Dir, Central and Eastern Europe Pavol Demes; Exec. Dir Brussels William Drozdiak.

Address: 1744 R St, NW, Washington, DC 20009.

Telephone: (202) 745-3950; **Fax:** (202) 265-1662; **Internet:** www.gmfus.org; **e-mail:** info@gmfus.org.

J. Paul Getty Trust

Founded in 1953 by J. Paul Getty (as the J. Paul Getty Museum); a private operating foundation dedicated to the visual arts and the humanities. The Getty Grant Program was established in 1984.

Activities: Operates through the J. Paul Getty Museum, and in the fields of conservation, education, research, information technology and grant-making, in order to provide opportunities for people to understand more fully, experience, value and preserve the world's artistic and cultural heritage.

Geographical Area of Activity: International.

Publications: Annual Report; *The Getty Grant Program Funding Priorities; Grants Awarded* (booklet); various museum and conservation publications.

Finance: Assets $8,793,485,757 (June 2001); grants disbursed $19,579,820 (2001).

Trustees: David P. Gardner (Chair.); Lewis W. Bernard (Vice-Chair.); Helene L. Kaplan (Vice-Chair.); J. H. Biggs; L. H. Bryson; R. W. Burkle; R. C. Cortines; L. E. Cotsen; B. G. Fleischman; A. Gund; B. Munitz; L. G. Nogales; B. J. Wilson.

Principal Staff: Pres. and CEO Barry Munitz; Vice-Pres. and Dir Getty Museum Deborah Gribbon; Vice-Pres. Finance and Admin. Bradley W. Wells; Vice-Pres., Gen. Counsel and Sec. Bd Trustees Peter Erichsen.

Address: 1200 Getty Center Dr., Los Angeles, CA 90049-1679.

Telephone: (310) 440-7300; **Fax:** (310) 440-7703; **Internet:** www.getty.edu; **e-mail:** info@getty.edu.

Gifts in Kind International

Established in 1984, in order to promote the donation of products from the private and commercial sectors to charitable causes around the world.

Activities: A global network that co-ordinates and distributes donated products from the private sector, providing quality services and goods for poorer communities in different countries. These donations include computers for education, clothing for the homeless, products for disaster relief and construction materials for the rehabilitation of residential areas.

Geographical Area of Activity: International.

Publications: Newsletter; Annual Report.

Finance: Total assets $51,708,535 (2000); revenue $460,709,932, expenditure $487,158,600 (2000).

Board of Directors: Jeffrey R. Rodek (Chair.); Thomas A. Dowling (Vice-Chair.); Robert J. Symon (Treas.); Mark A. Weinberger (Sec.); Susan Corrigan (Pres.); and 18 others.

Principal Staff: Pres. and CEO Susan Corrigan.

Address: 333 North Fairfax St, Suite 100, Alexandria, VA 22314.

Telephone: (703) 836-2121; **Fax:** (703) 549-1481; **Internet:** www.giftsinkind.org; **e-mail:** customerservice@giftsinkind.org.

Howard Gilman Foundation, Inc.

Established in 1981 by the Gilman Paper and Investment Corporation to nurture and conserve a vibrant natural and cultural environment.

Activities: Operates in the fields of the arts and humanities, conservation and the environment, and medicine and health, through research, offering grants to institutions and conferences.

Geographical Area of Activity: USA and the countries of the former USSR.

Restrictions: No grants are made to individuals.

Publications: Application guidelines.

Finance: Net assets $244,640,000 (Dec. 2001); annual expenditure approx. $5,725,656 (2001).

Trustees: Jeff Borer (Pres.); Steve Cropper (Vice-Pres.); Pierre Apraxine; Bernard Bergreen; Donald Bruce; Bob Burkett; Luigi Gaspalinetti; Marcello Guidi; John Lukas; Natalie Moody; Isabella Rossellini.

Principal Staff: Exec. Dir J. A. Smith; Programme Admin. Jen Amis.

Address: 111 West 50th St, 2nd Floor, New York, NY 10020.

Telephone: (212) 307-1073; **Fax:** (212) 262-4108; **Internet:** www.howardgilman.org; **e-mail:** jamis@gilman.com.

Elizabeth Glaser Pediatric AIDS Foundation

Founded in 1988 to support pediatric AIDS research.

Activities: Funds research into pediatric AIDS nationally and internationally. Support is given to study on the maternal–foetal transmission of HIV, opportunistic infection, growth and development, and the effect of the virus on the central nervous system, as well as providing grants to help families affected by HIV. Established International Leadership Awards in 2002 to support researchers in less-developed countries whose work will have direct impact on pediatric HIV and AIDS in their country.

Geographical Area of Activity: International.

Publications: Annual Report.

Finance: Total assets $38,299,502 (2001); annual revenue $13,965,835, expenditure $17,593,651 (2001).

Directors: Paul M. Glaser (Hon. Chair.); David Kessler (Chair.); Peter Benzian (Sec.); Sheri Babbio; Morton Bahr; Willow Bay; Bob Burkett; Mark Burnett; Kate Carr; Barry Edwards; Jeffrey Elton; Frank Fielding; Russ Hagey; Alexis Herman; Karen Jenkins; Cynthia Lewis; Cliff Gilbert-Lurie; David Kessler; Philip Pizzo; Paul G. Quie; Honey Jacobs Skinner; Sandy Thurman; Alexander Vreeland; Susan Zeegan; Lloyd S. Zeiderman; Bobbi Zifkin.

Principal Staff: Pres. and CEO Kate Carr.

Address: 2950 31st St, Suite 125, Santa Monica, CA 90405-3092.

Telephone: (310) 314-1459; **Fax:** (310) 314-1469; **Internet:** www.pedaids.org; **e-mail:** info@pedaids.org.

Global Alliance for Women's Health

Established in 1994 for the advancement of women's health world-wide.

Activities: Works in co-operation with national and international NGOs, women's groups and other organizations to advance women's health in all areas of the world. Promotes the implementation of improvements to health-care services and research into women's health. Distributes women's health-care information and organizes health conferences and symposia on a variety of health policy issues.

Geographical Area of Activity: International.

Publications: *Health for All Women in the 21st Century: How do we get there?; Smoking and Women's Health: Les Liaisons Dangereuses; Trachoma: A Women's Health Issue;* other books and booklets.

Board of Directors: E. M. Wolfson (Pres.); F. Mekbeb (Vice-Pres.); G. Iijima (Sec.).

Address: 823 United Nations Plaza, Suite 712, New York, NY 10017.

Telephone: (212) 286-0424; **Fax:** (212) 286-9561; **Internet:** www.gawh.org; **e-mail:** contactus@gawh.org.

Global Fund for Women

Founded in 1987 to promote the growth of women's groups and links between groups world-wide.

Activities: The Fund operates in the fields of economic affairs, education, human rights, medicine and health, and social welfare and studies, by assisting grass-roots women's organizations outside the USA.

Geographical Area of Activity: International.

Restrictions: Operates internationally but does not support individuals or groups based in the USA.

Publications: *Raising Our Voices* (newsletter); Annual Report; information brochure.

Finance: Total assets $12,340,000 (2001/2002); total revenue $13,600,000, grants disbursed $4,500,000 (2002).

Governing Board: Jacqueline Pitanguy (Chair.); Adele Smith Simmons (Treas.); Diane Jordan Wexler (Sec.); Lin Chew; Myrna Cunningham; Connie Evans; Sumaya Farhat-Naser; Stans Kleijnen; Idelisse Malavé; Amina Mama; Laurene Powell Jobs; Kavita N. Ramdas; Olena Suslova; Zene Tadesse; Mayan Villalba.

Principal Staff: Pres. and CEO Kavita Nandini Ramdas; Vice-Pres. of Devt and Communications Nicola McIntyre; Vice-Pres. of Programmes Misti Mukhopadhyay Sanjami.

Address: 1375 Sutter St, Suite 400, San Francisco CA 94109.

Telephone: (415) 202-7640; **Fax:** (415) 202-8604; **Internet:** www.globalfundforwomen.org; **e-mail:** gfw@globalfundforwomen.org.

Global Greengrants Fund

Established in 1993 by the Tides Foundation (q.v.), aiming to protect the global environment by strengthening the grass-roots environmental movement in developing countries.

Activities: Awards small grants of up to $5,000 throughout the world to grass-roots NGOs working in the field of conservation and the environment.

Geographical Area of Activity: International.

Restrictions: No unsolicited proposals accepted.

Publications: Annual Report.

Finance: Annual revenue $1,250,000, expenditure $1,100,000 (2000–01).

Directors: H. Seidler (Chair.); C. Brodsky, J. Harrison (Vice-Chair.); C. Porter (Sec.); D. Chatfield; A. Fazal; L. Grossman; B. Mayer; M. L. Smith; C. Tchozewski; S. Viederman.

Principal Staff: Exec. Dir Chet Tchozewski; Dir Programmes Chris Allan.

Address: 2840 Wilderness Place, Suite E, Boulder, CO 80301.

Telephone: (303) 939-9866; **Fax:** (303) 939-9867; **Internet:** www.greengrants.org; **e-mail:** info@greengrants.org.

Global Health Council

Established in 1971, as the National Council for International Health, a membership organization of individuals, organizations and communities working in the field of health internationally. Changed its name to the Global Health Council in 1999.

Activities: Operates in the field of health world-wide by working in collaboration with local partner organizations; its main areas of activity are HIV/AIDS (the Global AIDS Program), reproductive and maternal health, infectious diseases, child health and nutrition, disaster and refugee health, and health systems. Holds an annual conference to promote the exchange of ideas, practices and procedures on international health care and human development. The Global Aids Program includes a small grants fund to support networking initiatives, scholarships and the production of resource materials. Administers the Gates Award for Global Health, funded by the Bill and Melinda Gates Foundation (q.v.) and the Jonathan Mann Award for Global Health and Human Rights in partnership with Doctors of the World and the Association François-Xavier Bagnoud (q.v.), as well as making other awards recognizing excellence in global health issues.

Geographical Area of Activity: International.

Publications: *Best Practice Review; HealthLink* (every 2 months); *AIDSLink* (newspaper, every 2 months).

Finance: Assets $6,283,563 (Sept. 2001); annual revenue $7,314,914, expenditure $6,072,874 (2001).

Board of Trustees: William Foege (Chair.).

Principal Staff: Pres. and CEO Dr Nils Daulaire.

Address: 1701 K St, NW, Suite 600, Washington, DC 20006-1503.

Telephone: (202) 833-5900; **Fax:** (202) 833-0075; **Internet:** www.globalhealth.org; **e-mail:** ghc@globalhealth.org.

Global Impact

Established in 1956 as a federation of a number of US international relief and development organizations that aims to help people overseas and in the USA who are suffering the effects of poverty, disaster or disease.

Activities: Represents 59 humanitarian and development charities in the USA, working as a cost-effective fundraiser for these organizations, through workplace charitable contributions.

Geographical Area of Activity: International.

Publications: Annual Report.

Finance: Assets $14,717,332 (June 2002); annual revenue $3,020,520, expenditure $3,221,649 (2002).

Directors: D. J. Zuercher (Chair.); J. Beardsley (Vice-Chair.); R. Acosta (Pres.); H. K. Fleishman (Sec./Treas.); A. E. Brill; S. Jackson; K. R. Johnson; Gen. G. A. Joulwan; N. A. Kelly; M. Davies Lewis; S. F. Ristow; W. J. Underwood.

Principal Staff: Pres. R. S. Acosta; Vice-Pres. Operations S. S. Murphy.

Address: 66 Canal Center Plaza, Suite 310, Alexandria, VA 22314.

Telephone: (703) 548-2200; **Fax:** (703) 548-7864; **Internet:** www.charity.org; **e-mail:** isa@charity.org.

Global Links

Established in 1989 to assist health-care institutions in developing countries regardless of nationality, or religious or political affiliation.

Activities: Collects donations of a wide variety of surplus medical supplies, including equipment, instruments, sutures and other supplies and hospital furnishings from the USA and distributes them to health-care facilities in developing countries in order to improve the medical care received by those in need. Donations are currently sent to institutions in Bolivia, Cuba, Guyana, Honduras and Jamaica, although sutures are donated throughout the world.

Geographical Area of Activity: Mainly Central and South America and the Caribbean, although sutures are donated world-wide.

Publications: *Global Links News* (newsletter); Annual Report.

Directors: E. F. Lauer (Chair.); J. A. Ford (Vice-Chair and Treas.); C. R. Vargo (Sec.); D. Drawbaugh; R. J. Forsythe; G. A. Geibel; K. Herbert; K. G. Hower; G. J. Magovern; M. Marquez; B. L. Silverman; B. L. Smith; D. T. Wagner; R. L. Wholey.

Principal Staff: Exec. Dir Kathleen Hower.

Address: 4809 Penn Ave, 2nd Floor, Pittsburgh, PA 15224.

Telephone: (412) 361-3424; **Fax:** (412) 361-4950; **Internet:** www.globallinks.org; **e-mail:** info@globallinks.org.

Richard and Rhoda Goldman Fund

Established in 1989 by Richard N. Goldman and the late Rhoda H. Goldman to promote protection of the environment and for general charitable purposes.

Activities: The Foundation awards the Goldman Prize each year, to one person from each of the six inhabited continents deemed to have made a significant contribution in the field of environmental protection; each prize carries a monetary award of $125,000. Also operates in the areas of Jewish affairs, the prevention of violence, children and youth, the elderly, social and human services, population, health, education, democracy and civil society, and the arts and humanities. Apart from the environmental prize, grants are usually made within the San Francisco Bay area in California, USA.

Geographical Area of Activity: International.

Restrictions: No unsolicited proposals currently in the areas of the arts, education or health.

Publications: Newsletter; occasional report; informational brochure.

Finance: Assets $394,822,720 (2001); grants disbursed $29,990,937 (2001).

Officers and Directors: Richard N. Goldman (Pres.); Susan R. Gelman; Michael C. Gelman; Douglas E. Goldman; John D. Goldman; Lisa M. Goldman; Marcia L. Goldman; Donald H. Seiler.

Principal Staff: Exec. Dir Robert Gamble.

Address: 1 Lombard, Suite 303, San Francisco, CA 94111.

Telephone: (415) 788-1090; **Fax:** (415) 788-7890; **Internet:** www.goldmanfund.org; **e-mail:** info@goldmanfund.org.

Goldman Sachs Foundation

Established in December 1999 by the Goldman Sachs banking and security firm to assist in the creation of partnerships in the public, private and non-profit sectors in order to promote innovation and excellence in education and youth development throughout the world.

Activities: Operates nationally and internationally, supporting projects in the field of education through promoting partnerships between the public, private and non-profit sectors. Assistance is given to large projects which enhance academic outcomes and offer educational opportunities in the field of business and entrepreneurship. Major programme areas are Developing High Potential Youth, Promoting Entrepreneurship and Leadership, and Advancing Academic Achievement.

Geographical Area of Activity: International.

Publications: *Highlights of the Portfolio; Ideas into Action.*

Finance: A contribution of $200,000,000 was made by the Goldman Sachs group to launch the Foundation; total assets $211,943,536 (June 2001); total giving $12,322,000 (2001).

Board of Directors: John C. Whitehead (Chair.).

Principal Staff: Pres. Stephanie Bell-Rose.

Address: 375 Park Ave, Suite 1008, New York, NY 10152.

Telephone: (212) 902-8509; **Fax:** (212) 888-9482; **Internet:** www.gs.com.

Horace W. Goldsmith Foundation

Founded in 1955 by Horace W. Goldsmith to provide support for cultural activities, Jewish welfare funds and temple support, hospitals, particularly for the elderly, and education, especially higher education.

Activities: Operates in the USA and Israel to carry out its aims.

Geographical Area of Activity: USA and Israel.

Restrictions: No grants are made to individuals.

Finance: Assets $892,590,763 (Dec. 2001); total grants $40,112,467 (2001).

Directors: James C. Slaughter (CEO); Richard L. Menschel; Robert B. Menschel; Thomas Slaughter; William A. Slaughter.

Address: 375 Park Ave, Suite 1602, New York, NY 10152.

Telephone: (212) 319-8700.

Goodwill Industries International, Inc

Established in 1902 by Rev. Edgar Helms to assist in training and finding jobs for people who otherwise have difficulty in finding employment; with the long-term aim of helping ensure every person in the global community has the opportunity to achieve his/her fullest potential as an individual and to participate and contribute fully in all aspects of a productive life.

Activities: Operates internationally, running employment and training programmes to increase the self-sufficiency of people with barriers to work, for example people with disabilities, illiterate or homeless people. Seeks to create opportunities for vocational training and employment through its network of 206 autonomous, community-based agencies in the USA and Canada, and by creating alliances with other NGOs, foundations and companies. Runs a chain of more than 1,900 Goodwill charity shops in the USA and Canada to raise funds. Goodwill Global, with an office in Washington, DC, seeks to foster Goodwill's entrepreneurial efforts outside the USA and Canada.

Geographical Area of Activity: International.

Publications: *Working!* (quarterly magazine); Annual Report.

Finance: Total assets $6,883,806 (2001); annual revenue $21,629,912, expenditure $21,378,609 (2001).

Principal Staff: Pres. and CEO George W. Kessinger; Dir, Goodwill Global Howard Wallack; Dir, Development Anne P. Swire.

Address: 9200 Rockville Pike, Bethesda, MD 20814.

Telephone: (240) 333-5200; **Fax:** (301) 530-1516; **Internet:** goodwill.org; **e-mail:** contactus@goodwill.org.

Adolph and Esther Gottlieb Foundation, Inc

Founded in 1976 to assist artists in financial need.

Activities: Conducts two grant programmes to assist painters, sculptors and printmakers in a mature phase of their art who are in current financial need: the Emergency Assistance Programme available throughout the year and the Individual Support Programme awarded on an annual basis. Emergency Assistance programme grants are for a maximum of $10,000.

Restrictions: No grants to organizations, students, educational institutions, to those working in crafts, graphic artists or for projects.

Finance: Total assets $25,802,914 (June 2001); total grants $340,000 (2001).

Officers and Directors: Dick Netzer (Pres.); Lynda Benglis; Sanford Hirsch; Charlotte Kotik; Robert Mangold.

Principal Staff: Grants Man. Sheila Ross.

Address: 380 West Broadway, New York, NY 10012-5115.

Telephone: (212) 226-0581; **Fax:** (212) 226-0584.

Florence J. Gould Foundation

Founded in 1957 by Florence J. Gould to promote good relations between France and the USA, and for general charitable purposes.

Activities: The Foundation provides financial assistance to organizations furthering its aims with regard to French–US relations as well as supporting higher education, museums and the arts and humanities. Money is also donated to a hospital in Paris.

Geographical Area of Activity: USA and France.

Finance: Total assets $101,675,466 (2001); grants disbursed $6,592,672 (2001).

Officers and Directors: John R. Young (Pres.); Daniel P. Davison (Vice-Pres. and Treas.); Daniel Wildenstein (Vice-Pres.); Walter C. Cliff (Sec.).

Address: c/o Cahill Gordon and Reindel, 80 Pine St, Suite 1736, New York, NY 10005-1702.

Telephone: (212) 701-3400.

Graham Foundation for Advanced Studies in the Fine Arts

Founded in 1956 by Ernest R. Graham for research and study in the arts, particularly architecture and the built environment.

Activities: Grants, mainly for Americans working in the USA, are made in support of activities, including research, in relation to contemporary architecture, design and urban planning; also supports exhibitions, lectures, publications and the study of architecture and urban planning.

Geographical Area of Activity: Mainly USA.

Publications: Annual Report.

Finance: Assets $38,186,292 (2001); grants disbursed $1,345,845 (2001).

Officers and Trustees: Henry Kuehn (Pres.); Daniel Wheeler (Vice-Pres.); Jeffrey Jahns (Sec./Treas.); Thomas Beeby; Robert Bruegmann; Sally A. Kitt Chappell; Roberta Feldman; James Nagle; Martha Thorne; Ben Weese; Robert Wislow; Carter H. Manny (Dir Emeritus).

Principal Staff: Dir Richard Solomon.

Address: 4 West Burton Pl., Chicago, IL 60610-1416.

Telephone: (312) 787-4071; **Internet:** www.grahamfoundation.org; **e-mail:** info@grahamfoundation.org.

Grameen Foundation

Established by Prof. Muhammad Yunus with the aim of combating poverty in the USA and world-wide; the organization grew from the Grameen Bank, which began in Bangladesh in 1976, offering small amounts of credit, and has now become a world-wide movement.

Activities: Supports the Grameen Bank in its anti-poverty programmes; these programmes include support for micro-credit institutions, projects in the areas of education and technical assistance, establishing joint ventures with the private sector, marketing products produced by small enterprises, and educating the public and government in the USA about poverty and its alleviation through micro-credit. Has established the Grameen Technology Center in Bangladesh.

Geographical Area of Activity: International.

Finance: Net assets $1,512,776 (Dec. 2001); annual revenue $3,273,682, expenditure $2,718,614 (Dec. 2000).

Principal Staff: Chair. Susan M. Davis; Treas. Paul F. Kane; Sec. Robert G. Ottenhoff; Pres. and CEO Alex Counts.

Address: 1029 Vermont Ave, NW, Suite 400, Washington, DC 20005-3517.

Telephone: (202) 628-3560; **Fax:** (202) 628-3880; **Internet:** www.gfusa.org; **e-mail:** info@gfusa.org.

William T. Grant Foundation

Founded in 1936 by William T. Grant to promote the research capacity of promising scholars who investigate topics relevant to the understanding of, and promoting the well-being and healthy development of, children and adolescents.

Activities: The Foundation supports research in any medical or social-behavioural scientific discipline on the development of children and adolescents, particularly interdisciplinary research, employing multiple methods to investigate several problems simultaneously. There are four forms of support: Research on the Development of Children, Adolescents and Youth; Research to Evaluate Broadly-Based Social Interventions; Faculty Scholars Program; and Small Grants Program.

Restrictions: Does not give scholarships or fellowships or normally support building funds, fundraising drives, on-going operating budgets or endowments.

Publications: Annual Report; Foundation brochure; Faculty Scholars brochure.

Finance: Total assets $209,441,515 (2002); total income $3,377,473, total expenditure $15,471,176 (2002).

Officers and Directors: R. R. Winant (Chair.); A. M. Grumbach (Vice-Chair. and Sec.); K. Hein (Pres.); K. S. Rolland (Treas.); E. Dorann (Controller); J. Lawrence Aber; P. Allen-Meares; T. C. Barry; R. F. Boruch; R. A. Feldman; H. Gooss; K. Hall Jamieson; B. A. Macaskill; R. H. Price; K. S. Rolland; M. Tienda; G. Walker.

Address: 570 Lexington Ave, 18th Floor, New York, NY 10022-6837.

Telephone: (212) 752-0071; **Fax:** (212) 752-1398; **Internet:** www.wtgrantfoundation.org; **e-mail:** info@wtgrantfdn.org.

Grass Foundation

Founded in 1955 by Albert and Ellen Grass to support research and education in neuroscience.

Activities: Operates in the fields of medicine and science through two fellowship programmes: summer fellowships for young researchers conducting independent research at the Marine Biological Laboratory, Woods Hole, MA; and the Robert S. Morrison Fellowship in neuroscience, neurophysiology or psychiatry, providing one to two years of support for an outstanding young scientist in preparation for a career in academic medicine. There were no plans to offer the Morrison Fellowship in 2003. Also supports several courses in neuroscience and annual funding of lectureships.

Geographical Area of Activity: International.

Restrictions: Applicants from overseas are eligible for these fellowships, but the work must be carried out at a North American institution. No support for on-going research, full-time students, symposia or conferences.

Publications: Application guidelines; programme policy statement; information brochure.

Finance: Assets $8,074,800 (Dec. 2000).

Officers and Trustees: Steven Zottoli (Pres.); Henry J. Grass (Clerk); Richmond Woodward (Treas.); Bernice Grafstein (Vice-Pres.); John Burris; George Butterworth; R. Hoy; John Hildebrand; Eve Marder; James McNamara; Donald Price; Felix Schweizer; Janis Weeks.

Address: POB 850250, Braintree, MA 02185-0250.

Telephone: (781) 843-0219; **Fax:** (781) 843-0474; **Internet:** www.grassfoundation.org; **e-mail:** grassfdn@aol.com.

Grassroots International

Established in 1983 as an independent non-profit agency to work for social change.

Activities: Operates in the areas of human rights and social welfare in co-operation with partner organizations in Africa, Asia, the Middle East, and Central and South America and the Caribbean. Grassroots International works for progressive social change through community development work, making grants through partner NGOs. In the USA it draws media attention to issues of poverty, power and social change around the world and engages in educational and advocacy work on behalf of its partners.

Geographical Area of Activity: Africa (Horn), Middle East, Central and South America and the Caribbean.

Restrictions: Grants are only made to specific organizations in specific regions.

Publications: *Insights* (newsletter); *GrassrootsONLINE* (on-line news service); fact sheets; reports and summaries; Annual Report.

Finance: Financed by charitable donations. Total assets $959,182 (Oct. 2000); annual revenue $2,410,367, expenditure $2,395,298 (2000).

Directors: Leena Deevy; Anuradha Desai; Carla Johnston; Fernando Leiva; Judith Lockhart-Radtke; Keven Murray; Luis Prado; Byron Rushing; Joe Stork; Marlyn Tadros; Clark Taylor; Chris Tilly; Emira Woods; Katherine Yih.

Principal Staff: Exec. Dir Kevin Murray; Program Dir Maria Aguier; Devt Dir Daniel Moss.

Address: 179 Boylston St, 4th Floor, Boston, MA 02130.

Telephone: (617) 524-1400; **Fax:** (617) 524-5525; **Internet:** grassrootsonline.org; **e-mail:** info@grassrootsonline.org.

William and Mary Greve Foundation, Inc

Founded in 1964 by Mary P. Greve.

Activities: The Foundation operates in the fields of education, international relations, especially between the USA and Eastern Europe, the environment and the performing arts, through grants to organizations.

Restrictions: No grants are made to individuals, nor for scholarships or fellowships.

Finance: Assets $41,813,754 (2001); total grants $2,113,155 (2001).

Officers and Directors: John W. Kiser, III (Chair.); Anthony C. M. Kiser (Pres.); Victoria B. Bjorkland (Sec.); Robert E. Cohen; James W. Sykes, Jr.

Address: 630 Fifth Ave, Suite 1750, New York, NY 10111.

Telephone: (212) 307-7850.

Daniel and Florence Guggenheim Foundation

Founded in 1924 by Daniel and Florence Guggenheim to advance public welfare, civic betterment and the well-being of mankind throughout the world.

Activities: The Foundation's main interest is criminal justice and the bulk of its grants are made to relevant programmes. Also some donations in the field of medical research and to the Federation of Jewish Philanthropies annual campaign.

Geographical Area of Activity: International.

Restrictions: No grants are made to individuals.

Publications: Report.

Finance: Assets $7,870,723 (2001); total giving $556,000 (2001).

Officers and Directors: Oscar S. Straus, II (Chair.); Oscar S. Straus, III (Pres. and Treas.); Rowley Bialla (Sec.); Powell M. Cabot; Michael B. Davies; Dana Draper; Mrs Max A. Hart; Mrs Walter Metcalf, III; Kristin Miller; Henry H. Patton; Perry Preston; Oscar S. Schafer; Hon. Kenneth Taylor.

Address: 950 Third Ave, 30th Floor, New York, NY 10022.

Telephone: (212) 755-3199.

Harry Frank Guggenheim Foundation

Founded in 1929 by Harry Frank Guggenheim to study and research 'Man's Relation to Man', the Foundation supports specific and innovative projects which seek to promote understanding of human social problems related to violence, aggression and dominance.

Activities: Operates both nationally and internationally in the field of science, through research and grants to individuals for research; also makes awards for support during the writing of doctoral theses. Grants are available for holders of a doctorate or professional equivalent, and for doctoral candidates for the writing of their dissertation. Support is mainly given for basic research in the social, behavioural and biological sciences.

Geographical Area of Activity: International.

Restrictions: No grants to institutions nor for programmes.

Publications: *HFG Review;* research reports.

Finance: Assets $78,695,003 (2000); total expenditure $1,342,037 (2000).

Trustees: P. Lawson-Johnston (Chair.); James M. Hester (Pres.); W. O. Baker; J. Bunting; P. Cochran; D. Draper; J. B. Edwards; H. D. Graves; D. R. Griffin; D. C. Hood; C. Langstaff; L. H. Lapham; P. Lawston-Johnston, II; G. A. Lindt; T. D. Lockwood; T. L. J. McCleery; J. Millbank, III; A. Pifer; L. D. Rice; W. C. Westmoreland.

Principal Staff: Sr Programme Officer Karen Colvard; Programme Officer Joel Wallman.

Address: 527 Madison Ave, 15th Floor, New York, NY 10022-4304.

Telephone: (212) 644-4907; **Fax:** (212) 644-5110; **Internet:** www.hfg.org; **e-mail:** hfgacf@aol.com.

John Simon Guggenheim Memorial Foundation

Founded in 1925 by Senator and Mrs Simon Guggenheim to improve the quality of education and the practice of the arts and professions; to foster research; and to provide for the cause of better international understanding.

Activities: Operates nationally and internationally in all fields of science, the humanities and the creative arts, through fellowships and grants to individuals who have demonstrated exceptional capacity for productive scholarship or exceptional creative ability in the arts. Fellowships are open to all citizens and permanent residents of the USA, Canada, and Central and South America and the Caribbean.

Geographical Area of Activity: North, Central and South America and the Caribbean.

Restrictions: No grants to organizations or institutions, only to individuals. No grants for the performing arts.

Publications: Annual Report; information brochure.

Finance: Total assets $219,,610,673 (2001); total grants $7,576,807 (2001).

Officers and Trustees: Joseph A. Rice (Chair.); Joel Conarroe (Pres.); G. Thomas Tanselle (Sr Vice-Pres. and Sec.); Coleen P. Higgins-Jacob (Treas.); Peter F. Kardon (Vice-Pres.); Richard W. Hatter (Dir, Development and Public Relations); Sue Schwager (Assoc. Sec.); Joel Conarroe; Kenneth Lipper; A. Alex Porter; Richard A. Rifkind; Charles Andrew Ryskamp; Wendy Wasserstein; Ellen Taaffe Zwilich.

Address: 90 Park Ave, New York, NY 10016.

Telephone: (212) 687-4470; **Fax:** (212) 697-3248; **Internet:** www.gf.org; **e-mail:** fellowships@gf.org.

Habitat for Humanity International

Founded in 1976 by Millard and Linda Fuller to provide affordable homes for families in need by building and rehabilitating simple housing.

Activities: Operates in the USA and less-developed countries in the field of social welfare, in particular housing, by providing volunteers to work alongside those in need of shelter in order to build adequate basic houses. Homes are then sold to families at no profit or interest. Also promotes sustainable building, providing education and training to local affiliates.

Geographical Area of Activity: International.

Publications: *Habitat World Magazine*; Annual Report.

Finance: Funded by house payments, donations and no-interest loans provided by supporters; assets $112,911,649 (June 2002); annual revenue $162,080,768, expenditure $159,576,400 (2002).

Directors: Paul Leonard (Chair.); Lyle Hanna, Rey Ramsey (Co-Vice-Chair.); Sybout Vandermeer (Sec.); Chuck Thiemann (Treas.); and 25 others.

Address: 121 Habitat St, Americus, GA 31709.

Telephone: (229) 924-6935; **Internet:** www.habitat.org; **e-mail:** publicinfo@hfhi.org.

Hands Across Africa, Inc

Established in 1994, a non-profit charitable organization aiming to make health care and education accessible in poverty-stricken parts of Africa by donating education, medical and technical resources from the USA.

Activities: Operates in the fields of education and health care to create long-term solutions to the effects of poverty in Africa. Co-ordinates medical trips into remote parts of Africa to donate medical supplies, provide treatment in rural villages and to decrease the infant mortality rate. Donates and distributes books and other educational materials to schools to increase literacy levels. Also donates relief supplies of clothing and food.

Geographical Area of Activity: Africa.

Restrictions: Not a grant-making organization.

Finance: Total income $126,000 (2000).

Address: 417 Garfield Ave, Suite 4, Calumet City, IL 60409.

Telephone: (708) 832-0976; **Fax:** (708) 832-0975; **e-mail:** handsacross@voyager.net.

John A. Hartford Foundation, Inc

Founded in 1929 by John A. Hartford for general charitable purposes.

Activities: Operates two programmes in the field of Ageing and Health: the Academic Geriatrics and Training Initiative and the Integrating and Improving Services Initiative. These programmes provide grants to US organizations aiming to improve the efficacy and affordability of health care for the increasingly ageing population in the USA.

Geographical Area of Activity: USA.

Restrictions: No grants are made directly to individuals.

Publications: Annual Report; programme policy statement.

Finance: Assets $587,900,000 (Dec. 2001); total revenue $70,700,000, expenditure $30,400,000 (2001).

Officers and Trustees: Norman H. Volk (Chair.); Kathryn D. Wriston (Pres.); William D. Matteson (Sec.); Corinne H. Rieder (Exec. Dir and Treas.); Anson McBeard, Jr; William T. Comfort; James G. Kenan, III; Christopher T. H. Pell; Thomas A. Reynolds, Jr.

Principal Staff: Exec. Dir and Treas. Corinne H. Rieder.

Address: 55 East 59th St, 16th Floor, New York, NY 10022-1178.

Telephone: (212) 832-7788; **Fax:** (212) 593-4913; **Internet:** www.jhartfound.org; **e-mail:** mail@jhartfound.com.

Hasbro Children's Foundation

Founded in 1984 by Hasbro, Inc to improve quality of life for disadvantaged children aged 12 and under, their families and communities in the USA.

Activities: Operates in the areas of health, special and minority education, child abuse and neglect, literacy, homelessness and hunger. Current funding priorities focus on supporting the development and/or expansion of innovative programmes for disadvantaged children throughout the USA and the development of fully accessible playground facilities. In May 2003 the Foundation is set to launch new funding guidelines.

Geographical Area of Activity: USA.

Restrictions: No grants are made to individuals.

Publications: Annual Report.

Finance: Total assets $4,888,727 (2000); total grants $2,891,533 (2000).

Officers and Trustees: Ellen Block (Chair.); Barry J. Alperin (Sec.); Jane S. Englebandt (Exec. Dir); Carole L. Anderson; William Birenbaum; Roger Hart; Alan G. Hassenfeld; Sally Holm; Judith Jones; Samuel Katz; Richard Krugman; Jerome Lowenstein; Ralph Nuñez; B. J. Seabury; William Whaley.

Address: 32 West 23rd St, New York, NY 10010.

Telephone: (212) 645-2400; **Fax:** (212) 645-6815; **Internet:** www.hasbro.org.

Health Alliance International—HAI

Established in 1987 as the Mozambique Health Committee, name changed in 1993 to reflect the expanding reach of its activities. Aims to improve the health and welfare of those in need around the world; and to educate North Americans about social, economic and political issues that affect those in Southern Africa.

Activities: Operates in the field of health care internationally in a number of ways in collaboration with local organizations: works to identify economic, social and political factors causing poor health care for marginalized peoples, and to raise public awareness of these matters; provides direct technical and material assistance in support of basic health services; engages in research and training in public health care in the USA and abroad (including parts of sub-Saharan Africa, Central and South America, the Caribbean, Asia and the Middle East) and supports graduate training in public health at the University of Washington. Also tries to ensure the equal distribution and efficient delivery of quality health care world-wide and seeks to support policies that promote health, equality, social justice and self-sufficiency.

Geographical Area of Activity: International.

Publications: *National policies regarding congenital syphilis in sub-Saharan Africa; Prenatal Syphilis Screening*; newsletter.

Directors: Joshua Fliegel (Pres.); Jo Anne Myers-Ciecko (Vice-Pres.); Kathy Hubenet (Sec.); Edith Wolff (Treas.); and 6 others.

Principal Staff: Exec. Dir S. Gloyd; Deputy Dir M. A. Mercer; Country Co-ordinator K. Sherr.

Address: 1107 NE 45th St, Suite 410, Seattle, WA 98105.

Telephone: (206) 543-8382; **Fax:** (206) 685-4184; **Internet:** www.depts.washington.edu/haiuw; **e-mail:** hai@u.washington.edu.

Health Volunteers Overseas

A private non-profit organization established in 1986 to improve health care in developing countries through training and education.

Activities: Operates in the field of health care and international development, working to improve the accessibility and quality of health care in developing countries in a number of ways. Volunteer professionals train local people in pathologies and medical problems they might encounter in their area, thus providing a self-sustaining, long-term medical presence in under-developed areas using local available supplies and equipment. Programmes specialize in anaesthesia, dentistry, internal medicine, nursing, oral surgery, orthopaedics, paediatrics and physical therapy.

Geographical Area of Activity: Asia, Africa, Central and South America.

Restrictions: Not a grant-making organization.

Publications: *The HVO Guide to Volunteering Overseas; The Volunteer Connection* (newsletter, quarterly); Annual Report.

Finance: Assets $907,000 (2001).

Directors: B. Gainor (Chair); N. Kelly (Exec. Dir); P. Benson; S. Borden; W. Day; K. Dunleavy; R. Feinberg; D. Frost; J. Gerry; J. Jacobs.

Principal Staff: Exec. Dir N. Kelly.

Address: POB 65157, Washington, DC 20035.

Telephone: (202) 296-0928; **Fax:** (202) 296-8018; **Internet:** www.hvousa.org; **e-mail:** info@hvousa.org.

The Hearst Foundation, Inc

Founded in 1945 by William Randolph Hearst to support general charitable purposes in the USA. Shares an administration with the William Randolph Hearst Foundation (q.v.).

Activities: The Foundation supports programmes in the USA and its overseas dependencies in the fields of higher and private secondary education, health care, social welfare, and culture, through the provision of funds. Maintains an office in San Francisco, CA.

Geographical Area of Activity: USA and its dependencies.

Restrictions: Grants are not made to individuals.

Finance: Assets $271,400,000 (2001); total grants $13,385,000 (2001).

Officers and Directors: George R. Hearst, Jr (Pres.); Robert M. Frehse, Jr (Exec. Dir); Thomas Eastham (Western Dir).

Address: 888 Seventh Ave, 45th Floor, New York, NY 10106-0057.

Telephone: (212) 586-5404; **Fax:** (212) 586-1917; **Internet:** www.hearstfdn.org.

William Randolph Hearst Foundation

Founded in 1948 by William Randolph Hearst for general charitable purposes. Shares an administration with the Hearst Foundation, Inc (q.v.).

Activities: The Foundation provides financial assistance to organizations operating programmes in the fields of social welfare, health care, private education (secondary and higher) and culture. Also makes miscellaneous grants. Scholarships are offered under two schemes: the Journalism Awards Program and the United States Senate Youth Program. Grants are limited to the USA and its dependencies.

Geographical Area of Activity: USA and its dependencies.

Restrictions: Grants are not made to individuals.

Finance: Assets $624,456,279 (2001); grants disbursed $28,928,400 (2001).

Officers and Directors: Randolph A. Hearst (Pres.); Robert M. Frehse, Jr (Vice-Pres. and Exec. Dir); Thomas Eastham (Vice-Pres. and Western Dir).

Address: 888 Seventh Ave, 45th Floor, New York, NY 10106-0057.

Telephone: (212) 586-5404; **Fax:** (212) 586-1917; **Internet:** hearstfdn.org.

Heart to Heart International

Founded in 1992 by Dr Gary Morsch, an international development and relief organization which aims to alleviate human suffering.

Activities: Operates a number of programmes world-wide in the fields of international development and relief, including educational and medical supplies projects in developing countries, an international food programme, disaster relief for the victims of natural and man-made disasters, and on-going domestic projects to help the poor, neglected and abused in the USA. In 2002 supported projects in 50 countries.

Geographical Area of Activity: International.

Board of Directors: Sandra L. Panther (Chair.); Gary B. Morsch (Pres.).

Address: 401 S Clairborne, Suite 302, Olathe, KS 66062.

Telephone: (913) 764-5200; **Fax:** (913) 764-0809; **Internet:** www.hearttoheart.org; **e-mail:** info@hearttoheart.org.

Hebrew Immigrant Aid Society—HIAS

Founded in 1881, HIAS aims to assist oppressed people (both Jews and non-Jews) world-wide and to resettle them in a safe country.

Activities: Assists refugees, mainly Jews, under threat internationally and helps to resettle them. The organization works to fulfil its mission in a number of ways, including providing information and services for refugees throughout the migration process; communicating between clients, resettlement communities and government authorities; acting as an advocate for better policies affecting refugees and immigrants; and providing advice and orientation for resettled people in the USA and elsewhere. In the USA, HIAS also assists immigrants with documents such as applying for visas, provides training for the naturalization exam and interview, and legal advice and representation. Also runs a scholarship programme for American and Israeli students. Maintains offices in Israel, Moscow and Vienna.

Geographical Area of Activity: International.

Principal Staff: Pres. and CEO Leonard S. Glickman; Sec. Caryl Kligfeld; Treas. Jack Serber.

Address: 333 Seventh Ave, 17th Floor, New York, NY 10001-5004.

Telephone: (212) 967-4100; **Fax:** (212) 967-4483; **Internet:** www.hias.org; **e-mail:** info@hias.org.

Heifer International

Founded in 1944 by Dan West, with the aim of providing long-term solutions to hunger and poverty.

Activities: Operates in the field of aid to less-developed countries and social welfare, by providing animals that can be a source of food and income to families in need (including heifers, goats, llamas, geese, sheep, buffalos, rabbits and pigs) and any necessary training. In this way the family receives a nutritious long-term food source, a potential income to be used for better education, housing and health care, and learns sustainable agricultural techniques. Established the Heifer International Foundation in 1990, to provide an on-going endowment for the Heifer International and to educate people about charitable giving and estate planning.

Geographical Area of Activity: International.

Publications: *World Ark Magazine* (quarterly); *Project Profile* (annual); Annual Report.

Finance: Total assets $55,436,374 (June 2001); annual revenue $40,111,425, expenditure $37,103,356 (2001).

Board of Directors: Mark Lancaster (Chair.); Charles Stewart (Vice-Chair.); Rom McClean (Immediate Past Chair.); Thomas A. Bruce, Willie Jones Dell; Carol Hillard; Chuck Krouse.

Principal Staff: Pres. and Chief Exec. Jo Luck; Chief Operating Officer Dr Hans J. Hoyer; Vice-Pres., International Programmes James De Vries.

Address: POB 8058, Little Rock, AR 72203.

Telephone: (501) 907-2600; **Internet:** www.heifer.org; **e-mail:** info@heifer.org.

Howard Heinz Endowment

Founded in 1941 as the Howard Heinz Endowment and incorporating the Vera Heinz Endowment, established in 1986.

Activities: Works through five programme areas seeking innovative ways of improving the quality of life in Pennsylvania, supporting organizations which are concerned with the arts and culture, education, the environment, economic opportunity and children, youth and families.

Geographical Area of Activity: Pennsylvania, USA.

Restrictions: No grants to individuals; grants only to non-profit organizations with an emphasis on programmes either in South-Western Pennsyvania or of clear benefit to the region.

Publications: Annual Report; programme policy statement.

Finance: Assets $907,657,792 (Dec. 2001); total grants $41,130,518 (2001).

Trustees: Teresa F. Heinz (Chair.); Drue Heinz (Dir. Emeritus); Carol R. Brown; Frank V. Cahouet; H. John Heinz, IV; Howard M. Love; Shirley M. Malcom; William H. Rea; Barbara K. Robinson; Frederick W. Thieman; Mallory Walker.

Principal Staff: Exec. Dir Maxwell King; Chief Financial Officer Jack E. Kime.

Address: 30 Dominion Tower, 625 Liberty Ave, Pittsburgh, PA 15222-3115.

Telephone: (412) 281-5777; **Fax:** (412) 281-5788; **Internet:** www.heinz.org; **e-mail:** info@heinz.org.

Heiser Program for Research in Leprosy and Tuberculosis

Founded in 1972 by Dr Victor G. Heiser, to support biomedical research into leprosy (research into tuberculosis was added in 1992). Part of the New York Community Trust, a public non-profit organization.

Activities: Operates internationally, through post-doctoral research fellowships awarded to biomedical students beginning post-doctoral training in research in leprosy and/or tuberculosis at a stipend of $30,000–$35,000 a year; and research grants for one year of up to $30,000 (the same amount to apply should application for a second year be approved) made to laboratories conducting leprosy research, in order to accelerate World Health Organization efforts to eliminate leprosy as a public health problem throughout the world. Has also funded a project to determine the DNA sequence of the entire genome of *Mycobacterium leprae*.

Geographical Area of Activity: International.

Restrictions: Grants for research fellowships only.

Scientific Advisory Committee: Patrick J. Brennan (Chair.); Roy Curtiss, III; Jerrold J. Ellner; Gilla Kaplan.

Principal Staff: Dir Barbara M. Hugonnet.

Address: c/o New York Community Trust, 2 Park Ave, New York, NY 10016.

Telephone: (212) 686-0100; **Internet:** www.nycommunitytrust.org.

Help International

Established in 1999 with the aim of helping to eliminate poverty through humanitarian aid and promoting economic development.

Activities: Operates in the fields of aid to less-developed countries and social welfare, currently in Bolivia, Brazil, El Salvador and Peru, through sending volunteers to work in local communities, who assist with the setting up of village banks and with humanitarian and social projects.

Geographical Area of Activity: USA and Central and South America.

Principal Staff: Exec. Dir Jennifer Boehme.

Address: 363 North University Ave, Suite 110, Provo, UT 84601.

Telephone: (801) 374-0556; **Fax:** (801) 374-0457; **Internet:** www.help-international.org; **e-mail:** info@help-international.org.

William and Flora Hewlett Foundation

Founded in 1966 by William R. Hewlett, Flora Lamson Hewlett and Walter B. Hewlett to promote the well-being of humanity by supporting selected activities of a charitable, religious, scientific, literary or educational nature as well as organizations or institutions engaged in such activities.

Activities: Operates primarily in the fields of education, conflict resolution, environment, family and community development, performing arts, population and US–Central and South American relations, through the provision of grants to relevant institutions and regional grants. Activities are restricted to the USA. A proportion of the organization's funds are given to projects in the San Francisco Bay area.

Geographical Area of Activity: USA.

Publications: Annual Report; grants lists.

Finance: Total assets $6,080,721,309 (2001); total grants $119,955,933 (2001).

Officers and Directors: Walter B. Hewlett (Chair.); Paul Brest (Pres.); Robert F. Erburu; James C. Gaither; Eleanor H. Gimon; Mary H. Jaffe; Herant Katchadourian; Richard Levin; Jean G. Stromberg.

Principal Staff: Pres. Paul Brest.

Address: 2121 Sand Hill Rd, Menlo Park, CA 94025.

Telephone: (650) 234-4500; **Fax:** (650) 234-4501; **Internet:** www.hewlett.org; **e-mail:** info@hewlett.org.

Conrad N. Hilton Foundation and Conrad N. Hilton Fund

Founded in 1944 by Conrad N. Hilton, hotel entrepreneur, for the alleviation of the suffering of the world's most disadvantaged people, with a special emphasis on children and support for the work of the Roman Catholic Sisters.

Activities: In 1996, the Foundation established the annual Conrad N. Hilton Humanitarian Prize of $1,000,000, which honours a charitable or non-governmental organization that has made extraordinary contributions toward alleviating human suffering anywhere in the world. Each year the award is presented at an international humanitarian conference sponsored by the Foundation. Also initiates and develops long-term projects and seeks out organizations to implement them, in the priority funding areas of: world-wide blindness prevention and treatment through the Perkins School for the Blind, the Carter Center and Helen Keller Worldwide (q.v.); potable water development and sanitation in Africa (Ghana, Niger and Mali) through the West Africa Water Initiative; early childhood development through a public–private partnership with the Head Start Bureau and California Institute on Human Services; substance abuse prevention through the BEST Foundation for a Drug-Free Tomorrow, and its Project ALERT curriculum; hospitality management education through sponsorship of the Conrad N. Hilton College of Hotel and Restaurant Management at the University of Houston; and homeless and mentally ill people through funding of the Corporation for Supportive Housing. The Conrad N. Hilton Fund's principal beneficiary is the Conrad N. Hilton Fund for Sisters, established in 1986 and administered separately, which supports projects operated by Roman Catholic Sisters serving the economically disadvantaged world-wide.

Geographical Area of Activity: Africa, Asia and the Americas.

Restrictions: Does not accept unsolicited proposals; no grants to individuals.

Publications: Annual Report; annual humanitarian conference report.

Finance: Conrad N. Hilton Fund: Assets $373,900,000 (March 2002); total revenue $63,728,375 (2002). Conrad N. Hilton Foundation: Assets $682,500,000 (March 2002); total revenue $135,146,602 (2002). Total grants disbursed by the Fund and Foundation $23,500,000 (2002).

Directors: Donald H. Hubbs (Chair. and CEO); Robert Buckley (Man. Dir.); Gregory R. Dillon; James R. Galbraith; Barron Hilton; Conrad N. Hilton, III; Eric M. Hilton; Steven M Hilton; William B. Hilton, Jr.

Principal Staff: Chair and CEO Donald H Hubbs; Pres. Steven M. Hilton; Chief Financial Officer, Vice-Pres. and Admin. Patrick Modugno; Vice-Pres., Programmes Dyanne M. Hayes; Vice-Pres., Dir Humanitarian Prize Judy M. Miller.

Address: 10100 Santa Monica Blvd, Suite 1000, Los Angeles, CA 90067.

Telephone: (310) 556-4694; **Fax:** (310) 556-2301; **Internet:** www.hiltonfoundation.org; **e-mail:** foundation@hiltonfoundation.org.

Baron de Hirsch Fund

Founded in 1891 by Baron Maurice de Hirsch and Baroness Clara de Hirsch to assist in the economic assimilation of Jewish immigrants in the USA and Israel, and in providing them with vocational training in trade and agriculture.

Activities: Makes grants, primarily in the New York area and Israel, for the above purposes, and assists agencies helping to obtain education and employment for immigrants. Awards fellowships to Israeli agriculturalists.

Geographical Area of Activity: USA and Israel.

Finance: Total assets $8,863,108 (2000).

Trustees: Jennie Morgenthau (Pres); Linda Gerstel (Vice-Pres.); E. H. Stern, III (Treas.); Misha Ratner (Sec.); James A. Block; Valerie Block; Beverly S. Coleman; William M. Heineman; Abby Knopp; Erza P. Mager; Ellen Merlo; George W. Naumburg, Jr; Laura Scheuer; Christopher Schwabacher; Arthur Sporn; Seymour Zises.

Principal Staff: Man. Dir Lauren Katzowitz.

Address: 130 East 59th St, 12th Floor, New York, NY 10022.

Telephone: (212) 836-1358.

Hitachi Foundation

Founded in 1985 by Hitachi Ltd, Japan.

Activities: Makes awards in the three categories of General Grants, Matching Funds Program/ Community Action Committees, and the Yoshiyama Award for Exemplary Service to the Community. Aims to support grassroots non-profit organizations throughout America, through its general grants programme; work with employees of the Hitachi companies in its Matching Funds Program; and makes ten annual Yoshiyama Awards to senior school students in recognition of their community activities.

Geographical Area of Activity: USA.

Restrictions: The Foundation does not accept unsolicited proposals.

Publications: Annual Report.

Finance: Total assets $22,842,973 (2001); total income $1,648,079, total expenditure $3,893,695 (2001).

Governing Board: Dr Katushige Mita (Hon. Chair.); Joseph E. Kasputys (Chair.); Clara Apodaca; Sherry Salway Black; Hon. Charles Bowsher; Dr Patricia Albjerg Graham; David Dodson; Barbara Dyer.

Principal Staff: Pres. and CEO Barbara Dyer.

Address: 1509 22nd St, NW, Washington, DC 20037.

Telephone: (202) 457-0588; **Fax:** (202) 296-1098; **Internet:** www.hitachi.org.

Holt International Children's Services

Established in 1956, serves as an international adoption agency which has programmes in 10 countries.

Activities: Operates in the field of child welfare, specifically national and international adoption and family preservation. Has a network of its own offices, agencies and affiliated organizations around the world and is committed to successfully reuniting families and arranging adoptions, so that every child in their care is placed in a loving and secure family unit. Supports adopting families and funds staff training in child welfare and recommends policies related to children's rights and those of adoptive and birth parents to national governments and the United Nations.

Geographical Area of Activity: Asia, South America, Central America, Eastern Europe and the USA.

Principal Staff: Pres. J. Williams; R. Waite; G. Gamer; S. Soon-Keum Cox; C. Stiles; K. Sweeney.

Address: POB 2880, 1195 City View, Eugene, OR 97402.

Telephone: (541) 687-2202; **Fax:** (541) 683-6175; **Internet:** www.holtintl.org; **e-mail:** info@holtinternational.org.

Homeland Foundation

Founded in 1986 to provide funding in order 'to preserve individual rights to have a safe place to live, to organizations that work to preserve the world's natural resources'.

Activities: Operates in the field of environmental conservation and protection on the West Coast of the USA and in Central and South America and the Caribbean. The Foundation has a special interest in programmes promoting marine conservation. Also concerned with women's centres and services in California.

Geographical Area of Activity: USA and Central and South America.

Finance: Total assets $30,284,340 (2000); total grants $5,581,520 (2000).

Principal Staff: Admin. Glenda Menges.

Address: 412 North Coast Highway, PMB 359, Laguna Beach, CA 92651.

Telephone: (949) 494-0365.

Houston Endowment Inc

Founded in 1937 by Mr and Mrs Jesse H. Jones for the support of any charitable, educational or religious undertaking.

Activities: Operates nationally, with greatest priority on local and state needs, in the fields of education and health institutions, through grants to institutions, scholarships and the construction and equipping of educational establishments and hospitals. Also makes grants in the areas of arts and culture, community enhancement and medical facilities and research.

Geographical Area of Activity: USA.

Restrictions: No grants to individuals; grants only to non-profit organizations.

Publications: Annual Report and financial statement.

Finance: Assets $1,367,974,800 (2001); grants distributed $71,761,140 (2001).

Officers and Directors: D. Kent Anderson (Chair.); H. J. Nelson, III (Pres.); Sheryl L. Johns (Vice-Pres. and Treas.); David L. Nelson (Vice-Pres. and Sec.); Audrey Jones Beck; Anthony W. Hall, Jr; Harold Metts; L. E. Simmons; Melissa Jones Stevens; Rosie Zamora.

Address: 600 Travis, Suite 6400, Houston, TX 77002-3007.

Telephone: (713) 238-8100; **Fax:** (713) 238-8101; **Internet:** www.houstonendowment.org.

George A. and Eliza Gardner Howard Foundation

Founded in 1952 by Nicea Howard to aid the personal development of promising individuals at the crucial middle stage of their careers.

Activities: Awards a limited number of one-year fellowships for independent projects in various categories, selected on a rotational basis each year that awards are made. The categories are as follows: art history, painting and sculpture; music composition and musicology; history (including history of science and archaeology) and political science; creative writing (novel, short story, poetry, play-writing and essays in English); literary and film criticism; and sociology, anthropology and philosophy.

Geographical Area of Activity: USA.

Restrictions: The fellowships are tenable anywhere in the world, but are restricted to candidates who, regardless of their country of citizenship, are professionally based in the USA. Fellowships are not given to support degree candidates.

Finance: Awards average $20,000 each. Total grants awarded $260,000 (2001/02).

Board of Trustees: Gordon E. Cadwgan; Bradford Gorham; Robert W. Kenyon; William W. Kenyon; Arthur H. Parker.

Principal Staff: Admin. Dir Henry F. Majewski; Co-ordinator Susan M. Clifford.

Address: 42 Charlesfield St, 4th Floor, Brown University, Providence, RI 02912.

Telephone: (401) 863-2640; **Fax:** (401) 863-7341; **Internet:** www.brown.edu/divisions/graduate_school/howard/; **e-mail:** howard_foundation@brown.edu.

Howard Hughes Medical Institute

Founded in 1953 by Howard R. Hughes to support the field of science, particularly medical research and education. Also interested in minority issues, notably Asian/Pacific islanders, African Americans, Latinos and native Americans.

Activities: Operates a Medical Research Program conducting biomedical research in the USA in such fields as cell biology, genetics, immunology, neuroscience, structural biology and bioinformatics/computational biology. Makes grants to promote education in the biological sciences in the USA and supports research abroad, particularly in Central and South America, Canada, Europe (including the United Kingdom), Russia and Australia. Also assists scientists in the Czech Republic, Hungary and Poland through grants to the European Molecular Biology Organization. Fellowships are awarded for research training for medical students.

Geographical Area of Activity: International.

Restrictions: Grants are made primarily within defined competitive programmes; rarely funds unsolicited proposals.

Publications: Annual Report; occasional reports; quarterly magazine; grant programme announcements.

Finance: Assets $14,898,377,000 (Aug. 2002); disbursements $630,210,000 (2002).

Trustees: Hanna H. Gray (Chair.); James A. Baker, III; Alexander G. Bearn; Joseph L. Fordstein; Frank William Gay; James H. Gilliam, Jr; Garnett L. Keith; Jeremy Knowles; William R. Lummis; Anne M. Tatlock.

Principal Staff: Pres. Thomas R. Cech; Vice-Pres., Grants and Special Programmes Peter J. Bruns; Vice-Pres. and Chief Scientific Officer David A. Clayton; Vice-Pres. and Chief Financial Officer Stephen M. Cohen; Vice-Pres. and Gen. Counsel Joan S. Leonard; Vice-Pres. and Dir of Planning Gerald M. Rubin; Vice-Pres., Communications and Public Affairs Avice A. Meehan; Vice-Pres. and Chief Investment Officer Nestor V. Santiago.

Address: 4000 Jones Bridge Rd, Chevy Chase, MD 20815-6789.

Telephone: (301) 215-8500; **Fax:** (301) 215-8863; **Internet:** www.hhmi.org; **e-mail:** webmaster@hhmi.org.

Human Rights Watch

Established in 1978 as Helsinki Watch, with the aim of assisting in the protection of human rights world-wide; it does not accept direct or indirect funding from any government.

Activities: Operates in the field of human rights internationally in collaboration with other NGOs. Maintains three offices in the USA, and offices in London, Moscow and Brussels, which collect information on human rights, in areas such as executions, torture, restrictions on religious organizations, children's and women's rights, refugees, prisons, landmines and discrimination. Also carries out research; disseminates information; and lobbies national governments and international organizations.

Geographical Area of Activity: International.

Publications: *HRW World Report 2001;* Reports; and other publications.

Finance: Total revenue $16,140,811, expenditure $16,144,416 (March. 2000).

Directors: J. Fanton (Chair.); R. L. Bernstein (Founding Chair.).

Principal Staff: Exec. Dir K. Roth.

Address: 350 Fifth Ave, 34th Floor, New York, NY 10118-3299.

Telephone: (212) 290-4700; **Fax:** (212) 736-1300; **Internet:** www.hrw.org; **e-mail:** hrwnyc@hrw.org.

Humana Foundation, Inc.

Founded in 1981 by Humana, Inc for general charitable purposes.

Activities: Operates mainly in Kentucky in the fields of the arts and culture, health and human services, education, community development and international projects; awards scholarships; operates institutes for medical research and training, and funds medical schools. Operates a wide-spread humanitarian aid project in Romania.

Geographical Area of Activity: Currently USA, Romania and Poland.

Restrictions: Focuses on organizations supporting communities where Humana, Inc has a business presence.

Finance: Total assets $55,011,694 (2000); total grants $5,357,621 (2000).

Officers and Directors: David A. Jones (Chair., Pres. and CEO); Wayne T. Smith (Pres. and Chief Operating Officer); Arthur P. Hipwell, Sr, George G. Bauernfeind, Walter E. Neely, James E. Murray (Vice-Pres); James W. Doucette (Vice-Pres. and Treas.); Katherine Pellegrino (Sec.); William R. Drury (Chief Financial Officer and Foundation Man.).

Principal Staff: Pres. and CEO David A. Jones; Exec. Dir Virginia Kelly-Judd.

Address: Humana Bldg, 500 West Main St, POB 1438, Louisville, KY 40201.

Telephone: (502) 580-3041; **Internet:** www.humanafoundation.org; **e-mail:** cjackson@humana.com.

Humanitarian Law Project

Founded in 1985 with the aim of promoting the protection of human rights world-wide, and supporting the peaceful resolution of conflict through international human rights laws.

Activities: Operates internationally in the area of law and human rights. Monitors volatile situations around the world in order to identify abuses of human rights; holds consultative status with the United Nations; seeks to put pressure on countries that do not observe basic human rights; and promotes the non-violent resolution of conflict. Also dedicates itself to raising awareness of human rights issues.

Geographical Area of Activity: International.

Publications: Reports.

Address: 8124 West Third St, Suite 105, Los Angeles, CA 90048.

Telephone: (323) 653-0726; **Fax:** (323) 658-6306; **Internet:** hlp.home.igc.org/index.html; **e-mail:** hlp@igc.org.

The Hunger Project

Non-profit organization dedicated to eliminating chronic hunger around the world by focusing on the human issues that cause it.

Activities: Operates in the fields of aid to less-developed countries and social welfare, through seeking to empower disadvantaged people in Africa, Asia and Central and South America to improve their own health, education, nutrition and income in collaboration with local grass-roots organizations. Also committed to gender equality and the reduction of infant mortality. Awards the annual Africa Prize for Leadership for the Sustainable End of Hunger.

Geographical Area of Activity: Africa, South Asia, and Central and South America.

Publications: Newsletter (monthly); Annual Report.

Finance: Assets $5,059,432 (2000); annual revenue $6,891,467, expenditure $6,674,901 (2000).

Directors: Joan Holmes (Pres.); Dr P. G. Bourne (Chair.); V. Mohini Giri; Dr S. Wandira Kazibwe; G. Mathew; Chief Bisi Ogunleye; Queen Noor of Jordan; J. Pérez de Cuéllar; M. Robinson; A. Sen; S. J. Sherwood; G. M. Weiss; M. S. Swaminathan (Chair. Emer.).

Address: 15 East 26th St, New York, NY 10010.

Telephone: (212) 251-9100; **Fax:** (212) 532-9785; **Internet:** www.thp.org; **e-mail:** info@thp.org.

IAPA Scholarship Fund

Founded in 1955 by the Inter American Press Association to support the exchange of journalists and journalism students between Western hemisphere countries.

Activities: Operates internationally (in the Western hemisphere) in the field of journalism, through exchange programmes and scholarships (at least 10 a year) awarded to residents of North, Central and South America and the Caribbean for study at university schools of journalism abroad.

Geographical Area of Activity: North, Central and South America and the Caribbean.

Principal Staff: Pres. Alejandro Aguirre; Vice-Pres. Hilda O'Farrill; Treas. Jim Hampton; Sec. Bartolome Mitre; Exec. Dirs William P. Williamson, Jr, Julio E. Muñoz.

Address: 1801 SW Third Ave, Miami, FL 33129.

Telephone: (305) 634-2465; **Fax:** (305) 635-2272; **e-mail:** sipiapa@aol.com.

IBM International Foundation

Founded in 1985 for general charitable purposes in South Africa; in 1992 its charter was amended to allow charitable giving world-wide.

Activities: Operates nationally and internationally, mainly in the field of education; projects also include: global initiatives in early learning and the arts and culture; and grants to organizations working in Africa, Asia and Europe.

Geographical Area of Activity: International.

Publications: Information brochure.

Finance: Funded by IBM Corporation. Total assets $146,630,946 (Dec. 2000); total grants $10,148,618 (2000).

Officers and Directors: Stanley S. Litow (Pres.); Paula W. Baker (Vice-Chair.).

Address: c/o IBM Corporation, New Orchard Rd, Armonk, NY 10504-1709.

Telephone: (914) 766-1900; **Fax:** (914) 499-7624; **Internet:** www.ibm.com/ibm/ibmgives.

IDE—International Development Enterprises

Established in 1981 to assist in the development of the rural poor in less-developed countries through affordable technology.

Activities: Operates in Africa and Asia in the fields of aid to less-developed countries, science and technology and social welfare, through funding technology development and marketing of irrigation equipment so as to increase income for farmers, technicians and manufacturers, thus allowing people in less-developed countries to help themselves. Also provides consultancy services. Maintains country offices in Bangladesh, Cambodia, Canada, People's Republic of China, India, Nepal, UK, Vietnam and Zambia.

Geographical Area of Activity: Africa and Asia.

Publications: Newsletter.

Finance: Assets $842,065 (2001); annual revenue $4,247,046 (2001).

Principal Staff: Pres. Paul Polak.

Address: 10403 W Colfax Ave, Suite 500, Lakewood, CO 80215.

Telephone: (303) 232-4336; **Fax:** (303) 232-8346; **Internet:** www.ideorg.org; **e-mail:** ide@ideorg.org.

India Partners

Founded in 1984 to support self-help ministry projects in India through partner organizations, who are committed to providing long-term solutions to poverty for every individual, regardless of race, religion, caste or sex.

Activities: Supports work in the fields of development assistance, leadership training, disaster relief, education and health work. Also works on short-term projects (including programmes related to agriculture, construction and water resource management amongst others) and runs a child sponsorship programme.

Geographical Area of Activity: India.

Publications: Annual Report; *Partners Newsletter* (3 a year).

Finance: Annual revenue $435,654 (2001).

Directors: Brent Hample (Pres. and Exec. Dir); Nancy Olsen (Vice-Pres.); Eileen Miller (Sec.); Jay Nelapudi (Treas.); Deborah Hoopes.

Principal Staff: Exec. Dir Brent Hample.

Address: POB 5470, Eugene, OR 97405.

Telephone: (541) 683-0696; **Fax:** (541) 683-2773; **e-mail:** info@indiapartners.org.

INMED—International Medical Services for Health

Established to promote better health world-wide.

Activities: Operates in the field of medicine, health and education, through four main programmes: Mother Net America, which aims to provide advice and support for first-time mothers in the USA; Medical Supply, which procures and sends necessary supplies to less-developed countries at reduced cost; Children as Agents of Change, which seeks to improve health through educating children in health and welfare issues and through immunization; and Millennium Alliance for Social Investment, which brokers multi-sector partnerships in support of global development. Maintains field offices in Los Angeles, Mexico, Brazil and the Dominican Republic.

Geographical Area of Activity: International.

Publications: *Home Visitors Handbook; Women's Wellness Sourcebook; Curriculum Sourcebook; and other educational and training materials.*

Board of Directors: Paul C. Bosland (Chair.); Dr Linda Pfieffer (Pres.); Paul Grunder (Treas.); Linda Asay (Sec.); Dr George Armstrong; Wendy Balter; Dr Lynda Davis; Dr Thad M. Jackson; Eugene H. Rotberg; James R. Rutherford; Dr Paul Stern.

Principal Staff: Pres. Dr Linda Pfieffer; Exec. Vice-Pres. Dr Thad M. Jackson; Vice-Pres. and Dir Joyce Capelli.

Address: 45449 Severn Way, Suite 161, Sterling, VA 20166.

Telephone: (703) 444-4477; **Fax:** (703) 444-4471; **Internet:** www.inmed.org; **e-mail:** contact@inmed.org.

Institute for Cancer Prevention

Established in 1969 with the aim of preventing chronic diseases—especially cancer; formerly known as the American Health Foundation.

Activities: Promotes preventive medicine through research (in areas including nutrition, tobacco carcinogenesis, molecular biology, pathology and epidemiology), and clinical research (including clinical trials and intervention programmes). Supports education of the public, professionals and government officials in preventive medicine. Maintains the Naylor Dana Institute for Disease Prevention.

Geographical Area of Activity: USA.

Publications: *Preventive Medicine* (quarterly).

Finance: Annual budget approx. $20,000,000.

Board of Trustees: Thomas A. Moore (Chair.).

Principal Staff: Pres. and Dir Dr Daniel W. Nixon; Senior Vice-Pres., Medical Affairs Richard S. Rivlin; Dir Research Karam El-Bayoumy; Chief Operating Officer and Senior Vice-Pres. John Aufderheide.

Address: 390 Fifth Ave, New York, NY 10018.

Telephone: (212) 551-2500; **Fax:** (212) 697-2339; **Internet:** www.ifcp.us; **e-mail:** info@ifcp.us.

Institute of Current World Affairs, Inc—Crane–Rogers Foundation

Founded in 1925 by Charles R. Crane and Walter S. Rogers (and also known as the Crane–Rogers Foundation) to provide opportunity and full financial support to a few persons of high character and unusual promise to enable them to observe and study at first hand particular areas and problems of contemporary significance outside the USA.

Activities: Operates through the granting of a limited number of long-term fellowships with the purpose of promoting a thorough and balanced knowledge of particular areas or problems outside the USA and the effective communication of this knowledge. Fellowships are for study in Eastern Europe, the Middle East and sub-Saharan Africa and for outside these areas. Fellowships are not awarded to support work towards academic degrees, nor to underwrite specific studies or programmes of research as such, but for independent self-designed programmes of study.

Geographical Area of Activity: International, excluding USA.

Restrictions: Fellowship candidates must be fluent in the English language; fellowships are awarded only to candidates under 36 years of age.

Publications: Information brochure.

Finance: Endowment approx. $2,000,000 (2002); annual budget approx. $100,000 (2002).

Trustees: Paul A. Rahe (Chair.); Carol Rose (Vice-Chair.); Ann Mische (Sec.); Edmond H. Sutton (Treas.); Carole Beaulieu; Mary Lynne Bird; Steve Butler; William F. Foote; P. Jayapal; P. B. Martin; D. S. Patterson; C. Rosenberger; J. Spencer; D. Vandewalle; S. Wriggins.

Principal Staff: Exec. Dir Peter B. Martin; Programme Asst B. Jacobson; Publications Man. E. Kozak.

Address: 4 West Wheelock St, Hanover, NH 03755.

Telephone: (603) 643-5548; **Fax:** (603) 643-9599; **Internet:** www.icwa.org; **e-mail:** icwa@valley.net.

Institute for Development Research

Established as a non-profit research, education and consulting body dedicated to increasing the capacity of organizations which work to advance sustainable development and social justice; in 2002 merged with World Education.

Activities: Operates internationally, in co-operation with partner organizations, in the field of international development and co-operation, and the development of civil society, working to develop ways in which NGOs and other civil society groups can solve social and economic problems more effectively, by identifying and researching emerging issues affecting the non-profit sector, communicating with NGOs to identify innovative strategies and disseminating this information.

Publications: *Promoting Corporate Citizenship in the Global South: Towards a Model of Empowered Civil Society Collaboration With Business; Strengthening North-South Partnerships: Addressing Structural Barriers to Mutual Influence; Intersectoral Co-operation: Lessons for Practice; IDR Reports* (on-line series of working papers); and other specialist publications.

Finance: Assets $433,328 (1999); annual revenue $1,514,383, expenditure $1,506,557 (1999).

Principal Staff: Pres. J. G. Covey; Chair. L. David Brown; Dir of Programmes D. Ashman; D. Machado; J. Yanulis.

Address: 44 Farnsworth St, Boston, MA 02210-1211.

Telephone: (617) 482-9485; **Fax:** (617) 482-0617; **Internet:** www.jsi.com/idr; **e-mail:** idr@jsi.com.

Institute of International Education

Founded after the First World War by Dr Stephen Duggan, Dr Nicholas Murray Butler and Elihu Root, and based on the belief that the sharing of knowledge and skills is the only road to lasting peace and international understanding.

Activities: The Institute is an administrative agency with no funds of its own for distribution, administering over 250 funding programmes on behalf of its sponsors. It manages exchange programmes for students, faculty members and professionals sponsored by governments, foundations, corporations, universities and international organizations; assists the United States State Department with the exchange of US and foreign students and professionals (serving Fulbright Fellows from foreign countries, and administering the Hubert Humphrey North–South Fellowships Program for mid-career professionals from the developing world); and raises scholarship support for foreign undergraduates studying in the USA through programmes which it administers in co-operation with other agencies. It administers programmes for the US Agency for International Development (USAID), including the Energy Training Project (providing training in energy development to citizens of developing countries); the Zimbabwe Manpower Development Program; and projects in Central and South America and the Caribbean. It co-ordinates the South African Education Program, which assists black South African students through the resources of US universities, corporations, foundations and USAID. It offers counselling and information services on overseas study and scholarships, conducts statistical and policy-oriented research, and issues publications. Maintains overseas offices in Hong Kong, Hungary, Mexico, Russia, Thailand and Vietnam and is represented in Egypt, Indonesia, Namibia, the Philippines and Ukraine.

Geographical Area of Activity: International.

Restrictions: Does not make grants.

Publications: Annual Report; *Financial Resources for International Study; Funding for US Study; English Language and Orientation Programs* (every 2 years); *Academic Year Abroad* (annually); *Open Doors* (annually); *Vacation Study Abroad* (annually); studies, handbooks, surveys and leaflets on international education.

Finance: Assets $95,626,718 (Sept. 2002); annual revenue $170,569,389, expenditure $174,165,904 (2002).

Directors: Thomas S. Johnson (Chair.); Henry Kaufman (Chair. Emeritus); Allan E. Goodman (Pres. and CEO); Thomas S. Johnson (Chair., Exec. Cttee); Victor J. Goldberg, Diane J. Paton (Vice-Chair.); Henrik N. Vanderlip (Treas.).

Principal Staff: Pres. Allan E. Goodman.

Address: 809 United Nations Plaza, New York, NY 10017-3580.

Telephone: (212) 883-8200; **Fax:** (212) 984-5452; **Internet:** www.iie.org; **e-mail:** info@iie.org.

Institute for Sustainable Communities—ISC

Founded in 1991 by former Vermont Governor Madeleine M. Kunin, an independent non-profit organization which aims to help communities around the world to address environmental, economic and social challenges to build a better future shaped and shared by all.

Activities: Since its establishment ISC has managed international projects in more than 14 countries. It helps communities in existing and emerging democracies solve problems while building a better future for themselves and the world. ISC gives communities and the organizations that support them training, advice and grants needed to solve their own problems and shape their own long-term future. Programmes operate in the following fields: community action; education; civil society; environment; and business development. Maintains field offices in Macedonia, the Russian Federation and the Ukraine.

Geographical Area of Activity: Central and Eastern Europe, the republics of Central Asia, Japan and the USA.

Restrictions: Grants only to projects in Macedonia, Bulgaria and the Russian Federation.

Publications: *ISC Report*; published articles.

Finance: Supported by individual donors, private foundations and the US Government. Revenue and expenditure $7,100,000 (2000).

Board of Directors: Peter Clavelle (Chair.); Kevin Quigley (Vice-Chair.); Hon. Harry Barnes, Jr (Sec.); Janet C. Ballantyne; John A. Dooley; Dr Kristalina Georgieva; Jerry Greenfield; Hon. Madeleine M. Kunin; Jonathan Lash; Dr Joyce Malombe; Stephen Ramsey; Joanna Regulska; Aaron Williams; Douglas Costle (Chair. Emer.); George Hamilton (*ex officio*).

Principal Staff: Pres. George Hamilton.

Address: 535 Stone Cutters Way, Montpelier, VT 05602.

Telephone: (802) 229-2900; **Fax:** (802) 229-2919; **Internet:** www.iscvt.org; **e-mail:** isc@iscvt.org.

Inter-American Bar Foundation

Founded in 1957 to promote the study of law, advance the administration of justice in the West and strengthen inter-American legal relations.

Activities: Supports educational, literary, scientific and charitable projects promoting the study of law. Funds and organizes training and exchange programmes; provides finance for legal research; organizes seminars and workshops on matters of specific legal interest; advises the US Government, professional associations in the USA and Central and South America, and individuals about inter-American legal activities. Runs the Administration of Justice Program (Central and South America). Focus on conducting long term projects aimed at strengthening regional bar associations in Central America and the Andean countries, as well as creating alternative dispute resolution institutions in Bolivia's three major cities.

Geographical Area of Activity: USA, and Central and South America.

Finance: Annual budget approx. $200,000.

Principal Staff: Pres. and Dir Judd L. Kessler.

Address: Federal Bar Bldg, Suite 310, 1819 H St, NW, Washington, DC 20006.

Telephone: (202) 293-1455; **Fax:** (202) 828-0157.

Inter-American Foundation

Founded in 1969 by the US Congress (as an independent agency, so that its operations would not be affected by short-term US policy considerations) to support the self-help efforts of disadvantaged people in Central and South America and the Caribbean.

Activities: Makes grants through two programmes, the Resource Mobilization Program and the Local Development Program, to regional NGOs such as agricultural co-operatives, community associations and small urban enterprises, or to larger organizations that work with local groups, providing credit, technical assistance, training and marketing services. The Foundation's grants mainly fund programmes concerned with education and training, eco-development, community services, food production and agriculture, and small enterprise development and management. Fellowships are awarded for field research in Central and South America and the Caribbean by postgraduate scholars at US universities, and for advanced study in the USA by well-established researchers from Central and South America and the Caribbean.

Geographical Area of Activity: Central and South America and the Caribbean.

Publications: *Grassroots Development* (journal, 2 a year in English, Spanish and Portuguese); annual review; fact sheets.

Finance: The Foundation receives about 60% of its annual budget from the US Congress (appropriation of $20,600,000 in 1999); it also receives funding from the Social Progress Trust Fund of the Inter-American Development Bank ($44,000,000 for 1995–2000). Total grants $22,262,000 (1999).

Board of Directors: Frank Yturria (Chair.); Patricia Hill Williams (Vice-Chair.); Kay K. Arnold; Fred P. DuVal; Anita Perez Ferguson.

Principal Staff: Pres. George Evans; Sr Vice-Pres. and Gen. Counsel Adolfo Franco.

Address: Ballston Metro Center, 901 North Stuart St, 10th Floor, Arlington, VA 22203.

Telephone: (703) 306-4338; **Fax:** (703) 306-4365; **Internet:** www.iaf.gov; **e-mail:** correo@iaf.gov.

Interchurch Medical Assistance, Inc

Set up in 1960 to represent Protestant relief organizations and to improve the quality and availability of health care for the world's poorest people. Obtains medicines and medical supplies for emergency, health and development programmes on behalf of its 12 member Protestant relief and development agencies.

Activities: Acts on behalf of its 12 member organizations, co-ordinating the procurement and transportation of donated and purchased medical supplies to disaster relief areas; provides essential medicines to treat common illnesses in areas of need; and works in partnership with its members and other organizations to control parasitic diseases in less-developed countries.

Geographical Area of Activity: International.

Restrictions: Not a grant-making organization.

Address: 500 Main Street, Building Old Main, POB 429, New Windsor, MD 21776.

Telephone: (410) 635-8720; **Fax:** (410) 635-8726; **Internet:** www.interchurch.org; **e-mail:** imainfo@interchurch.org.

International Aid, Inc

Established in 1980, a non-profit organization aiming to bring compassion and relief to people in need around the world.

Activities: International Aid is a network of mission hospitals, clinics, orphanages and churches world-wide which operates in the fields of global relief, international development and local training. It supports missionaries and organizations providing emergency relief and development programmes in less-developed countries in crisis, while also acting as an agent linking available resources, people and organizations with situations and people that need their help. Incorporates Kids Hope USA, a national programme in which volunteers work to build the skills and self-esteem of at-risk children.

Geographical Area of Activity: International.

Publications: Annual Report.

Directors: Randall G. Veltkamp (Chair.); R. Wiersma (Vice-Chair); W. Olsson (Sec.); Myles Fish (Pres. and CEO); J. B. Wynsma (Treas.); J. G. Buick; T. Coan; D. L. Dull; P. Egbert; J. K. Haveman, Jr; D. Lane; C. Masamitsu; J. Mulder.

Principal Staff: Pres. and CEO Rev. Myles D. Fish; Exec. Vice-Pres. J. Bult DeJong.

Address: 17011 W Hickory, Spring Lake, MI 49456-9712.

Telephone: (616) 846-7490; **Fax:** (616) 846-3842; **Internet:** www.gospelcom.net/ia; **e-mail:** ia@internationalaid.org.

International Center for Not-for-Profit Law—ICNL

International organization established to support and facilitate the development of civil society world-wide, through promoting the development of laws and regulatory systems that encourage this sector.

Activities: Operates internationally, co-operating with national and international organizations in the area of third-sector law. Provides technical legal assistance, training and educational materials for legal professionals; organizes conferences; and carries out research. Maintains a library and resource centre. ICNL has offices in Budapest, Almaty and Kiev.

Geographical Area of Activity: International.

Publications: *The International Journal of Not-for-Profit Law* (quarterly online journal); *World Bank Handbook; International Reporter of Not-for-Profit Law; Country Reports.*

Principal Staff: Pres. Stephan Klingelhofer; Senior Vice-Pres. Programs Douglas Rutzen; Vice-Pres. NIS Natalia Bourjaily; Vice-Pres. Finance Darla Mecham.

Address: 733 15th St, NW, Suite 420, Washington, DC 20005.

Telephone: (202) 624-0766; **Fax:** (202) 624-0767; **Internet:** www.icnl.org; **e-mail:** infoicnl@icnl.org.

International Center for Research on Women

Established to carry out research on gender-related issues of the developing world.

Activities: Engages in research, advocacy and direct action on issues affecting women around the world, including poverty reduction and economic growth, HIV/AIDS, reproductive health and nutrition, social conflict and transformation, population and social transition, and policy and communications.

Geographical Area of Activity: International.

Publications: Research reports.

Directors: S. Levine (Chair.); J. Breyer; Hon. W. Byanyima; S. Byorum; P. Deutch; C. Dickert-Scherr; F. Friedman; H. Gayle; V. de Ladoucette; Y. C. Richardson; B. Shearer; J. Warner.

Principal Staff: Pres. Geeta Rao Gupta; Vice-Pres. Kathleen Barnett; Treas. Michael Lavelline.

Address: 1717 Massachusetts Ave, NW, Suite 302 Washington, DC 20036.

Telephone: (202) 797-0007; **Fax:** (202) 797-0020; **Internet:** www.icrw.org; **e-mail:** info@icrw.org.

International Child Art Foundation—ICAF

A charity founded in 1997 by Ashfaq Ishaq to inspire children to be creative, imaginative, innovative and artistic, and thus fostering communication and co-operation among the children of the world.

Activities: Operates world-wide in the areas of the arts and humanities and creativity, through Child Art and Creativity programmes, educational exhibitions and publications, creativity workshops and conferences. Children aged between eight and 12 years can participate in ICAF's Global Art Creation Program.

Geographical Area of Activity: International.

Restrictions: Global Art Creation Program restricted to children between the ages of eight and 12. No grants to individuals or non-profits.

Publications: *ChildArt* (quarterly).

Finance: Financed by donations, membership dues, grants and other contributions. Assets $302,794 (Dec. 1999); annual revenue $682,278, expenditure $988,064 (1999).

Trustees: Harriet Mayor Fulbright; Katty Guerami; Ashfaq Ishaq; Peter N. G. Schwartz.

Principal Staff: Chair. Harriet Mayor Fulbright; Exec. Dir Ashfaq Ishaq; Dir of Programmes Tim Bigelow; Dir of Corporate Relations Sharon Franklin.

Address: 1350 Connecticut Ave, NW, Suite 1225, Washington, DC 20036-1702.

Telephone: (202) 530-1000; **Fax:** (202) 530-1080; **Internet:** www.icaf.org; **e-mail:** childart@icaf.org.

International Child Health Foundation

Founded in 1986 to promote better health of children and their mothers in developing countries and medically underserved populations.

Activities: Operates mainly in the area of diarrhoeal diseases, malnutrition and poverty, through the development of low-cost technologies, conducting health, educational and training programmes, promoting research capabilities in institutions in developing countries, and through charitable activities. Maintains a speakers' bureau and through its Innovative Small Grant Program awards grants of up to $5,000 to research or service projects aiming to improve the health of children.

Geographical Area of Activity: International.

Publications: Annual Report; newsletter.

Finance: Annual revenue $166,664, expenditure $170,767 (2001).

Officers and Trustees: E. Marler (Chair.); W. Greenough (Pres.); M. R. Bashir (Vice-Pres.); L. D. Andrew (Sec. and Treas.); G. Arrowsmith; A. Bruchesi; R. Colwell; C. Dale-Riikonen; J. Deltito; H. Fleming; B. Lamont.

Address: 10630 Little Patuxent Parkway, Suite 126, Columbia, MD 21044.

Telephone: (301) 596-4514; **Fax:** (410) 992-5641; **Internet:** www.childhealthfoundation.org; **e-mail:** chf@erols.com.

International College of Surgeons

Founded in 1935 by Dr Max Thorek; a world-wide federation of organizations that aims to encourage world-wide surgical excellence through training, humanitarian work, education and fellowship.

Activities: Operates in the field of medicine and health, through the exchange of surgical knowledge and techniques, and assisting in surgical missions in developing countries around the world, including disaster relief work and providing surgical care alongside other humanitarian agencies. Offers scholarships for surgical training, funds surgical research and lectureships. There are 60 national sections, of which ICS–USA is the largest. Maintains the International Museum of Surgical Science, in Chicago, IL.

Geographical Area of Activity: International.

Publications: *International Surgery* (quarterly journal); Newsletter.

Principal Staff: World Pres. Dr Raymond A. Dieter, Jr; Pres. Elect Prof. Nadey Hakim; Exec. Dir Max Downham.

Address: 1516 N. Lake Shore Dr., Chicago, IL 60610-1694.

Telephone: (312) 642-3555; **Fax:** (312) 787-1624; **Internet:** www.icsglobal.org; **e-mail:** max@icsglobal.org.

International Education Research Foundation

Founded in 1969.

Activities: Evaluates international education credentials in terms of US equivalence for employment purposes, for colleges, universities, licensing agencies, professional organizations and the armed services. The Foundation also conducts workshops and research, and maintains a library on international education.

Geographical Area of Activity: USA and international.

Publications: *The Country Index*.

Principal Staff: Exec. Dir Susan J. Bidel.

Address: POB 3665, Culver City, CA 90231-3665.

Telephone: (310) 258-9451; **Fax:** (310) 342-7086; **Internet:** www.ierf.org; **e-mail:** info@ierf.org.

International Executive Service Corps

Established in 1964 by David Rockefeller, a private non-profit organization aiming to promote the development of free market economies and democracy in the developing world and emerging markets.

Activities: Promotes economic development world-wide by providing technical or managerial experts to assist in enterprise projects in the developing world, thus ultimately increasing employment and standards of living. Its services include preparing local firms for investment, delivering up-to-date business information at all times, strengthening infrastructures in order to develop a stronger private sector and free-market economies, and helping businesses to increase productivity through training. Also manages the Global Technology Network, assisting American companies to find markets overseas.

Geographical Area of Activity: International.

Publications: Newsletter; Annual Report; IESC Fact Sheet.

Finance: Funded by USAID, other US government departments, corporations and foundations. Total revenue $39,868,000, expenditure $39,852,000 (2000).

Directors: J. P. Birkelund (Chair.); R. McGrath (Sec.); L. W. Benson; R. L. Bornhuetter; N. F. Brady; D. Burke; F. Carlucci; H. L. Clark, Jr; R. M. Davis; G. M. Ferris, Jr; H. C. Gardiner; J. M. Kilts; D. K. McIvor; D. E. McKinney; C. H. Pforzheimer; W. P. Powell; R. Sabot; J. R. Torrell, III; J. C. Whitehead.

Principal Staff: Pres. and CEO Hobart C. Gardiner.

Address: 333 Ludlow St, POB 10005, Stamford, CT 06904-2005.

Telephone: (203) 967-6000; **Fax:** (203) 324-2531; **Internet:** www.iesc.org; **e-mail:** iesc@iesc.org.

International Eye Foundation

Founded in 1961 as the International Eye Bank by Dr John Harry King, Jr, to promote the prevention and cure of blindness in developing countries, through the provision of training; clinical, surgical and preventive services; equipment, supplies and medication; public education; and technical assistance in the development of health infrastructure. Present name adopted in 1969.

Activities: Operates internationally in the fields of medicine, public health and education, through co-operative programmes with health ministries and private indigenous organizations, as well as through fellowships for ophthalmic training and scientific conferences. Addresses the prevention and amelioration of conditions such as onchocerciasis (river blindness), xerophthalmia, glaucoma, cataracts and other major eye diseases, through projects in Africa, Asia, Central and South America, and Eastern Europe.

Geographical Area of Activity: Africa, Asia, Central and South America, and Eastern Europe.

Publications: *Eye to Eye; Eye Care in Developing Nations*; *IEF Fact Sheets*; Annual Report.

Board of Directors: Thomas H. Price, III (Pres.); Frank S. Ashburn, Jr (Vice-Pres.); Elizabeth Burt (Treas.); Rowland R. Bradley (Sec.); and 24 others.

Principal Staff: Exec. Dir Victoria M. Sheffield.

Address: 10801 Connecticut Ave, Kensington, MD 20895.

Telephone: (240) 290-0263; **Fax:** (240) 290-0269; **Internet:** www.iefusa.org; **e-mail:** ief@iefusa.org.

International Foundation

Founded in 1948 to assist people of developing countries in their endeavours to solve some of their problems, to attain a better standard of living and to obtain a reasonable degree of self-sufficiency.

Activities: Makes grants to US-based agencies or institutions engaged in aid to developing countries in Asia, Central and South America, the Caribbean, the Middle East, the South Pacific and Southern Africa, with priority given to agricultural research and production; medicine and health (including sanitation and nutrition); education and research; and social welfare and development (including the arts and humanities, business, refugees and population planning).

Geographical Area of Activity: Southern Africa, Asia, the Middle East, Central and South America, and the South Pacific.

Restrictions: No grants to individuals, nor for scholarships, conferences, operating budgets or endowment funds.

Publications: Information brochure.

Finance: Assets $31,739,914 (2001); total grants $1,446,800 (2001).

Principal Staff: Chair., Grant Applications Dr E. A. Holmes.

Address: 170 Changebridge Rd, C5-4, Montville, NJ 07045.

Telephone: (973) 227-6107; **Fax:** (973) 227-6821.

International Foundation for Art Research

Founded in 1969 by John de Menil, John Rewald and Harry Bober to research authentication problems and provide information to the art world.

Activities: Operates in the field of the arts and humanities, nationally through self-conducted programmes, and internationally through research, grants to institutions, publications and training courses. The Foundation has an Art Advisory Council and a Law Advisory Council. Provides an art authentication service.

Geographical Area of Activity: International.

Publications: *IFAR Journal* (incorporating *Stolen Art Alert,* quarterly, in co-operation with the Art Loss Register, the art community, insurance companies, the police, the Federal Bureau of Investigation—FBI and Interpol).

Board of Directors: J. A. Josephson (Chair.); D. M. Campbell; D. L. Dalva, II; L. M. Edwards; R. C. Graham, Jr; J. A. Josephson; T. N. Kaplan; V. P. Klein; A. M. Milrad; D. Nash; L. B. Polsky; J. Richardson; S. Sachs, II.

Principal Staff: Exec. Dir Dr Sharon Flescher; Chair., Art Advisory Council Donald Posner; Chair., Law Advisory Council Franklin Feldman.

Address: 500 Fifth Ave, New York, NY 10110.

Telephone: (212) 391-6234; **Fax:** (212) 391-8794; **Internet:** www.ifar.org; **e-mail:** kferg@ifar.org.

International Foundation for Education and Self-Help

Founded by the Rev. Leon H. Sullivan to reduce poverty and unemployment in sub-Saharan Africa and to improve links between Africa and the USA.

Activities: Operates in the fields of agriculture, business and economic development, democracy and governance, education and health in order to improve the quality of life in developing countries, with a particular focus on sub-Saharan Africa. Its programmes work in a number of areas including reducing hunger and poverty, increasing literacy levels through better education, providing training to the unemployed and unskilled, helping to reduce the spread of HIV/AIDS, providing basic health care, and encouraging cultural, social and economic relations between Africans and African-Americans.

Geographical Area of Activity: Sub-Saharan Africa.

Restrictions: Operates its own programmes.

Publications: Annual Newsletter; Annual Report.

Finance: Annual revenue (excluding in-kind donations) $1,000,000 (Sept. 2002).

Principal Staff: Pres. and Exec. Dir Dr C. T. Wright.

Address: 5040 East Shea Blvd, Suite 260, Scottsdale, AZ 85254-4687.

Telephone: (480) 443-1800; **Fax:** (480) 443-1824; **Internet:** www.ifesh.org; **e-mail:** ifesh@ifesh.org.

International Foundation for Election Systems—IFES

Established in 1987, a private non-profit organization which provides technical assistance in the promotion of democracy world-wide.

Activities: Operates world-wide in the fields of education, international affairs, law and human rights, politics and civil society, through self-conducted programmes, research, grants to institutions, scholarships and fellowships, conferences, training courses and publications. Also offers information about democratic development and elections. The Foundation has developed methodologies which promote the understanding of the political, social and economic background to international electoral events. It organizes training courses for election officials and NGOs; the Foundation supports civil society, rule of law and the strengthening of international governance. Has worked in more than 100 countries.

Geographical Area of Activity: International.

Restrictions: Not a grant-making institution, however, public funds are expended to carry out programmes internationally, and sub-grants are made to in-country partners.

Publications: Annual Report; *Elections Today* (quarterly); *International Directory of Election Offices; Buyer's Guide to Election Services, Supplies and Equipment*.

Board of Directors: W. J. Hybl (Chair.); P. G. Kelly (Vice-Chair.); L. J. Weil (Sec.); J. Napolitan (Treas.); and 12 others.

Principal Staff: Pres. Richard W. Soudriette.

Address: 1101 15th St, NW, 3rd Floor, Washington, DC 20005.

Telephone: (202) 828-8507; **Fax:** (202) 452-0804; **Internet:** www.ifes.org; **e-mail:** rrescenter@ifes.org.

International Foundation for Ethical Research

Founded in 1985 to support basic and applied research into valid alternatives to the use of live animals for research, testing and educational purposes.

Activities: Operates in the area of scientific research, through grants of up to $25,000 per award and renewal postgraduate fellowships of up to $15,000. Grants are awarded to scientists who are developing credible alternatives to live animal research, and to postgraduate students seeking to incorporate animal welfare issues into their studies. The Foundation also disseminates information designed to increase awareness of alternatives through seminars, publications and workshops.

Geographical Area of Activity: International.

Publications: Newsletter (quarterly); workshop proceedings.

Principal Staff: Exec. Dir Peter O'Donolan.

Address: 53 West Jackson Blvd, Suite 1552, Chicago, IL 60604.

Telephone: (312) 427-6025; **Fax:** (312) 427-6524; **Internet:** www.ifer.org; **e-mail:** ifer@navers.org.

International Foundation for Genetic Research—The Michael Fund

Founded in 1978 by Randy Engel and Dr Jerome Lejeune to promote cure and treatment research programmes for genetic disorders, including Down's Syndrome.

Activities: Operates in the area of medicine and health internationally, carrying out research and awarding grants to individuals for research and defending the rights of physically and mentally disabled people.

Geographical Area of Activity: International.

Publications: *The Friends of the Michael Fund* (newsletter).

Trustees: Fr Clifton Hill (Chair.); and eight others.

Principal Staff: Pres. Randy Engel; Dir, Medical Research Dr Marie Peeters-Ney.

Address: 500A Garden City Dr., Pittsburgh, PA 15146.

Telephone: (412) 823-6380; **Fax:** (412) 373-7713; **Internet:** www.michaelfund.org; **e-mail:** randy@michaelfund.org.

International Fund for Animal Welfare—IFAW

Founded in 1969 by Brian Davies to campaign for animal welfare.

Activities: Operates in the field of animal welfare, seeking to improve conditions for wild and domestic animals all over the world. Aims to reduce commercial exploitation of animals, protect natural habitats, and help animals in distress through campaigning and research. IFAW seeks to motivate the public to prevent cruelty to animals and promote animal welfare and conservation policies that advance the well-being of both animals and people. Works closely with a number of non-profit organizations, government leaders and volunteers to protect animals world-wide.

Geographical Area of Activity: International.

Publications: Annual report; *Animal Update* (quarterly magazine); Animal Education Pack for schools.

Finance: Funding mainly from supporter contributions. Net assets $35,200,000 (2000); annual revenue $60,800,000, expenditure $59,600,000 (2000).

Directors: Margaret Kennedy (Chair.); Stijn Albregts; Angelica Aragon; Karen I. Cotton; Anne Fitzgerald; John Garamendi; Atherton Martin; Thomas Ramey; Gary Tabor.

Principal Staff: Pres. Frederick M. O'Regan; Dir of Operations Azzedine Downes; Chief Financial Officer Christopher H. Tuite.

Address: 411 Main St, POB 193, Yarmouth Port, MA 02675.

Telephone: (508) 744-2000; **Fax:** (508) 744-2009; **Internet:** www.ifaw.org; **e-mail:** info@ifaw.org.

International League for Human Rights

Established in 1942, a non-profit NGO aiming to defend individual human rights advocates.

Activities: Operates in the field of human rights, seeking to keep human rights at the forefront of international affairs, and working to ensure that laws and treaties relating to human rights are adhered to at all times. Holds consultative status with the United Nations and other international organizations, and raises issues and cases before the UN and other regional organizations in order to co-ordinate strategies for human rights protection, and to bring attention to particular causes. Conducts regular seminars for policy-makers, government officials and NGO representatives concerning prominent issues in the field of human rights. Presents a Human Rights Award annually. Maintains a representative office in Geneva, and has affiliates and partner organizations world-wide.

Geographical Area of Activity: International.

Publications: *League Reports;* Newsletter.

Principal Staff: Pres. Scott Horton; Exec. Dir Louise Kantrow.

Address: 823 United Nations Plaza, Suite 717, New York, NY 10017.

Telephone: (212) 661-0480; **Fax:** (212) 661-0416; **Internet:** www.ilhr.org; **e-mail:** info@ilhr.org.

International Orthodox Christian Charities

Established in 1992 as the official humanitarian arm of the Standing Conference of Canonical Orthodox Bishops in the Americas.

Activities: Operates in the field of international and humanitarian development, identifying priority needs in countries overseas and working on aid programmes through the Orthodox Church and local groups. Programmes include working with orphans, refugees and displaced persons, the elderly, children, single-parent families, the disabled and in hospitals and schools. It is currently working in Central and Eastern Europe, Palestinian Autonomous Areas and Greece. International Orthodox Christian Charities is a member organization of InterAction (q.v).

Geographical Area of Activity: Africa, Central and Eastern Europe, the Middle East and Greece, USA and Central and South America.

Restrictions: Does not support programmes of church mission.

Publications: *News and Needs* (newsletter); Annual Report.

Finance: Net assets $9,563,748 (Dec. 2001); annual revenue $22,953,711, expenditure $38,083,140 (2001).

Directors: Bert W. Moyer (Chair.); and 22 others.

Principal Staff: Exec. Dir and CEO Constantine M. Triantafilou.

Address: 110 West Rd, Suite 360, Baltimore MD 21024.

Telephone: (410) 243-9820; **Fax:** (410) 243-9824; **Internet:** www.iocc.org; **e-mail:** relief@iocc.org.

International Relief and Development

Aims to improve the quality of life of people living in developing countries throughout the world.

Activities: Operates in the fields of international aid and development, implementing programmes in less-developed countries with the support of other aid organizations, government agencies and private business sources. Works in Central and Eastern Europe and Central and South-East Asia in the areas of food aid and production, agriculture, health care, emergency relief for refugees and displaced persons, promotion of democracy and providing information technology facilities to promote peace. Maintains field offices in Armenia, Azerbaijan, Georgia, Indonesia, Montenegro, Serbia and Ukraine.

Geographical Area of Activity: Central and Eastern Europe and Central and South-East Asia.

Restrictions: No grants are made.

Publications: Information bulletin.

Directors: Arthur B. Keys, Jr (Pres. and CEO); P. A. Tyson (Vice-Pres.); F. L. Howell (Sec.); Dr J. Mager (Treas.); Rev. Dr J. R. Deckenback; E. Scott Osborne; A. Rhee.

Principal Staff: Pres. and CEO Arthur B. Keys; Dir, Finance Yolanda Brumfield; Dir Programmes and Operations Joe Salsberry; Dir Audits, Grants, Contracts and Compliance Joseph Ferri.

Address: 1601 North Kent St, Suite 100, Arlington, VA 22209.

Telephone: (703) 248-0161; **Fax:** (703) 248-0194; **Internet:** www.ird-dc.org; **e-mail:** ird@ird-dc.org.

International Relief Teams

Established in 1988, a non-profit organization aiming to provide medical and non-medical relief to the victims of poverty and disaster around the world.

Activities: Organizes relief teams to travel to areas in which people are suffering through extreme poverty, or the effects of natural and man-made disasters. Much of the assistance lent is medical, including training programmes for doctors and medical staff in Central and Eastern Europe in order to improve quality of life and decrease infant mortality rates, the emergency provision of medical supplies, and surgical outreach programmes in Central and South America.

However, the relief teams also work to bring clean water and improved sanitation to many, and provide disaster relief both in the USA and abroad.

Geographical Area of Activity: International.

Publications: *Team News* (newsletter); Annual Report.

Finance: Total relief and aid sent approx. $4,800,000 (2002).

Directors: D. D. Tanner (Chair.); Barry La Forgia (Exec. Dir); S. Daly; H. J. Forney; J. Pierik.

Principal Staff: Exec. Dir Barry La Forgia.

Address: 3547 Camino del Rio South, Suite C, San Diego, CA 92108.

Telephone: (619) 284-7979; **Fax:** (619) 284-7938; **Internet:** www.irteams.org; **e-mail:** info@irteams.org.

International Rescue Committee—IRC

Voluntary organization founded in 1933 at the suggestion of Albert Einstein to help Germans suffering under the Nazi regime in Germany. Now works to provide relief, protection and assistance to refugees and victims of oppression or conflict internationally.

Activities: Works internationally to help those fleeing victimization, oppression and conflict. Resettles and rehouses refugees; and provides emergency shelter and supplies for homeless and displaced people, and health services and health-care training in areas suffering the effects of violent conflict.

Geographical Area of Activity: International.

Publications: Annual Report.

Finance: Assets $46,574,000 (Sept. 2001); annual revenue $147,694,000, annual expenditure $150,648,000 (2001).

Trustees: W. Lord, Dr J. C. Strickler (Co-Chair.); J. C. Whitehead (Chair. Emer.); L. Ullmann (Vice-Chair.); R. Levy (Pres. and CEO); A. Batkin (Treas.); G. F. Hritz (Counsel); C. Sternberg (Sec.); R. P. de Vecchi; N. Starr.

Principal Staff: Pres. and CEO Reynold Levy.

Address: 122 East 42nd St, New York, NY 10168-1289.

Telephone: (212) 551-3000; **Fax:** (212) 551-3180; **Internet:** www.theirc.org; **e-mail:** irc@theirc.org.

International Research & Exchanges Board—IREX

A non-profit organization established in 1968 and committed to international education in its broadest sense.

Activities: Operates in the field of education. Administers programmes in academic research, professional training, institution-building, technical assistance and policy-making, which operate collaboratively between the USA and the countries of Eastern Europe, the countries of the former USSR, Asia and the Middle East.

Geographical Area of Activity: USA, Central and Eastern Europe and the republics of Central Asia, Asia and the Middle East.

Publications: *Frontline* (newsletter); Annual Report; policy papers; on-line newsletter; conference reports.

Finance: Supported by public and private funds; annual budget approx. $50,000,000 (2002).

Principal Staff: Pres. Dr Mark G. Pomar.

Address: 2121 K St, NW, Suite 700, Washington, DC 20037.

Telephone: (202) 628-8188; **Fax:** (202) 628-8189; **Internet:** www.irex.org; **e-mail:** irex@irex.org.

International Rivers Network

Established in 1985 as a non-profit organization aiming to protect river systems and the communities that depend upon them and to fight for world-wide environmental integrity, social justice and human rights.

Activities: Works with environmental and human rights organizations around the world to campaign for community-based river development, and with people who are directly affected by dams and other large-scale water intervention projects. Fosters greater understanding and respect for rivers and participates in research and project analyses. Makes recommendations for alternative solutions to international environmental problems caused by governments' environmental policies.

Geographical Area of Activity: International.

Publications: *World Rivers Review; River Keepers Handbook;* working papers; videos; information resources; and other publications.

Directors: P. Strasburg (Chair.); D. P. Beard; P. W. Chang; G. Coe; R. Hass; D. Keehn; L. Tresnon Klein; J. Mailman; W. C. Sedgwick; B. Smith; F. Vietor.

Principal Staff: Exec. Dir Juliette Majot.

Address: 1847 Berkeley Way, Berkeley, CA 94703.

Telephone: (510) 848-1155; **Fax:** (510) 848-1008; **Internet:** www.irn.org; **e-mail:** irn@irn.org.

International Snow Leopard Trust

Established in 1981 by Helen Freeman, Stan Freeman, Douglas Fleming and Kathleen Braden.

Activities: The Trust is a non-profit organization, operating in Central Asia, dedicated to the conservation of the snow leopard and its mountain ecosystem, through conservation, research, education and information exchange, symposia, running projects in collaboration with local organizations, and publications. Certain environmental education, captive breeding and research programmes are carried out outside Central Asia.

Geographical Area of Activity: Mainly Central Asia.

Publications: *Snow Leopard Survey and Conservation Handbook;* symposia proceedings; scholarly articles; pamphlets.

Principal Staff: Exec. Dir Brad Rutherford; Dir of Conservation Thomas McCarthy.

Address: 4649 Sunnyside Ave North, Suite 325, Seattle, WA 98103.

Telephone: (206) 632-2421; **Fax:** (206) 632-3967; **Internet:** www.snowleopard.org; **e-mail:** info@snowleopard.org.

International Voluntary Services, Inc—IVS

Established in 1950 to help people suffering from the effects of poverty around the world.

Activities: Works internationally with grass-roots organizations. Sends teams of volunteers to developing areas to initiate change in the lives of the poor. Supports local projects engaged in teaching people transferable skills and knowledge in order to provide a long-term solution to the effects of poverty, and places skilled volunteers to work on development assistance projects at the request of local organizations and governments.

Geographical Area of Activity: International.

Board of Directors: Jeanette Goodstein (Chair.); Gary Alex; Richard Berliner; Ray Borton; Michael Fairley; Parker Hallberg; Lany Lang; Dr Charles Lockyear; Thomas Luche; Mark Lynch; Hugh Manke; Darla Mecham; Stephen Nichols; Richard Poole; Kimberly Schmidt; Anne Shirk; John Sommer; Paul Weatherly.

Principal Staff: Exec. Dir Anne Shirk.

Address: 1625 K St, NW, Suite 102, Washington, DC 20006.

Telephone: (202) 387-5533; **Fax:** (202) 387-4291; **Internet:** www.ivs-inc.org/IVS/Us/About.htm; **e-mail:** ivs.inc@erols.com.

International Women's Health Coalition

Founded in 1980 to improve reproductive and sexual education and health in the developing world.

Activities: Operates in the fields of medicine and health, and social welfare, in Bangladesh, Brazil, Cameroon, Chile, Nigeria and Peru to reduce preventable deaths and illnesses by providing better reproductive and sexual health information and services. Promotes women's rights; provides technical, practical and financial support to grass-roots organizations that work in reproductive and sexual health care and women's rights; holds meetings and conferences; publishes books and information papers; raises awareness in the USA of the problems facing women in these areas; acts as an advocate for new and improved health and population policies in order to benefit the lives of women and their communities; and provides grants for organizations engaging in innovative health-care schemes, training, public education and advocacy.

Geographical Area of Activity: Selected countries in Africa, Asia and Central and South America.

Board of Directors: Dr Ellen Chesler (Chair.); Jacqueline de Chollet, Thomas W. Merrick (Vice-Chair.); Paul S. Zuckerman (Sec. and Treas.); and 13 others.

Principal Staff: Pres. Adrienne Germain; Exec. Asst Carmen Díaz-Olivo.

Address: 24 East 21st St, New York, NY 10010.

Telephone: (212) 979-8500; **Fax:** (212) 979-9009; **Internet:** www.iwhc.org; **e-mail:** info@iwhc.org.

International Women's Rights Action Watch

Established in 1985 at the World Conference on Women in Nairobi, Kenya.

Activities: A network of activists, academics and organizations concerned with the advancement of women's rights internationally. Supports NGOs in developing countries in their work to improve women's role in society, advocating for positive change in government policy and law. Monitors the implementation of the Convention on the Elemination of All Forms of Discrimination Against Women.

Geographical Area of Activity: International.

Publications: *The Women's Watch* (newsletter, quarterly); reports, reviews, guidelines.

Address: Hubert Humphrey Institute of Public Affairs, University of Minnesota, 301 19th Ave South, Minneapolis, MN 55455.

Telephone: (612) 625-5557; **Fax:** (612) 624-0068; **Internet:** www.igc.org/iwraw; **e-mail:** iwraw@hhh.umn.edu.

International Youth Foundation

Founded in 1990 by Richard R. Little, with funds provided by the W. K. Kellogg Foundation and the Rockefeller Foundation (qq.v.), to support programmes which help children and youth world-wide to develop skills in learning and living, including skills related to the improvement of personal health, the alleviation of poverty, the elimination of drug abuse, and the improvement of education and other conditions which put children and youth at a disadvantage in building healthy lives.

Activities: The Foundation is dedicated to the positive development of children and youth, between the ages of five and 20. It operates internationally in the fields of aid to less-developed countries, conservation and the environment, education and health, working specifically in the areas of micro-enterprise development and children's and youth development. It identifies, strengthens and replicates effective programmes for young people, building a global network of independent, indigenous foundations committed to positive youth development, and increasing international philanthropy in support of such efforts. In 2003 there were 37 partner foundations operating in around 50 countries, including Argentina, Australia, Brazil, Canada, China, Colombia, the Czech Republic, Ecuador, Finland, Germany, India, Ireland, Israel, Mexico, Paraguay, the Philippines, Poland, Portugal, Russia, Slovakia, Thailand, South Africa, Uruguay and Venezuela.

Geographical Area of Activity: International.

Restrictions: Grants directed towards partner foundations.

Publications: Annual Report; brochures; newsletters, country reports and studies; Community Development series.

Finance: Total assets $56,014,829 (Dec. 2001); total revenue $16,803,566, total expenditure $25,297,987 (2001).

Board of Directors: David Bell (Chair.); Sten Akestam; Sari Baldauf; Maria Livanos Cattaui; Arnold Langbo; Rick Little; Helio Mattar; Penina Mlama; Queen Rania Al-Abdullah; Jaime Augusto Zobel de Ayala, II; Richard F. Schubert (Chair. Emer.).

Principal Staff: Founder and Pres. Rick Little.

Address: 32 South St, Suite 500, Baltimore, MD 21202.

Telephone: (410) 347-1500; **Fax:** (410) 347-1188; **Internet:** www.iyfnet.org; **e-mail:** youth@iyfnet.org.

James Irvine Foundation

Founded in 1937 by James Irvine for charitable purposes.

Activities: Operates within California in the fields of education, health, culture, youth services and community projects not receiving government support, through grants to institutions.

Geographical Area of Activity: California, USA.

Restrictions: No grants are made to individuals, private secondary schools, for sectarian religious activities, normal operating expenses, nor for general support.

Publications: Annual Report; information brochure; and publications relating to areas of interest.

Finance: Assets $1,378,433,649 (Dec. 2001); grants disbursed $59,017,797 (2001).

Officers and Directors: James C. Gaither (Chair.); Donn B. Miller (Vice-Chair.); Dennis A. Collins (Pres. and CEO); Larry R. Fies (Treas. and Chief Financial Officer); James E. Canales (Chief Admin. Officer and Corporate Sec.); Samuel A. Armacost; Camilla C. Frost; Joan F. Lane; Cheryl White Mason; Molly Munger; Patricia S. Pineda; Gary B. Pruitt; Toby Rosenblatt; Peter W. Stanley; Peter J. Taylor; Kathryn L. Wheeler.

Principal Staff: Pres. and CEO Mary G. F. Bitterman; Dir Grants Admin. Ann Clarke.

Address: 1 Market Plaza Steuart Tower, Suite 2500, San Francisco, CA 94105.

Telephone: (415) 777-2244; **Fax:** (415) 777-0869; **Internet:** www.irvine.org.

ISAR—Initiative for Social Action and Renewal in Eurasia

Established in 1983 by Harriett Crosby and Nancy Graham as the Institute for Soviet–American Relations.

Activities: Works to facilitate partnerships between NGOs in the former USSR and the USA in a number of ways. These include promoting citizen participation and development in the non-government sector in Eastern Europe and the republics of Central Asia, by providing financial and technical support to grass-roots NGOs and individuals; gathering and disseminating information; producing publications that promote NGOs and their work; encouraging information and dialogue within the NGO community; educating the public about the role that third-sector organizations play in improving community development, human rights and public participation; and administering a small grants programme funding former USSR organizations working on local projects. Has eight field offices in the former USSR.

Geographical Area of Activity: Countries of the former USSR.

Restrictions: Grants made through country offices only.

Publications: *Give & Take: A Journal on Civil Society in Eurasia* (newsletter, quarterly); 2ISAR in Focus .

Principal Staff: Pres. Harriett Crosby; Exec. Dir Eliza Klose.

Address: 1601 Connecticut Ave, NW, Suite 301, Washington, DC 20009.

Telephone: (202) 387-3034; **Fax:** (202) 667-3291; **Internet:** www.isar.org; **e-mail:** membership@isar.org.

Islamic American Relief Agency

Established in 1985, a non-profit humanitarian organization, which aims to support disadvantaged people around the world. Formerly known as the Islamic African Relief Agency.

Activities: Operates internationally in the fields of aid to less-developed countries, health and welfare, human rights and social welfare. Responds to emergency situations in co-operation with local partner organizations and NGOs to provide relief and development aid around the world. Operates programmes to provide emergency aid; support long-term development; promote gender equality; and provide clean water and sanitation, and education. Runs a child sponsorship programme; a Palestinian Children's Relief Fund; and an AIDS in Africa Children's Relief fund.

Geographical Area of Activity: International.

Directors: M. Hamed (Dir); A. O. Makki (Pres.); Dr A. Bagegni; A. Asibai; Dr M. Ismail; M. Dakhil; A. Latif Alqusari.

Address: POB 7084, Columbia, MO 65205-7084.

Internet: www.iara-usa.org; **e-mail:** iara@iara-usa.org.

Ittleson Foundation, Inc

Founded in 1932 by Henry Ittleson for the promotion of the well-being of humanity throughout the world, including, as means to that end, research, publication, the establishment and maintenance of charitable, religious and educational activities, agencies and institutions, and the aid of any such activities, agencies and institutions already established.

Activities: Operates nationally in the fields of the environment, health, welfare and education for health and welfare, with special emphasis on mental health and psychiatric research, through research grants to institutions, conferences, courses, publications and lectures. The Foundation's current main focus areas are AIDS, the environment and mental health.

Geographical Area of Activity: USA.

Restrictions: No fellowships or scholarships, travel grants or grants-in-aid to individuals.

Publications: Annual Report.

Finance: Assets $26,482,436 (2000); total grants $1,328,896 (2000).

Officers and Directors: H. Anthony Ittleson (Chair. and Pres.); Pamila Lee Syrmis (Vice-Pres.); Anthony C. Wood (Sec. and Exec. Dir); Lawrence O. Sneag (Treas.); Marianne S. Ittleson; Lionel I. Pincus; Victor Syrmis.

Address: 15 East 67th St, 5th Floor, New York, NY 10021.

Telephone: (212) 794-2008; **Fax:** (212) 751-2485; **Internet:** www.ittlesonfoundation.org.

Jewish Community Development Fund for Russia and Ukraine

Established by the American Jewish World Service (q.v.) to support grass-roots Jewish renewal and human rights programmes in Russia and Ukraine.

Activities: The Fund aims to revive Jewish religion, education and culture in Russia and Ukraine through supporting grass-roots projects conceived and developed by local activists involved in community and leadership development, including youth groups, schools, child-care centres and inter-religious dialogue programmes. The Fund also makes grants to non-Jewish human rights organizations that promote democratic reforms and mutual understanding among nationalities in Russia and Ukraine. Maintains regional offices in Moscow and Kiev.

Geographical Area of Activity: Russia and Ukraine.

Principal Staff: Dir Martin Horwitz; Jon Orren; Ruth R. Messinger; Ludmilla Milner.

Address: c/o American Jewish World Service, 45 West 36th St, New York, NY 10018.

Telephone: (212) 273-1642; **Fax:** (212) 736-3463; **Internet:** www.ajws.org/jcdf; **e-mail:** jcdf@jws.org.

The Johnson Foundation, Inc

Founded in 1958 by Herbert F. Johnson to promote international understanding, educational excellence, intellectual and cultural growth, and improvement of the human environment.

Activities: Operates nationally in the fields of social welfare and studies, the arts and humanities, and both nationally and internationally in the fields of education and sustainable development. Activities are carried out principally through planning and carrying out conferences at Wingspread, the Foundation's educational conference centre in Racine, WI.

Geographical Area of Activity: Mostly USA, some international.

Restrictions: Supports conference-related activities by non-profit organizations.

Publications: *Wingspread Journal*; Annual Report; information brochure.

Finance: Assets $33,014,788 (June 2002); expenditure $3,754,484 (2002).

Officers and Trustees: Samuel C. Johnson (Chair.); Boyd Gibbons (Pres.); Helen P. Johnson-Leipold (Vice-Pres.); Lois Y. Berg (Treas./Sec.); James D. Ericson; Howard L. Fuller; Gwen Ifill; Janice C. Kreamer; Paul R. Portney; Frank H. T. Rhodes; Paula Wolff.

Principal Staff: Programme Sec. Barbara J. Schmidt.

Address: 33 East Four Mile Rd, Racine, WI 53402.

Telephone: (262) 681-3343; **Fax:** (262) 681-3325; **Internet:** www.johnsonfdn.org; **e-mail:** bschmidt@johnsonfdn.org.

Lyndon Baines Johnson Foundation

Activities: Makes grants for living and travel expenses incurred by researchers of any nationality while conducting research on the life and career of Lyndon B. Johnson at the Johnson Library.

Geographical Area of Activity: USA.

Principal Staff: Contact: Tina Houston.

Address: 2313 Red River St, Austin, TX 78705.

Telephone: (512) 721-0200; **Fax:** (512) 478-9104; **Internet:** www.lbjlib.utexas.edu; **e-mail:** tina.houston@nara.gov.

Robert Wood Johnson Foundation

Founded in 1936 by Robert Wood Johnson for the improvement of health care in the USA.

Activities: The Foundation operates through grants to hospitals, medical, nursing and public schools, hospices, professional associations, research organizations, local and government agencies and community groups, and focuses on three primary concerns in its grant-giving: to ensure that Americans of all ages have access to basic health care at reasonable cost; to improve the organization and provision of services to people with chronic health conditions; and to promote health and reduce the personal, social and economic harm caused by substance abuse (tobacco, alcohol and illicit drugs).

Geographical Area of Activity: USA.

Publications: Annual Report; *Advance* (newsletter); occasional reports.

Finance: Assets $9,044,511,000 (Dec. 2001); annual expenditure $270,985,040 (2001).

Trustees: Robert E. Campbell (Chair.); R. de Tornyay; L. G. Foster; G. S. Frazza; J. R. Gavin, III; L. Griego; W. W. Hagen; E. J. Hartnett; R. W. Johnson, IV; J. Hon. T. H. Kean; E. E. Matthews; J. W. Owen; W. L. Roper; S. A. Schroeder; J. H. Steele; G. L. Warden; R. B. Worley; and 12 Trustees Emeritus.

Principal Staff: Dir, Office of Proposal Man. Richard J. Toth.

Address: College Rd East and Route 1, POB 2316, Princeton, NJ 08543-2316.

Telephone: (609) 452-8701; **Internet:** www.rwjf.org; **e-mail:** mail@rwjf.org.

Joyce Foundation

Independent foundation established in 1948 by Beatrice Joyce Kean to promote conservation, culture, economic development, education, finance reform and the prevention of violence in the Great Lakes area.

Activities: Awards grants to not-for-profit organizations whose aims are to improve public policies in the areas of education, employment, gun violence, campaign finances and culture. Also works to reduce poverty, to protect the natural environment of the Great Lakes and to prevent political corruption. Operates in the mid-Western states, and in Canada.

Geographical Area of Activity: USA and Canada.

Finance: Assets $868,298,527 (2001); grants $42,676,236 (2001).

Officers and Directors: J. T. Anderson (Chair.); R. K. Donahue (Vice-Chair); R. G. Bottoms; C. A. Clauss; C. U. Daly; A. Earl; R. R. Fross; C. L. Guthrie; M. T. Hall; B. Obama; P. Wolff.

Principal Staff: Acting Pres. Lawrence N. Hansen; Communications Officer Mary M. O'Connell.

Address: 70 West Madison St, Suite 2750, Chicago, IL 60602.

Telephone: (312) 782-2464; **Fax:** (312) 782-4160; **Internet:** www.joycefdn.org; **e-mail:** info@joycefdn.org.

Alfred Jurzykowski Foundation

Founded in 1960 by Alfred Jurzykowski for general charitable purposes.

Activities: Operates nationally and internationally in the fields of the arts and humanities, science and medicine, and social welfare, through grants to scientific, cultural and educational organizations in the USA, and through financial support for social services in Brazil.

Geographical Area of Activity: USA, Poland and Brazil.

Restrictions: The Foundation's international interests are limited to Poland and Brazil.

Finance: Assets $39,202,860 (2001); annual charitable expenditure $2,650,243 (2001).

Officers and Trustees: Yolande L. Jurzykowski (Exec. Vice-Pres.); Bluma D. Cohen (Vice-Pres. and Exec. Dir); M. C. Jurzykowski (Sec. and Treas.); K. Falencki.

Principal Staff: Exec. Dir Bluma D. Cohen.

Address: 15 East 65th St, New York, NY 10021.

Telephone: (212) 535-8930.

Juvenile Diabetes Research Foundation International

Founded in 1970 to support research into the causes, treatment, prevention and cure of diabetes and its complications.

Activities: Promotes research and education in the area of medicine and health, and counselling services for those affected by diabetes and the general public. Offers grants and awards including: the Career Development Award in diabetes research for post-doctoral study in any country; the New Training for Established Scientist Award to provide assistance for visiting scholars researching in any country, in a field different from, but related to, the diabetes-related area in which the applicant normally works; the Summer Student Program in diabetes research to assist colleges, universities, medical schools, etc., in supporting student research work; and fellowships and research awards tenable in any country for research into diabetes and its complications.

Geographical Area of Activity: International.

Publications: Annual Report; *Countdown Magazine; Countdown for Kids* ; publications about diabetes.

Finance: Research grants approx. $108,000,000 (2002).

Directors: M. Tyler Moore (Int. Chair.); R. Wood Johnson, IV (Chair.); G. Barker (Chair. of Board); K. Peterson (Sec.); C. Bowles (Treas.).

Principal Staff: Pres. and CEO P. Van Etten.

Address: 120 Wall St, New York, NY 10005-3904.

Telephone: (212) 785-9500; **Fax:** (212) 785-9595; **Internet:** www.jdrf.org; **e-mail:** info@jdrf.org.

Max Kade Foundation, Inc

Founded in 1944 by Max Kade for general charitable purposes.

Activities: Operates both nationally and internationally in the field of education, by sponsoring post-doctoral research exchange programmes between the USA and Europe in medicine and in the natural and physical sciences. Particular focus on developing relations between Germany and America.

Geographical Area of Activity: USA and Europe.

Restrictions: No grants or loans are made to individuals.

Finance: Assets $107,911,600 (2000); total expenditure $5,821,035 (2000).

Officers and Directors: Hans G. Hachmann (Pres.); Reimer Koch-Weser (Vice-Pres.); Lya Friedrich Pfeifer (Treas.); Berteline Baier-Dale (Sec.); Fritz Kade, Jr.

Address: 6 East 87th St, New York, NY 10128.

Telephone: (646) 672,4354.

Henry J. Kaiser Family Foundation

Founded in 1948 by Henry J. Kaiser and his family members principally to support medical care programmes.

Activities: The Foundation operates in the areas of health policy, media and public education, and health and development in South Africa, through the provision of funds for research grants, special projects, fellowships, scholarships, professorships, seminars, conferences and technical assistance. Grants in the Community Grants Program are limited to California, other grants are made in the USA and Canada.

Geographical Area of Activity: North America and South Africa.

Restrictions: No grants are made to individuals.

Publications: Annual Report; information brochure.

Finance: Total assets $597,891,506 (Dec. 2001); total grants $1,358,843 (2001).

Trustees: Gerry Rosberg (Chair.); Patricia King (Vice-Chair.); Drew Altman (Pres. and CEO); Sheila Burke; Jennifer Drobac; James Jones; Michael Kaiser; David Kessler; Charles J. Ogletree; Allan Rosenfield; Donna E. Shalala.

Address: 2400 Sand Hill Rd, Menlo Park, CA 94025.

Telephone: (650) 854-9400; **Fax:** (650) 854-4800; **Internet:** www.kff.org; **e-mail:** rwells@kff.org.

Mitchell Kapor Foundation

Founded by Mitchell Kapor to protect the environment, improve quality of life for all people and help sustain healthy ecosystems. Administered by the Jenifer Altman Foundation (q.v.).

Activities: Operates in the area of the environment, and science and technology, through two main programmes, relating to environmental health and the impact of information technology on society, by awarding grants to organizations and individuals carrying out work or research in these areas. Also helped found the Level Playing Fields Institute, which administers a small grants programme funding innovative projects on behalf of the Foundation.

Geographical Area of Activity: USA.

Publications: Biennial Report.

Finance: Total assets $208,387 (2000); total giving $2,260,944 (2000).

Officers and Directors: Mitchell Kapor (Chair.); Michael Lerner (Pres.); Amy McDevitt (Treas.); Thomas Silk (Sec.).

Address: POB 29209, San Francisco, CA 94129.

Telephone: (415) 561-2182; **Fax:** (415) 561-6480; **Internet:** www.mkf.org; **e-mail:** info@jaf.org.

Howard Karagheusian Commemorative Corporation

Founded in 1921 by Mihran Karagheusian and others to promote child welfare, public health services and international relief programmes in the Armenian refugee communities of Lebanon and Syria, and, on a smaller scale, in native Muslim Arab groups in the same communities.

Activities: Operates through self-conducted programmes, in Lebanon, Syria and Armenia, including establishing a health centre in Lebanon and offering related social and community services.

Geographical Area of Activity: Lebanon, Syria and Armenia.

Restrictions: No grants are made to individuals or organizations.

Publications: Annual Report.

Finance: Assets $43,843,862 (1999).

Directors: Walter C. Bandazian (Exec. Dir); Harry A. Dorian; Helene Irma Der Stepanian; Michael Haratunian; Edward Janjigian; Louis M. Najarian; Pergrouhi Svajian; Richard J. Varadian.

Address: 386 Park Ave South, Suite 1601, New York, NY 10016.

Telephone: (212) 725-0973; **Fax:** (212) 447-0378.

Helen Keller Worldwide

Founded in 1915 by George Kessler and with Helen Keller as a founding trustee, the agency has been previously known as the British French Belgian Permanent Blind Relief War Fund, the American Braille Press for War and Civilian Blind, the American Foundation for Overseas Blind, and Helen Keller International. The organization is dedicated to fighting and treating preventable blindness abroad, and providing free eye glasses to needy students in the USA.

Activities: Operates in 25 countries throughout Africa, Asia and the Americas, providing the technical assistance needed to establish blindness prevention, treatment and rehabilitation programmes within existing health-care systems. Current programmes combat cataract, trachoma, nutritional blindness and onchocerciasis (river blindness). Through ChildSight, the organization also improves the vision and educational performance of children living in urban and rural poverty in the USA. The agency benefits over 200,000,000 people each year.

Geographical Area of Activity: Africa, Asia and the Americas.

Restrictions: Does not distribute grants.

Publications: *Seeing is Believing* (teachers kit); Annual Report.

Finance: Net assets $12,666,448 (June 2002); annual revenue $37,485,657, expenditure $32,292,015 (2002).

Board of Trustees: Daniel G. Sisler (Chair.); Nancy W. Smith (Vice-Chair.); Mitchell Brock (Sec.); John N. Citron (Treas.); and 30 others.

Principal Staff: Pres. John M. Palmer.

Address: 352 Park Ave South, Suite 1200, New York, NY 10010.

Telephone: (212) 532-0544; **Fax:** (212) 532-6014; **Internet:** www.hkworld.org; **e-mail:** info@hkworld.org.

W. K. Kellogg Foundation

Founded in 1930 by W. K. Kellogg, the breakfast cereal pioneer, to build the capacity of individuals, communities and institutions to solve their own problems. Its activities 'centre around the common vision of a world in which each person has a sense of worth; accepts responsibility for self, family, community and societal well-being; and has the capacity to be productive, and to help create nurturing families, responsive institutions and healthy communities'.

Activities: Operates with the aim of improving human well-being in the USA, Central and South America, the Caribbean and Southern African countries (Botswana, Lesotho, Mozambique, South Africa, Swaziland and Zimbabwe). Support for the needs of young people is an area of major programming concentration. Limited world-wide involvement is achieved through Kellogg International Fellowship programmes. The Foundation also supports the needs of young people through its other areas for assistance: health, youth and education, rural development, food systems, philanthropy and volunteerism.

Geographical Area of Activity: USA (79% of funds), Central and South America and the Caribbean (12%) and Southern Africa (9%).

Restrictions: The Foundation does not support research or endowment projects, nor does it award grants for operational phases of established programmes, capital facilities, equipment, conferences, films, television or radio programmes (unless these are an integral phase of a project the Foundation is already supporting), planning and studies, religious purposes, nor to individuals except for fellowships in specific areas of Foundation programming.

Publications: Report of operations and financial statement.

Finance: Total assets $5,530,494,099 (Aug. 2002); annual charitable expenditure $200,745,771 (2002).

Officers and Trustees: William C. Richardson (Pres. and CEO); G. A. Lyman (Sr Vice-Pres. and Corporate Sec.); R. M. Foster, P. J. Lawler, G. D. McClure, C. H. Milligan, D. E. Moore, G. R. Smith (Vice-Pres); S. D. Bowser; C. T. Christ; D. A. Johnson; H. Liu; R. G. Mawby; W. W. Moore; H. F. Sims; J. T. Walton.

Principal Staff: Vice-Pres. and Chief Investment Officer Paul J. Lawler; Vice-Pres. for Finance and Treas. LaJune Montgomery-Talley; Sr Vice-Pres. A. C. Petersen.

Address: 1 Michigan Ave East, Battle Creek, MI 49017-4058.

Telephone: (616) 968-1611; **Fax:** (616) 968-0413; **Internet:** www.wkkf.org; **e-mail:** library@wkkf.org.

Kennan Institute

Established in 1974 to increase American understanding and knowledge of Russia and the former USSR.

Activities: The Institute hosts US-based scholars selected through a competition, so that they can conduct their individual research on the Newly Independent States (countries of the former USSR). Also provides scholarships to researchers from the Newly Independent States and also runs a public lecture series during the academic year. The Institute has a publication programme; and other activities include a junior scholar workshops series and a human rights fellowship in memory of former scholar Galina Starovoitova. Maintains offices in Moscow and Kiev.

Geographical Area of Activity: Russia and other countries of the former USSR (excluding the Baltic states).

Restrictions: Short-term grants only to individuals from the USA and former USSR.

Publications: Monthly calendar/meeting reports; occasional paper series; commercially published books.

Finance: Receives funding from the US Department of State, Carnegie Corporation of New York and Woodrow Wilson International Center for Scholars (qq.v.), federal appropriation and income from endowment.

Principal Staff: Dir Blair Ruble; Deputy Dir Nancy Popson.

Address: 1 Woodrow Wilson Plaza, 1300 Pennsylvania Ave, NW, Washington, DC 20004-3027.

Telephone: (202) 691-4100; **Fax:** (202)691-4247; **Internet:** wwics.si.edu/kennan/; **e-mail:** kiars@wwic.si.edu.

Joseph P. Kennedy, Jr Foundation

Founded in 1946 by Mr and Mrs Joseph P. Kennedy for the prevention of mental disability by identifying its causes, and for the improvement of the means by which society deals with its mentally-disabled citizens.

Activities: Makes grants for research, special projects, advisory services, conferences and seminars involving medicine and health, education and welfare of people with mental disability. Funds are limited to proposals in the field of mental disability. Awards scholarships for a one-week bioethics course held at the Kennedy Institute of Ethics at Georgetown University, and Public Policy Leadership Fellowships for professionals and parents involved in the field of mental disability.

Publications: Information brochure.

Finance: Assets $24,135,253 (June 2001); annual expenditure $2,379,854 (2001).

Officers and Trustees: Edward M. Kennedy (Pres.); Eunice Kennedy Shriver (Exec. Vice-Pres.); Joseph E. Hakim (Treas.); Patricia Kennedy Lawford; Jean Kennedy Smith.

Principal Staff: Exec. Dir Sue Swenson.

Address: 1325 G St, NW, Suite 500, Washington, DC 20005-4709.

Telephone: (202) 393-1250; **Fax:** (202) 824-0351; **Internet:** www.jpkf.org; **e-mail:** sswenson@jpkf.org.

Kettering Foundation

Founded in 1927 by Charles F. Kettering, the Foundation deals with questions associated with governing, educating and science, all in relation to one another and in an international perspective, with attention to both formal and informal institutions, in order to learn how democracy can work better.

Activities: The Foundation conducts projects aiming to find solutions to fundamental problems in the areas of governing, educating and science. Carries out research in six interrelated areas: citizens and public choice; community politics and community leadership; the public and public schools; institutions, professionals and the public; the public–government relationship; and the international and the civil. As an operating, rather than a grant-giving, foundation, it pursues its projects in collaboration with organizations sharing its interests. It maintains a publications programme and holds training workshops in the USA and abroad.

Geographical Area of Activity: Mainly USA.

Restrictions: This is not a grant-making organization.

Publications: Periodicals, publications and videos relating to the Foundation's research.

Finance: Assets $250,700,090 (2001).

Trustees: J. A. MacAllister (Chair.); J. R. Thomas; E. Dorn; M. Hatwood Futrell; V. Hodgkinson; A. F. Jones; D. Kemmis; Hon. J. A. Leach; L. C. Carter, Jr; D. Mathews; S. W. Morse.

Address: 200 Commons Rd, Dayton, OH 45459.

Telephone: (937) 434-7300; **Fax:** (937) 439-9804; **Internet:** www.kettering.org.

Koch Foundation, Inc

Established in 1979 by Carl E. Koch and Paula Koch to promote Roman Catholicism.

Activities: Awards grants to Catholic organizations nationally and internationally, that propogate the Catholic faith. Grants are made for different evangelization programmes, educational and spiritual formation of evangelists, resource-poor Catholic schools that are the principal means of evangelization in the community, a Catholic presence in the media, and capital expenditures. Priority is given to situations involving financially distressed, underdeveloped areas.

Geographical Area of Activity: International.

Restrictions: No grants are made to individuals; no loans or scholarships.

Publications: Annual Report.

Finance: Assets $130,799,599 (2002); grants disbursed $11,126,958 (2002).

Officers and Directors: C. L. Bomberger (Chair. and Pres.); I. L. Vraney (Vice-Pres.); L. E. Vraney, Jr (Treas.); R. A. Bomberger (Sec.); D. C. Bomberger; M. A. Bomberger; W. A. Bomberger; C. L. Spacinsky.

Principal Staff: Exec. Dir Michael A. Marconi.

Address: 2830 NW 41st St, Suite H, Gainesville, FL 32606.

Telephone: (352) 373-7491.

Susan G. Komen Breast Cancer Foundation

Established in 1982 by Nancy Brinker; aims to eradicate breast cancer as a life-threatening disease.

Activities: Funds breast cancer research, education, screening and treatment programmes, as well as operating a community-based grant programme, funding breast cancer health education and screening projects aimed at disadvantaged people. Funding is provided to non-profit organizations, educational institutions and government agencies. Also funds fellowships designed to improve the quality of care for breast cancer patients.

Geographical Area of Activity: USA.

Publications: Annual Report.

Finance: Total assets $59,610,641 (2001); total grants approx. $19,000,000 (2001).

Board of Directors: LaSalle D. Leffall (Chair.); Becky Haddad (Vice-Chair.); Norman Brinker; Ann Curry; Linda Custard; Connie O'Neill; Lynn Sellers; Robert Taylor; Barney Young.

Principal Staff: Chief Exec. Susan Braun.

Address: 5005 LBJ Freeway, Suite 250, Dallas, TX 75244.

Telephone: (972) 855-1600; **Fax:** (972) 855-1605; **Internet:** www.komen.org; **e-mail:** grants@komen.org.

Koret Foundation

Founded in 1966 by Joseph Koret and Stephanie Koret for general charitable purposes.

Activities: Operates in California, mainly in the San Francisco Bay area, and Israel, in the fields of community development and Jewish life and culture. Initiatives include the Koret Israel Economic Development Fund, the Koret Jewish Studies Publications Program, the Koret Jewish Book Awards, the Koret Synagogue Initiative, Routes to Learning, and the Koret Prize.

Geographical Area of Activity: USA (San Francisco Bay area) and Israel.

Restrictions: No support is given to private foundations, nor to individuals.

Publications: *Responding to Israel's Emergency and Economic Needs; Catalyst* (newsletter); and other publications and resource materials.

Finance: Total assets $315,112,125 (2001); annual revenue $14,555,326, grants disbursed $19,398,571 (2001).

Officers and Directors: Susan Koret (Chair.); Tad Taube (Pres.and Dir); Eugene L. Friend (Vice-Chair.); Richard Atkinson; Michael J. Boskin; William K. Coblentz; Richard L. Greene; Stanley Herzstein; Abraham Sofaer; Sandra J. Edwards (Dir of Grants); Claudia J. Hardin (Dir Finance and Admin.).

Address: 33 New Montgomery St, Suite 1090, San Francisco, CA 94105-4526.

Telephone: (415) 882-7740; **Fax:** (415) 882-7775; **Internet:** www.koretfoundation.org; **e-mail:** info@koretfoundation.org.

Kosciuszko Foundation

Founded in 1925 by Stephen P. Mizwa, Dr Henry Noble MacCracken, Willis H. Booth, Cedric E. Fauntleroy, Dr Robert H. Lord, Dr Paul Monroe and Samuel M. Vauclain, to promote a better knowledge of their Polish heritage among Americans of Polish descent, and thus to develop that sense of pride in the accomplishment of their ancestors which is basic to an appreciation of their American heritage; to promote understanding between the USA and Poland; to encourage the younger generation of Americans of Polish descent to secure higher education, and thus to contribute to the educational level in the USA; and to promote the growth of Polish studies in the USA.

Activities: Operates both nationally and internationally in the fields of education, science and medicine, and the arts and humanities, through grants to institutions and individuals, fellowships, scholarships, conferences, courses, publications and lectures. Grants are awarded to enable Polish Americans to enter medical schools in Poland, and to enable writers, artists and students to complete scholarly, artistic or literary projects that would serve to implement the purposes of the Kosciuszko Foundation. Scholarships are awarded to enable Polish Americans to go on to higher education, and to enable Americans of non-Polish background to undertake Polish studies. Chopin Piano Scholarship and Marcella Sembrich Scholarship in Voice competitions are held annually, as well as the Metchie J. E. Budka Award for outstanding scholarly work.

Geographical Area of Activity: Poland and the USA.

Publications: Newsletter; and other publications.

Finance: Scholarships approx. $1,000,000 (June 2002).

Trustees: Witold S. Sulimirski (Chair.); and 30 others.

Principal Staff: Pres. Joseph E. Gore; Treas. Henry Malon.

Address: 15 East 65th St, New York, NY 10021-6595.

Telephone: (212) 734-2130; **Fax:** (212) 628-4552; **Internet:** www.kosciuszkofoundation.org; **e-mail:** thekf@aol.com.

Kresge Foundation

Founded in 1924 by Sebastian S. Kresge for general charitable purposes.

Activities: Provides challenge grants only towards projects involving construction or renovation of facilities; purchase of major items of equipment or an integrated equipment at a cost of at least $300,000 (which may include computer software expenses, if applicable); or the purchase of real estate. Those eligible to apply are well-established, financially sound, tax-exempt charitable organizations operating in the fields of higher education (awarding baccalaureate and/or graduate degrees), health and long-term care, human services, science and the environment, the arts and humanities, and public affairs. Full accreditation is required for higher education and hospital applicants. Also supporting development at historically Black colleges and universities and makes local grants in Detroit and South-Eastern Michigan.

Geographical Area of Activity: Detroit, South-Eastern Michigan and other parts of the USA, Colombia, Kenya, Canada and the United Kingdom.

Restrictions: Requests towards debt retirement or completed projects are not eligible.

Publications: Annual Report.

Finance: Assets $2,415,971,841 (2001); grants disbursed $123,592,090 (2001).

Officers and Trustees: Bruce A. Kresge (Chair.); John E. Marshall, III (Pres. and CEO); Jill K. Conway; Jane L. Delgado; George D. Langdon, Jr; Robert C. Larson; Deborah E. McDowell; David K. Page; Robert D. Storey; Alfred H. Taylor, Jr.

Principal Staff: Pres. and CEO John E. Marshall, III.

Address: POB 3151, Troy, MI 48007-3151.

Telephone: (248) 643-9630; **Fax:** (248) 643-0588; **Internet:** www.kresge.org.

Samuel H. Kress Foundation

Founded in 1929 to promote education in the history of art and advanced training in fine arts conservation.

Activities: Provides grants for individuals and institutions to conduct research in European art from antiquity to 1850 and in the conservation of works of art; for the conservation and restoration of monuments in Western Europe; and for the development of scholarly resources in the areas of art history and conservation. Awards scholarships, fellowships for study and travel, and supports conferences and publications.

Geographical Area of Activity: USA, Europe and the Middle East.

Restrictions: No grants to living artists, for films, art history programmes below the pre-doctoral level, nor for the purchases of art. Grants only to organizations with non-profit status.

Publications: Annual Report.

Finance: Net assets $103,530,599 (2001); grants disbursed $4,873,012 (2001).

Trustees: Marilyn Perry (Pres.); John C. Fontaine (Chair.); Daniel Belin (Vice-Chair.); Frederick W. Beinecke (Sec. and Treas.); William B. Brider; Inmaculada de Habsburgo; Cheryl Hurley; Walter L. Weisman.

Principal Staff: Vice-Pres. Lisa M. Ackerman.

Address: 174 East 80th St, New York, NY 10021.

Telephone: (212) 861-4993; **Fax:** (212) 628-3146; **Internet:** www.kressfoundation.org.

KRS Foundation

Established by the KRS Group to support projects relating to the environment, education and development, mainly in India.

Activities: Aims to improve education and health conditions for women and children in rural parts of India. Sponsors activities in the USA to advance global awareness and human understanding. Runs the Centre for Environment, Education and Development, which carries out research and development, as well as providing consultancy and information and running training courses and seminars. Also manages the Centre for Environment, Education and Development.

Geographical Area of Activity: USA and India.

Address: POB 820392, Vicksburg, MS 39182.

Internet: www.krsfoundation.com; **e-mail:** info@krsfoundation.com.

La Leche League International

Established in 1956 to promote breastfeeding and to help breastfeeding mothers around the world.

Activities: Operates internationally in the area of health and social welfare. Provides encouragement, education and information on topics and issues related to breastfeeding. Holds local meetings in communities world-wide and acts as a network and resource for breastfeeding and parenting help, shared knowledge and support. Raises awareness of breastfeeding as an important element in the healthy development of the baby, the mother and the relationship between them.

Geographical Area of Activity: International.

Publications: Publishes a number of informative brochures, articles and leaflets.

Directors: Lynne Coates (Chair.); Anne Easterday, Nancy Jolly (Vice-Chair.); Trudy Hartt (Sec.); Marcia Lutostanski (Treas.); Jane Berendsen-Hill; Betty Crase; Susan Deo; Mimi de Maza; Donna Cookson Martin; Sharon Matuszek; Jean Moneyhon; Rachel O'Leary; Heidi Sloss; Carmen Vandenabeele; Sharon Vines.

Address: 1400 North Meacham Rd, Schaumburg, IL 60173-4808.

Telephone: (847) 519-7730; **Fax:** (847) 519-0035; **Internet:** www.lalecheleague.org; **e-mail:** lllibod@llli.org.

Lannan Foundation

Founded in 1960 by J. Patrick Lannan, supports the visual and literary arts and rural Native American communities.

Activities: The Foundation's visual arts programme makes awards, grants and fellowships with the aim of promoting, exhibiting, studying and discussing contemporary art. The literary programme fosters the writing of prose and poetry through grants and projects, and attempts to bring literature to a wider audience. The programme has awarded more than $3,400,000 to 75 writers of fiction, non-fiction and poetry since 1989 through its annual literary awards, which include a $200,000 Lifetime Achievement Award. It also awards the

Prize for Cultural Freedom. The Indigenous Communities Program supports the efforts of Native Americans to continue their traditions by funding projects which revive and preserve languages and culture.

Geographical Area of Activity: USA.

Publications: Programme Policy Statement.

Directors: J. Patrick Lannan, Jr (Pres.); Frank C. Lawler (Vice-Pres.); James G. Butler; Marian P. Day; Meghan Ferrill; Sharon Ferrill; William E. Johnston; Sharron L. Korybut; John J. Lannan; John R. Lannan; Lawrence P. Lannan, Jr; Anne Lannan; Mary M. Plauché.

Address: 313 Read St, Santa Fe, New Mexico 87501-2628.

Telephone: (505) 986-8160; **Fax:** (505) 986-8195; **Internet:** www.lannan.org; **e-mail:** jo@lannan.org.

Latter-day Saint Charities

Established in 1996 to provide life-sustaining resources to people in emergencies, help strengthen families to help them become self-reliant, and offer opportunities for giving and service.

Activities: Provides emergency relief response; builds self-reliance through health promotion and disease prevention initiatives; literacy, English language, and other training for teachers; gardening and food production; and assisting children to live within loving families, or in appropriate institutions when necessary.

Geographical Area of Activity: International.

Restrictions: No grants to individuals.

Finance: Funded by public donations and by the Church of Jesus Christ of Latter-day Saints. Assets $5,140,000 (Dec. 2000); annual revenue $15,119,000, expenditure $15,881,000 (2000).

Directors: H. D. Burton; H. C. Brown; R. C. Edgely; K. B. McMullin; M. E. Smoot.

Principal Staff: Dir Garry R. Flake.

Address: 50 East North Temple St, 7th Floor, Salt Lake City, UT 84150-6890.

Telephone: (801) 240-1201; **Fax:** (801) 240-1964; **e-mail:** lds-charities@ldschurch.org.

Laubach Literacy

Non-profit educational corporation established in 1955 by Dr Frank C. Laubach, aiming to increase adult literacy levels world-wide.

Activities: Operates world-wide to improve the quality of life of adults by helping them to learn reading, writing, mathematics and problem-solving skills. The organization runs teaching programmes in a number of communities in 36 countries of Africa, Asia, the Middle East and Central and South America. Laubach Literacy Action, the US division of the organization, runs programmes provided by volunteer teachers in the USA. Maintains a publishing division (*New Readers Press*) that publishes and disseminates books and educational materials to other literacy programmes and organizations around the world.

Geographical Area of Activity: International.

Publications: Books; educational materials; documentaries.

Board of Directors: Thomas E. Noel (Chair.).

Principal Staff: Pres. Robert Wedgeworth; Exec. Dir Peter A. Waite.

Address: 1320 Jamesville Ave, Syracuse, NY 13210.

Telephone: (315) 422-9121; **Internet:** www.laubach.org /home.html; **e-mail:** info@laubach.org.

The Ronald S. Lauder Foundation

Founded in 1987 by Ronald S. Lauder and Estee Lauder, Inc for the support of Central and Eastern Europe and the former Soviet Union, to promote Jewish education, and for the preservation of Jewish monuments and buildings.

Activities: Operates primarily in Central and Eastern Europe, in Austria, Belarus, Bulgaria, Czech Republic, Estonia, Germany, Hungary, Latvia, Lithuania, Moldova, Poland, Romania, Russia, Slovakia and Ukraine, making grants in the areas of Jewish welfare, religion, cultural programmes, conservation and education. Also supports a non-sectarian international student exchange.

Geographical Area of Activity: Central and Eastern Europe, and the former Soviet Union.

Restrictions: No applications for grants accepted.

Publications: Financial statement; information brochure; newsletter.

Officers and Directors: Ronald S. Lauder (Chair); Marjorie S. Federbush (Vice-Chair); Michael G. Berenbaum; Rabbi Chaskel O. Besser; Rabbi Jacob Biderman; Micki Edelsohn; Rabbi Pinchas Goldschmidt, Rabbi Irving Greenberg; Malcolm Hoenlein; Jo Carole Lauder; Richard D. Parsons; Menachem Z. Rosensaft; Steven Schwager; Israel Singer; Kalman Sultanik.

Principal Staff: Exec. Vice-Pres. and CEO George Bán; Vice-Pres. Joan Braunstein, P. Rachel Laufer; Treas. Jacob Z. Schuster.

Address: 767 Fifth Ave, 46th Floor, New York, NY 10153.

Telephone: (212) 319-6300; **Fax:** (212) 319-9411; **Internet:** www.rslfoundation.org; **e-mail:** rslf@rslfound.com.

L. S. B. Leakey Foundation

Founded to promote research into human origins, behaviour and survival.

Activities: Supports postgraduate research (principally doctoral candidates and scientists with professional qualifications and demonstrated capability) in human origins and evolution, and human behaviour and survival, especially in the areas of: the ecology, archaeology and human paleontology of the Miocene, Pliocene and Pleistocene eras; great apes and primate behaviour; and the ecology of contemporary hunter-gatherer societies. Also awards the Franklin Mosher Baldwin Memorial Fellowships to students with citizenship in an African country who wish to obtain an advanced degree or carry out specialist training in an area of study related to human origins research..

Geographical Area of Activity: Mainly USA.

Publications: *AnthroQuest* (quarterly newsletter).

Finance: Grants totalled $700,000 (2001).

Board of Trustees: Gordon P. Getty (Chair); Kay Harrigan Woods (Pres.); Joan C. Donner, C. Paul Johnson (Vice-Pres); William P. Richards, Jr (Treas.); George D. Smith (Sec.); Mary Gooch Armour; Edward Barlow; John L. Bradley; Nina Carroll; Philae Dominick; Carloyn Farris; John Hemingway; Dr Diana McSherry; Frank Montgomery Woods; Christine Murray; Barbara Newsom; Owen O'Donnell; Mason Phelps; Barry H. Sterling; Richard Thieriot.

Principal Staff: Programmes and Grants Officer Dr Alan Almquist; Exec. Dir Robert W. Lasher; Grants Manager Cary Roloson.

Address: 1002A O'Reilly Ave, POB 29346, San Francisco, CA 94129.

Telephone: (415) 561-4646; **Fax:** (415) 561-4647; **Internet:** www.leakeyfoundation.org; **e-mail:** info@leakeyfoundation .org.

Levi Strauss Foundation

Founded in 1941 by Levi Strauss & Co. for general charitable purposes in regions where the company operates, both in the USA and abroad.

Activities: The Foundation aims to promote social welfare through grants, and through the encouragement of employee volunteer activity; its main activities are in the areas of enhancing the economic opportunities of the disadvantaged through job creation and training, the prevention of AIDS and care of AIDS patients, and the promotion of youth empowerment and support for social justice/anti-racism efforts. Grants are mainly limited to areas of company operations in the states of Arkansas, California, Florida, Georgia, Kentucky, Mississippi, New Mexico, North Carolina, Tennessee, Texas and Virginia, although the Foundation also runs a global grant-making programme. Moreover, in 2000 the Foundation established a fund for organizations from seven European countries (Belgium, Germany, Italy, the Netherlands, Spain, Sweden and the United Kingdom), managed by the CAF (Charities Aid Foundation, q.v.) in the United Kingdom, for the benefit of non-profit organizations working in the areas of AIDS prevention and care, youth empowerment, social justice and economic empowerment. A programme is also co-ordinated by the Fondation de France (q.v.) and a Community Partnership Programme operates in other areas of Western and Central Europe and Turkey.

Geographical Area of Activity: Canada, Africa, Asia Pacific, Central and South America, East and West Europe, Middle East, and USA.

Restrictions: No grants are made to individuals.

Publications: Annual Report.

Finance: Assets $90,741,095 (Dec. 2001); grants disbursed $12,472,180 (2001).

Board of Directors: Robert D. Haas (Pres. and Chair.); Theresa Fay-Bustillos (Vice-Pres. and Sec.); Karen Duvall; Roy Edmondson; Elizabeth Eisenhardt; Gordon T. Geballe; Peter E. Haas; Peter E. Haas, Jr; Karen R. S. Hanna; Peter A. Jacobi; Lai Si Meng; Albert F. Moreno; Christine Haas Russell; Darryl Wilburn; Philip Marineau (Pres. and CEO, Levi Strauss & Co.).

Principal Staff: Exec. Dir Theresa Fay-Bustillos; Dir, Brussels Alan Christie; Dir, Singapore Kim Yang Lim.

Address: 1155 Battery St, 7th Floor, San Francisco, CA 94111; POB 7215, San Francisco, CA 94120-6906.

Telephone: (415) 501-6579; **Internet:** www.levistrauss.com.

Liberty Fund, Inc

Founded in 1960 by Pierre F. Goodrich.

Activities: The Fund, a private operating foundation, supports educational activity which promotes programmes concerned with human liberty, including the publication of deceased authors, and of current works deemed unprofitable by commercial publishers. Holds conferences annually in the USA, Canada, Central and South America, Europe and Australia.

Geographical Area of Activity: North, Central and South America, Europe and Australia.

Restrictions: Not a grant-making organization.

Finance: Assets $410,622,000 (April 2000).

Officers and Directors: T. Alan Russell (Chair.); Emilio J. Pacheco (Vice-Pres.); Chris L. Talley (Treas.); Manuel Ayau; George W. Carey; Roseda D. Decker; Richard W. Duesenberg; Joseph F. Johnston; Edward B. McLean; Irwin H. Reiss; Richard A. Ware.

Principal Staff: Dir of Grants William C. Dennis.

Address: 8335 Allison Pointe Trail, Suite 300, Indianapolis, IN 46250-1684.

Telephone: (317) 842-0880; **Fax:** (317) 577-9067; **Internet:** www.libertyfund.org.

Life Sciences Research Foundation

Founded in 1981 by Dr Donald D. Brown to administer an international programme of post-doctoral fellowships in all areas of life sciences.

Activities: Operates nationally and internationally in the fields of conservation and the environment, education, medicine and health, and science and technology. Provides grants to institutions and individuals, and funding for research. The Foundation accepts applications from American and foreign candidates conducting their research in US laboratories.

Geographical Area of Activity: USA.

Restrictions: Applications from non-US citizens must be for study in the USA.

Publications: Financial statement; information brochure.

Principal Staff: Chair. Steven L. McKnight; Pres. Donald D. Brown; Sec. Roger Redden; Treas. Patricia Englar.

Address: 115 West University Parkway, Baltimore, MD 21210; 305 Lewis Thomas Laboratory, Princeton University, Washington Rd, Princeton, NJ 08544.

Telephone: (410) 467-2597 (Baltimore); (609) 258-3551 (Princeton); **Internet:** www.lsrf.org; **e-mail:** sdirenzo@molbio.princeton.edu.

Lifebridge Foundation Inc

Set up to promote holistic living.

Activities: Funds organizations within the following general policy categories: arts and culture, youth and education, environment, science, community service, world goodwill, and interdimensional. In 2003, the grant-making programme was temporarily reduced.

Geographical Area of Activity: International, but 95 per cent of funded projects are in the USA.

Restrictions: Selects its own beneficiaries; no unsolicited funding applications, apart from brief introductory letters.

Publications: *The Bridging Tree* (newsletter, twice a year).

Finance: Total assets $4,900,000 (2001).

Principal Staff: Communications Manager Robert Silverstein.

Address: POB 793, Times Square Station, New York, NY 10108.

Telephone: (212) 757-9711; **Fax:** (212) 757-0246; **Internet:** www.lifebridge.org.

Lifewater International

Non-profit Christian organization founded by Bill Ashe in 1979, aiming to help poor people living in rural areas around the world to obtain safe water.

Activities: Operates in less-developed countries, through training local people in the technical skills necessary to improve water supplies, and donating equipment and financial support in order to assist communities to become self-sufficient and to provide a long-term solution to the problems caused by unclean water.

Geographical Area of Activity: International.

Publications: *Lifewater International Newsletter* (bi-monthly).

Finance: Assets $281,235 (Dec. 2001); annual revenue $837,804, expenditure $853,865 (2001).

Address: POB 3131, San Luis Obispo, CA 93403.

Telephone: (805) 772-0600; **Fax:** (805) 772-0606; **Internet:** www.lifewater.org; **e-mail:** info@lifewater.org.

Lilly Endowment, Inc

Founded in 1937 by the Lilly family for the promotion and support of religious, educational or charitable programmes.

Activities: Operates mainly in the fields of religion, education and community development (including social welfare and the arts and humanities). Special attention is given to programmes in Indianapolis and Indiana. Emphasis is on projects that depend on private support, but a limited number of grants are made to governmental institutions and tax-supported programmes. International projects supported by the Endowment are limited to a small number of emergency relief efforts and public policy programmes, mostly in Canada and Mexico. Projects in health care, biological and physical science research, housing, transport, environment and population are usually not funded.

Geographical Area of Activity: Mainly USA (Indiana); some funding to Canada and Mexico.

Restrictions: Grants are not made to individuals.

Publications: Annual Report; occasional report; newsletter.

Finance: Total assets $12,814,397,581 (2001); total grants $598,001,581 (2001).

Officers and Directors: Thomas M. Lofton (Chair.); N. Clay Robbins (Pres.); David D. Biber (Sec.-Treas.); William M. Goodwin (Vice-Pres., Community Devt); Ralph E. Lundgren (Vice-Pres., Education); Craig R. Dykstra (Vice-Pres., Religion); Otis R. Bowen; William G. Enright; Earl B. Herr, Jr; Byron J. Hollett; Thomas Lake; Eli Lilly, II; Eugene F. Ratcliff; Herman B. Wells.

Principal Staff: Communications Assoc. Sue Ellen Walker.

Address: 2801 North Meridian St, POB 88068, Indianapolis, IN 46208-0068.

Telephone: (317) 924-5471; **Fax:** (317) 926-4431.

Charles A. and Anne Morrow Lindbergh Foundation

Founded in 1977 by members of the Explorers Club, including Gen. James H. Doolittle and the astronaut Neil Armstrong, to further Charles and Anne Morrow Lindbergh's vision of a balance between the advance of technology and the preservation of the environment.

Activities: Operates nationally and internationally in the fields of conservation and the environment, the arts and humanities, education and medicine and health, through self-conducted programmes, research and grants to individuals. Makes about 10 Lindbergh Grants each year of amounts up to $10,580.

Geographical Area of Activity: International.

Restrictions: Grants to individuals only.

Publications: Newsletter (3 a year).

Finance: Funded by private, corporate and non-profit contributions; net assets $1,711,861 (Dec. 2001); annual revenue $402,385, expenditure $504,820 (2001).

Principal Staff: Pres. Reeve Lindbergh; Exec. Dir Marlene White.

Address: 2150 Third Ave North, Suite 310, Anoka, MN 55303.

Telephone: (763) 576-1596; **Fax:** (763) 576-1664; **Internet:** www.lindberghfoundation.org; **e-mail:** info@lindberghfoundation.org.

Lindesmith Center—Drug Policy Foundation

Founded in 1994 as the Lindesmith Center by George Soros, part of the Open Society Institute (q.v.). Promotes research and discussion of drug policy and related issues. Merged with the Drug Policy Foundation, an advocacy foundation dedicated to the reformation of current drug policy, in June 2000.

Activities: Awards grants and research fellowships; studies government drug policy and its consequences; promotes drug policy reform; maintains a library and information centre; and organizes seminars and conferences. Works on the Open Society Institute's International Harm Reduction Development programme, which aims to reduce the social and individual harm associated with drug use in Eastern Europe and the former USSR through awarding grants to projects.

Geographical Area of Activity: USA, Eastern Europe and the countries of the former USSR.

Publications: Working papers; briefings and monographs.

Principal Staff: Dir Ethan Nadelmann.

Address: 70 West 36th St, 16th Floor, New York, NY 10018.

Telephone: (212) 613-8020; **Fax:** (212) 613-8021; **Internet:** www.lindesmith.org; **e-mail:** nyc@drugpolicy.org.

Lucius N. Littauer Foundation, Inc

Founded in 1929 by Lucius N. Littauer 'to enlarge the realms of human knowledge to promote the general moral, mental and physical improvement of society'.

Activities: Provides grants to US institutions for study in the fields of the humanities, the environment, academic Jewish studies, Judaism and the Middle East, and medical ethics; establishes book funds at universities for the acquisition of Jewish collections.

Geographical Area of Activity: USA, Israel, Europe and South America.

Restrictions: No grants to individuals; grants only to non-profit organizations in the USA.

Publications: Guidelines.

Finance: Net assets $41,011,478 (2001); expenditure $1,337,396 (2001).

Trustees: William Lee Frost (Pres. and Treas.); Henry A. Lowet (Vice-Pres. and Sec.); George Harris (Asst Vice-Pres. and Sec.); Charles Berlin; Bertholt Bilski; Mark A. Bilski; Robert D. Frost; Peter J. Solomon; Noah Perlman.

Principal Staff: Programme Dir Pamela W. Brumberg.

Address: 60 East 42nd St, Suite 2910, New York, NY 10165.

Telephone: (212) 697-2677.

Long Now Foundation

Established in 1996 to found a long-term cultural institution, comprising a library and clock project.

Activities: Aims to create a long-term cultural institution, through the development of a special accurate clock which would keep time for millennia, and a library to house works important to humanity.

Principal Staff: Co-Chair. Stewart Brand, Danny Hillis; Exec. Dir Alexander Rose.

Address: POB 29462, San Francisco, CA 94129-0462.

Telephone: (415) 561-6582; **Fax:** (415) 561-6297; **Internet:** www.longnow.org; **e-mail:** services@longnow.org.

Henry Luce Foundation, Inc

Founded in 1936 by Henry Robinson Luce in order to make grants for specific projects in the broad areas of Asian affairs, higher education and scholarship, theology, American arts and public affairs.

Activities: The Luce Scholars Program gives a select group of young Americans, who are not Asian specialists, a year's work/study experience in East and South-East Asia. The Henry R. Luce Professorship Program provides six- to nine-year support for a limited number of integrative academic programmes in the humanities and social sciences at private colleges and universities. Funding in the arts focuses on research, scholarship and exhibitions in American art; direct support for specific projects at major museums and service organizations; and dissertation support for topics in American art history through the American Council of Learned Societies (q.v.). The Clare Boothe Luce Program is designed to enhance the careers of women in science and engineering by offering scholarships, fellowships and professorships at invited institutions. Grants are also available in the fields of public policy, the environment and theology.

Geographical Area of Activity: USA.

Publications: Biennial report; information brochure; grants list.

Finance: Assets $905,305,357 (2001); total grants $43,514,883 (2001).

Directors: Henry Luce, III (Chair. and CEO); Michael Gilligan (Pres.); Terrill E. Lautz (Vice-Pres. and Sec.); John C. Evans (Vice-Pres. and Treas.); Robert E. Armstrong; Anne d'Harnoncourt; Margaret Boles Fitzgerald; Claire L. Gaudini; Mrs. John N. Irwin II; James T. Laney; H. Christopher Luce; Thomas L. Pulling; David V. Ragone.

Address: 111 West 50th St, Room 4601, New York, NY 10020.

Telephone: (212) 489-7700; **Fax:** (212) 581-9541; **Internet:** www.hluce.org; **e-mail:** hlf@hluce.org.

Georges Lurcy Charitable and Educational Trust

Founded in 1985 by Georges Lurcy to support educational purposes.

Activities: The Trust provides grants to students of US and French universities and colleges for educational exchanges. Also supports cultural organizations and secondary education.

Geographical Area of Activity: France and the USA.

Finance: Assets $34,258,333 (June 2001); grants expenditure $1,862,234 (2001).

Trustees: Daniel L. Bernstein; George Lurcy Bernstein; Seth E. Frank.

Address: 125 West 55th St, New York, NY 10019.

Lutheran World Relief

Established to offer humanitarian aid around the world.

Activities: Operates in the fields of agriculture, health, housing, community work, gender equality, education and emergency aid, working to improve quality of life in communites in over 50 countries. Engages in long-term programmes in partnership with local organizations to overcome poverty and injustice, and in short-term relief work, aiming to alleviate human suffering resulting from natural disasters, war or famine.

Geographical Area of Activity: International.

Restrictions: No funding to US-based organizations.

Finance: Annual revenue $29,092,622, expenditure $28,434,978 (Sept. 2002).

Directors: E. Duda (Chair.); K. Betts (Vice-Chair.); L. Ishida (Sec.); M. Harrison; D. Hooks; B. Hewitt; B. Jensen; A. Larson; N. Lehr; E. Markquart; V. Peters; M. Sheie; W. Schumacher.

Principal Staff: Pres. Kathryn Wolford.

Address: 700 Light St, Baltimore, MD 21230.

Telephone: (410) 230-2700; **Fax:** (410) 230-2882; **Internet:** www.lwr.org; **e-mail:** lwr@lwr.org.

John D. and Catherine T. MacArthur Foundation

Founded in 1978 by John D. and Catherine T. MacArthur to foster lasting improvement in the human condition.

Activities: The Foundation operates four programmes: the Program on Human and Community Development supports improved access to economic opportunity, building the capacity of communities to advance human and community development and child and youth development; the Program on Global Security and Sustainability provides support in the areas of weapons control, population and ecosystem conservation and policy; the General Program supports initiatives that complement the Foundation's other work, and projects that promote diversity in the media; and the MacArthur Fellows Program awards fellowships to exceptionally creative people in their chosen field.

Geographical Area of Activity: USA.

Publications: Annual Report.

Finance: Assets $4,215,930,831 (2001); grants disbursed $167,945,326 (2001).

Directors: J. E. Corbally (Chair.); E. J. McCormack (Vice-Chair.); L. Axworthy; J. Seeley Brown; Drew Saunders Days, III; R. E. Denham; Jonathan F. Fanton; W. H. Foege; J. M. Furman; M. Gell-Mann; J. S. Gorelick; M. Graham; A. M. Hallene; P. Harvey; J. P. Holdren; S. M. Hufstedler; S. L. Lightfoot; M. E. Mahoney; G. A. Ranney, Jr; T. Theobald.

Principal Staff: Pres. Jonathon F. Fanton; Asst. Vice-Pres. Institutional Research and Grants Richard Kaplan.

Address: 140 South Dearborn St, Suite 1100, Chicago, IL 60603-5285.

Telephone: (312) 726-8000; **Fax:** (312) 920-6258; **Internet:** www.macfound.org; **e-mail:** 4answers@macfound.org.

Robert R. McCormick Tribune Foundation

Established as the Robert R. McCormick Charitable Trust in 1955 by Robert R. McCormick; became a foundation in 1990.

Activities: Aims to improve the social and economic development, encourage a free and responsible discussion of issues affecting the nation, enhance the effectiveness of American education and to stimulate responsible citizenship. Operates mainly in the Chicago metropolitan area supporting work in the fields of communities, citizenship, education and journalism. Operates a Journalism Program nationally and in Central and South America.

Geographical Area of Activity: USA, and Central and South America.

Restrictions: No grants are made to individuals.

Publications: Annual Report; information brochure.

Finance: Total assets $1,599,796,701 (2001); total grants $112,048,773 (2001).

Officers and Directors: J. W. Madigan (Chair.); R. A. Behrenhausen (Pres. and CEO); D. Grange (Exec. Vice-Pres.); N. Goodban (Senior Vice-Pres., Philanthropy); L. J. Marsico, Jr (Vice-Pres., Finance and Admin.); C. T. Brumback; J. C. Dowdle; D. J. FitzSimons; J. Fuller;.

Address: 435 North Michigan Ave, Suite 770, Chicago, IL 60611.

Telephone: (312) 222-3512; **Fax:** (312) 222-3523; **Internet:** www.rrmtf.org; **e-mail:** rrmtf@tribune.com.

James S. McDonnell Foundation

Founded in 1950 by James S. McDonnell, James S. McDonnell, III and John F. McDonnell for general charitable purposes and to contribute to the generation of new knowledge through supporting research and scholarships.

Activities: Operates in the fields of biological and behavioural sciences. Runs the 21st Century Science Initiative supporting individual and collaborative research in three areas: Bridging Brain, Mind and Behavior; Studying Complex Systems; and Brain Cancer Research. Individual grants are awarded over a three to six year period. International applications are invited.

Restrictions: Grants only to not-for-profit 501c3 organizations.

Finance: Assets $381,902,227 (2002).

Board of Directors: James S. McDonnell, III; Jeffrey M. McDonnell; John F. McDonnell.

Principal Staff: Pres. John T. Bruer; Vice-Pres. Susan M. Fitzpatrick.

Address: 1034 South Brentwood Blvd, Suite 1850, St Louis, MO 63117.

Telephone: (314) 721-1532; **Fax:** (314) 721-7421; **Internet:** www.jsmf.org; **e-mail:** info@jsmf.org.

McKnight Foundation

Founded in 1953 by William L. and Maude L. McKnight and Virginia M. and James M. Binger for general charitable purposes.

Activities: Gives funding in the fields of children, families and communities; the arts; environment; research and applied science; and international funding. Scientific research is divided into three main areas: neuroscience, particularly diseases affecting the memory; and crop research, particularly in developing countries. Has interests in Tanzania, Uganda, Zimbabwe, Cambodia, Laos and Vietnam.

Geographical Area of Activity: Mainly USA (Minnesota); some grants in Cambodia, Laos, Tanzania, Uganda, Vietnam and Zimbabwe.

Restrictions: Grants are rarely made outside the state of Minnesota.

Publications: Annual Report; grants list; occasional report; information brochure.

Finance: Assets $1,877,703,000 (2001); total grants $90,791,000 (2001).

Officers and Directors: Noa Staryk (Chair.); Virginia M. Binger (Hon. Chair.); Rip Rapson (Pres.); Carol Berde (Exec. Vice-Pres.); James M. Binger (Treas.); Patricia S. Binger (Asst

Sec. and Asst Treas.); Rick Scott (Vice-Pres., Finance and Admin. and Sec.); Benjamen Binger; Cynthia Binger Boynton; Erika Binger; Meghan Binger Brown.

Address: 710 Second St South, Suite 400, Minneapolis, MN 55401.

Telephone: (612) 333-4220; **Fax:** (612) 332-3833; **Internet:** www.mcknight.org; **e-mail:** info@mcknight.org.

Maclellan Foundation, Inc

Incorporated in 1945 by Robert J. Maclellan and family. Reincorporated in 1992. Provides funding for Christian education and agencies.

Activities: Makes grants for Christian higher education, supports Protestant missions abroad, youth agencies and religious associations. Active in the Tennessee area, and in Eastern Europe, Asia, Africa, and Central and South America.

Geographical Area of Activity: USA (Tennessee), Eastern Europe, Asia, Africa, and Central and South America.

Restrictions: No grants are made to individuals.

Finance: Assets $403,953,114 (2001); total grants $17,796,860 (2001).

Trustees: R. L. Maclellan; Hugh O. Maclellan, Jr; F. A. Brock; Ronald Blue; G. Richard Hostetter; Robert H. Maclellan; Pat MacMillan; Dudley Porter; Al Duke.

Principal Staff: Pres. Hugh O. Maclellan; Exec. Dir Thomas H. McCallie, III.

Address: Provident Bldg, Suite 501, Chattanooga, TN 37402.

Telephone: (423) 755-1366; **Fax:** (423) 755-1640; **Internet:** www.maclellanfdn.org; **e-mail:** info@maclellan.net.

Josiah Macy, Jr Foundation

Founded in 1930 by Kate Macy Ladd to advance medicine and health in the USA and abroad; the Foundation's major interest is in medical education.

Activities: Operates both nationally and internationally in the fields of science and medicine, through health programmes, grants to institutions, conferences and publications. Particularly concerned with African American, Latino and Native American health issues. Currently focusing on improvement in health professional education, increasing teamwork between and among multiple health professions, educational strategies that increase access and use of health-care facilities by underserved communities and increasing diversity amongst health-care professionals.

Geographical Area of Activity: Mainly USA.

Restrictions: No grants are given for building, endowment, annual fund appeals or individual travel.

Publications: Annual Report; occasional reports; conference papers; specialist publications.

Finance: Total assets $139,825,416 (June 2002); total grants $5,308,894 (2002).

Officers and Directors: Clarence F. Michalis (Chair.); June E. Osborn (Pres.); Martha Wolfgang (Vice-Pres. and Treas.); Rina Forlini (Sec.); Lawrence K. Altman; Harold Amos; Louis S. Auchinloss; J. Carter Bacot; Alexander G. Bearn; Jordan J. Cohen; E. Virgil Conway; John W. Frymoyer; S. Parker Gilbert; P. Albjerg Graham; Bernard W. Harleston; Arthur H. Hayes, Jr; Lawrence S. Huntington; John J. Iselin; David L. Luke, III; Mary Patterson McPherson; Walter N. Rothschild; William H. Wright, II.

Principal Staff: Pres. June E. Osborn; Vice-Pres. Martha Wolfgang.

Address: 44 East 64th St, New York, NY 10021.

Telephone: (212) 486-2424; **Fax:** (212) 644-0765; **Internet:** www.josiahmacyfoundation.org; **e-mail:** jmacyinfo@josiahmacyfoundation.org.

MADRE

Founded in 1983 by a group of women with the aim of advancing human rights in areas of conflict world-wide.

Activities: Operates in the field of international human rights by working with community-based women's organizations in areas of conflict around the world, focusing on health, education, economic development and other basic human rights. Provides financial and technical support for these partner groups, while raising awareness of prevalent issues within the USA. Programmes currently operate in Central and South America and the Caribbean, Palestinian Autonomous Areas, Kenya and Rwanda.

Geographical Area of Activity: International.

Restrictions: Grants only to partner organizations.

Publications: Newsletter.

Address: 121 West 27th St, Rm 301, New York, NY 10001.

Telephone: (212) 627-0444; **Fax:** (212) 675-3704; **Internet:** www.madre.org; **e-mail:** madre@madre.org.

A. L. Mailman Family Foundation

Founded in 1980 by Abraham Mailman to support families and communities in providing care and stability for young children.

Activities: The Foundation funds projects to benefit young children, both regionally and nationally, particularly those involved with improving care systems, helping to mitigate the effects of poverty in young children, fostering community support and improving the emotional and social development of children. The A. L. Mailman Family Foundation Early Childhood Leadership Award recognizes individuals who have made an extraordinary contribution towards the improvement of the lives and life chances of young children and their families.

Geographical Area of Activity: USA.

Finance: Assets $25,869,540 (2001); grants $1,532,569 (2001).

Directors: Marilyn Mailman Segal (Chair. Emer.); Betty S. Bardige (Chair.); Patricia S. Lieberman (Vice-Chair.); Richard D. Segal (Pres.); Wendy S. Masi (Vice-Pres.); Jonathan R. Gordon; Jay B. Langner.

Principal Staff: Exec. Dir Luba H. Lynch; Treas. Donna Tookmanian; Grant Admin. Barbara Enright.

Address: 707 Westchester Ave, White Plains, NY 10604.

Telephone: (914) 683-8089; **Fax:** (914) 686-5519; **Internet:** www.mailman.org; **e-mail:** almf@mailman.org.

MAP International

Established in 1954 by Dr J. Raymond Knighton, a non-profit Christian relief and development organization that aims to promote the health of people living in developing countries.

Activities: Operates in developing countries in Africa and Central and South America in the area of medicine and health, through working in partnership with other organizations to provide essential medicines to those in need, so as to prevent and eradicate diseases (particularly addressing the problem of HIV/AIDS) and to promote community health development in less-developed countries. Also provides emergency health care in areas suffering from the effects of natural and man-made disasters. Offers scholarships to medical students from North America to travel to developing countries to work at hospitals helping people in financial need.

Geographical Area of Activity: Africa, and Central and South America.

Principal Staff: CEO and Pres. Michael J. Nyenhuis.

Address: 2200 Glynco Parkway, POB 215000, Brunswick, GA 31521.

Telephone: (912) 265-6010; **Fax:** (912) 265-6170; **Internet:** www.map.org; **e-mail:** map@map.org.

March of Dimes Birth Defects Foundation

Founded in 1938 as the National Foundation for Infantile

Paralysis to combat polio; the Foundation's current aim is to help prevent birth defects and infant mortality through education and research.

Activities: Promotes the continuing education of professionals in the field of perinatal care, and the expansion of education programmes for the general public. Makes grants to organizations for research in aspects of birth defects; and various research awards for research in the USA, including Clinical Research Grants, Pre-doctoral Graduate Research Training Fellowships, Social and Behavioral Sciences Research Grants, the Summer Science Research Program for Medical Students, the Basil O'Connor Starter Scholar Research Award Program and the Research Support Program on Reproductive Hazards in the Workplace, Home, Community and Environment.

Geographical Area of Activity: USA.

Publications: Annual Report.

Finance: Total assets $138,198,000 (Dec. 2001); total expenditure $217,912,000 (2001).

Principal Staff: Pres. Jennifer Howse.

Address: 1275 Mamaroneck Ave, White Plains, NY 10605.

Telephone: (914) 428-7100; **Fax:** (914) 997-4650; **Internet:** www.modimes.org; **e-mail:** aedelstein@modimes.org.

John and Mary R. Markle Foundation

Founded in 1927 by John Markle and Mary Markle to promote the advancement and diffusion of knowledge and the general good of humanity. The Foundation is now concentrating on the potential of mass communications and information technology to enhance learning, and improving the mass media, including services growing out of new technologies for the processing and transfer of information.

Activities: Operates throughout the USA in the field of communications, through self-conducted programmes, research and grants to institutions. The Foundation has made substantial commitments to the following programme areas: developing policies for a networked society, developing interactive media for children, and promoting information technologies for better health.

Geographical Area of Activity: USA.

Restrictions: No grants are made to individuals.

Finance: Assets $141,565,543 (June 2002).

Board of Directors: J. L. Fleishman (Chair.); Zoë Baird (Pres.); Lewis W. Bernard; T. A. Bernstein; J. I. Cash, Jr.; L. B. Kaden; E. C. Lagemann; D. T. Murray; S. S. Shuman.

Principal Staff: Pres. Zoë Baird; Man. Dir and Chief Fin. Officer Karen D. Byers.

Address: 10 Rockefeller Plaza, 16th Floor, New York, NY 10020-1903.

Telephone: (212) 489-6655; **Fax:** (212) 765-9690; **Internet:** www.markle.org; **e-mail:** info@markle.org.

The Max Foundation

Established by Pedro José Rivarola in 1995, a non-profit organization that aims to improve the quality of life and the treatment of patients suffering from leukaemia and other blood diseases, especially children of Hispanic and Latino origin.

Activities: Operates in the USA and in Central and South America in the field of medicine and health. Provides information about treatment options; offers advice and emotional and financial support to sufferers of blood-related diseases; and raises awareness of the importance of becoming a bone marrow donor. Maintains regional offices in Argentina, Brazil and Peru. Also working to establish the VidaMax-MaxLife Bone Marrow and Cord Blood Registry to increase patients' chances of survival and successful treatment.

Geographical Area of Activity: Central and South America, and the USA.

Governers: Dr E. Donnall Thomas (Hon. Chair.); A. Di-Tolla (Vice-Pres.); C. Dominguez; N. Glick; H. Milla; J. Norton; K. Weyant.

Principal Staff: CEO Pedro Rivarola.

Address: 110 West Dayton, Suite 205, Edmonds, WA 98020.

Telephone: (425) 778-8660; **Fax:** (425) 778-8760; **Internet:** www.themaxfoundation.org; **e-mail:** info@themaxfoundation.org.

Craig and Susan McCaw Foundation

Activities: Operates in the fields of aid to less-developed countries, and health and welfare. Offers small loans to assist in the development of technology in Asia; and makes grants to organizations working in Africa, including the Nelson Mandela Foundation and the Foundation for Community Development (qq.v.).

Geographical Area of Activity: Africa and South-East Asia.

Finance: Assets $22,525,138 (Dec. 2000); annual grants expenditure $11,817,686 (2000).

Address: POB 2908, Kirkland, WA 98083.

The Andrew W. Mellon Foundation

Founded in 1969 through the merger of the Avalon Foundation (founded in 1940 by Ailsa Mellon Bruce) and the Old Dominion Foundation (founded in 1941 by Paul Mellon), to furnish support for higher education and cultural institutions.

Activities: Operates nationally in selected areas of the humanities, cultural activities, higher education, population, and conservation and the environment. Its graduate fellowships are administered by the Woodrow Wilson National Fellowship Foundation (q.v.).

Geographical Area of Activity: Mainly USA.

Restrictions: The Foundation makes very few grants to non-US organizations, and no grants to individuals.

Publications: Annual Report.

Finance: Assets $4,135,567,000 (2001); grants disbursed $182,321,993 (2001).

Trustees: Hanna H. Gray (Chair.); William G. Bowen (Pres.); C. E. Exley, Jr; H. H. Gray; W. E. Massey; T. Mellon; W. T. Reveley, III; C. A. Ryskamp; A. M. Tatlock.

Principal Staff: Pres. William G. Bowen, Sr; Vice-Pres. Harriet Zuckerman; Financial Vice-Pres. T. Dennis Sullivan; Vice-Pres. Mary Patterson McPherson; Sec. Michele S. Warman; Treas. and Asst Sec. Eileen M. Scott.

Address: 140 East 62nd St, New York, NY 10021.

Telephone: (212) 838-8400; **Fax:** (212) 223-2778; **Internet:** www.mellon.org.

Richard King Mellon Foundation

Founded in 1947 by Richard King Mellon for general charitable purposes. The major focus of the Foundation is on the quality of life in Pittsburgh and South-west Pennsylvania, however it also promotes national conservation programmes.

Activities: Operates programmes in the fields of conservation, wildlife, the environment, education (particularly primary and second level), medicine and health care, cultural activities and civic affairs.

Geographical Area of Activity: USA (particularly South-western Pennsylvania).

Restrictions: No grants are made to individuals.

Publications: Annual report and financial statement; information brochure.

Finance: Assets $1,661,919,000 (2001); grants disbursed $58,668,007 (2001).

Officers and Trustees: Richard P. Mellon (Chair.); Seward P. Mellon (Pres.); Michael Watson, Arthur D. Miltenberger (Vice-Pres); Robert B. Burr, Jr (Treas.); Lawrence S. Busch (Asst Treas.); Scott D. Izzo (Assoc. Dir and Sec.); Ann Marie Helms (Asst Sec.); John J. Turcik (Controller).

Address: 1 Mellon Bank Center, Suite 4106, 500 Grant St, Pittsburgh, PA 15219-2502.

Telephone: (412) 392-2800; **Internet:** http://fdncenter.org/grantmaker/rkmellon/.

Memorial Foundation for Jewish Culture

Founded in 1965 by Dr Nahum Goldmann with reparation funds from the Government of West Germany. Aims to encourage and assist Jewish scholarship and education; and to contribute to the preservation, enhancement and transmission of Jewish culture throughout the world.

Activities: Awards scholarships to prepare future scholars, researchers and rabbinical leaders, and fellowships to aid scholars, writers and artists. Supports special training programmes for rabbis, educators and Jewish communal workers for countries which do not have adequate training facilities. Also provides grants for Jewish research and publication, higher education and for programmes to commemorate and document the Holocaust.

Geographical Area of Activity: International.

Principal Staff: Asst Dir Dr Marc G. Brandriss; Exec. Vice-Pres. Dr Jerry Hochbaum.

Address: 15 East 26th St, Rm 1703, New York, NY 10010.

Telephone: (212) 425-6606; **Fax:** (212) 425-6602; **Internet:** www.mfjc.com; **e-mail:** jcult@aol.com.

John Merck Fund

Founded in 1970 by the late Serena S. Merck for charitable purposes.

Activities: Operates nationally and internationally in the areas of developmental disabilities, the environment, disarmament, reproductive health, providing job opportunities, and human rights, through awarding grants to medical teaching hospitals and small organizations; support for conferences and seminars; research; and fellowships.

Geographical Area of Activity: International, although mainly USA.

Publications: Annual Report.

Finance: Assets $225,690,000 (2000); grants disbursed $11,859,000 (2000).

Officers and Trustees: F. W. Hatch (Chair); H. C. Held (Treas.); Judith M. Buechner; Serena M. Hatch; Arnold Hiatt; Robert M. Pennoyer; Frederica Perera.

Principal Staff: Admin. Ruth G. Henning.

Address: 11 Beacon St, Suite 1230, Boston, MA 02108.

Telephone: (617) 723-2932; **Fax:** (617) 523-6029; **Internet:** www.jmfund.org; **e-mail:** info@jmfund.org.

Mercy Corps

Humanitarian organization founded in 1981 by Dan O' Neill and Ellsworth Culver to alleviate suffering around the world.

Activities: Operates as a network of organizations with offices in 25 countries working internationally in the fields of sustainable community development, civil society and emergency relief. Programmes are primarily targeted at providing long-term solutions for people suffering the effects of poverty, oppression and conflict, through health care, housing, education, economic and community development, material aid and micro-enterprise schemes. Provides emergency relief for those affected by natural and man-made disasters and also works to promote citizen participation, the accountability of governments, and conflict management.

Geographical Area of Activity: International.

Publications: Annual Report.

Finance: Annual revenue $87,839,852, expenditure $86,987,898 (2001).

Directors: Senator M. Hatfield (Hon. Chair.); J. A. Barber, Jr (Chair.); R. D. Newell (Vice-Chair.); D. W. O'Neill (Pres.); P. Dobyns (Sec./Treas.); N. Keny-Guyer (CEO); B. Alstead; E. Bartholomew; E. Goebel; A. Johnson; D. Kidd; L. Mason; R. S. Nicholson; R. E. Vath.

Principal Staff: Pres. D. W. O' Neill; CEO Neal L. Keny-Guyer; Chief Operating Officer S. Zimmerman; Senior Vice-Pres. E. Culver; Exec. Vice-Pres. N. Lindborg; M. De Galan; J. C. Salmonson.

Address: 3015 SW First Dept W, Portland, OR 97201.

Telephone: (800) 292-3355; **Internet:** www.mercycorps.org; **e-mail:** info@mercycorps.org.

Mercy-USA for Aid and Development—M-USA

Founded in 1986, Mercy-USA for Aid and Development (M-USA) is a non-profit international relief and development organization dedicated to alleviating human suffering and supporting individuals and their communities in their efforts to become more self-sufficient.

Activities: Operates in the areas of aid to less-developed countries, education, medicine and health, and social welfare, through a number of projects, including promoting economic and educational growth, disaster relief, reconstruction and rehabilitation, and international development projects.

Geographical Area of Activity: Africa, Central and South-Eastern Europe, Central and Southern Asia, the Middle East and the USA.

Restrictions: No grants are made to individuals.

Publications: *Mercy News* (newsletter).

Finance: Funded by donations from private individuals, grants and gifts-in-kind from agencies of the US Government, the United Nations and from various NGOs, and investment revenue. Assets $2,701,382 (2001); annual revenue $4,454,587, expenditure $4,660,219 (2001).

Board of Directors: Z. Mahasa (Chair.); S. Salman (Treas.); F. Baksh; Dr A. Elkadi; Dr S. Khan; Dr Ali El-Menshawi.

Principal Staff: Pres. and CEO U. al-Qadi; Int. Programme Dir M. Ahmed; Community Relations Dir A. Alhaidar.

Address: 44450 Pinetree Dr., Suite 201, Plymouth, MI 48170-3869.

Telephone: (734) 454-0011; **Fax:** (734) 454-0303; **Internet:** mercyusa.org; **e-mail:** mercyusa@mercyusa.org.

Mertz Gilmore Foundation

Founded in 1959 by Joyce Mertz-Gilmore for general charitable purposes.

Activities: Currently makes grants to non-profit organizations active in the following programme areas: International Human Rights; Immigrant Rights in the USA; Lesbian and Gay Rights in the USA, Israel and Palestine; Dance in New York City; New York City Human and Built Environment; and Energy. The International Human Rights programme supports efforts that bridge work on civil and political rights with work on economic, social and cultural rights and bring them to the same level. The Israel and Palestine programme makes capacity-building grants, both programmatic and institutional, to Israeli and Palestinian human rights groups. The Immigrant Rights, Lesbian and Gay Rights, Dance in New York City, New York City Built and Human Environment, and Energy programmes are all focused on the USA.

Geographical Area of Activity: International, including Israel, Palestine and the USA.

Restrictions: No grants are made for individuals, sectarian religious concerns, conferences, film or media projects, endowments, publications or for single country projects.

Publications: Report (every two years); information brochure; grants list.

Finance: Assets $106,330,553 (2001); expenditure $11,029,713 (2001).

Officers and Directors: Larry E. Condon (Chair.); Elizabeth Burke Gilmore (Vice-Chair. and Sec.); Robert Crane (Exec. Dir); Denise Nix Thompson (Treas.); Jay Beckner (Asst Treas.); Charles Bloomstein; Harlan Cleveland; Hal Harvey; Patricia Ramsay; Peggy Saika; Mikki Shepard; Franklin W. Wallin; C. Virgil Martin (Emer.).

Principal Staff: Exec. Dir Robert Crane.

Address: 218 East 18th St, New York, NY 10003-3694.

Telephone: (212) 475-1137; **Fax:** (212) 777-5226; **Internet:** www.mertzgilmore.org; **e-mail:** info@mertzgilmore.org.

Milbank Memorial Fund

Founded in 1905 by Elizabeth Milbank Anderson to improve the physical, mental and moral condition of humanity. The Fund's work in health policy now addresses three themes: improving health-care and related services for patients; protecting and improving the health of people in communities and workplaces; and improving the governance of public and private organizations so that they offer more effective care and health protection, as well as opportunities for health improvement.

Activities: The Fund is an endowed foundation that engages in non-partisan analysis, study, research and communication on significant issues in health policy. The results are made available in meetings with decision-makers and publications. Most of the Fund's work is collaborative, involving strategic relationships with decision makers in the public and private sectors. It uses its resources in ways that complement the resources of its partners, not making grants in the traditional sense.

Geographical Area of Activity: USA.

Publications: *The Milbank Quarterly;* reports and books.

Finance: Assets $78,520,800 (Dec. 2001).

Officers and Directors: Samuel L. Milbank (Chair.); Peter M. Gottsegen (Vice-Chair.); Daniel M. Fox (Pres.); Byron L. Knief (Treas.); J R. Ball; C. C. Clark; T. E. Harvey; C. Hooker Odim; L. J. Palmer; C. J. Schramm; R. A. Stevens; J. D. Stoeckle; J. M. Sullivan; C. Tucker.

Principal Staff: Vice-Pres. and Chief Operating Officer K. S. Andersen; Editorial Dir P. D. Cleary.

Address: 645 Madison Ave, 15th Floor, New York, NY 10022-1095.

Telephone: (212) 355-8400; **Fax:** (212) 355-8599; **Internet:** www.milbank.org; **e-mail:** mmf@milbank.org.

Mobility International

Founded in 1981 by Susan Sygall and Barbara Williams with the aim of empowering people with disabilities around the world.

Activities: Operates internationally to provide people with disabilities with equal opportunities, and promotes their inclusion in development programmes through international exchange, information, technical assistance and training. Also manages the National Clearinghouse on Disability and Exchange (NCDE).

Publications: Books, fact sheets and videos.

Address: POB 10767, Eugene, OR 97440.

Telephone: (541) 343-1284; **Fax:** (541) 343-6812; **Internet:** www.miusa.org; **e-mail:** info@miusa.org.

Ambrose Monell Foundation

Established to contribute to religious, charitable, scientific, literary and educational purposes in New York, the USA in general, and world-wide.

Activities: Operates in New York, the USA in general and internationally; makes grants to organizations operating in the above fields.

Geographical Area of Activity: International.

Restrictions: No grants are made to individuals.

Finance: Total grants $11,177,500 (2001).

Officers and Directors: George Rowe, Jr (Pres.); Joseph T. C. Hart (Treas.); Laura Naus (Sec.); Eugene P. Grisanti; Ambrose K. Monell; Henry G. Walter.

Address: 1 Rockefeller Plaza, Suite 301, New York, NY 10020-2002.

Telephone: (212) 586-0700; **Fax:** (212) 245-1863; **Internet:** www.monellvetlesen.org; **e-mail:** info@monellvetlesen.org.

Moody Foundation

Founded in 1942 by William Lewis Moody, Jr and Libbie Shearn Moody.

Activities: Operates in Texas in the fields of conservation and renovation, the arts and humanities, medicine and health, science, education, social welfare and religion, through research, grants to institutions, fellowships, scholarships, publications, conferences and lectures. Currently, however, approximately 95 per cent of the Foundation's grant-making is concentrated on the Moody Gardens in Galveston Island and the Transitional Learning Center, which offers facilities for the rehabilitation of people with brain injuries.

Geographical Area of Activity: USA (Texas).

Restrictions: No grants to individuals, except for scholarships to Galveston County students. Grants only to organizations in Texas.

Publications: Annual Report; application guidelines.

Finance: Assets $926,916,215 (2001); total expenditure $8,277,161 (2001).

Officers and Trustees: Frances Moody Newman (Chair.); Frances Ann Moody (Exec. Dir).

Principal Staff: Dir of Grants Peter M. Moore; Scholarship Admin. Sandy Griffin.

Address: 2302 Postoffice St, Suite 704, Galveston, TX 77550.

Telephone: (409) 763-5333; **Fax:** (409) 763-5564; **Internet:** www.moodyf.org.

John Motley Morehead Foundation

Founded in 1945 by John Motley Morehead, III for the advancement of education, learning and/or research for public benefit in the USA, particularly in North Carolina and the South.

Activities: Operates nationally in the field of education, through the allocation of scholarships. The activities of the Foundation are currently restricted to undergraduate study at the University of North Carolina at Chapel Hill, through offering scholarships to graduates of secondary schools in North Carolina, of selected preparatory schools in the USA and Canada, and of selected schools in the United Kingdom. All awards are based solely on merit, and are sufficient to cover the entire cost of attending the institution for four years.

Geographical Area of Activity: USA and United Kingdom.

Restrictions: Grants for study at specified educational institutions.

Publications: Annual Report; fact sheets on grants programmes.

Finance: Assets $111,735,815 (2001).

Trustees: A. T. Dickson (Chair.); L. H. Chatham (Vice-Chair.); T. B. Burnett; R. Cluett; J. Morehead Larkin; R. M. Robinson, II.

Principal Staff: Exec. Dir C. E. Lovelace; Treas. C. W. Johnston, Jr.

Address: POB 690, Chapel Hill, NC 27514-0690.

Telephone: (919) 962-1201; **Fax:** (919) 962-1615; **Internet:** www.moreheadfoundation.org; **e-mail:** morehead@unc.edu.

Charles Stewart Mott Foundation

Founded in 1926 by Charles Stewart Mott for charitable purposes.

Activities: Operates nationally and (on a limited basis) internationally, in the fields of social welfare, education, the environment and civil society, through grants to institutions. Supports projects which lead to better community and family relations, more inter-agency co-operation, and strengthening the non-profit sector. The Foundation, a pioneer in the concept of community education, now supports limited programme development in Canada, the United Kingdom, South Africa, Eastern and Central Europe and the countries of the former USSR, and other countries. The four main programme areas of the Foundation are: Civil Society; the Environment; the town of Flint, MI; and Pathways out of Poverty. Maintains an on-line grants database on grants made by the Foundation since 1993.

Geographical Area of Activity: North America, limited funding to projects in Western, Central and Eastern Europe, the countries of the former USSR, and South Africa.

Restrictions: Grants are not made to individuals, nor to religious organizations for religious purposes.

Publications: Annual report and financial statement; *Facts on Grants* (containing fact sheets); newsletter and magazine (occasional), grant guidelines, occasional report.

Finance: Assets approx. $2,460,169,524 (Dec. 2001); grants disbursed approx. $110,829,012 (2001).

Board of Trustees: William S. White (Chair, CEO and Pres.); William H. Piper (Vice-Chair.); A. Marshall Acuff Jr; Rushworth M. Kidder; Tiffany W. Lovett; Webb F. Martin; Olivia P. Maynard; John Morning; Maryanne Mott; Douglas X. Patiño; John W. Porter; Marise M.M. Stewart; Claire M. White; Willa B. Player.

Principal Staff: Pres. and Chief Exec. William S. White; Dir Grants Admin. and Asst Treas. Jimmy L. Krause; Man. Grants Admin. Mary Gailbreath.

Address: Office of Proposal Entry, Mott Foundation Bldg, 503 S. Saginaw St, Suite 1200, Flint, MI 48502-1851.

Telephone: (810) 238-5651; **Fax:** (810) 766-1753; **Internet:** www.mott.org; **e-mail:** infocenter@mott.org.

The Mountain Institute

Non-profit educational and scientific organization founded in 1972 that aims to help and protect mountain environments and cultures around the world.

Activities: Engages in conservation work in the Andes, the Himalayas and the Appalachians, protecting the habitat of mountain wildlife; funds programmes to improve the quality of life of people living in and around mountain parks and protected areas, including projects dedicated to economic development and the promotion of cultural heritage; established the Mountain Forum, an international alliance which acts as a base for information-sharing on issues which affect mountain environments.

Geographical Area of Activity: Asia, and North and South America.

Trustees: Robert H. Whitby (Chair.); Elsie Walker (Vice-Chair.); Walt Coward (Treas.); Jim Underwood (Sec.).

Principal Staff: Pres. and CEO Catherine Nixon Cooke.

Address: 1828 L St, NW, Suite 725, Washington, DC 20036.

Telephone: (202) 452-1636; **Fax:** (202) 452-1635; **Internet:** www.mountain.org; **e-mail:** summit@mountain.org.

Ms Foundation for Women

Founded in 1972 to improve the lives of women and girls.

Activities: So as to achieve its aims, the Foundation operates in three project areas: Women's Economic Security; Women's Health and Safety; and Girls, Young Women and Leadership, as well as making grants outside these areas through its Special Fund. It conducts advocacy and public education campaigns, provides technical assistance, and directs resources to organizations operating in these project areas. The Foundation established Take Our Daughters To Work Day.

Geographical Area of Activity: USA.

Restrictions: No grants to direct service organizations, individuals, for scholarships, university-based research, state agencies, religious institutions, cultural or media projects, publications or conferences.

Publications: Annual Report; newsletter.

Finance: Annual budget approx. $8,600,000.

Board of Directors: A. S. Levere (Chair.); Y. C. Richardson (Vice-Chair.); M. Campbell (Treas.); L. Shea (Sec.); J. Belk; C. Gilligan; K. Grover; G. R. Gupta; R. McKay; A. Taylor; Marie C. Wilson.

Principal Staff: Pres. Marie C. Wilson; Exec. Dir Sara K. Gould.

Address: 120 Wall St, 33rd Floor, New York, NY 10005.

Telephone: (212) 742-2300; **Fax:** (212) 742-1653; **Internet:** www.ms.foundation.org; **e-mail:** info@ms.foundation.org.

Muscular Dystrophy Association

Founded in 1950 by a group of New York parents and relatives of young people affected by muscular dystrophy, to fight the disease and related neuromuscular disorders, through world-wide research and a comprehensive programme of services available to residents of the USA, and a professional and public education programme.

Activities: Aims to combat neuromuscular disease through world-wide support of basic and clinical research directed at developing affective treatments for neuro-muscular disorders. Also operates a national programme of medical services and clinical care, including diagnostic services and rehabilitative follow-up care through a nationwide network of hospital-affiliated clinics; provides selected medical equipment; and offers support groups and summer camp programmes. It attempts to broaden public awareness of neuromuscular disease through its publications, video presentations and press releases and offer on-line information services.

Geographical Area of Activity: Conducts research internationally; services only available in the USA.

Restrictions: Grants only to those affiliated to a university or other educational facility.

Publications: Annual Report; brochures; *ALS Newsletter; Quest.*

Finance: Assets $190,030,405 (March 2002); annual revenue $155,570,924, expenditure $156,365,431 (2002).

Trustees: Jerry Lewis (Chair.); Robert M. Bennett (Chair., Board of Dirs).

Principal Staff: Pres. Robert Ross; Grants Man. Karen Mashburn.

Address: 3300 East Sunrise Dr., Tucson, AZ 85718-3208.

Telephone: (520) 529-2000; **Fax:** (520) 529-5300; **Internet:** www.mdausa.org; **e-mail:** mda@mdausa.org.

The ONDEO Nalco Foundation

Founded in 1953 by Nalco Chemical Co., now known as Ondeo Nalco, for general charitable purposes; formerly known as the Nalco Foundation.

Activities: Operates primarily in California, Illinois, Louisiana, New Jersey, Ohio and Texas, where the company has manufacturing operations, in the fields of private higher education, the arts and humanities, social welfare and medicine and health.

Geographical Area of Activity: USA (California, Illinois, Louisiana, New Jersey, Ohio and Texas).

Restrictions: No grants are made to individuals.

Publications: *Corporate Giving Report;* guidelines.

Finance: Total assets US $2,246,235 (Dec. 2000); total giving US $1,281,859 (2000).

Directors: James F. Lambe; Michael E. Kahler; Ellen B. DeLordo.

Principal Staff: Pres. Ellen B. DeLordo.

Address: 1601 West Diehl Rd, Naperville, IL 60563-1198.

Telephone: (630) 305-1566; **Fax:** (630) 305-2896; **Internet:** www.ondeo-nalco.com; **e-mail:** foundation@ondeo-nalco.com.

National Democratic Institute for International Affairs

Affiliated to the US Democratic Party and set up as an independent organization to expand and strengthen democracy world-wide; created as part of the 1984 statute which set up the National Endowment for Democracy.

Activities: Provides practical assistance to civic and political leaders advancing democratic values, practices and institutions. Provides support to build political and civic organizations, safeguard elections, and to promote citizen participation, openness and accountability in government through the provision of expert volunteers, technical resources and training. Programmes focus on citizen participation, civil–military relations, election and political processes, democratic governance, political party development and women's participation.

Geographical Area of Activity: International.

Restrictions: Not a grant-making organization.

Publications: *NDI Reports: a review of political developments in new democracies* (newsletter).

Board of Directors: Madeleine K. Albright (Chair.); Rachelle Horowitz (Vice-Chair.); Kenneth F. Melley (Sec.); Eugene Eidenberg (Treas.); Kenneth D. Wollack (Pres.); and 27 others.

Address: 2030 M St, NW, Fifth Floor, Washington, DC 20036-3306.

Telephone: (202) 728-5500; **Fax:** (202) 728-5520; **Internet:** www.ndi.org; **e-mail:** contactndi@ndi.org.

National Fish and Wildlife Foundation

Founded in 1984 by the US Congress for the conservation of natural resources through grant-making to effective and innovative projects.

Activities: Runs projects concerned with habitat protection, environmental education, public policy development, natural resource management, ecosystem rehabilitation and leadership training for conservation workers. Operates nationally and internationally, although with a focus on the USA, through grants to institutions and individuals.

Geographical Area of Activity: Mainly USA.

Restrictions: No awards for lobbying, political activism or litigation.

Publications: Annual Report.

Board of Directors: Stephen Peet (Chair.); Max C. Chapman, Jr, Carlton N. Owen (Vice-Chair.).

Principal Staff: Exec. Dir John Berry.

Address: 1120 Connecticut Ave, NW, Suite 900, Washington, DC 20036.

Telephone: (202) 857-0166; **Fax:** (202) 857-0162; **Internet:** www.nfwf.org; **e-mail:** fritts@nfwf.org.

National Foundation for Cancer Research

Founded in 1973 to fund basic scientific research and investigation of the structure and function of normal and abnormal cells.

Activities: Funds 40 laboratories in the USA and eight other countries. Holds conferences and symposia.

Geographical Area of Activity: Mainly USA.

Publications: *National Cancer Bulletin* (newsletter); booklets and papers.

Finance: Total assets $8,353,726 (Sept. 2002); total revenue $16,330,867, total expenditure $14,588,967 (2002).

Principal Staff: Pres. Franklin C. Salisbury.

Address: 4600 East West Highway, Suite 525, Bethesda, MD 20814.

Telephone: (301) 654-1250; **Internet:** www.nfcr.org.

National Humanities Center

Incorporated in 1976 by the American Academy of Arts and Sciences to support advanced post-doctoral scholarship in the humanities and to foster the influence of the humanities in the USA.

Activities: Awards 35–40 fellowships annually for post-doctoral scholars in the humanities, including history, philosophy, languages, literature, classics, religion, history of art, etc.; open to students of any nationality for study in the USA.

Geographical Area of Activity: USA.

Restrictions: Grants only for study in the USA.

Publications: *Ideas* (2 a year); Annual Report; conference reports; occasional papers.

Finance: Total assets $47,304,983 (June 2002); annual revenue $4,490,728, expenditure $8,325,905 (2002).

Trustees: John P. Birkelund (Chair.).

Principal Staff: Pres. Geoffrey Galt Harpham.

Address: 7 Alexander Dr., POB 12256, Research Triangle Park, NC 27709.

Telephone: (919) 549-0661; **Fax:** (919) 990-8535; **Internet:** www.nhc.rtp.nc.us; **e-mail:** lmorgan@ga.unc.edu.

National Kidney Foundation

Activities: Awards about 40 post-doctoral fellowships annually for kidney research in the USA by scholars of any nationality, who have not completed more than two years of research training at the start of the fellowship tenure; Young Investigator Grants in nephrology, urology and related disciplines, for students beginning a career in the faculty of a US medical school; and Clinical Scientist Awards to support investigators who have demonstrated outstanding research potential. Also operates in the fields of patient services and public health education.

Geographical Area of Activity: USA.

Restrictions: Grants only for study in the USA.

Publications: Periodicals and specific publications.

Finance: Total assets $91,251,814 (June 2001); annual revenue $48,987,317, annual expenditure $50,499,116 (2001).

Principal Staff: Chair. Andrew N. Baur; CEO John Davis.

Address: 30 East 33rd St, Suite 1100, New York, NY 10016.

Telephone: (212) 889-2210; **Fax:** (212) 689-9261; **Internet:** www.kidney.org; **e-mail:** info@kidney.org.

National Organization for Women Foundation—NOW Foundation

Established in 1986 to advance women's rights and promote equality in the USA and around the world.

Activities: Operates in the field of women's rights through education, advocacy, conferences, publications, training and leadership development. Runs projects in areas including women's reproductive rights, prevention of violence against women, sexual harassment, lesbian rights, global feminism and other related issues. Affiliated with the National Organization for Women (NOW).

Geographical Area of Activity: International.

Governing Board: Patricia Ireland (Pres.); Kim A. Gandy (Exec. Vice-Pres); Elizabeth Toledo (Education Vice-Pres.); Karen Johnson (Sec./Treas.).

Address: POB 1848, Merrifield, VA 22116-8048.

Fax: (202) 785-8576; **Internet:** www.nowfoundation.org.

National Science Foundation

Founded as an independent US Government agency to facilitate and fund research into solid-earth sciences.

Activities: Supports various scientific programmes: Archaeology Program; Arctic Research Program; Astronomy Support Programs, to promote fundamental research into matter, physical processes and other aspects of astronomy at one of the five National Astronomy Centers supported by the Foundation (located in the USA, Puerto Rico and Chile); Atmospheric Research Programs, to support research into the atmospheres of the sun, the earth and other planets at the National Center for Atmospheric Research, or at other institutions world-wide; Biomedical Engineering and Research to Aid Persons with Disabilities; Cultural Anthropology Program; Developmental Mechanisms Program; programmes in engineering, environmental biology, information and intelligent systems, molecular and cellular biosciences; the Earth Science Program to assist in the purchase of equipment for research and to support research in the structure and composition of the earth; Elementary,

Secondary and Informal Education programme; Human Cognition and Perception Program; International Opportunity for Scientists and Engineers programme; Linguistics Program; Mathematical and Physical Sciences Grant Program; Neuroscience Program; NSF Graduate Research Fellowships; NSF Minority Graduate Research Fellowships; NSF–NATO Post-doctoral Fellowships in Science and Engineering for closer collaboration between scientists of various countries (tenable in NATO member countries outside the USA); Oceanography Programs, supporting various research projects in the field of oceanographic sciences; Physical Anthropology Program, Physics Research Grants, Physiology and Ethology Program; Sensory Systems Program; Social Psychology Program; Teacher Enhancement Program; and US Antarctic Research Program.

Geographical Area of Activity: Mainly USA.

Publications: *Frontiers* (monthly newsletter).

Finance: Annual programmes budget approx. $5,480,000,000 (2004).

Principal Staff: Dir Dr Rita Colwell; Deputy Dir Dr Joseph Bordogna.

Address: 4201 Wilson Blvd, Arlington, VA 22230.

Telephone: (703) 292-8070; **Fax:** (703) 292-5090; **Internet:** www.nsf.gov; **e-mail:** info@nsf.gov.

National Wildlife Federation

Founded in 1936 to promote the study of wildlife, conservation and the environment, and to increase public awareness of such issues.

Activities: The organization provides fellowships, internships and awards. Environmental Conservation Fellowships are open to Canadian, Mexican and US citizens for advanced study in the USA or abroad. Internships are for work in the Resources Conservation Department in Washington, DC, and for research in the Institute for Wildlife Research. Environmental Publication Awards are offered to student publications in the field of environmental science. Runs various environmental educational programmes, including the Environmental Education Division Internships. Maintains the Institute for Wildlife Research.

Geographical Area of Activity: North America and Mexico.

Publications: *Conservation Directory* (annually); *Conservation Exchange* (quarterly); *EYAS* (newsletter, 3 a year); *International Wildlife* (6 year); *National Wildlife* (6 a year); *Ranger Rick* (monthly); *Your Big Backyard* (monthly); Annual Report; books, directories and reports.

Finance: Total revenue $112,009,000, total expenditure $124,811,000 (2001).

Directors: Bryan T. Pritchett (Chair.); and 27 others.

Principal Staff: Pres. and CEO Mark Van Putten.

Address: 11100 Wildlife Center Dr., Reston, VA 20190-5362.

Telephone: (703) 438-6000; **Internet:** www.nwf.org.

Nature Conservancy, Inc

Established in 1951 with the aim of saving the world's most beautiful areas for future generations.

Activities: Operates in the field of international conservation, working with governments, corporations and landowners as well as local people to help save and preserve land including forests, aquatic areas, prairies and deserts and the communities that support such areas.

Geographical Area of Activity: North, Central and South America and the Caribbean, USA, Asia and the Pacific.

Publications: *Nature Conservancy* (newsletter).

Finance: Assets $3,281,680 (June 2000); annual revenue $923,010, expenditure $1,031,808 (2002).

Governers: Anthony P. Grassi (Chair.); Carol E. Dinkins, Philip J. James, Leigh H. Perkins Jr (Vice-Chair.); Jan V. Portman (Sec.); John P. Morgridge (Treas.); and others.

Principal Staff: Pres. and Chief Exec. Stephen J. McCormick.

Address: 4245 N Fairfax Dr., Suite 100, Arlington, VA 22203-1606.

Telephone: (703) 841-5300; **Internet:** www.tnc.org; **e-mail:** comment@tnc.org.

NCSJ

Created in 1971 as the National Conference on Soviet Jewry; aims to safeguard the individual and communal political rights of Jews living in the former USSR as well as working to secure their religious and political freedoms.

Activities: Advocates on behalf of Jews in Russia, Ukraine, the Baltic states and the republics of Central Asia, and represents the American Jewish community abroad. Monitors compliance by the governments of the former USSR in the areas of free emigration and religious and cultural rights, and also monitors developments related to anti-Semitism in the former USSR. Runs Operation Lifeline, which provides materials, kosher food, and religious and cultural objects to Soviet Jews. Holds conferences, seminars and special events.

Geographical Area of Activity: Russia, Ukraine, Baltic states and the republics of Central Asia.

Restrictions: Not a grant-making organization.

Publications: *Newswatch*; Country Reports.

Trustees and officers: Dr Robert J. Meth (Chair.); Joel Schindler (Pres.); Terry Fisher, Sandra Goldberg, Yona Goldberg, Rabbi David Hill, Lesley Israel; Margery Kohrman (Vice-Pres.); Dr Judith Wolf (Treas.); Max R. Schrayer (Sec.).

Principal Staff: Exec. Dir Mark B. Levin.

Address: 1640 Rhode Island Ave, NW, Suite 501, Washington, DC 20036.

Telephone: (202) 898-2500; **Fax:** (202) 898-0822; **Internet:** www.ncsj.org; **e-mail:** ncsj@ncsj.org.

Near East Foundation

Founded in 1915 by Cleveland E. Dodge, Thomas Jesse Jones, Paul Monroe, Edwin M. Bulkley and Otis W. Caldwell, to offer people of developing nations technical assistance in the implementation of programmes of rural and community improvement.

Activities: Works in the Middle East and Africa on projects to increase food production, with related activities in rural and community development, and primary health care. The Foundation sends qualified technicians overseas to assist with transfer of technical skill and human resource development. It provides start-up funds for projects until support is available from local sources, and often works in co-operation with other donor agencies. The Foundation has offices in Egypt, Jordan, Lebanon, Lesotho, Mali, Morocco, Sudan, Swaziland and West Bank/Gaza.

Geographical Area of Activity: Middle East and Africa.

Restrictions: Operating rather than grant-making foundation.

Publications: Annual Report.

Finance: Net assets $6,921,981 (2002); annual revenue $1,492,524, expenditure $4,448,174 (2002).

Board of Trustees: Geoffrey A. Thompson (Chair.); David S. Dodge (Vice-Chair.); Antranig R. Sarkissian (Treas.); Richard H. Beahrs (Sec.).

Principal Staff: Pres. Ryan LaHurd; Pres. Emer. Richard C. Robarts; Chair. Geoffrey A. Thompson.

Address: 420 Lexington Ave, Suite 2516, New York, NY 10170-2599.

Telephone: (212) 867-0064; **Fax:** (212) 867-0169; **Internet:** www.neareast.org; **e-mail:** nef-hq@neareast.org.

Netaid.org Foundation

Established in 1999, an internet-based charity collaboration between the United Nations Development Programme (UNDP) and Cisco Systems that makes grants to alleviate poverty in developing countries. The Foundation is sponsored by a variety of companies and organizations.

Activities: Uses the internet to raise funds to alleviate extreme poverty. Makes grants to organizations carrying out innovative work in less-developed countries in the fields of aid, sustainable development, health care and education. All money donated to the Foundation is used to support programmes featured on the Netaid.org website.

Geographical Area of Activity: International.

Finance: Assets $12,114,462 (2000); total revenue $5,219,099, expenditure $4,172,725 (2000).

Board of Directors: Carol Bellamy; Mark Malloch Brown; Sharon Capeling-Alakija; John T. Chambers; Quincy Jones; Don Listwon; David Morrison.

Address: 267 5th Ave, 11th Floor, New York, NY 10016.

Telephone: (212) 537-0500; **Fax:** (212) 537-0501; **Internet:** www.netaid.org; **e-mail:** info@netaid.org.

New World Foundation

Founded in 1954 by Anita McCormick Blaine for the support of equal rights, public education, health care, community development and peaceful international relations.

Activities: The Foundation operates through four main programmes: Political Participation (including California Initiative and Southern Organizing); Environmental Justice; Economic Justice (the Phoenix Fund); and Media and Democracy. Emphasis is placed on youth, the community, enfranchisement of voters and democracy.

Restrictions: No grants are made to individuals.

Publications: Biennial Report.

Finance: Assets $40,977,065 (2000).

Board of Directors: Cindy C. Choi (Chair.); Scott Douglas (Vice-Chair.); George Friday (Sec.); Barbara Fiorito.

Principal Staff: Pres. Colin Greer.

Address: 666 West End Ave, New York, NY 10025.

Telephone: (212) 249-1023; **Fax:** (212) 472-0508; **Internet:** www.newwf.org; **e-mail:** info@newwf.org.

Newberry Library

Founded in 1887 at the bequest of Walter Loomis Newberry to collect, preserve and make available to readers books, journals, newspapers, maps, manuscripts and other library materials in history and the humanities; and to foster the use of these materials by all available means, including fellowships, lectures, seminars, exhibitions and publications.

Activities: Offers fellowships for scholars proposing to work in residence, and sponsors conferences, courses, publications, lectures and four research centres. The Library comprises more than one million volumes and five million manuscripts, and has strong general collections embracing history and the humanities within Western Europe and the Americas from the late Middle Ages to the early 20th century, and a specialization in genealogy.

Finance: Assets $77,549,000 (June 1999); annual revenue $10,116,000, expenditure $7,991,000 (1999).

Trustees: Charles C. Haffner, III (Chair.); Andrew W. McGhee, Kenneth Nebenzahl, Janis W. Notz (Vice-Chair.); Peter Van Cleave (Sec.); Cindy Mitchell (Acting Sec.); Roger S. Baskes (Treas.); and others.

Principal Staff: Pres. and Librarian Charles Cullen.

Address: 60 West Walton St, Chicago, IL 60610-3305.

Telephone: (312) 943-9090; **Internet:** www.newberry.org; **e-mail:** research@newberry.org.

Novartis US Foundation

Established in 1997 as part of Novartis Corporation's commitment to social investment in the USA. Aims to support social, health and education ventures initiated by communities and organizations.

Activities: Supports innovative biomedical science programmes and effective education in order to encourage the advancement of the life sciences. Also works to ensure that every young person in the USA has a good start in life with sufficient care and support for a healthy development.

Geographical Area of Activity: USA.

Restrictions: Grants only to US programmes.

Finance: Total assets $18,241,732 (Dec. 2000); total giving $794,220 (2000).

Principal Staff: Contact: Erin Hullstrum.

Address: Novartis Finance Corpn, 608 Fifth Ave, New York, NY 10020.

Internet: www.us.novartis.com/us_foundation.

Obor, The International Book Institute, Inc

International publishing support organization established in 1970, aiming to promote intellectual freedom.

Activities: Operates internationally in less-developed countries in the field of the arts and humanities. Encourages the translation, publication, and distribution of books in indigenous languages, by supporting small organizations that would not be able to succeed without financial assistance, and by providing training and advice. Involved in five major projects in Africa, Asia and the Middle East.

Geographical Area of Activity: Africa, Asia and the Middle East.

Principal Staff: Exec. Dir Donna K. Anderton.

Address: 1501 Cherry St, Philadelphia, PA 19102.

Telephone: (215) 636-0505; **Fax:** (215) 636-0705; **e-mail:** oborinc@aol.com.

John M. Olin Foundation

Founded in 1953 by John M. Olin to provide support for projects that reflect or are intended to strengthen the economic, political and cultural institutions upon which American democratic capitalism is based, and to promote understanding of these institutions through thoughtful study of the connections between economic and political freedoms and the cultural heritage that sustains them.

Activities: Operates through grant programmes for research, institutional support, fellowships, professorships, lectures, books, scholarly journals, conferences and seminars, and radio and television programmes, in the areas of justice and the law, economics, the media, communications, international studies, political science, weapons control, public policy and education and welfare.

Geographical Area of Activity: USA.

Restrictions: No unsolicited proposals; no grants for endowments, capital building work, annual giving programmes, individuals, nor for projects without a direct national impact.

Publications: Annual Report.

Finance: Total assets $71,196,916 (2001); total grants $20,486,946 (2001).

Officers and Trustees: Eugene F. Williams, Jr (Chair.); George J. Gillespie, III (Pres. and Treas.); James Piereson (Sec.); Peter M. Flanigan; Richard M. Furlaud; Charles F. Knight;.

Principal Staff: Exec. Dir James Piereson.

Address: 330 Madison Ave, 22nd Floor, New York, NY 10017.

Telephone: (212) 661-2670; **Fax:** (212) 661-5917; **Internet:** www.jmof.org; **e-mail:** inquiry@imof.org.

Pierre Omidyar Family Foundation

Founded by Pierre Omidyar, founder of eBay, in 1999; the Foundation aims to promote the importance of the community in improving quality of life for everyone.

Activities: Supports educational organizations and provides seed grants to non-profits to enable them to build sustainable income streams, followed by further support to enable organizations develop their activities in the long term.

Beneficiaries include New Profit Venture, Inc, Pittsburgh University, Tufts University and the Omidyar Institute. Also sponsors conferences.

Geographical Area of Activity: USA.

Restrictions: No unsolicited applications accepted.

Finance: Annual revenue $20,362,910, expenditure $2,326,015 (2000).

Trustees: Pierre Omidyar (Pres.); Michael Mohr (Treas.).

Principal Staff: CEO Iqbal Paroo; Vice-Pres. Direct Community Experience Deborah Alvarez-Rodriguez; Vice-Pres. Finance and Admin. Edward Diener; Vice-Pres. Strategic Technology Matt Hamilton; Vice-Pres. Civic Engagement Lisa Spinali.

Address: 2483 East Bayshore Rd, Suite 212, Palo Alto, CA 94303.

Telephone: (650) 846-2560; **Internet:** www.omidyar.org; **e-mail:** info@omidyar.org.

Open Society Institute

Founded in December 1993 by George Soros, the Open Society Institute assists the work of the national foundations in Central and Eastern Europe, promotes the development of open societies, encourages public debate on policy alternatives in controversial areas and manages many regional programmes conducted throughout Central and Eastern Europe and the countries of the former USSR. The New York office acts as the administrative, financial and communications headquarters of the Soros foundations network.

Activities: The Open Society Institute assists the network of Soros foundations world-wide, by providing administrative, financial and technical support, and by operating OSI initiatives which provide administrative, financial and technical support to the Soros foundations and also OSI initiatives, which address specific issues on a regional or network-wide basis, and other independent programmes. The Institute is also the home of a series of programmes that focus principally on the USA. In the American capital, the OSI Washington office engages in public education on a range of domestic and international issues, including criminal and civil justice reform, women's rights, US policy in Colombia, and Central Eurasia. The Open Society Policy Center, a separate organization that is incorporated as a 501(c)(4) non-profit, undertakes lobbying efforts on these and other public policy issues. The Institute's initiatives address specific issue areas on a regional or network-wide basis around the world. Most of the initiatives are administerd by OSI in New York or OSI–Budapest (q.v.) and implemented in co-operation with Soros foundations in various countries. The nearly 20 OSI initiatives cover a range of activities aimed at building free and open societies, including the strengthening of civil society; economic reform; education at all levels; human rights; legal reform and public administration; media and communications; public health; and arts and culture. OSI in New York also operates special initiatives such as the Central Eurasia Project, the Burma Project/Southeast Asia Initiative, and the European Union Accession Monitoring Program. The OSI's US programmes support initiatives in a range of social areas, including access to justice for low- and moderate-income people; independence of the judiciary; ending the death penalty; reducing gun violence and over-reliance on incarceration; drug policy reform; inner-city education and youth programmes; reproductive health and choice; campaigning on finance reform; and improved care of the dying.

Geographical Area of Activity: Central and Eastern Europe, the countries of the former USSR, Myanmar, Haiti, Guadeloupe, Southern and Western Africa, and the USA.

Publications: Annual Report; *Open Society News* (quarterly newsletter); leaflets and directory of Soros foundations.

Finance: Total network expenditure $452,666,000 (2001).

Trustees: George Soros (Chair.); Aryeh Neier (Pres.); Morton Abramowitz; Leon Botstein; Geoffrey Canada; Joan B. Dunlop; Lani Guinier; David J. Rothman; Thomas M. Scanlon, Jr; John G. Simon; Herbert Sturz.

Principal Staff: Pres. Aryeh Neier; Exec. Vice-Pres. Stewart J. Paperin.

Address: 400 West 59th St, New York, NY 10019.

Telephone: (212) 548-0600; **Fax:** (212) 548-4679; **Internet:** www.soros.org/osiny.html; **e-mail:** info@soros.org.

Operation Rainbow, Inc

Founded in 1978 by Dr William B. Riley, Jr to provide free reconstructive surgery for underprivileged children in the USA and in developing countries around the world.

Activities: Operates in the field of medicine and health care, by raising money from individuals, foundations and corporations to fund reconstructive surgery (plastic and orthopaedic) to be performed by volunteer sugeons on children with medical problems in Asia, Central and South America and the USA. Also provides teaching and training for local medical staff overseas, and runs a sponsorship programme, so that nurses and physicians from abroad are sponsored to come to the USA for additional training.

Geographical Area of Activity: Asia, Central and South America, and the USA.

Finance: Funded by donations and volunteer support.

Principal Staff: Pres. and CEO Bill Magee.

Address: POB 571017, Houston, TX 77257-1017.

Telephone: (281) 980-7800; **Fax:** (281) 960-7803; **Internet:** www.operationrainbow.org; **e-mail:** tinabreskamedlin@operationrainbow.org.

Operation USA

Established in 1979 as Operation California; aims to mitigate the effects of poverty and the results of natural and man-made disasters in the USA and abroad.

Activities: Provides emergency medical, nutritional and shelter supplies to victims of poverty and disaster throughout Asia, Africa, Central and South America and the Caribbean, Eastern Europe and the Balkans. Also runs a domestic disaster response programme, micro-enterprise initiatives, a community clinic support programme in the USA, and initiated Operation Landmine in 1995 in order to engage in de-mining activities around the world.

Geographical Area of Activity: International.

Finance: Assets $1,836,254 (June 2002); annual revenue $3,943,165, expenditure $7,574,933 (2002).

Directors: J. Estrin (Chair.); S. Frileck (Vice-Chair.); T. Adams; J. Andrews Edwards; B. Edwards; R. Joffé; G. Larsen; M. Mahdesian; T. Moore, Jr; Dr P. O'Rourke; P. Patri; D. Shearer; C. Sparv Kolber; M. Starr; L. Vernon; R. Walden; L. L. Whitney.

Principal Staff: CEO and Pres. Richard M. Walden.

Address: 8320 Melrose Ave, Suite 200, Los Angeles, CA 90069.

Telephone: (323) 658-8876; **Fax:** (323) 653-7846; **Internet:** www.opusa.org; **e-mail:** opusa@opusa.org.

Opportunity International

Established with the aim of transforming the lives of those living in chronic poverty, through job creation, small business development and community support; a network of 52 autonomous affiliated implementing partners in developing countries world-wide and seven support partners in developed countries.

Activities: Operates internationally in collaboration with indigenous partner organizations in the areas of aid to less-developed countries and social welfare, through promoting micro-enterprise schemes to combat poverty and offering loans and basic business training. Founded the Women's Opportunity Fund, which manages an annual buget of $1,650,000.

Geographical Area of Activity: Africa, Asia, Central and Eastern Europe, Central and South America and the Caribbean.

Board of Directors: David L. Simms (Chair.).

Principal Staff: Pres. and CEO Charles L. Dokmo.

Address: Network Office, 2122 York Rd, Suite 340, Oak Brook, IL 60523.

Telephone: (630) 645-4100; **Fax:** (630) 645-1458; **Internet:** www.opportunity.org; **e-mail:** getinfo@opportunity.org.

Orbis International

Established to reduce preventable blindness throughout the world through training, health education and improved access to eye care.

Activities: The organization started its work by building a mobile teaching eye hospital—a fully-equipped aeroplane—to travel around the world training doctors and medical staff in developing countries, transferring knowledge and skills through lectures and training. Since then, Orbis has expanded to include specialized training programmes and community health projects, in order to further improve the standard of eye care in less-developed countries where a large percentage of blindness is due to preventable conditions. Currently operates projects in Bangladesh, China, Ethiopia, India and Vietnam.

Geographical Area of Activity: International.

Finance: Annual budget $27,155,108.

Directors: A. L. Ueltschi (Chair.); P. P. Mullen (Sec.); L. P. Cook (Treas.); D. O. Barber; E. T. Cloonan; B. Trippe DeVecchi; D. FitzGerald; Hon. O. I. Foot; G. Greenwald; D. Merrill Hartley; T. Knight, Jr; R. T. Lewis; R. C. E. Morgan; A. D. Palmer; L. J. Ramer; J. Virgil Waggoner.

Principal Staff: Pres. and Exec. Dir Kathy Spahn.

Address: 520 8th Ave, 11th Floor, New York, NY 10018.

Telephone: (646) 674-5500; **Fax:** (646) 674-5599; **Internet:** www.orbis.org; **e-mail:** executive@ny.orbis.org.

Orentreich Foundation for the Advancement of Science, Inc

Founded in 1961 and classified as an operating private foundation in 1972, the Foundation carries out its own research and/or collaborates with other institutions on projects which aim to prevent or reverse disorders decreasing length of, or quality of, life.

Activities: Operates in the field of medicine and health, through conferences, seminars and research, which it carries out at its biomedical research centre in New York state.

Publications: Annual Director's Report.

Finance: Total assets $47,239,608 (2000).

Officers and Directors: Norman Orentreich (Pres.); Edward I. Klar, Sari Mass, Catherine Orentreich, David Orentreich (Vice-Pres); Fay Pines (Treas.).

Principal Staff: Dir Norman Orentreich; Assoc. Dir David Orentreich.

Address: 910 Fifth Ave, New York, NY 10021-4187.

Telephone: (212) 606-0877; **Internet:** www.orentreich.org.

Outreach International

Incorporated in April 1979; an international development organization that aims to alleviate suffering in the world.

Activities: Works to eliminate the poverty, hunger and disease suffered by people around the world by providing long-term solutions, through Participatory Human Development, a non-directive process designed to involve the poor in the decisions that affect them in order that they can learn to sustain themselves.

Geographical Area of Activity: North, Central and South America and the Caribbean, Africa and Asia.

Publications: *Outreach Developments* (quarterly newsletter).

Finance: Total assets $1,000,000 (2002); annual revenue $1,600,000, total expenditure $1,800,000 (2002).

Board of Directors: Prof. Steven L. Anders (Chair.).

Principal Staff: Pres. Dr William T. Higdon; Chief Financial Officer and Treas. Exec. Dir Russell R. Fletcher.

Address: POB 210, Independence, MO 64051-0210.

Telephone: (816) 833-0883; **Fax:** (816) 833-0103; **Internet:** www.outreach-international.org; **e-mail:** info@outreach-international.org.

Pacific Ocean Research Foundation

Founded in 1977 by Peter S. Fithian to promote research involving pelagic fish, with special emphasis on billfish, tuna and related species.

Activities: Operates nationally and internationally in the fields of conservation and the environment, education and science and technology, through research, grants to institutions and individuals, and publications. Has established tag and release programmes in the Pacific Basin, enabling the study of migratory patterns. Maintains a scientific laboratory and library. Works under the guidance of a scientific advisory board, which comprises internationally recognized experts in the fields of billfish and tuna biology.

Geographical Area of Activity: Pacific.

Publications: *Pacific Ocean Research News* (quarterly); over 65 scientific publications.

Address: POB 4800, 74–381 Kealakehe Parkway, Suite C, Kailua-Kona, HI 96740.

Telephone: (808) 329-6105; **Fax:** (808) 329-1148; **Internet:** holoholo.org/porf.

David and Lucile Packard Foundation

Founded in 1964 by David and Lucile Packard to support projects in the areas of child development and health, family planning, education, the environment and conservation, marine sciences and global population studies.

Activities: Primarily concerned with supporting local projects; however, the Foundation also offers support in the fields of conservation, population studies, children, family and communities, arts, science, organizational effectiveness and philanthropy in Central and South America, particularly Mexico and Colombia. In 1996 the Foundation received 46.6 million shares in the Hewlett Packard company; this extra income has allowed an expansion of geographical focus.

Geographical Area of Activity: North, Central and South America.

Restrictions: No grants are made to individuals.

Publications: Annual report; grants list; occasional report; information brochure; programme policy statement; programme area publications.

Finance: Assets $6,196,520,868 (Dec. 2001); expenditure $428,897,276 (Dec. 2001).

Trustees: Susan Packard Orr (Chair.); Nancy Packard Burnett, Carol S. Larson, Julie E. Packard (Vice-Chair.); George E. Vera (Vice-Pres. and Chief Financial Officer); Barbara P. Wright (Sec.); Colburn S. Wilbur; Robin Chandler Duke; Robert J. Glaser; Jane Lubchenko; Dean O. Morton; Franklin M. Orr, Jr; Lew Platt; William K. Reilly; Frank Roberts; Alan Rosenfield; Richard D. Schlosberg; Robert Stephens; E. van Bronkhorst.

Principal Staff: Pres. and CEO Richard D. Schlosberg III; Vice-Pres. Carol S. Larson.

Address: 300 Second St, Suite 200, Los Altos, CA 94022.

Telephone: (650) 948-7658; **Internet:** www.packfound.org.

Pact

Established in 1971 to assist indigenous organizations working for development.

Activities: Runs its own development programmes throughout Africa, Asia, and South America alongside partner organizations and local NGOs. Projects deal with areas including food security, education, health (HIV/AIDS), micro-credit and small enterprise, capacity building, women's empowerment, increasing the effectiveness of grass-roots civil society organizations, and rural development. Maintains 18 field offices.

Geographical Area of Activity: Africa, Asia, and South America.

Restrictions: This is not a grant-making organization, although does provide financial resources to local partner organizations.

Publications: Publishes a number of books related to the areas in which Pact works.

Board of Trustees: Dr Ruth Morgenthau (Chair.); Louis Stamberg (Vice-Chair.).

Principal Staff: Pres. and CEO Sarah Newhall; Vice-Pres. Programs Jeff Whisenant.

Address: 1200 18th St, NW, Suite 350, Washington, DC 20036.

Telephone: (202) 466-5666; **Fax:** (202) 466-5669; **Internet:** www.pactworld.org; **e-mail:** pact@pacthq.org.

Pan American Development Foundation—PADF

Founded in 1962 to promote social and economic development of the Americas.

Activities: The Foundation's primary objective is to assist in bringing technical expertise and resources to Central and South America and the Caribbean, as well as providing disaster assistance. Main project areas are the strengthening of local civic institutions, sustainable agricultural production, increasing family incomes, and family health promotion. The Foundation operates in partnership with local organizations, with multinational corporations, private businesses and NGOs in the region, along with the US Government and non-governmental inter-American organizations.

Geographical Area of Activity: Central and South America and the Caribbean.

Publications: Annual Report; *PADF Newsletter* (2 a year); technical publications.

Finance: Annual budget approx. $20,000,000.

Trustees and Officers: César Gaviria (Chair.).

Principal Staff: Exec. Dir John Sanbrailo.

Address: Organization of American States Bldg, 2600 16th St, NW, 4th Floor, Washington, DC 20009-4202.

Telephone: (202) 458-3969; **Fax:** (202) 458-6316; **Internet:** www.padf.org; **e-mail:** padf-dc@padf.org.

Pan American Health and Education Foundation

Founded in 1968 to promote and stimulate efforts to combat disease, lengthen life and promote physical and mental health in the Western hemisphere, and in particular Central and South America; to promote the improvement and expansion of health and medical care services, the expansion of water supplies and sanitation facilities, and the level of nutrition; to promote the education and training of health care workers; and to foster research, charitable, scientific and educational projects.

Activities: Operates, mainly in Central and South America, in the field of medicine and health, through self-conducted programmes, awarding prizes and issuing publications. Supports health and education projects (administers about 100 projects annually). Collaborates in a programme making textbooks and instructional materials available for the training of health personnel, and with similar organizations and governmental and international bodies sharing its objectives (primarily the Pan American Health Organization and the World Health Organization). The Foundation makes several awards: the Abraham Horwitz Award for Inter-American Health, the Clarence H. Moore Award for outstanding contribution in health by national or local not-for-profit organizations in Central and South America or the Caribbean, the Pedro Acha Award for Veterinary Public Health and the Fred L. Soper Award for outstanding contributions to health in the Americas.

Geographical Area of Activity: Central and South America.

Restrictions: The Foundation does not encourage unsolicited proposals.

Publications: *Medicamentos y Terapeutica* (quarterly); manuals for primary health care.

Finance: Net assets approx. $20,000,000.

Trustees and Directors: Malden C. Nesheim (Chair.) Dr Enrique J. Guardia (Vice-Chair.); Dr Nancy E. Moss (Sec.); Eric J. Boswell (Treas.); Dr William Bertrand; Sandra de Castro Buffington; Dr William Hubbard; Dr Margaret Marshall; Dr Mirta Roses; Dr Arnold Simonse.

Principal Staff: Exec. Dir Dr Mirta Roses Periago.

Address: 525 23rd St, NW, Washington, DC 20037.

Telephone: (202) 974-3000; **Fax:** (202) 974-3663; **Internet:** www.paho.org/english/pahef; **e-mail:** pahef@paho.org.

Panasonic Foundation

Established in 1984 by Matsushita Electrical Corporation of America (MECA), and formerly known as the Matsushita Foundation, a subsidiary company of the Japan-based Matsushita Electrical Industrial Co. Ltd.

Activities: The Foundation operates in the field of education, through partnerships with a small number of school districts, which are provided with direct technical assistance to bring about school reform.

Geographical Area of Activity: USA.

Restrictions: Does not make grants.

Publications: Newsletter.

Finance: Total assets $21,539,771 (2001); total grants $1,646,689 (2001).

Officers and Trustees: R. S. Ingersoll (Chair.); L. Levine (Sec.); R. Pagano (Treas.); S. Sa (Exec. Dir); R. LeFauve; P. Liao; D. Meier; M. Myerson; I. Perlman.

Principal Staff: Exec. Dir Sophie Sa; Asst Dir Scott Thompson; Programme Co-ordinator Jennifer Yousif; Financial Analyst Eileen Murphy; Sec. Kathleen Archetti.

Address: 1 Panasonic Way 1F-5, Secaucus, NJ 07094.

Telephone: (201) 392-4132; **Fax:** (201) 392-4126; **Internet:** www.panasonic.com/meca/foundation/foundation.html; **e-mail:** info@foundation.panasonic.com.

Parkinson's Disease Foundation, Inc

Founded in 1957 by William Black to raise funds in order to plan, undertake, support and promote investigation into the cause and cure of Parkinson's disease and related disorders, and to provide patients suffering from the disease with a better quality of life. Merged with the United Parkinson Foundation, Chicago in 1999.

Activities: Operates nationally and internationally; funds research into aspects of Parkinson's disease, makes grants to institutions and individuals, awards scholarships and fellowships, holds conferences, runs advisory services and issues publications. Programmes include an International Research Grants Program; H. Houston Merritt Fellowship Program; and Summer Fellowship Program; and a post-doctoral programme.

Geographical Area of Activity: Mainly USA, although international grants are available.

Publications: Annual Report; *PDF Newsletter; PDF Science Bulletin; Progress, Promise and Hope!; Exercises for the Parkinson Patient; The Parkinson Patient at Home;* leaflets and brochures.

Officers and Directors: Mrs William Black (Chair.); Lewis P. Rowland (Pres.); Edward M. Kalikow (Treas.); Isobel Robins Konecky (Sec.); Stanley Fahn (Scientific Dir); and 14 others.

Principal Staff: Exec. Dir Robert Elliot; Asst Dir Renay Crooms.

Address: William Black Medical Research Bldg, 710 West 168th St, New York, NY 10032-9982.

Telephone: (212) 923-4700; **Fax:** (212) 923-4778; **Internet:** www.pdf.org; **e-mail:** info@pdf.org.

Albert Parvin Foundation

Founded in 1960 by Albert B. Parvin to promote peace, understanding and goodwill among the nations of the world through education, enlightenment and recognition of achievements toward this objective.

Activities: Operates both nationally and internationally in the fields of social welfare and education, through grants for child welfare, social service agencies and medical research; and through fellowships tenable at Princeton University and the University of California at Los Angeles by students from new and less-developed nations. Also funds a journalism studies fellowship at the University of Hawaii for journalists from the People's Republic of China, in conjunction with the Freedom Forum (q.v.).

Restrictions: No loans or grants are made to individuals.

Finance: Total assets $8,420,821 (2001); total expenditure $381,156 (2001).

Officers and Directors: Phyllis Parvin (Pres.); Harvey G. Joffe (Chief Financial Officer); Stanley Parvin; Mary C. Rudin; Bernard Silbert; Steven Silbert.

Address: 10880 Wilshire Blvd, No. 520, Los Angeles, CA 90024.

Telephone: (310) 475-5676.

PATH—Program for Appropriate Technology in Health

Non-profit international organization that aims to improve health, especially that of women and children.

Activities: Operates in less-developed countries in the fields of medicine and health, and social welfare. Works to identify, develop and carry out solutions to global health problems, through programmes that aim to improve women's health, children's health, and to stop the spread of infectious diseases, largely through immunization (PATH operates the Bill and Melinda Gates Children's Vaccine Programme). This is done by the exchange of knowledge and technology with governments and local NGOs in developing countries. An emphasis is placed on improving the quality of reproductive health services available. Maintains offices in Cambodia, France, India, Indonesia, Kenya, the Philippines, Thailand, Ukraine, Vietnam, Seattle and Washington, DC, and an affiliated organization in Canada.

Geographical Area of Activity: International.

Directors: Dr Halida Hanum Akhter (Chair.); Dr Horacio B. Croxarro (Vice-Chair.); Christopher Hedrick (Treas.); Molly Joel Coyle; Steve Davis; Mahmoud Fahmy Fathalla; Vincent McGee; Jane Mutambirwa; Dr Kharma Odera Rogo; Ajarie Visessiri.

Address: 1455 NW Leary Way, Seattle, WA 98107-5136.

Telephone: (206) 285-3500; **Fax:** (206) 285-6619; **Internet:** www.path.org; **e-mail:** info@path.org.

Pathfinder International

Incorporated as the Pathfinder Fund in 1957 by Dr Clarence Gamble to introduce better family planning information and facilities around the world.

Activities: Works to improve reproductive health services in the developing world, aiming thereby to improve the lives of women and their families, particularly in the areas of improving access to services, advocacy work, AIDS and abortion services. Funds and participates in national family planning programmes in Africa, Central and South America and the Caribbean, and Asia.

Geographical Area of Activity: Africa, Central and South America and the Caribbean, and Asia.

Publications: Annual Report; medical training modules and organizational publications.

Finance: Total revenue $49,672,616, expenditure $47,892,202 (June 2001).

Directors: Mary B. Hewlett (Chair.); Dr Henry W. Foster, Jr (Vice-Chair.); Julia G. Kahrl (Sec.); Susan S. Swift (Treas.); and 29 others.

Principal Staff: Pres. Daniel E. Pellegrom.

Address: 9 Galen St, Suite 217, Watertown, MA 02472-4501.

Telephone: (617) 924-7200; **Fax:** (617) 924-3833; **Internet:** www.pathfind.org; **e-mail:** information@pathfind.org.

Alicia Patterson Foundation

Founded in 1965 by members of the Albright and Patterson families to support print journalists.

Activities: Awards one-year fellowships to journalists or photo-journalists with at least five years' experience who are US citizens. Fellowship recipients pursue independent projects of significant interest in the USA or overseas.

Geographical Area of Activity: USA.

Restrictions: Fellowships only open to US citizens, or non-US citizens who work on US print publications. No grants are made for academic study.

Publications: *APF Reporter* (quarterly); web magazine; Annual Report; information brochure.

Finance: Assets $5,278,000 (2003); annual revenue $345,000, expenditure $410,000 (2003).

Trustees: Joseph P. Albright (Chair); Alice Arlen (Pres.); Cathy Trost (Treas.); Adam M. Albright, Blandina Albright (Vice-Pres); M. Engel (Sec. and Exec. Dir); Kai Bird; Patrick Hoge.

Principal Staff: Exec. Dir Margaret Engel.

Address: 1730 Pennsylvania Ave, NW, Suite 850, Washington, DC 20006.

Telephone: (202) 393-5995; **Fax:** (301) 951-8512; **Internet:** www.aliciapatterson.org; **e-mail:** info@aliciapatterson.org.

Pax World Service

Founded in 1971 as Pax World Foundation; the organization is dedicated to the cause of world peace and international development.

Activities: Initiates and supports programmes that promote peace-making and reconciliation, diplomacy, human rights, civil society and sustainable development. It also provides disaster relief. Affiliated with Mercy Corps (q.v.). Operates through initiating and promoting student exchanges between US students wanting to study abroad and foreign students coming to the USA.

Geographical Area of Activity: International.

Publications: Annual Report.

Finance: Receives funding from the Pax World Balanced Fund social investment fund.

Standing Committee: W. Harvey Wise (Chair.); Ed Bartholomew; Malcolm Butler; Jack Corbett; Diana Dajani; Joseph Eldridge; Lois Herrmann; Arthur Johnson; Luke Lee; Douglas Nelson.

Principal Staff: Pres. Dr Landrum Bolling.

Address: 1400 16th St, NW, 7th Floor, Washington, DC 20036.

Internet: www.paxworld.org; **e-mail:** info@paxworld.org.

PepsiCo Foundation, Inc

Founded in 1962 by PepsiCo, Inc and Frito-Lay, Inc.

Activities: The Foundation provides financial support to non-profit organizations where employees of PepsiCo are involved as volunteers. Organizations involved in the areas of education, medicine and health, the arts and humanities, and social welfare are the most likely beneficiaries.

Geographical Area of Activity: USA.

Publications: Information brochure.

Finance: Assets $34,237,000 (Dec. 1999).

Officers and Directors: Roger A. Enrico (Chair.); Joseph F. McCann (Pres.); Jacqueline R. Millan (Vice-Pres., Contributions); Kathleen Luke (Sec.); D. Wayne Calloway; Ronald E. Harrison; Donald M. Kendall; Indra Nooyi; Stephen S. Reinemund.

Address: 700 Anderson Hill Rd, Purchase, NY 10577.

Telephone: (914) 253-2000.

Pesticide Action Network North America—PANNA

Founded in 1982 as a regional centre of the PAN International network, to campaign for safer forms of pest control in Canada, Mexico and the USA.

Activities: Promotes healthier and more effective methods of pest-control to replace harmful pesticides, through research, policy development, media coverage, education and international advocacy campaigns. Provides activists, researchers and policy-makers with technical information, analysis, training, campaign support and policy guidance. Enlists the support of numerous health, consumer, agricultural and environmental groups throughout North America to eliminate harmful pesticide use.

Geographical Area of Activity: North and Central America.

Publications: *Partners Update* (newsletter); *Global Pesticide Campaigner;* numerous articles, guides, reports, videos and databases.

Directors: Rajiv Bhatia; Dick Bunce; Ignacio H. Chapela; J. D. Doliner; John Harrinton; Reggie James; María Elena Martínez-Torrez; Rob McConnell; S. Ravi Rajan; Pat Scott; Kay Treakle.

Address: 49 Powell St, Suite 500, San Francisco, CA 94102.

Telephone: (415) 981-1771; **Fax:** (415) 981-1991; **Internet:** www.panna.org; **e-mail:** panna@panna.org.

The Pew Charitable Trusts

The Pew Charitable Trusts include the Pew Memorial Trust (founded in 1948), the J. N. Pew, Jr Charitable Trust (founded in 1956), the J. Howard Pew Freedom Trust, the Mabel Pew Myrin Trust and the Mary Anderson Trust (all founded in 1957), the Knollbrook Trust (founded in 1965) and the Medical Trust (founded in 1979).

Activities: The Trusts support non-profit activities in the areas of culture, education, the environment, health and human services, public policy and religion. Strategic investments are made to help organizations and citizens develop practical solutions to difficult problems. A Venture Fund invests in projects falling outside the six programme areas and typically involves significant risk combined with high potential for impact, leveraging opportunities and innovation.

Geographical Area of Activity: USA, with a special emphasis on the Philadelphia area.

Restrictions: No grants are made to individuals, for scholarships, nor for endowment funds.

Publications: *Program Resource Guide; Trust* (quarterly magazine); strategy papers; reports; and other publications.

Finance: Assets $3,821,000,000 (2002); grant commitments $166,033,000 (2002).

Officers and Directors: Rebecca W. Rimel (Pres. and CEO).

Address: 1 Commerce Sq., Suite 1700, 2005 Market St, Philadelphia, PA 19103-7017.

Telephone: (215) 575-9050; **Fax:** (215) 575-4939; **Internet:** www.pewtrusts.com; **e-mail:** info@pewtrusts.com.

Pfizer Foundation

Independent charitable organization founded in 1953 by Pfizer Inc.

Activities: Operates in areas where the Pfizer company has offices. Promotes access to health care and education, encourages and develops innovation, and supports the community involvement of Pfizer workers. Provides disaster relief in the form of funding and gifts-in-kind.

Geographical Area of Activity: International.

Restrictions: Unsolicited proposals are discouraged, but not refused.

Finance: Total assets $392,848,769 (Dec. 2000); total giving $17,228,882 (2000).

Principal Staff: Grants Assoc. Paget Walker.

Address: Philanthropy Programs, Pfizer Inc, 235 East 42nd St, New York, NY 10017.

Telephone: (212) 733-4250; **Internet:** www.pfizer.com /pfizerinc/philanthropy.

Carl and Lily Pforzheimer Foundation, Inc

Founded in 1942 by members of the Pforzheimer family for general charitable purposes.

Activities: Operates primarily in the field of American and English literature, in collaboration with libraries and educational institutions, through publications and through the Carl H. Pforzheimer Library. Support is given to certain selected institutions active in the fields of education, medicine, social welfare and the arts.

Geographical Area of Activity: USA.

Finance: Assets $42,081,769 (Dec. 2001); grants expenditure $6,908,349 (2001).

Officers and Directors: Carl H. Pforzheimer, III (Pres. and Treas.).

Address: 650 Madison Ave, 23rd Floor, New York, NY 10022.

Telephone: (212) 223-6500.

Physicians for Human Rights—PHR

Founded in 1986, PHR aims to mobilize members of the medical profession to encourage public support for global human rights issues.

Activities: Uses medical and scientific methods to research and expose human rights violations around the world and campaigns to stop such violations. Educates health professionals about these issues and encourages them to become active in the fight against human rights abuses.

Geographical Area of Activity: International.

Publications: *Measuring Landmine Incidents and Injuries; War Crimes in Kosovo: A Population Based Assessment of Human Rights Violations Against Kosovar Albanians; Endless Brutality: War Crimes in Chechnya; Women's Health and Human Rights in Afghanistan; The Record* (newsletter, 3 a year); audio tapes; journals.

Board of Directors: Holly G. Atkinson (Pres.); Frank Davidoff (Vice-Pres.).

Principal Staff: Exec. Dir Leonard Rubenstein.

Address: 100 Boylston St, Suite 702, Boston, MA 02116.

Telephone: (617) 695-0041; **Fax:** (617) 695-0307; **Internet:** www.phrusa.org; **e-mail:** phrusa@phrusa.org.

Plenty International

Established in 1974 by the Farm community, a non-government alternative organization aiming to help share the world's resources and knowledge.

Activities: Facilitates the exchange of technology, skills, information and friendship between communities and cultures by sending volunteers to areas of need around the world, who work on sustainable development projects relating to health care, education, food and nutrition (particularly soya nutrition). Works on long-term projects in Central America, West Africa and the USA, especially with Native Americans.

Geographical Area of Activity: North and Central America, and Mexico and the Caribbean.

Publications: *The Plenty Bulletin* (quarterly newsletter).

Finance: Funded by individuals and foundations; annual budget approx. $250,000.

Board of Trustees: Bruce Curtis (Chair.); Lisa Wartinger (Pres.); Carol Nelson (Sec. and Treas.); Sofia Casini; Tom Cook; Karen Heikkala; Kathryn Hutchens; Jeff Keating; Patricia O'Bannon.

Principal Staff: Exec. Dir Peter Schweitzer.

Address: POB 394, Summertown, TN 38483.

Telephone: (931) 964-4323; **Fax:** (931) 964-4864; **Internet:** www.plenty.org; **e-mail:** plenty@plenty.org.

Ploughshares Fund

Public foundation founded in 1981 to help prevent the spread of nuclear weapons, control the sale of conventional weapons, take steps toward preventing armed conflict, and to build global and regional security.

Activities: Operates on an international basis in the fields of weapons control and international conflict resolution, particularly in the USA, Europe, Asia, the Middle East, the Russian Federation, the Democratic People's Republic of Korea and Japan. Grants are made for projects, research, conferences and to individuals.

Geographical Area of Activity: International.

Publications: Annual Report; grants list; newsletter (quarterly).

Finance: Assets $22,061,594 (June 2002); income $14,524,610, expenditure $5,174,083 (2002).

Officers and Directors: Lewis H. Butler (Chair.); Sally Lilienthal (Pres.); Thomas C. Layton (Sec.); Patricia E. Sullivan (Treas.); James B. Blume; Anne H. Ehrlich; Mary Lloyd Estrin; Angela Foster; Roger L. Hale; David Holloway; Alastair Mactaggart; Lynda Palevsky; Michael L. Parker; Robert A. Rubinstein; Lynde B. Uihlein; Brooks Walker, III; Edith B. Wilkie.

Principal Staff: Exec. Dir Naila Bolus.

Address: Fort Mason Center, Bldg B, Suite 330, San Francisco, CA 94123.

Telephone: (415) 775-2244; **Fax:** (415) 775-4529; **Internet:** www.ploughshares.org; **e-mail:** ploughshares@ploughshares.org.

Pollock–Krasner Foundation, Inc

Founded in 1985 by Lee Krasner to support artists.

Activities: The Foundation awards grants to professional, working artists in the fields of sculpture, painting, works on paper and printmaking. Since 1985 the Foundation has awarded over 2,100 grants totalling over $30,000,000 to artists in 62 countries.

Geographical Area of Activity: International.

Restrictions: No grants are made for academic study, nor to commercial artists, photographers, performance artists, video artists, film-makers or artisans.

Publications: Annual Report.

Finance: Total assets $59,070,084 (June 2001); total grants $3,290,400 (2001).

Board of Directors: Charles C. Bergman (Chair.); Eugene Victor Thaw (Pres.); Kerrie Buitrago (Exec. Vice-Pres.).

Principal Staff: Programme Officer Caroline Black.

Address: 863 Park Ave, New York, NY 10021.

Telephone: (212) 517-5400; **Fax:** (212) 288-2836; **Internet:** www.pkf.org; **e-mail:** grants@pkf.org.

Poniecki Foundation

Founded in 1990 by W. I. Poniecki and previously known as the Wladyslaw Poniecki Charitable Foundation. Aims to enhance education through technology, and to support activities in developing countries, especially emerging market economies.

Activities: Operates in the fields of education and technology. Its main programmes concentrate on internet training for librarians, but other work includes the translation of workbooks relating to technology and software, publishing educational books in the areas of medicine, business, the environment and education, and the stimulation of grass-roots, professional, non-profit associations. Work is principally centered in Central and Eastern Europe, but the foundation is not restricted to this area and its expertise is also applicable to other parts of the developing world.

Geographical Area of Activity: Mainly Central and Eastern Europe.

Finance: Funded by private donations, corporate and government grants, and support from other foundations.

Directors: W. M. Grycz (Pres.); M. Dodds Grycz (Vice-Pres.); C. J. Grycz (Exec. Sec.); A. van der Vant; E. Witkowska.

Address: 8637 Arbor Dr., El Cerrito, CA 94530-2728.

Telephone: (415) 732-6172; **Fax:** (510) 527-4512; **Internet:** www.poniecki.org; **e-mail:** grycz@poniecki.org.

Population Action International

Established to promote voluntary family planning and reproductive health services so as to slow world-wide population growth.

Activities: Operates in the areas of health and welfare, through advocating voluntary family planning and related health services, particularly for women and girls. Also promotes educational and economic opportunities for women. Its work is carried out through research, publications, liaising with national and international governmental organizations and agencies, and international advocacy in collaboration with other organizations.

Geographical Area of Activity: International.

Publications: *A World of Difference: Sexual and Reproductive Health & Risks; What You Need to Know About the Global Gag Rule Restrictions: an Unofficial Guide; Meeting the Challenge: Securing Contraceptive Supplies;* newsletter; other fact sheets, books and charts.

Principal Staff: Chair. Constance Spahn; Pres. Amy Coen.

Address: 1300 19th St, NW, 2nd Floor, Washington, DC 20036.

Telephone: (202) 557-3400; **Fax:** (202) 728-4177; **Internet:** www.popact.org; **e-mail:** pai@popact.org.

Population Communications International

Founded in 1985, aims to work creatively with the media and other organizations in order to influence population trends.

Activities: Promotes sustainable development through the research, production and broadcast of locally-run and culturally-appropriate radio and television serial dramas. These productions inform and educate local communities in Africa, Asia, Central and South America, and the USA about population and development issues through popular entertainment, and work to enhance communications between NGOs. Issues covered include reproductive health and family planning, HIV prevention, gender equality, social welfare and the protection of the environment. Also acts as the Secretariat for the NGO Committee on Population and Development, which encourages co-operation between the United Nations and NGOs.

Geographical Area of Activity: International.

Restrictions: Does not make grants.

Publications: *Mónica en busca de amor; Jam Packed; Time to Act; The Cost of Cool; Telling Stories, Saving Lives* Annual Report; research papers.

Finance: Assets $3,190,927 (Dec. 2001); annual revenue $4,873,496, expenditure $4,732,502 (2001).

Directors: K. L. Henderson (Chair.); A. Albright (Hon. Chair.); A. J. Amor (Vice-Chair.); J. W. Sheffield (Sec.); V. A. Staebler (Treas.); H. Ando; H. Badran; H. Baudenet d'Annoux; S. Dawson; M. C. DeYoung; D. A. Gray-Felder; C. Haub; S. Koo;T. Mount; G. C. Morales; A. I. Mundigo; K. McBride Puckett; J. S. Reidy; M. Roberts Ripley; F. Sai; E. Sanga; T. Semmes; B. M. Silla; M. G. Tambala; A. Watson.

Principal Staff: Pres. David J. Andrews; Exec. Vice-Pres. Michael Tatu Castlen.

Address: 777 United Nations Plaza, Suite 7C, New York, NY 10017-3521.

Telephone: (212) 687-3366; **Fax:** (212) 661-4188; **Internet:** www.population.org; **e-mail:** pciny@population.org.

Population Council

International, non-profit NGO, founded in 1952 by John D. Rockefeller, III; seeks to improve the well-being and reproductive health of current and future generations around the world, and to help achieve a humane, equitable and sustainable balance between people and resources.

Activities: Operates in the social, health and biomedical sciences in the following specific areas: develops contraceptives and other products for the improvement of reproductive health; conducts fundamental biomedical research in reproduction; improves the quality and outreach of family planning and reproductive health services; conducts research on reproductive health and behaviour, family structure and function, and causes and consequences of population growth; strengthens professional resources in developing countries through collaborative research, awards, fellowships and training; and publishes innovative research in peer-reviewed journals, books and working papers. Research and programmes are carried out by the Center for Biomedical Research, the International Programs Division, and the Policy Research Division. Council headquarters are located in New York City; the Council also maintains an office in Washington, DC, and an international presence through its four regional offices (in Accra, Cairo, Mexico City and New Delhi) and 18 country offices.

Geographical Area of Activity: Africa, Asia, Central, North and South America and the Caribbean, Europe and Australia.

Restrictions: Grants only in the form of doctoral and post-doctoral fellowships in the biomedical, health and social sciences.

Publications: *Studies in Family Planning* (quarterly); *Population and Development Review* (quarterly); working papers; books; newsletters; regional monographs.

Finance: Assets $173,500,000 (Dec. 2001); annual budget $85,201,000 (2003).

Trustees: The Council is governed by a multinational Board of Trustees.

Principal Staff: Pres. Linda G. Martin.

Address: 1 Dag Hammarskjöld Plaza, New York, NY 10017.

Telephone: (212) 339-0500; **Fax:** (212) 755-6052; **Internet:** www.popcouncil.org; **e-mail:** pubinfo@popcouncil.org.

Pro Mujer (Pro Women)

Established by Lynne Patterson and Carmen Velasco, a private non-profit charitable organization that aims to help women in Central and South America to play a more effective role in their own personal development and that of their children, families, and society.

Activities: Works in Bolivia, Mexico, Nicaragua and Peru, providing loans and micro-enterprise training for women to start or improve businesses, empowering them to develop their business skills and to support their families. Also informs and trains women in health, family planning and child development.

Geographical Area of Activity: Bolivia, Mexico, Nicaragua and Peru.

Publications: Newsletter.

Finance: Assets $4,100,000 (1999); annual revenue $2,700,000, expenditure $1,800,000 (1999).

Directors: R. Werrett (Pres.); J. McCarthy (Vice-Pres.); C. H. Skodinski (Treas.); R. Cowan; S. R. Downes; E. Edgcomb; P. G. Hess; P. H. Johnson; B. L. Moyer; M. J. O'Neill; L. R. Patterson; A. Schroeder; D. Simon; M. B. Sudo; C. Velasco.

Principal Staff: Co-Exec. Dirs Lynne Patterson, Carmen Velasco; Programme Officer G. Figueroa; W. Linares; S. Porter; K. McMahan.

Address: 120 Wall St, 20th Floor, New York, NY 10005.

Telephone: (212) 952-0181; **Fax:** (212) 952-0183; **Internet:** www.promujer.org; **e-mail:** promujer@promujer.org.

Project Concern International

Established in 1961 by Dr James Turpin to help the world's vulnerable children, families and communities, to provide access to health resources, prevent disease and promote development through dynamic partnerships that build local capacity in efficient and measurable ways.

Activities: Works in four key areas, Women and Children's Health, including child survival interventions (immunizations, breastfeeding, control of diarrhoeal disease and acute respiratory infections, integrated management of childhood illnesses, provision of vitamin A) as well as family planning, reproductive health, prenatal care and men's health education; Food Security, improving access, availability and utilization of food resources, promoting home gardens, nutritional education programmes, community infrastructure development, school feeding programmes and food aid for households affected by HIV/AIDS; Disease Prevention and Mitigation, preventing the spread of communicable and vector-borne diseases, as well as the activities that mitigate their impact, home-based care for people with AIDS, community-based programmes that address the needs of orphans and vulnerable children, tuberculosis and leprosy screening and treatment; and Water and Sanitation, improving access to potable water and sanitation facilities, including the construction and training in community management of wells, gravity-fed arrangements and rain-water catchment systems, small-scale municipal sewerage systems and solid waste disposal systems.

Geographical Area of Activity: International, with an emphasis on Bolivia, Central America, Ghana, India, Indonesia, Romania, the USA and Zambia.

Restrictions: No grants to individuals.

Publications: *CONCERNews* (quarterly newsletter); Annual Report.

Finance: Net assets $3,916,269 (Sept. 2001); annual revenue $23,209,173, expenditure $23,634,648 (2001).

Directors: Gary Acosta; Barbara Burgess Van Aken; Norma Bustamante; John Collins; Ciaran Cosgrave; Julie Crockford; Judy Ettinger; Robert S. Gerber; Susan Hawken; Lon Henderson; Jeff Mangum; Philip R. Mathews; Sacha Millstone; Nancy Plaxico; Tom Saiz; Peter Shaw; Maxine Shearer; Chris Twomey; Larry Weitzen; Marshall Whiting; Michael Williams; Bert Young.

Principal Staff: Interim CEO and Pres. Mark O'Donnell; Chief Financial Officer and Vice-Pres. Jerry Ray.

Address: 3550 Afton Rd, San Diego, CA 92123.

Telephone: (858) 279-9690; **Fax:** (858) 694-0294; **Internet:** www.projectconcern.org; **e-mail:** postmaster@projectconcern.org.

Project Harmony

Founded in 1985 with the aim of empowering individuals to create healthier communities, through international exchange and training.

Activities: Co-ordinates cultural, educational and professional exchanges between Russia and other countries of the former USSR, and the USA, in order to enhance international understanding, strengthen communities and nurture personal friendships. Also carries out programmes to combat domestic violence, youth leadership programmes in Bosnia-Herzegovina, and projects to develop the use of the internet in the former USSR. There are 16 offices in the USA, Armenia, Azerbaijan, Georgia, the Russian Federation and Ukraine.

Geographical Area of Activity: USA, Central and Eastern Europe, and the republics of Central Asia.

Trustees: Tom MacLeay (Interim Chair., Pres. and Chief Exec.); P. R. Smith (Vice-Chair.); P. Benedict; P. Biggam; B. Bottamini; S. Carbon; M. Carr; A. Gardner; L. Jondahl; P. Richardson; P. Smith.

Principal Staff: Co-Dirs Jared Cadwell, Charlie Hosford, Barbara Miller.

Address: 5197 Main St, Suite 6, Waitsfield, VT 05673.

Telephone: (802) 496-4545; **Fax:** (802) 496-4548; **Internet:** www.projectharmony.org; **e-mail:** ph@projectharmony.org.

Project HOPE—People-to-People Health Foundation

Project HOPE (Health Opportunity for People Everywhere) is the principal activity of the People-to-People Health Foundation, founded in 1958 by William B. Walsh.

Activities: Promotes the development of health system infrastructure, the training of local health workers in modern medical techniques in developing countries world-wide, and assists in the development of medical facilities. Distributes medical textbooks and journals to institutions throughout the world. Holds conferences. The Foundation's Center for Health Affairs carries out research in health policy. Has established national organizations in Germany, Hong Kong, Japan, Switzerland, United Kingdom and the USA.

Geographical Area of Activity: Africa, Asia, Europe, the Russian Federation and the republics of Central Asia, Central, South and North America, and the Middle East.

Publications: Annual Report; newsletter; brochures.

Finance: Annual revenue $115,798,000, expenditure $117,701,000 (June 2002).

Trustees: Charles A. Sanders (Chair.).

Principal Staff: Pres. and CEO John P. Howe, III.

Address: 255 Carter Hall Lane, Millwood, VA 22646.

Telephone: (540) 837-2100; **Fax:** (540) 837-1813; **Internet:** www.projecthope.org; **e-mail:** cflynn@projecthope.org.

Prudential Foundation

Founded in 1977 by the Prudential Insurance Co. of America and the Prudential Property & Casualty Co. for general charitable purposes.

Activities: Involved in the fields of the arts and humanities, education, business, urban and community affairs, health and medicine, and social welfare, mainly in areas of company operations. Support is themed under the three areas of Ready to Learn; Ready to Work; and Ready to Live.

Geographical Area of Activity: USA.

Restrictions: No grants are made to individuals; generally no funding for capital campaigns or endowments.

Publications: Annual Report.

Finance: Total assets $1,178,000 (Dec. 2001); total giving $37,518,379 (2001).

Officers and Trustees: Michele S. Darling (Chair.); Gabriella Morris Coleman (Pres.); Peter J. Bushyeager (Vice-Pres.); Lata N. Reddy (Sec.); James J. Straine (Treas.); Martin Berkowitz (Comptroller); Carolyn K. Davis; Jean D. Hamilton; Jon F. Hanson; Rodger A. Lawson; Arthur F. Ryan; P. Roy Vagelos; Stanley C. Van Ness.

Address: 751 Broad St, 15th Floor, Newark, NJ 07102-3777.

Telephone: (973) 802-4791; **Internet:** www.prudential.com/community/foundation/cmfzz1000.html; **e-mail:** community.resources@prudential.com.

Public Welfare Foundation, Inc

Founded in 1949 by Charles Edward Marsh and others.

Activities: Operates mainly in the USA in eight programme areas: criminal justice; disadvantaged elderly; disadvantaged youth; environment; health; population and reproductive health; community economic development and participation; and human rights and global security. The Foundation provides grants to organizations.

Geographical Area of Activity: Mainly USA; limited international grants to Africa, Haiti, Mexico and Central and South America.

Restrictions: No grants to individuals, nor for scholarships, graduate work, government projects, research projects or foreign study.

Publications: Annual Report; Guidelines.

Finance: Assets $355,371,636 (Oct. 2002); annual expenditure $23,739,809 (2002).

Officers and Directors: T. J. Scanlon (Chair.); R. H. Haskell (Vice-Chair.); P. Taylor (Sec.); A. M. Haskell (Treas.); L. Kressley (Exec. Dir); P. Edelman; T. Ehrlich; J. Villareal Garcia; B. L. Henry; M. H. Powell; T. W. Scoville; J. W. D. Stokes; C. E. Warner; M. C. Williams.

Address: 1200 U St, NW, Washington, DC 20009.

Telephone: (202) 965-1800; **Fax:** (202) 265-8851; **Internet:** www.publicwelfare.org; **e-mail:** reviewcommittee@publicwelfare.org.

Rainforest Action Network

Founded in 1985 by Randy Hayes to protect the Earth's rainforests and support the rights of their inhabitants through education, local community organization and non-violent direct action.

Activities: A non-profit organization working nationally and internationally with other environmental and human rights organizations to protect rain forests. There are two primary campaigns: the Old Growth Campaign works to end the logging of old-growth forests; and the Beyond Oil Campaign works towards a moratorium on new fossil fuel projects in pristine and endangered areas. The Protect-an-Acre programme provides grant funding directly to organizations and communities in rain forest regions. The Network is also involved in negotiation, research, conferences and seminars, and consumer education. Issues publications and maintains a speakers' bureau and library. The Network organizes an annual strategic gathering for forest activists (Chautauqua). There are some 25,000 active members, and more than 175 Rainforest Action Groups world-wide.

Geographical Area of Activity: International.

Publications: *Cut Waste, Not Trees; a wood use reduction guide; Drilling to the Ends of the Earth; 500 Year Plan; Action Alerts* (bi-monthly); Annual Report; fact sheets and information packs.

Principal Staff: Dir Randall Hayes; Exec. Dir Christopher Hatch.

Address: 221 Pine St, Suite 500, San Francisco CA 94104.

Telephone: (415) 398-4404; **Fax:** (415) 398-2732; **Internet:** www.ran.org; **e-mail:** rainforest@ran.org.

RealNetworks Foundation

Established in 2000 as part of the RealNetworks company's commitment to donating five per cent of its annual net income to non-profits upon attaining sustained profitability, which it first achieved in the second quarter of 2000.

Activities: Supports projects, particularly those that involve an innovative use of the internet, in the fields of fostering the right to speech throughout the world, broadening access to technology among under-served communities world-wide and enhancing the quality of life in areas where the company has a presence.

Geographical Area of Activity: International.

Finance: Total assets $1,493,570 (Dec. 2001); total giving $593,401 (2001).

Board of Directors: Eileen Quigley (Pres. and Treas.); Rob Glaser (Vice-Pres.); Kelly Jo MacArthur (Sec.); Susan Coskey.

Principal Staff: Program Man. Ellen Stearns.

Address: 2601 Elliott Ave, Seattle, WA 98121.

Telephone: (206) 892-6644; **Fax:** (206) 956-8249; **Internet:** www.realnetworks.com/company/giving/rnfoundation.html; **e-mail:** info@realfoundation.org.

Christopher Reeve Paralysis Foundation

Established in 1999 following the merger of the American Paralysis Association (formed in 1982) and the Christopher Reeve Paralysis Foundation.

Activities: Operates in the field of medical research, especially in the area of spinal cord injury research. The Foundation offers two-year research awards of a maximum of $75,000 per award: to encourage new research on regeneration and recovery, in particular with regard to spinal cord injuries; to encourage established researchers to transfer their research efforts onto spinal cord research; and to assist researchers with new ideas to seek awards from other sources of funding. Funds activities that hold promise of identifying therapies for paralysis and other sequelae of spinal cord injury. Development of effective therapies for chronic injury is a priority for the organization, although funding is also provided for studies more relevant to the acute phase of injury. Basic research is supported if it has clear potential to accelerate progress at the applied end of the continuum and/or if it reflects a research change in direction. The Quality of Life Program includes health promotion programmes for people with paralysis-related disabilities; these programmes aim to remove societal and environmental barriers that limit an individual's ability to participate in life's activities; grants are made to regional and local organizations. The CRPF Consortium on Spinal Cord Injury assists international neuroscientists to collaborate in the development of therapies for recovery from chronic spinal cord injury.

Geographical Area of Activity: USA.

Publications: Annual Report; *Walking Tomorrow; Progress in Research;* reports.

Finance: Assets $27,284,604 (2000); annual revenue $31,287,154, expenditure $10,231,382 (2000).

Board of Directors: Christopher Reeve (Chair.); T. Blair; J. Chalsty; J. Faden; G. Fischbach; R. Francis; R. Frigerio; W. Guarino; K. Guyett; F. Hall; J. Hughes; P. Kiernan; D. Landrey; F. Le Frak; H. Liss; J. Melone; K. Nichols; R. Nichols; M. Pinney; D. Reeve; R. Schneidman; T. See; C. Stifel; H. Stifel; J. Welch; W. Wight; K. Yant; and 14 others.

Principal Staff: Pres. and CEO Mitchell R. Stoller; Chair., Science Advisory Council Oswald Steward; Dir, Research Susan P. Howley.

Address: 500 Morris Ave, Springfield, NJ 07081.

Telephone: (973) 225-0292; **Fax:** (973) 912-9433; **Internet:** crpf.org; **e-mail:** info@crpf.org.

Refugees International

Established in 1979 to act as an independent voice for humanitarian action on behalf of the least-known and most vulnerable victims of war, famine and disaster.

Activities: Operates in areas of war and crisis, providing direct aid to refugees and people who have been displaced from their homes, including emergency relief, repatriation and protection. Also provides on-site field assessments and reports to policy and opinion makers world-wide to mobilize help for the victims. Since 2000, the organization has been working towards reforms in six areas designed to help avoid or alleviate chronic, continuing refugee crises: improvement of the United Nations peacekeeping capability through the creation of an established rapid-reaction peace and security force; new protection for internally-displaced people; increased attention to the needs of refugee women; an end to the recruitment and use of child soldiers; more attention to the transition between relief operations and economic development; and building local capacity and institutions.

Geographical Area of Activity: International, particularly Africa, Asia and the Balkans.

Publications: Newsletter (monthly); Annual Report; bulletins; articles; videos.

Finance: Assets $2,540,640 (Dec. 2001); annual revenue $2,232,849, expenditure $2,218,589 (2001).

Directors: James V. Kimsey (Chair.); Trish Malloch Brown, Eileen Shields West (Vice-Chair.); Sandra Senett Tully (Sec.); Dr Jim Cobey (Treas.); and 22 members.

Principal Staff: Pres. Kenneth H. Bacon; Pres. Emer. Lionel A. Rosenblatt; Vice-Pres. Policy Joel Charny.

Address: 1705 N St, NW, Washington, DC 20036.

Telephone: (202) 828-0110; **Fax:** (202) 828-0819; **Internet:** www.refugeesinternational.org; **e-mail:** ri@refintl.org.

Rehabilitation International

Founded in 1922 to assist and act as an advocate for disabled people around the world.

Activities: The organization is a federation of 200 organizations in 90 countries, dedicated to preventing disabilities, rehabilitating those with disabilities and advocating equal opportunities for disabled people and their families. Acts as an open forum for the exchange of information and experience on research and practice. Offers Kessler International Fellowships and various awards. Maintains regional offices in Asia, Europe and Central America.

Geographical Area of Activity: International.

Publications: *International Rehabilitation Review* (annually); *One in Ten;* bulletins; reviews; catalogues; videos.

Executive Committee: L. Frieden (Pres.); G. Wilson (Treas.).

Address: 25 East 21st St, New York, NY 10010.

Telephone: (212) 420-1500; **Fax:** (212) 505-0871; **Internet:** www.rehab-international.org; **e-mail:** rehabintl@rehab-international.org.

Relief International

Non-profit humanitarian organization founded in 1990, aiming to reduce suffering world-wide.

Activities: Provides humanitarian assistance in the form of emergency relief, rehabilitation, development assistance and more long-term services to communities around the world, including health, shelter, reconstruction, education, community development, agriculture, food, income generation and conflict resolution. Promotes self-reliance in developing countries and empowers communities by maximizing local resources.

Geographical Area of Activity: International.

Principal Staff: Chief Exec. Farshad Rastegar.

Address: 1575 Westwood Blvd, Suite 201, Los Angeles, CA 90024.

Telephone: (310) 478-1200; **Fax:** (310) 478-1212; **Internet:** www.ri.org; **e-mail:** rihq@ri.org.

Renewable Natural Resources Foundation

Founded in 1972 to advance scientific and public education in renewable natural resources; to promote the application of sound scientific practices in managing and conserving renewable natural resources; and to foster co-operation among professional, scientific and educational organizations having leadership responsibilities for renewable natural resources.

Activities: Operates in the field of conservation and the environment, nationally through self-conducted programmes, and nationally and internationally by awarding prizes, organizing conferences and through publications.

Geographical Area of Activity: International.

Restrictions: Funds own activities.

Publications: *Renewable Resources Journal* (quarterly); *Promoting Sustainability in the 21st Century; Human Population Growth: Impact on the Sustainability of Renewable Natural Resources;* and other publications.

Board of Directors: Albert A. Grant (Chair.); and 20 representatives from natural resources associations and organizations.

Principal Staff: Exec. Dir Robert D. Day; Dir of Programmes Ryan M. Colker; Dir of Admin. and Finance Chandra Krishna.

Address: 5430 Grosvenor Lane, Bethesda, MD 20814-2193.

Telephone: (301) 493-9101; **Fax:** (301) 493-6148; **Internet:** www.rnrf.org; **e-mail:** info@rnrf.org.

Research Corporation

Founded in 1912 by Frederick Gardner Cottrell and others to receive and acquire inventions, patent rights and letters patent, and to render the same more available and effective in the useful arts and manufactures; to provide means for the advancement of technical and scientific investigation, research and experimentation, by contributing the net earnings of the Corporation to scientific and educational institutions and societies.

Activities: The Foundation's programmes, operating in the USA and Canada, aid research proposed by college and university faculty members. These programmes include the Cottrell College Science Awards (physics, chemistry and astronomy at undergraduate institutions); Research Opportunity Awards (to assist mid-career chemists, astronomers and physicists in doctoral departments to pursue new areas of research); Research Innovation Awards (to assist highly original research by faculty members at research universities); Cottrell Scholars Awards (research and teaching in physics, chemistry and astronomy at graduate institutions); and Special Opportunities in Science Awards (to assist projects with potential for advancing science that do not fall under other programme guidelines).

Geographical Area of Activity: USA and Canada.

Publications: Newsletter; Annual Report; occasional reports.

Finance: Assets $158,566,094 (2000); grants $6,405,684 (2000).

Board of Directors: J. P. Schaefer (Pres.); Ray Kellman (Vice-Pres.); Sherri R. Benedict (Sec.); Suzanne D. Jaffe (Treas.); Herbert S. Adler; S. B. Crampton; R. M. Gavin, Jr; R. Holland, Jr; J. S. Valentine; G. K. Walters; L. L. Wilkening.

Address: 101 North Wilmot Rd, Suite 250, Tucson, AZ 85711.

Telephone: (520) 571-1111; **Fax:** (520) 571-1119; **Internet:** www.rescorp.org; **e-mail:** awards@rescorp.org.

Christopher Reynolds Foundation

Founded by Libby Holman Reynolds in 1952 to support initiatives in the field of international relations.

Activities: The Foundation supports projects dealing with injustice in social, economic and environmental matters, provides funds to humanitarian organizations in the USA and in Cuba, and seeks to promote improved relations between the two countries.

Geographical Area of Activity: USA and Cuba.

Restrictions: Does not support individuals, capital or endowment funds, deficit financing, scholarships, or matching gifts.

Publications: Report (every 5 years).

Finance: Assets $35,680,927 (Jan. 2001); total grants $2,233,012 (2001).

Board of Directors: Michael Kahn (Pres.); John R. Boettiger, Suzanne Derrer (Vice-Pres); Andrea Panarities (Exec. Dir).

Principal Staff: Exec. Dir Andrea Panaritis.

Address: 267 Fifth Ave, Suite 1001, New York, NY 10016.

Telephone: (212) 532-1606; **Fax:** (212) 532-1403; **Internet:** ww.creynolds.org; **e-mail:** crfny@aol.com.

Smith Richardson Foundation, Inc

Founded in 1935 by H. S. Richardson, Sr and Grace Jones Richardson for the support of behavioural research relating to government operations; and for programmes promoting a better understanding of American society and the economy.

Activities: The Foundation aims to inform important public policy debates through supporting pragmatic, policy-relevant research, analysis and writing. Grants are provided in two main programme areas: the International Security and Foreign Policy Program, which supports research and policy projects on issues central to the strategic interests of the USA; and the Domestic Public Policy Program, researching the development of US economic, social and governmental institutions.

Restrictions: The majority of unsolicited applications are rejected. No grants are made for projects in the arts and humanities, physical sciences or historic restoration, nor are grants made to individuals.

Publications: Annual Report.

Officers and Directors: Peter L. Richardon (Pres. and Chair.); Dr Marin J. Strmecki (Sen. Vice-Pres.); Robert L. Coble (Vice-Pres. and Chief Financial Officer); Ross Hemphill (Treas.); Dr Arvid R. Nelson (Sec.); Diana B. Wasburn (Asst Sec.); W. Winburne King, III; Adele Richardson Ray; Lunsford Richardson, Jr; Stuart S. Richardson.

Principal Staff: Dir, Programs Dr Marin J. Stronechi; Sen. Program Officer Dr Phoebe Cottingham, Mark Steinmyer; Program Officer Nadia Schadlow, Allen Sony.

Address: 60 Jesup Rd, Westport, CT 06880.

Telephone: (203) 222-6222; **Fax:** (203) 222-6282; **Internet:** www.srf.org.

Righteous Persons Foundation

Established by Steven Spielberg in 1994 to receive a share of the profits from the film *Schindler's List* to make grants to organizations working to strengthen Jewish communal life, primarily in the USA.

Activities: Grants focus on the use of communications and technology, as well as history and archaeology, Jewish organizations and temples. Grants have been made to fund research fellowships, television shows and the Holocaust Museum, Washington, DC.

Geographical Area of Activity: Mainly USA.

Restrictions: No grants are made to individuals.

Publications: Application guidelines.

Finance: Assets $18,614,068 (2000); total grants $3,135,000 (2000).

Officers and Directors: Steven Spielberg (Chair.); Gerald Breslauer (Pres.); Michael Rutman (Sec. and Chief Financial Officer); Bruce Ramer.

Principal Staff: Exec Dir Margery Tabankin; Programme Office Rachel Levin.

Address: 1460 Fourth St, Suite 212, Santa Monica, CA 90401.

Telephone: (310) 395-3599; **Fax:** (310) 395-9676.

Rockefeller Brothers Fund

Founded in 1940 by John D. Rockefeller, Jr, Martha Baird Rockefeller, Abby Rockefeller Mauze, David Rockefeller, John D. Rockefeller, III, Laurance S. Rockefeller, Nelson A. Rockefeller and Winthrop Rockefeller to improve the well-being of all people through support of efforts in the USA and abroad that contribute ideas, develop leaders and encourage institutions in the transition to global interdependence. The Fund merged with the Charles E. Culpeper Foundation in July 1999.

Activities: Operates both nationally and internationally through grants to non-profit organizations. Occasionally conducts programmes of its own. Focuses on locally-based problems, but in the context of global concerns. To maximize resources, projects are concentrated from time to time in different geographic regions. The Fund makes grants in nine areas. The largest area of grant-making concerns Sustainable Resource Use (to encourage sustainable development world-wide, employing an approach that balances social, economic and ecological concerns). The Arts and Culture programme aims to build greater understanding and appreciation of various art forms and cultural activities. The Global Security programme supports constituency building and public education, transparency in the development of transnational policies and economic integration in order to achieve a more just, stable and peaceful world. The Health programme supports projects involving research and education in the field of human health. Other areas are: promoting and sustaining a vital non-profit sector; a three-year Balkans programme, focusing on Serbia and Montenegro, addressing building democratic capacity, dealing with questions of national identity and ethnic reconciliation and developing sustainable communities; improving the quality of life in New York City; strengthening the numbers and quality of teachers in public education, as well as supporting educational programmes in the USA that are directed towards undergraduate education in the liberal arts and sciences at private institutions of higher learning; and improving the quality and accessibility of basic education for children and adults in South Africa. Also distributes the annual Ramon Magsaysay Awards and administers the Asian Cultural Council, affiliated with the Fund since 1991, which awards fellowships and programme grants.

Geographical Area of Activity: International, excluding Central and South America.

Restrictions: No programmes operate in Central or South America.

Publications: Annual Report; *Voices of Insight and Poverty*; various books and papers.

Finance: Assets $684,464,383 (2001); annual revenue $14,962,336, annual expenditure $39,899,406 (2001).

Trustees: Steven C. Rockefeller (Chair.); Neva R. Goodwin (Vice-Chair.); David J. Callard; Richard Chasin; Peggy Dulany; Jessica P. Einhorn; Neva R. Goodwin; Stephen B. Heintz; James Moltz; John Morning; Robert B. Oxnam; Joseph A. Pierson; David Rockefeller, Jr; Richard Rockefeller; Steven C. Rockefeller; Frank Wisner; Edmond D. Villani; Tadataka Yamada.

Principal Staff: Pres. Steven B. Heintz; Exec. Vice-Pres. And Chief Operating Officer William F. McAlpin; Sec. Benjamin R. Shute, Jr; Treas. Boris A. Wessely.

Address: 437 Madison Ave, 37th Floor, New York, NY 10022-7001.

Telephone: (212) 812-4200; **Fax:** (212) 812-4299; **Internet:** www.rbf.org; **e-mail:** rock@rbf.org.

Rockefeller Foundation

Founded in 1913 by John D. Rockefeller, Sr to promote the well-being of mankind throughout the world.

Activities: Operates nationally and internationally through offering grants to organizations, and also scholarships and fellowships. The Foundation's programme strategies and guidelines were redefined in 1999, and projects in the following four areas were to be funded: Food Security, Global Inclusion Health Equity and Working Communities. Also funds the Africa Regional Program, Communication for Social Change, Public/Private Partnerships and Global Philanthropy. Maintains the Bellagio Study and Conference Center in Italy, for international conferences and residencies for artists and scholars. The Foundation maintains offices in Bangkok, Italy, Nairobi, Mexico City, San Francisco and Zimbabwe.

Geographical Area of Activity: International.

Restrictions: No grants are made for personal aid to individuals, nor for general institutional support or fund endowments, nor for building or operating funds.

Publications: Annual Report; programme policy statement.

Finance: Assets $3,100,000,000 (Dec. 2001); annual budget (grants and international operations) approx. $162,000,000 (2001).

Board of Trustees: James F. Orr, III (Chair.); Ela R. Bhatt; Gordon Conway; David de Ferranti; William H. Foege; Antonia Hernandez; Linda A. Hill; David Lawrence; Jessica T. Mathews; Mamphela Ramphele; Frederick Boyd williams; Dr Vo-Tong Xuan.

Principal Staff: Pres. Gordon Conway; Vice-Pres. Lincoln C. Chen.

Address: 420 Fifth Ave, New York, NY 10018-2702.

Telephone: (212) 869-8500; **Fax:** (212) 764-3468; **Internet:** www.rockfound.org.

Rotary Foundation

Founded in 1917 by Rotary International to further understanding and friendly relations between peoples of different nations.

Activities: Operates internationally in financing scholarships, grants for charitable and educational projects, cultural and educational exchanges of business and professional leaders, and grants for major health, hunger relief and humanitarian projects. Awards and grants are open to men and women with no restriction on race or creed. Programmes include: International Ambassadorial Scholarships; World Peace Scholarships; PolioPlus Program; Community Assistance Program; Group Study Exchange; Humanitarian Grants; Matching Grants; Grants for Rotary Volunteers; and Rotary Peace Programs.

Geographical Area of Activity: International.

Publications: Annual Report; programme brochures.

Address: One Rotary Center, 1560 Sherman Ave, Evanston, IL 60201.

Telephone: (847) 866-3000; **Fax:** (847) 328-8554; **Internet:** www.rotary.org/foundation; **e-mail:** scholarshipinquiries@rotaryintl.org.

The Judith Rothschild Foundation

Founded in 1993 with the purpose of promoting, presenting and interpreting the work of lesser-known American artists who have died after 12 September 1976.

Activities: Promotes lesser-known artists through support for exhibitions, the acquisition of their work by museums and the safe-keeping of paintings; cataloguing of works of art; scholarly research; operates programmes for study and interpretation of works of art.

Geographical Area of Activity: USA.

Finance: Assets $34,286,854 (Dec. 2000); annual grants $465,984 (2000).

Trustees: Harvey S. Shipley Miller.

Principal Staff: Chair., Grants Review Cttee Wilder Green; Vice-Pres. Grants Programme Elizabeth S. Slater.

Address: 1110 Park Ave, New York, NY 10128.

Telephone: (212) 831-4114; **Fax:** (212) 831-6222; **Internet:** http://fdncenter.org/grantmaker/rothschild/.

Edmond de Rothschild Foundation

Founded in 1963 by Edmond de Rothschild for general charitable purposes.

Activities: Operates primarily in New York and in France, but also makes grants in Israel, in the fields of Jewish social welfare, education, including business administration and religious education, science and medicine, and the arts and humanities, through grants to institutions.

Geographical Area of Activity: USA, France and Israel.

Restrictions: The Foundation makes grants only to pre-selected organizations. Unsolicited applications are not accepted.

Finance: Assets $71,359,526 (Feb. 2001); total grants $4,113,797 (2001).

Officers and Directors: Benjamin de Rothschild (Chair.); Paul H. Epstein (Pres.); Georges C. Karlweis (Vice-Pres.); Stanley Komaroff (Sec.); Roger Cukierman (Treas.); Nadine de Rothschild; Haim Stoessel.

Address: 1585 Broadway, 24th Floor, New York, NY 10036.

Telephone: (212) 969-3250.

Samuel Rubin Foundation, Inc

Founded in 1958 to promote peace and justice.

Activities: The Foundation provides grants to organizations concerned with human rights, justice, peace and the redistribution of resources in the world; promotes social, economic, political, civil and cultural rights. Operates in the fields of education, human rights and social welfare.

Geographical Area of Activity: USA and international.

Restrictions: No grants to individuals, for building funds or scholarships.

Publications: Programme policy statement.

Finance: Assets $13,499,092 (2002).

Officers and Directors: Cora Weiss (Pres.); Judy Weiss (Vice-Pres.); Charles L. Mandelstam (Sec.); Peter Weiss (Treas.); Daniel Weiss; Tamara Weiss.

Principal Staff: Grants Admin. Lauranne Jones.

Address: 777 United Nations Plaza, New York, NY 10017-3521.

Telephone: (212) 697-8945; **Fax:** (212) 682-0886; **Internet:** www.samuelrubinfoundation.org; **e-mail:** info@samuelrubinfoundation.org.

Damon Runyon Cancer Research Foundation

Founded in 1946 to support all theoretical and experimental research relevant to the study of cancer, and the search for its causes, mechanisms, treatment and prevention.

Activities: Awards up to 60 post-doctoral research fellowships per year for basic scientists and physician scientists, allowing scientists and medical practitioners beginning full-time post-doctoral research to carry out cancer research.

Restrictions: US citizens may study in any country; foreign researchers' study must be carried out in the USA.

Finance: Total assets $84,333,684 (2002); total revenue and expenditure $13,570,840 (2002).

Board of Directors: Dale F. Frey (Chair.); Leon G. Cooperman (Vice-Chair. Finance and Treas.); Kenneth G. Langone (Vice-Chair. Bd Development); David M. Livingston (Vice-Chair. Scientific Programmes); David Baltimore; Norman Eig; Thomas J. Fahey, Jr; Scott Greenstein; Margaret Brennan Hassett; Martha M. Kenny; John P. Keyser; Ronald Levy; Anthony F. LoFrisco; David G. Marshall; Sanford W. Morhouse; Richard J. O'Reilly; Katharine F. Plum; Gordon Ringold; Samuel C. Silverstein; Marsha M. Sterling; Craig B. Thompson; Virginia Ueberroth; Robert C. Wright.

Address: 675 Third Ave, 25th Floor, New York, NY 10017.

Telephone: (212) 697-9550; **Fax:** (212) 697-4950; **Internet:** www.cancerresearchfund.org; **e-mail:** crfinfo@cancerresearchfund.org.

Russell Sage Foundation

Founded in 1907 by Margaret Olivia Sage for the improvement of social and living conditions in the USA: now devoted exclusively to research in the social sciences, as a means to improve social policies.

Activities: The Foundation's professional staff of about 21 social scientists (Resident Scholars, Visiting Scholars, Visiting Post-doctoral Fellows and part-time advisers and consultants) conduct research on selected topics (including basic research in improvements in methodology, data and theory). The Foundation also provides support for the work of scholars at other academic and research institutions; sponsors special seminars; and publishes books and monographs. Research grants are made in the programme areas of: the future of work; the social analysis of poverty; immigration; cultural contact; trust; politics of social policy; and Census 2000.

Geographical Area of Activity: USA.

Restrictions: No grants are made internationally; no grants for pre-doctoral study or research; no scholarships or other types of grants for support of college funding.

Publications: Biennial Report; books and monographs.

Finance: Total assets $245,524,614 (Aug. 2001); total grants $6,434,951 (2001).

Board of Directors: I. Katznelson (Chair.); P. C. Ellsworth (Vice-Chair.); A. S. Blinder; C. K. Cassel; T. D. Cook; R. E. Denham; J. L. Hochschild; T. A. Hultquist; M. Konger; E. Condliffe Lagemann; C. B. Marrett; E. Smolensky; M. Tienda; E. Wanner.

Principal Staff: Pres. E. Wanner; Vice-Pres. and Sec. M. Spitaleri; Chief Financial Officer Christopher Brogna.

Address: 112 East 64th St, New York, NY 10021.

Telephone: (212) 750-6000; **Fax:** (212) 371-4761; **Internet:** www.russellsage.org; **e-mail:** info@rsage.org.

Rutherford Institute

Non-profit organization founded by John Whitehead in 1982. It is dedicated to the defence of civil and human rights.

Activities: Provides lawyers to help people whose civil rights or human rights have been violated. Also provides educational opportunities to improve standards of social justice in the USA.

Geographical Area of Activity: International.

Publications: *Insider* (e-mail newsletter); various pamphlets, books and videos.

Principal Staff: Pres. John Whitehead.

Address: POB 7482, Charlottesville, VA 22906-7482.

Telephone: (804) 978-3888; **Fax:** (804) 978-1789; **Internet:** www.rutherford.org; **e-mail:** staff@rutherford.org.

Sabre Foundation, Inc

Founded by Josiah Lee Auspitz in 1969 to promote the philosophy and practice of free institutions.

Activities: Primary activities include donating large quantities of new books and other educational materials to needy individuals in developing regions of the world, and assisting organizations to take advantage of internet and related information technologies through conducting training workshops. The Foundation operates through NGO partner organizations, libraries, universities, schools, research institutes and other similar organizations.

Geographical Area of Activity: Africa, Asia, Central and Eastern Europe, the countries of the former USSR, and Central and South America and the Caribbean.

Publications: Annual Report; *Foundation Update* (2 a year).

Finance: Total revenue $27,274,238, expenditure $27,406,530 (2001).

Principal Staff: Pres. and Treas. Kenneth G. Bartels; Vice-Pres. and Dir Anne D. Neal; Sec. Charles Getchell; Exec. Dir Tania Vitvitsky.

Address: 872 Massachusetts Ave, Suite 2-1, Cambridge, MA 02139.

Telephone: (617) 868-3510; **Fax:** (617) 868-7916; **Internet:** www.sabre.org; **e-mail:** sabre@sabre.org.

Samaritan's Purse

International non-denominational Christian organization founded in 1970 by Dr Robert Pierce. Aims to help people suffering around the world.

Activities: Provides aid and assistance to victims of war, disasters, disease, famine and poverty, as well as promoting the Gospel world-wide. The organization is active in many countries, engaging in a number of programmes, including emergency health care and improving existing medical facilities, providing emergency supplies including food and clothing, funding community development projects, and providing shelters for abandoned children. Also organizes evangelical festivals throughout the world. Has offices in Australia, Canada, Germany, Ireland, the Netherlands and the United Kingdom.

Geographical Area of Activity: International.

Publications: Newsletter; Annual Report.

Address: POB 3000, Boone, NC 28607.

Telephone: (828) 262-1980; **Fax:** (828) 266-1053; **Internet:** www.samaritanspurse.org; **e-mail:** info@samaritan.org.

San Francisco Foundation

Founded in 1948 for the support of philanthropic undertakings in the San Francisco Bay area.

Activities: Makes grants to organizations in the San Francisco Bay area in the fields of arts, education, environment, community health, humanities, social services and urban affairs, to improve the quality of life, promote greater equality of opportunity and help those in need or at risk in the area. Initiatives include the Koshland Program, which makes awards to grass-roots social innovators in the San Francisco Bay Area.

Geographical Area of Activity: USA, mainly the San Francisco Bay Area.

Publications: Annual Report; newsletter (2 a year); *Koshland Program Newsletter* (annual); *Who's Funding the Digital Connect?*.

Finance: Assets $672,512,115 (June 2002); net annual revenue $12,661,639, expenditure $77,995,227 (2002).

Trustees: Leslie P. Hume (Chair.); Rolland C. Lowe (Vice-Chair.); Sandra R. Hernandez (Sec.); Gay P. Cob; Peter E. Haas, Jr; F. Warren Hellman; James Hormel; Stephanie Di Marco; Hugo Morales; Ted J. Saenger; David J. Sanchez, Jr; Gladys Thacher.

Principal Staff: CEO Sandra R. Hernandez.

Address: 225 Bush St, Suite 500, San Francisco, CA 94104.

Telephone: (415) 733-8500; **Fax:** (415) 477-2783; **Internet:** www.sff.org; **e-mail:** rec@sff.org.

Margaret Sanger Center International—MSCI

Established as the international arm of Planned Parenthood of New York City to improve quality of life world-wide by improving standards of reproductive and sexual health.

Activities: Operates in around 50 countries in Africa, Asia and the Pacific, and Central and South America and the Caribbean in collaboration with local leaders and organizations around the world, to plan, develop and implement improved administrative, managerial and financial systems for reproductive and sexual health programmes; carries out technical training programmes in family life, sexuality, peer and parent education for local family health practitioners; and improves existing facilities and abilities to deliver high-quality reproductive health care. Also provides an annual Leadership Training Course for senior-level international professionals to design and develop programmes relating to sex education, the prevention of HIV/AIDS and reproductive health care. Maintains offices in South Africa and Mongolia.

Geographical Area of Activity: Africa, Asia and the Pacific, Central and South America, and the Caribbean.

Address: 26 Bleecker St, New York, NY 10012–2413.

Telephone: (212) 274-7200; **Fax:** (212) 274-7299; **Internet:** www.ppnyc.org/services/msci.html; **e-mail:** msci@ppnyc.org.

Scaife Family Foundation

Established by the Scaife family; shares administrative offices with the Carthage Foundation and the Sarah Scaife Foundation (qq.v.).

Activities: The Foundation supports projects that aim to strengthen families, address issues surrounding the health and welfare of women and children, promote animal welfare, demonstrate the beneficial interaction between humans and animals, and encourage private conservation. Grants are also made to organizations working in the area of early intervention and prevention efforts in the area of drug and alcohol addiction.

Geographical Area of Activity: USA (emphasis on Florida and Pennsylvania).

Restrictions: No grants for events, capital campaigns nor renovations, nor for government agencies. No grants for individuals.

Publications: Annual Report.

Finance: Net assets $91,422,568 (2001); annual revenue $8,719,217, grants disbursed $3,429,400 (2001).

Trustees: Jennie K. Scaife (Chair.); Barbara M. Sloan (Pres.); Beth H. Genter, Mary T. Walton (Vice-Pres.).

Principal Staff: Pres. Barbara M. Sloan.

Address: Phillips Point, 777 S. Flagler Dr., West Tower, Suite 903, West Palm Beach, FL 33401.

Telephone: (561) 659-1188; **Internet:** www.scaifefamily.org.

Sarah Scaife Foundation, Inc

Founded in 1941 by Sarah Mellon Scaife for broad charitable purposes; present name adopted in 1974.

Activities: Supports public policy programmes which address major domestic and international issues, in areas such as education, government, economics, international law, crime and law enforcement, international affairs, etc. Makes grants for fellowships, research, projects, conferences and publications.

Geographical Area of Activity: International.

Restrictions: No grants are made to individuals nor to nationally-organized fundraising groups.

Publications: Annual Report.

Finance: Total assets $232,029,669 (2001); total grants paid $18,331,500 (2001).

Officers and Trustees: Richard M. Scaife (Chair.); Michael Gleba (Exec. Vice-Pres.); Barbara L. Slaney (Vice-Pres. and Treas.); R. Daniel McMichael (Sec.); Yvonne Marie Bly (Asst Treas.).

Address: 1 Oxford Center, Suite 3900, 301 Grant St, Pittsburgh, PA 15219-6401.

Telephone: (412) 392-2900; **Internet:** www.scaife.com/sarah .html.

Robert Schalkenbach Foundation, Inc

Founded in 1925 by Robert Schalkenbach to promote the social and economic philosophy of Henry George, especially his views concerning the single tax on land values and international free trade. Also promotes sustainable economic development, human rights, the resolution of conflicts regarding land rights, wealth redistribution, ecological use of the earth's resources and the public sharing of land values (including electromagnetic, oceanic, mineral, forest, agricultural and urban location values).

Activities: Operates through research, publications, seminars and conferences, and grants to educational institutions.

Geographical Area of Activity: Europe, USA, Russian Federation and People's Republic of China.

Restrictions: No grants are made to individuals; grants are made only to specific organizations.

Publications: *Progress and Poverty* (by Henry George); *Land Value Taxation Around the World* (by R. V. Andelson); *The American Journal of Economics and Sociology* (quarterly); numerous monographs.

Finance: Assets $12,012,255 (June 2001); annual expenditure $208,300 (2001).

Officers and Directors: F. K. Peddle (Pres.); N. Tideman (Vice-Pres.); L. R. Abele; R. V. Andelson; H. Barry, III; M. Cleveland; C. W. Cobb; S. B. Cord; J. A. Coughlan; G.

Erickson; K. Feder; M. Gaffney; T. Gwartney; D. L. Harris; A. Hartheimer; B. Howells; G. Nixon; R. Noyes; H. Remoff; W. Samuels; T. Smith.

Principal Staff: Exec. Dir Christopher E. Williams.

Address: 149 Madison Ave, Suite 601, New York, NY 10016-6713.

Telephone: (212) 683-6424; **Fax:** (212) 683-6454; **Internet:** www.schalkenbach.org; **e-mail:** cwilliams@schalkenbach.org.

Dr Scholl Foundation

Founded in 1947 by William M. Scholl, and formerly known as the William M. Scholl Foundation, for general charitable purposes.

Activities: Operates in the fields of culture, social welfare and economic affairs, through awarding grants and providing support primarily for private education, medical and nursing institutions; medical and scientific research; programmes for children, young people, the developmentally disabled and older people; civic, cultural, social services, economic and religious institutions; and for conferences and seminars.

Restrictions: No grants are made to individuals.

Publications: Information brochure; grant guidelines.

Finance: Assets $186,645,652 (Dec. 2000); grants expenditure $12,815,494 (2000).

Officers and Directors: W. H. Scholl (Chair.); Pamela Scholl (Pres.); Jack E. Scholl (Vice-Pres. and Sec.); David L. Royalty (Treas.); Neil Flanagin; Richard B. Patterson; Jeanne M. Scholl; Michael W. Scholl; Susan Scholl; Douglas C. Witherspoon.

Address: 1033 Skokie Blvd, Suite 230, Northbrook, IL 60062.

Telephone: (847) 559-7430; **Internet:** www.drschollfoundation.com.

Florence and John Schumann Foundation

Founded in 1961 by Florence F. Schumann and John J. Schumann, Jr to operate in the fields of effective governance, the environment and international relations.

Activities: Active in the areas of education, foreign and public policy, the environment and citizenship. Supports projects which expose the effect of money on democratic governance and encourage citizen activism in seeking to correct the problem of privately funded public elections.

Geographical Area of Activity: USA.

Restrictions: No grants are made to individuals; support is currently confined to programmes within the USA.

Publications: Biennial Report.

Finance: Assets $82,395,690 (Dec. 2000); grants disbursed $15,248,890 (2000).

Principal Staff: Vice-Pres. and Admin. Lynn Welhorsky.

Address: 33 Park St, Montclair, NJ 07042.

Telephone: (201) 783-6660; **Fax:** (201) 783-7553; **e-mail:** welhorsky.scmd@verizon.net.

Charles and Lynn Schusterman Family Foundation

Founded in 1987, exclusively for charitable, religious, literacy, scientific and educational purposes.

Activities: Operates nationally and internationally, in Israel and the former USSR, to support and expand Jewish communities; gives grants to institutions, offers scholarships and fellowships, runs conferences and training courses, all with the aim of promoting education, child development and community service.

Geographical Area of Activity: USA, Israel and the former USSR.

Restrictions: No grants to: individuals, non-sectarian groups outside Tulsa, local Jewish programmes in communities outside Tulsa, endowments, deficits, programmes appropriately funded by government, nor for permanent financing.

Finance: Assets $74,302,600 (2001); total giving $7,908,683 (2001).

Officers and Trustees: Lynn Schusterman (Pres.); Stacy H. Schusterman (Vice-Pres. and Treas.); Jay Schusterman (Sec.).

Principal Staff: Exec. Dir Sanford R. Cardin.

Address: POB 51, Tulsa, OK 74101-0051.

Telephone: (918) 591-1090; **Fax:** (918) 591-1758; **Internet:** www.schusterman.org; **e-mail:** ahughes@schusterman.org.

Albert Schweitzer Institute for the Humanities

Established by Harold Robles, the Institute is committed to the ethics and philosophy of Dr Schweitzer.

Activities: The Institute has collaborated with the Open Society Institute (q.v.) on a series of health-care development conferences and seminars in Central and Eastern Europe, subjects including tuberculosis control, HIV/AIDS prevention, micro-nutrient deficiencies, palliative care, substance abuse and data collection. Distributes humanitarian aid, including shipments to Bulgaria and Macedonia, Has established a Youth Ethical Education initiative in the USA in conjunction with the School for Ethical Education, involving workshops, inter-school projects and action packs. Also has established an educational initiative involving volunteers in its humanitarian aid programme; and supports special initiatives reflecting Dr Schweitzer's dedication to music, philosophy, human rights and world peace.

Geographical Area of Activity: USA, Central and Eastern Europe and the former USSR.

Publications: *Legacy* (newsletter); books and pamphlets by and about Dr Albert Schweitzer.

Board of Directors: D. Croteau (Chair.); S. Lindberg (Vice-Chair.); A. Alexander (Sec.); R. Schweitzer Miller (Hon. Chair.); and others.

Principal Staff: Exec. Dir David T. Ives.

Address: Quinnipiac University CL–SCH, 275 Mount Carmel Ave, Hamden, CT 06518.

Telephone: (203) 582-3144; **Fax:** (203) 582-8478; **Internet:** www.schweitzerinstitute.org; **e-mail:** info@schweitzerinstitute.org.

William G. Selby and Marie Selby Foundation

Founded in 1954 by William G. Selby and Marie Selby for general charitable purposes.

Activities: Operates in Florida in the fields of education, social welfare, health, culture and community development. Programmes are carried out through grants and scholarships for students and organizations in Florida.

Geographical Area of Activity: Florida only.

Restrictions: No grants are made to individuals.

Finance: Assets $78,520,228 (May 2001); total grants $3,706,228 (2001).

Principal Staff: Pres. Debra M. Jacobs.

Address: 1800 Second St, Suite 750, Sarasota, FL 34236.

Telephone: (941) 957-0442.

SERRV International—Sales Exchange for Refugee Rehabilitation Vocation

Established in 1949 by the Church of the Brethren to help refugees in Europe after the Second World War; became SERRV International in 1999, aiming to promote the economic and social progress of people living in developing countries and to alleviate poverty through fair trade.

Activities: Acts as a fair trade, non-profit organization, through advancing money to low-income artisans in developing countries so they can buy raw materials to make crafts. SERRV then purchases and markets the finished items, selling them through more than 3,000 churches, non-profit groups and retail outlets.

Geographical Area of Activity: International.

Publications: *SERRV Catalogue*.

Address: 122 State St, Suite 600, Madison, WI 53703.

Telephone: (608) 255-0440; **Fax:** (608) 255-0451; **Internet:** www.serrv.org; **e-mail:** admin@serrv.org.

Seva Foundation

Founded to help relieve and prevent suffering in the world and to generate hope through compassionate action.

Activities: Operates internationally to promote health, nutrition, education, economic development and self help, native Americans, and social and economic justice. The Foundation works in partnership with organizations in the USA and in Cambodia, Guatemala, India, Mexico, Nepal and Tibet.

Geographical Area of Activity: International.

Restrictions: No unsolicited grant requests accepted.

Publications: Annual report; newsletters; special programme reports.

Finance: Net assets $1,700,870 (June 2002); annual revenue $3,123,735, expenditure $3,026,460 (2002).

Directors: Jahanara Romney (Chair.); Stephen Miller (Chair. Elect); Mary LaMar (Treas.); Girija Brilliant (Sec.).

Principal Staff: Exec. Dir James O'Dea.

Address: 1786 Fifth St, Berkeley, CA 94710.

Telephone: (510) 845-7382; **Fax:** (510) 845-7410; **Internet:** www.seva.org; **e-mail:** admin@seva.org.

Sierra Club Foundation

Founded in 1960 to advance the preservation and protection of the natural environment.

Activities: Promotes environmental protection through education, research, litigation and social services. Active at grass-roots level, providing funding for more than 900 volunteer environmental organizations nationally and internationally.

Geographical Area of Activity: Mainly USA.

Publications: *Foundation News* (monthly supporters newsletter); Annual Report; information brochure; financial statement.

Finance: Annual revenue $25,911,512, expenditure $19,866,417 (2001).

Trustees: Marlene Fluharty (Pres.); Charles E. Frank (Vice-Pres.); Robert B. Flint, Jr (Treas.); Marilyn Brown (Sec.); Robert Perkowitz (Fifth Officer); Richard Cellarius; Harry Dalton; Jennifer Ferenstein; Michael Loeb; Michael McCloskey; Chuck McGrady; Albert Meyerhoff; William Newsom; Michael Rigney; Guy Saperstein; J. Rand Sparling.

Principal Staff: Exec. Dir John DeCock.

Address: 85 Second St, Suite 750, San Francisco, CA 94105.

Telephone: (415) 995-1780; **Fax:** (415) 995-1791; **Internet:** www.tscf.org; **e-mail:** sierraclub.foundation@sierraclub.org.

L. J. Skaggs and Mary C. Skaggs Foundation

Founded in 1967 by L. J. Skaggs and Mary C. Skaggs for general charitable purposes; the Foundation's interest is in the alleviation of social problems and concerns, and the enrichment and preservation of cultural and historic heritages, both in the USA and abroad.

Activities: Operates nationally and internationally, making grants under four main programme categories: Performing Arts, Projects of Historic Interest, Environment/Ecology and Special Projects. Emphasis is given to projects proposing unusual and untried solutions or innovative processes. Also awards discretionary grants to projects relating to the Foundation's interests.

Geographical Area of Activity: United Kingdom and USA.

Restrictions: No grants are made to individuals.

Publications: Report of operations and financial statement.

Finance: Assets $2,390,588 (2001); annual expenditure $1,076,395 (2001).

Officers and Directors: Mary C. Skaggs (Pres.); Jayne C. Davis, Georgia A. Fulstone (Vice-Pres); Philip M. Jelley (Sec. and Man.); Joseph W. Martin, Jr (Dir and Treas.).

Principal Staff: Dir Joseph W. Martin, Jr.

Address: 1221 Broadway, 21st Floor, Oakland, CA 94612-1837.

Telephone: (510) 451-3300; **Fax:** (510) 451-1527; **Internet:** www.skags.org; **e-mail:** skaggs@fablaw.com.

Alfred P. Sloan Foundation

Founded in 1934 for general charitable purposes.

Activities: Operates mainly nationally in the fields of science and technology, economic affairs, management and related fields, including economic growth and industrial competitiveness, through self-conducted programmes and grants to institutions. The Foundation sponsors the Sloan Fellowships for Basic Research for young chemists, physicists, mathematicians, neuroscientists and economists in institutions in the USA and Canada.

Geographical Area of Activity: USA.

Restrictions: Only rarely supports activities outside the USA and does not normally support projects in areas of religion, creative or performing arts, elementary or secondary education, medical research or health care. No grants for endowments, buildings or equipment.

Publications: Annual Report; information brochure.

Finance: Assets $1,314,367,357 (Dec. 2001); grants disbursed $60,852,714 (2001).

Officers and Directors: Harold T. Shapiro (Chair.); Ralph E. Gomory (Pres.); Stephen L. Brown; S. Parker Gilbert; William E. Hoglund; Donald N. Langenberg; Sandra O. Moose; Richard E. Salomon; Philip A. Sharp; Roger B. Smith; Roger M. Solow; Dennis Weatherstone; Sheila E. Widnall.

Principal Staff: Pres. Ralph E. Gomory.

Address: 630 Fifth Ave, Suite 2550, New York, NY 10111.

Telephone: (212) 649-1649; **Fax:** (212) 757-5117; **Internet:** www.sloan.org.

Smithsonian Institution

Created by Act of Congress in 1846 in accordance with the terms of the will of James Smithson of England, who in 1826 bequeathed his property to the USA to found at Washington, under the name of the Smithsonian Institution, an establishment for the increase and diffusion of knowledge among men.

Activities: Operates both nationally and internationally in the fields of education, science, the arts and humanities, and the conservation of natural resources. The Institution performs basic research, publishes results of studies, explorations and investigations, maintains study and reference collections in the sciences, culture and history, and exhibitions in the arts, American history, technology, aeronautics, space exploration and natural history. It administers various museums, art galleries and other institutions including the Anacostia Museum and Center for African American History and Culture; Archives of American Art; Arts and Industries Building; Cooper-Hewitt, National Design Museum; Freer Gallery of Art; Hirshhorn Museum and Sculpture Garden; National Air and Space Museum; National Museum of African Art; Smithsonian American Art Museum; National Museum of American History; National Museum of the American Indian; National Museum of Natural History/Museum of Man; National Portrait Gallery; National Postal Museum; National Zoological Park; Renwick Gallery; Arthur M. Sackler Gallery; Smithsonian Astrophysical Observatory; Smithsonian Environmental Research Center; Smithsonian Institution Building; Smithsonian Tropical Research Institute. A new National Air and Space Museum Steven F. Udvar-Hazy Center was to open in 2003. Fellowships are offered to students of all nationalities to study at Smithsonian Institution facilities. Through the National Museum Act, grants are made to museum professionals for museum studies. The Smithsonian Institution Travelling

Exhibition Service organizes exhibitions which circulate to museums around the USA, while the Smithsonian Affiliates Program establishes links and affiliations across the country.

Geographical Area of Activity: USA.

Publications: Annual report and financial statement; *Smithsonian Opportunities for Research and Study; Smithsonian Magazine*; various scholarly and popular publications.

Finance: The Smithsonian is approx. 72% funded by an annual appropriation from the US Congress. Direct federal appropriation $455,000,000 (2000–01).

Board of Regents: Wesley S. Williams, Jr (Chair. Exec. Cttee); William H. Rehnquist, Alan G. Spoon (Members of Exec. Cttee); and 17 others.

Principal Staff: Chancellor William H. Rehnquist; Sec. Lawrence Small; Under-Sec. for American Museums and Nat. Programmes Sheila Burke; Under-Sec. for Science J. Dennis O'Connor; Under-Sec. for Finance and Admin Robert Bailey; Smithsonian Business Ventures CEO Gary Beer; Dir of the Int. Art Museums Division Thomas Lentz.

Address: POB 37012, SI Bldg, Rm 153, MRC 010, Washington, DC 20013-7012.

Telephone: (202) 357-1729; **Internet:** www.si.edu; **e-mail:** info@si.edu.

Spencer Foundation

Founded in 1962 by Lyle M. Spencer to support research leading to the improvement of education.

Activities: Supports research into all aspects of education, in the USA and abroad. The Foundation is interested in a wide variety of disciplinary and interdisciplinary approaches, though by direction of its charter it gives emphasis to the behavioural sciences; it defines education broadly to include all the situations and institutions in which education proceeds, regardless of age. The Foundation is interested in a wide variety of research formats, from relatively low-cost efforts extending over a few months to more expensive collaborative efforts extending over several years.

Geographical Area of Activity: International.

Publications: Annual Report.

Finance: Assets $414,367,000 (2002); grants disbursed $22,509,000 (2002).

Officers and Directors: Derek C. Bok (Chair.); Kenji Hakuta (Vice-Chair.); Michael McPherson (Pres.); Paul Goren (Vice-Pres.); H. E. Gardner; C. Greenleaf; M. Lampert; L. Logan, Sr.; J. S. Reed; R. J. Shavelson.

Principal Staff: Sen. Prog. Officers Margaret J. Braatz; Susan L. Dauber; Mark E. Rigdon; Lauren Jones Young.

Address: 875 North Michigan Ave, Suite 3930, Chicago, IL 60611-1803.

Telephone: (312) 337-7000; **Fax:** (312) 337-0282; **Internet:** www.spencer.org; **e-mail:** information@spencer.org.

Stanley Foundation

Founded in 1956 by C. Maxwell and Elizabeth M. Stanley to encourage study, research and education in the field of international policy that contributes to secure peace with freedom and justice. Emphasis is placed upon activities related to international institutions and US foreign policy.

Activities: Operates nationally and internationally in the fields of education and international relations, through self-conducted programmes, conferences, publications, seminars and a weekly radio series on world affairs (Common Ground). Within the field of Global Education, the Foundation organizes various youth education programmes designed to ensure global perspectives are taught at schools. Within the area of US Foreign Policy, there are two main programmes: Emerging From Conflict which works to improve US relations with current and recent adversaries; and Euro-Atlantic Initiatives, which seeks to build transatlantic communities committed to security. Also organizes off-the-record conferences for policy-makers to discuss global issues and global security. Reports from conferences and seminars are published periodically and distributed free.

Geographical Area of Activity: International.

Restrictions: The Foundation is not a grant-making organization.

Publications: *World Press Review* (monthly); *Courier* (newsletter, three a year); *Common Ground* (radio transcripts); conference reports; books on global change, the United Nations, security and disarmament, human rights and global education.

Finance: Total assets $103,534,998 (2001).

Directors: Richard H. Stanley (Pres. and Chair.); Donna J. Buckles; Brian T. Hanson; Michael L. McNulty; Lynne E. Stanley; Sarah C. Stanley; Jane A. Stephenson; Mary Jo Stanley (Dir Emer.).

Address: 209 Iowa Ave, Muscatine, IA 52761.

Telephone: (563) 264-1500; **Fax:** (563) 264-0864; **Internet:** www.stanleyfdn.org; **e-mail:** stanley@stanleyfdn.org.

Starr Foundation

Founded in 1955 by Cornelius V. Starr.

Activities: Makes grants largely in the area of education, particularly higher education. Also active in culture, medicine and health, public policy in international relations, welfare and social services. Offers funding for scholarships, professorships, fellowships and endowment funds.

Geographical Area of Activity: USA.

Restrictions: No grants are made to individuals.

Finance: Assets $4,781,056,809 (2001); total grants $245,469,098 (2001).

Officers and Directors: Maurice R. Greenberg (Chair.); Florence A. Davis (Pres.); Marlon I. Breen, Gladys Thomas (Vice-Pres); Ida E. Galler (Sec.); Frank R. Tengi (Treas.); Houghton Freeman; Edwin A. G. Manton; John J. Roberts; Ernest E. Stempel.

Address: 70 Pine St, New York, NY 10270.

Telephone: (212) 770-6881; **Fax:** (212) 425-6261; **Internet:** http://fdncenter.org/grantmaker/starr/; **e-mail:** grants@starrfoundation.org.

Stewardship Foundation

Founded in 1962 by the C. Davis Weyerhaeuser Irrevocable Trust.

Activities: Concerned with funding evangelical religious organizations whose ministries operate over a wide area. Areas of involvement include education, mental health, youth development, international economic development and peace. Grants are made to international development organizations, foreign missions and youth ministries.

Geographical Area of Activity: International.

Restrictions: No grants are made to individuals; grants are made only to US public non-profit organizations.

Finance: Assets $110,000,000 (Nov. 2000).

Board of Trustees: W. T. Weyerhaeuser (Chair.); Charles L. Anderson; Wesley J. Anderson; Carl T. Fynboe; Donald W. Mowat; Annette B. Weyerhaeuser.

Principal Staff: Exec. Dir Cary A. Paine; Grants Coordinator Amy Alva.

Address: POB 1278, Tacoma, WA 98402.

Telephone: (253) 620-1340; **Fax:** (253) 572-2721; **Internet:** www.stewardshipfdn.org; **e-mail:** info@stewardshipfdn.org.

Barbra Streisand Foundation

Founded in 1986 by Barbra Streisand to provide funding in the fields of AIDS research, child and youth welfare, civil liberties, voting rights, international human rights and women's issues.

Activities: Makes grants to US-based organizations working on a national level.

Geographical Area of Activity: USA (Los Angeles and New York).

Restrictions: No grants are made to individuals, nor to local organizations.

Publications: Application guidelines.

Finance: Total assets $3,833,146 (2001); total grants $670,970 (2001).

Trustees: Richard Baskin; Alan Bergman; Marilyn Bergman; Marvin Goldberger; Jason Gould; Page Jenkins; Stanley K. Sheinbaum; Barbra Streisand.

Principal Staff: Exec. Dir Margery Tabankin; Programme Assoc. Suzy de Blois.

Address: 1460 Fourth St, Suite 212, Santa Monica, CA 90401-2329.

Telephone: (310) 535-3767; **Fax:** (310) 395-9676.

Sun Microsystems Foundation, Inc

Founded in 1990 to promote community development in disenfranchised areas where Sun Microsystems is located.

Activities: Operates nationally and internationally, making grants through four world-wide corporate affairs programmes: Education and Employment Training; Open Gateways; Employee Matching Gifts; and Community Partnership.

Geographical Area of Activity: International.

Publications: Brochures and information on programmes.

Finance: Total assets $4,763,906 (June 2000); total giving $1,963,808 (2000).

Principal Staff: Exec. Dir Gary F. Serda.

Address: 901 San Antonio Rd, Palo Alto, CA 94303.

Telephone: (650) 336-0545; **Fax:** (650) 856-2114; **Internet:** www.sun.com; **e-mail:** corpaffrs@corp.sun.com.

Surdna Foundation, Inc

Founded in 1917 by John E. Andrus for general charitable purposes.

Activities: Operates in the following areas: the environment (in particular energy, transportation, urban and suburban land use, human systems, and biological and cultural diversity); community revitalization (taking a comprehensive and holistic approach to restoring communities in the USA, in particular through entrepreneurial programmes offering solutions to difficult systemic problems); building an effective citizenry (promoting a civil society through character development, ethical behaviour, social and emotional learning and conflict resolution); and the arts, focusing on arts education and young people. Also provides funding to support the development of the non-profit sector in the US and grants for organizational capacity building.

Restrictions: No grants are made to individuals.

Publications: Annual Report; reports.

Finance: Total assets $639,562,016 (June 2001); total grants $39,531,216 (2001).

Board of Trustees: Chair. Elizabeth Andrus; Vice-Chair. Christopher Davenport; Treas. Frederick Moon, III; Sec. John L. Lynagh.

Principal Staff: Exec. Dir Edward Skloot.

Address: 330 Madison Ave, 30th Floor, New York, NY 10017-5001.

Telephone: (212) 557-0010; **Fax:** (212) 557-0003; **Internet:** www.surdna.org; **e-mail:** request@surdna.org.

Survivors of the Shoah Visual History Foundation

Established by Steven Spielberg in 1994 to videotape and preserve the testimonies of Holocaust survivors and other witnesses, and to overcome prejudice, ignorance and bigotry, and the suffering they cause, through the educational use of visual history testimonies. The Shoah Foundation has collected more than 51,000 videotaped testimonies of Holocaust survivors and other witnesses in 57 countries.

Activities: The Foundation works to develop partnerships to support three main strategic goals: to use the archive to create educational projects for classrooms and broader dissemination; to build and support educational programmes; and to preserve the archive and provide access to it.

Geographical Area of Activity: International.

Restrictions: Does not make grants.

Publications: *Past Forward* newsletter; documentary films; CD-ROMs; study guides; and books.

Finance: The Foundation is partially financed by a $6,000,000 donation from Steven Spielberg, as well as receiving donations from other individuals, foundations, companies and government agencies.

Trustees and Directors: Steven Spielberg (Founder and Chair.); Gerald Breslauer; Michael Rutman; Bruce Ramer.

Principal Staff: Pres. and CEO Dr Douglas Greenberg; Vice-Pres., Admin. Ari Zev; Vice-Pres., Development Steve Klappholz.

Address: POB 3168, Los Angeles, CA 90078-3168.

Telephone: (818) 777-7802; **Fax:** (818) 866-0312; **Internet:** www.vhf.org; **e-mail:** webmaster@vhf.org.

TechnoServe

Founded in 1968 to help increase the income of rural farmers and business people in developing countries.

Activities: Runs its own projects to help rural families to create their own local businesses, giving them advice, sharing technical expertise, and providing the marketing and capital needed to create prosperity and a long-term sustainable solution to poverty.

Geographical Area of Activity: Central and South America, and Africa.

Restrictions: Runs own projects. No unsolicited applications for grants accepted. This is not a grant-making foundation.

Finance: Total assets $19,828,401 (2002); annual revenue $16,596,319, expenditure $16,749,533 (2000).

Directors: P. E. Tierney (Chair.); Peter A. Reiling (Pres. and CEO); S. N. Johnson (Treas.); G. Baldwin; J. Bullard Broggini; B. A. Brooke; M. J. Bush; J. B. Caron; J. W. Donley; P. A. Flaherty; T. Hardy; B. Heerema; H. Howe, Jr; T. S. Kaplan; S. D. Lindsay; R. L. Lumpkins; W. E. Mayer; J. C. Orr; J. A. Riessen; P. Soros; H. A. Verfaillie; R. G. Viault; C. Williams.

Principal Staff: Pres. and CEO Peter A. Reiling.

Address: 49 Day St, Norwalk, CT 06854.

Telephone: (203) 852-0377; **Fax:** (203) 838-6717; **Internet:** www.technoserve.org; **e-mail:** technoserve@tns.org.

Thrasher Research Fund

Founded in 1977 by E. W. Thrasher to support meritorious, innovative research projects that seek to improve child health and well-being.

Activities: Grants are made to institutions in any country for research, without restriction as to geographical location, ethnicity, gender, creed or nationality. The Fund gives priority to practical applied research with the potential to benefit large numbers of children and find sustainable solutions to major problems of child health and well-being. The main focus is currently on gaps in paediatric medical research most likely to have an impact on the treatment of children with critical illnesses and major health problems. Grants range from $10,000–$400,000 and generally run for one to three years.

Geographical Area of Activity: International.

Restrictions: No grants for general operations, construction or renovation of buildings or facilities, nor for general donations, loans, student aid, scholarships, or support of other funds or institutions.

Publications: Biennial Report and application brochure.

Executive Committee: Keith B. McMullin (Chair.).

Principal Staff: Pres. A. Dean Byrd; Sec. Allison F. Martinez.

Address: 15 East South Temple St, Salt Lake City, UT 84150-6910.

Telephone: (801) 240-4753; **Fax:** (801) 240-1625; **Internet:** www.thrasherresearch.org; **e-mail:** martinezaf@thrasherresearch.org.

Tides Foundation

Founded in 1976, a grant-making organization dedicated to positive social change.

Activities: Acts as a mediator between donors and charitable organizations in need of resources, promoting human rights, social justice and a healthy environment. Strengthens community non-profit organizations, and awards grants in a large number of areas, including the arts and culture; economic development; the environment; gay and lesbian issues; HIV/AIDS; Native American communities; gender equality; reproductive health; and youth. Current programmes include the Death Penalty Mobilization Fund, Bridging the Economic Divide, Rapid Response Initiative and a Democracy Fund. Offers a number of services to donors to ensure that their money makes a lasting social impact. These include: flexible and personalized grant-making programmes; expert advice; and the opportunity to network. In 2003 launched the Tides Peace Strategies Fund to make grants to domestic and international organizations working to advocate for peace and oppose military aggression; protect civil liberties and immigrant rights in the United States; and respond to humanitarian and social crises in ways that promote equity and sustainability.

Geographical Area of Activity: USA.

Finance: Total revenue $93,224,126, grants $84,604,356 (2001).

Directors: D. Pike (Pres.); J. Bronfman; E. Cobell; Q. Delaney; A. Kydd; J. A. Powell; W. Rathke; C. C. Savitt; J. Solomon.

Principal Staff: Pres. Drummond Pike; Exec. Dir Idelisse Malavé; Vice-Pres. Ellen Friedman.

Address: The Presidio, POB 29903, San Francisco, CA 94129.

Telephone: (415) 561-6400; **Fax:** (415) 561-6401; **Internet:** www.tides.org; **e-mail:** info@tides.org.

Timken Foundation of Canton

Founded in 1934 by the Timken family to promote community development and improve civic amenities.

Activities: Operates nationally and internationally, in areas where the Timken Co. has manufacturing facilities, through the Timken International Fund (q.v.), in the fields of education, the arts, science and technology, and social welfare; provides capital fund grants for colleges, schools, hospitals, cultural centres, conservation and recreation centres, and other charitable institutions.

Geographical Area of Activity: International.

Restrictions: No grants are made to individuals, or for operating expenditures.

Finance: Assets $152,869,005 (Sept. 2002); total giving $4,537,943 (2002).

Officers and Directors: Ward J. Timken (Pres.); W. R. Timken, Jr (Vice-Pres.); Don D. Dickes (Sec./Treas.); Nancy S. Knudsen.

Principal Staff: Programme Dir Nancy S. Knudsen.

Address: 200 Market Ave N, Suite 210, Canton, OH 44702.

Telephone: (330) 452-1144; **Fax:** (330) 452-2306.

Timken International Fund

Founded in 1959 by H. H. Timken, Jr, W. R. Timken and J. M. Timken for general charitable purposes.

Activities: Makes capital grants primarily internationally in areas where the Timken Co. has manufacturing facilities, through grants to educational and charitable institutions.

Geographical Area of Activity: International.

Restrictions: No grants are made to individuals, nor for operating expenditures.

Trustees: Ward J. Timken (Pres.); W. R. Timken, Jr (Vice-Pres.); D. D. Dickes (Sec./Treas.).

Address: c/o The Timken Co., 1835 Dueber Ave, SW, Canton, OH 44706.

Telephone: (330) 455-5281; **Fax:** (330) 455-1752.

Tinker Foundation, Inc

Founded in 1959 by Edward Larocque Tinker to promote better understanding between the peoples of the Americas, Portugal and Spain, and for the support of work in, or directly related to, Antarctica.

Activities: Operates in the following fields: social sciences, with particular emphasis on economic and political matters having strong public policy implications; and natural resources, with major support allocated for those projects focusing on environmental policy. The Foundation supports research projects, conferences and workshops. The Foundation also promotes collaboration between organizations in the USA and Central and South America, Portugal and Spain, and among institutions in those regions.

Geographical Area of Activity: Central and South America, Mexico, Portugal, Spain and Antarctica.

Restrictions: No grants are made to individuals.

Publications: Annual report.

Finance: Assets $74,589,872 (Dec. 2001); annual grant expenditure $3,371,523 (2001).

Officers and Directors: Martha T. Muse (Chair.); Renate Rennie (Pres.); John A. Luke, Jr (Treas.); Richard de J. Osborne (Sec.); William R. Chaney; Sally Grooms Cowal; Kenneth R. Maxwell; Charles McC. Mathias; Susan L. Segal; Alan Stoga.

Principal Staff: Pres. Renate Rennie.

Address: 55 East 59th St, New York, NY 10022.

Telephone: (212) 421-6858; **Fax:** (212) 223-3326; **Internet:** http://fdncenter.org/grantmaker/tinker; **e-mail:** tinker@tinker.org.

The Trull Foundation

Founded in 1967 by R. B. Trull, Florence M. Trull, Gladys T. Brooking, Jean T. Herlin and Laura Shiflett for general charitable purposes.

Activities: Focuses its grants on four priority areas: local health-care and other local projects in the Matagorda County area, Texas, where the Foundation has its roots; children and families, particularly in the fields of child abuse, hunger relief and poverty; people and families affected by substance abuse; and the coastal environment of Texas, including farming, ranching, aquaculture and birds.

Geographical Area of Activity: USA (mainly Texas).

Publications: Report (every 2 years); application guidelines.

Trustees: Colleen Claybourn (Chair.); Rose C. Lancaster (Vice-Chair.); J. Fred Huitt (Sec./Treas.); Sarah H. Olfers; R. Scott Trull.

Principal Staff: Exec. Dir E. Gail Purvis.

Address: 404 Fourth St, Palacios, TX 77465.

Telephone: (512) 972-5241; **Fax:** (512) 972-1109; **Internet:** www.trullfoundation.org; **e-mail:** trullfdn@wcnet.net.

Trust for Mutual Understanding

Founded in 1984 to provide support to American non-profit cultural and environmental organizations for professional exchanges between the USA and Central Europe and the countries of the former USSR.

Activities: Some three-quarters of funds are directed at cultural exchanges, with the remaining one-quarter allocated to environmental projects. Grants are made for exchange progammes that include a significant amount of professional interaction and collaboration between the two countries involved.

Geographical Area of Activity: USA, Eastern and Central Europe and the countries of the former USSR.

Restrictions: Grants only to American non-profit organizations for international travel, and related expenses of Russian, Eastern and Central European, and American exchange participants.

Publications: Annual Report.

Finance: Funding from anonymous donor. Endowment $52,000,000; annual grant budget approx. $3,500,000.

Directors and Trustees: Richard S. Lanier (Dir); Elizabeth J. McCormack; Donal C. O'Brien, Jr. *Board of Advisors:* Ruth Adams; Wade Green; Julie J. Kidd; William H. Luers; Joseph Polisi; Blair Ruble; Isaac Shapiro.

Principal Staff: Dir Richard S. Lanier; Programme Assoc. Wendy S. Newton; Programme Asst Carrie E. Thompson; Exec. Sec. Jacie L. Almira.

Address: 30 Rockefeller Plaza, Rm 5600, New York, NY 10112.

Telephone: (212) 632-3405; **Fax:** (212) 632-3409; **Internet:** www.tmuny.org; **e-mail:** tmu@tmuny.org.

TRW Foundation

Founded in 1953 as the Thompson Products Foundation, present name adopted in 1965.

Activities: Operates mainly in the field of education, primarily in areas where the company operates, and especially in Cleveland, Ohio. Grants are made for education, in particular for engineering, science and technology, and business administration programmes, and for scholarships, professorships and fellowships; funds are also given for social welfare, especially community funds, hospitals, youth and general welfare agencies, cultural organizations and selected national and international agencies. Awards the TRW Presidential Young Investigators Award.

Geographical Area of Activity: USA (mainly Cleveland, OH).

Publications: Annual Report; programme policy statement; grants list.

Finance: Assets $19,075,833 (Dec. 2000); total giving $8,922,230 (2000).

Officers and Trustees: H. V. Knicely (Pres.); A. F. Senger (Exec. Vice-Pres. and Chief Financial Officer); C. G. Miller (Vice-Pres. and Controller); William C. Seeger, Jr (Vice-Pres. and Treas.); R. M. Hamje, W. A. Warren (Vice-Pres); J. Powers (Sec.).

Address: 1900 Richmond Rd, Cleveland, OH 44124.

Telephone: (216) 291-7160.

Turner Foundation, Inc

Founded in 1990 to prevent damage to the environment and to support those institutions working to protect the environment and promote sustainable practices.

Activities: The Foundation focuses on the areas of conservation and protection of natural resources, preservation of the environment, protection of wildlife and population management, and supports education and activism in these areas. The primary environmental concerns of the foundation are: energy efficiency and renewables, the protection of forests and other habitats and the protection of water from toxic pollution.

Geographical Area of Activity: International.

Restrictions: No funding for buildings, land acquisition, endowments, or start-up funds, nor to fund films, books, magazines, or other specific media projects. No support for individuals. Some programmes are restricted to certain states of the USA..

Finance: Total assets $148,222,535 (2001); total grants $68,089,432 (2001).

Officers and Directors: Michael Finley (Pres.).

Principal Staff: Exec. Dir. Peter Bahouth; Programme Man. Jonathan Roseman.

Address: One CNN Center, Suite 1090, South Tower, Atlanta, GA 30303.

Telephone: (404) 681-9900; **Fax:** (404) 681-0172; **Internet:** www.turnerfoundation.org; **e-mail:** turnerfi@turnerfoundation.org.

Desmond Tutu Peace Foundation

Established in 2001 to advance the philosophy and practices of Archbishop Desmond Tutu.

Activities: Establishes leadership academies in the USA and Africa. The academies focus on developing emerging leaders who act for peace, reconciliation and restorative justice.

Geographical Area of Activity: Africa and the USA.

Address: 1245 10th Ave East, Seattle, WA 98102.

Telephone: (206) 323-7566; **Fax:** (206) 323-4018; **Internet:** www.tutufoundation-usa.org; **e-mail:** info@tutfoundation-usa.org.

Unitarian Universalist Service Committee

Established in 1939, a non-sectarian organization committed to human rights and social justice.

Activities: Works in the field of human rights internationally, through advocacy, education and partnerships with grass-roots organizations. Maintains partnerships in the USA, South and South-East Asia, Central Africa, and Central and South America and the Caribbean, and sponsors programmes related to the rights of children, indigenous people, oppressed groups and the empowerment of women. Also provides financial and technical support to areas suffering the effects of disaster, especially where human rights are threatened.

Geographical Area of Activity: International.

Directors: D. Mohler (Pres.); Rick Van Dyke, Jr (Vice-Pres.); D. E. Arnink (Sec.); A. W. Bradburd (Treas.); B. Cheatham; S. Corfman; G. Guengerich; J. Gunning; L. Herrick; F. Lee; N. Nowak; J. Hubbard Robinson; R. van Dyke, Jr; I. Dugger Vargas; L. D. Whealey.

Principal Staff: Interim Exec. Dir Nancy Moore.

Address: 130 Prospect St, Cambridge, MA 02139.

Telephone: (617) 868-6600; **Fax:** (617) 868-7102; **Internet:** www.uusc.org; **e-mail:** programs@uusc.org.

United Nations Development Fund for Women—UNIFEM

Created in 1976, UNIFEM is dedicated to gender equality and the empowerment of women throughout the developing world.

Activities: Supports projects and initiatives related to the social, political and economic empowerment of women in over 130 countries, through advocacy and financial and technical support. Projects range from national education programmes to small grass-roots programmes to improve working conditions for women. Also plays an active role in influencing the United Nations system of development co-operation.

Geographical Area of Activity: International.

Publications: *Currents* (electronic monthly newsletter); Annual Report; and other publications.

Principal Staff: Exec. Dir Dr Noeleen Heyzer.

Address: 304 East 45th St, 15th Floor, New York, NY 10017.

Telephone: (212) 906-6400; **Fax:** (212) 906-6705; **Internet:** www.unifem.undp.org; **e-mail:** unifem@undp.org.

United Nations Foundation

Established in 1997 along with its sister organization, the Better World Fund (q.v.), following a gift of $1,000,000,000 to the United Nations by R. E. (Ted) Turner; the Foundation seeks to support the goals and objectives of the United Nations and its Charter in order to promote a more peaceful, prosperous and just world, with special emphasis on the work of the United Nations, especially on behalf of economic, social, environmental and humanitarian causes.

Activities: Invests in United Nations-sponsored agencies and programmes. Its four current main areas of activity are: peace, security and human rights; women and population; the environment; and children's health. Selective assistance is also provided to humanitarian causes, and to activities strengthening the United Nations. Projects receiving funding include the United Nations Population Fund (UNFPA) and the United Nations High Commissioner for Refugees (UNHCR), which have received grants to develop and distribute emergency reproductive health information and services to refugees in Asia, Africa and South-Eastern Europe (especially Kosovo). The Foundation also provides grants to the UNAIDS programme to assist in the prevention of the spread of HIV and AIDS in Botswana and Zimbabwe and, in partnership with organizations such as the World Health Organization (WHO), is working to eliminate polio. In conjunction with the Better World Fund, the Foundation sponsors the daily *UN Wire* news summary on United Nations and global affairs.

Geographical Area of Activity: International.

Finance: Total assets $58,024,985 (2000); annual revenue $51,185,581, expenditure $91,527,199 (2000).

Board of Directors: R. E. (Ted) Turner (Chair.); Timothy E. Wirth (Pres.); Ruth Correa Leite Cardoso; Liang Dan; Graça Machel; Hisashi Owada; Emma Rothschild; Dr Nafis Sadik; Andrew Young; Muhammad Yunus.

Address: 1225 Connecticut Ave, NW, Fourth Floor, Washington, DC 20036.

Telephone: (202) 887-9040; **Fax:** (202) 887-9021; **Internet:** www.unfoundation.org.

United States–Central and Eastern European Environment Foundation

Established in 2000 with the aim of improving the environment in Central, Eastern and South-Eastern Europe.

Activities: Operates in Central, Eastern and South-Eastern Europe in the field of conservation and the environment, through promoting collaboration between US organizations and local partners in the region. Aims to extend its area of operation to countries of the former USSR. Promotes exchange programmes for professionals; provides advisory services to Eastern European environmental organizations; facilitates the exchange of information between environmental organizations; and informs the American people about the state of the environment in Eastern European countries.

Geographical Area of Activity: Central, Eastern and South-Eastern Europe (Albania, Bosnia-Herzegovina, Bulgaria, Croatia, Czech Republic, Estonia, Hungary, Latvia, Lithuania, the Former Yugoslav Republic of Macedonia, Poland, Romania, Slovakia, Slovenia and Yugoslavia).

Restrictions: Currently no grants are being made.

Publications: Newsletter (by e-mail).

Board of Directors: Toni Popovski (Pres.); Robert Herbst (Chair.); and eleven other members.

Principal Staff: Exec. Dir Betsy Hoffmeister; Assoc. Dir Frana Milan.

Address: 6723 48th Ave, SW, Seattle, WA 98136.

Telephone and Fax: (206) 932-9973; **e-mail:** info@useuroenvirofoundation.org.

United States–Japan Foundation

Founded in 1980 by Ryoichi Sasakawa to strengthen co-operation and understanding between the people of the USA and Japan.

Activities: The Foundation supports improved teaching about Japan in US schools, and about the USA in Japanese schools, and the improvement of Japanese language instruction in US secondary schools. It also supports policy study groups in the fields of international finance, development assistance, multilateral crisis management and regional security, environmental protection and energy, and science and technology. Operates a programme of interaction by future leaders in Japan and the USA. Grants are also made to non-profit organizations for projects involving US–Japanese co-operation, as well as journalist exchanges, media programmes and/or documentary film. Maintains an office in Tokyo.

Geographical Area of Activity: USA and Japan.

Restrictions: No grants to individuals or for-profit organizations.

Publications: Annual Report.

Finance: Net assets $99,914,586 (Dec.2000); annual expenditure $8,658,600 (2000).

Board of Trustees: T. S. Johnson (Chair.); Shinji Fukukawa (Vice-Chair.); Yusuke Saraya (Sec.); Dr G. R. Packard (Pres.); Dr J. Brademas; Prof. G. L. Curtis; R. Chandler Duke; T. S. Foley; Hon. W. Frenzel; M. S. Izumi; T. S. Johnson; Yotaro Kobayashi; T. T. Ryan; Yohei Sasakawa; Takeo Takuma; Jiro Ushio.

Principal Staff: Dir, Tokyo Office T. Takuma; Treas. and Asst. Sec. C. Manapat-Sims; J. L. Schhoff; D. P. Janes; T. Sham; J. C. Villatoro.

Address: 145 East 32nd St, 12th Floor, New York, NY 10016.

Telephone: (212) 481-8753; **Fax:** (212) 481-8762; **Internet:** www.us-jf.org; **e-mail:** info@us-jf.org.

United Way International

Established in 1974 as a support organization, helping to build community capacity for a better quality of life worldwide, through voluntary giving and action.

Activities: Operates in the area of community development, working with corporations, foundations and other donors to assist them with their global philanthropic needs.

Geographical Area of Activity: International.

Publications: Newsletter; Annual Report.

Finance: Total assets $5,732,384 (2001); annual revenue $9,432,595, expenditure $8,567,660 (2001).

Address: 701 North Fairfax St, Alexandria, VA 22314.

Telephone: (703) 519-0092; **Fax:** (703) 519-0097; **Internet:** www.uwint.org; **e-mail:** uwi@unitedway.org.

UPS Foundation

Established by United Parcel Service in 1951 to support higher education and social welfare projects and charities.

Activities: Provides funding for programmes internationally in the following areas: families and children in crisis; adult illiteracy; food distribution; programmes for disabled people; economic opportunities for minorities; community development; higher education; disaster relief; and research. Awards scholarships and grants for research projects, equipment and special projects.

Geographical Area of Activity: International.

Publications: Information brochure.

Finance: Assets $109,825,000 (2000); grants disbursed approx. $40,300,000 (2001).

Officers and Trustees: Lea Soupata (Chair.); Thomas H. Weidemeyer (Sec.); Robert J. Clanin (Treas.); Evern Cooper (Exec. Dir); Mike Eskew; James P. Kelly; Joe Pyne.

Principal Staff: Pres. Evern D. Cooper; Exec. Dir Evern Cooper.

Address: 55 Glenlake Parkway, NE, Atlanta, GA 30328.

Telephone: (404) 828-6374; **Fax:** (404) 828-7435; **Internet:** www.community.ups.com/community/resources/foundation/index.html.

US-Baltic Foundation

Established in 1990 to promote the social and economic development of the Baltic states.

Activities: Operates in the Baltic states in the areas of education and training, in order to fulfil its aims. Established offices in Estonia, Latvia and Lithuania, which now operate as independent foundations. Programmes support the development of democracy and an independent media. The Foundation has also funded three Schools of Public Admnistration in Estonia, Latvia and Lithuania.

Geographical Area of Activity: Estonia, Latvia and Lithuania.

Board of Directors: William Altman (Chair.); Hamid Ladjevardi (Vice-Chair.); George Ramonas (Treas.); Eric Harkna (Sec.).

Principal Staff: Man. Dir Jeff Nelson; Dir Program Development Karina Donnelly.

Address: 733 15th St, NW, Suite 1026, Washington, DC 20005.

Telephone: (202) 393-3338; **Fax:** (202) 393-3388; **Internet:** www.usbaltic.org; **e-mail:** info@usbaltic.org.

US-Ukraine Foundation

The Foundation was established in 1991 to facilitate democratic development, encourage free market reform, and enhance human rights in Ukraine.

Activities: Supports democratic development in Ukraine through its own projects, including the Community Partnerships Project; the Ukraine Education Project; Health Care and Humanitarian Aid; the Petrach Project; Kennan Kyiv Project; Chernobyl 2000; Parliamentary Development Project; Constitutional Court Project; and an NGO Project. Also established the Pylyp Orlyk Institute for Democracy in the Ukraine to carry out policy research. Activities include sponsoring workshops and seminars, providing support, training and technical resources, publishing and disseminating information; and providing emergency and development relief to certain sectors of the population in Ukraine. Maintains an office in Kiev.

Geographical Area of Activity: Ukraine.

Restrictions: Does not make grants.

Publications: *Infolink* (quarterly newsletter).

Finance: Funded by USAID and the Charles Stewart Mott Foundation (q.v.) and individual donors.

Board of Directors: Nadia K. McConnell (Pres.); George Sierant (Treas.); Walter Baranetskyj; Bohdan Burachinksky; Tamara Denysenko; George F. Hamm; Michael Kostiw; William Green Miller; Robert A. McConnell; Yaromyr Oryshkevych.

Principal Staff: Pres. Nadia K. McConnell; Vice-Pres. and Chief Operating Officer John A. Kun.

Address: 733 15th St, NW, Suite 1026, Washington, DC 20005.

Telephone: (202) 347-4264; **Fax:** (202) 347-4267; **Internet:** www.usukraine.org; **e-mail:** usuf@usukraine.org.

Lawson Valentine Foundation

Founded in 1989 for general charitable purposes.

Activities: Primarily concerned with the fields of sustainable agriculture and food systems, environment, human rights, race relations, and community programmes. Operates nationally and internationally, in Africa, Central and South America, and Asia.

Geographical Area of Activity: Africa, North, Central and South America, and Asia.

Publications: Application guidelines.

Finance: Assets $16,550,414 (2001); total grants $763,700 (2001).

Trustees: Allen Doyle; Valentine Doyle; Lucy Miller; Jay Vawter; William D. Zabel.

Address: 1000 Farmington Ave, West Hartford, CT 06107.

Telephone and Fax: (860) 570-0728.

G. Unger Vetlesen Foundation

Founded in 1955 by Georg Unger Vetlesen to contribute to religious, charitable, scientific, literary and educational causes world-wide.

Activities: Operates in New York, the USA in general and internationally in education and other fields; grants are mainly made in the areas of oceanographies, climate studies and other earth sciences; offers an international science award every two years for discoveries in the earth sciences; and makes grants for biological, geophysical and environmental scientific research, higher education and cultural activities, with an emphasis on Norwegian–US relations and maritime issues. Also supports public policy research and libraries.

Geographical Area of Activity: International.

Restrictions: No grants are made to individuals.

Finance: Total grants $4,730,000 (2001).

Officers and Directors: George Rowe, Jr (Pres.); Maurizio J. Morello (Sec. and Asst Dir); Gary Beauchamp; Eugene P. Grisanti; Ambrose K. Monell.

Address: 1 Rockefeller Plaza, Suite 301, New York, NY 10020-2002.

Telephone: (212) 586-0700; **Fax:** (212) 245-1863; **Internet:** www.monellvetlesen.org; **e-mail:** info@monellvetlesen.org.

Virtual Foundation

Founded in 1996 by ECOLOGIA (q.v.), an international non-profit organization, to support local projects in the areas of the environment, sustainable development and health; and to encourage philanthropy by fostering partnerships between local groups and on-line donors.

Activities: The Foundation works in collaboration with NGOs world-wide to fund projects in the fields of the environment, health and sustainable economic activity. Project proposals submitted to the Virtual Foundation are posted on the Virtual Foundation's web-site for evaluation by visitors to the site, who may make a donation to the project of their choice. The Foundation maintains offices in various countries, including Japan and the Czech Republic.

Geographical Area of Activity: International, including Central Europe, Russia, Africa, Central Asia, China and Central and South America.

Restrictions: No grants for emergency crisis aid or academic projects.

Directors: Randy Kritskausky (Pres.); Carolyn Schmidt (Sec.); Ed Shoener (Treas.); Alene N. Case; Dr Mike Case; Aleg Cherp; Rachel Golden; Paul Soler-Sala.

Principal Staff: Exec. Dir Jürgen Hess; Grants Co-ordinator Giedre Donauskaite; Prog. Man. Carolyn Schmidt.

Address: 4 Mill St, POB 268, Middlebury, VT 05753.

Telephone: (802) 388-8075; **Fax:** (802) 388-8069; **Internet:** www .virtualfoundation.org; **e-mail:** cschmidt@ecologia.org.

Vollmer Foundation, Inc

Founded in 1965 by Alberto F. Vollmer for general charitable purposes.

Activities: Operates in the fields of medicine and health, education and social welfare, through grants to hospitals and institutions of higher education in Venezuela. Also supports the Catholic Church in Venezuela. No grants are made to individuals.

Geographical Area of Activity: South America.

Finance: Assets $14,133,943 (2001); total grants $276,050 (2001).

Officers and Directors: G. J. Vollmer (Pres.); A. L. Wallis (Vice-Pres. and Treas.); C. V. de Eseverri (Sec.); G. A. Vollmer.

Principal Staff: Asst Sec. Albert J. Ennist.

Address: 217 Gravel Hill Rd, Kinnelon, NJ 07405.

Telephone: (201) 492-2309.

DeWitt Wallace—Reader's Digest Fund, Inc

Founded in 1965 by DeWitt Wallace to foster fundamental improvement in the quality of opportunities for education and career development for all school-age young people, and to increase access to these improved services for young people in low-income communities. Shares an administration with the Lila Wallace—Reader's Digest Fund, Inc.

Activities: Operates primarily nationally in the field of education, through improving services in schools (including investing in the Pathways to Teaching Careers programme to recruit non-traditional candidates for teaching, improving school library services and reforming vocational education); improving services in community-based organizations (including after-school care systems and services for young people); and improving services through school–community collaboration (career guidance and school services in low-income communities). Also makes grants to cultural organizations through the LEAP (Leadership and Excellence in Arts Participation) initiative ($31,000,000 since the project's inception in 1999). Resources are allocated to organizations which are invited to apply for grants.

Geographical Area of Activity: USA.

Restrictions: Grants are rarely made for unsolicited projects.

Publications: Annual Report; education reports.

Finance: Assets $737,000,000 (Dec. 2001); grants approved $24,895,683 (2001).

Officers and Directors: George V. Grune (Chair.); M. Christine DeVita (Pres.); Rob D. Nagel (Dir, Investments); Mary E. Geras (Dir, Finance); Gordon M. Ambach; W. Don Cornwell; Peter C. Marzio; Laraine S. Rothenberg; Joseph Shenker; Walter G. Shipley; C. J. (Pete) Silas.

Principal Staff: Communications Dir Lucas Held.

Address: 2 Park Ave, 23rd Floor, New York, NY 10016.

Telephone: (212) 251-9700; **Fax:** (212) 679-6990; **Internet:** www.wallacefunds.org; **e-mail:** wrdf@wallacefunds.org.

Lila Wallace—Reader's Digest Fund, Inc

Founded in 1956 by Lila Acheson Wallace and formerly known as the L.A.W. Fund, Inc. The Fund supports programmes which promote art and culture as an everyday part of life. Shares an administration with the DeWitt Wallace—Reader's Digest Fund, Inc (q.v.).

Activities: Promotes programmes and projects which aim to enhance the cultural life of communities and bring culture and art into people's everyday lives. Attempts to increase audiences for the performing, visual and folk arts. Funds adult literacy projects and urban park programmes.

Geographical Area of Activity: USA.

Publications: Annual Report; financial statement; newsletter; occasional report; brochure.

Finance: Assets $566,000,000 (Dec. 2001); grants approved $10,028,201 (2001).

Officers and Directors: George V. Grune (Chair.); M. Christine DeVita (Pres.); Rob D. Nagel (Dir, Investments); Mary E. Geras (Dir, Finance); Gordon M. Ambach; W. Don Cornwell; Peter C. Marzio; Laraine S. Rothenberg; Joseph Shenker; Walter G. Shipley; C. J. (Pete) Silas.

Principal Staff: Communications Dir Lucas Held.

Address: 2 Park Ave, 23rd Floor, New York, NY 10016.

Telephone: (212) 251-9700; **Fax:** (212) 679-6990; **Internet:** www.wallacefunds.org; **e-mail:** wrdf@wallacefunds.org.

Miriam G. and Ira D. Wallach Foundation

Founded in 1956 to support general charitable purposes, mainly in New York.

Activities: The Foundation provides financial assistance in the fields of international affairs, education, the humanities, social welfare and Jewish organizations.

Restrictions: Grants are made to pre-selected organizations only, applications are not accepted.

Finance: Assets $18,873,979 (Oct. 2001); total grants $1,163,933 (2001).

Officers and Directors: Kenneth L. Wallach (Pres.); Ira D. Wallach (Chair.); Edgar Wachenheim, III (Vice-Pres.); Kenneth L. Wallach, Miriam G. Wallach (Vice-Chair.); Peter C. Siegfried (Sec.); Reginald Reinhardt (Treas.); Kate W. Cassidy; Martin W. Cassidy; Sue W. Wachenheim; Mary K. Wallach; Susan S. Wallach.

Address: 3 Manhattanville Rd, Purchase, NY 10577-2110.

Telephone: (914) 696-9060; **Fax:** (914) 696-1066; **e-mail:** purchase@cng-inc.com.

Andy Warhol Foundation for the Visual Arts

Founded in 1987 by Andy Warhol for the promotion of the visual arts.

Activities: Operates nationally and (on a limited scale) internationally in the areas of the visual arts, aspects of performing arts incorporating the plastic arts, education and historic preservation and urban development. Gives grants for curatorial programmes in museums, universities and other organizations to assist in the presentation of the visual arts in innovative ways and to support artists themselves and their work; and to organizations assisting in the preservation of historic properties and parks, and promoting public participation in urban planning. Also running a project on Arts, Culture and Society, aimed at ensuring a public debate about global, economic and societal forces affecting the arts.

Geographical Area of Activity: Mainly USA, but organizations elsewhere are eligible to apply.

Restrictions: Unable to make grants directly to individuals.

Publications: Annual Report.

Finance: Total assets $169,345,457 (April 2001); total grants $8,972,102 (2001).

Officers and Directors: Archibald L. Gillies (Pres.); John Warhol (Vice-Pres.); Peter P. McN. Gates (Sec.); K. H. Conwill; R. J. Denison; V. N. Desai; R. Gluckman; K. Halbreich; F. W. Hughes; S. T. Leval; A. M. Solomon; J. Wachs.

Principal Staff: Programme Dir Pamela Clapp.

Address: 65 Bleeker St, 7th Floor, New York, NY 10012.

Telephone: (212) 387-7555; **Fax:** (212) 387-7560; **Internet:** www.warholfoundation.org.

Web Lab—Digital Innovations Inc.

Established in 1997 by Marc N. Weiss as a not-for-profit think tank that encourages and supports innovation on the Web, with a special emphasis on developing the potential of the medium to bring people together to explore both personal and public issues in powerful, transforming ways.

Activities: The organization's principal projects include Small Group Dialogues, which aims to provide an innovative alternative to conventional on-line dialogue models; Crossover, which aims to stimulate collaboration and experimentation across communications disciplines and develop groundbreaking ideas for new projects through convening filmmakers, interactive artists, designers, animators, writers, technologists, game designers, web producers and cultural theorists; and the Web Development Fund, which provides funding to committed new media innovators to create groundbreaking Web projects addressing public and/or private issues.

Geographical Area of Activity: International.

Restrictions: Proposals are not currently accepted.

Publications: Newsletter.

Advisory Board: M. Bowe; J. McCabe Calacanis; C. Clark; D. Crocker; G. Davenport; S. Horn; A. Clayton Powell, III; J. Singh; M. Stahlman; C. Varley; R. Wakkary; T. Watson; B. Weil; M. Wilhelm; J. Wilson.

Principal Staff: Exec. Producer Marc N. Weiss.

Address: 853 Broadway, Suite 608, New York, NY 10003.

Telephone: (212) 353-0080; **Fax:** (212) 353-0572; **Internet:** www.weblab.org; **e-mail:** info@weblab.org.

Weeden Foundation

Founded in 1963 by Frank Weeden to address concerns about the destruction of natural resources and the problems associated with a growing global population.

Activities: Operates nationally and internationally in the field of conservation and the environment through three programme areas: bio-diversity, population and consumption. The Foundation's areas of interest are Western North America, Chile, Bolivia and Central Siberia (Russian Federation).

Geographical Area of Activity: International, with focus on Western North America, Chile, Bolivia and Central Siberia (Russian Federation).

Restrictions: No grants for individuals, marine conservation, elementary education, museums, capital construction, endowments, animal rights, toxic contamination, films, universities, fellowships or research.

Publications: Funding guidelines and Annual Report (on website only).

Finance: Net assets $37,000,000 (2000); annual expenditure $2,400,000 (2000).

Governing Board: Norm Weeden (Pres.); William Weeden (Vice-Pres.); John Weeden (Sec.); Elizabeth Barek; David Davies; Donald A. Weeden; Donald E. Weeden; Alan Weeden.

Principal Staff: Exec. Dir Donald A. Weeden; Research Asst Melissa Mahony.

Address: 747 Third Ave, 34th Floor, New York, NY 10017.

Telephone: (212) 888-1672; **Fax:** (212) 888-1354; **Internet:** www.weedenfdn.org; **e-mail:** weedenfdn@weedenfdn.org.

Robert A. Welch Foundation

Founded in 1954 by Robert A. Welch.

Activities: Supports a programme of basic research in chemistry with grants to faculty members at colleges and universities in Texas. Also sponsors a conference, a lectureship series yearly and scholarships and professorships in chemistry. Awards the Welch Award in Chemistry and the Norman Hackerman Award in Chemical Research.

Geographical Area of Activity: USA.

Publications: Annual Report.

Finance: Assets $537,748,201 (2001); total revenue $15,800,166, total expenditure $4,406,652 (2001).

Officers and Directors: Richard J. V. Johnson (Chair.); Norbert Dittrich (Pres. and Chief Operating Officer); J. Evans Attwell (Vice-Chair. and Sec.); Charles W. Duncan, Jr; Dennis Hendrix (Treas.); Jack S. Josey (Chair. Emer.).

Address: 5555 San Felipe, Suite 1900, Houston, TX 77056-2732.

Telephone: (713) 961-9884; **Fax:** (713) 961-5168; **Internet:** www.welch1.org; **e-mail:** dittrich@welch1.org.

Rob and Bessie Welder Wildlife Foundation

Founded in 1954 by Mr and Mrs R. H. Welder and others to promote graduate-level education in wildlife conservation, and to support research into wildlife and methods for increasing wildlife populations.

Activities: Operates in the field of conservation and the environment, through funding research, fellowships and internships, open to US citizens or to foreigners registered at a US university for a graduate degree; and the operation of the Welder Foundation Refuge.

Geographical Area of Activity: USA, particularly Texas.

Restrictions: No grants for work outside continental USA.

Publications: Report (every 2 years).

Trustees: H. C. Weil; J. J. Welder, V; P. H. Welder.

Principal Staff: Dir Dr D. Lynn Drawe; Asst. Dir Dr Terry L. Blankenship, Dr Selma N. Glasscock.

Address: POB 1400, Sinton, TX 78387.

Telephone: (512) 364-2643; **Fax:** (512) 364-2650; **Internet:** hometown.aol.com/welderwf/welderweb; **e-mail:** welderwf@aol.com.

Wenner-Gren Foundation for Anthropological Research, Inc

Founded in 1941 as the Viking Fund, Inc, by Dr Axel L. Wenner-Gren to support research in all branches of anthropology, including cultural and social anthropology, ethnology, biological and physical anthropology, archaeology, anthropological linguistics, and in closely related disciplines concerned with human origins, development and variation.

Activities: Operates an individual research grants programme, awarding up to approximately $25,000 for basic research in anthropology to holders of a doctorate degree and doctoral candidates undertaking dissertation projects; and offers the following awards and scholarships: Richard Carley Hunt Post-doctoral Fellowships, up to a maximum of approximately $15,000, to aid the writing up of research results for publication; Professional Development International Fellowships of up to approximately $15,000 per year, to PhD scholars and $35,000 to post-PhD scholars and advanced students from developing countries seeking additional training in anthropology; Conference Grants, of up to approximately $15,000, to organizers of conferences; and International Collaborative Research Grants, of up to approximately $30,000, to assist anthropological research projects undertaken jointly by two or more investigators from different countries, with priority given to projects involving at least one principal investigator from outside the countries of North America and Western Europe. Sponsor of Current Anthropology journal.

Geographical Area of Activity: International.

Restrictions: No scholarships.

Publications: Biennial Report.

Finance: Assets $113,541,000 (1999).

Trustees: R. Hackney (Chair.); F. Wadsworth (Vice-Chair.); D. Alexander; D. Brigham; B. Chase; D. Cobb; J. Immerwahr; R. Kennedy; G. Langdon; S. Masters; E. Milckiewicz; D. Patterson; D. Robinson; C. Williams.

Principal Staff: Pres. Dr Richard Fox.

Address: 220 Fifth Ave, 16th Floor, New York, NY 10001-7780.

Telephone: (212) 683-5000; **Fax:** (212) 683-9151; **Internet:** www.wennergren.org; **e-mail:** inquiries@wennergren.org.

Weyerhaeuser Family Foundation, Inc

Founded in 1950, and formerly known as the Weyerhaeuser Foundation, by F. K. Weyerhaeuser, E. W. Davis, Margaret W. Driscoll, Sarah-Maud W. Rosenberry, Frederick Weyerhaeuser, G. F. Jewett, Elizabeth W. Titcomb, Carl A. Weyerhaeuser, C. Davis Weyerhaeuser and John P. Weyerhaeuser, Jr, for the relief of the poor, the advancement of the Christian religion, the advancement of education and science, including medical science, and the application of the same through hospitals, clinics and research institutions. Since the 1960s emphasis has been placed on the support of programmes of national and international significance that attempt to identify and correct the causes of maladjustment in our society.

Activities: Operates both nationally and internationally in the fields of the arts and humanities (through programmes that assist the public to understand various art forms), education (opportunities for minority groups, religious training, youth development projects and private higher education), health (mental health, alcoholism, psychiatry), social welfare, international activities, religion and the environment, science and technology (environmental preservation, utilization of scarce resources and forestry), through grants to institutions. The Foundation supports international projects that enable people to help themselves via population planning, agricultural improvements, self-government and peace education.

Geographical Area of Activity: International.

Restrictions: The Foundation does not normally make grants for projects with limited geographical emphasis, operating budgets, annual campaigns, building and equipment, elementary and secondary education, lobbying or propaganda. Nor does it make grants to individuals, for scholarships, fellowships or for travel.

Publications: Annual Report.

Finance: Assets $13,826,707 (2001); total grants $564,760 (2001).

Officers and Trustees: Lucy R. Jones (Pres.); Kathleen McGoldrick (Vice-Pres.); Margaret R. King (Sec.); Peter C. Titcomb (Treas.); M. G. Carr; M. L. Driscoll; L. M. Fremont; B. P. Phares; L. W. Piasecki; E. V. Rasmussen; P. R. Rosenberry; K. Z. Titcomb; F. J. Weyerhaeuser; J. H. Weyerhaeuser; M. W. Weyerhaeuser; N. N. Weyerhaeuser; R. M. Weyerhaeuser; W. T. Weyerhaeuser.

Address: 322 Minnesota St, Suite 100, St Paul, MN 55101.

Telephone: (612) 228-0935; **Internet:** www.wfamilyfoundation.org; **e-mail:** jmo@fidcouns.com.

Whirlpool Foundation

Founded in 1951 by Louis and Frederick Upton (Co-Founders of the Whirlpool Corporation) to improve the quality of life in the communities where the corporation operates.

Activities: Operates world-wide, particularly in the USA and Canada, Western and Eastern Europe, and Asia, within three programme areas: the quality of family life; cultural diversity; and lifelong learning. Principally aimed at projects likely to have an impact in communities where the company has a presence. Also runs a programme of citizenship grants within the USA, aimed at organizations supporting general education, health and human services, arts and culture and civic and community; and employee-directed programmes.

Geographical Area of Activity: International.

Restrictions: No grants are given to religious or labour organizations.

Finance: Total giving $7,000,000 (2001).

Address: 2000 North M-63, Benton Harbor, MI 49022-2692.

Telephone: (269) 923-5580; **Fax:** (269) 925-0154; **Internet:** www.whirlpoolcorp.com/whr/foundation/foundation.html.

Whitehall Foundation, Inc

Founded in 1937 by George M. Moffett, Jeremiah Milbank, Willis D. Wood, Frederick T. Fisher, Morris Sayre, Frank H. Hall and Linus C. Coggan, to give financial aid to charitable, benevolent or educational work through such agencies or institutions as the Trustees may determine.

Activities: Assists scholarly work in the life sciences, through a programme of grants and grants-in-aid primarily targeting dynamic areas of basic biological research that are not generally supported by Federal agencies or other foundations with specialized missions. Currently interested in basic research in neurobiology: invertebrate and vertebrate neurobiology, exclusive of human beings, including investigation into the neural mechanisms involved in sensory, motor and other complex functions of the whole organism as these relate to behaviour. Research grants are for up to three years, awarded to established scientists working at accredited institutions in the USA. Grants-in-aid are for a one year period and are designed especially for young postgraduate investigators who have not yet established themselves, as well as to senior scientists.

Geographical Area of Activity: USA.

Restrictions: Funds are not awarded to investigators who have substantial existing or potential support. The Foundation does not consider grant applications from outside the USA.

Publications: Report of operations and financial statement.

Finance: Assets $108,960,000 (2000). Research grants range from $30,000–$75,000 per year; grants-in-aid do not exceed $30,000.

Trustees: George M. Moffett, II (Pres. and Treas.); J. Wright Rumbough, Jr, (Vice-Pres.); L. T. Baker (Sec.); W. S. Adams; K. S. Beall, Jr; H. A. Brooks; M. V. Dawes; Peter Gibbons-Neff; E. A. Newton; M. M. Rumbough.

Address: POB 3423, Palm Beach, FL 33480.

Telephone: (561) 655-4474; **Fax:** (561) 659-4978; **Internet:** www.whitehall.org; **e-mail:** email@whitehall.org.

Wilbur Foundation

Established in 1975 by Marguerite Eyer Wilbur.

Activities: Operates in the fields of the arts and humanities, education, political science and religion, through support for programme development, organizing seminars and conferences, publications, fellowships and for research.

Restrictions: No grants are made to individuals, with the exception of Residential Writing Grants fellowships at the Russell Kirk Center, Mecosta, MI.

Finance: Assets $3,075,775 (2001); total giving $113,500 (2001).

Officers and Trustees: Gary R. Ricks (Pres.); Annette Kirk (Vice-Pres.); Gleaves Whitney (Treas.); John Engler; Dr Regis C. Ginn.

Address: POB 3370, Santa Barbara, CA 93130-3370.

Fax: (805) 563-1082; **Internet:** www.wilburfoundation.org; **e-mail:** info@wilburfoundation.org.

WILD Foundation—International Wilderness Leadership Foundation

Founded in 1974 by Ian Player as the International Wilderness Leadership Foundation, to protect and sustain critical wild areas, wilderness values and endangered wildlife throughout the world, with a special emphasis on Southern Africa, by initiating or assisting environmental education, experiential projects and programmes.

Activities: Operates internationally in the field of conservation and the environment. Runs programmes on wilderness and wildlife, ecotourism and education and training; projects are conducted in Southern Africa and elsewhere. Promotes the wise use of wildland resources and provides environmental education and training. Works in partnership with other organizations world-wide.

Geographical Area of Activity: International, with an emphasis on Southern Africa.

Publications: *The Leaf* (newsletter, 2 a year); *Wilderness Management; International Journal of Wilderness;* internet newsletter; educational promotions and other publications.

Officers and Directors: Robert C. Baron (Chair.); Michael Sweatman (Vice-Chair. and Treas.); Vance G. Martin (Pres.); Dr Robert Cleaves (Gen. Counsel and Sec.); Dr Ian Player (Founder); David Barron; Magalen Bryant; Ulf Doerner; Robert B. Haas; Dr John Hendee; Carl Hilker; Cathryn Hilker; Paul G. Irwin; M. A. Partha Sarathy.

Principal Staff: Pres. Vance G. Martin.

Address: POB 1380, Ojai, CA 93024.

Telephone: (805) 640-0390; **Fax:** (805) 640-0230; **Internet:** www.wild.org; **e-mail:** info@wild.org.

Wildlife Trust

Founded in 1971 by Gerald M. Durrell, and until 2000 known as the Wildlife Preservation Trust International, to seek to save endangered species from extinction through creative, small-scale projects in collaboration with local scientists and educators.

Activities: Makes grants to more than 60 projects in 18 countries in North, Central and South America and the Caribbean, Africa and Asia. Supports research in the field of captive breeding of endangered species, the reintroduction of captive-bred animals to the wild, conservation, and associated environmental education programmes. The Trust aims to train local conservation professionals. Jointly administers the Gerald Durrell Memorial Funds in conjunction with the Durrell Wildlife Conservation Trust and the Wildlife Preservation Trust Canada, supporting endangered species conservation projects by International Conservation Center graduates.

Geographical Area of Activity: North, Central and South America and the Caribbean, Africa and Asia.

Publications: Annual Report; *The Wild Times* (3 a year); information sheets, posters, maps and monographs.

Finance: Annual budget approx. $1,800,000.

Principal Staff: Pres. Virginia C. Mars; Vice-Pres. Martin S. Kaplan, Cynthia R. Stebbins; Exec. Dir Mary Pearl.

Address: 61 Route 9w, Palisades, NY 10964-8000.

Telephone: (845) 365-8337; **Fax:** (845) 365-8177; **Internet:** www.wpti.org; **e-mail:** homeoffice@wildlifetrust.org.

Woodrow Wilson International Center for Scholars

Founded in 1968 as a memorial to President Woodrow Wilson, to symbolize and strengthen the fruitful relation between the world of learning and the world of public affairs. The Center is part of the Smithsonian Institution (q.v.), but is administered by its own Board of Trustees.

Activities: Awards 20–25 annual post-doctoral fellowships for full-time research to be conducted at the Center by scholars from any country. Fellowships are awarded for within the broad themes of governance, including the key issues of the development of democratic institutions, democratic society, civil society and citizen participation; the US role in the world and issues of partnership and leadership; and key long-term future challenges confronting the United States and the world.

Geographical Area of Activity: International.

Publications: Annual Report; *The Wilson Quarterly; Scholar's Guides* (to Washington); working papers, conference reports.

Trustees: Joseph B. Gildenhorn (Chair.): David A. Metzner (Vice-Chair.); Joseph A. Cari, Jr; Carol Cartwright; Donald E. Garcia; Bruce S. Gelb; Daniel L. Lamaute; Tami Longaberger; Thomas R. Reedy; and seven state representatives.

Principal Staff: Dir Lee H. Hamilton.

Address: 1 Woodrow Wilson Plaza, 1300 Pennsylvania Ave, NW, Washington, DC 20004-3027.

Telephone: (202) 691-4000; **Fax:** (202) 691-4001; **Internet:** wwics.si.edu; **e-mail:** wwics@wwic.si.edu.

Windstar Foundation

Founded by John Denver and Tom Crum in 1976 to promote an holistic approach to global issues through encouraging people to make responsible choices and take responsibility for a peaceful and environmentally sustainable future.

Activities: The Foundation aims to raise environmental awareness and develop leadership potential in all people. Programmes include the Environmental Studies Scholarship awarded to first year university students in the fields of environmental studies or environmental engineering; and the Trees from Grass-Roots project which raises funds for the Foundation, reforests areas damaged by natural disaster, erosion, or excessive logging in the USA and abroad, and aims to involve all its members in a common project.

Geographical Area of Activity: International.

Restrictions: Does not make grants.

Publications: *Windstar Vision.*

Board of Trustees: Cheryl Charles; Ron Deutschendorf; Jim Leary; Dan McCormick; Marge MacDonald.

Principal Staff: Communications Dir Janet Rasmussen.

Address: POB 656, Snowmass, CO 81654.

Telephone: (970) 927-5435; **Internet:** www.wstar.org.

Winrock International

Formed in 1985 by the merger of the Agricultural Development Council (founded in 1953 by John D. Rockefeller, III), the International Agricultural Development Service (founded in 1975 by the Rockefeller Foundation, q.v.) and the Winrock International Livestock Research and Training Center (founded in 1975 by the bequest of Winthrop Rockefeller). The Institute's aim is to reduce poverty and hunger in the world through sustainable agricultural and rural development.

Activities: Operates in Asia, Africa, the Middle East, Central and South America, the Caribbean and the USA by strengthening agricultural institutions, developing human resources, designing sustainable agricultural systems and strategies, and improving policies for agricultural and rural development. Maintains a library on agriculture.

Geographical Area of Activity: Asia, Africa, the Middle East, and North, Central and South America and the Caribbean.

Publications: *Innovations (e-mail newsletter); Annual Report; project profiles; development education series books; research papers.*

Principal Staff: Pres. and CEO Frank Tugwell.

Address: 38 Winrock Dr., Morrilton, AR 72110.

Telephone: (501) 727-5435; **Fax:** (501) 727-5242; **Internet:** www.winrock.org; **e-mail:** communications@winrock.org.

Women for International Peace and Arbitration

Non-profit, public benefit organization that aims to promote the peaceful settlement of international disputes, and gender equality.

Activities: Acts as an advocate for peace and non-violence, and supports programmes which work to eliminate human rights abuses, especially those affecting the rights of women and children. Recent projects have included building schools and funding university education for girls in the People's Republic of China. Affiliate organizations are based in Canada, Liberia, Rwanda, Sierra Leone, Switzerland and Zambia.

Address: POB 9619, Glendale, CA 91226-0619.

Internet: www.wipa.org; **e-mail:** information@wipa.org.

Women, Law and Development International

Women's human rights organization, originally established in 1979 as a programme of OEF International. It became an independent organization in 1993, aiming to improve the rights of women world-wide.

Activities: Operates in the field of human rights, specifically women's rights, around the world by identifying and seeking to overcome barriers to women's education and human rights. This is done through collaboration with international advocates, researchers and activists. Also trains women's groups to advocate for human rights, and has launched independent regional women's rights organizations in Africa, Asia and Central and South America. Offers fellowships for the New Voices Fellowship Program—a capacity-building and leadership development grant programme for non-profit organizations and professionals entering the human rights field.

Geographical Area of Activity: International.

Publications: *A Women's Rights Agenda for the 90's and Beyond; Women's Human Rights Step by Step; Becoming an Advocate Step by Step;* newsletter; case studies; fact sheets.

Directors: S. Huq (Chair.); M. A. Schuler (Pres.); G. A. Vargas (Vice-Chair.); J. Lyons Wolf (Vice-Chair./Sec./Treas.); F. Butegwa; N. Duff Campbell; W. Campbell; R. Clarke; R. Coomaraswamy; K. Dharmaraj; D. Dourado; J. Eldridge; N. Heyzer; A. Jahangir; N. Katjasungkana; H. Kijo-Bisimba; A. Kuenyehia; A. Molokomme; M. Pisklakova; S. Picado Sotela; D. Q. Thomas.

Address: 1050 Connecticut Ave, NW, Tenth Floor, Washington, DC 20036.

Telephone: (202) 463-7477; **Fax:** (202) 463-7480; **Internet:** www.wld.org; **e-mail:** wld@wld.org.

Women's Environment and Development Organization

An international advocacy network established in 1990 by Bella Abzug and Mim Kelber to increase the power of women world-wide as policy-makers in governance and policy-making institutions.

Activities: Works in three programme areas: the Gender and Governance Program aims to raise awareness about the under-representation of women in decision-making positions, runs a global campaign called 50/50 by 2005: Get the Balance Right!, and develops information resources and advocacy tools; the Sustainable Development Program aims to strengthen international networking between women's and environmental organizations and work towards women's representation at international forums; and the Social and Economic Justice Program works to advance women's social and economic rights generally and strengthen the capacity of the global women's economic and social justice movement. Established the Women's Caucus, an advocacy organization participating at United Nations and other inter-governmental conferences.

Geographical Area of Activity: International.

Restrictions: Not a grant-making organizations; carries out its own projects.

Publications: *News & Views* (newsletter); *Women and Sustainable Development: a Local Agenda; The First Step: Getting in the Door; Getting the Balance Right: Strategies for Change; Women's Equality: an Unfinished Agenda; Women's Action Agenda for a Healthy and Peaceful Planet; Women Challenging Globalization; Untapped Connections: Gender, Water and Poverty;* and other publications on gender and development issues.

Board of Directors: Srilatha Batliwala (Chair.); Thais Corral (Vice-Chair. Brazil); Chief Bisi Ogunleye (Vice-Chair. Nigeria); Jocelyn Dow (Guyana); Robert Bissio (Uruguay); Hellen Wangusa (Uganda); Elizabeth Calvin (Treas.).

Principal Staff: Exec. Dir June Zeitlin; Assoc. Dir Tracy Dolan.

Address: 355 Lexington Ave, 3rd Floor, New York, NY 10017-6603.

Telephone: (212) 973-0325; **Fax:** (212) 973-0335; **Internet:** www.wedo.org; **e-mail:** wedo@wedo.org.

Women's International League for Peace and Freedom—WILPF

Founded in 1915 to create an environment of political, economic, social and psychological freedom for all members of humanity.

Activities: Operates campaigns and advocacy projects world-wide on a variety of issues including peace and disarmament, empowerment of women and racial justice. WILPF has an international office located in Geneva, Switzerland, a United Nations office in New York City, and sections in 37 countries world-wide.

Geographical Area of Activity: International.

Restrictions: Not a grant-making organization.

Trustees and Officers: Phyllis Yingling (Chair.); Sandy Silver (Treas.).

Principal Staff: Exec. Dir Mary Day Kent.

Address: 1213 Race St, Philadelphia, PA 19107-1691.

Telephone: (215) 563-7110; **Fax:** (215) 563-5527; **Internet:** www.wilpf.org; **e-mail:** wilpf@wilpf.org.

World AIDS Foundation

Established in 1988 by the US Department of Health and Human Services and the Institut Pasteur (q.v.) to support AIDS-related research and education in developing countries, to facilitate information exchange and to assist developing countries responding to the AIDS pandemic.

Activities: Main area of interest is education for health professionals in developing countries, particularly in-country training. Training includes highly-focused workshops which enhance the scientific process and transfer knowledge needed in the efforts against HIV and AIDS. Grants generally range from $50,000 to $150,000. The Foundation is incorporated in Geneva and maintains an office in Paris.

Geographical Area of Activity: International.

Restrictions: In 2000 the Foundation was no longer accepting unsolicited proposals; it was to be closed down by 2004.

Board of Governors: Dr Raymond Dedonder; Dr Robert Gallo; Alain Gallochat; Dr Luc Montagnier; Richard Risebert; Dr Harold Varmus.

Address: Fogarty International Center, National Institute of Health, Bldg 31, Rm B2C02, Bethesda, MD 20892; Institut Pasteur, 28 rue du Docteur Roux, 75724 Paris Cedex 15, France.

Telephone: (301) 496-2516 (Bethesda); **Fax:** (301) 402-2056 (Bethesda); **Internet:** www.fic.nih.gov/textonly/programs/WAF.html.

World Concern

International relief and development organization founded in 1955 to alleviate human suffering in the world.

Activities: Operates in the field of aid to less-developed countries, through emergency relief, rehabilitation and long-term development programmes. Projects have included vocational training, in order to equip people with the skills to support themselves; providing emergency food supplies to famine victims; training farmers in improved agricultural methods of food production; supplying survivors of disasters with food, clothing and critical aid.

Geographical Area of Activity: Africa, Asia, Central and South America, Haiti, and Eastern Europe.

Restrictions: Not a grant-making organization.

Finance: Funded through individual donations, foundation and government grants.

Principal Staff: Pres. Paul C. Kennel.

Address: 19303 Fremont Ave North, Seattle, WA 98133.

Fax: (206) 546-7269; **Internet:** www.worldconcern.org; **e-mail:** info@worldconcern.org.

World Education

Non-profit organization dedicated to improving the lives of the poor through economic and social development.

Activities: Operates in the field of development aid, with an emphasis on education and capacity building. Provides training and technical assistance for adults and children who are not in formal education, to help generate an income for themselves and their families; provides relief and assistance to refugees and displaced people; runs an enterprise development programme; and educates people about the environment, reproductive and family health, including HIV/AIDS prevention. Projects aim to develop individual growth as well as contributing to the community and the nation.

Geographical Area of Activity: Africa, Asia, North, Central and South America, and Eastern Europe.

Publications: *Reports Magazine*; training manuals; development resources.

Address: 44 Farnsworth St, Boston, MA 02210.

Telephone: (617) 482-9485; **Fax:** (617) 482-0617; **Internet:** www.worlded.org; **e-mail:** wei@worlded.org.

World Emergency Relief

Established in 1991, a Christian, non-profit organization aiming to help people in need around the world, especially children and families.

Activities: Responds to aid requests from around the world, delivering emergency supplies to people in need, including food, clothing, medical care, shelter, education and emotional and spiritual support. Assistance is particularly directed towards children, and the organization has supported many orphanages and child refugees. Runs a domestic programme, focusing on the needs of Native Americans. Currently prefers to direct its work towards its own projects or to partner projects in the areas supported. Has partner organizations in Germany, Hong Kong, the Netherlands and the United Kingdom.

Geographical Area of Activity: International.

Restrictions: Does not currently accept unsolicited requests for support.

Publications: Annual Report.

Finance: Total assets $551,433 (2001); annual revenue $29,454,922, expenditure $29,245,720 (2001).

Principal Staff: Pres. Rev. Joel MacCollam.

Address: POB 131570-W, Carlsbad, CA 92013.

Telephone: (760) 930-8001; **Fax:** (760) 930-9085; **Internet:** www.wer-us.org; **e-mail:** info@wer-us.org.

World Federation for Mental Health

Non-profit organization founded in 1948 to advance the prevention of mental illnesses around the world, to promote the cause of mental health and raise public awareness, and to improve the treatment and care of mental and emotional disorders.

Activities: Works through public education programmes. Holds a World Congress every two years, alternating with a smaller conference on evidence-based prevention of mental and behavioural disorders and promotion of mental health. Works through nine regional Vice-Presidents (Africa, Eastern Mediterranean, Europe, Mexico and Central America, North America and the Caribbean, Oceania, South America, South-East Asia and Western Pacific) to promote regional and local programmes and activities. Eight academic Collaborating Centres at universities provide advice. Established World Mental Health Day in 1992.

Geographical Area of Activity: International.

Restrictions: Does not make grants.

Publications: Newsletter (quarterly); Annual Report; World Mental Health Day planning kit (distributed internationally).

Executive Committee: Pirkko Lahti (Pres.); L. Patt Franciosi (Pres.-Elect); Ahmed Abou El Azayem (Immediate Past Pres.); John R. M. Copeland (Treas.); Janet Meagher (Hon. Sec.).

Principal Staff: Pres. and CEO Preston J. Garrison.

Address: POB 16810, Alexandria, VA 22302-0810.

Telephone: (703) 838-7543; **Fax:** (703) 519-7648; **Internet:** www.wfmh.org; **e-mail:** wfmh@erols.com.

World Learning

Founded in 1932 as The Experiment in International Living to promote inter-cultural understanding and community development.

Activities: Operates in the fields of education, training, international exchange and international development, through projects including: Projects in International Development and Training; the School for International Training; World Learning Business Solutions; and the Experiment in International Living.

Principal Staff: Pres. James A. Cramer.

Address: Kipling Rd, POB 676, Brattleboro, VT 05302-0676.

Telephone: (802) 257-7751; **Fax:** (802) 258-3248; **Internet:** www.worldlearning.org; **e-mail:** info@worldlearning.org.

World Monuments Fund

Founded in 1965 by private citizens concerned about the accelerating destruction of important artistic treasures world-wide, to encourage the restoration of monuments.

Activities: The Fund provides financial assistance and technical expertise for the restoration of architectural monuments. Since 1965 the Fund has completed major projects in over 69 countries; current projects include conservation and development work in Albania, Armenia, Cambodia, the Czech Republic, France, Hungary, Italy, Poland, Romania, the United Kingdom, Mexico and Easter Island (Chile). The World Monuments Watch programme supports cultural heritage preservation world-wide and compiles a 'List of 100 Most Endangered Sites' every two years; selected projects from the list receive financial assistance from the World Monuments Watch. Grants are also available from the Kress Foundation European Preservation Program, the Robert W. Wilson Challenge Grant, the Jewish Heritage Grants Program and the Ralph E. Ogden Foundation President's Discretionary Fund. There are Fund offices in Paris and Venice (Italy), and independent affiliates in France, Portugal, Spain and the United Kingdom.

Geographical Area of Activity: International.

Publications: *ICON* (quarterly newsletter); reports on projects.

Trustees: M. Perry (Chair.); Hon. Ronald S. Lauder, H. Peter Stern (Vice-Chair.); Robert W. Wilson (Vice-Chair. and Treas.); Robert J. Geniesse (Sec.); and 20 others.

Principal Staff: Pres. Bonnie Burnham.

Address: 95 Madison Ave, 9th Floor, New York, NY 10016.

Telephone: (646) 424-9594; **Fax:** (646) 424-9593; **Internet:** www.wmf.org; **e-mail:** wmf@wmf.org.

World Neighbors

Founded in 1952 by Dr John L. Peters. Aims to improve the lives of those living in rural communities in developing countries through long-term development.

Activities: Works to improve agriculture, health care and family planning, conservation, water and sanitation, and small business development through 75 programmes in 18 countries in Asia, Africa and Central and South America. This is done through programmes that focus on helping individuals and communities determine their own solutions to poverty, through long-term sustainable development projects.

Geographical Area of Activity: Asia, Africa, and Central and South America.

Restrictions: Not a grant-making organization. Works directly with selected partners in the regions in which it operates.

Publications: Books; videos; papers; financial statements.

Finance: Assets $9,123,550 (2002); annual revenue $5,147,018, expenditure $5,801,539 (2002).

Trustees: Susan Chambers (Chair.); Jim Morley (Vice-Chair.); Kathy Edwards (Sec.); Richard Donaldson (Treas.); R. E. Olds Anderson; Carol Blackwood; Anthea George; Betty Harris; Jeanne Haws; Barbara Henderson; John Hirschi; Hari John; Harold Massey; Frank Merrick; Paul Milburn; Dan Pellegrom; Leo Portman; Anne Powell; Martin Seldman; John Swift.

Principal Staff: Exec. Dir Ron Burkard; Dir Int. Programmes Peter Gubbels; Dir Finance Richard Williamson; Chief Dev. Officer Alice Mae Britt.

Address: 4127 NW 122 St, Oklahoma City, OK 73120.

Telephone: (405) 752-9700; **Fax:** (405) 752-9393; **Internet:** www.wn.org; **e-mail:** info@wn.org.

World Peace Foundation

Founded in 1910 by Edwin Ginn to encourage international peace and co-operation.

Activities: Seeks to advance the cause of world peace through study, analysis and the advocacy of wise action. The Foundation, through a series of interrelated projects, aims to examine how the forces of world order may most effectively engage in preventive diplomacy, create early warning systems leading to early preventive action, engage in regional conflict avoidance and attack the underlying causes of enmity and war. The Foundation is active in Cyprus and Puerto Rico as well as carrying out other projects in Africa, Central Asia and South East Asia.

Geographical Area of Activity: Africa, Central Asia, Cyprus, Puerto Rico and South East Asia.

Restrictions: Support only for its self-initiated projects.

Board of Trustees: Richard H. Ullman (Chair.).

Principal Staff: Pres. Robert I. Rotberg.

Address: 79 John F. Kennedy St, Cambridge, MA 02138.

Telephone: (617) 496-2258; **Fax:** (617) 491-8588; **Internet:** www.worldpeacefoundation.org; **e-mail:** world_peace@harvard.edu.

World Research Foundation

Founded in 1980 to work in the field of medicine and health.

Activities: Makes information available to the public on the latest developments in health and environmental issues; informs the public and health care professionals about technology unavailable in the USA; maintains a library; organizes International Health Congresses; and conducts data searches in the fields of health and the environment. Also maintains offices in Germany and the Far East.

Geographical Area of Activity: International.

Publications: *Proceedings* (annually); newsletter; quarterly journal and scientific reports.

Principal Staff: Pres. Steven A. Ross.

Address: 41 Bell Rock Plaza, Sedona, AZ 86351.

Telephone: (520) 284-3300; **Fax:** (520) 284-3530; **Internet:** www.wrf.org; **e-mail:** info@wrf.org.

World Resources Institute

Founded in 1982 with a grant from the John D. and Catherine T. MacArthur Foundation (q.v.) as a centre for policy research seeking to discover how the world's people and nations can meet their basic needs and economic requirements without at the same time undermining the earth's ability to provide the natural resources and environmental quality on which life, growth and security depend.

Activities: Carries out specific policy research in five major areas: Climate, Energy and Pollution; Biological Resources and Institutions; Economics and Population; Technology and the Environment; and Resource and Environmental Information. In developing countries the Institute's Center for International Development and Environment provides policy advice, technical assistance and other supporting services to governments, NGOs and local groups charged with managing natural resources and economic development. Research is conducted by the Institute's own staff or by visiting fellows, or may be undertaken in collaboration with other institutions and affiliated groups throughout the USA and abroad. The Institute organizes conferences and seminars, issues publications and offers material for use in the media.

Geographical Area of Activity: International.

Publications: Annual Report; books, reports, studies, papers, handbooks, videos and computer diskettes.

Finance: Total assets $53,885,349 (2002); annual revenue $25,326,401, annual expenditure $20,040,994 (2002).

Board of Directors: William D. Ruckelshaus (Chair.); Julia Marton-Lèfevre (Vice-Chair.).

Principal Staff: Pres. Jonathan Lash; Exec. Vice-Pres. and Man. Dir Paul Faeth.

Address: 10 G St, NE, Suite 800, Washington, DC 20002.

Telephone: (202) 729-7600; **Fax:** (202) 729-7610; **Internet:** www.wri.org.

World SHARE—Self Help and Resource Exchange

Founded to improve the lives of individuals and communities through a self-help initiative.

Activities: Works in Guatemala, Mexico and the USA as a non-profit 'social business', to generate revenue for people to engage in self-help activities, through serving their local communities as volunteers and then receiving food and aid in return for their participation. Aid areas include health care, economic development, agriculture and education.

Geographical Area of Activity: USA, Mexico and Guatemala.

Restrictions: This is not a grant-making organization.

Address: 6950 Friars Rd, San Diego, CA 92108.

Telephone: (619) 686-5818; **Fax:** (619) 686-5816; **e-mail:** info@wshare.org.

World Vision

International Christian organization founded in 1950, which aims to help the poor through humanitarian programmes and relief.

Activities: Engages in emergency relief, providing aid for victims of disaster, including food, clothing and shelter; and long-term development and advocacy work. Programmes are carried out in the areas of education, health care, agriculture, micro-enterprise and clean water and sanitation. The majority of World Vision's work is child-focused.

Geographical Area of Activity: International.

Finance: Total revenue $525,350,000, total expenditure $527,600,000 (2001).

Principal Staff: Pres. Rich Stearns.

Address: POB 9716, Weyerhaeuser Way South, Federal Way, WA 98001-9716.

Telephone: (253) 815-1000; **Fax:** (253) 815-3446; **Internet:** www.worldvision.org; **e-mail:** info@worldvision.org.

Worldwatch Institute

Founded in 1974 as a non-profit research organization that aims to inform policy-makers and the public about emerging global problems, and the implications of links between the world economy and its environmental support systems.

Activities: Works to foster an environmentally sustainable society, through the provision of information. Disseminates the results of research regarding global environmental issues through a number of publications, thus raising public awareness of environmental threats. Focuses on issues such as climate change, depletion of the ozone layer, pollution of the oceans, population growth, bio-diversity, eco-systems, sustainable agriculture and economics, the impact of globilization on the environment, and energy.

Geographical Area of Activity: International and USA.

Restrictions: Does not make grants to individuals or organizations.

Publications: *World Watch Reader on Global Environmental Issues; State of the World* (annual publication); *Vital Signs* (annual); *Worldwatch Database and Downloadable Datasets;* (CD-ROM, every 2 months); *Environmental Alert Series;* books; papers.

Finance: Funded by grants from foundations, individual donations and earned income from publication sales, royalties, honoraria and investment income.

Directors: Oystein Dahle (Chair.); Tom Crain (Treas.); L. Minear (Sec.); A. Albright; C. Flavin; C. Crain; J. Dehlsen; L. Gallagher; I. van Melle; W. Wirth; J. L. Witt.

Principal Staff: Pres. Christopher Flavin; Vice-Pres. Communications Richard C. Bell; Vice-Pres. Business Development Elizabeth Nolan; Dir Research Gary Gardener; Vice-Pres. Development Adrianne Greenlees; Dir of Foundation Relations Kevin Parker; Dir of Finance and Admin. Barbara Fallin; Dir of Communications Leanne Mitchell.

Address: 1776 Massachusetts Ave, NW, 8th Floor, Washington, DC 20036-1904.

Telephone: (202) 452-1999; **Fax:** (202) 296-7365; **Internet:** www.worldwatch.org; **e-mail:** worldwatch@worldwatch.org.

Helene Wurlitzer Foundation of New Mexico

Founded in 1954 by Mrs Howard E. Wurlitzer to promote the arts and humanities.

Activities: Provides free housing in Taos, New Mexico to literary and visual artists, musicians and composers, in order to encourage and stimulate work in the creative arts.

Geographical Area of Activity: South-Western USA.

Finance: Assets $10,057,700 (2000).

Trustees and Officers: T. Rainbolt (Pres.); R. Rosenquist (Vice-Pres.); M. Alexander (Treas.); H. Hahn (Sec.); M. Knight (Exec. Dir); J. Caldwell; B. Ebie; T. Naranjo.

Principal Staff: Exec. Dir M. Knight; Office Man. Jessica Crowley; Facilities Man. Jerry Rea.

Address: POB 1891, Taos, NM 87571.

Telephone: (505) 758-2413; **Fax:** (505) 758-2559; **e-mail:** hwf@taosnet.com.

Irvin L. Young Foundation

Founded in 1949 by Irvin L. Young.

Activities: The Foundation assists medical programmes in Africa through grants to Christian missionary organizations.

Geographical Area of Activity: Africa.

Finance: Assets $2,888,728 (2001); total grants $308,500 (2001).

Principal Staff: Pres. David S. Fisher.

Address: 15535 St Therese Blvd, Brookfield, WI 53005-2627.

Telephone: (262) 495-2485.

Zonta International Foundation

Founded in 1919, Zonta International is a world-wide service organization of executives in business and the professions working together to advance the status of women. There are approximately 34,000 members in more than 1,200 clubs in 70 countries and geographic areas, supporting women's advancement, rights, education and leadership.

Activities: Has awarded Amelia Earhart Fellowship Awards annually since 1938. These grants support graduate study by women in aerospace-related sciences and engineering. Since 1938, over $5,000,000 has been raised to support these awards. Other awards include the Young Women in Public Affairs Awards encouraging women's leadership and careers in public policy, government and volunteer organizations; the Jane M. Klausman Women in Business Scholarships supporting undergraduate business study and the Michael J. Freeman Scholarships expanding educational opportunity for Irish women. Other work includes the Zonta International Stategies to Eradicate Violence Against Women and Children, a global violence prevention programme of education, advocacy and awareness, and a series of international women's development projects primarily in conjunction with the United Nations, providing more than $6,000,000 since 1956, for projects in 25 countries.

Geographical Area of Activity: International, operating in 70 countries and geographic areas.

Restrictions: No grants to individuals except for established scholarships; international development projects for women primarily through UN agencies.

Finance: Financed by contributions from members and associates. Net assets $6,000,000 (May 2002); annual expenditure $2,000,000 (May 2002).

Principal Staff: Exec. Dir Janet Halstead; Dir, Programs and Foundation Admin. Maureen Powers; Dir, Development Cathe Wood.

Address: 557 West Randolph St, Chicago, IL 60661-2206.

Telephone: (312) 930-5848; **Fax:** (312) 930-0951; **Internet:** www.zonta.org; **e-mail:** zontafdtn@zonta.org.

Uruguay

FOUNDATION CENTRE AND CO-ORDINATING BODY

Instituto del Tercer Mundo—ITeM (Third World Institute)

Established in 1989 to promote civil society internationally, in particular with the aim of building democratic and environmentally sustainable societies.

Activities: Aims to promote the development of civil society nationally and internationally, through communication, information, research and education. Encourages networking between organizations. Publishes books on the subject of the third sector. Has consultative status at the United Nations.

Geographical Area of Activity: International.

Restrictions: No grants to individuals; grants made only in specific countries or regions.

Publications: *The World Guide* (every 2 years); *Revista del Sur; Tercer Mundo Económico;* books and magazines; and CD-ROMs.

Finance: Financed by grants from international organizations, and from the sale of its own products and services.

Principal Staff: Pres. Clara Píriz; Sec. Luis Alvarez; Exec. Dir Dr Carlos Abin de Maria.

Address: POB 1539, Montevideo 11000.

Telephone: (2) 4196192; **Fax:** (2) 4119222; **Internet:** www.item.org.uy; **e-mail:** item@item.org.uy.

FOUNDATIONS, TRUSTS AND NON-PROFIT ORGANIZATIONS

Foro Juvenil

Established in 1981 to promote opportunities for young people in Uruguay.

Activities: Promotes programmes and policies that expand social, cultural and economic opportunities for all young people in Uruguay, through managing programmes, raising awareness, and influencing national public institutions and policies. Since 1985 it has been experimenting with alternative approaches to combating the problem of youth unemployment and under-employment, working to have the best practices adapted and replicated in the formal education system. Also provides support to small- and medium-sized companies run by young people; space for youth cultural exhibitions; services for the defence of young people's civil rights; programmes for young people living in poverty, without homes, and in disadvantageous situations; and programmes focusing on young women, domestic violence and sexual abuse.

Geographical Area of Activity: Uruguay.

Principal Staff: Exec. Dir Dardo Rodríguez.

Address: Maldonado 1260, CP 11000, Montevideo AP 6288.

Telephone: (2) 930029; **Fax:** (2) 927300; **Internet:** www.forojuvenil.org.uy; **e-mail:** info@forojuvenil.org.uy.

Uzbekistan

FOUNDATIONS, TRUSTS AND NON-PROFIT ORGANIZATIONS

Open Society Institute Assistance Foundation —Uzbekistan

Founded in 1996; the Institute is an independent organization, part of the Soros foundations network, which aims to foster political and cultural pluralism and reform economic structures in order to encourage free enterprise and a market economy.

Activities: Operates nationally in the fields of the arts and humanities, conservation and the environment, economic affairs, law and human rights, medicine and health, science and technology, and social welfare and social studies, through self-conducted programmes, research, grants to institutions and individuals, scholarships, conferences, training courses and publications. The Institute also participates in region-wide projects, including the East–East Programme.

Geographical Area of Activity: Uzbekistan.

Publications: Produces more than 300 publications.

Finance: Annual expenditure US $4,813,000 (2001).

Board of Directors: Mikhail Gasanov (Chair.); Babaniyazo vich Djumaev; Sakhibakhon Ergasheva; Alisher Ilkhamov; Mikhail Perper; Galina Vinogradova.

Principal Staff: Exec. Dir Alain Deletroz.

Address: Zarbog St 31, 700031 Tashkent.

Telephone: (71) 152-36-98; **Fax:** (71) 120-68-54; **e-mail:** osi@osi.freenet.uz.

Soholm Avlod Uchun Charitable Foundation

Founded in 1993 to promote improved health for future generations.

Activities: Conducts programmes and carries out research in the following areas: immunization, family planning, hygiene, talented children, and health and nutrition for mothers and infants. Operates a network of centres for the distribution of donated medicines and 'Starting Points' centres, which distribute humanitarian assistance and conduct health and other educational programmes. Works in co-operation with AmeriCares.

Geographical Area of Activity: Uzbekistan.

Principal Staff: Pres. Gulnora Yuldasheva.

Address: 15 Akhunbabayeva St, 700000 Tashkent.

Telephone: (71) 268-92-85; **Fax:** (71) 268-92-86.

Vatican City

FOUNDATION CENTRE AND CO-ORDINATING BODY

Caritas Internationalis—International Confederation of Catholic Organizations for Charitable and Social Action

Founded in 1950 by national Caritas organizations to study the problems arising from poverty in the world, to investigate the causes and to propose adequate solutions; to foster the foundation of a national charitable organization in all countries where no such organization exists, and, if necessary, to support its development; to promote the collaboration of member organizations and the co-ordination of their international activities without infringing on their autonomy; to participate in the endeavours of peoples to better their individual and collective standards of living in order to achieve total fulfilment of the human person; to stimulate and co-ordinate the relief activities of its members in cases of disaster; to represent at interconfessional and international levels members having adhered to the present statutes; and to realize, as far as possible, co-operation with other international aid and development organizations.

Activities: Acts as a co-ordinating and representative body for its member organizations, and does not itself distribute funds or conduct programmes. The 154 national member organizations are active in the fields of social welfare, development and emergency relief. There are permanent committees for emergency aid and legal questions. There are regional commissions or zone co-ordinators in Belgium, Ecuador, Kenya, Togo, Mozambique, Mauritius, the Philippines and France (representative to UNESCO). Helped set up African Caritas and Euro-Caritas, which represent member organizations in their regions. Caritas has consultative status with a number of international organizations, including ECOSOC (United Nations) and UNICEF.

Geographical Area of Activity: International.

Publications: *Bulletin* (monthly); information sheets, reports and monographs.

Principal Staff: Pres. Archbishop Youhanna-Fouad El-Hage; Sec.-Gen. Duncan MacLaren; Dir, Global Issues Jacques Bertrand.

Address: Palazzo San Calisto 16, 00120 Vatican City.

Telephone: (06) 69879799; **Fax:** (06) 69887237; **Internet:** www.caritas.org; **e-mail:** caritas.internationalis@caritas.va.

FOUNDATIONS, TRUSTS AND NON-PROFIT ORGANIZATIONS

Foundation 'Populorum Progressio'

Established in February 1992 by Pope John Paul II to promote solidarity with the poor in the developing countries of Central and South America and the Caribbean, and to support the work of other charities working in the region, in order to contribute to the development of populations which are marginalized, especially indigenous and mixed-race peoples, in accordance with the social teaching of the Church.

Activities: Operates in the field of aid to less-developed countries through financing projects nominated by national socio-pastoral institutions, and which conform to the aims of the Foundation. Maintains an Administration Council in Colombia.

Geographical Area of Activity: Central and South America and the Caribbean.

Finance: Grants disbursed since 1992 US $9,000,000.

Council of Administration: Comprises six bishops from different Central and South American countries, and a representative of Pontifical Council 'Cor Unum'.

Address: Pontificio Consiglio Cor Unum, 00120 Vatican City.

Telephone: (06) 69887331; **Fax:** (06) 69887301; **e-mail:** corunum@corunum.va.

Venezuela

FOUNDATION CENTRE AND CO-ORDINATING BODY

Sinergia

Founded in 1996 to support the development of civil society organizations in Venezuela.

Activities: Provides and publishes information on civil society organizations in Venezuela; provides technical assistance for establishing civil society organizations; and promotes philanthropy in Venezuela.

Geographical Area of Activity: Venezuela.

Publications: Information Bulletin.

Principal Staff: Pres. Armando Janssens; Vice-Pres. Jacobo Rubinstein; Treas. Morella Ramírez.

Address: Avda Andrés Bello, Edf. Las Fundaciones, Caracas.

Telephone: (212) 576-27-44; **Internet:** www.sinergia.org.ve; **e-mail:** info@sinergia.org.ve.

FOUNDATIONS, TRUSTS AND NON-PROFIT ORGANIZATIONS

Fundación para la Defensa de la Naturaleza—FUDENA (Foundation for the Defence of Nature)

Founded in 1975 to promote the conservation of the environment through the preservation of natural resources and sustainable development.

Activities: The Foundation conducts research; organizes the planning and management of protected areas and endangered species; runs environmental education and community participation projects; promotes co-operation between environmental groups; and disseminates information to the public.

Geographical Area of Activity: Venezuela.

Publications: *Guidelines for Mangrove; Venezuelan Waterfowl; Do it and show it: Guide for youngsters;* newsletters; research reports; technical reports.

Board of Directors: Luisa Abad; Andrés Barsumian; Vicente Carrillo; Albino Ferreras; Luisa Himiob; Federico Kurowski; Raúl Maestres; Ramón Piñango; Ramón Sosa; Victor de Yavorsky.

Principal Staff: Exec. Dir Deborah Bigio; Programme Man. Ernesto Estévez.

Address: Apdo Postal 77076, Centro Empresarial Senderos, 6°, Oficinas 611 y 612, Avda Principal de Los Cortijos de Lourdes con 2A Transversal, Caracas 1071.

Telephone: (212) 238-17-93; **Fax:** (212) 239-65-47; **Internet:** www.fudena.org.ve; **e-mail:** fudena@fudena.org.ve.

Fundación La Salle de Ciencias Naturales—FLASA (La Salle Foundation for Natural Sciences)

Founded in 1957 by Pablo Mandazen Soto to contribute to the nation's integral development through scientific research concerning the Venezuelan population and natural resources, and technical training of the young; to disseminate the acquired knowledge by means of specialized publications, lectures, seminars and museums; to assist the marginal population, mainly the tribal Indians and fishermen, by direct action such as the setting up of communal farms and co-operatives.

Activities: Operates nationally, and in the border zones between Venezuela and Colombia, Brazil and Guyana, in the fields of education, social welfare and studies, science and medicine, and the conservation of natural resources, through self-conducted programmes, research, scholarships, conferences, courses, publications and lectures. Maintains a Marine Research Station at Margarita, on the eastern coast, to increase knowledge of the Venezuelan sea and its resources and to help to establish an education system adapted to the needs of the fishing industry. The Foundation has also pioneered the development of technical schools whose programmes combine academic preparation with technical training—courses are of six years' duration, and embrace a wide range of subjects from mechanics and refrigeration to fishing and marine biology. In this area the Foundation established three schools, at Margarita Island, Ciudad Guayana and San Carlos (Edo. Cojedes); also at Margarita the Instituto Universitario de Tecnología del Mar (IUTEMAR) was created. Other specialized institutes established by the Foundation are the Instituto Caribe de Antropología y Sociología (Caribbean Institute of Anthropology and Sociology) and the Centro de Desarrollo Indígena (Centre for Indigenous Development), whose aims are to ease the shock of cultural transition and to provide Indian communities with a basic training that will enable them to raise their standard of living by their own efforts. Maintains offices in Cojedes, Isla de Margarita and Trujillo, and in Guyana.

Geographical Area of Activity: Venezuela.

Publications: Report of operations and financial statement; *Antropológica* (review); *Memoria*; monographic series.

Address: Edif. Fundación La Salle, Avda Boyacá, Cota Mil, Apdo 1930, Caracas 1010-A.

Telephone: (2) 793-42-55; **Fax:** (2) 793-74-93; **Internet:** www.fundacionlasalle.org.ve; **e-mail:** publicacionesflasa@hotmail.com.

Fundación Eugenio Mendoza (Eugenio Mendoza Foundation)

Founded in 1951 by Eugenio Mendoza and Luisa R. de Mendoza to promote studies and the creation of centres dedicated to scientific experimental research for the development of agriculture and breeding in Venezuela; to improve the living conditions, education and recreation of young people (including aid to the Venezuelan Foundation for Infantile Paralysis); and to organize artistic and cultural activities and other work of a charitable, social or scientific nature.

Activities: The Foundation's Community Development Programme supports micro-enterprises, primarily aiming to promote the social and economic development of low-income families through an educational programme in management skills, in order that they may improve their economic activities as well as the quality of life of their families. It has recently been extended to rural areas of the country, and the Foundation is working with new entrepreneurs. In co-operation with other organizations, the Foundation has created *Bangente*, the first private Venezuelan Bank in microfinances. A programme to support community day-care centres was set up in 1992 to assist people engaged in running child-care centres in their own homes or at local community centres; this support programme includes six teacher-training workshops in early childhood education. The Foundation's Cultural Committee co-operates in activities of interest to the country, and the Foundation publishes various literary works. The Art Gallery promotes the work of Venezuelan artists. The Foundation's library co-ordinates its cultural programmes.

Geographical Area of Activity: Venezuela.

Restrictions: No grants are made to individuals or organizations.

Publications: Report of operations and financial statement.

Trustees: Luisa R. de Mendoza (Pres.).

Principal Staff: Exec. Pres. Luisa E. M. de Pulido; Gen. Man. Morella Ramírez.

Address: Edif. 'Las Fundaciones', 9°, Avda Andrés Bello, Apdo 332, Caracas 1010.

Telephone: (212) 573-63-80; **Fax:** (212) 576-08-47; **Internet:** www.fundacionmendoza.org.ve; **e-mail:** femlmp@cantv.net.

Fundación Polar (Polar Foundation)

Founded in 1977 to contribute to the social development of Venezuela.

Activities: Collaborates with other public and private development institutions; conducts projects in the fields of agriculture, the environment, science, culture, food economy, education and community development, history, and health and social welfare. Develops its own projects and works in partnership with other organizations.

Geographical Area of Activity: Venezuela.

Publications: Environmental publications; science magazine; and publications within other interest areas.

Directors: Leonor Gimenez de Mendoza (Pres.); Morella Pacheco Ramella (Vice-Pres.); Leopoldo Márquez Áñez; Alfredo Guinand Baldó; Asdrúbal Baptista; Vicente Pérez Dávila; Gunther Faulhaber; Orlando Perdomo Gómez; Alfredo Fernández Porras; Carlos Eduardo Quintero.

Principal Staff: Gen. Man. Graciela Pantin.

Address: Apdo Postal 70934, Los Ruices, 1071-A Caracas.

Telephone: (212) 202-75-30; **Fax:** (212) 202-75-22; **Internet:** www.fpolar.org.ve; **e-mail:** webmaster@fpolar.org.ve.

Fundación Venezolana para la Conservación de la Diversidad Biológica—Fundación Bioma (Venezuelan Foundation for the Conservation of Biological Diversity)

Founded in 1986 by Dr Aldemaro Romero Díaz to improve the quality of life of the Venezuelan people through the preservation of biological diversity and ecosystems of Venezuela.

Activities: Involved in the identification, protection and management of significant natural areas; the collation of ecological information in order to identify Venezuela's environmental problems and propose solutions; and the dissemination of information through courses, lectures, national and international conferences, and publications. Awards scholarships and fellowships.

Geographical Area of Activity: Venezuela.

Publications: *Bioma en Acción* (quarterly); *Auditoría Ambiental de Venezuela* (annually); monographs.

Principal Staff: Exec. Dir Yves Lesenfants.

Address: Edif. Cámara de Comercio de Caracas, 4°, Avda Este 2, Los Caobos, Apdo 1968, Caracas 1010-A.

Telephone: (212) 571-88-31; **Fax:** (212) 571-14-12.

Fundación una Vivienda para cada Familia—FUNDAVICAF (A House for Every Family Foundation)

Founded in 1990 to promote world-wide changes in housing systems by declaring housing the first obligation of government and the priority for the allocation of taxes, advocating that families only pay the market value of a property.

Activities: Proposes a new model of society whereby the provision of adequate housing is the first priority of governments, and families pay for housing in the course of their working lives. Aims to motivate people to vote for politicians committed to its cause.

Geographical Area of Activity: Currently Venezuela, with the aim of expanding to other Central and South American countries.

Publications: *Plan PRIMHOGAR: PRIMEHOUSE Plan* (a publication describing how to implement housing changes in any country).

Finance: Annual budget approx. US $200,000.

Principal Staff: Hemogenes Huerfano.

Address: Apdo 60034, Chacao, Caracas 1060-A.

Telephone: (212) 234-02-87; **Fax:** (212) 235-61-54.

Fundación de la Vivienda Popular (Foundation for Low-Cost Housing)

Founded in 1958 by Eugenio Mendoza, with the support and participation of 41 eminent persons, 59 business concerns and four foundations, to contribute to the solution of the housing problem facing the lower-income sections of the community.

Activities: Operates nationally in the field of housing in two areas: Social Action, and Research and Development. The Social Action programme has the aim of stimulating community self-management, supporting low-income families and motivating them to organized participation in the amelioration of their housing and environment through the creation of a housing association (Asociación Civil de Vivienda); it also advises businesses wishing to contribute a solution to housing problems experienced by their workers, and trains public and private institutions interested in setting up housing associations. The Research and Development programme aims to carry out research in areas associated with housing, especially families with few economic resources; its support programmes seek to advance knowledge of housing and the environment, and it promotes the Eugenio Mendoza Chair in Housing at national universities, and the Eugenio Mendoza Prize for Research in Housing. The Foundation also maintains a documentation and information centre which offers information on housing and the environment.

Geographical Area of Activity: Venezuela.

Publications: The Foundation is the main publisher of housing literature in Venezuela.

Governing Board: Eugenio Antonio Mendoza (Pres.).

Principal Staff: Exec. Vice-Pres. Jacobo Rubinstein Gelman; Gen. Man. Oswaldo Carrillo Jiménez.

Address: Calle Junín, entre Sojo y Ayacucho, El Rosal, Caracas 1060.

Telephone: (212) 952-93-61; **Fax:** (212) 953-22-26; **e-mail:** viviendaenred@cantv.net.

FUNDAPILDE—Fundación de Apoyo a las Iniciativas Locales de Desarrollo (Foundation in Support of Local Development Initiatives)

Founded in 1997 to promote economic development and improved standards of living in Venezuela and the countries of Central and South America, especially in the areas of providing support for local development initiatives and projects which benefit women and young people.

Activities: Programmes include a training programme for people running small businesses and a Skills Promotion Plan for craftspeople in the Simón Bolívar del Estado Miranda municipality. These programmes are intended to help small businesses in the area improve the quality of their work and develop new markets. Also operates a programme of short courses for local children during their summer holidays.

Geographical Area of Activity: Mainly Venezuela.

Address: POB 14852, Caracas 1011-A.

Internet: www.members.tripod.com/~handmade/index.html; **e-mail:** cablanco@zeus.ucab.edu.ve.

Zambia

FOUNDATIONS, TRUSTS AND NON-PROFIT ORGANIZATIONS

Inter-African Network for Human Rights and Development—Afronet

Charitable organization founded in 1993 by Ngande Mwanajiti and others to promote human rights in Africa.

Activities: Operates in the field of human rights, through networking, sharing information, advocacy work, action-oriented programmes and campaigns, and publications.

Geographical Area of Activity: Africa.

Publications: *Afronet File; Southern Africa Human Rights Review; Southern Africa Human Rights Observer; Zambia Human Rights Report.*

Board of Directors: Olisa Ogbakoba (Pres.); Joe Ghartey (Chair.); Ngefa Atondoko; Rahim Khan.

Principal Staff: Exec. Dir Ngande Mwanajiti; M. Muuba; G. Mudonda.

Address: POB 31145, Lusaka.

Telephone: (1) 251813; **Fax:** (1) 251776; **Internet:** www.afronet.org.za; **e-mail:** afronet@zamnet.zm.

Mindolo Ecumenical Foundation

Founded in 1958 by Rev. Peter Mathews to promote, develop and train lay and ordained church leaders.

Activities: The Foundation serves as an ecumenical training centre, organizing courses for African churches, church-related organizations and NGOs. Programmes operated by the Foundation include: women's training; youth leadership; ecumenical church ministries; pre-school teachers and trainers; peace building and conflict transformation; and community development. It awards scholarships, organizes conferences and training courses, operates mobile schools, and issues publications. A library of 45,000 books is maintained. The Foundation has recently acquired 4,000 hectares of agricultural land which will be used for practical agricultural training and commercial farming. There are members in Angola, Botswana, Sierra Leone, Tanzania and Zambia.

Geographical Area of Activity: Africa.

Publications: *Mindolo World* (2 a year); conference reports.

Board of Governors: A pan-African board consisting of 22 representatives from national and regional religious and educational bodies, including the All Africa Conference of Churches.

Principal Staff: Dir Charley Thomas.

Address: POB 21493, Kitwe.

Telephone: (2) 214572; **Fax:** (2) 211001; **Internet:** www.mindolo.org; **e-mail:** info@mindolo.org.

Zimbabwe

FOUNDATION CENTRE AND CO-ORDINATING BODY

African Forum and Network on Debt and Development—AFRODAD

Activities: Network of African NGOs, organizations, churches and individuals that promotes debt relief, and raises awareness of debt and development issues within Africa. Takes part in conferences in the Northern hemisphere in order to promote empathy with the African position regarding international debt. Currently developing a database of poverty information on five African countries: Burkina Faso, Mauritania, Mozambique, Tanzania and Uganda.

Geographical Area of Activity: Africa.

Principal Staff: Co-ordinator Opa Kapijimpanga.

Address: POB MR 38, Marlborough, Harare.

Telephone: (4) 702093; **Fax:** (4) 702143; **Internet:** www.afrodad.org; **e-mail:** afrodad@afrodad.co.zw.

FOUNDATIONS, TRUSTS AND NON-PROFIT ORGANIZATIONS

African Capacity Building Foundation/Fondation pour le Renforcement des Capacités en Afrique

Founded in 1991 through a collaboration between the African Development Bank, the World Bank and the UN Development Programme to help the countries and regional organizations of Africa build and strengthen indigenous capacity in order to reduce poverty.

Activities: The Foundation promotes and supports the improvement of human and institutional capacities in the areas of policy analysis and development management in sub-Saharan Africa. It awards fellowships to improve research and training skills and to expand in-service training for professionals. The ACB Fund has been established to provide direct funding for capacity building projects. The Partnership for Capacity Building in Africa (PACT) initiative aims to provide an integrated framework for capacity building, good governance and sustainable development in Africa; promote a partnership between African governments, the private sector, civil society and development partners in order to strengthen Africa's ownership, leadership and responsibility in the capacity-building process; and provide a forum for sharing experiences and best practices, and discussing issues and problems.

Geographical Area of Activity: Africa, South of the Sahara.

Finance: The PACT initiative has a fund of US $1,000,000,000.

Executive Board: Kwesi Botchwey (Chair.); Joan Corkery (Vice-Chair.); Winnie Byanyima; Abdoulaye Mar Dieye; Poul Engberg-Pedersen; Gerald K. Helleiner; Henock Kifle; Brian Levy; Thandika Mkandawire; Soumana Sako.

Principal Staff: Exec. Sec. Dr Soumana Sako.

Address: Intermarket Life Towers, 7th Floor, Jason Moyo Ave/Second St, POB 1562, Harare.

Telephone: (4) 790398; **Fax:** (4) 702915; **Internet:** www.acbf-pact.org; **e-mail:** root@acbf-pact.org.

African Development Foundation

Established in 1986, the Foundation works in three main areas: small enterprise development; agribusiness; and environment, sanitation and water.

Activities: Co-ordinates community development programmes in Africa, and promotes the active participation of the community in socio-economic development programmes. Promotes sustainable employment and income generation, through micro- and small-enterprise development; encourages improved resource management for scarce natural resources; and develops models for participation and capacity building.

Geographical Area of Activity: Africa.

Publications: *Advanced* (journal); *Beyond Relief* (newsletter).

Finance: Annual revenue approx. US $720,000 (2000).

Principal Staff: Country Representative Japhet Mtukwa.

Address: POB 5150, Harare; Bush House, 2nd Floor, 72 Cameron St, Harare.

Telephone: (4) 750254; **Fax:** (4) 795525; **e-mail:** adf-zim@id.co.zw.

Amani Trust

Founded in 1993 to provide services for the rehabilitation of victims of human rights violations.

Activities: Provides a range of services to victims of human rights abuses, particularly torture, repressive violence and institutionalized violence, through education and training programmes, liaising with national and international bodies which share Amani's objectives, carrying out research into the effects of torture and human rights violations, and providing information and documentation on the effects of torture and psychosocial trauma.

Geographical Area of Activity: Zimbabwe.

Address: Suite 3, 1 Raleigh St, Kopje, Harare.

Telephone: (263-4) 792222; **Fax:** (263-4) 731660; **e-mail:** amani@echo.icon.co.za.

Self Help Development Foundation

Established in 1963 by Francis Waddelove for the reduction of poverty through food security.

Activities: Operates in Zimbabwe and Southern Africa in the areas of economic affairs, education and social welfare, through providing credit; education for self-survival; mobilization of savings; civic education; and social welfare in the area of food security. The Foundation makes grants and loans to groups and individual members, and carries out projects.

Geographical Area of Activity: Zimbabwe and Southern Africa.

Trustees: Prof. Chimedza; A. Masuku; G. F. Munyoro; M. T. Mutambira; S. Zimbiti.

Principal Staff: Man. Dir M. T. Mutambira.

Address: POB 4576, Harare.

Telephone: (4) 570130; **Fax:** (4) 570139; **e-mail:** shdf@pci.co.zw.

Select Bibliography

ANHEIER, H. K. AND TOEPLER, S. (EDS) *Private Funds, Public Purpose: Philanthropic foundations in international perspective.* Kluwer Academic/Plenum Publishers, USA, 1999.

ARIAS FOUNDATION FOR PEACE AND HUMAN PROGRESS. *The State of Philanthropy in Central America.* San José, 1992.

ASSOCIATION OF MEDICAL RESEARCH CHARITIES. *The Association of Medical Research Charities Handbook 2001.* London, 2001.

BAINE, S., BENINGTON, J. and RUSSELL, J. (Editors). *Changing Europe: Challenges Facing the Voluntary and Community Sectors in the 1990s.* National Council for Voluntary Organisations, London, 1992.

BALDWIN, LEONIE (Researcher and Compiler). *The Irish Funding Handbook.* CAFE/CAN/Combat Poverty Agency, in association with the Directory of Social Change, 3rd edn, 1994.

BALOGLU, Z. (EDITOR). *The Foundations of Turkey.* TÜSEV, Istanbul, 1996.

BERKEL, UTE, NEUHOFF, KLAUS, SCHINDLER, AMBROS and STEINSDÖRFER, ERICH (Editors). *Stiftungshandbuch.* Nomos Verlagsgesellschaft, Baden-Baden, 3rd edn, 1989.

BERTELSMANN FOUNDATION (Editor) *The Future of Foundations in an Open Society.* Bertelsmann Foundation, Gütersloh, 1999.

BERTELSMANN FOUNDATION (Editor). *Foundations in Europe.* Directory of Social Change, London and Bertelsmann Foundation, Gütersloh, 2001.

R. R. BOWKER. *Annual Register of Grant Support.* New Providence, NJ, 35th edn, 2002.

BREMNER, ROBERT H. *Giving: Charity and Philanthropy in History.* Rutgers University Press, New Brunswick, NJ, 1995.

BUNDESVERBAND DEUTSCHER STIFTUNGEN EV (Editor). *Verzeichnis Deutscher Stiftungen.* Verlag Hoppenstedt GmbH, 4th edn, 2000.

BURNELL, PETER. *Charity, Politics and the Third World.* Harvester Wheatsheaf, Hemel Hempstead, 1991.

CACHO, MYRNA GIMENA, DE QUIROS, CONRADO and RAGRAGIO, CONCHITA MANONGDO (Editors). *Directory of Philippine Foundations 1990.* Association of Foundations, Manila, 1990.

CANADIAN CENTRE FOR PHILANTHROPY. *Canadian Directory to Foundations and Grants.* 17th edn, Toronto, 2003.

CENTRO DE FUNDACIONES. *Fundaciones Españolas.* Madrid, 1985.

CENTRO ITALIANO DI RICHERCHE E D'INFORMAZIONE SULL'ECONOMIA DELLE IMPRESE PUBBLICHE E DI PUBBLICO INTERESSE. (CIRIEC). *Le Fondazione Italiane.* Franco Angeli Editore, Milan, 1973.

CENTRO MEXICANO PARA LA FILANTROPÍA, AC. *Directorio de Instituciones Filantrópicas.* México.

CENTRO PORTUGUÊS DE FUNDAÇÕES. *Guia das Fundações Portuguesas / Portuguese Foundations Guide* 1996.

CHILDERS, ROBERTA, and TRZYNA, THADDEUS C. (Editors). *World Directory of Environmental Organizations.* California Institute of Public Affairs, Sacramento, CA, 5th edn, 1996.

CUNNINGGIM, MERRIMON. *Private Money and Public Service: The Role of Foundations in American Society.* Herder & Herder, New York, 1972.

DIRECTORY OF SOCIAL CHANGE. *The Directory of Grant Making Trusts 2003–2004* (2 vols, London 2003, in association with CAF); *A Guide to the Major Trusts (3 vols, London, 2003); Trust Monitor (3 a year).*

LES EDITIONS SA2. *GAFA—Guide Annuaire des Fondations et des Associations.* Vincennes, 1997.

EUROPA PUBLICATIONS. *The International Directory of Corporate Philanthropy.* London, 2002.

EUROPEAN FOUNDATION CENTRE (EFC). *Cultural Funding in Europe.* (Orpheus Programme Publication, Brussels); *Education Funding in Europe.* (Orpheus Programme Publication, Brussels, 2 vols, 1998); *Environmental Funding in Europe 1998.* (Orpheus Programme Publication, Brussels, 1st edn, 1998); *European Foundation Centre Profiles.* (Orpheus Programme Publication, Brussels, 1995–96 edn); *European Grants Index.* (Orpheus Programme Publication, Brussels, 1998); *Independent Funding.* (Orpheus Programme Publication, Brussels, 2002); *International Guide to Funders Interested in Central and Eastern Europe.* (Orpheus Programme Publication, Brussels, 1993); *Mediterranean Funding.* (Orpheus Programme Publication, Brussels, 1999); *Selected Bibliography on Foundations and Corporate Funders in Europe.* (Orpheus Programme Publication, Brussels, 1994); *Typology of Foundations in Europe.* (Orpheus Programme Publication, Brussels); *Funding Minorities and Multiculturalism in Europe: Funders' Activities against Racism and for Equality in Diversity* (Orpheus Programme Publication, Brussels, 2001); *Funding Vocational Training and Employment for People with Disabilities in Europe* (Orpheus Programme Publication, Brussels, 2002); *Disaster Grantmaking: A Practical Guide for Foundations and Corporations; Select Legislative Texts & Commentaries on Central and Eastern European Not-for-Profit Law.*

FERRARA, MIRANDA H. and JASZCZAK, SANDRA (Editors). *The Awards Almanac.* St James Press, Detroit, MI, 1996.

FONDAZIONE GIOVANNI AGNELLI. *Guide to European Foundations.* Edizioni della Fondazione. SM, Turin, 3rd edn, 1978.

FOUNDATION CENTER. *The Foundation Directory.* (New York, 2003, also CD-ROM and on-line); *The Foundation 1000* (2002); *Foundation Fundamentals: A Guide for Grantseekers* (6th edn, 1999); *Foundation Grants to Individuals* (12th edn, 2001, also CD-ROM and online); *Guide to Funding for International and Foreign Programs* (6th edn, 2002); *National Directory of Corporate Giving* (8th edn, 2002); *Philanthropy News Digest* (weekly, by e-mail).

FREEMAN, DAVID F. and the COUNCIL ON FOUNDATIONS. *Handbook on Private Foundations.* Foundation Center, New York, 1991.

FUNDACIÓN JOSÉ MARÍA ARAGÓN. *Primer Directorio de Fundaciones de la República Argentina.* (Buenos Aires, 1980); *Guía de Becas de Postgraduado 1991–92.* (Buenos Aires, 7th edn, 1991).

FUNDACIÓN ARIAS PARA LA PAZ Y EL PROGRESO HUMANO. *Guía de Fundaciones y Organisaciones Afines de CA.* San José.

GALLEGOS, HERMAN E. and O'NEILL, MICHAEL. *Hispanics and the Nonprofit Sector.* Foundation Center, New York, 1991.

THE HAGUE CLUB. *Foundation Profiles.* Helsinki, 1998.

HOLLY, KARINA (Editor). *Philanthropy in Europe.* Philanthropy in Europe Ltd, www.philanthropyineurope.com, Bristol, 6 a year.

INTERNATIONAL SOCIETY FOR THIRD-SECTOR RESEARCH. *Voluntas (International Journal of Voluntary and Nonprofit Organisations).* Plenum Publishing Corpn, New York, quarterly.

ISTITUTO NAZIONALE DELL'INFORMAZIONE—INI. *Documenti Italia: Annuario degli Enti di Studio, Cultura, Ricerca Scientifica e Tecnologica 1998/99.* Editoriale Italiana, Rome, 7th edn, 1998.

JAPAN ASSOCIATION OF CHARITABLE CORPORATIONS. *Philanthropy in Japan.* Tokyo, 1983.

JAPAN FOUNDATION CENTER. *Directory of Grantmaking Foundations: Summary of Current Grant Awards; Directory of Grantmaking Foundations: Guide to Private Grant Sources.* Tokyo.

JOSEPH, JAMES A. (Editor). *The Charitable Impulse: Wealth and Social Conscience in Communities and Cultures Outside the United States.* Foundation Center, New York, 1989.

KEELE, HAROLD M. and KIGER, JOSEPH C. (Editors). *Foundations.* Greenwood—Encyclopedia of American Institutions, Westport, CT, 1984.

LEHSMANN, KURT and ODELBERG, WILHELM. *Kulturfonder i Sverige.* P. A. Norstedt & Söners Förlag, Stockholm, 9th edn, 1999.

MAGAT, RICHARD (Editor). *An Agile Servant: Community Leadership by Community Foundations.* Foundation Center, New York, 1989.

MARTIN, MIKE W. *Virtuous Giving: Philanthropy, Voluntary Service, and Caring.* Indiana University Press, Bloomington, IN, 1995.

MARTIN, SAMUEL A. *An Essential Grace: Funding Canada's Health Care, Education, Welfare, Religion and Culture.* McClelland and Stewart, Toronto, 1984.

MORRIS MAXFIELD, DORIS. *Charitable Organizations in the U.S.* Gale Research Inc, Detroit, MI, 2nd edn, 1992.

NAGAI, A., LERNER, R. and ROTHMAN, R. (Editors). *Giving for Social Change: Foundations, Public Policy, and the American Political Agenda.* Praeger Publishers, Westport, CT, 1994.

NATIONAL COUNCIL FOR RESEARCH AND DEVELOPMENT (Israel). *Scientific Research in Israel.* Jerusalem, every 2 years.

NEW ZEALAND COUNCIL FOR EDUCATIONAL RESEARCH. *A Directory of Philanthropic Trusts.* Wellington, 4th edn, 1994.

O'CONNELL, BRIAN (Editor). *America's Voluntary Spirit: A Book of Readings.* Foundation Center, New York, 1983.

ODENDAHL, TERESA J., BORIS, ELIZABETH T. R. and DANIELS, ARLENE K. *Working in Foundations: Career Patterns of Women and Men.* Foundation Center, New York, 1985.

ORGANIZATION FOR ECONOMIC CO-OPERATION AND DEVELOPMENT (OECD). *Directory of Non-Governmental Development Organizations in OECD Member Countries.* Paris, 1997.

ORYX PRESS. *Directory of Grants in the Humanities 2002/03.* Phoenix, AZ, 2002.

OWEN, DAVID. *English Philanthropy 1660–1960.* Harvard University Press, Cambridge, MA, 1964.

PALGRAVE MACMILLAN. *The Grants Register 2003.* London, 21st edn, 2002.

PHILANTHROPY AUSTRALIA INC. *The Australian Directory of Philanthropy 2002/03.* (Melbourne, 11th edn, 2002, also on-line); *The Australian Guide to Scholarships and Awards.* (Melbourne, 1st edn, 1997).

PIFER, ALAN. *Philanthropy in an Age of Transition.* Foundation Center, New York, 1984.

POMEY, MICHEL. *Traité des Fondations d'Utilité Publique.* Presse Universitaire de France, 1980.

SALAMON, LESTER M. *The Global Associational Revolution: The Rise of the Third Sector on the World Scene.* Johns Hopkins University, Institute for Policy Studies, Baltimore, MD, 1993.

SALAMON, LESTER M. and ANHEIER, H. K. *The Emerging Sector: The Nonprofit Sector in Comparative Perspective: An Overview.* Johns Hopkins University, Institute for Policy Studies, Baltimore, MD, 1994.

SALAMON, LESTER M. and ANHEIER, H. K. *The Emerging Nonprofit Sector: An Overview.* Manchester University Press, Manchester, 1996.

SALAMON, LESTER M. and ANHEIER, H. K.(Editors). *Defining the Nonprofit Sector: A Cross-National Analysis.* Manchester University Press, Manchester, 1997.

SALAMON, LESTER M., ANHEIER, H. K., LIST, R., TOEPLER, S. and SOKOLOWSKI, W. (Editors). *Global Civil Society: Dimensions of the Nonprofit Sector.* Johns Hopkins Institute for Policy Studies, Baltimore, MD, 1999.

SCHWEIZERISCHE AKADEMIE DER MEDIZINISCHEN WISSENSCHAFTEN. *Schweizerische Stiftungen.* Basle.

SHEETS, T. and MAURER, C. (Editors). *Encyclopedia of Associations, International Organizations.* Gale Research Inc, Detroit, MI, 40th edn, 2003.

SIEGEL, DANIEL and YANCEY, JENNY. *The Rebirth of Civil Society: The Development of the Nonprofit Sector in East Central Europe and the Role of Western Assistance.* Rockefeller Brothers Fund, New York, 1992.

SOLIDARIOS—CONSEJO DE FUNDACIONES AMERICANAS DE DESAROLLO. *Catálogo de Instituciones de Desarrollo sin Fines de Lucro en América Latina.* Santo Domingo, 1981.

STUBBS, L. *The Third World Directory.* Directory of Social Change, London, 3rd edn, 1997.

THOMAS, RALPH LINGO. *Policies Underlying Corporate Giving.* Prentice-Hall, Inc, Englewood Cliffs, NJ, 1966.

UNION OF INTERNATIONAL ASSOCIATIONS. *Yearbook of International Organizations 2002/2003.* K. G. Saur, Munich, 39th edn, 5 vols, 2002 (also CD-ROM and on-line).

URAL, ENGIN (Editor). *Foundations in Turkey.* Development Foundation of Turkey, Ankara, 1978.

VERENIGING VAN FONDSEN IN NEDERLAND. *Fondsenboek 2001/2002.* The Hague, 2001 (also CD-ROM).

VINCENT, JEREMY and PHAROAH, CATHY. *Patterns of independent grantmaking in the UK.* CAF Publications, CAF, West Malling, 2000.

WEAVER, WARREN. *U.S. Philanthropic Foundations: Their History, Structure, Management and Record.* Harper & Row, New York, 1967.

PART THREE

Indexes

Index of Foundations

Index of Main Activities

AID TO LESS-DEVELOPED COUNTRIES; DEVELOPMENT STUDIES

ARTS AND HUMANITIES

CONSERVATION AND THE ENVIRONMENT

ECONOMIC AFFAIRS

EDUCATION

INTERNATIONAL AFFAIRS

LAW AND HUMAN RIGHTS

MEDICINE AND HEALTH

SCIENCE AND TECHNOLOGY

SOCIAL WELFARE AND STUDIES

FOUNDATION CENTRES AND CO-ORDINATING BODIES

Index by Area of Activity

AFRICA (SOUTH OF THE SAHARA)

ASIA AND THE PACIFIC

CENTRAL AND SOUTH-EASTERN EUROPE

EASTERN EUROPE AND THE REPUBLICS OF CENTRAL ASIA

MIDDLE EAST AND NORTH AFRICA

SOUTH AMERICA, CENTRAL AMERICA AND THE CARIBBEAN

USA AND CANADA

WESTERN EUROPE